REAL ESTATE FINANCE LAW

REAL ESTATE FINANCE LAW

Third Edition

By

Grant S. Nelson
Professor of Law
University of California, Los Angeles

Dale A. Whitman
Guy Anderson Professor of Law
J. Reuben Clark Law School
Brigham Young University

Volume 2
Chapters 10–End
Appendix
Table of Cases
Index

PRACTITIONER TREATISE SERIES

WEST PUBLISHING CO.
ST. PAUL, MINN., 1993

Practitioner Treatise Series, Westlaw, the West Publishing Co. Logo and the Hornbook Series Logo appearing on the front cover and spine are registered trademarks of West Publishing Co. Registered in the U.S. Patent and Trademark Office.

COPYRIGHT © 1951, 1970, 1979 WEST PUBLISHING CO.
COPYRIGHT © 1985 GRANT S. NELSON & DALE A. WHITMAN
COPYRIGHT © 1994 GRANT S. NELSON & DALE A. WHITMAN
All rights reserved
Printed in the United States of America

Library of Congress Cataloging-in-Publication Data
Nelson, Grant S.
    Real estate finance law / by Grant S. Nelson, Dale A. Whitman. — 3rd ed.
       p.   cm. — (Practitioner treatise series)
    Includes index.
    ISBN 0–314–02296–1 (vol. 1). — ISBN 0–314–02434–4 (vol. 2)
    1. Mortgages—United States. I. Whitman, Dale A. II. Title.
III. Series.
KF695.N45 1993c
346.7304′364—dc20
[347.3064364]
                                                            93–28748
                                                                CIP

ISBN 0–314–02434–4 (vol. 2)
ISBN 0–314–02435–2 (set)

(N. & W.) Real Est.Fin. 3d PTS
        Vol. 2
1st Reprint—1994

PRINTED ON 10% POST CONSUMER RECYCLED PAPER

WESTLAW® Overview

Nelson and Whitman's *Real Estate Finance Law*, 3d edition, offers a detailed and comprehensive treatment of principles and issues in real estate finance law. To supplement the information in this book, you can access WESTLAW, a computer-assisted legal research service of West Publishing Company. WESTLAW contains a broad library of real estate finance law resources, including case law, federal and state statutes, law reviews, texts and journals, and portions of the Practicing Law Institute's Course Handbook Series on continuing legal education in real estate law.

Learning how to use these materials effectively will enhance your legal research. To help you coordinate your book and WESTLAW research, this volume contains an appendix listing WESTLAW databases, search techniques and sample problems.

THE PUBLISHER

*

Summary of Contents

Volume 1

Chapter		Page
1.	An Introduction to the Law of Mortgages	1
2.	The Necessity and Nature of the Obligation	15
3.	Mortgage Substitutes	31
	A. Restricting the Right to Redeem	32
	B. The Absolute Deed	44
	C. The Conditional Sale	72
	D. Tripartite Transactions	82
	E. The Installment Land Contract	91
	F. The Negative Covenant as a Mortgage Substitute	144
4.	Rights and Duties of the Parties Prior to Foreclosure	149
	A. Theories of Title and the Right to Possession	150
	B. Tortious Injury to Land by Mortgagor or Third Persons	159
	C. Rights in the Product of the Res	175
	D. Escrows or Reserves for Taxes and Insurance	191
	E. Right to Rents	205
	F. Mortgagee in Possession	213
	G. Receiverships	235
	H. Acquisition of Title in Breach of Duty	274
	I. Mortgagee Liability for Environmental Problems	282
5.	Transfer by the Mortgagor and the Mortgagee	293
	A. Transfer by the Mortgagor	294
	B. Restrictions on Transfer by the Mortgagor	356
	C. Transfer by the Mortgagee	404
6.	Discharge of the Mortgage	478
	A. Payment	479
	B. Statutes of Limitation	523
	C. Merger	536
	D. The Deed in Lieu of Foreclosure	547
7.	Foreclosure	550
	A. Redemption From the Mortgage	551
	B. Accrual of the Right to Foreclosure	561
	C. Strict Foreclosure	575
	D. Judicial Foreclosure	580
	E. Power of Sale Foreclosure	609
	F. Disposition of Surplus	669
8.	Statutory Impacts on Foreclosure	675
	A. Regulation of Deficiency Judgments	676
	B. Statutory Redemption	707

Chapter		Page
8.	Statutory Impacts on Foreclosure—Continued	
	C. The Soldiers' and Sailors' Civil Relief Act	724
	D. Bankruptcy	731
9.	Some Priority Problems	800

Volume 2

10.	Subrogation, Contribution and Marshaling	1
	A. Subrogation and Contribution	1
	B. Marshaling	20
11.	Government Intervention in the Mortgage Market	45
12.	Financing Real Estate Construction	147
13.	Financing Condominiums and Cooperatives	272
14.	Residential Financing Forms	314
15.	Commercial Financing Forms	442

Appendix: Real Estate Finance Law Research on WESTLAW	705
TABLE OF CASES	725
INDEX	817

Table of Contents

Volume 1

CHAPTER 1. AN INTRODUCTION TO THE LAW OF MORTGAGES

Sec.		Page
1.1	The Basic Mortgage Transaction	1
1.2	The Impact of English History	6
1.3	The Intervention of Equity	7
1.4	The American Development	9
1.5	The Title, Lien, and Intermediate Theories of Mortgage Law	10
1.6	The Deed of Trust as a Mortgage Variant	11
1.7	Mortgage Substitutes and Clogging the Equity of Redemption	13

CHAPTER 2. THE NECESSITY AND NATURE OF THE OBLIGATION

2.1	Necessity of Obligation	15
2.2	Nature of the Obligation	19
2.3	The Necessity of Consideration	22
2.4	Description of the Debt	26

CHAPTER 3. MORTGAGE SUBSTITUTES

A. RESTRICTING THE RIGHT TO REDEEM

3.1	Clogging the Equity of Redemption	32
3.2	The Option to Purchase as a Clog on the Equity of Redemption	38
3.3	Subsequent Transactions	41

B. THE ABSOLUTE DEED

3.4	The Absolute Deed With Separate Instrument of Defeasance	44
3.5	The Absolute Deed Coupled With an Oral Understanding—Reasons for Frequent Use	47
3.6	Parol Evidence—Admissibility	49
3.7	Burden of Proof	50
3.8	Factors Establishing an Absolute Deed as a Mortgage	52
3.9	Effect of Absolute Deed Between the Parties	56
3.10	Grantee's Title	57
3.11	Rights of Grantor on Sale by the Grantee	59
3.12	Creditors of Grantee	60

Sec.		Page
3.13	The Absolute Deed as a Fraudulent Conveyance	61
3.14	Recordation	62
3.15	Objections to Parol Evidence	62
3.16	Parol Mortgage vs. Parol Trust or Parol Condition Subsequent to a Written Contract	69

C. THE CONDITIONAL SALE

3.17	Nature of the Transaction	72
3.18	Extrinsic Evidence	74
3.19	Factors Establishing Conditional Sale as a Mortgage	77

D. TRIPARTITE TRANSACTIONS

3.20	Purchase Money Resulting Trusts	82
3.21	____ Security Agreements	83
3.22	Statute of Frauds in Tripartite Cases	84
3.23	Continuing Equitable Ownership in the Borrower	86
3.24	Effect of Statutory Abolition of Purchase Money Resulting Trusts	87
3.25	Contract or Option to Purchase	90

E. THE INSTALLMENT LAND CONTRACT

3.26	An Introduction to the Installment Land Contract	91
3.27	The Forfeiture Remedy—Some General Considerations	93
3.28	Statutory Limitations on Forfeiture	94
3.29	Judicial Limitations on Forfeiture	98
3.30	Constitutionality of Forfeiture	115
3.31	The Deed in Escrow as an Aid to Vendor Forfeiture Remedy	118
3.32	Other Remedies for Vendors	119
3.33	Title Problems for Vendees	125
3.34	Title Problems for Vendors	130
3.35	Mortgaging the Vendee's Interest—Problems for Mortgagees	135
3.36	Judgments Against Parties to Installment Land Contracts	138
3.37	Mortgaging the Vendor's Interest—Problems for Mortgagees	140

F. THE NEGATIVE COVENANT AS A MORTGAGE SUBSTITUTE

3.38	The Negative Covenant and the "Coast Bank" Mortgage	144

CHAPTER 4. RIGHTS AND DUTIES OF THE PARTIES PRIOR TO FORECLOSURE

A. THEORIES OF TITLE AND THE RIGHT TO POSSESSION

4.1	The Title Theory	150
4.2	The Lien Theory	154
4.3	The Intermediate Theory	158

B. TORTIOUS INJURY TO LAND BY MORTGAGOR OR THIRD PERSONS

Sec.		Page
4.4	Tortious Injury by the Mortgagor	159
4.5	Injury by Third Parties	165
4.6	Severed Property—Mortgagee's Rights	167
4.7	Injunction Against Removal of Severed Property	168
4.8	Injury by Third Persons—Mortgagor's Rights	169
4.9	Relation of Rights of Mortgagor and Mortgagee Against Third Parties	169
4.10	Equitable Relief Against the Mortgagor for Threatened Injury	171
4.11	Enforcing Specific Covenants Against Waste	173

C. RIGHTS IN THE PRODUCT OF THE RES

4.12	Eminent Domain	175
4.13	Insurance—Some General Considerations	179
4.14	____ Types of Policies	182
4.15	____ Restoration of Premises	186
4.16	____ Effect of Foreclosure Purchase by Mortgagee	188

D. ESCROWS OR RESERVES FOR TAXES AND INSURANCE

4.17	Escrow Accounts—Some General Considerations	191
4.18	Judicial Scrutiny of Escrow Accounts	193
4.19	Statutory and Related Regulation	199

E. RIGHT TO RENTS

4.20	General Considerations	205
4.21	Lease Before Mortgage—Title States	205
4.22	Mortgage Before Lease—Title States	207
4.23	Lien States	211

F. MORTGAGEE IN POSSESSION

4.24	"Mortgagee-in-Possession" Rule	213
4.25	What Constitutes Possession	218
4.26	Liability of Mortgagee to Third Parties	219
4.27	The Mortgagee's Duty to Account—Nature and Scope	220
4.28	The Duty to Account for Rents	223
4.29	Maintenance and Improvements	224
4.30	Compensation for Services	230
4.31	Reimbursement for Insurance and Taxes	231
4.32	Annual Rests	234

G. RECEIVERSHIPS

4.33	General Considerations	235
4.34	Basis for Appointment—Title and Lien Jurisdictions	236

Sec.		Page
4.35	Agreements for Rents, Profits, and Receiverships	242
4.36	Ex Parte Receivership—Constitutional Problems	253
4.37	Effect of Receivership on Rents—General Considerations	255
4.38	Receivership—Lease Prior to Mortgage	255
4.39	____ Lease Subsequent to Mortgage	258
4.40	____ Mortgagor in Possession	263
4.41	____ Mortgagor Conducting Business	264
4.42	____ "Milking" by the Mortgagor	267
4.43	Priorities Between Mortgagees as to Rents	271

H. ACQUISITION OF TITLE IN BREACH OF DUTY

4.44	Acquisition by Mortgagor	274
4.45	Acquisition of Tax Title by Mortgagee	277
4.46	Tax Payment by Subsequent Mortgagee—Effect on Prior Mortgagee	280

I. MORTGAGEE LIABILITY FOR ENVIRONMENTAL PROBLEMS

4.47	Introduction	282
4.48	Mortgagee Liability Under CERCLA	284
4.49	The 1992 E.P.A. Lender Liability Regulation	287
4.50	The CERCLA Lien	290
4.51	Environmental Problems—Suggestions for Mortgagees	291

CHAPTER 5. TRANSFER BY THE MORTGAGOR AND THE MORTGAGEE

A. TRANSFER BY THE MORTGAGOR

5.1	Transferability of Mortgagor's Interest	294
5.2	Methods of Sale of Mortgaged Land	295
5.3	Transfer "Subject To" the Mortgage	297
5.4	Assumption of the Mortgage—In General	299
5.5	____ Deed Provisions	302
5.6	____ Statute of Frauds	303
5.7	____ Parol Evidence Rule	305
5.8	Implied Personal Obligations	307
5.9	Rights of Transferor—Non-assuming Grantee	310
5.10	____ Assuming Grantee	314
5.11	Mortgagee vs. Assuming Grantee—In General	318
5.12	____ Third Party Beneficiary	319
5.13	____ "Suretyship" Subrogation	321
5.14	____ Miscellaneous Theories	323
5.15	Successive Purchasers	325
5.16	Assumption by Second Mortgagee	329
5.17	Grantee's Defenses Against Mortgagee	331
5.18	Subsequent Discharge or Modification of Rights Between Grantor and Grantee	334

Sec.		Page
5.19	Extension, Release and other Modification—Suretyship and the Mortgagor	337
5.20	Effect of the Uniform Commercial Code, pre–1990 Official Text, on Suretyship Defenses	353

B. RESTRICTIONS ON TRANSFER BY THE MORTGAGOR

5.21	The Due-on Clauses—Introduction	356
5.22	Due-on Clauses—Pre–Garn–St. Germain Act State Judicial and Legislative Response	363
5.23	___ Pre–Garn–St. Germain Act Federal Regulation	371
5.24	___ The Garn–St. Germain Act	373
5.25	___ Concealment of Transfers	397
5.26	___ Conclusion	401

C. TRANSFER BY THE MORTGAGEE

5.27	Introduction—Nature of the Mortgagee's Interest	404
5.28	Methods of Transfer	408
5.29	Negotiability and Negotiation	418
5.30	Statutory and Regulatory Limitations on the Holder in Due Course Doctrine	427
5.31	Rights of Holders in Due Course	433
5.32	Rights of Assignees Who Are Not Holders in Due Course	437
5.33	Payment to Assignor as a Defense	442
5.34	Impact of Recording Acts	451
5.35	Partial Assignments and Participations	463

CHAPTER 6. DISCHARGE OF THE MORTGAGE

A. PAYMENT

6.1	Prepayment—General Considerations	479
6.2	Prepayment Clauses—Judicial Treatment	483
6.3	___ Involuntary Prepayment	489
6.4	___ Legislative and Other Nonjudicial Regulation	493
6.5	Prepayment Penalties—Collection Incident to Due-on-Sale Enforcement	500
6.6	Acceptance of Payment—Effect	503
6.7	Tender on or After Maturity	508
6.8	Late Payment Charges—Introduction	514
6.9	___ Judicial Interpretation	515
6.10	___ Legislative and Other Regulatory Impact	520

B. STATUTES OF LIMITATION

6.11	Relationship of Obligation and Mortgage	523
6.12	Effect of Acts of Mortgagor Upon Junior Interests	529
6.13	Effect of Acts of Grantees or Junior Interests on Mortgagor	532
6.14	Statutory Trends	534

C. MERGER

Sec.		Page
6.15	Merger—General Considerations	536
6.16	____ Between the Parties to the Mortgage	537
6.17	____ Intervening Interests	543

D. THE DEED IN LIEU OF FORECLOSURE

6.18	Reasons for Use	547
6.19	Potential Pitfalls for the Mortgagee	547

CHAPTER 7. FORECLOSURE

A. REDEMPTION FROM THE MORTGAGE

7.1	Redemption From the Mortgage and Statutory Redemption—Definitions	551
7.2	Who May Redeem	552
7.3	Amount to Be Paid	554
7.4	The Procedure of Redemption	556
7.5	Limitations on the Right to Redeem	558

B. ACCRUAL OF THE RIGHT TO FORECLOSE

7.6	Acceleration Clauses—In General	561
7.7	Limitations on Acceleration	564
7.8	The Absence of an Acceleration Clause—Effect on Foreclosure	573

C. STRICT FORECLOSURE

7.9	The Nature of Strict Foreclosure	575
7.10	Use of Strict Foreclosure	576

D. JUDICIAL FORECLOSURE

7.11	Judicial Foreclosure—General Characteristics	580
7.12	Parties Defendant and the "Necessary-Proper" Party Distinction	581
7.13	Joinder—Effect of Recording Acts and Lis Pendens	586
7.14	Senior Lienors and Adverse Interests	589
7.15	Omitted Parties	593
7.16	Conduct of the Sale	600
7.17	Position of Purchaser	605
7.18	Judicial Foreclosure—Defects and Title Stability	608

E. POWER OF SALE FORECLOSURE

7.19	General Considerations	609
7.20	Defective Power of Sale Foreclosure—The "Void–Voidable" Distinction	613

Sec.		Page
7.21	____ Specific Problems	616
7.22	____ Remedies	632
7.23	Constitutionality of Power of Sale Foreclosure—Introduction	641
7.24	Constitutional Problems—Notice	642
7.25	____ Hearing	647
7.26	____ Waiver	652
7.27	____ State Action	655
7.28	____ Federal Action	661
7.29	____ Title Difficulties	665
7.30	____ Conclusion	666

F. DISPOSITION OF SURPLUS

7.31	Surplus—General Rules	669
7.32	____ Some Special Problems	672

CHAPTER 8. STATUTORY IMPACTS ON FORECLOSURE

A. REGULATION OF DEFICIENCY JUDGMENTS

8.1	Deficiency Judgments—In General	676
8.2	The "One Action" Rule	679
8.3	Anti-deficiency Legislation	682

B. STATUTORY REDEMPTION

8.4	General Characteristics	707
8.5	Who May Redeem—Nature of Interest	710
8.6	Effect of Redemption—By Mortgagor or Successor	712
8.7	____ By Lienors	717
8.8	Reforming the Foreclosure Process	720

C. THE SOLDIERS' AND SAILORS' CIVIL RELIEF ACT

8.9	General Considerations	724
8.10	The "Stay" Provisions	726
8.11	Default Judgments	730

D. BANKRUPTCY

8.12	General Considerations	731
8.13	Straight Bankruptcy	732
8.14	The Chapter 11 Reorganization	738
8.15	The Chapter 13 "Wage Earner" Plan	753
8.16	Chapter 12 (Family Farmer Bankruptcy Act of 1986)	768
8.17	Setting Aside Pre-bankruptcy Foreclosures	774
8.18	Rents in Bankruptcy	788
8.19	Installment Land Contracts in Bankruptcy	797

CHAPTER 9. SOME PRIORITY PROBLEMS

9.1	Purchase Money Mortgage Priority Concepts	800

Sec.		Page
9.2	Purchase Money Mortgages—Recording Act Problems	806
9.3	After–Acquired Property Clauses	810
9.4	Replacement and Modification of Senior Mortgages—Effect on Intervening Lienors	814
9.5	Fixtures—Introduction	819
9.6	Fixtures—Pre–UCC Law	820
9.7	Fixtures Under the UCC	822
9.8	Wraparound Mortgages	830

Volume 2

CHAPTER 10. SUBROGATION, CONTRIBUTION AND MARSHALING

A. SUBROGATION AND CONTRIBUTION

10.1	General Principles	1
10.2	Payment as Surety	4
10.3	Payment to Protect an Interest—Contribution	7
10.4	The Volunteer Rule	9
10.5	Loans to Pay the Mortgage	10
10.6	___ Subrogation Against Intervening Interests	12
10.7	Payments by Grantees—Subrogation Against Intervening Interests	16
10.8	Compelling an Assignment	19

B. MARSHALING

10.9	General Principles	20
10.10	Grantees—Inverse Order Rule	26
10.11	Effect of Assumption or Taking "Subject" to the Mortgage	30
10.12	Gift Conveyances	33
10.13	Second Mortgages	33
10.14	Marshaling by Mortgagor—Exemptions	40
10.15	Effect of Release by Mortgagee	42

CHAPTER 11. GOVERNMENT INTERVENTION IN THE MORTGAGE MARKET

11.1	The Mortgage Market, Institutional Lenders, and Their Regulators	45
11.2	Mortgage Insurers and Guarantors	53
11.3	Government–Sponsored Mortgage Market Support Agencies	69
11.4	Alternative Mortgage Instruments	83
11.5	Discrimination in Mortgage Lending	107
11.6	Federal Preemption of State Mortgage Law	118
11.7	Resolution of Insolvent Financial Institutions: Impact on Mortgage Transactions	135

CHAPTER 12. FINANCING REAL ESTATE CONSTRUCTION

Sec.		Page
12.1	Construction Lending—An Overview	147
12.2	Construction Contracts and Bonds	155
12.3	Mortgage Loan Commitments	166
12.4	Mechanics' Liens	183
12.5	___ Constitutionality	192
12.6	The Stop Notice and the Equitable Lien	200
12.7	Future Advances	209
12.8	Dragnet Clauses	227
12.9	Subordination Agreements	234
12.10	Improper Disbursement of Loan Proceeds	249
12.11	Lender Liability for Construction Defects or Other Wrongful Acts of Contractors	262

CHAPTER 13. FINANCING CONDOMINIUMS AND COOPERATIVES

13.1	An Overview of Condominiums and Cooperatives	272
13.2	Financing Condominiums and Cooperatives	277
13.3	Construction Financing of Condominiums	281
13.4	Financing Conversions to Condominium and Cooperative Status	298
13.5	Permanent Financing of Condominium Units	301
13.6	Permanent Financing of Cooperative Units	308

CHAPTER 14. RESIDENTIAL FINANCING FORMS

14.1	Introduction	314
14.2	FNMA/FHLMC Multistate Fixed Rate Note—Single Family	316
14.3	FNMA/FHLMC Uniform Mortgage—Deed of Trust Covenants—Single Family	319
14.4	FNMA/FHLMC Deed of Trust—Single Family—California	326
14.5	FNMA/FHLMC Mortgage—Single Family—Kansas	329
14.6	FNMA/FHLMC Mortgage With Power of Sale—Single Family—Minnesota	331
14.7	FNMA/FHLMC Adjustable Rate Note	333
14.8	FNMA/FHLMC Graduated Payment Note	339
14.9	FNMA/FHLMC Growing Equity Note	344
14.10	FNMA/FHLMC Fixed/Adjustible Rate Note	348
14.11	FNMA/FHLMC Condominium Rider	353
14.12	FNMA/FHLMC Uniform Instrument—1–4 Family Rider	355
14.13	FHA Note and Deed of Trust—Fixed Rate Home Loan—Missouri	358
14.14	FHA Adjustable Rate Note	367
14.15	Department of Veterans Affairs Note and Deed of Trust—Fixed Rate Home Loan—Missouri	371

Sec.		Page
14.16	FNMA/FHLMC Note, Deed of Trust and Rider—Fixed Rate Multifamily Loan—Texas	377
14.17	Promissory Note, Combination Deed of Trust, Security Agreement and Fixture Filing, Assignment of Leases and Unsecured Indemnity Agreement—Multifamily Residential	399

CHAPTER 15. COMMERCIAL FINANCING FORMS

Sec.		Page
15.1	Introduction	442
15.2	Construction Loan Agreement	443
15.3	___ Condominium Development	459
15.4	Subordination Agreement	469
15.5	Loan Agreement With Lender Participation in Cash Flow and Appreciation	472
15.6	Promissory Note—Incorporating Construction and Long-term Financing	479
15.7	Combination Mortgage, Security Agreement, and Fixture Financing Statement	482
15.8	Promissory Note With Lender Participation in Project Income and Appreciation	501
15.9	Construction Loan Agreement—Homes in Subdivision	510
15.10	Guaranty—Personally Guaranteeing Mortgage Debt	597
15.11	Assignment of Leases and Rents—As Additional Security for Note and Mortgage	600
15.12	Subordination, Nondisturbance and Attornment Agreement—For Lessee	613
15.13	Tenant Estoppel Certificate	621
15.14	Leasehold Mortgage—On Ground–Leased Income Property	624
15.15	Lease Language Crucial to the Mortgageability of a Leasehold Interest	647
15.16	Shopping Center Lease	657

	Page
APPENDIX: REAL ESTATE FINANCE LAW RESEARCH ON WESTLAW	705
TABLE OF CASES	725
INDEX	817

REAL ESTATE FINANCE LAW

Third Edition

*

Chapter 10

SUBROGATION, CONTRIBUTION AND MARSHALING

Table of Sections

A. SUBROGATION AND CONTRIBUTION

Sec.
10.1 General Principles.
10.2 Payment as Surety.
10.3 Payment to Protect an Interest—Contribution.
10.4 The Volunteer Rule.
10.5 Loans to Pay the Mortgage.
10.6 ⎯⎯ Subrogation Against Intervening Interests.
10.7 Payments by Grantees—Subrogation Against Intervening Interests.
10.8 Compelling an Assignment.

B. MARSHALING

10.9 General Principles.
10.10 Grantees—Inverse Order Rule.
10.11 Effect of Assumption or Taking "Subject" to the Mortgage.
10.12 Gift Conveyances.
10.13 Second Mortgages.
10.14 Marshaling by Mortgagor—Exemptions.
10.15 Effect of Release by Mortgagee.

A. SUBROGATION AND CONTRIBUTION

§ 10.1 General Principles

Subrogation occurs when someone, termed the subrogee, satisfies the claims of a creditor and thereby succeeds to all the rights, priorities, liens and securities of the creditor in relation to the debt.[1] It amounts

---

§ 10.1
1. See generally Restatement, Second, Restitution § 31 (Tent. Draft No. 2, 1984). See Stafford Metal Works, Inc. v. Cook

to an assignment by operation of law of the original creditor's position to the subrogee. Subrogation is derived from Roman and civil law,[2] but there is some doubt as to how much those systems have influenced the Anglo–American development of the doctrine.[3] It is an equitable doctrine designed to prevent unjust enrichment and is closely related to the principles of suretyship and restitution.[4] Like the doctrine of constructive trust,[5] it is a device designed "to compel ultimate payment of a debt by one who in justice, equity and good conscience should pay it."[6] The facts and circumstances of each case determine whether the doctrine is applicable.[7]

The question of subrogation arises in mortgage law in three distinct situations: (1) When a person who is obligated as a surety for a mortgage debt pays that debt; (2) when a person pays a debt for which he or she is not liable, for the purpose of protecting some interest in the property; and (3) when a person makes a payment voluntarily or at the request of the principal obligor to pay off another mortgage or encumbrance on the property. Subrogation in the first two situations has been termed "legal" subrogation and is said to arise by operation of

Paint & Varnish Co., 418 F.Supp. 56 (N.D.Tex.1976); First National City Bank v. United States, 548 F.2d 928 (Ct.Cl.1977); Liberty Mutual Insurance Co. v. Davis, 52 Ohio Misc. 26, 6 O.O.3d 108, 368 N.E.2d 336 (1977). Rights of the original mortgagee against guarantors are included; U.S. Steel Homes Credit Corp. v. South Shore Development Corp., 277 Pa.Super. 308, 419 A.2d 785 (1980).

While the focus of this chapter is on subrogation to the primary creditor's mortgage security, the term subrogation also describes the payor/subrogee's acquisition of the simple right to enforce the debt against a party who is principally liable on it. See, e.g., Cole v. Hotz, 758 P.2d 679 (Colo.App.1987) (mortgagor on wraparound mortgage who makes payments on underlying mortgage because wraparound mortgagee has failed to do so is subrogated to underlying mortgagee's debt claim against wraparound mortgagee).

But see First Vermont Bank v. Kalomiris, 138 Vt. 481, 418 A.2d 43 (1980), noted 7 Vt.L.Rev. 71, 82 (1982), in which the court refused to give the subrogee (a junior mortgagee) the benefit of the decree of strict foreclosure that had been granted to the senior mortgagee; the subrogee was required to reforeclose.

2. United States v. Commonwealth of Pa., Department of Highways, 349 F.Supp. 1370 (E.D.Pa.1972); D.W. Jaquays & Co. v. First Security Bank, 101 Ariz. 301, 419 P.2d 85 (1966); 24 Va.L.Rev. 771 (1938).

3. Marasinghe, An Historical Introduction to the Doctrine of Subrogation: The Early History of the Doctrine, 10 Val. U.L.Rev. part 1 at 45, part 2 at 275 (1975–76); Jones, Roman Law Bases of Suretyship in Some Modern Civil Codes, 52 Tulane L.R.Rev. 129 (1977); Comment, 31 Mich.L.Rev. 826 (1933).

4. Reese v. AMF–Whitely, 420 F.Supp. 985 (D.Neb.1976); Ray v. Donohew, 177 W.Va. 441, 352 S.E.2d 729 (1986); Rock River Lumber Corp. v. Universal Mortgage Corp. of Wisconsin, 82 Wis.2d 235, 262 N.W.2d 114 (1978); Garrity v. Rural Mutual Insurance Co., 77 Wis.2d 537, 253 N.W.2d 512 (1977).

5. Cole v. Morris, 409 S.W.2d 668 (Mo. 1966). "The doctrines of subrogation and constructive trust are analogous. The creditor is regarded as holding his claim against the principal debtor and his securities therefor in trust for the subrogee." New York Casualty Co. v. Sinclair Refining Co., 108 F.2d 65, 71 (10th Cir.1939). See First National Bank v. Huff, 441 So.2d 1317 (Miss.1983).

6. Skauge v. Mountain States Telephone & Telegraph Co., 172 Mont. 521, 565 P.2d 628 (1977).

7. Mellon Bank v. Barclays American/Business Credit, Inc., 527 F.Supp. 251 (W.D.Pa.1981); Cagle, Inc. v. Sammons, 198 Neb. 595, 254 N.W.2d 398 (1977); U.S. Fidelity and Guaranty Co. v. Maryland Casualty Co., 186 Kan. 637, 352 P.2d 70 (1960); Burgoon v. Lavezzo, 92 F.2d 726, 113 A.L.R. 944 (D.C.Cir.1937).

§ 10.1 **SUBROGATION AND CONTRIBUTION** **3**

law.[8] Subrogation in the third case is called "conventional" subrogation and is sometimes said to arise from contract, the agreement between the subrogee and either the debtor or the creditor,[9] although there is serious doubt that its real basis is contractual.[10] An agreement between the debtor and the person claiming subrogation clearly does not in itself transfer the right of the creditor to such person.[11] And if there is really a contract between the subrogee and the creditor, the result may be an assignment or an agreement to assign enforceable in equity, of either a legal or an equitable chose in action—a perfectly valid idea, but not a part of the doctrine of subrogation.[12] In some cases equity will take into consideration the presence of an agreement in determining whether to allow subrogation,[13] and the extent of the

---

8. See Harrington v. Harrington, 427 A.2d 1314, 1316, n. 3 (R.I.1981); Skauge v. Mountain States Telephone & Telegraph Co., 172 Mont. 521, 565 P.2d 628 (1977); Lawyers' Title Guaranty Fund v. Sanders, 571 P.2d 454 (Okl.1977).

9. Hoppe v. Phoenix Homes, Inc., 211 Neb. 419, 318 N.W.2d 878 (1982); Rock River Lumber Corp. v. Universal Mortgage Corp. of Wisconsin, 82 Wis.2d 235, 262 N.W.2d 114 (1978); Lentz v. Stoflet, 280 Mich. 446, 273 N.W. 763 (1937).

"From our study we may draw the following conclusions: (1) That where a lender, in no way related to the property nor in any way required to protect an interest, advanced the money to pay off a lien, it could not be a case for legal subrogation, but must, if anything, come within the principles of conventional subrogation. (2) That in conventional subrogation there must be an agreement, express or implied, that the lender whose money pays off a lien will have the same status as the lien his money releases to the extent of the debt secured by that lien. (3) That equity applies the doctrine of subrogation in such cases, not in exacting a performance of the contract, but as a matter of doing justice under the circumstances; the so-called agreement only being of value showing such a situation where the doctrine should be applied in order to do justice and as evidence that the lender was not a volunteer." Martin v. Hickenlooper, 90 Utah 150, 179, 59 P.2d 1139, 1152, 107 A.L.R. 762 (1936), rehearing denied 90 Utah 185, 61 P.2d 307 (1936).

See Restatement, Second, Restitution § 31 comment c. (Tent. Draft No. 2, 1984).

10. "[S]ubrogation arises, not as a direct legal consequence of the contract of the parties, but rather as a matter of doing justice after a balancing of the equities, and * * * the agreement is merely a consideration—although an important consideration—in determining whether subrogation is appropriate." Rock River Lumber v. Universal Mortgage Corp. of Wis., 82 Wis.2d 235, 241, 262 N.W.2d 114, 117 (1978). "Even when there is an agreement to subrogate, the so-called right of subrogation is not one inherent in the contract, but arises in equity and can therefore be withheld or applied as in equity seems meet according to sound judicial discretion, which is another way of saying, according to the dictates of justice. The doctrine of subrogation has its roots in the soil of justice and equity, and not in contract." Martin v. Hickenlooper, 90 Utah 150, 161, 59 P.2d 1139, 1143, 107 A.L.R. 762 (1936), rehearing denied 90 Utah 185, 61 P.2d 307 (1936).

11. "Even where a definite agreement for subrogation is shown, therefore, subrogation will be denied where it would lead to an uncontemplated and inequitable result." Rock River Lumber Corp. v. Universal Mortgage, supra, 262 N.W.2d at 117.

12. The difference between subrogation and assignment is illustrated by the question discussed in § 10.8, infra, as to whether one who is entitled to subrogation may compel an assignment.

13. "In the case of *conventional* subrogation, equity says: Where the lender of money did it with the intention and understanding that he was to be placed in the position of the creditor whose debt he paid, but without taking an assignment of the credit, equity, where no innocent parties will suffer or no right has intervened, will treat the matter as if an assignment had been executed." Martin v. Hickenlooper, 90 Utah 150, 157, 59 P.2d 1139, 1141, 107 A.L.R. 762 (1936) rehearing denied 90 Utah 185, 61 P.2d 307 (1936). See note 10, supra. Note, 21 Col.L.Rev. 470 (1971).

right will be determined by the agreement.[14] But unless an assignment has been executed,[15] subrogation is always by operation of law.

The payor, in order to obtain subrogation to the principal creditor's security rights, must pay the entire debt. Partial payments will not suffice.[16] The reason is the burden that the creditor would bear if the security were divided. As a well-known opinion put it, "the creditor cannot be equitably compelled to split up his securities and give up control of any part until he is fully paid." [17]

§ 10.2 Payment as Surety

Where a principal obligor and a surety are liable on a debt, if the surety pays the debt, he or she is clearly entitled to be subrogated to the rights of the creditor against the principal obligor.[1] Thus if a mortgagor sells the property to a grantee who assumes the mortgage, the mortgagor who is later obliged to pay off the mortgage is entitled to be subrogated to all rights of the mortgagee, both against the assuming grantee personally and against the mortgaged property.[2] Similarly, if

---

14. Millers Mutual Fire Insurance Co. of Tex. v. Farmers Elevator Mutual Insurance Co., 408 F.2d 776 (5th Cir.1969); Tennessee Farmers' Mutual Insurance Co. v. Rader, 219 Tenn. 384, 410 S.W.2d 171 (1966).

15. The assignment may be informal; see Tilden v. Beckmann, 203 Neb. 293, 278 N.W.2d 581 (1979). In such cases the line between conventional subrogation and assignment may be hard to distinguish.

16. In re Cavalier Homes, 102 B.R. 878 (Bkrtcy.Ga.1989); Western Coach Corp. v. Rexrode, 130 Ariz. 93, 634 P.2d 20 (App. 1981); Jessee v. First Nat. Bank, 154 Ga. App. 209, 267 S.E.2d 803 (1980); United States Fidelity & Guaranty Co. v. Maryland Casualty Co., 186 Kan. 637, 352 P.2d 70 (1960). A partial or pro tanto subrogation is possible if the entire debt is paid, partly by the subrogee and partly from other sources; Ray v. Donohew, 177 W.Va. 441, 352 S.E.2d 729 (1986).

17. Standard Surety & Casualty Co. v. Standard Accident Insurance Co., 104 F.2d 492 (8th Cir.1939), certiorari denied 308 U.S. 598, 60 S.Ct. 129, 84 L.Ed. 500 (1939), rehearing denied 308 U.S. 638, 60 S.Ct. 259, 84 L.Ed. 530 (1939). See also Erwin v. Brooke, 159 Ga. 683, 126 S.E. 777 (1924): "The reason for this rule is that if the surety upon making a partial payment became entitled to subrogation pro tanto, and thereby became entitled to the position of an assignee of the property to the extent of such payment, it would operate to place such surety upon a footing of equality with the holders of the unpaid part of the debt, and, in case the property was insufficient to pay the remainder of the debt for which the guarantor was bound, the loss would logically fall proportionately upon the creditor and upon the surety. Such a result would be grossly inequitable."

§ 10.2

1. Aultman v. United Bank, 259 Ga. 237, 378 S.E.2d 302 (1989); St. James Bank v. S & H Enterprises, Inc., 532 So.2d 915 (La.App.1988); Barnes v. Hampton, 198 Neb. 151, 252 N.W.2d 138 (1977); Langeveld v. L.R.Z.H., 74 N.J. 45, 376 A.2d 931 (1977); Ray v. Donohew, 177 W.Va. 441, 352 S.E.2d 729 (1986). Cf. Fluke Capital & Mgmt. Serv. Co. v. Richmond, 106 Wash.2d 614, 724 P.2d 356 (1986) (surety was not entitled to subrogation to first mortgage, where surety did not in fact pay first mortgage but merely suffered a loss of its second mortgage position when first mortgage was foreclosed).

2. See supra § 5.4 note 2; First Vermont Bank v. Kalomiris, 138 Vt. 481, 418 A.2d 43 (1980); Konoff v. Lantini, 111 R.I. 691, 306 A.2d 176 (1973); French v. May, 484 S.W.2d 420 (Tex.Civ.App.1972); Malone v. United States, 326 F.Supp. 106 (N.D.Miss.1971), affirmed 455 F.2d 502 (5th Cir.1971); Toler v. Baldwin County Savings & Loan Association, 286 Ala. 320, 239 So.2d 751 (1970); Sanders v. Lackey, 59 Tenn.App. 207, 439 S.W.2d 610 (1968); Finance Co. of America v. Heller, 247 Md. 714, 234 A.2d 611 (1967). See also Edwards v. Columbia, S.C. Teachers Federal Credit Union, 276 S.C. 89, 275 S.E.2d 879 (1981) and Stanford v. Aulick, 124 Ariz. 487, 605 P.2d 465 (1979), where one of the original mortgagors died and her credit life insurance policy paid part of the loan.

§ 10.2 SUBROGATION AND CONTRIBUTION

the mortgagor sells the property subject to the mortgage and is forced to pay, he or she is subrogated to the creditor's security interest in the property now owned by the grantee—the property being regarded as the principal and the mortgagor the surety.[3] The suretyship relation can run the other way as well: Suppose the purchaser buys for the full value of the property, with the mortgagor being bound to pay off the mortgage. Should the purchaser be forced to pay, he is entitled to subrogation to the mortgagee's claim against the mortgagor.[4]

It is equally clear that a principal obligor who pays is not entitled to subrogation against a person acting as surety. Such a payment would be merely the performance of the principal obligor's own duty. Hence neither an assuming grantee [5] nor a mortgagor who had agreed to pay the mortgage to protect a grantee [6] would be entitled to subrogation upon paying the mortgage. A grantee who took subject to the mortgage and pays the debt plainly cannot have subrogation against the mortgagor unless the amount of payment exceeds the value of the land, for up to that extent the grantee is obviously paying on behalf of the principal, the land.[7] Whether such a grantee may have subrogation as to the excess of the debt paid over the value of the land has already been discussed in connection with merger.[8] Even there, no subrogation against the mortgagor should be recognized. The reason is that the amount of the debt was included in the original purchase price

---

3. See supra § 5.3 note 1. Johnson v. Zink, 51 N.Y. 333, 336–37 (1873): "This relation between the mortgagor and his grantee does not deprive the obligee from enforcing the bond against the obligor. He is entitled to his debt, and has a right to avail himself of all his securities. Equity however requires that the obligor, on the payment of the debt out of his own funds, should be subrogated to the rights of the obligee, so that he can reimburse himself by a recourse to the mortgaged premises for that purpose. This cannot prejudice the creditor, and it is clearly equitable as between the debtor and the owner of the land." See also Wright v. Estate of Valley, 827 P.2d 579 (Colo.App.1992); Howard v. Burns, 279 Ill. 256, 116 N.E. 703 (1917); Woodbury v. Swan, 58 N.H. 380 (1878); University State Bank v. Steeves, 85 Wash. 55, 147 P. 645, 2 A.L.R. 237 (1915).

4. United States Steel Homes Credit Corp. v. South Shore Development Corp., 277 Pa.Super. 308, 419 A.2d 785 (1980); Simpson v. Ennis, 114 Ga. 202, 39 S.E. 853 (1901); Hazle v. Bondy, 173 Ill. 302, 50 N.E. 671 (1898); Wadsworth v. Lyon, 93 N.Y. 201, 45 Am.R. 190 (1883); Hudson v. Dismukes, 77 Va. 242 (1883). See Martynes & Associates v. Devonshire Square Apartments, 680 P.2d 246 (Colo.App.1984) and Cox v. Wooten Brothers Farms, Inc., 271 Ark. 735, 610 S.W.2d 278 (1981) for analogous situations.

The concept in the text is one possible explanation for MGIC Financial Corp. v. H.A. Briggs Co., 24 Wash.App. 1, 600 P.2d 573 (1979). See supra § 5.20 note 6.

5. Dodds v. Spring, 174 Cal. 412, 163 P. 351 (1917); Drury v. Holden, 121 Ill. 130, 13 N.E. 547 (1887); Lydon v. Campbell, 204 Mass. 580, 91 N.E. 151, 134 Am.St.Rep. 702 (1910); Pee Dee State Bank v. Prosser, 295 S.C. 229, 367 S.E.2d 708 (App.1988). Cf. Lackawanna Trust & Safe Deposit Co. v. Gomeringer, 236 Pa. 179, 84 A. 757 (1912). See 15 Col.L.Rev. 171 (1915).

6. Wadsworth v. Williams, 100 Mass. 126 (1868); Byles v. Kellogg, 67 Mich. 318, 34 N.W. 671 (1887); Hooper v. Henry, 31 Minn. 264, 17 N.W. 476 (1883).

7. Drury v. Holden, 121 Ill. 130, 13 N.E. 547 (1887); Northwestern National Bank v. Sloan, 97 Iowa 183, 66 N.W. 91 (1896); In re Wisner's Estate, 20 Mich. 442 (1870); Guernsey v. Kendall, 55 Vt. 201 (1880). Cf. Fortier v. Fortier, 200 So.2d 901 (La.App.1967), writ refused 251 La. 59, 202 So.2d 661 (La.1967), appeal after remand 221 So.2d 653 (1969) application refused 254 La. 292, 223 So.2d 412 (Sup.1969); See 5 Hous.L.Rev. (1967) for catalogue of surety-principal relationships in all types of sales of encumbered property.

8. See supra § 6.16 notes 25–26.

of the land. Even though the agreement imposed no personal duty to pay, nevertheless the payment of the mortgage was a condition to the grantee's retention of the land and the grantee should not be able, by paying it, to recover any portion of it from the mortgagor, through the help of subrogation or otherwise. The fact that at the time the mortgage debt is paid the land is no longer equal in value to the amount of the debt would not justify a recovery from the seller, and would contradict the intent of the original bargain.

Where the debt is in the form of a negotiable instrument, the UCC may arguably prevent subrogation in any case in which the ownership of the instrument passes into the hands of its maker; the Code (§ 3–601) indicates that when this occurs the debt no longer exists. However, the drafters of the Code almost certainly did not intend to affect subrogation rights by this provision, and it should not be so read.[9]

Great controversy has developed in recent years concerning the subrogation rights of banks that issue standby letters of credit. Such a letter is payable upon the creditor's draft or demand for payment and certification that there has been a default by the debtor;[10] it is thus distinguishable from an unconditional letter of credit, which is payable on demand without regard to whether the debtor has defaulted. Obviously a standby letter of credit is similar in practical terms to a guaranty or suretyship agreement, and some courts have held on this basis that the issuing bank is entitled to subrogation.[11] On the other hand, the letter is technically a direct and primary obligation of the bank which matures when certain objective conditions are met. Under this view, the bank cannot have subrogation because that doctrine applies only when the subrogee pays the debt of another, not its own debt.[12] The cases are divided on the point, but the majority deny subrogation.

---

9. In Best Fertilizers of Arizona, Inc. v. Burns, 116 Ariz. 492, 570 P.2d 179 (1977), subrogation was denied where the mortgagor-maker paid the holder of the note and took an assignment of it after an assuming grantee had defaulted. The court held that under the UCC all liability on the note was discharged when the maker reacquired the note and therefore the mortgage was released. See § 5.9 for a summary of the case and authors' view that it was decided erroneously.

10. See J. White & R. Summers, Uniform Commercial Code § 19–1, at 809 (3d ed. 1988).

11. In re Valley Vue Joint Venture, 123 B.R. 199 (Bkrtcy.Va.1991); In re Air One, Inc., 80 B.R. 145 (Bkrtcy.Mo.1987); National Service Lines, Inc., 80 B.R. 144 (Bkrtcy.Mo.1987); In re Sensor Systems, Inc., 79 B.R. 623 (Bkrtcy.Pa.1987); In re Minnesota Kicks, Inc., 48 B.R. 93 (Bkrtcy.Minn.1985); In re Glade Springs, Inc., 47 B.R. 780 (Bkrtcy.Tenn.1985).

12. In re Carley Capital Group, 119 B.R. 646 (D.Wis.1990); In re Agrownautics, Inc., 125 B.R. 350 (Bkrtcy.Conn.1991); Berliner Handels–Und Frankfurter Bank v. East Texas Steel Facilities, Inc., 117 B.R. 235 (Bkrtcy.Tex.1990); In re St. Clair Supply Co., Inc., 100 B.R. 263 (Bkrtcy.Pa.1989); Bank of America v. Kaiser Steel Corp., 89 B.R. 150 (Bkrtcy.Colo.1988); In re Munzenrieder Corp., 58 B.R. 228 (Bkrtcy.Fla.1986); Merchants Bank v. Economic Enterprises, Inc., 44 B.R. 230 (Bkrtcy.Conn.1984). See U.C.C. § 5–103 official comment 3 ("The issuer is not a guarantor of the performance of these underlying transactions"); Avidon, Subrogation in the Letter of Credit Context, 56 Brooklyn L.Rev. 129, 136 (1990). Even under this view, the bank may have subrogation if the parties have agreed in advance to that effect; see The Wichita Eagle and Beacon Pub. Co. v. Pacific Nat. Bank, 493 F.2d 1285 (9th Cir. 1974).

§ 10.3 Payment to Protect an Interest—Contribution

Another instance in which the right of subrogation is not questioned is where a person, although not personally bound to pay, is compelled to do so in order to protect his or her own interest.[1] This right may apply to a variety of interests in property subject to a mortgage.[2] Following are some examples:

1. A junior mortgagee may pay off a prior mortgage and be subrogated to all rights under it against the mortgagor.[3]

2. A wife who has joined in the mortgage, thus subjecting her dower interest to it, may pay off the entire mortgage but keep the mortgage alive through subrogation as against the other owners who have been benefitted by her payment.[4]

3. A remainder holder may pay off the mortgage, where both the life interest and remainder were mortgaged, and be subrogated as against the life tenant.[5]

4. A creditor of the mortgagor who has levied an attachment or execution on the redemption interest may pay off the debt and have subrogation.

5. A cotenant of the mortgaged property whose cotenancy is subject to the mortgage is entitled to pay and be subrogated for the purpose of obtaining contribution from the other cotenant.[6]

§ 10.3

1. Martynes & Associates v. Devonshire Square Apartments, 680 P.2d 246 (Colo.App.1984); Harrington v. Harrington, 427 A.2d 1314, 1316, n. 3 (R.I.1981); Cagle, Inc. v. Sammons, 198 Neb. 595, 254 N.W.2d 398 (1977); Cobb v. Osman, 83 Nev. 415, 433 P.2d 259 (1967). See cases cited § 10.2 note 4, supra.

2. See Hope, Officiousness, 15 Corn. L.Q. 25, 205, 239 (1930), for a survey of such interests. See also 93 A.L.R. 89 (1934) for a collection of authorities on the right to compel an assignment by one who has an interest to protect and pays.

In In re Keil's Estate, 51 Del. (1 Storey) 351, 145 A.2d 563, 76 A.L.R.2d 996 (1958), reargument denied 51 Del. (1 Storey) 351, 146 A.2d 398 (1958), discussed in 58 Mich. L.Rev. 137, 1959, 73 Harv.L.Rev. 425, the surviving mortgagor of entireties property given to secure a joint debt, the proceeds of which were used to improve the property, was held entitled to contribution against the estate of the deceased tenant.

See also Dolan v. Borregard, 466 So.2d 11 (Fla.App.1985) (senior mortgagee may pay off *junior* lien, in order to make the senior mortgage more marketable, and will be subrogated.)

3. In re Forester, 529 F.2d 310 (9th Cir.1976); C.T.W. Co. v. Rivergrove Apartments, Inc., 582 So.2d 18 (Fla.App.1991) (payment made by corporation formed by junior mortgagees); Rock River Lumber v. Universal Mortgage Corp. of Wisconsin, 82 Wis.2d 235, 262 N.W.2d 114 (1978). But see Frago v. Sage, 737 S.W.2d 482 (Mo.App. 1987), refusing to grant subrogation rights to a junior mortgagee who foreclosed his own mortgage, taking title, and then paid off the senior mortgage; the opinion seems erroneous in characterizing the payor as a "volunteer."

4. Swaine v. Perine, 5 Johns. Ch. 482, 9 Am.Dec. 318 (N.Y.1821), Osborne, Cases Property Security, 2nd Ed., 546; cf. Gibson v. Crehore, 22 Mass. (5 Pick.) 146 (1827); Fitcher v. Griffiths, 216 Mass. 174, 103 N.E. 471 (1913); Harrington v. Harrington, note 1 supra.

5. See Mosely v. Marshall, 22 N.Y. 200 (1860), life tenant; Wunderle v. Ellis, 212 Pa. 618, 62 A. 106 (1905), tenant for years pays; cf. also Federal Land Bank v. Newsom, 175 Miss. 134, 166 So. 346 (1936), discussed, 50 Harv.L.Rev. 534 (1937).

6. Aiello v. Aiello, 268 Md. 513, 302 A.2d 189 (1973); Taylor v. Jones, 285 Ala. 353, 232 So.2d 601 (1970); A.F.C., Inc. v. Brockett, 257 Cal.App.2d 40, 64 Cal.Rptr. 771 (1967); Eloff v. Riesch, 14 Wis.2d 519, 111 N.W.2d 578 (1961) holds that right of

6. A lessee may pay off a mortgage debt to prevent foreclosure and may be subrogated to the rights of the holder of the lien.[7]

Since the payor in most the foregoing cases benefits to some extent by the payment, he or she does not have a claim for the entire amount paid. Instead, the payor will be entitled to recover a ratable contribution from the other parties proportional to their shares of the value of the interest in the property from which the mortgage has been removed.[8] The evaluation of the interest is not always easy, but the right to contribution is well-recognized.[9]

The listing above surely does not exhaust the possibilities for subrogation of a party who pays a mortgage debt to protect an interest. For example, in one recent case[10] a bonding company had issued construction bonds on projects being built by a real estate developer. When the projects ran into financial difficulty, the bonding company paid off an existing mortgage on the properties, thereby hoping to stave off the foreclosure and failure of the projects, which would have triggered liability on the bonds. The bonding company in fact took a formal assignment of the mortgage it paid, but there seems little doubt that principles of subrogation would have led to the same result even without the assignment. While the bonding company did not have a legal interest in the real estate, it plainly had a financial and business interest to protect in paying the mortgage.

In another case, a lessee obtained a mortgage loan, and persuaded the lessor to "subordinate" his fee interest by joining in the execution

---

subrogation exists even where joint tenants are husband and wife. In Walters v. Walters, 1 Wash.App. 849, 466 P.2d 174 (1970), subrogation was denied where one tenant in common was made primarily liable for obligations by divorce decree.

7. G.B. Seely's Son, Inc. v. Fulton–Edison, Inc., 52 A.D.2d 575, 382 N.Y.S.2d 516 (1976); Dominion Financial Corp. v. 275 Washington St. Corp., 64 Misc.2d 1044, 316 N.Y.S.2d 803 (1970).

8. "What rule should then govern the parties in adjusting the common burdens resting upon the property, in different parts of which they have respectively acquired an interest? We think the parties should contribute to the payment of the burden in proportion to the value of the property in which they are respectively interested." Tarbell v. Durant, 61 Vt. 516, 519, 17 A. 44, 45 (1889). See Carpenter v. Koons, 20 Pa. 222 (1852). Cf. McLaughlin v. Estate of Curtis, 27 Wis. 644 (1871).

9. E.g., the evaluation of a dower interest. See Swaine v. Perine, supra note 4. A similar question arises between a life tenant and remainderman. "A tenant for life is bound to keep down the current interest, * * * but not to pay any part of the principal. Now if, for example, there is a tenant for life, and a remainderman in fee of an estate, subject to a mortgage which is due and must be paid at once to save foreclosure, and the remainderman, to save the estate, pays the mortgage, he is not obliged to take the share of the tenant for life in annual installments of interest to continue as long as he shall live. He is entitled, as equitable assignee of the mortgagee, to immediate payment; and the sum which he thus has a right to claim is whatever the present worth of an annuity equal to the amount of the annual interest would be, computed for the number of years which the tenant will live." 2 Washburn, Real Prop., 6th Ed., § 1142. See also Todd's Executor v. First National Bank, 173 Ky. 60, 67, 190 S.W. 468 (1917); Damm v. Damm, 109 Mich. 619, 67 N.W. 984, 63 Am.St.Rep. 601 (1896); Tindall v. Peterson, 71 Neb. 160, 98 N.W. 688, 99 N.W. 659, 8 Ann.Cas. 721 (1904); Moore v. Simonson, 27 Or. 117, 39 P. 1105 (1895); Wilder's Executrix v. Wilder, 75 Vt. 178, 53 A. 1072 (1903); 3 Pomeroy, Eq.Jur., 4th Ed., § 1223. Cf. Leach v. Hall, 95 Iowa 611, 619, 64 N.W. 790 (1895).

10. Heller Financial v. Insurance Co. of N. America, 410 Mass. 400, 573 N.E.2d 8 (1991).

of the mortgage. When the lessee subsequently defaulted on the loan, the lessor paid it off and was held subrogated to the lender's rights in the mortgage and note, as against parties who had guaranteed the loan. While the lessor had no personal liability on the loan, his payment was obviously necessary to protect his fee title from loss by foreclosure.[11]

§ 10.4 The Volunteer Rule

Courts repeatedly state that a volunteer is not entitled to subrogation.[1] A person who is obligated as a surety, or who pays to protect his or her own interest, is not a volunteer.[2] Even a moral obligation has been considered sufficiently compelling to entitle the payor to subrogation,[3] but one who pays with no obligation but merely to preserve goodwill will be held to be a volunteer.[4] Where the payment was made pursuant to an agreement or understanding with the debtor or creditor, the court may deny subrogation on the ground that the payor was a volunteer unless the particular agreement is one which falls within the limits of "conventional" subrogation as recognized in that jurisdiction.[5] It is therefore necessary to determine just which agreements will bring about subrogation. For example, it is sometimes held that the person paying the debt must have believed that he or she would receive the prior security.[6]

---

11. Brown v. Bellamy, 170 A.D.2d 876, 566 N.Y.S.2d 703 (1991).

§ 10.4

1. Cox v. Wooten Brothers Farms, Inc., 271 Ark. 735, 610 S.W.2d 278 (1981); Lawyers Title Insurance Corp. v. Edmar Construction Co., 294 A.2d 865 (D.C.App.1972); Southwest Title & Trust Co. v. Norman Lumber Co., 441 P.2d 430 (Okl.1968); Zapata v. Torres, 464 S.W.2d 926 (Tex.Civ.App. 1971).

2. Cagle, Inc. v. Sammons, 198 Neb. 595, 254 N.W.2d 398 (1977); Cobb v. Osman, 83 Nev. 415, 433 P.2d 259 (1967); First National City Bank v. United States, 537 F.2d 426 (Ct.Cl.1976); Indemnity Insurance Co. v. Lane Contracting Corp., 227 F.Supp. 143 (D.Neb.1964). A payor whose payment was induced by fraud, or whose security was dissipated by fraud, is not a volunteer; see Rees v. Craighead Investment Co., 251 Ark. 336, 472 S.W.2d 92 (1971); Bunge Corp. v. St. Louis Terminal Field Warehouse Co., 295 F.Supp. 1231 (N.D.Miss.1969). Cf. Photomagic Industries, Inc. v. Broward Bank, 526 So.2d 136 (Fla.App.1988) (guarantor not entitled to subrogation, where the debt paid by guarantor was otherwise more than adequately secured by other property, so that the payment was as a mere volunteer); Matter of Munzenrieder Corp., 58 B.R. 228 (Bkrtcy. Fla.1986) (bank issuing letter of credit for corporation's debt may not claim subrogation, where the letter of credit was procured by a party who was not the debtor corporation and had no formal relationship with it).

3. Springham v. Kordek, 55 Md.App. 449, 462 A.2d 567 (1983); Commercial Standard Insurance Co. v. American Employers Insurance Co., 209 F.2d 60 (6th Cir.1954).

4. Lawyers Title Insurance Corp. v. Edmar Construction Co., 294 A.2d 865 (D.C.App.1972).

5. "[T]he facts or circumstances from which the agreement will be implied vary in the different courts, some requiring evidence from which an actual understanding between the parties may be inferred, while others hold that payment under such circumstances as show that the lender 'supposed' or 'intended' to get security of the same dignity as that released by his payment is sufficient; and some go as far as holding that such intention may be inferred from the mere fact that the money was advanced for the purpose of paying off another lien." Martin v. Hickenlooper, 90 Utah 150, 179, 59 P.2d 1139, 1152, 107 A.L.R. 762 (1936), rehearing denied 90 Utah 185, 61 P.2d 307 (1936).

6. Metropolitan Life Insurance Co. v. First Security Bank, 94 Idaho 489, 491 P.2d 1261 (1971), rehearing denied 94 Idaho 527, 492 P.2d 1400 (1972); Southwest Title & Trust Co. v. Norman Lumber Co., 441 P.2d 430 (Okl.1968).

The limits as well as the rationale of the volunteer rule are a matter of dispute. It has been asserted that whenever courts for any reason deny subrogation, they characterize the unsuccessful applicant as a volunteer.[7] Even when the rule is used with more discrimination it has sometimes been unclear whether subrogation was denied because the court found that the plaintiff did not intend any legal consequences to flow from the act (that is, a gift was intended), or that the intervention was unsolicited and therefore officious.[8] A critical examination of the reasons [9] offered for using the rule to deny subrogation on payment of a creditor by a third person has revealed them to be so lacking in force as to make reasonable the suggestion that, in order for such a payment to be officious, it must be unnecessary and confer no benefit.[10] Because of the variety and unpredictability of its application,[11] the voluntary payment test is of little value. Except in cases in which the payor clearly intended a gift, it should be discarded.

§ 10.5 Loans to Pay the Mortgage

The problem of the volunteer rule and subrogation in mortgage law has occurred most frequently in the case of lenders whose money is used to pay off a mortgage or other encumbrance. Where the payor already holds a lien junior to that of the creditor being paid off, the payment obviously protects the payor's own position and the courts have no difficulty giving subrogation.[1] In other cases, whether subroga-

---

7. Pomeroy, Equity Juris., 4th ed., § 2348n.

"A good deal of the confusion concerning the volunteer rule has arisen because courts have carelessly termed the payor a volunteer in cases involving a situation where payment would ordinarily be considered not voluntary but subrogation is denied because of a superior intervening equity. It is submitted that these cases have misapplied the term and must be sharply distinguished." 32 Minn.L.Rev. 183, 185 (1948).

8. See Frago v. Sage, 737 S.W.2d 482 (Mo.App.1987); 31 Mich.L.Rev. 826, 830 (1933).

9. The three basic reasons for not permitting subrogation on the ground that the person asking it is a volunteer are: "(1) he is able to elect whether he is to pay or not, and knowing the facts he should protect himself by contract, (2) a debt paid without any agreement to keep it alive is extinguished, and (3) one cannot become a creditor of another against the other's will." 32 Minn.L.Rev. 183 (1948), citing Hope, Officiousness, 15 Corn.L.Q. 25 (1929), and note 24 Va.L.Rev. 771, 776 (1938).

10. Hope, Officiousness, 15 Cornell L.Q. 25, 205 (1929). A comment on this as a criterion stated, "Indeed, there would seem to be no great difference in principle in the case where a person theretofore unconnected with a transaction purchases a debt, which he can obviously do against the express will of the debtor, and where he pays the debt absent any intention to make a gift." 24 Va.L.Rev. 771, 776 (1938).

11. "All courts subscribe to the rule that subrogation will not be permitted a mere 'volunteer'. But there is no general agreement as to the personification of the word. A minority of courts is prone to call everyone a volunteer who was not in the position of a surety or who did not have some previous interest to protect in the subject matter in question. At the other extreme, the liberal view leads to the result that the only volunteer would be one who, without invitation from any other party and purely as a philanthropist, relieved another from an obligation." Note, 48 Yale L.J. 683, 686 (1939). See Photomagic Industries, Inc. v. Broward Bank, 526 So.2d 136 (Fla.App.1988), characterizing even a guarantor of the debt as a volunteer.

§ 10.5

1. First Vermont Bank v. Kalomiris, 138 Vt. 481, 418 A.2d 43 (1980), noted 7 Vt.L.Rev. 71, 82 (1982).

tion will be given depends both on the terms of the arrangement and the attitude of the particular court toward subrogation.[2] Subrogation of the lender is based on the general principle that one who advances money upon a justifiable expectation of receiving security is entitled to the security.[3] When the question is one of the lender's rights as against the parties to the mortgage, the outcome depends on whether the lender relied only on the general credit of the mortgagor,[4] or whether the loan was made on the understanding that the lender was to have the benefit of the existing mortgage or a mortgage having at least equal rank with that which was paid.[5] Where the lender takes a new mortgage, the latter intent is obvious.

Even if the lender pays off a prior encumbrance and receives a void or defective mortgage, it will be subrogated to the discharged encumbrance.[6] Subrogation has also been invoked where the loan that pays off the old mortgage is on the faith of a promise of a new mortgage

---

2. See Burgoon v. Lavezzo, 68 App.D.C. 20, 92 F.2d 726, 113 A.L.R. 944 (1937); Martin v. Hickenlooper, 90 Utah 150, 59 P.2d 1139, 107 A.L.R. 762 (1936), rehearing denied 90 Utah 185, 61 P.2d 307 (1936); Means v. United Fidelity Life Insurance Co., 550 S.W.2d 302 (Tex.Civ.App.1977), error refused n.r.e. Some cases require that the payoff be made at the debtor's instance; see Collateral Investment Co. v. Pilgrim, 421 So.2d 1274 (Ala.Civ.App.1982).

3. Leonard v. Brazosport Bank, 628 S.W.2d 216 (Tex.App.1982), error refused n.r.e.; Rock River Lumber Corp. v. Universal Mortgage Corp. of Wisconsin, 82 Wis.2d 235, 262 N.W.2d 114 (1978).

4. Southwest Title & Trust Co. v. Norman Lumber Co., 441 P.2d 430 (Okl.1968); Citizens State Bank v. Pittsburg County Broadcasting Co., 271 P.2d 725 (Okl.1954), commented on by Updike, Mortgages, in 1954 Annual Survey of American Law, 30 N.Y.U.L.Rev. 805, 809 (1955), followed this test in a chattel mortgage case.

5. Hughes Co. v. Callahan, 181 Ark. 733, 27 S.W.2d 509 (1930); G.R.W. Engineers, Inc. v. Elam, 557 So.2d 725 (La.App. 1990), writ denied 563 So.2d 884 (La.1990); Home Owners' Loan Corp. v. Collins, 120 N.J.Eq. 266, 184 A. 621 (1936); Federal Union Life Insurance Co. v. Deitsch, 127 Ohio St. 505, 189 N.E. 440 (1933); Martin v. Hickenlooper, 90 Utah 150, 59 P.2d 1139, 107 A.L.R. 762 (1936), rehearing denied 90 Utah 185, 61 P.2d 307 (1936); discussed in notes, 36 Mich.L.Rev. 151 (1937); 6 Fordham L.Rev. 138 (1937); 107 A.L.R. 785 (1937); Federal Land Bank of Baltimore v. Joynes, 179 Va. 394, 18 S.E.2d 917 (1942); Home Owners' Loan Corp. v. Dougherty, 226 Wis. 8, 275 N.W. 363 (1937). Cf. Boley v. Daniel, 72 Fla. 121, 72 So. 644, L.R.A.1917A, 734 (1916), denying recovery because lender did not stipulate for the original mortgage, only a "first lien." Where a lender advanced money to pay a valid encumbrance on a homestead, "under circumstances from which an understanding is to be implied that at least part of the advancement made is to be secured by a first lien on the land encumbered," he was subrogated to rights of prior encumbrancer which were superior to homestead rights and was allowed to foreclose the homestead. Means v. United Fidelity Life Insurance Co., 550 S.W.2d 302, 309 (Tex.Civ.App.1977).

In Fleetwood v. Med Center Bank, 786 S.W.2d 550 (Tex.App.1990), a tenant held both a mortgage and a lease in the same real estate project. The tenant had subordinated the lease to the mortgage so that it could preserve the lease in the event it needed to foreclose the mortgage. The owner of the real estate then obtained a new mortgage loan, proceeds from which were used to pay off the tenant's mortgage. The new lender argued that it was subrogated to that mortgage, and thus that it had priority over the lease. The court rejected the argument, holding that subrogation would unfairly prejudice the tenant, whose lease position was originally subordinate to a mortgage over which the tenant had full control.

6. Union Savings Bank of Patchogue v. Dudine, 40 Misc.2d 155, 242 N.Y.S.2d 692 (1963); Means v. United Fidelity Life Insurance Co., note 4 supra.

which the owner subsequently refuses to execute,[7] or on an oral agreement to convey title of the land to the lender.[8] Going beyond these are cases in which the money is loaned and used for the express purpose of paying off an encumbrance but the expectation of security does not relate to the particular property freed from the prior lien.[9] Finally, the most liberal cases allow subrogation simply where money is loaned and used for paying off an encumbrance.[10]

While lenders who have advanced money to pay the claims of laborers and suppliers on construction projects have sometimes been subrogated to their claims,[11] other cases have denied them subrogation rights on the ground that the mechanics lien statutes were not intended to protect them.[12]

§ 10.6 Loans to Pay the Mortgage—Subrogation Against Intervening Interests

A more difficult question is whether the lender who has loaned money to pay off an encumbrance will be subrogated to the encumbrance when there are intervening junior liens on the property. Since the basis for subrogation in this context is the lender's justified expectation of receiving security, most of the cases hold that actual knowledge of the intervening lien will bar subrogation.[1] Where there is construc-

---

7. Smith v. Sprague, 244 Mich. 577, 222 N.W. 207 (1928); Baker v. Baker, 2 S.D. 261, 49 N.W. 1064, 39 Am.St.Rep. 776 (1891); see 21 Cal.L.Rev. 471 (1921); 31 Mich.L.Rev. 826, 835 (1933).

8. Dobbs v. Bowling, 339 So.2d 985 (Miss.1976).

9. In Elmora & West End Building & Loan Association v. Dancy, 108 N.J.Eq. 542, 155 A. 796 (1931), commented on in 45 Harv.L.Rev. 390 (1931), M loaned the widow of his mortgagor, A, money, part of which was used to pay off the mortgage held by him, taking as security a mortgage on her dower interest in the property. M marked the mortgage "paid" and sent it to his solicitor for cancellation but it was never cancelled of record. Before the new debt was paid the widow died, thus extinguishing the security. M sued to foreclose on his original mortgage, and the land was sold. A's heirs petitioned to open the decree and set aside the sale. M was held entitled to foreclose the original mortgage to the extent that the money borrowed from him was applied thereto.

10. Turney v. Roberts, 255 Ark. 503, 501 S.W.2d 601 (1973); Chrisman v. Daniel, 134 Neb. 326, 278 N.W. 565 (1938); see Martin v. Hickenlooper, 90 Utah 150, 170, 178, 59 P.2d 1139, 1148, 1152, 107 A.L.R. 762 (1936), rehearing denied 90 Utah 185, 61 P.2d 307 (1936); 36 Mich.L.Rev. 151, 152 (1937).

11. A contractor who paid materials suppliers and laborers was subrogated to their claims under the payment bond in Cagle, Inc. v. Sammons, 198 Neb. 595, 254 N.W.2d 398 (1977).

12. "The object of the Legislature was to secure to a very meritorious but helpless class of persons the payment of the wages of their toil, and to that end to give them, personally, a paramount lien on the assets of the employer. It did not contemplate giving to creditors from whom the company might borrow money on its own credit with which to pay its workmen, such a lien or the assets for their reimbursement." Board of Educ. of City of Bayonne v. Kolman, 111 N.J.Super. 585, 270 A.2d 64 (1970) citing In re North River Construction Co., 38 N.J.Eq. 433, 437–438 (Ch. 1884), affirmed 40 N.J.Eq. 340 (E & A 1885).

§ 10.6

1. See Herberman v. Bergstrom, 168 Ariz. 587, 816 P.2d 244 (App.1991) (priority over intervening homestead declaration denied, where paying lender had actual knowledge of homestead claim); Louisiana Nat. Bank v. Belello, 577 So.2d 1099 (La. App.1991); Restatement, Second, Restitution § 31 comment f & Illustration 10 (Tent.Draft No. 2, 1984); 70 A.L.R. 1396, 1414 (1931). This may be the basis for denial of subrogation in Plymouth Fertiliz-

§ 10.6 SUBROGATION AND CONTRIBUTION

tive notice, the courts are divided.[2] The better view is that constructive notice should be disregarded, since it is irrelevant to the question whether the lender actually expected to get priority of security in the property.[3]

Where the lender's ignorance is a result of its own negligence, many courts will consider that factor in balancing the equities between the lender and the parties holding intervening liens.[4] Some courts

er Co. v. Pitt–Greene Production Credit Association, 58 N.C.App. 207, 292 S.E.2d 732 (1982).

A minority view, which the present authors find quite appealing, holds that the payor may have subrogation even if the payment was made with *actual* knowledge of the intervening lien. See Klotz v. Klotz, 440 N.W.2d 406 (Iowa App.1989); Chicago Title Ins. Co. v. Lawrence Investments, Inc., 782 S.W.2d 332 (Tex.App.1989) (payor apparently had actual knowledge); Providence Institution for Savings v. Sims, 441 S.W.2d 516, 520 (Tex.1969): "We hold that under these circumstances neither actual nor constructive knowledge of the intervening lien will defeat the right of subrogation to which the debtor agreed in the later deed of trust."

Occasionally counsel will miss the subrogation argument entirely, and instead will treat the case as merely raising the issue whether the payor intended to pay off the senior mortgage or to purchase an assignment of it; see, e.g., First Security Bank v. Banberry Devel. Corp., 786 P.2d 1326 (Utah 1990).

2. Id.; Peterman Donnelly Engineers & Contractors Corp. v. First National Bank, 2 Ariz.App. 321, 408 P.2d 841 (1965); Castleman Construction Co. v. Pennington, 222 Tenn. 82, 432 S.W.2d 669 (1968). See Pipola v. Chicco, 274 F.2d 909 (2d Cir.1960), granting subrogation. Cases denying subrogation on the basis of constructive notice from the records include Pelican Homestead & Savings Ass'n v. Security First Nat. Bank, 532 So.2d 397 (La.App.1988), writ denied 533 So.2d 381 (La.1988) (based on Louisiana's public records doctrine); Landmark Bank v. Ciaravino, 752 S.W.2d 923 (Mo.App.1988); Cheswick v. Weaver, 280 S.W.2d 942 (Tex.Civ.App.1955).

3. Mutual Life Insurance Co. v. Grissett, 500 F.Supp. 159 (M.D.Ala.1980); Potter v. United States, 111 F.Supp. 585 (D.R.I.1953); Brooks v. RTC, 599 So.2d 1163 (Ala.1992); Davis v. Johnson, 241 Ga. 436, 246 S.E.2d 297 (1978); Boston Trade Bank v. Kuzon, 154 Misc.2d 217, 584 N.Y.S.2d 994 (Sup.Ct.1992) (unclear whether paying lender had notice of intervening liens); Rusher v. Bunker, 99 Or.App. 303, 782 P.2d 170 (1989); Pee Dee State Bank v. Prosser, 295 S.C. 229, 367 S.E.2d 708 (App. 1988). Cf. Collateral Investment Co. v. Pilgrim, 421 So.2d 1274 (Ala.Civ.App.1982) (subrogee may not take priority over mechanics liens, where it had constructive notice from work in progress); Blaylock v. Dollar Inns of America, Inc., 548 S.W.2d 924 (Tex.Civ.App.1977), modified 576 S.W.2d 794 (Tex.1978) (subrogee given priority over intervening mechanics lien). See Comment, 20 So.Tex.L.J. 326, 330–32 (1979). See 48 Yale L.J. 683, 688 (1939); 21 Col.L.Rev. 471, 472, (1921) n. 18. But cf. 31 Mich.L.Rev. 826, 834 (1933).

See also Han v. United States, 944 F.2d 526 (9th Cir.1991) (purchasers of real estate who paid off prior mortgage at closing were subrogated to its priority as against intervening federal tax lien of which they had constructive but not actual notice). Cf. Fidelity Nat. Title Ins. Co. v. Department of the Treasury, 907 F.2d 868 (9th Cir.1990) (purchaser at foreclosure sale has not "paid off" the mortgage being foreclosed, and is not subrogated to it as against an intervening federal tax lien that was omitted in the foreclosure).

See 21 Col.L.Rev. 471, (1921) "Constructive notice, which is intended to protect the rights of an equitable lienor, cannot be invoked to increase those rights by imputing to the new mortgagee a knowledge of facts and a consequent expectation which he did not in fact possess." Id. at 472 n. 18.

4. Negligence on the part of one seeking subrogation is of some importance when the right is wholly dependent on equitable principles; see Providence Institution for Savings v. Sims, 441 S.W.2d 516 (Tex.1969). Some courts hold that ordinary negligence by the subrogee may be taken into consideration in determining whether he or she is entitled to subrogation, but "[o]rdinary negligence alone will not be held as a complete bar to subrogation where in spite of such negligence the equities are still in favor of the subrogee;"

distinguish between negligence that is inexcusable and negligence that is only ordinary.[5] In connection with the negligence issue courts will consider whether the intervening lienors will be prejudiced by the subrogation.[6] A few courts have suggested that intervening lienors would be prejudiced simply because subrogation would prevent their being able to enforce their liens.[7] However, most cases have held that the junior lienors are not prejudiced unless they have changed their position in reliance on extinguishment of the debt.[8] Where the junior lienor occupies the same position as before the prior lien was paid and discharged, to deny subrogation and permit the lienor to advance would give it a windfall advantage at the expense of the justifiable expectation of the lender.[9] This would defeat the purpose of subrogation, which is

Castleman Construction Co. v. Pennington, 222 Tenn. 82, 432 S.W.2d 669, 677 (1968); Rusher v. Bunker, 99 Or.App. 303, 782 P.2d 170 (1989): "We *might* agree that a failure to search the record by a lender on record notice would be a significant negative factor in a comparison of equities. However, [the lender] here did have the record searched." Cf. Eastern Nat. Bank v. Glendale Fed. Sav. & Loan Ass'n, 508 So.2d 1323 (Fla.App.1987), granting subrogation to the lender despite the fact that its lack of knowledge may have been the result of its negligence in failing to examine title before making the loan.

5. Castleman Construction Co. v. Pennington, 222 Tenn. 82, 432 S.W.2d 669 (1968); Martin v. Hickenlooper, 90 Utah 150, 178, 59 P.2d 1139, 1152, 107 A.L.R. 762 (1936), rehearing denied 90 Utah 185, 61 P.2d 307 (1936): "[A]ccording to the modern view, indiligence in searching the record will not prevent equity from applying the doctrine unless it is culpable or unjustifiable negligence." See also Banta v. Vreeland, 15 N.J.Eq. 103, 82 Am.Dec. 269 (1862).

6. See Federal Land Bank v. Joynes, 179 Va. 394, 18 S.E.2d 917 (1942), "the negligence should be chiefly of significance when there are subsequently intervening rights involved which would be prejudiced if subrogation were allowed."

"[I]n a case where the court feels the negligence so culpable that the junior lienor should advance to the senior position in preference to the payer, it will refuse to imply an agreement for subrogation of the payer; but where no harm is done and the payer's negligence only 'ordinary,' the courts are prone to find an implied agreement. * * * That is, in a case involving no change of position by the junior lienor in reliance on the discharge of the original first lien, the courts will strain the concept of implied intent to the breaking point in order to prevent the junior lienor from claiming a windfall and advancing to the position of first encumbrancer, whereas their real reason for giving subrogation to the payer is that they feel he has superior equities on his side." Note, 36 Mich.L.Rev. 151, 153–154 (1937).

7. Landmark Bank v. Ciaravino, 752 S.W.2d 923 (Mo.App.1988); Carl H. Peterson Co. v. Zero Estates, 261 N.W.2d 346 (Minn.1977).

8. Rock River Lumber v. Universal Mortgage Corp. of Wisconsin, 82 Wis.2d 235, 262 N.W.2d 114 (1978); Credit Bureau Corp. v. Beckstead, 63 Wash.2d 183, 385 P.2d 864, 866 (1963): "The doctrine however will not be applied if it would work injustice to the rights of those having equal or superior equities; nor will it be enforced against a bona fide purchaser for value without notice or one who, in good faith, has changed his position in reliance upon the act which subsequently is claimed to have been a mistake."

9. Equity Savings & Loan Association v. Chicago Title Insurance Co., 190 N.J.Super. 340, 463 A.2d 398 (1983). Where intervening lienor remains with a lien prior to all claims except a mortgage given before he began work on the project, "Equity requires that appellee be afforded that security for which he obviously bargained." Peterman–Donnelly Engineers & Contractors Corp. v. First National Bank, 2 Ariz. App. 321, 408 P.2d 841, 846 (1965). "There is no reason for advancing [the junior lienor] to the position of a senior lienor, since all he ever contracted for was a junior encumbrance." 21 Col.L.Rev. 471, 472 (1921). "His advancement to first mortgagee on extinguishment of the prior lien is a purely fortuitous benefit, to which he

§ 10.6 SUBROGATION AND CONTRIBUTION

to prevent unjust enrichment and grant an equitable result between the parties.

In most modern transactions involving payment by a lender of a prior debt, the paying lender will obtain title insurance. Hence, quibbles over the lender's degree of negligence or notice really come down to a decision whether to cast the loss on the title insurance underwriter. Cases that impute constructive notice of the intervening lien to the paying lender, even though the title company missed the lien in its search of the records, have precisely this effect.[10] But while it is certainly true that title companies should bear the losses resulting from their negligent searches, it is hard to see why they should be compelled to pay merely to promote the priority of an intervening lienor who has suffered no loss and who has no reason to expect or claim such a promotion. Such decisions have the long-run effect of raising title insurance costs in order to give windfalls to a few lienholders.

The volunteer rule is not an obstacle to subrogation where the lender has paid the prior debt at the request of the mortgagor. If it has advanced money with the understanding, or under circumstances which would give rise to an understanding, that the loan would be secured by a first lien on the property, the lender is not a mere volunteer and should be subrogated to the prior liens that the advance was made to discharge.[11]

A special case of payment by a lender of a prior mortgage arises when the prior mortgage is held by the very lender who makes the payment. This is nothing more than a refinancing of the lender's original loan, and is usually accompanied by some modification of its terms, such as an extension of the term or a change in interest rate. From a procedural viewpoint, the lender may be ill-advised to cancel or satisfy the original mortgage and replace it with a new one; a simple amendment to the note would serve as well and would not raise the risk

---

has no equitable or legal right." Id. at n. 20.

10. One recent decision appeared to reject subrogation precisely because doing so would place the loss on the title company; see Landmark Bank v. Ciaravino, 752 S.W.2d 923 (Mo.App.1988): "The status of Chicago Title as the insurer of Landmark and its status as the ultimate beneficiary of a decree in favor of Landmark is relevant. It is strange equity indeed, which would protect Chicago Title from the results of its negligence at the expense of [the intervening lienor], which is totally innocent in the matter." The court gave the fact of lack of harm to the intervening lienor short shrift: "The only fact supporting equitable subrogation in this case is that possibly [the intervening lienor] may have sustained no diminution in the value of its security from the actions of Landmark. That fact, if true, is not alone sufficient to invoke the doctrine."

See also Universal Title Ins. Co. v. United States, 942 F.2d 1311 (8th Cir.1991): "* * * it is difficult to think of a situation in which a title insurance company could not claim unjust enrichment as to someone who might inadvertently benefit by their negligence. Either they insure or they don't. It is not the province of the court to relieve a title insurance company of its contractual obligation."

11. Pee Dee State Bank v. Prosser, 295 S.C. 229, 367 S.E.2d 708 (App.1988); Blaylock v. Dollar Inns of America, Inc., 548 S.W.2d 924 (Tex.Civ.App.1977). See 48 Yale L.J. 683, 686; 1933, 31 Mich.L.Rev. 826, 830 (1939). The same is true of one who pays as part of the purchase price. Burgoon v. Lavezzo, 92 F.2d 726, 113 A.L.R. 944 (D.C.Cir.1937).

of a total loss of priority to intervening liens. If the lender does employ a new note and mortgage, they should state plainly that they are mere replacements or modifications of the original documents. Where this is the intent, and especially if the intent is stated in the instruments, the priority of the original mortgage will be retained except to the extent that the modification of terms causes harm to junior interests.[12]

Occasionally the counsel and judges in a case will simply miss the "replacement mortgage" argument outlined above, and will instead treat the matter as one of subrogation. Sometimes this theory works,[13] but unfortunately the "fit" is poor. The court may conclude that one cannot be subrogated to his or her own prior mortgage, that the lender was negligent in not discovering the intervening lien of record, or that the payment was as a "volunteer" because the lender had no interest to protect in discharging its prior debt or lien. Hence the lender may entirely lose priority to intervening liens, an absurd and lamentable result.[14] This situation is one in which the subrogation theory is neither necessary nor helpful, and courts should instead readily impute the intention to make the later mortgage a replacement for the earlier one, with the same priority except as noted above.

§ 10.7 Payments by Grantees—Subrogation Against Intervening Interests

Where a grantee of the mortgagor assumes the payment of a prior mortgage in actual ignorance of the existence of a later encumbrance, even though it might be of record, the question arises as to whether, on paying the earlier lien, the grantee is entitled to be subrogated to it as against the later lienors.[1] A strong line of cases permits subrogation in such a case.[2] There are, however, a considerable number of authorities that refuse it.[3]

Those denying subrogation do so on several grounds. One is that the assuming grantee has become primarily liable for the debt and the

---

12. See supra § 9.4.

13. See Boston Trade Bank v. Kuzon, 154 Misc.2d 217, 584 N.Y.S.2d 994 (1992); Davis v. Johnson, 241 Ga. 436, 246 S.E.2d 297 (1978).

14. See Carl H. Peterson Co. v. Zero Estates, 261 N.W.2d 346 (Minn.1977); Dedes v. Strickland, 414 S.E.2d 134 (S.C.1992)

§ 10.7

1. See 113 A.L.R. 958 (1925); 87 U.Pa. L.Rev. 1012 (1939); 48 Yale L.J. 683 (1939). The same question is involved if the grantee, rather than assuming the senior debt, simply discharges it as part of the purchase transaction, provided that the grantee is unaware of the existence of intervening liens. See Burgoon v. Lavezzo, 92 F.2d 726 (D.C.Cir.1937).

2. E.g., Johnson v. Tootle, 14 Utah 482, 47 P. 1033 (1897); Capitol National Bank v. Holmes, 43 Colo. 154, 95 P. 314, 16 L.R.A.,N.S., 470, 127 Am.St.Rep. 108 (1908); Young v. Morgan, 89 Ill. 199 (1878); Smith v. Dinsmoor, 119 Ill. 656, 4 N.E. 648 (1887), recorded junior incumbrance; Federal Land Bank v. Smith, 129 Md. 233, 151 A. 420 (1930); Dixon v. Morgan, 154 Tenn. 389, 285 S.W. 558 (1926).

Compare the discussion of merger in §§ 6.15, 6.17, supra.

3. Citizens' Mercantile Co. v. Easom, 158 Ga. 604, 123 S.E. 883, 37 A.L.R. 378 (1924) noted in 38 Harv.L.Rev. 266 (1924); Goodyear v. Goodyear, 72 Iowa 329, 33 N.W. 142 (1887); Kuhn v. National Bank, 74 Kan. 456, 87 P. 551, 118 Am.St.Rep. 332 (1906); Smith v. Feltner, 259 Ky. 833, 83 S.W.2d 506 (1935).

general rule applies that one paying his or her own debt is not entitled to subrogation. Coupled with this is the idea that by assuming the mortgagor's debt, the grantee must be regarded as having stepped into the grantor's shoes and therefore the payment has the same effect as if it had been made by the grantor before parting with the property.[4] Where the grantee assumes any junior mortgages as well as a senior mortgage, as is the case when the assumption is of "all" encumbrances, no objection can be taken to this reasoning and the courts uniformly deny subrogation in such cases.[5] Since the grantee has a duty to pay the junior liens, he or she cannot complain if payment and discharge of the earlier mortgage advances them in priority. If only the first mortgage is assumed and the grantee has actual knowledge of the junior liens at the time of assumption, it is arguable that the same result is justified,[6] although there are authorities to the contrary.[7] In such a case, the grantee pays under no mistake, and it is at least arguably reasonable to elevate the junior lien, just as would have occurred if the original mortgagor had made the payment.

The same is not true when the grantee assumes only the first mortgage, and pays and discharges it without knowledge of any junior lien. In such a case the grantee owes a duty to the mortgagor to pay off the first mortgage, but has entered into no agreement with the second mortgagee to discharge it for the latter's benefit. The only possible claim to heightened priority that the second lienor may urge is through the duty of the original mortgagor to pay off the prior mortgage for the second lienor's benefit. But between the mortgagor and the grantee, the mortgagor has a duty to pay off the second mortgage entirely, not to let it rise to a position of priority on the land now owned by the grantee. This being so, it would seem to follow that the mortgagor could not claim that the grantee owed any duty to the mortgagor, which could accrue derivatively to a second mortgagee, to

---

4. Kuhn v. National Bank, 74 Kan. 456, 87 P. 551, 118 Am.St.Rep. 332 (1906); Goodyear v. Goodyear, 72 Iowa 329, 33 N.W. 142 (1887); Poole v. Kelsey, 95 Ill. App. 233 (1900). See also a similar line of reasoning in 87 U. of Pa.L.Rev. 1012 (1939).

5. E.g., Stastny v. Pease, 124 Iowa 587, 100 N.W. 482 (1904); Martin v. C. Aultman & Co., 80 Wis. 150, 49 N.W. 749 (1891); Morris v. Twichell, 63 N.D. 747, 249 N.W. 905 (1933), commented on in 19 Iowa L.Rev. 629 (1934), denied subrogation to a purchaser who assumed the first mortgage with knowledge of the second mortgage and who, when he paid the first mortgage, asked for and thought he had received an assignment instead of the cancellation which actually was executed. Although the purchaser did not expressly assume payment of the second mortgage the court stressed the fact that its amount had been deducted from the purchase price. The court said, "The rule is that when payment has been made by one primarily liable, it operates as an absolute satisfaction. * * * Neither by assignment nor by subrogation can he keep the mortgage alive as against other liens on the land."

6. In some of the cases in which the courts stress the grantee's assumption as the basis of the decision, the grantee had actual notice of the intervening liens. E.g., Lackawanna Trust & Safe Deposit Co. v. Gomeringer, 236 Pa. 179, 84 A. 757 (1912); De Roberts v. Stiles, 24 Wash. 611, 64 P. 795 (1901); Willson v. Burton, 52 Vt. 394 (1880); Cady v. Barnes, 208 Fed. 361 (D.C.Ohio 1913), reversed 232 Fed. 318 (1913). Cf. Kitchell v. Mudgett, 37 Mich. 81 (1877).

7. Joyce v. Dauntz, 55 Ohio St. 538, 45 N.E. 900 (1896); see Young v. Morgan, 89 Ill. 199, 202 (1878); cf. Stantons v. Thompson, 49 N.H. 272 (1870). See § 10.2, supra.

pay off the first mortgage in order that the second mortgage might rise to a preferred position on the land. To permit the second mortgage to rise to priority under these circumstances would give its holder an unwarranted enrichment at the expense of the grantee.[8]

Cases sometimes arise in which the grantee had no actual knowledge of the intervening liens, but either failed to search the records or searched them negligently under circumstances in which a careful search would have disclosed the liens in question. By analogy to the discussion of loans to pay mortgages in the preceding section, negligence [9] or constructive notice [10] should be irrelevant. Here, as there, the issue is only whether the payor expected that the payment would free the property;[11] if this was the grantee's understanding, subrogation should be available. A contrary result would give the intervening lienors an unjustified and unearned windfall, advancing their priority for no good reason. Clearly this should be done only when the payor actually knew of them and failed to protect against them by obtaining an appropriate assignment of the senior debt.

The principles discussed above with respect to assuming grantees apply equally, and perhaps even more readily, to grantees who merely take subject to the senior mortgage.[12] On these facts it cannot even be

8. Tibbetts v. Terrill, 26 Colo.App. 64, 140 P. 936 (1914), commented on in 15 Col.L.Rev. 171 (1915), in which an assuming grantee was subrogated to the lien of the first mortgage which he paid, although he had actual knowledge of the recordation of a lis pendens claim against the property at the time he bought it but bona fide, after legal advice, thought the claim invalid. The court made the point that to allow subrogation would work no hardship to the junior claimant. His security interest in the property when he acquired it was subject to this superior lien, and he should not reap the benefit of the grantee's innocent mistake.

9. Lamoille County Savings Bank & Trust Co. v. Belden, 90 Vt. 535, 98 A. 1002 (1916); see Burgoon v. Lavezzo, 68 App. D.C. 20, 23, 92 F.2d 726, 729, 113 A.L.R. 944 (1937).

10. Ragan v. Standard Scale Co., 128 Ga. 544, 58 S.E. 31 (1907); Goodyear v. Goodyear, 72 Iowa 329, 33 N.W. 142 (1887); Kitchell v. Mudgett, 37 Mich. 81 (1877); see Stastny v. Pease, 124 Iowa 587, 591, 592, 100 N.W. 482, 483, 484 (1904). In Duke v. Kilpatrick, 231 Ala. 51, 163 So. 640 (1935), criticized in note, 14 N.Car.L.Rev. 295 (1936), subrogation for the purpose of obtaining contribution from his co-owner was denied to an assuming grantee who paid off the entire first mortgage on property which he had bought honestly thinking that he was getting full title when actually he was obtaining only a one-half interest in it. The fact of joint ownership of his grantor with another was on record and also appeared in the deed he received. See also Hieber v. Florida Nat. Bank, 522 So.2d 878 (Fla.App.1988), refusing subrogation because the grantee had constructive notice from the recordation of the second mortgage.

Other courts allowing subrogation have expressly considered constructive notice as an obstacle and rejected it. See In re Hubbard, 89 B.R. 920 (Bkrtcy.Ala.1988); Prestridge v. Lazar, 132 Miss. 168, 177, 95 So. 837, 838 (1923); Burgoon v. Lavezzo, 68 App.D.C. 20, 24, 92 F.2d 726, 730, 113 A.L.R. 944 (1937). See also Smith v. Dinsmoor, 119 Ill. 656, 4 N.E. 648 (1887); Neff v. Elder, 84 Ark. 277, 105 S.W. 260, 120 Am.St.Rep. 67 (1907). Compare Belcher v. Belcher, 161 Or. 341, 87 P.2d 762 (1939), noted 24 Minn.L.Rev. 121 (1939).

11. See § 10.6, supra.

12. Darrough v. Herbert Kraft Co. Bank, 125 Cal. 272, 57 P. 983 (1899) (recorded junior encumbrance); Barnes v. Mott, 64 N.Y. 397, 21 Am.R. 625 (1876) (recorded junior encumbrance); Ryer v. Gass, 130 Mass. 227 (1881); Hudson v. Dismukes, 77 Va. 242 (1883); see Burgoon v. Lavezzo, 68 App.D.C. 20, 23, 24, 92 F.2d 726, 729, 730, 113 A.L.R. 944 (1937). See also 14 N.Car.L.Rev. 295, 297 (1936); 15 Col.L.Rev. 171 (1915). Contra: Hayden v. Huff, 60 Neb. 625, 83 N.W. 920 (1900),

argued that the grantee who discharges the senior mortgage is paying his or her own debt, since there is no personal obligation to do so. At the same time, both assuming and "subject to" grantees must be considered well outside the "volunteer" classification, since they clearly have a property interest to protect by payment.[13]

§ 10.8 Compelling an Assignment

Subrogation is similar to an assignment of the mortgage creditor's rights, but since it is only an equitable right, it does not give as complete protection as does an assignment.[1] Therefore, frequently one who has a right to be subrogated upon payment of the mortgage debt desires instead a formal assignment. The question arises whether the payor is entitled to it.

The objection to compelling a mortgage creditor to execute an assignment under such circumstances is that the mortgagee's only duty under the mortgage agreement is to cancel the debt upon payment and to discharge the mortgage on the land—not to keep the mortgage alive by assigning it. But there are many legal incidents which attach to a relationship regardless of the agreement between the parties, simply because equity courts have believed it desirable and fair. Where the claimant shows a substantial need for an assignment as opposed to subrogation, an assignment should be compelled.[2] The burden on the mortgagee under an assignment as compared to subrogation is not onerous, and the duty to transfer the debt and mortgage without recourse imposes no additional risk on the mortgagee.

While courts have given varying answers on the question of compelling an assignment,[3] most of the cases have granted it if the person paying the mortgage debt stands in the relation of surety for its payment.[4] Some courts have gone beyond this and granted it where the person paying did so to protect an interest[5] and even in favor of

affirmed 63 Neb. 99, 88 N.W. 179 (1900), negligence in failure to examine records; cf. Storer v. Warren, 99 Ind.App. 616, 192 N.E. 325 (1934).

13. Kahn v. McConnell, 37 Okl. 219, 220, 131 P. 682, 683, 47 L.R.A.,N.S., 1189 (1913); Clute v. Emmerich, 99 N.Y. 342, 2 N.E. 6 (1885); cf. Weidner v. Thompson, 69 Iowa 36, 28 N.W. 422 (1886).

§ 10.8

1. Liberty Mutual Insurance Co. v. Thunderbird Bank, 113 Ariz. 375, 555 P.2d 333 (1976). See § 10.1, supra. See also Pardee v. Van Anken, 3 Barb. 534, 541 (N.Y.1848); Cantor v. Union Mutual Life Insurance Co., 547 S.W.2d 220, 225 (Mo. App.1977): "When there is an assignment of an entire claim there is complete divestment of all rights from the assignor and a vesting of those same rights in the assignee; but, in a case of subrogation, only an equitable right passes to the subrogee and the legal right to the claim is not removed from subrogor."

2. "[W]here justice requires, the payment of a mortgage note will be considered not as a discharge, but as an assignment of both instruments; [particularly if] it is the intention of the person making payment to take an assignment of the instruments for his own protection." United States v. Boston and Berlin Transportation Co., 237 F.Supp. 1004, 1008 (D.N.H.1964).

3. For collections of authorities, see Ann.Cas.1914B, 562; 2 A.L.R. 242 (1919) (chattel mortgage); 93 A.L.R. 89 (1934).

4. E.g., Johnson v. Zink, 51 N.Y. 333 (1873). See 93 A.L.R. 89, 99 (1934).

5. Global Realty Corp. v. Charles Kannel Corp., 9 Misc.2d 241, 170 N.Y.S.2d 16 (1958) (tenant who held valuable long term lease which was subordinate to second

lenders who are entitled to subrogation because they paid a prior mortgage debt.[6] On the other hand, some courts deny the assignment even though the payment was made to protect an interest in the property[7] or when the payor was in the position of a surety.[8]

B. MARSHALING

§ 10.9 General Principles

Marshaling is an equitable principle applied by the courts in determining the order in which mortgaged parcels are foreclosed upon, thus adjusting the rights of the various parties having an interest in mortgaged property.[1]

Frequently a single tract of land consisting of several lots or parcels is mortgaged to secure one debt. Or it may be that two or more

---

mortgage was entitled upon payment or tender of amount due on mortgage to demand an assignment of bond and mortgage from its holder); Payne v. Foster, 284 App. Div. 1058, 135 N.Y.S.2d 819 (1954) (where remainderman tendered payment he could compel life tenant's execution and delivery of an assignment of mortgage rather than a discharge); Averill v. Taylor, 8 N.Y. 44 (1853). In Simonson v. Lauck, 105 App. Div. 82, 93 N.Y.S. 965 (1905), the mortgagor, owner of the fee simple as tenant-in-common with four others, obtained an assignment to a third person who had tendered payment of the entire mortgage at the request of the mortgagor. Motes v. Roberson, 133 Ala. 630, 32 So. 225 (1902), accord. Cf. Fears v. Albea, 69 Tex. 437, 6 S.W. 286, 5 Am.St.Rep. 78 (1887). In Bayles v. Husted, 40 Hun. 376 (N.Y.1886), the widow of a deceased mortgagor tendered to the mortgagee the amount of the secured debt and demanded that the mortgage be assigned to X. The court compelled the mortgagee to make the assignment.

6. French v. Grand Beach Co., 239 Mich. 575, 215 N.W. 13 (1927), noted 12 Minn.L.Rev. 189 (1927). Cf. Arant, Suretyship, 360–367; 34 Harv.L.Rev. 792 (1921); 20 Va.L.Rev. 917 (1934). Lackawanna Trust & Safe Deposit Co. v. Gomeringer, 236 Pa. 179, 84 A. 757 (1912) is contra.

7. Lamb v. Montague, 112 Mass. 352 (1873); Butler v. Taylor, 71 Mass. (5 Gray) 455 (1855); Hamilton v. Dobbs, 19 N.J.Eq. 227 (1868). Cf. Holland v. Citizens' Savings Bank, 16 R.I. 734, 19 A. 654, 8 L.R.A. 553 (1890). See Updike, Mortgages, in 1954 Annual Survey of American Law, 30 N.Y.U.L.Rev. 805, 812 (1955), noting Marine View Savings & Loan Association v. Andrulonis, Ch., 31 N.J.Super. 378, 106 A.2d 559 (1954).

8. Fitcher v. Griffiths, 216 Mass. 174, 103 N.E. 471 (1913). Cf. Heighe v. Sale of Real Estate, 164 Md. 259, 164 A. 671, 93 A.L.R. 81 (1933).

§ 10.9

1. Marshaling is "the ranking or ordering of several estates or parcels of land for the satisfaction of a judgment or mortgage to which all are liable." 1 Black, Judgments, § 440. For collections of authorities on various aspects of the problem of marshaling see, 5 L.R.A. 280 (1889); 12 L.R.A.,N.S. 965 (1908); id. 359 (1912); id. 302 (1914); Ann.Cas.1914A., 715; id. 1916D, 1119; 35 A.L.R. 1307 (1925); 44 id. 608 (1926); 77 id. 371 (1932); 101 id. 618 (1936); 106 id. 1102 (1937); 110 id. 65 (1937); 119 id. 1109 (1939); 131 A.L.R. 4 (1941). This last is a long and comprehensive survey of the inverse order of alienation rule.

While marshaling originated in realty mortgage cases, it is often applied in modern times to personal property security as well; see In re Payne & Haddock, Inc., 103 B.R. 166 (Bkrtcy.Tenn.1988); Labovitz, Marshaling Under the U.C.C.: The State of the Doctrine, 99 Banking L.J. 440 (1982).

Whether marshaling should be recognized at all in bankruptcy proceedings is controversial. Bankruptcy courts have a variety of other equitable powers and tools which may often be used to accomplish similar objectives. See In re Packard Properties, Ltd., 112 B.R. 154 (Bkrtcy.Tex. 1990); Averch & Prostok, The Doctrine of Marshaling: An Anachronistic Concept under the Bankruptcy Code, 22 U.C.C.L.J. 224 (1990); Comment, 1983 B.Y.U.L.Rev. 639.

separate tracts are subject to a single mortgage debt. The various lots or tracts may then be sold or further mortgaged to different parties, either simultaneously or successively, with one or more of the lots or tracts being retained by the mortgagor. In such cases there are two or more pieces of property as security for the same debt and more than one person has an interest in the properties under the mortgage.

For convenience in the following discussion the foregoing situation may be stated in hypothetical terms in which R is the mortgagor and E the mortgagee of the single tract, Blackacre, which is composed of three lots, X, Y and Z. T-1 and T-2 represent later purchasers or second mortgagees, as the case may be, of lots X and Y. Lot Z remains in the hands of R. If the transfers of X and Y are by sale, T-1 and T-2 may have bought in any one of three types of transactions: they may have assumed the mortgage, taken subject to it, or paid the full value of the parcel with R bound to pay off the mortgage on it. Or there may be agreements apportioning the debt in specified amounts or percentages among the various parcels transferred or retained by the mortgagor. The transfer to T-1 may or may not have been recorded. T-2, whether a purchaser or a mortgagee, may have actual notice of the prior transfer to T-1.

If there were no principles of marshaling, in the event of a default on the mortgage E could proceed against the three parcels in any order he or she wished. This would endow E with the power, to be exercised at whim, of wiping out the interest of T-1 or T-2 even though foreclosure against R's parcel alone might suffice to satisfy E's debt. The purpose and effect of marshaling is to prevent this result.

The term marshaling is used to cover two principles which are commonly given the separate titles of the "inverse order of alienation" rule and the "two funds" doctrine.[2] Under the inverse order of alienation rule, a mortgagee holding a paramount lien on an entire tract of land which has been sold successively in separate parcels must satisfy the debt out of the land retained by the mortgagor-grantor, if possible, and if that is insufficient must resort to the parcels aliened in the inverse order of their alienation.[3] The rule has been traced back to

---

[2] See Fidelity & Casualty Co. v. Massachusetts Mutual Life Insurance Co., 74 F.2d 881 (4th Cir.1935); Restatement, Second, Restitution § 44 (Tent.Draft No. 2, 1984). For applications of the principles of marshaling in subdivision financing, see Melli, Subdivision Control in Wisconsin, Wis.L.Rev. 389 (1953). See also Green, Marshaling Assets in Texas, 34 Texas L.Rev. 1054 (1956). For a discussion of subdivision financing problems, see Storke and Sears, Subdivision Financing, 28 Rocky Mt.L.Rev. 1 (1956). See Note, The Rights of a Junior Lienholder in Wisconsin, 43 Marq.L.Rev. 89, 94 (1959).

[3] Mobley v. Brundidge Banking Co., 347 So.2d 1347 (Ala.1977); Commonwealth Land Title Co. v. Kornbluth, 175 Cal. App.3d 518, 220 Cal.Rptr. 774 (1985) (based on West's Ann.Cal.Civ.Code § 2899); Bartley v. Pikeville National Bank & Trust Co., 532 S.W.2d 446 (Ky.1975); Seasons, Inc. v. Atwell, 86 N.M. 751, 527 P.2d 792 (1974); Broughton v. Mount Healthy Flying Service, Inc., 104 Ohio App. 479, 143 N.E.2d 597 (1957); Haueter v. Rancich, 39 Wash. App.2d 328, 693 P.2d 168 (1984); Note, Marshaling: Equitable Rights of Holders of Junior Interests, 38 Rutgers L.Rev. 287 (1986).

Coke in England,[4] and was first enunciated in this country by Chancellor Kent[5] and later approved by the great weight of authority.[6]

The two funds rule requires that where two creditors have claims upon the assets of a common debtor and one of the creditors can resort to two funds but the other can reach only one, the doubly secured creditor must first seek satisfaction out of the fund which he or she alone can reach, before resorting to the fund upon which both creditors have claims.[7] For example, lots X and Y are mortgaged to E. T–1 then

---

4. Harbert's Case, 3 Co.Rep. 11b (1584). Cf. Lord Eldon in Aldrich v. Cooper, 8 Ves. 382 (1803), and Sugden, in Averall v. Wade, L1. & G. 252 (1825), on the "two funds" doctrine. See Clowes v. Dickenson, N.Y., 5 Johns.Ch. 235 (1821). See also Sanford v. Hill, 46 Conn. 42 (1878); National Savings Bank of District of Columbia v. Creswell, 100 U.S. (10 Otto) 630, 25 L.Ed. 713 (D.C.1880).

5. In Clowes v. Dickenson, supra note 4.

6. Brown v. Simons, 44 N.H. 475 (1863); Cumming v. Cumming, 3 Ga. 460 (1847); Clowes v. Dickenson, note 4, supra; Sanford v. Hill, note 4, supra; National Savings Bank v. Creswell, note 4, supra; see Iglehart v. Crane & Wesson, 42 Ill. 261, 265, 269 (1866). See 5 L.R.A. 276, 282 (1889); Ann.Cas.1916D, 1119.

7. In re Beacon Distributors, Inc., 441 F.2d 547 (1st Cir.1971); In re Hansen, 77 B.R. 722 (Bkrtcy.D.N.D.1987); All American Holding Corp. v. Elgin State Bank, 17 B.R. 926 (Bkrtcy.Fla.1982); Shedoudy v. Beverly Surgical Supply Co., 100 Cal. App.3d 730, 733, 161 Cal.Rptr. 164 (1980); Bartley v. Pikeville National Bank & Trust Co., 532 S.W.2d 446 (Ky.1975); Pongetti v. Bankers Trust Savings & Loan Association, 368 So.2d 819 (Miss.1979); Lineham v. Southern New England Production Credit Ass'n, 122 N.H. 179, 442 A.2d 585 (1982); Waff Brothers, Inc. v. Bank of North Carolina, 289 N.C. 198, 221 S.E.2d 273 (1976); Community Bank v. Jones, 278 Or. 647, 566 P.2d 470 (1977); First Wisconsin Trust Co. v. Rosen, 143 Wis.2d 468, 422 N.W.2d 128 (1988), review denied 144 Wis.2d 957, 428 N.W.2d 554 (1988); Annot., 76 A.L.R.3d 327 n. 2 (1977). But see Valparaiso Bank and Trust Co. v. Royal Trust Bank, N.A., 512 So.2d 298 (Fla.App.1987) (marshaling in favor of a junior lienor denied, where the junior had already foreclosed its lien and collected a deficiency judgement calculated on assumption that the entire senior debt would be charged against the parcel the junior had acquired by foreclosure).

In general, the debtor must be identical as to both properties; see SAC Construction Co. v. Eagle National Bank, 449 So.2d 301 (Fla.App.1984); Janke v. Chace, 487 N.W.2d 301 (Neb.App.1992); Allstate Financial Corp. v. Westfield Serv. Mgt. Co., 62 Ohio App.3d 657, 577 N.E.2d 383 (1989). Even if one parcel of mortgaged property is owned by a corporation and the other by its principal or sole shareholder, marshaling is not ordinarily imposed; see In re C & B Oil Co., Inc., 72 B.R. 228 (Bkrtcy.Ohio 1987); In re Coors of North Mississippi, Inc., 66 B.R. 845 (Bkrtcy.Miss.1986); In re Rich Supply House, Inc., 43 B.R. 68 (Bkrtcy.Ill.1984). But in this context at least three exceptions to the common debtor requirement exist.

> One exception occurs where a shareholder has treated the corporation as an "alter ego" thus allowing piercing of the corporate veil to hold the stockholder liable for corporate debts. * * * The second exception occurs where a stockholder holds property or a claim against the corporation that equitably should be deemed a contribution to the capital of the corporation. * * * A third, but narrower exception arises when the stockholder has engaged in some inequitable conduct."

In re Muir, 89 B.R. 157 (Bkrtcy.Kan.1988). In that case a trust had obtained a mortgage loan, and one of the trustees had guaranteed the loan, collateralizing the guarantee with certain oil properties. The court held that the guarantor had the right to require the lender to exhaust the mortgaged property before resorting to the guarantor's collateral. Because the guarantor was bankrupt, the marshaling effectively aided his general creditors. Contra, see In re Bay Metro Glass Co., Inc., 101 B.R. 50 (Bkrtcy.Wis.1989).

See also In re Jack Green's Fashions for Men—Big and Tall, 597 F.2d 130 (8th Cir. 1979) (marshaling ordered against guarantor's assets, to aid general creditors of bankrupt principal debtor); In re Vermont Toy Works, Inc., 82 B.R. 258 (Bkrtcy.Vt. 1987), reversed on other grounds, but expressing doubt as to the need to pierce the

takes a second mortgage on lot X. Unless lot X is sufficient to pay both mortgages, if E should foreclose by taking payment out of it first, there will be nothing left for T–1, who will be reduced to the status of an unsecured creditor. On the other hand, if E takes payment out of Y first before resorting to X, some or all of the latter is likely to be available for T–1. To prevent the caprice of the doubly secured creditor, E, from determining where the loss shall fall in such a case, the "two funds" rule may be invoked by T–1 to compel E to realize first on Y.[8]

In application the two rules are not always clear and separable. The doctrine of inverse alienation, while generally thought of in situations where the mortgagor-owner has sold parcels successively, may also apply in other circumstances. As one court noted, it "not only applies to a vendee, but to any one having a substantial and valuable interest in any of the separate parcels of land. It has been applied in favor of a wife's dower and homestead rights. It has been applied in favor of judgment creditors, and in fact to almost all the transactions of business in which the rights of creditors, mortgagees, grantees, and lienees are involved before a court of equity."[9] There are times when the court discusses the "two funds" rule but, where more than one junior mortgagee is involved, may consider the inverse order of their encumbrances.[10] The court may recognize the inverse order rule as

veil 135 B.R. 762 (D.Vt.1991); In re Tampa Chain Co., Inc., 53 B.R. 772 (Bkrtcy.N.Y. 1985); DuPage Lumber Co. v. Georgia–Pacific Corp., 34 B.R. 737 (Bkrtcy.Ill.1983); Moser Paper Co. v. North Shore Publishing Co., 83 Wis.2d 852, 266 N.W.2d 411 (1978). See generally Restatement, Second, Restitution § 44(2) (Tent.Draft No. 2, 1984).

Marshaling of assets as between a principal debtor and a surety or guarantor is not ordinarily ordered, since the "common debtor" concept is not satisfied. See, e.g., First Interstate Bank v. H.C.T., 108 Nev. 242, 828 P.2d 405 (1992); Marsh v. National Bank of Commerce of El Dorado, 37 Ark.App. 41, 822 S.W.2d 404 (1992). It is the close relationship between the debtor and the guarantor that makes marshaling appropriate in cases like those cited in the preceding paragraphs.

8. "Its purpose is to prevent the arbitrary action of a senior lienor from destroying the rights of a junior lienor or a creditor having less security." Meyer v. United States, 375 U.S. 233, 237, 84 S.Ct. 318, 321, 11 L.Ed.2d 293 (1963). The rule goes back to Culpepper v. Aston, 2 Ch.Cas. 115, 117 (1682). As to the justice of this rule, which operates to the prejudice of general creditors, see Duck v. Wells Fargo Bank, 28 B.R. 397 (9th Cir. BAP 1983); Langdell, A Brief Survey of Equity Jurisdiction, 15; Note, 43 Harv.L.Rev. 501 (1930).

9. Mack v. Shafer, 135 Cal. 113, 67 P. 40, 41 (1901). See 53 Am.Jur.2d, Marshaling Assets § 61.

10. See § 10.13. Indeed some states have statutes providing that the order of inverse alienation be applied within the two funds rule.

West's Ann.Cal.Civ.Code § 2899 provides that "Where one has a lien upon several things, and other persons have subordinate liens upon, or interest in, some but not all of the same things, the person having the prior lien, if he can do so without risk of loss to himself, or of injustice to other persons, must resort to the property in the following order, on the demand of any party interested:

"1. To the things upon which he has an exclusive lien;

"2. To the things which are subject to the fewest subordinate liens;

"3. In like manner inversely to the number of subordinate liens upon the same thing; and,

"4. When several things are within one of the foregoing classes, and subject to the same number of liens, resort must be had—

"(1) To the things which have not been transferred since the prior lien was created;

valid between grantees but refuse to apply it between junior mortgagees.[11]

Because of this confusion the orthodox classifications have been criticized and some commentators have suggested that the cases be grouped under the two heads, "Suretyship Marshaling" and "Lien Marshaling". "The first group is made up of cases in which there are two owners of separate tracts liable for the same mortgage debt, with a real suretyship relation existing between the owners. The second group consists of cases in which there are two mortgagees, one of whom has a mortgage on two tracts, and the other a junior mortgage on one of these tracts."[12] These commentators recognize that there may be complex cases which would involve both suretyship marshaling and lien marshaling.

Regardless of which of these two marshaling principles is applicable, it is clear that marshaling will not be applied in such a way as to prejudice the rights of the paramount mortgagee to have the debt satisfied. All fractional interests remain bound by the first mortgage. The mortgagor can no more divest a portion of the mortgaged property by conveying it away or giving a second mortgage on it than to free the entire property by the same means[13] (provided that the first mortgage is properly recorded). And although restrictions may be placed upon E's enforcement of foreclosure rights for the purpose of ordering or ranking the relative positions of T–1, T–2 and R, those restrictions must stop short of prejudicing E's paramount rights as first mortgagee.[14]

"(2) To the things which have been so transferred without a valuable consideration; and,

"(3) To the things which have been so transferred for a valuable consideration in the inverse order of the transfer."

See also 42 Okl.St.Ann. § 17.

11. Bryson v. Newtown Real Estate & Development Corp., 153 Conn. 267, 216 A.2d 176 (1965). See also Platte Valley Bank of North Bend v. Kracl, 185 Neb. 168, 174 N.W.2d 724 (1970).

12. Storke and Sears, Transfer of Mortgaged Property, 38 Corn.L.Q. 185, 201 et seq. (1953).

13. "[E]very portion of the real estate embraced within the mortgage was equally burdened with the debt. No part could be relieved of the burden without consent of the mortgagee." Broughton v. Mount Healthy Flying Service, Inc., 104 Ohio App. 479, 481, 143 N.E.2d 597, 599 (1957).

14. Caplinger v. Patty, 398 F.2d 471 (8th Cir.1968); In re Payne & Haddock, Inc., 103 B.R. 166 (Bkrtcy.Tenn.1988); In re Oransky, 75 B.R. 541 (Bkrtcy.Mo.1987); Charles White Co. v. Percy Galbreath & Sons, Inc., 563 S.W.2d 478 (Ky.App.1978) (court refused to sell leasehold estate separate from fee; despite the benefits of doing so to junior lienors, such sale would have prejudiced senior mortgagee's position); Lieberman Music Co. v. Hagen, 394 N.W.2d 837 (Minn.App.1986) (marshaling refused where it would have required senior mortgagee to take judicial action, otherwise unnecessary, to foreclose its mortgage); Lincoln First Bank v. Spaulding Bakeries, Inc., 117 Misc.2d 892, 459 N.Y.S.2d 696 (1983); First National Bank of Omaha v. First Cadco Corp., 189 Neb. 553, 203 N.W.2d 770 (1973), appeal after remand 191 Neb. 678, 217 N.W.2d 93 (1974). "The doctrine is never enforced where it will operate to suspend or put in peril the claim of the paramount creditor, or cause him risk of loss, or where the fund to be resorted to is one which may involve such creditors in litigation, especially if final satisfaction is somewhat uncertain." Platte Valley Bank of North Bend v. Kracl, 185 Neb. 168, 174, 174 N.W.2d 724, 729 (1970) citing 55 C.J.S. Marshaling Assets and Securities § 4, p. 963. In S. Lotman & Son, Inc. v. Southeastern Financial Corp., 288 Ala. 547, 263 So.2d 499 (1972), the court would not require creditor to attempt satisfaction from 3rd mortgage on land

Even risk of loss to E will preclude marshaling.[15] It has been held that the junior creditor has the burden to show that the senior creditor has sufficient collateral to satisfy his or her claims.[16]

In some cases the protection to the mortgagee can be accomplished by the decree itself.[17] After directing that the parcels shall be offered for sale in the inverse order of alienation, beginning with that part of the tract still in the hands of the mortgagor, it may then provide that "[I]f the aggregate amount bid for the said lands so offered in severalty shall be insufficient to satisfy this decree, then the said master shall offer for sale said lots * * * together as one parcel * * *; and if the amount bid for the said lands so offered together shall exceed the aggregate of the amounts bid for said lands when offered in severalty * * * then said master shall sell said lands together".[18] It may be that such a procedure would add to the costs of the action. If so, those costs could be allocated to those for whose benefit the marshaling is ordered.

It is generally held that one entitled to marshaling has a right only to require a certain order of realization out of the various parcels under the mortgage when foreclosure occurs. Consequently a grantee or junior encumbrancer who has such a right must properly assert it before sale or other foreclosure of his or her parcel takes place.[19] This may be done by bill in equity if the attempted foreclosure is under power of sale,[20] or by cross-bill, answer or the like in the case of judicial foreclosure.[21] Even where the mortgagee's suit is for strict foreclosure the same result can be obtained. In such an action an equity court will always order a sale if the equities of the junior parties in interest require it. And it has even been held that a grantee of one of two mortgaged tracts, in a proper case for marshaling, may require the mortgagee who is seeking strict foreclosure to confine the remedy to the

where he also held security interest in equipment. See Matter of St. Cloud Tool & Die Co., 533 F.2d 387 (8th Cir.1976), holding that the creditor requesting marshaling must act promptly so as not to prejudice others by inaction.

See generally Restatement, Second, Restitution § 44(4) (Tent.Draft No. 2, 1984).

15. Victor Gruen Associates, Inc. v. Glass, 338 F.2d 826 (9th Cir.1964). See also Matter of Mills, 40 B.R. 72 (Bkrtcy. 1984) (marshalling denied in bankruptcy where it would affect unsecured creditors adversely.)

16. Id. Pankow Construction Co. v. Advance Mortgage Corp., 618 F.2d 611, 617 (9th Cir.1980); Grise v. White, 355 Mass. 698, 247 N.E.2d 385 (1969) (record did not establish existing collateral.) But see Continental Oil Co. v. Graham, 8 S.W.2d 719 (Tex.Civ.App.1928) where mortgagee failed to show that marshaling would cause hardship.

17. E.g., Hyde Park Thomson–Houston Light Co. v. Brown, 172 Ill. 329, 50 N.E. 127 (1898).

18. Id. This procedure was followed even in the absence of the contractual provision in Conneaut Building and Loan Co. v. Felch, 100 Ohio App. 52, 135 N.E.2d 480 (1955).

19. Matter of Mills, 40 B.R. 72 (Bkrtcy. N.C.1984); Monegan v. Pacific National Bank of Washington, 16 Wash.App. 280, 556 P.2d 226 (1976); Vines v. Wilcutt, 212 Ala. 150, 102 So. 29, 35 A.L.R. 1301 (1925).

20. Vines v. Wilcutt, note 19 supra.

21. Black v. Suydam, 81 Wash. 279, 142 P. 700 (1915), Ann.Cas.1916D, 1113. See 35 A.L.R. 1307, 1310 (1924). Control of all of the parcels by the foreclosing court is essential. Hence marshalling cannot be ordered if part of the mortgaged property is outside of the state. Drexler v. Commercial Savings Bank, 5 F.2d 13 (8th Cir.1925), noted, 25 Col.L.Rev. 974 (1925).

other tract where the net value of that tract is clearly equal to the mortgage debt.[22]

While the foregoing are the usual ways in which principles of marshaling are applied, others should be mentioned. One is to utilize the right of subrogation. Instead of having the land sold on foreclosure by the mortgagee in the order to which a subsequent grantee or mortgagee is entitled, such a transferee may elect to pay off the underlying first mortgage and be subrogated to it.[23] Another is by an action to redeem, in which the reciprocal rights of the parties may be adjusted by the decree.[24] Alternatively, the mortgagee may be permitted to sell all of the mortgaged property and the subsequent grantee or mortgagee may assert a priority right to the proceeds after the foreclosing mortgagee has been satisfied and before general creditors are paid.

With these principles of marshalling before us, we may now turn to specific instances and applications in the following sections. In doing so we shall consider the problem as it arises where subsequent purchasers from the mortgagor are concerned, where junior encumbrancers are interested, where general creditors assert a claim, and the occasional case where the mortgagor personally is seeking protection, as where a homestead is subject to the mortgage.

§ 10.10 Grantees—Inverse Order Rule

The basis of the inverse order of alienation rule is that each of the successive purchasers has bought his or her parcel on terms which impose upon the mortgagor and the remaining property in the mortgagor's hands the primary obligation of paying the mortgage debt. The property in the hands of the grantee, although still liable, stands merely in the position of surety.[1] This situation occurs where the full price of the parcel is paid without deduction of the whole or any part of

---

22. Markham v. Smith, 119 Conn. 355, 366, 367, 176 A. 880, 885 (1935); New England Mortgage Realty Co. v. Rossini, 121 Conn. 214, 183 A. 744 (1936). "On the other hand, the mortgagor, or a grantee or junior incumbrancer of *both* tracts, not being entitled to marshalling, is denied such relief on the ground that application should have been made to the court for an order of foreclosure by sale, in which event, by the usual practice, the tracts would have been sold separately, unless used as a whole." Campbell, Cases on Mortgages, 2d ed., 620 n. 7, citing New Haven Bank N.B.A. v. Jackson, 119 Conn. 451, 453, 455, 177 A. 387, 388 (1935).

23. Taylor v. Jones, 285 Ala. 353, 232 So.2d 601 (1970); Sanders v. Lackey, 59 Tenn.App. 207, 439 S.W.2d 610 (1968); Cobb v. Osman, 83 Nev. 415, 433 P.2d 259 (1967). See §§ 10.2, 10.3, 10.7, supra.

24. Taylor v. Jones, note 23 supra. See §§ 7.1–7.3, supra.

§ 10.10

1. Gribble v. Stearman & Kaplan, Inc., 249 Md. 289, 239 A.2d 573 (1968). "[T]he doctrine of marshaling confers upon the grantee * * * an equitable right to require the mortgagee to seek satisfaction of the underlying obligation from the mortgagor's remaining properties which are subject to the blanket mortgage, before resorting to the premises conveyed. This equitable right on the part of the grantee is, of course, independent of and in addition to its rights against the grantor mortgagor." In re Penn Central Transportation Co., 346 F.Supp. 1323, 1326 (E.D.Pa.1972), motion denied 346 F.Supp. 1333 (1972). See also Storke & Sears, Transfer of Mortgaged Property, 38 Cornell L.Q. 185, 202 n. 69 (1953).

the debt secured by the blanket mortgage.[2] Persons who had notice of the underlying mortgage through searching the records or otherwise[3] probably would not enter into such a transaction if they possessed business experience or had consulted a competent lawyer,[4] since it places them at risk of losing their property as a result of a default by someone whose actions they cannot control. But one who purchases under these conditions has a right to have the remaining property in the hands of the mortgagor foreclosed first in order to protect the parcel he or she bought.

Since the agreement of purchase creates an equity of marshaling which attaches to the rest of the property under the mortgage remaining in the mortgagor's hands, that equity will follow the remaining land into the hands of anyone who has notice of it.[5] When T-2 buys Y with notice of T-1's equity, T-2 will, of course, take subject to it. Thus after T-1 buys parcel X, parcels Y and Z are subject in R's hands to T-1's equity that they are to be applied to E's debt before X is touched. But if T-2 bought on the same terms as T-1, T-2 in turn has a similar equity against parcel Z which stays in R's hands. If R subsequently sells Z to T-3 who takes with notice, T-3 will take Z subject to the prior equitable rights of T-1 and T-2. When E seeks to foreclose, T-1 can compel E to proceed first against Y and Z before seeking to realize on X; and T-2 in turn can demand that, as between Y and Z, Z go first.

---

2. This is true even though the purchaser does not receive a deed until after sale of a second parcel. The equity attaches when the consideration is paid. Libbey v. Tufts, 121 N.Y. 172, 24 N.E. 12 (1890). This equity would be defeated, of course, if the purchaser of the second parcel did not have notice of the first sale and could qualify as a bona fide purchaser in other respects.

3. Their ignorance is as to the existence of the mortgage, not its legal consequences. It cannot, therefore, be urged against helping them that their plight is the result of a mistake of law. See Note, 23 Va.L.Rev. 298 (1937).

4. In subdivision financing it is customary to provide in the underlying mortgage agreement that the mortgagee is required "to release any lot from the lien of the mortgage on payment of a specified amount * * *. The contract between the subdivision company and the purchaser should contain a clause requiring the former, upon full payment by the latter, to pay the mortgagee the required amount and procure the release of lien. It is unwise to purchase a lot in a subdivision without first checking the mortgage and contract to see that these provisions are present." Storke and Sears, Transfer of Mortgaged Property, 38 Cornell L.Q. 185, 211 (1953). The language of such provisions has not been standardized, and in construing it there is a divergence of authority as to whether the partial release privilege is personal to the mortgagor or can be taken advantage of by purchasers of portions of the property. See 31 Col.L.Rev. 894, 895 (1931). The agreement between mortgagee and mortgagor gave the grantee the mortgagor's rights to demand a partial release in Conway v. Andrews, 286 Ala. 28, 236 So.2d 687 (1970).

5. National Savings Bank v. Creswell, 100 U.S. 630, 637, 25 L.Ed. 713 (1879); Taylor v. Jones, 285 Ala. 353, 232 So.2d 601 (1970); Clowes v. Dickenson, 5 Johns, Ch. 235 (N.Y.1821); Brown v. Simons, 44 N.H. 475, 478 (1863): "In the case of the sale by the mortgagor of all the mortgaged property to different purchasers at the same time, their equities must be regarded as equal, and each must contribute ratably to the discharge of the common burthen * * *." Carpenter v. Koons, 20 Pa. 222, 226 (1852): "The second purchaser sits in the seat of his grantor, and must pay the whole value of what he bought towards the extinguishment of the mortgage, before he can call on the first purchaser to pay anything. The first sale having thrown the whole burden on the part reserved, it cannot be thrown back again by the second sale. In other words the second purchaser takes the land he buys subject to all the liabilities under which the grantor held it."

Thus we have the rule of inverse order of alienation, which is, as was stated earlier, the great weight of authority in the United States.[6]

It has sometimes been asserted that the grantee's right to marshaling is dependent upon having received a deed with covenants of warranty.[7] Historically this was not true,[8] and it is analytically incorrect. Since marshaling is an equitable concept, the vital question is whether the duty of paying off the debt rests upon the mortgagor rather than the grantee.[9] On that question, the presence or absence of covenants in the deed may have value as evidence in determining the question of fact,[10] but otherwise it is immaterial.

While the courts in Iowa and Kentucky will apply the doctrine of marshaling to the extent that the residue of property remaining in the hands of the mortgagor will be used to exonerate a grantee or second mortgagee, they reject the doctrine which would require that the debt be satisfied out of portions of the property sold or mortgaged in the order of inverse alienation. In those jurisdictions the debt is pro-rated against the tracts sold or mortgaged or their proceeds, in proportion to

---

6. Seasons, Inc. v. Atwell, 86 N.M. 751, 527 P.2d 792 (1974); Taylor v. Jones, 285 Ala. 353, 232 So.2d 601 (1970); In re Penn Central Transportation Co., 346 F.Supp. 1323 (E.D.Pa.1972); Ellickson v. Dull, 34 Colo.App. 25, 521 P.2d 1282 (1974); Voltin v. Voltin, 179 N.W.2d 127 (N.D.1970) (portion given to wife in divorce decree to go last); Broughton v. Mount Healthy Flying Service, Inc., 104 Ohio App. 479, 143 N.E.2d 597 (1957) (where parcels had been leased, creditor must look first to residue). See 131 A.L.R. 103 at n. 11 for authorities applying the rule.

"It appears from the precedents and authorities dealing with the Rule of Inverse Order of Alienation that whether jurisdictions have adopted the rule in its entirety or with some modifications, they are virtually unanimous in holding that where a mortgagor conveys a portion and retains a portion of the encumbered property, the property so retained should first be subjected to the payment of the debt before resorting to the portion conveyed." Seasons, Inc. v. Atwell, 86 N.M. 751, 756, 527 P.2d 792, 797 (1974).

7. See, e.g., Pomeroy, Equity Juris, 5th ed., § 1225, "This relation * * * results from the form of the conveyance, which, being a warranty deed, or equivalent to a warranty, shows conclusively an intention between the two that the grantor is to assume the whole burden of the encumbrance as a charge upon his own parcel, while the grantee is to take and hold his portion entirely free."

8. "We are unable to find a case deciding, * * * that the equity could not be founded upon a quitclaim deed; * * * neither can we find a case which affirmatively decides that the rule depends upon the existence or nonexistence of covenants of warranty." Biswell v. Gladney, 182 S.W. 1168, 1172 (Tex.Civ.App.1916), modified on other grounds 213 S.W. 256 (1919). In Wadsworth v. Lyon, 93 N.Y. 201, 45 Am. Rep. 190 (1883), in spite of the absence of covenants of title, the grantee of mortgaged property who had paid the full value of the property was held entitled to exoneration. In Wilcox v. Campbell, 106 N.Y. 325, 12 N.E. 823 (1887), although the grantee took a quitclaim deed he was held entitled to marshal against a prior grantee of another parcel who assumed the mortgage.

9. "It [the rule requiring sale in inverse order of alienation] rests chiefly, perhaps, upon the grounds that where one who is bound to pay a mortgage confers upon others rights in any portion of the property, retaining other portions himself, it is unjust that they should be deprived of their rights, so long as he has property covered by the mortgage, out of which the debt can be made. * * * The rule cannot, therefore, depend upon the existence or nonexistence of covenants of warranty." Cooper v. Bigly, 13 Mich. 463, 474 (1865). See 131 A.L.R. 103 (1941).

10. A warranty deed may show intent of the mortgagor to remain liable on the whole mortgage. Seasons, Inc. v. Atwell, 86 N.M. 751, 527 P.2d 792 (1974); Taylor v. Jones, 285 Ala. 353, 232 So.2d 601 (1970).

their respective values.[11] The argument in favor of this minority approach is that "as between two grantees purchasing different parcels of the incumbered premises at different times, there is no more obligation on the one to pay than on the other. Both of them have purchased premises that are alike affected by a lien which neither created nor undertook to pay. The purchased premises are liable to be sold because of the failure of their grantor to discharge his undertaking, and not because of any failure on their part. In such cases, their interest is common, their rights are equal, and there should be equality of burden."[12]

This argument is plausible, but there are answers to it. First, it is widely accepted that a grantee, unless qualifying as a bona fide purchaser, takes the property subject to the equities held in it by third persons.[13] Thus T-2 takes parcel Y subject to an existing equity in favor of T-1 that arose when T-1 bought X. Second, under the Iowa and Kentucky view a mortgagor, who by transferring a part of the mortgaged land had established an equity in a grantee to have the residue applied first in satisfaction of the debt, could divest this equity at pleasure by transferring such residue to another.[14] This would be an undesirable and anomalous result.

To return to the majority view, if T-2 and T-3 have actual notice of T-1's marshaling rights there is no question that the rule operates. If they lack actual notice, should they be charged with constructive notice by reason of the fact that T-1 recorded his or her conveyance? Most states say yes.[15] The rule has been criticized, however, as placing an undue burden upon later purchasers, and as being contrary to the spirit of the recording acts.[16] There is an additional objection where the

---

11. Bartley v. Pikeville National Bank & Trust Co., 532 S.W.2d 446 (Ky.1975); Bronaugh v. Burley Tobacco Co., 212 Ky. 680, 280 S.W. 97 (1926); Bates v. Ruddick, 2 Iowa 423, 2 Coles 423, 65 Am.Dec. 774 (1856); Huff v. Farwell, 67 Iowa 298, 25 N.W. 252 (1885). "Even in Kentucky marshaling is granted if the mortgagor agreed with the first grantee to confine the mortgage to the retained tract by procuring a release from its operation (Calhoun v. Federal Land Bank, 230 Ky. 460, 465, 20 S.W.2d 72, 74 [1929]), or, probably, if the mortgagor expressly agreed with him that he might have marshaling, and the subsequent grantee or mortgagee had knowledge of the agreement." Campbell, Cases on Mortgages, 2d ed., 619 n. 6.

12. Bates v. Ruddick, 2 Iowa 423, 430, 65 Am.Dec. 774, 779 (1856).

13. See Commonwealth Land Title Co. v. Kornbluth, 175 Cal.App.3d 518, 220 Cal. Rptr. 774 (1985); Huston, Enforcement of Decrees in Equity, 127-131.

14. See Tiffany, Real Prop., 3d ed., § 1446. Cf. Shenkin, Marshaling of Securities, 79 U. of Pa.L.Rev. 785, n. 14 (1931).

15. Brown v. Simons, 44 N.H. 475 (1863); see Iglehart v. Crane & Wesson, 42 Ill. 261, 265, 269, Ann.Cas.1916D, 1119 (1866).

16. "The court, in effect, is imposing upon C [the subsequent grantee from the mortgagor of a part of the mortgaged property] a duty of running back every chain of title connected with a blanket mortgage, to ascertain whether any latent equities exist. To impose such a duty is contrary to the spirit of our Recording Acts, the policy of which is to remove secret liens. * * * Prospective purchasers or mortgagees of real estate are rightly considered to be on notice of prior liens on the property concerned, but the equity to marshal is one that can only be uncovered after, what may be in some cases, a most exhaustive and unreasonable search." Note, 79 U. of Pa.L.Rev. 782, 787 n. 28 (1931). See Cunningham, Stoebuck & Whitman, Property § 11.11 (1984), at 801-02.

terms of the recorded conveyance between the mortgagor and the first grantee did not make clear whether the mortgagor or the grantee was expected to pay the mortgage, as will often be the case. Should a later purchaser of part or all of the rest of the property be put upon inquiry to find out the real terms of the bargain? If so, the burden on the purchaser is compounded.[17]

Where T–1, the first grantee, fails to record the deed of parcel X and T–2 takes parcel Y without actual or constructive notice of T–1, it has been held that T–2 has an equity to have X sold before Y.[18] This seems correct if the rule of constructive notice by recordation is accepted. Having no notice of any prior conveyance, T–2 legitimately expects to be considered the first grantee and to be exonerated out of the land he or she believed was a residue in the hands of the grantor.

There is, however, a situation in which it would seem that T–1's failure to record should not cause T–2 to advance to T–1's position. Where E has a mortgage on two separate parcels of land securing one debt and T–1 takes a second mortgage on parcel X, the recording of the lien on X would have nothing to do with parcel Y and would not put T–2 who takes a second mortgage on Y on notice. Hence the recording acts would not apply to T–1's recording as giving notice to T–2, and if T–1 fails to record T–2 should not be given a windfall by advancing to T–1's priority position. It would seem that the proper result in this case would be to pro-rate the debt between the two parcels according to their respective values.

§ 10.11 Effect of Assumption or Taking "Subject" to the Mortgage

Where a mortgagor sells part of a mortgaged tract to a grantee who assumes the payment of the mortgage, the parcel conveyed becomes primarily liable for the payment of the mortgage and the part retained is only secondarily liable.[1] The grantee is also personally liable as principal for the payment of the debt and the mortgagor and the rest of the mortgaged land is only a surety as to this personal obligation.[2] As

---

17. See note 16, supra.

18. In Gray v. H.M. Loud & Sons Lumber Co., 128 Mich. 427, 87 N.W. 376, 54 L.R.A. 731 (1901), the lower court had pro-rated the mortgage between two tracts, each of which had been sold by warranty deed with each purchaser paying the full value of the property. The first grantee failed to record, and the subsequent grantee had no actual notice of the first. The upper court reversed the decision and held that the entire mortgage should be paid out of the part first sold. See also LaFarge Fire Insurance Co. v. Bell, 22 Barb. 54 (N.Y.1856); Bode v. Tannehill, 119 Wash. 98, 204 P. 802 (1922).

§ 10.11

1. Sanders v. Lackey, 59 Tenn.App. 207, 439 S.W.2d 610 (1968); Cobb v. Os-man, 83 Nev. 415, 433 P.2d 259 (1967); Chancellor of New Jersey v. Towell, 80 N.J.Eq. 223, 82 A. 861, 39 L.R.A.,N.S., 359, Ann.Cas.1914A, 710 (1912); Wilcox v. Campbell, 106 N.Y. 325, 12 N.E. 823 (1887); Reid v. Whisenant, 161 Ga. 503, 131 S.E. 904, 44 A.L.R. 599 (1926).

2. Id. Prudential Savings and Loan Association v. Nadler, 37 Ill.App.3d 168, 345 N.E.2d 782 (1976); Toler v. Baldwin County Savings & Loan Association, 286 Ala. 320, 239 So.2d 751 (1970); Smith v. Olney Federal Savings & Loan Association, 415 S.W.2d 515 (Tex.Civ.App.1967).

a consequence, not only does the inverse order of alienation rule not apply,[3] but the rule is reversed. Since both the grantee and the parcel conveyed have the duty to exonerate the residue in the hands of the mortgagor, the mortgagee can be compelled to foreclose first on the parcel transferred to the grantee.[4] Where the mortgagor afterwards sells the remainder of the tract to a subsequent purchaser who pays the full price on the remaining portion, all of the mortgagor's rights with respect to the assuming grantee's duty in respect to this remaining part inure to the benefit of the second purchaser.[5]

These rights give the second purchaser a choice of several courses. In a foreclosure action by the mortgagee, the purchaser may insist that the parcel held by the prior assuming grantee be sold first.[6] If the proceeds of this sale are insufficient to pay the mortgage, the subsequent purchaser may either pay the balance due upon the mortgage in order to save the land, or let the land be sold.[7] In either event he or she has an action against the prior grantee for failing to perform the promise to pay the mortgage.[8] The damages would be the amount the second purchaser paid to stave off the threatened foreclosure,[9] or if the

3. In re Beacon Distributors, Inc., 441 F.2d 547 (1st Cir.1971); Cobb v. Osman, note 1 supra; Sanders v. Lackey, note 1, supra. See 131 A.L.R. 4, 62 (1941). Where the first grantee of a portion of mortgaged land assumes or takes subject to the mortgage and other parcels are then sold to grantees who pay full value with an agreement that the mortgagor shall pay off the mortgage, although the parcel in the hands of the first grantee is subject to being sold first, the inverse order of alienation rule would apply to the other grantees. Moore v. Shurtleff, 128 Ill. 370, 21 N.E. 775 (1889).

4. Chancellor of New Jersey v. Towell, 80 N.J.Eq. 223, 82 A. 861, 39 L.R.A.,N.S., 359, Ann.Cas.1914A, 710 (1912); Epperson v. Cappellino, 113 Cal.App. 473, 298 P. 533 (1931). Contra: Ewing v. Bay Minette Land Co., 232 Ala. 22, 26, 166 So. 409, 413 (1936), on the ground that marshaling cannot be invoked by a debtor. See § 10.14, infra. This right of the mortgagor to marshaling will be available against subsequent transferees from the grantee if they are not bona fide purchasers. E.g., Costa v. Sardinha, 265 Mass. 319, 163 N.E. 887 (1928).

5. Sanders v. Lackey, note 1, supra; Reid v. Whisenant, note 1, supra. See 44 A.L.R. 608 (1926). By way of analogy, see Valparaiso Bank v. Royal Trust Bank, 512 So.2d 298 (Fla.App.1987). There a second mortgage holder as to one of the parcels foreclosed, acquiring title, and then sought marshaling as against the foreclosing first mortgagee. The court denied marshaling, since the second mortgagee had also collected a deficiency judgment which was computed on the assumption that the entire senior debt would be charged against the second mortgagee's parcel.

6. Wilcox v. Campbell, 106 N.Y. 325, 329, 12 N.E. 823, 826 (1887); Dieckman v. Walser, 114 N.J.Eq. 382, 386, 168 A. 582, 583 (1933), affirming 112 N.J.Eq. 46, 163 A. 284 (1932); Union Central Life Insurance Co. v. Cates, 193 N.C. 456, 463, 464, 137 S.E. 324, 327, 328 (1927); Welch v. Beers, 90 Mass. (8 Allen) 151 (1864). Although the subsequent grantee may compel the mortgagee to foreclose first on the property held by the assuming grantee, in the event of a deficiency the mortgagee may sell the remainder of the tract in the hands of the mortgagor or subsequent grantee. Vanderspeck v. Federal Land Bank, 175 Miss. 759, 765, 167 So. 782, 783 (1936). See 39 L.R.A.,N.S., 359, 360 (1912).

7. See Wilcox v. Campbell, note 6, supra. The second purchaser might also pay off the entire mortgage before any of the property is sold. In that case he or she would be subrogated to the rights of the mortgagee and could enforce the mortgage against the assuming grantee and, if the property is insufficient, take a judgment for the deficiency.

8. Sanders v. Lackey, note 1, supra.

9. See Cooley v. Murray, 11 Colo.App. 241, 52 P. 1108 (1898); Wilcox v. Campbell, 106 N.Y. 325, 12 N.E. 823 (1887).

foreclosure went forward, either the value of the parcel lost [10] or the amount of the proceeds from its sale that were applied in discharge of the mortgage foreclosure decree.[11]

As stated by one court: "[W]here the mortgagor sells part of the mortgaged property 'subject to' the pre-existing mortgage without an agreement about payment of the mortgage, it is generally held that the mortgage lien remains an equal charge against all the mortgaged tract and that either mortgagor-vender or his vendee may enforce pro-rata application of the separate tracts to the satisfaction of the mortgage." [12] If it were clear that the purchase of the part was subject to the entire amount of the mortgage which was deducted from its purchase price, the part sold would be primarily liable for the entire debt. In such a case the mortgagor and subsequent purchasers for full value of portions of the tract left in the hands of the mortgagor could insist that the mortgagee, on foreclosing, resort first to the parcel sold subject to the mortgage.[13] Or if there were an explicit provision or clear evidence that the conveyance of the first parcel was subject to a specified portion of the mortgage, the parties' intent would govern.[14] In many cases, however, there is no evidence of any express or implied agreement about payment of the mortgage. When such is the situation, where one parcel of a mortgaged tract is sold subject to the mortgage and a later portion is also sold subject to the mortgage, the weight of authority is that the debt will be prorated between the two grantees in proportion to the value of their respective lots.[15] The same result has been reached where the mortgagor first conveyed one parcel of the mortgaged land to T–1 who assumed the payment of the mortgage, and later

---

10. Reid v. Whisenant, 161 Ga. 503, 131 S.E. 904, 44 A.L.R. 599 (1926).

11. Wilcox v. Campbell, 106 N.Y. 325, 12 N.E. 823 (1887). This opinion sets forth clearly the various alternative remedies and the underlying reasons for them.

12. Meadowlands National Bank v. Court Development, Inc., 192 N.J.Super. 579, 471 A.2d 801 (1983), certification denied 96 N.J. 303, 475 A.2d 595 (1984); Sanders v. Lackey, 59 Tenn.App. 207, 219, 439 S.W.2d 610, 616 (1968).

13. See 39 L.R.A.,N.S., 361 (1912).

14. Mickle v. Gould, 42 Mich. 304, 3 N.W. 961 (1879); Engle v. Haines, 5 N.J.Eq. 186, 43 Am.Dec. 624 (1945), affirmed 5 N.J.Eq. 632 (1847); Moore v. Shurtleff, 128 Ill. 370, 21 N.E. 775 (1889); New England Loan & Trust Co. v. Stephens, 16 Utah 385, 52 P. 624 (1898). If such an agreement is put into the mortgage it clearly will be binding upon all later transferees of any part of the property; see Mickle v. Gould, supra; Maurer v. Arab Petroleum Corp., 134 Tex. 256, 135 S.W.2d 87, 131 A.L.R. 1 (1940). The same result can be accomplished by inserting a common provision in all deeds transferring fractional interests in the property. Moore v. Shurtleff, supra; New England Loan & Trust Co. v. Stephens, supra.

15. Briscoe v. Power, 47 Ill. 447 (1868); Carpenter v. Koons, 20 Pa. 222 (1852); Stephens v. Clay, 17 Colo. 489, 30 P. 43 (1892); Hooper v. Capitol Life Insurance Co., 92 Colo. 376, 384, 20 P.2d 1011, 1014 (1933); Markham v. Smith, 119 Conn. 355, 363, 176 A. 880, 884 (1935); Hall v. Morgan, 79 Mo. 47 (1883); Hoy v. Bramhall, 19 N.J.Eq. 563, 97 Am.Dec. 687 (1868); Stuyvesant Security Co. v. Dreyer, 103 N.J.Eq. 457, 461, 143 A. 616, 617 (1929), affirmed 105 N.J.Eq. 585, 148 A. 920 (1930) (values at time of conveyance taken); Dieckmann v. Walser, 112 N.J.Eq. 46, 53, 55, 163 A. 284, 287, 288 (1932), affirmed 114 N.J.Eq. 382, 168 A. 582 (1933). Cf. Savings Investment & Trust Co. v. United Realty & Mortgage Co., 84 N.J.Eq. 472, 94 A. 588 (1915), Ann. Cas.1916D, 1134 ("subject to" clause in second mortgage).

conveyed another parcel to T–2 subject to it.[16]

§ 10.12 Gift Conveyances

Where the mortgagor makes a gift conveyance of a portion of a mortgaged tract with no covenants protecting the grantee against the mortgage, some decisions hold that the donee takes it subject to a primary liability for a part of the mortgage debt proportional to the respective values of the land conveyed and retained.[1] It has been questioned whether this should be true where the grantor is personally liable for the debt.[2] In such cases, it is urged, the presumption should be that the transferor is to pay his or her own debt and, consequently, the land retained would be primarily liable.[3] If there is a covenant against encumbrances covering the mortgage, this has been held to be sufficient evidence of intention that the land under the gift conveyance shall not be liable for the debt as to throw the primary liability upon the residue in the hands of the grantor.[4]

§ 10.13 Second Mortgages

Let us return to our hypothetical involving Blackacre. If T–1 is a mortgagee rather than a purchaser, T–1 and E are both creditors of a common debtor. This is a situation to which the two funds rule applies.[1] In the simple example where R has made only one conveyance to T–1 or given one second mortgage to T–1 the result is the same, but it is reached by a different rationale. The reasoning under the inverse order doctrine is that the mortgagor who incurred the debt should be the one to pay it. Under the two funds doctrine, it is reasoned that E, the senior encumbrancer, should not be able to

---

16. Pearson v. Bailey, 177 Mass. 318, 58 N.E. 1028 (1901).

§ 10.12

1. Mills v. Kelley, 62 N.J.Eq. 213, 215, 50 A. 144, 145 (1901) ("Where the conveyance is voluntary, and there are no covenants, then equality is equity. There is no reason why the voluntary grantee should not take the land with any charge that may rest upon it, except in so far as the parties themselves have otherwise stipulated."); Jackson v. Condict, 57 N.J.Eq. 522, 526, 41 A. 374 (1898). But see 131 A.L.R. 4, 88 (1941).

2. See Tiffany, Real Property, 3d ed., § 1446.

3. Id. In re Darby's Estate, 2 Ch. 465 (1907) (devisees of balance of mortgagor's property denied contribution against donee-grantee of mortgaged property by deed containing no reference to the mortgage and no covenants for title, express or implied).

4. Harrison v. Guerin, 27 N.J.Eq. 219 (1876); Howser v. Cruikshank, 122 Ala. 256, 25 So. 206, 82 Am.St.Rep. 76 (1898). The covenant would serve only as evidence of intent. See 5 Houston L.Rev. 221 (1967). Since covenants cannot be effective without consideration, a warranty deed without exception is unenforceable and the donee has no recourse against the mortgagor should the mortgagee foreclose and wipe out the donee.

§ 10.13

1. Generally the funds must be in the hands of a common debtor of both creditors. Dixieland Realty Co. v. Wysor, 272 N.C. 172, 158 S.E.2d 7 (1967); Little v. United Investors Corp., 157 Conn. 44, 245 A.2d 567 (1968); Markman v. Russell State Bank, 358 F.2d 488 (10th Cir.1966). See 135 A.L.R. 739–40 for additional cases. But there are exceptions. See § 10.14 note 7, supra. In Charles Construction Co., Inc. v. Leisure Resources, Inc., 1 Mass.App. 755, 307 N.E.2d 336 (1974), the court found the reasoning underlying the two funds doctrine had equal application where there is only one fund. See also 8 L.R.A.,N.S., 965 (1912).

foreclose first on the only fund available to T–1. However, the equities that really must be considered are not between E and T–1. E will ultimately have access to the entire property in any case, and it does not matter to E whether he or she proceeds first against the property upon which T–1 has a second mortgage or the property upon which E alone holds a mortgage. So the equity to be considered is actually the same as that considered under the inverse rule of alienation—should R, who incurred the debt, bear the burden of paying it off as opposed to T–1, who took the second mortgage as security expecting that R would pay off the first mortgage? Where there are no other junior lienholders involved or where their rights will not be prejudiced, the two funds rule will be applied.[2]

If there has been a subsequent second mortgage or conveyance to T–2, does T–1 have the same right to marshal as against T–2 that T–1 would have under the inverse order rule if he purchased a parcel for full value with the agreement that the duty of discharging the mortgage would fall upon the residue of the land retained by R? Where the

2. In re Forester, 529 F.2d 310 (9th Cir.1976); Zellerbach Paper Co. v. Valley National Bank of Arizona, 18 Ariz.App. 301, 501 P.2d 570 (1972); Charles Construction Co., Inc. v. Leisure Resources, Inc., 1 Mass.App. 755, 307 N.E.2d 336 (1974); SCD Chemical Distributors, Inc. v. Maintenance Research Laboratory, Inc., 191 Mich.App. 43, 477 N.W.2d 434 (1991); In re Estate of Hansen, 458 N.W.2d 264 (N.D.1990) (marshaling applied despite "order of sale" statute that purported to give debtor power to determine sequence of sale); Associates Realty Credit Limited v. Brune, 89 Wash.2d 6, 568 P.2d 787 (1977). In Waff Brothers, Inc. v. Bank of North Carolina, N.A., 289 N.C. 198, 221 S.E.2d 273 (1976), a preliminary injunction was granted so that the trial court could determine whether the creditor did have security in a second fund. In Columbia Bank for Cooperatives v. Lee, 368 F.2d 934 (4th Cir.1966), certiorari denied 386 U.S. 992, 87 S.Ct. 1308, 18 L.Ed.2d 338 (1967), the doubly secured bank was required to satisfy its debt from the stock rather than the real property because the stock was worth more in the bank's hands than it would be in the hands of the competing creditor. In United States v. Herman, 310 F.2d 846 (2d Cir.1962), certiorari denied 373 U.S. 903, 83 S.Ct. 1291, 10 L.Ed.2d 199 (1963) and United States v. Stutsman County Implement Co., 274 F.2d 733 (8th Cir.1960) the courts refused to subject the government to the requirement to marshal assets in favor of junior lienors. But the court enforced the requirement in United States v. LeMay, 346 F.Supp. 328 (E.D.Wis.1972), citing United States Fidelity & Guaranty Co. v. Long, 214 F.Supp. 307, 319 (D.Or.1963), "In the application of the doctrine, the United States and its agencies are on an equal basis with other creditors."

For an excellent collection of authorities, see 106 A.L.R. 1102 (1937). See Gest, Marshalling Assets with Reference to the Rights of Successive Part Purchasers and Incumbrancers, 27 Am.L.Reg.,N.S., 739 (1888); Strachan, The Marshalling of Mortgages, 22 L.Q.Rev. 307 (1906); See also notes, 79 U. of Pa.L.Rev. 782 (1931); 18 Harv.L.Rev. 453 (1905); 24 Iowa L.Rev. 328 (1939); 106 A.L.R. 1102 (1937); 5 L.R.A. 280 (1889); 12 L.R.A.,N.S., 965 (1908); 119 A.L.R. 1109 (1939).

If T–1 does not request marshaling, E may have the entire property sold in bulk. If a surplus is produced by the foreclosure, T–1 is entitled only a fraction of it equal to the ratio of the value of the land covered by T–1's mortgage to the value of the entire land sold. William H. Metcalfe & Sons, Inc. v. Canyon Defined Benefit Trust, 318 Md. 565, 569 A.2d 669 (1990).

Under California's "one-action" rule, the Court of Appeal has held that a junior mortgagee who brought an action on the debt rather than foreclosing the mortgage effectively waived its right to require marshaling by a senior mortgagee; see O'Neil v. General Sec. Corp., 4 Cal.App.4th 587, 5 Cal.Rptr.2d 712 (1992); § 8.2 supra. See also Valparaiso Bank v. Royal Trust Bank, 512 So.2d 298 (Fla.App.1987), refusing to marshal at the request of a junior mortgagee when it had received a deficiency judgment based on a much higher balance on the senior mortgage than actually existed.

§ 10.13 MARSHALING 35

question involves competing holders of second mortgages or a second mortgagee and a later transferee, two divergent lines of authority have developed. The major difference between the two lines of cases under the two funds rule is the same distinction that has been offered to explain the difference between the inverse order rule and the two funds doctrine.[3] One group of courts holds that T–1 acquires a fixed and established right in equity at the time he or she acquires the second mortgage on lot X to require E to look primarily to lots Y and Z, and to sell them before resorting to lot X held by T–1,[4] provided that E's rights will not be prejudiced by so doing.[5] Or where both lots must be sold to satisfy E's mortgage T–1 will have the first right to any surplus from the sale.[6] This equity would be the same as the equity acquired by T–1 if T–1 were a purchaser rather than a second mortgagee, and under this line of authority the inverse order of alienation is applied.[7] Consequently any subsequent taker of lots X or Y by way of purchase for full value or as second mortgagee will take subject to T–1's prior equity unless that taker can qualify as a bona fide purchaser for value without notice.[8] T–1 can effectively guard against such a possibility by recording the second mortgage on parcel X, which will then give constructive notice of T–1's equity to any later taker of Y or Z.[9] If the subsequent

---

3. "[T]he two doctrines are quite distinct. The equity of marshaling, until it is asserted, is a mere inchoate equity subject to displacement, whereas the equity of the purchaser of land subject to a lien to have that lien satisfied out of land remaining in the grantor and then out of the parcels subsequently conveyed in inverse order of alienation, where it exists at all, is a fixed indefeasible right." Fidelity & Casualty Co. v. Massachusetts Mutual Life Insurance Co., 74 F.2d 881, 884 (4th Cir.1935).

4. See note 7, infra.

5. See note 14, § 10.9, supra.

6. Banks-Miller Supply Co. v. Smallridge, 154 W.Va. 360, 175 S.E.2d 446 (1970).

7. Fidelity & Casualty Co. v. Massachusetts Mutual Life Insurance Co., 74 F.2d 881 (4th Cir.1935) (paramount tax lien on the various parcels); In re Shull, 72 B.R. 193 (Bkrtcy.S.C.1986); Bank of Commerce of Evansville v. First National Bank of Evansville, 150 Ind. 588, 594, 50 N.E. 566, 568 (1898) (senior judgment lien on both properties; mortgage on one, followed by conveyance of other to trustee to pay creditors); Sibley v. Baker, 23 Mich. 312 (1871); Sanborn, McDuffee Co. v. Keefe, 88 N.H. 236, 187 A. 97, 106 A.L.R. 1097 (1936); Hunt v. Townsend, 4 Sandf. Ch. 510 (N.Y. 1847); Riverside Apartment Corp. v. Capitol Construction Co., 107 N.J.Eq. 405, 413, 152 A. 763, 769 (1930), affirmed 110 N.J.Eq. 67, 158 A. 740 (1952) (probably constructive notice from recording); Ingersoll v. Somers Land Co., 82 N.J.Eq. 476, 89 A. 288 (1913); Robeson's Appeal, 117 Pa. 628, 12 A. 51 (1888) (senior judgment lien on both properties; recorded mortgage on one followed by mortgage on the other; later mortgagee charged with constructive notice of the earlier). See 76 A.L.R.3d 333, § 4.

8. As to the rule where the transferees of other parcels have not parted with value cf. quotation from Newby v. Fox, note 20, infra, decided in a jurisdiction following the second view in respect to marshaling by a junior mortgagee on the first parcel.

9. Harron v. Du Bois, 64 N.J.Eq. 657, 54 A. 857 (1903); Ingersoll v. Somers Land Co., note 7, supra; Appeal of Robeson, note 7, supra. If T–1 fails to record he or she cannot invoke the doctrine against one without actual notice. Birch River Boom & Lumber Co. v. Glendon Boom & Lumber Co., 71 W.Va. 139, 76 S.E. 167 (1912). Some cases do not even mention notice. See 106 A.L.R. 1102, 1103 (1937).

If the paramount lien arises against each of the two or more parcels by separate instruments, only the most exhaustive search of all deeds or mortgages to or from the mortgagor could reveal to T–2 the prior junior mortgage on lot X to T–1; such a burden is much too onerous to impose. See 5 Duke B.A.J. 35, 39 (1937); Green v. Ramage, 18 Ohio 428 (1849).

taker is not a bona fide purchaser, the priority of T–1 is said to rest upon the fact that T–1's equity is prior in time and that the later equity is inferior either by reason of notice or lack of value being given for it.[10] If T–2, the subsequent purchaser or mortgagee of Y or Z, can qualify under the bona fide purchase rule, T–2 and T–1 would have equal positions, and the paramount mortgage would then be apportioned between them according to the value of their respective lots.[11]

The rule in England [12] and that followed by many cases in this country [13] is that the equity of marshaling acquired by T–1 who takes a second mortgage on X is not a fixed equitable right when T–1 acquires the lien, but remains inchoate until the right is invoked by actual proceedings to enforce it; [14] and if at that time the rights of third

---

10. Conrad v. Harrison, 30 Va. 532 (1832); Ingersoll v. Somers Land Co., 82 N.J.Eq. 476, 89 A. 288 (1913) (constructive notice by record and later mortgage of other parcel was to secure pre-existing debt); Harron v. Du Bois, 64 N.J.Eq. 657, 54 A. 857 (1903) (later encumbrance was judgment lien acquired with constructive notice of prior recorded mortgage). See Newby v. Fox, 90 Kan. 317, 319, 133 P. 890, 891 (1913); Bank of Commerce v. First National Bank, note 7, supra (second parcel conveyed to trustee to pay creditors); Sanborn, McDuffee Co. v. Keefe, 88 N.H. 236, 187 A. 97, 106 A.L.R. 1097 (1936). See also 106 A.L.R. 1102, 1103 (1937). Cf. Sager v. Tupper, 35 Mich. 133 (1876); Reilly v. Mayer, 12 N.J.Eq. 55 (1858).

11. Cf. Green v. Ramage, 18 Ohio 428 (1849). Of course both T–1 and T–2 would have an equity to have lot Z in the hands of R sold before touching either X or Y. In such a case any deficiency would be prorated between the latter. See Newby v. Fox, quoted n. 20, infra.

12. Aldrich v. Cooper, 8 Ves. 381 (1803); Barnes v. Racster, 1 Younge & C.Ch.Cas. 401 (1842); Bugden v. Bignold, 2 Y. & C.C.C. 377 (1843). Shenkin, Marshaling of Securities, 79 U. of Pa.L.Rev. 782, 784 (1931): "This disposition of the problem * * * is perhaps attributable to the absence of a recording system at the time the law crystallized. This fact kept the English courts from dealing with the question of presumed notice * * *." See Kay, L.J., in Flint v. Howard, 2 Ch. 54, 73 (1893); Barnes v. Racster, 1 Younge & C.C.C. 401 (1842). See also 106 A.L.R. 1102, 1109 (1937). But cf. Falconbridge, Mortgages § 139 (2d ed. 1931).

13. "The decided cases in this country are in conflict. Many jurisdictions adopt the English view, while equally as many courts * * * have reached a contrary result, and have practically accorded the equity to marshal the effect of a lien." Shenkin, supra note 12.

14. In some cases either of two junior creditors is in a position to demand marshaling. In In re Forester, 529 F.2d 310 (9th Cir.1976), a junior lienor was competing with the trustee in bankruptcy (in behalf of the mortgagor's creditors) where each had claims against one fund and the bank as paramount mortgagee had claims against two funds. The majority held that the junior lienor's right to marshaling became vested at the point when he demanded that the first mortgagee marshal its liens. The dissent pointed out that the trustee had already demanded of the bank that it marshal its liens in favor of the bankruptcy estate and that the junior lienor should lose the marshaling contest because its demand for marshaling was later in time than the trustee's and its equities were inferior to those of the trustee. The dissent continued:

"The demand is an essential step in perfecting a right to marshal, good against a superior lienor or creditor upon whom the demand is made and against others who are also entitled to marshaling, but the demand does not itself create a lien or interest in any asset. A right to marshal does not ripen into an interest in the nature of an equitable lien until the court, applying equitable principles, enforces it."

Id. at 319. Both majority and dissent cite Harrington v. Taylor, 176 Cal. 802, 169 P. 690 (1917) which states: "This inchoate right or equity is not a lien, and is therefore subject to defeat at any time before it is attempted to be enforced."

persons are involved, it will not be enforced to their prejudice.[15] As a consequence, the paramount mortgage is prorated between the two junior mortgagees in proportion to the value of the parcel to which each has claim.[16] In some of the American cases marshaling is refused by simply denying that when T–2 takes an interest in Y he or she is charged with constructive notice of T–1's inchoate equity of T–1 through the recorded second mortgage on X.[17]

The English courts prorate even though the later second mortgagee of lot Y has actual notice of the prior junior lien on lot X.[18] There is American authority that T–1's prior equity, even though regarded as inchoate, will prevail over T–2 if the latter did not part with value for it.[19] However, if T–2 paid value, doubt has been expressed as to whether T–1 should prevail over T–2 even if the latter actually knew of the existence of T–1's mortgage but had no reason to anticipate that T–1 would invoke the doctrine of marshaling.[20] Under this view, if T–2

15. Vandever Investment Co., Inc. v. H.E. Leonhardt Lumber Co., 503 P.2d 185, 76 A.L.R.3d 315 (Okl.1972); Platte Valley Bank of North Bend v. Kracl, 185 Neb. 168, 174 N.W.2d 724 (1970); St. Clair Savings Association v. Janson, 40 Ohio App.2d 211, 318 N.E.2d 538, 69 O.O.2d 196 (1974). Two funds denied when it would prejudice general creditors, Langel v. Moore, 119 Ohio St. 299, 164 N.E. 118 (1928); Bronaugh v. Burley Tobacco Co., 212 Ky. 680, 685, 280 S.W. 97 (1926) (junior mortgage on one tract, followed by execution lien on other tract); Richards v. Cowles, 105 Iowa 734, 75 N.W. 648 (1898).

16. Omaha National Bank v. Continental Western Corp., 203 Neb. 264, 278 N.W.2d 339 (1979); Vandever Investment Co., Inc. v. H.E. Leonhardt Lumber Co., n. 64, supra; Bryson v. Newtown Real Estate and Development Corp., 153 Conn. 267, 216 A.2d 176 (1965); Conneaut Building & Loan Co. v. Felch, 100 Ohio App. 52, 135 N.E.2d 480, 60 O.O. 15 (1955); Green v. Ramage, 18 Ohio 428, 51 Am.Dec. 458 (1849). See 76 A.L.R.3d 351, § 5 (1977). The proration approach is adopted by Restatement (Second) of Restitution § 44(3) and Illustration 4 (Tent.Draft No. 2, 1984).

17. See Gilliam v. McCormack, 85 Tenn. 597, 4 S.W. 521 (1887); Bronaugh v. Burley Tobacco Co., note 15, supra; Cf. last sentence quoted from Shenkin, note 12, supra.

18. Barnes v. Racster, 1 Younge & C.C.C. 401 (1842). See note 12, supra.

19. E.g., Ingersoll v. Somers Land Co., 82 N.J.Eq. 476, 89 A. 288 (1913), later mortgage of other parcel was to secure preexisting debt; Harron v. Du Bois, 64 N.J.Eq. 657, 54 A. 857 (1903) (later encumbrance was judgment lien); Humphries v. Fitzpatrick, 253 Ky. 517, 69 S.W.2d 1058 (1934) (attachment creditor as to second parcel); Bank of Commerce of Evansville v. First National Bank of Evansville, 150 Ind. 588, 594, 50 N.E. 566, 568 (1898) (later conveyance of second parcel to trustee to pay creditors). See quotation from Newby v. Fox, note 20, infra. General creditors of the mortgagor have been regarded as falling within this class, First National Bank of Boston v. Proctor, 40 F.2d 841 (1930), certiorari denied 282 U.S. 863, 51 S.Ct. 36, 75 L.Ed. 764 (1930), in spite of a suggestion that this was unfair to them. See Langdell, A Brief Survey of Equity Jurisdiction, 15. Compare Langel v. Moore, 32 Ohio App. 352, 168 N.E. 57 (1928), affirmed 119 Ohio St. 299, 164 N.E. 118 (1928) commented on, 43 Harv.L.Rev. 501 (1930). Cf. Shewmaker v. Yankey, 23 Ky.L.Rep. 1759, 66 S.W. 1 (1902) (general creditors for whose benefit an assignment has been made); Bronaugh v. Burley Tobacco Co., 212 Ky. 680, 280 S.W. 97 (1926) (judgment creditor).

20. "One who acquires title through the debtor without parting with value (as a judgment creditor or a grantee in a voluntary conveyance) cannot thereby gain any superior standing. Even a purchaser for value who becomes such with notice of a proceeding to enforce the right to have the securities marshaled must be deemed to have acted at his peril. But it might unduly extend this merely equitable right to allow its enforcement against one who has bought and paid for the singly mortgaged land, knowing, to be sure, of the existence of the two mortgages, but having no particular reason to anticipate that the doctrine of marshaling securities will ever be invoked." Newby v. Fox, 90 Kan. 317, 323,

has notice of a proceeding by T-1 to enforce marshaling, T-2 will take subject to it.[21]

The doctrine of the first group of cases has been vigorously criticized as a mistaken and improper application of the doctrine of sale in the inverse order of alienation.[22] It is said that a second mortgagee on X, unlike a purchaser of it for full value, does not pay to get the land free and clear of the first mortgage, but merely bargains for a security interest in it subordinate to the first mortgage. So far as other portions of the tract are concerned, since T-1 did not stipulate for any security interest in them, it even has been argued that as to them T-1 should have no better right than general creditors and should come in, *pari passu*, with them.[23] And it is contended that T-1 should have no priority over T-2, who has acquired an interest in those other parcels without notice as purchaser for full value or as mortgagee.

In answer it is urged that "Second mortgages upon portions of mortgaged premises are rarely taken without considering and relying upon the equity which will arise in favor of the second mortgagee to have the first mortgage charged upon the residue of the property; * * *."[24] Furthermore, it has been pointed out that the English rule opens a door to the practice of fraud by the mortgagor-transferor.[25] One scholar also pointed out that it is hard to understand how the right of a second mortgagee to marshaling, which at the time the mortgage is taken exists against the mortgagor and the owner of the paramount mortgage of the whole tract,[26] "can be lost by the intervention of a second mortgagee, over whom, and over the mortgagor, the second mortgagee has no control; nor is it easy to understand why a second mortgagee should be obliged to keep constant watch upon the registry of deeds and assert his equity by litigation against every casual purchaser who records a deed fixing a later lien upon the mortgaged land."[27]

133 P. 890, 892 (1913). Cf. text at note 8, supra.

21. Id.

22. "If this doctrine is applied to successive second mortgages in these cases, and the second lot so mortgaged is sold first on foreclosure of the blanket mortgage to the exoneration of the second mortgage on the first lot, the result is almost surely to destroy altogether the second mortgage on that lot. * * * It should be clear that it never can be applied without such injury where the second parcel has been mortgaged instead of conveyed outright." Walsh & Simpson, Cas. Security Transactions, 376. See also Newby v. Fox, 90 Kan. 317, 325, 133 P. 890, 893 (1913).

23. "As between secured and unsecured creditors, equity clearly ought to favor the latter class, if either." Langdell, A Brief Survey of Equity Jurisdiction, 15.

24. La Farge Fire Insurance Co. v. Bell, 22 Barb. 54, 65 (N.Y.1856). As to the duty of a mortgagor to pay off a first mortgage for the benefit of a second mortgagee and the latter's justifiable expectation of advancement in that event see § 10.6, supra.

25. "There is nothing to stop him from giving C, a friend, a mortgage on the second property, reducing to that extent the amount that B would otherwise get. Of course, if a court of equity even suspects the presence of fraud in the case, B and C will not be treated equally, but the possibility is still present, and it may be for this reason that a number of American jurisdictions have reached an opposite result." Shenkin, op.cit. supra note 12, 785 n. 14.

26. See note 20, supra.

27. Keigwin, Cas.Morts., 583 n. 49.

The English rule of pro-ration even though the subsequent second mortgagee of Y had notice of the prior junior mortgage on X seems wrong. Very clearly T–1 did acquire an equity of marshaling against lots Y and Z at the time T–1 took the second mortgage on X. The equity acquired at that time may well be regarded as "so weak that the rights of a bona fide purchaser for value without notice could displace it, but the equity should be sufficiently virile not to be defeated by the rights of a subsequent taker with notice of its existence."[28] On the other hand, the rule of pro-ration if T–2 takes without notice of any sort seems entirely fair and prevents the caprice of E from determining where any loss shall fall. If notice is only constructive through recordation of T–1's second mortgage, it is difficult to decide between the two results. The preferable solution would seem to be a compromise. Where the "two funds" rule of marshaling is proper it should not be regarded as creating in the first sub-mortgagee of a parcel a fixed indisplaceable equity as does the inverse order of alienation rule.[29] To this extent there is merit in the attitude of the courts in the second group of cases. So regarded, however, it seems desirable to accept the view of the first group to the extent that T–1's right to marshaling against the other parcels be recognized as the general rule but that relief will be refused in the particular case if it would work injustice.[30] This gives to the "two funds" doctrine to some extent the greater certainty of the inverse order rule and yet preserves to it sufficient flexibility to deal with the individual case, if this should be necessary, at the date the right is invoked by action. This flexibility, unimportant where the inverse rule is properly applicable, i.e., in case of successive purchases of portions of the mortgaged property for full value, is of consequence where sub-mortgages on different parcels are concerned. As has been pointed out, the reason is that the lienor on lot X may be amply secured whereas the lienor on lot Y is insufficiently margined.[31]

The last point has relevancy also where one of the sub-mortgagees of part of the property subject to a paramount mortgage has taken, in addition, a piece of property not under that mortgage.[32] That is, lots X and Y only are mortgaged to E. T–1 takes a second mortgage on lot X and also takes a first mortgage on lot Z. T–2 then takes a second mortgage on lot Y with knowledge of the situation. T–1 as well as E is a doubly secured creditor, and any equity of marshaling T–1 may have

---

28. Shenkin, Marshaling of Securities, 79 U. of Pa.L.Rev. 782, 787 (1931).

29. Shenkin, op.cit. supra note 28, at 785.

30. E.g., Bernhardt v. Lymburner, 85 N.Y. 172 (1881), although recognizing the general rule of marshaling as being established, refused to apply it where it would work injustice. See also Sternberger v. Sussman, 69 N.J.Eq. 199, 60 A. 195 (1905), affirmed 85 N.J.Eq. 593, 98 A. 1087 (1916); Payne v. Avery, 21 Mich. 524 (1870); Milligan's Appeal, 104 Pa. 503 (1883).

31. Glenn, Morts., § 298. The learned author adds: "The fact that one may have such a case in front of him does not require a general rule that there shall never be marshalling in the case of liens, but it will justify an exception in this case of hardship." Ibid.

32. In general assets will not be marshaled where there are different funds, or the funds are not in the hands of a common debtor, but there are exceptions to this. See note 1, supra.

as against E and Y would seem to be limited to the excess of T–1's debt over the value of the outside security, Z. T–2, if T–1 is disregarded, has an equity to have E go first against X. The proper solution, therefore, would seem to be that T–2 should be able to have marshaling, limited only by T–1's superior claim to be able to reach X ahead of T–2 as to any deficiency T–1 would have after applying the value of lot Z. If T–1 is amply secured by Z alone, there is authority for the indicated result.[33] Even if T–1 is not, the principle suggested seems properly applicable and could be used without difficulty if T–1's debt was due at the time of E's foreclosure. Even if it was not, T–1 might be protected by requiring clear proof of the minimum amount Z would yield and reserving out of the sale of X an amount equal to the difference until T–1's debt matured.[34]

§ 10.14 Marshaling by Mortgagor—Exemptions

In general a debtor is not entitled to invoke the doctrine of marshaling,[1] but there are many circumstances in which the mortgagor can compel a doubly secured creditor to resort to one fund rather than to another. Even where the mortgagor is primarily liable for the debt a court may, at the mortgagor's request, restrict the mortgagee to selling only so much of the property as is necessary to pay off the mortgage,[2] or may order the selling of the property by parcels or en masse as will be most advantageous to the mortgagor.[3] If the mortgagor is only secondarily liable she or he can force the mortgagee to proceed against the person or property primarily liable if that will not prejudice the mortgagee.[4] Similarly, if the mortgagor in selling part of a mortgaged tract takes back a mortgage on the portion sold so that he or she now occupies the position of a singly secured creditor as well as being debtor-mortgagor of the doubly secured creditor, the court will

---

33. Worth v. Hill, 14 Wis. 559 (1861). See Glenn, Morts., § 299.

34. Cf. Worth v. Hill, 14 Wis. 559 (1861). The court said that where the adequacy of T–1's outside security could not be tested by sale, the court might nevertheless grant marshaling to T–2 upon testimony of witnesses provided that such testimony clearly established the entire adequacy of lot Z.

§ 10.14

1. See Peterson v. Brent Banking Co., 514 So.2d 888 (Ala.1987); Rogers v. Meyers, 68 Ill. 92, 97 (1873); Newby v. Fox, 90 Kan. 317, 320, 133 P. 890, 891 (1913); Dolphin v. Aylward, 4 Eng. & Irish.App.L.Rev. 486, 505. See Schwartz, Marshaling Assets for Benefit of Mortgagor, 5 Not.D.Law. 208 (1930); 47 L.R.A.,N.S., 302 (1914).

2. See text at § 7.21 supra.

3. Id. Security Savings Bank v. King, 198 Iowa, 1151, 199 N.W. 166 (1924); McClintic-Marshall Co. v. Scandinavian-American Building Co., 296 Fed. 601 (9th Cir.1924).

As to the right of the maker of a negotiable instrument to compel the marshaling of securities in his or her favor, see Sowell v. Federal Reserve Bank of Dallas, 268 U.S. 449, 45 S.Ct. 528, 69 L.Ed. 1041 (1925), discussed in note, 39 Harv.L.Rev. 256 (1925). See also note, 34 Col.L.Rev. 779 (1934).

4. Konoff v. Lantini, 111 R.I. 691, 306 A.2d 176 (1973); Bartley v. Pikeville National Bank & Trust Co., 532 S.W.2d 446 (Ky.1975); Cook v. American States Insurance Co., 150 Ind.App. 88, 275 N.E.2d 832 (1971); Sanders v. Lackey, 59 Tenn.App. 207, 439 S.W.2d 610 (1968); Champlain Valley Federal Savings & Loan Association v. Ladue, 35 A.D.2d 888, 316 N.Y.S.2d 19 (1970).

order marshaling under the two funds doctrine.[5]

Perhaps the most frequent case where the question of a mortgagor's right to marshal has arisen is where one of the mortgaged parcels, X, is subject to a homestead exemption which was waived[6] in favor of E when R gave the mortgage on the entire tract of which X is a part.[7] Later R may have given a second mortgage on parcel Y on which R had no exemption. Where the question arises between the two creditors E and T–1, the weight of authority refuses to apply the usual two funds rule of marshaling in favor of T–1 even though the result may be that E will collect out of Y leaving T–1 unsecured.[8] The justification for this result is found in the policy of protecting homesteads from forced sales. In some states legislation expressly protects the mortgagor and his or her family in such a situation.[9] There are, however, some cases which have held that T–1 may have marshaling even against X, the homestead parcel, this being the fund to which T–1 had no access.[10]

Where the question arises between the mortgagor and two creditors, E and T–1, the majority rule is that the mortgagor may compel E on foreclosure to sell first the property to which the homestead exemption does not apply; thus the mortgagor may have marshaling against T–1.[11] There are a few statutory provisions to the same effect.[12]

---

5. Newby v. Fox, note 1, supra.

6. A debtor may waive his or her homestead in property by language in the mortgage; Thomas v. Wisner, 66 Colo. 243, 180 P. 744 (1919); Cleve v. Adams, 222 N.C. 211, 22 S.E.2d 567 (1942).

7. For discussions and collections of cases, see 46 Harv.L.Rev. 1035 (1933); 12 Tex.L.Rev. 514 (1934); 23 Minn.L.Rev. 692 (1939), reprinted, 23 Or.L.Rev. 204 (1944); 44 A.L.R. 758 (1926); 77 A.L.R. 371 (1932); 17 Ann.Cas. 1061; 47 L.R.A.,N.S., 302, 303 (1913).

8. Lee v. Mercantile First Nat. Bank, 27 Ark.App. 11, 765 S.W.2d 17 (1989); McLaughlin v. Hart, 46 Cal. 638 (1873), appeal after remand 31 Ark.App. 169, 790 S.W.2d 916 (1990) approved on its special facts by Glenn, Mortgages, § 37.3; Bowers v. Norton, 175 Minn. 541, 222 N.W. 71 (1928) (T–1 being an attaching creditor); McArthur v. Martin, 23 Minn. 74 (1876); Douglas County State Bank v. Steele, 54 N.D. 686, 210 N.W. 657 (1926). Cf. In re Estate of Hansen, 458 N.W.2d 264 (N.D. 1990), refusing to apply marshaling where the mortgagor had not requested it and where only mineral homestead estate and not surface homestead estate had been foreclosed upon). See 44 A.L.R. 758 (1926); 77 A.L.R. 371 (1932).

9. E.g., Ill.St. Ch. 735 § 5/2–904; S.C. Const. Art. 3, § 28 (subsequently amended); Wis.Stat.Ann. 815.20; Iowa Code of 1950, § 561.21, discussed in Gaumer v. Hartford–Carlisle Sav. Bank, 451 N.W.2d 497 (Iowa 1990). See 44 A.L.R. 758, 761 (1926); 77 A.L.R. 371, 372 (1932).

10. E.g., State Savings Bank of Anderson v. Harbin, 18 S.C. 425 (1883); cf. Plain v. Roth, 107 Ill. 588 (1883). See 44 A.L.R. 758, 761, 762 (1926). Statutory enactments have overcome most of this authority. E.g., White v. Polleys, 20 Wis. 503, 91 Am.Dec. 432 (1866), later nullified by Wis.Stat.Ann. § 272.20.

11. Alston v. Bitely, 252 Ark. 79, 477 S.W.2d 446 (1972). In Sims v. McFadden, 217 Ark. 810, 233 S.W.2d 375 (1950), the state refused to apply marshaling where exemption would be destroyed even though it entailed a loss to general creditors. Boykin v. First State Bank, 61 S.W.2d 126 (Tex.Civ.App.1933), T–1 being a second mortgagee; In re Tucker's Estate, 160 Or. 362, 85 P.2d 1025 (1938); Frick Co. v. Ketels, 42 Kan. 527, 22 P. 580, 16 Am.St.Rep. 507 (1889). See 44 A.L.R. 758, 763 (1926); 77 A.L.R. 371, 373 (1932).

Where there are other interests exempt under state policy or statute, courts will protect such interests held by a mortgagor by refusing to apply the principle of marshaling in favor of a junior lienor. Dower was protected in Alston v. Bitely, supra this note; Bowen v. Brockenbrough, 119 Ind. 560, 20 N.E. 534 (1889); Stokes v. Stokes, 206 N.C. 108, 173 S.E. 18 (1934).

12. See note 12 on page 42.

However, there is also authority that the mortgagor cannot compel marshaling in such a case.[13]

Where the case arises only between R and E, the majority rule permitting R to save the homestead if E can get paid out of non-exempt property seems a desirable result.[14] Where exercise of the right to compel marshaling will result in saving the mortgaged homestead at the expense of a creditor whose hold is on non-exempt property, the question moves into doubtful area. Perhaps T-1 should be granted marshaling against a homestead if T-1's lien is a second mortgage, but not if the lien was acquired by way of judgment or attachment.[15]

§ 10.15 Effect of Release by Mortgagee

The paramount mortgagee of a tract, having knowledge of parcels which have been transferred or mortgaged to persons under circumstances giving to them a right of marshaling against other portions of the property, must not do anything to defeat the rights of such persons.[1] The knowledge must be actual, not constructive through the recordation of subsequent conveyances or mortgages of portions of the mortgaged property.[2] If the paramount mortgagee has actual notice of subsequent alienations of or mortgages on parcels of the mortgaged property, he or she acts in peril in releasing from the mortgage any

Beneficiaries of life insurance policies may have the right to protection, Meyer v. United States, 375 U.S. 233, 84 S.Ct. 318, 11 L.Ed.2d 293 (1963); Barbin v. Moore, 85 N.H. 362, 159 A. 409, 83 A.L.R. 62 (1932). Marshaling was not applied where the effect would have been to defeat rights of survivorship of debtor's widow in mortgaged realty held in tenancy by the entirety; see First National City Bank v. Phoenix Mutual Life Insurance Co., 364 F.Supp. 390 (S.D.N.Y.1973).

12. See note 9, supra. See 44 A.L.R. 758, 766 (1926); 77 A.L.R. 371, 374 (1932).

13. Booker v. Booker, 225 Ala. 626, 144 So. 870 (1932), discussed 46 Harv. L.Rev. 1034 (1933); Searle v. Chapman, 121 Mass. 19 (1876). See 44 A.L.R. 758, 766 (1926).

14. First National Bank v. Powell, 212 Mont. 468, 689 P.2d 255 (1984) (R may have marshaling only if she demands it at the foreclosure sale). See 46 Harv.L.Rev. 1035 (1933); 12 Tex.L.Rev. 515 (1934). Cf. State Bank of Hartland v. Arndt, 129 Wis.2d 411, 385 N.W.2d 219 (App.1986) (recognizing the rule protecting the homestead, but refusing to apply it because the mortgagee had no valid lien on non-homestead property).

15. E.g., in Merchants' National Bank v. Stanton, 55 Minn. 211, 56 N.W. 821, 43 Am.St.Rep. 491 (1893), a mortgagee was granted marshaling on the ground that his interest arose by contract and not *in invitum*. But cf. Boykin v. First State Bank, 61 S.W.2d 126, 129 (Tex.Civ.App.1933).

§ 10.15

1. See Broughton v. Mount Healthy Flying Service, 104 Ohio App. 479, 143 N.E.2d 597, 5 O.O.2d 224 (1957). In General Builders Supply Co. v. Arlington Cooperative Bank, 359 Mass. 691, 271 N.E.2d 342 (1971) reformation of release was denied where it would prejudice rights of subsequent lienors.

2. Iglehart v. Crane & Wesson, 42 Ill. 261, 268 (1866); Woodward v. Brown, 119 Cal. 283, 51 P. 2, 63 Am.St.Rep. 108 (1897), modified 119 Cal. 283, 51 P. 542, 63 Am.St. Rep. 108 (1897); Ocean County National Bank v. J. Edwin Ellor & Sons, Inc., 116 N.J.Eq. 287, 290, 173 A. 138, 139 (1934); Balen v. Lewis, 130 Mich. 567, 90 N.W. 416, 47 Am.St.Rep. 499 (1902); Bridgewater Roller-Mills Co. v. Strough, 98 Va. 721, 37 S.E. 290 (1900); Clarke v. Cowan, 206 Mass. 252, 92 N.E. 474, 138 Am.St.Rep. 388 (1910), accord. See also Stuyvesant v. Hall, 2 Barb.Ch. 151, 158 (N.Y.1847); 110 A.L.R. 65, 70 (1937); 131 A.L.R. 4, 109 (1941); Ann.Cas.1916D, 1119, 1133; Bridgewater Roller-Mills v. Receivers of Baltimore Building & Loan Association,

part of the property against which the marshaling equity runs.[3] When releasing a parcel under such circumstances, the paramount mortgagee must deduct from the debt, before enforcing the lien against the property in the hands of these persons, the value of the property released which they had a right to have applied to the debt before resorting to the property held by them.[4] If the right was to have the entire parcel applied first, its entire value must be deducted.[5] On the other hand, if the right was only that the released lot should be used to satisfy its pro rata share of the debt, the mortgagee must abate the debt only to such a proportion of it as the value of released parcel bore to the value of the entire tract.[6]

If the property released is one against which there is no right of marshaling, e.g., if it is the parcel first aliened in cases where the inverse order of alienation rule applies, the mortgagee does not have to make any deduction of its value before enforcing the mortgage against the other parcels.[7] Further, if in giving a release of a parcel the mortgagee received a consideration which was applied upon the mortgage debt, he or she may enforce the balance of the debt against the remaining property provided the amount received was equal to the fair value of the lot in question.[8] And if, as is provided in modern

124 Fed. 718 (C.C.Va.1903). See 110 A.L.R. 65, 70, 75 (1937).

3. Charles Construction Co., Inc. v. Leisure Resources, Inc., 1 Mass.App.Ct. 755, 307 N.E.2d 336 (1974). See Brooks v. Benham, 70 Conn. 92, 97, 38 A. 908, 910, 66 Am.St.Rep. 87 (1897).

See also Green, Marshaling Assets in Texas, 34 Texas L.Rev. 1054 (1956).

4. The discharge has been rested upon an impairment of the grantee or mortgagee's right of subrogation. Brooks v. Benham, note 3, supra. Cf. § 5.19, supra, for the cognate problem where not just a portion, but the entire property has been sold. The doctrine of discharge here rests upon an application of the same basic principles applied, however, pro tanto. A junior encumbrancer is entitled to have proceeds of sale of mortgaged property applied upon the senior indebtedness, even though the property sold was not covered by the junior mortgage. See Continental Supply Co. v. Marshall, 152 F.2d 300 (10th Cir.1945), certiorari denied 327 U.S. 803, 66 S.Ct. 962, 90 L.Ed. 1028 (1946).

5. Manufacturers & Traders Trust Co. v. Miner Homes, Inc., 71 A.D.2d 826, 419 N.Y.S.2d 381 (1979), appeal denied 48 N.Y.2d 603, 421 N.Y.S.2d 1027, 396 N.E.2d 206 (1979); Pongetti v. Bankers Trust Savings & Loan Association, 368 So.2d 819 (Miss.1979); Brown v. Simons, 44 N.H. 475 (1863); Hill v. Howell, 36 N.J.Eq. 25 (1882); Schrack v. Shriner, 100 Pa. 451 (1882); New South Bldg. & Loan Association v. Reed, 96 Va. 345, 31 S.E. 514, 70 Am.St. Rep. 858 (1898); Schaad v. Robinson, 50 Wash. 283, 97 P. 104 (1908); Deuster v. McCamus, 14 Wis. 307 (1861)—accord. See also Iglehart v. Crane & Wesson, 42 Ill. 261 (1866); Pomeroy, Eq.Jur., 4th Ed., § 1226, note 4; 110 A.L.R. 65, 67, 73 (1937); 131 A.L.R. 4, 108, 109 (1941). Cf. Gaskill v. Sine, 13 N.J.Eq. 400, 78 Am.Dec. 105 (1861); Snyder v. Crawford, 98 Pa. 414 (1881). Contra: McCoy v. Wynn, 215 Ala. 172, 174, 110 So. 129, 130 (1926).

6. Home Unity Savings & Loan Association v. Balmos, 192 Pa.Super. 542, 162 A.2d 244 (1960); Brooks v. Benham, 70 Conn. 92, 97, 38 A. 908, 910, 66 Am.St.Rep. 87 (1897). See Taylor v. Short's Administrator, 27 Iowa 361, 1 Am.Rep. 280 (1869); Parkman v. Welch, 36 Mass. (19 Pick.) 231 (1837).

7. Clark v. Kraker, 51 Minn. 444, 53 N.W. 706 (1892); Lyman v. Lyman, 32 Vt. 79, 76 Am.Dec. 151 (1859). As to the effect of the mortgagee's release of the mortgagor's personal liability, by dealings with a purchaser of part of the mortgaged property who assumed the mortgage debt, upon the lien of the mortgage upon another part which has been conveyed by the mortgagor to a third person, see 101 A.L.R. 618 (1936).

8. Beardsley v. Empire Trust Co., 96 N.J.Eq. 212, 124 A. 457 (1924), noted 24 Col.L.Rev. 804. See Taylor v. Short's Administrator 27 Iowa 361, 362, 1 Am.Rep. 280 (1869).

mortgages in which subdivisions are contemplated, the mortgagee is given permission to execute partial releases, he or she may release portions without further liability to other holders provided the terms of authorization are followed.[9]

[9]. Thompson v. Thomas, 43 Cal.App. 588, 185 P. 427 (1919). See 110 A.L.R. 65, 72, 77 (1937).

§§ 10.16–11.0 are reserved for supplementary material

Chapter 11

GOVERNMENT INTERVENTION IN THE MORTGAGE MARKET

Table of Sections

Sec.
11.1 The Mortgage Market, Institutional Lenders, and Their Regulators.
11.2 Mortgage Insurers and Guarantors.
11.3 Government–Sponsored Mortgage Market Support Agencies.
11.4 Alternative Mortgage Instruments.
11.5 Discrimination in Mortgage Lending.
11.6 Federal Preemption of State Mortgage Law.
11.7 Resolution of Insolvent Financial Institutions: Impact on Mortgage Transactions.

§ 11.1 The Mortgage Market, Institutional Lenders, and Their Regulators

About thirty percent of the outstanding debt in the United States is secured by real estate mortgages.[1] Because the United States is a nation of homeowners, it is not surprising that more than two-thirds (68.5%) of this mortgage debt is secured by 1-to-4 family homes. (Loans on buildings containing four or fewer residential units are conventionally lumped together and termed "home loans.") Another 20.8% of this mortgage debt is secured by commercial properties, 8.4% by multifamily apartment buildings, and 2.3% by farm properties. Mortgage financing is particularly important in the development of

§ 11.1

1. Economic data in this section are derived from Economic Report of the President (1990) at 372. A further useful source is the Savings and Loan Fact Book, published annually by the United States League of Savings Associations. On the demand for mortgage credit, see Markstein, Crowding Out? An Analysis of Credit Supply and Demand, Mortgage Banking, June 1984, at 35; Aldrich & Kopcke, Real Estate Consequences of the New Credit Markets, 12 Real Est.Rev. 25 (No. 4, Winter 1983).

new real estate projects, and it is quite rare for one to be constructed without mortgage debt.

About 43% of the mortgage debt in the United States is held by private institutional lenders, such as banks and savings and loan associations. Federally-chartered corporations and the mortgaged-backed securities they have issued or guaranteed account for another 41%, with various miscellaneous lenders, including life insurance companies, pension funds, and individuals, holding the remainder. Since private lending institutions are so important in the American mortgage market, they and the regulatory agencies under whose rules they operate are the subject of this section; a subsequent section will discuss the federally-supported agencies active in the mortgage market.

Most mortgage debt consists of relatively long term loans—say, ten to thirty years. Construction lending, which ties up the institution's funds for a relatively short time but requires close on-site supervision, is handled mainly by commercial banks and savings associations.[2] Some real estate investment trusts are also active in the construction lending field, but the federally sponsored agencies, pension funds, and life insurance companies, lacking the necessary local offices and personnel, are almost totally absent from construction lending.

One type of lending organization not mentioned above is the mortgage banker (sometimes simply called a mortgage company). This sort of firm is organized to originate loans, not for retention in its own portfolio, but almost exclusively for sale or assignment to other private investors or government-sponsored agencies that will hold the loans for the long term. All of the types of financial institutions discussed above are active from time to time as investors purchasing loans originated by mortgage bankers. They may also act, in effect, as mortgage bankers themselves, originating loans which they do not expect to hold in portfolio, but rather which will be sold to other investors. Some institutional lenders, particularly commercial banks, have also established mortgage banking subsidiaries.

An important feature of a mortgage banker's activity (as well as that of any other financial institution that happens to be acting in a mortgage banking capacity) is the "servicing" of the loan. Most investors that purchase mortgage loans on the secondary market lack local offices in the area in which the real estate is located. Consequently they usually contract with the originating lender for "servicing" to be provided by that local organization. Servicing includes collecting the regular payments of principal and interest, maintaining an appropriate escrow account for taxes and insurance, following up on any delinquency, and if necessary, arranging for foreclosure. The servicer maintains proper records, remits the loan payments to the investor which holds the loan, and communicates with the investor if problems arise. For

---

2. See Mason & Leaffer, The Preferences of Financial Institutions for Construction and Permanent Mortgage Lending, 4 Am.Real Est. & Urb.Econ.Ass'n J. 41 (1976). On construction lending generally, see infra § 12.1.

performing this work the servicer receives a fee from the investor, commonly an annual amount of three-eighths of one percent of the average outstanding balance of the loan—for example, $150 on a $40,000 loan. Servicing is considered a profitable and attractive activity by mortgage bankers, and they are usually eager to retain servicing when a loan is sold. In recent years an active market in the "sale" of servicing rights has developed; hence, the borrower who originally dealt with a local mortgage company may be notified to send future payments to different company, perhaps many miles away. There was a good deal of consumer dissatisfaction in such cases, and Congress addressed the problem in 1990 by requiring at least a minimal degree of borrower notification concerning transfers of servicing.[3]

The lending activities of mortgage bankers were traditionally unregulated, but in the 1980s a majority of the states adopted licensing laws. Many of them establish only minimal requirements, such as payment of fees, registration of the officers and managers, and the obtaining of surety bonds. A few, however, impose much more far-reaching state regulation of lending and loan servicing operations, including regular on-site examinations.[4] In addition mortgage bankers must, of course, comply with the requirements and guidelines set down by the investor institutions to whom they sell loans, and the requirements of FHA and VA to the extent that they originate loans of those types.

For the other major types of institutional mortgage lenders, intense regulation has been a fact of life since the 1930s. Each of them must comply with the requirements of at least one, and sometimes several, specialized regulatory agencies at the federal or state level. A brief review of this regulatory system follows.

Savings and Loan Associations

The Office of Thrift Supervision (OTS) is the federal regulator of the "thrift industry," which consists of savings and loan associations and their close relations, mutual savings banks. Such associations may be either federally or state chartered; about half of the associations are of each type. All federal charters are issued by the OTS, and federal

3. § 6, Real Estate Settlement Procedures Act, 12 U.S.C.A. § 2605; see HUD's implementing regulations, 24 CFR 3500.21. The statute requires that at the time of loan application, the borrower must be informed as to how likely it is that servicing will be transferred. In addition, if an actual transfer of servicing occurs, the borrower must be given notice by the transferor 15 days before, and by the transferee 15 days after the transfer. The statute contains a grievance procedure and provisions for civil damages and penalties against lenders who fail to comply.

4. See, e.g., West's Fla.Stat.Ann. ch. 521, adopted in 1990. A complete and convenient summary of state laws regulating mortgage banking is found in Negroni & Pfaff, A License to Lend, Mortgage Banking, Aug. 1991, at 33. See also Mancuso & Cooper, New York Mortgage Banker Regulations: A Guide to Understanding the Purposes and Avoiding the Pitfalls, 38 Syracuse L.Rev. 879 (1987); Negroni, Traps for the Unwary: Recent Trends in Mortgage Banking, Mortgage Banking, Oct. 1987, at 166.

associations are closely supervised by the OTS in virtually all areas of activity.[5]

The thrift industry experienced a remarkable upheaval during the 1980s. The industry's financial strength was battered at the beginning of the decade by a period of extremely high interest rates. This forced the institutions to pay savings depositors high rates in order to retain their deposits, while at the same time the institutions' revenues, primarily from fixed interest mortgage loans made in earlier years at lower rates, moved upward only slowly. The result was insolvency for many institutions and a major loss of net worth for nearly all of them. A second stage of difficulty for the industry occurred during the mid-1980s, and resulted from a combination of reduced federal regulation, improvident investments in both residential and commercial mortgage loans, and a major downturn in the real estate markets in many areas of the nation, especially in oil-producing states. The combination of these two waves of crisis took a terrible toll on the industry. The number of thrift institutions declined from more than 4,000 at the beginning of the 1980s to well below 3,000 by the end of the decade, and to about 2,200 by the beginning of 1993.[6]

Congress responded to these problems by enacting the Financial Institutions Reform, Recovery, and Enforcement Act of 1989 (FIRREA)[7]. The act drastically modified the regulatory environment in

---

5. Traditionally the lines between banks and savings and loan associations were tightly drawn, and the transfer of an institution from one category to the other was rare and approved only in unusual circumstances. However, §§ 501–502 of the FDIC Improvement Act of 1991, 12 U.S.C.A. §§ 1815(d)(3), 1467a(t), grants a greatly liberalized authority to the applicable federal banking agencies to approve such changes in status, as well as mergers and consolidations, transfers of assets, and assumptions of liability between one type of institution and another. See OTS proposed regulation implementing this new authority, 57 Fed.Reg. 37112 (1992).

In addition, savings and loan association conversions from mutual to stock form were permitted under Federal Home Loan Bank Board approval beginning in 1976, and numerous conversions have occurred; see 12 CFR Parts 552 and 563b (OTS regulations of mutual-to-stock conversions); Charter Federal Sav. & Loan Ass'n v. OTS, 912 F.2d 1569 (11th Cir.1990). See also Lovell v. One Bancorp, 690 F.Supp. 1090 (D.Me.1988) (conversion of state-chartered mutual savings bank to stock form); Home Mortgage Bank v. Ryan, 768 F.Supp. 330 (D.Utah 1991), affirmed 986 F.2d 372 (10th Cir.1993) (requiring approval of such a conversion by OTS, where institution had been placed in receivership by OTS); Saba & Robbins, Savings and Loan Associations—Mutual to Stock Conversion Under the Revised Regulations, 17 Ark.L.Rev. 413 (1984).

6. The events leading to the enactment of FIRREA are detailed in U.S. Gen. Accounting Office, Thrifts and Housing Finance: Implications of a Stricter Qualified Thrift Lender Test (1991), at 20–32. See also Tammen, The Savings and Loan Crisis: Which Train Derailed—Deregulation or Deposit Insurance?, 6 J.Law & Politics 311 (1990).

7. Pub.L.No. 101–73, 103 Stat. 183, codified in various sections of 12 U.S.C.A. and other titles. FIRREA was further amended by the Comprehensive Thrift and Bank Fraud Prosecution and Taxpayer Recovery Act of 1990, Pub.L.No. 101–647, 104 Stat. 4859. See Providenti, Playing with FIRREA, Not Getting Burned: Statutory Overview of the Financial Institutions Reform, Recovery and Enforcement Act of 1989, 59 Ford.L.Rev. 323 (1991); Wood, Young, Frost & Nichols, An Overview of FIRREA, Prac.Real Estate Law. 43 (July, 1990); Gail & Norton, A Decade's Journey from "Deregulation" to "Supervisory Reregulation": The Financial Institutions Reform, Recovery & Enforcement Act of 1989, 45 Bus.Law. 1103 (1990); Malloy, Nothing to Fear but FIRREA Itself: Revising and

which the thrift industry operates. It terminated operation of both the Federal Home Loan Bank Board, which had been the industry's principal federal regulator, and the Federal Savings and Loan Insurance Corporation, which had provided deposit insurance to thrift institutions. The regulatory functions were transferred to the newly-created Office of Thrift Supervision, an agency of the Department of the Treasury.[8] The FSLIC's deposit insurance functions were assumed by a new Savings Associations Insurance Fund (SAIF), created under the control of the Federal Deposit Insurance Corporation, which had long provided deposit insurance for the banking industry; the preexisting FDIC insurance program for banks became known as the Bank Insurance Fund (BIF). FIRREA also imposed major new restrictions on the lending powers and capital requirements of thrift institutions,[9] and created the Resolution Trust Corporation to manage and dispose of the assets of insolvent thrifts.[10]

The federal government also exercises considerable authority over most state-chartered savings and loan associations by virtue of their membership in the FDIC's Savings Association Insurance Fund (SAIF), which insures depositors against loss up to a statutory maximum, currently $100,000. This deposit insurance is, of course, an extremely attractive drawing card for institutions seeking deposits, so most state-chartered institutions obtain it, as do all federal associations. The scope of the regulations governing state-chartered institutions through the FDIC is somewhat more limited than the regulations governing federal associations, but it has grown under FIRREA. For example, the federal regulations governing real estate lending traditionally applied only to federally-chartered institutions, while state associations were governed in this respect by state law. However, the FDIC Improve-

Reshaping the Enforcement Process of Federal Bank Regulation, 50 Ohio St.L.J. 1117 (1989).

8. The transfer of these functions was fraught with problems. Members of the industry pointed to various assurances made to them by FHLBB, especially concerning accounting and capital requirements, but OTS generally rejected any duty to comply with those assurances. The courts generally favored OTS, but the cases are mixed. See, e.g., Security Sav. & Loan Ass'n v. OTS, 960 F.2d 1318 (5th Cir.1992); Transohio Savings Bank v. OTS, 967 F.2d 598 (D.C.Cir.1992); Carteret Saving Bank v. OTS, 963 F.2d 567 (3d Cir. 1992); Ensign Financial Corp. v. FDIC, 785 F.Supp. 391 (S.D.N.Y.1992); Security Fed. Sav. & Loan Ass'n v. FSLIC, 796 F.Supp. 1435 (D.N.M.1991); Security Sav. and Loan Ass'n v. OTS, 761 F.Supp. 1277 (S.D.Miss. 1991); Security Federal Sav. Bank v. OTS, 747 F.Supp. 656 (N.D.Fla.1990).

9. Regulations issued under FIRREA adopted "risk-based" capital requirements; in effect, they demanded greater net worth for institutions engaging in lending considered relatively more risky; see Costello, The Qualified Thrift Lender Test of FIRREA: Reregulation, 36 Fed.B.News & J. 477 (1989); Note, FIRREA: Controlling Savings and Loan Association Credit Risk Through Capital Standards and Asset Restrictions, 100 Yale L.J. 149 (1990).

10. See Day, Gregory & Nelson, Purchasing Real Property Assets from the Resolution Trust Corporation, 41 Mercer L.Rev. 1157 (1990); Simpson, Scaling Back FIRREA: Federal Judges Begin to Place Limits on RTC's Conservatorship/Receivership Powers, 25 Ga.L.Rev. 1375 (1991); Adams, Is the Power of the RTC Unlimited? Federal Preemption of State Banking Law, 18 Fla.St.U.L.Rev. 995 (1991); Tucker, Meire & Rubinstein, The RTC: A Practical Guide to the Receivership/Conservatorship Process and the Resolution of Failed Thrifts, 25 U.Rich.L.Rev. 1 (1990).

ment Act of 1991 authorized all four of the principal federal banking agencies (FDIC, OTS, the Federal Reserve Board, and the Office of the Comptroller of the Currency, which regulates national banks) to issue consistent regulations on mortgage lending.[11] Under these regulations, for example, the maximum loan-to-value ratios on real estate loans are the same for all federally-regulated lenders.

In most states, state-chartered associations are also subject to the supervision of a state banking or savings and loan commission or board. This agency's regulations or some applicable state statute often regulates lending powers and other operational activities of state-chartered associations that are not governed by FDIC's regulations. In many states, state-chartered associations are subject to periodic on-site examinations by both the federal and state authorities. In other states, however, a cooperative arrangement has been negotiated under which the state supervisory agency merely receives copies of the federal examiners' reports and does not attempt to perform independent examinations except in unusual or emergency cases.

Commercial Banks

The regulation of commercial banks is far more complex than that of any other form of financial institution. Part of the complexity derives from the fact that both federal and state charters are possible, a feature commonly termed the "dual banking" system.[12] More important is the fact that three federal agencies are charged with commercial bank supervision.[13] All federally-chartered (so-called "national") banks are supervised by the Comptroller of the Currency, a division of the U.S. Treasury Department. State-chartered banks that are members of the Federal Reserve System, and are thereby privileged to draw funds at the credit windows of the Federal Reserve Banks, are supervised by the Board of Governors of the Federal Reserve System, commonly called the Federal Reserve Board (FRB) or the "Fed." Many large state banks fall in this category, and all federally-chartered banks are automatically members of the Federal Reserve System. State-chartered banks that are not members of the Federal Reserve System ("nonfed-member" banks) may nonetheless have their deposits insured (currently up to $100,000) by the Federal Deposit Insurance Corporation

---

11. § 304, FDIC Improvement Act, Pub.L.No. 102–242, codified at 12 U.S.C.A. § 1828. The resulting regulations are found in 57 Fed.Reg. 62890 (Dec. 31, 1992).

12. See Scott, The Dual Banking System: A Model of Competition in Regulation, 30 Stan.L.Rev. 1 (1977); Brown, The Dual Banking System in the United States (American Bankers Assoc. undated), reprinted in Subcomm. on Financial Institutions, Senate Comm. on Banking, Housing and Urban Affairs, Compendium of Issues Relating to Branching by Financial Institutions, 94th Cong., 2d Sess. (1976) at 239.

13. See Mitchell–Lockyer, The Federalization of Banking–Due-on-Sales, A Case in Point, 15 Pac.L.J. 217 (1984); Gorinson & Manishin, Garn–St. Germain: A Harbinger of Change, 40 Wash. & Lee L.Rev. 1313 (1983); Note, Deregulation of the Banking Industry in the 1980's, 86 W.Va. L.Rev. 189 (1983); Via, Some Thoughts on Evaluating the Tripartite Federal Bank Regulatory System, 93 Banking L.J. 509 (1976); Kreider, American Banking: Structure, Supervision, and Strengths, 92 Banking L.J. 437 (1975).

(FDIC), which in turn exercises supervisory authority over them. The great majority of state-chartered non-fed-member banks are FDIC-insured, as are all fed-member banks and national banks.[14]

In addition to this complex federal regulatory structure, state-chartered banks are all at least potentially subject to regulation by a state agency.[15] In some jurisdictions the state supervision is intense, while in others the state regulators rely principally upon the examination and supervision efforts of the relevant federal agencies except with respect to the small number of banks which are not even FDIC-insured.

The banking regulatory system has fairly been called "baffling."[16] It is quite possible, for example, for a fed-member state bank to be subject to the regulations of at least three agencies—the FRB, the FDIC, and the state banking commissioner—with respect to various phases of its operations. Coordination among the multitude of agencies involved is not as extensive as might be desired. The system has obvious inefficiencies built into it, and it is not unusual for an institution to engage in a sort of "agency-shopping," changing its status in order to align itself with a regulatory agency that will better fit its desires.[17]

The mortgage lending powers of national banks were traditionally governed by Section 24 of the Federal Reserve Act.[18] However, in 1982 the Garn–St. Germain Act removed all statutory restrictions on real estate lending by national banks.[19] The Office of Comptroller of the Currency then amended its rules to leave these banks essentially unrestricted.[20] This situation continued until 1993, when the banking agencies, acting under the authority of the FDIC Improvement Act of 1991, instituted a uniform system of real estate lending regulations for all federally-insured and federally-chartered banks and savings and loan associations.[21]

Many proposals for reform of the federal banking regulatory system have been made over the years,[22] most of them recommending some

---

14. See Murane, The FDIC and Bank Regulation, 89 Banking L.J. 483 (1972); Scott & Mayer, Risk and Regulation in Banking: Some Proposals for Federal Deposit Insurance Reform, 23 Stan.L.Rev. 857 (1971).

15. See Vestner, Trends and Developments in State Regulation of Banks, 90 Banking L.J. 464 (1973); Bell, State Regulation of Commercial Banks, 26 Bus.Law. 109 (1970).

16. See Hackley, Our Baffling Banking System, Part I, 52 Va.L.Rev. 565 (1966); Part II, 52 Va.L.Rev. 771 (1966).

17. See Changing Charters—Did the Bank Switch Rather Than Fight the Fed. Examiners? Wall St.J., Apr. 26, 1976, at p. 1, col. 6.

18. 12 U.S.C.A. § 371.

19. Pub.L.No. 97–320, at § 403.

20. 12 CFR Part 34, added by 48 Fed. Reg. 40698.

21. See supra note 11.

22. See Blueprint for Reform: The Report of the Task Group on Regulation of Financial Services (1984); Report of the President's Commission on Housing 131–33 (1982); Report of the President's Commission on Financial Structure and Regulation (the "Hunt Commission," after its chair, Reed O. Hunt) (1972), at 87–95; the Federal Bank Commission Act, S. 684, 95th Cong., 1st Sess. (1977), proposing a single federal banking agency. See Fischel, Rosenfield & Stillman, The Regulation of Banks and Bank Holding Companies, 73 Va.L.Rev. 301 (1987); Miller, The Future of the Dual Banking System, 53 Brooklyn

form of consolidation of the plethora of regulators. Prior to 1989 commercial banks and savings and loan associations were regulated by entirely separate sets of agencies with little coordination. FIRREA changed that picture, and today two agencies operating under the umbrella of the Department of the Treasury, the OCC and the OTS, regulate respectively federally-chartered banks and federal savings and loan associations. Likewise, the FDIC issues federal deposit insurance regulations applicable both to banks (through the BIF) and savings and loan associations (through the SAIF). Hence, a great deal of consolidation and coordination has been accomplished.

Pensions Funds and Life Insurance Companies

Unlike savings and loan associations and banks, life insurance companies and pension funds are not depository institutions. Instead, their assets come from premium payments on life policies and contributions to various retirement and annuity programs. These comprise a relatively stable and predictable source of funds compared with savings deposits. Hence, these companies have a preference for long-term large-dollar mortgage loans. Since they are regulated only at the state level by insurance commissions or departments, and since the legal constraints on their lending are not very restrictive, they are generally able to make loans of precisely this type. Moreover, in most jurisdictions they are permitted to invest in real estate financings other than standard mortgage loans. These include sale-leasebacks, sale-salebacks, leasehold mortgages, and other innovative financing methods. These investments are often called "basket" loans since the applicable law or regulation usually provides for a maximum percentage of assets which can be devoted to these relatively unusual types of financings.[23]

Real Estate Investment Trusts

A real estate investment trust (REIT) is much like a mutual fund, except that it invests in mortgages or equity positions in real estate rather than in marketable securities. If seventy-five percent of the trust's income is derived from real estate, and if 95 percent of its profits are distributed annually to shareholders, the trust is taxed only on its retained earnings; in effect, the profits can be passed through to the shareholders without tax.[24] There are two basic types of REITs: mort-

L.Rev. 1 (1987); Ginsberg, An Idea for a Modified Dual Banking System, 53 Brooklyn L.Rev. 23 (1987); Note, The Federal Bank Commission Act: A Proposal to Consolidate the Federal Banking Agencies, 25 Cleve.St.L.Rev. 475 (1977); Keeffe and Head, What is Wrong with the American Banking System and What to do About It, 36 Md.L.Rev. 788 (1977); Verkuil, Perspectives on Reform of Financial Institutions, 83 Yale L.J. 1349 (1974). See also Hearings on Financial Institutions and the Nation's Economy (FINE) "Discussion Principles" before the Subcomm. on Financial Institutions, House Comm. on Banking, Currency and Housing, 94th Cong., 1st & 2d Sess., pts. 1–4 (1975).

23. See Gunning and Roegge, Contemporary Real Estate Financing Techniques: A Dialogue on Vanishing Simplicity, 3 Real Prop.Prob. & Tr.J. 322, 325 (1968).

24. See Englebrecht and Kramer, Tax Breaks for REITs Under the Tax Reform Act, 7 Real Est.Rev. 33 (No. 1, Spring 1977).

gage REITs, which concentrate on making mortgage loans, principally on large income projects, and equity REITs, which take ownership positions in such projects. Shares of REIT's are generally traded on the national and regional stock exchanges and are widely held.

Many mortgage REITs, especially those engaged in short-term construction lending, have experienced financial difficulties. To a great extent they employed bank lines of credit as a source of capital from which to make construction loans. Increases in interest rates on this credit, construction delays and cost overruns, and the inability of their developer-borrowers to market the projects were all important factors in producing losses.[25] For these reasons, many investment advisors see equity REITs, or mortgage REITs specializing in long-term loans on carefully selected properties, as more attractive investments.

§ 11.2 Mortgage Insurers and Guarantors

From the viewpoint of a mortgage lender, each loan represents a risk of loss. In order for an actual loss to be sustained, two or perhaps three occurrences must eventuate. First, there must be a default in payment by the mortgagor or his or her successor which is uncured. Second, the foreclosure of the mortgage (and the ultimate marketing of the property by the lender if it is the successful bidder at the foreclosure sale) must produce insufficient funds to cover the outstanding debt, accrued interest, and costs and fees associated with the foreclosure. Third, the deficiency must be uncollectable (either because of a legal prohibition on its collection or because the borrower is unable to pay the judgment) or inadequate to cover the loss resulting from foreclosure.[1]

Lenders attempt to assess the risk of loss for each loan they make. This process is termed "underwriting" the loan. For a home mortgage, it consists of appraising the property, obtaining a credit history on the borrower, verifying the borrower's employment and income, and obtaining a variety of other information thought to be useful in predicting risk. While this process is routinized in the offices of most institutional lenders, and while various rules of thumb have been developed to determine whether a proposed borrower is acceptable, the scientific basis for mortgage risk assessment is surprisingly rudimentary. Some factors commonly considered—length of time on the present job or in residence in the community, for example—are probably of marginal relevance. One factor, however, stands out as a highly reliable indicator: the higher the loan-to-value ratio, the greater the risk.[2]

25. See Winston, Choosing Between Publicly Traded Partnerships and Real Estate Investment Trusts, 2 Prac.Real Estate Law. 19 (No.2, Mar. 1986); Stevenson, Lessons From the Mortgage Trust Experience, 6 Real Est.Rev. 72 (No.3, Fall 1976).

§ 11.2
1. On antideficiency statutes, see generally § 8.3, supra.
2. See, e.g., Holloway, Economic Trends, Mortgage Banking, May 1989, at 81; Aylward, Residential Mortgages: Lining Up the Customers, Mortgage Banking, Mar. 1984, at 20; von Furstenberg &

This relation between loan-to-value ratio and risk is intuitively easy to understand. If the borrower has little or no "equity"—that is, excess value above the mortgage debt—in the property, it is relatively easy for him or her to decide simply to walk away when financial difficulties arise; there is nothing to protect by persisting in the face of adversity. The borrower is also unlikely to attempt to sell the property in the event of trouble, since the sales proceeds would be inadequate, after payment of the mortgage, to cover a brokerage commission and other selling expenses. Finally, if the lender forecloses or obtains a deed in lieu, there is obviously a strong probability that the ultimate marketing of the property will produce insufficient funds to cover the debt, interest, and expenses. For these reasons, loan-to-value ratio is highly correlated to mortgage risk.

Logically, lenders making a high volume of mortgage loans might simply charge a somewhat increased interest rate on loans they judged to be relatively risky, thus hedging against the losses that they expected to incur. In modern American mortgage lending, however, lenders attempt to do this only to a modest extent. For reasons of preference and regulation, they tend to a much greater degree to rely on contracts of indemnification with outside entities, usually termed mortgage insurers, to shift the risk of loss.[3] Such insurance contracts are commonly executed on loans in which the loan-to-value ratio exceeds eighty percent, although some lenders employ an even lower threshold ratio. Mortgage insurers charge premiums for executing these contracts, and the cost is generally passed on to the mortgagor, even though the mortgagee is the insured.

Three types of mortgage insurance are commonly written in the United States. The first and oldest is provided by the Federal Housing Administration (FHA), established in 1934 by the National Housing Act[4] and currently a part of the Department of Housing and Urban Development (HUD). The predecessor of the present Department of Veterans Affairs, the Veterans Administration, was given authority to guarantee home loans for GI's by the Servicemen's Readjustment Act in 1944.[5] (Technically, the VA program is termed guaranty rather than insurance, since the agency does not maintain a fund that is actuarially designed to pay future claims.) Finally, private mortgage insurance companies (PMI's) have become a major force, beginning with the chartering of Mortgage Guaranty Insurance Company in Wisconsin in

Green, Estimation of Delinquency Risk for Home Mortgage Portfolios, 2 Am.Real Est. & Urban Econ. Ass'n J. 5 (Spring 1974); von Furstenberg, Technical Studies of Mortgage Default Risk (1971); Herzog and Earley, Home Mortgage Delinquency and Foreclosure (1970); Kendall, Anatomy of the Residential Mortgage (1964).

3. See generally Rapkin, The Private Insurance of Home Mortgages (1973); Griffith, Mortgage Guaranty Insurance is What?, 48 Cal.B.J. 683 (1973).

4. 12 U.S.C.A. §§ 1701–1742.

5. 38 U.S.C.A. § 1801 et seq. The Department of Veterans Affairs also has authority to make direct loans to veterans under 38 U.S.C.A. § 1811, but few such loans are made.

1957;[6] there are now more than a dozen such companies writing mortgage insurance on a national scale. The Farmers Home Administration (FmHA), a division of the Department of Agriculture, also operates home mortgage insurance and guaranty programs.[7] However, FmHA mortgage insurance is available only in towns of 20,000 or less, and the program is relatively small in scale; it will not be discussed in further detail.

FHA's mortgage insurance programs are much more complex than the activities of VA and the PMIs. The latter confine themselves almost exclusively to mortgages on homes (i.e., one-to-four family buildings) and condominiums, while FHA has a vast range of programs covering homes, condominiums, cooperatives, apartment buildings, hospitals, and other types of real estate. FHA's programs are commonly identified by the relevant sections of the National Housing Act: Section 203(b) for ordinary home loans, Section 207 for apartments, Section 234 for condominiums, and so on.

It is instructive to see how the market in home mortgages is divided among the major groups of mortgage insurers.[8] At the end of 1991 about 87 percent of all home loans outstanding were "conventional"—that is, neither insured by FHA nor guaranteed by VA. FHA and VA insured about 8% and 4% of all outstanding home mortgages respectively. The annual volume of home mortgages insured by FHA and VA has fluctuated widely, but the overall trend over the past several decades has been downward as a proportion of all home loans. Roughly 30% of all conventional loans have loan-to-value ratios exceeding 80%, and it is probable that the great majority of this group are PMI-insured.

The major classes of institutional lenders have definite preferences for particular types of mortgage insurance. Savings and loan associations, for example, have generally had little interest in making FHA and VA loans, but have been very active customers of the PMI's. Mortgage bankers, by contrast, have been strong participants in the FHA and VA markets for many years, in part because they developed the pattern of selling many mortgages to the Federal National Mortgage Association (FNMA) during the pre–1972 period when it did not purchase conventional loans. In more recent years, mortgage bankers have also become active in PMI usage.

Lending institutions and particular loans must meet relevant criteria and rules in order to be eligible for mortgage insurance through any

---

6. See Rapkin, supra note 3, at 38ff; The Arthur D. Little Study of the Private Mortgage Insurance Industry (1975); Graaskamp, Development and Structure of Mortgage Loan Guaranty Insurance in the United States, 34 J. Risk & Ins. 47 (1967); Reppe, Why Residential Lenders Like Mortgage Guaranty Insurance, 3 Real Estate Rev. 58 (No. 3, Fall 1973).

7. See Sec. 417, Housing Act of 1949, 42 U.S.C.A. § 1487.

8. The data in this paragraph are derived from Economic Report of the President 382–83 (1992). The data reflect third quarter 1991 conditions, and the reader may readily update them from more recent editions of the same source.

of the three main types of insurers. First, the institution must be approved as such by the insurer or insurers with which it wishes to do business. In the case of FHA and VA, this poses little problem for most lenders. Federally insured financial institutions qualify virtually automatically; "non-supervised" (mainly mortgage bankers) must demonstrate a minimum net worth of $100,000, as well as compliance with certain internal financial procedures.[9] Historically, PMI's were eager to attract new institutional customers and their requirements for approval were not difficult to meet. However, major losses during the 1980s made them much more particular about the solvency and credibility of the lenders with whom they are willing to do business.[10]

In addition, the particular loan in question must conform to the applicable insurer's guidelines. For FHA and VA, the loan's parameters are fixed by statute, and have been subject to constant "tinkering" by Congress. The result is an unduly complex set of rules. For example, a single-family FHA loan cannot (with certain exceptions) exceed 95 percent of the median 1–family house in the area. The loan-to-value ratio is limited to 97% of the first $25,000 of appraised value, 95% of the amount between $25,000 and $125,000, and 90% of the excess above $125,000. In addition to these limitations, the loan may not in any case exceed 98.75% of the appraised value, or 97.75% in the case of a property appraising for more than $50,000.[11]

VA has no specific limits on loan amount, and loans for 100% of value (i.e., with no down payment) are common. Instead, Congress sets a guaranty amount for VA loans. At this writing, the guaranty is computed using a complex sliding scale based on the original principal loan amount. For loans between $56,250 and $144,000, the guaranty is the lesser of $36,000 or 40% of the loan amount.[12] For loans in this range and above $90,000, the $36,000 figure is controlling. Loans exceeding $144,000 receive a guaranty of the lesser of $46,000 or 25% of the loan amount. The guaranty acts in effect as a substitute for the veteran's down payment. Thus, it determines the maximum loan a lender will make with no money down. Since for large loans the

---

9. 24 CFR 203.2–203.4. In 1992 HUD imposed a major increase in these requirements; see 57 Fed.Reg. 58326 (Dec. 9, 1991).

10. See Lacy, MIs: After the Losses, a Second Chance, Mortgage Banking, Sept. 1988, at 79; DeZube, Feeling the Squeeze, Mortgage Banking, Aug.1989, at 12.

11. 12 U.S.C.A. § 1709(b), as most recently amended at this writing by § 503, Housing and Community Devel. Act of 1992, Pub.L.No. 102–550; 24 CFR 203.18. HUD publishes the applicable dollar limits, based on its surveys of housing prices, in the Federal Register from time to time.

FHA borrowers were traditionally permitted to include their closing costs in the appraised value for purposes of calculating the loan amount. In 1991, however, HUD adopted a regulation limiting this privilege to 57% of the closing costs, a move designed to require borrowers to make larger cash investments, and thereby to reduce the risk of default. See 56 Fed.Reg. 24628. This change was met with heavy protest from mortgage lenders, who charged that the cutback was not authorized by Congress and that it would raise the cost of home acquisition for many families. Congress agreed with the lenders, and directed that the limitation be repealed in the 1992 HUD appropriations act, Pub.L.No. 102–389.

12. 38 CFR 36.4302.

guarantee is limited to $46,000, a lender that would require a 25% down payment on an unguaranteed conventional loan (e.g., a 75% loan-to-value ratio) would be willing to make a VA loan of 4 times $46,000, or $184,000. This is roughly the practical limit of VA loans.

PMI's may impose maximum loan amounts or loan-to-value ratio limits as a consequence of their own internal policies or the statutes and regulations of the states in which they are chartered and operate.[13] In addition, PMI-insured conventional loans must comply with the regulations governing the financial institutions that make them,[14] and with the guidelines of the purchasing investor if they are sold on the secondary mortgage market. For these reasons, PMI loans are generally limited to 95% loan-to-value ratios or lower.

For many years both FHA and VA fixed a maximum interest rate on the loans they insured or guaranteed. FHA discontinued this practice for most of its programs in 1983,[15] and in 1992 VA was authorized to discontinue it, at the election of the Secretary of Veterans Affairs.[16] These changes were highly desirable. Under the old system both FHA and VA consistently set their maximum rates at levels below those of conventional loans. Hence, lenders would make FHA and VA loans only at a discount—that is, with the note showing a higher face amount than the amount actually disbursed. Since the regulations of the agencies prohibited the borrower from paying the discount, it was generally paid by the builder or seller of the real estate, who of course attempted to recapture it in the price of the housing. The result was a rather silly system that tended to distort housing prices while saving borrowers nothing in the long run.[17] It was widely criticized by virtually all responsible commentators, and the nation is well rid of it.[18]

Mortgage Insurance Premiums

The premiums charged for mortgage insurance are almost invariably paid by the mortgagor, either in cash at the time the loan is made

13. See Rapkin, supra note 3, at 31–37.

14. See supra § 11.1 note 11.

15. § 424(b)(2), Housing and Urban-Rural Recovery Act of 1983, Pub.L. No. 98–181.

16. 38 U.S.C.A. § 3703, as amended by the Veterans Home Loan Program Revitalization Act of 1992, Pub.L.No. 102–547. It was in fact discontinued immediately.

17. See Hood & Kushner, Real Estate Finance: The Discount Point System and its Effect on Federally Insured Home Loans, 40 U.Mo.K.C.L.Rev. 1 (1971). The problem of limiting rates is well illustrated by Brown v. Tuttle, 189 Ill.App.3d 123, 136 Ill.Dec. 553, 544 N.E.2d 1328 (1989). The purchaser of a house obtained a VA loan, and the seller paid $1,760 in discount points. The purchaser signed a note promising to reimburse the seller, but subsequently refused to pay it. The court held that the note was enforceable despite the prohibition in the VA regulations against the borrower's paying the discount points directly.

18. See Report of the President's Commission on Housing 164 (1982); U.S. Dep't of Housing and Urban Development, Final Report of the Task Force on Housing Costs 54, 62 (1978); Testimony of Secretary James Lynn, Hearings on Administration's 1973 Housing Proposals before the Senate Banking, Housing, and Urban Affairs Comm., 93d Cong., 1st Sess. (1973), at 8 (recommendation derived from National Housing Policy Review Task Force); Report of the President's Commission on Financial Structure and Regulation 77 (1972); Report of the Commission on Mortgage Interest Rates 10 (1969).

or divided into equal monthly installments and paid along with the principal and interest payments. For many years FHA charged a mortgage insurance premium (MIP) of ½ percent per year on the average outstanding balance of the loan, divided into 12 installments and paid with each mortgage payment. However in 1983, acting under new authority from Congress,[19] FHA shifted to a system for most of its programs under which the MIP was paid entirely at the loan closing.[20] It established a premium of 3.8% of the initial loan amount for loans with terms of 25 years or more; slightly smaller premiums were fixed for shorter terms. In 1990, as a result of concerns about the solvency of the FHA's mortgage insurance reserves, the ½ percent per year premium was reinstated on top of the 3.8% front-end MIP.[21] The front-end MIP may be either paid in cash or financed by adding it to the normal mortgage amount. If a group of loans has a favorable loss experience, its mortgagors may receive a refund of a portion of the premiums they have paid.

The VA's loan guarantee program operated for many years at no cost to the veteran-mortgagor; its losses were borne by the federal treasury as a veterans' benefit. However, it now charges a "funding fee" of up to 1.25 percent of the loan amount,[22] which is directed to the VA's Home Loan Guaranty Fund. While not designed to make the VA program actuarially sound, the fee does serve to offset losses from claims.

Premiums charged by the PMIs vary considerably from one company to another, and may also depend on whether the loan-to-value ratio is 85% or below, between 86% and 90%, or between 91% and 95%. Many PMIs give the borrower a choice between a single front-end charge with no payments thereafter, and a combination of front-end and monthly charges. The latter approach is probably more common. A typical premium for a loan with a 90% loan-to-value ratio would be

---

19. § 201, Omnibus Budget Reconciliation Act of 1982, Pub.L. No. 97–253, amending National Housing Act § 203(c), 12 U.S.C.A. § 1709(c).

20. 24 CFR 203.259a, 203.280 et seq., added by 48 Fed.Reg. 28794. See Herzog, Single Premium Plan Premiere, Mortgage Banking, Apr. 1984, at 84; 50 Fed.Reg. 2779 (Jan. 22, 1985), giving further detail on the calculation of the one-time premium.

21. See § 325, Cranston–Gonzalez National Affordable Housing Act of 1990, Pub.L.No. 101–625, introducing the change on a temporary basis; § 2103, Omnibus Budget Reconciliation Act of 1990, Pub.L.No. 101–508, making the change permanent. See HUD's final rule implementing the change, 57 Fed.Reg. 15208 (24 Apr. 1992). The up-front premium is scheduled to decline from 3.8% to 3.0% for fiscal years 1993 and 1994, and to 2.25% thereafter. The duration of the 0.5% annual premium varies with the loan-to-value ratio. For example, for fiscal years 1993 and 1994 it will be payable for 7 years for loan-to-value ratios below 90%, for 12 years if the ratio is between 90% and 95%, and for 30 years if the ratio exceeds 90%. The whole scheme (which we have described only superficially here) seems a model of unnecessary complexity. On the adequacy of FHA's insurance reserves to cover its losses, see Allen & Van Order, High–LTV Lending: Lessons from FHA's Efforts to Shore Up Its Insurance Fund, Secondary Mortgage Markets, Winder 1991/92, at 20.

22. 38 CFR 36.4312(e). The fee is based on the size of the down payment. If the down payment is less than 5%, the fee is 1.25% of the loan amount; if the down payment is 5% or more, but less than 10%, the fee is 0.75%; if the down payment is 10% or more, the fee is 0.5%.

0.9% at closing and 0.55% per year (in monthly installments) for the next ten years.[23] The advent of graduated-payment loans and adjustable rate loans in the early 1980s caused many PMIs to reevaluate their premium schedules, since these new mortgage forms appeared to carry significantly greater risk of default and loss. Higher premiums were established by most companies for such mortgages.

Claims Procedures

The objective of all mortgage lenders in participating in mortgage insurance programs is to shift the loss to the insurer. To accomplish this, some procedure for making and paying claims is necessary. FHA's procedure differs from those of VA and the PMIs; of the three, FHA's is most likely to shift fully to the insurer even the most severe losses. The VA and PMI procedures are similar to one another, and leave open a greater potential for loss by the lender.

Under the traditional approach to FHA claims,[24] still available under limited circumstances, the lender under the single-family programs must acquire title to the property (by foreclosure or deed in lieu) and transfer the property to FHA. It then receives the full loan balance (including out-of-pocket expenses for taxes, assessments, repairs, and the like) in payment of the claim. Under the project mortgage (e.g., multifamily apartment) programs, the lender may either transfer title, or may assign the unforeclosed mortgage to FHA, leaving it to worry about working out the default or acquiring title.[25] If the lender chooses the latter approach, FHA will pay only 99% of the loan balance.[26] Whether the loan is foreclosed or assigned, FHA also includes in the loan balance the expenses of the lender for taxes, assessments, insurance, repairs, and other out-of-pocket costs.[27] FHA also pays two-thirds of the foreclosure expenses if the lender forecloses.

Under the single-family programs, FHA will approve an assignment of a mortgage only if the default was due to circumstances beyond the mortgagor's control.[28] The purpose of permitting assignment on such facts is to allow FHA to engage in forbearance or recasting of

---

23. See Rapkin, supra note 3, at 135. Fairly typical rates for fixed-interest loans are about as follows:

    91% to 95% loan-to-value, 30% coverage: 1.3% at closing plus 0.7% per year.

    86% to 90% loan-to-value, 30% coverage: 0.9% at closing plus 0.55% per year.

    81% to 85% loan-to-value, 25% coverage: 0.5% at closing plus 0.5% per year.

24. 24 CFR 200.155; see generally Note, 49 Bos.U.L.Rev. 717, 722–23 (1969).

25. 24 CFR 207.258.

26. 24 CFR 207.259(b)(2)(iv).

27. 24 CFR 203.402. Accrued interest is not a direct element of the claim, but is compensated for to some extent by the fact that the claim includes interest at the debenture rate, beginning one month following the date of the first delinquent payment. See 24 CFR 203.410, 203.331. Interest at the debenture rate is also paid on out-of-pocket expenses, but only from the date the lender actually expends the funds. See HUD's proposed rule on this point, which nicely summarizes the various expenses for which reimbursement is made, 49 Fed.Reg. 31444 (Aug. 7, 1984); final rule, 50 Fed.Reg. 3891 (Jan. 29, 1985).

28. See 24 U.S.C.A. § 1715u(b); 24 CFR 203.350.

payments under circumstances in which the mortgagee is unwilling to do so.[29] FHA has construed its duty to accept such assignments very narrowly, and several cases have found it to have abused its discretion in refusing to accept assignments.[30]

The traditional approach to FHA claims payment results in acquisition by the government of large numbers of vacant houses. They pose serious problems of maintenance, vandalism, and the blighting of surrounding neighborhoods. FHA attempts to put the houses in marketable condition and lists them for sale, but the process is slow and costly. In 1987 FHA adopted an alternative method of satisfying lenders' claims, termed "claim without conveyance of title" (CWCOT). The government can require its use for all mortgages insured by FHA after November 30, 1983, and it is available at the lender's option for earlier mortgages as well.[31] In fact, however, CWCOT is currently used only in cases in which FHA plans to seek a deficiency judgment, and in other cases at FHA's discretion.

CWCOT works as follows: FHA appraises the property prior to the foreclosure, adjusts the appraised value by deducting an estimate of FHA probable costs of maintenance, holding, and sale, and arrives at a "Commissioner's adjusted fair market value." The lender is informed of this amount and instructed to bid it at the foreclosure sale. If the lender in fact bids that amount, and acquires title as the successful bidder, the lender is in effect considered to have an asset equal in value to the bid. The lender's claim against FHA is then computed by subtracting the bid amount from the balance owing on the debt (includ-

---

29. An alternative form of relief for defaulting homeowners, the Temporary Mortgage Assistance Program (TMAP), was finally implemented by HUD in 1987. It had been authorized by § 341, Housing and Community Development Act of 1980, Pub.L.No. 96–399, 24 U.S.C.A. § 1715u(a), but HUD's original regulations under it were enjoined in Ferrell v. Pierce, 560 F.Supp. 1344 (N.D.Ill.1983), affirmed 743 F.2d 454 (7th Cir.1984). TMAP differs from the assignment program: the lender retains the mortgage and HUD makes assistance payments to make up for the borrower's nonpayment; the borrower executes a note and second mortgage promising to reimburse HUD. See the explanation of the two programs in the preamble to HUD's final TMAP rule, 52 Fed.Reg. 6908 (Mar.5, 1987).

Yet a third form of default relief is termed "special forbearance." The lender retains the loan and has authority to enter into a forbearance agreement with the borrower, providing for suspension or reduction of payments for up to 18 months. HUD makes no assistance payments, but does make certain minor financial concessions to the lender if foreclosure ultimately occurs. See 24 CFR 203.614; Whitacre, Resurrecting Special Forbearance, Mortgage Banking, Nov. 1992, at 85, arguing that this program is the most efficient way of resolving most mortgagor defaults and deserves much more widespread use.

30. These cases typically raise the question whether HUD was arbitrary and capricious in its refusal to find that the default was caused by "circumstances which are beyond the mortgagor's control." Cases so finding include Cronkhite v. Kemp, 741 F.Supp. 828 (E.D.Wash.1990); Butler v. HUD, 595 F.Supp. 1041 (E.D.Pa. 1984); FNMA v. Rathgens, 595 F.Supp. 552 (S.D.Ohio 1984); In re Armstead, 97 B.R. 798 (Bkrtcy.Pa.1989); In re Huderson, 96 B.R. 541 (Bkrtcy.Pa.1989). Contra, see Western & Southern Life Ins. Co. v. Smith, 859 F.2d 407 (6th Cir.1988) and In re Madison, 60 B.R. 837 (E.D.Pa.1986), sustaining HUD's refusal to accept an assignment. It seems clear that Congress intended HUD to take risks that a prudent lender would not accept; see FNMA v. Rathgens, supra.

31. See 24 CFR 203.368 and 24 CFR 203.401, as amended 52 Fed.Reg. 1320 (Jan. 13, 1987); HUD Handbook 4330.1. REV–3 (4/92).

ing the lender's out-of-pocket foreclosure expenses). The lender keeps the property and can market it as it chooses. If the lender can indeed dispose of it for the amount of the "Commissioner's fair market value," the lender will be made whole. If the lender bids more than the "Commissioner's fair market value," it is in effect opining that it can sell the property for more than FHA estimates. That is the lender's privilege, but the burden of actually doing so is then on the lender, and its claim against FHA is only the difference between its actual bid and the loan balance plus expenses.

If a third party outbids the lender and takes title at the foreclosure sale, the calculation of the lender's claim is obvious: the proceeds of the sale are subtracted from the outstanding balance on the loan (including expenses, as above), and FHA must pay the lender the difference. The same principle applies if the property is redeemed from the mortgagee after foreclosure; the proceeds of the redemption are analogous to the proceeds of the sale itself, and the FHA claim is limited to the difference between the redemption amount and the loan balance.

FHA pays claims either in cash or in the form of debentures. Cash payment is more desirable from the lender's viewpoint, since the debentures carry interest rates, fixed by FHA, which are typically lower than those of comparable government obligations; they must therefore be sold by the lender at a discount if it wishes to liquidate them. The option to pay in debentures is intended to help FHA avoid large and unanticipated lump sum cash outflows. For many years FHA has paid claims on single-family home loans in cash,[32] but that policy is subject to change.

Upon acquiring the property, FHA has the option to hold and rent it, or to place it on the market for sale; the former is generally done only in the case of multifamily projects which are already tenanted, and for which no responsible buyer is immediately available. Single-family homes are usually marketed as rapidly as possible, often at a substantial loss. FHA has the right to require the mortgagee to seek a deficiency judgment against the mortgagor in states where this is permitted. For many years FHA rarely exercised this right, but it reversed this policy in 1988 and now requires mortgagees to pursue deficiencies where their collection appears practical, at least with regard to "worst-case" offenders.[33] If a judgment is obtained by the mortgagee it is then assigned to HUD, which undertakes the ultimate responsibility for collecting it. The mortgagee's expenses in seeking the deficiency judgment are fully reimbursed by HUD.

VA's claim procedure is quite different than FHA's. Upon notification by the lender that it intends to foreclose, VA appraises the property to determine its fair market value. It then subtracts from that value the amount VA estimates it will spend in disposing of the

---

32. See preamble, 52 Fed.Reg. 1320 (Jan.13, 1987).

33. 24 CFR 203.369, added by 53 Fed. Reg. 4384 (Feb.16, 1988).

property, including property taxes, assessments, other liens, maintenance, resale commissions and other costs, and a factor for VA's administrative expenses.[34] The result of this computation is termed the "net value" of the property; in effect, it is the amount VA expects to "clear" after disposing of the property.

VA then determines whether to authorize the lender to bid at the foreclosure in VA's behalf, with a concomitant right to convey the property to VA in return for VA's payment of the debt and foreclosure expenses in full.[35] Of course, this is the procedure lenders invariably prefer. But whether VA will authorize it depends on the property's value in relation to the amount of the VA guaranty. In effect, the guaranty represents VA's maximum financial exposure. Computation of the guaranty is based on a complex sliding scale; as mentioned above,[36] for most loans up to $144,000, it is the lesser of $36,000 or 40% of the original loan amount, while loans exceeding $144,000 receive a guaranty of the lesser of $46,000 or 25% of the loan amount. If the difference between the lender's full claim (the loan balance and costs) and the property's net value is less than the guaranty amount, VA will authorize the lender to bid a "specified amount," which is the lesser of the loan balance and the net value. If the lender is the successful bidder, it conveys the property to VA which pays the full claim. If a third party outbids the lender, the lender retains the proceeds of the sale and VA pays the lender the additional amount (if any) needed to make the lender whole.

However, if the amount VA would pay under this procedure exceeds the guaranty, VA simply pays the guaranty amount to the lender, which is then free to buy the property in foreclosure and dispose of it in the most advantageous manner possible. Such cases are referred to as "no-bids," and lenders do not like them. Conceivably the lender will come out whole in a no-bid case, if the property's net value is only a little lower than the debt balance minus the guaranty; the lender may be able to acquire and market the property more efficiently than VA. But in the great majority of cases, a "no-bid" means a loss to the lender.

To illustrate VA's procedure, assume a loan with an original balance of $75,000, a current balance including interest and expenses of $70,000, and an appraised value of $60,000. The VA guaranty would be $30,000 on these facts. VA would calculate the net value by subtracting the currently applicable percentage—say, 15% or $9,000, giving a net value of $51,000. VA would authorize the lender to bid this

---

34. See 38 CFR 36.4323. The amount deducted for these items varies from year to year, and is published by VA in the Federal Register annually, based on its cost experience during the previous three fiscal years. At this writing the deduction for fiscal year 1993 is 14.16% of the fair market value; see 57 Fed.Reg. 58548. The percentage has generally been rising in recent years on account of increasing VA costs.

35. 38 CFR 36.4320.

36. See supra text at note 12.

amount at foreclosure. Upon conveyance of the property to VA,[37] the lender would receive its full $70,000 claim.

On the other hand, suppose the property had been badly vandalized by the mortgagor, and its appraised value was only $40,000. VA would again subtract, say, 15% or $6,000, representing its probable expenses in holding and marketing the property, giving a "net value" of only $34,000. If VA accepted the property and paid the full claim on these facts, it would sustain an overall loss of $70,000 (the claim) minus $34,000 (recovery from the property), or $36,000. Since this exceeds the $30,000 guaranty amount, VA will instead simply "no-bid" the case, pay the $30,000 guaranty to the lender and wash its hands of the transaction.[38] The lender is likely to suffer a loss on the order of $6,000 (70,000 minus $30,000 from VA, minus $34,000 from marketing the property), unless the lender is able to sell the house for a higher price or with lower carrying and marketing costs than VA expected to incur. Obviously the VA system results in losses to lenders only when the property has dropped rather severely in value, but such declines have not been unusual.[39]

In 1984 the Administration recommended legislative changes that would have eliminated entirely VA's activity in acquiring and marketing houses, imposing that duty on lenders in all cases.[40] But it was by no means clear to Congress that such a change would save the government money, and it was not enacted. However, Congress did direct the VA to take its probable administrative costs into account in determining net value,[41] and to make case-by-case determinations as to which method of claims payment would be most economical to the government. VA continued to attempt to find ways of minimizing its payouts; in 1989, for example, it proposed to begin taking into consideration an

37. Incidentally, the lender is not required to convey the property to VA in order to make a claim; it may instead retain the property and have the claim payment reduced by the specified amount; this would make sense to the lender if it felt that it could market the property at a net sale price greater than the VA-computed net value. However, in most cases the property is conveyed to VA, which then attempts to market it in much the same fashion as FHA.

The U.S. General Accounting Office has criticized VA for failing to make greater use of alternatives to foreclosure that are generally less costly to the government. They include acceptance of deeds in lieu of foreclosure, accepting an assignment of the loan from the lender and recasting its term to permit the borrower to cure the default, and entering into a compromise agreement under which VA provides cash to the veteran to permit him or her to sell the property. See General Accounting Office, Housing Programs: Increased Use of Alternatives to Foreclosure Could Reduce VA's Losses (Dec.1989).

38. 38 CFR 3620(b).

39. The percentage of VA claims that result in no-bids is a good indicator of the health of the residential real estate market. In 1981 only 2.9% of VA loan foreclosures were no-bids; by 1988 they had risen to 23.9%, but they subsequently declined. See VA proposed regulation, 54 Fed.Reg. 30207; Gates, The VA Home Loan Program, Prospects for the Future, Secondary Mortgage Markets, Spring 1991, at 16.

40. The mortgage banking industry, in particular, objected to the proposed change; it is not well organized to dispose of foreclosed properties and did not want this burden. See WG & L Hsg. & Devel. Rptr., Feb. 13, 1984, at 797.

41. See Deficit Reduction Act of 1984, Pub.L. No. 98–369, amending 38 U.S.C.A. § 1816.

imputed interest factor representing the government's cost of borrowing funds in computing the net value it would assign to each house it accepted. There is plainly logic in doing so, since the government's funds are tied up during the period each house is held on the market by VA from the time of acquisition to the time of sale. But the effect of this change would have been to reduce net values and thereby to increase the number of cases in which VA would "no-bid" the property, leaving it with the lender. Lenders opposed this proposal vigorously, and Congress responded to their lobbying to instructing VA not to adopt it.[42]

VA traditionally pursued deficiencies aggressively. Unlike FHA, which asks the lender to obtain the deficiency judgment, VA brings its own actions. It has a right of subrogation to the lender's position,[43] and an additional direct action against the borrower under a statutory right of indemnification.[44] Each veteran loan applicant also signs a specific indemnity agreement.[45] But for loans made in 1990 or thereafter, Congress has directed VA to pursue deficiency claims against original borrowers only if they engaged in fraud, misrepresentation, or bad faith in obtaining the loan or in defaulting on it.[46] Borrowers under older loans do not have this specific protection, but may request waivers of liability on the ground that collection of the debt would be "against equity and good conscience."[47] When a VA borrower sells the real estate without paying off the loan, VA authorizes the lender to give the borrower a release of liability, provided the assuming grantee's credit and income are satisfactory.[48] Of course, if no release is obtained (as is

42. § 308, Veterans' Benefits Amendments of 1989, Pub.L.No. 101-237; see VA's capitulation on the point, 55 Fed.Reg. 27465 (Jul. 3, 1990). See also 38 U.S.C.A. § 3732 note, added by VA, HUD & Independent Agencies Appropriations Act of 1993, Title I, expressly providing that VA, in determining "net value," is to take into consideration losses sustained on the resale of the property. The U.S. General Accounting Office advocated VA's inclusion of imputed interest in its calculations; see U.S. General Accounting Office, Housing Programs: VA Can Reduce Its Guaranteed Home Loan Foreclosure Costs (July 1989).

43. 38 U.S.C.A. § 3732; see, e.g., Jensen v. Turnage, 782 F.Supp. 1527 (M.D.Fla. 1990); United States v. Whitney, 602 F.Supp. 722 (W.D.N.Y.1985).

44. Both subrogation and indemnity rights are set out in 38 CFR 36.4323. See United States v. Shimer, 367 U.S. 374, 81 S.Ct. 1554, 6 L.Ed.2d 908 (1961), upholding the VA's direct indemnity right; Vail v. Derwinski, 946 F.2d 589 (8th Cir.1991), modified 956 F.2d 812 (8th Cir.1992); Connelly v. Derwinski, 961 F.2d 129 (9th Cir. 1992).

45. See United States v. Davis, 961 F.2d 603, 606 n. 5 (7th Cir.1992). Prior to March 1, 1988, the veteran borrower had no federal right to notice of default and foreclosure, and was relegated to whatever notice rights might be provided by state law; this posed particular problems in cases in which the veteran had sold the home without obtaining a release of liability from VA. See Jensen v. Turnage, 782 F.Supp. 1527 (M.D.Fla.1990). However, under amendments made by the Veterans' Home Loan Program Improvements and Property Rehabilitation Act of 1987, Pub. L.No. 100-198, the veteran is now entitled to notice and counseling from VA when VA is notified of a default; see 38 U.S.C.A. § 3732(a)(4)(A).

46. 38 U.S.C.A. § 3703(e)(1).

47. 38 U.S.C.A. § 5302(b).

48. See 38 CFR 36.4285. The standards the grantee must meet are set out in 38 U.S.C.A. § 3713(a). The lender is permitted to charge a fee of up to $300 for performing these underwriting services; see 38 CFR 36.4275. VA charges a 0.5% fee for the assumption; 38 CFR 36.4232. See generally VA's final regulations on

often the case), the original borrower remains personally liable under the principles set out above. However, the veteran may obtain a retroactive release, even after the grantee's default, if one would have been given by VA at the time of the sale.[49] The assuming grantee is liable to VA for any deficiency irrespective of fraud or bad faith.[50]

PMI claims procedures are roughly similar to VA's. The maximum PMI loss or guaranty is usually fixed at 25% (or if a higher premium is paid, 30%) of the current loan balance plus costs and expenses.[51] Upon foreclosure or the taking of a deed in lieu, the lender will contact the PMI for further instructions. The PMI has two choices: either to take a conveyance of the property (or authorize the lender to sell it as the PMI's agent) and pay the lender the full loan balance plus costs and expenses, or to pay the guaranty amount and allow the lender to keep the property. Obviously the PMI will elect the latter route only if the lender's total claim exceeds the property's current value plus the guaranty. If the value of the property is lower than the debt balance, the PMI will generally instruct the lender to bid the lower amount at the foreclosure sale in order to preserve the deficiency claim, if available under state law. When the PMI pays the lender's claim, it is subrogated to the lender's right to a deficiency against the borrower, and that right is usually supplemented by a formal assignment of the note and mortgage to the PMI.[52]

While the basic economic decisions that PMIs must make are similar to those of VA, the guaranty amount is usually smaller than with VA. Consequently the potential for unreimbursed losses is greater. In the VA claims example given above, if PMI insurance had been employed instead, the guaranty amount would be only $17,500 (assuming a 25% policy) and the lender would sustain a loss if the property's value dropped below $52,500. Of course, even value diminutions of this magnitude are relatively uncommon, a fact that may explain why most

loan assumptions, 55 Fed.Reg. 37468 (Sept. 12, 1990).

49. 38 U.S.C.A. § 3713(b). See Travelstead v. Derwinski, 978 F.2d 1244 (Fed.Cir. 1992), holding that VA may not base a denial of a retroactive release simply on the fact that the grantee defaulted shortly after buying the property, but must instead consider the credit and income information that would have been available to VA at the time of the transfer.

50. 38 U.S.C.A. § 3703(e)(2)(A).

51. See, e.g., Mortgage Guaranty Insurance Corp., Default and Claims Manual.

52. See Pineda v. PMI Mortgage Ins. Co., 843 S.W.2d 660 (Tex.App.1992), upholding the PMI's subrogation claim. Cf. Commonwealth Mortgage Assur. Co. v. Superior Court, 211 Cal.App.3d 508, 259 Cal. Rptr. 425 (1989) (PMI could not recover from borrower on subrogation theory or express indemnity agreement; to allow recovery would violate antideficiency statute). The Commonwealth case also held that, where the lender made a full credit bid at the foreclosure sale, it had established that it suffered no loss; hence, the PMI could not proceed against the borrower on a fraud theory. See also Twin City Fed. Sav. & Loan Ass'n v. Zimmerman, 411 N.W.2d 294 (Minn.App.1987) (borrower cannot compel lender to resort to mortgage insurance rather than seeking deficiency judgment); Sandusky v. First Nat. Bank, 299 Ark. 465, 773 S.W.2d 95 (1989) (lender's failure to obtain mortgage insurance, despite having collected premium from borrowers, did not bar lender from obtaining deficiency judgment against borrowers).

lenders seem to perceive little difference in effective coverage as among FHA, VA, and the PMI's.

During the mid-1980s the PMI industry was battered by severe losses. Many PMI underwriters stopped (or were prohibited by their state insurance commissions from) writing new business, and only about a dozen continued to do so by the end of the decade.[53] A large share of the losses were paid to thrift institutions in energy-producing states that were themselves suffering massive losses. A significant number of losses resulted from fraud by borrowers as well.[54] The industry searched for ways of reducing the damage. PMIs became much more cautious in selecting lenders with whom they did business, and many of them began offering preferential rates to lenders whose loans produced the lowest claim rates.[55] At the same time, many lenders became more particular about which PMIs they would use, since no lender wanted to find itself in the awkward position of submitting claims to an insolvent mortgage insurer.[56]

From a legal viewpoint, perhaps the most significant result of the losses suffered by PMIs during the 1980s was that they began scrutinizing the claims submitted to them with greater care. In cases where some representation in a loan or insurance application was found to be untrue, most commonly an overstatement of the borrower's down payment or the property's selling price, the PMIs adopted a policy of denying coverage. Policy language typically purported to grant the insurers that option. The result was a spate of litigation between PMIs and insured lenders. Of course, if the lender was a party to the fraud or had notice of it the time of the insurance application, it is easy to decide the case for the insurer.[57] But many lenders argued that they, too, were innocent and unaware of the misrepresentations made by their borrowers. The results of these cases depend on somewhat

---

53. See Lacy, MIs: After the Losses, a Second Chance, Mortgage Banking, Sept. 1988, at 79; Blood, Taking Stock, Secondary Mortgage Markets, Summer 1987, at 29. The PMI industry lobbied vigorously for the elimination or privitization of FHA, which it saw as an unfair competitor. This misguided effort failed completely; see DeZube, Feeling the Squeeze, Mortgage Banking, Aug.1989, at 12. For a view of FHA's defense, see An Assessment of FHA's Section 302(B) Program: A Comparison with Private Mortgage Insurance, Office of Policy Devel. & Research, U.S. Dep't of HUD (1987); Temple, Barker & Sloan, Inc., Comparison of the Markets Served by Private Insurers and the Federal Housing Administration (1987).

54. See Calvelli, Flimflams and Real Estate Scams, Probate & Property, Mar./Apr. 1988, at 31.

55. See Simon, MIs View Price, Underwriting Changes, Real Estate Finance Today, May 5, 1989, at 1; Dickey, Performance Sets the Price, Mortgage Banking, Dec. 1987, at 42 (describing a system of performance ratings used by PMIs to evaluate lenders); Blood, Taking Stock, Secondary Mortgage Markets, Summer 1987, at 29; Lacy, Gearing up for New Challenges, Mortgage Banking, Feb. 1987, at 22. Data in the latter article illustrate the sensitivity of PMI claims both to the carefulness of lender processing and to economic conditions in the locality.

56. See How Are Today's Lenders Choosing Mortgage Insurance?, Mortgage Banking, Feb.1988, at 35; Molesky, How Moody's Rates MIs, Mortgage Banking, Feb.1987, at 55. A number of large lenders also moved, at least temporarily, toward self-insurance as a result of their dissatisfaction with the PMIs; see DeZube, supra note 53.

57. See In re TMIC Ins. Co., 207 Cal. App.3d 981, 255 Cal.Rptr. 175 (1989).

variable state statutes and insurance policy language, but the PMIs have prevailed in nearly all of them.[58]

Mortgage insurance has only short-term value. As the loan-to-value ratio declines over time, through amortization of the principal balance and possibly through appreciation in property value or improvements, the insurance becomes increasingly less necessary. There is obviously no point in a borrower's paying mortgage insurance premiums for 30 years. Both FNMA and FHLMC have adopted guidelines permitting cancellation of the insurance after as little as two years if the original loan-to-value ratio has been reduced to 80% or less by amortization, or after five years if such a reduction has been achieved by a combination of amortization and market appreciation.[59] Several states have statutes requiring lenders to notify borrowers at closing of the right to cancel when a specified loan-to-value ratio has been achieved,[60] and in California lenders must also send annual notices reminding borrowers of the right and advising them of their current loan-to-value ratio.[61]

58. Firstier Mortg. Co. v. Investors Mortg. Ins. Co., 930 F.2d 1508 (10th Cir. 1991) (under Oklahoma statute, PMI can rescind irrespective of lender's knowledge of borrower's misrepresentations); Citizens Savings Bank v. Verex Assur., Inc., 883 F.2d 299 (4th Cir.1989) (fraud by attorney for borrowers was attributable to lender, thereby permitting PMI to rescind); FDIC v. Verex Assur., Inc., 795 F.Supp. 404 (S.D.Fla.1992) (under Florida statute, PMI can rescind despite lender's innocence); Twin City Bank v. Verex Assur. Inc., 733 F.Supp. 67 (E.D.Ark.1990) (PMI can rescind regardless of lender's knowledge or good faith); Wisconsin Mortgage Assur. Corp. v. HMC Mortgage Corp., 712 F.Supp. 878 (D.Utah 1989) (under Utah statute, PMI can rescind); TCF Mortgage Corp. v. Verex Assur., Inc., 709 F.Supp. 164 (D.Minn.1989) (under Minnesota statute, PMI can rescind); Centrust Mortgage Corp. v. PMI Mortgage Ins. Co., 166 Ariz. 50, 800 P.2d 37 (App.1990) (fraudulent representations of borrowers presumed to be within lender's knowledge; PMI permitted to rescind); RTC v. Urban Redevelopment Authority of Pittsburgh, 412 Pa.Super. 351, 603 A.2d 618 (1992) (PMI can rescind even though lender was unaware of falsity of information submitted). Cf. Verex Assur., Inc. v. John Hanson Sav. & Loan, Inc., 816 F.2d 1296 (9th Cir.1987) (PMI can rescind unless it had notice of the misrepresentations at the time it issued the insurance; such notice would constitute a waiver of the right to rescind); Centrust Mortgage Corp. v. PMI Mortgage Ins. Co., supra (same). See generally Note, The Private Mortgage Insurer's Action for Rescission for Misrepresentation: Limiting a Potential Threat to Private Sector Participation in the Secondary Mortgage Market, 47 Wash. & Lee L.Rev. 587 (1990).

The most notable refusal of a court to permit PMI rescission occurred in the well-publicized EIPC Mortgage case, Foremost Guaranty Corp. v. Meritor Savings Bank, 910 F.2d 118 (4th Cir.1990). EPIC, which was the parent corporation of the lender, was also a general partner in numerous limited partnerships set up to buy houses from builders, rent them for several years, and then sell them at a profit. The scheme was economically unsound and the partnerships all defaulted on their mortgage loans. The PMIs denied coverage on the basis of oral misrepresentations made by EPIC and its lender subsidiary. However, the court held that documents in the possession of the PMIs showed or strongly suggested that the representations were false, or at least required further investigation. Since the PMIs failed to investigate, they were held to have waived their right of rescission. State statutes that generally permit insurers to deny coverage for fraud were found inapplicable in light of the information available to the PMIs.

59. See FHLMC Allows Earlier MI Cancellations, Real Estate Finance Today, Apr. 21, 1989, at 7.

60. West's Ann.Cal.Civ.Code § 2954.7; Conn.Gen.Stat.Ann. § 36–442bb(a)(2); Md. Code, Fin.Inst., § 9–903.

61. West's Ann.Cal.Civ.Code §§ 2954.6–2954.65.

Risk Sharing and Mortgagee Processing

In principle, a mortgage insurance system in which the risk is shared between insurer and lender, as is the case to some degree with VA and the PMIs, can reasonably delegate more underwriting responsibility to the lender than can a system like FHA's in which the lender has virtually no risk. This is so because the lender can be expected to exercise more care in appraising, checking credit, and so forth if its determinations bear on its own potential loss. In fact, VA and the PMIs do delegate more underwriting decision-making to mortgagees than does FHA.[62] However, FHA has also delegated increasing processing authority to lenders in recent years. Its "direct endorsement" program, instituted in 1983, allows larger, more experienced lenders that meet certain standards to underwrite FHA single-family home loans without prior review of each loan by HUD.[63] The program proved extremely popular, and by 1988 direct endorsement loans accounted for 90% of FHA's home loan volume.[64]

During the 1980s[65] FHA introduced a much more novel approach, termed "co-insurance," under which rather complete underwriting authority was delegated to lenders on apartment projects and certain nursing care facilities, in return for the lenders' acceptance of twenty percent of the risk of loss.[66] The co-insurance program seemed conceptually sound, and it was fairly popular; 39 lenders were approved to use it, and co-insured loans totalling about $10 billion were made.[67] But in practice it was disastrous, producing very high losses to FHA as a result of poor underwriting, imprudent lending, weak capitalization of the lenders involved, and inadequate oversight by the government. In 1990 FHA concluded that the program was irredeemably flawed and

---

62. See, e.g., 38 CFR 36.4348, VA's requirements for "automatic processing" by lenders, which include (for other than "supervised" lenders—that is, federally insured financial institutions) $50,000 in working capital, three years of VA lending experience, and access to a minimum $1 million line of credit).

63. 24 CFR 200.163–200.164a, adopted 48 Fed.Reg. 11928.

64. See Face to Face with FHA & VA, Mortgage Banking, Feb. 1988, at 20.

65. The program was authorized by the Housing and Urban Development Act of 1974, which added § 244 to the National Housing Act, but it did not become operational until 1983.

66. 24 CFR Parts 250, 251, 252, and 255. For a good overall summary of HUD's coinsurance efforts, see the proposed rule on 24 CFR Part 251, 49 Fed.Reg. 9084. See also Puller, Fuller & Graham, New Financing from Old Programs, Mortgage Banking, Mar. 1985, at 64; McGavin, Overcoming the Risks in FHA Co-insured Mortgage Loans, Nat'l Law J., Oct. 31, 1983, at 15.

One of the ironies of the program was that FHA bore 100% rather than 80% of the loan losses in many cases. The reason was that the lenders frequently obtained their capital by issuing mortgage-backed securities guaranteed by the Government National Mortgage Association (GNMA), an agency of HUD. When the loans went into default, the lenders in turn defaulted to the securities holders. GNMA then stepped in under its guaranty contract, made up the payments to the bondholders, and assigned the defaulted mortgages to FHA (as is GNMA's statutory right) for full indemnity! See GNMA Takes Over $2.1 Million Coinsurance Portfolio, Real Estate Finance Today, Jul.20, 1990, at 6.

67. See 55 Fed.Reg. 41312 (Oct.10, 1990), announcing the termination of all FHA multifamily coinsurance programs.

terminated it, notwithstanding the protests of lenders who argued that the worst was over and that the concept could be salvaged.[68]

§ 11.3 Government–Sponsored Mortgage Market Support Agencies

In an effort to improve the functioning of the market for residential mortgages, the federal government has created several agencies and institutions. Among these are FHA and VA, discussed in the preceding section; other entities, which do not insure or guarantee mortgages, will be described here.[1] They include the Federal National Mortgage Association (FNMA or "Fannie Mae") and the Federal Home Loan Mortgage Corporation (FHLMC or "Freddie Mac"), both of which purchase mortgage loans on the secondary market. This section will also discuss the Government National Mortgage Association (GNMA or "Ginnie Mae"), which operates several mortgage market assistance programs, and the Federal Home Loan Bank System, which makes loans to its member institutions, primarily savings and loan associations. Finally, state agencies which provide support for the residential mortgage market will be described.[2]

Secondary Market Agencies—FNMA and FHLMC

Both of these agencies are primarily engaged in purchasing on the secondary market residential mortgages originated by local lending institutions. Their impact on the U.S. mortgage market is enormous; together they hold or have outstanding securities representing about $1 trillion in mortgages. FNMA is by far the older, having been organized

---

68. Id. HUD's efforts to get out of the co-insurance business were fraught with legal conflict between the government and approved lenders; see Housing Study Group v. Kemp, 739 F.Supp. 633 (D.D.C. 1990), holding that HUD had provided inadequate notice and comment period before making a final decision to terminate co-insurance program, and requiring it to extend the comment period.

§ 11.3

1. Discussions of the secondary mortgage market, which is the principal governmental support system, include Bradner, The Secondary Mortgage Market and State Regulation of Real Estate Financing, 36 Emory L.J. 971 (1987); Malloy, The Secondary Mortgage Market: A Catalyst for Change in Real Estate Transactions, 39 Sw.L.J. 991 (1986); McNulty, Secondary Mortgage Markets: Recent Trends and Research Results, 17 FHLBBJ 10 (Apr. 1984); Miles, Housing Finance: Development and Evolution in Mortgage Markets, in House Comm. on Banking, Finance & Urban Affairs, Housing—A Reader, 98th Cong., 1st Sess., at 45; Report of the President's Commission on Housing 166–73 (1982); Hender-shott & Villani, Secondary Mortgage Markets and the Cost of Mortgage Funds, 8 J.Am.Real Est. & Urb. Econ. Ass'n 50 (1980); Browne, The Private Mortgage Insurance Industry, the Thrift Industry, and the Secondary Mortgage Market: Their Interrelationships, 12 Akr.L.Rev. 631 (1979).

An older but highly insightful study is Grebler, The "New System" of Residential Mortgage Finance, Mortgage Banker, Feb. 1972, at 4, reprinted in Federal Reserve Staff Study, Ways to Moderate Fluctuations in Housing Construction 177 (1972).

See also all issues of Secondary Mortgage Markets, a quarterly published by FHLMC, beginning in Feb. 1984; and the annual reports of FNMA, FHLMC, and GNMA (from which most data in the text are taken).

2. Other institutions supporting the mortgage market, not discussed in the text because of their relatively small impact on mortgage lending, include the Federal Land Banks, Federal Intermediate Credit Banks, Banks for Cooperatives, and Farmers Home Administration.

in 1938 as a corporation wholly owned and administered by the federal government.[3] In 1954 it became a "mixed ownership" corporation, owned partly by private shareholders.[4] Finally, by the Housing and Urban Development Act of 1968, FNMA was divided into two separate entities, each of which inherited a portion of the original FNMA's duties.[5] One of these was the Government National Mortgage Association (GNMA), which became a pure federal agency within the Department of Housing and Urban Development, and which retained the management of FNMA's pre–1954 mortgage portfolio and took over certain of its "special assistance" functions, described below. At the same time, FNMA was re-created as a privately owned and managed corporation, although with certain ties to the federal government; its function is to continue to purchase residential and other mortgages from originating institutions.

Two years after the "privatization" of FNMA, FHLMC was created by the Emergency Home Finance Act of 1970.[6] Its mission is substantially similar to that of FNMA, although it carries out its functions in a somewhat different fashion. Both FNMA and FHLMC are expected to contribute to the effective operation of the mortgage market in several ways:[7] (1) They facilitate the flow of capital from areas of the country where funds are plentiful to places in which mortgage money is in short supply. (2) By means of the sale of debt paper, mortgage-backed securities, and other instruments to persons and institutions who would not ordinarily invest in mortgages, they shift capital investment from other sectors of the national economy into the mortgage market. The instruments they sell typically have term and repayment structures that are different than mortgages, and thus are more attractive to certain types of investors, such as individuals, life insurers and pension funds. (3) By issuing advance commitments to purchase mortgages at fixed interest rates or yields, they assist local lenders and homebuilders in hedging against the risk of rising interest rates in the future. (4) By purchasing mortgages when credit is tight and selling them when funds are readily available, they may assist in smoothing the flow of mort-

---

3. FNMA's original charter was contained in Title III of the National Housing Act, 48 Stat. 1246 (1938).

4. Title II of the Housing Act of 1954, 68 Stat. 612.

5. Title VIII of the Housing and Urban Development Act of 1968, 82 Stat. 503, 536. The FNMA General Counsel's Office provides a booklet entitled "Federal National Mortgage Association Charter Act" which contains complete legislative history details of the Association. The charter's present citation is 12 U.S.C.A. § 1716ff. An excellent historical summary of FNMA is found in 43 Fed.Reg. 36200.

6. 12 U.S.C.A. § 1451. FHLMC was originally capitalized by the issuance of $100 million in nonvoting common stock to the 12 Federal Home Loan Banks. In 1990 FHLMC redeemed this stock at its original par value; see 55 Fed.Reg. 4907. This move outraged the management of the Federal Home Loan Banks, who argued (in vain) that the stock was then worth far more than its par value. See McGarity, Dispute Over Freddie Mac Stock Remains Unresolved, Real Estate Finance Today, Feb.23, 1990, at 9.

7. See Villani, The Secondary Mortgage Markets: What They Are, What They Do, and How to Measure Them, 1 Secondary Mortgage Markets 24 (Feb. 1984); Federal National Mortgage Ass'n, A Guide to Fannie Mae 9 (1975).

gage funds during the extreme cycles of credit fluctuation which have characterized the post-war American economy.

Both FNMA and FHLMC have been authorized to purchase FHA/VA and conventional mortgages since 1970, when FHLMC was created. Prior to that time, FNMA was permitted to purchase only government-insured or -guaranteed mortgages. The authority to purchase conventional loans has had several important consequences. FNMA and FHLMC cooperated during 1970 in developing a set of standard forms for use with conventional mortgages throughout the United States. These forms have gained wide-spread acceptance and are now often used even in transactions in which the lender does not anticipate a sale of the loan to either FNMA or FHLMC. Another consequence has been the reviewing and approval of private mortgage insurance companies by FNMA and FHLMC. Each agency maintains an approved list, an essential activity since weak or unreliable private mortgage insurers could endanger the security of the conventional mortgages which the two secondary market entities purchase. For both agencies, private mortgage insurance is legally essential on any portion of a loan which exceeds an 80% loan-to-value ratio.

While FNMA and FHLMC began life quite differently, they have become increasingly similar. Since 1968 FNMA's board of directors has consisted of 18 persons, 5 of whom are appointed by the president of the United States and the other 13 elected by the shareholders in the conventional corporate manner.[8] Prior to the enactment of the Financial Institutions Reform, Recovery, and Enforcement Act of 1989 (FIRREA), FHLMC was governed by the Federal Home Loan Bank Board; but FIRREA abolished the FHLBB and gave FHLMC a new board structure virtually identical to FNMA's.[9] Both are subject to broad regulatory authority of the Secretary of Housing and Urban Development.[10]

Both FNMA and FHLMC need huge amounts of capital to finance their mortgage purchasing operations, and they raise it in three distinct ways. First, they issue stock (both common and preferred), which is traded on the national securities markets and is widely held.[11] Second, they issue debt instruments (bonds and notes); increasingly in

8. 12 U.S.C.A. § 1723(b).

9. 12 U.S.C.A. § 1452(a).

10. 12 U.S.C.A. § 1723a(h) (FHMA); 12 U.S.C.A. § 1452(b) (FHLMC). This authority is confirmed by § 1321 of the Federal Housing Enterprises Financial Safety and Soundness Act of 1992, Pub.L.No. 102–550: "The Secretary of Housing and Urban Development shall have general regulatory power over each enterprise and shall make such rules and regulations as shall be necessary and proper to ensure that this part and the purposes of the Federal National Mortgage Association Charter Act and the Federal Home Loan Mortgage Corporation Act are accomplished." The authority includes control of annual dividends, increases in total debt, and the issuance of particular debt or equity securities; id. In addition, the debt securities of the two entities are subject to approval by the Secretary of the Treasury.

11. Both companies are highly "leveraged," and FNMA, because of its traditional reliance on debt capital, is particularly so. HUD regulations require FNMA to maintain a debt-to-capital ratio of less than 20–to–1; at the end of 1991 it was about 16:1. See FNMA, 1991 Annual Report, at 22.

recent years, they have employed "callable" debt, which may have a fairly long term, say 5 to 10 years, but which they have the right to prepay as soon as one year. The call feature makes the debt more costly to FNMA and FHLMC, but gives them the very desirable opportunity to refinance at a lower interest cost if market rates fall.[12] While the debt is not technically a full-faith-and-credit liability of the United States government, the capital markets appear to assume that the government would remedy any default, and the instruments command interest rates nearly as low as government agency debt.

The third approach to capital formation used by both entities is the issuance of mortgage-related securities, primarily pass-through participation certificates on which FNMA and FHLMC guarantee payment.[13] Legally, these certificates represent shares of ownership in pools of underlying mortgages held by FNMA and FHLMC. To the extent the certificates are sold to private investors, the mortgages no longer appear on the agencies' balance sheets, and there is technically no corresponding debt liability owed by the agencies, despite their guarantee of payment on the securities. Historically FNMA relied heavily on debt paper as a source of capital, while FHLMC from the outset pooled and securitized about 90% of the mortgages it acquired, making its debt needs much smaller. FNMA began issuing mortgage-backed securities in 1981, and has been particularly energetic in doing so since 1987; it currently has outstanding about three times as many securitized mortgages as it has mortgages in portfolio.[14]

Both agencies issue a substantial share of their mortgage-backed securities as "swaps" with private lending institutions. In a "swap" transaction, the private lender creates a pool of mortgages and exchanges them with FNMA or FHLMC for mortgage-backed securities based on the same pool. From the lender's viewpoint, the advantage of the swap is that it now has a highly liquid, readily marketable security, guaranteed by a government-sponsored corporation, rather than a pool

12. See Dougherty & McManus, The Preferred Approach to Capital, Secondary Mortgage Markets, Spring/Summer 1992, at 2. FNMA traditionally issued relatively short-term debt and used it to purchase mortgages, which are fairly long-term instruments. When market rates rose rapidly to unprecedented heights during 1980–81, FNMA was compelled to refinance its short-term debt at very high rates, putting itself in a position to suffer major losses during the early and mid–1980s. It subsequently embarked on an effort to lengthen the average maturity of its debt paper in order to reduce the risk of a recurrence of this disastrous episode. From 1981 to 1990 it reduced the "duration gap" between mortgage portfolio maturity and debt maturity from 3 years to about 3 months. See FNMA, 1990 Annual Report, at 12–13; 1985 Annual Report at 14. It also began emphasizing the techniques described next in the text much more heavily.

13. See Hu, Secondary Market: The American Model, Mortgage Banking, Apr. 1991, at 14; Bradner, The Secondary Mortgage Market and State Regulation of Real Estate Financing, 36 Emory L.J. 971 (1987) at nn. 49–68; Malloy, The Secondary Mortgage Market: A Catalyst for Change in Real Estate Transactions, 39 Sw.L.J. 991 (1986) at nn. 48–62.

14. At the end of 1991, FNMA held mortgage assets worth $126 billion and had $371 billion in outstanding mortgage-backed securities. FNMA, 1991 Annual Report at 8, 25. For a historical perspective on the agencies' issuance of mortgage-backed securities, see U.S. General Accounting Office, The Federal National Mortgage Association in a Changing Economic Environment (Apr.1985), at 10–12.

of relatively illiquid mortgages. FHMA and FHLMC earn very substantial fees for providing this service. But not all of their mortgage-backed securities are swaps; they also purchase mortgages in the ordinary course of business and sell the corresponding securities on the national securities markets.[15]

While FHLMC has been consistently profitable since its inception, and FNMA has made money except during the early 1980s, concern nevertheless grew in Congress during the early 1990s about the adequacy of the government's oversight of the two corporations. It seemed clear that if either found itself in serious financial trouble, Congress would be compelled as a political matter to rescue it. The massive failures in the savings and loan industry during the late 1980s doubtless fueled these worries. HUD's regulation of FNMA and FHLMC was widely regarded as ineffective.[16] The General Accounting Office issued several reports that were highly critical of the effectiveness of the oversight effort, and observed that HUD did not have clear legal authority to do a good job.[17]

Congress responded by passing the Federal Housing Enterprises Financial Safety and Soundness Act of 1992.[18] It tightened oversight of both FNMA and FHLMC in a number of ways. It established within HUD (but largely independent of the HUD Secretary) an Office of Federal Housing Enterprises Oversight (OFHEO) with authority to examine and audit FNMA and FHLMC, to require various reports from them, and most importantly, to fix various capital levels which the enterprises must maintain, depending on the credit risk (the risk of default on mortgages held) and interest rate risk (the risk that market rate fluctuations will result in losses) with which they are faced.[19] The

15. For example, in 1991 FHLMC issued $52.8 billion in swap securities and $39.7 billion in cash securities (sold on the open market). In the same year, FNMA issued $7.1 billion in swap securities and $112.8 billion in cash securities. See Database, Secondary Mortgage Markets, Spring/Summer 1992, at Table 2.

16. The regulatory authority of the Secretary of HUD was regarded as having relatively little significance until 1978, when the Secretary proposed a set of far-reaching regulations which would, among other things, have operated to allocate a certain portion of FNMA's mortgage purchase activity for inner-city and other low-income areas. See 43 Fed.Reg. 7659. FNMA, which had already created certain inner-city programs, vigorously opposed the regulations, and their more objectional features were ultimately withdrawn by HUD; see 24 CFR Part 81, as amended 43 Fed.Reg. 36200.

17. U.S. General Accounting Office, Government-Sponsored Enterprises: The Government's Exposure to Risks (Aug. 1990); U.S. General Accounting Office, The Federal National Mortgage Association in a Changing Economic Environment (Apr. 1985). See also Brendsel, Market Insight: Tailoring Regulation for GSEs, Secondary Mortgage Markets, Summer 1991, at 21; Golding, Regulating the Secondary Market, Secondary Mortgage Markets, Fall 1990, at 3.

18. Title XIII of the Housing and Community Development Act of 1992, Pub. L.No. 102–550.

19. Id. at § 1361. The director is also authorized to contract with private rating agencies (such as Moody's and Standard & Poor's) to provide reviews of FNMA and FHLMC. See id. at § 1319; U.S. General Accounting Office, Government-Sponsored Enterprises: Using Private Risk Ratings for Exemptions from Federal Regulations (Nov.1991).

director of this office may even place the enterprises in conservatorship if they become "critically" undercapitalized.[20]

The 1992 Act also made the HUD Secretary's supervisory authority much more specific. While he or she has no power to regulate capital standards (a task which, as mentioned above, falls to the new OFHEO), the Secretary was given authority to require certain reports of the enterprises, to insure non-discrimination in their activities, and to establish and enforce certain goals with respect to their support of low- and moderate-income housing.[21] Both the Secretary of HUD and the Director of OFHEO may conduct cease-and-desist hearings, issue orders, and enforce them in court if necessary.[22] They may even impose civil money penalties.[23]

The Government National Mortgage Association (GNMA)

When FNMA was reorganized as a private corporation in 1968, GNMA was created simultaneously to take over the "special assistance" functions that FNMA had previously handled, and also to manage and liquidate the existing FNMA portfolio of special assistance loans.[24] For example, during the 1961–1968 period FNMA had purchased a large number of below-market-interest-rate mortgages under FHA's 221(d)(3) moderate-income subsidized apartment program. These mortgages, most of which bore only a 3% interest rate, were transferred to GNMA, which continues to hold some of them today. GNMA also holds and continues to purchase from time to time mortgages of a variety of types that are deemed important to national housing policy but that would have difficulty attracting private investors. These include loans in urban renewal projects, in disaster areas, on Indian reservations, and in Guam.[25]

The GNMA activity that has had the greatest impact on the mortgage market in recent years is its program for guaranteeing mortgage-backed securities.[26] These securities are issued by mortgage lending institutions, including thrifts, banks, and mortgage bankers. The securities are in registered form and are actively traded among investors. They represent the obligation of the issuer, collateralized by

---

20. Id. at § 1369.
21. Id. at §§ 1324–25, 1331–38.
22. Id. at §§ 1341–44, 1374–76.
23. Id. at §§ 1345, 1376.
24. See 12 U.S.C.A. § 1717(a)(2)(A).
25. For details, see any current GNMA annual report. During the 1970's GNMA operated another assistance program, known as the "tandem plan." It involved GNMA's purchasing of FHA and VA mortgages, made at below-market interest rates, from originating lenders at relatively small discounts, and then reselling them on the secondary market at the much deeper discounts the market demanded. The resulting loss was absorbed by appropriations from Congress; the result was to keep mortgage interest rates lower and more affordable.

See also Note, The GNMA Securities Market: An Analysis of Proposals for a Regulatory Scheme, 9 Ford.Urb.L.Rev. 457 (1980).

26. 12 U.S.C.A. § 1721(g). See MortgageAmerica Corp. v. American National Bank, 651 S.W.2d 851 (Tex.Civ.App.1983), error refused n.r.e., an interesting case growing out of a mortgage company's efforts to market GNMA MBS which it had issued.

a pool of FHA-insured, FmHA-insured, or VA-guaranteed mortgages. The GNMA guarantee behind such securities represents the full faith and credit of the United States government, so the securities are considered highly desirable by the market.

Several types of GNMA-guaranteed securities have been issued, but by far the largest volume has been of the "fully modified pass-through" type. This means that GNMA guarantees that the holders of the securities will receive their respective shares of the regular monthly principal and interest payments which are due and owing on the underlying mortgages, even if the mortgage payments are in fact delinquent or the issuer fails to remit the payments to the holders. All additional payments resulting from the mortgage foreclosures or prepayments are also passed through to the holders immediately. The minimum size of a pass-through issue is one million dollars, with minimum individual security denominations of $25,000.

The mortgages that collateralize a GNMA-backed issue must all be federally insured or guaranteed. Under the original GNMA program (now termed GNMA I) they must all bear the same interest rate, and must have approximately the same maturity. The mortgages themselves are transferred to a bank or trust company to hold as a custodian. In the event the issuer of the securities defaults in payments, the mortgages are transferred to GNMA, which may in turn place them with another lender to manage and service. The diagram below indicates the relationships of the various parties in a GNMA-backed security issue. The great majority of the securities issued thus far have been collateralized by single family mortgages, but multi-family project and mobile home loans have also been used.

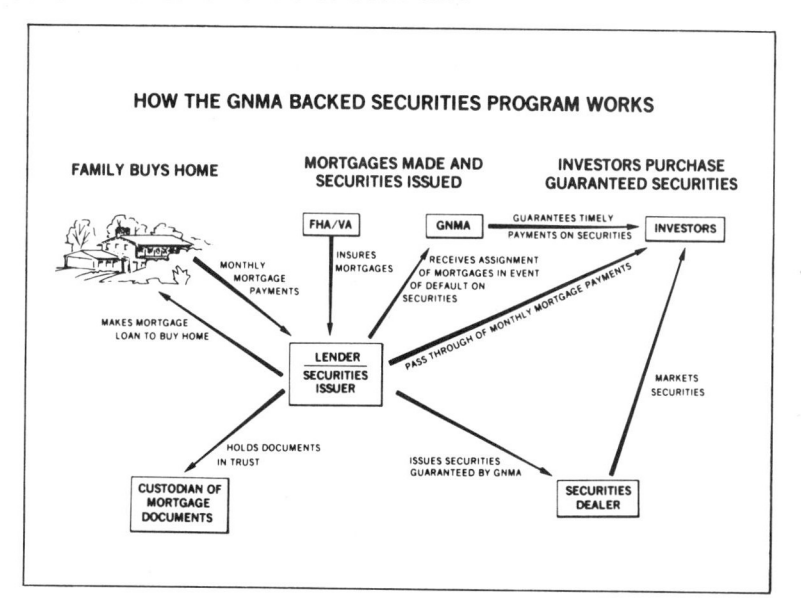

Under GNMA I, the issuing lender deals directly with the investors, remitting the mortgage payments to them monthly. Beginning in 1983, a new program, known as GNMA II, was instituted.[27] It is fundamentally similar to the GNMA I program described above, and does not replace it. But GNMA II is characterized by very large ("jumbo") mortgage pools which are composed of packages of loans from many different originating lenders, as contrasted with GNMA I pools, which are created by a single lender. Loans with different interest rates, within a 1% range, can be mixed in a GNMA II pool. Each individual lender is responsible for marketing a share of the pool's securities based on that lender's contribution to the mortgages in the pool; but the investors who buy the securities are acquiring an interest in the entire pool, which does not correspond to the mortgages originated by any one lender.

Under GNMA II a central paying agent (Chemical Bank of New York) handles all processing of the securities, including original issuance, transfers, accounting, payments to investors, and income tax withholding and reporting. Since these functions are centralized, an investor who owns securities in several GNMA II pools receives a single check and payment advice each month. The individual lenders remain responsible for servicing the underlying mortgages and for remitting the loan collections to the paying agent each month. If a lender defaults in doing so GNMA will, of course, step in under its guarantee obligation and make those payments.

Many GNMA-guaranteed securities are purchased by institutions that are already in the mortgage lending business, but a major share is bought by pension funds, trusts, profit-sharing plans, and other entities that seldom invest directly in mortgages. In this way the program has been successful in attracting large quantities of new funds to the mortgage market. The fact that the securities carry monthly payments of principal and interest is attractive to many investors, such as pension funds, who have monthly cash flow needs. At the same time, the securities are far simpler investments than mortgages themselves, and require no effort on the part of the investor to satisfy itself with regard to title, appraised value, credit worthiness, or the other factors about which a direct investor in mortgages must be concerned. In addition, the securities are highly liquid, and a secondary market for them is made by many investment banking houses.

The GNMA MBS program's impact has been vast, and it must be regarded as an outstanding success. It is a particularly strong source of financing for FHA and VA home loans, 86% of which are funded through GNMA-guaranteed securities. It is interesting to compare the GNMA program with the activities of FNMA and FHLMC discussed above. By way of illustration, in 1991 GNMA guaranteed about $63 billion in mortgage securities, while FNMA purchased $144 billion in

---

27. See Lasko, GNMA II: New Entrees, Mortgage Banking, June 1983, at 19.

mortgages and FHLMC purchased $100 billion in the same year. The aggregate impact of the three programs was thus more than $300 billion.[28]

The success of the GNMA MBS program has inspired numerous imitators. As mentioned above, both FNMA and FHLMC now issue their own mortgage-backed securities, guaranteeing them directly rather than relying on a GNMA guarantee. Numerous private and public institutional lenders also issue securities collateralized by non-FHA/VA mortgages. Some have been of the pass-through type, but with reliance on the institution's own full faith and credit, private mortgage insurance, or a combination of the two, rather than on GNMA (which is not permitted by law to guarantee conventional mortgage pools).[29]

These privately-issued mortgage securities have become increasingly sophisticated. In 1983 lenders began issuing "collateralized mortgage obligations" or CMOs.[30] Like GNMA-guaranteed securities, they were backed by pools of mortgages, but they were not of the pass-through type. Instead, they typically paid interest semiannually, but principal payments from the mortgages were restructured so as to produce several groups of bond-like securities with varying maturities. For example, a CMO might consist of three packages of securities, with maturities of approximately 3, 5, and 10 years. All payments of principal on all of the mortgages would be applied in the early years to retire the first group of bonds, then the second group, and so on. The result was a security that was backed by mortgages but closely resembled an industrial bond—an instrument which is attractive to some types of investors who would be disinterested in a pass-through of mortgage payments. Consumer borrowers benefitted because the increased market demand for CMOs over conventional pass-through securities resulted in lower interest rates.

But until 1986 CMOs were subject to a serious limitation. Because they were issued in multiple classes and their cash flows were actively managed by the issuer, CMOs were required by applicable Federal income tax rules to be treated as balance-sheet debt, rather than off-balance-sheet sales of assets like conventional pass-through mortgage-backed securities. Many issuers wanted to combine the market efficiencies of CMOs with the off-balance-sheet treatment of pass-throughs.

28. Data in this paragraph are derived from Database, Secondary Mortgage Markets, Spring/Summer 1992.

29. See Malloy, The Secondary Mortgage Market: A Catalyst for Change in Real Estate Transactions, 39 Sw.L.J. 991 (1986); Budd & Wasserman, The Yankee Mac Mortgage Pass–Through Program, 15 Conn.L.Rev. 385 (1983). Privately-issued mortgage pool securities have also provided fertile opportunities for fraud by unscrupulous lenders; see, e.g., Mercer v. Jaffe, Snider, Raitt & Heuer, 736 F.Supp. 764 (W.D.Mich.1990); In re National Mortgage Equity Corporation Mortgage Pool, 636 F.Supp. 1138 (C.D.Cal.1986), subsequent opinion 723 F.Supp. 497 (Cal.1989); United States v. Butler, 704 F.Supp. 1338 (E.D.Va.1989); Martin, Fighting Fraud, Secondary Mortgage Markets, Spring 1990, at 24.

30. See Cholewicki, CMOs Transform Mortgage Credit Markets, Mortgage Banking, Feb.1985, at 61; Street Talk on the CMO, Secondary Mortgage Markets, Feb. 1984, at 45; Use of CMO Structure Grows Rapidly, Freddie Mac Reports, Jan. 1984, at 1.

The Tax Reform Act of 1986 finally gave them that right by creating the concept of a Real Estate Mortgage Investment Conduit (REMIC).[31] Since its enactment, the vast majority of the new multiple-maturity mortgage-backed securities have qualified as REMICs, which proved extremely popular.[32]

During recent years REMICs have become far more complex than the early CMOs. They are often issued with large numbers of specialized classes. The principal and interest payments expected on the underlying mortgages can be restructured in a variety of ways, producing, for example, interest-only and principal-only securities. Some classes may be subordinated to others in terms of priority of payout in the event of mortgage default. Private mortgage insurance may be called upon to enhance the creditworthiness of some or all classes. Some classes may carry adjustable-rate coupons indexed to some external interest rate, such as the London Interbank Offered Rate (LIBOR). In addition, some REMICs have been issued on pools of adjustable-rate mortgages. Not only home first mortgages, but also second mortgages,[33] multifamily apartment project mortgages,[34] and mortgages on commercial projects have been securitized, although growth in the latter area has been slow because of the individually-negotiated character and lack of standardization of the commercial mortgage market.[35] Both FNMA and FHLMC have "resecuritized" some of their mortgage-backed securities as REMICs to gain the greater marketing advantages associated with multi-class issues.

The Federal Home Loan Bank System

The Federal Home Loan Bank System is organized in a manner similar to the Federal Reserve System. It consists of twelve Federal Home Loan Banks located in districts covering the United States and about 2,000 member financial institutions, most of which are savings and loan associations.[36] The district banks serve as central credit

31. §§ 671–675, Tax Reform Act of 1986, enacting Int.Rev.Code §§ 860A–860G. See final regulations, 57 Fed.Reg. 40319 (Sept.3, 1992); Treas.Reg. §§ 1.67–3, 1.1275–3.

32. See Hu, Secondary Market: The American Model, Mortgage Banking, Apr. 1991, at 14, estimating that $350 billion in REMICs were issued during the 1987–90 period; Latimer, Regarding REMICs, Secondary Mortgage Markets, Fall 1991, at 2.

33. Swartz, Securitizing Seconds, Secondary Mortgage Markets, Spring 1991, at 12.

34. Stevenson, Securitizing Low–Income Multifamily Mortgages, Mortgage Banking, May 1992, at 81; Godner & Rosen, Mobilizing the Multifamily Secondary Market, Secondary Mortgage Markets, Summer 1989, at 2.

35. See Kane, Fundamentals of Commercial Securitization, Mortgage Banking, July 1992, at 18; Healy, A Promising Outlook, Mortgage Banking, July 1990, at 27; Franzetti, Growing the Market for Commercial MBS, Mortgage Banking, July 1989, at 32; Richards, "Gradable and Tradable": The Securitization of Commercial Real Estate Mortgages, 16 Real Est.L.J. 99 (No.2, Fall 1987).

36. See the Federal Home Loan Bank Act, 47 Stat. 725 (1932), 12 U.S.C.A. § 1421. Under FIRREA, commercial banks and credit unions may also become FHLB members if they hold at least 10% of their assets in residential mortgage loans. See 12 U.S.C.A. § 1424, as amended by FIRREA § 704; 12 CFR Parts 931–932; proposed regulation, 57 Fed.Reg. 58732 (Dec. 11, 1992).

banks for the member institutions and do not do business directly with the public. They are instrumentalities of the federal government, and were originally under the control and regulation of the Federal Home Loan Bank Board in Washington, D.C. When FIRREA abolished the FHLBB in 1989, the oversight of the Federal Home Loan Banks was assigned to a new agency, the Federal Housing Finance Board (FHFB).[37] This agency is governed by five directors; one is *ex officio* the Secretary of HUD, and the other four are private citizens appointed by the President for seven-year terms. However, each of the banks has issued capital stock which is owned by its members. Hence the banks are an unusual hybrid of federal control and private ownership. Each bank has its own staff and board of directors; six of the board members of each bank are appointed by the FHFB to represent the public interest, two of whom must be from consumer or community organizations;[38] the other directors (at least eight, and as many more as needed to equal the number of states in the bank's district) are elected by the member institutions.

Congress seems to have been dissatisfied with the beginning efforts of the FHFB; in the 1992 it amended the FHFB's legislation to make clear that the agency's highest priority was ensure that the banks operate in a financially safe and sound manner. Its other duties, as indicated above, are to supervise the banks, to ensure that they carry out their housing finance mission, and to ensure that they remain adequately capitalized and able to raise funds in the capital markets.[39]

The banks provide a variety of benefits to their members, including the acceptance of interest-bearing deposits and the provision of computer services. By far the most important activity of the banks is the making available of credit to their members. Loans from the banks to their members are known as "advances."[40] The funds the banks use to make advances are obtained primarily from two sources: deposits made by member institutions (currently about one-fourth of the banks' liabilities), and more importantly, "consolidated obligations"—that is, notes, debentures, and other debt instruments issued in the general capital markets. These obligations must be approved by the FHFB's Office of Finance, which also assists the banks in marketing them.[41]

---

37. Title VII of FIRREA, Pub.L.No. 101–73, 103 Stat. 183 (1989).

38. 12 U.S.C.A. § 1427. If the number of elected directors is expanded beyond eight, the number of appointed directors is also enlarged to three-fourths of the elected directors.

39. § 1391, Housing and Community Development Act of 1992, Pub.L.No. 102–550, codified at 12 U.S.C.A. § 1422a(a)(3).

40. See 12 CFR Parts 935, 940; proposed regulation, 57 Fed.Reg. 45338 (Oct. 1, 1992). See Fidelity Financial Corp. v. Federal Home Loan Bank of San Francisco, 792 F.2d 1432 (9th Cir.1986), certiorari denied 479 U.S. 1064, 107 S.Ct. 949, 93 L.Ed.2d 998 (1987) (member institution had no property right to advances that was violated when FHLB discontinued making them to member).

41. See 12 CFR 900.30 (delegation of authority to Office of Finance); 12 U.S.C.A. § 1431(b) and 12 CFR Parts 932, 941 (issuance of consolidated obligations). The amount of obligations, in relation to the banks' equity, is limited by a "leverage ratio"; see 12 CFR 910.1; proposed regulation, 57 Fed.Reg. 20061 (May 11, 1992).

The savings and loan industry has tended to use advances from the banks as a substitute for funds withdrawn by depositors from savings accounts when tight credit and high interest rates in other markets have resulted in reductions in savings account balances. For this reason the total level of advances has fluctuated widely, tending to reach peak levels when interest rates are highest and dropping off as credit becomes more available. During the spate of savings and loan failures during the 1980s, institutions that were insolvent or nearly so tended to make heavy use of advances.[42] FIRREA consequently narrowed the preexisting definitions of eligible collateral for advances, eligible institutions, and uses of advances.[43]

Since the consolidated obligations of the banks are purchased by a wide variety of institutional investors, most of which are not primarily mortgage investors, the bank system has the effect of shifting funds from the general capital markets into the mortgage market. In this respect, and also in its counter-cyclical tendencies, the bank system serves much the same function as FNMA and FHLMC. However, it differs from the secondary market agencies in that no mortgages are actually purchased by the Federal Home Loan Banks from their member institutions. The associations that borrow from the banks continue to hold the mortgages in their portfolios, although these mortgages serve as collateral for advances made.

State and Local Housing Finance Agencies

The creation by state governments of mortgage market support agencies is a relatively recent phenomenon. In 1960 New York became the first state to do so; by 1970 twelve more states had acted, and now nearly all states have such agencies.[44] The underlying concept of all of the agencies is similar. They sell bonds and other debt issuances that, because of their state government status, are exempt from federal and often state income taxation, and which therefore bear relatively low interest rates. The funds raised by these bond and note sales are then used to finance housing for low-income and moderate-income families and individuals, with the lower interest rates being passed on in the form of lower mortgage interest to the home-buyers (in the case of single-family housing) or sponsors (in the case of rental apartments).

The mechanisms by which the state agencies funnel their money into the residential mortgage market are varied. Some make direct loans to housing developers, sponsors, and individual buyers. Others act as secondary market purchasers, issuing advance commitments to

---

42. See U.S. General Accounting Office, Thrift Industry: The Role of Federal Home Loan Bank Advances (Sept.1989); U.S. General Accounting Office, Thrift Industry: Federal Home Loan Bank Board Advances Program (Mar.1988).

43. FIRREA § 714, codified in 12 U.S.C.A. § 1430.

44. See State Housing Finance Agencies: The Iowa Blueprint, 62 Iowa L.Rev. 1524 (1977). Only Arizona and Kansas have no state agencies. The WG & L Housing and Development Reporter contains a thorough summary of state agency techniques and a current listing of the individual agencies and the programs they operate.

lending institutions to purchase loans which meet prescribed criteria.[45] Still others make loans to lending institutions on the condition that the funds be employed in mortgage lending on housing of the type the agency desires to assist. Some employ two or more of the foregoing methods. Whether single-family or multi-family housing is involved, the agencies usually impose limitations on the household income of the occupants and on the cost of the housing.

Other programmatic variations exist. In a few states, legislatures have appropriated subsidy funds which the agencies administer, sometimes employing them to further lower interest rates. In addition, many of the agencies have worked cooperatively with the Department of Housing and Urban Development, supplying mortgage loans for projects subsidized by HUD under its Section 8 program.[46] The advantage of the state agency's lower interest rate when used in conjunction with HUD subsidies is that it may make otherwise infeasible projects feasible by lowering the sponsor's debt service, or may permit the construction of apartment buildings with somewhat greater amenities than would otherwise be possible.

As the success of the state housing finance agencies grew in the late 1970's, cities and counties began to emulate their example, either creating local financing agencies or issuing mortgage-backed bonds themselves. In most of these situations, single-family home loans to owner-occupants were involved. One result of this increased activity was a growing concern on the part of Congress that the implicit federal subsidy was being abused. There were reports of loans to wealthy individuals to buy expensive houses. Since the bonds represented a significant loss of revenue to the federal government, they could hardly be justified in social policy terms except in cases of needy borrowers who could not otherwise afford decent housing.

Congress' objections to this free-wheeling use of tax-free financing found expression in the Mortgage Subsidy Bond Tax Act of 1980,[47] which added Section 103A to the Internal Revenue Code.[48] It deems the interest on mortgage subsidy bonds to be taxable income unless the criteria set out in the Act are met. To qualify, 90% of the mortgage loans in the program must be to persons who have not owned a home during the previous three years, and 20% of the funds must be directed to economically distressed areas. Each state is given an annual "quota" in terms of dollar volume of bonds that can be issued; half of this amount is allocated to the state agency, and half to local agencies, unless the state chooses a different allocation. Prices of the homes

---

45. See Lupis v. Peoples Mortg. Co., 107 Idaho 489, 690 P.2d 944 (1984).

46. See Sangster, For Section 8 Housing—New Financing Relationship Between LHA's and State Housing Finance Agencies Proposed, 32 J. Housing 67 (1975).

47. Pub.L. No. 96–499, adding I.R.C. § 103A. On the inefficiency of using mortgage bonds to subsidize housing, see U.S. General Accounting Office, The Costs and Benefits of Financing with Tax–Exempt Bonds (Feb.1986); U.S. General Accounting Office, Mortgage Bonds are Costly and Provide Little Assistance to Those in Need (Mar.1988).

48. See I.R.C. Temp.Reg. § 6a.103A.

financed must not exceed certain limits, and the IRS is authorized to publish "safe harbor" figures for these limits.[49]

The Tax Reform Act of 1984 added a new twist in an attempt to respond to the long-expressed criticism that tax-exempt bonds are an inherently inefficient and costly technique for subsidizing housing, since much of the lost federal revenue benefits wealthy bond-holders and the various underwriters, lawyers, and other professionals who create and market the bonds. The 1984 Act allows state housing finance agencies to "trade in" a portion of their unused tax-exempt bond-issuing authority in return for authority to issue taxable bonds tied to "mortgage credit certificates", or MCC's. The MCC's can then be issued to qualified home buyers, and allow them to take a tax *credit* (not merely a deduction) for a portion of the interest they pay on their mortgage loans.[50] The credit may vary from 10% to 50% of the interest paid, and has the obvious effect of reducing the cost of home ownership.[51] Thus, the benefit to the home buyer is economically analogous to that which results from issuance of tax-free bonds. But under the MCC program, the interest on the agency's corresponding bonds is taxable rather than tax-exempt.

The MCC program was further complicated by the Technical and Miscellaneous Revenue Act of 1988,[52] which set in place a system for recapturing the tax credits of homeowners whose incomes rise or who sell their houses at a profit. The recapture amount may be as great as the lesser of 6.25% of the highest mortgage balance or 50% of the mortgagor's gain on disposition of the property. The 6.25% figure is a maximum percentage, and is adjusted downward depending on the time the mortgagor has held the home; only 20% of it is applied if the home is disposed of in the first year; that percentage rises by 20% a year to 100% in the fifth year, and then declines by 20% per year through the ninth year. If the home is held for ten years or more, there is no recapture. A downward adjustment in the recapture amount is also made for low-income families.

A final important program operated by state housing finance agencies is known as the low income housing tax credit program.[53] The agencies are authorized to allocate tax credits to developers and investors for the construction and rehabilitation of apartments for tenants with incomes of 60 percent or loss of the area median income. Each state has a tax credit cap based on its population. The credit may be taken only in lieu of various other tax incentives for low-income

49. See Rev.Proc. 91–17, 1991–7 Cum. Bull. 23.

50. § 611, Pub.L. No. 93–369, codified in I.R.C. § 25.

51. See I.R.C. Temp.Reg. 26 CFR 1.25, adopted 50 Fed.Reg. 19344 (May 8, 1985).

52. Pub.L.No. 100–646, codified as I.R.C. § 143(m). The law also requires mortgage lenders to explain the recapture system to borrowers, no small task in itself! See Drummond, Lenders Clarifying MRB Recapture Provision, Real Estate Finance Today, Feb. 4, 1991, at 7.

53. See U.S. General Accounting Office, Observations on the Low–Income Housing Tax Credit Program (Aug.1990); McEvoy, The Growing Importance of HFAs, Freddie Mac Reports, Apr. 1991.

housing developers, such as accelerated cost recovery and rapid deduction of construction-period interest and taxes. The credit is claimed over a ten-year period, and requires the developer to set aside the housing units in question for low-income use for 15 years.[54]

§ 11.4 Alternative Mortgage Instruments

The great majority of mortgage loans made in America since the great depression are of the level-payment self-amortizing type described in Section 1.1. Interest is fixed for the life of the loan and payments are the same each month or other period, and fully amortize the debt with no "balloon" payment upon maturity. While this format has resolved the problem of mandatory refinancing that existed in pre-depression mortgage loans, in which only interest was paid monthly,[1] it also has certain disadvantages. The disadvantages fall into two basic categories, as do various approaches to reform.

The first troublesome aspect of the standard loan format is its failure to take into account changes in the ability of the mortgagors to make payments over their life spans. For example, young families purchasing a first house are likely to experience significant increases in income as they grow older.[2] Yet the standard loan provides for level payments in terms of nominal dollars; in an inflationary economy, the real value of the monthly payments will decline over time, even though the mortgagors' ability to pay will probably be increasing. Hence their maximum initial loan amount will be fixed by an income that is likely to become irrelevant with the passage of time;[3] after a few years they will easily be able to afford payments on a larger home, but can make

---

54. The mortgage revenue bond and low-income tax credit programs described in the text expired on June 30, 1992. The efforts of the industry groups to get them extended and made permanent were successful in Congress, but the President vetoed the bill (H.R. 11). Nevertheless, many state agencies had "stockpiled" both bond funds and tax credits prior to the expiration date, and continued to use them. It was widely believed that the programs would probably be revived in 1993. See Haas, State Agencies Seem Prepared to Weather Tax Credit, MRB Hiatus, WG & L Housing & Devel. Rptr., Nov. 23, 1992, at 538.

§ 11.4

1. Pre-depression mortgages were usually written for relatively short periods—five to fifteen years—and made no provision for amortization of principal balance; thus, when the loan matured, the borrower was expected either to pay the principal out of accumulated savings, or to refinance for an additional period with the same or another lender. During the depression many borrowers found both alternatives impossible, and large-scale foreclosures resulted. See Harr, Federal Credit and Private Housing 58 (1960). As Harr describes, the Federal Housing Administration was primarily responsible for popularizing the long-term, level-payment, fully-amortizing loan.

2. Life-cycle incomes are discussed in Weinrobe, Whatever Happened to the Flexible Payment Mortgage?, FHLBBJ, Dec. 1975, at 16. See also Hu, In Search of the Ideal Mortgage, FNMA Seller–Servicer, Apr.-Jun. 1981, at 21.

3. Lenders usually "qualify" borrowers by permitting them to borrow only the amount which can be repaid by monthly installments (including principal, interest, taxes, and insurance) no larger than 25% to 28% of monthly income. See, e.g., FNMA Guide Servicers–Lending, ch. 2, § 102.06 (1984); Federal Home Loan Mortgage Corp., Sellers' Guide Conventional Mortgages § 3.403(a) (1984). FHA uses a guideline of 35% of "net effective income;" see HUD Handbook 4000.2 (1982) at sec. 5–7. Thus income often fixes the maximum amount a mortgagor can borrow, even if he or she would prefer a larger loan.

such a change only through the rather costly method of selling the existing house and buying another.

Toward the end of the mortgagors' life span an opposite mismatch occurs. They usually retire and experience a sharp drop in income, but their monthly mortgage payment obligation remains constant despite the fact that principal amortization and inflating house values have combined to produce a very low loan-to-value ratio. The mortgagors might prefer to reduce their payments, or even to stop them entirely, but the standard loan format makes no provision for doing so.

The second major problem with the standard loan relates not to the preferences and incomes of mortgagors, but to the ability of lenders, particularly thrift institutions, to retain deposits and hence to continue lending during periods of sharply increasing interest rates. The United States economy has experienced a series of large fluctuations in interest rates during the post-war period, especially since 1966. These credit cycles are produced by the interaction of a complex set of factors, including consumer behavior, federal and state borrowing demands, domestic and international trade and economic conditions, and the periodic efforts of the Federal Reserve Board to tighten the supply of money in the economy in order to slow inflation. Interest rate peaks can be clearly discerned in 1966, 1969–70, 1974, 1978, 1981, and 1984. In each case rates have subsequently fallen, but usually not as low as pre-peak levels.[4]

The effect of these credit cycles on thrift institutions has been highly damaging. When short-term rates on alternative investments, such as Treasury bills and commercial paper, rise above the rates being paid on savings deposits by thrift institutions, many sophisticated depositors withdraw their funds from savings accounts and place them in these alternative investments. The institutions may literally run out of money to lend, and the housing market suffers. This phenomenon is known as disintermediation, since it involves the removal of funds from the thrift institutions, which are financial intermediaries.[5] To forestall disintermediation, thrift institutions may attempt to raise the interest rates on their own deposits, thereby inducing investors to keep their funds on deposit. Until recently, one major barrier to such an effort was Regulation Q, under which the Federal Reserve Board and the Federal Home Loan Bank Board set legal limits on deposit

---

4. See the statistical series in any current issue of Mortgage Banking magazine or in the annual Economic Report of the President. The post–1984 downward cycle was an exception; by early 1992 rates had fallen to the levels of twenty years earlier. See Are Mortgage Rates Really Low?, Secondary Mortgage Markets, Winter 1991/92, at back cover.

5. Disintermediation and its effects are discussed in The Report of the President's Commission on Housing 118–20 (1982); Klaman, Maintaining Deposit Inflows When Interest Rates Rise: The Impossible Dream, 38 Mortgage Banker 46 (No. 7, Apr. 1978); Gramley, Short–Term Cycles In Housing Production: An Overview of the Problem and Possible Solutions, in Federal Reserve Staff Study: Ways to Moderate Fluctuations in Housing Construction (1972), at 1; Schechter, The Residential Mortgage Financing Problem, Committee Print, House Housing Subcommittee, 92d Cong., 1st Sess., 1971.

§ 11.4   GOVERNMENT INTERVENTION

interest rates payable by both banks and thrift institutions.[6] In principle, Regulation Q was intended to prevent damaging rate wars among institutions. But whatever the merits of that policy, Regulation Q had the practical effect of keeping rates paid to small savers at below-market levels. Moreover, because it maintained a small interest differential between thrifts and commercial banks (with the former typically being permitted to pay one-fourth percent higher interest), it also served to divert funds into the thrifts, and thus into housing investment.

Regulation Q was persistently criticized by economists as anticompetitive, unfair to small savers, and inefficient.[7] In the Depository Institutions Deregulation and Monetary Control Act of 1980, Congress directed the financial regulatory agencies to phase out Regulation Q and eliminate all deposit rate ceilings by March 31, 1986.[8] But even without Regulation Q, depository lenders that invest primarily in standard mortgages will still have difficulty raising their deposit interest rates to competitive levels during periods of generally rising rates. The reason is that their mortgage portfolios consist of mortgages made in prior years as well as those made in the current year. Even if the institution raises the interest rates on mortgage loans currently being made to very high levels, that action has relatively little impact on the overall yield of the portfolio, since it consists largely of fixed-interest loans made in earlier periods when rates were lower. This "portfolio lag" phenomenon virtually precludes the institutions from raising deposit interest rates quickly, no matter how much they would like to do so. Thus thrift institutions may be caught in a fundamental structural dilemma; by their nature they violate the well-known axiom of finance: "Never borrow short and lend long." In an economy characterized by volatile interest rates, their problem is an acute one.[9]

Two approaches to this problem can be taken, and the thrift institutions and their regulators moved toward both. The first is to change the maturity structure of the institutions' liabilities—that is, their deposits—in order to make them less volatile. A number of regulatory changes were made to allow thrifts to offer a broader range

---

6. See 12 U.S.C.A. §§ 3502–3509, added by Pub.L. No. 96–221, §§ 203–210. The repeal of the previous authority of the individual agencies to fix deposit ceilings is found in 12 U.S.C.A. § 3506. See 12 CFR Part 217 (Federal Reserve Bd.); 12 CFR Part 329 (Federal Deposit Ins. Corp.); 12 CFR Part 526 (Federal Home Loan Bank Bd.). All federally-chartered and federally-insured state-chartered banks and S & Ls are controlled by these regulations.

7. See, e.g., The Report of The President's Commission on Financial Structure and Regulation (the "Hunt Commission") (1972) recommending abolition of Regulation Q. Cf. Dunne, Scott & Barrett, The Swan Song of Regulation Q—A Rejoinder, 92 Banking L.J. 219 (1975).

8. See note 6 supra.

9. The portfolio lag concept is discussed in Ashley, Use of "Due–On" Clauses to Gain Collateral Benefits: A Common-Sense Defense, 10 Tulsa L.J. 590 (1975). The problem is illustrated by the fact that, in 1980, when current mortgage rates were typically above 15%, 67% of the mortgages held by savings and loan associations carried rates below 10%. See Report of the President's Commission on Housing 129 (1982).

of longer-term instruments to savers.[10] But this solution has limited impact; many depositors want immediate access to their funds, and are unwilling to commit them to certificates of deposit for fixed terms.

The other approach is to shorten the effective maturity of the institutions' assets, their mortgage loans. Although most home mortgages today have nominal maturities of twenty-five to thirty years, they are typically prepaid in ten to twelve years or less.[11] These early payments have historically been in part a result of inflating housing prices, which tend to make property sales with assumptions and subject-to transfers impractical within a few years after a mortgage loan has been placed on a home. The widespread use of due-on-sale clauses is also an important factor in causing early payoffs. But most portfolio lenders wish to reduce the effective term of the average home mortgage loan a great deal more than the reduction that results from ordinary prepayments associated with home sales. Hence, since the beginning of the 1980s they have engaged in a major shift away from the standard fixed-rate loan and toward instruments with adjustable rates, with the adjustment indexed to short-term or medium-term market rates such as those on United State government securities. Such mortgages are viewed as the economic equivalent of short-term loans, even though their monthly payment schedules might continue to be based on twenty-five or thirty year amortization of principal.

There are, then, two reasons for the development in recent years of alternative mortgage instruments: the desire to conform payment schedules to borrowers' abilities to pay, and the desire to make mortgage loans which are not locked into fixed interest yields for long time periods, but on which yields will tend to match those available in the current market from time to time. Certain types of new mortgage formats are associated with each of these two objectives.[12]

Mortgages That Address The Borrower's Ability to Pay

The *graduated payment mortgage (GPM)* is intended to be attractive to mortgagors who expect to have rising incomes in the near future. The interest rate on a GPM is fixed, but the payments start out at a relatively low level and gradually rise to a predetermined higher amount. The payments are not keyed to the borrower's actual income, but rather follow a rising schedule which the mortgagor expects to be

10. See President's Commission on Housing 124–26 (1982); Olin, Changes in Deposit Account Structure, September 1982—March 1983, 16 FHLBBJ 32 (Aug. 1983); regulations cited note 6 supra.

11. See Boykin, Implications of the 12-Year Prepayment Assumption, Mortgage Banker, Nov. 1976, at 38; Kinkade, Mortgage Prepayments and Their Effects on S & Ls, FHLBBJ, Jan. 1976, at 12.

12. See generally Iezman, Alternative Mortgage Instruments: Their Effect on Residential Financing, 10 Real Est.L.J. 3 (1981); Thomas, Alternative Residential Mortgages for Tomorrow, 26 Prac.Law 55 (Sept.1980); Federal Home Loan Bank Board, Alternative Mortgage Instruments Research Study (3 vols. 1977) (hereafter cited AMIRS Study); Smith, Reforming the Mortgage Instrument, FHLBBJ, May 1976, at 2; Follain & Struyk, Homeownership Effects of Alternative Mortgage Instruments, 5 Am.Real Est. & Urb.Econ.Ass'n J. 1 (1977).

§ 11.4 GOVERNMENT INTERVENTION 87

able to meet without difficulty. The objective is to permit the borrower to qualify for a larger loan than would be permitted if the payments were level.[13]

The first federal encouragement for the GPM came in 1974, when the Federal Home Loan Bank Board authorized federal savings and loan associations to make "flexible payment mortgage loans."[14] Such loans were required to be structured so that each payment would cover at least the entire interest due. In addition, by the end of the fifth year the payments had to be high enough for the loan to be fully self-amortizing. The full-interest requirement meant, for example, that the initial payments on an 8.5 percent "flexible payment" mortgage could, at best, be about 8% lower than payments on a standard mortgage. The reduction in payments was not very great, and the program was not widely used.[15]

The enactment of the Housing and Community Development Act of 1974 added a new Section 245 to the National Housing Act,[16] authorizing HUD to insure mortgages "with provisions for varying rates of amortization corresponding to anticipated variations in family income." After some uncertainty as to how to proceed,[17] HUD in 1976 issued regulations under the authority of Section 245 (now Section 245(a)),[18] approving the insurance by FHA of graduated payment mortgages. The regulations permit monthly payments to be increased in annual steps over either the first five years or the first ten years of the loan; under the five-year plan the payments may rise by 2.5%, 5%, or 7.5% each year, while under the ten-year plan payments may increase annually by either 2% or 3%. There is no requirement that all payments cover interest owed, and the FHA program often involves "negative amortization" in the early years. If the early payments do not cover the full interest, the difference is added to principal; thus, it is entirely possible for the outstanding balance to rise rather than decline for the first few years. The program requires that the outstanding balance never exceed 97% of the original appraised value of the property.

To illustrate the operation of the GPM concept, assume the mortgagor borrows $50,000 for a 30-year term at an interest rate of 12%. The monthly payment on a standard level-payment loan would be $514.31. Suppose the mortgagor instead elects a GPM under the most popular of the FHA plans mentioned above—Plan III, which provides for payments increasing at 7.5% per year for the first five years of the loan.

13. See note 3, supra.

14. 12 CFR 541.14(c); see Cassidy & McElhone, The Flexible Payment Mortgage: An Opportunity for Experimentation by S & Ls, FHLBBJ, Aug. 1974, at 7.

15. See Weinrobe, Whatever Happened to the Flexible Payment Mortgage?, FHLBBJ, Dec. 1975, at 16.

16. 12 U.S.C.A. §§ 1715z–1710.

17. See 40 Fed.Reg. 34625, in which HUD solicited public comments as to what it should do under its Section 245 authority.

18. 12 CFR 203.45, 203.436; condominium financing is also made available under the GPM by virtue of 12 CFR 234.75, 234.-259. See McFarlin & Vitek, The HUD GPM Program: An Evaluation, Mortgage Banker, Mar. 1980, at 27.

The payments in the first year will be only $395.69, and for the first five years, will rise as follows: [19]

Year 1	395.69 per month
Year 2	425.37 per month
Year 3	457.27 per month
Year 4	491.56 per month
Year 5	528.43 per month

All payments in later years will remain at the same level as the fifth year. The advantages to the borrower in terms of initial qualification for the loan are obvious; the first-year payment is about 23% lower than under a level-payment plan. Of course, this is offset by the higher payments that must be made in years five through thirty, but that is a price many borrowers are willing to pay.

This example also illustrates the negative amortization that many GPM's produce. Here the $50,000 outstanding balance on the loan does not begin to decline with the first payment, as is the case with level payment mortgages. Instead, because the early payments are insufficient to cover the accrued interest, the balance rises steadily until the 60th month, at which point it "peaks" at $53,935.41. Not until the 151st month does the balance decline below its original level of $50,000. The decline continues, and the loan is fully amortized by the 360th month's payment.

In addition to the Section 245(a) plans described above,[20] Congress also adopted Section 245(b), which permitted FHA to insure GPMs with even more liberal terms. Under this plan monthly payments could rise by 4.6% per year for ten years, or by 7.5% per year for five years. The mortgage amount could be higher under Section 245(b) than under 245(a), since the "peak" outstanding balance could be as great as the lesser of 113% of the original appraised value of the house, or 97% of appraised value, inflated by 2.5% per year during the period the outstanding balance is rising. FHA's default experience with this program was unsatisfactory, and it terminated it by regulation in 1987.[21]

The Veterans Administration also operates a GPM plan for VA-guaranteed home mortgages. It is essentially identical to FHA's Plan III described above.[22] While the authorizing statute permitted VA to allow negative amortization up to a "peak" of the original appraised

---

19. The financial tables from which this example was computed are found in HUD Handbook 4240.2 CHG 2, issued Jan. 29, 1980.

20. Section 442 of the Housing and Urban–Rural Recovery Act of 1983, Pub.L. No. 98–181, added a new Section 245(c) to the National Housing Act. It authorized FHA to insure graduated payment mortgages on multifamily housing. Such a GPM would have varying rates of amortization corresponding to anticipated variations in project income. FHA proposed regulations to implement this program, see 49 Fed.Reg. 41068, but has never finalized them.

21. See 24 CFR 203.46; 52 Fed.Reg. 32754 (Aug. 28, 1987).

22. See 38 CFR 36.4309(e); DVB Circular 26–81–36, published in 46 Fed.Reg. 60124.

value inflated by 2.5% per year (with a maximum of 115% of appraised value),[23] VA did not implement this concept and instead insists that the loan balance never exceed the original appraised value.

Federally-chartered lenders are empowered by their regulators to make conventional GPM loans with few limitations. For federal savings and loan associations, the regulations of the Office of Thrift Supervision allow the loan contract to provide for payment adjustments "pursuant to a formula, or to a schedule specifying the percentage or dollar change in the payment as set forth in the loan contract."[24] The loan term may not exceed 40 years, and if negative amortization causes the loan balance to exceed 125% of the property's original appraised value, the contract must provide for an adjustment in payments at least every five years (beginning no later than the 10th year of the loan) to an amount that will fully amortize the loan over its remaining term.[25]

For national banks, whose lending practices are subject to regulation by the Comptroller of the Currency, the legal environment is even more liberal. In 1983 the Comptroller, responding to the congressional deregulation of bank lending found in the Garn–St. Germain Depository Institutions Act of 1982,[26] eliminated all of its rules and interpretive rulings with respect to amortization and maturity of real estate loans.[27] Hence, a national bank can make virtually any type of GPM loan.

A second type of new mortgage instrument is designed for the other end of the life cycle: retirement. Its thesis is that many elderly persons have accumulated large equity values in their homes, but will suffer substantial income reductions upon retirement. Under the *reverse annuity mortgage (RAM)*,[28] sometimes termed a home equity conversion mortgage (HECM), the mortgagor in this situation can be given a large cash advance by the lender, and can immediately use this cash to purchase an annuity. The monthly cash flow from the annuity can be used, in part, to pay the interest (and perhaps some principal amortization) on the enlarged mortgage debt; the remainder of the annuity stream would be paid directly to the mortgagor to augment his or her income.

---

23. 38 U.S.C.A. § 1803(d)(2), as amended by the Veterans' Disability Compensation, Housing and Memorial Benefits Amendments of 1981, Pub.L. No. 97–66, 95 Stat. 1026.

24. 12 CFR 545.33(e).

25. 12 CFR 545.33(d).

26. § 403, Pub.L. No. 97–320, 96 Stat. 1469, removing all statutory restrictions on real estate lending by national banks.

27. 48 Fed.Reg. 40698. The regulation preempts any state law which would limit national banks as to loan amount, repayment schedule, or term; see 12 CFR Part 34.

28. See U.S. Dept. of HUD, Home Equity Conversion Mechanisms (1986); Note, Effects of Legislation on the Reverse Annuity Mortgage as a Means of Home Equity Conversion, 13 Ford.Urb.L.J. 909 (1985); Comment, The Effect of Reverse Annuity Mortgages on SSI, 16 U.Cal.Davis L.Rev. 435 (1983); Shaman, New Hope for the Elderly: Home Equity Conversion, Real Estate Today, May 1982, at 36; Comm. on Aging, U.S. House of Representatives, Home Equity Conversion, 98th Cong., 1st Sess. (1983); Edwards, Reverse Annuity Mortgages, AMIRS Study at XIX; Guttentag, Reverse Annuity Mortgages: How S & Ls Can Write Them, AMIRS Study at XVIII.

Under an alternative and simpler approach, the mortgagee makes monthly installment payments directly to the mortgagor, thereby regularly increasing the outstanding balance on the debt; interest would also continue to accrue and be added to principal. No annuity is purchased under this approach; it can termed simply a "reverse mortgage." Obviously this results at some future point in the reaching of an unacceptable loan-to-value ratio if the mortgagor lives long enough; the lender will then insist on payoff, presumably achieved only by selling the house, or would foreclose.[29] The advantage of the annuity approach, by contrast, is that it will continue to pay as long as the mortgagor lives, so there is no risk of the mortgagor being forced to vacate the property.

Other variants on the RAM or HECM are possible. For example, the lender might offer more favorable terms in return for a share in the property's future appreciation in value. Under another option, the so-called "split equity contract"[30] the homeowner might sell the house to an investor (possibly the mortgagee), reserving a life estate. The sale proceeds could be paid in installments over a number of years, or the vendor might take the proceeds in cash and purchase an annuity. Numerous other permutations may also be conceived.[31]

In recent years most regulatory barriers to the making of reverse mortgage loans have been swept away. As mentioned above, the real estate lending powers of national banks are now almost fully deregulated, so they may readily engage in reverse mortgage lending.[32] Reverse lending by savings and loan associations is governed by the OTS regulations, which provide that associations may agree to defer and capitalize "all interest on loans to natural persons secured by borrower-occupied property and on which periodic advances are being made."[33] Thus the classic reverse mortgage, with regular payments to the borrower and accrual of all interest, is authorized. There has also been a good deal of state legislative activity, approving or encouraging and regulating the use of reverse mortgages by state-chartered lending institutions.[34] Nevertheless they continue to be seen as radical or even dangerous by many lenders, and their growth is likely to be slow.[35]

Reverse mortgages were given a significant boost by the adoption of a pilot FHA home equity conversion mortgage (HECM) program in

---

29. See Quinn, Let the Mortgagor Beware, Forbes, Mar. 20, 1978, at 77, criticizing this type of RAM.

30. See Edwards, Reverse Annuity Mortgages, AMIRS Study, at XIX–5.

31. See Garnett & Guttentag, The Reverse Shared–Appreciation Mortgage, 3 Housing Fin.Rev. 63 (1984); Chen, Alternative Reverse Mortgages: A Simulation Analysis of Initial Benefits in Baltimore, 2 Housing Fin.Rev. 295 (1983); Note, Reverse Annuity Mortgages and the Due–on–Sale Clause, 32 Stan.L.Rev. 143 (1979).

32. See notes 27–28 supra.

33. 24 CFR 545.33(c). See the previous regulations in 46 Fed.Reg. 51893.

34. See, e.g., Ill.Stat. Ch. 205 § 5/6.1; Minn.Stat.Ann. § 47.58(4); N.Y.—McKinney's Banking Law § 6–h; N.C.Gen.Stat. § 53–255 et seq.

35. See DeZube, A Slow Start for Reverse Mortgages, Mortgage Banking, Dec. 1990, at 33.

1989.[36] It is remarkably complex, and perhaps cannot successfully be explained to consumers.[37] Three options are provided for drawing down the funds: payments for a fixed term, payments until the mortgagor ceases to occupy the home, and a line of credit with no scheduled advances. Interest may be fixed or adjustable, and the mortgagee may include a right to share in the appreciation, if any, of the house. One of the mortgagors must be at least 62 years old, and they must own the property and occupy it as their principal residence. The loans are nonrecourse, with no deficiency liability.

Lack of affordability of housing, especially for young families, has given rise to several other innovative mortgage formats. One of these is the *shared-equity mortgage, or SEM*. It involves at least two parties who are liable on the mortgage loan. One of them will occupy the house; the other is an investor who owns a share of the equity, typically as a tenant in common, and makes a portion of the down payment and monthly payments, but does not occupy the property. Since each contributes a portion of the investment, they are entitled to share, on the basis of agreed percentages, in the proceeds of a subsequent sale or other disposition.

The objective of the SEM is to reduce the owner-occupant's initial down payment and monthly outlays to manageable levels, while providing an investment opportunity for the non-occupant party.[38] There is nothing unique about the mortgage itself, but the agreement between the owning parties is complex and requires careful drafting.[39] Since 1982 FHA has encouraged the development of the SEM by treating the house as owner-occupied, and thus eligible for a higher loan-to-value

---

36. Originally 2,500 loans were authorized by Congress, but this was later expanded by § 2107 of the Omnibus Budget Reconciliation Act of 1990 (Pub.L.No. 101-508), to 25,000, a level that FHA is far from exhausting at this writing. See DeZube, note 35 supra, citing criticisms of HUD's program by the chief executive of American Homestead, Inc. of Mt. Laurel, N.J., which has made more than 5,500 conventional reverse mortgages since 1982; Sichelman, A Tough Sell, Mortgage Banking, Nov. 1991, at 22; Wise, HUD's Reverse Mortgages: Alive and Expanding, Real Estate Finance Today, Feb. 4, 1991, at 6; 56 Fed.Reg. 16002 (Apr. 19, 1991), eliminating the reservations system for mortgagees wishing to make FHA reverse mortgage loans, on the ground that the 25,000-loan authority is likely to last for several years.

37. 24 CFR Part 206, added by 54 Fed. Reg. 24822 (Jun. 9, 1989), technical corrections 54 Fed.Reg. 32059 (Aug. 4, 1989). See May & Szymanoski, Reverse Mortgages: Risk Reduction Strategies, Secondary Mortgage Markets, Spring 1989, at 16; Black, Reverse Mortgages: Making Equity Work for the Elderly, Mortgage Banking, Sept. 1989, at 67.

38. See McCartney, Sharing Home Ownership, Sylvia Porter's Personal Finance, Mar. 1986, at 59; All-in-the-Family Mortgages Start to Show Some Promise, Wall St.J., May 29, 1985, at 31 col.1; Fields, Real Estate Interests as Investment Contracts: An Update and a New Application—the Shared-Equity Program, 12 Real Est.L.J. 307 (1984); Alper, Equity Sharing in Florida, Fla.B.J., Dec. 1984, at 701. If the occupant pays rent to the investor, the latter may claim depreciation on his or her interest in the house; I.R.C. § 280A(d)(3) and proposed IRS Reg. § 1.280A-1.

39. See, e.g., Keith v. El-Kareh, 729 P.2d 377 (Colo.App.1986), in which the equity-sharing agreement provided for forfeiture of the occupants' interest to the investor-owner if the occupants defaulted on their portion of the mortgage payments. The court refused to enforce the forfeiture clause, and instead ordered partition of the property, engaging in complex calculations to determine the size of their respective interests.

ratio, if the agreement meets certain tests.[40] However, FHA became dissatisfied with abuses in this program and eliminated it except for related co-mortgagors in 1988.[41]

Another mortgage technique that came into common use during the 1980s as a way of improving housing affordability is the "*buy-down.*"[42] Here a builder or home-seller makes a substantial payment to the mortgage lender in return for the latter's reducing the interest rate (and hence the monthly payments) on the loan to the buyer. Such a payment is, of course, costly to the seller, but it can be a useful and sometimes powerful tool for marketing the housing. In some cases, the seller requires the buyer to repay in future years the amount advanced to accomplish the buy-down, and may take a junior mortgage on the property to secure this repayment obligation.[43] In most recent buy-down programs, the interest rate reduction has been on the order of 1% to 3%, and has been scheduled to phase out (i.e., to rise to market rate) over a period of one to three years. Such a buy-down is much less costly to the seller than would be the case if the interest rate were to be reduced for the entire life of the loan. The mortgagor may or may not undertake an obligation to repay the buydown; FHA specifically authorizes such repayment obligations, with certain restrictions, and permits

---

40. For non-owner-occupied properties, the maximum loan-to-value ratio is only 85%; 24 CFR 203.18. Under the FHA SEM guidelines, the co-mortgagor's (i.e., investor-owner's) proportion of the monthly payment obligation must be the same as his share of equity ownership; the occupant must pay at least 55% of the monthly payment; the occupant must have the right to buy out the co-mortgagor on 30 days' notice, with the price to be determined by an FHA-approved appraiser; and either party may sell his or her interest after giving the other a 30-day option to purchase it. See also FHLMC Sellers' Guide Conventional Mortgages § 3.201(a)(7), providing guidelines for FHLMC purchase of mortgages on shared-equity properties.

41. FHA Mortgagee Letter 88-24.

42. See Wang and Peterson, Toward Affordability: Buydown and Pledged Account Loans, 42 Mortgage Banking 9 (Aug. 1982). The pledged account is similar to a buy-down, except that the funds needed to reduce the loan interest come from a savings or escrow account rather than being paid in cash. The account balance may be assigned outright to the lender at the closing of the loan, or may be "pledged" or assigned under an agreement by which the lender draws down the funds over a period of time—generally the same period as that during which the interest rate reduction is in effect. See FHLMC Sellers' Guide Conventional Mortgages § 3.201(a)(6), describing FHLMC's policies on purchase of mortgages that have been bought down; where the seller provides the funds, they may not exceed 10% of the original loan amount. See also FNMA Guide Services—Lending, ch. 1, § 417, limiting seller buy-downs to 10% of the appraised value of the property if the loan-to-value ratio is 90% or less, and otherwise to 6% of appraised value.

Until deregulation of the FHA interest rate in 1983, see supra § 11.2 at notes 20–21, nearly all FHA loans were made at below-market rates, with the seller compensating the lender by payment of "discount points"—in effect, a buydown of the interest rate. This practice has now been discontinued for both FHA and VA loans; see supra § 11.2 note 16. These buy-downs differed from those discussed in the text in that the interest rate remained at the lower level for the entire mortgage term. See Agarwal & Phillips, Mortgage Rate Buy-downs: Further Evidence, 3 Housing Fin. Rev. 191, 1984, discussing the extent to which FHA and VA discounts were passed back to home buyers via increased house selling prices.

43. See 49 Fed.Reg. 14113 (proposed amendment to FHA regulation, 24 CFR 203.32, which would authorize such junior mortgages to secure buy-down repayments).

them to be secured by a second mortgage on the home.[44]

A final innovation described here is the *growing equity mortgage, or GEM*. Unlike the other techniques described above, its primary thrust is not the lowering or eliminating of monthly payment amounts; indeed, it increases them. Rather, the objective of the GEM is to produce earlier loan pay-offs, and thus to shorten the effective term of the mortgage. The GEM is similar to a GPM in structure: it involves monthly payments that increase by a prearranged percentage each year for, say, the first five or ten years of the loan. But unlike the GPM, a GEM's first-year payments are identical to those which would be required for a level-payment 30-year mortgage. Since this amount is more than sufficient to cover all accruing interest, the entire added amount of the higher payments in later years is applied to retire the principal of the loan. The result is much more rapid pay-off, typically in the range of 12 to 20 years.[45]

From the mortgagor's viewpoint, the GEM has several advantages. Most obviously, the home will be debt-free at a much earlier date than under a standard mortgage. In addition, because the effective maturity of the debt is shorter, the lenders generally offer such loans at lower interest rates than would be demanded on level-payment loans.[46] To the extent that any discount or buy-down is involved, the short effective maturity accentuates its impact in further reducing the interest rate.[47] The result is that a GEM can bear a much more attractive rate to the borrower than a standard loan under the same market conditions. On the other hand, the quick amortization is not always an advantage; after only a few years, if the original mortgagor wishes to sell the property on an assumption basis, the balance on the loan may be too low to be attractive to most buyers.

FHA has approved GEM loans as a variant of the GPM since 1982,[48] and the Government National Mortgage Association (GNMA) is empowered to guarantee mortgage-backed securities that are supported by pools of GEM loans.[49] Like the GPM, the GEM recognizes that many mortgagors will experience increasing incomes, and thus increasing ability to pay, over time. By conforming to their expected economic life cycles, it allows them to gain significant economic advantages.

44. See 24 CFR 203.32, as amended by 50 Fed.Reg. 20903 (May 21, 1985).

45. See Hill, Growing-Equity Home Loans Are Gaining Popularity Because of Quick Repayments, Wall St.J., Oct. 6, 1982, at 52 col. 1.

46. Under most economic conditions, the "yield curve," which represents interest rates as a function of loan term, slopes upward, indicating that long-term investors usually demand higher rates than short-term investors because their funds are at risk for a longer period. See Weggeland, Understanding the ARMs Indexes, Mortgage Banking, Oct. 1984, at 105.

47. In general, the shorter the loan term, the greater the effect of any discount or buy-down; see Lederman, Pricing Discount ARMs in the Secondary Market, Mortgage Banking, Aug. 1984, at 57.

48. See 49 Fed.Reg. 19451, adding 24 CFR 203.47. The FHA regulations were also amended, in the above Federal Register entry, to make GEMs available for condominium and cooperative share loans.

49. See 24 CFR Part 390, subpart D, as amended by 48 Fed.Reg. 3588.

Mortgages that Address the Term Mismatch Problem of Portfolio Lenders

As discussed above, lenders who make or purchase mortgage loan assets to hold in portfolio, and whose capital comes primarily from short-term or medium-term liabilities, such as savings deposits, are faced with a problem of mismatched terms. If rates rise on the liability side of the ledger, the lender's cost of funds may approach or even exceed its earnings from its mortgage portfolio. This happens because so much of the portfolio is comprised of mortgage loans made in earlier years at lower rates.[50] The result is serious financial stress for the lender, and in some cases even insolvency.[51]

At least three types of mortgage formats have been developed in recent years in an attempt to solve this problem. By far the most widely-used and discussed is the *adjustable rate mortgage, or ARM*. It provides for periodic readjustments to the interest rate, based on fluctuations in some external index of rates on financial instruments.[52] Because of these regular rate changes, the lender views the ARM as the approximate economic equivalent of a series of short-term mortgages, each made at approximately the current market rate.

The ARM has a checkered regulatory history. The Federal Home Loan Bank Board was a leader in proposing regulations to authorize ARMs (which were usually termed VRMs, or variable rate mortgages, until the 1980s). But its proposals in 1972[53] and 1975[54] met with strenuous political objection[55] and were withdrawn. Finally in 1978 the FHLBB adopted rules allowing such loans by federal savings associations, but they were initially applicable only in states where the Board determined they were necessary to meet competitive pressures

---

50. For a thorough discussion of these phenomena, see FHLBB, Proposed Amendments Relating to Interest Rate Adjustments, 40 Fed.Reg. 6870.

51. During the early 1980s this is precisely what occurred to the savings and loan industry.

52. While the vast majority of ARMs are tied to a specific index, one court has upheld an ARM in which rate adjustments were entirely discretionary with the lender and unconnected with any index. Murello Constr. Co. v. Citizens Home Savings Co., 29 Ohio App.3d 333, 505 N.E.2d 637 (1985).

53. 37 Fed.Reg. 16201, withdrawn 38 Fed.Reg. 17023.

54. 40 Fed.Reg. 6870.

55. See Hearings on the Financial Institutions Act of 1975 before the Subcomm. on Financial Institutions, Senate Banking, Housing & Urban Affairs Comm., 94th Cong., 1st Sess. (1975), at 725–49; Hearings on Alternative Mortgages before the Senate Comm. on Banking, Housing & Urban Affairs, 95th Cong., 2d Sess. (1978); Comment, Adjustable Interest Rates in Home Mortgages: A Reconsideration, 1975 Wisc. L.Rev. 742.

During 1984 a new spate of political concern with the risks of ARMs to consumers surfaced; see Adjustable-Rate Mortgage Attacked, Defended at House Panel Hearing, BNA Hsg. & Devel. Rptr., July 2, 1984, at 100; Mortgage Lenders, Others Defend ARMs at Hearing, Legislation Unlikely, BNA Hsg. & Devel. Rptr., Aug. 13, 1984, at 217.

Consumers have seemed a good deal less concerned than politicians; see Consumer Acceptance of ARMs Reported Up; Lenders Concerned about "Payment Shock," BNA Hsg & Devel. Rptr., Apr. 9, 1984, at 978; Thompson, All Quiet on the Western VRM Front, FHLBBJ, Oct. 1978, at 10; Colton, Lessard & Solomon, Borrower Attitudes Toward Alternative Mortgage Instruments, 7 J.Am.Real Est. & Urb.Econ. Ass'n 581 (1979).

from state-chartered associations;[56] California was the initial example. Not until mid-1979 were the geographic limits removed, and adjustable rate lending approved nationwide.[57]

During these years there was considerable concern about the possible adverse impact of ARMs on consumers. Hence the initial FHLBB regulations contained a number of detailed provisions to protect borrowers from unfair or unduly onerous ARMs.[58] They included a minimum time period between rate changes, a maximum percentage rate change per year, a cap on total rate increases over the life of the loan, a minimum adjustment percentage to avoid trivial or harassing changes, a requirement of notice some minimum time before the effective date of any rate adjustment, and detailed disclosure to borrowers before loan closing. In addition, the FHLBB specified the rate index which all ARMs were required to employ.[59]

Over time, virtually all of these restrictions on lender behavior have been relaxed or have disappeared.[60] Under the FHLBB's last codification of its lending-power regulations, published in 1983 and still in effect under the auspices of the Office of Thrift Supervision, the remaining restrictions apply only to loans secured by homes owned by borrower-occupants. The same is true of the Office of the Comptroller of the Currency's restrictions on ARM loans by national banks. In the case of both agencies, the index can be any rate that is "readily available to and verifiable by the borrower and is beyond the control"

56. 43 Fed.Reg. 59336; the geographic restriction was made a part of then 12 CFR 545.6–2(c)(2). This same rule authorized GPMs and RAMs by federal S & Ls as well.

57. 44 Fed.Reg. 32199.

58. See Cassidy, Comparison and Analysis of the Consumer Safeguards of Variable Rate and Renegotiable Rate Mortgage Instruments, FHLBB Research Working Paper No. 95 (1980). Note that the regulation itself used the term "VRM." The text here employs "ARM" for the sake of conceptual consistency.

59. In the 1978 geographically-limited regulations, the index was the current cost-of-funds index published by the district Federal Home Loan Bank in which the property was located. When the regulations were applied nation-wide in 1979, the FHLBB's national index of cost of funds to FSLIC-insured associations was substituted. See 44 Fed.Reg. 32199.

60. See Buckley & Villani, Problems with the Adjustable–Rate Mortgage Regulations, 2 Housing Fin.Rev. 183 (1983), suggesting that the liberalization of federal regulation of ARMs may have gone too far, shifting excessive risk to borrower households; Miller, Adjustable Rate Mortgages: A Proposed Statutory Reform, 26 Santa Clara L.Rev. 253 (1986). The original OCC rules were much more protective of consumers; see 46 Fed.Reg. 18932. See generally Parks, Adjustable-rate Mortgages— New Regulations for National Banks and Federal Savings and Loan Associations, 70 Ill.B.J. 126 (1981). The preemptive effect of the OCC regulations was upheld in Conference of State Bank Supervisors v. Conover, 710 F.2d 878 (D.C.Cir.1983).

Numerous states have adopted statutes or regulations governing ARM lending by state-chartered institutions. See, e.g., West's Ann.Cal.Civ.Code § 1916.5; Minn. Stat.Ann. § 51A.02. See also Note, Alternative Mortgage Instruments: The Oklahoma Experience, 8 Okla.C.U.L.Rev. 121 (1983); Bucki, Variable Rate Instruments in New York State, 54 N.Y.St.B.J. 510 (1982); Note, Variable Rate Mortgages: Texas Savings & Loan Associations Authorized to Offer Flexible Financing Alternatives, 12 St. Mary L.J. 1144 (1981); Washburn, Alternative Mortgage Instruments in California, 12 Akron L.Rev. 599 (1979). However, under the federal Alternative Mortgage Parity Act, 12 U.S.C.A. § 3801 et seq., much of this legislation is irrelevant, since state-chartered lenders can make any sort of alternative mortgage loan (including ARMs) that would be available to the same type of federally-chartered lender.

of the lender.[61] There are no longer any regulated minimum or maximum rate adjustments, either annually or during the loan's life, nor is there any minimum time between adjustments. By federal statute, ARMs on homes must include a maximum rate, but the law is virtually meaningless since the rate may be as high as the parties agree.[62] For a time each of the federal banking regulators had its own ARM disclosure requirements, but in 1988 a uniform system of disclosure for home loans was promulgated by all of the agencies.[63]

How does the borrower pay when the rate increases? There are essentially three methods. The most obvious is simply to increase the monthly payments to correspond to the new rate. The only problem with this approach is a practical one: will the borrower be able to afford the higher monthly outlay? In the parlance of the lending industry, will the "rate shock" encourage an unacceptable level of delinquency and ultimate default and foreclosure?

A second alternative is to leave the payment amount at its initial level, but to increase the term of the loan. However, this works only with small rate increases. For example, a fully-amortizing 30-year loan of $50,000, with a 12 percent interest rate, carries monthly payments of $514.31. If the rate is raised to 12.5 percent, the interest alone would amount to $520.83 per month, even if no principal were paid at all. Hence, no conceivable lengthening of the loan's maturity will allow the monthly payment to remain constant with this (relatively small) rate increase. Since most home loans (including ARMs) are made initially with 30-year terms, and 40 years is typically the maximum term permitted under applicable regulations,[64] the greatest rate increase that can be accommodated by lengthening the 30-year maturity is about one-fourth of one percent.

---

61. See 12 CFR 545.33(e) (OTS); 12 CFR 34.7 (OCC). Even these restrictions do not apply to non-home loans, and general legal limitations on indexes based on contract law appear to be minimal. See, e.g., Murello Constr. Co. v. Citizens Home Savings Co., 29 Ohio App.3d 333, 505 N.E.2d 637 (1985) (loan agreement enforceable despite having no index at all). Apparently contra, but arguably based on the Truth-in-Lending Act, see Preston v. First Bank of Marietta, 16 Ohio App.3d 4, 473 N.E.2d 1210 (1983), holding unenforceable as lacking mutuality an adjustable rate clause with no index rate and no restriction on the lender's power to increase the rate. See also Rent America, Inc. v. Amarillo Nat. Bank, 785 S.W.2d 190 (Tex.App. 1990) (index equal to 2% over prime rate of another bank sustained); Columbus Production Credit Ass'n v. Weeks, 54 Ohio App.3d 149, 561 N.E.2d 984 (1988) (index equal to rate currently being charged by mortgagee sustained).

62. 12 U.S.C.A. § 3806, adopted by § 1204, Competitive Equality Banking Act of 1987, Pub.L.No. 100–86.

63. Disclosures at the time of loan origination are described in Regulation Z, promulgated by the Federal Reserve Board under the Truth–in–Lending Act; see 12 CFR 226.19. The other banking agencies have adopted these disclosure rules; see, e.g., 12 CFR 563.99 (OTS); 12 CFR 34.10 (OCC). FHA has also adopted them for its ARM program; FHA Mortgagee Letter 88–26. The OTS rules also prescribe disclosures to be given when notices of rate change are issued; 12 CFR 563.99(c). See generally Bylsma, Less ARMtwisting, Mortgage Banking, May 1988, at 63; Lee & Schmelzer, Adjustable Rate Mortgages: Continued Debate over Disclosure and Underwriting Standards, 41 Bus.Law. 1065 (1986).

64. See, e.g., 12 CFR 545.33(a) (1984) (40 years, federal savings and loan associations); 24 CFR 203.17(d) (35 years, FHA-insured mortgages).

The foregoing assumes that the loan will continue to be self-amortizing despite the rate increase. The third method of accommodating a rate increase does not make this assumption; instead of raising monthly payments to meet the increased interest rate, the payments are held constant and the unpaid interest is simply added to principal, producing "negative amortization" each month in much the same way as do many GPM plans.[65] The difference, of course, is that here there is no specific schedule of rising payments to which the borrower is obligated, and that will eventually "catch up" the capitalized interest. Lenders and regulators have been deeply concerned with this fact, since it raises the prospect that in the event of default the loan may be seriously under-secured by the mortgaged property. Until 1981 federal savings and loan associations were not permitted to use negative amortization in ARMs.[66] The current OTS rules limit the use of negative amortization: the loan balance may never exceed 125 percent of the original appraised value of the property unless the contract provides for readjustment of the payments at least once every five years, beginning no later than the 10th year of the loan, to a level sufficient to amortize the loan fully over its remaining term at the then-existing interest rate.[67]

During the early 1980s ARMs were extremely popular among portfolio lenders, who had been badly burned by the "stickiness" of the yields on their fixed-rate portfolios during the high-interest swing of 1979–81. However, borrower resistance to ARMs soon became apparent. When fixed-rate loans carry high rates, borrowers are attracted to ARMs because of their relatively lower rates—commonly 1.5% to 2% below fixed rates. But when fixed rates are relatively low, consumers see ARMs as unduly risky, and a larger interest rate advantage is necessary to convince borrowers to opt for them.[68] As a result, the ARM share of home loans closed in the United States since ARMs were first widely available in the early 1980s has fluctuated from nearly 70% to a low of about 20%, and has been highly dependent on rates being offered on fixed-rate mortgages.[69] They have fallen far short of providing the thrift industry with a reliable hedge against the risks of a sharp and sustained future increase in interest rates.

The inherent complexity of ARMs has also proven problematic for lenders. The difficulties of training loan officers, explaining ARMs to borrowers, ensuring that loan documents are consistent and correctly

---

65. See supra text at notes 18–25.

66. See 46 Fed.Reg. 24148.

67. 12 CFR 545.33(d). National banks operating under OCC rules have no similar limits on negative amortization.

68. See Khazeh, Decker & Winder, Consumer Preferences Toward Adjustable and Fixed Rate Mortgages, 7 Real Estate Finance 65 (No. 2, Summer 1990); Brueckner & Follain, Tracking ARMs, Secondary Mortgage Markets, Winter 1986–87, at 2.

69. See ARM Share of Home Loans Closed, Real Estate Finance Today, Mar.25, 1991, at 1. See also Khazeh, Decker, Winder & Neat, Who Has ARMs?, 7 Real Estate Finance 57 (No. 4, Winter 1991), discussing survey data showing that ARM borrowers were wealthier, older, and bought more costly houses than fixed-rate borrowers.

completed, and calculating and collecting rate changes are manifold. In 1989 John Geddes, a former FSLIC employee, issued a report based on an audit of 7,000 ARMs originated by thrift institutions in the midwest. He claimed an error rate of more than 50% in adjustments made on these loans. The U.S. General Accounting Office reviewed his study and concluded that his figures were somewhat inflated, but nonetheless estimated error rates between 20% and 31%. Whatever the precise numbers, it is clear that errors are common.[70]

The acceptance by FNMA and FHLMC of ARMs as suitable instruments for purchase has been critical to their success.[71] These agencies have been a major force in standardizing ARMs; they have accomplished this by adopting standard forms [72] and identifying the characteristics of instruments they are willing to buy, and the market has responded by creating instruments which meet these specifications. As a result, FMNA and FHLMC have become *de facto* regulators of ARMs.

It is not feasible to describe here the detailed programs currently being operated by FNMA and FHLMC. In general, they have attempted to encourage ARMs with annual and lifetime caps on interest rate increases, payment increases, or both; to discourage the use of so-called "teaser rates" (in which the initial interest rate on an ARM is made artificially low by means of a buy-down or a rate concession by the lender, raising the possibility of serious "payment shock" to the borrower in later years); to discourage negative amortization; and to adopt fairly conservative standards for qualifying borrowers under ARMs.[73] They have also encouraged experimentation with ARM conversion options—loans that begin life as ARMs, but that may be converted to fixed-rate mortgages at the borrower's option on a specified date.[74] The converted mortgage may bear interest at the then-prevailing rate, an

---

70. See Badger, Adjusting to the Perils of ARMs, Mortgage Banking, Aug. 1991, at 53; Fortney, ARMed and Dangerous, Mortgage Banking, June 1991, at 53.

71. See Colton & Lea, ARMs and the Secondary Markets: The Next Boom?, Secondary Mortgage Markets, May 1984, at 2. In 1991 about 14% of the conventional mortgages purchased by FNMA were ARMs; see FNMA, 1991 Annual Report, at 20.

72. See Browne, Development and Practical Application of the Adjustable Rate Mortgage Loan: The Federal Home Loan Mortgage Corporation's Adjustable Rate Mortgage Loan Purchase Program and Mortgage Loan Instruments, 47 Mo. L.Rev. 179 (1982). Eskridge, One Hundred Years of Ineptitude: The Need for Mortgage Rules Consonant with the Economic and Psychological Dynamics of the Home Sale and Loan Transaction, 70 Va.L.Rev. 1083, 1183 (1984).

73. See Freddie Mac Announces New ARM, GPM Purchase Programs, BNA Hsg. & Devel.Rptr, Feb. 11, 1985, at 726; Thomas, Freddie Mac ARM Guidelines, Mortgage Banking, Oct. 1984, at 85; Lederman, Pricing Discount ARMs in the Secondary Market, Mortgage Banking, Aug. 1984, at 57; Standard Rate–Capped ARMs Announced by Fannie Mae, BNA Hsg. & Devel. Rptr., Oct. 22, 1984, at 430; Thomas, Pricing and Analysis of Adjustable Rate Mortgages, Mortgage Banking, Dec. 1984, at 61.

74. See Nothaft, Vetrano & Stamper, Designing ARMs, Secondary Mortgage Markets, Winter 1987/88, at 2; Young & Matthiesen, The Long, Strong ARM: Legal Issues Attendant to Negative Amortization, ARM Loans with Conversion Options, 38 Consumer Fin.L.Q.Rpt. 43 (1984).

average of rates that have prevailed since the ARM was made, or some combination of the two.

The Federal Housing Administration was a late-comer to ARM activity; its Congressional authority to insure ARMs was not granted until 1983,[75] and was limited by statute to ten percent of the aggregate number of mortgages insured by FHA in any fiscal year. Unlike the financial regulatory agencies discussed above, which elected to approve a broad spectrum of ARM formats for institutional lenders, FHA defined the parameters of its ARM rather strictly.[76] This is an understandable approach, since FHA ultimately bears the full risk of default on loans it insures.[77]

Under FHA's ARM rules, adjustments must be made annually, and may not result in rate increases of more than one percent.[78] The rate may not change more than 5 percent (up or down) over the life of the loan. The index selected by FHA is the weekly average yield on U.S. Treasury securities, adjusted to a constant maturity of one year. While the statute allows rate changes to be paid by increased monthly payments, extensions of loan maturity up to 40 years, or increases in principal balance, FHA's regulations permit only payment increases. This eliminates any possibility of negative amortization, which FHA obviously felt would be unacceptably risky. However, the rule allows the lender to "carry over" index changes that would produce a rate increase greater than one percent, and apply them in a future year. The rule also contains provisions on disclosure and notice of adjustment.

Many of the conventional ARM loans made in recent years have incorporated a GPM feature; that is, the documents contain a schedule of rising monthly payments for the first five or ten years of the loan, which must be followed irrespective of any interest rate changes.[79] The

---

75. See § 443, Housing and Urban-Rural Recovery Act of 1983, Pub.L.No. 98-181.

76. See interim rule, 49 Fed.Reg. 23560, codified in 24 CFR 203.49; FHA Mortgagee Letter 84-16, July 18, 1984; Bak, Introduction to the FHA ARM, Mortgage Banking, Nov. 1984, at 24.

77. See supra § 11.2, note 23.

78. The adjustment in the mortgage rate under the FHA rule must be the same as the *absolute* change in the index (subject to the 1% per year and 5% lifetime caps, of course); it is not based on the *proportionate* change in the index. To illustrate, assume the initial mortgage rate is 12% and the initial index rate is 11%. On the date of the first adjustment, the index rate has risen to 11.75%. The mortgage rate will then be adjusted to 12.75%.

Some non-FHA ARMs are adjusted on the basis of proportionate changes in the index. Under such a system, using the numbers in the preceding example, the index would have risen from 11% to 11.75%, a proportionate increase of .06818. The mortgage interest would then be adjusted upward by .06818 of its original 12% level, or to 12.8172%. Hence, the absolute change in the mortgage rate under this method is greater than the absolute change in the index.

79. The FHLBB at one point adopted a specific regulation approving loans with both graduated payments and adjustable rates; it was termed the Graduated Payment Adjustable Mortgage Loan (GPAML). See 46 Fed.Reg. 37625 (July 22, 1981). The present OTS rule, however, treats ARMs, GPMs, and a variety of other instruments under the same section of the regulations (12 CFR 545.33), allows great flexibility in combining features, and avoids such distinctions in terminology entirely.

On GPARMs, see generally Cortes, Everything You Always Wanted to Know

FHA ARM, however, appears not to contemplate such a feature, but instead provides for payment changes only in accordance with fluctuations in the index rate.[80]

The advent of the FHA ARM set the stage for introduction of an ARM mortgage-backed security guaranteed by the Government National Mortgage Association (GNMA).[81] (GNMA is empowered to guarantee only securities backed by FHA and VA mortgages, and thus could take no action on conventional ARM loans.)[82] GNMA introduced its ARM security program in 1984.[83]

A second new type of mortgage instrument that is intended to help lenders shift interest rate risk to borrowers, and thus to hedge against the prospect of mismatched short-term and long-term rates, is the *shared appreciation mortgage, or SAM.*[84] In a SAM, the lender charges both fixed interest and contingent interest. The fixed component of interest is typically a good deal lower than current market rates on standard mortgages. The contingent interest is computed as a percentage (perhaps in the range of 10% to 40%) of the amount of price appreciation in the property. The contingent interest is not paid until the property is sold or transferred by the borrower, or until the loan matures at some specified date, say ten years from its inception.[85]

About ARMs, Mortgage Banking, June 1984, at 21; Hu, In Search of the Ideal Mortgage, FNMA Seller/Servicer, Apr.-Jun. 1981, at 21, discussing the design of graduated payment adjustable rate loans.

80. See 24 CFR 203.49(h) ("This section does not apply to a mortgage that meets the requirements of * * * § 245 (graduated payment mortgages) * * *"); FHA Mortgagee Letter 84–16, July 18, 1984 (ARMs may be originated only under National Housing Act Sections 203(b) (1–4 family fixed payment), 203(k) (rehabilitated housing), and 234(c) (condominiums)).

81. See 24 CFR Part 390, Subpart D, added by 49 Fed.Reg. 23580 (Jun. 6, 1984) (interim rule).

82. See § 11.3 supra at note 17.

83. The ARM program was established under the GNMA type II plan, which involves the creation of large national pools of mortgages by GNMA, with participation by many different lenders. See Carrel, The GNMA Adjustable Rate Security, Mortgage Banking, Oct. 1984, at 99.

84. See generally Burnes, The Shared Appreciation Mortgage—A Joint Venture, A Relationship Between Debtor and Creditor, or Both?, 12 J.Real Est.Tax. 195 (1991); Boyd & O'Dell, The Tax Consequences of Shared Appreciation Mortgages After Tax Reform, 4 J.Partnership Tax. 302 (1988); Friend, Shared Appreciation Mortgages, 34 Hast.L.J. 329 (1982); Iezman, The Shared Appreciation Mortgage and the Shared Equity Program: A Comprehensive Examination of Equity Participation, 16 Real Prop. Prob. & Tr.J. 510 (1981); Angell & Wardrep, Evaluating the Shared Appreciation Mortgage, Mortgage Banker, Apr. 1981, at 31; Hu, How to Build a SAM, FNMA Seller/Servicer, Apr.-Jun. 1981, at 30.

Note that we have elsewhere discounted the notion, raised by some writers, that the SAM may constitute a clog on the equity of redemption; see § 3.1 supra. Cf. Preble & Cartwright, Convertible and Shared Appreciation Loans: Unclogging the Equity of Redemption, 20 Real Prop.Prob. & Tr.J. 821 (1985); Comment, The Shared Appreciation Mortgage: A Clog on the Equity of Redemption?, 15 J.Marsh.L.Rev. 131 (1982).

85. If there is no sale at the time the loan must be paid, the appreciation is normally determined by an appraisal. If the loan is paid at maturity, there will usually be a substantial "balloon" payment due, since the loan term is typically ten years while monthly payments are based on a 30–year amortization schedule. If no sale of the property occurs at that time, the documents may obligate the lender to refinance the loan, typically with a new fixed-interest mortgage; otherwise, there is no assurance that the borrower will have funds available to make the cash payment. Moreover, if there has been substantial appreciation, the payments on the new

From the borrower's viewpoint, the SAM's advantage is its lower monthly payment level, and thus easier qualification for the loan; in return, the borrower gives up some of the expectation of possible profit which might otherwise have been experienced upon resale of the property. From the lender's viewpoint, if a period of high inflation ensues while the loan is outstanding, the contingent interest will be substantial. Since there is generally a rough correspondence between the inflation level and interest rates, the lender's right to a share of inflation in the property's value may be an attractive substitute for a higher fixed contract interest. On the other hand, the rate of return to the lender on a SAM is obviously speculative, since future inflation cannot be predicted. Moreover, the SAM provides a much lower cash flow to the lender prior to maturity than does a standard loan of the same amount; this is disadvantageous to institutions that have large cash needs.

The FHLBB proposed a specific rule authorizing SAM's in 1980;[86] it was never made final, but the present broader OTS lending regulations clearly permit federal savings associations to make SAM loans.[87] The FHA was authorized by Congress in 1983 to insure SAM's on both one-to-four-family housing and multifamily housing.[88]

The SAM does not make the lender an equity owner of the property. Arrangements doing so are quite possible, of course, but they have not been much used to finance owner-occupied housing. On the other hand, in commercial real estate lending the taking by the lender of an equity participation interest in the property has been common for many years.[89] The fundamental difference between such a loan and a SAM is that the contingent return on the SAM is based solely on appreciation above the original price of the real estate,[90] while an equity participation loan gives the lender a share of the entire property value at the time the loan is paid.[91]

loan may be sharply higher than under the old SAM; see Iezman, Alternative Mortgage Instruments: Their Effect on Residential Financing, 10 Real Est.L.J. 3 (1981).

86. See 45 Fed.Reg. 66801 (Oct. 8, 1980).

87. A federal savings association "may receive a portion of the consideration for making a real estate loan in the form of a percentage of the amount by which the current market value of the property, during the loan term or at maturity, exceeds the original appraised value." 12 CFR 545.32(b)(3).

See also West's Ann.Cal.Civ.Code § 1917.010 et seq., authorizing investment in SAMs by pension funds and containing detailed rules regarding their structure.

88. See §§ 444–45, Housing and Urban–Rural Development Act of 1983, Pub.L. No. 98–181, adding §§ 252–53 to the National Housing Act.

89. See Comment, Lender Participation in the Borrower's Venture: A Scheme To Receive Usurious Interest, 8 Hous.L.Rev. 546 (1971); Comment, Equity Participation in Real Estate Finance, 7 N.C.Cent.L.J. 387 (1976).

90. Of course, SAM mortgages generally give the mortgagor credit, against the appreciation, for any improvements he or she has made during the term of the loan, such as construction of a swimming pool, an added room, or the like.

91. See Gallagher, Computing the Lender's Yield on an Equity Participation Mortgage, Mortgage Banker, Feb. 1981, at 33.

From the perspective of the present day, the SAM seems to have arrived on the scene too late. During the 1960s and 1970s there was persistent inflation in housing prices in most areas of the nation, and SAM loans might have served lenders well. But by the time the SAM began to receive serious consideration by lenders, about 1980, housing inflation had dropped to a fraction of its earlier level, and housing prices have risen slowly (or even declined) throughout most of the country ever since. In such a market, the SAM offers no advantage to lenders, and hence has been little used.

The third, and in many ways, most interesting of the new efforts to shift interest rate risk to the borrower is the *price-level adjusted mortgage, or PLAM,* sometimes termed the *indexed mortgage, or IM.* To understand it, one must begin with the notion that mortgage interest rates are a composite of two factors: a *real* rate, which represents the return a lender would demand on this sort of investment (given the perceived risk of nonpayment, the supply of and demand for lendable funds, and other relevant market conditions) in a non-inflationary economy; and an *inflation premium* which reflects the lender's expectation about probable inflation in price levels over the life of the loan. The real rate is generally assumed to be about 3% to 4.5% for residential first mortgages.[92] Any amount beyond this represents the inflation premium, the purpose of which is to take account of the fact that the loan will be repaid in dollars having less purchasing power than those lent. Of course, the lender cannot predict future inflation with certainty, and the inflation premium may in fact turn out to be higher or lower than the actual inflation.

The problem with standard fixed-payment loans (as PLAM proponents view them) is that the monthly payments, from the outset, are based on an interest rate that includes the inflation premium. If inflation actually occurs, the real value of the monthly payments will steadily decline, despite the fact that the borrower's income in real terms may be static or rising.

Under a PLAM, the lender charges only the real rate by way of contract interest. However, the outstanding principal balance on the loan is adjusted periodically (say, annually) to reflect actual changes in the overall price levels of the nation. For example, the U.S. Department of Labor's Consumer Price Index could be used for this purpose.[93] The result is that payments are very low in the early years of the mortgage, since they are based on the real rate of only, say, 4.5%. If actual inflation occurs, however, nominal payments will rise each year because the 4.5% rate will be applied to a higher outstanding balance than would otherwise be the case, and the payments must be increased

---

92. See Note, Alternative Mortgage Instruments: Authorizing and Implementing Price Level Adjusted Mortgages, 16 U.Mich.J.L.Reform 115, 121 n. 28 (1982); Barnes, A Proposal for "Indexed" Mortgage Financing, Mortgage Banker, Oct. 1980, at 32; Cassidy, Price–Level Adjusted Mortgages Versus Other Mortgage Instruments, 14 FHLBBJ 3 (1981).

93. This is in fact the index proposed by FHA; see 49 Fed.Reg. 23063 (Jun. 4, 1984).

to the level needed to fully amortize the new balance over the remaining term.

PLAMs have been very widely used in countries such as Brazil and Israel, in which inflation is rampant. Whether they will be attractive to American consumers is still unclear, as they have been little used in residential finance in this country. They present the possibility of extremely sharp increases in nominal dollar payment levels in their later years, although in real terms the payments are constant, and should not pose a problem for mortgagors whose incomes rise as rapidly as inflation. For young borrowers with strong potential for increased earnings, the PLAM may be even more attractive than the GPM in solving the "life cycle" problem and permitting earlier home ownership. At the same time it has the effect, even more directly than the ARM, of shifting the risk of inflation from lender to borrower. If high inflation ensues, the PLAM probably presents a greater default risk than the ARM or any other plan discussed in this section.

The OTS lending regulations clearly approve of PLAMs for federal savings associations,[94] and in 1983 Congress authorized the FHA to insure PLAM mortgages, which it referred to as "indexed mortgages." The FHA's proposed rule implementing this authority has never been made final. However, it contains a thoughtful analysis of the policy issues raised by PLAMs. It also describes the possibility of a modified PLAM, in which the contract rate consists of the real rate plus a "buffer rate" of an additional, say, 5 percent. Only inflation that exceeds the "buffer rate" would be reflected in adjustments to the loan's balance. The result is an instrument that carries a higher initial payment than a "pure" PLAM (although still much lower than a standard mortgage), but in which the impact of future inflation on later-year payments is greatly ameliorated.

Like the SAM, the PLAM seems to have missed its opportunity, at least for the time being. It is designed to cope with high levels of inflation, but inflation has been well-controlled in the United States since the early 1980s. Hence, there is little need for the PLAM. Because it is such a novel concept, with doubtful market acceptability and some unresolved legal questions,[95] it is doubtful that the PLAM will soon become a significant feature of the American mortgage market.

94. "Adjustments to the payment and the loan balance * * * may be made if (i) the adjustments reflect a change in a national or regional index that measures the rate of inflation or the rate of change in consumer disposable income, is readily available to and verifiable by the borrower, and is beyond the control of the association." 12 CFR 545.33(e)(2).

95. In Aztec Properties, Inc. v. Union Planters National Bank, 530 S.W.2d 756 (Tenn.1975), certiorari denied 425 U.S. 975, 96 S.Ct. 2175, 48 L.Ed.2d 799 (1976), noted in 11 Tulsa L.J. 450 (1976), and discussed in Hyer & Kearl, Legal Impediments to Mortgage Innovation, 6 Real Est.L.J. 211, 228–31 (1978), the Tennessee Supreme Court held the PLAM concept violated the Gold Clause Resolution, by which Congress in 1933 prohibited loan clauses requiring payment in a particular form of currency or coin. The case seems wrongly decided, as the Gold Clause Resolution was surely not intended to prohibit indexing of mortgage loan principals. In any event, the Resolution was repealed by Congress in 1983 for all obligations entered into after October 27, 1977; see 31 U.S.C.A.

The Priority of Alternative Mortgage Instruments

As we have seen above, several types of newly-developed mortgage instruments, including the GPM, RAM, ARM, SAM, and PLAM may involve negative amortization—the process of adding unpaid interest to the loan's original balance. Lenders have a practical concern about negative amortization, since it may reduce their margin of security and, in extreme cases, leave them with a loan balance which exceeds the property's value. But negative amortization also raises a difficult priority issue in mortgage law. In substance, capitalizing unpaid interest is the equivalent of making the debtor an additional loan with which to pay the accrued interest. Thus, it can be viewed as a future advance. In general, a future advance loses priority as against any intervening lien (one created between the date of the original mortgage and the date of the advance in question) if the lender had no contractual obligation to make the advance and, at the time it was made, had notice of the intervening lien.[96]

In some types of alternative mortgages the negative amortization is the contractual obligation of the lender, and hence seems to be in no danger of loss of priority. This is most obviously the case with the GPM and RAM, in which the original mortgage documents set out the disbursement and payment schedules precisely, so that there can be no doubt from the outset about the amount of negative amortization that will occur. Suppose, however, that the lender under a RAM reserves discretion to discontinue disbursements to the borrower if it becomes dissatisfied with the property's condition or if the borrower places junior liens on the property. Under these circumstances, further disbursements (and resulting increments to the loan balance) might well be considered optional, and thus to suffer a priority loss.[97] Lenders generally have a tendency to give themselves broad discretion in their loan documents, but in this situation such discretion could be extremely dangerous.

§ 5118(d)(2); Fay Corp. v. Bat Holdings I, Inc., 646 F.Supp. 946 (W.D.Wash.1986); Dom, From the Gold Clause to the Gold Commission: A Half Century of American Monetary Law, 50 U.Chi.L.Rev. 504 (1983).

It is quite likely that a PLAM note cannot be negotiable. U.C.C. § 3–104(1)(b) requires a sum certain, and U.C.C. § 3–106 provides that the sum is certain even though it is to be paid with a stated rate of interest. Query whether the interest can be said to be "stated" where it depends on future inflation. See Note, Alternative Mortgage Instruments: Authorizing and Implementing Price Level Adjusted Mortgages, 16 U.Mich.J.L.Reform 115, 128–29 (1982); Dawson & Coultrap, Contracting by Reference to Price Indices, 33 Mich.L.Rev. 685 (1935). On the other hand, it is not particularly obvious that negotiability is essential to a well-functioning primary or secondary mortgage market; see § 5.29 supra.

The taxation of the lender's receipts under a PLAM is problematic. See Temp. Treas. Reg. § 1.125–6T, 55 Fed.Reg. 729 (Jan. 9, 1990).

96. See generally § 12.7 infra.

97. This problem would not exist if the RAM were of the type involving immediate disbursement by the lender of the full loan balance, which is then used to purchase a commercial annuity for the borrower. See Brodkey, AMIs: Let The Lawyers Work Out The Details, 45 Legal Bull. 133, 139–41 (1979).

With ARMs and PLAMs, the amount of negative amortization which will occur over the loan's life is obviously not predictable when the loan is made, since it will depend on future economic conditions. But this fact alone is insufficient to render the negative amortization "optional," and thus to risk loss of priority. Rather, the question is whether the lender has discretion to add to the loan principal. For example, under an ARM, if the *borrower* has the right to determine whether increased interest will be capitalized or will be covered by increased monthly payments, the lender's priority is not in jeopardy; but if it is the *lender* which is empowered by the documents to make this decision, the risk to priority is raised.[98] Similarly, an ARM lender may believe that it is doing the borrower a favor by permitting negative amortization under documents that do not compel the lender to do so; but the favor may be a costly one, for it may place the lender's priority at risk. The lender is safe only if the documents compel the lender to use negative amortization, either automatically or at the borrower's option.

With the SAM, the problem is somewhat different. The contingent interest does not accrue until the loan is paid off. If the lender is obligated to refinance with a new (non-SAM) loan at that point, there should be no priority problem.[99] If the lender is under no duty to refinance, but does so anyway, it may attempt to rely, for priority purposes, on the doctrine that treats replacement mortgages as retaining the priority of their predecessors.[100] However, it is unclear whether the courts will treat the "predecessor" here as the SAM's balance before or after the addition of the contingent interest.

All of these priority problems, of course, could be resolved by statute. But they are issues of state law, and the current federal statutes do not appear to preempt them. Neither do the federal banking agencies' regulations; in the case of ARMs, they provide that the federally-chartered lenders may *make* ARM loans notwithstanding contrary state law,[101] but it is very hard to read into such language any intent to preempt state priority rules,[102] particularly now that the

---

98. See Hyer & Kearl, Legal Impediments to Mortgage Innovation, 6 Real Est. L.J. 211, 232–34 (1978). Earlier versions of the FHLBB's and Comptroller's regulations on ARMs appeared virtually to force their constituent lenders into an optional position; they provided explicitly that the lender could elect whether or not to implement rate increases. See 12 CFR 545.6-2(a)(2)(i) (FHLBB); 12 CFR 29.5(c)(1) (OCC). These provisions have been deleted from the current versions of the regulations.

99. The FHLBB's proposed SAM regulations did require the lender to refinance; see 45 Fed.Reg. 66801 (Oct. 8, 1980). The present broader OTS rule, however, does not. Of course, the lender may undertake a refinancing duty in the original SAM documents, whether compelled to do so by regulation or not.

100. See § 9.4 supra.

101. See 12 CFR 29.2 (OCC) (ARMs only); 12 CFR 545.2 (OTS) (all lending authority); 12 CFR 701.21-6B(b)(2) (NCUA) (ARMs only).

102. Interestingly, the former FHLBB regulation governing GPMs contained an explicit statement that capitalization of interest would not result in a loss of first-lien status; see 12 CFR 545.6-4(b)(3) (1980). See Broadkey, AMIs—Let the Lawyers Work Out the Details, 45 Legal Bull. 133, 139 n. 20 (1979). This language was dropped in the FHLBB's 1982 amendments.

former federal rules confining the lenders to first lien investments have been largely eliminated. In a few states the legislatures have addressed this issue,[103] but preemptive federal legislation would be a useful and desirable addition.[104]

The Alternative Mortgage Transaction Parity Act of 1982

In 1982 Congress addressed the problem of inconsistency between state and federal regulation of institutional lending on alternative mortgage instruments. It enacted the Alternative Mortgage Transaction Parity Act,[105] which permits state-chartered lenders to "make, purchase, and enforce alternative mortgage transactions" on the same basis as the analogous federally-chartered institutions. Thus, state banks may follow the regulations of the Comptroller of the Currency, state credit unions may follow the NCUA's regulations, and all other lenders (including savings and loan associations and mortgage bankers) may lend under the rules of the Federal Home Loan Bank Board.[106] Any conflicting state law or regulation is preempted. On the other hand, a state-chartered lender that prefers to follow state law is free to do so; lenders may select whichever regulatory scheme is more liberal.

The definition of "alternative mortgage" is very broad, and includes adjustable-rate loans, re-negotiable loans with balloon payments, and loans:

> "involving any similar type of rate, method of determining return, term, repayment, or other variation not common to traditional fixed-rate, fixed-term transactions, including without limitation, transactions that involve the sharing of equity or appreciation." [107]

This seems to cover every sort of new mortgage format discussed above, as well as others not yet devised.

A state may opt out of the federal preemption scheme by statute or initiative vote adopted prior to October 15, 1985.[108] Several states have done so, and thus have "recaptured" control of mortgage lending by non-federally-chartered institutions within their borders.[109]

Perhaps the most interesting legal question raised by the Parity Act is whether it preempts state priority rules. As discussed above, a mortgage that involves negative amortization raises the risk that priority will be lost if the additions to principal are deemed optional future

103. See, e.g., S.C.Code § 29-3-50.

104. It is arguable that the Alternative Mortgage Transaction Parity Act accomplishes such a preemption; see infra text at note 111.

105. See Title VIII, Garn–St. Germain Depository Institutions Act of 1982, Pub.L. No. 97–320, enacting 12 U.S.C.A. § 3801 et seq.

106. See 12 U.S.C.A. § 3803. The Act does not preempt general state-law restrictions on mortgage lending that apply to both state-chartered and federally-chartered lenders. See First Gibralter Bank v. Morales, 815 F.Supp. 1008 (W.D.Tex.1993).

107. 12 U.S.C.A. § 3802(1).

108. 12 U.S.C.A. § 3804.

109. See, e.g., 9–A Maine Rev.Stat. Ann. § 1–110; New York—McKinney's Banking Law § 6–g.

advances.[110] The Parity Act gives non-federally-chartered lenders the power "to enforce" mortgages "made in accordance with regulations governing alternative mortgage transactions as issued by" the applicable federal agencies.[111] If a mortgage conforms to the relevant federal regulation, does the Parity Act mean that it can be "enforced" with first priority, notwithstanding contrary state law relating to future advances? Such an argument is tenuous, both because the Parity Act says nothing about priority *per se*, and also because to override state priority rules would actually give such mortgages more than *parity*; it would grant them a sort of "super priority" that identical mortgages made by federally-chartered lenders would not have, since their federal regulators have not attempted to preempt state priority rules. This is neither a likely nor a plausible interpretation. Of course, the federal regulators may well amend their regulations in the future to accomplish just such a preemption, and if they do so the Parity Act will obviously bring the state-chartered lenders within that umbrella.

§ 11.5 Discrimination in Mortgage Lending

A wide range of federal statutes prohibit racial discrimination in mortgage lending. Some of these statutes also bar discrimination on other bases as well; the coverage of each will be described in turn. The oldest statutory provisions are those of the Civil Rights Act of 1866, now codified in 42 United States Code at Sections 1981 and 1982. Section 1982 provides that "all citizens * * * shall have the same right * * * as is enjoyed by white citizens * * * to inherit, purchase, lease, sell, hold and convey real and personal property." Section 1981 makes similar provisions regarding the right to make and enforce contracts. Until 1968 it was generally assumed that these statutes applied only to actions of the federal or state governments, but in Jones v. Alfred H. Mayer Co.,[1] the Supreme Court held them applicable to private acts of discrimination as well. There is little question that the language of these sections would ban racial discrimination by a mortgage lender.[2] They apply to all transactions, not merely those relating to housing; a commercial mortgage loan, for example, would be covered. However, they provide no administrative enforcement mechanism, and a suit for damages or conceivably an injunction would be the only remedy. They apply only to discrimination based on race.

Two more recent enactments also prohibit racial discrimination in the provision of mortgage financing. Section 805 of the Civil Rights Act of 1968 (the "Fair Housing Act")[3] makes illegal the discriminatory

---

110. See text at notes 96–104 supra.

111. 12 U.S.C.A. § 3803.

§ 11.5

1. 392 U.S. 409, 88 S.Ct. 2186, 20 L.Ed.2d 1189 (1968).

2. See Baker v. F & F Investment Co., 489 F.2d 829 (7th Cir.1973).

3. 42 U.S.C.A. § 3605. Discriminatory enforcement of mortgages, as by selective foreclosure, is also illegal; Harper v. Union Savings Association, 429 F.Supp. 1254 (N.D.Ohio 1977). Cf. Shipley v. First Fed. Sav. & Loan Ass'n, 703 F.Supp. 1122 (D.Del.1988) (discrimination in foreclosure would violate 42 U.S.C.A. § 1982, but plaintiffs failed to show either discrimina-

denial of a loan or discrimination in respect to loan amount, interest rate, duration, or other terms or conditions. Under the original version of the statute, only discrimination based on race, color, religion, or national origin was barred, but a 1974 amendment included sex as well, and also required all persons making "federally related mortgage loans" to married couples to "consider without prejudice the combined income of both husband and wife for the purpose of extending mortgage credit." This last clause was inserted to stop the prevalent practice of discounting a working wife's income in determining the amount of loan for which the couple was qualified. The Fair Housing Act was further amended in 1988 to prohibit discrimination on the basis of handicapped status or "familial status," defined as households having children under the age of 18.[4]

Section 805 has certain inherent limitations. It applies only to institutional lenders and others in the business of making real estate loans. In addition, the loan in question must be "for the purpose of purchasing, constructing, improving, repairing, or maintaining a dwelling." Thus, loans for non-housing purposes, even if secured by mortgages on housing, are not covered.[5] The statute expressly directs all federal agencies to administer their programs in a manner that will further the objectives of the law,[6] and it gives the Department of Housing and Urban Development authority to administer the act and to receive, investigate, and attempt to resolve complaints of violations.[7] Amendments adopted in 1988 also give the Secretary of HUD authority to issue regulations enforcing and interpreting the Act.[8] United States district courts are given jurisdiction over suits for violations,[9] and the Attorney General is empowered to file injunctive actions when he or

tory intent or effect). The Fair Housing Act is probably violated by the discriminatory withholding of services, such as hazard insurance, that are ordinarily essential to the securing of mortgage financing, but the point is still debatable; compare N.A.A.C.P. v. American Family Mut. Ins. Co., 978 F.2d 287 (7th Cir.1992) and Dunn v. Midwestern Indemnity, Mid-American Fire & Casualty Co., 472 F.Supp. 1106 (S.D.Ohio 1979) (redlining by hazard insurer violates Fair Housing Act, since it makes housing "unavailable") with Mackey v. Nationwide Insurance Cos., 724 F.2d 419 (4th Cir.1984) (hazard insurer's "redlining" of minority neighborhoods is not within Fair Housing Act). HUD's regulations take the position that insurance discrimination violates the Act; see 24 CFR 100.70. See also United States v. American Inst. of Real Estate Appraisers, 442 F.Supp. 1072 (N.D.Ill.1977), appeal dismissed 590 F.2d 242 (7th Cir.1978) (settlement agreement of Dep't of Justice with real estate appraisers' organization.)

4. § 808, Housing and Community Development Act of 1974, Pub.L.No. 93-383, 88 Stat. 633, 728, adding § 527 to the National Housing Act; The Fair Housing Act Amendments of 1988, Pub.L.No. 100-430 (1988). See Dennis, The Fair Housing Act Amendments of 1988: A New Source of Lender Liability, 106 Banking L.J. 405 (1989).

5. Evans v. First Fed. Sav. Bank, 669 F.Supp. 915 (N.D.Ind.1987) (mortgage loan on existing house, for purchase of automobile and college education, was not covered by Title VIII).

6. § 1808(d), Fair Housing Act, 42 U.S.C.A. § 3608(d).

7. §§ 808, 810, Fair Housing Act, 42 U.S.C.A. §§ 3608, 3610.

8. 42 U.S.C.A. § 3614a; see 24 CFR Part 100; N.A.A.C.P. v. American Family Mut. Ins. Co., 978 F.2d 287 (7th Cir.1992); Fenwick-Schafer v. Sterling Homes Corp., 774 F.Supp. 361 (D.Md.1991).

9. § 810(d), Fair Housing Act, 42 U.S.C.A. § 3610(d).

she has reasonable cause to believe a person or group is engaged in a pattern or practice of resistance to the act.[10]

A third statute explicitly prohibiting mortgage credit discrimination is the Equal Credit Opportunity Act (ECOA).[11] Originally enacted in 1974 to prohibit discrimination based on sex or marital status, it was expanded in 1976[12] to cover race, color, religion, national origin, and age discrimination as well. Unlike the Fair Housing Act, ECOA is not confined to housing finance, but applies to all extensions of credit, whatever the purpose. Violations may result in civil liability in federal or state courts. The Federal Reserve Board is given the general power to enact regulations under ECOA, and the principal enforcement power is vested in the various federal banking regulatory agencies with respect to each type of institutional lender.[13] Only persons and institutions which "regularly" extend or renew credit and their assignees are covered by ECOA.

Under the three statutes discussed above, both racial and sex discrimination in lending are broadly prohibited, and it is likely that in their most overt forms they have to a great extent disappeared from the American scene. Two significant issues remain, however. The first is the general problem of loan underwriting criteria which are facially neutral but which in fact have a disproportionate impact on one race or sex; the second is the refusal by institutional lenders to make loans, or the willingness to make loans only on more onerous terms, in certain geographic areas, a practice often termed "disinvestment" or "redlining." The second issue is sometimes an illustration of the first, for a refusal to lend in an area of residential concentration by a minority racial group will plainly have a disproportionate impact on members of a particular race, but redlining may also be considered objectionable as a consequence of its impact on the housing stock and property values, even when no minorities are affected.

The concept that a disproportionate racial *effect* may be illegal, even absent intent to discriminate, is derived from Griggs v. Duke Power Co.,[14] in which the Supreme Court in 1971 considered certain intelligence and aptitude tests administered by an employer to its employees as a condition of promotion. Black employees generally made lower scores on the tests than whites, and hence were not promoted as frequently, but there was no evidence that the employer intended to use the tests to screen out blacks. In response to an attack based on Title VII of the Civil Rights Act of 1964, the Court held that a

10. § 813, Fair Housing Act, 42 U.S.C.A. § 3613; see, e.g., United States v. American Institute of Real Estate Appraisers, 442 F.Supp. 1072 (N.D.Ill.1977) (suit by Dep't of Justice; settlement agreement; discriminatory appraisal practices violate Fair Housing Act.)

11. 15 U.S.C.A. § 1691ff.

12. Equal Credit Opportunity Act Amendments of 1976, Pub.L. No. 94–239, 90 Stat. 251.

13. § 704, Equal Credit Opportunity Act, 15 U.S.C.A. § 1691c (enforcement powers given to OCC, FRB, FDIC, OTS, and NCUA).

14. 401 U.S. 424, 91 S.Ct. 849, 28 L.Ed.2d 158 (1971).

violation had been made out. The Court's opinion articulated what is commonly called the "effects test": if the plaintiffs can show that the defendant's practices have the effect of disproportionately barring minorities in a substantial manner, the burden shifts to the defendant to show that those practices are required by "business necessity" or "genuine business need." [15] Later cases have generally held that to make a successful defense, the defendant must show that no other procedure with a lesser discriminatory impact could be used to accomplish the same business goal.[16]

For some time after *Griggs* there was doubt as to whether the disparate impact test applied to the Fair Housing Act or other non-employment discrimination statutes,[17] but in 1977 the Supreme Court appeared to resolve that issue affirmatively.[18] However, there are still

---

15. 401 U.S. at 432, 91 S.Ct. at 854.

16. See, e.g., Williams v. Matthews Co., 499 F.2d 819 (8th Cir.1974), certiorari denied 419 U.S. 1021, 95 S.Ct. 495, 42 L.Ed.2d 294 (1974): to rely on the "business necessity" defense the defendant must show "the absence of any acceptable alternative that will accomplish the same business goal with less discrimination."

17. Compare United States v. City of Black Jack, 508 F.2d 1179 (8th Cir.1974), certiorari denied 422 U.S. 1042, 95 S.Ct. 2656, 45 L.Ed.2d 694 (1975), rehearing denied 423 U.S. 884, 96 S.Ct. 158, 46 L.Ed.2d 115 (1975) and Stingley v. City of Lincoln Park, 429 F.Supp. 1379 (E.D.Mich.1977) (applying *Griggs* to housing discrimination) with Boyd v. Lefrak Organization, 509 F.2d 1110 (2d Cir.1975), certiorari denied 423 U.S. 896, 96 S.Ct. 197, 46 L.Ed.2d 129 (1975), (*Griggs* inapplicable to housing). See Note, Applying the Title VII Prima Facie Case to Title VIII Litigation, 11 Harv.Civ.Rts.—Civ.Lib.L.Rev. 128 (1976).

18. In Village of Arlington Heights v. Metropolitan Housing Development Corp., 429 U.S. 252, 97 S.Ct. 555, 50 L.Ed.2d 450 (1977), the town had refused to rezone certain land on which the plaintiffs proposed to build a low-income housing project. The evidence showed no discriminatory purpose or intent on the part of the town, but it did show a discriminatory impact, since 40% of the population eligible for the project were black, as opposed to only 18% of the overall area population. The Court held that the Fourteenth Amendment did not prohibit municipal actions with such discriminatory effects unless intent was also shown, citing its previous opinion in Washington v. Davis, 426 U.S. 229, 96 S.Ct. 2040, 48 L.Ed.2d 597 (1976). However, it remanded the case for further consideration as to the application of the Fair Housing Act to the town's action, thus clearly implying that a racial effect could form the basis for a Fair Housing Act complaint. See 558 F.2d 1283 (7th Cir.1977) (on remand to Seventh Circuit Court of Appeals), holding that the town's action may violate the Act if certain additional facts are shown, and applying *Griggs*. See also Resident Advisory Board v. Rizzo, 564 F.2d 126 (3d Cir.1977), certiorari denied 435 U.S. 908, 98 S.Ct. 1457, 55 L.Ed.2d 499 (1978).

The Court's most recent comment on the matter appears in Town of Huntington v. Huntington Branch, N.A.A.C.P., 488 U.S. 15, 109 S.Ct. 276, 102 L.Ed.2d 180 (1988), in which the Second Circuit had applied the disparate impact test to invalidate a zoning decision that prevented the construction of a low-income housing project. The Court's approach to the test was a bit elliptical:

> Since [the city] conceded the applicability of the disparate impact test for evaluating the zoning ordinance under Title VIII, we do not reach the question whether that test is the appropriate one. Without endorsing the precise analysis of the Court of Appeals, we are satisfied on this record that disparate impact was shown, and that the sole justification proffered to rebut the prima facie case was inadequate.

Id. at 18, 109 S.Ct. at 277. While this language led one Court of Appeals to comment that "the Supreme Court has yet to decide whether practices with disparate impact violate Title VIII," see N.A.A.C.P. v. American Family Mut. Ins. Co., 978 F.2d 287 (7th Cir.1992), the comment seems unwarranted. Most of the federal courts have consistently held since *Arlington Heights* that disparate impact analysis applies under Title VIII. See, e.g., Oxford House, Inc. v. Township of Cherry Hill, 799

few reported cases dealing directly with loan underwriting practices that have a discriminatory impact. One reported case dealt with the application of appraisal standards; it upheld the rejection by the lender of a loan application by black borrowers on the ground that the appraisal was too low to support the amount requested, even though the appraiser had commented that it would have been worth much more if it had been located anywhere else.[19] The court specifically sustained the use of the loan-to-value ratio as an underwriting standard; it "is a legitimate business criterion and its use is not a violation of section 3605," the court held.

Clearly many common underwriting rules bear more heavily on minority than on white loan applicants, including the usual 28% housing expense-to-income ratio and probably such requirements as previous homeownership, a specific time in the present residence or on the present job, and the like. The relatively lower incomes and higher mobility of minorities in the United States mean that such criteria will result in more loan rejections than will be experienced by whites. The issue then becomes the nature of the proof that a lender must offer to rebut the prima facie case. Perhaps most of the underwriting guidelines now in use have *some* predictive validity in assessing risk of future default, but some of them are far weaker than others.[20] The courts are

F.Supp. 450 (D.N.J.1992); Stewart B. McKinney Foundation, Inc. v. Town Plan and Zoning Com'n of Town of Fairfield, 790 F.Supp. 1197 (D.Conn.1992); Association of Relatives and Friends of AIDS Patients (A.F.A.P.S.) v. Regulations and Permits Admin. or Administracion de Reglamentos y Permisos (A.R.P.E.), 740 F.Supp. 95 (D.P.R. 1990); Tinsley v. Kemp, 750 F.Supp. 1001 (W.D.Mo.1990).

It remains unclear whether the disparate impact test applies under 42 U.S.C.A. §§ 1981–1982; most of the cases have held that evidence of discriminatory intent must be shown. See, e.g., Watson v. Pathway Financial, 702 F.Supp. 186 (N.D.Ill. 1988); Thomas v. First Fed. Sav. Bank, 653 F.Supp. 1330 (N.D.Ind.1987); Evans v. First Fed. Sav. Bank, 669 F.Supp. 915 (N.D.Ind.1987).

It is generally agreed that the disparate impact test applies under ECOA. See Miller v. American Express Co., 688 F.2d 1235 (9th Cir.1982) (applying effects test to sex discrimination under ECOA); Cherry v. Amoco Oil Co., 490 F.Supp. 1026 (N.D.Ga. 1980) (recognizing under ECOA the possible application of effects test to a zip-code credit scoring system, but finding evidence insufficient). See also United States v. American Future Systems, 743 F.2d 169 (3d Cir.1984).

The disparate impact test is recognized as applicable to discrimination in mortgage lending by both the FRB under ECOA and the OTS in its lending guidelines for thrift institutions. See 12 CFR 202.6, at n.2 (FRB); 12 CFR 571.24(b) (OTS):

"The use of lending standards which have no economic basis and which are discriminatory in effect is a violation of law even in the absence of an actual intent to discriminate. However, a standard which has a discriminatory effect is not necessarily improper if its use achieves a genuine business need which cannot be achieved by means which are not discriminatory in effect or less discriminatory in effect."

19. Thomas v. First Fed. Sav. Bank, 653 F.Supp. 1330 (N.D.Ind.1987). The court held that the appraiser was merely referring to the overimproved condition of the home when compared with other houses in the area. It also conceded that appraisals are inherently somewhat subjective and discretionary, but nonetheless found no evidence of discrimination.

20. See Holloway, Economic Trends, Mortgage Banking, May, 1989, at 81, summarizing various economic studies and concluding, "Surprisingly, much of the information on the loan application often thought to be relevant in determining a borrower's credit worthiness may have little value in predicting loan defaults;" The Arthur D. Little Study of the Private Mortgage Insurance Industry (summary 1975), at 11–14. In Watson v. Pathway Finan-

likely to hold that those with only marginal predictive power cannot be used if they produce a disparate impact on racial minorities.

A court confronting this issue is faced with serious problems. Should the judicial standard of business necessity be implemented by inquiring whether the underwriting standards in question are "reasonably predictive" of default, or some such test?[21] What is a reasonably acceptable level of default risk? Suppose it is shown that use of a few relatively noncontroversial criteria, such as loan-to-value ratio, income, and credit rating, provide reasonably adequate predictability, but the addition of other, more objectionable factors such as those mentioned in the preceding paragraph make the underwriting process more accurate. What is called for here is the drawing of fine lines based on complex empirical evidence—a task for which administrative agencies are much better equipped than courts. Yet the most comprehensive federal regulations on the subject, originally promulgated by the Federal Home Loan Bank Board and now issued under the auspices of the Office of Thrift Supervision, applicable to all federally-insured savings and loan associations, stop short of drawing the necessary lines. Instead, they merely warn that lenders should "take into consideration" that some common underwriting standards, including favoring previous homeowners, those with high educational attainments, those with stable job or residence histories, and those who have previously done business with the lender, may be legally questionable.[22] The guidance provided by the regulations on these points is ambiguous, although they might conceivably provide some evidence of improper practices in a litigated case. The lenders themselves would probably have preferred a clear cut statement of permissible and impermissible practices. The validity of many frequently-employed standards is still open to doubt.[23] The

cial, 702 F.Supp. 186 (N.D.Ill.1988), the court found that the plaintiffs had made out a prima facie case of discrimination by showing that numerous white applicants had received loans despite having credit histories of late payment similar to the plaintiffs. The facts do not require a "disparate impact" analysis, since the institution had not applied its own criteria consistently.

21. See Mass.Gen.Laws Ann. c. 183, § 64: Lenders shall not discriminate "on a basis that is arbitrary or unsupported by a reasonable analysis of the lending risks," but may exercise "the judgment and care * * * which men of prudence, discretion and intelligence exercise in the management of their affairs." Cf. Bishop v. Pecsok, 431 F.Supp. 34 (N.D.Ohio 1976), holding that criteria imposed by a landlord on tenant applicants must be a "reasonable measure of the applicant's ability to be a successful tenant."

22. 12 CFR 571.24, added by 43 Fed. Reg. 22338 (May 25, 1978).

23. The regulations promulgated by the California Savings and Loan Commissioner provide an instructive point of comparison with those of the OTS. The "effects test" is explicitly stated in the California regulations; see 10 Cal.Admin.Code § 245.2(c). An accompanying set of guidelines lists a number of common practices that are deemed to have a disproportionate racial impact and to lack business justification, and hence to be impermissible; see 10 Cal.Admin.Code § 246.3. These include the rejection of persons who have had isolated credit problems in the past, those with prior arrest records, those who have not previously owned a home, and those below a certain minimum income or who are buying houses below a specific purchase price or loan amount. Housing expense-to-income ratios below 25% are prohibited, and income from overtime, part-time or other usual work or from alimony or child support payments may not arbitrarily be disregarded.

OTS rules are, however, quite helpful in another way; they require lenders to prepare written loan underwriting standards, review them annually, and make them available to the public and to loan applicants.[24]

Redlining

Much of the thrust of recent legislation and regulation has been to combat geographically-based discrimination or redlining.[25] This issue is complicated by the difficulty of separating cause and effect. To some extent, withdrawal by mortgage lenders is a cause of neighborhood deterioration and ultimate abandonment, for the lack of mortgage financing impedes market sales transactions and makes maintenance and rehabilitation more difficult. But other factors also operate to cause neighborhood decline: crime and social disorder, lack of maintenance of public services and facilities such as street cleaning and lighting, trash removal, schools and parks, and the general aging of a housing stock that may have been substandard even when constructed. Some areas that lenders have abandoned are sound and attractive (although now threatened by the lack of mortgage funds), while others are so dilapidated and dangerous that lending on properties there would be insane. In an era in which the supply of mortgage funds has rarely been adequate to meet demand, lenders have generally preferred "safe" loans in the suburbs to loans of even moderate and manageable risk in inner-city neighborhoods.

Further complicating the picture is the fact that lenders may withdraw investment from a neighborhood for reasons that have nothing to do with the characteristics of the housing or its residents. For example, they may identify other markets, perhaps hundreds of miles away, where mortgage interest rates are higher, or they may shift out of residential lending in favor of commercial or consumer loans.

The articulation of a workable distinction between reasonable and unreasonable geographic discrimination in mortgage lending is no simple matter, and it is doubtful that any existing law or regulation has yet done so successfully. Some principles, however, are clear. One of these is that a refusal to lend because of the race of the neighborhood's occupants is illegal; this follows from the Fair Housing Act and from a number of state statutes as well.[26] In Laufman v. Oakley Building and

---

24. 12 CFR 528.2a(b) & 528.3(b), added by 43 Fed.Reg. 22335 (May 25, 1978); see also Mich.Comp.Laws Ann. § 445.1601.

25. See generally Lucey, The Redlining Battle Continues: Discriminatory Effect v. Business Necessity Under the Fair Housing Act, 8 Bos.Coll.Env.Aff.L.Rev. 357 (1979); Redlining, Disinvestment and the Role of Mutual Savings Banks: A Survey of Solutions, 9 Ford.Urb.L.J. 89 (1980); Givens, The "Antiredlining" Issue: Can Banks Be Forced to Lend?, 95 Banking L.J. 515 (1978); Wisniewski, Mortgage Redlining (Disinvestment): The Parameters of Federal, State and Municipal Regulation, 54 U.Det.J.Urb.L. 367 (1977); Comment, Redlining in Mortgage Lending: California's Approach to Getting the Red Out, 8 Pac.L.J. 699 (1977).

26. See, e.g., Ill.St. Ch. 775 § 5/3–101 et seq.; West's Ann.Cal.Health & Safety Code § 35812; Mass.Gen.Laws Ann. c. 183, § 64; Mich.Comp.Laws Ann. § 445.1601. See Ring v. First Interstate Mortgage, Inc.,

Loan Co.,[27] the lender declined to loan to a white applicant because the neighborhood in which he proposed to live was racially integrated. The court found violations of both Section 805 of the Fair Housing Act, discussed above, and Section 804, which prohibits the making "unavailable" of housing because of race. The point is virtually incontestible that racially-motivated redlining, if provable, is prohibited.

In many cases, however, no evidence of the type of racial motivation shown in *Laufman* will be available. In several recent cases, the plaintiff foundered on this ground; the lender provided a plausible, nonracial reason for refusing to lend, and the court accepted it.[28] In such cases the plaintiff is left to rely on the "effects test;" the area being excluded "happens" to be populated by minorities, but it is also characterized by deteriorated or abandoned housing or other structures, poor public facilities, and the like. Refusal to lend in such an environment, absent a showing of racial motive, has not yet been tested judicially in any reported case. Presumably the lender would be obliged to offer business justifications for its decision, and the court would be faced with deciding whether they were sufficiently compelling to justify the withdrawal of financing. Again, the question "how compelling?" is presently unresolved.

Of the federal regulatory agencies, the Office of Thrift Supervision has the most specific guidelines designed to deal with the redlining problem. Their thrust is generally to discourage discrimination based on property age or location, and to require lenders to focus on the particular real estate that will secure the proposed loan, rather than on the characteristics of the neighborhood as a whole. In simplistic terms, then, a lender may be expected to make a loan on a good house in a bad neighborhood. But the problem is more complex, for it is well known that neighborhood factors have a strong influence on the value of any given parcel of land, and neighborhood trends can reasonably be expected to bear on its future value, as the OTS rules recognize:

> Loan decisions should be based on the present market value of the property offered as security (including consideration of specific improvements to be made by the borrower) and the likelihood that the property will retain an adequate value over the term of the

---

984 F.2d 924 (8th Cir.1993) (white apartment developer stated a claim under Fair Housing Act, where he alleged that lender refused to make loan because of race of tenants of properties or neighborhoods in question).

27. 408 F.Supp. 489 (S.D.Ohio 1976). See also Harrison v. Otto G. Heinzeroth Mortgage Co., 414 F.Supp. 66 (N.D.Ohio 1976).

28. See Thomas v. First Fed. Sav. Bank, 653 F.Supp. 1330 (N.D.Ind.1987) (refusal based on inadequate appraised value); Cartwright v. American Sav. & Loan Ass'n, 880 F.2d 912 (7th Cir.1989) (refusal based on fact that house was much more costly than others in neighborhood). Cf. Steptoe v. Savings of America, 800 F.Supp. 1542 (N.D.Ohio 1992) (summary judgment for lender denied, where lender's refusal to loan was based on appraisal practices with arguably discriminatory effect); Old West End Ass'n v. Buckeye Fed. Sav. & Loan Ass'n, 675 F.Supp. 1100 (N.D.Ohio 1987) (summary judgment for lender denied, where lender's refusal to loan was based on dubious interpretation of FNMA "predominant value" guidelines and dubious objections to appraisal, and where statistical evidence tended to show redlining).

loan. Specific factors which may negatively affect its short-range future value (up to 3–5 years) should be clearly documented. Factors which in some cases may cause the market value of a property to decline are recent zoning changes or a significant number of abandoned homes in the immediate vicinity of the property. However, not all zoning changes will cause a decline in property values, and proximity to abandoned buildings may not affect the market value of a property because of rehabilitation programs or affirmative lending programs, or because the cause of abandonment is unrelated to high risk. Proper underwriting considerations include the condition and utility of the improvements, and various physical factors such as street conditions, amenities such as parks and recreation areas, availability of public utilities and municipal services, and exposure to flooding and land faults. However, arbitrary decisions based on age or location are prohibited, since many older, soundly constructed homes provide housing opportunities which may be precluded by an arbitrary lending policy.[29]

Two federal statutes enacted in the mid–1970s also bear on the redlining problem. The first is the Home Mortgage Disclosure Act,[30] which requires depository financial institutions to maintain and publish records showing, by census tract, the locations of the properties securing their residential loans. The Act's thesis is that local citizens and groups will, by analyzing this data, be able to identify lenders guilty of redlining and will apply the pressures of publicity and deposit withdrawals to bring them into line.[31] The data are also useful to the federal and state agencies that examine depository institutions. Thus far, however, the Act has proved of only limited value to those opposing discrimination. It has made possible the identification of gross disparities in lending patterns—and in a number of cities such disparities have

---

29. 12 CFR 571.24, promulgated 43 Fed.Reg. 22338 (May 25, 1978). See also 12 CFR 701.31 (Nat'l Credit Union Admin.); 12 CFR Part 338 (FDIC); 12 CFR Part 27 (Office of Comptroller of the Currency). Consider by contrast the considerably stronger terms of the California statute:

No financial institution shall discriminate in the availability of, or in the provision of, financial assistance for the purpose of purchasing, constructing, rehabilitating, improving, or refinancing housing accommodations due, in whole or in part, to the consideration of conditions, characteristics, or trends in the neighborhood or geographic area surrounding the housing accommodation, unless the financial institution can demonstrate that such consideration in the particular case is required to avoid an unsafe and unsound business practice.

West's Ann.Cal.Health & Safety Code § 35810. The California Savings and Loan Commissioner's regulations interpret the "unsafe or unsound business practice" rather narrowly; see 10 Cal.Admin.Code § 245.3(b).

30. 12 U.S.C.A. § 2801 et seq. The HMDA was scheduled to expire on June 28, 1980, but was made permanent by § 318, Pub.L.No. 96–399, 94 Stat. 1659 (1980).

31. See An Analysis of the Effectiveness of the Home Mortgage Disclosure Act of 1975, 28 Case W.Res.L.Rev. 1074 (1978); The Home Mortgage Disclosure Act of 1975: Will It Protect Urban Consumers from Redlining?, 12 N.Eng.L.Rev. 957 (1977); Red-lining and The Home Mortgage Disclosure Act of 1975: A Decisive Step Toward Private Urban Redevelopment, 25 Emory L.J. 667 (1976).

been shown to exist.[32] But HMDA data cannot directly prove discrimination, since they do not include the underwriting data (payment-to-income ratio, credit history, net worth, income stability, and the like) on which the lenders' decisions were based.

HMDA was considerably strengthened in 1989 by FIRREA. It previously applied only to depository institutions, but was expanded to cover nondepository lenders, such as mortgage bankers, provided they or their parent corporations have assets of $10 million or more.[33] The law was also changed to require reporting of all loan applications, not merely loans actually closed. In addition to the pre-1989 requirements of data on loan amount, property location, and loan type, data on race, sex, and income of applicants must also be reported.

HMDA's goals are complemented by the requirements of the Community Reinvestment Act of 1977 (the CRA).[34] This statute requires the federal financial regulatory agencies to consider, in their examinations and in evaluating applications by lenders for new deposit facilities and for mergers and acquisitions, each institution's record in meeting the credit needs of its entire community, including low- and moderate-income neighborhoods. Presumably lenders who have been guilty of unjustifiable redlining will be subject to criticism by the federal examiners, and may not be able to get permission to open new branches, close offices, or take other actions they desire.[35] The statute and the early regulations of the federal banking agencies were criticized as vague and ineffectual.[36] But in the late 1980s there were indications that the regulators were beginning to take the CRA seriously. Some

---

32. See Fuchs, Discriminatory Lending Practices: Recent Developments, Causes, and Solutions, 10 Ann.Rev.Banking L. 461 (1991), reviewing numerous studies showing that minority communities are underserved by mortgage lenders; Glenn B. Canner & Dolores S. Smith, Home Mortgage Disclosure Act: Expanded Data on Residential Lending, 77 Fed.Res.Bull. 859, 868–76 (1991); Federal Home Loan Mortgage Corp., The Secondary Market and Community Lending Through Lenders' Eyes (Feb. 1991); Nothaft & Perry, Home Mortgage Disclosure Act Data, Secondary Mortgage Markets, Winter 1991/92, at 2, summarizing data showing much greater rejections of loan applications from minorities than from whites; Thomas, Behind the Figures: Federal Data Detail Pervasive Racial Gap in Mortgage Lending, Wall.St.J., Mar.31, 1992, at A1 col.1; Research Suggests Thrifts Shun Lower Income Markets, Real Estate Finance Today, Jun.30, 1989, describing a study done by the Center for Community Change; Minorities Continue to Receive Fewer Home Loans, Says Fed, WG & L Housing & Devel. Rptr., Nov. 9, 1992, at 507.

33. 12 U.S.C.A. § 2802(2)(B), as amended by § 1211(d) & (e) of FIRREA, Pub.L.No. 101–79 (1989). See Federal Financial Institutions Examination Council, disclosure statement samples, 55 Fed.Reg. 27886 (1990); OTS amendments to regulations on nondiscrimination, 55 Fed.Reg. 1386 (1990); Ulrich, Home Mortgage Disclosure Act Developments, 46 Bus.Law. 1077 (1991); Schieber, HMDA: New Reporting Burdens, Mortgage Banking, Mar. 1990, at 23.

34. 12 U.S.C.A. § 2901 et seq.

35. For the applicable regulations under the CRA, see 12 CFR Part 25 (Comptroller of the Currency); 12 CFR 345 (FDIC); 12 CFR Part 563e (OTS).

36. McCluskey, The Community Reinvestment Act: Is It Doing the Job?, 100 Bank.L.J. 33 (1983); Community Reinvestment Act Regulations: Another Attempt to Control Redlining, 28 Cath.U.L.Rev. 635 (1979). See also Hicks v. RTC, 970 F.2d 378 (7th Cir.1992), a case in which a savings and loan executive was fired for his reporting to the FHLBB of his employer's CRA violations, and who unsuccessfully sought damages for wrongful discharge.

applications for branches and mergers were actually denied because of poor CRA performance,[37] and the Federal Financial Institutions Examination Council, which consists of all the federal financial regulatory agencies, released a set of guidelines detailing the evaluation procedures, assessment criteria, and performance expectations of the agencies in examining lenders for CRA compliance.[38] FIRREA strengthened the CRA in 1989, creating a four-tiered descriptive rating system for community reinvestment evaluations and adding a requirement for public disclosure of each institution's CRA rating and of portions of its regulatory agency's evaluation.[39] But CRA is fundamentally an instruction to the regulatory agencies, not a substantive antidiscrimination law, and it gives rise to no private right of action.[40]

A number of states have statutes prohibiting lending discrimination and redlining, and imposing record-keeping and disclosure duties on lenders.[41] Both the substantive standards and procedural duties under state law may vary from those imposed by the federal agencies. The HMDA itself provides that state-chartered financial institutions are exempt from state disclosure rules to the extent that they are inconsistent with the federal act.[42] However, the HMDA is silent on the question whether federally-chartered institutions (national banks and federal savings and loan associations) are required to follow state law. The case law on this issue has regarded the federal regulations as pervasive and fully preemptive so far as record-keeping, reporting, disclosure, and discipline are concerned; the institutions are free to disregard state law with respect to such matters. With regard to the

---

37. See Wilsker, The Community Reinvestment Act of 1977: The Saga Continues ..., 46 Bus.Law. 1083 (1991), at n.6, describing such actions by the FRB and FHLBB; 36 Fed.Res.Bull. 304 (1989). A more complete list of CRA-motivated actions of the FRB appears in Traiger, Federal Community Reinvestment Act Compliance, 1990 WL 357782 (published only on Westlaw).

38. Final Guidelines for Disclosure of Written Evaluations and Revised Assessment Rating System, 55 Fed.Reg. 18163 (1990). The factors the regulators consider are (1) the institution's efforts to ascertain community credit needs and reach out to fulfill them; (2) the extent of marketing and other efforts to make the community aware of the institution's services; (3) the geographic distribution of the institution's credit and branches; (4) any evidence of discrimination or other illegal practices; and (5) the institution's participation in community development projects or programs.

39. 12 U.S.C.A. § 2906, as amended by § 1212 of FIRREA, Pub.L.No. 101–79 (1989). The public release of CRA evaluations has become a potent weapon in the hands of community groups who wish to pressure institutions toward more active CRA compliance; see Schrader, Competition and Convenience: The Emerging Role of Community Reinvestment, 67 Ind.L.J. 331 (1992); Cowell & Hagler, The Community Reinvestment Act in the Decade of Bank Consolidation, 27 Wake For.L.Rev. 83 (1992); Tomes, The "Community" in the Community Reinvestment Act: A Term in Search of a Definition, 10 Ann.Rev.Banking L. 225 (1991); Snow, The Community Reinvestment Act Business, Mortgage Banking, May 1990, at 75 (with a subtitle observing that "New legal requirements to lend in ways that help communities may actually be good business"); Kane, CRA: Getting Good Grades, Mortgage Banking, June 1992, at 52.

40. See Hicks v. RTC, 970 F.2d 378 (7th Cir.1992); Harambee Uhuru School, Inc. v. Kemp, 1992 WL 274545 (S.D.Ohio 1992, not reported in F.Supp.)

41. See, e.g., Iowa Code Ann. tit. 535A; N.J.Stat.Ann. 17:16F–1 to 17:16F–11.

42. 12 U.S.C.A. § 2805.

substantive rules of state law, such as those prohibiting discrimination or redlining, the cases hold that their application and enforcement is exclusively a matter for the relevant federal agencies to determine. Any state enforcement mechanisms are inapplicable.[43]

Other approaches to the redlining problem have developed. One is the concept of a "mortgage review board," composed of community representatives and lending institution employees, which considers appeals of loan denials. In some cities lenders have cooperated voluntarily in forming such groups, and in others they have done so under pressure from legislation or state regulators.[44] The board may have authority to order the loan granted, or it may refer the applicant to a central pool of funds set up by the lenders of the area for the purpose of making higher-risk loans. Exhaustion of the appeal may also be a prerequisite to the filing of suit by a disappointed applicant.[45]

§ 11.6 Federal Preemption of State Mortgage Law

Under the Supremacy Clause of the United States Constitution, federal law that is validly adopted and within the constitutional power of the federal government is the supreme law of the land and supersedes state law.[1] This preemption concept has several applications in mortgage law. The most clearcut is the situation in which a congressional enactment or a valid regulation of a federal agency speaks directly to the point. Numerous illustrations may be cited. The Home Mortgage Disclosure Act requires institutional lenders to assemble and release to the public certain data on the amounts and locations of their residential loans.[2] The Fair Housing Act limits lenders' discretion in

---

43. National State Bank v. Long, 630 F.2d 981 (3d Cir.1980); Conference of Federal Savings and Loan Associations v. Stein, 604 F.2d 1256 (9th Cir.1979), affirmed 445 U.S. 921, 100 S.Ct. 1304, 63 L.Ed.2d 754 (1980); Glen Ellyn Savings & Loan Association v. Tsoumas, 71 Ill.2d 493, 17 Ill.Dec. 811, 377 N.E.2d 1 (1978), certiorari denied 439 U.S. 927, 99 S.Ct. 311, 58 L.Ed.2d 320 (1978). See also Michigan Savings & Loan League v. Francis, 683 F.2d 957 (6th Cir.1982) (where lenders asserted federal law as a defense to a suit enforcing state anti-redlining statute, there was no federal court jurisdiction.)

See Annot., 57 A.L.R. Fed. 322 (1982); Lechner, National Banks and State Anti-redlining Laws: Has Congress Preempted the Field?, 99 Bank.L.J. 388 (1982) (arguing that the panoply of federal legislation constitutes a complete preemption of state law, both substantive and procedural, for federally-chartered institutions); Federal Preemption of the Illinois Financial Institutions Disclosure Act, 28 DePaul L.Rev. 805 (1979); State Regulation of Federally Chartered Financial Institutions: Washington's Anti-redlining Act, 54 Wash. L.Rev. 339 (1979).

44. The Michigan and Massachusetts statutes expressly authorize the creation of such review boards; Mass.Gen.Laws Ann. c. 167, § 73; Mich.Comp.Laws Ann. § 445.-1609(1). The Boston Board is described in Comment, The Home Mortgage Disclosure Act of 1975: Will It Protect Urban Consumers From Redlining?, 12 N.Eng.L.Rev. 957, 988 (1977).

45. See Mass.Gen.Laws Ann. c. 183, § 64.

§ 11.6

1. U.S. Const. Art. VI, § 2; see McCulloch v. Maryland, 17 U.S. (4 Wheat.) 316, 4 L.Ed. 579 (1819).

2. 12 U.S.C.A. § 2801; see Comment, The Home Mortgage Disclosure Act of 1975: Will It Protect Urban Consumers From Redlining?, 12 N.Eng.L.Rev. 957 (1977); § 11.5, supra, at note 34. See also Glen Ellyn Savings & Loan Association v. Tsoumas, 71 Ill.2d 493, 17 Ill.Dec. 811, 377 N.E.2d 1 (1978).

rejecting loan applicants because of race, sex, or other factors,[3] and the Office of Thrift Supervision's regulations supplement the Act by requiring the maintenance of records on loan applications and by delimiting the criteria that can be employed by savings associations in screening applicants and properties.[4] The Truth–In–Lending Act [5] mandates that certain disclosures concerning interest and finance charges be made to borrowers, and the Real Estate Settlement Procedures Act (RESPA)[6] requires disclosures concerning settlement charges, prescribes a standard form of settlement statement, and prohibits certain types of kickbacks and rebates between mortgage lenders and other providers of settlement services. In 1973 Congress considered, but did not enact, a comprehensive federal mortgage foreclosure bill which would have applied to all federally-owned, -insured, or -guaranteed loans;[7] the bill would have preempted state foreclosure procedures in numerous respects, and would perhaps have represented a high-water mark in federal preemption.[8] A somewhat similar bill, but with a much narrower scope, was enacted in 1981.[9] It authorizes nonjudicial power-of-sale foreclosure of mortgages held by the Department of Housing and Urban Development on multifamily housing projects. The act specifically preempts any state law granting post-foreclosure redemption rights.

Beginning in 1980 Congress enacted three statutes that preempt state law in a particularly direct and forceful manner. Each was a product of the extremely high interest rates that prevailed in the early 1980s, and of the resultant financial stress with which mortgage lenders were beset. The first, effective March 31, 1980, preempted state usury laws for all "federally-related" loans secured by first liens on residential real estate.[10] Interest rate ceilings as well as restrictions on discount points and other finance charges were covered. Second, Congress passed Section 341 of the Garn–St. Germain Depository Institu-

3. 42 U.S.C.A. § 3605; § 11.5, supra, at note 4. See also Equal Credit Opportunity Act, 15 U.S.C.A. § 1691 et seq.

4. 12 CFR 528.6; see supra § 11.5, at note 29 et seq. The preamble to the regulations, 43 Fed.Reg. 22335 (May 25, 1978), states that federal savings associations are not required to observe more stringent state law regarding lending discrimination.

5. 15 U.S.C.A. § 1601 et seq.; 12 CFR Part 226.

6. 12 U.S.C.A. § 2601 et seq.; 24 CFR, Part 3500, as amended 57 Fed.Reg. 49600 (1992). See generally Field, RESPA in a Nutshell, 11 Real Prop.Prob. & Trust J. 447 (1976); Payne, Conveyancing Practice and the Feds: Some Thoughts About RESPA, 29 Ala.L.Rev. 339 (1978).

7. The Federal Mortgage Foreclosure Act, Title IV, S. 2507, 93d Cong., 1st Sess., 1973.

8. See Pedowitz, Current Developments in Summary Foreclosure, 9 Real Prop. Prob. & Trust J. 421, 422–25 (1974).

9. The Multifamily Mortgage Foreclosure Act of 1981, 12 U.S.C.A. §§ 3701–3717. For HUD's regulations implementing the Act, see 24 CFR Part 27. See the more extended discussion, § 7.19 supra, at notes 13–20.

10. § 501, Depository Institutions Deregulation and Monetary Control Act of 1980, Pub.L. No. 96–221, 94 Stat. 161, as amended, §§ 308, 324, Pub.L. No. 96–399, 94 Stat. 1641, 1647–48, codified at 12 U.S.C.A. § 1735f–7. The FHLBB regulations issued under authority of the statute are found in 12 CFR Part 590. See McInnis v. Cooper Communities, Inc., 271 Ark. 503, 611 S.W.2d 767 (1981), recognizing the validity of the federal act; Alexander, Federal Intervention in Real Estate Finance: Preemption and Federal Common Law, 71 N.C.L.Rev. 293, 313–18 (1993).

tions Act of 1982.[11] Effective October 15, 1982, it preempted (with certain exceptions) state law that restricted exercise by lenders of due-on-sale clauses in mortgage instruments.[12]

The third prong of this preemptive effort was the Alternative Mortgage Transactions Parity Act of 1982, also effective October 15, 1982.[13] It authorized state-chartered financial institutions to make alternative forms of mortgage loans (such as ARMs, GPMs, and RAMs) that were approved by the federal financial regulatory agencies for federally-chartered lenders, even though such loans might be contrary to state law.[14] Its purpose was to place federal and state institutions on an equal footing in respect to their ability to experiment with new mortgage types.

In each of these preemptive statutes, Congress attempted to mitigate the inevitable political objections to federal intrusion into what were traditionally matters exclusively of state concern. It did so by permitting state law-makers to adopt, within a limited time period (three years from the federal law's effective date),[15] statutes or constitutional provisions rejecting the federal preemption and recapturing state control.[16] With respect to each of the three, some states took advantage of this opportunity;[17] thus, the federal preemption is not entirely uniform across the nation.

In addition to these statutes, several federal agencies issue regulations governing the operation of federally-chartered financial institutions. Many of these rules (which have the same weight as statutes for preemption purposes) directly contradict state law. The most significant of these are promulgated by the Office of Thrift Supervision [18] and apply to federally-chartered savings and loan associations. It is well-established that federal law governs the internal affairs of such associations "from the cradle to the grave," [19] fully occupying the field. If

---

11. Pub.L. No. 97–320, 96 Stat. 1505, codified at 12 U.S.C.A. § 1701j–3.

12. For an extended discussion, see §§ 5.22–5.24 supra.

13. Title VIII of the Garn–St. Germain Depository Institutions Act of 1982, Pub.L. No. 97–320, 96 Stat. 1545, codified at 12 U.S.C.A. § 3801 et seq.

14. For an extended discussion see supra § 11.4, at note 105 et seq.

15. With respect to the preemption of usury ceilings, the states' power to reregulate discount points and other loan charges is not limited by time; see § 501(b)(4), Pub.L. No. 96–221. Such reregulation may apparently be accomplished by considerably less specific language than a reregulation of interest rates.

16. In the case of the due-on-sale preemption, the states were empowered only to continue the restrictions on due-on-sale enforcement that they had adopted prior to enactment of the federal law. States with no such previous restrictions could not adopt them subsequently and thereby override the federal preemption. See Nelson & Whitman, Congressional Preemption of Mortgage Due–on–Sale Law: An Analysis of the Garn–St. Germain Act, 35 Hast.L.J. 241, 296–98 (1983).

17. See notes 12, 14 supra.

18. See generally § 11.1 supra, at notes 4–7; Bartlett, The Federal–State Preemption Conflict, 44 Legal Bull. 1 (1978).

19. See Meyers v. Beverly Hills Federal Savings & Loan Association, 499 F.2d 1145 (9th Cir.1974). When state courts "deal with the internal affairs of federal savings and loan associations * * * they are nonetheless applying federal law." Murphy v. Colonial Federal Savings and Loan Association, 388 F.2d 609, 612 (2d Cir.1967). See Community Title Co. v. Roosevelt Federal Savings & Loan Associa-

there is no specific regulation on a matter affecting the internal governance of an association, such as branching,[20] proxy solicitations,[21] employment of officers,[22] or directors' fiduciary duties,[23] the federal courts will supply a rule of federal common law.[24]

In external transactions, such as the content and enforcement of mortgages and notes and the institution's liability to its borrowers for lending-related action that violate state law, however, the picture is much less clear. In recent years the OTS and its predecessor, the FHLBB, have been quite active in attempting to resolve by regulation certain controversial issues in mortgage law as applied to federal associations. Its regulations concerning prepayment penalties[25] and interest on tax escrow accounts[26] on home loans were held to prevail over contrary state law, as were its rules preempting state due-on-sale law for federal associations[27] until Congress fully occupied that field.[28] And of course its regulations governing types of loans, repayment

tion, 670 S.W.2d 895, 903 (Mo.App.1984). Much the same conclusion is warranted as to national banks, at least when they are taken over by FDIC; see Gaff v. FDIC, 919 F.2d 384 (6th Cir.1990).

On control by OTS' predecessor, the FHLBB, of S & L mergers, see Federal Home Loan Bank Board: Preemptive Rights or Unbridled Powers?, 12 Cap. U.L.Rev. 529 (1983).

20. Lyons Savings & Loan Association v. Federal Home Loan Bank Board, 377 F.Supp. 11 (N.D.Ill.1974); Washington Federal Savings and Loan Association v. Balaban, 281 So.2d 15 (Fla.1973); Springfield Institution for Savings v. Worcester Federal Savings & Loan Association, 329 Mass. 184, 107 N.E.2d 315 (1952), certiorari denied 344 U.S. 884, 73 S.Ct. 184, 97 L.Ed. 684 (1952).

21. Kupiec v. Republic Federal Savings & Loan Association, 512 F.2d 147 (7th Cir.1975); Murphy v. Colonial Federal Savings & Loan Association, 388 F.2d 609 (2d Cir.1967); City Federal Savings & Loan Association v. Crowley, 393 F.Supp. 644 (E.D.Wis.1975).

22. Community Federal Savings & Loan Association v. Fields, 128 F.2d 705 (8th Cir.1942).

23. FSLIC v. Kidwell, 716 F.Supp. 1315 (N.D.Cal.1989) (federal law governed liability of former officers and directors to the institution; court found a federal common law action existed for breach of fiduciary duty but not for negligence); First Hawaiian Bank v. Alexander, 558 F.Supp. 1128 (D.Haw.1983); Rettig v. Arlington Heights Federal Savings & Loan Association, 405 F.Supp. 819 (N.D.Ill.1975); City Federal Savings and Loan Association v. Crowley, 393 F.Supp. 644 (E.D.Wis.1975).

24. In Murphy, supra note 19, the court was obliged to devise a common-law rule regarding the availability of lists of members to persons planning a proxy fight; by the time Kupiec, supra note 21, was decided, the FHLBB had promulgated a regulation on the point, thereby superseding the Murphy court's common-law rule.

25. Toolan v. Trevose Federal Savings & Loan Association, 501 Pa. 477, 462 A.2d 224 (1983); Meyers v. Beverly Hills Federal Savings and Loan Association, 499 F.2d 1145 (9th Cir.1974); see generally § 6.4, supra.

26. First Federal Savings & Loan Association v. Greenwald, 591 F.2d 417 (1st Cir.1979); Wisconsin League of Financial Institutions, Ltd. v. Galecki, 707 F.Supp. 401 (W.D.Wis.1989); Olsen v. Financial Federal Savings & Loan Association, 105 Ill.App.3d 364, 61 Ill.Dec. 253, 434 N.E.2d 406 (1982); see generally § 4.19 supra. Cf. Derenco, Inc. v. Benjamin Franklin Federal Savings & Loan Association, 281 Or. 533, 577 P.2d 477 (1978), certiorari denied 439 U.S. 1051, 99 S.Ct. 733, 58 L.Ed.2d 712 (1978).

27. Fidelity Federal Savings & Loan Association v. de la Cuesta, 458 U.S. 141, 102 S.Ct. 3014, 73 L.Ed.2d 664 (1982). See also Haugen v. Western Federal Savings & Loan Association, 633 P.2d 497 (Colo.App. 1981), affirmed 649 P.2d 323 (Colo.1982).

28. See § 5.24 supra.

schedules, and the like supersede state law.[29]

Where there is a specific OTS regulation on the point in issue, there can be no serious doubt that federal preemption has occurred. But suppose there is none; can federal preemption be implied? There is some authority that the OTS has completely occupied the field of relations with borrowers, thereby making state law respecting the content of notes and mortgages inapplicable. The earliest case taking this view is Kaski v. First Federal Savings and Loan Association;[30] there the plaintiffs were borrowers who sought to have a variable interest rate clause in their mortgage declared invalid under the Wisconsin statute regulating such clauses.[31] The loan had been made prior to the 1972 FHLBB regulatory amendments that effectively prohibited variable rate clauses,[32] and the parties conceded that there was no FHLBB regulation dealing with the subject. Nonetheless, the Wisconsin Supreme Court held that the scheme of federal regulations was pervasive and fully occupied the field, thereby making the Wisconsin statute inapplicable. Virtually all of the cases cited by the court involved the internal governance of associations rather than relationships with borrowers, but the court thought the two spheres of activity were intimately tied together: "The regulation of loan practices directly affects the internal management and operations of federal associations and therefore requires uniform control. The present litigation ought, therefore, be resolved as a matter of federal law."[33] The case was remanded for a determination of the content of the federal (presumably common) law and an assessment of whether exhaustion of FHLBB remedies, if any, should be required.

Kaski is anomalous and should not be followed. The OTS regulations governing dealings between associations and borrowers are extensive, but far from comprehensive,[34] and actually reflect ad hoc responses by the Office and its predecessor, the Federal Home Loan Bank Board, to a few specific issues. They do not purport to exhaust the field, and leave far more issues uncovered than covered. State law has customarily governed such matters as the interpretation of notes and mortgages, the negotiability of notes, and procedures for foreclosure, redemption, and collection of deficiencies by federal associations. To invent federal common law to control all of these issues would require extensive litigation and introduce great uncertainty, and it would be entirely unnecessary. There is no significant need for uniformity in such matters, since most federal associations originate few loans across

---

29. See Beal v. First Federal Savings & Loan Association, 90 Wis.2d 171, 279 N.W.2d 693 (1979). See also Conference of State Bank Supervisors v. Conover, 710 F.2d 878 (D.C.Cir.1983) (OCC regulation on adjustable rate mortgages is a valid preemption of state law).

30. 72 Wis.2d 132, 240 N.W.2d 367 (1976).

31. Wis.Stat.Ann. 138.055.

32. See 12 CFR 541.14(a), as amended 37 Fed.Reg. 5118 (Mar. 10, 1972). The loan in the Kaski case was made in 1967.

33. 240 N.W.2d at 373.

34. The principal regulations are those discussed in the sources cited at notes 25 through 29 supra, and those dealing with security property, loan-to-value ratios, and maturities; see 12 CFR 545.32–545.53.

state lines, and their secondary market purchasing activity is generally quite modest in scope. The training of employees and the education of customers are both likely to be simplified by the application of state law. To infer a new legal basis for perhaps one-eighth of all home loans made in the United States from the OTS's silence is absurd.[35] Federal law should govern federal institutions' lending activities only when there is an applicable federal regulation.[36]

This conclusion is consistent with the United States Supreme Court's opinion in Fidelity Federal Savings and Loan Association v. de la Cuesta,[37] in which the Court upheld the validity and preemptive effect of the FHLBB's due-on-sale regulation. The California Court of Appeal had held that the Board's regulation was outside the authority granted it by Congress under the Home Owners Loan Act,[38] insofar as it purported to preempt state due-on-sale law. In this respect the Court of Appeal was wrong, and the Supreme Court properly reversed it.

But the lender also argued that the existence of the Board's plenary authority to regulate federal associations amounted to an

---

35. S & Ls hold about one-fourth of all home loans, and federal S & Ls's have about half of the assets of all associations; see Economic Report of the President 337 (1991).

36. The position or the FHLBB, OTS's predecessor, on the scope of its preemption of state mortgage law was ambiguous. In Schott v. Mission Federal Savings & Loan Association, Civ. 75–366, D.Cal.1975 (unreported), the plaintiffs attacked the due-on-sale clause in a federal association's mortgage; at that time there was no express FHLBB regulation on the subject. The Board filed an advisory opinion with the court arguing that the topic was preempted because it related to the "internal" affairs of the association. This assertion was based principally on the view that only by use of due-on-sale clauses could federal associations provide the maximum amount of financing at reasonable interest rates to credit-worthy borrowers, thus fulfilling the purpose of their charters. The case was settled, and the FHLBB subsequently issued regulations explicitly preempting the due-on clause issue, so the particular issue is moot. The Board's distinction between internal and external affairs, as expressed in its advisory opinion in *Schott*, is nonetheless interesting:

> We are discussing here only Board regulation and control over the affairs, business, business powers and authority, internal and external expansion, supervisory matters, internal operations and affairs, *relationships between the association, its management and its members*, and all similar and related matters respecting federal associations. The Board does not seek to regulate wholly unrelated matters of purely local concern, such as zoning for federal association property, methods of recording title, etc., which are left by the Board to state and local authorities, since they do not impinge upon the regulatory areas under Board control, or interfere with the Board's overall regulatory scheme. (italics added)

As a statement of the delineation between preempted and non-preempted matters, the foregoing is inept and offers little meaningful guidance for the courts. Since the Board's successor, the OTS can readily preempt any matter within its competence merely by issuing a regulation (as it ultimately did regarding due-on-sale clauses), it can hardly expect the courts to read its collective mind and to decide matters that OTS itself has not articulated. It is hard to avoid the conclusion that the Board's position in the Schott case was inconsistent with its own statement quoted above, and was merely result-oriented; that is, that it had concluded that due-on-sale clauses were desirable by the time the litigation was filed.

For sources of the foregoing materials, see Bartlett, The Federal–State Preemption Conflict, 44 Legal Bull. 1, 8–13 (1978).

37. 458 U.S. 141, 102 S.Ct. 3014, 73 L.Ed.2d 664 (1982), reversing 121 Cal. App.3d 328, 175 Cal.Rptr. 467 (1981). See § 5.23 supra.

38. 12 U.S.C.A. §§ 1461–1468.

"occupation of the field," superseding all state law even as to matters of real property and mortgages.[39] The Court of Appeal correctly rejected this view, observing that it was contrary to longstanding practice and that it would require the development of a vast body of federal common law which did not then exist.[40] The Supreme Court did not contradict this conclusion. While it cited the *Kaski* court's conclusion that regulation of loan practices affects internal operations and "therefore requires uniform federal control," [41] it did so in a context in which the FHLBB had issued a specific regulation on the subject in controversy. The Court's use of the *Kaski* phraseology is unfortunate, but it cannot fairly be understood to endorse the notion that federal common law governs all real property and mortgage issues for federal savings associations when there is no federal regulation on the point. Only on matters of corporate governance does this sort of occupation of the field prevail.

The matter is well put in Shea v. First Federal Savings and Loan Association,[42] in which an attorney sued the savings association for violations of the Connecticut antitrust laws. The association had distributed to its loan customers a list of closing attorneys whom it considered acceptable, thereby allegedly steering clients away from the plaintiff. While there were some FHLBB regulations touching the matter of attorney representation in closings, the court concluded that they did not directly treat the problem at hand. It rejected the notion of total "occupation of the field," and held that since this was not a question of internal governance, federal associations were bound by state law unless "compliance actually conflicts with federal law, jeopardizes congressional purposes, or Congress or a federal regulatory body unmistakably indicates otherwise." [43]

Two more recent cases lead to the same conclusion. In Flanagan v. Germania, F.A.,[44] the plaintiff, a prospective buyer of suntanning beds, sued Germania for tortious interference with his contract rights growing out of Germania's loan collection practices. The Eighth Circuit rejected Germania's argument that FHLBB regulations preempted the plaintiff's state law claims. It pointed out that there was no specific federal regulation on the matter, and refused to conclude that the FHLBB's regulations generally preempted the field of lending practices. *de la Cuesta* did not help Germania, the court noted, since it had involved a "direct and actual conflict between state law and federal regulations."

The California Court of Appeal reached a similar conclusion in Siegel v. American Savings & Loan Association,[45] in which a group of borrowers brought a class action against American because of its

---

39. 121 Cal.App.3d at 335–36, 175 Cal. Rptr. at 471.

40. 121 Cal.App.3d at 337, 175 Cal. Rptr. at 472.

41. 458 U.S. 152, 170 n. 23, 102 S.Ct. 3015, 3031 n. 23.

42. 184 Conn. 285, 439 A.2d 997 (1981).

43. 439 A.2d at 1005.

44. 872 F.2d 231 (8th Cir.1989).

45. 210 Cal.App.3d 953, 258 Cal.Rptr. 746 (1989).

practice of collecting deed of trust reconveyance fees from borrowers at the time of loan closing, even though in many cases the fees were never earned and the practice violated FNMA guidelines. The plaintiffs' claims were based on such state law theories as breach of contract and fraud. American asserted that governance of its activities was preempted by FHLBB regulations, but the court could find no regulation on reconveyance fees. Like the Eighth Circuit in *Germania*, it rejected the assertion that American's lending practices were part of the field that the FHLBB had occupied to the exclusion of state law. Reflecting on the due-on-sale regulations that had been held preemptive in *de la Cuesta*, it observed that the FHLBB knew how to engage in preemption when it wanted to do so. Cases like *Germania* and *Siegel* should help put to rest the misbegotten notion that federal institutions' relations with their borrowers can automatically be swept under federal law.[46]

Federally-held Mortgages

Perhaps the most perplexing cases in which federal preemption of state mortgage law is asserted are those in which the United States is a party, usually as holder and foreclosor of the mortgage. Often the government appears in the guise of the Federal Housing Administration (FHA), the Veterans Administration (VA) or the Small Business Administration (SBA); the mortgage may have been originally made to the federal agency, or it may have been assigned to the agency upon the mortgagor's default. It is well-settled that the federal courts have jurisdiction to foreclose mortgages held by the government.[47] The question arises, however, to what extent state rules governing such matters as appointment of receivers, redemption following sale, and protection against deficiency judgments are binding against the government, which frequently would prefer to be unfettered by them.

The preemption concept asserted by federal agencies in these cases originated in Clearfield Trust Co. v. United States,[48] in which the government sought recovery from Clearfield on account of a check, issued by the United States and drawn on the Treasury, which Clearfield had collected. An endorsement had been forged on the check, but under state law the government had not given notice of the forgery in a timely fashion after its discovery, and hence would have been barred

---

46. See also People v. Highland Fed. Sav. & Loan, 14 Cal.App.4th 1692, 19 Cal. Rptr.2d 555 (1993). The notion of broad-scale implied preemption seems to die hard in Wisconsin. In Wisconsin League of Financial Institutions, Ltd. v. Galecki, 707 F.Supp. 401 (W.D.Wis.1989), the court correctly held that the FHLBB regulations on mortgage escrow accounts expressly preempted contrary state law. Unfortunately, it could not resist the further assertion that, even if the express preemption were absent, "state law would be preempted because it stands as a barrier to the accomplishment of the objectives of the federal regulations." The statement is dictum, of course, and is unfortunate indeed.

47. See 28 U.S.C.A. § 1345 (jurisdiction over cases in which the United States is a plaintiff); United States v. Belanger, 598 F.Supp. 598 (D.Me.1984), adopting state foreclosure process as the federal rule.

48. 318 U.S. 363, 63 S.Ct. 573, 87 L.Ed. 838 (1943).

from recovery against Clearfield. The Supreme Court, however, held that the federal common law preempted the state rule:

> The application of state law, even without the conflict of laws rules of the forum, would subject the rights and duties of the United States to exceptional uncertainty. It would lead to great diversity in results by making identical transactions subject to the vagaries of the laws of the several states. The desirability of a uniform rule is plain.

The *Clearfield Trust* holding was first applied to a mortgage transaction in 1959 in United States v. View Crest Garden Apartments, Inc.[49] An FHA mortgage had been assigned to the government after default. The government filed an action in federal court to foreclose the mortgage and sought the appointment of a receiver pending foreclosure. The trial court held that under the law of the state of Washington, no sufficient showing had been made to justify a receiver, but the Ninth Circuit reversed. It held that after default the question of remedies should be determined by federal law, and remanded the case for a determination as to whether federal law would justify appointment of a receiver. The court purported to reach its conclusion by weighing the policies underlying the state and federal rules, but it strongly emphasized the federal need to protect the treasury and promote the security of the federal investment, and it gave little weight to the policies underlying the Washington law of receiverships.

For a time, it appeared that state law respecting mortgage remedies was entirely preempted by the federal government when acting as mortgage holder. However, the seeds of a reconsideration of this trend were sown in 1966 in United States v. Yazell,[50] in which the SBA had made a disaster loan secured by a chattel mortgage to a Texas couple. Upon default and foreclosure, the wife claimed that the Texas law of coverture insulated her separate property from execution by the government to satisfy the deficiency. The Supreme Court agreed, rejecting the SBA's claim that federal common law (which presumably would not recognize the coverture defense) should apply. The Court relied to some extent on the fact that the loan had been individually negotiated with specific reference to state law, and that the documents gave no clue that the government would attempt to overcome the coverture doctrine; in this way it distinguished the *View Crest* case. But the Court's principal rationale involved a weighing of the respective interests of state and federal governments. It held the state law was a significant manifestation of Texas' overall allocation of family property rights and obligations, and noted that the coverture doctrine could

---

49. 268 F.2d 380 (9th Cir.1959), certiorari denied 361 U.S. 884, 80 S.Ct. 156, 4 L.Ed.2d 120 (1959); see also United States v. Queen's Court Apartments, Inc., 296 F.2d 534 (9th Cir.1961); Midwest Sav. Ass'n v. Riversbend Assoc. Partnership, 724 F.Supp. 661 (D.Minn.1989); United States v. Mountain Village Co., 424 F.Supp. 822 (D.Mass.1976).

50. 382 U.S. 341, 86 S.Ct. 500, 15 L.Ed.2d 404 (1966). See Note, The Role of State Deficiency Judgment Law in FHA Insured Mortgage Transactions, 56 Minn. L.Rev. 463 (1972).

hardly be a serious impediment to SBA collections generally, since it was obsolete in most states. The Court thus concluded that Texas law should apply, although it declined to decide whether through adoption into federal common law or by virtue of the fact that the parties contracted with reference to it.

The balancing approach of *Yazell* was further developed and formalized in 1979 by the Supreme Court in United States v. Kimbell Foods, Inc.[51] The *Kimbell* opinion involved two consolidated cases in which federal agencies (the Farmers Home Administration and the Small Business Administration) asserted lien priority in personal property against competing private lienholders. The Court reaffirmed that federal law invariably applies to cases in which the government is asserting or foreclosing a lien, but it articulated a three-pronged test for determining whether the courts should adopt state law as the federal rule of decision. In summary form, the test is as follows: (1) Is the nature of the federal program such that a nationally-uniform rule of law is needed? (2) Would the application of the state rule frustrate specific objectives of the federal program? (3) Would application of a federal rule disrupt commercial relationships that are predicated on state law?

On the facts of *Kimbell*, the Court determined that state law provided an appropriate rule. It emphasized that the federal agencies involved were already organized to take account of and comply with state law, and that their handbooks and procedures made abundant references to state rules. If they had used greater care in lending, they could readily have protected themselves from the losses they suffered under state law. Thus, the state rules would not generally frustrate the objectives of the programs in question. On the other hand, to substitute new federal rules would be highly disruptive, the Court concluded.

If the Court believed that its new test provided enough specificity to produce consistent results in the lower federal courts, it was mistaken. Consider the cases that have dealt with post-sale statutory redemption and antideficiency legislation, features of the state mortgage fore-

---

51. 440 U.S. 715, 99 S.Ct. 1448, 59 L.Ed.2d 711 (1979), on remand 600 F.2d 478 (5th Cir.1979). Neither of the cases consolidated in *Kimbell* involved real estate security. In one case, the debtor had given Kimbell Foods a chattel mortgage containing a dragnet clause; later it executed a security agreement to a bank on the same property in return for an SBA-guaranteed loan. The District Court held that under Texas law the SBA would prevail because the dragnet mortgage was not "choate" until Kimbell reduced its claim to judgment. 401 F.Supp. 316, 324–35 (N.D.Tex. 1975). The Court of Appeals held that under Texas law the dragnet security given to Kimbell would have priority; but instead of following Texas law, it created a federal common law rule that reached the same result; 557 F.2d 491, 503–05 (5th Cir.1977).

In the other case, the debtor gave FmHA a security interest in his tractor. Later he had the tractor repaired by a mechanic who, when unpaid, asserted a possessory lien on it. The Court of Appeals held that, under Georgia law, the FmHA's lien was unperfected because the description of the tractor was inadequate. However, it adopted a federal common law rule which limited the priority of the mechanic's lien to only a portion of the total repair bill. See 563 F.2d 678 (5th Cir. 1977).

closure in many jurisdictions that the federal mortgage-holding agencies usually find objectionable.[52] The Ninth Circuit has been extremely active in preemption cases of these types, deciding nearly as many as all of the other circuits combined. In 1970 in United States v. Stadium Apartments, Inc., it refused to recognize Idaho's post-sale redemption statute as controlling in an FHA foreclosure.[53] But even before *Kimbell* it had begun to retreat from this position, adopting state antideficiency and statutory redemption rules in an SBA foreclosure [54] and distinguishing *Stadium Apartments* on the ground that the documents there were non-negotiated "boilerplate" which included a waiver by the debtor of the state-law protections.[55]

Some pre-*Kimbell* Ninth Circuit cases seemed to suggest that choice-of-law clauses or waivers of state protective rules in the documents themselves were highly significant, and perhaps controlling.[56] And in a case in which no clause in the documents bore on the issue, the Ninth Circuit devised a federal rule allowing the FHA to recover for waste following its foreclosure of an apartment building;[57] such an action would have been barred under the California antideficiency statute,[58] which the court felt would have interfered with the FHA's goals of eliminating substandard housing.

52. United States v. Stadium Apartments, Inc., 425 F.2d 358 (9th Cir.1970), cert. denied 400 U.S. 926, 91 S.Ct. 187, 27 L.Ed.2d 185 (1970). See generally §§ 8.4–8.8 supra (statutory redemption); § 8.3 (antideficiency legislation). See Alexander, Federal Intervention in Real Estate Finance: Preemption and Federal Common Law, 71 N.C.L.Rev. 293 (1993); Note, Toward Adoption of State Law as the Federal Rule of Decision in Cases Involving Voluntary Federal Creditors, 73 Minn.L.Rev. 171 (1988); Note, Federal Housing Loans: Is State Mortgage Law Preempted?, 19 Santa Clara L.Rev. 431 (1979).

53. United States v. Stadium Apartments, Inc., 425 F.2d 358 (9th Cir.1970), certiorari denied 400 U.S. 926, 91 S.Ct. 187, 27 L.Ed.2d 926 (1970). The decision was based principally on the high cost to the government of holding the property, with little practical opportunity to dispose of it, during the redemption period. The court also emphasized the meager value, in its view, of the debtor's redemption right.

54. United States v. MacKenzie, 510 F.2d 39 (9th Cir.1975). The court opined that the state rules actually tended to fulfill the federal program's goal of helping small businesses—a conclusion that must have astonished the SBA itself, normally considered the best authority on how its programs should be administered.

55. This distinction between individually-negotiated and boilerplate documents was unconvincing to Judges Ely and Browning, concurring in *MacKenzie;* they asserted that *Stadium Apartments* had been effectively overruled.

56. See United States v. Stewart, 523 F.2d 1070 (9th Cir.1975) (California antideficiency rule applied, where documents stated that California law governed the transaction); United States v. Gish, 559 F.2d 572 (9th Cir.1977), certiorari denied 435 U.S. 996, 98 S.Ct. 1648, 56 L.Ed.2d 85 (1978) (rejecting application of the Alaska antideficiency statute, where both the documents and an SBA regulation stated that federal law would control).

But the documents have not always been controlling; see United States v. Crain, 589 F.2d 996 (9th Cir.1979), in which the SBA sued guarantors on a note. Arizona law required creditors to exhaust their remedies against the principal debtor, but a clause in the guarantee purported to waive those rights. The court declined to follow the documents, and adopted state law, again asserting, as in *MacKenzie,* supra note 54, that it was consistent with the SBA's goals of protecting small businesses.

57. United States v. Haddon Haciendas Co., 541 F.2d 777 (9th Cir.1976).

58. See Cornelison v. Kornbluth, 15 Cal.3d 590, 125 Cal.Rptr. 557, 542 P.2d 981 (1975).

§ 11.6　　　GOVERNMENT INTERVENTION　　　129

The Ninth Circuit seems to have taken *Kimbell* as *carte blanche* to embrace state redemption law when federal agencies foreclose, irrespective of the other factors in the case. In United States v. Ellis,[59] it adopted the Washington state statutory redemption process in a Farmers Home Administration foreclosure. It refused to follow *Stadium Apartments* despite the fact that the documents in *Ellis*, like those in *Stadium*, were standard forms with no individualized negotiation.[60] It held that the "overriding federal purpose is not adversely affected, and may even be advanced, by adopting state law."[61]

In United States v. Pastos,[62] the Ninth Circuit took an additional step, applying the Montana mortgage redemption statute to an SBA foreclosure despite both the nonnegotiated nature of the loan documents and the fact that they contained an express waiver by the debtors of their redemption rights. The *Pastos* opinion suggests that the only factor that might have produced a different result would have been an express statutory provision or SBA regulation preempting state redemption law—and there was no such provision.[63]

With respect to antideficiency legislation, the Ninth Circuit has not quite been willing to adopt state law in its entirety, but it has nonetheless gone a long way in that direction. The difference in treatment between redemption and antideficiency statutes is easy to see: if the government is subject to a redemption statute, it may be inconvenienced and may suffer some losses while holding the property during the redemption period, but if the redemption right is exercised it will ultimately collect its debt. An antideficiency statute, on the other hand, stands firmly in the way of collection in every case in which the real estate is inadequate security. The Ninth Circuit had this distinc-

59. 714 F.2d 953 (9th Cir.1983). See also United States v. Hargrove, 494 F.Supp. 22 (D.N.M.1979) (semple).

60. See also United States v. Crain, 589 F.2d 996 (9th Cir.1979) (Arizona equitable subrogation doctrine applied against SBA despite form language purporting to give SBA direct right of action without subrogation, and despite fact that form was standardized and nonnegotiated).

61. *Stadium Apartments* was distinguished on the unconvincing ground that it had involved the National Housing Act, the primary objective of which was to maximize the amount of housing produced, while *Ellis* involved a direct loan to a farmer from the Farmers Home Administration, which presumably had differing (but unstated) objectives.

62. 781 F.2d 747 (9th Cir.1986). See also Dupnik v. United States, 848 F.2d 1476 (9th Cir.1988), applying to the SBA Arizona's rules regarding the filing of notice by a junior lienholder who wishes to exercise a statutory right of redemption. The case is considerably easier for the government to stomach than *Pastos*, since the cost to the government as junior lienor of complying with the notice requirements should be trivial, while the cost to the government as foreclosing party, as in *Pastos*, of enduring the post-foreclosure redemption period could be very substantial. But in *Pastos* the Ninth Circuit appeared to regard the cost as unimportant, or at least as not overriding the state's concern with protecting debtors.

63. The court pointed out that SBA had adopted an express preemptive regulation with respect to state antideficiency statutes, and that it had previously given due respect to that regulation; see United States v. Gish, 559 F.2d 572 (9th Cir.1977). See also Ayers v. Philadelphia Housing Authority, 908 F.2d 1184 (3d Cir.1990), certiorari denied ___ U.S. ___, 111 S.Ct. 1003, 112 L.Ed.2d 1086 (1991) (HUD regulation directly conflicted with and therefore preempted state law with respect to notice of foreclosure).

tion in mind as long ago as 1965 when, in United States v. Rossi,[64] it held that California's antideficiency law was preempted by the VA's regulations that expressly permitted the government to collect by way of a personal action against the borrower.

In Whitehead v. Derwinski [65] the court declined to apply the same reasoning to the Washington antideficiency statute. The difference between the two states is that, under California law, all deficiency judgments on purchase-money home loans are barred irrespective of the foreclosure method used. In Washington, by contrast, foreclosing lenders have a choice: they may employ non-judicial power of sale and give up the right to a deficiency, or alternatively may foreclose judicially (with some attendant delays and added costs) and preserve their deficiency claims. The Ninth Circuit concluded that because these choices were open to the VA in Washington, it was properly subjected to state law, which the court found was "consistent" with the federal regulations. In effect, the VA had made its bed by instructing its lenders to use power-of-sale foreclosure, and now had to lie in it by losing its deficiency claims. The court recognized that the statute and regulations give VA both a right of subrogation to the lender's position and also a direct right of action against the borrower, but found the latter right to be "secondary" and insufficient to override the antideficiency statute.[66] The opinion gave scant attention to *Kimbell*. Three years later in Carter v. Derwinski,[67] the circuit en banc overruled *Whitehead*, concluded that there was nothing "secondary" about the VA's right of indemnity, and held that VA could exercise it after a nonjudicial foreclosure despite state law restricting deficiency judgments to judicial foreclosure situations.

The other federal circuits have had far less to say about preemption than the Ninth, but what they have said has usually been more favorable to the government. The Eighth Circuit, in United States v. Victory Highway Village, refused to recognize the Minnesota statutory redemption scheme in an FHA foreclosure.[68] The court simply cited pre-*Kimbell* holdings to the same effect and avoided even mentioning *Kimbell*, much less analyzing the case under the *Kimbell* test! [69] The

64. 342 F.2d 505 (9th Cir.1965).

65. 904 F.2d 1362 (9th Cir.1990). *Rossi* remained the law in states where deficiency judgments were absolutely prohibited; see Connelly v. Derwinski, 961 F.2d 129 (9th Cir.1992) (Oregon law); Jones v. Turnage, 699 F.Supp. 795 (N.D.Cal.1988), affirmed without opinion 914 F.2d 1496 (9th Cir.1990), certiorari denied ___ U.S. ___, 111 S.Ct. 1309, 113 L.Ed.2d 243 (1991) (California law); Shepherd v. Derwinski, 961 F.2d 132 (9th Cir.1992) (Arizona law). See also Great Southwest Life Ins. Co. v. Frazier, 860 F.2d 896 (9th Cir.1988) (Idaho UCC governs borrower's assertion of impairment of collateral as a defense in SBA's deficiency action).

66. See supra § 11.2 notes 43–45.

67. 987 F.2d 611 (9th Cir.1993).

68. 662 F.2d 488 (8th Cir.1981).

69. See John Hancock Mutual Life Insurance Co. v. Bruening Farms Corp., 537 F.Supp. 936 (N.D.Iowa 1982), following *Victory Highway Village*, supra note 61. See also United States v. Curry, 561 F.Supp. 429 (D.Kan.1983), following *Victory Highway Village* and refusing to adopt Kansas law prohibiting waivers of statutory redemption, but nonetheless giving the debtors an equitable period of redemption as is allowed under Kansas law.

Sixth Circuit employed similarly disappointing judicial craftsmanship in United States v. Scholnick,[70] reaching an identical conclusion with no thoughtful *Kimbell* analysis.

The Ninth Circuit's pre-1993 approach to state antideficiency law, discussed above, has also received a cool reception elsewhere. Declining to follow *Whitehead*, the Eighth Circuit distinguished Minnesota law from Washington's, concluding that the former recognized VA's right of direct action against the borrower notwithstanding the antideficiency statute.[71] But it also disagreed with *Whitehead's* assertion that VA's direct right of action was somehow "secondary" or of lesser importance than the right of subrogation. The Seventh Circuit, dealing with Wisconsin antideficiency law, was more blunt. It found the state statute to be essentially identical to Washington's, but disagreed with the *Whitehead* analysis: "There is no basis in the statute and regulations ... that compels us to force the VA to privilege its subrogation right over its indemnification right."[72] Hence VA could employ Wisconsin power-of-sale foreclosure without giving up its action against the borrower. The court rejected the notion that the antideficiency statute was "consistent" with federal law merely because VA could avoid it by using judicial foreclosure. These cases currently have much less direct practical importance than heretofore, since for loans made in and after 1990 Congress drastically reduced the probability that VA will seek deficiency judgments from veteran borrowers.[73] But they remain significant in reflecting sharply divergent attitudes about the burdens the government should be required to bear under state debtor-protection laws.

Cases on other legal issues have been much more consistent in adopting state law as the rule of decision. Where the question is lien priority, the courts have usually followed state law under *Kimbell* faithfully,[74] although often with little analysis.[75] The Ninth Circuit held that VA was subject to a state 3–month limitation period in obtaining a deficiency judgment.[76] The Fifth Circuit held that the SBA

---

70. 606 F.2d 160 (6th Cir.1979). The level of the court's analysis is aptly represented in its dictum: "Local rules that limit the effectiveness of remedies available to the United States are not to be adopted." One could scarcely imagine a statement more out of character with the spirit of *Kimbell*.

71. Vail v. Derwinski, 946 F.2d 589 (8th Cir.1991), opinion on rehearing 956 F.2d 812 (8th Cir.1992).

72. United States v. Davis, 961 F.2d 603 (7th Cir.1992). Accord, Boley v. Principi, 144 F.R.D. 305 (E.D.N.C.1992).

73. Deficiencies are now sought against the original borrower only if he or she engaged in fraud, misrepresentation, or bad faith. See supra § 11.2 note 46.

74. See, e.g., United States v. Tipton, 898 F.2d 770 (10th Cir.1990); More v. United States, 505 F.Supp. 612 (N.D.Fla.1980) (FmHA); Sims v. Smith, 502 F.Supp. 609 (N.D.Fla.1980) (FmHA).

75. But see United States v. Dansby, 509 F.Supp. 188 (N.D.Ohio 1981), applying Ohio law to recognize the priority of a state property tax lien, as against an FmHA mortgage, and carefully analyzing FmHA's decentralized administration and capacity to operate efficiently without a uniform federal rule.

76. Carter v. Derwinski, 758 F.Supp. 603 (D.Idaho 1991). Several other cases have refused to impose state statutes of limitations on the federal government; see, e.g., Westnau Land Corp. v. SBA, 785 F.Supp. 41 (E.D.N.Y.1992) (New York 6–

must follow the Georgia rule requiring judicial confirmation of foreclosure sales;[77] in another case it applied Georgia law to determine the standard of reasonableness which SBA must meet in disposing of a leasehold upon which it holds a lien.[78] Here the Court took *Kimbell* seriously, discussing the test at length and commenting particularly on the local title difficulties that would result if a new federal rule were adopted.

One of the best-crafted opinions is that of the First Circuit in Chicago Title Insurance Co. v. Sherred Village Associates.[79] There a mortgage on a multifamily housing project was insured by, and subsequently assigned to, the Department of Housing and Urban Development. During construction a subcontractor on the project was unpaid, and it subsequently filed a mechanics' lien. Under Maine law, such liens relate back for priority purposes to the date of the claimant's contract,[80] which was earlier than the HUD-held mortgage. HUD argued strenuously for a federal common law rule of "first in time, first in right," which would have negated the relation back of the lien. But the First Circuit concluded that HUD's program, which is administered on a local basis with careful case-by-case scrutiny of mortgage insurance applications, would not be burdened significantly by the state rule, while employment of a federal rule would seriously interfere with the expectations of local contractors.[81]

State law has also been adopted in recent cases in the face of arguments by government agencies urging federal common law treatment of dragnet clause enforcement,[82] general mortgage foreclosure procedure,[83] and general contract law.[84] On the other hand, federal common law has been held to control the HUD Secretary's right to

year statute of limitations on actions to foreclose mortgage); United States v. Freidus, 769 F.Supp. 1266 (S.D.N.Y.1991) (same); United States v. Copper, 709 F.Supp. 905 (N.D.Iowa 1988) (Iowa rule barring mortgage foreclosure when debt was barred by statute of limitation did not apply against SBA).

77. United States v. Dismuke, 616 F.2d 755 (5th Cir.1980).

78. United States v. Irby, 618 F.2d 352 (5th Cir.1980).

79. 708 F.2d 804 (1st Cir.1983). See also Federal Land Bank v. Ferguson, 896 F.2d 1244 (10th Cir.1990); Yankee Bank for Finance & Savings v. Task Assoc., 731 F.Supp. 64 (N.D.N.Y.1990).

80. See 10 Maine Rev.Stat.Ann. § 3251; § 12.4 supra.

81. Id. at 810–813.

82. United States v. Vahlco Corp., 720 F.2d 885 (5th Cir.1983).

83. Johnson v. United States Department of Agriculture, 734 F.2d 774 (11th Cir.1984); United States v. Mikolaitis, 682 F.Supp. 798 (M.D.Pa.1988) (SBA is bound by state foreclosure statute requiring pre-foreclosure notice to mortgagors informing them of rights under emergency assistance program). Contra, see United States v. Spears, 859 F.2d 284 (3d Cir.1988) (state notice requirements not binding on FmHA, where it employed equivalent or better notice procedures and where no rights of commercial third parties were at stake, so that there was no compelling reason to adopt state law); Ayers v. Philadelphia Housing Authority, 908 F.2d 1184 (3d Cir. 1990) (same, where state law directly conflicted with HUD regulations).

84. United States v. Stump Home Specialties Mfg., Inc., 905 F.2d 1117 (7th Cir. 1990) (Indiana contract law adopted); First Interstate Bank v. SBA, 868 F.2d 340 (9th Cir.1989) (general state law, including Restatement of Contracts, adopted; but it is unclear that local Idaho law would have led to different results); Curry v. SBA, 679 F.Supp. 966 (N.D.Cal.1987) (California contract law adopted).

become a mortgagee in possession and to perfect an assignment of rents,[85] and (prior to the Congressional preemption of the matter) to preempt state law limiting enforcement of a due-on-sale clause by FmHA.[86]

It is not easy to find a thread of consistency in the preemption decisions. The strongest cases for adoption of state law as the rule of decision are those involving lien priority, as in *Kimbell* itself. In most such instances state law is neither pro-debtor nor pro-creditor,[87] and in no sense discriminates against the government. It is essentially neutral, and merely establishes ground rules involving filing, possession, and notice that the government can observe as readily as any private party. Moreover, displacement of state priority rules by rules invented by a federal court can be extremely disruptive to local businesses. For these reasons, *Kimbell* makes excellent sense on its facts.

But extending *Kimbell* to other areas of mortgage law, such as statutory redemption and antideficiency legislation, which are quite overtly pro-debtor, is a harder question, as the diversity of judicial decisions illustrates. The government would like to collect its money, and these rules stand in its way. Is preemption "needed?" Will state law frustrate the objectives of the federal program? Only in the sense that the public fisc will suffer added losses, and private debtors will be benefitted, if there is no preemption.[88]

The question is fundamentally one of policy, and it ought to be resolved by the political branches—the Congress and the agencies that administer the programs. It is within their power to preempt state law by statute or regulation, and in some instances they have done so.[89] It makes little sense for federal judges to speculate about how obnoxious the state rule is to a federal program, when those who devised and administer the program can decide for themselves and announce the

85. United States v. St. Paul Missionary Public Housing, Inc., 575 F.Supp. 867 (N.D.Ohio 1983) (mortgagee in possession); United States v. Landmark Park & Assoc., 795 F.2d 683 (8th Cir.1986) (perfection of assignment of rents).

86. United States v. Med O Farm, Inc., 701 F.2d 88 (9th Cir.1983).

87. One exception, arguably, is the mechanics' lien relation-back doctrine involved in the *Sherred Village* case, supra note 79, which seems inherently adverse to the interest of the government in its capacity as assignee of an institutional lender. But even here there are numerous methods by which the government can minimize or eliminate its risk.

88. Thus, the Ninth Circuit's effort to predicate different preemption results on a distinction, for example, between the objectives of the SBA (to aid small businesses), which are advanced by antideficiency and redemption statutes, and those of HUD (to clear slums and build housing), which are retarded by antideficiency and redemption statutes, is wholly unconvincing. Both agencies are fundamentally in the business of making federal credit available to the private sector, and both have an equal interest in being repaid.

89. For example, the Multifamily Mortgage Foreclosure Act, 12 U.S.C.A. §§ 3701–3717 specifically preempts any state post-sale redemption rights following a foreclosure under the Act. See United States v. Shimer, 367 U.S. 374, 81 S.Ct. 1554, 6 L.Ed.2d 908 (1961) (VA regulations fully preempt inconsistent state foreclosure rules); Cf. United States v. Whitney, 602 F.Supp. 722 (W.D.N.Y.1985). See also notes 10–17 supra, discussing other preemptive federal statutes.

extent to which state law should govern it.[90] Unless they have done so, or the impairment of the program is obvious and egregious, state law should be followed by the courts.

There is a further question, not yet answered in the cases, concerning the extent to which the preemption doctrines discussed above should apply when the mortgage is held by a federally-sponsored entity, such as the Federal National Mortgage Association (FHMA) or the Federal Home Loan Mortgage Corporation (FHLMC), rather than by a direct federal agency. Rust v. Johnson[91] provides some guidance, although its facts are distinguishable. There FNMA held a mortgage on realty which was the subject of a city's lien foreclosure action for a delinquent street improvement assessment. The Ninth Circuit held that FNMA was a "federal instrumentality," and thus was entitled to "protection of the federal interest" in its defense against the city's foreclosure. This result seems inconsistent with the cases holding that FNMA is not sufficiently "governmental" to be subject to the burdens of the Due Process Clause when foreclosing mortgages by power of sale.[92] Nevertheless, Rust v. Johnson suggests that FNMA and FHLMC may be treated as direct instrumentalities of the federal government when their mortgage foreclosures come into conflict with state law.[93]

Some of the cases discussed above have considered significant, in deciding whether to adopt state law, the extent to which an agency's programs are administered at the local level, so that it would not be burdensome to impose local law upon them.[94] But it is doubtful that any federal agency's programs are so fully centralized that compliance with state law would present difficult burdens. FHMA and FHLMC illustrate the point well. One can hardly imagine more centralized operations. They deal with thousands of lenders and have purchased millions of mortgages, while employing relatively small staffs operating only at the national and regional levels.[95] Yet they have at the same time been acutely conscious of the variations in mortgage law from one state to another, and have meticulously drafted state-by-state versions of their "standard" instruments in order to comply with those varia-

90. See the excellent analysis in Alexander, Federal Intervention in Real Estate Finance: Preemption and Federal Common Law, 71 N.C.L.Rev. 293, 360–370 (1993). We suggest that the announcement ought to be by way of statute or regulation, and not merely by language in the documents. This will encourage consistency in administration, and will subject the decision to public scrutiny in a way that document drafting does not.

91. 597 F.2d 174 (9th Cir.1979), certiorari denied 444 U.S. 964, 100 S.Ct. 450, 62 L.Ed.2d 376 (1979).

92. See § 7.28 supra.

93. Cf. FHLMC v. Superior Court, 224 Cal.App.3d 218, 273 Cal.Rptr. 531 (1990) (FHLMC is not a federal instrumentality so as to be entitled to have the priority accorded to the federal government for its claims against an insolvent insurance company); Rockford Life Ins. Co. v. Department of Revenue, 128 Ill.App.3d 302, 83 Ill.Dec. 470, 470 N.E.2d 596 (1984), affirmed 112 Ill.2d 174, 97 Ill.Dec. 405, 492 N.E.2d 1278 (1986) (mortgage-backed securities guaranteed by GNMA and other government entities are not direct federal obligations immune from state taxation).

94. See, e.g., Chicago Title Insurance Co. v. Sherred Village Associates, 708 F.2d 804, 810–11 (1st Cir.1983); United States v. Dansby, 509 F.Supp. 188 (N.D.Ohio 1981).

95. Cf. United States v. Dansby, id., distinguishing FmHA's highly localized operations from FNMA's centralized ones.

tions.[96] When spread over so many transactions, the cost of this individualization cannot be very great. Arguments by other agencies that they need not do as much, or that the federal courts ought to protect them from their own lack of careful drafting of loan documents and regulations, are not very persuasive.

§ 11.7 Resolution of Insolvent Financial Institutions: Impact on Mortgage Transactions

When a bank or a savings and loan association becomes insolvent, the Federal Deposit Insurance Corporation [1] must decide whether to attempt to maintain it as a going business, to transfer its assets to an existing institution, or to create a new institution (a "bridge bank") to receive its assets. (A fourth option, closing the association and putting nothing in its place, is rarely used, since it undermines confidence in the banking system.) The FDIC most commonly "resolves" an insolvent institution by means of a *purchase and assumption* ("P & A") transaction.[2]

At the inception of this process, FDIC is appointed receiver for the institution. It assumes control, replaces existing management, and assesses the institution's financial condition.[3] FDIC then decides whether to operate the institution, close and liquidate it, or engage in a P & A transaction. If a P & A is the course elected, the purchasing and assuming institution may be one already in existence and ready to take on the role. If no suitable purchaser can be located, FDIC may set up a "bridge bank" for the purpose.[4] A bridge bank is a temporary federally chartered bank, with a charter issued by the Comptroller of the Currency (or, in the case of a thrift institution, the Office of Thrift Supervision). It is authorized by law to engage in P & A transactions

---

96. See Randolph, The FHMA/FHLMC Uniform Home Improvement Loan Note: The Secondary Market Meets the Consumer Movement, 60 N.C.L.Rev. 365 (1982); Browne, Development of the FHMA/FHLMC Plain Language Mortgage Documents—Some Useful Techniques, 14 Real Prop.Prob. & Tr.J. 696 (1979).

§ 11.7

1. Federally insured savings and loan associations were previously resolved by the Federal Savings and Loan Insurance Corporation (FSLIC), but its operation was terminated in 1989 by the Financial Institutions Reform, Recovery & Enforcement Act (FIRREA); see FIRREA § 401, Pub. L.No. 101–73 (1989). FIRREA established the Resolution Trust Corporation (RTC) to administer the assets of insolvent thrifts that were previously insured by FSLIC and that were placed in conservatorship or receivership between January 1, 1989 and August 9, 1992; see FIRREA § 501. All other savings and loan association resolutions are under the jurisdiction of the Federal Deposit Insurance Corporation (FDIC), which prior to FIRREA insured and resolved only banks; see FIRREA § 401. RTC continues at this writing to be active in resolving pre-August 9, 1992 insolvencies, but will eventually phase out of operation. Hence, for the sake of simplicity, the text refers only to FDIC. RTC's powers and duties are essentially identical to those of FDIC; see FIRREA § 501; Castleglen, Inc. v. Commonwealth Sav. Ass'n, 728 F.Supp. 656 (D.Utah 1989), affirmed 984 F.2d 1571 (10th Cir. 1993).

2. See Note, Unsecured Creditors of Failed Banks: It's Not a Wonderful Life, 104 Harv. L.Rev. 1052 (1991).

3. Such assumption of control by FDIC is not a compensable taking under the Fifth Amendment; California Housing Securities, Inc. v. United States, 959 F.2d 955 (Fed.Cir. 1992), certiorari denied ___ U.S. ___, 113 S.Ct. 324, 121 L.Ed.2d 244 (1992).

4. See 12 U.S.C.A. § 1821(n).

and is eligible to receive assistance funds from FDIC in its corporate capacity. The bridge bank terminates on the earliest of the following events: the passage of two years; the merger of the bridge bank with another bank; the sale of the stock of the bridge bank to another bank; or the assumption of substantially all of the assets of the bridge bank by another bank.[5]

The purchasing bank [6] assumes the deposit and secured liabilities of the insolvent institution. It also receives the "good" or performing assets. It does not assume the *unsecured* liabilities, and they generally become uncollectible. The "bad" or unacceptable assets are assigned to FDIC-corporate, which in turn pays the purchasing bank a sum sufficient to make the transaction acceptable to it. It is clear that the bridge bank or other purchaser under a P & A agreement has no liability for the debts or torts of the insolvent institution except to the extent that they are expressly assumed.[7] If the P & A transaction involves a bridge bank, FDIC will, at some time in the two-year period following the P & A transaction, locate a permanent purchaser. This institution may either merge with the bridge bank, acquire its stock and continue to operate it as a separate entity, or purchase its assets and assume its liabilities (after which the bridge bank will be closed).

A P & A transaction can be employed only if FDIC first determines that it will be less costly to the government than a liquidation of the insolvent institution, but this is generally the case.[8] The P & A has several advantages over a liquidation. Public confidence in the banking system is not undermined, since the purchasing institution or bridge bank will continue to operate at the same location without any noticeable disruption. Often the transaction occurs overnight and the public is only vaguely aware that something has changed. FDIC funds are saved, since the "going business" value of the insolvent institution is preserved. In addition, it is not necessary to engage in a complex payout of cash to the insured depositors of the insolvent institution. Normally even deposits in excess of the $100,000 insurance ceiling are assumed by the purchasing bank. Nonetheless, P & A transactions can be very costly. FDIC's corporate (insurance reserve) funds are spent in several ways: Paying the purchasing institution to engage in the transaction; sustaining losses in attempting to collect the "bad" assets which were not transferred to the purchasing institution; and subsidizing the operations of the bridge bank if it is unable to operate profit-

---

5. See 12 U.S.C.A. § 1821(n)(10).

6. The purchasing institution may be a savings and loan association; "bank" is used in the text in the interest of brevity.

7. See, e.g., First Indiana Fed. Sav. Bank v. FDIC, 964 F.2d 503 (5th Cir.1992) (insolvent institution's obligations under loan participation agreements it had sold were unsecured obligations, and were not transferred to purchaser under purchase and assumption agreement); Deposit Guaranty Bank v. Hall, 741 F.Supp. 1287 (S.D.Tex.1990). Unliquidated obligations of the closed institution are not ordinarily assumed by the bridge bank. See Santopadre v. Pelican Homestead & Sav. Ass'n, 937 F.2d 268 (5th Cir.1991). For an example of a recent P & A transaction involving a bridge bank, see Texas American Bancshares, Inc. v. Clarke, 954 F.2d 329 (5th Cir.1992).

8. See 12 U.S.C.A. § 1821(n)(10).

ably. It may also be necessary for FDIC to subsidize the later purchase of the bridge bank by another institution, if the bridge bank does not have a positive net worth at that time.

In the complex P & A scenario just described, there are typically several entities (in chronological order) that may acquire the institution's assets. They include FDIC as receiver, FDIC in its corporate capacity (taking ownership of the "bad" assets such as nonperforming loans), the purchasing and assuming institution, and later purchasers from the original purchasing and assuming institution. Each of these may hold mortgages and notes that were originally the property of the insolvent institution. The insolvent institution's mortgagors, junior lienholders, and other parties who have an interest in the security real estate may thus have to deal with each of them. These dealings take on a unique cast because of the special immunities federal law gives to FDIC and its successors. Those immunities are the subject of the remainder of this section.

The D'Oench, Duhme Doctrine and § 1823(e)

The case of D'Oench, Duhme & Co. v. FDIC[9] established as a matter of federal common law that when the government or its transferees attempt to collect on an asset acquired from an insolvent financial institution, the obligor may not raise certain defenses that could have been asserted against the original institution. The doctrine is largely codified in 12 U.S.C. § 1823(e).[10] The statute is arguably

---

9. 315 U.S. 447, 62 S.Ct. 676, 86 L.Ed. 956 (1942), rehearing denied 315 U.S. 830, 86 L.Ed. 1224 (1942).

10. The statute provides:
No agreement which tends to diminish or defeat the interest of the Corporation in any asset acquired by it under this section or section 1821 of this title, either as security for a loan or by purchase or as receiver of any insured depository institution shall be valid against the Corporation unless such agreement (1) is in writing, (2) was executed by the depository institution and any person claiming an adverse interest thereunder, including the obligor, contemporaneously with the acquisition of the asset by the depository institution, (3) was approved by the board of directors of the depository institution or its loan committee, which approval shall be reflected in the minutes of said board or committee, and (4) has been, continuously, from the time of its execution, an official record of the depository institution.

Prior to the enactment of FIRREA in 1989, § 1823(e) applied only to FDIC in its corporate capacity. However, FIRREA expanded it to apply both the FDIC and RTC in both their corporate and receivership capacities. See FDIC v. McCullough, 911 F.2d 593 (11th Cir.1990); RTC v. Camp, 965 F.2d 25 (5th Cir.1992) (§ 1823 codified the D'Oench doctrine); FDIC v. Orrill, 771 F.Supp. 777 (E.D.La.1991); Castleglen, Inc. v. Commonwealth Sav. Ass'n, 728 F.Supp. 656 (D.Utah 1989), affirmed 984 F.2d 1571 (10th Cir. 1993). Some recent cases have held this expansion to be retroactive to pre-FIRREA transactions; see, e.g., FDIC v. Engel, 746 F.Supp. 1223 (S.D.N.Y.1990).

The National Credit Union Administration operates under statutes with wording virtually identical to § 1823(e); see 12 U.S.C.A. § 1787(p)(2) (NCUA as receiver); 12 U.S.C.A. § 1788(a)(3) (NCUA as conservator). See Savoy v. White, 788 F.Supp. 69 (D.Mass.1992). Cf. National Credit Union Admin. Board v. Regine, 795 F.Supp. 59 (D.R.I.1992) (§ 1823(e) applies to NCUA in its capacity as receiver, but not as conservator). Both of the foregoing cases agree that the common-law *D'Oench* doctrine also applies to NCUA.

In FIRREA Congress did not specifically extend § 1832(e) to FSLIC. The federal common law of *D'Oench* was generally applied to FSLIC even before FIRREA; see

somewhat broader than the *D'Oench* doctrine, which has sometimes been limited to cases involving either a "secret agreement" or participation by the borrower in a scheme likely to mislead the banking authorities.[11] "At the same time, however, the statute is narrower than *D'Oench, Duhme* in that it applies only to *agreements*, and not to other defenses the borrower might raise."[12] Despite these distinctions, the great bulk of the cases treat *D'Oench* and § 1823(e) as virtually synonymous, lumping them together to reach the announced result.

§ 1823(e) is extremely protective of the government, and seems almost Draconian in the demands it makes on borrowers who wish to raise defenses to collection of their loans.[13] Any defense must be based on a writing,[14] must have been approved by institution's directors or loan committee[15] (not merely by a loan officer, for example), and must

---

FSLIC v. Murray, 853 F.2d 1251 (5th Cir. 1988). However, there is currently a split of authority as to whether the pre-FIRREA application of the *D'Oench* doctrine continues to apply to FSLIC, or whether the intent of Congress in FIRREA was to make it clear that FSLIC does not have the protection of the doctrine. See Gray, Limitation on the FDIC's D'Oench Duhme Doctrine of Federal Common Law Estoppel: Congressional Preemption and Authoritative Statutory Construction, 31 S.Tex. L.Rev. 245 (1991). Compare In re Woodstone Ltd. Partnership, 133 B.R. 678 (Bkrtcy. N.Y.1991), reversed 149 B.R. 294 (E.D.N.Y.1993) (*D'Oench* does not apply to FSLIC) with FSLIC v. McCullough, 911 F.2d 593 (11th Cir.1990) (*D'Oench* applies to FSLIC); Hall v. FDIC, 920 F.2d 334 (6th Cir.1990), certiorari denied ___ U.S. ___, 111 S.Ct. 2852, 115 L.Ed.2d 1020 (1991) (same); Carteret Savings Bank v. Compton, Luther & Sons, Inc., 899 F.2d 340 (4th Cir.1990) (same).

11. See, e.g., Garrett v. Commonwealth Mortg. Corp., 938 F.2d 591 (5th Cir.1991); Adams v. Walker, 767 F.Supp. 1099 (D.Kan.1991).

12. FDIC v. Sather, 488 N.W.2d 260 (Minn.1992).

13. See generally Comment, Banking Law: The D'Oench Doctrine and 12 U.S.C.A. § 1823(e): Overextended, But Not Unconstitutional, 43 Okla.L.Rev. 315 (1990); Hymanson, Note, Borrower Beware: D'Oench, Duhme and Section 1823 Overprotect the Insurer when the Banks Fail, 62 S.Cal.L.Rev. 253 (1988); Norcross, The Bank Insolvency Game: FDIC Superpowers, the D'Oench Doctrine, and Federal Common Law, 103 Banking L.J. 316 (1986).

14. See FDIC v. Hamilton, 939 F.2d 1225 (5th Cir.1991) (memorandum in borrower's credit file was insufficient writing);

FDIC v. Mr. "T's", Inc., 764 F.Supp. 1087 (M.D.La.1991) (ledger card, while reflecting payments under modification of loan, did not spell out the terms of modification and hence did not satisfy requirement of a written agreement); RTC v. Toler, 791 F.Supp. 649 (N.D.Tex.1991) (signed letter from institution to borrower, promising lender would resort to letter of credit before accelerating the loan, was not part of lender's official records and was not a sufficient writing); FDIC v. Gemini Management, 921 F.2d 241 (9th Cir.1990) (unsigned letter from lender, discussing a larger loan than indicated by promissory note, was insufficient writing); Tuxedo Beach Club Corp. v. City Fed. Sav. Bank, 749 F.Supp. 635 (D.N.J.1990) (discussing the difficulty plaintiffs are likely to experience in attempting to piece together a written agreement from various separate writings in the institution's files); Oliver v. RTC, 955 F.2d 583 (8th Cir.1992) (sustaining dismissal of borrowers' complaint, where they merely hoped that discovery of the institution's files might produce some relevant writing).

The written agreement need *not* be the promissory note itself, but may be a separate document, provided it meets the other tests outlined below; see FDIC v. Laguarta, 939 F.2d 1231 (5th Cir.1991) (where promissory note clearly referred to separate loan agreement, agreement was binding on FDIC); FDIC v. Sather, 488 N.W.2d 260 (Minn.1992) (FDIC bound by separate but written line of credit agreement).

15. See Stiles v. RTC, 831 S.W.2d 24 (Tex.App.1992) ("write-off" of loan by bank on its internal accounting records was not binding on RTC, where there was no proof that the accounting records were signed or approved by the board or the loan committee).

have been continuously part of the institution's official records.[16] Obviously these are matters in which the average borrower takes little interest, since they seem to relate only to the lender's internal operations, but they can turn out to be of crucial importance to the borrower if the institution becomes insolvent. But the clause of § 1823(e) that seems most harsh to borrowers provides that the agreement on which the defense is based must have been executed "contemporaneously with the acquisition of the asset by the depository institution."[17] Taken at face value, this would mean that an accord and satisfaction (such as a forbearance agreement or an agreement restructuring an outstanding loan's terms or reducing its interest rate or balance), even if written, approved, and recorded properly, would not bind the FDIC, since by its nature such an agreement is non-contemporaneous with the original loan agreement.[18] There is surprisingly little authority on this point, possibly because FDIC has been reluctant to assert the "non-contemporaneous" concept as a sole ground for resisting a borrower's defenses. Most of the cases that refer to the "contemporaneously" requirement also involve other lapses of compliance with § 1823(e), such as failure of the lender to sign the agreement or to have the directors or loan committee properly approve it.[19] Can Congress really have meant that loan restructurings are *never* binding on the government? Might such a position raise serious constitutional questions? The decisions are mixed,[20] and will have to await Supreme Court resolution.[21]

16. See RTC v. McCrory, 951 F.2d 68 (5th Cir.1992) (letter in "draft document" file of outside attorney representing bank was not part of an "official record" of the bank). But see Agri Export Cooperative v. Universal Sav. Ass'n, 767 F.Supp. 824 (S.D.Tex.1991) (*D'Oench* not applicable when the document was missing from the institution's records merely because it used poor record-keeping procedures).

17. 12 U.S.C.A. § 1823(e)(2).

18. Somewhat less troublesome is the case of a forbearance or modification agreement executed *before* the loan itself is entered into. Here the case law seems quite clear that § 1823(e) means what it says, and that the non-contemporaneous agreement is not binding on FDIC. See FDIC v. Virginia Corssings Partnership, 909 F.2d 306 (8th Cir.1990); FDIC v. La Rambla Shopping Center, Inc., 791 F.2d 215 (1st Cir.1986); RTC v. Dubois, 771 F.Supp. 154 (M.D.La.1991).

19. FDIC v. Wright, 942 F.2d 1089 (7th Cir.1991), certiorari denied ___ U.S. ___, 112 S.Ct. 1937, 118 L.Ed.2d 544 (1992), rehearing denied ___ U.S. ___, 112 S.Ct. 3058, 120 L.Ed.2d 923 (1992) (agreement not properly approved); Twin Constr., Inc. v. Boca Raton, Inc., 925 F.2d 378 (11th Cir. 1991) (agreement not binding on FSLIC, even though found in the institution's records, since not signed by the institution);

FDIC v. Friedland, 758 F.Supp. 941 (S.D.N.Y.1991) (agreement not properly approved); Tax Inv. Ltd. v. FDIC, 763 F.Supp. 1452 (N.D.Ill.1991) (letter signed only by debtor and not by institution held not enforceable against FDIC); In re Ajootian, 119 B.R. 749 (Bkrtcy.Cal.1990) (escrow instruction never signed by institution).

20. See RTC v. Crow, 763 F.Supp. 887 (N.D.Tex.1991) (statute construed literally; letter agreements modifying loan were not binding on RTC); FDIC v. Waldron, 472 F.Supp. 21 (D.S.C.1979), affirmed 630 F.2d 239 (4th Cir.1980) ("The defendants have also argued that 12 U.S.C.A. § 1823(e) does not apply to agreements which are made after the asset affected has been acquired by the bank. The statute contains no such exception, and this court cannot, by judicial fiat, create a class of cases to which the statute does not apply.") Compare the majority opinion of Judge Floyd R. Gibson ("We doubt that Congress intended that section 1823(e)(2)'s contemporaneousness requirement would defeat a valid accord and satisfaction entered into by the bank") with the concurring opinion of Judge John R. Gibson ("This interpretation may make accord and satisfaction inapplicable when the FDIC purchases a bank's assets, since parties can never reach an accord and sat-

21. See note 21 on page 140.

The rationale offered by the courts for this protection of the government banking agencies has traditionally focused on the nature of P & A transactions. It is essential that they be completed quickly, often overnight or over a weekend, in order to keep the doors of the institution's facilities open for business. Failure to do so, it is argued, would undercut public confidence in the banking system. Since the government must act quickly, it cannot be expected to interview the institution's officers and employees or search in a variety of places for miscellaneous side agreements that might bear on the status of outstanding loans. Instead, it is entitled to rely on what is found in the official loan files. In light of this rationale, it is perhaps strange, but nonetheless well established, that even the government's actual knowledge of a borrower's defense at the time it acquires the loan will not subject it to the defense.[22]

The reach of § 1823(e) and *D'Oench* are long. They can be raised not only by the government, but by any party who acquires assets from FDIC or RTC, including institutions that enter into purchase and assumption transactions and their successors.[23]

isfaction that compromises a debt at the same time they create an original debt obligation.... [W]hen the bank fails and must be taken over by the government as insurer of the bank's depositors, public concerns then arise.... The wisdom of the Act of Congress is an issue we do not consider.") in FDIC v. Manatt, 922 F.2d 486 (8th Cir.1991), certiorari denied ___ U.S. ___, 111 S.Ct. 2889, 115 L.Ed.2d 1054 (1991).

21. Langley v. FDIC, 484 U.S. 86, 108 S.Ct. 396, 98 L.Ed.2d 340 (1987) contains some oblique dictum on the point:

> A second purpose of § 1823(e) is implicit in its requirement that the "agreement" not merely be on file in the bank's records at the time of an examination, but also have been executed and become a bank record "contemporaneously" with the making of the note and have been approved by officially recorded action of the bank's board or loan committee. These latter requirements ensure mature consideration of unusual loan transactions by senior bank officials, and prevent fraudulent insertion of new terms, with the collusion of bank employees, when a bank appears headed for failure.

While the requirements of official approval and recording may serve the purpose of preventing fraud, it is hard to see how the "contemporaneously" requirement does so; loan restructuring agreements are extremely common and usually entirely legitimate. In any event, the quoted language is dictum, since the borrower's defense in *Langley* was based on alleged oral, unapproved, unrecorded misrepresentations by the lender's employees. There is thus far no discussion in any reported case of the possibility that the "contemporaneously" requirement might violate the Contract Clause.

22. See, e.g., Victor Hotel Corp. v. FCA Mortg. Corp., 928 F.2d 1077 (11th Cir.1991); Timberland Design, Inc. v. First Service Bank for Sav., 932 F.2d 46 (1st Cir.1991); Shuler v. RTC, 757 F.Supp. 761 (S.D.Miss. 1991); Northwest Land & Inv., Inc. v. New West Fed. Sav. & Loan Ass'n, 64 Wash. App. 938, 827 P.2d 334 (1992).

23. See, e.g., Bell & Murphy & Assoc. v. Interfirst Bank Gateway, 894 F.2d 750 (5th Cir.1990), certiorari denied 498 U.S. 895, 111 S.Ct. 244, 112 L.Ed.2d 203 (1990) (bridge bank is protected by *D'Oench*); New Maine Nat'l Bank v. Seydler, 765 F.Supp. 770 (D.Me.1991) (same); Webb v. Superior Court, 225 Cal.App.3d 990, 275 Cal.Rptr. 581 (1990) (same); Porras v. Petroplex Sav. Ass'n, 903 F.2d 379 (5th Cir. 1990) (private entity purchasing assets of failed institution from FSLIC is protected by D'Oench); Willow Tree Investments, Inc. v. Wagner, 453 N.W.2d 641 (Iowa 1990). Compare Cockrell v. Republic Mortg. Ins. Co., 817 S.W.2d 106 (Tex.App. 1991) (*D'Oench* does not apply to notes sold directly by one financial institution to another, notwithstanding financial assistance by FSLIC, where the notes never passed through FSLIC's hands).

Section 1823(e) applies both to *affirmative claims* that might be made against the government as a successor or receiver of the insolvent institution, and to *defenses* that a party might attempt to raise when sued by the government or its successors.[24] The sorts of claims barred include those based loan commitments,[25] fraudulent statements,[26] and various breaches of legal duty.[27] Typical defenses barred include fraud in the inducement,[28] failure of consideration,[29] breach of fiduciary duty or duty of good faith and fair dealing,[30] negligence,[31] breach of contract,[32] and waiver or estoppel.[33]

Notwithstanding the apparent comprehensiveness of § 1823(e)'s language, there is authority that certain claims and defenses can be raised without compliance with the statute. For example, while the cases are not entirely consistent, some of them hold that defenses based

---

24. See Sunchase Apartments v. Sunbelt Service Corp., 596 So.2d 119 (Fla.App. 1992).

25. See RTC v. Dubois, 771 F.Supp. 154 (M.D.La.1991) (commitment was entered into before and not contemporaneously with promissory notes; hence commitment was not binding on RTC, and notes were not subject to adjustment of interest as provided in commitment); FDIC v. Hamilton, 939 F.2d 1225 (5th Cir.1991) (commitment was based on "implied understanding," not on an unambiguous writing); Hall v. FDIC, 920 F.2d 334 (6th Cir. 1990), certiorari denied __ U.S. __, 111 S.Ct. 2852, 115 L.Ed.2d 1020 (1991) (collateral agreement that borrower would not have to supply all collateral required by the loan documents); FSLIC v. Murray, 853 F.2d 1251 (5th Cir.1988); FSLIC v. Two Rivers Assoc., 880 F.2d 1267 (11th Cir.1989) (alleged promise by S & L to fund construction of condominium project).

26. See Bohm v. Forum Resorts, Inc., 762 F.Supp. 705 (E.D.Mich.1991); Glen Johnson, Inc. v. RTC, 598 So.2d 81 (Fla. App.1990).

27. See Garrett v. Coastal Financial Mgmt. Co., 765 F.Supp. 351 (S.D.Tex.1990), reversed on other grounds 938 F.2d 591 (5th Cir.1991) (failure of lender to maintain insurance on security property); McCullough v. FDIC, 788 F.Supp. 626 (D.Mass. 1992), affirmed 987 F.2d 870 (1st Cir.1993) (breach of duty to inform investors in a condominium project of a notice of contamination issued by a state environmental agency); Newton v. Uniwest Financial Corp., 967 F.2d 340 (9th Cir.1992) (tying agreement violating federal anti-tying statutes).

28. Armstrong v. RTC, 234 Ill.App.3d 162, 175 Ill.Dec. 195, 599 N.E.2d 1209 (1992); FDIC v. Virginia Crossings Partnership, 909 F.2d 306 (8th Cir.1990); FDIC v. Bertling, 751 F.Supp.1235 (E.D.Tex. 1990); FSLIC v. Locke, 718 F.Supp. 573 (W.D.Tex.1989); RTC v. Maldonado, 595 So.2d 774 (La.App.1992).

29. FDIC v. McCullough, 911 F.2d 593 (11th Cir.1990); FDIC v. Sarvis, 697 F.Supp. 1161 (D.Colo.1988).

30. FSLIC v. T.F. Stone–Liberty Land Associates, 787 S.W.2d 475 (Tex.App.1990) (breach of fiduciary duty); Pelican Homestead & Sav. Ass'n v. Campbell, 588 So.2d 179 (La.App.1991) (breach of duty of fair dealing); FDIC v. Texas Country Living, Inc., 756 F.Supp. 984 (E.D.Tex.1990) (same).

31. But see New Connecticut Bank v. Stadium Management Corp., 132 B.R. 205 (D.Mass.1991) (tort claim of borrower based on lender's negligent impairment of collateral was not barred by *D'Oench*, since no secret agreement was involved).

32. See Desmond v. FDIC, 798 F.Supp. 829 (D.Mass.1992) (institution's oral agreement to accept less than face amount of loan, and to refrain from seizing collateral of debtor, not binding on FDIC); Raymond L. Sabbag, Inc. v. FDIC, 1991 WL 146876 (not reported in F.Supp.) (construction subcontractor barred by *D'Oench* from recovery against FDIC for alleged breach of construction loan agreement by insolvent savings association).

33. See Abrams v. FDIC, 944 F.2d 307 (6th Cir.1991) (bank president's oral promise to borrower not to collect deficiency was not binding on FDIC); New Maine Nat'l Bank v. Seydler, 765 F.Supp. 770 (D.Me.1991) (workout and forbearance agreement not binding on bridge bank created by FDIC).

on tort, rather than on contract or agreement, can be raised.[34] Fraud in the factum (in which the borrower is deceived about the nature of the transaction or the documents) is a viable defense.[35] There is also limited authority that the borrower can raise defenses if he or she was "completely innocent" of any wrongdoing or negligence in the transaction that formed the basis of the defense, and did nothing to contribute to misleading the government.[36] Some cases, although of doubtful validity, hold that if the lender's claim against a private party has *already* been barred by the lender's action before the government takes over as receiver, *D'Oench* and § 1823(e) are inapplicable.[37] Finally,

---

34. See, e.g., RTC v. Liberty Homes, Inc., 941 F.2d 1213 (10th Cir.1991) (unpublished opinion; text available on Westlaw) (defenses based on institution's tortious interference with borrower's contractual relations was not barred by *D'Oench*); New Connecticut Bank v. Stadium Management Corp., 132 B.R. 205 (D.Mass.1991) (tort claim for lender's negligent impairment of collateral permitted).

35. See Patterson v. FDIC, 918 F.2d 540 (5th Cir.1990) (court found that no such fraud was actually proved); FSLIC v. Gordy, 928 F.2d 1558 (11th Cir.1991) (same). See also Brogdon v. Exterior Design, 781 F.Supp. 1396 (W.D.Ark.1992) (violation of state "doing business" law made note and mortgage void *ab initio*, and such defense could be raised against RTC; analogous to fraud in the factum). But see FDIC v. McClanahan, 795 F.2d 512 (5th Cir.1986) (where borrower signs note in blank and bank officer fills it in without authorization, *D'Oench* applies); FDIC v. Caporale, 931 F.2d 1 (1st Cir.1991) (same).

Fraud in the inducement arguably can be raised if the fraud was committed by someone other than the insolvent financial institution, in a transaction in which it was not involved. See Park Tuscon Investors Ltd. Partnership v. Ali, 770 F.Supp. 531 (D.Ariz.1991) (where investors were induced by fraud to give notes to limited partnerships, and partnerships later assigned the notes to a financial institution, § 1823(e) and *D'Oench* do not bar the investors from raising the defense of fraud). Contra, see Adams v. Madison Realty & Devel., Inc., 937 F.2d 845 (3d Cir.1991) (where institution acquired notes on secondary market, RTC can enforce them despite makers' claims of fraud in the inducement in the original note transactions).

Economic duress may arguably be raised against the government, although the authorities are mixed. See Desmond v. FDIC, 798 F.Supp. 829 (D.Mass.1992) (borrower permitted to raise the claim that the institution asserted at the last minute that borrower's attorney had a conflict of interest, as a way of pressuring borrower to sign loan agreement in haste and without counsel). Cf. Newton v. Uniwest Financial Corp., 967 F.2d 340 (9th Cir.1992); FDIC v. Meyer, 755 F.Supp. 10 (D.D.C.1991) (economic duress is a "personal" defense barred by § 1823(e)); FDIC v. Gettysburg, 760 F.Supp. 115 (S.D.Tex.1990), affirmed without opinion, Unitedbank v. Gettysburg Corp., 952 F.2d 400 (5th Cir.1992) (same). Economic duress must be shown by more than mere hard bargaining or the lender's taking advantage of the borrower's financial straits; it must involve wrongful or illegal actions by the lender. See RTC v. Ruggiero, 756 F.Supp. 1092 (N.D.Ill.1991).

36. See FDIC v. Meo, 505 F.2d 790 (9th Cir.1974); In re C.P.C. Development Co. No. 5, 113 B.R. 637 (Bankr.Cal.1990); Agri Export Cooperative v. Universal Sav. Ass'n, 767 F.Supp. 824 (S.D.Tex.1991); Reisig v. RTC, 806 P.2d 397 (Colo.App. 1991). The vitality of this exception outside the Ninth Circuit is doubtful. See FDIC v. Municipality of Ponce, 904 F.2d 740 (1st Cir.1990) and Northwest Land & Inv., Inc. v. New West Fed. Sav. & Loan Ass'n, 64 Wash.App. 938, 827 P.2d 334 (1992), both rejecting the "completely innocent" exception.

D'Oench does not bar the raising of defenses based on the actual agreement that FDIC/RTC seeks to enforce affirmatively. First Texas Sav. Ass'n v. Comprop Invest. Properties Ltd., 752 F.Supp. 1568 (M.D.Fla.1990); Howell v. Continental Credit Corp., 655 F.2d 743 (7th Cir.1981); Riverside Park Realty Co. v. FDIC, 465 F.Supp. 305 (M.D.Tenn.1978).

37. See FDIC v. Percival, 752 F.Supp. 313 (D.Neb.1990) (where lender failed to notify guarantor before selling collateral at auction, lender's claim against guarantor was barred by state law; hence, FDIC acquired nothing when it later became receiver of lender). This theory is much stronger if the lender's claim has been

§ 11.7   GOVERNMENT INTERVENTION   143

only defenses based on transactions with the insolvent institution prior to its government takeover are barred; post-receivership conduct by the institution in receivership, or other conduct of the government agency, may be raised by a private litigant without regard to *D'Oench* or § 1823(e).[38]

The operation of the D'Oench doctrine and § 1823 are perhaps difficult to appreciate in the abstract; an example may help. In FDIC v. McClanahan,[39] a farmer applied for a loan from the bank to buy a tractor. At the request of the loan officer, the farmer signed a blank note form. Later the loan officer told the farmer that the loan application had been rejected by the bank, and the farmer obtained financing elsewhere. The loan officer filled in the note form, filed it with the bank, caused it to disburse $62,500 in purported loan proceeds, and pocketed the money. The bank failed and FDIC sued the farmer to collect the note. Despite the farmer's attempt to raise such defenses as fraud in the inducement and failure of consideration, the court held him liable, calling his conduct in signing the blank note "reckless."

Perhaps even more shocking is **FDIC v. Kasal**.[40] It seems obvious that a debtor who has actually made a payment on a debt to an insolvent institution should be credited with that payment in litigation with the federal banking agencies. This has been held to follow even if the institution's records do not reflect the payment.[41] But in *Kasal* certain accommodation makers, relatives of the borrower, made payments to the president of the bank, who simply embezzled the funds and never deposited them in the bank. The court treated the payments as "unwritten side agreements" within the meaning of *D'Oench*, and held that the FDIC was required to give the debtor no credit for them.

barred by a state court judgment prior to the receivership; see First RepublicBank Fort Worth v. Norglass, 751 F.Supp. 1224 (N.D.Tex.1990), affirmed 958 F.2d 117 (5th Cir. 1992). See also RTC v. 1601 Partners, Ltd., 796 F.Supp. 238 (N.D.Tex.1992) (where note was originally made to a private payee, and that payee released the makers from personal liability on it before transferring to the financial institution, *D'Oench* does not apply).

On the other hand, *D'Oench* and § 1823(e) apply to cases in which a party's claim or defense against an insolvent financial institution is based on the acts of a *subsidiary* of the institution. See, e.g., Alexandria Assoc. v. Mitchell Co., 800 F.Supp. 1412 (S.D.Miss.1992); Oliver v. RTC, 955 F.2d 583 (8th Cir.1992); Victor Hotel Corp. v. FCA Mortg. Corp., 928 F.2d 1077 (11th Cir.1991); Garrett v. Coastal Financial Mgmt. Co., 765 F.Supp. 351 (S.D.Tex. 1990), reversed on other grounds 938 F.2d 591 (5th Cir.1991); FSLIC v. T.F. Stone—Liberty Land Assoc., 787 S.W.2d 475 (Tex.App.1990).

38. See FDIC v. Byrne, 736 F.Supp. 727 (N.D.Tex.1990); FDIC v. Harrison, 735 F.2d 408 (11th Cir.1984). However, claims against the government may be subject to the Federal Tort Claims Act, which imposes formidable barriers to affirmative recovery. See Rauscher Pierce Refsnes, Inc. v. FDIC, 789 F.2d 313 (5th Cir.1986).

39. 795 F.Supp. 512 (5th Cir.1986). See also FSLIC v. Murray, 853 F.2d 1251 (5th Cir.1988) (borrower who signs note in blank cannot assert fraud against FSLIC).

40. 913 F.2d 487 (8th Cir.1990), certiorari denied 498 U.S. 1119, 111 S.Ct. 1072, 112 L.Ed.2d 1178 (1991).

41. See Breaux Bridge Bank & Trust Co. v. Simon, 570 So.2d 156 (La.App.1990), writ denied 575 So.2d 375 (La.1991) (payment does *not* tend to "defeat or diminish" FDIC's interest, and hence is not governed by § 1823(e)).

There was a vigorous dissent.[42]

As these cases illustrate, the federal courts have gone very far in protecting the banking agencies and their successors, broadly reading § 1823(e) and expanding the scope of *D'Oench* make loans collectible. It is arguable that they have gone too far, imposing heavy costs on relatively innocent individual borrowers in order to conserve the public fisc. From the viewpoint of counsel representing borrowers, one message stands out plainly: when the terms of a loan are modified in any way, it is essential that the agreement be written, properly approved by the institution, and recorded in its official files.

Federal Holder–in–Due–Course Status

Many (but not all) federal courts have held, as a matter of federal common law, that the federal banking agencies and their transferees who acquire negotiable promissory notes are entitled to holder-in-due-course status under the Uniform Commercial Code, despite the fact that they acquire the notes in a bulk transaction and arguably pay no value for them. The details of this concept have been discussed earlier in this volume.[43]

The Consent and Redemption Statutes and the Policy of FDIC and RTC

Both FDIC and RTC, when they hold title to or mortgages on real estate, are protected by two federal statutes that impose significant burdens on the holders of other interests in the real estate. The first, generally termed the Consent Statute,[44] provides:

---

42. Cf. FDIC v. Sather, 488 N.W.2d 260 (Minn.1992), in which the payments made to the crooked bank officer were reflected in the records of the bank; hence, *D'Oench* and § 1823(e) were inapplicable, and the party making the payments was permitted to raise them as a defense.

43. See infra § 5.29 at notes 28–40. See FDIC v. Wood, 758 F.2d 156 (6th Cir. 1985), cert. denied 474 U.S. 944, 106 S.Ct. 308, 88 L.Ed.2d 286 (1985); Gunter v. Hutcheson, 674 F.2d 862 (11th Cir.1982); FDIC v. Caledonia Inv. Corp., 725 F.Supp. 90 (D.P.R. 1989). Compare In re Woodstone Ltd. Partnership, 133 B.R. 678 (Bkrtcy.N.Y.1991), reversed on the basis of the *D'Oench* doctrine, 149 B.R. 294 (E.D.N.Y.1993), refusing to recognize the federal HDC doctrine. Normally the federal banking agencies would not qualify for HDC status, since they acquire the institution's notes and other assets by bulk transfer rather than in the ordinary course of business. However, the federal HDC doctrine applies irrespective of the bulk nature of the transfer. See FSLIC v. Cribbs, 918 F.2d 557 (5th Cir.1990); FSLIC v. Murray, 853 F.2d 1251 (5th Cir.1988).

The federal HDC doctrine and the *D'Oench* doctrine coexist, and while many cases could readily be resolved identically under both approaches, either alone may be sufficient to bar a defense to a promissory note or other instrument. See, e.g., RTC v. Associated Investment Group, 792 F.Supp. 796 (S.D.Fla.1991).

44. 12 U.S.C.A. § 1825(b)(2). Although the consent statute appears to bar only involuntary liens (e.g., property tax liens, mechanics' liens, etc.) that attach *after* the government acquires the property, FDIC has argued vigorously that *pre-acquisition* involuntary liens are extinguished when it acquires the property. Most courts have rejected this argument; see Irving Independent School Dist. v. Packard Properties, Ltd., 762 F.Supp. 699 (N.D.Tex.1991), affirmed 970 F.2d 58 (5th Cir. 1992); Carrollton–Farmers Branch Independent School Dist. v. FDIC, 776 F.Supp. 1180 (N.D.Tex.1991). But see FDIC v. Shain, Schaffer & Rafanello, 1991 WL 84469 (D.N.J.1991, not reported in F.Supp.), affirmed on other grounds 944 F.2d 129 (3d Cir.1991), in which the court in dictum agreed with FDIC's position.

> No property of the Corporation shall be subject to levy, attachment, garnishment, foreclosure or sale without the consent of the Corporation, nor shall any involuntary lien attach to the property of the Corporation.

Further problems are raised by the Redemption Statute,[15] which provides:

> A sale to satisfy a lien inferior to one of the United States shall be made subject to and without disturbing the lien of the United States, unless the United States consents ... and (2) the United States shall have one year from the date of sale within which to redeem.

These statutes proved problematic for the mortgage lending and title insurance industries. The Consent Statute raises difficulties when the government holds title to real estate or a junior lien on it, since foreclosure against the government is conditioned on its consent. By contrast, the Redemption Statute becomes an issue when the government holds a first lien on real estate, and the private holder of a junior lien wishes to foreclose; the one-year redemption period may effectively chill bidding at the foreclosure sale, and potentially diminishes the property's value even if the junior lienor buys at the sale, since it is impractical to improve or further dispose of the property until the redemption period has expired.[46] This may come as a particular shock to junior lienholders in states where there is no statutory redemption.

Obviously FDIC and RTC, in acquiring assets from insolvent lending institutions, may find themselves in any one of these positions: as holder of a senior lien, a junior lien, or title to the real estate. When they do so, the first question is how private parties can discover that the government has entered on the scene. Mortgage assignments are often unrecorded, so that even though it is clear from the records that a lien exists, it will not be obvious that the government has acquired it; nothing compels FDIC or RTC to record an assignment when a receivership takes effect or a purchase and assumption transaction is consummated.

Moreover, even if the private lender detects the government's presence and seeks its consent to foreclosure or its waiver of redemption rights, there may be a significant delay before the government's decision is made and communicated. The property may suffer addition-

---

45. 28 U.S.C.A. § 2410(c). FDIC's right to redeem under the statute has been repeatedly upheld; see FDIC v. Bennett, 898 F.2d 477 (5th Cir.1990); FDIC v. Thompson, 753 F.Supp. 190 (W.D.La.1989). But see Cooley v. Fredinburg, 114 Or.App. 532, 836 P.2d 162 (1992), in which FDIC held a junior lien and failed to obtain a judgment in the senior lender's foreclosure action. The senior mortgagor subsequently redeemed under Oregon law, which would have had the effect of reviving FDIC's junior lien if FDIC had obtained a judgment. Since the revived lien would have given FDIC a state law right to redeem (which would have been the equivalent of the federal statutory right of redemption), the court held that FDIC's failure to take advantage of state law barred it from claiming the federal redemption right.

46. See infra § 8.4.

al deterioration and interest and costs may continue to accrue in the interim.

In 1992, in an attempt to alleviate some of the concerns described above, both RTC and FDIC issued policy statements detailing the manner in which they expected to assert their rights under the Consent and Redemption Statutes.[47] These statements apply whether the agencies are holding interests in property as conservators, receivers, or in their corporate capacities. In their statements, both agencies give a blanket consent to foreclosure of senior mortgages and other voluntary liens. Hence, private lenders no longer need seek specific consent to a foreclosure. However, the agencies retain whatever rights are granted to titleholders and junior lienholders under state law or under the terms of the mortgage being foreclosed, such as rights to notice of the sale, state statutory redemption, and the like. RTC's policy statement provides that, where it holds *title* (as distinct from a junior lien) on real estate, its blanket consent to foreclosure depends on its receiving *mailed notice* of the individual foreclosure. Details of the notice procedure are set out. FDIC did not include this requirement in its policy statement, and presumably felt safe in relying on state law foreclosure notice requirements.

If the senior lien is "involuntary," and if the agency's junior interest is of record, no blanket consent is given, and the lienor must obtain specific consent prior to foreclosing. "Involuntary" liens include mechanics liens, judgment liens, property tax liens, etc. A lien is "of record" if the local land records show that the government agency holds the lien, or if they show that the lien is held by a financial institution, and the agency has published in the Federal Register a notice that it has been appointed receiver for that institution. For purposes of determining whether the agency's lien is "of record," the relevant date is the date on which all persons who are entitled to notice under local law have been given notice of the foreclosure action, in the case of judicial foreclosure, or the foreclosure sale, in the case of power-of-sale foreclosure.

Finally, both agencies' policy statements provide that, if the guidelines described above regarding consent are complied with, they will waive their rights under the Redemption Statute.

47. See 57 Fed.Reg. 29491 (July 2, 1992) (FDIC); 57 Fed.Reg. 19651 (May 7, 1992) (RTC).

§§ 11.8–12.0 are reserved for supplementary material.

Chapter 12

FINANCING REAL ESTATE CONSTRUCTION

Table of Sections

Sec.
12.1 Construction Lending—An Overview.
12.2 Construction Contracts and Bonds.
12.3 Mortgage Loan Commitments.
12.4 Mechanics' Liens.
12.5 ____ Constitutionality.
12.6 The Stop Notice and the Equitable Lien.
12.7 Future Advances.
12.8 Dragnet Clauses.
12.9 Subordination Agreements.
12.10 Improper Disbursement of Loan Proceeds.
12.11 Lender Liability for Construction Defects or Other Wrongful Acts of Contractors.

§ 12.1 Construction Lending—An Overview

The purpose of a construction loan is to provide funds with which the owner of a parcel of land can construct improvements upon it.[1] The construction loan is superficially similar to a long-term mortgage loan; the borrower's obligation to repay will be represented by a promissory note or similar instrument, and will be secured by a

---

§ 12.1

1. See generally U.S. League of Sav. Associations, Constr. Lending Guide; Livingston, Current Business Approaches—Commercial Construction Lending, 13 Real Prop.Prob. & Tr.J. 791 (1978); Kesler, Construction Lending Risks & Returns, Mortgage Banking, Jan.1989, at 62; Storke & Sears, Subdivision Financing, 28 Rocky Mt. L.Rev. 549 (1956); Albright, Processing the Construction Mortgage, 3 Real Est.Rev. 72 (No. 3, Fall 1973); Gallaher, Protecting the Construction Loan, 5 Real Est.Rev. 114 (No. 1, Spring 1975); Tockarshewsky, Reducing the Risks in Construction Lending, 7 Real Est.Rev. 59 (No. 1, Spring 1977); Hall, How to Build Lender Protection into Construction Loan Agreements, 6 Real Est. L.J. 21 (1977).

mortgage, deed of trust, or comparable document. In addition, the lender and borrower will usually enter into a construction loan agreement, spelling out the obligations of each with regard to the construction process. The borrower (who is usually the owner of the land on which the project will be built) may perform the construction personally, or may employ a separate general contractor with whom the borrower enters into a construction contract. The discussion below will refer to the borrower as a "developer," and will assume that no separate general contractor is involved unless specifically mentioned. Most of this chapter is equally applicable to construction projects that will be sold upon completion (such as detached-house subdivisions) and to projects that the developer will retain upon completion, either for personal use (such as an individual's own home or a business warehouse or office) or for rental purposes (such as the usual apartment building). Where distinctions among these types of projects are important, they will be noted.

Construction lending is far more critical and exacting, and presents far greater risks to the mortgagee, than does lending on completed structures. This is so because the value of the real estate for security purposes is entirely dependent upon the happening of a future event: the completion of the building or project as agreed by the parties. If the construction is not completed by the mortgagor, or is completed late or defectively, or if the project's value upon completion is less than anticipated, the construction lender may find itself in the unhappy position of being inadequately secured. Such a situation is viewed even more seriously by junior lienors, such as the vendor from whom the present owner purchased the land (and who has not yet been fully paid), or claimants under mechanics and materialmen's liens. These parties are frequently present in construction lending situations, and their roles will be discussed presently. Because of their junior security position, their risk of being wiped out by the mortgagor's failure to complete the project as agreed, or the project's lack of value despite its completed status, is even more serious than that of the construction lender.

A critical concern of every construction lender (and of knowledgeable junior lienors as well) is that the funds disbursed by the lender actually find their way into labor and materials used in the project. To some extent this is a matter for negotiation between the borrower and lender; in addition to covering the "hard costs," such as materials and direct labor, the construction lender may be willing to cover certain "soft costs" such as legal and accounting services directly related to the project, insurance, real estate taxes, and possibly even interest on the construction loan itself, as well as charges made by permanent lenders for their commitments. Other negotiable points include whether the construction loan will cover any portion of the land acquisition or site development costs, such as the extension of utility lines, roads and streets, storm and sanitary sewers, and the like to the project. The most conservative position, taken by many construction lenders, is to insist that all land acquisition, site development, and "soft" costs be covered by the developer through cash outlays or other financing separate from (and junior to) the construction loan. In some cases the lender is required by law to limit its construction loans to "hard" construction costs.[2]

The construction lender will be particularly concerned that no construction loan funds be diverted to other uses. Such diversions occur often, and can obviously be devastating to the construction lender, since they greatly increase the probability that the property's security value will be less than the indebtedness it secures. Diversion of funds by a developer does not always imply outright dishonesty. In some cases, the developer may have other projects under construction which are in serious trouble, and he or she may be tempted to "rob" one project in order to "bail out" another. Diversion of funds is almost always a sign of serious trouble to the construction lender, and wise lenders take careful precautions to insure that it does not occur.

Institutional Construction Lenders

Construction lending cannot be successfully handled by remote control. The lender must be intimately familiar with local circumstances and practices, and must be represented by an on-site inspector. In addition, construction loans tend to be of relatively short duration, since the construction periods for most types of real estate projects are measured in months or small numbers of years. Finally, construction lending tends to be risky but profitable, with fees and interest rates significantly higher than are normally demanded on long-term loans on completed real estate developments. Given these constraints, it is not surprising that the two principal types of local lending institutions, commercial banks and savings and loan associations, together account for nearly 90% of all construction lending in the United States.[3] Commercial banks make more than half of all construction loans, displaying some preference for loans on commercial property, while savings and loan associations have a somewhat heavier activity in the residential construction area. The remaining construction lending is attributable largely to real estate investment trusts, although these entities have often suffered significant losses on such loans, largely as a consequence of poor underwriting and inspection.[4]

National banks. The authority of national banks to make real estate construction loans is derived from Section 24 of the Federal

2. See, e.g., Sharp Lumber Co. v. Manus Homes, Inc., 189 N.E.2d 447, 90 O.L.A. 421 (Ohio App.1961), holding a construction loan valid despite its noncompliance with an applicable regulation limiting such loans to construction costs.

3. See U.S. Dep't of Commerce, Statistical Abstract of the United States 776 (1992) (commercial banks held 58% of all construction loans in 1991; savings and loan associations held 29%.)

4. See, e.g., Stevenson, Lessons from the Mortgage Trust Experience, 6 Real Est. Rev. 72 (No. 3, Fall 1976).

Reserve Act.[5] For many years this section imposed rather rigid limitations on loan-to-value ratios, amortization, and other features of real estate loans, but it was amended by the Garn–St. Germain Depository Institutions Act of 1982[6] to provide that such loans are subject only to whatever regulatory limitations may be imposed by the Comptroller of the Currency; the Comptroller, in turn, removed all such regulatory requirements in 1983.[7] However, in a reaction to increased concern about lending risk for all institutional lenders, the four principal federal regulatory agencies (the Comptroller, the Federal Reserve Board, FDIC, and OTS) issued in 1992 a new set of "Interagency Guidelines for Real Estate Lending Policies,[8] the principal function of which was to establish maximum loan-to-value ratios for virtually all banks and savings associations nationwide. For construction loans, the applicable ratios are 85% for one-to-four-family homes and 80% for all other types of property.

Federal savings and loan associations. The regulations of the Office of Thrift Supervision govern construction lending by federal savings and loan associations. They have been substantially liberalized in recent years, and impose maximum terms for such loans ranging from two years for a single-family dwelling to six years for nonresidential buildings and eight years for land development loans.[9] Loan-to-value ratios are governed by the Interagency Guidelines mentioned above.[10]

State-chartered lenders. Each state regulates the lending powers of state-chartered banks and savings and loan associations, as well as mutual savings banks in those states in which they are authorized. The construction lending powers of these institutions vary considerably from one jurisdiction to another, but for those whose deposits are insured by FDIC, the same Interagency Guidelines just mentioned impose a ceiling; state regulations may set lower limits.

FHA and VA. Neither the Federal Housing Administration (FHA) nor the Veterans Administration (VA) normally insures or guarantees construction loans to developers of single-family homes. However, between 1965 and 1989, under Title X of the National Housing Act,[11] FHA had authority to insure land development loans to finance the installation of such improvements as water and sewer systems, other utilities, street paving, and facilities for public or common use by the residents of the development. Title X could not be used to finance the construction of dwelling units; developers had to obtain separate con-

---

5. 12 U.S.C.A. § 371. For the former regulations under this section, see 12 CFR 7.2000 et seq.

6. Pub.L. No. 97–320, § 403.

7. See 48 Fed.Reg. 40698 (Sept. 30, 1983), repealing 12 CFR 7.2000–7.2700 and adopting 12 CFR Part 34.

8. 57 Fed.Reg. 62890 (Dec. 31, 1992).

9. 12 CFR 545.36.

10. Supra note 8.

11. 12 U.S.C.A. § 1749aa et seq. See 24 CFR Part 205.

struction loans for that purpose, and it was usually necessary to release lots from the Title X mortgage as they were placed within the coverage of the construction loan, since most construction lenders require that their loans be secured by first liens. Title X was never highly popular; it averaged only 5 loans per year, representing a tiny fraction of all subdivisions developed.[12] In 1989 Congress terminated the program.[13] Its loss went virtually unnoticed.

FHA also insures construction loan mortgages on multi-family housing projects under many of its programs.[14] In such cases, a single set of mortgage documents is frequently used for both the construction and permanent loan periods. In FHA's terminology, the agency's activity during the construction period is known as "insurance of advances." Generally, developers (or "sponsors," as they are called by FHA) who wish the advantages of permanent financing under one of the FHA multi-family programs may elect insurance of advances or not, as they choose.

Although FHA does not insure construction loans on housing subdivisions that are to be owner-occupied, the agency nonetheless has historically been heavily involved in the construction of such projects. This occurred because, under applicable statutes, a house is eligible for a permanent FHA-insured loan with the highest available loan-to-value ratio only if it was "approved for mortgage insurance prior to the beginning of construction," unless it is covered by a HUD-approved warranty plan or is more than one year old.[15] Thus, if a builder wishes the advantage of offering customers high-ratio FHA financing, he or she must obtain advance approval of the development, with its attendant paperwork (which is substantial) and FHA inspections during construction. The advent of 95% privately-insured conventional permanent financing made FHA a less attractive approach to many developers,[16] but some are still willing to seek the FHA's "conditional commitment" and concomitant involvement. Over time FHA has steadily reduced its degree of supervision of subdivision house construction, delegating increasing authority to local lenders and local governments.[17] In 1992 it proposed [18] to virtually eliminate its prior review with respect to loans originated under the "direct endorsement" pro-

12. See HUD commentary on termination of Title X program, 55 Fed.Reg. 18873 (1990).

13. § 133, Housing and Urban Development Reform Act of 1989, Pub.L.No. 101–235; 24 CFR 205.2.

14. These include Section 207 (unsubsidized rental projects); Section 213 (cooperative housing projects); Section 221(d)(2) and 221(d)(4) (moderate-income rental projects); and Section 236 (subsidized rental projects for lower-income families). The numbers refer to sections of the National Housing Act.

15. National Housing Act § 203(b)(2), 12 U.S.C.A. § 1709(b)(2).

16. For example, in 1991 FHA and VA home loans combined were only about 11% of all home loans originated in the U.S. See Database, Secondary Mortgage Markets, Spring/Summer 1992.

17. See, e.g., 50 Fed.Reg. 20096 (1985), codified in 24 CFR 203.12. To avoid duplication, FHA also refrains from subdivision review in all cases in which VA or FmHA has reviewed the same subdivision.

18. See 57 Fed.Reg. 13592 (1992).

gram,[19] which accounts for the great majority of FHA loans.

The Farmers Home Administration (FmHA), a division of the U.S. Department of Agriculture, operates several programs to finance both single-family and multi-family housing in rural areas.[20] FmHA guarantees loans made by other institutional lenders, and also makes some direct loans. FmHA will provide necessary construction financing for developers, although it strongly prefers that construction loans be made by other institutions.[21]

Underwriting Construction Loans

From the mortgagee's point of view, successful construction lending depends on the interplay of several activities, including thorough underwriting of the proposed loan, inspection during the construction period, and the use of careful controls to insure that disbursed funds are not diverted from the construction project. "Underwriting" means a careful evaluation of all of the factors that could result in a risk of loss to the construction lender. Not all of these factors are legal in nature, although many have legal ramifications. Underwriting a construction project is complex,[22] and the material given here should be taken only as a brief summary of the items with which the lender will be concerned.

The proposed borrower's reputation, experience, credit rating, and capitalization are all important to the lender. Success in previous smaller projects is usually a prerequisite to obtaining financing for a major enterprise. If the borrower is a limited partnership or closely-held corporation, its partners or shareholders will usually be asked to take personal liability for the debt.[23] Most lenders will require that the borrower put a substantial amount of cash—in many cases on the order of ten percent of the project's construction cost—rather than borrowing the entire amount. This cash investment requirement may be a result of the regulations applicable to the particular lender, or it may derive from the lender's internal policies; in either event, the assetless developer or one whose assets are illiquid (such as other land holdings) does not present an attractive risk.

The marketability of the project is also critical. If the completed structures will be sold or rented, the lender needs some assurance that they will be in demand. A careful market survey will usually be required for a large project.[24] In the case of a project that can be leased

---

19. See supra § 11.2 notes 62–63; proposed regulations, 56 Fed.Reg. 29202 (1991).

20. The principal programs are Section 502 (rural home loans) and Section 515 (rural rental project loans) of the Housing Act of 1949, 42 U.S.C.A. §§ 1472, 1485.

21. 7 CFR 1822.7(g), 1822.94(a).

22. For an excellent description of underwriting gone awry, see Kesler, Construction Lending Risks and Returns, Mortgage Banking, Jan.1989, at 62.

23. See Cook, Guaranties in Construction Loans, Probate & Property, Jan. 1991, at 6; Branning v. Morgan Guar. Trust Co., 739 F.Supp. 1056 (D.S.C.1990).

24. See White, How to Plan and Build a Major Office Building, 10 Real Est.Rev. 87 (No. 1, 1980); Siegelaub & Meistrich, How the Professional Shopping Center De-

to an identifiable business tenant prior to construction (as is often the case with large store space in shopping centers), the lender will usually wish to verify the tenant's credit worthiness.

The architectural and engineering design and the soil tests for the project will be carefully reviewed by the construction lender to make sure that they are technically sound, are in compliance with local codes, and will result in a marketable project. The lender will perform an appraisal of the project prior to granting the construction loan, and will carefully analyze the developer's proposed budget and schedule of costs to determine that the project can be completed with the available funds. The lender will also give close scrutiny to the developer's proposed timing and completion date.

A variety of legal matters will be of direct interest to the construction lender, including the quality of the developer's title and compliance with local zoning and building codes, environmental regulations, and all other local, state, and federal laws which might bear on the construction. The lender will usually require a survey and a plot plan to verify that the property's location and size are as represented by the developer and that the project will comply with any applicable set-back lines.

Finally, the lender will wish to review other documents associated with the project, including the construction contract if a separate general contractor is being used, the lease forms if the project is to be rented after completion, the forms of any bonds required, and the permanent loan commitment if the construction lender is not also to carry the permanent financing.

Of course, not all construction lenders are as uniformly careful and deliberate as the foregoing list suggests. Some are willing to take underwriting shortcuts when dealing with developers with whom they have had prior good experience. But failure to consider any of these details increases the potential risk.

Documentation

When the underwriting process has been completed and the construction lender has determined to make the loan, it will usually execute, with the developer, three basic documents: a promissory note or bond, a construction loan mortgage or deed of trust, and a construction loan agreement. This agreement [25] will generally incorporate by reference the entire plans and specifications for the project, will contain a budget to which the developer agrees to adhere, and will fix a

veloper Obtains a Mortgage, 9 Real Est. Rev. 50 (No. 1, 1979).

25. An excellent example is reprinted in § 15.2. See J. Krasnowiecki, Housing and Urban Development Cases and Materials 30, 82 (1969). See also Burger, Negotiating Construction Loan Agreements: Selected Issues, 53 Legal Bull. 202 (Mar. 1987); Nellis, A Construction Loan Agreement, 1 Prac.Real Est.Law. 65 (No.4, July 1985); ALI–ABA, Modern Real Estate Transactions 284 (5th ed. 1984) and subsequent editions of that workbook; Florida Bar, I. Florida Real Property Practice § 17.56 (1965); Calif.Cont.Ed. of Bar, California Land Security and Development § 30.29 (1960).

completion date for the project.[26] It will define the specific "hard" and "soft" costs the loan will cover, and will determine the extent to which land acquisition and development costs (grading, site preparation, utilities, streets, and the like), as distinct from direct construction, are to be funded by the loan.[27] It will explain the method of disbursing funds as construction progresses; events that constitute a default on the part of the borrower will be set forth in detail, and the agreement will specify the lender's remedies for such defaults. The developer's responsibility for such matters as bonds, insurance, and permits from government agencies will be spelled out in detail. The lender's draw inspector may be identified and his or her right of access to the project assured.

The agreement will usually create a construction loan account out of which funds will be disbursed as construction moves forward;[28] the developer may also be required to deposit an agreed amount of his or her own cash in this account, as discussed above. From the lender's viewpoint, it is essential that the account, including the loan amount plus the developer's deposit, contain sufficient funds at the commencement of construction to complete the project, and that the account remain "in balance"—that this sufficiency continue throughout the construction period. The agreement may contain language requiring the borrower to deposit additional funds at any time if the account becomes inadequate to complete construction.[29] The account itself will usually be assigned to the lender as additional security for the loan.

In a subdivision development or a condominium, the lender may take a separate construction loan mortgage on each lot, or may take a blanket mortgage on the entire project. The latter is obviously simpler in terms of initial documentation, but if it is employed, it is necessary to include a "partial release" clause in the mortgage to permit the developer to sell individual houses free of the construction loan. Such clauses ordinarily require the lender to release the lot only upon the receipt of somewhat more than a pro-rata payment on the loan; in this way the lender tries to build up its "equity cushion" as sales progress.

---

26. See Sharp v. Machry, 488 So.2d 133 (Fla.App.1986) (loan was to mature "one year from the date of the first construction draw," but construction never occurred); American National Bank v. Norris, 368 So.2d 897 (Fla.App.1979), certiorari denied 378 So.2d 342 (1979) (time was not of the essence of construction loan agreement).

27. During the 1980s many institutional lenders began making land acquisition, development, and construction (ADC) loans, as distinct from "pure" construction loans. These loans proved highly risky, and by the end of the decade many lenders ceased making them. See Berger, Left, Lichterman, Opelka & Pfeiler, Acquisition, Development and Construction Lending: A Transactional Approach, 53 Legal Bull. 99 (Mar.1987); Panel Discussion, 53 Legal Bull. 153 (Mar.1987); Lack of ADC Funding Foremost Topic for Homebuilders, Real Estate Finance Today, Jan. 26, 1990, at 8.

28. Lenders sometimes attempt to charge interest on the funds they have placed in the account, including the portion not yet disbursed. This can raise serious usury issues; see Hoffman v. Key Federal Savings & Loan Association, 286 Md. 28, 416 A.2d 1265 (1979).

29. For cases in which the developer was held in default on the construction loan for failure to keep the account in balance, see, e.g., Quail Ridge Assoc. v. Chemical Bank, 185 A.D.2d 522, 586 N.Y.S.2d 155 (1992); Jackson County Fed. Sav. & Loan Ass'n v. Urban Planning, Inc., 95 Or.App. 598, 771 P.2d 629 (1989), review denied 308 Or. 197, 777 P.2d 410 (1989).

The drafting of partial release clauses is not simple,[30] and their interpretation is often disputed.[31]

Control of Disbursements

Several methods have been developed by which the construction lender may insure that the funds being disbursed under the loan are in fact being used for improvements in the project.[32] Perhaps the oldest method, now commonly used alone only for the construction of detached houses, is the "progress payment" method under which some previously agreed fraction of the funds is disbursed as each stage of construction is completed. The stages of "progress" may be defined either as percentages of total construction cost or as phases of the building's completion: grading, foundation, framing, roof, etc. Either approach requires periodic inspections by the lender.

A more sophisticated method, termed the voucher system, requires the lender to disburse funds only when presented with bills or vouchers for work actually done on the site. The lender may require the developer to pay the bills directly and may issue a single check, say monthly, to the developer to cover them, or it may issue separate checks to the suppliers and subcontractors directly. On large projects, the voucher system is usually supplemented by site inspections by the lender or an inspecting architect employed by the lender. None of these methods is foolproof, but they tend to discourage attempts by the developer to divert loan funds to non-construction uses.

§ 12.2 Construction Contracts and Bonds

Both of the topics covered in this section are very broad and can be treated only briefly here. They are mentioned primarily because of their relation to financing issues and in order to present a reasonably comprehensive picture of the construction process.

Construction Contracts

It is rare for a landowner to have the skills and the personnel to construct substantial improvements on his or her own land. Occasion-

---

30. Such clauses sometimes fail to deal with the case of a tender by the developer of prepayment of the entire loan; see Admiral Builders v. South River Landing, 66 Md.App. 124, 502 A.2d 1096 (1986) (where clause required a "release fee" for the release of each unit, the fee was not required upon prepayment of the entire loan); Sears v. Riemersma, 655 P.2d 1105 (Utah 1982) (upon prepayment of entire loan, lender had obligation to release all lots). The statute of frauds applies to release clauses, and oral release promises are unenforceable; see Casey v. Travelers Ins. Co., 585 So.2d 1361 (Ala.1991). See generally supra § 6.6 notes 28–30.

31. See, e.g., Epic Assoc, 80–XX v. Wasatch Bank, 725 P.2d 1369 (Utah 1986); Eichorn v. Lunn, 63 Wash.App. 73, 816 P.2d 1226 (1991) (developer could exercise rights under release clause despite fact that he was in default).

32. See Ridloff, Smoothing Out the Mechanics of Construction Loan Advances, 10 Real Est.Rev. 83 (No. 1, 1980); Hall, How to Build Lender Protection into Construction Loan Agreements, 6 Real Est.L.J. 21 (1977); Halper, People and Property: Controlling Construction Contractors, 10 Real Est.Rev. 74 (No. 1, 1980); Livingston, Current Business Approaches—Commercial Construction Lending, 13 Real Prop. Prob. & Tr.J. 791, 799–800 (1978); Walker v. First Pennsylvania Bank, 518 F.Supp. 347 (E.D.Pa.1981).

ally an owner will build a personal residence, but for larger projects, some form of construction contracting is usually necessary.[1] A principal decision that the owner must make is whether to delegate total responsibility for construction to a single entity—a prime or general contractor—or whether the owner has the skill and time to assume overall management and enter into separate contracts with those who will perform the major elements of work, such as structural, electrical, plumbing and heating, and the like. The separate contract system has several advantages: (1) The owner has the opportunity to select individual firms that are, in his or her opinion, best qualified; (2) the owner can pay them directly for their work or arrange for disbursements to them from the construction lender, thereby obviating the possibility that funds will be diverted by a general contractor; and (3) the owner need not be concerned that a general contractor will attempt to "squeeze" the subcontractors to do more work for less money, increasing the general contractor's profits at the expense of quality.

Despite these advantages, the single contract system, involving a general contractor, is much more widely used. As suggested, the primary reason is that it permits full delegation of responsibility to a single entity to whom the owner can look in the event there are problems. If the general contractor is honest, competent, and financially responsible, the owner can sign the contract and then forget about the project until it is finished—in theory, at least. In major projects, the owner's architect or engineer will inspect the work frequently, call discrepancies to the general contractor's attention, and inform the owner if they are not corrected. Thus, the single contract system isolates the owner fairly well from continual administrative concerns with the construction work.

Pricing and Bidding

By far the most widely used pricing system is the fixed price or "lump sum" contract. The general contractor contracts that the project will be built for an agreed dollar figure. If the work costs less than anticipated, the contractor pockets the savings; if it costs more, the contractor's profits are reduced and he or she may ultimately sustain a loss. In principle, this provides maximum protection to the owner; in practice, however, if cost overruns threaten to force the general contractor into insolvency or induce abandonment the project, the owner may be virtually compelled to increase the contract price; a lawsuit, particularly against a financially disabled contractor, is a poor substitute for a completed building.

§ 12.2

1. The discussion here draws upon J. Sweet, Legal Aspects of Architecture, Engineering, and the Construction Process 428–94 (3d Ed.1985). See also Sweet, Your First Construction Contract, 21 Prac.Law. 27 (No. 2, Mar. 1975); E. Colby, Practical Legal Advice for Builders and Contractors 19 (1972); Prac.L.Inst., Construction Contracts 1–58 (1977); Prac.L.Inst., Real Estate Construction Current Problems 45–174 (1973); Simpkin & Nielsen, The Rise of Project/Construction Management, 6 Real Est.Rev. 46 (No. 4, Winter 1977).

An alternative form of contract in fairly wide use is the "guaranteed maximum," in which the owner cannot be charged more than an agreed amount, but if the contractor's costs are lower than estimated, the owner and contractor share in the savings according to some agreed percentage—often 50–50. This gives the contractor an incentive to hold costs down, and at the same time protects the owner to some degree against extravagant overruns.

Another approach is the "cost-plus" contract, in which the owner agrees to pay the contractor's costs plus some agreed percentage or dollar amount. This sort of arrangement is rarely used in real estate development; unless coupled with some maximum or "upset" price it obviously has the potential for wreaking financial devastation on the owner, since it gives the contractor no incentive to hold costs down. The cost-plus contract is usually found only in projects that are so unusual or technologically innovative that no reasonable advance estimate of their costs can be made.

All of the types of contracts discussed above may be entered into either through bidding or negotiation. Normally negotiation is feasible only if the owner is quite skilled in construction matters, or employs people with such skills; otherwise he or she will have difficulty in knowing whether the contractor's proposed price is a reasonable one. The competitive aspect of bidding tends to eliminate this problem. On the other hand, bidding has its disadvantages. It is often slower and requires more administrative effort to get the contract executed. Additionally, bidders may tend to reduce their bids below feasible levels in order to get the job, anticipating that they will be able to get additional money from the owner when it becomes apparent that the work cannot be completed for the original price. Nonetheless, in large projects bidding is more widely used than negotiation.

The owner usually solicits bids through some sort of invitation or advertisement. Often the invitations will be limited to contractors who, on the basis of reputation, experience, and financial position, appear to have the capacity to do the job well. Each prospective bidder will be given a package consisting of the complete plans, specifications, and drawings for the project; the proposed construction contract; and a set of rules outlining the bidding process itself—when bids are due, whether the owner is obligated to select the lowest (or any) bid, and the like. Bidders may be required to post some security to assure that they will actually enter into the contract if their bid is accepted. All of these matters are often covered by statutes on public contracts, frequently in rather inflexible terms.

Obviously, bidding a general contract requires that detailed plans and specifications have first been developed. This is less true in a negotiated contract, in which the prospective contractor may actually work with the owner's architects and engineers in producing the final plans and specifications. A radically different approach is the "package" or "turnkey" contract, in which the owner provides merely a set of general performance specifications. The contractor is responsible for the detailed design as well as the construction of the buildings. In such a transaction the contractor may even supply the land and may be expected to obtain his or her own financing during construction.

Construction bonds—An Introduction

Construction is a volatile and uncertain business; perhaps more than any other, it follows Murphy's Law: If anything can go wrong, it will.[2] Some types of problems are clearly attributable to the contractor: weak capitalization, poor planning or management, and outright dishonesty are illustrative. Other perils are beyond the contractor's control: strikes, shortages, natural disasters, concealed soil problems, changes in government regulations—all may slow construction or make it more costly. In many cases general contractors are financially weak and are unable to respond in damages even when it is clear that they have breached their contracts. Thus, owners and lenders frequently seek the participation of some financially responsible third party who can step in to rectify the contractor's breach or compensate them for the damage it causes.[3]

The third party is usually a commercial surety company, and the instrument that binds it is a surety bond. Several types of surety bonds are commonly used in construction. These are described below, but first some basic terminology is necessary.[4] In the usual case, it is the general contractor whose default is to be protected against;[5] he or she is termed the *principal.* The owner of the land on which the project is to be constructed, and who employs the contractor, is the *obligee,* the person to whom the principal's obligation is owed. The *surety* is obligated to perform if the principal does not,[6] or to pay damages instead. The bond will contain a *"penal sum,"* the maximum amount the surety company will be obliged to pay out. The amount is usually as high as the price affixed to the underlying contract between

---

2. An axiom of engineers and scientists whose origin is obscure; see American Heritage Dictionary of the English Language 863 (1973).

3. Bonds are often required by statute on public projects, but seldom on private work; an exception is Utah Code Ann. 1953, 14–2–1.

4. See generally J. Sweet, Legal Aspects of Architecture, Engineering, and the Construction Process 363 (1970); Prac. L.Inst., Construction Default: The Contractor's Bond (1976); Surety Ass'n of America, Bonds of Suretyship (1959); R. Kratovil & R. Werner, Modern Mortgage Law & Practice § 25.27(f) (2d ed. 1981); G. Osborne, Law of Suretyship (1966); L. Simpson, Suretyship (1950); Hart & Kane, What Every Real Estate Lawyer Should Know About Payment and Performance Bonds, 17 Real Prop.Prob. & Tr.J. 674 (1982).

5. On a large project, the general contractor may also insist that the major subcontractors obtain bonds; in that case, the general contractor is the obligee and the subs are principals.

6. Technically, a surety's obligation may or may not be conditioned upon the default of the principal; if it is so conditioned, it is properly termed a guaranty. See L. Simpson, Suretyship §§ 4–6 (1950). The typical construction bond is conditioned upon the principal's default; see, e.g., American Institute of Architects Document A311, Performance Bond and Labor and Material Payment Bond, Feb. 1970 edition, reprinted in Prac.L.Inst., Real Estate Construction Current Problems 525–28 (1973).

owner and contractor, but it may be less—perhaps only 50 percent or 25 percent. This is a point of negotiation between the contracting parties, except in some public or governmentally-financed projects, in which it is fixed by statute or regulation.[7]

Construction bonds are generally purchased directly by the contractor, who pays the premium (a lump sum amount) and who usually selects the surety (although the construction contract may give the owner a veto or approval power). The premium is usually stated as a percentage of the contract amount, which may vary with the size and type of project, as well as other factors, including the surety company's perception of the risk the particular contractor presents.[8] From the contractor's viewpoint, the bond premium is a cost of constructing the project, and will therefore be taken into account in preparing the bid on the job. The owner thus pays it indirectly. Some contractors may be deemed so unreliable, inexperienced, or financially weak that they cannot qualify for a bond from any company at any price; indeed, this is usually the case with small homebuilding companies, which consequently are seldom required by their customers to obtain bonds. In a project of substantial size, however, a prospective contractor's inability to obtain a bond is an important warning signal to the owner.[9]

Three principal types of bonds are used in the modern construction industry: the bid bond, the performance bond, and the payment bond. Each of these is explained briefly below.[10]

The bid bond. The purpose of this bond is to pay the damages if the contractor who is awarded the contract fails to enter into it or is unable to obtain the other bonds required for the job. In some cases a bid bond is not used; instead each bidder is required to post a cash deposit to assure that he or she will enter into the contract if selected. The bond, however, has the added advantage of serving as a screening

---

7. See, e.g., the Miller Act, 40 U.S.C.A. § 270a-d (1964), requiring both a payment and a performance bond in federal construction projects; the amount of the latter is in the discretion of the contracting officer, but the payment bond is fixed by statute at 50 percent of the contract amount for contracts under $1 million, 40 percent for contracts between $1 million and $5 million, and $2.5 million for larger contracts.

8. A typical fee is 1 percent of the first $100,000 (of contract amount), 0.65 percent of the next $2.4 million, and 0.525 percent of the next $3.5 million. On this basis the fee for a $5 million bond would be $29,725. Both payment and performance bonds would be provided for this single fee; a bid bond, if required, would be priced and obtained separately. See Prac.L.Inst., Real Estate Construction Current Problems 231 (1973).

9. See Miller v. Safeco Title Ins. Co., 758 F.2d 364 (9th Cir.1985), in which the builder was unable to qualify for a commercial bond and gave a deed of trust on his home instead.

Sometimes an owner will attempt to save the expense of the bond by requiring that the contractor qualify for it and then waiving it. The thesis is that a contractor who qualifies is sufficiently responsible that the bond itself adds little to the owner's protection. If the surety's evaluation was incorrect in such a case, however, the owner will have learned a costly lesson.

10. An excellent summary of these types of bonds and their legal aspects is Pierce, Rights and Responsibilities of the Contractor's Surety—What Happens When the Contractor Defaults, in Prac.L.Inst., Construction Contracts 435 (1977); see also Rodimer, Use of Bonds in Private Construction, 7 Forum 235 (1972).

mechanism, since bidders who are seriously underqualified probably will not be able to obtain bonds.

The amount of the claim the owner may make in the event of a default varies with the provisions of the bond. In some cases the bond or the applicable statute provides that the entire penalty amount is forfeited, irrespective of the owner's ability to show actual damages in that amount.[11] Other bond forms limit the owner to actual damages,[12] with the penal sum as a maximum.[13]

In some circumstances the law will excuse a bidder from liability for an inadvertent mistake in calculating the bid. Typically, the courts require proof that the mistake was unintentional and of substantial size, and that the owner was notified of the mistake as early as possible, and will not be irreparably injured by the court's excusing the bidder.[14] In such cases, the owner is usually denied recovery, both against the bidder and the issuer of the bond.[15] Such holdings follow the general rule that a surety can raise all defenses that would have been available to the principal.[16] From the owner's viewpoint, however, this doctrine makes the bid bond less satisfactory and inclusive than would be desired.

The performance bond. In the event that the contractor fails to complete the project as agreed, the surety under a performance bond must make good the default. The surety usually has the option of taking over the construction and completing it (usually hiring a new general contractor) or of paying for the completion by the owner or a new general contractor hired by the owner.[17] The surety's liability, of course, does not exceed the bond's penal sum. In addition, the surety

---

11. See, e.g., City of Lake Geneva v. States Improvement Co., 45 Wis.2d 50, 172 N.W.2d 176 (1969), holding valid as liquidated damages both bond and statutory clauses which provided for forfeiture of the full bond amount, irrespective of actual damages.

12. See Board of Education v. Sever-Williams Co., 22 Ohio St.2d 107, 258 N.E.2d 605 (1970), certiorari denied 400 U.S. 916, 91 S.Ct. 175, 27 L.Ed.2d 155 (1970), in which the bond's terms limited the obligee's recovery to its actual damages, measured by the difference between the bid amount and the amount of the contract ultimately entered into with another contractor.

13. The claim cannot exceed the penal sum, even if actual damages are greater. Bolivar Reorg. School District No. 1 v. American Surety Co., 307 S.W.2d 405 (Mo. 1957).

14. Ruggiero v. United States, 190 Ct. Cl. 327, 420 F.2d 709 (1970). See Smith & Lowe Construction Co. v. Herrera, 79 N.M. 239, 442 P.2d 197 (1968); M. F. Kemper Construction Co. v. City of Los Angeles, 37 Cal.2d 696, 235 P.2d 7 (1951). Grimes & Walker, Unilateral Mistakes in Construction Bids: Methods of Proof and Theories of Recovery—A Modern Approach, 5 B.C.Indus. & Com.L.Rev. 213 (1964); Annot., 52 A.L.R.2d 792 (1957). Cf. Board of Education v. Sever-Williams Co., supra note 12.

15. White v. Berenda Mesa Water Dist., 7 Cal.App.3d 894, 87 Cal.Rptr. 338 (1970); Boise Junior College District v. Mattefs Construction Co., 92 Idaho 757, 450 P.2d 604 (1969).

16. See L. Simpson, Suretyship §§ 52–62 (1950).

17. Granite Computer Leasing Corp. v. Travelers Indemnity Co., 894 F.2d 547 (2d Cir.1990). But the owner can recover on the bond even if he or she does not in fact complete the project or correct the defects; see Lake View Trust v. Filmore Construction Co., 74 Ill.App.3d 755, 30 Ill.Dec. 678, 393 N.E.2d 714 (1979).

has a legal right to the undisbursed portion of the contract price;[18] otherwise the owner would get a windfall, having the building completed without paying the price originally agreed upon.

Common types of contractor defaults that will trigger the performance surety's obligation include serious delays in the scheduled progress of the work, deviation from the contract's plans and specifications,[19] abandonment by the contractor, and failure to pay for labor and materials in order to keep the property lien-free. Since the surety is only obligated to the performance originally agreed to by the contractor, not all problems in construction will necessarily give rise to bond claims. The construction contract or applicable law, for example, may excuse the builder (and the surety) for defaults resulting from natural calamities[20] or undisclosed subsoil conditions which make the project more costly.[21] The surety may have a defense based on the owner's fraud,[22] the illegality of the contract,[23] or most other standard contract defenses. The owner may also be denied recovery on the bond if he or she has failed to perform conditions precedent to the contractor's duties[24] or has made advances to the contractor without the surety's consent for work not yet done.[25] Such premature or excessive payments, particularly if they are not actually used in the construction work, harm the surety's position, both by reducing the contractor's incentive to perform and by diminishing the fund available to complete the building if the contractor defaults.

Another defense available to the surety is the existence of facts, known to the owner and not revealed to the surety, that materially increase the risk of default. If the owner should have perceived the increased risk, realized that the facts were unknown to the surety, and

18. Henningsen v. United States Fidelity & Guar. Co., 208 U.S. 404, 28 S.Ct. 389, 52 L.Ed. 547 (1908); Mid–Continent Cas. Co. v. First National Bank & Trust Co., 531 P.2d 1370 (Okl.1975).

19. See, e.g. Carrols Equities Corp. v. Villnave, 57 A.D.2d 1044, 395 N.Y.S.2d 800 (1977), appeal denied 42 N.Y.2d 810, 399 N.Y.S.2d 1026, 369 N.E.2d 775 (1977).

20. See Barnard–Curtiss Co. v. United States, 257 F.2d 565 (10th Cir.1958), certiorari denied 358 U.S. 906, 79 S.Ct. 230, 3 L.Ed.2d 227, and 358 U.S. 906, 79 S.Ct. 233, 3 L.Ed.2d 227 (1958); cf. Barnard–Curtiss Co. v. United States, 157 Ct.Cl. 103, 301 F.2d 909 (1962).

21. See Scherrer Construction Co. v. Burlington Memorial Hospital, 64 Wis.2d 720, 221 N.W.2d 855 (1974).

22. See United Bonding Insurance Co. v. Donaldson Engineering, Inc., 222 So.2d 447 (Fla.App.1969).

23. See Wheaton v. Ramsey, 92 Idaho 33, 436 P.2d 248 (1968); Medina v. Title Guaranty & Surety Co., 152 App.Div. 307, 136 N.Y.S. 786 (1912), affirmed 211 N.Y. 24, 104 N.E. 1118 (1914).

24. See Kanters v. Kotick, 102 Wash. 523, 173 P. 329 (1918).

25. National American Bank v. Southcoast Contractors, Inc., 276 So.2d 777 (La. App.1973), writ refused 279 So.2d 694 (La. 1973); Gibbs v. Hartford Accident & Indemnity Co., 62 So.2d 599 (Fla.1952); Pacific Coast Engineering Co. v. Detroit Fidelity & Surety Co., 214 Cal. 384, 5 P.2d 888 (1931). The more recent cases tend to discharge the surety only pro tanto, to the extent of the harm caused by the advance payment; see Restatement, Security § 128(b)(ii) (1941); L. Simpson, Suretyship § 78 (1950). Some cases treat advance payments as a species of the contract modification problem (see text at note 27, infra), but this may be misleading; the discharge occurs even if the overpayment was unilateral and voluntary.

had a reasonable opportunity to reveal them, the failure to warn may bar the owner's recovery on the bond.[26]

A recurring problem in the enforcement of performance bonds is the modification of construction contracts as work progresses. In every large project numerous changes are made as a result of unavailability of materials, impracticalities in the original design, or innovations that will improve the building's usefulness. Traditionally the law of suretyship provided for a complete release of the surety in the event of any unconsented material alteration in the principal's contract with the obligee.[27] In theory, the modification increased the surety's risk unjustifiably. Courts today have grown less receptive to this doctrine. Only major changes in the scope of work are likely to result in a release of the surety, and even then, it will probably be held a pro tanto release, only to the extent that the change caused damage to the surety, rather than a complete discharge.[28] Additionally, many performance bonds contain language that expressly permits changes in details of the project, so long as the overall concept remains the same.[29]

The performance bond should not be confused with the *completion bond*, an instrument which is now largely obsolete. The completion bond differs in two important respects.[30] First, the surety is absolutely bound to complete the project; it has no option to pay a penal amount to the obligee instead. Second, completion bonds are normally written in favor of lending institutions and obligate the surety irrespective of the performance or good faith of the owner. Thus, the surety is bound even if the owner has squandered or diverted the construction funds. The obvious risks associated with this sort of instrument have led most commercial sureties to discontinue issuing them.

The payment bond. This is an undertaking by the surety that all persons supplying labor or materials to the project will be paid. It is arguable that the contractor's duty to pay such persons is a part of the

---

26. See Sumitomo Bank v. Iwasaki, 70 Cal.2d 81, 73 Cal.Rptr. 564, 447 P.2d 956 (1968); Rocky Mountain Tool & Machine Co. v. Tecon Corp., 371 F.2d 589 (10th Cir.1966).

27. See United States v. Freel, 186 U.S. 309, 22 S.Ct. 875, 46 L.Ed. 1177 (1902); William J. Morris, Inc. v. Lanzilotta & Teramo Construction Corp., 63 A.D.2d 969, 405 N.Y.S.2d 508 (1978), affirmed 47 N.Y.2d 901, 419 N.Y.S.2d 494, 393 N.E.2d 488 (1979).

28. See, e.g., Carrols Equities Corp. v. Villnave, supra note 19; McLaughlin Electric Supply v. American Empire Insurance Co., 269 N.W.2d 766 (S.D.1978); Zuni Construction Co. v. Great American Insurance Co., 86 Nev. 364, 468 P.2d 980 (1970); Verdugo Highlands, Inc. v. Security Insurance Co., 240 Cal.App.2d 527, 49 Cal.Rptr. 736 (1966); Hochevar v. Maryland Casualty Co., 114 F.2d 948 (6th Cir.1940); cf. Brunswick Nursing & Convalescent Center, Inc. v. Great American Insurance Co., 308 F.Supp. 297 (S.D.Ga.1970). See Restatement, Security § 128(b) (1941).

29. See, e.g., the unusually pro-obligee language in the performance bond appearing at Prac.L.Inst., Real Estate Construction Current Problems 522–25 (1973):

> The Surety hereby waives notice of any and all modifications, omissions, additions, changes and advance or deferred payments in and about the Agreement and agrees that the obligations of this Bond shall not be impaired in any manner by reason of any such modifications, omissions, additions, changes or advanced or deferred payments.

30. Id. at 224, 229–30.

obligation under the construction contract and hence is guaranteed by the performance bond.[31] However, the payment bond obviates the need for this argument and also makes it clear that subcontractors and material suppliers themselves may bring an action on the bond.[32] Thus the bond serves two purposes: it assures the owner a lien-free project, and it induces suppliers and subcontractors to accept work on the project, perhaps at a lower price, because of the assurance that they will be paid. Since no additional charge is generally made for a payment bond when a performance bond is being purchased, the two are usually issued simultaneously.

In public projects, in which the filing of mechanics and materialmen's liens is usually prohibited, the payment bond is even more important and is frequently required by statute.[33] It provides a fund for payment if the general contractor has been dishonest, and thus avoids petitions by subcontractors to legislative bodies for more money to cover the contractor's default.

It is necessary for the payment bond to define the extent of its coverage in terms of layers of subcontractors and suppliers. The 1970 AIA form, for example, defines a "claimant" as "one having a direct contract with the Principal or with a Subcontractor of the Principal for labor, material, or both * * *."[34] Thus, second-tier claimants (sub-subs) are covered, while third-tier claimants (sub-sub-subs) are not.

The payment bond surety is generally entitled to raise as against the owner-obligee the various defenses discussed above in connection with performance bonds. Against third-party beneficiaries of the bond, such as subcontractors and suppliers, however, it is likely that only defenses as to which the claimant has some fault can be asserted. For example, a subcontractor can generally maintain an action on a payment bond despite the fraud of the general contractor or the owner in inducing the surety to write the bond, or the default of the owner in complying with the bond's terms.[35]

---

31. See Cretex Companies v. Construction Leaders, Inc., 342 N.W.2d 135 (Minn. 1984); Dealers Electrical Supply v. United States Fidelity & Guaranty Co., 199 Neb. 269, 258 N.W.2d 131 (1977); Amelco Window Corp. v. Federal Insurance Co., 127 N.J.Super. 342, 317 A.2d 398 (1974); Restatement, Security § 166 (1941).

32. See R. C. Mahon Co. v. Hedrich Construction Co., 69 Wis.2d 456, 230 N.W.2d 621 (1975); Byler v. Great American Insurance Co., 395 F.2d 273 (10th Cir. 1968); Restatement, Security § 165 (1941). There is no necessity that the claimant even knew of the bond at the time the work or materials were supplied; Air Temperature, Inc. v. Morris, 63 Tenn.App. 90, 469 S.W.2d 495 (1970). See also Sukut-Coulson, Inc. v. Allied Canon Co., 85 Cal. App.3d 648, 149 Cal.Rptr. 711 (1978) (public project).

33. See Cedar Vale Co-op Exch. v. Allen Utilities, Inc., 10 Kan.App.2d 129, 694 P.2d 903 (1985); note 7, supra.

34. See note 6, supra. More specialized payment bonds are also sometimes used; see, e.g., Southern Steel Co. v. Hobbs Const. & Devel., Inc., 543 So.2d 843 (Fla. App.1989) (supply contract bond did not cover steel company that furnished materials to steel door supplier).

35. See United States Fidelity & Guaranty Co. v. Borden Metal Products Co., 539 S.W.2d 170 (Tex.Civ.App.1976); Guin & Hunt, Inc. v. Hughes Supply, Inc., 335 So.2d 842 (Fla.App.1976); Filippi v. McMartin, 188 Cal.App.2d 135, 10 Cal. Rptr. 180 (1961); Williams v. Baldwin, 228 S.W. 554 (Tex.Com.App.1921); Culligan Corp. v. Transamerica Insurance Co., 580 F.2d 251 (7th Cir.1978).

The dual obligee bond. Construction lenders sometimes feel a need for the same type of protection that performance and payment bonds afford to owners. The dual obligee bond, which names both the lender and the owner as obligees, accomplishes this.[36] However, nearly every dual obligee bond contains a so-called "savings clause" or "Los Angeles clause," which in substance provides that any default by either obligee will release the surety from its obligation to both.[37] The surety's main concern here is the same as that which led to the disuse of the completion bond—that one of the obligees will interfere with the flow of funds to the contractor. The surety fears that the construction lender might refuse to make proper disbursements, or the owner might intercept disbursements and divert them. The consequence of the savings clause is that the dual obligee bond protects the lender against the defaults of the contractor, but not those of the owner. This fact has great impact, since trouble on the job may well lead the owner to commit a technical default as well: for example, the owner may advance funds to the contractor prematurely, or may grant a contract modification or extension of time without the surety's consent. Although there are few cases,[38] it seems probable that under the savings clause this sort of behavior will discharge the surety (at least pro tanto, and perhaps absolutely) as to both obligees. To the lender, then, the dual obligee bond does not constitute very adequate protection.[39]

Surety's priority in undisbursed funds. Space does not permit comprehensive treatment here of another common problem with con-

36. Other parties may also be made obligees, although the practice is infrequent: a title company, a major tenant of the project, or a permanent lender. See Leake, Contract Bond Co-obligees—Rights and Responsibilities, 37 Ins.Counsel J. 554 (1970).

37. A simple, although quite ambiguous, form of the clause states:

> Any default by either or both of the obligees will automatically relieve the principal and the surety from the performance of the contract.

A more comprehensive form is:

> The surety shall not be liable under this bond to the obligees, or either of them unless the said obligees, or either of them, shall make payments to the principal, strictly in accordance with the terms of said contract as to payments and shall perform all other obligations to be performed under said contract at the time and in the manner therein set forth.

The latter clause above was used in the bond litigated in New Amsterdam Casualty Co. v. Bettes, 407 S.W.2d 307 (Tex.Civ.App. 1966), error refused n.r.e. See R. Kratovil & R. Werner, Modern Mortgage Law & Practice § 25.27(f)(1) (2d ed. 1981); Robinson, The Multiple Obligee Construction Bond: A Problem for the Surety, 15 So. Tex.L.J. 181 (1974); Franklin, Dual Obligee Bond—What Constitutes "Default" of an Obligee, 17 Federation Ins.Coun.Q. 51 (No. 4, Summer 1967).

38. In New Amsterdam Casualty Co. v. Bettes, 407 S.W.2d 307 (Tex.Civ.App.1966), error refused n.r.e., the court held that the owner's knowledge that funds were being disbursed to the contractor on the basis of falsified affidavits would not be attributable to the lender; thus, the lender's rights against the surety on the dual obligee bond were preserved.

39. See Kratovil & Werner, Mortgages for Construction and the Lien Priorities Problem—the "Unobligatory" Advance, 41 Tenn.L.Rev. 311, 321 (1974); sources cited note 37, supra.

The loss of coverage is only as to the performance aspect of the bond, and not as to the payment aspect; see Aetna Insurance Co. v. Maryland Cast Stone Co., 254 Md. 109, 253 A.2d 872 (1969); Elliott, Dual Obligee Bonds—Some Practical and Legal Considerations, 11 The Forum 1229 (1976).

struction bonds: the priority as between the surety and other claimants with respect to the undisbursed construction funds. Frequently the other claimant is a lending institution (not the construction lender) that has advanced money to the contractor. The issue may arise as follows. The contractor is midway through the project and finds that, despite the receipt of regular progress payments from the owner or construction lender, he or she is unable to meet the obligations to subcontractors and suppliers. To solve this problem the contractor obtains a bank loan, assigning as security for its repayment the payments to be received in the future from the owner. Subsequently the contractor is unable to complete the job or to pay the subcontractors, and the surety steps in and does so. As between the surety and the bank, which is entitled to first priority in the remainder of the contract price, as represented by the balance in the construction loan account?

In Prairie State Nat. Bank v. United States,[40] the Supreme Court held for the surety on similar facts, reasoning that the surety was subrogated to the rights of the owner against the defaulting contractor, and that this subrogation dated, in effect, from the time the contract and bond were signed, thus being prior to the bank's assignment.[41] The bank's argument, however, is also appealing, particularly if it can show that the loan it made was used to pay for labor or materials on the job, and perhaps was even required by the bank to be so used. On these facts, the bank loan has reduced the surety's potential liability. This argument, however, is typically rejected on the ground that the bank was a mere volunteer in this role, while the surety was contractually bound by its bond.

While the federal courts have followed *Prairie* quite consistently,[42] state courts have shown more variability. Surveying these cases, one commentator concluded that "while the surety generally wins, assignee banks prevail just often enough to maintain the flow of litigation."[43] It now is settled that the surety need not file a financing statement under

---

40. 164 U.S. 227, 17 S.Ct. 142, 41 L.Ed. 412 (1896). See also Henningsen v. United States Fidelity & Guaranty Co., 208 U.S. 404, 28 S.Ct. 389, 52 L.Ed. 547 (1908) and Pearlman v. Reliance Ins. Co., 371 U.S. 132, 83 S.Ct. 232, 9 L.Ed.2d 190 (1962), reaffirming the rule of *Prairie*. The development of the law in the federal courts is well summarized in American Fidelity Fire Insurance Co. v. Construcciones Werl, 407 F.Supp. 164, 191–97 (D.V.I. 1975). See also Franks & Evans, A Defense of Established Landmarks: Claims of Construction Sureties to Contract Funds under Chapter 11, 25 Tort & Ins.L.J. 28 (1989); Mungall, The Buffeting of the Subrogation Rights of the Construction Contract Bond Surety by United States v. Munsey Trust Co., 46 Ins. Couns.J. 607 (1979); Dauer, Government Contractors, Commercial Banks, and Miller Act Bond Sureties—A Question of Priorities, 14 B.C.Indus. & Com.L.Rev. 943 (1973); Rudolph, Financing on Construction Contracts Under the Uniform Commercial Code, 5 B.C.Indus. & Com.L.Rev. 245 (1964); Jordan, The Rights of a Surety Upon the Default of its Contractor–Principal, 41 Ore.L.Rev. 1 (1961).

41. The bond or bond application will frequently contain language by which the contractor purports to assign to the surety the funds expected under the contract, but even in the absence of such language the subrogation theory of *Prairie* still applies.

42. See, e.g., Great American Insurance Co. v. United States, 203 Ct.Cl. 592, 492 F.2d 821 (1974); Framingham Trust Co. v. Gould–National Batteries, Inc., 427 F.2d 856 (1st Cir.1970); American Fidelity Fire Insurance Co. v. Construcciones Werl, supra note 40 and cases cited therein.

43. Rudolph, Financing on Construction Contracts Under the Uniform Commercial Code, 5 B.C.Indus. & Com.L.Rev. 245 (1964); Friedberg, Construction Sure-

the Uniform Commercial Code, even if the competing creditor does so.[44] Cases sometimes turn on whether the surety knew of or approved the obtaining of the bank loan, whether the fund being contested consists of percentage retainages or of earned but undisbursed progress payments, whether the bank insisted that its loan be used on the job, or whether the project is public or private.[45] Since both claimants are innocent, and both have contributed to the completion of the work, a choice between them is difficult.

The surety may sometimes find itself in a contest with others for the undisbursed contract funds. Mechanics' and material suppliers' lien claimants may assert a priority, particularly in those states which give such claimants a statutory right in the undisbursed contract funds.[46] Other creditors of the contractor may make similar claims; even the owner may seek a setoff against the contract price, perhaps because of defective work done or damage caused by the contractor.[47] Again, these cases defy generalization, and the reader is referred to detailed discussions of them in the literature.[48]

§ 12.3 Mortgage Loan Commitments

A loan commitment is a promise by a lender to make a loan at some future time. Both construction and permanent loans are frequently preceded by written commitments.[1] For the developer of a new project, the construction loan commitment is the signal that the search

ties: Don't Put All Your Eggs in the Equitable Subrogation Basket, 41 Case W.Res. L.Rev. 305 (1990). See First Vermont Bank v. Village of Poultney, 134 Vt. 28, 349 A.2d 722 (1975).

44. See Balboa Ins. Co. v. Bank of Boston, 702 F.Supp. 34 (D.Conn.1988); First Alabama Bank v. Hartford Accident & Indemnity Co., Inc., 430 F.Supp. 907 (N.D.Ala.1977); Transamerica Ins. Co. v. Barnett Bank, 540 So.2d 113 (Fla.1989); Finance Co. of America v. United States Fidelity & Guaranty Co., 277 Md. 177, 353 A.2d 249 (1976); Argonaut Insurance Co. v. C and S Bank of Tipton, 140 Ga.App. 807, 232 S.E.2d 135 (1976); cf. United States Fidelity & Guaranty Co. v. Leach, 438 F.Supp. 295 (M.D.Ga.1977); Interfirst Bank Dallas v. U.S. Fidelity & Guar. Co., 774 S.W.2d 391 (Tex.App.1989). See Note, Equitable Subrogation—Too Hardy a Plant to be Uprooted by Article 9 of the U.C.C.? 32 U. of Pitts.L.R. 580 (1971).

45. See Rudolph, supra note 43 at 248–49. See, e.g., Fidelity & Casualty Co. of New York v. Central Bank of Birmingham, 409 So.2d 788 (Ala.1982); Himes v. Cameron County Construction Corp., 289 Pa.Super. 143, 432 A.2d 1092 (1981), affirmed 497 Pa. 637, 444 A.2d 98 (1982); First National Bank v. McHasco Electric, Inc., 273 Minn. 407, 141 N.W.2d 491 (1966). In National Surety Co. v. State National Bank, 454 S.W.2d 354 (Ky.App.1970), the court held for the assignee bank on the ground that the surety had acquiesced in the contractor's seeking the bank loan, which occurred after the surety had taken over the project.

46. See General Acrylics v. United States Fidelity & Guaranty Co., 128 Ariz. 50, 623 P.2d 839 (App.1980); § 12.4, infra.

47. In United States v. Munsey Trust Co., 332 U.S. 234, 67 S.Ct. 1599, 91 L.Ed. 2022 (1947), the Court held that the set-off claim of the United States as owner had priority over the claim of the surety; see Mungall, supra note 40; see also Fireman's Insurance Co. v. New York, 91 Misc.2d 183, 397 N.Y.S.2d 524 (1977), affirmed 65 A.D.2d 241, 412 N.Y.S.2d 206 (1979); Safeco Insurance Co. v. State, 89 Misc.2d 864, 392 N.Y.S.2d 976 (1977); American Fidelity Fire Insurance Co. v. Construcciones Werl, supra note 40 and cases cited therein.

48. See sources cited note 40 supra.

§ 12.3

1. Calif.Cont.Ed. of Bar, California Real Estate Sales Transactions § 10.42 (1967). The most fundamental element of the commitment is the promise to lend

for construction financing is over. Before the commitment is issued, the developer has usually completed most or all of the other arrangements for construction, including land acquisition, basic project design, and the preliminary negotiation of the construction contract. Construction will typically commence within a short time after the commitment is issued, after the developer has made whatever modifications and final touches the committing lender requires.

money; see International Minerals & Mining Corp. v. Citicorp North America, Inc., 736 F.Supp. 587 (D.N.J.1990) (where letter stated plainly that it was not a commitment, the lender incurred no obligation to lend); Runnemede Owners, Inc. v. Crest Mortg. Corp., 861 F.2d 1053 (7th Cir.1988) (letter bound lender only to consider making the loan). The commitment must include at least the essential terms of the loan to be made; see Peterson Devel. Co. v. Torrey Pines Bank, 233 Cal.App.3d 103, 284 Cal.Rptr. 367 (1991); T.O. Stanley Boot Co. v. Bank of El Paso, 847 S.W.2d 218, 19 UCC Rep.Serv.2d 514 (Tex.1992). Cf. Teachers Ins. & Annuity Ass'n v. Ormesa Geothermal, 791 F.Supp. 401 (S.D.N.Y. 1991) (commitment binding despite omission of certain terms); Teachers Ins. & Annuity Ass'n v. Coaxial Communications of Central Ohio, Inc., 799 F.Supp. 16 (S.D.N.Y.1992) (same).

A writing is required under the Statute of Frauds in most jurisdictions; see Linsker v. Savings of America, 710 F.Supp. 598 (E.D.Pa.1989); United of Omaha Life Insurance Co. v. Nob Hill Associates, 450 So.2d 536 (Fla.App.1984), petition for review dismissed 458 So.2d 273 (Fla.1984), petition for review denied 458 So.2d 274 (1984) and Fremming Construction Co. v. Security Savings & Loan Ass'n, 115 Ariz. 514, 566 P.2d 315 (1977). Contra, see Martyn v. First Federal Savings & Loan Association, 257 So.2d 576 (Fla.App.1971), certiorari denied 262 So.2d 446 (Fla.1992) (oral loan commitment enforceable). See also Silverdale Hotel Associates v. Lomas & Nettleton Co., 36 Wash.App. 762, 677 P.2d 773 (1984), review denied 101 Wash.2d 1021 (1984) (parol testimony admitted to supplement written agreement); Towers Charter & Marine Corp. v. Cadillac Insurance Co., 894 F.2d 516 (2d Cir.1990) (under New York law, if loan commitment states that it can be modified only in writing, an oral modification is not binding). Compare OMP v. Security Pacific Business Finance, Inc., 716 F.Supp. 239 (N.D.Miss.1988) (agreement not taken out of Statute of Frauds by estoppel) with First National Bank v. Logan Mfg. Co., 577 N.E.2d 949 (Ind.App.1991) (agreement taken out of Statute of Frauds by estoppel) and Seattle First National Bank v. Siebol, 64 Wash. App. 401, 824 P.2d 1252 (1992), review denied 119 Wash.2d 1010, 833 P.2d 386 (1992) (same). If the commitment is in writing, it need not necessarily be accepted in writing to make it binding; see McKee v. First Nat. Bank, 220 Ill.App.3d 976, 163 Ill.Dec. 389, 581 N.E.2d 340 (1991), appeal denied 143 Ill.2d 639, 167 Ill.Dec. 401, 587 N.E.2d 1016 (1992) (borrower's efforts to satisfy conditions in commitment constituted acceptance).

Even an oral commitment may be used by the borrower to show that the terms of the written note and mortgage differ from the parties' actual agreement and hence are unenforceable; see Peoples Trust & Savings Bank v. Humphrey, 451 N.E.2d 1104 (Ind.App.1983). In addition, an oral statement, such as "I see no problems in approving this loan," may form the basis of an action, not on the loan commitment itself, but for misrepresentation or fraudulent concealment; see, e.g., Anderson v. Beneficial Mortg. Corp., 699 F.Supp. 1075 (D.Del.1988); Frame v. Boatmen's Bank, 824 S.W.2d 491 (Mo.App.1992); Federal Land Bank Ass'n v. Sloane, 825 S.W.2d 439 (Tex.1991). See generally Shadur, Avoiding Lender Liability at the Loan Commitment Stage, 6 Prac.Real Est.Law. 47 (no.6, May 1990); Williamson & Redfern, Lender Liability in Mississippi: Part II, Loan Agreements and Commitments, 59 Miss. L.J. 71 (1979).

The person issuing the commitment must be authorized to do so; Labor Discount Center, Inc. v. State Bank & Trust Co., 526 S.W.2d 407 (Mo.App.1975). In Walter Harvey Corp. v. O'Keefe, 346 So.2d 617 (Fla.App.1977), the construction lender advanced an additional $450,000, over and above its original loan commitment, in order to cover cost overruns. Even this amount was not sufficient to complete the project, and the developer claimed that the lender was legally obligated to advance even more funds. The court held that the making of one optional advance did not impliedly obligate the lender to make another, and that the lender was entitled to foreclose.

The permanent loan commitment, a promise by a lender to make a long-term loan on the property when construction is completed, is of critical importance. From the developer's viewpoint, it represents assurance that marketing of the project can be financed (if sales-type development, such as a residential subdivision, is involved), or that funds will be available to pay the construction loan when it is due at the time of completion. This sort of assurance is at least as important to the construction lender as to the developer. As a result of regulatory requirements,[2] internal policies, or both, the great majority of construction lenders will not issue *their* commitment until a permanent or "take-out" loan commitment has first been obtained.[3] The permanent commitment may call either for payoff of the construction loan and execution of a new note and mortgage, or for the permanent lender to purchase the construction loan, under a "buy-sell agreement," when construction is completed.[4]

The permanent loan commitment will usually be based on the same underwriting considerations as the construction loan: the borrower's credit, the project's design and technical feasibility, an appraisal of its completed value and marketability, and the satisfaction of various title and other legal requirements.[5] Neither the construction nor permanent lender can afford to leave the evaluation of these matters to the other; both must do a thorough underwriting job if they are prudent, since it is impossible to tell at the commitment stage which of them might eventually foreclose on the property. The requirements of the two lenders must not be inconsistent, and the construction commitment will usually require that the developer comply with all terms of the permanent commitment.

In most cases the construction lender will seek to have the permanent loan commitment assigned to it. Ideally, the construction lender would prefer this assignment to be sufficiently broad that, in the event the construction loan is foreclosed and it winds up owning and completing the project, it will be able to enforce the permanent loan commitment and demand funding of the permanent loan. The permanent lender, however, may resist approving such an assignment. Even a less extensive assignment is useful, since it can ensure that no renegotiation

---

2. See, e.g., N.Y.—McKinney's Banking Law § 103:4(c)(3)(iv); § 12.1 at notes 5–10 supra.

3. See Texas Bank v. Lone Star Life Insurance Co., 565 S.W.2d 353 (Tex.Civ. App.1978); Ridloff, A Construction Lender Looks at Permanent Loan Commitments, 10 Real Est.Rev. 60 (No. 2, 1980); Haggerty, Procedures, Forms and Safeguards in Construction Lending with a Permanent Takeout, 85 Bank.L.J. 1035 (1968). Alternatively, the construction lender may accept a commitment from a high-credit purchaser to *buy* the project (not merely the mortgage) upon completion.

4. See text at notes 36–38 infra; Douglas v. United States, 217 Ct.Cl. 97, 576 F.2d 887 (1978); BA Mortgage Co. v. Unisal Development, Inc., 469 F.Supp. 1258 (D.Colo.1979); Reed & Ridloff, The Buy-sell or Tripartite Agreement, Mortgage Banker, Dec.1980, at 33. For an illustrative buy-sell agreement, see ALI–ABA, Modern Real Estate Transactions 324 (5th ed. 1984); Berks Title Ins. Co. v. Haendiges, 772 F.2d 278 (6th Cir.1985).

5. See United California Bank v. Prudential Insurance Co., 140 Ariz. 238, 681 P.2d 390 (1983); § 12.1 at note 17 supra.

§ 12.3 FINANCING REAL ESTATE CONSTRUCTION 169

of the permanent loan commitment occurs without the construction lender's approval. The assignment may also have the effect of allowing the construction lender to cure any default by the borrower, a very useful right if the default would otherwise excuse the permanent lender from its commitment.[6]

Loan commitments are usually hedged with numerous conditions to protect the lender's interests.[7] In a sales-type project such as a subdivision or a condominium, the evaluation of the credit-worthiness of the future purchasers of the units is impossible at the outset of construction; thus the permanent loan commitment for such a project is invariably conditioned upon the purchasers' compliance with the lender's customary standards (which may be articulated in the commitment itself), or the standards of the Federal Housing Administration or other insurance or guaranty agency.[8] Other common conditions include submission to the lender of final plans and specifications (if the commitment is issued on the basis of preliminary versions or if the

---

6. See Ridloff, A Checklist for the Construction Lender's Attorney, 11 Real Est. Rev. 103 (No. 4, 1982); Ridloff, A Sample Construction Loan Commitment, 10 Real Est.Rev. 87 (No. 4, 1981); FDIC v. Connecticut National Bank, 916 F.2d 997 (5th Cir. 1990) (construction lender to whom permanent commitment was assigned can enforce it). Cf. American Fletcher Mortgage Co. v. First American Investment Corp., 463 F.Supp. 186 (N.D.Ga.1978) (construction lender that received no assignment is not third-party beneficiary of standby commitment and cannot recover for its breach); Homer National Bank v. Tri-District Devel. Corp., 534 So.2d 154 (La.App.1988), writ denied 536 So.2d 1236 (La.1989) (same).

7. See Walsh, A Practical Guide to Mortgage Loan Commitments, 8 Real Est. L.J. 195 (1980); Garfinkel, Negotiation of Construction and Permanent Loan Commitments, 25 Prac.Law 13 (Mar.1979), 37 (Apr.1979); R. Kratovil, Modern Real Estate Documentation 185–197 (1975); ALI-ABA, Modern Real Estate Transactions 267 (5th ed. 1984) (document prepared by Noel R. Nellis); Ridloff, A Sample Construction Loan Commitment, supra note 6. The conditions inserted in the commitment are ordinarily for the lender's benefit, and failure by the lender to enforce them is not a breach for which other parties may recover. See Buehner Block Co. v. UWC Assoc., 752 P.2d 892 (Utah 1988) (lender's failure to require adequate bonds, as stated in its commitment letter, did not give rise to liability to owner or subcontractors who would have benefitted from bonds); McKee v. First Nat. Bank, 220 Ill.App.3d 976, 163 Ill.Dec. 389, 581 N.E.2d 340 (1991), appeal denied 143 Ill.2d 639, 167 Ill.Dec. 401, 587 N.E.2d 1016 (1992) (borrower's failure to satisfy conditions excused lender's performance).

The courts readily imply a condition that there are no material misrepresentations in the borrower's loan application; thus, their existence will discharge the lender's duty under the commitment. See Simmons v. Prudential Constr., Inc., 533 So.2d 808 (Fla.App.1988); FDIC v. W.R. Grace & Co., 877 F.2d 614 (7th Cir.1989), certiorari denied 494 U.S. 1056, 110 S.Ct. 1524, 108 L.Ed.2d 764 (1990) (lender who honored commitment despite borrower's was entitled to damages). A false statement in a loan application may also be a crime; see United States v. Thompson, 811 F.2d 841 (5th Cir.1987); United States v. Lueben, 812 F.2d 179 (5th Cir.1987), vacated in part 816 F.2d 1032 (1987), appeal after remand 838 F.2d 751 (1988).

8. The FHA itself issues conditional commitments to insure permanent loans based on its approval of plans and specifications and its inspections as houses are constructed. The relevant form, FHA 2800–5, provides:

> The mortgage amount and term set forth in the heading are the maximum approved for this property assuming a satisfactory owner-occupant mortgagor. The maximum amount and term in the heading may be changed depending upon FHA's rating of the borrower, his income and credit. * * * A firm commitment to insure a loan will be issued upon receipt of an Application for Credit Approval, FHA form 2900, executed by an approved mortgagee and a borrower satisfactory to the Commissioner.

lender has required changes) and submission of other documentation, including the executed construction contract, the documents creating the developer entity (if a corporation, partnership, or trust), leases executed by the major tenants, the title insurance report and binder, the permanent loan commitment if a construction loan is being made, fire and hazard insurance policies, the building permit, and perhaps an opinion of counsel respecting the validity of the developer entity's creation, its power to undertake the project, and the validity of the other documents. In a permanent loan commitment on a project to be built, lien-free completion in accordance with the agreed plans and specifications will be made a condition.[9]

The permanent commitment on a rental project, such as an apartment or office building, may also be conditioned upon some specified fraction of the project being rented. More complex arrangements are sometimes used, so that a portion of the permanent loan will be funded at a given rental level (the "floor"), and the remainder when a higher rental level (the "ceiling") has been achieved.[10] Obviously a permanent commitment conditioned upon rent-up is less satisfactory to the construction lender than an unconditional commitment, but such conditions are commonly accepted. If the construction lender demands payment before a sufficient number of tenants has been found to meet the permanent lender's rent roll requirements, the developer may be able to obtain an interim or "bridge" loan to carry through the rent-up period.

A permanent loan commitment will often be conditioned on the developer's continued solvency during the construction period, or that the developer's financial condition not suffer any "material adverse change."[11] The commitment will, of course, fully identify the project and the parties, including the general contractor, if any. It will state the amount of the loan and the period within which the loan closing

---

9. See Penthouse International, Ltd. v. Dominion Fed. Sav. & Loan Ass'n, 855 F.2d 963 (2d Cir.1988), certiorari denied 490 U.S. 1005, 109 S.Ct. 1639, 104 L.Ed.2d 154 (1989), permitting a participating lender to refrain from entering into the participation because various conditions in the loan commitment were not met; United California Bank v. Prudential Insurance Co., supra note 4, construing the commitment to require only a title insurance policy insuring a first lien, rather than a first lien in fact; Boucher v. Eastern Sav. Bank, 145 A.D.2d 520, 536 N.Y.S.2d 463 (1988) (condition that parking spaces be available for duration of the mortgage).

In general, substantial rather than strict performance is sufficient; see First National State Bank v. Commonwealth Federal Savings & Loan Association, 610 F.2d 164 (3d Cir.1979); Whalen v. Ford Motor Credit Co., 475 F.Supp. 537 (D.Md. 1979). See Ridloff, supra note 3, at 61.

Not every loan commitment is as well-drafted as it might be in terms of conditions. See FDIC v. Connecticut National Bank, 916 F.2d 997 (5th Cir.1990): "the Agreement is absolutely devoid of any conditions to the obligations of the Permanent Lenders. Remarkably, there is no condition to the Permanent Lenders' commitment that the condominium project even be completed in accordance with the plans and specifications. In fact, there is no reference to the plans and specifications."

10. See Brown–Marx Associates v. Emigrant Savings Bank, 703 F.2d 1361 (11th Cir.1983) (strict rather than substantial performance of rental levels required.)

11. See Mellon Bank v. Aetna Business Credit, Inc., 619 F.2d 1001 (3d Cir. 1980); Ridloff, supra note 3.

§ 12.3 FINANCING REAL ESTATE CONSTRUCTION 171

must occur. The plans and specifications, the construction loan agreement, and the form of note and mortgage which the lender proposes to require will usually be incorporated by reference in the commitment on a construction loan. The interest rate and fees to be charged for the loan will be specified, as well as the fee for the commitment itself. Such fees vary with the duration, type, and amount of the commitment, but are frequently in the 1 to 2 percent range. In some cases permanent loan commitments on residential subdivisions are issued and are acceptable to construction lenders without stipulation of the interest rate. Since such commitments do not shift the risk of fluctuating rates to the permanent lender, they may be obtained at a lower cost than is usually charged for a fixed-interest commitment and may even be issued free or at a nominal charge.

Many lenders who issue fixed-interest permanent loan commitments on housing do so on the basis of commitments which they, in turn, have obtained from the Federal National Mortgage Association (FNMA) or the Federal Home Loan Mortgage Corporation (FHLMC). Both of these federally-chartered organizations give advance commitments to local lenders to purchase mortgages in the future. A lender who has such commitments can make equivalent commitments to its loan customers, secure in the knowledge that the mortgages, when originated, can be resold immediately on the secondary market at a known price.[12]

FNMA and FHLMC, like many other mortgage investors, issue both mandatory commitments, under which the originating lender is contractually bound to deliver the mortgages to the secondary market purchaser, and optional commitments, under which the lender is under no obligation to deliver the loans.[13] The optional commitments extend over longer time periods, and are mainly intended to allow the lender to offer commitments to residential builders to cover purchase loans for their home-buying customers.

In the past both FNMA and FHLMC have used a "free market auction" system for determining the yields (or effective interest rates)[14]

---

12. For a more complete discussion of these agencies and their operations in the secondary mortgage market, see § 11.3 supra; Garrett, How Home Builders Use Conventional Forward Take-out Commitments, 10 Real Est.Rev. 72 (No. 4, Winter 1981).

13. See LaMalfa & Griesbach, Wholesale Commitments, Mortgage Banking, Sept. 1992, at 59.

14. Note that this effective yield is normally higher than the contract interest rate shown on the face of the promissory note signed by the borrower. The loan will ordinarily be sold to FNMA or FHLMC at a discount—that is, an amount lower than the loan's original or outstanding balance. The effect of the discount is to raise the effective yield to FNMA or FHLMC above the contract rate. A standard formula is used to convert yields on loans sold on the secondary market into equivalent discount prices. The prices are often expressed as percentages of face amount. Thus, if FNMA pays a price of 95 on a $80,000 mortgage, the dollar price would be $76,000 and the loan is said to be sold at a "five point" discount. The conversion formula for most loan programs is based on the assumption that the loan will be prepaid in 12 years from the date its first payment is due.

To illustrate the formula's operation, assume a 30-year fixed-rate loan of $80,000 is made at a contract interest rate of 12%. Such a loan will require monthly payments

at which they would make commitments. These auctions were conducted on announced days at regular intervals by telephone; lenders called and offered to sell mortgages at specified yields, and the secondary market agency then decided how many such offers to accept, starting, of course, with those carrying the highest yields. Neither FHMA nor FHLMC is presently using an auction system; instead, both agencies simply establish and announce periodically the yields at which they will issue commitments to buy mortgage loans of various types. The details of these purchase programs are complex and are changed constantly, so it is not feasible to provide detailed descriptions of them here. They vary in terms of the commitment period, the seller's legal obligation to deliver mortgages under them, and the fees required. The interested reader should obtain the most recent Sellers' Guides and other literature from FNMA and FHLMC.

A unique form of commitment, the "standby" commitment, is one that the borrower does not expect to draw upon. The developer of commercial or income-producing properties may seek a standby commitment from an interim lender, even on very onerous terms, in order to allow more time to locate permanent financing.[15] The standby commitment will often carry a costly fee, as much as 3 to 5 percent of the amount committed, and will bear a high interest rate and a short maturity if it is ever actually funded. But its real purpose is to satisfy the construction lender's requirement that a take-out commitment exist; the developer has no intention of using it. Rather, he or she hopes that more attractive permanent financing will be available at some time during construction or by completion, either because of changes in money market conditions or because the building will then be fully built and rented and thus appear less risky to a permanent lender. The standby lender's position is obviously risky, and this fact accounts for the commitment's high cost. Sometimes a construction lender will itself issue a standby commitment as well; in substance,

---

of $822.89, and after 12 years will have an outstanding balance of 72,697. Assume also that the yield required by FNMA when it purchases the loan is 13%. The applicable formula simply computes the present value (at a 13% rate) of (a) the right to receive the regular monthly payments on the loan until it is 12 years old, plus (b) the right to receive the outstanding balance on the loan when it is 12 years old. Thus:

Present value of right to receive $822.89 per month for 12 years	= $59,863
Present value of right to receive $72,697 12 years in the future	= $15,405
TOTAL price paid by FNMA	= $75,268

Thus, in this example the discount would be $4,732, or 5.92 "points" on the $80,000 loan. The procedure for computing secondary market prices on adjustable rate loans is somewhat more complex. See generally FNMA, Selling Guide § 301 (1984). The originating lender normally does not absorb the discount, but instead passes it on (along with any commitment fee it has paid) to the borrower, builder, or seller of the property. For a discussion of legal limitations on the imposition of the discount on the borrower in VA-guaranteed loans, see § 11.2, supra.

15. See, e.g., B.F. Saul Real Est. Inv. Trust v. McGovern, 683 S.W.2d 531 (Tex. App.1984); Hidalgo Properties, Inc. v. Wachovia Mortgage Co., 617 F.2d 196 (10th Cir.1980); Prac.L.Inst., Real Estate Financing: Contemporary Techniques 313 (No. 14, 1973).

this is its way of contracting for substantially increased interest and fees if the construction loan is not paid off immediately upon completion.[16]

Lender's fees and enforcement rights. The cost to the prospective borrower of obtaining a loan commitment varies widely. On permanent commitments for existing owner-occupied houses, some lenders charge nothing and others charge only appraisal and credit report fees of a few hundred dollars. At the other extreme are construction and permanent loan commitments on large income-producing properties where the borrower will usually be required to cover all of the lender's out-of-pocket costs, such as the appraiser's, attorney's, architect's and engineer's fees. These fees are typically nonrefundable, irrespective of whether a satisfactory commitment is ever issued or a loan ever made. Since such fees can add up substantially, the developer is often well-advised to obtain the appraisal as early as possible, so that other financing can be sought without much loss if the appraisal is too low to make possible an attractive loan.[17]

In addition to these expenses, the borrower on a large project may be charged a substantial application fee, and upon the issuance of the commitment, a further nonrefundable commitment fee. The latter's apparent purpose is to compensate the lender for the opportunity cost and administrative burden of underwriting the loan and holding the funds available for the borrower's use.[18]

Finally, many lenders, especially permanent lenders on new income properties, require that the borrower post a "good faith deposit," sometimes termed a "security" or "standby" deposit, when the commitment is issued.[19] If the loan is actually made, the deposit is refunded or

---

16. See Prac.L.Inst., Real Estate Construction 225 (No. 5, 1969).

17. R. Kratovil, Modern Real Estate Documentation § 434 (1975).

18. See First National Mortgage Co. v. Arkmo Lumber & Supply Co., 277 Ark. 298, 641 S.W.2d 31 (1982), holding such a fee to be interest for usury purposes. Cf. Stedman v. Georgetown Savings & Loan Association, 595 S.W.2d 486 (Tex.1979). See United States v. Grissom, 814 F.2d 577 (10th Cir.1987), in which a loan officer was convicted of embezzlement for making personal use of a loan application fee; Schwartz v. Federated Realty Group, Inc., 148 Wis.App. 419, 436 N.W.2d 34 (1988), holding that a lender may be liable for accepting a loan application fee and thereafter failing to process the application with reasonable diligence.

While no borrower likes to pay fees, they may actually serve the borrower's legal purposes. In Security Bank v. Bogard, 494 N.E.2d 965 (Ind.App.1986) a farmer obtained without charge an oral loan commitment from a bank loan officer. The bank subsequently refused to make the loan, and the court held that since the farmer had paid no consideration and had not made a promise to borrow the funds, the contract lacked mutuality and was unenforceable by the farmer.

19. See Prac.L.Inst., Real Estate Construction 327–31 (No. 5, 1969); Douglas v. United States, 217 Ct.Cl. 97, 576 F.2d 887 (1978). Note that the term "standby" here is unrelated to the concept of the "standby commitment" discussed earlier. See United States v. Ellzey, 874 F.2d 324 (6th Cir. 1989), a criminal prosecution of a mortgage broker who collected commitment fees in return for commitments made by a coconspirator that had neither the capability nor the intention of funding the loans.

Efforts of loan applicants who ultimately did not draw down the loan to recover these deposits have generally been unsuccessful; see First Fed. Savings & Loan Association v. Sailboat Key, Inc., 375 So.2d 625 (Fla.App.1979), certiorari denied 386

applied against the borrower's obligations toward interest and other loan fees; but if the borrower does not draw down the loan, the deposit will be forfeited. Obviously, the deposit is intended to discourage the borrower from "walking away"—i.e., seeking financing from another source on more attractive terms.

The commitment-related fees just discussed should not be confused with interest and fees on the loan itself.[20] In many cases the lender will charge a "processing fee" or "origination fee" if and when the loan is made, ostensibly to cover the administrative cost and overhead of putting the loan "on the books." In some cases, however, these fees substantially exceed the lender's costs, and amount to a form of prepaid interest, raising the lender's overall yield on the loan. Such fees are common in a wide range of loan types, from single-family residences to large commercial projects. In addition, in VA-guaranteed home loan transactions, in which the face interest rate on the note is limited to a below-market level by government regulation, the lender will usually charge "discounts" or "points" to the builder or seller in order to raise the effective yield on the loan to a competitive level.[21]

A loan commitment usually makes it clear that the lender is legally obligated to loan in the event all of the stated conditions are fulfilled. Rather surprisingly, many commitments are so poorly drafted that they leave unclear whether the borrower has a corresponding obligation to follow through and obtain the loan.[22] In most single-family home loan commitments, certain commitments issued to lenders by FNMA and FHLMC,[23] and in standby commitments,[24] it is apparent that the party receiving the commitment has no obligation to use it; in

So.2d 641 (Fla.1980); Levenson v. Barnett Bank of Miami, 330 So.2d 192 (Fla.App. 1976); Oran v. Canada Life Assur. Co., 194 Ga.App. 518, 390 S.E.2d 879 (1990); White Lakes Shopping Center, Inc. v. Jefferson Standard Life Insurance Co., 208 Kan. 121, 490 P.2d 609 (1971); Joseph v. Lake Michigan Mortgage Co., 106 Ill.App.3d 988, 62 Ill.Dec. 637, 436 N.E.2d 663 (1982); Walker v. First Pennsylvania Bank, 518 F.Supp. 347 (E.D.Pa.1981); B.F. Saul Real Est. Inv. Trust v. McGovern, 683 S.W.2d 531 (Tex. App.1984); Annot., 93 A.L.R.3d (1979). Of course, recovery of the fee is an appropriate remedy if the lender breaches the commitment; see Hidalgo Properties, Inc. v. Wachovia Mortgage Co., 617 F.2d 196 (10th Cir.1980). See Annot., supra.

Occasionally, however, a borrower is able to take advantage of poor drafting to recover a standby commitment. See Woodbridge Place Apartments v. Washington Square Capital, Inc., 965 F.2d 1429 (7th Cir.1992), in which the court characterized the standby fee as a liquidated damages provision, which the lender was not entitled to enforce under Indiana law because the borrower did not breach the commitment, but merely failed (without bad faith) to fulfill certain conditions upon which the commitment depended.

20. The distinction between commitment fees and loan fees was significant for usury purposes in Gonzales County Savings & Loan Association v. Freeman, 534 S.W.2d 903 (Tex.1976), holding the former outside the usury statute. Contra, see Henslee v. Madison Guaranty Sav. & Loan Ass'n, 297 Ark. 183, 760 S.W.2d 842 (1988). See also People v. Central Federal Savings & Loan Association, 46 N.Y.2d 41, 412 N.Y.S.2d 815, 385 N.E.2d 555 (1978); 1980 Op.Wis.Att'y Gen. No. 9–80, reported in 1974–80 CCH Cons.Cred.Guide ¶ 97,553; Meadow Brook National Bank v. Recile, 302 F.Supp. 62 (E.D.La.1969).

21. See note 13, supra; § 11.2 infra.

22. See, e.g, Woodbridge Place Apartments v. Washington Square Capital, Inc., 965 F.2d 1429 (7th Cir.1992).

23. See text at notes 12–15 supra.

24. See Prac.L.Inst., Real Estate Financing: Contemporary Techniques 177–78 (No. 14, 1973).

§ 12.3 FINANCING REAL ESTATE CONSTRUCTION 175

effect, the commitment gives the prospective mortgagor an option to borrow. But in loans on income properties, it is often ambiguous whether the borrower has an obligation to borrow the funds.[25]

If a developer to whom a commitment has been issued declines to borrow (presumably because he or she has found a better deal elsewhere), what remedies can the lender assert? If the loan applicant has deposited fees that, by the commitment's terms, are nonrefundable, the courts have uniformly allowed the lender to retain them.[26] But if the lender seeks additional relief, it has several barriers to overcome. First, it must persuade the court that the borrower has an affirmative obligation to borrow, and not merely an option; this is typically a matter of construction of the commitment.[27] Second, it may be faced with the argument that the "good faith deposit" is, in substance, a liquidated damages clause, and that its retention is the sole valid remedy at law for the prospective borrower's default. The situation is arguably analogous to a buyer's "earnest money deposit" in a contract to purchase a house; if the seller reserves the right to retain the deposit, it is often held that he or she can recover no additional damages.[28] In principle, this issue is also a matter of interpretation of

---

25. See, e.g., Lowe v. Massachusetts Mutual Life Insurance Co., 54 Cal.App.3d 718, 127 Cal.Rptr. 23 (1976); Goldman v. Connecticut General Life Insurance Co., 251 Md. 575, 248 A.2d 154 (1968). Both cases hold the commitment to be an option to the borrower, but with no clear language in the documents to support the conclusion. A set of letters that read much like a construction loan commitment was held too vague to be enforced in Willowood Condominium Association, Inc. v. HNC Realty Co., 531 F.2d 1249 (5th Cir. 1976); see also Wheeler v. White, 385 S.W.2d 619 (Tex.Civ.App.1964) reversed 398 S.W.2d 93 (Tex.1965).

26. B.F. Saul Real Est. Inv. Trust v. McGovern, 683 S.W.2d 531 (Tex.App.1984); Lowe v. Massachusetts Mutual Life Insurance Co., 54 Cal.App.3d 718, 127 Cal.Rptr. 23 (1976); Suitt Construction Co. Inc., v. Seaman's Bank for Savings, 30 N.C.App. 155, 226 S.E.2d 408 (1976), holding the applicable law is that of the place at which the lender receives the borrower's signed acceptance of the commitment. Other cases are collected in Groot, Specific Performance of Constructs to Provide Permanent Financing, 60 Cornell L.Rev. 719, 729 n. 49. In Levenson v. Barnett Bank of Miami, 330 So.2d 192 (Fla.App.1976), the court held that the developer could recover his "standby" deposit if he could show that the lender had not in fact been able and prepared to make the loan, since the very purpose of that deposit had been to compensate the lender for holding itself "in readiness." The court distinguished and denied the developer's attempt to recover his commitment fee, which the agreement expressly made nonrefundable; it found that this fee's purpose was to compensate the lender for its time and expense in underwriting the loan.

27. The "option" interpretation has been adopted frequently; see Financial Federal Savings & Loan Association v. Burleigh House, Inc., 305 So.2d 59 (Fla.App. 1974), certiorari denied 429 U.S. 1042, 97 S.Ct. 742, 50 L.Ed.2d 754 (1977); D & M Development Co. v. Sherwood & Roberts, Inc., 93 Idaho 200, 457 P.2d 439 (1969); cases cited note 25, supra. But see Lincoln Nat'l Life Ins. Co. v. NCR Corp., 603 F.Supp. 1393 (N.D.Ind.1984), affirmed 772 F.2d 315 (7th Cir.1985), admitting parol evidence and finding an enforceable promise to borrow, but finding no damages in light of the general upward trend of interest rates which occurred following the borrower's breach.

28. See, e.g., Brewer v. Myers, 545 S.W.2d 235 (Tex.Civ.App.1976); Coca-Cola Bottling Works (Thomas) Inc. v. Hazard Coca-Cola Bottling Works, Inc., 450 S.W.2d 515 (Ky.1970); Alois v. Waldman, 219 Md. 369, 149 A.2d 406 (1959); Andreasen v. Hansen, 8 Utah 2d 370, 335 P.2d 404 (1959); C. McCormick, Damages § 152 (1935). Of course, this conclusion is easy if the contract provides that the vendor's sole damages remedy is retention of the deposit, as is usually the case in California, see

the commitment agreement,[29] but if the good faith deposit is substantial, it may well be held the lender's exclusive remedy.[30]

Assuming the lender can overcome these barriers, it is rather clearly entitled to damages against the defaulting commitment-holder. Presumably damages can be shown only if mortgage market conditions have changed so that the lender must place the loan funds with another borrower at lower interest or fees. Damages would then be computed as the difference between the discounted present values of the stream of loan fees and payments the lender would have received if the original loan had been made and the stream of such fees and payments it will be able to earn on alternate investments available at the time of the breach. Discounting should be at the interest rate prevailing in the relevant mortgage market at the date of the breach.[31] Interest on the sum thus computed should be added, again preferably at prevailing mortgage market rates, to the date of judgment.[32] The formulation suggested here presumes that the lender has mitigated its damages by re-lending at prevailing rates the money which the original loan appli-

Calif.Cont.Ed. of Bar, California Real Estate Sales Transaction §§ 4.67, 11.50 (1967), or if the contract provides that the vendor must elect between retention and other remedies, and the vendor in fact retains the deposit, see G.H. Swope Building Corp. v. Horton, 207 Tenn. 114, 338 S.W.2d 566 (1960); McMullin v. Shimmin, 10 Utah 2d 142, 349 P.2d 720 (1960). See generally Cunningham, Stoebuck & Whitman, Property § 10.4 (2d ed.1993) at 651–53; M. Friedman, Contracts and Conveyances of Real Property § 12.1(c) (3d ed. 1975); D. Dobbs, Remedies § 12.5 (1973), at 825.

29. In well-drafted commitments, language is employed to clarify the existence of additional remedies (usually in favor of their existence, since the lender is generally the drafter). For example:

> It is understood that the foregoing provision for retention of the deposit shall not constitute an option on Borrower's part not to complete the Loan transaction herein contemplated, but that Lender reserves any and all rights which it may have in law or in equity, including but not limited to specific performance.

ABA Sec. of Real Prop., Probate & Trust Law, The Lawyer's Role in Financing the Real Estate Development 36 (Probate & Prop. Cassette Series, Vol. 1, No. 3, 1975). See also Goldman v. Connecticut General Life Ins. Co., 251 Md. 575, 248 A.2d 154 (1968).

30. Capital Holding Corp. v. Octagon Devel. Co., 757 S.W.2d 202 (Ky.App.1988). See Groot, Specific Performance of Contracts to Provide Permanent Financing, 60 Cornell L.Rev. 718, 730 n. 50 (1975).

31. Lincoln Nat'l Life Ins. Co. v. NCR Corp., 603 F.Supp. 1393 (N.D.Ind.1984), order affirmed 772 F.2d 315 (7th Cir.1985). The cases that deal with discounting of future income streams contribute little on the appropriate discount rate. See generally D. Dobbs, Remedies 178 (1973). Some courts use statutory or arbitrary rates, but when the breach is so intimately tied to a particular money market, it seems fairest to use the rate prevailing in that market. One may think of the lender as receiving its damages award at the moment of breach and immediately investing it at the then-available rate. In addition, the rate at the date of breach will usually be lower than the rate specified in the commitment (the fall in rates frequently being the very reason for the commitment-holder's breach); the lower rate will produce a larger measure of damages for the lender, which seems reasonable, since the lender is the non-breaching party. Cf. Groot, supra note 30, at 732, advocating interest at mortgage market rates as of the date of judgment.

32. The damages in this sort of case are sufficiently analogous to "liquidated" damages that a court should have no difficulty in awarding interest on them from the date of breach to the date of judgment; see D. Dobbs, Remedies 165–74 (1973). Again, the prevailing rate for mortgages of the type involved should be used in computing interest on the damages, since this is probably how the lender would have invested the funds if it had been awarded them on the date of breach.

cant did not draw down; whether the lender actually re-lends at inferior rates, or not at all, is immaterial. The lender can presumably claim its out-of-pocket expenses, such as legal and architect's fees, as additional damages, but it must obviously offset against this claim all such amounts paid to or for it by the loan applicant.

The fact that damages are readily computable suggests that specific performance will not be available to the lender;[33] its remedy at law is usually entirely adequate.[34] The lender might argue that it had bargained for an interest in land, and that by analogy to land contract cases which hold every parcel of realty to be unique, specific performance should be granted.[35] But the situations are not analogous, for the lender's concern is only with the land's value as security, and not with its individual characteristics as such. Even an express clause in the commitment making it enforceable in specie is unlikely to impress an equity court. Perhaps the only situation imaginable in which specific performance should be awarded is upon a showing by the lender that no comparable investment alternatives were available to it at the time of the breach. If this is the case (which is exceedingly improbable), damages will be more difficult to compute and specific performance arguably the only feasible remedy. Even here, specific performance is both literally impossible and nonsensical if the developer has actually obtained a permanent first mortgage loan from another lender, so that the original lender cannot have the prior lien for which it contracted, or if the project has been abandoned prior to completion, so that the conditions of the original commitment cannot be fulfilled.

Lenders rarely sue holders of loan commitments for breach. The right to recover is tenuous under many commitment forms, the fees and deposits retained by lenders are often adequate recompense for their damages, and in the case of incompleted projects, the prospective borrowers are usually insolvent. In an effort to avoid the necessity of suit, while maximizing the probability that the permanent loan will actually be drawn down, some lenders enter into a "buy-sell agreement" rather than issuing a loan commitment.[36] The buy-sell agree-

---

33. An argument that the good faith deposit is a liquidated damages clause, and thus bars other remedies, will be unavailing as a defense to a specific performance suit by the lender; only damage actions are barred by this theory. See D. Dobbs, Remedies § 12.5 (1973), at 825.

34. City Centre One Assoc. v. Teachers Insurance & Annuity Ass'n, 656 F.Supp. 658 (D.Utah.1987). See Groot, supra note 30, at 727–36; Annot., 82 A.L.R.3d 1116 (1978); cf. Draper, The Broken Commitment: A Modern View of the Mortgage Lender's Remedy, 59 Cornell L.Rev. 418 (1974). Groot effectively dispatches Draper's arguments that damages are an inadequate remedy.

35. See D. Dobbs, Remedies § 12.10 (1973); Kitchen v. Herring, 42 N.C. 190 (1851). Cf. Centex Homes Corp. v. Boag, 128 N.J.Super. 385, 320 A.2d 194 (1974), denying specific performance to the vendor-builder of a unit in a large condominium project on the ground that the property was not unique.

36. See Haggarty, Procedures, Forms and Safeguards in Construction Lending with a Permanent Takeout, 85 Banking L.J. 1035, 1053 (1968); Prac.L.Inst., Real Estate Construction 327 (No. 5, 1969). The buy-sell agreement is executed by the construction and permanent lenders, and is usually endorsed by the borrower. Such agreements are illustrated in Equity Associates v. Society for Savings, 31 N.C.App.

ment contemplates that upon completion of construction, the construction loan itself will begin to require regular payments of interest and amortization and will be purchased by the permanent lender from the construction lender. The permanent lender has the added advantage of a priority dating from the commencement of construction, which in most states means that any mechanics' liens filed during construction will be subordinate if all construction advances have been obligatory.[37] There is thus no opportunity for the developer to find better permanent financing during the construction period; he or she is locked into the agreement contained in the original documents. If the permanent lender must sue, it will do so to recover on the note or to foreclose the mortgage; a "walk away" by the developer is most unlikely. From the construction lender's viewpoint, the buy-sell agreement is as satisfactory as a permanent loan commitment in most respects, although it does mean that the construction loan documents must be fully acceptable to the permanent lender. There is rarely a problem of unwillingness of the construction lender to sell the loan upon completion, since most construction lenders have little desire to get into the long-term loan business. Finally, it should be noted that loan commitments and buy-sell agreements are fundamentally different types of contracts, and a court is unlikely to rewrite the former to make it the latter.[38] The permanent lender should make it perfectly clear whether it is promising to make a new loan or purchase an existing one.

Borrower's enforcement rights. Suppose a lender, despite having issued a loan commitment to a borrower, refuses to make the loan. Assuming that the borrower has met all conditions in the commitment, so that the refusal constitutes a breach, what remedies are available to the borrower?[39] The answer seems to depend on whether the borrower has obtained another loan from an alternate source. If so, and if the interest and fees on the new loan are not higher than under the old commitment, the borrower needs no remedy, aside from possible compensation for incidental or consequential damages.[40] More frequently, however, the new loan will carry higher interest and fees, a reflection of the fact that market rates have risen since the commitment was issued—the very fact which may have induced the committing lender to breach. On these facts damages are an appropriate and adequate remedy. Their computation is similar to the calculation of lender's

182, 228 S.E.2d 761 (1976), certiorari denied 291 N.C. 711, 232 S.E.2d 203 (1977), and Goldstein v. Lincoln Sav. Bank, 144 A.D.2d 281, 534 N.Y.S.2d 164 (1988), in both of which the permanent lender refused to purchase the loan.

37. See Selective Builders, Inc. v. Hudson City Savings Bank, 137 N.J.Super. 500, 349 A.2d 564 (1975); § 12.7, infra.

38. See Exchange Bank & Trust Co. v. Lone Star Life Insurance Co., 546 S.W.2d 948 (Tex.Civ.App.1977).

39. The borrower is not the only possible plaintiff. In Silverdale Hotel Associates v. Lomas & Nettleton Co., 36 Wash. App. 762, 677 P.2d 773 (1984), review denied 101 Wash.2d 1021 (1984), a general contractor recovered damages from a defaulting construction lender on a promissory estoppel theory.

40. Sparks v. Farmers Fed. Sav. & Loan Ass'n, 183 W.Va. 315, 395 S.E.2d 559 (1990) (where borrower obtained other financing on more favorable terms, borrower could recover commitment fee from breaching lender).

damages discussed above: the difference between the present values of the payments the borrower would have made under the original commitment and those that must be made under reasonable alternative financing.[41] Obviously, the terms of the actual substitute loan obtained will usually be excellent evidence of what is reasonably available in the market, particularly if the borrower shopped diligently for it.

The cases dealing with consequential damages suffered by erstwhile borrowers display a surprising diversity. Each element of damages must meet three initial tests: (1) it must have been "foreseeable" or "within the contemplation" of the parties to the loan commitment, (2) it must have been caused by the lender's breach, and (3) it must be provable with reasonable precision. Clearly the borrower should recover commitment fees already paid to the breaching lender. Direct expenditures related to obtaining a substitute loan, such as architects', abstract, and title attorneys' fees, recording and notary charges, etc., usually qualify without difficulty.[42] Lost rents or profits have been allowed,[43] but usually only upon rather convincing proof that they

---

41. See supra text at note 31; Lester v. RTC, 125 B.R. 528 (D.C.Ill.1991); Bridgkort Racquet Club, Inc. v. University Bank, 85 Wis.2d 706, 271 N.W.2d 165 (1978); United of Omaha Life Insurance Co. v. Nob Hill Associates, 450 So.2d 536 (Fla.App. 1984), petition for review dismissed 458 So.2d 273 (Fla.1984), petition for review denied 458 So.2d 274 (1984); Pipkin v. Thomas & Hill, Inc., 298 N.C. 278, 258 S.E.2d 778 (1979); Annot., 4 A.L.R.4th 682, 690 (1981); 36 A.L.R. 1408 (1925); 44 A.L.R. 1486 (1926); Quail, Wallace, Gallo & Hogan, Remedies for Breach of Commitment, Probate & Property, Sept./Oct. 1989, at 47.

Many of the cases state the measure of damages too loosely, as the "difference in the interest rates" or the "increased interest," and provide no discussion of the present value aspect of the computation. See, e.g., Rubin v. Pioneer Federal Savings & Loan Association, 214 Neb. 364, 334 N.W.2d 424 (1983); Consolidated American Life Insurance Co. v. Covington, 297 So.2d 894 (Miss.1974); Archer–Daniels–Midland Co. v. Paull, 188 F.Supp. 277 (W.D.Ark. 1960) reversed 293 F.2d 389 (8th Cir.1961), on remand 199 F.Supp. 319 (W.D.Ark. 1961), affirmed 313 F.2d 612 (8th Cir.1963); Annot., 36 A.L.R. 1408 (1925). At least one opinion expressly approves discounting the stream of damages to present value, but provides no indication of the appropriate interest rate or method; Financial Fed. Sav. & Loan Assoc. v. Continental Enterprises, Inc., 338 So.2d 907 (Fla.App.1976); see particularly the dissent of Pearson, J., arguing that the discount should not be at the statutory rate, but at a rate which is fair and just under the circumstances, taking into account current rates in the relevant money market.

If the lender's breach has caused the owner to lose his or her equity in the land, as by foreclosure of a construction loan, the measure of damages is the lost value; see United California Bank v. Prudential Insurance Co., 140 Ariz. 238, 681 P.2d 390, 447–48 (App.1983). See also Lincor Contractors, Ltd. v. Hyskell, 39 Wash.App. 317, 692 P.2d 903 (1984), review denied 103 Wash.2d 1036 (1985) (damages in amount of equity that borrower would have had in building never built due to construction lender's breach.)

42. Pipkin v. Thomas & Hill, Inc., 298 N.C. 278, 258 S.E.2d 778 (1979); Coastland Corp. v. Third National Mortgage Co., 611 F.2d 969 (4th Cir.1979) (damages for breach of construction loan commitment include amount developer paid for permanent loan commitment, which was never used due to defendant's breach); Culp v. Western Loan & Building Co., 124 Wash. 326, 214 P. 145 (1923), affirmed 127 Wash. 249, 220 P. 766 (1923). See Annot., 4 A.L.R.4th 682, 695–98 (1981). Note that the borrower who seeks damages is not entitled to recover the commitment fee on the original loan as well, since he or she is affirming the contract; see Rubin v. Pioneer Fed. Sav. & Loan, 214 Neb. 364, 334 N.W.2d 424 (1983).

43. W–V Enterprises, Inc. v. Federal Sav. & Loan Ins. Corp., 234 Kan. 354, 673 P.2d 1112, 1123 (1983) (also awarding punitive damages for fraud); Pasadena Associates v. Connor, 460 S.W.2d 473 (Tex.Civ. App.1970), error refused n.r.e.; Archer–

would have been earned if the loan had been granted.[44] More remote damages,[45] such as the loss of favorable relations with subcontractors, damage to the borrower's credit standing, loss of a contractor's license, and even mental suffering,[46] are conceivable, though difficult to prove.

If the prospective borrower has been unable or unwilling to obtain another loan, the remedial picture is quite different. The borrower may, of course, seek damages, and they will presumably be measured in the same fashion as described above.[47] It is more probable, however, that he or she will pray for specific performance of the commitment, hoping thereby to salvage ownership of the property. Manifold authorities hold that this remedy is unavailable for breach of a loan commitment, the remedy at law being fully adequate,[48] but in fact numerous cases have granted specific performance. Nearly all of these can be explained by the fact that the lender had already closed the loan, recorded the mortgage, and even made some disbursements before closing the credit window.[49] On such facts, the lender's actions will have made alternative first mortgage financing impossible; the mortgage encumbers the borrower's title, and no other lender will be able to

Daniels–Midland Co. v. Paull, 188 F.Supp. 277 (W.D.Ark.1960), reversed in part 293 F.2d 389 (8th Cir.1961), order on remand 199 F.Supp. 319 (W.D.Ark.1961), affirmed 313 F.2d 612 (8th Cir.1963). See Annot., 4 A.L.R.4th 682, 698–708 (1981).

44. The evidence has often been unconvincing to the courts; see First Mississippi Bank v. Latch, 433 So.2d 946 (Miss. 1983); Coastland Corp. v. Third National Mortgage Co., 611 F.2d 969, 977–78 (4th Cir.1979); Davis v. Small Business Investment Co., 535 S.W.2d 740 (Tex.Civ.App. 1976); Stanish v. Polish Roman Catholic Union, 484 F.2d 713 (7th Cir.Ind.1973); St. Paul at Chase Corp. v. Manufacturers Life Insurance Co., 262 Md. 192, 278 A.2d 12 (1971), certiorari denied 404 U.S. 857, 92 S.Ct. 104, 30 L.Ed.2d 98 (1971); Archer–Daniels–Midland Co. v. Paull, note 43 supra. See also A.M.R. Enterprises v. United Postal Savings Ass'n, 567 F.2d 1277 (5th Cir.1978) (construction loan commitment breached; developer can recover fees paid and costs paid toward construction).

45. See Bank of New Mexico v. Rice, 78 N.M. 170, 429 P.2d 368 (1967), modified after remand 79 N.M. 115, 440 P.2d 790 (1968).

46. See Westesen v. Olathe State Bank, 78 Colo. 217, 240 P. 689, 44 A.L.R. 1484 (1925).

47. See text at note 40, supra; Northwest Land & Investment, Inc. v. New West Fed. Sav. & Loan Ass'n, 57 Wash.App. 32, 786 P.2d 324 (1990), review denied 115 Wash.2d 1013, 797 P.2d 513 (1990) (denying deficiency judgment after foreclosure by lender who breached commitment). But see Commerce Financial v. Markwest Corp., 806 P.2d 200 (Utah App.1990) (damages denied, where borrower failed to mitigate damages by attempting to obtain substitute financing); cf. Davis v. First Interstate Bank, 115 Idaho 169, 765 P.2d 680 (1988) (mitigation by rancher borrowers not required, where bank assured them that it would not let their sheep starve).

48. The classic case is Rogers v. Challis, 54 Eng.Rep. 68 (Ch.1859). See Towers Charter & Marine Corp. v. Cadillac Insurance Co., 894 F.2d 516 (2d Cir.1990); American Bancshares Mortg. Co. v. Empire Home Loans, Inc., 568 F.2d 1124 (5th Cir. 1978); Investment Service Co. v. Smither, 276 Or. 837, 556 P.2d 955 (1976); Kent v. Walter E. Heller & Co., 349 F.2d 480 (5th Cir.1965); Steward v. Bounds, 167 Wash. 554, 9 P.2d 1112 (1932), modified 170 Wash. 698, 15 P.2d 1119 (1932). See Annot., 82 A.L.R.3d 1116 (1978).

49. Vandeventer v. Dale Construction Co., 271 Or. 691, 534 P.2d 183 (1975), appeal after remand 277 Or. 817, 562 P.2d 196 (1977); Cuna Mutual Insurance Society v. Dominguez, 9 Ariz.App. 172, 450 P.2d 413 (1969); Southampton Wholesale Food Terminal, Inc. v. Providence Produce Warehouse Co., 129 F.Supp. 663 (D.Mass. 1955); Jacobson v. First National Bank, 129 N.J.Eq. 440, 20 A.2d 19 (1941), affirmed, 130 N.J.Eq. 604, 23 A.2d 409 (1942); Columbus Club v. Simons, 110 Okl. 48, 236 P. 12 (1925).

secure a first lien until the old mortgage is satisfied. Several of these cases have involved construction loans, with the additional difficulty of refinancing a partially completed project. If the borrower is precluded from access to the mortgage market, the traditional measure of damages, which requires proof of the availability and cost of alternative loans, becomes meaningless, and specific performance is entirely appropriate.

Even if the prospective borrower has not executed a mortgage to the committing lender, he or she might be able to obtain a decree of specific performance if efforts to obtain an alternate loan have been unsuccessful. It is difficult to apply the traditional measure of damages with confidence on these facts: what is the interest rate on reasonably available mortgage financing if the borrower has been able to come up with no financing at all? Moreover, if the breached commitment is for a permanent loan at the completion of construction, the lender's default may result in consequential damages which will be difficult to quantify but are nonetheless harsh, including the besmirching of the developer's reputation and credit and the possible inability of subcontractors and materials suppliers to collect for their contributions to the project.[50] Several recent cases have recognized these factors [51] and granted specific performance even though no mortgage had been executed to the lender.[52]

Not many specific performance cases have been decided, probably because the remedy is usually unattractive from the borrower's viewpoint. The delay inherent in litigation suggests that it is economically feasible only if the borrower has access to some interim financing while the case is pending (such as a construction loan which can be extended until the permanent financing becomes available as a result of the court's decree.) [53] Generally, an alternative loan and a suit for damages

50. See generally Groot, Specific Performance of Contracts to Provide Permanent Financing, 60 Cornell L.Rev. 718, 741 (1975). Other damages in this situation, such as the loss of the project due to construction loan foreclosure, and a possible deficiency judgment, are more readily measurable. See St. Paul at Chase Corp. v. Manufacturers Life Insurance Co., 262 Md. 192, 278 A.2d 12 (1971), certiorari denied 404 U.S. 857, 92 S.Ct. 104, 30 L.Ed.2d 98 (1971).

51. First National State Bank v. Commonwealth Fed. Sav. & Loan Ass'n, 610 F.2d 164 (3d Cir.1979) (specific performance granted because damages would be difficult to ascertain); Selective Builders, Inc. v. Hudson City Savings Bank, 137 N.J.Super. 500, 349 A.2d 564 (1975). Specific performance of a sales contract is routinely granted to the purchaser, even when the contract calls for the seller to finance the sale by taking back a purchase-money mortgage; see Turley v. Ball Associates Limited, 641 P.2d 286 (Colo.App.1981).

52. In Leben v. Nassau Savings & Loan Association, 40 A.D.2d 830, 337 N.Y.S.2d 310 (1972), affirmed 34 N.Y.2d 671, 356 N.Y.S.2d 46, 312 N.E.2d 180 (1974), the permanent lender insisted on a higher interest rate at closing than had been agreed to in the commitment. The borrower signed the documents, but sought and obtained judicial reformation to readjust the interest rate downward. Some dicta in the opinion might be read as approving specific performance, but on the facts the case is similar to those cited in note 47, supra, with reformation of future payments as a substitute for damages. See Groot, supra note 50, at 725-27.

53. Compare Selective Builders, Inc. v. Hudson City Savings Bank, 137 N.J.Super. 500, 349 A.2d 564 (1975), in which the construction lender gave such an extension, making a specific performance suit

are more appealing to the borrower, and if the project or the borrower is so weak that no other financing can be obtained, a court might infer that a decree of specific performance would also be inefficient and bad policy, constituting a futile effort to shore up an economically fatal situation; this risk would have to be balanced against the arguments favoring specific performance mentioned in the preceding paragraph.

The Securities and Exchange Act of 1934

In United States v. Austin,[54] the Tenth Circuit Court of Appeals considered a charge of criminal fraud against a lender based on the antifraud provisions of Section 10(b) of the Securities and Exchange Act of 1934.[55] In substance, the government argued that the lender had issued a mortgage loan commitment and charged a commitment fee with no intention of ever making the loan. The court concluded that the commitment letter was a "security" within the meaning of the Act, and upheld the defendants' conviction. If the holding were sound, civil remedies would be available as well.[56]

The decision, however, is of dubious validity, and its logical implications would cut a wide swath indeed: virtually every executory bilateral contract in which one party pays money consideration in return for the other's future performance would be a security. Plainly the commitment fee paid by a loan applicant is in no sense an "investment;" the applicant does not expect "profits to come solely from the efforts" of the lender.[57] Indeed, the lender's performance of its commitment will ordinarily be entirely independent of its internal profitability during the commitment period. The commitment will yield the applicant neither capital appreciation nor a participation in earnings, but only a loan of money upon previously agreed terms. Any profits earned by the borrower will be attributable to his or her own entrepreneurial and managerial efforts, not those of the lender.[58]

The Tenth Circuit appears to have repented of its holding in *Austin*. In McGovern Plaza Joint Venture v. First of Denver Mortgage Investors,[59] it held that neither the construction loan nor permanent loan commitments on hotel construction project were securities, lamely

feasible, with St. Paul at Chase Corp. v. Manufacturers Life Insurance Co., 262 Md. 192, 278 A.2d 12 (1971), certiorari denied 404 U.S. 857, 92 S.Ct. 104, 30 L.Ed.2d 98 (1971), in which the construction lender foreclosed and purchased the project, leaving the developer with only a suit for damages against the reneging permanent lender.

54. 462 F.2d 724 (10th Cir.1972), certiorari denied 409 U.S. 1048, 93 S.Ct. 518, 34 L.Ed.2d 501 (1972).

55. 15 U.S.C.A. § 78j(b).

56. See J.I. Case v. Borak, 377 U.S. 426, 84 S.Ct. 1555, 12 L.Ed.2d 423 (1964); Kardon v. National Gypsum Co., 73 F.Supp. 798 (E.D.Pa.1947), supplemented 83 F.Supp. 613 (1947).

57. S.E.C. v. W. J. Howey Co., 328 U.S. 293, 301, 66 S.Ct. 1100, 1104, 90 L.Ed. 1244 (1946), rehearing denied 329 U.S. 819, 67 S.Ct. 27, 91 L.Ed. 697 (1946).

58. See United Housing Foundation, Inc. v. Forman, 421 U.S. 837, 95 S.Ct. 2051, 44 L.Ed.2d 621 (1975), rehearing denied 423 U.S. 884, 96 S.Ct. 157, 46 L.Ed.2d 115 (1975). See generally Sonnenschein, Federal Securities Law Coverage of Note Transactions: The Antifraud Provisions, 35 Bus.Law 1567 (1980).

59. 562 F.2d 645 (10th Cir.1977).

distinguishing *Austin* on the ground that it involved a "large-scale, advance fee loan swindle" in which the "entire procedure was fraudulent." It is difficult to see the relevance of the scale or gravity of the fraud in determining whether a security is being sold. *Austin* should be regarded as overruled,[60] although it has attracted some following.[61] While its securities aspect is a red herring, the case nevertheless contains a useful lesson. The issuance of a loan commitment may well be fraud under state law, if at the time of issuance the lender intends to breach. Both criminal and civil penalties may be applicable in many jurisdictions.

§ 12.4 Mechanics' Liens

Mechanics' and materialmen's liens, created by statute, give unpaid contractors, workers, and materials suppliers a security interest in the real estate which they have improved; they may foreclose such liens as an aid to the recovery of the payment owed them. Although the legal scholar can find authority that a form of mechanics' lien existed in the Roman law,[1] was well developed in the civil law [2] and was incorporated in the Code Napoleon,[3] it was unknown in England, either at common law or in equity [4] and, so far as our present laws are concerned, is of native origin in the United States, dating back to the Maryland statute of 1791.[5] Today in every state in the Union such

---

60. The *Austin* holding was rejected explicitly by Cocklereece v. Moran, 532 F.Supp. 519 (N.D.Ga.1982); Lee v. Navarro Savings Association, 416 F.Supp. 1186 (N.D.Tex.1976), reversed on other grounds 597 F.2d 421 (5th Cir.1979), affirmed 446 U.S. 458, 100 S.Ct. 1779, 64 L.Ed.2d 425 (1980); and FBS Financial, Inc. v. Cleve-Trust Realty Investors, CCH Fed.Sec. L.Rep.Par. 96,341 (1977), and implicitly by United States v. Namer, 680 F.2d 1088, 1096 n. 16 (5th Cir.1982), on remand 1987 WL 6576 (E.D.La.1987), affirmed 835 F.2d 1084 (5th Cir.1988), certiorari denied 486 U.S. 1006, 108 S.Ct. 1731, 100 L.Ed.2d 195 (1988) and McClure v. First National Bank, 352 F.Supp. 454 (N.D.Tex.1973), affirmed 497 F.2d 490 (5th Cir.1974), certiorari denied 420 U.S. 930, 95 S.Ct. 1132, 43 L.Ed.2d 402 (1975). See also Sanders v. John Nuveen & Co., Inc., 463 F.2d 1075 (7th Cir.1972), certiorari denied 409 U.S. 1009, 93 S.Ct. 443, 34 L.Ed.2d 302 (1972); LTV Federal Credit Union v. UMIC Government Securities, Inc., 523 F.Supp. 819 (N.D.Tex.1981), affirmed 704 F.2d 199 (5th Cir.1983), certiorari denied 464 U.S. 852, 104 S.Ct. 163, 78 L.Ed.2d 149 (1983) (standby commitment to purchase GNMA mortgage-backed securities is not itself a security); First Federal Savings & Loan Association v. Mortgage Corp. of the South, 467 F.Supp. 943 (N.D.Ala.1979), affirmed on the other grounds 650 F.2d 1376 (5th Cir.1981).

61. See FSLIC v. Provo Excelsior Ltd., 664 F.Supp. 1405 (D.Utah 1987); State v. Gates, 325 N.W.2d 166 (N.D.1982) (state securities act).

§ 12.4

1. Mackeldy, Handbook of the Roman Law, Dropsie's Translation, 274.

2. See South Fork Canal Co. v. Gordon, 73 U.S. (6 Wall.) 561, 571, 18 L.Ed. 894 (1867); Jones v. Great Southern Fireproof Hotel Co., 86 Fed. 370, 386 (6th Cir.1898), reversed 177 U.S. 449, 20 S.Ct. 690, 44 L.Ed. 842 (1900); 1 Domat, Civil Law, 1861 ed., 681–4, arts. 1736, 1741–5.

3. Code Napoleon, Privileges and Mortgages, § 2 (2103).

4. See South Fork Canal Co. v. Gordon, supra note 2; Van Stone v. Stillwell & Bierce Manufacturing Co., 142 U.S. 128, 136, 12 S.Ct. 181, 183, 35 L.Ed. 961 (1891); Durling v. Gould, 83 Me. 134, 137, 21 A. 833 (1890).

5. Acts of General Assembly of Maryland, c. 45, § 10 (1791). "The origin of such laws, in America, arose from the desire to establish and improve, as readily as possible, the city of Washington. In 1791, at a meeting of the commissioners appointed for such purpose, both Thomas Jefferson and James Madison were present, and a memorial was adopted urging the General

legislation exists,[6] but because the liens are wholly statutory, because the laws creating them are extremely varied both in their provisions and in the courts' construction of them, and because legislatures have been prolific with amendments, generalizations are extremely difficult and always must be checked against local enactments.[7] Furthermore, case law is unreliable in the field because the decisions are meaningful only with reference to the particular statute under which each arose and the precise language of the act at that time. This variability has been justified on the ground that the problems involved are dissimilar in different parts of the country,[8] even perhaps from state to state. This assertion is dubious, but efforts to secure the adoption of uniform legislation on the subject have thus far failed.[9] Because of the result-

Assembly of Maryland to pass an act securing to *master-builders,* a lien, on houses erected, and land occupied. The requested law was enacted December 19, 1791." Moore–Mansfield Const. Co. v. Indianapolis New Castle & Toledo Railway Co., 179 Ind. 356, 369, 101 N.E. 296, 44 L.R.A.,N.S. 816, Ann.Cas.1915D, 917 (1913). See Barry Properties v. Fick Bros., 277 Md. 15, 353 A.2d 222 (1976). The next statute was in Pennsylvania in 1803. Act of April 1, 1803, P.L. 791; see Cushman, Proposed Mechanics' Lien Law, 80 U.Pa.L.Rev. 1083 n. 3 (1932).

6. See Armour & Co. v. Western Const. Co., 36 Wash. 529, 78 P. 1106 (1905). In at least two states mechanics' liens are provided for by constitution. West's Ann.Cal. Const. Art. 14, § 3; Vernon's Ann.Tex. Const. Art. 16, § 37; see Youngblood, Mechanics' and Materialmen's Liens in Texas, 26 Sw.L.J. 665, 687 (1972).

7. General (and necessarily cursory) summaries of mechanics' lien law from a national perspective include Introductory Comment, Art. 5, Uniform Simplification of Land Transfers Act, 14 Uniform Laws Annot. 271 (1980); Comment, Mechanics' Liens and Surety Bonds in the Building Trades, 68 Yale L.J. 138 (1968); Report of the Standard State Mechanics' Lien Act Committee of the U.S. Dept. of Commerce 19–25 (1932).

Numerous articles and comments analyze the mechanics' lien laws of particular states. Among these (omitting title and author for the sake of brevity) are: 6 Cumb.L.Rev. 243 (Ala.1975); 7 Ariz.L.Rev. 296 (Ariz.1966); 25 Hast.L.J. 1043 (Cal. 1974); 47 L.A.Bar.Bull. 299 (Cal.1972); 9 Santa Clara L. 101 (Cal.1968); Colo.Law., Feb.1979, at 196 (Colo.1979); 39 U.Colo. L.Rev. 105 (Colo.1966); 62 Fla.B.J. 21 (Fla., Mar.1988); 18 Fla.St.U.L.Rev. 257 (Fla. 1991); 29 U.Fla.L.Rev. 411 (Fla.1977); 47 Chi.-Kent L.Rev. 157 (Ill.1970); 36 Ind.L.J. 526 (Ind.1921); 51 Iowa L.Rev. 862 (Iowa, 1966); 47 Iowa L.Rev. 144 (Iowa 1961); 62 Ky.L.J. 278 (Ky.1972); 44 Tul.L.Rev. 326 (La.1970); 6 U.Balt.L.Rev. 180 (Md.1977); 28 Md.L.Rev. 225 (Md.1968); 37 Miss.L.J. 385 (Miss.1966); J.Mo.Bar, Apr.-May 1990, at 201 (Mo.1990); 52 Mo.L.Rev. 989 (Mo. 1987); 54 U.M.K.C.L.Rev. 109 (Mo.1985); 42 Mo.L.Rev. 53 (Mo.1976); 12 Wake For. L.Rev. 283 (N.C.1976); 38 Ohio St.L.J. 3 (Ohio 1977); 3 Akron L.Rev. 1 (Ohio 1969); 29 Ohio St.L.J. 917 (Ohio 1968); 74 Dick. L.Rev. 740 (Pa.1970); 35 U.Pitt.L.Rev. 265 (Pa.1963); 36 Rh.Is.B.J. 14 (R.I.1988); 25 S.C.L.Rev. 817 (S.C.1974); 6 Memph.St. L.Rev. 519 (Tenn.1976); 5 Memph.St.L.Rev. 359 (Tenn.1975); 26 Southwest L.J. 665 (Tex.1972); 1966 Ut.L.Rev. 181 (Utah 1966); 25 U.Rich.L.Rev. 291 (Va.1991); 49 Wash.L.Rev. 685 (Wash.1974).

On title insurance coverage of mechanics liens, see Jordan, What You Should Know About Mechanics' Lien Coverage In 1989, Title News, Jan.1989, at 5; Jones & Ressall, Mechanic's Lien Title Insurance Coverage for Construction Projects, 16 Real Est.L.J. 291 (1988).

8. See Glenn, Mortgages § 351.

9. The proposed Uniform Mechanics Lien Law, drafted by the Commissioners on Uniform State Laws in 1932, was adopted only by Florida, and was withdrawn in 1943; see Handbook of Comm. on Uniform State Laws 150 (1943); Cushman, The Proposed Uniform Mechanics' Lien Law, 80 U.Pa.L.Rev. 1083 (1932). The Florida law, which persists today with modifications, is discussed in Note, Lien Rights and Construction Lending: Responsibilities and Liabilities in Florida, 29 U.Fla.L.Rev. 411 (1977). In 1976 the Commissioners on Uniform State Laws promulgated the Uniform Simplification of Land Transfers Act, Article 5 of which deals with "construction liens," and is partially based, in turn, on the Florida statute. This new proposal

§ 12.4 FINANCING REAL ESTATE CONSTRUCTION 185

ing state-by-state complexity, a comprehensive treatment of mechanics' liens is impossible here. However, the principal groups of statutes and their general features can be outlined.

The basic idea of the mechanics' lien is that those whose work or materials go into an improvement to real estate [10] should be permitted, in fairness, to satisfy their unpaid bills out of that real estate.[11] Beginning with the original Maryland statute, "[t]hese laws grew, and their validity became established, as the courts held that the building business did not have the protection inherent in the widespread distribution of credit risk common to other businesses, and therefore needed this broader and special protection. Contractors, subcontractors, materialmen, and other building groups were frequently obliged to extend credit in larger amounts, and for longer time, than other businesses. Such parties might have their entire capital, or a substantial part of it, tied up in one or two, or ten or twenty, projects under construction." [12]

To begin with only general contractors or master-builders were given protection under the acts.[13] But by a process of amendment and enlargement of the similar acts that were passed in other states, today "practically every segment composing the construction industry—including contractors, subcontractors, material dealers, laborers, artisans, architects, landscape architects, engineers, surveyors—is granted liens of varying extent under varying conditions for the labor, services, or materials furnished or contracted to be furnished for the particular improvement." [14]

contains some of the features of the 1932 Act, including a requirement that the lien claimant give notice to the owner of his or her potential claim. It has been adopted only in Nebraska at this writing; see Neb. Rev.Stat. §§ 52-125 to 52-159.

10. See John Wagner Assoc. v. Hercules, Inc., 797 P.2d 1123 (Utah App.1990), certiorari denied 815 P.2d 241 (Utah 1991) (modular buildings, although removable, were part of real estate and gave rise to mechanics lien); Alaska Cascade Financial Services, Inc. v. Doors Northwest, Inc., 52 Wash.App. 588, 762 P.2d 362 (1988) (modular buildings lienable, even though constructed off-site). Even work done off-site may be lienable if it directly benefits the property; see Vulcraft, a Div. of Nucor Corp. v. Midtown Business Park, Ltd., 110 N.M. 761, 800 P.2d 195 (1990) (steel fabrication performed off-site); Northlake Concrete Products, Inc. v. Wylie, 34 Wash.App. 810, 663 P.2d 1380 (1983) (sewer line).

11. This does not necessarily mean the contract price can be recovered; if the work was done badly or improperly, the lien may be for less, or even zero. See Summit–Top Devel., Inc. v. Williamson Constr., Inc., 203 Ga.App. 460, 416 S.E.2d 889 (1992); Ed Hackstaff Concrete, Inc. v. Powder Ridge Condominium "A" Owners' Association, 679 P.2d 1112 (Colo.App.1984); Tighe v. Kenyon, 681 P.2d 547 (Colo.App. 1984); Cashway Concrete & Materials v. Sanner Contracting Co., 158 Ariz. 81, 761 P.2d 155 (App.1988) (lien is for reasonable value of materials furnished; contract price is evidence of reasonable value). If a valid contract is proved, the contractor may get a personal judgment even though he or she failed properly to perfect a lien; see Douglas Northwest, Inc. v. Bill O'Brien & Sons Construction, Inc., 64 Wash.App. 661, 828 P.2d 565 (1992); Paro v. Biondo, 105 App.Div.2d 577, 481 N.Y.S.2d 518 (1984).

12. Stalling, Mechanics' Lien Laws As They Exist Today, 4 F.H.L.B.Rev. 232 (1938); see Cook v. Carlson, 364 F.Supp. 24 (D.S.D.1973).

13. Acts of General Assembly of Maryland, c. 45, § 10 (1791).

14. Stalling, supra note 12; Note, Mechanics Lien Priority Rights for Design Professionals, 46 Wash. & Lee L.Rev. 1035 (1989); Survey of Illinois Law, 1951–1952: Mechanics Liens—Fixtures, 31 Chi.Kent L.Rev. 71 (1952). See Mark Twain Kansas City Bank v. Kroh Bros. Development Co.,

If the mechanics' lien were limited to those with whom the owner dealt with directly, little question would arise as to the amount of the lien upon the property—it would be for the unpaid amount still owing under the contract. When the acts extended the coverage to persons who had no direct dealings with the owner, the statutes divided into two main classes. One, generally designated the "Pennsylvania" type,[15] gives the subcontractor or materialman a direct right of his own regardless of the existence of any indebtedness between the owner and general contractor[16] and measured by the value of his contribution. Conceivably,[17] under such statutes the claims of the ancillary contractors could exceed the contract price or could still exist even though the owner had paid the general contractor in full; nevertheless they are generally upheld when attacked as unconstitutional.[18] The other type

14 Kan.App.2d 714, 798 P.2d 511 (1990) (architect may have lien only if building is constructed); Kenneth D. Collins Agency v. Hagerott, 211 Mont. 303, 684 P.2d 487 (1984); Stern v. Great Plains Fed. Sav. & Loan Ass'n, 778 P.2d 933 (Okl.App.1989) (same); Branecky v. Seaman, 688 S.W.2d 117 (Tex.App.1984), error refused n.r.e. (same); Stratford v. Boland, 306 Pa.Super. 475, 452 A.2d 824 (1982) (architect may have lien only if he supervises construction.)

As to the right to mechanic's lien as for "labor" or "work" in case of preparatory or fabricating work done on materials intended for use and used in particular building or structure, see 25 A.L.R.2d 1370 (1952). In Nolte v. Smith, 189 Cal.App.2d 140, 11 Cal.Rptr. 261 (1961), a civil engineer who surveyed, planned and prepared a subdivision map for recording and erected permanent markers and monuments on the property was held to be entitled to a mechanic's lien. See also Torkko/Korman/Engineers v. Penland Ventures, 673 P.2d 769 (Alaska 1983). Cf. Nevada Nat. Bank v. Snyder, 108 Nev. 151, 826 P.2d 560 (1992) (architectural, soil testing, and survey work not sufficient to establish lien); Laurence J. Rich & Assoc. v. First Interstate Mortg. Co., 807 P.2d 1199 (Colo.App.1990) (legal services performed for developer were not lienable). Engineers' and architects' liens are sometimes provided by statute; see, e.g., Utah Code Ann. § 38–1–3 (1981).

Compare Anderson v. Breezy Point Estates, 283 Minn. 490, 168 N.W.2d 693 (1969) (surveyor may not have lien for cutting brush and staking lots); Rotta v. Hawk, 756 P.2d 713 (Utah App.1988) (cutting brush is not lienable); and George A.Z. Johnson, Jr., Inc. v. Barnhill, 279 S.C. 242, 306 S.E.2d 216 (1983) (surveying and laying out lots not lienable) with Midland Mortgage Co. v. Sanders England Investments, 682 P.2d 748 (Okl.1984) (surveying work is lienable). See also Fortune v. Superior Court, 159 Ariz. 549, 768 P.2d 1194 (App.1989) (where contract was terminated before completion, contractor not entitled to lien for overhead or expected profit); Big S Trucking Co. v. Gervais Favrot, Inc., 450 So.2d 369 (La.App.1983) (lien allowed for hauling away trash or dirt); Hardin Const. Group, Inc. v. Carlisle Const. Co., 300 S.C. 456, 388 S.E.2d 794 (1990) (no lien allowed to lessor of rental equipment used in construction). See Annot., 32 A.L.R.4th 1130 (1984).

15. See 49 Pa.Stat. § 1301. Approximately 30 states adopt the Pennsylvania approach; see Comment, Mechanics' Liens and Surety Bonds in the Building Trades, 68 Yale L.J. 138, 144 n. 30 (1958); Annot., 75 A.L.R.3d 505 (1977).

16. Cf. Baldwin Locomotive Works v. Edward Hines Lumber Co., 189 Ind. 189, 125 N.E. 400 (1919), holding that an express stipulation between owner and general contractor could negative a direct lien.

17. Statutes usually fix the contract price as the uppermost limit for such claims. See Prince v. Neal–Millard Co., 124 Ga. 884, 53 S.E. 761, 4 Ann.Cas. 615 (1906).

18. E.g., Jones v. Great Southern Fireproof Hotel Co., 86 Fed. 370, 30 C.C.A. 108 (1898), certiorari granted 173 U.S. 704, 19 S.Ct. 885 (1899), reversed 177 U.S. 449, 20 S.Ct. 690, 44 L.Ed. 842 (1900); AMI Operating Partners Ltd. v. JAD Enterprises, Inc., 77 Md.App. 654, 551 A.2d 888 (1989), certiorari denied 315 Md. 307, 554 A.2d 393 (1989); Hightower v. Bailey, 108 Ky. 198, 56 S.W. 147, 22 Ky.Law Rep. 88, 49 L.R.A. 255, 94 Am.St.Rep. 350 (1900); Becker v. Hopper, 22 Wyo. 237, 138 P. 179, Ann.Cas. 1916D, 1041 (1914), affirmed on rehearing 23 Wyo. 209, 147 P. 1085, Ann.Cas.1918B, 35 (1915). But contra, see Selma Sash,

of statute, usually referred to as the "New York" system, measures the liability of the owner's property by the price stated in the original contract with the general contractor less payments properly made to the contractor.[19] The theory of these statutes is that all lien rights are based directly or derivatively upon the contract between the owner and general contractor.[20]

The procedure which a lien claimant must follow varies widely, but he or she is typically required to file a notice of the claim within some fixed period of time, commonly 60 to 180 days, after completing the work.[21] The notice is usually required to be recorded, served personally on the owner, published in a newspaper, or made effective by some combination of these methods. If the claim is not paid within some additional period, the claimant must usually bring a judicial action to foreclose the lien in a manner similar to mortgage foreclosures.[22]

Door & Blind Factory v. Stoddard, 116 Ala. 251, 22 So. 555 (1897); Gibbs v. Tally, 133 Cal. 373, 65 P. 970 (1901). An amended version of the California statute was upheld in Roystone Co. v. Darling, 171 Cal. 526, 154 P. 15 (1915).

19. See N.Y.Cons.Laws, Cahill, c. 34, §§ 4, 14 (now N.Y.—McKinney's Lien Law, §§ 4, 14). West's Fla.Stat.Ann. § 713.-06(1); Official Code Ga.Ann. § 44–14–361(b). See Justice v. Arab Lumber and Supply, Inc., 533 So.2d 538 (Ala.1988); Dallas Bldg. Material, Inc. v. Rose, 191 Ga. App. 783, 383 S.E.2d 151 (1989); Ace Contracting Co. v. Garfield & Arma Associates, 148 Misc.2d 475, 560 N.Y.S.2d 382 (1990); Electric Supply Co. v. Swain Electrical Co., 328 N.C. 651, 403 S.E.2d 291 (1991); A.V.A. Construction Corp. v. Palmetto Land Clearing, Inc., ___ S.C.App. ___, 418 S.E.2d 317 (1992); Sewer Viewer, Inc. v. Shawnee Sunset Developers, Inc., 454 So.2d 701 (Fla. App.1984) (statute's limitation does not apply if there is no specific price stated in general contract).

20. See Electric City Concrete Co. v. Phillips, 100 A.D.2d 1, 473 N.Y.S.2d 608 (1984). Commonly there are additional provisions making it the duty of the owner, on receiving notification of unpaid obligations by the contractor to subcontractors, to withhold payments to the contractor for the benefit of the notifying lien claimant. Other statutes make it the duty of the owner, on making payments under the contract, to require a statement under oath from the contractor of the sums owed to subcontractors and then to withhold those sums.

21. See Bailey Mortg. Co. v. Gobble-Fite Lumber Co., Inc., 565 So.2d 138 (Ala. 1990) (notice must also be given to construction lender, if the lender's identity can reasonably be obtained); First Federal Savings & Loan Association v. Connelly, 97 Ill.2d 242, 73 Ill.Dec. 454, 454 N.E.2d 314 (1983); Wavetek Indiana, Inc. v. K.H. Gatewood Steel Co., 458 N.E.2d 265 (Ind.App. 1984); AAA Electric & Neon Serv., Inc. v. R–Design Co., 364 N.W.2d 869 (Minn.App. 1985); Preferred Sav. & Loan Ass'n v. Royal Garden Resort, Inc., 301 S.C. 1, 389 S.E.2d 853 (1990); D.T. McCall & Sons v. Seagraves, 796 S.W.2d 457 (Tenn.App. 1990).

The date of completion is not always easy to determine. Suppose the owner calls the mechanic back to correct defective workmanship which has been discovered after nominal completion? See Southwest Paving Co. v. Stone Hills, 206 Cal. App.2d 548, 24 Cal.Rptr. 48 (1962). See also Daily v. Mid–America Bank, 130 Ill. App.3d 639, 85 Ill.Dec. 828, 474 N.E.2d 788 (1985); Eisenhut v. Steadman, 13 Kan. App.2d 220, 767 P.2d 293 (1989). A sale of the property was held not tantamount to completion in Anderson v. Taylor, 55 Wash.2d 215, 347 P.2d 536, 78 A.L.R.2d 1161 (1959). See Hartman, Creditors' Rights and Security Transactions, 8 Vand. L.Rev. 989 (1955).

22. See Reisterstown Lumber Co. v. Royer, 91 Md.App. 746, 605 A.2d 980 (1992), certiorari denied 327 Md. 626, 612 A.2d 257 (1992) (recognizing interlocutory lien pending trial); Bonner Building Supply, Inc. v. Standard Forest Products, Inc., 106 Idaho 682, 682 P.2d 635 (1984).

The action is ordinarily filed in state court, but may be in federal bankruptcy court; RDC, Inc. v. Brookleigh Builders, Inc., 309 N.C. 182, 305 S.E.2d 722 (1983).

Once the lien is filed, the running of the limitations period for the bringing of a

When the lien is perfected by the giving of appropriate notice, however, its date for priority purposes generally relates back to some earlier time. This concept is critically important to mortgagees, who frequently must attempt to establish their own priority as against competing mechanics' liens.[23] Nearly half of the states treat the lien as taking its priority from the time of commencement of the building project.[24] In theory this rule seems unobjectionable, since an inspection of the property will presumably disclose whether construction has begun or not.[25] As a practical matter, however, commencement is often an ambiguous event, with courts disagreeing as to whether it has occurred when lumber is piled on the property,[26] clearing of trees and brush or grading has begun,[27] or an electrical service pole and box are erected.[28] Well-advised construction lenders often photograph the property on the date they record their mortgages in order to establish that construction has not commenced; thus they hope to ensure their

foreclosure action is tolled under the automatic stay if the owner files bankruptcy; see Major Lumber Co. v. G & B Remodeling, 817 S.W.2d 474 (Mo.App.1991); Depner Architects and Planners, Inc. v. Nevada Nat. Bank, 104 Nev. 560, 763 P.2d 1141 (1988).

23. The priority date of the mortgage is normally the date it was recorded; see Blue Spot, Inc. v. Rakower, 120 Misc.2d 150, 465 N.Y.S.2d 493 (1983). However, it may lose priority if the mortgagee had notice of the claim of lien when taking the mortgage; see Palmer v. Forrest, Mackey & Associates, 251 Ga. 304, 304 S.E.2d 704 (1983). Similarly, actual notice of an unrecorded mortgage may defeat the priority of a lienor; see Comstock & Davis, Inc. v. G.D.S. & Assoc., 481 N.W.2d 82 (Minn.App. 1992).

24. See Kratovil, Modern Mortgage Law and Practice § 214 (1972); Republic Bank v. Bohmar Minerals, Inc., 661 P.2d 521 (Okl.1983); M.D. Marinich, Inc., v. Michigan National Bank, 193 Mich.App. 447, 484 N.W.2d 738 (1992), appeal denied ___ Mich. ___, 497 N.W.2d 184 (1993); Dixie Heating & Cooling Co. v. Bank of Gadsden, 437 So.2d 576 (Ala.Civ.App.1983). Under this view, it is immaterial whether the particular lienor did his work before or after the mortgage was recorded; see Barker's Inc. v. B.D.J. Development Co., 308 N.W.2d 78 (Iowa 1981). Cf. Strouss v. Simmons, 66 Hawaii 32, 657 P.2d 1004 (1982) (if mortgage recites it is for construction, it has priority over liens if recorded any time before completion).

25. A common, but not universal, requirement is that the work of improvement must be "visible"; see Strouss v. Simmons, 66 Hawaii 32, 657 P.2d 1004 (1982); Security Bank v. Pocono Web Press, Inc., 295 Pa.Super. 455, 441 A.2d 1321 (1982); Kloster–Madsen, Inc. v. Tafi's, Inc., 303 Minn. 59, 226 N.W.2d 603 (1975); Ketchum, Konkel, Barrett, Nickel & Austin v. Heritage Mountain Devel. Co., 784 P.2d 1217 (Utah App. 1989), certiorari denied 795 P.2d 1138 (Utah 1990); Cook v. Carlson, 364 F.Supp. 24, 29 (D.S.D.1973).

26. Compare James v. Van Horn, 39 N.J.L. 353, 363 (1877), with Kansas Mortgage Co. v. Weyerhaeuser, 48 Kan. 335, 29 P. 153 (1892).

27. See Diversified Mortgage Investors v. Gepada, Inc., 401 F.Supp. 682 (S.D.Iowa 1975); Clark v. General Electric Co., 243 Ark. 399, 420 S.W.2d 830 (1967); Wooldridge Const. Co. v. First Nat. Bank, 130 Ariz. 86, 634 P.2d 13 (App.1981) (earthwork and site preparation constituted commencement); Rupp. v. Earl H. Cline & Sons, Inc., 230 Md. 573, 188 A.2d 146, 1 A.L.R.3d 815 (1963); Lacentra Trucking Inc. v. Flagler Fed. Sav. & Loan Ass'n, 586 So.2d 474 (Fla.App.1991) (surveying, flagging, and staking site is commencement of improvement); Carlson Grefe Const., Inc. v. Rosemount Condominium Group Partnership, 474 N.W.2d 405 (Minn.App.1991) (placement of trailer on site and ceremonial groundbreaking did not constitute commencement of improvement); Ketchum, Konkel, Barrett, Nickel & Austin v. Heritage Mountain Devel. Co., 784 P.2d 1217 (Utah App.1989), certiorari denied 795 P.2d 1138 (Utah 1990) (off-site architectural work did not constitute commencement of improvement).

28. Jim Walter Homes, Inc. v. Bowling, 258 Ark. 28, 521 S.W.2d 828 (1975).

§ 12.4 FINANCING REAL ESTATE CONSTRUCTION 189

priority over mechanics' liens that might be filed later.[29]

The second most popular priority date is the time at which the particular lienor began furnishing labor or materials.[30] The difficulties under such statutes of determining commencement of service or supplies are considerably greater than those of being sure when the whole building operation started. There is also the possibility of an intervening mortgage dividing the lien claimants into prior and subsequent groups, creating a problem of concern where the mechanics' lien statute provides that all lien claimants shall, as among themselves, be on a parity.[31] In third place come some half dozen jurisdictions that make the lien attach from the time of filing the claim. In a few states the liens attach at the date of the general contract, or the lienor's contract,[32] or when a notice of the contract is recorded. In some states the liens attach at different times depending upon various factors involved. In Missouri, all construction loans are apparently subordinate to mechanics' liens, regardless of the dates of commencement or recording.[33]

The statutes usually provide that property is lienable only if the improvements were constructed with the consent of the owner.[34]

29. See Shade v. Wheatcraft Industries, Inc., 248 Kan. 531, 809 P.2d 538 (1991); Jesco, Inc. v. Home Life Ins. Co., 357 N.W.2d 123 (Minn.App.1984). In Indiana the lien will not relate back to achieve priority over a recorded mortgage unless the mortgage loan was for construction purposes; see In re Venture Properties, Inc., 139 B.R. 890 (Bkrtcy.N.D.Ind. 1990). A similar issue may arise if a bona fide purchaser buys the property; see Starek v. TKW, Inc., 410 So.2d 35 (Ala.1982). But some statutes give BFPs priority over mechanics' liens, despite the "relation back" feature of the lien; see Anderson v. Streck, 190 Ga.App. 224, 378 S.E.2d 526 (1989); Mass. Gen.L. c.254, § 2, construed in J & W Wall Systems, Inc. v. Shawmut First Bank & Trust Co., 413 Mass. 42, 594 N.E.2d 859 (1992).

30. See Comment, Mechanics' Liens and Surety Bonds in the Building Trades, 68 Yale L.J. 138, 152 n. 69 (1968); Metropolitan Federal Bank of Iowa v. A.J. Allen Mechanical Contractors, Inc., 477 N.W.2d 668 (Iowa 1991); Geiser v. Permacrete, Inc., 90 So.2d 610, 612 (Fla.1956); Hulinsky v. Parriott, 232 Neb. 670, 441 N.W.2d 883 (1989); Hickey v. Polachek, 63 Or.App. 784, 666 P.2d 294 (1983); In re Williamson, 43 B.R. 813, 827 (Bkrtcy.Utah 1984).

31. Pacific States Savings, Loan & Building Co. v. Dubois, 11 Idaho, 319, 83 P. 513 (1905); Ward v. Yarnelle, 173 Ind. 535, 91 N.E. 7 (1910); Henry & Coatsworth Co. v. Fisherdick, Administrator, 37 Neb. 207, 55 N.W. 643 (1893), and Meister v. J. Meister, Inc., 103 N.J.Eq. 78, 142 A. 312 (1928), permit the intervening encumbrance to create two different classes of mechanics' liens. See, accord, Conn.Pub.Acts, 3905–6, (now Conn.G.S.A. § 49–33) (1925). Gardner v. Leck, 52 Minn. 522, 54 N.W. 746 (1893), preferred all the lien claimants to the mortgagee. Cf. Finlayson v. Crooks, 47 Minn. 74, 49 N.W. 398 (1891), rehearing denied 47 Minn. 74, 49 N.W. 645 (1891).

32. Chicago Title Insurance Co. v. Sherred Village Associates, 708 F.2d 804 (1st Cir.1983) (Maine law); FirstSouth, F.A. v. LaSalle Nat. Bank, 766 F.Supp. 1488 (N.D.Ill.1991) (Illinois law).

33. The theory is that, by making a construction loan, the mortgagee has waived its priority; see Dave Kolb Grading, Inc. v. Lieberman Corp., 837 S.W.2d 924 (Mo.App.1992); Kranz v. Centropolis Crusher Inc., 630 S.W.2d 140 (Mo.App. 1982); Drilling Service Co. v. Baebler, 484 S.W.2d 1 (Mo.1972). But see Union Electric Co. v. Clayton Center Limited, 634 S.W.2d 261 (Mo.App.1982), suggesting that the waiver will not necessarily be found in every case; Genesis Engineering Co. v. Hueser, 829 S.W.2d 579 (Mo.App.1992) (where loan was for land acquisition cost, not construction, waiver is a question of fact).

34. See R. Powell, Real Property, ¶ 486 (1977). Under some statutes the owner's consent is presumed if he or she has knowledge of the work, unless the owner posts or records a "notice of non-responsibility"; see Falcon Holdings, Limited v. Isaacson, 66 Or.App. 614, 675 P.2d 501 (1984).

"Owner" is variously defined, and often a leaseholder or life tenant will not have the requisite power to consent.[35] With respect to "consent", it is obviously present if the owner has signed a construction contract, but some courts hold that no formal contract is required, and that the owner's acquiescence or even mere knowledge of the construction will suffice.[36] A number of these latter jurisdictions incorporate procedures under which an owner who has not contracted for the improvement may, within some fixed time after commencement of construction, file of record or post on the property a notice or disclaimer of responsibility.[37] The effect of such a notice, depending on the statute, may be to

35. Express language in the lease may authorize the tenant to consent for the landlord, see American Seating Co. v. Philadelphia, 434 Pa. 370, 256 A.2d 599 (1969), or the court may imply such authority from the fact that the lease requires the tenant to construct the improvements, see Lentz Plumbing Co. v. Fee, 235 Kan. 266, 679 P.2d 736 (1984); Ott Hardware Co. v. Yost, 69 Cal.App.2d 593, 159 P.2d 663 (1945); D & N Electric, Inc. v. Underground Festival, Inc., 202 Ga.App. 435, 414 S.E.2d 891 (1991); Harner v. Schecter, 105 A.D.2d 932, 482 N.Y.S.2d 124 (1984) (owner's consent implied from course of conduct); Christensen v. Idaho Land Developers, Inc., 104 Idaho 458, 660 P.2d 70 (1983); Stern & Son, Inc. v. Gary Joint Venture, 530 N.E.2d 306 (Ind.App.1988) (landlord's consent not implied from lease language detailing improvements tenant was to make); Landas Fertilizer Co. v. Hargreaves, 206 N.W.2d 675 (Iowa 1973); Bell v. Tollefsen, 782 P.2d 934 (Okl.1989); Kelly v. Hannan, 388 Pa.Super. 638, 566 A.2d 310 (1989) (landlord estopped to deny consent for work contracted by tenant); Dunlap v. Hinkle, 173 W.Va. 423, 317 S.E.2d 508 (1984) (mere authority in lease for tenant to construct improvements is insufficient to impose lien on lessor). See note, 1952 Wash.U.L.Q. 453 (1952). The lien may well be valid against the limited interest of the tenant, even absent the landlord's consent; see Lentz Plumbing Co. v. Fee, 235 Kan. 266, 679 P.2d 736 (1984); Tropic Builders, Limited v. United States, 52 Hawaii 298, 475 P.2d 362 (1970); Cabana, Inc. v. Eastern Air Control, Inc., 61 Md.App. 609, 487 A.2d 1209 (1985), certiorari denied 302 Md. 680, 490 A.2d 718 (1985); Adams v. B & D, Inc., 297 S.C. 416, 377 S.E.2d 315 (1989). See also Carolina Builders Corp. v. Howard-Veasey Homes, Inc., 72 N.C.App. 224, 324 S.E.2d 626 (1985), review denied 313 N.C. 597, 330 S.E.2d 606 (1985) (contract vendee has sufficient interest to be considered "owner").

36. See Bailey v. Call, 767 P.2d 138 (Utah App.1989), certiorari denied 773 P.2d 45 (Utah 1989); Crowley Brothers v. Ward, 322 Ill.App. 687, 54 N.E.2d 753 (1944). Cf. Beaudet v. Saleh, 149 A.D.2d 772, 539 N.Y.S.2d 567 (1989), appeal denied 74 N.Y.2d 610, 546 N.Y.S.2d 554, 545 N.E.2d 868 (1989) (no consent implied from landlord's knowledge nor from fact that tenant was credited toward rent with cost of improvements); Petrillo v. Pelham Bay Park Land Co., 119 Misc. 146, 196 N.Y.S. 124 (1922).

37. See, e.g., Minn.Stat.Ann. § 514.06; similar provisions are found in California, Nevada, New Mexico, Oregon, and South Dakota. See comment, supra note 30, at 158 n. 99; Calif.Cont.Ed. of Bar, California Mechanics' Liens §§ 6.4–6.10 (1972); Annot., 123 A.L.R. 7. In some states, such as California and Florida, the owner is aided in learning of the proposed construction by the requirement that subcontractors and materials suppliers send him or her written notice of their activities before, or within a fixed number of days after, commencement of the work or supplying of materials; West's Ann.Cal.Civ.Code § 3097; see Calif.Cont.Ed. of Bar, California Mechanics' Liens §§ 3.8–3.15 (1972); Note, 21 Hast.L.J. 216 (1969); Westside Galvanizing Services, Inc. v. Georgia-Pacific Corp., 921 F.2d 735 (8th Cir.1990) (under Arkansas law, owner's actual knowledge was not a substitute for required notice); Westfour Corp. v. California First Bank, 3 Cal.App.4th 1554, 5 Cal.Rptr.2d 394 (1992) (no such notice need be given by general contractor); Aetna Cas. & Sur. Co. v. Buck, 594 So.2d 280 (Fla.1992) (no notice need be sent to owner if owner already knows subcontractor is working on the job, or where owner and contractor share common identity); Urrey Ceramic Tile Co., Inc. v. Mosley, 304 Ark. 711, 805 S.W.2d 54 (1991) (statute requiring such notice, but exempting contractors doing commercial and industrial construction, was irrational and unconstitutional); Fischer-Flack, Inc. v. Churchfield, 180 Mich.App. 606, 447 N.W.2d 813 (1989) (notice was proper un-

shift to the lienor the burden of proving actual consent, or entirely to bar the filing of liens on the owner's interest.[38]

Waivers of mechanics' liens are widely permitted, but must be analyzed in two separate contexts. The first is the purported waiver or "no-lien" clause in the original general contract. States which follow the derivative theory of lien liability generally enforce such clauses, treating them as barring liens filed both by the general contractor and by subcontractors and materialmen.[39] States which follow the direct liability approach usually treat no-lien clauses as unenforceable against the latter groups,[40] reasoning that since their rights are not derived from the general contract, it cannot adversely affect them. However, the results in both groups of jurisdictions are frequently affected by specific statutes, which often validate no-lien clauses against subcontractors and materialmen if the contract is filed for record. An intermediate group of states recognizes the validity of the no-lien clause as binding the contractor, but as having no effect upon subcontractors or materialmen unless they have clearly assented to be bound by it.[41]

Waivers given by individual lien claimants during the course of construction are unquestionably valid,[42] and are extremely useful to

der statute, although it was given more than three months prior to furnishing of materials). See also C & C Tile & Carpet Co. v. Aday, 697 P.2d 175 (Okl.App.1985) (special notice to owners who reside on the liened property).

38. Under some statutes, however, the lienor may be permitted to remove the improvement notwithstanding the owner's notice of nonresponsibility; in effect, this may compel the owner to pay for the improvement in order to keep it. See, e.g., American Transit Mix Co. v. Weber, 106 Cal.App.2d 74, 234 P.2d 732 (1951).

39. Jurisdictions recognizing such contractual waivers include Connecticut, Illinois, Indiana, Iowa, Maryland, Minnesota, Missouri, Nebraska, Oregon, Pennsylvania, and Wisconsin. See Ridgeview Const. Co. v. American Nat. Bank, 205 Ill.App.3d 1045, 150 Ill.Dec. 859, 563 N.E.2d 986 (1990). Such clauses are binding as to subcontractors but not as to the general contractor in Idaho, Illinois, and Massachusetts. See Wavetek Indiana, Inc. v. K.H. Gatewood Steel Co., 458 N.E.2d 265 (Ind. App.1984); Comment, supra note 30, at 158 n. 102; Annot., 75 A.L.R.3d 505, 543–48 (1977); Annot., 76 A.L.R.2d 1097 (1961).

New Jersey law permits the owner to avoid all liens merely by filing for record the contract and specifications. However, subcontractors and suppliers may file "notices of intention" to furnish materials or labor, and the owner is then legally bound to ensure that such claimants receive what is due them from each construction disbursement. See Solondz Bros. Lumber Co. v. Piperato, 28 N.J.Super. 414, 101 A.2d 33 (1953). A similar procedure is followed in Florida, although recordation of the contract is not required; see Fla.Stat. § 713.-06; Note, Lien Rights and Construction Lending: Responsibilities and Liabilities in Florida, 29 U.Fla.L.Rev. 411, 417–21 (1977).

40. See Annot., 75 A.L.R.3d 505, 533–43 (1977), listing Alabama, Arkansas, Montana, Nebraska, and Ohio cases as following this view.

41. See Steel Suppliers, Inc. v. Ehret, Inc., 486 A.2d 32 (Del.Super.1984); Aetna Casualty & Surety Co. v. United States, 228 Ct.Cl. 146, 655 F.2d 1047 (1981) (Calif. law); Con Co., Inc. v. Wilson Acres Apartments, Limited, 56 N.C.App. 661, 289 S.E.2d 633 (1982), certiorari denied 306 N.C. 382, 294 S.E.2d 206 (1982); Higby v. Hooper, 124 Mont. 331, 221 P.2d 1043 (1950).

42. See Halbert's Lumber, Inc. v. Lucky Stores, Inc., 6 Cal.App.4th 1233, 8 Cal.Rptr.2d 298 (1992) (waiver bars all recovery for materials delivered through date of waiver, whether supplier had actually been paid for them or not); Santa Clara Land Title Co. v. Nowack & Associates, Inc., 226 Cal.App.3d 1558, 277 Cal. Rptr. 497 (1991); Anchor Concrete Co. v. Victor Savings & Loan Association, 664 P.2d 396 (Okl.1983); Durant Construction, Inc. v. Gourley, 125 Mich.App. 695, 336 N.W.2d 856 (1983). Some courts regard

owners and construction lenders. It is a wise and common practice for the owner to insist upon a sworn list of subcontractors and suppliers from the general contractor, and to require partial lien waivers from each party on the list prior to each disbursement of construction funds. Construction lenders also usually require such waivers,[43] which serve to indicate that the prospective claimant has been fully paid for work done or materials furnished to that date. When construction of the project is completed, the owner will usually require a final waiver, the effect of which will be to bar the filing of any lien on the project, even if the particular subcontractor must return to the site later to correct defects in workmanship, for example.[44]

Sometimes waivers obtained during the course of construction are broadly worded to cover not only work performed to date but also all work to be done in the future. The cases are divided on the validity of such prospective waivers; some courts readily hold them valid,[45] while others construe them strongly against the party obtaining the waiver [46] or hold them unenforceable as against public policy.[47]

§ 12.5 Mechanics' Liens—Constitutionality

Several courts have examined the constitutionality of mechanics' lien statutes; most have held them constitutional. Recent constitutional attacks on these statutes have usually featured a due process analysis of the variety involved in the line of Supreme Court cases beginning with Sniadach v. Family Finance Corp.[1] and running through

the recitation of nominal consideration as adequate support for a lien waiver; see Ramsey v. Peoples Trust and Savings Bank, 148 Ind.App. 167, 264 N.E.2d 111 (1970). In jurisdictions in which this is not sufficient, the cases are divided as to whether a waiver is valid in favor of the owner of the property if the subcontractor has not actually been paid; compare Gerard C. Wallace Co. v. Simpson Land Co., 267 Md. 702, 298 A.2d 881 (1973) (waiver valid) with Cook v. Metal Building Products Inc., 297 Minn. 330, 211 N.W.2d 371 (1973) (waiver invalid absent detrimental reliance). Most courts would probably hold the waiver valid in favor of the construction lender on detrimental reliance grounds if it released funds on the basis of the waiver.

43. See First National Bank v. Smith, 331 N.W.2d 120 (Iowa 1983), narrowly construing a waiver as against a construction lender; cf. Frank Maio General Contractor, Inc. v. Consolidated Electric Supply, Inc., 452 So.2d 1092 (Fla.App.1984). If joint checks are issued by the owner or construction lender to a subcontractor and its materials supplier, and the supplier endorses the check, it will be regarded as having been paid the amount of the check, and hence to have waived its lien to that extent; Brown Wholesale Elec. Co. v. Beztak of Scottsdale, Inc., 163 Ariz. 340, 788 P.2d 73 (1990); Post Bros. Const. Co. v. Yoder, 20 Cal.3d 1, 141 Cal.Rptr. 28, 569 P.2d 133 (1977).

44. See R. Kratovil, Modern Mortgage Law and Practice § 214 (1972).

45. Townsend v. Barlow, 101 Conn. 86, 124 A. 832 (1924).

46. Southwestern Electrical Co. v. Hughes, 139 Kan. 89, 30 P.2d 114 (1934); Bruce Construction Corp. v. Federal Realty Corp., 104 Fla. 93, 139 So. 209 (1932). See also P & C Const. Co. v. American Diversified/Wells Park II, 101 Or.App. 51, 789 P.2d 688 (1990) (where waiver was for labor and material furnished as of June 30, it waived lien only for items billed as of that date, and not for items furnished by that date but billed later).

47. Boise Cascade Corp. v. Stephens, 572 P.2d 1380 (Utah 1977); Brimwood Homes v. Knudsen Builders Supply Co., 14 Utah 2d 419, 385 P.2d 982 (1963).

§ 12.5

1. 395 U.S. 337, 89 S.Ct. 1820, 23 L.Ed.2d 349 (1969).

§ 12.5 FINANCING REAL ESTATE CONSTRUCTION

North Georgia Finishing, Inc. v. Di-Chem, Inc.[2] However, mechanics' lien statutes were subjected to constitutional scrutiny long before *Sniadach*. The older cases generally found the statutes to be constitutional[3] as against a variety of constitutional objections, including due process,[4] equal protection,[5] freedom of contract,[6] and impairment of contractual obligations.[7] The early due process cases are perhaps the most interesting. Typically it was asserted that allowing a subcontractor not in contractual privity with the landowner to assert a lien on the owner's property amounted to an unauthorized deprivation of property in violation of due process. Cases holding the statutes constitutional

---

2. 419 U.S. 601, 95 S.Ct. 719, 42 L.Ed.2d 751 (1975). The other cases in the series of Supreme Court decisions articulating notice and hearing standards in the debtor-creditor context are Fuentes v. Shevin, 407 U.S. 67, 92 S.Ct. 1983, 32 L.Ed.2d 556 (1972), rehearing denied 409 U.S. 902, 93 S.Ct. 177, 34 L.Ed.2d 165 (1972), and Mitchell v. W. T. Grant Co., 416 U.S. 600, 94 S.Ct. 1895, 40 L.Ed.2d 406 (1974). As to the issue of state action, see also Flagg Brothers, Inc. v. Brooks, 436 U.S. 149, 98 S.Ct. 1729, 56 L.Ed.2d 185 (1978).

3. Cases holding mechanics' lien statutes constitutional include: Jones v. Great Southern Fireproof Hotel Co., 86 Fed. 370 (C.C.A.Ohio 1898), reversed on other grounds 177 U.S. 449, 20 S.Ct. 690, 44 L.Ed. 842 (1900); Hollenbeck-Bush Planing Mill Co. v. Amweg, 177 Cal. 159, 170 P. 148 (1917); Stimson Mill Co. v. Nolan, 5 Cal. App. 754, 91 P. 262 (1907); Chicago Lumber Co. v. Newcomb, 19 Colo.App. 265, 74 P. 786 (1903); State v. Tabasso Homes, Inc., 42 Del. (3 Terry) 110, 28 A.2d 248 (1942); State v. Chillingworth, 126 Fla. 645, 171 So. 649 (1936); Summerlin v. Thompson, 31 Fla. 369, 12 So. 667 (1893); Prince v. Neal-Millard Co., 124 Ga. 884, 53 S.E. 761 (1906); Boyer v. Keller, 258 Ill. 106, 101 N.E. 237 (1913); Barrett v. Millikan, 156 Ind. 510, 60 N.E. 310 (1901); Smith v. Newbaur, 144 Ind. 95, 42 N.E. 40 (1895), rehearing denied 144 Ind. 95, 42 N.E. 1094 (1896); Aalfs Wall Paper & Paint Co. v. Bowker, 179 Iowa 726, 162 N.W. 33 (1917); Stewart v. Gardner-Warren Implement Co., 70 S.W. 1042 (Ky.1902), 24 Ky.Law Rep. 1216; Hightower v. Bailey, 108 Ky. 198, 56 S.W. 147 (1900); Bardwell v. Mann, 46 Minn. 285, 48 N.W. 1120 (1891); Chears Floor & Screen Co. v. Gidden, 159 Miss. 288, 131 So. 426 (1930); Colpetzer v. Trinity Church, 24 Neb. 113, 37 N.W. 931 (1888); Baldridge v. Morgan, 15 N.M. 249, 106 P. 342 (1910); Gardner & Meeks Co. v. New York, Central & Hudson River Railroad Co., 72 N.J. Law 257, 62 A. 416 (1905); Chapel State Theatre Co. v. Hooper, 123 Ohio St. 322, 175 N.E. 450 (1931), affirmed 284 U.S. 588, 52 S.Ct. 137, 76 L.Ed. 508 (1931); Title Guarantee & Trust Co. v. Wrenn, 35 Or. 62, 56 P. 271 (1899); Cole Manufacturing Co. v. Falls, 90 Tenn. 466, 16 S.W. 1045 (1891); Spokane Manufacturing & Lumber Co. v. McChesney, 1 Wash. 609, 21 P. 198 (1889); Mallory v. La Crosse Abattoir Co., 80 Wis. 170, 49 N.W. 1071 (1891).

Cases finding provisions of mechanics' lien statutes unconstitutional include: Selma Sash, Door & Blind Factory v. Stoddard, 116 Ala. 251, 22 So. 555 (1897); Stimson Mill Co. v. Braun, 136 Cal. 122, 68 P. 481 (1902); Santa Cruz Rock Pavement Co. v. Lyons, 117 Cal. 212, 48 P. 1097 (1897); Cameron-Schroth-Cameron Co. v. Geseke, 251 Ill. 402, 96 N.E. 222 (1911); Kelly v. Johnson, 251 Ill. 135, 95 N.E. 1068 (1911); John Spry Lumber Co. v. Sault Savings Bank, Loan & Trust Co., 77 Mich. 199, 43 N.W. 778 (1889); Meyer v. Berlandi, 39 Minn. 438, 40 N.W. 513 (1888); Masterson v. Roberts, 336 Mo. 158, 78 S.W.2d 856 (1934); Waters v. Wolf, 162 Pa. 153, 29 A. 646 (1894).

4. See, e.g., Stimson Mill Co. v. Nolan, 5 Cal.App. 754, 91 P. 262 (1907); State v. Chillingworth, 126 Fla. 645, 171 So. 649 (1937); Baldridge v. Morgan, 15 N.M. 249, 106 P. 342 (1910).

5. See, e.g., Hollenbeck-Bush Planing Mill Co. v. Amweg, 177 Cal. 159, 170 P. 148 (1917); Barrett v. Millikan, 156 Ind. 510, 60 N.E. 310 (1901).

6. See, e.g., Jones v. Great Southern Fireproof Hotel Co., 86 Fed. 370 (C.C.A.Ohio 1898), reversed on other grounds 177 U.S. 449, 20 S.Ct. 690, 44 L.Ed. 842 (1900); Boyer v. Keller, 258 Ill. 106, 101 N.E. 237 (1913).

7. See, e.g., State v. Tabasso Homes, Inc., 42 Del. (3 Terry) 110, 28 A.2d 248 (1942); Colpetzer v. Trinity Church, 24 Neb. 113, 37 N.W. 931 (1888); Chapel State Theatre Co. v. Hooper, 123 Ohio St. 322, 175 N.E. 450 (1931), affirmed 284 U.S. 588, 52 S.Ct. 137, 76 L.Ed. 508 (1931).

frequently responded that authorization was implicit in the owner's formation of the original construction contract, with the statute becoming in effect part of the contract.[8]

Some of these early cases did find certain statutory provisions unconstitutional. In Kelly v. Johnson,[9] for example, the statute was held unconstitutional as depriving a landowner of liberty of contract to the extent it vested a subcontractor with the right to a lien despite a lien waiver agreement in the construction contract. In Meyer v. Berlandi,[10] a provision of Minnesota's statute was held unconstitutional that conclusively presumed the landowner's consent to a subcontractor's work if the landowner failed to enjoin the work. The court reasoned that the provision violated due process because it permitted a lien to be filed even when no actual consent to work had been given. In Selma Sash, Door & Blind Factory v. Stoddard,[11] the Alabama statute was found violative of due process because it permitted subcontractors to have a lien on property even when the owner fulfilled his or her contractual duties to the general contractor.

Notwithstanding these holdings, the vast majority of the older cases upheld the validity of lien statutes. Regardless of the results, however, the older cases have had little precedential impact on recent court considerations of the constitutionality of mechanics' liens. The reason is that modern attacks on constitutionality have employed a due process analysis unknown in earlier years. Between 1969 and 1975, the Supreme Court examined statutory prejudgment procedures in the debtor-creditor context and established notice and hearing standards that must be met for such procedures to comport with due process. In three of these cases—Sniadach v. Family Finance Corp.,[12] Fuentes v. Shevin,[13] and North Georgia Finishing, Inc. v. Di–Chem Inc.[14]—prejudgment procedures were found violative of due process. In one case—Mitchell v. W. T. Grant Co.[15]—due process standards were found to be met. There is considerable uncertainty as to the precise state of the law in this area—even among justices of the Court[16]—but at least this much seems clear: absent extraordinary circumstances, statutory prejudgment creditor remedies that deprive a debtor of a significant property interest without notice and a prior opportunity for hearing are unconstitutional unless sufficient safeguards are present to ensure that

8. See, e.g., Stimson Mill Co. v. Nolan, 5 Cal.App. 754, 91 P. 262 (1907).

9. 251 Ill. 135, 95 N.E. 1068 (1911).

10. 39 Minn. 438, 40 N.W. 513 (1888).

11. 116 Ala. 251, 22 So. 555 (1897).

12. 395 U.S. 337, 89 S.Ct. 1820, 23 L.Ed.2d 349 (1969).

13. 407 U.S. 67, 92 S.Ct. 1983, 32 L.Ed. 556 (1972), rehearing denied 409 U.S. 902, 93 S.Ct. 177, 34 L.Ed.2d 165 (1972).

14. 419 U.S. 601, 95 S.Ct. 719, 42 L.Ed.2d 751 (1975).

15. 416 U.S. 600, 94 S.Ct. 1895, 40 L.Ed.2d 406 (1974).

16. Compare North Georgia Finishing, Inc. v. Di–Chem, Inc., 419 U.S. 601, 608–09, 95 S.Ct. 719, 723, 42 L.Ed.2d 751 (1975) (concurring opinions) with Mitchell v. W. T. Grant Co., 416 U.S. 600, 623–29, 629–36, 94 S.Ct. 1895, 1907–10, 1910–14, 40 L.Ed.2d 406 (1974) (concurring and dissenting opinions).

§ 12.5   FINANCING REAL ESTATE CONSTRUCTION   195

the debtor's interests are protected.[17]

The U.S. Supreme Court has not yet decided a case applying these due process standards to mechanics' liens;[18] consequently, it is not entirely clear what safeguards would be required. Other courts, however, have struggled with the constitutional issue. Most have upheld the statutes examined,[19] but two have held otherwise.[20] To some extent, of course, the differences in result reflect differences in the statutes examined, but they also reflect differences in approach. A brief survey of prominent cases will make this clear.[21]

The leading case upholding the constitutionality of a mechanics'

17. See, e.g., North Georgia Finishing, Inc. v. Di–Chem, Inc., 419 U.S. 601, 95 S.Ct. 719, 42 L.Ed.2d 751 (1975); Catz & Robinson, Due Process and Creditor's Remedies: From Sniadach and Fuentes to Mitchell, North Georgia and Beyond, 28 Rutgers L.Rev. 541 (1975).

18. The Court did, however, summarily affirm the decision of a three judge district court upholding the constitutionality of Arizona's mechanics' lien statute. See Spielman–Fond, Inc. v. Hanson's, Inc., 379 F.Supp. 997 (D.Ariz.1973) (per curiam), affirmed 417 U.S. 901, 94 S.Ct. 2596, 41 L.Ed.2d 208 (1974). The degree to which this summary affirmance should be binding on other courts has been the subject of considerable discussion. See, e.g., B & P Development v. Walker, 420 F.Supp. 704 (W.D.Pa.1976); Bankers Trust Co. v. El Paso Pre–Cast Co., 192 Colo. 468, 560 P.2d 457 (1977); Barry Properties, Inc. v. Fick Brothers Roofing Co., 277 Md. 15, 353 A.2d 222 (1976).

19. See B & P Development v. Walker, 420 F.Supp. 704 (W.D.Pa.1976); In re Thomas A. Cary, Inc., 412 F.Supp. 667 (E.D.Va.1976), affirmed 562 F.2d 47 (4th Cir.1977); Ruocco v. Brinker, 380 F.Supp. 432 (S.D.Fla.1974); Spielman–Fond, Inc. v. Hanson's, Inc., 379 F.Supp. 997 (D.Ariz. 1973) (per curiam), affirmed 417 U.S. 901, 94 S.Ct. 2596, 41 L.Ed.2d 208 (1974); Cook v. Carlson, 364 F.Supp. 24 (D.S.D.1973); Nelson–American Developers, Limited v. Enco Engineering Corp., 337 So.2d 729 (Ala.1976); Connolly Development, Inc. v. Superior Court, 17 Cal.3d 803, 132 Cal. Rptr. 477, 553 P.2d 637 (1976), appeal dismissed 429 U.S. 1056, 97 S.Ct. 778, 50 L.Ed.2d 773 (1977); Bankers Trust Co. v. El Paso Pre–Cast Co., 192 Colo. 468, 560 P.2d 457 (1977); Tucker Door & Trim Corp. v. Fifteenth Street Co., 235 Ga. 727, 221 S.E.2d 433 (1975); Carl A. Morse, Inc. v. Rentar Industrial Development Corp., 56 A.D.2d 30, 391 N.Y.S.2d 425 (1977), order affirmed 43 N.Y.2d 952, 404 N.Y.S.2d 343, 375 N.E.2d 409 (1978), appeal dismissed 439 U.S. 804, 99 S.Ct. 59, 58 L.Ed.2d 96 (1978); Silverman v. Gossett, 553 S.W.2d 581 (Tenn.1977); Home Building Corp. v. Ventura Corp., 568 S.W.2d 769 (Mo.1978); Keith Young & Sons Construction Co. v. Victor Senior Citizens Housing, Inc., 262 N.W.2d 554 (Iowa 1978); Williams & Works, Inc. v. Springfield Corp., 81 Mich. App. 355, 265 N.W.2d 328 (1978), reversed on other grounds 408 Mich. 732, 293 N.W.2d 304 (1980); South Central District of the Pentecostal Church v. Bruce–Rogers Co., 269 Ark. 130, 599 S.W.2d 702 (1980); Mobile Components, Inc. v. Layon, 623 P.2d 591 (Okl.1980), certiorari denied 454 U.S. 963, 102 S.Ct. 502, 70 L.Ed.2d 378 (1981); Kloos v. Jacobson, 30 B.R. 965 (Bkrtcy.Idaho 1983).

20. Roundhouse Construction Corp. v. Telesco Masons Supplies Co., 168 Conn. 371, 362 A.2d 778 (1975), vacated and remanded 423 U.S. 809, 96 S.Ct. 20, 46 L.Ed.2d 29 (1975), reaffirmed 170 Conn. 155, 365 A.2d 393 (1976), certiorari denied 429 U.S. 889, 97 S.Ct. 246, 50 L.Ed.2d 172 (1976); Barry Properties Inc. v. Fick Brothers Roofing Co., 277 Md. 15, 353 A.2d 222 (1976).

21. See Frank & McManus, Balancing Almost Two Hundred Years of Economic Policy Against Contemporary Due Process Standards—Mechanics' Liens in Maryland after Barry Properties, 36 Md.L.Rev. 733 (1977); Levine, Due Process of Law in Pre–Judgment Attachment and the Filing of Mechanics' Liens, 50 Conn.B.J. 335 (1976); Note, The Constitutional Validity of Mechanics' Liens Under the Due Process Clause—A Reexamination after Mitchell and North Georgia, 55 B.U.L.Rev. 263 (1975); Note, Mechanics' Liens Subject to Fourteenth Amendment Guarantees, 26 Cath.U.L.Rev. 129 (1976); 8 Conn.L.Rev. 744 (1976).

lien is Spielman–Fond, Inc. v. Hanson's, Inc.[22] In that case, a three-judge district court evaluated the Arizona mechanics' lien statute in light of *Sniadach* and *Fuentes*. The court focused on whether the filing of a mechanics' lien constituted a constitutionally cognizable deprivation of property that would require proper notice and hearing. While the court conceded that a mechanics' lien reduced the owner's ability to alienate the property, it ruled that lien filing did "not amount to a taking of a significant property interest."[23] Accordingly, said the court, due process was not violated by the absence of notice and hearing prior to lien filing. The Supreme Court summarily affirmed the ruling of this three-judge panel.[24]

Several cases have followed the *Spielman–Fond* decision in finding that a mechanics' lien filing does not involve the taking of a significant property interest.[25] For example, in Carl A. Morse, Inc. v. Rentar Industrial Development Corp.,[26] the due process challenge to the New York statute was asserted by a landowner whose property was subjected to lien claims of over a million dollars. The court analyzed the *Sniadach* line of cases through *North Georgia,* focusing particularly on how the New York statutory scheme differed from the one invalidated in the *North Georgia* case. The court averred that the New York provision effected no deprivation of use or possession of property. Although it admitted that a mechanics' lien impinges on the economic interests of a landowner, the court found this insufficient to bring the Fourteenth Amendment into play. It was, said the court, a "minimal intrusion." In addition, the court reasoned that even though the value of the property is diminished by the amount of a lien, the loss is offset by the value of the improvements contributed by a lienor. The court also examined the particular provisions of the lien statute, and found them to constitute a constitutional accommodation of the competing interest of owners, materialmen, and purchasers. Among the safeguards contained within these provisions, the court noted that the lienor was required in filing the lien to state under oath the facts giving rise to the claim, that the owner could discharge the lien by posting a

---

22. 379 F.Supp. 997 (D.Ariz.1973) (per curiam), affirmed 417 U.S. 901, 94 S.Ct. 2596, 41 L.Ed.2d 208 (1974).

23. Id. at 999.

24. 417 U.S. 901, 94 S.Ct. 2596, 41 L.Ed.2d 208 (1974).

25. See B & P Development v. Walker, 420 F.Supp. 704 (W.D.Pa.1976); In re Thomas A. Cary, Inc., 412 F.Supp. 667 (E.D.Va.1976), affirmed 562 F.2d 47 (4th Cir.1977); Ruocco v. Brinker, 380 F.Supp. 432 (S.D.Fla.1974); Bankers Trust Co. v. El Paso Pre–Cast Co., 192 Colo. 468, 560 P.2d 457 (1977); Tucker Door & Trim Corp. v. Fifteenth Street Co., 235 Ga. 727, 221 S.E.2d 433 (1975); C.J. Richard Lumber Co. v. Melancon, 476 So.2d 1018 (La.App.1985), writ denied 478 So.2d 1236 (La.1985); Carl A. Morse, Inc. v. Rentar Industrial Development Corp., 56 A.D.2d 30, 391 N.Y.S.2d 425 (1977), order affirmed 43 N.Y.2d 952, 404 N.Y.S.2d 343, 375 N.E.2d 409 (1978); Silverman v. Gossett, 553 S.W.2d 581 (Tenn.1977).

A pre-*Spielman-Fond* decision upheld the constitutionality of the South Dakota mechanics' lien provisions on the grounds that the deprivation of property was de minimus. See Cook v. Carlson, 364 F.Supp. 24 (D.S.D.1973).

26. 56 A.D.2d 30, 391 N.Y.S.2d 425 (1977), order affirmed 43 N.Y.2d 952, 404 N.Y.S.2d 343, 375 N.E.2d 409 (1978), appeal dismissed 439 U.S. 804, 99 S.Ct. 59, 58 L.Ed.2d 96 (1978).

bond, that the owner could compel an expeditious determination on the merits by demanding foreclosure, and that the lien could remain in force no longer than a year from filing unless a foreclosure action were commenced or a continuance granted.[27]

A different analytical approach to the due process question was taken by the California Supreme Court in Connolly Development, Inc. v. Superior Court.[28] The statutory scheme under attack in *Connolly* required a potential lienor to follow certain procedures in order to obtain a lien. One such requirement was the filing of a preliminary notice of claim with the owner, general contractor, and construction lender within twenty days of furnishing materials. In addition, the actual lien claim had to be recorded within ninety days after completion of the improvement or within thirty days after recordation of a notice of completion of the project. The lien could be released if the owner posted a bond, and it was discharged unless a foreclosure suit was begun within ninety days of recordation. These particular provisions ultimately convinced the court to conclude that a constitutional accommodation of competing interests was achieved by the California lien provisions.

Unlike the two cases discussed earlier, the court in *Connolly* determined that a constitutionally cognizable taking of property was involved in the recordation of a mechanic's lien. "A deprivation," said the court, "need not reach the magnitude of a physical seizure of property in order to fall within the compass of the due process clause." [29] Here, the constraints imposed on the owner's ability to sell or encumber his property were held sufficient to constitute a taking under the Fourteenth Amendment.

Having crossed this threshold, the court was then forced to decide whether state action was present. The court had no difficulty finding state action—a mechanics' lien is a creature of statute, and it can only be recorded and enforced under the power of the state.

The final question before the court was whether the statutory provisions comported with due process. The court held that they did. In reaching this conclusion, the court noted that California law provided more safeguards than the Arizona statute upheld in *Spielman-*

---

27. The court did not mention the fact that a lien could be filed up to four months following completion of the contract or the furnishing of materials. Id. at 35–36, 391 N.Y.S.2d at 432 (dissenting opinion).

28. 17 Cal.3d 803, 132 Cal.Rptr. 477, 553 P.2d 637 (1976), appeal dismissed 429 U.S. 1056, 97 S.Ct. 778, 50 L.Ed.2d 773 (1977). The case also deals with the constitutionality of California's statutory "stop notice" provision; see infra § 12.6.

29. Id. at 812, 132 Cal.Rptr. at 483, 553 P.2d at 643. The Court of Appeal subsequently held that filing of a mechanic's lien as against a construction *lender*, as distinct from an owner, was not a deprivation of property; the lien might ultimately be held to take priority over the construction mortgage, but the filing itself did not establish priority, and hence was not a taking. Thus a lien claimant could properly make an initial filing against a "Doe" lender, and subsequently substitute the name of the actual lender despite the fact that the 90-day limitations period had expired. Grinnell Fire Protection Systems Co. v. American Sav. & Loan Ass'n, 183 Cal.App.3d 352, 228 Cal.Rptr. 292 (1986).

Fond.[30] It also observed that the problematic garnishment provisions invalidated in *North Georgia* were different from the provisions of California law. In this regard, the court emphasized that the California statute did not effect a total deprivation of the owner's property, that the lienor had a legitimate interest in that property, and that the landowner had adequate statutory protection. The court noted that modern due process analysis was flexible, requiring a weighing of affected interests. In light of the statutory safeguards, the balance of interest pointed in favor of constitutionality.

Two courts have held mechanics' lien provisions unconstitutional under due process analysis. The first decision was that of the Supreme Court of Connecticut in Roundhouse Construction Corporation v. Telesco Masons Supplies Company.[31] The Maryland Supreme Court decided the second in Barry Properties, Inc. v. Fick Bros. Roofing Company.[32] Each of these decisions merits discussion.

Beginning its analysis in *Roundhouse*, the Connecticut court reviewed the statutory provisions under attack. These provisions required that, in order to have a valid lien, a potential lienor must file a sworn statement of amount claimed with the town clerk within sixty days after completing the work. The provisions also required subcontractors and materialmen not privy to the original construction agreement to give notice to the owner against whose property liens are claimed. The owner could apply for dissolution of the lien by filing a bond, or request a discharge on grounds of invalidity. If the request were not honored within thirty days, the owner could then bring a court action for discharge. In no case could a lien remain in force longer than four years unless the lienor commenced a foreclosure action within two years of filing.

The court found that these provisions failed to meet due process hearing standards. Although acknowledging that an early post-taking hearing instead of a prior hearing seemed acceptable after *North Georgia*, the court was concerned that it was possible for a lien to continue for two years without any hearing at all. This was different, said the court, from the Arizona statute upheld in *Spielman–Fond*, under which the lien could last no longer than six months without a foreclosure action. "Such a provision," said the court, "would seem to offer the bare minimum of due process protection consistent with the

---

30. One such protection is the California requirement that the lien claimant give a preliminary notice to the "owner or reputed owner" within 20 days of commencing work. The court acknowledged that the owner would not always get actual notice. See Brown Co. v. Superior Court, 148 Cal.App.3d 891, 196 Cal.Rptr. 258 (1983). Another protection is the owner's right to contest the validity of the lien by filing a motion in the lien claimant's action to enforce the lien; see Lambert v. Superior Court, 228 Cal.App.3d 383, 279 Cal.Rptr. 32 (1991).

31. 168 Conn. 371, 362 A.2d 778 (1975), vacated and remanded 423 U.S. 809, 96 S.Ct. 20, 46 L.Ed.2d 29 (1975), reaffirmed 170 Conn. 155, 365 A.2d 393 (1976), certiorari denied 429 U.S. 889, 97 S.Ct. 246, 50 L.Ed.2d 172 (1976).

32. 277 Md. 15, 353 A.2d 222 (1976).

extent of deprivation present."[33] On the issue of deprivation itself the court noted that even though a mechanics' lien does not absolutely prevent the alienation of property, it does restrict the practical opportunity to alienate. This was sufficient, in the court's view, to constitute a significant taking of property.[34]

A similar analysis pointed to unconstitutionality in *Barry Properties*. The Maryland statutory provisions under attack allowed for creation of a mechanics' lien by a general contractor without prior notice to the owner. Although a subcontractor was required to give the owner a notice of intent to make a lien claim, the claim could be filed before the notice was given. In any case, this notice had to be given within ninety days after furnishing work or material.[35] No hearing was required concerning the lien prior to foreclosure. After recordation, the lien could last for one year, unless enforcement were sought within that period. During this year, the owner could sue to compel the claimant to prove the lien's validity or could post a bond and secure a release. The court, in reasoning reminiscent of *Connolly*, found that state action was involved and that there was a significant taking of property.[36] The only remaining question was whether the statutory scheme provided "protections such as those discussed in *Mitchell* and *North Georgia Finishing* or is deemed to be within the "extraordinary circumstances' exception."[37]

The court noted that there was no requirement of a sworn statement by the creditor, setting forth facts upon which the lien was based, that there was no requirement of a bond to protect the debtor, nor was there an opportunity for a prompt post-lien hearing. The owner's opportunity to compel the claimant to prove the lien's validity was subject to the usual strictures of the trial calendar. In view of these findings, the court said the requirements of *Mitchell* and *North Georgia* were unmet. It also concluded that the extraordinary circumstances exception did not apply. *Spielman–Fond* was distinguishable, said the court, because the Arizona statute provided for safeguards not reflected in Maryland law.[38]

33. 168 Conn. at 381, 362 A.2d at 783. The court was also concerned that the lien statute permitted the ex parte filing, without judicial supervision, of a conclusory statement and that there was no requirement of posting a bond by the lienor.

34. The Connecticut statute was subsequently amended to give the owner notice and the right to a prompt hearing; see Conn.Gen.Stat.Ann. § 49–33 et seq. It has been held constitutional as to owners, but may be invalid as to general contractors, who must post bond to obtain a hearing. See General Electric Supply Co. v. Southern New England Telephone Co., 185 Conn. 583, 441 A.2d 581 (1981).

35. A general contractor was not required to give any such notice, but had to file a lien claim within 180 days of the completion of work or the furnishing of materials. 277 Md. at 19–20, 353 A.2d at 226.

36. The court said that the existence of a lien diminishes an owner's equity, severely impairs alienability of property, and makes additional financing problematical.

37. 277 Md. at 31, 353 A.2d at 232.

38. The court specifically referred to the Arizona provisions requiring that the claimant make a sworn statement upon filing the lien claim, that the owner be notified within a reasonable time of the filing, that the claimant institute enforcement proceedings within six months of fil-

After *Barry Properties* was decided, the Maryland legislature revised the statute to require notice to the owner and a judicial hearing before attachment of the lien.[39] This statute was attacked as well, on the ground that since the lien claimant was required to give notice to the owner only within 90 days after the date the last work or materials were supplied, the notice was not "meaningful" in terms of assisting the owner in avoiding liability for double payment—to the general contractor and to a subcontractor or supplier as well. But the Maryland Court of Special Appeals upheld the statute;[40] it conceded that some risk of double liability remained, but pointed out several methods by which owners could protect themselves from liens, including the use of payment bonds, retaining a percentage of each payment due to the general contractor, paying subcontractors and suppliers directly, and issuing joint checks to the general contract and the subcontractors or suppliers.[41]

Modern due process challenges to statutory provisions have usually failed, either because courts have been unwilling to find a significant deprivation of property or because appropriate constitutional accommodations have been found within the statutory scheme itself. Some well reasoned recent opinions, however, have discerned a significant deprivation of property in the imposition of mechanics' liens. Once this threshold is crossed, state action is easily found; the remaining question is whether adequate safeguards exist. Precisely what safeguards will be found adequate is not clear, but it appears that a statute may be in constitutional trouble if it permits a potential lienor to file without notice long after work's completion or if it allows a lien to subsist beyond six months without requiring a hearing. The *Spielman–Fond* case has become something of a standard in this area; courts have thus far been unwilling to invalidate statutory provisions like those upheld in that case.

§ 12.6 The Stop Notice and the Equitable Lien

The mechanics' lien, the traditional refuge of unpaid subcontractors and suppliers, is often useless to them in construction projects. Construction lenders have learned to record their mortgages before any

---

ing, and permitting the owner to discharge the lien by filing a bond. Id. at 34, 353 A.2d at 233–34.

39. See 1976 Md.Laws ch. 349, amending Md.Code, Real Prop., §§ 9–101 to 9–113; Cabana, Inc. v. Eastern Air Control, Inc., 61 Md.App. 609, 487 A.2d 1209 (1985), cert. denied 302 Md. 680, 490 A.2d 718 (1985); Tyson v. Masten Lumber & Supply, Inc., 44 Md.App. 293, 408 A.2d 1051 (1979); Note, 6 U.Balt.L.Rev. 181 (1976).

40. AMI Operating Partners Ltd. v. JAD Enterprises, Inc., 77 Md.App. 654, 551 A.2d 888 (1989), cert. denied 315 Md. 307, 554 A.2d 393 (1989). The court also summarily rejected the rather fatuous claim that the mechanic's lien statute accomplished a "taking" of private property for a non-public use. "The State isn't taking the debtor's property for either public or private use; it is merely creating an orderly process for the satisfaction of a debt that has a basis in law and that has been found by a court to be due and owing." 551 A.2d at 893.

41. 551 A.2d at 892.

§ 12.6   FINANCING REAL ESTATE CONSTRUCTION   201

work is done,[1] and to avoid optional advances;[2] under these circumstances the mechanics' lien claimants are almost certain to be subordinate to the construction loan, and its foreclosure will seldom produce any surplus for them. An alternative source of payment to the subcontractors and suppliers is the payment bond, but its use is generally confined to large commercial projects and those being built with public funds.[3] In residential subdivisions and small apartment projects, neither the lien nor the bond is likely to be available.

At least eleven states have attempted to provide another route to the unpaid subcontractors and suppliers (though usually not to general contractors): the stop notice.[4] In essence, it is a right to make and enforce a claim against the construction lender (or in some states, the owner)[5] for a portion of the undisbursed construction loan proceeds, if any. It is somewhat like a garnishment of the loan funds, although the analogy is not entirely accurate; a stop notice may be effectively filed, for example, even if the borrower-developer has defaulted and is therefore not entitled to any further construction loan draws.[6] Obviously the stop notice is effective only if some funds remain in the lender's or owner's hands.[7] The remedy is statutory, and specific time require-

§ 12.6

1. Mechanics' liens generally relate back in priority to the time the work was commenced; if the construction loan mortgage is recorded first, it will have priority over such liens. See § 12.4, supra, at notes 23–29.

2. An optional advance under a construction loan, if made by a lender having actual notice of intervening liens, will generally be subordinate to them. See § 12.7, infra.

3. See § 12.2, supra, at notes 31–35; Sarshik, Recovering Construction Losses from HUD: The Rights of Contractors on Troubled Projects with HUD–Insured Mortgages, 15 Urb.Law. 291 (1983).

4. Ala.Code 1975, § 35–11–210; Alaska Stat. 34.35.062; West's Cal.Civ.Code §§ 3156–3172; West's C.R.S.A. § 38–22–102; Burns Ind.Ann.Stat. § 32–8–3–9; Miss.Code 1972, § 85–7–181; N.C.Gen.Stat. § 44A–18; N.J.S.A. 2A:44–77, 78; R.I. Gen. L.1956; § 34–27.1–1; Vernon's Texas Code Ann., Property Code §§ 53.081–53.084; Wis.Stat.Ann. 779.036; West's Rev.Code Wash.Ann. 60.04.210. See Coatings Manufacturers, Inc. v. DPI, Inc., 926 F.2d 474 (5th Cir.1991) (stop notice procedure unavailable to supplier of rental equipment used in construction); Diamond Int'l Corp. v. Bristol County Builders Corp., 468 A.2d 282 (R.I.1983) (state statute providing for payment of undistributed loan funds held by construction lender directly to subcontractors, held not to extend that remedy to materials suppliers). See generally Comment, Mechanics Liens: The "Stop Notice" Comes to Washington, 49 Wash.L.Rev. 685, 694 (1974); Comment, California's Private Stop Notice Law: Due Process Requirements, 25 Hast.L.J. 1043, 1054–57 (1974).

5. See, e.g., West's Ann.Cal.Civ.Code §§ 3158–3159; under California law, the claimant need not file a bond if the stop notice is directed to the owner. See also Matter of Hull, 19 B.R. 501 (Bkrtcy.Ind. 1982) (Indiana statute confers personal right against owner, but not a lien on funds); Matter of Valairco, Inc., 9 B.R. 289 (Bkrtcy.N.J.1981) (New Jersey, semple); Exchange Savings & Loan Association v. Monocrete Pty, Limited, 629 S.W.2d 34, 37 (Tex.1982).

Some of the statutes also provide for the filing of stop notices against governmental entities for whom public works projects are being constructed.

6. See A–1 Door & Materials Co. v. Fresno Guarantee Savings & Loan Association, 61 Cal.2d 728, 40 Cal.Rptr. 85, 394 P.2d 829 (1964).

7. See Familian Corp. v. Imperial Bank, 213 Cal.App.3d 681, 262 Cal.Rptr. 101 (1989) (where lender had deducted amounts from the construction loan account for bank fees, interest reserves, and accrued interest, it was required to add these sums back to the account upon the filing of a stop notice. See also International Telephone & Telegraph Corp. v. Envirco Services, Inc., 144 N.J.Super. 31, 364 A.2d 549 (1976) (owner not liable on stop

ments must be met;[8] often the claimant must file a bond to indemnify the lender against damages which might result from a wrongful claim.[9] The lender may simply pay the claim and discharge the stop notice,[10] but if the claim is disputed or there are insufficient funds to pay all stop notice claims, litigation may be necessary.[11]

The statutes commonly make the stop notice unavailable if a payment bond has been filed, and some also do so if conventional mechanics' lien recovery is available.[12] Thus the foreclosure of the construction loan is not a bar to the assertion of a stop notice, and in some states may actually be helpful by establishing that the mechanics' lien has been destroyed.

The stop notice remedy generally makes lenders more careful in administration of construction loans. There are two reasons for this. One is that if claimants are unpaid and therefore file stop notices, they may bring the entire project to a halt;[13] this is especially true if it is

notice where general contractor's breach has terminated owner's liability on contract.

8. See, e.g., Moss, The Stop Notice Remedy in California—Updated, 47 L.A.Bar.Bull. 299 (1972). Under the California statute, the claimant must give a notice to the construction lender within 20 days after commencing work, or it is ineligible to file a stop notice; see Romak Iron Works v. Prudential Insurance Co., 104 Cal.App.3d 767, 163 Cal.Rptr. 869 (1980). See In re Aspen Homes, Inc., 54 B.R. 541 (Bkrtcy.Wash.1985), in which the court construed the Washington statute to obligate the lender to withhold funds only to cover *future* work or materials supplied by the stop notice claimant, and not work that had been performed prior to the filing of the notice. On the facts of the case, the supplier did not deliver any further materials after filing the stop notice; hence, the lender's failure to withhold funds was proper. See also Donnybrook Bldg. Supply Co. v. Alaska National Bank, 736 P.2d 1147 (Alaska 1987), similarly construing the Alaska statute.

9. E.g., West's Ann.Cal.Civ.Code § 3083. In order to free up the funds that the stop notice has frozen, the lender or owner can file a corresponding bond and discharge the stop notice; id. at § 3171. See Manos v. Degen, 203 Cal.App.3d 1237, 250 Cal.Rptr. 493 (1988) (where bond submitted by stop notice claimant was for less than statutory amount, lender had no duty to withhold any funds at all); Winick Corp v. General Ins. Co. of America, 187 Cal. App.3d 142, 231 Cal.Rptr. 606 (1986) (stop notice release bond was obtained by public agency as owner of the project; statute of imitations on bond ran against subcontractor despite the fact that it did not know bond had been obtained).

10. The lender or owner is generally personally liable if he or she fails to set aside, from the construction loan account, the amount claimed by the stop notice (or the amount set by the statute, if different from the claim); see West's Rev.Code Wash.Ann. 60.04.210(4), setting forth a rather complex and confusing formula for determining the amount to be withheld; see, Comment, Wash.L.Rev., supra note 4, at 697 n. 68). The Washington statute's withholding formula is explained in In re Aspen Homes, Inc., 54 B.R. 541 (Bkrtcy. Wash.1985). In Washington if the lender wrongfully refuses to comply with the stop notice, it is subordinated to the potential lien claimant to the extent of the funds improperly disbursed; West's Rev.Code Wash.Ann. § 60.040.221(6). See also Flintkote Co. v. Presley of Northern California, 154 Cal.App.3d 458, 201 Cal.Rptr. 262 (1984).

11. The stop notice claimants usually share pro-rata if the funds are insufficient to pay all claims. The statutes may provide a procedure for adjudication of disputed claims; see, e.g., West's Ann.Cal.Civ. Code §§ 3172–3173.

12. See Colorado, New Jersey, and Wisconsin statutes, supra note 4. Cf. Cordell v. Regan, 23 Wash.App. 739, 598 P.2d 416 (1979) (claimant may simultaneously file stop notice and foreclose mechanic's lien).

13. See Idaco Lumber Co. v. Northwestern Savings & Loan Association, 265 Cal.App.2d 490, 71 Cal.Rptr. 422 (1968); Ilyin, Stop Notice—Construction Loan Officer's Nightmare, 16 Hast.L.J. 187 (1964).

necessary to litigate the validity of the claims and there are many of them, for they may tie up the entire construction loan account for a long period.[14] A second reason is that negligent or wrongful disbursal of funds may come back to haunt the lender; the stop notice claimants may assert that such money should be regarded, for stop notice purposes, as still held in the hands of the lender and amenable to the claims.[15] Lenders in stop notice jurisdictions are likely to take a fairly active role in project supervision, and often use the voucher or direct-payment system of loan disbursement rather than the looser progress-payments system.[16] By this they hope to make certain that all subcontractors and suppliers are paid on time, and that no funds are diverted to non-construction uses.

Since the stop notice amounts to a garnishment of funds without a prior notice or hearing, it might be held a violation of due process under the *Sniadach–North Georgia* line of cases discussed in the preceding section. The California Supreme Court held its state's statute valid against such an attack in Connolly Development, Inc. v. Superior Court.[17] While the court conceded that the stop notice resulted in more than *de minimis* takings of property, and that it involved state action, it concluded that the interest of stop notice claimants in a rapid and efficient remedy outweighed the relatively limited deprivation visited upon the owner. In other states, however, this issue may yet be resolved differently.

The Equitable Lien

It often happens that neither the stop notice nor the mechanics' lien provides an adequate remedy to one who has supplied labor or materials to a construction project. As we have already indicated, foreclosure of the construction loan mortgage will usually wipe out the mechanics' lien, and the stop notice may be unavailable in the jurisdiction or the claimant may have omitted some essential procedural element in filing the lien claim, or may be outside the scope of the statute. For example, the claimant may be a remote materials supplier (one who has furnished materials to another supplier), an architect (in a jurisdiction in which architects are protected by neither mechanics'

---

14. See Note, 13 Cal.West.L.Rev. 489, 531–33 (1977). The California statute provides a speedy summary procedure for litigating the validity of stop notices on public projects, but it does not apply to private projects; West's Ann.Cal.Civ.Code §§ 3197–3205. In Connolly Development, Inc. v. Superior Court, 17 Cal.3d 803, 132 Cal.Rptr. 477, 553 P.2d 637 (1976), appeal dismissed 429 U.S. 1056, 97 S.Ct. 778, 50 L.Ed.2d 773 (1977), the court expressed approval of the summary procedure and suggested that the statute might be amended to cover private work as well, but concluded that its unavailability on private projects did not make the stop notice unconstitutional; id. at 17 Cal.3d 828 n. 26, 132 Cal.Rptr. at 494 n. 26.

15. See Moss, The Stop Notice Remedy in California—Updated, 47 L.A. Bar Bull. 299, 303–04 (1972); Miller v. Mountain View Savings & Loan Association, 238 Cal. App.2d 644, 48 Cal.Rptr. 278 (1965).

16. See Lubell, Changes in Construction Lenders' Policies—1958–1969, A Lender's Viewpoint, 44 L.A.Bar Bull. 346 (1969).

17. 17 Cal.3d 803, 132 Cal.Rptr. 477, 553 P.2d 637 (1976), appeal dismissed 429 U.S. 1056, 97 S.Ct. 778, 50 L.Ed.2d 773 (1977). See Note, 13 Cal.West L.Rev. 489 (1977).

liens nor stop notices, as is common), or a general contractor [18] (a class not covered by most stop notice laws).

On such facts, the claimant who has supplied materials or labor may assert an equitable lien on either the land itself or the undisbursed portion of the construction loan funds, if any.[19] Several barriers exist which may cause this claim to fail, however. One is the argument that the mechanics' lien and stop notice statutes were intended by the legislature to constitute the sole remedies for such claimants, and that any extra-statutory remedy is out of order.[20] This argument is sound if the legislature has said as much,[21] but in most jurisdictions there is no indication that the statutory remedies are intended to be exclusive, and such a result should not be easily inferred.[22]

To analyze the other barriers to recovery on an equitable lien theory, we must focus on lien claims to the undisbursed loan funds.[23]

---

18. General contractors are usually within the class of persons who can claim equitable liens of the type described in the text below; see Swinerton & Walberg Co. v. Union Bank, 25 Cal.App.3d 259, 101 Cal.Rptr. 665 (1972).

19. See Comment, Owner/Lender Liability to Unpaid Subcontractors, 29 Duquesne L.Rev. 661 (1991); Reitz, Construction Lenders' Liability to Contractors, Subcontractors, and Materialmen, 130 U.Pa. L.Rev. 416 (1981); Lefcoe & Schaffer, Construction Lending and the Equitable Lien, 40 So.Cal.L.Rev. 439 (1967); Smith & Cobbe, Questions of Priority Between Mechanics' Lienors and Construction Loan Mortgages, 38 Ohio St.L.J. 3, 15–17 (1977).

20. Compare Donnybrook Bldg. Supply Co. v. Alaska National Bank, 736 P.2d 1147 (Alaska 1987) (mechanic's lien and stop notice statutes held to exclude equitable lien) with Town Concrete Pipe of Washington, Inc., v. Redford, 43 Wash.App. 493, 717 P.2d 1384 (1986) (stop notice statute did not preclude contractor from asserting equitable lien on construction funds in lender's hands). See also Trane Co. v. Randolph Plumbing & Heating, 44 Wash.App. 438, 722 P.2d 1325 (1986) (on government construction project, supplier could recover against prime contractor on theory of unjust enrichment); Guarantee Electric Co. v. Big Rivers Electric Corp., 669 F.Supp. 1371 (W.D.Ky.1987) (mechanic's lien statute was not an exclusive remedy and did not preclude subcontractor's personal recovery against landowner on a theory of unjust enrichment).

21. See West's Ann.Cal.Civ.Code § 3264, enacted in 1967, which expressly declared the stop notice the exclusive remedy as against undisbursed construction loan funds, thereby wiping out a long line of California equitable lien cases; see Boyd & Lovesee Lumber Co. v. Modular Marketing Corp., 44 Cal.App.3d 460, 118 Cal.Rptr. 699 (1975); Pankow Construction Co. v. Advance Mortgage Co., 618 F.2d 611 (9th Cir.1980); Gutierrez, California Civil Code Section 3264 and the Ghost of the Equitable Lien, 30 Hast.L.J. 493 (1979). Compare Sofias v. Bank of America, 172 Cal.App.3d 583, 218 Cal.Rptr. 388 (1985) (West's Ann. Cal.Civ.Code § 3264 precludes contractor's action against construction lender on third-party-beneficiary theory; mechanic's lien and stop notice statutes are exclusive remedies of contractor) with Cal–West Nat. Bank v. Phillips, 185 Cal.App.3d 96, 229 Cal.Rptr. 431 (1986) (contractor may pursue action against construction lender for conspiracy to defraud contractor in the manner of disbursement of loan funds, notwithstanding Civ.Code § 3264) and Nibbi Bros., Inc. v. Brannan Street Investors, 205 Cal.App.3d 1415, 253 Cal.Rptr. 289 (1988) (court may impose equitable lien, notwithstanding Civ.Code § 3264, upon proof that construction lender made fraudulent misrepresentations to contractor; mere assurance that contractor would get paid was not a misrepresentation of fact, and did not give rise to lien).

22. See Crane Co. v. Fine, 221 So.2d 145 (Fla.1969), conformed to 222 So.2d 36 (Fla.App.1969), recognizing the equitable lien as an alternative to the mechanics' lien.

23. See Aetna Casualty & Surety Co. v. United States, 228 Ct.Cl. 146, 655 F.2d 1047 (1981) (Court of Claims has no jurisdiction of claimed equitable lien against HUD as assignee of construction loan). Cf. Bor–Son Building Corp. v. Heller, 572 F.2d 174 (8th Cir.1978) (federal district courts

§ 12.6 FINANCING REAL ESTATE CONSTRUCTION

While claims to a lien on the land itself are also entirely possible,[24] they are analytically much simpler and will be discussed later. Courts dealing with lien claims to the loan funds have explained the lien as based on either of two theories: the equitable concept of unjust enrichment[25] or the contract doctrine of third-party beneficiary,[26] with the lien claimant as the beneficiary of the construction loan agreement. Some courts have dealt with these concepts separately while others have merged them together, sometimes adding a dose of estoppel; the cases are difficult to synthesize. Depending on which of these theories is employed, the equitable lien claimant may be required to satisfy one or more of the criteria discussed below.

Commonly, the courts will recognize an equitable lien only if the construction lender has made some representation to the claimant during the course of construction.[27] One type of representation usually considered sufficient is an assurance that the claimant will be paid, or will be "made whole" or "taken care of."[28] Such a statement seems to

---

have jurisdiction of such claims.) But see Marcus Garvey Square, Inc. v. Winston Burnett Construction Co., 595 F.2d 1126 (9th Cir.1979).

24. See note 33, infra.

25. S.S. Silberblatt, Inc. v. East Harlem Pilot Block, 608 F.2d 28 (2d Cir.1979); Dave Kolb Grading, Inc. v. Lieberman Corp., 837 S.W.2d 924 (Mo.App.1992); Embree Const. Group, Inc. v. Rafcor, Inc., 330 N.C. 487, 411 S.E.2d 916 (1992); Irwin Concrete, Inc. v. Sun Coast Properties, Inc., 33 Wash.App. 190, 653 P.2d 1331 (1982); In re Monroe County Housing Corp., 18 B.R. 741 (Bkrtcy.Fla.1982). Cf. Taylor Woodrow Blitman Construction Co. v. Southfield Gardens Co., 534 F.Supp. 340 (D.Mass.1982) (no unjust enrichment, where owner was solvent and where a valid mechanic's lien could be filed by contractor); Van–Tex v. Pierce, 703 F.2d 891 (5th Cir.1983) (no unjust enrichment where owner was solvent); Mursor Builders, Inc. v. Crown Mountain Apartment Associates, 467 F.Supp. 1316, 1334–35 (D.V.I.1978) (same); D.A. Hill Co. v. Clevetrust Realty Investors, 524 Pa. 425, 573 A.2d 1005 (1990) (no unjust enrichment, in absence of proof that property was worth more than lender had disbursed).

26. Cf. Knight Construction Co. v. Barnett Mortgage Trust, 572 S.W.2d 381 (Tex. Civ.App.1978), error refused n.r.e., rejecting the third party beneficiary approach on the ground that contractor was merely an incidental beneficiary; Merchants National Bank v. Professional Constructors, Inc., 579 S.W.2d 100 (Ky.1979), noted 68 Ky.L.J. 689 (1980); R.M. Shoemaker Co. v. Southeastern Pennsylvania Economic Development Corp., 275 Pa.Super. 594, 419 A.2d 60 (1980). See Sofias v. Bank of America, 172 Cal.App.3d 583, 218 Cal.Rptr. 388 (1985) (construction loan agreement expressly denied that anyone other than borrower was a beneficiary; contractor could not claim third-party-beneficiary status); Volpe Const. Co. v. First National Bank, 30 Mass. App.Ct. 249, 567 N.E.2d 1244 (1991) (same).

27. See Swansea Concrete Products, Inc. v. Distler, 126 Ill.App.3d 927, 81 Ill. Dec. 688, 467 N.E.2d 388 (1984); Watson Construction Co. v. Amfac Mortgage Corp., 124 Ariz. 570, 606 P.2d 421 (App.1979); D.A. Hill Co. v. Clevetrust Realty Investors, 524 Pa. 425, 573 A.2d 1005 (1990) (lien might be based either on unjust enrichment or on misleading statements by lender, but neither shown by the facts); Town Concrete Pipe of Washington, Inc., v. Redford, 43 Wash.App. 493, 717 P.2d 1384 (1986) (denying equitable lien in part because of absence of any promise by lender to contractor).

28. See F.W. Eversley & Co. v. East New York Non–Profit HDFC, Inc., 409 F.Supp. 791 (S.D.N.Y.1976); J. G. Plumbing Service, Inc. v. Coastal Mortgage Co., 329 So.2d 393 (Fla.App.1976), certiorari dismissed 339 So.2d 1169 (Fla.1976); Gee v. Eberle, 279 Pa.Super. 101, 420 A.2d 1050 (1980); In re Monroe County Housing Corp., 18 B.R. 741 (Bkrtcy.Fla.1982); First National State Bank v. Carlyle House, Inc., 102 N.J.Super. 300, 246 A.2d 22, affirmed 107 N.J.Super. 389, 258 A.2d 545 (1968); Wahl v. Southwest Savings & Loan Association, 12 Ariz.App. 90, 467 P.2d 930 (1970) vacated in part 106 Ariz. 381, 476 P.2d 836 (1970) (representations by borrower not sufficient; lender must make representa-

satisfy the supposed requirement, in third-party-beneficiary law, that the parties have intended the claimant to have the benefits of the contract.[29] Yet this test reflects a misconception, for the modern majority view is that only the obligee to whom the direct promise was made must have intended that the third party be benefitted by it;[30] under this view the intent of the obligor—the construction lender in the present discussion—is immaterial, and its statements to the lien claimant should be deemed irrelevant. Since in virtually every case all of the parties understand from the outset that the owner or developer plans to contract for the construction of the improvements and to pay for them with borrowed funds, it seems crystal clear that the owner intends to benefit the contractor and the subcontractors and suppliers.[31] No further demonstration of intent should be required.

Other courts tend to focus on whether the construction lender has made some false statement to the lien claimant which has misled him or her into continuing to furnish labor or materials.[32] The usual statement of this type is an assurance that sufficient funds remain in the construction loan account to complete the project or to pay the claimant.[33] Such a statement, if false, seems to satisfy the "unjust"

---

tions to lien claimant); Liberty National Bank v. Kaibab Industries, Inc., 591 P.2d 692 (Okl.1978) (same); United Plumbing v. Gibralter Savings & Loan Association, 7 Ariz.App. 540, 441 P.2d 575 (1968); G. L. Wilson Building Co. v. Leatherwood, 268 F.Supp. 609 (W.D.N.C.1967); Demharter v. First Federal Savings & Loan Association, 412 Pa. 142, 194 A.2d 214 (1963).

Cf. Morgen–Oswood & Associates, Inc. v. Continental Mortgage Investors, 323 So.2d 684 (Fla.App.1975), certiorari dismissed 342 So.2d 1100 (Fla.1977) (equitable lien imposed with no discussion of lender's representations); Spring Construction Co. v. Harris, 614 F.2d 374 (4th Cir.1980) (lien imposed despite lack of evidence that contractors were "lulled" into continuing work). Compare Chase Manhattan Bank v. S/D Enterprises, Inc., 353 So.2d 131 (Fla.App.1977), appeal after remand 374 So.2d 1121 (1979), in which a statement of precisely this type was held to be insufficient to establish a lien; Nibbi Bros., Inc. v. Brannan Street Investors, 205 Cal.App.3d 1415, 253 Cal.Rptr. 289 (1988) (same). See also Rinker Materials Corp. v. Palmer First National Bank, 361 So.2d 156 (Fla. 1978); Coke Lumber & Manufacturing Co. v. First National Bank, 529 S.W.2d 612 (Tex.Civ.App.1975).

29. Cf. United States v. Chester Heights Associates, 406 F.Supp. 600, 604 (D.S.C.1975).

30. Williston, Contracts § 356A (3d Ed.1959).

31. The later California cases took this position; see McBain v. Santa Clara Sav. & Loan Association, 241 Cal.App.2d 829, 51 Cal.Rptr. 78 (1966); but see note 21, supra. See also Trans–Bay Engineers & Builders, Inc. v. Hills, 551 F.2d 370 (D.C.Cir.1976) (no express representation, but "expectation" of lien claimant was reasonable); United States v. Mill Association, Inc., 480 F.Supp. 3 (E.D.N.Y.1978) (intent to benefit contractor inferred from statement in building loan agreement that, in compliance with N.Y. lien law, lender would hold funds in trust for contractor).

32. The contractor's false statements to the lender, on the other hand, may cause a court to charge him or her with "unclean hands" and deny an equitable lien; see Mursor Builders, Inc. v. Crown Mountain Apartment Associates, 467 F.Supp. 1316, 1334–35 (D.V.I.1978).

33. Chase Manhattan Bank v. S/D Enterprises, Inc., 353 So.2d 131 (Fla.App. 1977), appeal after remand 374 So.2d 1121 (1979); Hall's Miscellaneous Ironworks, Inc. v. All South Investment Co., 283 So.2d 372 (Fla.App.1973) (lien on land imposed in favor of subcontractor; misrepresentations by general contractor). Cf. In re 200 Woodbury Realty Trust, 99 B.R. 184 (Bkrtcy.N.H.1989) (equitable subordination of construction loan denied, where court was unconvinced that lender's representations had induced suppliers to continue to work with project); Edd Helms Electrical Contracting, Inc. v. Barnett Bank, 531 So.2d 238 (Fla.App.1988) (equitable lien denied, where claimant made no allegations

§ 12.6 FINANCING REAL ESTATE CONSTRUCTION 207

element of the unjust enrichment concept. Here again, however, the lender's statement is quite arguably irrelevant. The essence of unjust enrichment is that the lender is receiving something (in this case, the improvements on the real estate, upon foreclosure) for which it has not paid (as is shown by the presence of undisbursed loan funds.) The enrichment, it would seem, is equally unjust whether the lender duped the lien claimant or not. The equitable lien claim should not be dependent upon a showing of false communications by the lender to the contractors or suppliers.

If the third-party-beneficiary theory is employed by the court, the lien claim may be barred by the owner-borrower's default. Such a default—for example, failure to obtain a permanent loan commitment or failure to pay interest on the construction loan when due—may permit the lender to argue that it no longer has any obligation to make additional disbursements of loan funds; since this is true as against the owner-borrower, the lender will assert it is also true of third party beneficiaries, since their rights are derivative of the owner-borrower's.[34] This defense by the lender is a formidable one. Some courts have thought it inapplicable if the lien claimant completed work before the borrower's default, so that the right to payment could be said to have "vested."[35] If the lender has encouraged the contractors and suppliers to continue with their work on the project despite the default, the court might find that the lender waived the default, at least so far as the lien claimants are concerned.[36] And at least one court has quite consciously disregarded the borrower's default and granted a lien on a third-party-beneficiary theory.[37] Yet it must be conceded that such a default is in general a serious impediment to the establishment of a lien on this theory. By comparison, the unjust enrichment theory is not impaired by the borrower's default, so long as it can be shown that the foreclosing lender will nonetheless get more than it has paid for while the lien claimants go unpaid.

Some Florida courts have required that the project be substantially completed as a condition of imposing a lien on the loan funds.[38] The

of misconduct, deception, or misrepresentation by construction lender). See also FDIC v. Key Biscayne Devel. Ass'n, 858 F.2d 670 (11th Cir.1988) (court refused to subordinate construction loan mortgage to mechanic's lien, where there was no evidence that lender misled contractor into believing he would be paid before lender); In re Commercial Investments, Ltd., 92 B.R. 488 (Bkrtcy.N.M.1988) (same).

34. Van-Tex Inc. v. Pierce, 703 F.2d 891 (5th Cir.1983); Trans–Bay Engineers & Builders, Inc. v. Hills, 551 F.2d 370 (D.C.Cir.1976); Pioneer Plumbing Supply Co. v. Southwest Savings & Loan Association, 102 Ariz. 258, 428 P.2d 115 (1967).

35. See Trans–Bay Engineers & Builders, Inc., supra note 34; Travelers Indemnity Co. v. First National State Bank, 328 F.Supp. 208 (D.N.J.1971).

36. Spring Construction Co. v. Harris, 562 F.2d 933 (4th Cir.1977) appeal after remand 614 F.2d 374 (4th Cir.1980).

37. Bennett Construction Co. v. Allen Gardens, Inc., 433 F.Supp. 825 (W.D.Mo. 1977).

38. Giffen Industries v. Southeastern Associates, Inc., 357 So.2d 217 (Fla.App. 1978); J. G. Plumbing Service Co. v. Coastal Mortgage Co., 329 So.2d 393 (Fla.App. 1976), certiorari dismissed 339 So.2d 1169 (1976). See also Urban Systems Development Corp. v. NCNB Mortgage Corp., 513 F.2d 1304 (4th Cir.1975), discussed in Urban, Future Advances Lending in North

rationale seems to be that if the project is incomplete, the lender will be forced to foreclose and liquidate the property at a loss; hence it will not be enriched at all, and no lien should be imposed.[39] This analysis is far too simplistic, however. In some cases, the lender will itself complete the project before liquidating it, and may eventually earn a tidy profit from doing so. And even if the project is immediately resold by the lender at a price below the outstanding balance on the debt, that by no means establishes that the lender has not been enriched; but for the labor or materials contributed by the lien claimant, the project would almost certainly have sold for an even lower price, and the lender would have sustained a greater loss. In effect, the lender is mitigating its loss at the expense of the unpaid contractor or supplier. It may well be that the lender's enrichment is less than the unpaid bill, and perhaps the former figure should serve as an upper limit of the lien, but the fact that the project is uncompleted should not act as an absolute barrier to imposition of the lien.[40]

The foregoing discussion assumes that the lender has not disbursed the funds which would have gone to pay the lien claimant. Suppose the lender has in fact done so, but the disbursement was made in a fashion which allowed the owner-borrower or some other person, such as the general contractor, to divert the money. On these facts, one of two innocent parties must bear the loss. Neither the lender nor the lien claimant is at fault. It might be argued that the lender has a better opportunity to control the ultimate disposition of the funds or to select reliable borrowers, or that it should have employed a more reliable (although probably more costly) disbursement system—perhaps the voucher system rather than progress payments. Still, it is hard to maintain that unjust enrichment of the lender has occurred. Perhaps the lien should still be imposed, in effect throwing the loss onto the lender's shoulders, in order to encourage lenders to use the best feasible methods of controlling funds and to mitigate damages in the event of default. Yet some authors have argued that lenders are likely to be little influenced in either respect by the decisions of the courts in this matter.[41] In cases in which the lender has not been enriched, and where a default bars the third-party-beneficiary theory, the imposition of the lien should probably depend on whether the lender acted in accordance with reasonable standards in administering the loan; if it did, no lien should be found to exist. From a policy viewpoint, this case

Carolina, 13 Wake For.L.Rev. 297, 339–43 (1977). The California courts rejected this requirement; Miller v. Citizens Savings and Loan Association, 248 Cal.App.2d 655, 56 Cal.Rptr. 844 (1967); McBain v. Santa Clara Savings & Loan Association, 241 Cal. App.2d 829, 51 Cal.Rptr. 78 (1966). But see note 12, supra.

39. See Mortgage Associates, Inc. v. Monona Shores, Inc., 47 Wis.2d 171, 177 N.W.2d 340 (1970).

40. See S.S. Silberblatt, Inc. v. East Harlem Pilot Block, 608 F.2d 28, 40–41 (2d Cir.1979); Town Concrete Pipe of Washington, Inc. v. Redford, 43 Wash.App. 493, 717 P.2d 1384 (1986) (where project was uncompleted, court found insufficient evidence of unjust enrichment to warrant imposition of equitable lien).

41. Lefcoe & Schaffer, Construction Lending and the Equitable Lien, 40 So.Cal. L.Rev. 439 (1967).

is much like that of the priority dispute between the construction lender and the mechanics' lien claimant, discussed in the next section.

As indicated above, equitable liens can also be asserted against the improved real estate.[42] In this context the equitable lien is merely being employed as a substitute for a conventional mechanic's lien.[43] The analysis is relatively straightforward, since in most cases there is a contractual relationship between the owner of the land and the lien claimant or those with whom the claimant dealt. So long as the debt is proved and the land that was improved is identifiable, no great difficulty should be experienced in obtaining a judgment imposing the lien. The problems arise in determining its priority. As against bona fide purchasers of the land, the equitable lien is usually not discoverable through the public records and must consequently take a subordinate position.[44] As against the construction lender, the lien is also likely to be subordinate unless there is evidence that the lender's statements or assurances of payment induced the claimant to refrain from filing an ordinary mechanic's lien,[45] and that such a lien, if filed, would have had priority.

§ 12.7 Future Advances

There are many transactions in which it is desirable from a business viewpoint for the parties to enter into a present mortgage even though some portion of the loan funds is not to be advanced to the mortgagor until some future date.[1] The most common examples are

---

42. See United States v. Francis, 623 F.Supp. 535 (D.V.I.1985); Architectonics v. Salem–American Ventures, Inc., 350 So.2d 581 (Fla.App.1977); Syring v. Sartorious, 28 Ohio App.2d 308, 277 N.E.2d 457, 57 O.O.2d 477 (1971); Fibkins v. Fibkins, 303 S.C. 112, 399 S.E.2d 158 (1990) (lender holding first mortgage was equitably subordinated to lien of second lender from whom first lender had concealed information about borrower). See generally Note, The Equitable Lien Alternative in Ohio, 44 U.Cin.L.Rev. 265 (1975).

43. See Burman & Wieher v. Holzkamper, 700 F.Supp. 957 (N.D.Ill.1988) (attorney awarded equitable lien for work done to reduce property taxes on the land, despite the fact that a mechanic's lien would presumably have been unavailable); cf. Security Pacific Mortg. & Real Estate Services, Inc. v. Republic of the Philippines, 962 F.2d 204 (2d Cir.1992) (where contractor's mechanic's lien had been wiped out by foreclosure of construction loan mortgage, it was not entitled to equitable lien on proceeds of foreclosure sale in the absence of a specific agreement giving it a security interest in the real estate).

44. Divine Homes, Inc. v. Gulf Power Co., 352 So.2d 115 (Fla.App.1977); Jacobsen v. Conlon, 14 Ill.App.3d 306, 302 N.E.2d 471 (1973).

45. All State Plumbing, Inc. v. Mutual Security Life Ins. Co., 537 So.2d 598 (Fla. App.1988), review denied 545 So.2d 1366 (Fla.1989); Architectonics v. Salem–American Ventures, Inc., 350 So.2d 581 (Fla.App. 1977); Hall's Miscellaneous Ironworks, Inc. v. All South Investment Co., 283 So.2d 372 (Fla.App.1973). In Indiana Mortgage & Realty Investors v. Peacock Construction Co., 348 So.2d 59 (Fla.App.1977), certiorari denied 353 So.2d 677 (Fla.1977), the lender's telephone statement to the contractor that sufficient funds remained in the construction loan account to complete the project was held insufficient to give the contractor an equitable lien on the property superior to that of the lender.

§ 12.7

1. See Restatement (Third) of Property—Security (Mortgages) §§ 2.1–2.4 (Tentative Draft No.1, 1991); Comment, Priority Disputes In Future Advance Mortgages: Picking the Winner in Arizona, 1985 Ariz. St. L.J. 537; Comment, Future Advances in Missouri, 49 Mo.L.Rev. 103 (1984); Comment, Future Advances Under the ULTA and USLTA: The Construction Lender Receives a New Status, 34 Wash. & Lee

construction loans and other loans to improve real property, in which the funds are advanced in installments as work progresses and the property becomes more valuable security.[2] Another illustration is the "open-end" mortgage, typically a permanent home loan in which the lender reserves the option, after the principal balance has been partially reduced, to advance additional funds up to the original balance to pay for needed remodeling of the house or other purposes.[3] Other transactions involving future advances include mortgages to secure letters of credit, guarantees, or accommodations of commercial paper to be issued by the mortgagor;[4] fluctuating balances under "home equity loans" or commercial lines of credit established with an institutional lender, such as a bank;[5] and as security for a corporate bond issue, or series of issues.[6]

The advantages of such arrangements, in which the borrower takes only a portion of the loan to begin with but will receive more in the future, are substantial. The mortgagor saves interest on the surplus until there is a need for it, and escapes the burden of proper investment of it for the interim. Both parties avoid the expense and paperwork inherent in refinancing the initial loan, or in executing a series of junior mortgages. With construction loans, the mortgagee has the advantage of seeing that construction is progressing satisfactorily before committing larger sums of money to the project, and of making sure that the growth in value represented by the construction is reasonably adequate to secure the additional advances.

Ideally, construction loans and other mortgages to secure future advances should state explicitly the amount initially advanced, the amounts of additional advances to be made in the future, and the terms and conditions on which those advances will be made. Frequently, however, neither the mortgage nor the note is so specific. Instead, two

L.Rev. 1027 (1977); Urban, Future Advances Lending in North Carolina, 13 Wake For.L.Rev. 297 (1977); Comment, Mortgages to Secure Future Advances: Problems of Priority and the Doctrine of Economic Necessity, 46 Miss.L.J. 433 (1975); Comment, The Priority Problem Between Construction Mortgages and Mechanics' Liens in Alabama, 6 Cumb.L.Rev. 243 (1975); Kratovil & Werner, Mortgages for Construction and the Lien Priorities Problem—The "Unobligatory" Advance, 41 Tenn.L.Rev. 311 (1974); Meek, Mortgage Provisions Extending the Lien to Future Advances and Antecedent Indebtedness, 26 Ark.L.Rev. 423 (1973); Note, Mortgages for Future Advances: The Need for Legislation in Wisconsin, 1965 Wisc.L.Rev. 175 (1965); Blackburn, Mortgages to Secure Future Advances, 21 Mo.L.Rev. 209 (1956).

2. See § 12.1, supra; Lefcoe & Schaffer, Construction Lending and the Equitable Lien, 40 So.Cal.L.Rev. 439 (1967).

3. See Note, the Open–End Mortgage—Future Advances: A Survey, 5 DePaul L.Rev. 76 (1955); Note, Refinements in Additional Advance Financing: The "Open End" Mortgage, 38 Minn.L.Rev. 507 (1954). See also FNMA–FHLMC 1 to 4 family mortgage, clause 21, for future advances language not limited to the original principal amount of the loan.

4. See Ackerman v. Hunsicker, 85 N.Y. 43, 39 Am.Rep. 621 (1881); Robinson v. Williams, 22 N.Y. 380 (1860).

5. McDaniels v. Colvin, 16 Vt. 300, 42 Am.Dec. 512 (1844). See Ill.Rev.Stat.1977, ch. 17 § 6405, a provision aimed at facilitating the use of mortgages to secure revolving lines of consumer credit.

6. Reed's Appeal, 122 Pa. 565, 16 A. 100 (1888); Claflin v. South Carolina Railway Co., 8 Fed. 118, 4 Hughes 12 (C.C.S.C. 1880); In re Sunflower State Refining Co., 183 Fed. 834 (D.Kan.1911); 11 Col.L.Rev. 459.

§ 12.7 FINANCING REAL ESTATE CONSTRUCTION 211

other forms [7] are common. (1) The mortgage may name a certain total sum as if it were being advanced simultaneously with the execution of the mortgage, although in reality (and as may be shown by extrinsic, perhaps oral, evidence) some of the funds are not intended to be advanced until a later time. (2) The mortgage may name only the amount of the initial advance but state that it secures future advances as well, although their amounts and the conditions on which they will be made are left indefinite. One common version of the latter type is the "dragnet" or "anaconda" clause, which purports to make the mortgaged land security for "all debts, past, present, or future, which the mortgagor may owe to the mortgagee." Dragnet clauses are discussed in the next section. In construction lending, there will commonly be a separate written construction loan agreement that fills in the terms and conditions of the future advances which both of these forms omit.

The first form, which seems to pretend that the whole amount has already been advanced, can be misleading. Nevertheless, in the absence of fraud, it is clearly enforceable between the parties, although only for the amount actually advanced plus interest, of course.[8] It is valid even as against third party creditors or encumbrancers.[9] This makes sense with respect to subsequent creditors; they can hardly complain of the fact that the mortgage overstated the debt, since the usual effect will have been to make them even more conservative in giving the mortgagor further credit. On the other hand, there is a real danger to pre-existing unsecured creditors; because the recorded mortgage gives them the misimpression that the mortgagor's property is fully encumbered, they may forego efforts to obtain judgment liens or otherwise improve their position. Nonetheless, the law has generally disregarded this problem and upheld the mortgage as against all creditors.[10]

---

7. See Commercial Bank v. Rockovits, 499 N.E.2d 765 (Ind.App.1986); First National Bank v. Bain, 237 Ala. 580, 188 So. 64 (1939); Tapia v. Demartini, 77 Cal. 383, 19 P. 641 (1888).

8. See Note, Future Advance Clauses in Tennessee—Construction and Effect, 5 Memphis St.L.Rev. 586 (1975); Note, 23 U.Kan.L.Rev. 745 (1975). The amount stated is generally taken to represent the maximum in terms of principal advances that the mortgage will secure, even if it also contains a general future advances clause; see Home State Bank v. Johnson, 240 Kan. 417, 729 P.2d 1225 (1986) (advances in excess of maximum stated were unsecured).

9. Peterson Bank v. Langendorf, 136 Ill.App.3d 537, 90 Ill.Dec. 961, 483 N.E.2d 279 (1985); Hemmerle v. First Federal Savings & Loan Association, 338 So.2d 82 (Fla. App.1976).

10. Shirras v. Caig, 11 U.S. (7 Cranch) 34, 3 L.Ed. 260 (1812); Griffin v. New Jersey Oil Co., 11 N.J.Eq. 49 (1855); Whelan v. Exchange Trust Co., 214 Mass. 121, 100 N.E. 1095 (1913); Witczinski v. Everman, 51 Miss. 841 (1876); Kramer v. Trustees of Farmers' & Mechanics' Bank of Steubenville, 15 Ohio 253 (1846); Savings & Loan Society v. Burnett, 106 Cal. 514, 39 P. 922 (1895) (trust deed); Tully v. Harloe, 35 Cal. 302, 95 Am.Dec. 102 (1868); Straeffer v. Rodman, 146 Ky. 1, 141 S.W. 742, Ann.Cas. 1913C, 549 (1911); Merchants' State Bank of Fargo v. Tufts, 14 N.D. 238, 103 N.W. 760, 116 Am.St.Rep. 682 (1905)—accord. Contra, see Tyler v. Butcher, 84 Or.App. 656, 734 P.2d 1382 (1987) (where mortgage lacked future advances clause, it was valid for future advances as between the parties, but not as against intervening lienors who had no notice of the parties' agreement with respect to future advances, despite the fact that the advances were within the

The second format, which states no total debt at all, might be thought open to attack on grounds of its vagueness. However, the courts have been readily willing to admit extrinsic documents (i.e., a construction loan agreement) or parol evidence in order to clarify the parties' obligations, and to enforce the mortgage as the parties are found to have intended.[11] One reason for the courts' willingness to enforce such broad mortgage language is that it is often difficult to predict at the outset the exact amount which will be needed in a complex construction job; the same is true of mortgages given to secure performance of public obligations, such as those given by land developers to local governments to guarantee completion of street paving and other required improvements. Moreover, the very vagueness of the mortgage is a warning to third party creditors that they had better inquire of the mortgagee about the status of the debt. Hence, there is little or no risk that they will be misled.

The courts' liberality with regard to the validity of mortgages securing future advances is not boundless, however. If the mortgage

---

stated maximum amount); Sadd v. Heim, 143 Conn. 582, 124 A.2d 522 (1956) (same); Youngs v. Wilson, 27 N.Y. 351 (1863); Winchell v. Coney, 54 Conn. 24, 5 A. 354 (1886) (contra.)

11. The courts are liberal in construing the parties' agreement as including future advances. See House of Carpets, Inc. v. Mortgage Investment Co., 85 N.M. 560, 514 P.2d 611 (1973); Industrial Supply Corp. v. Bricker, 306 So.2d 133 (Fla.App. 1975); Potwin State Bank v. J.B. Houston & Son Lumber Co., 183 Kan. 475, 327 P.2d 1091 (1958); McDaniels v. Colvin, 16 Vt. 300, 42 Am.Dec. 512 (1844); Citizens' Savings Bank v. Kock, 117 Mich. 225, 75 N.W. 458 (1898); Huntington v. Kneeland, 102 App.Div. 284, 92 N.Y.S. 944 (1905), affirmed 187 N.Y. 563, 80 N.E. 1111 (1907); Blackmar v. Sharp, 23 R.I. 412, 50 A. 852 (1901); Lamoille County Savings Bank & Trust Co. v. Belden, 90 Vt. 535, 98 A. 1002 (1916).

Cf. Hendricks v. Webster, 159 Fed. 927, 87 C.C.A. 107 (1908); First National Bank v. Manser, 104 Me. 70, 71 A. 134 (1908). See also 1 A.L.R. 1586 (1919). Parol evidence may be used to show that future advances are included. Turner v. Houston Agricultural Credit Corp., 601 S.W.2d 61 (Tex.Civ.App.1980); Western Pennsylvania Nat'l Bank v. Peoples Union Bank, 439 Pa. 304, 266 A.2d 773 (1970); Gosselin v. Better Homes, Inc., 256 A.2d 629 (Me.1969); Clark v. Howard, 192 So.2d 302 (Fla.App. 1966); Rinaldo v. Holdeen, 20 A.D.2d 745, 246 N.Y.S.2d 807 (1964); Ferguson v. Mueller, 115 Colo. 139, 169 P.2d 610 (1946); Langerman v. Puritan Dining Room Co., 21 Cal.App. 637, 132 P. 617 (1913).

Contra, excluding oral agreement on the basis of the Parol Evidence Rule, see Barnhart v. Edwards, 5 Cal.Unrep. 558, 47 P. 251 (1896); Matz v. Arick, 76 Conn. 388, 56 A. 630 (1904); Central Prod. Credit Ass'n v. Reed, 805 S.W.2d 300 (Mo.App. 1991); Akron Savings & Loan Co. v. Ronson Homes, Inc., 15 Ohio St.2d 6, 238 N.E.2d 760, 44 O.O.2d 4 (1968); Willamette Production Credit Ass'n v. Day, 167 Or. 451, 118 P.2d 1058 (1941); Schmitz v. Grudzinski, 141 Wis.2d 867, 416 N.W.2d 639 (1987); Glenn, Mortgages § 399.1 (1943); Jones, Mortgages § 118 (1928). See also Weatherwax v. Heflin, 244 Ala. 210, 12 So.2d 554 (1943) (parol agreement would violate Statute of Frauds).

In Wisconsin no statement of maximum amount is required, and in its absence the amount of future advances is limited only by the parties' agreement; Bank of Barron v. Gieseke, 169 Wis.2d 437, 485 N.W.2d 426 (1992). See also Commercial Bank v. Rockovits, 499 N.E.2d 765 (Ind.App.1986) (mortgage that did not state a dollar amount was held to secure amount of loan initially advanced as well as subsequent indebtedness that was created when mortgagors became sureties). See Mortgages for Future Advances: The Need for Legislation in Wisconsin, 1965 Wis.L.Rev. 175, 179; Thomson, Titles as Affected by Liens: Open-End Mortgages and Mortgages to Secure Future Advances, 28 Tenn.L.Rev. 354 (1961); Comment, The Extent of the Debts Secured By a Mortgage in Arkansas, 9 Ark.L.Rev. 45 (1954).

neither states the full amount (including future advances) nor warns that future advances are contemplated, it will probably be held unenforceable, at least as against third party creditors.[12]

Optional vs. obligatory advances. Thus far we have not discussed whether advances made in the future under a mortgage are obligatory or optional. Certainly the mortgage itself or collateral documents (such as a construction loan agreement) can be drafted to read either way. If the mortgagee has no contractual duty, but may elect to make the additional advances and include them within the security of the mortgage if it chooses, they are said to be optional. The distinction seems simple, but in practice it is often hard to draw, as will be seen below.

So far as enforcement between the parties is concerned, the obligatory-optional distinction is irrelevant. Even if the advance is clearly optional, its acceptance by the mortgagor signifies a willingness to have it included in the mortgage. However, when a subsequent third-party creditor enters the picture, it becomes critically important to determine whether the advance is obligatory or not. The rule widely followed in the United States is this: if the advance is obligatory, it takes its priority from the date of the original mortgage, and the subsequent creditor is junior to it.[13] (This is, of course, subject to the operation of the recording acts; it is assumed in this discussion that the mortgage was recorded immediately upon execution.) However, if the advance is optional, and if the mortgagee has notice when the advance is made that a subsequent mortgagee or lienor has acquired an interest in the land, then the advance loses its priority to that creditor.[14] "Notice," as

12. Leche v. Ponca City Prod. Credit Ass'n, 478 P.2d 347 (Okl.1970).

13. National Lumber Co. v. Advance Development Corp., 293 Ark. 1, 732 S.W.2d 840 (1987) (obligation to lend must be stated in the mortgage); Potwin State Bank v. J.B. Houston & Son Lumber Co., 183 Kan. 475, 327 P.2d 1091 (1958); House of Carpets, Inc. v. Mortgage Investment Co., 85 N.M. 560, 514 P.2d 611 (1973); Earnshaw v. First Federal Savings & Loan Association of Lowell, 109 N.H. 283, 249 A.2d 675 (1969); Briarwood Towers 85th Co. v. Guterman, 136 A.D.2d 456, 523 N.Y.S.2d 98 (1988); Thompson v. Smith, 420 P.2d 526 (Okl.1966); Kemp v. Thurmond, 521 S.W.2d 806 (Tenn.1975); Western Mortgage Loan Corp. v. Cottonwood Construction Co., 18 Utah 2d 409, 424 P.2d 437 (1967). The English roots of the doctrine are found in Lord Chancellor Campbell's opinion in Hopkinson v. Rolt, 9 H. of L. 514, 11 Eng.Rep. 829 (1861). See generally Annot., 80 A.L.R.2d 179 (1961). For a listing of cases and jurisdictions following this view, see Case Note on Future Advances, Restatement (Third) of Property—Security (Mortgages) § 2.1 (Tentative Draft No.1, 1991), at 72. See the excellent discussion in Korngold, Construction Loan Advances and the Subordinated Purchase Money Mortgagee: An Appraisal, A Suggested Approach, and the ULTA Perspective, 50 Ford.L.Rev. 313, 329–39 (1981).

14. Poulos Investment, Inc. v. Mountainwest Sav. & Loan Ass'n, 680 P.2d 1073 (Wyo.1984) (doctrine inapplicable to accrued interest); Wilson v. Ripley County Bank, 462 N.E.2d 263 (Ind.App.1984); Watson Construction Co. v. Amfac Mortgage Co., 124 Ariz. 570, 606 P.2d 421 (App.1979) (dictum); Liberty National Bank v. Kaibab Industries, Inc., 591 P.2d 692 (Okl.1978); Percy Galbreath & Son, Inc. v. Watkins, 560 S.W.2d 239 (Ky.App.1977); Idaho First National Bank v. Wells, 100 Idaho 256, 596 P.2d 429 (1979); Trustees of C.I. Mortgage Group v. Stagg of Huntington, Inc., 484 Pa. 464, 399 A.2d 386 (1979); National Bank of Washington v. Equity Investors, 81 Wash.2d 886, 506 P.2d 20 (1973), appeal after remand 83 Wash.2d 435, 518 P.2d 1072 (1974); J.I. Kislak Mortgage Corp. v. William Matthews Builder, Inc., 287 A.2d 686 (Del.Super.1972), affirmed 303 A.2d 648 (Del.1973); Colonial Mortgage Service Co. v. Southard, 56 Ohio St.2d 347, 384 N.E.2d 250 (1978); Wayne Building & Loan

used here, is a concept requiring further explanation and will be discussed later.[15]

How can this rule be explained? Some earlier decisions and texts employed a highly formalistic approach: in a mortgage to secure future advances, each advance is in reality a separate mortgage which would normally take its priority only from the date it was made, but an equitable "relation back" will occur to the date of the original mortgage if the advance was obligatory or if the mortgage lacked notice of the intervening creditor.[16] This explanation is highly dubious; realistically, there is only one mortgage involved.[17] But more important, the "relation back" concept provides no policy rationale. Why should obligatory advances be treated as relating back, while optional ones are not? What does notice to the mortgagee have to do with whether relation back will occur?

Perhaps the best explanation attributes the rule denying the first mortgagee's priority as to later advances to a concern over the marketability of the mortgagor's title, either for the purpose of obtaining loans from additional mortgagees by others or of sale. This concern is compounded by the traditional solicitude of the courts for the mortgagor as a person who needs unusual protection, the deepseated policy in favor of free alienability of land, and, most of all, by a desire to make the mortgage device an effective one in securing the various economic and business advantages for which it was invented.

Under this theory, it is argued that if optional advances had an absolute preference, the mortgagor, although having no right to demand the contemplated additional loan funds, would be unable to obtain financing elsewhere, for no one else would lend on security that could be cut down by subsequent action by the first mortgagee. For the same reason, the mortgagor would be unable to sell the property subject

Co. v. Yarborough, 11 Ohio St.2d 195, 228 N.E.2d 841, 40 O.O.2d 182 (1967); Housing Mortgage Corp. v. Allied Construction, 374 Pa. 312, 97 A.2d 802 (1953); Yost–Linn Lumber Co. v. Williams, 121 Cal.App. 751, 9 P.2d 324 (1932); Home Savings & Loan Association v. Sullivan, 140 Okl. 300, 284 P. 30 (1929). See also In re Kirk, 133 B.R. 914 (Bkrtcy. Ohio 1991) (under Ohio statute, a optional advance under a mortgage that fails to identify itself as an "open-end mortgage" loses its priority even if the lender has no notice of the intervening lien).

15. See text at notes 35–37, infra.

16. Ladue v. Detroit & Milwaukee Railroad Co., 13 Mich. 380, 87 Am.Dec. 759 (1865), is probably the leading authority for this view. See also Ter–Hoven v. Kerns, 2 Pa. 96 (1845) ("Every future advancement is, in reality, a new debt * * *"); Walsh, Mortgages, 77 ("Mortgages given to secure advances to be made in the future create no lien either at law or in equity until such advances are made. As money is advanced under a mortgage of this kind of lien at law arises thereunder to the extent of the advance actually made. This lien relates back in equity to the original date of the mortgage * * *."); 4 Pomeroy, Eq.Juris. 594; Bank of Montgomery County's Appeal, 36 Pa. 170, 3 Grant 300 (1860); Alexandria Savings Institution v. Thomas, 70 Va. (29 Grat.) 483 (1877). See also 11 Col.L.Rev. 459 (1911). Similarly, Second National Bank of Warren v. Boyle, 155 Ohio St. 482, 99 N.E.2d 474, 44 O.O. 440 (1951), noted, 13 U. of Pitt.L.Rev. 431 (1952), took the position that a mortgage for optional future advances was only an offer to provide security if and when such advances were made. Further, such advances must be made in reliance upon the mortgage.

17. See Osborne, Mortgages 114–17 (2d Ed. 1970).

to the mortgage. It is true that even if the advances are obligatory the mortgagor may have a claim which is quite empty practically. Nevertheless he or she does have a legal right to performance by the mortgagee and a greater practical probability of getting further credit from the mortgagee than from another lender, even if this other were given power to end the priorities of the first. So long as the mortgagor and the property constitute a good risk, the mortgagee will fulfill its contract; when the risk becomes so bad that the mortgagee refuses to continue, the chance of successful financing elsewhere would be remote as well.

This explanation for the optional-obligatory distinction makes good sense. The problem is that distinction is so difficult to apply in the context in which disputes most often arises: a contest between a construction lender that recorded before work commenced, but has made some arguably optional advances, and a subordinate lienholder, commonly a subcontractor or supplier who has filed a mechanic's lien. In effect, the lien claimant has supplied credit to the mortgagor, albeit in the form of labor and materials rather than cash, with full knowledge that there is a prior construction mortgage on record, and with no expectation that the lender would take any action which would subordinate its mortgage to the lien. In effect the lien claimant has, to paraphrase the argument of the preceding paragraph, lent on a security that he or she knew could be cut down by subsequent action by the first mortgagee.

Why are mechanics' lienors willing to assume such a risk? The answers are several: custom in the industry dictates it; they trust the developer's honesty and business judgment; and they expect that the construction lender will carefully supervise the job and the loan disbursements to guard against difficulty. When they are disappointed in these expectations, perhaps because the developer and lender underestimated costs or construction problems, or because the developer was able to divert funds away from the project, they try to advance their priority by showing that some of the loan advances were optional. If they succeed in finding such evidence, they thereby enhance their chances of collecting on their lien claims. Yet this success can only be regarded as a windfall—indeed, a fluke. It is most improbable that its eventuation was a factor in inducing them to work on the project in the first place, or that the owner would have been in a weaker position to obtain labor and materials for the project if the law gave original priority to all construction loan advances, optional or not.

Most construction lenders and their title insurers, as might be expected, despise the optional advance doctrine.[18] They argue that it tends to drive out construction capital and thereby to discourage

18. See M. Jones & R. Messall, Mechanic's Lien Title Insurance Coverage for Construction Projects, 16 Real Est.L.J. 291 (No. 4, Spring 1988); Skipworth, Should Construction Lenders Lose Out on Voluntary Advances If a Loan Turns Sour?, 5 Real Est.L.J. 221 (1977); Kratovil & Werner, Mortgages for Construction and the Lien Priorities Problem—The "Unobligatory" Advance, 41 Tenn.L.Rev. 311 (1974).

needed real estate development. It is hard to find any empirical evidence for this argument; the legal interpretations of the doctrine in particular states do not appear to have much bearing on the decisions of financial institutions to make or not to make construction loans there.

The one feature of the doctrine that cannot be doubted is its uncertainty in application; as will be seen below, it is often hard to tell whether an advance is obligatory or not, and litigation frequently results. Professor Grant Gilmore has argued that this very uncertainty is the principal virtue of the rule:

> Nevertheless, the conceptually nonsensical distinction between "obligatory" and "voluntary" has had the result (which is not in the least nonsensical) of preserving (or creating) a wide area of judicial discretion. There are few, if any, future advance clauses which an astute judge cannot, at will, classify on one side or the other of the line between obligatory and voluntary. When he has picked his label, he has also picked his priority rule. The distinction amounts to an absence of rule; the judges are invited to pick and choose, case by case, ad hoc or ad hominem. This is a recurrent phenomenon in a common law system when the arguments for or against a given position balance each other exactly. There is much to be said for giving the mortgagee an absolute priority. There is much to be said for allowing other creditors a chance at the assets (or the debtor's equity in the assets). There is much to be said for allowing the mortgagor freedom to choose new sources of financing and for allowing new lenders to come in with secure liens. Only a very wise or a very foolish man would be willing to state, categorically, where truth lies and to propose a rule for application in all possible situations. There is, then, much to be said for having no rule at all, or only a make-believe rule, and for letting the judges decide: judges are not necessarily wiser than other people, but they are paid to decide things.[19]

Gilmore's argument is superficially appealing but ultimately unconvincing. The cost of learning the answer in a particular case, stated in terms of attorneys' fees, court costs, the time of witnesses, and other litigation expenses, is far too high. A rule which could be applied with certainty would be far preferable.

As between construction lenders and mechanics' lien claimants, there is really no ground for a strong preference; each is usually innocent of any wrongdoing, and each is a potential victim of the poor judgment, bad luck, or dishonesty of the developer/mortgagor. The lender is usually in a better position to guard against these misfortunes,[20] but on the other hand if it has made advances which were

---

19. G. Gilmore, Security Interests in Personal Property § 35.4 (1965).

20. But see Skipworth, supra n. 18, at 224; Lefcoe & Schaffer, Construction Lending and the Equitable Lien, 40 So.Cal. L.Rev. 439, 447–49 (1967); First Nat. State Bank of N.J. v. Carlyle House, Inc., 102 N.J.Super. 300, 246 A.2d 22 (1968), af-

genuinely optional, it has typically done so in a good faith effort to stave off the developer's default and the foreclosure of the mortgage, an effort which surely redounds to the benefit of the prospective lien claimants as well. In an ideal world perhaps the law would grant the lienors and the lender equal priority, allowing them to share pro-rata in the foreclosure proceeds,[21] but no American statute or case seems to take this view. An arbitrary rule favoring either the lender or the lien claimants, irrespective of the obligatory character of the advances, would be much more desirable than the unpredictability and ultimate fortuity of the present system. The experience of a number of states bears this out. Missouri case law gives virtually automatic priority to mechanics' lien claimants over construction loans,[22] while at least 14 states, most by statute, accord automatic priority to future advances over intervening liens for some types of loans and lenders.[23] There is no evidence that either rule has much practical effect on the availability of construction financing or labor and materials.

What is an "optional" advance? Construction lenders frequently attempt, by language in their construction loan agreements, to reserve fairly broad discretion in making later determinations as to whether a mortgagor/developer is making satisfactory progress on the project. While lenders are generally not eager to cut off further payments or to foreclose, they often prefer to have the apparent right to do so if they sense trouble developing. This is well illustrated in National Bank of

---

firmed without opinion 107 N.J.Super. 389, 258 A.2d 545 (1969).

21. This suggestion is advanced in Comment, The Priority Problem Between Construction Mortgages and Mechanics' Liens in Alabama, 6 Cumb.L.Rev. 243 (1975).

22. Dave Kolb Grading, Inc. v. Lieberman Corp., 837 S.W.2d 924 (E.D.Mo.1992) and Kranz v. Centropolis Crusher, Inc., 630 S.W.2d 140 (Mo.App.1982).

23. West's Ann.Cal.Civ.Code § 3136 (but only for advances to pay lien claims and costs of improvements, and only against mechanics' lien claimants); Conn. Gen.Stat.Ann. § 49-3 (construction loans only); Del.Code Tit. 25 § 2118; West's Fla. Stat.Ann. § 697.04; Commercial Bank v. Readd, 240 Ga. 519, 242 S.E.2d 25 (1978); Courson v. Atkinson & Griffin, Inc., 230 Ga. 643, 198 S.E.2d 675 (1973); Hurst v. Flynn-Harris-Bullard Co., 166 Ga. 480, 143 S.E. 503 (1928); Haw.Rev.Stat. § 506-1; Idaho Code § 26-1931 (savings & loan associations only); Kan.Stat.Ann. 58-2336, as construed in Fidelity Sav. Ass'n v. Witt, 8 Kan.App.2d 640, 665 P.2d 1108 (1983); Md.Code, Real Prop., § 7-102; Mich.Stat. Ann. § 570.1119(4) (construction loans only, if proper lien waivers are obtained); Shutze v. Credithrift of America, Inc., 607 So.2d 55 (Miss.1992); N.H.Rev.Stat.Ann. 479:3-5 (financial institutions only); N.J. Stat. Ann. 46:9-8.1 to 46:9-8.4 (not applicable to construction loans); N.M.Stat.Ann. § 48-7-9, discussed in Styles, Mortgages In New Mexico, 20 N.M.L.Rev. 585, 590-92 (1990); N.Y.—McKinney's Real Prop.Law § 281 ("credit line" mortgage only; not applicable to construction loans); S.D.Codified L.Ann. § 44-8-26 (applicable only if statute is referred to in mortgage); Coke Lumber & Manufacturing Co. v. First National Bank in Dallas, 529 S.W.2d 612 (Tex. Civ.App.1975); Wood v. Parker Square State Bank, 390 S.W.2d 835 (Tex.Civ.App. 1965), reversed 400 S.W.2d 898 (Tex.1966); M.S. Foundations, Inc. v. Perma-Crete Bldg. Systems, Inc., 666 S.W.2d 568 (Tex. App.1984); West's Wash.Code Rev.Ann. 60.04.220 (caption refers to "interim or construction loans," but text of statute is not so limited); Wis.Stat.Ann. 706.11(1) (mortgages to state or national banks); Marine Bank Appleton v. Hietpas, Inc., 149 Wis.2d 587, 439 N.W.2d 604 (Wis.App.1989) (statute covers, but is not limited to, construction loans).

Washington v. Equity Investors,[24] in which the agreement made the bank's duty to advance the construction loan conditional upon a current appraisal, retention of an architect, and progress on the project, all of which were to be "satisfactory" to the bank. Moreover, funds were "to be advanced at such times and in such amounts as the Lender shall determine." No advance was due unless, in the judgment of the lender, all work which the advance covered had been done in a good and workmanlike manner. The Washington Supreme Court concluded that under this language the bank had no definite obligation to advance *any* funds; hence all advances were optional. By reserving too much discretion, the bank had defeated its own priority. The discretionary language may have represented sound banking practice, but the court found it legally insufficient to obligate the bank.[25]

A different problem is represented by J.I. Kislak Mortgage Corp. v. William Matthews Builder, Inc.,[26] in which the lender's agreement provided that it was not obligated to make construction advances unless the mortgagor provided evidence that all of the preceding advances had actually been disbursed to subcontractors or materialmen. Notwithstanding this language, the lender made advances without requiring receipts or other such evidence; the court held that these advances were optional and consequently subordinate to filed mechanics' liens.

These and similar cases can be synthesized into three principles which a construction lender should carefully observe. First, it must not reserve too much discretion, but must have a genuine contractual obligation to lend; if it makes the obligation conditional, the conditions must be objectively defined and not subject to the lender's control or whim.[27] Second, the lender must use the controls and assert the conditions that it has reserved in the loan agreement. Even if those procedural controls and conditions are far more restrictive than most prudent lenders require, so that its failure to assert them could in no wise be regarded as negligence, it may still be charged with making optional advances if it does not make the mortgagor hew to the line.[28]

24. 81 Wash.2d 886, 506 P.2d 20 (1973), appeal after remand 83 Wash.2d 435, 518 P.2d 1072 (1974). The rule was subsequently reversed by statute in Washington; see West's Rev.Code Wash.Ann. 60.04.220.

25. Compare Dempsey v. McGowan, 291 Ark. 147, 722 S.W.2d 848 (1987) (reasonable conditions and reservations of discretion by the construction lender to protect its loan do not render its advances optional). See Moore, Seeking Firmer Ground: Mortgages to Secure Future Advances and the Priorities Quagmire, 12 Suff.L.Rev. 445, 463 (1978).

26. 287 A.2d 686 (Del.Super.1972), affirmed 303 A.2d 648 (Del.1973); see also Trustees of C.I. Mortgage Group v. Stagg of Huntington, Inc., 247 Pa.Super. 336, 372 A.2d 854 (1977), reversed 484 Pa. 464, 399 A.2d 386 (1979); First National Bank v. Worthley, 714 P.2d 1044 (Okl.App.1985) (bank's advances were not obligatory, where it had notice that suppliers and subcontractors were not being paid).

27. The advances were held to be obligatory, despite the reservation of significant discretion by the mortgagee in the construction loan agreement, in Irwin Concrete, Inc. v. Sun Coast Properties, Inc., 33 Wash.App. 190, 653 P.2d 1331 (1982); Dempsey v. McGowan, 291 Ark. 147, 722 S.W.2d 848 (1987); National Lumber Co. v. Advance Development Corp., 293 Ark. 1, 732 S.W.2d 840 (1987).

28. For example, if progress payments are made ahead of schedule, they are optional; Housing Mortgage Corp. v. Allied

Third, the lender must make no further advances after the occurrence of any event is defined by the documents as a default of the mortgagor; if the lender has the *right* to cease making advances, it had better exercise it.[29] Since the construction loan agreements frequently contain broad and ambiguous pro-lender language, it is frighteningly easy to make, in the ordinary course of business, what turns out to be an optional advance. Better drafting may help, but it is only a partial solution.[30]

The lender may be put to an extremely difficult choice if it is obvious that any further advances will be optional. If construction is only partially completed and the construction loan account has been exhausted, it may make excellent business sense for the lender to provide further funds in the hope of getting the building completed; the increment in value that can be added by the investment of further money may far outstrip the amount invested. Moreover, completing the project so that it can be marketed is in everyone's interest if it can be accomplished at a reasonable added cost; the developer, the lender, prospective lien claimants, and the public at large will be benefitted. But if the optional/obligatory rule induces the lender to foreclose at that point, the lien claimants will be wiped out (as will the developer), to no one's advantage. Hence, the net result of the rule that deprives optional advances of their priority may well be to give a few lien

---

Construction, Inc., 374 Pa. 312, 97 A.2d 802 (1953).

29. Central Pennsylvania Savings Association v. Carpenters of Pennsylvania, Inc., 298 Pa.Super. 250, 444 A.2d 755 (1982), affirmed 502 Pa. 17, 463 A.2d 414 (1983); New York & Suburban Federal Savings & Loan Association v. Fi–Pen Realty Co., 133 N.Y.S.2d 33 (Sup.Ct.1954); Planters' Lumber Co. v. Griffin Chapel M.E. Church, 157 Miss. 714, 128 So. 76 (1930). Cf. N.C.Gen.Stat. § 45–70(a), defining an advance as obligatory even though it might have been withheld because of the borrower's default. See Urban, Future Advances and Title Insurance Coverage, 15 Wake For.L.Rev. 329, 356 n. 97 (1979).

It is quite likely that any advance made after exhaustion of the originally-committed construction funds will be held optional, even in the absence of relevant contractual language, since the law does not obligate the lender to fund the building to completion; Walter Harvey Corp. v. O'Keefe, 346 So.2d 617 (Fla.App.1977); Kinner v. World Savings & Loan Ass'n, 57 Cal.App.3d 724, 129 Cal.Rptr. 400 (1976). See also First Federal Savings & Loan Association of Rochester v. Green–Acres Building Corp., 38 Misc.2d 149, 236 N.Y.S.2d 1009 (1963), holding that a charge against the loan account to cover interest or fees on the loan is *per se* optional, since the lender could not sue itself for them. Cf. Mortgage Guarantee Co. v. Hammond Lumber Co., 13 Cal.App.2d 538, 57 P.2d 164 (1936).

30. One approach is to provide in the construction loan agreement that no default will be deemed to exist until the lender sends a formal notice of default to the borrower; another is to provide that all advances reasonably made by the lender to complete the improvements or to protect its security are deemed obligatory. The success of either of these techniques is problematic; see Urban, supra note 29; Skipworth, supra note 16, at 226–27.

Still another approach is to place the entire construction loan amount in an escrow or trust account, thus giving the appearance that the lender has made only a single obligatory advance; the trustee or escrowee is then charged with administration of the loan. The Maryland courts have accepted this technique enthusiastically, probably as a reaction to the extremely restrictive Maryland statute regarding future advance mortgages which prevailed until 1972; see Toney Schloss Properties Corp. v. Union Federal Saving & Loan Association, 233 Md. 224, 196 A.2d 458 (1964). However, if the lender has effective control of the escrowee or trustee, the ruse is so obvious that its success in other jurisdictions is doubtful.

claimants windfalls (in cases in which the lender is ignorant of the rule or misjudges its applicability), but to harm the great majority of lien claimants by encouraging knowledgeable lenders to foreclose immediately when a default occurs or the loan account is exhausted.

In a case in which further (albeit optional) advances represent the only sensible course to the lender, it may argue that those advances are economically if not contractually obligatory,[31] and should therefore retain their priority. Some support for this view may be drawn from the cases which hold that advances to cover delinquent property taxes or insurance, or to pay for necessary repairs, are deemed obligatory because they are essential to protect the lender's security.[32] Over-budget advances to complete construction might conceivably be viewed in a similar light.[33] One commentator has even recommended that before a construction lender makes an optional advance, it should obtain an appraisal of the property in order to show that the advance does make business sense and is in effect economically compelled.[34] Unfortunately, most courts that have considered the economic compulsion argument have rejected it.[35] If a lender acts in an economically reasonable manner to protect or enhance the security by making further advances, and makes them by means of a non-negligent mechanism—that is, one reasonably calculated to ensure that the funds are actually employed in improvements to the realty—the courts ought to protect loan's priority irrespective of the optional nature of the advances. Such a rule would better serve all parties, although only a few cases thus far support it.[36]

31. See Skipworth, supra note 18; Comment, Mortgages to Secure Future Advances: Problems of Priority and the Doctrine of Economic Necessity, 47 Miss.L.J. 433 (1975).

32. See United States v. Seaboard Citizens National Bank, 206 F.2d 62 (4th Cir. 1953); Blackburn, Mortgages to Secure Future Advances, 21 Mo.L.Rev. 209, 220–21 (1956); Gilmore, Security Interests in Personal Property 929 (1965) But see United States v. First National Bank of Crestview, 513 So.2d 179 (Fla.App.1987), where an advance by mortgagee for the purpose of settling an unrelated civil suit was held to be an optional advance; Heller v. Gate City Building & Loan Association, 75 N.M. 596, 408 P.2d 753 (1965).

33. A few cases adopt this view; see Central Pennsylvania Savings Association v. Carpenters of Pennsylvania, Inc., 502 Pa. 17, 463 A.2d 414 (1983); First National Bank v. Zook, 50 N.D. 423, 196 N.W. 507 (1923); Hyman v. Hauff, 138 N.Y. 48, 33 N.E. 735 (1893); Rowan v. Sharps' Rifle Manufacturing Co., 29 Conn. 282 (1860). But see Poulos Investment, Inc. v. Mountainwest Savings & Loan Association, 680 P.2d 1073 (Wyo.1984). There are also numerous cases upholding the priority of optional advances to farmers to prevent loss of growing crops; see Cedar v. W.E. Roche Fruit Co., 16 Wash.2d 652, 134 P.2d 437 (1943); Hamilton v. Rhodes, 72 Ark. 625, 83 S.W. 351 (1904); Comment, supra note 31, at 446–47.

34. Skipworth, supra note 18, at 238–39.

35. See, e.g., Elmendorf–Anthony Co. v. Dunn, 10 Wash.2d 29, 116 P.2d 253 (1941); Althouse v. Provident Mutual Building Loan Association, 59 Cal.App. 31, 209 P. 1018 (1922).

36. The Mississippi cases require that the mortgagee use reasonable diligence to ensure that the funds advanced actually pay for improvements to the property, but this requirement is in addition to, not in lieu of, the requirement that they be obligatory; see Wortman & Mann, Inc. v. Frierson Building Supply Co., 184 So.2d 857 (Miss.1966); Southern Life Insurance Co. v. Pollard Appliance Co., 247 Miss. 211, 150 So.2d 416 (1963); Comment, supra note 31, at 458–60. Under the Arkansas rule, the lender must disburse the advances for construction purposes, but has no absolute

§ 12.7 FINANCING REAL ESTATE CONSTRUCTION 221

Notice. An optional advance loses its priority only to intervening liens of which the mortgagee has notice at the time the advance is made. By the weight of authority, the notice must be actual;[37] in the case of mechanics' liens, this presumably means not merely knowledge that contractors have done work or supplied materials to the site, but that they are unpaid and their bills are overdue.[38] A minority view holds that the mortgagee is also charged with constructive notice from the public records, so that recordation of the appropriate form of notice of lien would postpone the priority of all further advances whether the lender had actual knowledge or not.[39] The basic policy choice regarding notice is whether it is more reasonable to impose on the lender the burden of searching the records before each disbursement which might be deemed optional, or to impose on the intervening lienor the duty to inform the lender of this claim? Technical arguments, based on whether each advance is the equivalent of a new mortgage, are of only academic interest, and do not assist in the resolution of the policy question.

From the viewpoint of the intervening lienor, it may be observed that the title search the lender would be required to make before each advance under the minority rule is not a very extensive one; it would

duty to ensure that they are so used; see House v. Scott, 244 Ark. 1075, 429 S.W.2d 108 (1968). The California statute gives even optional advances on a construction loan priority if they are applied against filed mechanics' lien claims or actually used to pay for improvements to the realty; West's Ann.Cal.Civ.Code § 3136; see Turner v. Lytton Savings & Loan Association, 242 Cal.App.2d 457, 51 Cal.Rptr. 552 (1966). Cf. Coast Central Credit Union v. Superior Court, 209 Cal.App.3d 703, 257 Cal.Rptr. 468 (1989), which appears to misread the California statute as giving priority only to obligatory advances. On the general duty of construction lenders to use reasonable care in disbursing advances, see infra § 12.10.

37. See Union National Bank v. First State Bank, 16 Ark.App. 116, 697 S.W.2d 940 (1985); Central Pennsylvania Savings Association v. Carpenters of Pennsylvania, Inc., 298 Pa.Super. 250, 444 A.2d 755 (1982), affirmed 502 Pa. 17, 463 A.2d 414 (1983); Idaho First National Bank v. Wells, 100 Idaho 256, 596 P.2d 429 (1979); Security Trust Co. v. Graney, 89 Misc.2d 290, 391 N.Y.S.2d 46 (1977); McMillen Feed Mills, Inc. v. Mayer, 265 S.C. 500, 220 S.E.2d 221 (1975); Alston v. Bitely, 252 Ark. 79, 477 S.W.2d 446 (1972); Pike v. Tuttle, 18 Cal. App.3d 746, 96 Cal.Rptr. 403 (1971); Leche v. Ponca City Production Credit Association, 478 P.2d 347 (Okl.1970); Biersdorff v. Brumfield, 93 Idaho 569, 468 P.2d 301 (1970); Rochester Lumber Co. v. Dygert, 136 Misc. 292, 240 N.Y.S. 580 (1930); Colonial Bank v. Marine Bank, 152 Wis.2d 444, 448 N.W.2d 659 (1989); Annot., 138 A.L.R. 566 (1942). The Ohio statute requires written notice; see Ohio Rev.Code § 5301.232; see In re Kirk, 133 B.R. 914 (Bkrtcy.Ohio 1991); Four Seasons Developers, Inc. v. Security Federal Savings & Loan Association, 8 Ohio App.3d 300, 456 N.E.2d 1344 (1983).

38. See Grider v. Mutual Federal Savings & Loan Association, 565 S.W.2d 647 (Ky.App.1978) (" * * * mortgagee must know that there are unpaid claims for which a lien may be asserted and that the debtor is unable to pay such claims or that the claimant intends to file a lien.")

39. See, e.g., Tyler v. Butcher, 84 Or. App. 656, 734 P.2d 1382 (1987); Lincoln Federal Savings & Loan Association v. Platt Homes, Inc., 185 N.J.Super. 457, 449 A.2d 553 (1982); People's Savings Bank v. Champlin Lumber Co., 106 R.I. 225, 258 A.2d 82 (1969), following Ladue v. Detroit & Milwaukee Railroad Co., 13 Mich. 380, 87 Am.Dec. 759 (1865). See also R.B. Thompson, Jr. Lumber Co. v. Windsor Development Corp., 374 N.W.2d 493 (Minn. App.1985) (date of attachment of mechanics lien, which is the date of visible commencement of the improvement, imparts notice to the prior mortgagee). See generally Green, Search Real Estate Records Before Making Future Advances, 58 Fla. B.J. 704–705 (Dec.1984).

need only to update its examination from the date of the previous advance. Moreover, there may be cases in which the junior lienor cannot readily locate the senior in order to give it actual notice, so that recording is the only practical alternative. Such cases must, however, be quite rare; the vast majority of mortgages to secure future advances, and particularly construction loans, are made by institutional lenders to which notice may readily be given. From the lender's perspective, there can be no doubt that there is a real cost implicit in the necessity of making even a partial title search. The burden is magnified by the difficulty of knowing whether an advance is optional, probably causing most conservative lenders to obtain such searches before every advance in minority rule states.[40] The cost, of course, will be passed on to the developer and ultimately to the public. A more even-handed rule would require that actual notice be given except in cases in which the junior lienor could show inability to locate the lender by a reasonable effort; the needs of both parties would thereby be accommodated. A number of states have legislated on the notice issue; they typically provide that all advances will have priority over intervening liens unless the senior lender has been given written notice of the subordinate lien.[41]

Waiver and Estoppel. Even if the advances made by a construction lender are clearly obligatory, several cases indicate that the lender's priority may be lost if it makes statements to prospective lien claimants that mislead them with respect to potential problems with the project.[42] For example, suppose a subcontractor, in the midst of construction, inquires of the lender about the economic soundness of the project, and is told that sufficient funds remain in the construction loan account to permit completion, or that the subcontractor will be paid; in fact, the account is badly depleted and it is unlikely that the project can be

---

40. See Note, Mortgages for Future Advances: The Need for Legislation in Wisconsin, 1965 Wisc.L.Rev. 175, 181 (1965).

41. Alaska Stat. 06.30.560–06.30.565, 34.35.060; Me.Rev.Stat.Ann. tit. 9B, § 436; Neb.Rev.Stat. § 76–238.01; N.D.Cent.Code 6–03–05.1; Ohio Rev.Code § 5301.232; R.I. Gen.Laws §§ 34–25–8 to 34–25–14; Tenn. Code Ann. §§ 47–28–01 to 47–28–110; Vt. Stat.Ann. tit. 8, § 1207; W.Va.Code, 38–14–1.

42. See In re 5000 Skelly Corp., 142 B.R. 442 (Bkrtcy.Okl.1992); Dave Kolb Grading, Inc. v. Lieberman Corp., 837 S.W.2d 924 (Mo.App.1992); Trout's Investments, Inc. v. Davis, 482 S.W.2d 510 (Mo. App.1972); H.B. Deal Construction Co. v. Labor Discount Center, Inc., 418 S.W.2d 940 (Mo.1967); Apex Siding & Roofing Co. v. First Fed. Sav. & Loan Ass'n, 301 P.2d 352 (Okl.1956). Most of the Missouri cases do not depend on any showing of an actual deceptive statement, but are based on the notion that a construction lender, by the very act of knowingly lending on a project to be built, has waived its priority. See, e.g., Genesis Engineering Co. v. Hueser, 829 S.W.2d 579 (Mo.App.1992). Cases recognizing waiver or estoppel in principle, but finding none on the facts, include FDIC v. Key Biscayne Dev. Ass'n, 858 F.2d 670 (11th Cir.1988); In re 200 Woodbury Realty Trust, 99 B.R. 184 (Bkrtcy.D.N.H.1989); In re Commercial Investments, Ltd., 92 B.R. 488 (Bkrtcy.D.N.M.1988); Liberty National Bank v. Kiabab Industries, Inc., 591 P.2d 692 (Okl.1978); Palmer First National Bank v. Rinker Materials Corp., 348 So.2d 1234 (Fla.App.1977); Gancedo Lumber Co. v. Flagship First National Bank, 340 So.2d 486 (Fla.App.1976); First National State Bank v. Carlyle House, Inc., 102 N.J.Super. 300, 246 A.2d 22 (1968), affirmed without opinion 107 N.J.Super. 389, 258 A.2d 545 (1969); Utah Savings & Loan Association v. Mecham, 12 Utah 2d 335, 366 P.2d 598 (1961).

§ 12.7 FINANCING REAL ESTATE CONSTRUCTION

completed with the funds available. Relying on this false impression, the subcontractor continues work, in effect throwing good money after bad. On such facts, it is hard to deny that the lien ultimately filed [43] should have priority over advances made after the misleading statement. A duty of candor to junior lienors should accompany the right of priority which the law awards to the construction lender.

Statutory modifications. As noted above, a number of states have reversed the traditional doctrine by legislation and permit all future advances to take the same priority as the original mortgage, regardless of their optional character.[44] Most of these statutes also require a definite statement in the mortgage of the maximum amount that will be advanced under it, and withdraw priority for advances which exceed the amount stipulated together with costs, fees, and accrued interest.[45] The statutes usually exalt the mortgage above all types of intervening liens; the California statute appears on its face to grant priority only over mechanics' liens, but has been held to give a construction loan priority over a vendor's purchase money mortgage as well.[46] While a few of the statutes apply only if the future advances are for improve-

43. The representations may be so convincing that the subcontractors or suppliers do not file their liens until after the applicable statutory period has run; they should nonetheless be granted liens (and priority) as against the construction lender. See also § 12.6, supra, regarding the possibility of such lien claimants being awarded equitable liens on any undisbursed construction loan funds.

44. See cases cited note 23 supra. The Maryland statute has a fascinating and checkered history. It was originally enacted in 1825; see Md.Laws, 1825, c. 50; Md. Code, 1957, Art. 66, §§ 2, 3 (repealed). Its apparent purpose was to prevent serious abuses of the future advances mortgage. Language in such mortgages was so broad as to permit the mortgagee to acquire the mortgage, then proceed to buy up at depreciated prices debts owed by the mortgagor to third parties, and assert them against the mortgagor's land. See Watkins, Maryland Mortgages for Future Advances, 4 Md.L.Rev. 111 (1940); comment, Md.Ann. Real Property Code § 7–102 (1974). The statute, which was modified numerous times, in effect held that no future advance, optional or obligatory, would have priority but from the date it was made.

By its terms the law did not apply to Baltimore or Prince George's counties, and in the rest of the state a practice grew up among construction lenders, sanctioned by the courts, of evading the statute by depositing the entire loan amount into an escrow or trust account from which the escrowee or trustee would administer the disbursements. See, e.g., Toney Schloss Properties Corp. v. Union Fed. Sav. & Loan Association, 233 Md. 224, 196 A.2d 458 (1964); Comment, Md.Code, Real Prop., § 7–102 (1974). Finally in 1972 the statute was repealed and replaced with an express endorsement of priority for all future advances, irrespective of their obligatory character; Md.Code, Real Prop. § 7–102 (1974). The Maryland statute thus shifted from one of the most restrictive (although easily evaded) in the country to one of the most liberal.

45. Most of the statutes cited supra note 23, as well as most of the "cut-off notice statutes cited infra note 54, require some binding statement of the maximum loan amount. Under the Connecticut statute, however, the parties may amend the advances schedule (including, presumably, the maximum amount) at any future time. The Florida statute appears to require an express statement that the mortgage is given for future advances, but a mortgage referring only to a stated principal sum, with no reference to further advances, was given priority over intervening liens in Snead Construction Co. v. First Federal Savings & Loan Association, 342 So.2d 517 (Fla.App.1976). For a general review of the Florida law, see Silver Waters Corp. v. Murphy, 177 So.2d 897 (Fla.App.1965).

46. Turner v. Lytton Savings & Loan Association, 242 Cal.App.2d 457, 51 Cal. Rptr. 552 (1966).

ments to the real estate or for similar purposes,[47] most make no requirement concerning the use of the advances.

Another statutory variation, mentioned above, is to redefine "notice" to make it clear that only actual written notice delivered to the mortgagee will be sufficient to jeopardize its priority position. This approach places the onus on the prospective intervening lienor to take affirmative steps to ensure that the senior mortgagee is aware of its position.[48] Most of the statutes permit the delivery of notice by a junior lienor to act only as a subordination of *optional* advances, following the common-law approach, but several of them inexplicably appear to subordinate *all* advances to an intervening lienor who gives written notice.[49]

In a few statutes, "obligatory" is redefined as "pursuant to commitment, ... whether or not a default ... has relieved or may relieve [the mortgagee] from its obligation." [50] The quoted language appears in Uniform Land Security Interest Act (ULSIA), which takes this approach.[51] This approach permits the mortgagee to safely continue funding the loan despite the borrower's default under the mortgage, note, or loan agreement. Under the traditional "obligatory" concept, by comparison, a material default by the borrower would excuse the lender from the duty to make further advances, so that any advances actually made thereafter might be regarded as "optional" and subject to loss of priority.[52] This could follow despite the fact that, from an economic viewpoint, continuing to supply funds (for example, to complete a construction project) was the only sensible course for the lender.

These same statutes, again following ULSIA, also provide that an advance is regarded as being made "pursuant to commitment ... whether or not ... [an] event not within [the mortgagee's] control has relieved or may relieve it from its obligation." This language is intended to deal with the fact that loan agreements, particularly for construction loans, are frequently hedged with multiple conditions. For example, the lender need not disburse funds unless the project is proceeding within budget, is constructed in conformity with approved plans and specifications, and the like. If some conditions are not met, and the lender continues (as a matter of economic good judgment) to fund the loan, we have already seen that case law under the "optional/obligatory" distinction suggests that the further advances might lose priority.[53] Under the reformulation found in these statutes, however, loss of priority would be a risk only if the lender had control of the conditions.

47. E.g., Conn., Cal., Mich.
48. See supra note 41.
49. See the statutes of Alaska, Maine, and Vermont, supra note 41.
50. See S.H.A. 735 ILCS 5/15–1302; N.C.Gen.Stat. §§ 45–67 to 45–74; R.I.Gen. Laws §§ 34–25–8 to 34–25–14.
51. Uniform Land Security Interest Act § 111(19) (1985). The language was originally drawn from U.C.C. § 9–105(1)(k).
52. See supra text at note 29.
53. See supra text at notes 27–28.

These redefinitions of "notice" and "obligatory" may be somewhat helpful in clarifying the optional/obligatory muddle, but they are by no means an adequate solution. First, they fail to deal with the situation in which the mortgagee has simply reserved too much discretion, or has too much control of the relevant conditions, so that its advance cannot be regarded as "pursuant to commitment." Second, and more significantly, they lose sight of the original purpose of the optional/obligatory doctrine: to protect the mortgagor's right to use his or her unencumbered equity in the real estate as security for additional borrowing.

It is easy to illustrate this. Assume, under a statute containing the features described above, that ME1 makes a line-of-credit mortgage loan to MR for business purposes. ME1 promises to fund the loan up to a maximum of $100,000, but only upon certain conditions, one of which is that MR maintain a specific credit rating. After MR borrows $50,000 under this loan, MR's credit rating falls below the specified level and ME1 refuses to make further advances. The real estate's value is still well above $100,000, so MR approaches ME2 and attempts to arrange a second mortgage loan. ME2 is willing, and can easily give ME1 actual notice that second loan is about to be made. However, ME2 realizes that ME1 might in the future relax its position and make further advances to MR. If ME1 did so, those advances would quite plainly be "pursuant to commitment" as defined in the statutory language discussed above, despite the fact that, as a consequence of the credit condition's being unsatisfied, ME1 could not be compelled to make them. Hence, they would have priority over ME2. Since ME2 cannot be sure that such advances will not be made by ME1, ME2 will consider the real estate inadequate security and will refuse to make the second mortgage loan. Thus MR is in precisely the awkward and unfair position that the optional-obligatory doctrine was designed to avoid: he or she has plenty of unencumbered equity in the realty, but cannot get a loan from any source on its security. Thus these statutory attempts to make the optional/obligatory doctrine more palatable to lenders have the effect of defeating the doctrine's objective.

The most interesting statutory development, found in about a dozen states, takes an entirely different and much more effective approach to reconciling the interests of construction and other future advance lenders with the borrower's need to use the equity in the property as security for further financing. It does this by providing a procedure for the future advances borrower to give a "cut-off notice."[54] Such a notice is served on the lender, not by the junior lien-holder, but by the borrower. Its effect is to limit the amount of the advances having priority to the amount that has actually been disbursed as of

---

54. Alaska Stat. 06.30.560–06.30.565; West's Fla.Stat.Ann. § 697.04; Me.Rev.Stat.Ann. tit.9B, § 436; Vernon's Ann.Mo.Stat. § 443.055; Mont.Code Ann. 71–1–206; Neb.Rev.Stat. § 76–238.01; Nev.Rev.Stat. 106.300–106.400; N.C.Gen.Stat. §§ 45–67 to 45–74; Ohio Rev.Code § 5301.232; Or.Rev.Stat. 86.155; R.I.Gen.Laws §§ 34–25–8 to 34–25–14; Tenn.Code Ann. §§ 47–28–01 to 47–28–110; Va.Code §§ 55–58.2, 55–59. See Green, Search Real Estate Records Before Making Future Advances, Fla.B.J., Dec.1984, at 704.

the notice's date. These statutes provide an ingenious answer to the argument that if optional advances are given priority the debtor may be entirely foreclosed from obtaining additional financing, having no right to demand more funds from the original mortgagee and no apparent equity to pledge as security with a new lender. The borrower in the states mentioned who is in such a predicament can file the applicable notice, thereby freeing his or her equity in the property for junior financing.

The cut-off notice is a simple and effective solution to the dilemma of the borrower who needs additional financing. If the cut-off procedure is adopted, there is simply no need for the law to subordinate optional advances, for a properly-advised junior lender will insist that a cut-off notice be given, and there will not *be* any further advances by the senior lender, optional or otherwise.

The statutory cut-off notice provisions vary in their effect. Some of them render advances made after receipt of the notice unsecured.[55] Others merely subordinate the priority of further advances to any intervening liens.[56] It is difficult to see any strong policy ground for preferring one approach over the other; either will adequate protect the borrower's opportunity to get subordinate financing, and it seems reasonable to permit the notice to have either effect, according to its tenor.

It should be observed that a borrower who issues a cut-off notice may free his or her land from the lien of any further advises, but is not necessarily free of other liability. If the borrower has an affirmative contractual duty to draw down the advances (as will almost surely be the case with a construction loan), the cut-off notice will not eliminate that duty, and the borrower may well be liable for damages for breaching it. Nevertheless, damages constitute the only remedy; specific performance is not available to the lender.[57] The risk of a suit for damages suggests that construction loan borrowers will issue cut-off notices only rarely, perhaps when the project is on schedule and budget or nearly so, but the lender-borrower relationship has broken down. Even then a full refinancing is more probable than the use of a cut-off notice as a route to the obtaining of junior financing.

There are also some situations in which the issuance of a cut-off notice would be intolerably unfair to the lender, and should not be permitted. For example, if the loan is for construction purposes, and because of the nature of the construction work done to date the cut-off would place the lender in an undersecured position, the notice should not be considered effective. Likewise, if the mortgage secures the lender's obligation to advance funds to a third party, and the lender cannot escape the duty to make those advances, it would be unjust for the borrower to cut off the expansion of the lender's lien to accommo-

---

55. See the Alaska, Florida, Maine, Missouri, Nebraska, Nevada, North Carolina, Ohio, and Rhode Island statutes cited supra note 54.

56. See the Montana, Tennessee, and Virginia statutes cited supra note 54.

57. See supra § 12.3 text at note 34.

date the additional advances. This would be the case, for example, if the mortgage secured a guaranty or an irrevocable letter of credit issued by a bank to a third party. The Missouri statute does the best job of attempting to take these circumstances into account;[58] any court that adopted a common-law version of the cut-off notice would also need to consider them.

Thus far the cut-off notice procedure has been embraced only by statute, but there is nothing to stop a court from adopting it as a common-law development. It is plainly superior to any of the alternatives with which the courts and legislatures have struggled. The tentative draft of the Restatement (Third) of Property—Security (Mortgages) adopts it,[59] and it deserves serious judicial consideration.

Eliminating the optional/obligatory advance doctrine has one significant disadvantage. The doctrine has sometimes been used by the courts as a tool, albeit a somewhat blunt one, to prevent unfair hardship to junior mortgagees and mechanics' lienors in construction projects. If the senior construction lender employs sloppy loan disbursement practices that permit the borrower to divert funds from the project, thus increasing the balance on the construction loan without a commensurate increase in the value of improvements on the property, junior lienors are obviously unfairly disadvantaged. Courts have sometimes come to their aid by labeling the diverted disbursements "optional," thus giving the intervening lienors a priority they would not otherwise have had.

If the optional/obligatory advance doctrine is eliminated, this means of assisting victimized junior lienors is no longer available. However, other and more appropriate means of helping them continue to exist. Perhaps the most effective, adopted by several courts, is the imposition of a duty of good faith and fair dealing on construction lenders, so that those who injure junior lienors by the use of negligent or lax disbursement procedures are held liable for the losses they cause.[60] Elevation of the junior lienors' priority is a good way to impose that liability.

§ 12.8 Dragnet Clauses

The dragnet clause is a mortgage provision that purports to make the real estate security for other, usually unspecified, debts that the

58. Vernon's Ann.Mo.Stat. § 443.-055(1). See Comment, Future Advances in Missouri, 49 Mo.L.Rev. 103 (1984).

59. See Restatement (Third) of Property Property—Security (Mortgages) § 2.3 (Tentative Draft No.1, 1991). Although there is no Mississippi statutory cut-off notice procedure, the court mentions the cut-off notice with approval in dictum in Shutze v. Credithrift of America, Inc., 607 So.2d 55 (Miss.1992), at n.13.

60. Cases imposing a duty of this sort on construction lenders include Security & Inv. Corp. v. Droege, 529 So.2d 799 (Fla. App.1988); Peoples Bank v. L & T Devel., Inc., 434 So.2d 699 (Miss.1983), noted 53 Miss. L.Rev. 691 (1983); Fikes v. First Fed. Sav. & Loan Ass'n, 533 P.2d 251 (Alaska 1975); Commercial Standard Ins. Co. v. Bank of America, 57 Cal.App.3d 241, 129 Cal.Rptr. 91 (1976); and Cambridge Acceptance Corp. v. Hockstein, 102 N.J.Super. 435, 246 A.2d 138 (1968). See Kratovil, Mortgage Lender Liability—Construction Loans, 38 DePaul L. Rev. 43 (1989). See generally infra § 12.10.

mortgagor may already owe or may owe in the future to the mortgagee. The clause is not functionally related to construction lending and is discussed at this point only because it is conceptually a mortgage to secure future advances. In a sense the dragnet clause is just the opposite of a construction loan; the lender usually has no particular future advances in mind, and merely "throws in" the clause in the hope that it might come in handy later.

A simple form of dragnet clause reads as follows:

This mortgage is given to secure the payment of a promissory note (described in detail), and also the payment of any additional sums and interest thereon now or hereafter due or owing from mortgagor to mortgagee.[1]

A more carefully-drafted form, which attempts to resolve some questions implicit in the foregoing clause, is:

This mortgage is given to secure the payment of a promissory note (described in detail), and any other indebtedness or obligation of the mortgagor, or any of them, and any present or future demands of any kind or nature which mortgagee or its successor may have against the mortgagor or any of them, whether created directly, or acquired by assignment, whether absolute or contingent, whether due or not, whether otherwise secured or not, or whether existing at the time of the execution of this instrument or arising thereafter.[2]

Dragnet clauses are frequently included in the printed language of mortgages drafted by mortgagees. They are seldom the subject of negotiation, and may go entirely unnoticed by the mortgagor until the mortgagee attempts to enforce them. The rule making optional advances subordinate to intervening liens[3] is highly relevant in this context. Advances secured by dragnet clauses are almost never obligatory; the only factual issue is generally whether the mortgagee had the requisite notice of intervening liens, and this is usually not hard to determine.[4] Moreover the rule, which was severely criticized in the

§ 12.8

1. The language is adapted from Union Bank v. Wendland, 54 Cal.App.3d 393, 126 Cal.Rptr. 549 (1976). See Emporia State Bank & Trust Co. v. Mounkes, 214 Kan. 178, 179, 519 P.2d 618, 620 (1974); In re Scranes, Inc., 67 B.R. 985 (Bkrtcy.Ohio 1986) (dragnet clause must be in mortgage, not in unrecorded promissory note); First Nat. City Bank v. Tara Realty Corp., 64 A.D.2d 460, 410 N.Y.S.2d 71 (1978) (dragnet clause found not in mortgage, but in unrecorded side agreement, is not effective to give priority against junior lienors); Note, Future Advance Clauses in Tennessee—Construction and Effect, 5 Memph.St. L.Rev. 586 (1975); Note, Enforceability of "Dragnet Clauses" in Deeds of Trust: The Current State of the Law in Texas, 56 Tex.L.Rev. 733 (1978); Annot., 3 A.L.R.4th 690 (1980).

2. Wong v. Beneficial Savings & Loan Association, 56 Cal.App.3d 286, 128 Cal. Rptr. 338 (1976).

3. See § 12.7, supra, at notes 11–15.

4. See Bank of Ephriam v. Davis, 559 P.2d 538 (Utah 1977), requiring actual notice on the part of the lender to subordinate its lien deriving from a dragnet clause. Since no such notice was shown, the lender was held to have priority despite the optional nature of the advances. Under some statutes, a future advances clause may never have priority for more than the original balance, irrespective of

§ 12.8 FINANCING REAL ESTATE CONSTRUCTION 229

preceding section as applied to construction loans, makes rather good sense in the dragnet clause case; in its absence, a mortgagor might naively execute a home mortgage containing a dragnet clause and consequently be locked to that particular lender for the rest of time he or she occupied the house.[5]

Dragnet clauses are generally enforced,[6] but because their apparent coverage is so broad, and because the mortgagor is often unaware of their presence or implications, the courts tend to construe them narrowly against the mortgagee.[7] Generalizations are difficult, since the language of the particular clause may be a decisive factor. However, the following illustrations show numerous ways in which the courts have narrowed the application of dragnet clauses. Sometimes such holdings are said to be based on the intention of the parties, but in reality they usually represent the court's conceptions of fairness and equity.[8] These illustrations are not intended to represent any majority rule, as there are many conflicting or contrary cases. They merely show the sort of judicial treatment dragnet clauses often receive.

1. The mortgage will only secure advances made or debts incurred in the future. If the mortgagor already owes debts to the mortgagee at the time the mortgage is executed, it would supposedly be easy enough to identify those existing debts specifically; if they are not so identified, it is assumed that the parties did not intend to secure them.[9]

notice of intervening liens; see New Mexico Bank v. Lucas Brothers, 92 N.M. 2, 582 P.2d 379 (1978); supra § 12.7 note 45.

5. See Dicus v. Ripley County Bank, 471 N.E.2d 1257 (Ind.App.1984); Meek, Mortgage Provisions Extending the Lien to Future Advances and Antecedent Indebtedness, 26 Ark.L.Rev. 485 (1973).

6. In re Ferguson, 85 B.R. 89 (Bkrtcy.Ark.1988) (mortgagee was forced to purchase mortgage insurance because the mortgagor failed to do so; the cost of the insurance was secured by the mortgage by virtue of its dragnet clause); Fazio v. Alan Sinton, Limited, 41 B.R. 865 (Bkrtcy.Pa.1984); Clovis Nat'l Bank v. Harmon, 102 N.M. 166, 692 P.2d 1315 (1984); O'Neill Production Credit Association v. Mitchell, 209 Neb. 206, 307 N.W.2d 115 (1981); North Park Bank v. Nichols, 645 P.2d 620 (Utah 1982); Whiteway Finance Co. v. Green, 434 So.2d 1351 (Miss.1983); Smith v. Union State Bank, 452 N.E.2d 1059 (Ind.App.1983); First National Bank v. Rozelle, 493 F.2d 1196 (10th Cir.1974); Lammey v. Producers Livestock Credit Corp., 463 P.2d 491 (Wyo.1970). See generally Annot. 3 A.L.R. 4th 690 (1980).

7. In re Continental Country Club, Inc., 108 B.R. 327 (Bkrtcy.Fla.1989); In re Bonner, 43 B.R. 261 (Bkrtcy.Ala.1984); Badger State Agri–Credit & Realty, Inc. v. Lubahn, 122 Wis.2d 718, 365 N.W.2d 616 (1985); Everett Credit Union v. Allied Ambulance Serv., Inc., 12 Mass.App. Ct. 343, 424 N.E.2d 1142 (1981); First v. Byrne, 238 Iowa 712, 28 N.W.2d 509 (1947); Annot., 172 A.L.R. 1072 (1948). The courts of Tennessee tend to be an exception, construing dragnet clauses rather consistently in favor of the lender; see Note, Future Advances Clauses in Tennessee—Construction and Effect, 5 Memph.St.L.Rev. 586 (1975). See also Bank of Kansas v. Nelson Music Co., 949 F.2d 321 (10th Cir.1991) (dragnet clauses between commercial entities, and involving only personal property security, are not disfavored in Kansas).

8. See Justice, Secured Transactions—What Floats Can Be Sunk, 24 Vill.L.Rev. 867, 896–99 (1979).

9. National Bank v. Blankenship, 177 F.Supp. 667 (E.D.Ark.1959), affirmed sub nom. National Bank v. General Mills, 283 F.2d 574 (8th Cir.1960); Lundgren v. Nat. Bank of Alaska, 742 P.2d 227 (Alaska 1987); Bank of Searcy v. Kroh, 195 Ark. 785, 114 S.W.2d 26 (1938); First v. Byrne, 238 Iowa 712, 28 N.W.2d 509 (1947); First National Bank v. Lygrisse, 231 Kan. 595, 647 P.2d 1268 (1982); Durham v. First Guaranty Bank, 331 So.2d 563 (La.App. 1976), writ denied 334 So.2d 431; Ruidoso State Bank v. Castle, 105 N.M. 158, 730

2. Only debts of the same type or character as the original debt are secured by the mortgage.[10] For example, if the original loan is for

P.2d 461 (1986), refusing to apply a dragnet clause to preexisting debts in the absence of a showing that the parties so intended, or that the preexisting debts and the dragnet mortgage were related to one another; Iser v. Herbert Mark Building Corp., 253 N.Y. 499, 171 N.E. 757 (1930); Farmers National Bank v. DeFever, 177 Okl. 561, 61 P.2d 245 (1936).

Contra, see United States v. Automatic Heating & Equipment Co., 181 F.Supp. 924 (E.D.Tenn.1960), affirmed 287 F.2d 885 (6th Cir.1961); Guilmette v. Peoples Savings Bank, 12 B.R. 799 (Bkrtcy.R.I.1981); Robert C. Roy Agency, Inc. v. Sun First Nat'l Bank, 468 So.2d 399 (Fla.App.1985) (preexisting debts are secured where dragnet clause clearly expresses intent to include them, even though they are not specifically identified); Kamaole Resort Twenty–One v. Ficke Hawaiian Investments, Inc., 60 Hawaii 413, 591 P.2d 104 (1979) (preexisting debts are not covered by dragnet clause unless they are specifically identified or relate to the same transaction or series of transactions); Clovis Nat'l Bank v. Harmon, 102 N.M. 166, 692 P.2d 1315 (1984); Johnson v. Midland Bank, 715 S.W.2d 607 (Tenn.App.1986); Mercer v. Daoran Corp., 662 S.W.2d 382 (Tex.App.1983), judgment reversed 676 S.W.2d 580 (1984); Badger State Agri–Credit & Realty, Inc. v. Lubahn, supra note 7. See also Ram Co. v. Estate of Kobbeman, 236 Kan. 751, 696 P.2d 936 (1985) (dragnet clause covers pre-existing advances growing out of same transaction). See Restatement (Second) of Property—Security (Mortgages) § 2.4(b) (Tent. Draft No.1, 1991).

10. Paul Rochester Investment Co. v. United States, 692 F.Supp. 704 (N.D.Tex. 1988), reversed without opinion, 869 F.2d 1485 (5th Cir.1989) (commercial loan mortgage containing dragnet clause did not secure later personal loan); Sowers v. FDIC, 96 B.R. 897 (S.D.Iowa 1989) (home mortgage containing dragnet clause did not secure later farm loan); In re Cox, 57 B.R. 290 (Bkrtcy.Tenn.1986) (mortgage loan on wife's land to rebuild her residence did not secure subsequent business loan to husband); In re Continental Resources Corp., 43 B.R. 658 (Bkrtcy.Okl.1984) (where both debts were for working capital, dragnet clause in first mortgage covered second debt); In re Grizaffi, 23 B.R. 137 (Bkrtcy. D.Colo.1982) (dragnet clause in mortgage for business purposes does not cause it to secure later personal note); Lundgren v. National Bank of Alaska, 742 P.2d 227 (Alaska 1987); L.B. Nelson Corp. v. Western American Financial Corp., 150 Ariz. 211, 722 P.2d 379 (App.1986) (dragnet clause was triggered by other notes, where all notes contained "cross-default" provisions and all were related to same construction project); Security Bank v. First National Bank, 263 Ark. 525, 565 S.W.2d 623 (1978); Hendrickson v. Farmers' Bank & Trust Co., 189 Ark. 423, 73 S.W.2d 725 (1934); Akamine & Sons, Limited v. American Security Bank, 50 Hawaii 304, 440 P.2d 262 (1968); Decorah State Bank v. Zidlicky, 426 N.W.2d 388 (Iowa 1988) (dragnet clause in farm operations loan mortgage did not cause it to secure subsequent residential purchase); Mark Twain Kansas City Bank v. Cates, 248 Kan. 700, 810 P.2d 1154 (1991) (mortgage for construction of borrower's house did not secure later loan for investment in apartment project); Garnett State Savings Bank v. Tush, 232 Kan. 447, 657 P.2d 508 (1983); Emporia State Bank & Trust Co. v. Mounkes, 214 Kan. 178, 519 P.2d 618 (1974), noted 23 U.Kan. L.Rev. 745 (1975) (original mortgage loan apparently to purchase realty; note signed eight years later to buy car and start son in restaurant business not covered by dragnet clause); Dalton v. First Nat'l Bank, 712 S.W.2d 954 (Ky.App.1986) (dragnet clause in security agreement for purchase of mobile home did not cause it to secure payment of an overdraft on bank account); Canal National Bank v. Becker, 431 A.2d 71 (Me.1981) (issue of fact existed as to whether later notes were sufficiently related to 1976 mortgage loan for acquisition of boat inventory, so that dragnet clause in mortgage would secure later notes); Trapp v. Tidwell, 418 So.2d 786 (Miss.1982) (clause does not cover claims in tort); First Security Bank v. Shiew, 609 P.2d 952 (Utah 1980) (quoting treatise); Airline Commerce Bank v. Commercial Credit Corp., 531 S.W.2d 171 (Tex.Civ.App.1975, writ ref'd n.r.e.)

Cf. First National Bank v. Rozelle, 493 F.2d 1196 (10th Cir.1974); Thorp Sales Corp. v. Dolese Brothers Co., 453 F.Supp. 196 (W.D.Okl.1978); In re Dorsey Electric Supply Co., 344 F.Supp. 1171 (E.D.Ark. 1972); In re Stone, 49 B.R. 25 (Bankr.Tex. 1985) (dragnet clause covered second loan, where parties were identical and both loans were for similar business purpose); Union National Bank of Little Rock v. First State Bank & Trust Co. of Conway, 16 Ark.App.116, 697 S.W.2d 940 (1985) ("rela-

home repairs, a future loan or advance for additional repairs would be secured by the mortgage but a loan for an automobile purchase would not. It is easy to imagine grey areas in such a test. For example, what if the second loan were for adding a room to the house? The resolution of the matter is made easier if the documents on the second loan state that it is to be secured under the dragnet clause of the existing mortgage.

The position of the tentative draft of the Restatement (Second) of Property—Security (Mortgages) on this matter is a compromise. It provides that, unless the future advances are similar in character to the original mortgage loan, the mortgage will secure them only if the dragnet clause describes them with reasonable specificity, or if the parties agree at the time of the advances that the mortgage will secure them.[11] Under this view, the mortgagee can draft a dragnet clause so detailed that virtually any future advance will be secured; but at least the clause will provide the borrower some warning that this can occur.

3. As an extension of the foregoing concept, it is sometimes held that the dragnet clause will cover future debts only if the documents evidencing those debts specifically refer back to the clause.[12]

4. If the future debt is separately secured, whether by another mortgage or by a personal property security agreement, it may be assumed that the parties did not intend that it also be secured by the dragnet mortgage.[13]

tionship of loans test" was not applicable, where dragnet clause specifically covered all debts, whether or not for related purposes and whether or not later debt instruments referred to dragnet mortgage); Wong v. Beneficial Savings & Loan Association, 56 Cal.App.3d 286, 128 Cal.Rptr. 338 (1976); Financial Acceptance Corp. v. Garvey, 6 Mass.App.Ct. 610, 380 N.E.2d 1332 (1978) (dragnet clause, in mortgage securing note made by mortgagor, also secures later note guaranteed by mortgagor); Fleming v. First American Bank, 171 Ga. App. 295, 319 S.E.2d 119 (1984) (same); Rogers v. First Tennessee Bank, 738 S.W.2d 635 (Tenn.App.1987) (dragnet clause in mortgage on nonresidential property for business purpose caused it to secure later loan on residential property); Murdock Acceptance Corp. v. Jones, 50 Tenn.App. 431, 362 S.W.2d 266 (1961).

11. Restatement (Second) of Property—Security (Mortgages) § 2.4(c) (Tent. Draft No. 1, 1991).

12. Uransky v. First Federal Savings & Loan, 684 F.2d 750 (11th Cir.1982); In re Rude, 122 B.R. 533 (Bkrtcy.Wis.1990) (dragnet clause by its terms applied only to future advances that expressly referred to the dragnet mortgage); In re Continental Country Club, Inc., 108 B.R. 327 (Bkrtcy. Fla.1989); In re Mills, 39 B.R. 564 (Bkrtcy. N.D.1984); Nutting v. Bradford Nat. Bank, 44 B.R. 233 (Bkrtcy.D.Vt.1984) (dragnet clause will secure future loans only if the parties to the future loan so intend); In re Resnick, 9 B.R. 891 (Bkrtcy.D.Mass.1981); Pearll v. Williams, 146 Ariz. 203, 704 P.2d 1348 (App.1985); Hawkeye Bank & Trust Co. v. Michel, 373 N.W.2d 127 (Iowa 1985) (dragnet clause in deed of trust on debtor's homestead was triggered by later notes given by debtors to finance "spec" house, where notes specifically referred to the deed of trust); Stockyards National Bank v. Capitol Steel & Iron Co., 201 Kan. 429, 441 P.2d 301 (1968); First National Bank v. Lygrisse, 231 Kan. 595, 647 P.2d 1268 (1982). North Carolina follows this rule by statute; see N.C.Gen.Stat. § 45–68(2); Matter of Mills, 39 B.R. 564 (Bkrtcy.N.C.1984). Cf. Cabot, Cabot & Forbes Land Trust v. First National Bank, 369 So.2d 89 (Fla. App.1979).

13. In re Titus, 13 B.R. 447 (Bkrtcy. D.Vt.1980); Lundgren v. National Bank of Alaska, 742 P.2d 227 (Alaska 1987); Moran v. Gardemeyer, 82 Cal. 102, 23 P. 8 (1889); Vaughn & Co., Limited, v. Saul, 143 Ga. App. 74, 237 S.E.2d 622 (1977); Second

5. The clause is inapplicable to debts that were originally owed by the mortgagor to third parties, and that were subsequently assigned to or purchased by the mortgagee.[14]

6. If there are several joint mortgagors, only future debts on which all of the mortgagors are obligated[15] (or at least of which all were aware)[16] will be covered by the dragnet clause.

7. Once the original debt has been fully discharged, the mortgage is extinguished and cannot secure future loans.[17]

National Bank v. Boyle, 155 Ohio St. 482, 99 N.E.2d 474, 44 O.O. 440 (1951). Cf. United States v. Vahlco Corp., 720 F.2d 885, 892 n. 14 (5th Cir.1983).

See also In re Magers, 83 B.R. 685 (Bkrtcy.Mo.1988) (dragnet clause in mortgage does not cause it to secure a later note which recites that it is "unsecured"). Cf. Johnson v. Midland Bank, 715 S.W.2d 607 (Tenn.App.1986) (dragnet clause causes mortgage to secure later notes despite the fact that they recited they were "unsecured;" court refused to consider whether later notes were for a purpose similar to that of the original loan).

14. Pongetti v. Bankers Trust, 368 So.2d 819 (Miss.1979); Wood v. Parker Square State Bank, 400 S.W.2d 898 (Tex. 1966); Thorp Sales Corp. v. Dolese Brothers Co., note 10 supra. Cf. Georgia Railroad Bank v. McCullough, 241 Ga. 456, 246 S.E.2d 313 (1978) (clause may be enforced by bank into which original mortgagee is merged.) See also Bowen v. Kicklighter, 124 Ga.App. 82, 183 S.E.2d 10 (1971) (assignee of mortgage may not assert dragnet clause to secure advances made to mortgagor before assignment.) See Official Code Ga.Ann. § 44–14–1(b) (clause limited to debts arising " * * * between the original parties to the security agreement.")

15. United States v. American National Bank, 255 F.2d 504 (5th Cir.1958), certiorari denied 358 U.S. 835, 79 S.Ct. 58, 3 L.Ed.2d 72 (1958), rehearing denied 359 U.S. 1006, 79 S.Ct. 1135, 3 L.Ed.2d 1034 (1959); Paul Rochester Investment Co. v. United States, 692 F.Supp. 704 (N.D.Tex. 1988); In the Matter of Ladner, 50 B.R. 85 (Bkrtcy.Miss. 1985); Mohler v. Buena Vista Bank, 42 Colo.App. 4, 588 P.2d 894 (1978); Citizens Bank v. Gibson, 490 N.E.2d 728 (Ind.1986); Loudermilk v. Citizens Bank of Mooresville, 505 N.E.2d. 107 (Ind.App. 1987); Farmers Trust v. Manning, 311 N.W.2d 285 (Iowa 1981); First v. Byrne, 238 Iowa 712, 28 N.W.2d 509 (1947); Holiday Inns, Inc. v. Susher–Schaefer Investment Co., 77 Mich.App. 658, 259 N.W.2d 179 (1977); O'Neill Production Credit Association v. Mitchell, 209 Neb. 206, 307 N.W.2d 115 (1981); Woodson v. Hibbitts, 626 S.W.2d 133 (Tex.App.1981, writ ref'd n.r.e.). This result is required by statute in Vermont; see Bellows Falls Trust Co. v. Gibbs, 148 Vt. 633, 534 A.2d 210 (1987) (since tenancy by entirety is considered a separate legal entity, a dragnet clause in a mortgage executed by the entirety is not triggered by a later debt incurred by either spouse individually).

Contra, see Martin v. First National Bank, 279 Ala. 303, 184 So.2d 815 (1966); Sutton v. Atlantic Bank, 167 Ga.App. 861, 307 S.E.2d 746 (1983); Willis v. Rabun County Bank, 249 Ga. 493, 291 S.E.2d 715 (1982); Citizens Bank v. Gibson, 463 N.E.2d 276 (Ind.App.1984); Newton County Bank v. Jones, 299 So.2d 215 (Miss.1974); Wright v. Lincoln County Bank, 62 Tenn.App. 560, 465 S.W.2d 877 (1970).

16. Lomanto v. Bank of America, 22 Cal.App.3d 663, 99 Cal.Rptr. 442 (1972); Gates v. Crocker–Anglo National Bank, 257 Cal.App.2d 857, 65 Cal.Rptr. 536 (1968); Capocasa v. First Nat. Bank., 36 Wis.2d 714, 154 N.W.2d 271 (1967).

17. In the Matter of Ladner, 50 B.R. 85 (Bkrtcy.Miss.1985); Underwood v. Jarvis, 358 So.2d 731 (Ala.1978); Jacobs v. City National Bank, 229 Ark. 79, 313 S.W.2d 789 (1958); cf. Padgett v. Haston, 279 Ark. 367, 651 S.W.2d 460 (1983); McGluan v. Southwest Georgia Production Credit Association, 256 Ga.App. 648, 352 S.E.2d 558 (1987); Tedesco v. CDC Federal Credit Union, 167 Ga.App. 337, 306 S.E.2d 397 (1983) (debtor may have mortgage cancelled only by giving up right to any further advances); State Bank of Albany v. Fioravanti, 51 N.Y.2d 638, 435 N.Y.S.2d 947, 417 N.E.2d 60 (1980). Contra, see Ranier v. Security Bank & Trust Co., 182 Ga.App. 171, 354 S.E.2d 882 (1987) (dragnet clause permits lender to continue to hold interest in pledged property, even after original debt has been paid); Ashburn Bank v. Reinhardt, 183 Ga.App. 292, 358 S.E.2d 675 (1987) (cancellation of certain dragnet mortgages did not impair the effec-

8. If the real estate is transferred by the mortgagor to a third party, any debts which the original mortgagor incurs thereafter are not secured by the mortgage.[18] This is the position taken by the drafters of the Uniform Land Transfer Act.[19]

9. If the real estate is transferred by the mortgagor to a grantee, advances subsequently made by the mortgagee to the grantee are not secured by the mortgage, even if the grantee expressly assumed the mortgage.[20]

In addition to these judicial limitations, most of the statutes relating to future advances discussed in the preceding section [21] limit the amount of such advances to the maximum amount stated in the original mortgage. This limitation is important in the construction of dragnet clauses since the clauses on their face are usually unlimited as to amount.

While the dragnet clause is usually regarded as advantageous to mortgagees, that is not necessarily the case. One reason is that the judicial limitations on the clause discussed above are very much open to debate and further development in most states; in this sense, the clause is an invitation to litigation. Moreover, even if the clause is held to be valid, it may be turned against the mortgagee. Union Bank v. Wendland,[22] a California intermediate appellate decision, provides an inter-

---

tiveness of a dragnet clause in a mortgage which was not cancelled); Central Production Credit Association v. Page, 268 S.C. 1, 231 S.E.2d 210 (1977) (dragnet clause remains valid even after principal debt is fully paid.)

18. Citizens National Bank v. Coates, 509 So.2d 103 (La.App.1987) (whether debt incurred by mortgagor after transferring title to the property is secured by dragnet mortgage is a question of intent, and is not necessarily controlled even by strongly-worded dragnet clause); Trapp v. Tidwell, 418 So.2d 786 (Miss.1982) (mortgagee gave permission for grantee to assume loan; is estopped to assert dragnet clause); Vaughn v. Crown Plumbing & Sewer Service, Inc., 523 S.W.2d 72 (Tex.Civ.App.1975), error refused n.r.e. Restatement (Second) of Property—Security (Mortgages) § 2.4(d) (Tent. Draft No.1, 1991) agrees, with respect to advances made after the mortgagee gains actual knowledge that the real estate has been transferred; see State Bank of Albany v. Fioravanti, 51 N.Y.2d 638, 435 N.Y.S.2d 947, 417 N.E.2d 60 (1980) (advances made before the mortgagee gains knowledge of the real estate transfer will continue to be secured by the mortgage). See also Official Code Ga.Ann. § 67–1316 (dragnet clauses are limited to debts arising between the original parties to the security instrument).

A question may also arise as to whether a later debt, incurred by the *transferee* after a transfer of the mortgaged property is covered by the mortgage's dragnet clause. See Uransky v. First Fed. Sav. & Loan Ass'n, 684 F.2d 750 (11th Cir.1982) (where subsequent note executed by transferee specifically states that it is secured by prior dragnet mortgage, it is so secured); Walker v. Whitmore, 165 Ark. 276, 262 S.W. 678 (1924) (where dragnet clause refers to future debts "owing by grantor" of mortgage, debts incurred by transferee of property are not covered); Citizens Fed. Sav. & Loan Ass'n v. Andrews, 114 Ga. App. 94, 150 S.E.2d 301 (1966) (under Ga. Code Ann. § 67–1316, dragnet clause applies only to debts between original parties to the mortgage).

19. U.L.T.A. § 3–205(d).

20. Uransky v. First Federal Savings & Loan Association, 1 B.R. 640 (Bkrtcy.Fla. 1979); Walker v. Whitmore, 165 Ark. 276, 262 S.W. 678 (1924). But see Cochran v. Deposit Guaranty National Bank, 509 So.2d 1045 (Miss.1987), where a dragnet clause was held to secure extension and renewal of note by grantee of the property.

21. See supra § 12.7 note 45; Mark Twain Kansas City Bank v. Cates, 248 Kan. 700, 810 P.2d 1154 (1991).

22. 54 Cal.App.3d 393, 126 Cal.Rptr. 549 (1976).

esting example. The Wendlands borrowed a sum from the bank and gave a deed of trust (containing a dragnet clause) on their house as security. Subsequently, they borrowed an additional amount from the same bank to remodel the house, giving a second note and another deed of trust on the same real estate. Upon their default the bank foreclosed the first deed of trust by power of sale. It then brought a suit upon the second note. The antideficiency statute, by its terms, barred any personal judgment on a note secured by a deed of trust which had been foreclosed by power of sale.[23] The Wendlands argued, and the court held, that the second note was in fact secured by the first deed of trust (through the operation of its dragnet clause) and thus could not be collected by way of personal suit.

Dragnet clauses can also be dangerous to title insurers. In Southwest Title Insurance Co. v. Northland Building Corp.,[24] the title company issued a policy that specifically excepted two existing mortgages disclosed by the company's search. The policy language recited that those mortgages secured certain specific promissory notes which were carefully identified in the policy. However, the mortgages also contained dragnet clauses that caused them to secure other loans made to the mortgagors as well, a fact not mentioned in the policy. The Texas Supreme Court held that, as to the loans covered by the dragnet clauses, the policy exceptions were ineffective and the title company was liable. More careful drafting of the policy exceptions could probably have produced a different result, but the case illustrates how dragnet clauses can have unanticipated and undesired results.

§ 12.9 Subordination Agreements

Mortgagees may enter into subordination agreements altering the relative priorities that the applicable law and documents would otherwise give their mortgages.[1] Subordination agreements are subject to

---

23. West's Ann.Cal.Civil Proc.Code § 580(d); see § 8.3, supra.

24. 552 S.W.2d 425 (Tex.1977).

§ 12.9

1. See generally McNamara, Subordination Agreements as Viewed by Sellers, Purchasers, Construction Lenders, and Title Companies, 12 Real Est.L.J. 347 (1984). A mortgagee must personally agree to be subordinated; see Dime Sav. Bank v. Roberts, 167 A.D.2d 674, 563 N.Y.S.2d 253 (1990), appeal dismissed 77 N.Y.2d 939, 569 N.Y.S.2d 612, 572 N.E.2d 53 (1991). The trustee under a trust deed has no power to subordinate without the consent of the beneficiary unless the trust instrument so provides. Tuscarora, Inc. v. B.V.A. Credit Corp., 218 Va. 849, 241 S.E.2d 778 (1978); First Funding Corp. v. Birge, 220 Va. 326, 257 S.E.2d 861 (1979); Belknap Savings Bank v. Lamar Land and Canal Co., 28 Colo. 326, 64 P. 212 (1901). See also Fierst v. Commonwealth Land Title Insurance Co., 499 Pa. 68, 451 A.2d 674 (1982). Persons dealing with a trustee must take notice of the scope of his or her authority. But if the trustee has power to subordinate, a third party acting in good faith is protected unless apprised of facts that should reasonably give notice that a breach of trust is involved. Dye v. Lincoln Rochester Trust Co., 40 A.D.2d 583, 334 N.Y.S.2d 402 (1972), affirmed 31 N.Y.2d 1012, 341 N.Y.S.2d 619, 294 N.E.2d 207 (1973).

Subordination of a mortgage's priority may occur without a written agreement. Examples include loss of priority because of failure to record a mortgage; partial loss of priority of a senior mortgage because it is modified to make its terms on the property more onerous (see supra § 9.4); and partial loss of priority of a mortgage as a consequence of the making of optional future advances (see supra § 11.7).

§ 12.9 FINANCING REAL ESTATE CONSTRUCTION 235

recording statutes and are used in many kinds of transactions.[2] It is well established that parties may use a subordination agreement to establish the priority of two or more mortgages executed on the same property at the same time.[3] A senior mortgage can be subordinated to a specific junior mortgage.[4] A subordination may be for an indefinite

2. It is widely assumed that, since the recording acts apply to subordinations, the parties can forego an express agreement and accomplish a subordination merely by ensuring that the prior mortgage is first. Unfortunately, in many cases this assumption is demonstrably false except in the few states that have pure "race" recording statutes. See Carolina Builders Corp. v. Howard–Veasey Homes, Inc., 72 N.C.App. 224, 324 S.E.2d 626 (1985) (order of recording determines priority under "race" type statute). The reason is that the recording acts, except in those states, operate to avoid an unrecorded mortgage only as against subsequent bona fide purchasers and creditors. This means that an unrecorded mortgage is valid and prior to a subsequent mortgagee who takes with notice of the first. Since in many, perhaps most, subordination cases each of the competing mortgagees if fully aware of the other's mortgage, the order of recording is entirely irrelevant to their priorities. The fallacy of the "order of recording" view of subordination is recognized in FDIC v. Republicbank, 883 F.2d 427 (5th Cir.1989) and Colonial Villas, Inc. v. Title Ins. Co. of Minnesota, 145 Ariz. 590, 703 P.2d 534 (App.1985). See also Community Title Co. v. Crow, 728 S.W.2d 652 (Mo.App.1987): the parties instructed the title company to record the construction mortgage before the purchase-money mortgage, but because an error the documents were recorded in the opposite order. The court held the vendor, who had plainly intended and agreed to subordinate, was estopped to claim priority. While recording order will not usually determine priority among mortgages recorded more or less simultaneously, a court may nonetheless consider the parties' instructions to their closing agent about the order of recording as evidence of their intent to subordinate; see, e.g., In re Mihalko, 87 B.R. 357 (Bkrtcy.Pa. 1988); Community Title Co. v. Crow, 728 S.W.2d 652 (Mo.App.1987).

Like other contracts, a subordination agreement will be unenforceable if made without consideration; see Dugan v. First National Bank, 227 Kan. 201, 606 P.2d 1009 (1980); Cameron v. Churchill Mortgage Corp., 249 Ga. 362, 290 S.E.2d 474 (1982). However, consideration is usually easy to find; see In re Cliff's Ridge Skiing Corp., 123 B.R. 753 (Bkrtcy.Mich.1991) (consideration satisfied by making of loan by lender who was benefitted by subordination agreement); Miller v. Wines, 197 Ill. App.3d 447, 143 Ill.Dec. 849, 554 N.E.2d 784 (1990) (advance of funds to seller by lender who was benefitted by subordination was sufficient consideration for subordination agreement).

The Statute of Frauds is also applicable to subordination agreements; see Troj v. Chesebro, 30 Conn.Sup. 30, 296 A.2d 685 (1972). Nonetheless, oral subordination agreements are often enforced on a variety of theories; see Poyzer v. Amenia Seed and Grain Co., 409 N.W.2d 107 (N.D.1987) (part performance); In re Mihalko, 87 B.R. 357 (Bkrtcy.Pa.1988) (enforced on basis of instructions to settlement clerk); Community Title Co. v. Crow, 728 S.W.2d 652 (Mo. App.1987) (same). Cf. In re Red Cedar Construction Co., 63 B.R. 228 (Bkrtcy.Mich. 1986) (letter constituted insufficient evidence of intent to subordinate liens on inventory and accounts receivable).

A subordination agreement induced by fraud is, of course, subject to rescission, provided that no innocent third parties have relied on it; see Perkins v. Coombs, 769 P.2d 269 (Utah App.1988).

3. Gautney v. Gautney, 253 Ala. 584, 46 So.2d 198 (1950); Collins v. Home Savings & Loan Association, 205 Cal.App.2d 86, 22 Cal.Rptr. 817, 822 (1962); Hagen v. Butler, 83 Idaho 427, 363 P.2d 712 (1961). Neither the consent nor execution of the subordination by the mortgagor is necessary; see Graydon v. Colonial Bank—Gulf Coast Region, 597 So.2d 1345 (Ala.1992). Likewise, it is unnecessary that the lienholder benefitted by the subordination be a party to it; Southern Floridabanc Fed. Sav. & Loan Ass'n v. Buscemi, 529 So.2d 303 (Fla.App.1988).

4. Conshohocken Federal Savings & Loan Association v. Period & Country Homes, Inc., 287 Pa.Super. 520, 430 A.2d 1173 (1981); Olds Bros. Lumber Co. v. Marley, 72 Ariz. 392, 236 P.2d 464 (1951); State Savings & Loan Association v. Kauaian Dev. Corp., 50 Hawaii 540, 445 P.2d 109 (1968).

time, or may be limited to a fixed period.[5] It may be made subject to the fulfillment of certain conditions, and if so will be ineffective if they are not met.[6] If a first mortgage is subordinated to a third mortgage, the first mortgage also becomes subordinate to the second mortgage.[7] In general, an agreement to subordinate a mortgage to another mortgage to be made in the future is enforceable,[8] although as we will see below, enforcement may be denied if the future mortgage is not sufficiently described.

Subordination of Vendors to Construction Lenders

Subordination agreements are frequently used in mortgages relating to new real estate developments because they make it possible for developers to finance subdivisions and other construction projects without investing large amounts of their own capital. First, the developer persuades the original land seller to accept a purchase money mortgage

---

5. Williams v. Vestman, 668 P.2d 957 (Colo.App.1983); Campanella v. Rainier National Bank, 26 Wash.App. 418, 612 P.2d 460 (1980) (party given priority by subordination for one year must complete foreclosure within the year).

6. See In re Sunset Bay Assoc., 944 F.2d 1503 (9th Cir.1991); Citizens & Southern Nat. Bank v. Smith, 277 S.C. 162, 284 S.E.2d 770 (1981); Life Savings & Loan Association v. Bryant, 125 Ill.App.3d 1012, 81 Ill.Dec. 577, 467 N.E.2d 277 (1984); Riggs National Bank v. Wines, 59 Md.App. 219, 474 A.2d 1360 (1984), certiorari denied 301 Md. 43, 481 A.2d 802 (1984); Bank v. Crumley, 699 S.W.2d 164 (Tenn.App.1985) (subordination limited to loans for working capital); Blanton v. Federal Deposit Insurance Corp., 706 P.2d 1111 (Wyo.1985) (subordination to loan not exceeding $200,000 to be used for certain purposes. See also Guarantee Bank v. Magness Construction Co., 462 A.2d 405 (Del.1983) (agreement to subordinate to a loan to be made to a corporation does not subordinate to a loan made to a related individual); RTC v. Niagara Asset Corp., 598 So.2d 1074 (Fla.App. 1992) (mortgage gave mortgagor power to subordinate it to future first liens, but mortgagor failed to follow the procedure set out to accomplish this, and no subordination occurred); Credithrift, Inc. v. Knowles, 556 So.2d 775 (Fla.App.1990) (agreement required mortgagee to subordinate only if it were given adequate substitute collateral); Security Trust Fed. Sav. & Loan Ass'n v. Gill Sav. Ass'n, 197 Ga. App. 242, 398 S.E.2d 382 (1990) (subordination was unconditional, despite the fact that it referred to prior agreement containing conditions); National Bank of Waterloo v. Moeller, 434 N.W.2d 887 (Iowa 1989) (senior mortgagee's statement that it was "agreeable" to subordination "provided no unexpected problems arise" was not an unconditional promise to subordinate, and did not act as a subordination).

Of course, the subordinating party may waive conditions inserted for his or her benefit, in which case the subordination will be effective despite the nonfulfillment of the conditions; see, e.g., See Aetna Life Insurance Co. v. McElvain, 221 Mont. 138, 717 P.2d 1081 (1986) (subordination valid, although mortgage gaining priority was for much larger amount than subordinating vendors had agreed to, where their broker had knowledge of the larger amount).

7. Shaddix v. National Surety Co., 221 Ala. 268, 128 So. 220 (1930); Old Stone Mortgage & Realty Trust v. New Georgia Plumbing, Inc., 239 Ga. 345, 236 S.E.2d 592 (1977); Union Bank v. Farmwald Devel. Corp., 181 Mich.App. 538, 450 N.W.2d 274 (1989); Ladner v. Hogue Lumber & Supply Co., 229 Miss. 505, 511, 91 So.2d 545, 547 (1956); ITT Diversified Credit Corp. v. First City Capital Corp., 737 S.W.2d 803 (Tex.1987) (personal property security interests). A contrary result may follow if the subordination agreement is limited expressly to a specific junior lien; see Colorado Nat'l Bank v. F.E. Biegert, 165 Colo. 78, 438 P.2d 506 (1968). Once the junior lien to which the mortgage was subordinated has been discharged, the mortgage resumes its original priority as against any intermediate liens. See Commercial Bank v. Stratford, 149 Ga.App. 736, 256 S.E.2d 69 (1979).

8. Ray Thomas Enterprises v. Fox, 128 Cal.App.3d 361, 180 Cal.Rptr. 253 (1982).

§ 12.9 FINANCING REAL ESTATE CONSTRUCTION 237

or trust deed for all or a large part of the purchase price.[9] Then, using the land as security, the developer arranges a construction loan from an institutional lender to finance the construction of the houses, apartments, condominiums, or some other project. A subordination agreement with the seller makes this financing scheme possible by reordering the lien priorities between the purchase money mortgage and the construction loan. Institutional lenders are often required by law or their own internal policies to secure real estate loans with first liens,[10] but in the absence of an explicit reversal of priorities, the law presumes that the purchase money mortgage is intended to have priority.[11] The purchase money mortgage is usually recorded first, as well, so an enforceable subordination agreement is necessary to give the institutional lender the first lien.[12]

There has been much recent litigation on the enforceability of subordination agreements, especially in relation to indefiniteness.[13] The validity and effectiveness of subordination agreements have been challenged at two points in the transaction: (1) while the agreement is

---

9. Sellers are often willing to accept a purchase money mortgage because of the tax benefits from receiving payments spread over a number of years (Internal Revenue Code § 453). Sellers will often subordinate their purchase money mortgages if they are convinced that the sale depends upon the developer being able to obtain first lien construction financing. They are usually compensated by receiving a higher purchase price. See generally Korngold, Construction Loan Advances and the Subordinated Purchase Money Mortgagee: An Appraisal, A Suggested Approach, and the ULTA Perspective, 50 Ford.L.Rev. 313, 319–328 (1981); Note, The Subordination of Purchase–Money Security, 52 Cal.L.Rev. 157 (1964). See Statland Holliday, Inc. v. Stendig Development Corp., 46 A.D.2d 135, 362 N.Y.S.2d 2 (1974).

10. Until the early 1980s, National banks were required to take first liens under 12 U.S.C.A. § 1371, and federal savings and loans under 12 U.S.C.A. § 1464(c). These requirements have been repealed, although state-chartered institutions may be bound by similar rules. Many lenders demand first liens as a matter of internal policy. The Interagency Guidelines for Real Estate Lending Policies issued by the OTS, OCC, and Federal Reserve Board, and FDIC limit construction loans by federally-chartered lenders to 80% loan-to-value ratio (85% on 1-to-4-family homes). The Guidelines do not specifically require the taking of a first lien, but do require the lender to count the amount of any prior liens along with its own in calculating the ratio. See 57 Fed.Reg. 62890 (31 Dec. 1992), codified, e.g., in 12 CFR Part 563, Subpart D, Appendix A. Hence as a practical matter, the construction loan obtainable is severely limited if the lender does not acquire a first lien.

11. See § 9.1 supra; West's Ann.Cal. Civ.Code § 2898. In the few states that have "race" type recording statutes, this presumption may be rebutted by an intentional recording of the construction mortgage before the purchase-money mortgage; see supra note 2.

12. See McNamara, Subordination Agreements as Viewed by Sellers, Purchasers, Construction Lenders, and Title Companies, 12 Real Est.L.J. 347 (1984); Dreckshage v. Community Federal Savings & Loan Association, 555 S.W.2d 314 (Mo. 1977), enforcing subordinations although the developer lied about the content of the agreements and the vendors never read them. Even if the subordination is valid and the land vendor's lien is destroyed by foreclosure of the lien of the superior construction loan, the land vendor has a personal action against the defaulting developer; see Hoyle v. Dickinson, 155 Ariz. 277, 746 P.2d 18 (App.1987).

13. See generally, Lambe, Enforceability of Subordination Clauses, 19 Real Prop. Prob. & Tr.J. 631 (1984); Annotation, Requisite Definiteness of Provision in Contract for Sale or Lease of Land, that Vendor or Landlord Will Subordinate His Interest to Permit Other Party to Obtain Financing, 26 A.L.R.3d 855 (1969); Miller, Starr and Regalia, Subordination Agreements in California, 13 U.C.L.A.L.Rev. 1298 (1966).

still executory and (2) after the construction loan has been made and a contest over priority develops between the seller and the construction lender as a result of the developer's default.

When litigation arises while the agreement is still executory, it is typically because a developer brings suit against a seller seeking specific performance of a contract for the sale of land. The executory agreement to subordinate is used because it is not considered feasible to negotiate the terms of the construction loan at the time the contract for the purchase of the land is entered into. The clause in the contract, or in the purchase-money mortgage, may be phrased as a promise to execute a subordination agreement in the future or may purport to be a self-sufficient subordination that requires no further documentation.[14] In either case, the problem is that the clause is more or less indefinite concerning the terms of the construction loan to be obtained. Then the seller reneges on the whole transaction or refuses to enter into a specific subordination agreement that would subordinate the purchase-money lien to the particular loan that the purchaser has arranged.[15] When the purchaser seeks specific performance of the contract, the seller usually attempts to avoid performance by showing that the subordination clause is too vague and indefinite to be enforced. When the courts have ruled for the seller, they have usually held the entire contract unenforceable, since the clause is considered a material part of the contract. However, it has been suggested that an absolute and unconditional waiver of the subordination clause by the purchaser could save the rest of the contract.[16]

When the subordination agreement is challenged after a default has occurred and a contest over priority has developed, sellers attempt to raise these same arguments. But because the contract has been at least partially performed, other issues prevent the question from being decided simply by determining if the contract is indefinite or unjust and unreasonable on its face.

Actions to Enforce Executory Subordination Agreements

In California, where most of the litigation related to subordination agreements has occurred, the courts have been sympathetic to the

---

14. See Rockhill v. United States, 288 Md. 237, 418 A.2d 197 (1980).

15. "The agreement altering priority may be contained in a separate writing or it may be set forth in the recorded security instrument. In either case the provisions of the subordination agreement are regulated, in part, by statute, and it must be recorded in order to impart constructive notice of its contents. By the terms of the 'automatic' subordination agreement the seller's lien is recorded with an agreement that the lien of a subsequent lender will automatically be senior to the seller's lien without further acts on his part. By the terms of the other common form, the seller promises to execute a subsequent instrument which will subordinate his lien to that of the lender. However, even under the 'automatic' subordination agreement, a title company will usually require the seller to execute another document at the time the new lien is recorded, in order specifically to subordinate the seller's lien to the new lien." Miller, Starr and Regalia, Subordination Agreements in California, 13 U.C.L.A.L.Rev. 1298, 1299 (1966).

16. See Reeder v. Longo, 131 Cal. App.3d 291, 182 Cal.Rptr. 287 (1982); Spellman v. Dixon, 256 Cal.App.2d 1, 4, 63 Cal.Rptr. 668, 671 (1967).

seller, whom they generally regard as an unsophisticated party in need of protection. They have held that "an enforceable subordination clause must contain terms that will define and minimize the risk that the subordinating lien will impair or destroy the seller's security." [17] Although the California courts have not specified a minimum set of terms that will make a subordination agreement enforceable, they have provided some guidance.[18]

In 1967 the California Supreme Court was asked to decide in Handy v. Gordon if a subordination clause specifying maximum loan amounts per unit, maximum interest rates, and maximum loan periods could be enforced by specific performance. In addition to arguing that the subordination clause was too indefinite to enforce, the seller raised a defense based upon a statute [19] which prohibited the enforcement of a contract by specific performance if the contract is not just and reasonable to the party against whom enforcement is sought. The court denied the suit for specific performance, saying that the contract was not fair and reasonable to the seller because it did not adequately define and minimize his risk. Specifically, the clause did not limit the buyer's use of the loan proceeds to construction on the land. Nor did it provide assurance that the amounts of the loans would not exceed the value the improvements added to the land; the loan maximums were expressed in terms of absolutes and did not limit the loan amounts to percentages of the building costs. Finally, the loan limits were maximums per lot and the developer had discretion to determine the number of lots.

While the court in Handy v. Gordon appeared to decide the case on the basis of whether the contract was just and reasonable to the seller, it would seem that the indefiniteness of the clause was the defect that made it unjust and unreasonable. It probably makes no difference that

---

17. Roskamp Manley Associates, Inc. v. Davin Development and Investment Corp., 184 Cal.App.3d 513, 229 Cal.Rptr. 186 (1986); Handy v. Gordon, 65 Cal.2d 578, 55 Cal.Rptr. 769, 422 P.2d 329, 26 A.L.R.3d 848 (1967). See Stockwell v. Lindeman, 229 Cal.App.2d 750, 40 Cal. Rptr. 555 (1964); Magna Development Co. v. Reed, 228 Cal.App.2d 230, 39 Cal.Rptr. 284 (1964); Burrow v. Timmsen, 223 Cal. App.2d 283, 35 Cal.Rptr. 668, 100 A.L.R.2d 544 (1963); Roven v. Miller, 168 Cal.App.2d 391, 335 P.2d 1035 (1959).

18. In Stockwell v. Lindeman, supra note 17, a California court of appeal held a subordination clause that specified a maximum loan amount and a maximum interest rate, and that provided that repayment should be made upon the terms required by the lender, could be enforced by specific performance. The court said the terms of repayment could be supplied by the lender or by custom but that the contract would not be valid if the terms of repayment were left for future agreement between the parties themselves. Although Stockwell is cited with apparent approval in Handy v. Gordon, supra note 17, Stockwell's reliance on custom or the future loan agreement to supply additional terms providing essential protection to the vendor is of questionable validity after *Handy*.

19. West's Ann.Cal.Civ.Code § 3391(2). See also West's Ann.Cal.Civ.Code §§ 2953.1–2953.5 which provides that where the secured loan to be subordinated is less than $25,000, the subordination agreement or clause must contain a prominent warning that the agreement may subordinate the holder of the note to another security which would normally have a lower priority. If the warning is not given and the subordinating party has no actual knowledge of the subordination, he or she can void the agreement any time within two years by recording notice.

the statutory defense relied upon in Handy v. Gordon technically applies only to suits for specific performance: if a subordination agreement is so indefinite that it is unfair to require a seller to perform under it, it probably would not be definite enough to support a suit for damages either.

In Malani v. Clapp [20] the Supreme Court of Hawaii followed reasoning like that of *Handy*, holding that a subordination agreement must adequately protect the subordinating party. There a lessor sued a lessee for breach of contract, and the lessee tried to avoid the contract by showing that the lease's subordination clause [21] was too indefinite to enforce. The subordination agreement limited the term of subordination to two years, required the lessee to be personally liable to the lessor, and required the lessee to show an aggregate net worth of $2,000,000. In addition to the clause itself, the court looked at the entire context of the transaction to determine if the lessor was adequately protected. The court concluded that because of the protections in the subordination clause and because the type of construction was specified in a building permit, the lessor was adequately protected.[22]

Most of the other courts that have been asked to decide the validity of subordination agreements have similarly held that terms limiting the seller's risk are necessary to make the agreement enforceable. While these courts have not uniformly designated certain terms as essential, the terms they most often mention are maximum loan amounts, maximum interest rates, maximum loan periods, and requirements that the loan proceeds be used for improvements on the land.[23]

---

20. 56 Hawaii 507, 542 P.2d 1265 (1975).

21. Under this agreement the lessor was to subordinate her fee estate to a construction loan to be procured by the lessee. While this is commonly called a subordination agreement, it is technically inaccurate to call it such. In reality the "subordination clause" is an agreement by the lessor to join in the lessee's mortgage, thereby subjecting the fee title to the mortgage. See McKee v. First Nat. Bank, 220 Ill. App.3d 976, 163 Ill.Dec. 389, 581 N.E.2d 340 (1991); Halper, Planning and Construction Clauses in a Subordinated Ground Lease, 17 Real Est.L.J. 48 (1988); Halper, Mortgagability of Unsubordinated Ground Leases, 16 Real Est.Rev. 60 (Winter 1987); Committee on Leases, Ground Leases and Their Financing, 4 Real Prop. Prob. & Trust J. 437 (1969). The misuse of the term "subordination" in this context irritated the court in Pearlman v. National Bank of New York City, 600 So.2d 5 (Fla. App.1992). Incorrect use of the term can be dangerous; see Old Stone Capital Corp. v. John Hoene Implement Corp., 647 F.Supp. 916 (D.Idaho 1986) (landlord's promise to "subordinate" to leasehold mortgage was not sufficient to subject the fee title to the mortgage; this could be accomplished only by the landlord's formally executing the mortgage).

If the "subordinating" lessor in such a transaction is considered a surety, a later agreement between the mortgagee and the lessee/mortgagee, modifying the terms of the loan, might be held to "unsubordinate" the lessor's interest, freeing it from the mortgage. Compare State of Wisconsin Investment Board v. Hurst, 410 N.W.2d 560 (S.D.1987) (lessor was a principal, not a surety), with Samuelson v. Promontory Investment Co., 85 Or.App. 315, 736 P.2d 207 (1987) (parties agreed that lessor was a surety, but court found lessor had consented to modifications in loan terms, and hence was not discharged).

22. The court might not have been so willing to find that the lessor was adequately protected if it had been the lessor who was trying to avoid the contract.

23. Lahaina-Maui Corp. v. Tau Tet Hew, 362 F.2d 419 (9th Cir.1966); Stenehjem v. Kyn Jin Cho, 631 P.2d 482 (Alaska 1981); Troj v. Chesebro, 30 Conn.Sup. 30, 296 A.2d 685 (1972); Hux v. Raben, 74

§ 12.9 FINANCING REAL ESTATE CONSTRUCTION 241

Contrary to the general trend toward requiring terms of limitation in subordination agreements, a few recent cases have ruled that construction loans do not have to be described in detail.[24]

Action to Reverse Priorities After a Default

A contest over priorities after a default is quite different from an action to enforce an executory subordination agreement. First, the parties usually have executed a second subordination agreement describing the specific construction loan, thus curing any indefiniteness in the original agreement.[25] Miller v. Citizens Savings and Loan Association[26] provides an example of such a situation. This case revolved around a term limiting the use of the loan proceeds that was in the first agreement but not in the second. The court merged the agreements and enforced the clause in the first agreement that required the construction loans to be used only for certain purposes.[27] But even absent the first agreement, the court noted that "a subordination agreement should be construed, unless it expressly provides otherwise, as permitting the loan proceeds to be used only for * * *" purposes which will improve the seller's security position.[28] The seller was

Ill.App.2d 214, 219 N.E.2d 770 (1966), affirmed 38 Ill.2d 223, 230 N.E.2d 831 (1967); Grooms v. Williams, 227 Md. 165, 175 A.2d 575 (1961); American Federal Savings & Loan Association v. Orenstein, 81 Mich. App. 249, 265 N.W.2d 111 (1978); MCB Limited v. McGowan, 86 N.C.App. 607, 359 S.E.2d 50 (1987), noted 23 Wake For.L.Rev. 575 (1988) (agreement to subordinate to future construction loan "in such amount as may reasonably be requested" held void for indefiniteness, whether or not it contained sufficient terms to protect vendor's security interest).

24. Provident Fed. Sav. & Loan Ass'n v. Idaho Land Developers, Inc., 114 Idaho 453, 757 P.2d 716 (App.1988); Hyatt v. Maryland Federal Savings & Loan Association, 42 Md.App. 623, 402 A.2d 118 (1979); Rivers v. Rice, 233 Ga. 819, 213 S.E.2d 678 (1975); Ideal Realty Co. v. Reese, 122 Ga. App. 707, 178 S.E.2d 564 (1970); Campbell Inns v. Banholzer, Turnure & Co., 148 Vt. 1, 527 A.2d 1142 (1987) (where subordinated vendor was fully aware of the nature of the new financing to which it was subordinating, and where purchaser relied upon subordination agreement, it was specifically enforceable despite its rather vague terms); White & Bollard, Inc. v. Goodenow, 58 Wash.2d 180, 361 P.2d 571 (1961). See also Dorothy Edwards Realtors, Inc. v. McAdams, 525 N.E.2d 1248 (Ind.App.1988), appeal after remand 591 N.E.2d 612 (1992) upholding an extremely broad subordination clause in an installment sale contract.

25. In Roberts v. Harkins, 292 So.2d 603 (Fla.App.1974), certiorari denied 302 So.2d 417 (Fla.1974), a later specific subordination was held to supersede an earlier promise to subordinate that was much more protective of the subordinating mortgagee's interests.

26. 248 Cal.App.2d 655, 56 Cal.Rptr. 844 (1967). See discussion in The California Supreme Court 1966–1967: X. Secured Transactions, A. Subordination Agreements, 1967, 55 Cal.L.Rev. 1184–1187.

27. But see Fandel, Inc. v. First of Denver Mortgage Investors, 522 S.W.2d 721 (Tex.Civ.App.1975).

28. Miller v. Citizens Savings and Loan Association, 248 Cal.App.2d 655, 663, 56 Cal.Rptr. 844, 851 (1967). See also B.J.I. Corp. v. Larry W. Corp., 183 N.J.Super. 310, 443 A.2d 1096 (1982), taking a similar approach; Ban–Co Investment Co. v. Loveless, 22 Wash.App. 122, 587 P.2d 567 (1978); Finest Investments v. Security Trust Co., 96 A.D.2d 227, 468 N.Y.S.2d 256 (1983), affirmed 61 N.Y.2d 897, 474 N.Y.S.2d 481, 462 N.E.2d 1199 (1984).

See Schneider v. Ampliflo Corp., 148 Cal.App.3d 637, 196 Cal.Rptr. 172 (1983), upholding a subordination which very clearly provided that the proceeds of the loan gaining priority need not be used for improvements on the subject property.

But see Back v. Union Life Insurance Co., 5 Ark.App. 176, 634 S.W.2d 150 (1982) (if subordinating vendor wishes proceeds of senior loan to go to improvements on land, the agreement must so provide); Hyatt v. Maryland Federal Savings & Loan Associa-

granted reestablishment of the superiority of his lien over that part of the construction loan not used for authorized purposes. Thus the case, and several other decisions in California and elsewhere, raise the startling possibility that a court will imply reasonable conditions in a subordination agreement even when the parties did not include them expressly.[29]

Even when a second agreement has not cured indefiniteness, courts have held that the seller was estopped from asserting that the subordination agreement was invalid. In *First Connecticut Small Business Investment Co. v. Arba*[30] the seller contended that a subordination agreement violated the Statute of Frauds because it contained neither the interest rate nor the maturity date of the construction loan. Although Connecticut courts had earlier accepted the Statute of Frauds as a defense against the enforcement of a similar subordination agreement,[31] in *Arba* the court held that the seller was estopped because the agreement had been executed and a lender had relied to its detriment on the subordination.[32] Similarly, in *Republic National Life Insurance Co. v. Lorraine Realty Corp.*,[33] the Minnesota Supreme Court upheld the validity of a rather vague subordination agreement because all of the parties had operated under it without questioning it for fourteen years.

When a subordination agreement contains conditions and the vendor attempts to use them as a basis for a reversal of priorities after default, several difficult questions arise. One is how the lender is expected to know the content of the conditions. Two recent cases based on California law suggest that the lender is on inquiry notice of the conditions, even if they do not appear of record.[34] In substance, these

tion, 42 Md.App. 623, 402 A.2d 118 (1979); Grenada Ready–Mix Concrete, Inc. v. Watkins, 453 F.Supp. 1298 (N.D.Miss.1978).

29. For a more thorough discussion of implied conditions in subordination agreements, see infra § 12.10 notes 25–33. See also Connecticut Gen. Life Ins. Co. v. Dredge, 746 F.2d 1420 (10th Cir.1984), reversing the priorities set up in a subordination agreement because it was procured by an agent who had a conflict of interest and who withheld pertinent information from the subordinating vendors; Pastor v. Lafayette Bldg. Ass'n, 567 So.2d 793 (La.App. 1990) (lender held liable for misrepresentation, when it advised subordinating vendor that his position would not be harmed by subordination, and then proceeded to disburse construction funds in a lump sum with no precautions to ensure that they would be used for improvements on the property).

A somewhat analogous situation was presented in Ranier v. Mount Sterling Nat. Bank, 812 S.W.2d 154 (Ky.1991). A private mortgagee subordinated her lien to a new bank mortgage loan. Subsequently the bank made a further unsecured loan to the borrower, and thereafter credited the borrower's payments to the unsecured loan rather than the mortgage loan. The court held the lender had a duty of good faith and fair dealing that required it to apply the payments toward the mortgage loan, thereby reducing its balance and improving the position of the subordinated mortgagee.

30. 170 Conn. 168, 365 A.2d 100 (1976).

31. Troj v. Chesebro, supra note 23.

32. See also American Century Mortgage Investors v. Unionamerica Mortgage and Equity Trust, 355 A.2d 563 (D.C.App. 1976).

33. 279 N.W.2d 349 (Minn.1979).

34. In re Sunset Bay Assoc., 944 F.2d 1503 (9th Cir.1991) (subordination was accomplished by recording construction loan mortgage first; court held construction lender to have inquired about conditions in

cases hold that when a lender knows a subordination is occurring, it has a responsibility to obtain and review the conditions of the subordination. Since this can easily be accomplished simply to contacting the subordinating vendor, the burden it imposes is slight. Indeed, it is hard to credit a lender's statement that it failed to do so in fact and obtain actual knowledge of the conditions.

Another question arises when the conditions are not met by the construction lender. Should the lender lose priority only to the extent of the loss caused by the failure to meet the conditions, or is the construction loan's priority entirely lost? The Ninth Circuit, addressing this question under California law in In re Sunset Bay Associates,[35] concluded that the answer depended on whether the conditions were express or implied. Several earlier California cases involving implied conditions had imposed only a pro tanto loss of priority,[36] but the court concluded that where the conditions were express, substantial failure to comply with them produced a complete reversal of priorities.[37] The different treatment of the two kinds of conditions follows from the fact that implied conditions exist as an equitable tool to help a court avoid unjust enrichment, which may be accomplished merely by a partial reversal of priority. An express condition, on the other hand, represents the subordinating party's considered decision about the circumstances under which he or she is willing to accept a loss of priority, and a court has no business rewriting that decision. The distinction drawn by the court makes considerable sense.

Drafting Subordination Agreements in Sales to Developers

The developer will want a self-executing subordination agreement that contains enough terms to be enforceable. To be safe the developer should see that the agreement includes (1) the maximum loan amount

---

vendor's mortgage, although it was recorded second); Protective Equity Trust No. 83 v. Bybee, 2 Cal.App.4th 139, 2 Cal.Rptr.2d 864 (1991). See also Dickens v. First American Title Ins. Co., 162 Ariz. 511, 784 P.2d 717 (App.1989) (where lender's closing agency had actual knowledge of conditions in subordination agreement, that knowledge would be imputed to lender).

35. 944 F.2d 1503 (9th Cir.1991).

36. United States Cold Storage of Calif. v. Great Western Sav. & Loan Assoc., 165 Cal.App.3d 1214, 212 Cal.Rptr. 232 (1985); Miller v. Citizens Sav. & Loan Assoc., 248 Cal.App.2d 655, 56 Cal.Rptr. 844 (1967), discussed supra note 26. Note that *Miller* can be read as either an express or an implied condition.

See also Electric M & R, Inc. v. Banco Popular de Puerto Rico, 863 F.2d 1055 (1st Cir.1988), in which the lender who gained priority from the subordination agreement failed to comply with its covenant to notify the subordinating lender of the borrower's subsequent defaults. The court held that this breach could in principle give rise to damages, but that the subordinated lender had not shown any actual loss, since it was not clear that it could have taken any effective action even if it had received the notice.

37. See Protective Equity Trust No. 83 v. Bybee, 2 Cal.App.4th 139, 2 Cal.Rptr.2d 864 (1991); Jones v. Sacramento Savings and Loan Assoc., 248 Cal.App.2d 522, 56 Cal.Rptr. 741 (1967); Collins v. Home Savings and Loan Assoc., 205 Cal.App.2d 86, 22 Cal.Rptr. 817 (1962); Mercantil Intercontinental, Inc. v. Generalbank, 601 So.2d 293 (Fla.App.1992) (where each lot in subdivision was covered by a separate subordination agreement, court declared a complete loss of priority with respect to the lots on which the express conditions had not been met); Citizens & Southern Nat. Bank v. Smith, 277 S.C. 162, 284 S.E.2d 770 (1981).

both as an absolute and as a percentage of the cost of construction, (2) the maximum interest rate, (3) the payment provisions and the minimum and maximum terms of years over which the construction loan is to be repaid, and (4) a clause stating the purposes for which the loan will be used. The terms should not be so restrictive that the developer cannot obtain financing meeting the conditions described.

The seller will want all of the terms mentioned above, and may also bargain for other safeguards that will protect against unreasonable risk. For example, the seller should consider prohibiting refinancing, future advances, dragnet clauses and assignments of the senior loan. The agreement should require that all proceeds be used for permanent improvements on the land.[38] The seller may want to require that all documents, plans and specifications be submitted for his or her approval, and that the lender make all disbursements through a voucher or progress payment system that assures that the funds pay only for materials and labor that improve the land. The seller may want to reserve the right to inspect the premises or the records of the other parties at any time. He or she may also want to require the construction lender to give some reasonable notice—say, 30 days—before the lender files a notice of default, thus giving the seller an opportunity to cure the default. The seller should make sure that the subordination agreement is recorded in full, and should try to get the construction lender to sign it. In general, he or she should investigate the project thoroughly and bargain for any safeguards that will insure the project's successful completion.

Subordination of Vendees' Rights

A contract purchaser of real estate may make a claim against the land in the event the seller breaches the contract. This claim may be either for specific performance, or for foreclosure of an equitable "vendee's lien" as an aid to restitution of the down payment or earnest money.[39] If improvements are to be constructed on the land after the contract of sale is entered into, the seller/developer may place a construction loan mortgage on the land to finance this development activity. In the event of a subsequent default by the developer on both

---

38. A lawyer was successfully sued by the seller he had represented for failing to draft a subordination agreement that required that all loan proceeds be used for permanent improvements on the property; Starr v. Mooslin, 14 Cal.App.3d 988, 92 Cal.Rptr. 583 (1971). See also Roskamp Manley Associates v. Davin Development & Investment Corp., 184 Cal.App.3d 513, 229 Cal.Rptr. 186 (1986) (enumerating elements of the agreement which would help protect a subordinating land vendor); Long & Foster Real Estate, Inc. v. Clay, 231 Va. 170, 343 S.E.2d 297 (1986) (real estate broker breached fiduciary duty to vendor by failing to give adequate explanation of significance of subordination clause).

If funds are diverted and the condition is thereby breached, the subordinating party will be restored to priority to that extent. See National Mortgage Co. v. American Title Insurance Co., 299 N.C. 369, 261 S.E.2d 844 (1980), refusing to hold the construction lender's title insurer liable for such loss of priority.

39. See R. Cunningham, W. Stoebuck & D. Whitman, Property (2d ed. 1993) at § 10.5 (specific performance), § 10.8 (vendee's lien).

the sale contract and the construction loan, the question arises whether the lender's or vendee's rights have priority.

Application of the recording acts usually fails to resolve the issue. Typically the sales contract is unrecorded, while the subsequent construction mortgage is placed of record. Thus, the mortgagee is in a position to claim priority over the vendee if it has the characteristics of a bona fide purchaser for value.[40] However, in most cases the lender will be fully informed of any preexisting sales contracts, and hence will have no priority claim based on the recording act.[41]

Construction lenders may attempt to solve this problem by insisting that developers with whom they do business employ subordination clauses in their sale contracts. One form of clause provides that:

> "The Purchaser agrees that all terms and provisions of this contract are and shall be subject and subordinate to the lien of any building loan mortgage heretofore or hereafter made and any advances heretofore or hereafter made * * *."[42]

Such a clause is at least potentially enforceable.[43] However, the sort of broad language quoted, which contains no limitations on the amount, interest rate, or use of funds from the loan to which the contract is subordinated, may be subject to the same sort of objections on the basis of fairness and specificity discussed above in connection with subordinations by land vendors.[44]

---

40. Id.; Garcia v. Atmajian, 113 Cal. App.3d 516, 169 Cal.Rptr. 845 (1980) (vendee's lien vs. optional advance under prior mortgage); Hillblom v. Ivancsits, 76 Ill. App.3d 306, 32 Ill.Dec. 172, 395 N.E.2d 119 (1979) (vendee's lien); Cohen v. Thomas & Son Transfer Line, Inc., 196 Colo. 386, 586 P.2d 39 (1978) (specific performance).

41. See State Savings & Loan Association v. Kauaian Development Co., 50 Hawaii 540, 445 P.2d 109 (1968). In a later decision in the same case, 62 Hawaii 188, 613 P.2d 1315 (1980), the court held the construction lender to be subordinate to the rights of vendees who entered into contracts of purchase *after* the construction mortgage was recorded. It construed language in the mortgage, reciting that it was "subject to" the condominium declaration, as making the mortgage subordinate to the rights of all condominium unit purchasers. See also Caribank v. Frankel, 525 So.2d 942 (Fla.App.1988) (construction lender on single-family house is subordinate to the equitable lien of a contract vendee of which the lender had actual knowledge at the time it recorded its mortgage). See the discussion infra at § 13.3 note 21.

42. Olympic Towers Purchase Agreement, reprinted in 1A P. Rohan & M. Reskin, Condominium Law & Practice ¶ 118.17 (Appendix 1976). See Dorothy Edwards Realtors, Inc. v. McAdams, 525 N.E.2d 1248 (Ind.App.1988), appeal after remand 591 N.E.2d 612 (1992) upholding a broad clause in an installment sale contract that subordinated the vendee's position to any mortgage which the vendor might place on the premises. The propriety of this decision is open to serious question.

43. State Savings & Loan Association v. Kauaian Development Co., 50 Hawaii 540, 445 P.2d 109 (1968), expressly endorses such use of subordination clauses. See also Dunson v. Stockton, Whatley, Davin & Co., 346 So.2d 603 (Fla.App.1977), holding that an owner who deeds land to a developer to build a house, with the understanding that the developer will obtain a construction loan mortgage, impliedly subordinates to the construction lender the owner's contract right to repurchase the property; Life Savings & Loan Association v. Bryant, 125 Ill.App.3d 1012, 81 Ill.Dec. 577, 467 N.E.2d 277 (1984) (subordination clause in purchase contract was ineffective, since its conditions were never fulfilled.)

44. See B.J.I. Corp. v. Larry W. Corp., 183 N.J.Super. 310, 443 A.2d 1096 (1982) holding that, under such a broad clause, a court might deny priority as to advances which were not actually used to benefit the property, unless the purchaser understood

Subordination Between Mortgages and Leases

The priority relationship that exists between a lease and a mortgage usually depends upon the order in which they are recorded,[45] unless their priorities have been altered by a subordination agreement.[46] In large developments such as shopping centers that involve mortgages and leases, subordination agreements are frequently negotiated carefully because the priorities of the mortgages and leases are very important to the parties involved. For instance, an institutional lender may insist on having a first lien on the property securing its mortgage, and while a lease is an encumbrance rather than a lien, the lender may still consider it unacceptable for the mortgage to be junior to a lease. On the other hand, because foreclosure of a senior mortgage will usually destroy all leases subordinate to it,[47] a major tenant in a shopping center may have a great deal to lose if its lease is subordinate to a mortgage.

In some states the mortgagee has the option of keeping junior leases in force by omitting joinder of the lessees in the foreclosure proceeding.[48] In these states it is never a disadvantage to a mortgagee to be senior to important leases.[49] But in other states where foreclosure permits omitted junior lessees to terminate, it may be a serious detriment to a mortgagee to have its mortgage senior to important leases. The leases of major tenants often form a very important part of the security value of a shopping center. A mortgagee may desire to have its mortgage subordinate to them so that it can foreclose with no risk of destroying these leases.[50] It is possible for a mortgagee to agree with a tenant to subordinate its mortgage to a lease after the mortgagor is in default,[51] but the mortgagee cannot accomplish this result unilaterally.

and bargained for the clause. Cf. Dorothy Edwards Realtors, Inc. v. McAdams, supra note 42.

45. Notice also plays a role in determining priorities, of course. A recorded mortgage may not have priority over an unrecorded prior lease if the mortgagee has notice of the lease. Republic National Life Insurance Co. v. Marquette Bank and Trust Co., 312 Minn. 162, 251 N.W.2d 120 (1977).

46. In re the Lantana Motel, 124 B.R. 252 (Bkrtcy.Ohio 1990); Hand v. Pelham Banking Co., 186 Ga.App. 520, 368 S.E.2d 129 (1988); Wright v. Home Beneficial Life Insurance Co., 155 Ga.App. 241, 270 S.E.2d 400 (1980); Prudential Insurance Co. v. Bull Market, Inc., 66 Ohio Misc. 9, 420 N.E.2d 140 (1979). See Oakes v. Michigan Oil Co., 476 So.2d 618 (Ala.1985) (where same party holds both mortgage and lease, a subordination agreement adjusting priorities as between the two is both impossible and unnecessary).

47. See id.; Dover Mobile Estates v. Fiber Form Products, Inc., 220 Cal.App.3d 1494, 270 Cal.Rptr. 183 (1990); T.D. Bickham Corp. v. Hebert, 432 So.2d 228 (La. 1983).

48. See § 7.12, supra; Gearen, Vranicar & Becker, Into *Harm's* Way: Now That *Harms v. Sprague* Has Established the Lien Theory of Mortgages in Illinois, Does Foreclosure Cut Off Junior Leases or Can a Mortgagee Elect to Preserve Them?, 34 DePaul L.Rev. 449 (1985); Hyde, The Real Estate Lease as a Credit Instrument, 20 Bus.Law. 359, 389 (1965).

49. Anderson, The Mortgagee Looks at the Commercial Lease, 10 U. of Fla.L.Rev. 484, 495 (1957).

50. See Dover Mobile Estates v. Fiber Form Products, Inc., 220 Cal.App.3d 1494, 270 Cal.Rptr. 183 (1990).

51. Landau v. Western Pennsylvania National Bank, 445 Pa. 217, 282 A.2d 335 (1971).

Before a mortgagee chooses to have its mortgage subordinate to a lease on the mortgaged premises, it should examine the lease carefully to be sure that it does not contain onerous duties for the landlord to perform.[52] It should also be sure that the lease does not give the lessee an option to buy that will cut off the mortgage if the option is exercised.

If the lender does assume priority, whether by order of recording or by agreement, it can insure that it will have the option of keeping the leases in force by having the mortgagor procure attornment agreements from the lessees. In an attornment agreement the lessee agrees to accept the purchaser at a foreclosure sale as landlord and to be bound to the purchaser by the lease. The attornment agreement per se does not bind the mortgagee or the sale purchaser to refrain from cancelling junior leases.

It is a simple matter for the lessor to put a subordination clause and an attornment clause in the form leases signed by minor tenants who have little bargaining power. But it is more difficult to negotiate an attornment clause or subordination clause in a lease with a major tenant. Nonetheless it is often less expensive to negotiate the clauses into the original lease than to get a later lease amendment from a powerful tenant.[53] In order for the mortgagor to get a subordination agreement from a major tenant it will usually be necessary for the mortgagee to agree to a nondisturbance clause, guaranteeing that as long as the lessee conforms to the lease it will be allowed to remain in possession of the property even if a foreclosure occurs. If the lessee is given a nondisturbance clause, the mortgagee should make sure that the lessee also has an obligation under an attornment clause to remain bound by the lease after a foreclosure.[54]

As was mentioned earlier, a major tenant may suffer a severe loss if the lease is destroyed by a foreclosure, especially if the tenant has made expensive improvements on the property. A powerful tenant, such a major "anchor" tenant in a shopping center, may be able to demand that the lease be prior to all mortgages on the property. If it is not practical for the tenant to negotiate an absolute priority, considerable protection can be obtained by the tenant's agreeing to subordinate the lease only to mortgages that meet certain standards. A lessee who

---

52. If the mortgagee feels that some of the landlord's covenants in the lease would be objectionable, it may be able to reach an agreement with the tenant that those clauses will not be enforceable against the mortgagee if it takes possession, or against a buyer at the mortgage foreclosure sale. The tenant, in turn, may bargain with the mortgagee for notice of the landlord's default and some reasonable time period in which the tenant may cure it, thus minimizing the risk of default to the tenant. This right to cure, however, is attractive to the tenant only if the debt service on the mortgage plus the other operating and carrying costs of the building do not exceed the rent which the tenant is obligated to pay under the lease. Moreover, the right to cure is binding against the lessor only if he or she expressly agrees to it in the lease or in a later agreement. Anderson, supra note 49, at 495.

53. See Committee on Leases, Drafting Shopping Center Leases, 2 Real Property, Probate and Trust Journal 222, 247 (No. 2 Summer 1967).

54. Hyde, The Real Estate Lease as a Credit Instrument, 20 Bus.Law. 359, 392 (1965).

occupies the entire premises may negotiate a clause limiting prior mortgages to those having debt service costs, including payments for taxes and other reserves, that do not exceed the gross rent.[55] If a clause in lease allows the tenant to cure mortgage defaults, the tenant will then be able to prevent a foreclosure.

Another way that the lessee can be protected, as suggested above, is by obtaining a nondisturbance clause [56] prohibiting eviction after a foreclosure as long as the tenant honors the lease. Depending upon the wording of the clause, the tenant may have the option in the event of foreclosure to remain under the lease or to treat it as destroyed. If the lease grants this option, the tenant may prefer this position to having the lease superior to the mortgage. However, a mortgage that is technically senior will still have the advantage of priority in the event of conflicts between the mortgage and the lease. For example, suppose the lease requires the landlord to use fire insurance proceeds for rebuilding, while under the provisions of the mortgage the proceeds can or must be used to pay off part of that mortgage. The lessee should make sure that the agreements in the lease with regard to fire insurance, condemnation awards and removal of fixtures will be honored by the mortgagee.[57]

Often subordination clauses in form leases state only that the lease will be subordinate to all present and future mortgages on the property. Earlier this section pointed out that, under many decisions, a subordination agreement in a purchase money mortgage must define the terms of future construction loans with considerable specificity in order to be enforceable. Reasoning by analogy from the purchase money situation, a court might require that a subordination agreement in a lease contain language limiting future mortgages to terms which the lessor-mortgagor is reasonably likely to be able to perform. If a lease contains a clause subordinating the lease to a future mortgage that is not adequately described or limited, the tenant may be able to attack the subordination clause on the grounds that it is (1) too indefinite to enforce, (2) unjust and unreasonable, or (3) invalid under the Statute of Frauds.[58]

There are two points in time at which a tenant may be able to attack a subordination clause in the lease: while the lease is still executory, and after a foreclosure. If the tenant successfully attacks the subordination clause while the lease is still executory, the court

---

55. M. Friedman, Preparation of Leases, 61 (1962).

56. See KVR Realties, Inc. v. Treasure Star, Inc., 58 N.Y.2d 793, 459 N.Y.S.2d 258, 445 N.E.2d 641 (1983). A lease covenant of quiet enjoyment will not keep the foreclosure of a superior mortgage from cutting off the lessee's right of possession. 220 West 42 Associates v. Ronbet Newmark Co., 53 A.D.2d 829, 385 N.Y.S.2d 304 (1976), modified 40 N.Y.2d 1000, 391 N.Y.S.2d 107, 359 N.E.2d 701 (1976). Only a clause to which the mortgagee is a party will guarantee nondisturbance; see Dover Mobile Estates v. Fiber Form Products, Inc., 220 Cal.App.3d 1494, 270 Cal.Rptr. 183 (1990).

57. M. Friedman, supra note 55 at 64; Committee on Leases, supra note 53 at 247.

58. See text at notes 9 to 33, supra.

might declare the lease void. After a foreclosure, the only reason a tenant will wish to attack the clause will be to restore the priority of the lease so that it cannot be cut off by the foreclosure. If the subordination clause is so indefinite that it has exposed the tenant to unreasonable risk, a court may be willing to reinstate the priority of the tenant's lease.[59] The tenant's argument is more likely to succeed if the lease was a printed form, while if the lease was negotiated with the help of counsel, the court may not be as sympathetic. The value of the leasehold may also make a difference in whether the court considers the subordination clause a material term.[60]

§ 12.10 Improper Disbursement of Loan Proceeds

Once a construction loan is obtained, the distribution of loan funds becomes a critical concern of all parties interested in the project, since improper disbursement can result in non-payment of subcontractors and material suppliers and the collapse of the entire project. This potential for severe economic loss emphasizes the importance of care on the part of the construction lender.

Suppose, for example, that the construction lender fails to supervise the course of construction and advances more money than the construction progress warrants. Suppose also that the owner or general contractor who receives the advances diverts them to other projects or to personal use. If the amount of the original loan accurately reflected the cost of construction, diversion of funds will probably cause the project to go unfinished and the subcontractors to go unpaid. When the owner-borrower defaults on the loan, the lender may foreclose. In the usual case, the lender's lien will be superior to the mechanics' liens filed by unpaid subcontractors and the lender will take the proceeds of the sale.[1] The lender will also have priority over any land vendors or ground lessors who subordinated their liens to enable the developer to secure a construction loan.[2] Other parties may be injured as well. The surety on the payment and performance bond (if any) will be liable for the losses resulting from the non-completion.[3] Purchasers of interests in the project may be unable to realize their expectations. Finally, any guarantors on the construction loan may be liable to the lender for the default.

In light of the catastrophic consequences that can result from improper disbursement of the funds by construction lenders, the question of lender liability naturally arises. In a preceding section of this chapter we observed that lenders can suffer a partial loss of priority in

---

59. Such an argument was rejected, despite an extremely vague lease clause, in T.D. Bickham Corp. v. Hebert, 432 So.2d 228 (La.1983).

60. In valuing a leasehold on commercial property many factors must be considered, including the bonus value of the lease (the present value of the difference between the fair market value of the lease and the rent), the value of the location to the tenant's business, and the value of the improvements that the tenant has made on the property.

§ 12.10

1. See § 12.7, supra.
2. See § 12.9, supra.
3. See § 12.2, supra.

many jurisdictions if their loan disbursements are found to be "optional" instead of "obligatory."[4] That theory is helpful to junior lienholders in some cases, but its application depends on such subtle vagaries of interpretation of the construction loan agreement and the conduct of the parties that it is at best an unreliable basis for reversal of priorities.[5] This section will focus on other theories used by courts to grant relief to parties injured by improper loan distributions.[6] However, cases denying relief to injured parties are numerous; unless express covenants of the loan agreement or conditions of a subordination agreement have been breached by the lender, most jurisdictions are unwilling to impose liability for wrongful distribution of loan proceeds in the absence of fraud or collusion.[7]

Express Agreement

The most widely accepted basis for lender liability for improper disbursements is the lender's breach of an express agreement to disburse the loan in a particular manner. Such agreements are not easy to find, since most construction loan documents are drafted by the lender and carefully avoid imposing specific duties upon it. But where an agreement can be made out, it is a powerful weapon.

---

4. § 12.7, supra.

5. See Korngold, Construction Loan Advances and the Subordinated Purchase Money Mortgagee: An Appraisal, A Suggested Approach, and the ULTA Perspective, 50 Ford.L.Rev. 313, 329–39 (1981): the optional advance doctrine is "too crude a vehicle for the task."

6. See Smith & Cobbe, Questions of Priority Between Mechanics' Lienors and Construction Loan Mortgagees, 38 Ohio St. L.J. 3, 13–18 (1977).

A novel theory was the basis of Sundance Land Corp. v. Community First Fed. Sav. & Loan Ass'n, 840 F.2d 653 (9th Cir. 1988). A mortgagee agreed to subordinate its lien on a fruit orchard to that of another mortgagee, who was to make advances for improvements to the orchard. The latter lender in fact *required* the borrower to divert part of the funds advanced to construction of two motels on other land. The subordinated mortgagee (who, by deed in lieu of foreclosure, had become the owner of the land) was held to have stated proper claim for an injunction of foreclosure of the prior mortgage. The ground for the injunction was that the prior lender had violated the anti-tying provisions of the Home Owners Loan Act, 12 U.S.C.A. § 1464(q)(1)(B), by requiring the diversion of the funds to the motel construction.

7. See e.g., Carlsberg Resources Corp. v. Cambria Savings & Loan Association, 413 F.Supp. 880 (W.D.Pa.1976), affirmed 554 F.2d 1254 (3d Cir.1977); Weiss v. Brentwood Savings & Loan Association, 4 Cal.App.3d 738, 84 Cal.Rptr. 736 (1970); Gill v. Mission Savings & Loan Association, 236 Cal.App.2d 753, 46 Cal.Rptr. 456 (1965); Drobnick v. Western Federal Savings & Loan Association, 479 P.2d 393 (Colo.App. 1970); First Connecticut Small Business Investment Co. v. Arba, Inc., 170 Conn. 168, 365 A.2d 100 (1976); Roberts v. Harkins, 292 So.2d 603 (Fla.App.1974), certiorari denied 302 So.2d 417 (Fla.1974); Hyatt v. Maryland Federal Savings & Loan Association, 42 Md.App. 623, 402 A.2d 118 (1979); Kennedy v. Betts, 33 Md.App. 258, 364 A.2d 74 (1976); Conshohocken Federal Savings & Loan Association v. Period & Country Homes, Inc., 287 Pa.Super. 520, 430 A.2d 1173 (1981); Forest Inc. v. Guaranty Mortgage Co., Inc., 534 S.W.2d 853 (Tenn.App.1975); Fandel, Inc. v. First of Denver Mortgage Investors, 522 S.W.2d 721 (Tex.Civ.App.1975) (per curiam); Tuscarora, Inc. v. BVA Credit Corp., 218 Va. 849, 241 S.E.2d 778 (1978); National Bank of Washington v. Equity Investors, 81 Wash.2d 886, 506 P.2d 20 (1973), appeal after remand 83 Wash.2d 435, 518 P.2d 1072 (1974); 42 Yale L.J. 980 (1933); Grenada Ready–Mix Concrete, Inc. v. Watkins, 453 F.Supp. 1298 (N.D.Miss.1978). See generally Korngold, supra note 5, at 319–29.

§ 12.10 FINANCING REAL ESTATE CONSTRUCTION 251

The concept is illustrated by Modesto Lumber Co. v. Wylde.[8] In extending a building loan to the owners of residential property, the lender promised that no claim would become a lien on the property and that the construction contractor would not be paid until all claims for labor and materials were satisfied. In fact, however, the lender disbursed funds directly to the contractor, instructing him to apply the funds to the accounts of materials suppliers. The contractor did not do so and the suppliers were not paid. In the ensuing litigation, a trial court awarded damages to the suppliers and allowed them to have two liens against the owner's property. The landowners were granted a personal judgment against the lender. On appeal, the court discharged one lien and reduced the amount of the other, but upheld the lender's liability to the owner to the extent of the materialman's lien. The court reasoned that "the loan association accepted a trusteeship to disburse these funds first to the laborers and materialmen and the balance to the contractor. It fairly appears that the loan association paid sums direct to the contractor."[9]

The utility of this approach is quite limited. Even if the construction loan agreement contains provisions which obligate the lender to employ a specific type of disbursement or to use a certain level of care, the borrower who signs that agreement may not be the party principally harmed by improper disbursal. Indeed, in the typical case, it is subordinating vendors[10] and subcontractors who have the most to lose when improper disbursements are made. Yet since they are not parties to the construction loan agreement, they find it difficult to use it as a basis for recovery.[11] In such cases an argument based on the third

8. 217 Cal. 421, 19 P.2d 238 (1933). See also Great Western Sav. Bank v. George W. Easley Co., 778 P.2d 569 (Alaska 1989) (construction lender made promise to general contractor that it would be paid directly; as remedies for breach, court subordinated construction mortgage to contractor's mechanic's lien, and also held lender liable for damages for failure to disburse all funds as promised); Dunson v. Stockton, Whatley, Davin & Co., 346 So.2d 603 (Fla.App.1977); Prudential Insurance Co. v. Executive Estates, Inc., 174 Ind.App. 674, 369 N.E.2d 1117 (1977) (lender's employee orally promised borrower "there would be no liens or encumbrances on that real estate because Prudential would take care of it."); Falls Lumber Co. v. Heman, 114 Ohio App. 262, 181 N.E.2d 713 (1961); Mason v. Western Mortgage Loan Corp., 705 P.2d 1179 (Utah 1985), opinion on remand following appeal after remand 754 P.2d 984 (Utah App. 1988) (construction loan agreement provided that lender would disburse funds "in amounts respectively equal to the value of the labor and materials actually incorporated in the improvements;" lender held liable for disbursing funds for other purposes). But see Laight v. Idaho First Nat'l Bank, 108 Idaho 211, 697 P.2d 1225 (1985), refusing to find lender liability where the loan agreement explicitly relieved the lender from any responsibility for payment to subcontractors; Woodall v. Citizens Banking Co., 503 N.E.2d 427 (Ind.App.1987), rehearing denied 507 N.E.2d 999 (1987), in which the court took the garden-variety covenant of title in the mortgage as evidence that there was no express agreement on the lender's part to disburse funds with care or to avoid mechanics' liens).

9. Id. at 428, 19 P.2d at 240.

10. Cambridge Acceptance Corp. v. Hockstein, 102 N.J.Super. 435, 439, 246 A.2d 138, 140 (1968) (per curiam), certification denied 53 N.J. 81, 248 A.2d 434 (1968).

11. See, e.g., United States v. Chester Heights Associates, 406 F.Supp. 600 (D.S.C. 1975); Ross v. Continental Mortgage Investors, 404 F.Supp. 922 (E.D.La.1975); Lampert Yards, Inc. v. Thompson–Wetterling Construction & Realty, Inc., 302 Minn. 83, 223 N.W.2d 418 (1974); Forest, Inc. v. Guaranty Mortgage Co., Inc., 534 S.W.2d 853 (Tenn.App.1975).

party beneficiary concept may be availing, and may permit a third person to enforce a promise made in the construction loan agreement even though he or she is a stranger to the contract.[12]

The plaintiff most likely to benefit from the third party beneficiary theory is a subordinated land vendor. While numerous courts have concluded that the parties to a construction loan agreement did not *intend* to benefit a subordinating vendor,[13] it is clear that the vendor is, in practical terms, a beneficiary of the agreement. Given the circumstances and equities involved in a typical subordination situation, it is likely that some courts would be responsive to the theory's use. Certainly those courts that view the subordination agreement as creating a "common enterprise" between the vendor, construction lender, and developer could approve of this approach.

No court has yet granted recovery on a third party beneficiary theory to a party injured by lender negligence. Several have rejected the theory's application when asserted by an injured contractor or materialman.[14] Nonetheless, it is conceivable that it could be asserted, particularly for a subordinating vendor. At least one case has suggested the legitimacy of such a cause of action.[15] Its chances of success have probably dimmed as lenders have begun inserting clauses in their construction loan agreements specifically disclaiming the intent to benefit anyone other than the borrower.[16]

We suggest that the courts have been excessively parsimonious in applying the third party beneficiary concept. It is clear that subordinated vendors and mechanics' lien claimants rely heavily on the construction lender's care and competence, and the lender and borrower are usually fully aware of their reliance. It is hard to see why the

---

12. See Restatement (Second) of Contracts § 302 (1981), defining a beneficiary as "intended" and therefore able to enforce the contract " * * * if recognition of the right to performance in the beneficiary is appropriate to effectuate the intention of the parties and * * * the circumstances indicate that the promisee intends to give the beneficiary the benefit of the promised performance."

13. See Home Sav. Ass'n v. State Bank, 763 F.Supp. 292 (N.D.Ill.1991); Inversiones Inmobiliarias Internacionales de Orlando Sociedad Anomina v. Barnett Bank, 584 So.2d 110 (Fla.App.1991); Chicago Title & Trust Co. v. First Arlington National Bank, 118 Ill.App.3d 401, 73 Ill. Dec. 626, 454 N.E.2d 723 (1983); Rockhill v. United States, 288 Md. 237, 418 A.2d 197 (1980); United States v. Chester Heights Associates, 406 F.Supp. 600 (D.S.C.1975).

14. See Light v. Equitable Mortgage Resources, 191 Ga.App. 816, 383 S.E.2d 142 (1989); cases cited note 13, supra. One typical opinion observed that successful assertion of such a third party claim required a demonstration that the "contracting parties intended to create a direct, not incidental or consequential benefit to the third party." See United States v. Chester Heights Associates, supra note 13, at 606–07. The court did not find such a demonstration.

15. See Middlebrook-Anderson Co. v. Southwest Savings & Loan Association, 18 Cal.App.3d 1023, 1038, 96 Cal.Rptr. 338, 347 (1971).

16. See, e.g., Inversiones Inmobiliarias Internacionales de Orlando Sociedad Anomina v. Barnett Bank, 584 So.2d 110 (Fla. App.1991):

The Lender shall in no event be responsible or liable to any person other than the Borrower for its disbursement of or failure to disburse the funds or any part thereof, and neither the contractor nor any subcontractor nor materialmen or craftsmen nor laborers nor others shall have any claim or right against the Lender under this Agreement for the Lender's administration thereof.

need exists for any further evidence that the borrower and lender intend these parties to be benefitted by the lender's agreement to disburse funds in a particular manner or with particular care. Even a specific disclaimer of intent to benefit third parties should carry little weight; it flies in the face of the obvious facts.

Conditional Subordination

A second theoretical approach to the problem of improper disbursements stresses the notion of conditional subordination. Under this theory, the focus is on the agreement by which a land vendor's lien is subordinated to that of a subsequent construction lender. If the agreement is conditioned on application of loan proceeds to construction costs, the courts will recognize the lender's priority only to the extent disbursements actually go to construction. When the condition is spelled out in sufficiently explicit terms in the subordination agreement, this theory is very widely accepted,[17] although it seems impossible to apply it in favor of those who were not parties to the subordination agreement, such as mechanics' lien claimants.[18]

An example of conditional subordination can be seen in the 1962 decision in Collins v. Home Savings & Loan Association.[19] There a land vendor agreed to subordinate his interest to a "construction loan for the purpose of constructing on each lot a dwelling house with the usual appurtenances."[20] This provision was contained in the vendor's deed of trust, which was recorded before the construction loan was obtained. At the request of the title company the vendor signed a subsequent subordination provision that identified more accurately the trust deeds to which his interest was subordinated. However, the second provision did not contain the limiting language of the provision in the vendor's trust deed. When the project failed, the construction lender foreclosed and sold the property to third parties. The subordinating vendor then sued the lender, alleging that three of the disbursements were for non-construction purposes and therefore not within the terms of the subordination agreement. The lender's defense was that there was no requirement in the later subordination agreement that disbursements go to any particular purpose.

Despite the failure of the second subordination provision to repeat the conditions of the first, judgment was for the vendor. The court observed that the lender had actual as well as constructive knowledge

---

17. Some courts refuse to allow the vendor to recover under this theory when the subordination conditions appear in the vendor's trust deed, but not in the lender's trust deed. See e.g., Gill v. Mission Savings & Loan Association, 236 Cal.App.2d 753, 46 Cal.Rptr. 456 (1965); Fandel, Inc. v. First of Denver Mortgage Investors, 522 S.W.2d 721 (Tex.Civ.App.1975) (per curiam). Contra, see In re Sunset Bay Assoc., 944 F.2d 1503 (9th Cir.1991) (if construction lender knows that vendor is subordinating, it has a duty to inquire as to the conditions of the subordination); Protective Equity Trust No. 83 v. Bybee, 2 Cal.App.4th 139, 2 Cal.Rptr.2d 864 (1991)(same).

18. See discussion at notes 12–16 supra.

19. 205 Cal.App.2d 86, 22 Cal.Rptr. 817 (1962).

20. Id. at 89, 22 Cal.Rptr. at 819.

of the language in the earlier subordination clause. It also suggested that the two subordination provisions were "executed contemporaneously" and should be read together. Finally, the court noted that it was possible to infer "that the only reason for respondents' subordination of their lien was the expectation that if payments were advanced by the appellant solely for construction purposes, the liens superior to their own would increase in value only as the property under development enjoyed a corresponding increase in value because of the accompanying progress in the work of construction." [21] The court concluded that subordination conditions were unsatisfied and that the vendor's lien retained its priority. Because the property had been sold to third parties, damages were allowed against the lender for the principal amount of the vendor's deed of trust plus interest. It is noteworthy that this result was not one of partial priority; rather, the vendor's entire lien was held superior to that of the lender for purposes of calculating damages.[22]

A later California case, Miller v. Citizens Savings & Loan Association,[23] went further in liberalizing the construction of subordination agreements; it held that even without an explicit reference in the agreement to the construction use of the funds, it "should be construed, unless it expressly provides otherwise, as permitting the loan proceeds to be used only for such purposes." [24]

Additional complexities arise when the subordination agreement fails to state any conditions protecting the land vendor, or when there is no explicit subordination agreement at all. What should be the consequences of the lender's disbursement of loan proceeds to nonconstruction purposes? This was the issue facing the court in Middlebrook–Anderson Co. v. Southwest Savings & Loan Association.[25] There the plaintiff agreed to sell 28 lots to developers, with part of the purchase price to be secured by a deed of trust. It was understood that the deed of trust was to be second to a construction loan the developers would obtain. In order to have first priority, the lender recorded its trust deeds first. When the developer abandoned the project, the lender foreclosed, purchasing the property itself.[26] The vendor was "wiped out" by the foreclosure, and brought suit, complaining that the lender had permitted the developers to use $300,000 of the loan dis-

---

21. Id. at 99, 22 Cal.Rptr. at 825.

22. The court did not discuss the reason for this result, but it did point out that the amount of the improper disbursements was greater than the value of the vendor's deed of trust. As a general proposition, absolute priority or damages would appear to be in order when partial priority results in no benefit to the vendor, i.e., when the foreclosure sale would provide no excess over that portion of the lender's lien given priority under the terms of the conditional subordination. See the discussion supra § 12.9 note 37.

23. 248 Cal.App.2d 655, 56 Cal.Rptr. 844 (1967).

24. Id. at 663–64, 56 Cal.Rptr. at 851.

25. 18 Cal.App.3d 1023, 96 Cal.Rptr. 338 (1971). For discussions of this case see Lambe, Enforceability of Subordination Agreements, 19 Real Prop.Prob. & Tr.J. 631, 639–47 (1984); Note, Purchase Money Subordination Agreements in California: An Analysis of Conditional Subordination, 45 So.Cal.L.Rev. 1109 (1972).

26. Ultimately, the property was sold to third parties.

§ 12.10   FINANCING REAL ESTATE CONSTRUCTION   255

bursements for non-construction purposes. In consequence, the vendor argued, it was entitled to a restoration of priority and damages. The cause of action depended, of course, on a conclusion that the agreement to take a second trust deed was the equivalent of a subordination agreement—otherwise there was no priority to be restored. The court ruled "that the duties owed by a lender to a seller under a formal subordination agreement do not differ from the duties owed by a lender to a seller when the lender obtains priority over the seller under an agreement by the seller to record after the lender."[27] The lender's main defenses were that it had no duty to supervise the loan distributions and that there was no privity of contract between it and the vendor. These defenses, held the court, were insufficient to prevent a trial on the merits.

The court was persuaded that there were "strong public policy reasons to protect the seller in subordination situations."[28] To be enforceable, a subordination clause "must contain terms that will define and minimize the risk that the subordinating liens will impair or destroy the seller's security."[29] Given the lender's superior ability to prevent loan misappropriations and its greater ability to absorb loss, the court held that an implied agreement to disburse loan proceeds for construction purposes "should be spelled out from the lender's alleged actual knowledge of the provisions of the seller's lien in general, and of the subordination therein in particular."[30] Furthermore the court said:

> In the superior position of a financial institution constantly engaged in professional construction lending, Southwestern had no reason to believe their trust deed conferred any lien to which the fee was subordinate other than to the extent of money spent for construction purposes. Its loan under the circumstances cannot be viewed other than as subject to the fair application of the construction funds. Accordingly, we conclude that such lien as the trust deed might have conferred on the lender should not be advanced or preferred over the seller.[31]

---

27. 18 Cal.App.3d at 1029, 96 Cal.Rptr. at 341. For a contrary view, see Spaziani v. Millar, 215 Cal.App.2d 667, 30 Cal.Rptr. 658 (1963); Miller, Regalia & Starr, Subordination Agreements in California, 13 U.C.L.A.L.Rev. 1298 (1966).

28. 18 Cal.App.3d at 1036, 96 Cal.Rptr. at 346. In United States Cold Storage of California v. Great Western Sav. & Loan Ass'n, 165 Cal.App.3d 1214, 212 Cal.Rptr. 232 (1985), the court expressly limited *Middlebrook's* implied subordination theory to construction loans. In a subsequent case the public policy requiring protection of subordinating sellers persuaded a California Court to rule that lender and borrower may not make modifications in their loan agreement without the knowledge and consent of the subordinating seller if the modifications materially affect the seller's rights; Gluskin v. Atlantic Savings & Loan Association, 32 Cal.App.3d 307, 108 Cal. Rptr. 318 (1973). See also Citizens & Southern Nat. Bank v. Smith, 277 S.C. 162, 284 S.E.2d 770 (1981).

29. 18 Cal.App.3d at 1036, 96 Cal.Rptr. at 346; Handy v. Gordon, 65 Cal.2d 578, 55 Cal.Rptr. 769, 422 P.2d 329 (1967); see § 12.9, supra.

30. Id. at 1038, 96 Cal.Rptr. at 347.

31. Id. A subsequent decision carved out an exception to the *Middlebrook-Anderson* rule when the subordinating vendor is also a part owner of the developer and participates in the construction pro-

The approach taken by the court in *Middlebrook–Anderson* is far more activist than many courts can swallow. It has been followed by some [32] and explicitly rejected by others.[33]

Breach of Duty of Care

The theories of recovery considered thus far have focused on lender liability arising out of the breach of express agreements or reversal of priority for failure to meet conditions in subordination agreements. These theories are not helpful, of course, when there is no express language in the construction loan agreement and there are no conditions, express or implied, on the subordination. A third approach has been taken by some courts: lenders have occasionally been found liable for improper disbursals because they have breached a duty of care, evidently arising in tort. This is a fairly radical step, and most courts have been unwilling to take it.[34]

ject. Woodworth v. Redwood Empire Savings & Loan Association, 22 Cal.App.3d 347, 99 Cal.Rptr. 373 (1971).

32. See B. J. I. Corp. v. Larry W. Corp., 183 N.J.Super. 310, 443 A.2d 1096 (1982) (implying conditions in subordination clause in purchase contract); Peoples Bank v. L & T Developers, Inc., 434 So.2d 699 (Miss.1983), judgment corrected 437 So.2d 7 (1983) (approving *Middlebrook* but adopting a direct "duty" approach). See also Burkons v. Ticor Title Ins. Co., 168 Ariz. 345, 813 P.2d 710 (1991), holding an escrow agent liable for failing to disclose to the vendor the fact that his subordination agreement contained no condition that the funds from the senior loan must be used for construction. The vendor never requested such language of condition, but the court found the duty to warn the vendor because "no rational seller would agree to subordinate his or her purchase money lien to a loan like" the one involved in the case; id. at 715. In Pastor v. Lafayette Bldg. Ass'n, 567 So.2d 793 (La.App.1990) the construction lender was held liable for misrepresentation, when it advised the subordinating vendor that his position would not be harmed by subordination, and then proceeded to disburse construction funds in a lump sum with no precautions to ensure that they would be used for improvements on the property.

33. See Home Sav. Ass'n v. State Bank, 763 F.Supp. 292, 298–99 (N.D.Ill. 1991) ("to impose a duty of cautious loan administration on the lender where none is expressed in the executed subordination agreement, thereby making subordination conditional, would amount to judicial redrafting of the parties' agreement, an exercise of power soundly rejected by the Illinois courts"); Owens–Corning Fiberglas Corp. v. Texas Commerce Bank, 104 Nev. 556, 763 P.2d 335 (1988) (no conditions will be implied in favor of a knowledgable and sophisticated party); Grenada Ready–Mix Concrete, Inc. v. Watkins, 453 F.Supp. 1298 (N.D.Miss.1978); Colonial Villas, Inc. v. Title Ins. Co. of Minnesota, 145 Ariz. 590, 703 P.2d 534 (App.1985); Provident Fed. Sav. and Loan Ass'n v. Idaho Land Developers, Inc., 114 Idaho 453, 757 P.2d 716 (App. 1988) (refusing to imply conditions protective of subordinated vendors); Rockhill v. United States, 288 Md. 237, 418 A.2d 197 (1980); Nevis v. Fidelity New York, 104 Nev. 576, 763 P.2d 345 (1988) (no liability where lender "unknowingly disbursed loan proceeds for work that was incomplete and improvements that were not properly constructed"); Conshohocken Federal Savings & Loan Association v. Period & Country Homes, Inc., 287 Pa.Super. 520, 430 A.2d 1173 (1981) (subordination conditions will not be implied, where there is no evidence of fraud in the lender's disbursements and funds were not diverted from the project, but merely spent for unscheduled items); Tuscarora, Inc. v. B.V.A. Credit Corp., 218 Va. 849, 241 S.E.2d 778 (1978). See also Crum v. AVCO Financial Services, 552 N.E.2d 823 (Ind.App.1990), in which the lender disbursed the loan funds without obtaining marketable title or recording a deed for the borrowers; the court held that these matters were outside the scope of the lender's duty and exonerated it from liability.

34. Professor Robert Kratovil urged adoption of a duty of care in disbursement, based on the general contract duty of good faith and fair dealing; see Kratovil, Mortgage Lender Liability—Construction

§ 12.10   FINANCING REAL ESTATE CONSTRUCTION   257

One variation on the breach of duty theme may be seen in Fikes v. First Federal Savings & Loan Association.[35] The case involved a foreclosure action by the lender of a construction loan. Fikes, who owned an unrecorded equitable interest [36] in the project, challenged the lender's priority on the ground that the developer diverted loan disbursements to other projects during the course of construction, and did so with the lender's knowledge. The court recognized the validity of the equitable interest asserted, and found that the lender had knowledge of Fikes' existence before construction funds were loaned. The central issue facing the court was whether a lender has a duty to protect such third party interests of which it has knowledge.[37] The lender argued that no such duty existed because there was no privity of contract between it and Fikes. The court rejected this contention and held that a duty, founded in equity, did exist.

The court observed that when the plaintiff allowed the developer to take legal title to the property, Fikes had the reasonable expectation that First Federal would perform its role as interim construction lender in a conventional manner. If First Federal had disbursed the construction loan proceeds according to normal secured-lending practices, the property which Fikes had contracted to buy would have been enhanced in value.[38] By failing to follow such ordinary disbursement procedures, First Federal breached its duty to Fikes.[39] In consequence of this

Loans, 38 Depaul L.Rev. 43 (1989). Cases holding that a lender owes no duty of care in loan disbursements to parties lacking contractual privity or a fiduciary relationship with the lender include Ross v. Continental Mortgage Investors, 404 F.Supp. 922 (E.D.La.1975); Baldwin v. Bright Mortgage Co., 791 P.2d 1182 (Colo.App.1989); Comet Devel. Corp. v. Prudential Ins. Co., 579 So.2d 355 (Fla.App.1991); Armetta v. Clevetrust Realty Investors, 359 So.2d 540 (Fla. App.1978), certiorari denied 366 So.2d 879 (Fla.1978); Equitable Mortgage Resources, Inc. v. Carter, 199 Ga.App. 866, 406 S.E.2d 494 (1991); Rockhill v. United States, supra note 33; Parker v. Columbia Bank, 91 Md.App. 346, 604 A.2d 521 (1992); Lampert Yards, Inc. v. Thompson–Wetterling Construction & Realty Inc., 302 Minn. 83, 223 N.W.2d 418 (1974); Marine Midland Bank v. Cafferty, 174 A.D.2d 932, 571 N.Y.S.2d 628 (1991); Shankle Equipment Co. v. Liberty National Bank, 569 P.2d 965 (Okl.1977); Thormahlen v. Citizens Sav. and Loan Ass'n, 73 Or.App. 230, 698 P.2d 512 (1985), review denied 299 Or. 443, 702 P.2d 1111 (1985); Forest Inc. v. Guaranty Mortgage Co. Inc., 534 S.W.2d 853 (Tenn. App.1975). See also Grenada Ready–Mix Concrete, Inc. v. Watkins, 453 F.Supp. 1298 (N.D.Miss.1978), rejecting a duty of care to a "subordinated" ground lessor.

In Woodall v. Citizens Banking Co., 503 N.E.2d 427 (Ind.App.1987) the court held the mortgagee had no duty to protect mortgagors from mechanics' liens, absent express agreement or agency relationship. The Woodalls later petitioned for a rehearing under a theory of promissory estoppel, see Woodall v. Citizens Banking Co., 507 N.E.2d 999 (Ind.App.1987), which the court denied on the basis that an oral assurance by the mortgagee that construction bills were paid was not a commitment to act in the future and did not constitute a promise under the doctrine of promissory estoppel.

35. 533 P.2d 251 (Alaska 1975). See also Big Land Investment Corp. v. Lomas & Nettleton Financial Corp., 657 P.2d 837, 839 n. 5 (Alaska 1983); Stenehjem v. Kyn Jin Cho, 631 P.2d 482, 488 (Alaska 1981).

36. The equitable interest arose out of an earnest money agreement between Fikes and the property owner's agent. Fikes allowed the developer to have legal title in order to facilitate construction financing. The arrangement was entered into on the lender's advice. Id. at 256.

37. Id. at 260.

38. Id. at 261.

39. Id.

breach, the court ruled that the lender's security interest encompassed only those funds spent for construction.

A similar result was reached in Cambridge Acceptance Corp. v. Hockstein.[40] In that case the subordinated ground lessor challenged a foreclosure action brought by the construction lender's assignee, alleging that the loan disbursements were expended for nonconstruction purposes. Unable to find an agreement between owner and lender that limited subordination to funds advanced for construction, the court said that there was at most an "intent and expectation" on the owner's part that the subordination would be to a construction loan. The court then noted the general view that "absent an express stipulation between the subordinator and the construction lender conditioning the scope of the subordination, diversion of construction money by the borrower from its contemplated use will not dislodge the advanced lienor from his bargained-for priority in the absence of collusion with the mortgagor in diverting the money from its purpose."[41] Despite the general rule, judgment was for the landowner. Equitable principles, said the court, required the construction lender "to make and administer the loan in the conventional manner of a construction lender rather than mask what is essentially a loan on the general credit and reliability of the borrower and the security of the land value as a construction loan, and act accordingly in disbursing the funds."[42] The lender failed to observe this standard. It was "totally oblivious of and seemingly disinterested in what the borrower actually did with the money."[43] Because the landowner was equitably entitled to rely on the expectation that the lender would comply with conventional practices, the lender's failure to do so estopped it from asserting the subordination of the owner's interest.

The Mississippi courts have imposed a direct duty of reasonably careful disbursement on construction lenders, in favor both of mechanics' lien claimants[44] and subordinated land vendors.[45] In the latter situation, the Mississippi Supreme Court described the rule recently in these terms:

> Absent an express agreement to the contrary, a construction lender owes a duty to the landowner who subordinates his purchase money deed of trust. That duty is to exercise reasonable diligence to see that the funds loaned are in fact used in the construction project. If the construction lender fails to exercise reasonable

---

40. 102 N.J.Super. 435, 246 A.2d 138 (1968) (per curiam), certification denied 53 N.J. 81, 248 N.E.2d 434 (1968).

41. Id. at 438, 246 A.2d at 140.

42. Id. at 440, 246 A.2d at 141.

43. Id. at 440, 246 A.2d at 141.

44. Cook v. Citizens Savings & Loan Association, 346 So.2d 370 (Miss.1977). But see Riley Building Supplies v. First Citizens National Bank, 510 So.2d 506 (Miss.1987), where the court found no duty of reasonable diligence owed by construction lender to materialman holding an *unperfected* lien.

45. Peoples Bank v. L & T Devel., Inc., 434 So.2d 699 (Miss.1983), noted 53 Miss. L.Rev. 691 (1983), remanded for determination of property values, 437 So.2d 7 (Miss. 1983); Home Federal Savings & Loan Association v. DePass, 287 S.C. 600, 340 S.E.2d 545 (1986).

§ 12.10 FINANCING REAL ESTATE CONSTRUCTION 259

diligence in this regard, its deed of trust will be prior in right to the landowner's purchase money deed of trust only to the extent that proceeds of the construction loan actually went into the construction project.[46]

Several other cases have adopted a breach of duty analysis.[47] One in particular deserves mention. In Commercial Standard Insurance Co. v. Bank of America[48] the court focused more on the policy considerations and the need to protect the plaintiff than on any strict search for duty. The issue was whether the lender could be liable to the surety on a performance bond for improperly disbursing loan proceeds to a construction contractor. The surety, which was forced to cover the losses on the project when the contractor defaulted, sought to be subrogated to the landowner's claims against the lender for negligent disbursement of loan proceeds. The court held that the surety could be subrogated to the owner's claims. It also found that inasmuch as the lender had agreed to disburse loan proceeds in accordance with the value of construction progress, the lender owed the owner a duty to exercise reasonable care. The lender contended, however, that even if it owed a duty to the owner, it owed none to the surety. The court's examination of this duty question reflected a negligence analysis founded in policy considerations. "Duty," observed the court, "is not sacrosanct in itself, but only an expression of the sum total of those considerations of policy which lead the law to say that the particular plaintiff is entitled to protection."[49] The policy considerations considered were:

> the foreseeability of harm to the plaintiff, the degree of certainty that the plaintiff suffered injury, the closeness of the connection between the defendant's conduct and the injury suffered, the moral blame attached to the defendant's conduct, the policy of preventing future harm, the extent of the burden to the defendant and consequences to the community of imposing a duty to exercise care

---

46. Id. at 713. Some earlier Mississippi case law appeared to impose an absolute duty to prevent diversion of loan proceeds; see Weiss, Dreyfous & Seiferth, Inc. v. Natchez Investment Co., 166 Miss. 253, 260, 140 So. 736, 738 (1932). But it is now clear that only reasonable care is required; see Guaranty Mortgage Co. v. Seitz, 367 So.2d 438 (Miss.1979); Southern Life Insurance Co. v. Pollard Appliance Co., 247 Miss. 211, 150 So.2d 416 (1963).

47. See, e.g. Radunich v. Basso, 235 Cal.App.2d 826, 45 Cal.Rptr. 824 (1965); Essex Savings Bank v. Leeker, 2 Conn.App. 98, 476 A.2d 1071 (1984); Security & Investment Corp v. Droege, 529 So.2d 799 (Fla.App.1988) (dictum); Prudential Insurance Co. v. Executive Estates, Inc., 174 Ind.App. 674, 369 N.E.2d 1117 (1977); Westland Homes Corp. v. Hall, 193 Neb. 237, 226 N.W.2d 622 (1975); Western Mortgage Loan Corp. v. Cottonwood Construction Co., 18 Utah 2d 409, 424 P.2d 437 (1967) (dictum). An "agreement to the contrary" may eliminate the lender's duty of care; see, e.g., Laight v. Idaho First Nat. Bank, 108 Idaho 211, 697 P.2d 1225 (App. 1985). But see Garbish v. Malvern Federal Savings and Loan Association, 358 Pa.Super. 282, 517 A.2d 547 (1986), appeal denied 516 Pa. 641, 533 A.2d 712 (1987) (exculpatory clause in the construction contract deemed unenforceable on the grounds that the lender was not a party to the contract and that there was no consideration for the exculpation).

48. 57 Cal.App.3d 241, 129 Cal.Rptr. 91 (1976).

49. Id. at 248, 129 Cal.Rptr. at 95 (quoting Dillon v. Legg, 68 Cal.2d 728, 734, 69 Cal.Rptr. 72, 76, 441 P.2d 912, 916 (1968)).

with resulting liability for breach, and the availability, cost, and prevalence of insurance for the risk involved.[50]

After analyzing these factors in the context of the facts alleged, the court imposed a duty on the lender, running to the surety, to exercise reasonable care in disbursing loan proceeds.

Several courts have used a principal-agent theory to find a duty of careful disbursement in the construction lender.[51] Since lenders generally insist on supervising the disbursements themselves rather than permitting their borrowers to do so, the lender can be viewed as the borrower's agent for this purpose, with a corresponding fiduciary obligation to see that the funds are distributed with due care.

It may be possible to find in state statutes a standard of care in disbursement of construction loan proceeds. For example, the Ohio code provides that no payment may be made by a lending institution to a contractor unless the latter has given the lender its affidavit setting forth any unpaid claims of subcontractors, materials suppliers, and laborers. This duty obviously runs to the borrower,[52] and the statutory language suggests that subcontractors can also assert liability under it. The Ohio Supreme Court recently appeared to agree in principle, but held that the "gross negligence or fraud" required for lender liability under the statute had not occurred on the facts before it, notwithstanding that the lender had closed on permanent loans on the houses in question with knowledge that they were not completed, and had used affidavits that were improperly executed.[53]

The Arkansas statutes provide limited protection for mechanics' lien claimants against misdisbursement by construction lenders. They recognize the priority to the construction mortgage (if it was recorded before construction commenced, and if disbursements were obligatory) only if the mortgage "was given or executed for the purpose of raising money or funds with which to make the ... improvements."[54] The Arkansas courts have read this language as denying mortgage priority

---

50. Id., 129 Cal.Rptr. at 95 (quoting Rowland v. Christian, 69 Cal.2d 108, 70 Cal.Rptr. 97, 443 P.2d 561 (1968)).

51. See Prudential Insurance Co. v. Executive Estates, Inc., 174 Ind.App. 674, 369 N.E.2d 1117 (1977); Falls Lumber Co. v. Heman, 114 Ohio App. 262, 181 N.E.2d 713 (1961); Garbish v. Malvern Federal Savings & Loan Association, 358 Pa.Super. 282, 517 A.2d 547 (1986), appeal denied 516 Pa. 641, 533 A.2d 712 (1987). Cf. Woodall v. Citizens Banking Co., 503 N.E.2d 427 (Ind.App.1987), rehearing denied 507 N.E.2d 999 (1987), refusing to find an agency relationship where the lender did not exercise exclusive control of disbursements); Gardner Plumbing, Inc. v. Cottrill, 44 Ohio St.2d 111, 117, 338 N.E.2d 757, 760–61 (1975), noted 45 U.Cin.L.Rev. 492 (1976). Cf. Inversiones Inmobiliarias Internacionales de Orlando Sociedad Anomina v. Barnett Bank, 584 So.2d 110 (Fla.App. 1991), refusing to find such a fiduciary relationship.

52. See Plumbing Connections, Inc. v. Kostelnik, 69 Ohio Misc. 11, 430 N.E.2d 1340, 23 O.O.3d 77 (1980), affirmed 1981 WL 4409 (Ohio App.1981).

53. Thompson Electric, Inc. v. Bank One, 37 Ohio St.3d 259, 525 N.E.2d 761 (1988), rehearing denied 38 Ohio St.3d 718, 533 N.E.2d 788 (1988). See also Takach v. Williams Homes, 6 Ohio St.3d 357, 453 N.E.2d 656 (1983), holding that the statute ran in favor of a party who had contracted to buy the property upon completion of construction, and who had obtained a long-term loan commitment from the same lender.

54. Ark.Code Ann. § 18–44–110.

§ 12.10   FINANCING REAL ESTATE CONSTRUCTION   261

if the lender has "permitted or known that funds were not to be used for the improvements."[55] Mere negligence in disbursement is not enough; the lender must have actual knowledge of the diversion of funds. Even where such knowledge is shown, the lender suffers only a *pro tanto* loss of priority, in the amount diverted.[56]

Note that even if a duty of reasonable care is found, it may not provide a remedy for every diversion of construction funds. In Daniels v. Big Horn Federal Savings & Loan Association,[57] the lender conceded it owed a duty of due care. However, since it was not common at that time for construction lenders in Wyoming to obtain lien waivers from subcontractors before making each disbursement, the court held that the defendant's failure to do so gave rise to no liability.

Assuming that lenders must use reasonable care to ensure that the loan funds find their way into improvements to the land, questions can arise as to what items constitute "improvements." There is obviously no difficulty with labor and materials expended on the site, and most courts would have little difficulty approving off-site infrastructure, such as extension of water and sewer lines, storm drains, and roads leading to the site.[58] Architects' and engineers' fees are more debatable, since the work products of these professionals may or may not enhance the property's value, depending on their quality and whether or not they can be used in completing the project after default and foreclosure.[59] Even more dubious are fees or interest on the construction loan and payments on junior financing, ground lease rentals, and the like.[60] Obviously, it is desirable to cover these details in a carefully-drafted construction loan agreement or subordination clause.

It is not clear that there is currently any trend in the courts toward holding construction lenders to a standard of reasonable care in dis-

55. Spickes Bros. Painting Contractors, Inc. v. Worthen Bank, 299 Ark. 79, 771 S.W.2d 258 (1989).

56. See the concurring opinion of Justice Jacoway in *Spickes Bros.*, id. at 261, arguing that a lender who misleads mechanics' lienors is acting in bad faith and should lose full priority, and suggesting that in a foreclosure action, where "unclean hands" and equitable estoppel could be considered, the court might reach that result.

57. 604 P.2d 1046 (Wyo.1980). See also Wooden v. First Security Bank of Idaho, 121 Idaho 98, 822 P.2d 995 (1991) (lender had no duty to avoid mechanics' liens, where all disbursements were made directly to borrower); Spurlock v. Fayette Federal Savings & Loan Association, 436 N.E.2d 811, 30 A.L.R.4th 125 (Ind.App.1982) (same); Essex Savings Bank v. Leeker, 2 Conn.App. 98, 476 A.2d 1071 (1984) (construction lender is not required to be an expert on modular housing, but only to use reasonable care in disbursement).

58. See B. J. I. Corp. v. Larry W. Corp., 183 N.J.Super. 310, 443 A.2d 1096 (1982) (approving house, off-site roads, gutter, sewers); Hyatt v. Maryland Federal Savings & Loan Association, 42 Md.App. 623, 402 A.2d 118 (1979) (approving preliminary engineer and architectural work, water and sewer systems).

59. See Hyatt v. Maryland Federal Savings & Loan Association, id.; G. Credit Co. v. Mid–West Land Development, Inc., 207 Kan. 325, 485 P.2d 205 (1971) (approving engineers' and architects' plans and specifications, construction loan interest, and rental payments on ground lease).

60. See Hyatt v. Maryland Federal Savings & Loan Association, id.; cf. Ban–Co Investment Co. v. Loveless, 22 Wash. App. 122, 587 P.2d 567 (1978) (disapproving prepayment of rent on ground lease and payments for developer's overhead and profit).

bursement. The cases that do so are plainly a minority. Yet several factors argue for their soundness. One is the enormous power that construction lenders hold, by virtue of their priority position, to wreak economic havoc on owners, purchase-money mortgagee, and mechanics' lienors if they act irresponsible in making disbursements.[61] Another is the common understanding of these subordinate parties that the construction lender will use good practices to protect itself, and that they too will be benefitted by these practices.[62] Arguably these considerations apply only where the lender has notice of the junior parties' existence and potential claims, but that is nearly always the case.

Adoption by the courts of a general duty of reasonable care has the advantage of avoiding the vagaries of interpretation of construction loan agreements and subordination agreements, and the uncertainties of the third party beneficiary doctrine, discussed earlier in this section. It also benefits junior parties who do not have the sophistication and knowledge of construction loan practices which would lead them to insist on contractual protection from sloppy disbursements. In light of the construction lender's broad legal and economic control of the entire transaction, imposition of this sort of duty is reasonable and commendable.

§ 12.11 Lender Liability for Construction Defects or Other Wrongful Acts of Contractors

If a lender becomes more than ordinarily involved in a construction project, its additional activities may form the basis for liability for negligent or illegal acts committed by the borrower. The principal case so holding is Connor v. Great Western Savings and Loan Association.[1] This 1969 decision by the California supreme court, which generated considerable concern and commentary,[2] held a construction lender liable to subdivision home purchasers for construction defects in their homes. In *Connor* an inexperienced and undercapitalized builder borrowed construction funds from Great Western Savings and Loan Association. In addition to lending these funds, Great Western "warehoused" the land upon which the subdivision was to be constructed, purchasing it in bulk and reselling it to the developer as he was able to use it. The lender also obtained from the builder a right of first refusal to make

---

61. See Korngold, Construction Loan Advances and the Subordinated Purchase Money Mortgagee: An Appraisal, A Suggested Approach, and the ULTA Perspective, 50 Ford.L.Rev. 313, 354–56 (1981).

62. Id. at 357.

§ 12.11

1. 69 Cal.2d 850, 73 Cal.Rptr. 369, 447 P.2d 609 (1969).

2. See e.g., Annot., Financing Agency's Liability to Purchaser of New Homes or Structures for Consequences of Construction Defects. 39 A.L.R.3d 247 (1971); Jordan, Construction Lender Liability to Third Parties, Probate & Property, Mar./Apr. 1991, at 45; Note, Mortgage Lender Liability to the Purchaser of New or Existing Homes, 1988 Ill.L.Rev. 191; Note, the Expanding Scope of Enterprise Liability, 69 Colum.L.Rev. 1084 (1969); Comment, New Liability in Construction Lending: Implications of Connor v. Great Western Sav. & Loan, 42 So.Cal.L.Rev. 353 (1969); Comment, Liability of the Institutional Lender for Structural Defects in New Housing, 35 U.Chi.L.Rev. 739 (1968); 6 Houston L.Rev. 580 (1969); 5 Real Property, Prob. & Tr.J. 495 (1970).

the permanent loans to subdivision homebuyers. The agreement between lender and developer provided that if Great Western met the terms of a competing lender and still lost the loan, the developer would have to pay Great Western the fees it otherwise would have earned.[3] Great Western reviewed the developer's plans, but failed to follow its usual procedure and examine the foundation specifications. When the defectively constructed foundations later cracked, the purchasers brought suit against several defendants, including Great Western. In reversing a judgment of nonsuit against Great Western, the California supreme court said:

> Great Western became much more than a lender content to lend money at interest on the security of real property. It became an active participant in a home construction enterprise. It had the right to exercise extensive control of the enterprise. Its financing, which made the enterprise possible, took on ramifications beyond the domain of the usual money lender.[4]

Because of this extensive involvement in the subdivision project, the court found that the lender had a duty to purchasers to exercise reasonable care in preventing defective construction. In so ruling, the court created a new theory of construction lender liability.

In a few cases decided after *Connor,* the courts have found highly intimate connections between developer and lender, and thus have imposed liability. For example, in Central Bank v. Baldwin,[5] the Nevada supreme court noted that the lender's wholly-owned subsidiary owned half of the developer corporation's stock, provided it with a generous line of credit, and inspected all of its construction work. This sort of involvement seems even more extensive than that in *Connor,* and was sufficient to support a judgment against the lender for defective construction.

In Dunson v. Stockton, Whatley, Davin & Co.,[6] *Connor* was used as the basis for a reordering of normal mortgage priorities. A housing developer had contracted to sell a completed house to the Dunsons. Ordinarily, the developer's construction loan mortgage on the property would have had priority over the Dunsons' contract rights, and its

---

3. This sort of referral arrangement may be an illegal tying agreement under the Sherman Act; see Fortner Enterprises, Inc. v. United States Steel Corp., 394 U.S. 495, 89 S.Ct. 1252, 22 L.Ed.2d 495 (1969), appeal after remand 452 F.2d 1095 (6th Cir.1971), certiorari denied 406 U.S. 919, 92 S.Ct. 1773, 32 L.Ed.2d 119 (1972).

4. 69 Cal.2d at 864, 73 Cal.Rptr. at 376, 447 P.2d at 616. See Note, 73 Va. L.Rev. 243 (1987), describing the "acquisition, development, and construction (ADC) loan," in which the lender typically finances the entire process of land acquisition and development and also takes an equity position in the project. The note author suggests that in such loans the lender's involvement is so extensive that *Connor*-type liability may be triggered.

5. 94 Nev. 581, 583 P.2d 1087 (1978). See also Kincaid v. Landing Devel. Corp., 289 S.C. 89, 344 S.E.2d 869 (App.1986) (lender liable if it is so amalgamated with developer to blur the legal distinction between the two). But see Starfish Condominium Association v. Yorkridge Service Corp., 295 Md. 693, 458 A.2d 805 (1983), refusing to hold the lender liable on very similar facts, and summarily dismissing *Connor* as having "no application," 458 A.2d at 819.

6. 346 So.2d 603 (Fla.App.1977).

foreclosure would have destroyed their interest.[7] However, prior to foreclosure the lender had become so concerned about the developer's shaky operation that it assumed control of the partially completed construction, placing its own employee in charge of the project. Because of this close tie between developer and lender, the court held that all advances made after the lender had taken control were subordinate to the vendee's interest.

Connor has also been a factor in some cases that otherwise would probably have been decided against the landowner. For example, ordinarily a construction lender's policy of making routine inspections during the course of construction is assumed to be for the lender's benefit alone, and does not form the basis for a claim by the owner if the inspection is carelessly done,[8] even if the owner has paid an "inspection fee." However, a combination of the *Connor* theory and an explicit promise by the lender produced a contrary result in Rudolph v. First Southern Federal Savings and Loan Association.[9] While the court did not find the sort of general control by the lender which existed in *Connor*, it noted a statement by an officer of the lender to the owners that the lender "had its own inspector who would not approve a draw * * * until the work was performed properly."[10] The court found this a sufficient basis for allowing the jury to decide whether the lender had assumed a duty to make inspections for the owner's benefit, and thus would be liable for substandard work by the contractor.

However, the great majority of recent cases have distinguished *Connor*, permitting lender defendants to avoid liability.[11] The distinc-

---

7. The Dunsons had initially conveyed the lot by deed to the developer in order to facilitate its arrangement of construction financing; the court took this conveyance to be the equivalent of a voluntary subordination of the Dunsons' interest to the construction loan. On subordination by vendees generally, see § 12.9, supra, at notes 39–44; § 13.3, infra.

8. See, e.g., Raynor v. United States, 604 F.Supp. 205 (D.N.J.1984); Meyers v. Guarantee Savings & Loan Association, 79 Cal.App.3d 307, 144 Cal.Rptr. 616 (1978); Rice v. First Federal Savings & Loan Association, 207 So.2d 22 (Fla.App.1968), certiorari denied 212 So.2d 879 (Fla.1968); Butts v. Atlanta Federal Savings & Loan Association, 152 Ga. 40, 262 S.E.2d 230 (1979); Charter Mortgage Co. v. Gray, 174 Ga.App. 502, 330 S.E.2d 440 (1985); First Family Mortgage Corp. of Florida v. Lubliner, 113 A.D.2d 868, 493 N.Y.S.2d 598 (1985); Goodman v. Pate Construction Co., 305 Pa.Super. 147, 451 A.2d 464 (1982); Eckman v. Centennial Sav. Bank, 757 S.W.2d 392 (Tex.App.1988).

The courts have usually adopted the same position with respect to inspections by permanent or long-term lenders; see Rzepiennik v. U.S. Home Corp., 221 N.J.Super. 230, 534 A.2d 89 (1987) (permanent lender's inspection of house as part of loan underwriting process gave rise to no liability to purchasers for construction defects); Holland Mortgage & Inv. Corp. v. Bone, 751 S.W.2d 515 (Tex.App.1987), error refused n.r.e. (same); Stempler v. Frankford Trust Co., 365 Pa.Super. 305, 529 A.2d 521 (1987) (permanent lender on condominium unit owed no duty to borrower to inspect property and identify defects).

9. 414 So.2d 64 (Ala.1982).

10. Id. at 71. Cf. Butts v. Atlanta Federal Savings & Loan Association, 152 Ga. App. 40, 262 S.E.2d 230 (1979), rejecting, on the basis of the parol evidence rule, a similar claim deriving from the statement of the lender's officer "that all work would be checked and approved for good workmanship before any funds were disbursed."

11. Drake v. Morris Plan Co., 53 Cal. App.3d 208, 125 Cal.Rptr. 667 (1975) (no lender liability for wrongful death for financing sale of automobile for incompetent unlicensed driver); Fox & Carskadon Financial Corp. v. San Francisco Federal

tion has usually been based on the lack of extensive involvement of the lender in the project,[12] although neither *Connor* nor its progeny make it very clear just how far a lender's activity must go to move within the zone of liability. Perhaps most courts would track the facts of *Connor* itself, requiring both land warehousing and a referral scheme for permanent loans, or some similarly intimate involvement. Although one court has suggested that the *Connor* theory represents a minority view,[13] several decisions have adopted the *Connor* rationale—or at least suggested that it might be applied—to subject lenders to liability in a variety of circumstances not involving physical defects in new construction as *Connor* did.

In Jeminson v. Montgomery Real Estate and Co.[14] a Michigan home purchaser who had abandoned her home as uninhabitable sued the real estate broker and the mortgagee for fraudulent misrepresentation in the sale. The plaintiff alleged that the lender knew she was on welfare and was relatively uneducated and commercially inexperienced. She further alleged that the lender both knew that the real estate broker was unscrupulous and was aware of facts giving rise to the fraud. Relying on *Connor,* the plaintiff concluded that since the lender "knew or should have known all of these facts, it made itself an integral and necessary part of the fraudulent transaction when it entered into the mortgage loan agreement with plaintiff."[15] Reversing the appellate court, the Michigan supreme court indicated that these allegations stated a cause of action against the lender.

Savings & Loan Association, 52 Cal.App.3d 484, 125 Cal.Rptr. 549 (1975) (no lender liability to apartment building purchaser who lost equity in foreclosure); Skerlec v. Wells Fargo Bank National Association, 18 Cal.App.3d 1003, 96 Cal.Rptr. 434 (1971) (no lender liability in tort to plaintiff injured in collision where lender knew automobile purchaser could not comply with financial responsibility laws); Bradler v. Craig, 274 Cal.App.2d 466, 79 Cal.Rptr. 401 (1969) (no liability in lender for construction defects in house in the absence of extraordinary lender involvement in the project); First Federal Savings Bank v. Hart, 185 Ga.App. 304, 363 S.E.2d 832 (1987) (construction lender on condominium project owned no duty to unit purchasers to disclose construction defects to them); Callaizakis v. Astor Development Co., 4 Ill.App.3d 163, 280 N.E.2d 512 (1972) (no lender liability to condominium purchasers for structural defects in the absence of *Connor*-like facts); Bill Stremmel Motors, Inc. v. IDS Leasing Corp., 89 Nev. 414, 514 P.2d 654 (1973) (financing agent not liable for acts of equipment seller unless agent knows of wrongful acts and induces others to utilize services of the seller); L.A. Christiansen v. Philcent Corp., 226 Pa.Super. 157, 313 A.2d 249 (1973) (no lender liability to home purchasers for construction defects in absence of *Connor*-like facts). See also Flamingo Drift Fishing, Inc. v. Nix, 251 So.2d 316 (Fla.App.1971) (lender's employment of inspector to supervise construction of fishing vessel did not impose obligation on bank toward the purchaser).

12. Wierzbicki v. Alaska Mutual Savings Bank, 630 P.2d 998 (Alaska 1981); Murry v. Western American Mortgage Co., 124 Ariz. 387, 604 P.2d 651 (1979); Armetta v. Clevetrust Realty Investors, 359 So.2d 540, 543 (Fla.App.1978), certiorari denied 366 So.2d 879 (Fla.1978); Harden v. Akridge, 193 Ga.App. 736, 389 S.E.2d 6 (1989); Butts v. Atlanta Fed. Sav. & Loan Ass'n, 152 Ga.App. 40, 262 S.E.2d 230 (1979); Clark v. Grover, 132 Mich.App. 476, 347 N.W.2d 748 (1984); Allison v. Home Savings Association, 643 S.W.2d 847 (Mo.App. 1982); DeBry v. Valley Mortg. Co., 835 P.2d 1000 (Utah App. 1992).

13. See Wright v. United States, 428 F.Supp. 782, 789 (D.Mont.1977), affirmed 599 F.2d 304 (9th Cir.1979).

14. 396 Mich. 106, 240 N.W.2d 205 (1976). The facts are reported at 47 Mich. App. 731, 210 N.W.2d 10 (1973).

15. 210 N.W.2d at 15 (dissenting opinion).

Another application of the *Connor* rule was suggested in Morrocco v. Felton.[16] In that case, a New Jersey landlord brought a summary dispossession action against several tenants. The tenants responded by filing a motion to remove the dispossession action and by suing the landlord and mortgagees for breach of an implied warranty of habitability. The court focused on procedural matters, but it observed by way of dicta that, under the *Connor* rationale, liability for maintaining decent dwellings may extend to the lender. "[I]t may well be necessary," said the court, "to join third parties. Especially where the property in question is heavily mortgaged, some determination on the mortgagee's liability appears appropriate."[17]

Without explicitly relying on *Connor*, a federal court ruled that construction lenders can be liable for fraud in connection with the purchase of subdivision lots. In Timmreck v. Munn,[18] 328 plaintiffs alleged fraud in the sale of subdivision lots, arguing that investment contracts were involved and that a violation of federal securities laws had occurred. They also claimed violations of the Interstate Land Sales Full Disclosure Act.[19] The plaintiffs alleged that the bank financing the project's construction had entered into an accord with the developers and had allowed itself to be held out to the public as the financial backer of the project. In moving to dismiss the action under the Disclosure Act, the bank contended that section 1709 of the Act limited actions to those brought against developers and their agents. The bank claimed it was neither. Responding to this defense, the court noted that a bank would not be subject to the Act in the normal course of its business, but that if it went beyond this, the bank could be liable.[20] The court ruled that

> plaintiffs are therefore entitled to attempt to show that the Bank exceeded the normal scope of financing practices and actively participated in and aided the advancement of a fraudulent scheme, or otherwise assisted in the luring of purchasers for an allegedly dubious project.[21]

Lender liability could arise in other contexts as well.[22] Tort actions might be brought against lenders heavily involved in construction

---

16. 112 N.J.Super. 226, 270 A.2d 739 (1970).

17. 270 A.2d at 743.

18. 433 F.Supp. 396 (N.D.Ill.1977).

19. 15 U.S.C.A. § 1701 et seq.

20. Essentially the same rule was suggested in Zachery v. Treasure Lake of Georgia, Inc., 374 F.Supp. 251 (N.D.Ga. 1974). In *Zachery*, the court found that only a lender-borrower relationship existed between the lender and the developer. The lender was therefore not liable for misrepresentation under the Interstate Land Sales Full Disclosure Act. Even a public financing agency can be found to be a developer; see California Housing Finance Agency v. Elliott, 17 Cal.3d 575, 131 Cal.Rptr. 361, 551 P.2d 1193 (1976).

21. 433 F.Supp. at 406.

22. A similar theory of close-connectedness has been used to prevent financial institutions from achieving holder in due course status. See, e.g., Commercial Credit Corp. v. Orange County Machine Works, 34 Cal.2d 766, 214 P.2d 819 (1950); see § 5.29 supra.

§ 12.11   FINANCING REAL ESTATE CONSTRUCTION   267

projects when construction defects contribute to personal injuries.[23] Governmental agencies might cite lenders for building code violations if they go beyond the usual scope of financing in connection with a non-complying structure. Creative plaintiffs could imagine other approaches. The potential for lender liability under a *Connor* theory is real.[24] Even though the case has been frequently distinguished, its theory has been occasionally applied to impose liability on financial institutions who operate outside the scope of normal lending activity.

Even if the construction lender's involvement in the project is not sufficient to actuate *Connor*-type liability, a lender who is making disbursement to a party other than the borrower (typically the general contractor) may still have a duty to terminate making draws available when the borrower so demands. The lender's failure to respond to the borrower's urgings resulted in its being held liable in Davis v. Nevada National Bank,[25] in which the borrower made repeated complaints that the contractor was performing defective work. The court held the lender liable for the cost of correcting the defects.

When a lender conceals from a buyer information about the property that the lender has obtained from third parties, there is considerable precedent for lender liability. These cases usually involve long-term lenders, not construction loans. In one case a lender was charged for not revealing the results of a termite inspection;[26] in another, for not disclosing that the property was in a federally-designated flood hazard

---

23. For a case rejecting application of the *Connor* rule in such a situation, see Wright v. United States, 428 F.Supp. 782 (D.Mont.1977), affirmed 599 F.2d 304 (9th Cir.1979).

24. The California legislature made a somewhat ambiguous attempt to reverse or limit *Connor*:

A lender who makes a loan of money [for construction purposes] * * * shall not be held liable to third persons for any loss or damage occasioned by a defect in the * * * property * * * unless such loss or damage is a result of an act of the lender outside the scope of the activities of a lender of money or unless the lender has been a party to misrepresentations with respect to such * * * property.

West's Ann.Cal.Civ.Code § 3434. The statute may be read as merely restating the result in *Connor*, but if this is its intent it is superfluous. In any event it is hardly a model of legislative drafting, and adds nothing to the clarity of the law in California.

See Gutierrez, Liability of a Construction Lender Under Civil Code Section 3434: An Amorphous Epitaph to Connor v. Great Western Savings & Loan Association, 8 Pac.L.J. 1 (1977).

Equally opaque is Nev.Rev.Stat. 41.590, also apparently enacted as a response to *Connor*. It provides that a construction lender shall not be liable for construction defects "unless the loss or damage is the result of some other action or activity of the lender than the loan transaction." The Nevada statute was held inapplicable in Davis v. Nevada Nat. Bank, 103 Nev. 220, 737 P.2d 503 (1987), discussed infra at note 25. See also Vernon's Ann.Mo.Stat. § 369.264; U.L.T.A. § 2–310 (construction lender is not liable, "solely by reason of making the loan," for construction defects).

25. 103 Nev. 220, 737 P.2d 503 (1987). See also Daniels v. Army Nat. Bank, 249 Kan. 654, 822 P.2d 39 (1991), agreeing with the rationale of the *Davis* case but distinguishing it on the ground that the plaintiff in *Daniels* had never specifically requested that the lender withhold further disbursements.

26. Miles v. Perpetual Sav. & Loan Co., 58 Ohio St.2d 93, 388 N.E.2d 1364 (1979).

area.[27] On the other hand, the cases have consistently refused to impose on lenders a duty to advise borrowers about the business risks of transactions.[28] Where an appraiser or inspector employed by the lender has negligently failed to identify or report defects in the property, the cases are divided; California and Vermont have taken the view that the work is done only to protect the lender's interests, so that no duty is owed to the borrower.[29] On the other hand, courts in Iowa and Wisconsin have concluded that the borrower's reliance on the appraisal is to be expected, and have held the lender responsible for the appraiser's negligence.[30] The latter holdings are probably counterproductive to borrowers' interests in the long run; their likely effect is to cause lenders to withhold all appraisal and inspection reports and data from their borrowers, thus reducing the amount of useful information available to real estate purchasers.[31]

Finally, a construction lender who takes over a project upon the borrower's default, and who completes and markets it in order to liquidate the debt, is subject to a high risk of liability for building defects that arise after the lender assumes control, assuming that the original developer would have been liable for such defects under applicable law.[32] A Florida court extended this liability to "patent" defects in the project arising before the lender took over as well.[33] This is a

---

27. Small v. South Norwalk Sav. Bank, 205 Conn. 751, 535 A.2d 1292 (1988). But see Holland Mortg. & Invest. Corp. v. Bone, 751 S.W.2d 515 (Tex.App.1987), error refused n.r.e. (where lender's inspection did not reveal flood risk, and lender made no representations whatever to buyer, lender was not liable).

28. Wagner v. Benson, 101 Cal.App.3d 27, 34–35, 161 Cal.Rptr. 516 (1980); Fox & Carskadon Financial Corp. v. San Francisco Fed. Sav. & Loan Ass'n, 52 Cal.App.3d 484, 488, 489, 125 Cal.Rptr. 549 (1975); Shea v. H.S. Pickrell Co., 106 N.M. 683, 686, 748 P.2d 980, 983 (App.1987); Northeast Savings v. Rodriguez, 159 A.D.2d 820, 553 N.Y.S.2d 490 (1990), appeal dismissed 76 N.Y.2d 889, 561 N.Y.S.2d 550, 562 N.E.2d 875 (1990).

29. Nymark v. Heart Fed. Sav. & Loan Ass'n, 231 Cal.App.3d 1089, 283 Cal.Rptr. 53 (1991); Hughes v. Holt, 140 Vt. 38, 435 A.2d 687 (1981).

30. Larsen v. United Fed. Sav. & Loan Ass'n, 300 N.W.2d 281 (Iowa 1981); Costa v. Neimon, 123 Wis.2d 410, 366 N.W.2d 896 (App.1985). See also Barry v. Raskov, 283 Cal.Rptr. 463, 232 Cal.App.3d 447 (1991), holding a mortgage loan broker to have a fiduciary duty to the *lender*, an inexperienced private investor, and hence imposing liability for the broker's failure to warn the lender that the property's appraisal was inflated.

31. Indeed, the Iowa supreme court relied specifically on the fact that the borrower was given access to the appraisal report:

> Even though the appraisal might be made primarily for the benefit of the lending institution, the appraiser should also reasonably expect the home purchaser, who pays for the appraisal and to whom the results are reported (and who has access to the written report on request), will rely on the appraisal to reaffirm his or her belief the home is worth the price he or she offered for it.

300 N.W.2d at 287.

32. See Kennedy v. Columbia Lumber & Mfg. Co., 299 S.C. 335, 384 S.E.2d 730 (1989); Van Atta, What Every Developer's Successor Should Know (with Form), Prac. Real Est.Law., July 1990, at 25; Ferguson, Lender's Liability for Construction Defects, 11 Real Est.L.J. 310 (1983). See also Roundtree Villas Ass'n, Inc. v. 4701 Kings Corp., 282 S.C. 415, 321 S.E.2d 46 (1984) (construction lender's mere monitoring of project, and selling units after taking deed in lieu of foreclosure, did not give rise to lender liability).

33. Port Sewall Harbor and Tennis Club Owners Association v. First Federal Savings & Loan Association of Martin County, 463 So.2d 530 (Fla.App.1985).

heavy burden, for the lender may be quite unaware of errors made by the project's designers and contractors before the borrower's default. It is not yet clear whether all courts would go so far.[34]

Government Agency Liability for Construction Defects

When government agencies such as the Federal Housing Administration (FHA), Veterans Administration (VA), and Farmers Home Administration (FmHA) make direct loans to home buyers, or guarantee or insure loans made by private lenders,[35] they generally appraise and inspect the property to ensure that it meets their standards of physical quality. Since the agency in question may well end up owning the property and attempting to market it,[36] this concern is entirely logical as a matter of self-protection. However, the buyer of the property may also claim to have relied on the government inspection, and if it was done carelessly or improperly, may bring an action against the agency for damages in the amount necessary to correct the defects that the appraisal or inspection should have disclosed.

Until recently, such actions nearly always failed. The agencies' defenses were generally based on (1) the notion that the government's inspections were only made on its own behalf, and were not intended to benefit the buyer;[37] and (2) that the Federal Tort Claims Act (FTCA),[38] which provides a limited waiver of sovereign immunity for actions against the Federal government, contains an exception for torts based on misrepresentation, and that claims for inadequate inspection fell within that exception.[39]

---

34. See McKnight v. Board of Directors, 32 Ohio St.3d 6, 512 N.E.2d 316 (1987), where a mortgagee who accepted a deed in lieu of foreclosure was held to have assumed the role of developer when it became engaged in the development and promotion of the property beyond those steps necessary to salvage its interest in the property. As a result, the mortgagee was held bound by the Ohio statute limiting the number of association directors who could be elected by the developer.

35. See generally § 11.2, infra, concerning the mortgage insurance and guaranty functions of these agencies.

36. In the case of an insured or guaranteed loan, the agency will usually pay the claim and take title to the property from the foreclosing lender; it will then attempt to remarket the property. Obviously construction defects may impair the agency's ability to sell for an adequate price.

37. See, e.g., Davis v. Romney, 490 F.2d 1360 (3d Cir.1974); Stanley v. Veterans Administration, 454 F.Supp. 9 (E.D.Pa. 1978); Baker v. Surman, 361 N.W.2d 108 (Minn.App.1985). See Mallory, Lender Liability for Negligent Real Estate Appraisals, 1984 U.Ill.L.Rev. 53.

38. 28 U.S.C.A. § 2680.

39. The landmark case is United States v. Neustadt, 366 U.S. 696, 81 S.Ct. 1294, 6 L.Ed.2d 614 (1961). See also Schneider v. United States, 936 F.2d 956 (7th Cir.1991), certiorari denied ___ U.S. ___, 112 S.Ct. 965, 117 L.Ed.2d 131 (1992); Summers v. United States, 510 F.2d 123, 125 (8th Cir.1975), certiorari denied 423 U.S. 851, 96 S.Ct. 95, 46 L.Ed.2d 75 (1975); Scott v. First Investment Co., 556 F.Supp. 782 (W.D.Pa.1983); Provencal v. Michel Construction, Inc., 505 F.Supp. 770 (W.D.Mich.1980); Cason v. United States, 381 F.Supp. 1362, 1367 (W.D.Mo.1974), affirmed 510 F.2d 123 (8th Cir.1975), certiorari denied 423 U.S. 851, 96 S.Ct. 95, 46 L.Ed.2d 75 (1975); Emmons v. Brown, 600 N.E.2d 133 (Ind.App.1992); Gay v. Broder, 109 Cal.App.3d 66, 167 Cal.Rptr. 123 (1980). See generally Annot., 30 A.L.R.Fed. 421.

However, two theories developed in recent years have the potential for overcoming these objections. One of them is based on a contract, inferred from the agency's regulations, to make the necessary inspections in a proper manner. For a claim sounding in contract, the FTCA and its limitations are irrelevant.[40] However, only the regulations of FmHA have been held to comprise such a contract,[41] and even those regulations have subsequently been amended to negate the contract theory quite effectively.[42]

A more fruitful attack may be based on the tort of negligent performance of an assumed duty, the so-called "Good Samaritan" doctrine. Even though the agency has no duty to inspect, if it undertakes to do so voluntarily, it may be liable for negligence in carrying out the inspection.[43] In Block v. Neal,[44] the Supreme Court held that the gravamen of this sort of tort claim lay in the faulty performance of the inspection rather than in faulty communication to the borrower of its results. Hence, it was not barred by the FTCA's exception for misrepresentation. But subsequent plaintiffs have not had much success in relying on *Block*; the federal courts have limited it to cases in which the government actively and negligently supervised construction of the improvements on the real estate, and thereby failed to prevent the defects from arising.[45]

40. For contract claims, the relevant waiver of sovereign immunity is the Tucker Act, 28 U.S.C.A. § 1346. Claims thereunder must be brought in the Court of Claims if the amount in controversy exceeds $10,000.

41. Kipf v. United States, 501 F.Supp. 110 (D.Mont.1980). See also Navarro v. United States, 586 F.Supp. 799 (D.V.I. 1984), apparently acknowledging the contract claims but declining jurisdiction because they exceeded the $10,000 Tucker Act limit. Cf. Scott v. First Investment Corp., 556 F.Supp. 782 (W.D.Pa.1983), distinguishing the HUD regulations from those of FmHA and rejecting the contract theory of agency liability.

42. See 7 CFR 1924.9, effective June 12, 1980; the amended regulations state explicitly that "FmHA's inspections are not to assure the borrower that the house is built in accordance with the plans and specifications. The inspections create or imply no duty or obligation to the particular borrower * * *."

43. See Restatement (Second) of Torts § 323 (1965); cf. Raynor v. United States, 604 F.Supp. 205 (D.N.J.1984), in which the Department of Housing and Urban Development was held not liable under the "Good Samaritan Doctrine" for improperly performed winterizing of a house, where HUD had inspected the property and either found no defect or failed to inform prospective purchasers of the defect; Clark v. Grover, 132 Mich.App. 476, 347 N.W.2d 748 (1984).

44. 460 U.S. 289, 103 S.Ct. 1089, 75 L.Ed.2d 67 (1983). See also Kirk v. United States, 604 F.Supp. 1474 (D.N.H.1985); Martin v. Block, 571 F.Supp. 1180 (D.V.I. 1983); Park v. United States, 517 F.Supp. 970 (D.Or.1981). The doctrine applies only if the plaintiff actually relied on the faulty inspection; see Bonuchi v. U.S., 827 F.2d 377 (8th Cir.1987). In Schneider v. United States, 936 F.2d 956 (7th Cir.1991), certiorari denied ___ U.S. ___, 112 S.Ct. 965, 117 L.Ed.2d 131 (1992), the plaintiff's counsel conceded that the inspection of the builder's factory approximately two times per year for two to three hours by a HUD official was "irrelevant" to the disposition of the case. The court concluded that it was the *communication* of false information, and not the inspections, that formed the basis of the plaintiff's case; hence, the misrepresentation exemption in the FTCA controlled, and the dismissal of the complaint was affirmed.

45. Luckinbill v. United States, 735 F.Supp. 155 (M.D.Pa.1990) (finding that FmHA took over active supervision of construction, and holding the government liable). Cases finding no liability include Hamre v. United States, 799 F.2d 455 (8th Cir.1986): "Any negligent inspection of the premises could not have caused their inju-

§ 12.11 FINANCING REAL ESTATE CONSTRUCTION

Moreover, the benefits to plaintiffs of the *Block* case have been largely eliminated by regulatory amendments. Both FHA and FmHA have declared that their inspections are solely for the government's protection and give rise to no duty or obligation to the mortgagor.[46] This languages appears to exclude quite effectively any duty of careful inspection, whether based on tort or contract, and several courts have so held.[47] Tort claims against VA may still be viable.

Other barriers stand in the way of aggrieved plaintiffs as well. A claim under the FTCA must be filed within a defined period after it arises, in written form, and with specific supporting evidence.[48] Moreover, Congress has enacted provisions giving monetary relief to homebuyers who purchase new houses under the principal federal programs and discover that they have serious structural defects.[49] There are many constraints on recovery under these provisions, and no judicial review is available. Several decisions have held that if a claim is within their scope, they constitute the exclusive remedy and no action for improper inspection will lie.[50] The Supreme Court expressly left this issue undecided in Block v. Neal. Ideally, it should be resolved by Congress.

---

ries, for the defects, if any, were present before the inspection was made."; Maple Hill Apartment v. Pierce, 798 F.2d 1415 (6th Cir.1986): "The District Court found no evidence that HUD undertook to inspect for Maple Hill's benefit, foreclosing the possibility of a good samaritan argument."; Kynerd v. U.S. Dept. of Housing and Urban Development, 607 F.Supp. 117 (D.Miss.1985), affirmed 806 F.2d 259 (5th Cir.1986) (no reliance, where plaintiff did not examine government reports until four years after purchasing the house). But see Pierre v. United States, 741 F.Supp. 306 (D.Mass.1990) (HUD liable for negligence in not properly removing lead-based paint from house before selling it to plaintiff).

46. See 7 CFR 1924.9 (FmHA); 24 CFR 200.145 (FHA).

47. Moody v. United States, 585 F.Supp. 286 (E.D.Tenn.1984), affirmed 774 F.2d 150 (6th Cir.1985), certiorari denied 479 U.S. 814, 107 S.Ct. 65, 93 L.Ed.2d 24 (1986); Cash v. United States, 571 F.Supp. 513 (N.D.Ga.1983).

48. See 28 CFR Part 14; Navarro v. United States, 586 F.Supp. 799 (D.V.I. 1984), rejecting a claim against FmHA because it was not filed with agency within the prescribed 2 year period.

49. See 12 U.S.C.A. § 1735b (FHA); 38 U.S.C.A. § 1827 (VA); 42 U.S.C.A. § 1479(c) (FmHA). See Note, Federal Compensation for Victims of the "Homeownership for the Poor" Program, 84 Yale L.J. 294 (1974).

50. See Summers v. United States, 510 F.2d 123 (8th Cir.1975), certiorari denied 423 U.S. 851, 96 S.Ct. 95, 46 L.Ed.2d 75 (1975). Cf. Martin v. Block, 571 F.Supp. 1180 (D.V.I.1983), suggesting that the compensation scheme is not the exclusive remedy.

§§ 12.12—13.0 are reserved for supplementary material.

Chapter 13

FINANCING CONDOMINIUMS AND COOPERATIVES

Table of Sections

Sec.
13.1 An Overview of Condominiums and Cooperatives.
13.2 Financing Condominiums and Cooperatives.
13.3 Construction Financing of Condominiums.
13.4 Financing Conversions to Condominium and Cooperative Status.
13.5 Permanent Financing of Condominium Units.
13.6 Permanent Financing of Cooperative Units.

§ 13.1 An Overview of Condominiums and Cooperatives

This chapter deals with legal issues relating to the financing of condominiums and cooperatives. While space does not permit a detailed treatment of the non-financing aspects of these forms of ownership, a brief overview of the legal relationships involved will preface discussion of the central topic.[1]

Both condominiums and cooperatives are legal formats for "unit ownership"—that is, the ownership of a physically defined portion of a larger parcel of (usually improved) real property. In the majority of cases, the "unit" is a residential apartment in a multifamily housing project. Condominiums are much more tightly controlled by state legislation than are cooperatives, and in most states the original stat-

---

§ 13.1

1. The most complete and useful treatment of such non-financing areas is P. Rohan & M. Reskin, Condominium Law & Practice (1976). Other works include D. Clurman & E. Hebard, Condominiums and Cooperatives (1969); A. Ferrer & K. Stecher, Law of Condominium (1967); P. Rohan & M. Reskin, Cooperative Housing Law and Practice (1975); and K. Romney, Condominium Development Guide (1974). Law journal symposia on condominium issues include 55 Fla.B.J. (Feb.1981); 10 Wm.Mitch.L.Rev. 1 (1984); and 48 St. John's L.Rev. 677 (1974).

utes, which date in most cases from the 1960s, recognized only residential condominium projects. More recently, many states have amended their statutes to permit the creation of condominiums in non-residential property, including commercial and industrial buildings, and even on unimproved land.[2] There are no significant legal barriers to non-residential cooperative ownership, although it is quite rare.

In most cases the owner of a condominium or cooperative unit is also a participant in an organization of owners that has responsibility for the operation, maintenance, and management of the "common areas"—features of the building or project which are used or available for use by all unit owners, such as exterior walls, roofs, lobbies, stairwells, elevators, grounds and landscaping, and often recreational facilities. The principal distinctions between condominiums and cooperatives are discussed below.

The Condominium

The term "condominium" is variously used to refer to the underlying concept, the building, or the individual unit; in this chapter, it refers to the building. In a condominium, each owner holds fee simple title to his or her unit directly. In addition, each unit owner holds an undivided fractional share in the common areas of the project as a tenant in common.[3] Management and maintenance of these common facilities are performed by an owners' association, which may be incorporated or unincorporated.[4] The fractional shares in the common areas and the vote of each member of the association are assigned on some equitable basis, such as the number of square feet in the unit or its proportionate share of the original value of all units.[5] The associa-

---

2. The model act on which many early American statutes were based used the term "apartment," presumably implying residential use; see Federal Housing Administration, Model Statute for the Creation of Apartment Ownership § 2(a), reprinted in G. Nelson & D. Whitman, Real Estate Transfer, Finance and Development 901 (1981) [hereinafter cited as FHA Model Act]. Examples of much broader definitions that permit non-residential uses include Uniform Condominium Act ("U.C.A.") § 1–103(25) (1980); Alaska Stat. 34.07.450(1); 60 Okl.Stat.Supp.1976, § 503(b); Va.Code 1950, § 55–79.2(a). See P. Rohan & M. Reskin, Condominium Law and Practice § 5.01[2] (1976). On non-residential condominiums, see generally, D. Clurman, The Business Condominium (1973); Note, Commercial Condominiums: Statutory Roadblocks to Development, 34 U.Fla.L.Rev. 432 (1982); Lundquist, Mixed Use Condominiums under the Minnesota Uniform Condominium Act, 10 Wm.Mitch. L.Rev. 97 (1984).

Condominiums on raw land are still problematic under some statutes; see Bonner Properties, Inc. v. Planning Board, 185 N.J.Super. 553, 449 A.2d 1350 (1982); Prestwick Landowners' Association v. Underhill, 69 Ohio App.2d 45, 429 N.E.2d 1191 (1980).

3. This distinguishes the condominium from the planned unit development ("P.U.D."), in which the owners association holds title to the common areas. See Country Greens Village One Owner's Association v. Meyers, 158 Ga.App. 609, 281 S.E.2d 346 (1981).

4. Most associations are incorporated; see Hyatt, Condominium and Home Owner Associations: Formation and Development, 24 Emory L.J. 977 (1975); Jackson, Why You Should Incorporate a Homeowners Association, 3 Real Est.L.J. 311 (1975); Krasnowiecki, Townhouses with Homes Association: A New Perspective, 123 U.Pa.L.Rev. 711 (1975).

5. See Reichman, Residential Private Governments: An Introductory Survey, 43 U.Chi.L.Rev. 253 (1976). Under the Uniform Condominium Act, expenses, voting

tion may assert a lien on each unit to enforce the owner's obligation to pay his or her share of the assessments levied by the association for management, maintenance, insurance, reserves for replacements, and the like.[6]

There is little question that a form of unit ownership similar to the condominium concept can be developed by careful structuring of documents in the absence of an authorizing statute. This has been done in many countries and continues today in England.[7] However, every jurisdiction in the United States has enacted a condominium statute that attempts to regularize procedures, spell out the duties and obligations of the unit owners and the association, provide for such eventualities as damage, destruction, and condemnation of the condominium, and provide legal confirmation of the association's lien rights against delinquent unit owners.[8] The statutes also provide for separate property tax assessment on each unit and prohibit partitioning of the common areas. Most of the original statutes were based heavily on model legislation drafted by the Federal Housing Administration. The statutes were helpful in standardizing relationships and protecting unit owners from some forms of overreaching, but they were unnecessarily restrictive in many respects and a "second generation" of statutes, which generally provide far greater flexibility in the legal structuring of the development, as well as more extensive consumer protection, has been enacted in many states.[9] In 1977 the Commissioners on Uniform Laws promulgated the Uniform Condominium Act, a second-generation statute that attracted widespread interest. They followed it in 1985 with the Uniform Common Interest Ownership Act, which largely repeats the provisions of the UCA but also governs real estate cooperatives and planned unit developments.[10]

rights, and common area ownership can each be based on a different formula; see U.C.A. § 2–107 (1980).

6. See Jackson, Homeowners Associations: Remedies to Enforce Assessment Collections, 51 L.A.B.J. 423 (1976).

7. See 1 P. Rohan & M. Reskin, Condominium Law and Practice, ch. 4 (1976); Leyser, The Ownership of Flats—A Comparative Study, 7 Int'l & Comp.L.Q. 31 (1958).

8. In several recent cases, unit owners have attempted to raise the homestead exemption as a defense to foreclosure of the association's lien. See Inwood North Homeowners' Ass'n v. Harris, 736 S.W.2d 632 (Tex.1987) (homestead statute provides no defense against foreclosure of non-condominium homeowners association lien, where the lien preexisted the homestead status of the property); Johnson v. First Southern Properties, 687 S.W.2d 399 (Tex. App.1985) (accord, condominium association lien). But see Pinebrook Homeowners Ass'n v. Owen, 48 Wash.App. 424, 739 P.2d 110 (1987), review denied 48 Wash.App. 424 (1987), rejecting the position of the Texas cases, concluding that there is no applicable exemption in the Washington statute, and holding that a homestead claim is a valid defense to foreclosure of a non-condominium homeowners association lien.

9. Leaders in this movement include West's Fla.Stat.Ann. §§ 718.101–718.508, discussed in Comment, 8 U.Mich.J.L.Ref. 387 (1975) and 27 U.Miami L.Rev. 451 (1973); Utah Code Ann.1953, 57–8–1 through 57–8–36; Va.Code §§ 55–79.01 to 55–79.103 discussed in Comment, 9 U.Richmond L.Rev. 135 (1974) and Johnakin, A Second Generation of Condominium Statutes, Lawyers Title News, May–June 1974, at 3. See generally Cannella, Recent Innovations in State Condominium Legislation, 48 St.John's L.Rev. 994 (1974).

10. The UCA and its successor, the Uniform Common Interest Ownership Act (UCIOA), which applies to cooperatives and

The Cooperative

In a cooperative the entire project, including the individual units and the common areas, is owned by a single entity, usually a corporation (often organized on a non-profit basis).[11] Persons who purchase units in the cooperative receive, as evidence of their interests, two documents: a "proprietary lease" establishing the member's right of possession in the particular apartment, and a stock certificate, evidencing ownership of a share or shares in the corporation. The documents usually provide that ownership of the stock and the tenant's interest in the proprietary lease are inseparable.

In most cooperatives, each apartment's owners have a single vote, rather than a vote apportioned by value or size as with condominiums. The functions of the corporation are similar to those of the owners' association in a condominium, but are more extensive. Since the cooperative corporation owns the project, it will normally be the mortgagor on one or more blanket mortgages covering the building. The "rent" paid by tenants under their proprietary leases must be sufficient to cover the cost of servicing this debt and the property taxes on the project in addition to such management, maintenance, and other expenses and reserves as would be expected in a condominium. Both condominium [12] and cooperative unit owners are entitled to deduct the portion of their monthly payments attributable to mortgage interest and real estate taxes, although this privilege is available to cooperative members only if at least 80% of the gross income of the corporation is derived from payments by tenant-stockholders.[13]

planned unit developments as well as condominiums, has been adopted in Alaska, Arizona, Colorado, Connecticut, Maine, Minnesota, Missouri, Nebraska, New Mexico, North Carolina, Pennsylvania, Rhode Island, and West Virginia. See Geis, Beyond the Condominium: The Uniform Common–Interest Ownership Act, Part I, Fla.B.J., Feb.1985, at 67; Part II, Fla.B.J., Mar.1985, at 35; Note, North Carolina Adopts the Uniform Condominium Act, 66 N.C.L.Rev. 199 (1987); Fisher, The Model Real Estate Cooperative Act: A Critique, 12 Real Est.L.J. 53 (1983). In addition, several jurisdictions have "borrowed" the UCA's or UCIOA's treatment of specific issues and incorporated it into their existing statutes; see, e.g., D.C.Code 1981, § 45–1853.

11. Although corporate ownership of cooperatives is by far the most common format, trust and tenancy-in-common ownership are also possible and have been used occasionally. See Future Federal Savings & Loan Association v. Daunhauer, 687 S.W.2d 871 (Ky.App.1985); P. Rohan & M. Reskin, Cooperative Housing Law and Practice § 201 (1975). I.R.C. § 216(b)(1)(c), which permits deduction of mortgage interest and property taxes by cooperative owners, is satisfied only if "no stockholder * * * is entitled to receive any distribution not out of earnings and profits of the corporation except on a complete or partial liquidation of the corporation." See the description of Co-op City by the Court in United Housing Foundation, Inc. v. Forman, 421 U.S. 837, 840, 95 S.Ct. 2051, 2054, 44 L.Ed.2d 621 (1975), rehearing denied 423 U.S. 884, 96 S.Ct. 157, 46 L.Ed.2d 115 (1975).

For a readable brief history of the cooperative housing movement in New York, see Gray, The "Revolution" of 1881 Is Now In Its 2d Century, New York Times, Oct. 28, 1984, at 61.

12. Rev.Rul. 64–31, 1964–1 C.B. 300.

13. See I.R.C. § 216, which imposes numerous other requirements on co-ops in addition to the 80% test; Short, Cooperative and Condominium Ownership Offers Benefits to Associations and Owners, 17 Tax. for Law. 208 (1989); Miller, The Impact of a Housing Cooperative's "Bad" Income on Its Members' Section 216(a) Deduction, Now and Under Proposed Legislation, 10 J.Real Est.Tax. 99 (1983); Cowan,

For federal tax purposes a cooperative member is treated much like the owner of a condominium or a detached house, assuming the requirements of the Internal Revenue Code are met. But for many other purposes the question remains: Is the cooperator's interest real or personal property? Since the cooperative is a unique kind of hybrid, answers to this question vary, depending on the view the courts take of the underlying policies. The characterization of the interest may be relevant for a wide variety of reasons, including the doctrine of restraints on alienation, rent control, ad valorem taxes, transfer taxes, conveyancing doctrines, construction of wills and of intestacy and judgment lien statutes, availability of title insurance, institutional financing,[14] summary eviction proceedings against members, and determination of the proper procedures for registering or recording transfers and creations of security interests, whether under the Uniform Commercial Code or realty recording acts. The answers of the courts in these contexts are far from uniform,[15] although there is no reason why the interest of a cooperative member should not be treated on a par with a condominium unit owner—as the owner of real property—for most purposes.

It is apparent that each member of a cooperative is somewhat more reliant upon the financial strength and honesty of his or her fellow members than is a condominium unit owner. If many members of a cooperative default, it may be impossible to meet the regular debt service payments on the blanket mortgage, which may consequently be foreclosed. In a condominium, by contrast, each unit owner arranges his own permanent financing on his apartment, and defaults by one's neighbors in the payment of monthly assessments, while possibly endangering the solvency of the owners' association, cannot directly trigger foreclosure by a lender of the unit belonging to a non-delinquent owner. On the other hand, it is probably easier for the member's

Working With New Rules for Condominiums, Cooperatives, and Homeowners Associations, 46 J.Taxation 204 (1977).

14. Whether cooperative financing involves real or personal property under the rules of financial regulatory agencies, and the procedures for perfecting liens on cooperative members' interests, are discussed in the text accompanying § 13.6, notes 14–28 infra.

15. See Comment, Legal Characterization of the Individual's Interest in a Cooperative Apartment: Realty or Personalty, 73 Colum.L.Rev. 250 (1973); P. Rohan & M. Reskin, Cooperative Housing Law and Practice, § 2.01[5] (1975). See Shulkin v. Dealy, 132 Misc.2d 371, 504 N.Y.S.2d 342 (1986) (UCC governs liquidated damages clause in contract to sell cooperative unit); Weiss v. Karch, 62 N.Y.2d 849, 477 N.Y.S.2d 615, 466 N.E.2d 155 (1984) (same). Cf. California Coastal Commission v. Quanta Investment Corp., 113 Cal.App.3d 579, 170 Cal.Rptr. 263 (1980) (cooperative conversion is a "division of land"); McMunn v. Steppingstone Mgmt. Corp., 131 Misc.2d 340, 500 N.Y.S.2d 219 (1986) (the usual landlord's duties of repair may be shifted to the tenant of a cooperative apartment by a clause in the proprietary lease); Penokie v. Colonial Townhouses Cooperative, Inc., 140 Mich.App. 740, 366 N.W.2d 31 (1985) (landlord-tenant act is inapplicable to cooperative apartments).

There is a further question: Is the cooperative member a tenant or an owner? See, e.g., Linden Hill No. 1 Cooperative Corp. v. Kleiner, 124 Misc.2d 1001, 478 N.Y.S.2d 519 (1984) (statute protecting tenant ownership of pets applies to cooperative member); Penokie v. Colonial Townhouses Cooperative, Inc., 140 Mich.App. 740, 366 N.W.2d 31 (1985) (statute governing refunds of tenants' security deposits does not apply to cooperative member).

organization to evict a delinquent owner and to realize on the security of the unit for unpaid assessments in a cooperative than in a condominium.[16]

Condominiums and cooperatives share many of the same economic and social advantages: economies of scale in the initial cost and maintenance of recreation, parking, and other community facilities; the potential for competent management of the common areas; and the benefits of security and social contact that result from relatively high-density occupancy, as well as the concomitant problems.[17] Since the advent of condominium statutes in most American jurisdictions, lending institutions and developers (and consequently consumers) have tended to prefer condominiums in most jurisdictions, and except in New York, relatively few new cooperatives are being built or converted from rental use.

§ 13.2 Financing Condominiums and Cooperatives

Condominium and cooperative financing differ from one another in important respects. A condominium project is much like a subdivision of detached houses; financing of construction is usually independent of the permanent or long-term financing of the sales of individual units.[1] The construction loan is typically secured by a blanket mortgage on the entire property, with provision for the release of each unit from that

---

16. The cooperative can treat the delinquent member as a tenant, terminate the lease for breach, and use unlawful detainer or other summary process to evict him or her; Martin v. Villa Roma, Inc., 131 Cal.App.3d 632, 182 Cal.Rptr. 382 (1982); Sun Terrace Manor v. Municipal Court, 33 Cal.App.3d 739, 108 Cal.Rptr. 307 (1973); Green v. Greenbelt Homes, Inc., 232 Md. 496, 194 A.2d 273 (1963). Cf. Moss v. Elofsson, 194 Ill.App.3d 256, 141 Ill.Dec. 182, 550 N.E.2d 1228 (1990) (tenant's lease may be terminated only upon a showing of a clear right to do so, and upon proof that forfeiture will not result in injustice). See Rohan, Cooperative Housing: An Appraisal of Residential Controls and Enforcement Procedures, 18 Stan.L.Rev. 1323 (1966), questioning whether such a severe remedy should be available for minor defaults or violations of the co-op's rules. Some cooperatives have not attempted to remove delinquent members from the project by declaring a strict foreclosure of the tenant's proprietary lease and stock under U.C.C. Article 9; see Saada v. Master Apts., Inc., 152 Misc.2d 861, 579 N.Y.S.2d 536 (1991), recognizing this remedy only if the cooperative corporation could show the existence of a specific security agreement actuating Article 9 remedies, but recognizing that possibly the proprietary lease itself could constitute such a security agreement.

In a condominium, by contrast, the usual remedy is foreclosure of the association's lien on the unit, an action which normally enjoys no calendar preference and may take many months to complete. In either case, of course, the association must follow its own rules and bylaws, and may also be subject to local statutes or ordinances; see Clydesdale, Inc. v. Wegener, 372 A.2d 1013 (D.C.App.1977).

17. See Shlopack, Condominium or Cooperative: Issues Facing the Developer, 55 Fla.B.J. 105 (1981); Comment, Community Living Condominium Style: Bed of Roses— Or Bed of Thorns?, 6 Univ.W.L.A.L.Rev. 121 (1974).

§ 13.2

1. See Pfeiler, Condominium Financing: Some Legal Basics, 38 Legal Bull. 249, 255–62 (1972) [hereinafter cited as Pfeiler]. Like most subdivision lenders, the condominium construction lender will usually require that a "take-out" or permanent loan commitment be obtained from another lender (or the permanent loan department of the same institution) before approving the construction loan. See Fegan, Condominium Financing, 48 St.John's L.Rev. 799 (1974) [hereinafter cited as Fegan].

mortgage as the units are sold by the developer to customers; the "partial release clause" in the construction mortgage will spell out the circumstances under which units will be released and the amount that must be applied toward retirement of the construction indebtedness for each unit sold.[2] The permanent mortgages placed on individual units by their purchasers are often arranged by the developer through a single lender, which may or may not be the mortgagee on the construction loan.[3] Alternatively, the purchasers may arrange their own financing through institutional lenders of their choice.

In the early years of American condominium development, it was often difficult for a unit purchaser to obtain a long-term loan from any lender other than the one with whom the developer had arranged the original permanent financing, since institutions were generally reluctant to undertake an extensive review of the complex documents unless they were certain that they could place numerous loans as a result.[4] However, since 1978, both the Federal National Mortgage Association (FNMA) and the Federal Home Loan Mortgage Corporation (FHLMC) have greatly simplified and streamlined their requirements for condominium loan purchases.[5] Once a project has been approved by these agencies, many lenders are usually willing to make loans on individual units in that project, since a secondary market for them is assured. Thus, the FNMA/FHLMC guidelines have become a *de facto* standard for permanent loans on condominium units.

Cooperatives are also financed with construction mortgages, but there are generally no individual loans to those who purchase the units

---

2. A common provision requires "presales" (executed contracts of sale to customers) on some fixed percentage of the units (say, 35% to 75%) before the construction lender will release the lien on any of the units. See Vishny, Financing the Condominium, 1970 Ill.L.F. 181 (1970). Similarly, the permanent lender may refuse to disburse funds until a specified percentage of the units have been presold; Fegan, supra note 1. The FNMA and FHLMC guidelines generally require 51% to 75% presales; see note 5 infra.

In imposing such requirements, lenders are concerned that they not be committed to financing the project as a condominium until they have substantial evidence of consumer demand; if the demand does not materialize, they may insist that the building be converted to rental use.

3. As an alternative to financing unit sales with new permanent mortgages, it is theoretically possible for the construction lender to take a separate mortgage on each unit, and to convert those mortgages to permanent status by loan assumptions as the units are sold to customers. This procedure is fairly common in some areas of the nation with subdivision development, but is not widely used with condominiums. It arguably violates § 14 of the FHA Model Act, which provides: "At the time of the first conveyance of each apartment, every mortgage and other lien affecting such apartment * * * shall be paid and satisfied of record * * *." There is no policy reason to prohibit assumptions of construction loans by unit purchasers, and the Model Act should not be so construed.

4. See Gose, Strum & Zinman, Real Estate Financing Techniques: What Now?, 9 Real Prop., Prob. & Tr.J. 617, 634 (1974). This lack of support from other institutions made it difficult for the original permanent lender to diversify its portfolio by declining to make resale loans as the units turned over later.

5. The current guidelines are discussed in Buck, Lending to PUDs—New Federal Guidelines, Prob. & Prop., Feb. 1990, at 25. See also Rosenthal, Condominium and P.U.D. Projects: Steps to Approval, Mortgage Banker, May 1984, at 57.

when construction is completed.[6] Instead, the construction loan may simply be converted to a permanent loan by the mortgagee—which means that it will begin to draw regular (usually monthly) payments of amortization and interest. At that point the construction loan may also be sold by the original mortgagee to another investor, particularly if the construction lender is a type of institution that prefers not to invest in long-term mortgages. Alternatively, the cooperative corporation may obtain a new blanket loan from a permanent lender and use the proceeds to discharge the construction loan. In either event, the permanent mortgage on a cooperative project is a blanket mortgage covering the entire property. Unit purchasers make down payments equal to the difference between the unit's market sales value and its pro-rata share of the blanket mortgage; in effect, they assume their shares of the mortgage.

The subsequent resale of an individual unit by one occupant to another also involves different treatment in condominiums than in cooperatives. In a condominium unit sale the existing mortgage may be assumed, taken subject to, or paid off by the unit purchaser with the proceeds of a new loan, just as in the sale of a detached house. By contrast, the sale of a cooperative unit amounts to an implicit "assumption" by the purchaser of that unit's pro rata share of the blanket mortgage on the project. Hence the cash paid by the purchaser of a resale cooperative unit may represent three components: (1) the original unit purchaser's down-payment; (2) the amortization of the blanket mortgage that has occurred since payments were commenced on it; and (3) any increase in value since the project was completed due to inflation or to improvements.[7]

Obviously, the longer the project is occupied the higher the cash investment required of a resale purchaser is likely to be, and the greater the difficulty the seller can anticipate in finding a buyer with sufficient cash and a willingness to invest it in the unit. The seller may be willing to take a promissory note from the purchaser in lieu of some part of this cash, and may be able to secure such a note with an interest in some real or personal property belonging to the purchaser.

---

6. Berger, Condominium: Shelter on a Statutory Foundation, 63 Colum.L.Rev. 987 (1963).

7. Some cooperatives limit the resale price by bylaw to the original down payment made by the seller, and others allow the seller to recoup only the cost of any improvements made (less depreciation), the seller's share of the blanket mortgage amortization, and some cost-of-living adjustment factor. These projects are usually termed "limited equity" cooperatives. The FHA insists on such resale price limits on the cooperatives whose mortgages it insures under some programs. The New York Supreme Court upheld these limits in Katz v. Nostrand Gardens Cooperative, Inc., May 2, 1984, reported in BNA Hsg & Devel. Rptr 1145 (May 21, 1984). See Bernstein–Baker, Cooperative Conversion: Is it Only for the Wealthy? Proposals that Promote Affordable Cooperative Housing in Philadelphia, 61 Temp. L. Rev. 393 (1988); FHA Model Form of Bylaws § 8(d), reproduced in J. Krasnoweicki, Housing and Urban Development 317, 323 (1969); National Comm'n. on Urban Problems, Building the American City 137 (1968). Many cooperatives impose no restrictions on resale prices at all.

But an installment sale by the unit owner may jeopardize the standing of the purchaser under I.R.C. § 216.[8]

The alternative, of course, is institutional financing for the resale purchaser. For a number of reasons, chiefly relating to questions about their statutory authority to do so, institutional lenders were traditionally reluctant to make loans on individual cooperative apartments. Starting with the New York legislation in 1971, a number of states have clarified that authority, and such loans are now widely available in states where housing cooperatives are popular.[9]

Whether the financing is provided by a financial institution or the seller of the unit, the creditor will normally desire a security interest in the unit. The usual approach involves a pledge of the proprietary lease and the stock—a transaction analogous to a mortgage on real estate. Since the blanket mortgage on the project cannot be disturbed, any security interest in an individual unit is economically analogous to a second mortgage. However, the legal effect of such a pledge is still uncertain on several points.[10]

It is quite possible that the corporation might decide to refinance the original blanket mortgage on the project; this might be done because the original mortgage is of the balloon type and has reached maturity,[11] because lower interest rates have become available, or because additional cash is needed for repairs or improvements. This

---

8. I.R.C. § 216(b)(2) defines a "tenant-shareholder" as one "whose stock is fully paid-up in an amount" reasonably related to the unit's share of the corporation's equity in the project. The applicable regulation, Treas.Reg. § 1.216–1(e), appears to say that this relationship is to be determined "as of the date of the original issuance of the stock". Arguably, an installment sale would qualify if the purchaser made a cash payment equal to the unit's share of the original equity, but this is not clear. Alternatively, the purchaser might structure the transaction so as to "fully pay" for the *stock* with cash, but to pay some additional amount, by way of a promissory note, for the assignment of the *proprietary lease*. The difficulty with this argument is that the stock and lease are invariably required by their own terms or the applicable corporate charter or bylaws to be held by the same person. In sum, whether any installment sale can qualify under § 216 is problematic. This is unfortunate, since there seems to be no policy reason whatever to make the tax benefits of § 216 hinge on an all-cash sale. See Miller, Tax Problems of the Housing Cooperative Under the 80% Income Rule, 18 Prac.Lawyer 81 (No. 4, Apr.1972); Jacobs & Kurfist, Cooperative Apartment Living and Loving—Part I, 7 J.Real Est.Tax. 307 (1980).

Since an installment purchaser is arguably not a "tenant-shareholder" it is entirely conceivable that a single installment sale could so reduce the total income from tenant-shareholders that the cooperative would cease to qualify under the 80% test of § 216.

9. See Goldstein, Institutional Purchase Money Financing of Cooperative Apartments, 46 St.Johns L.Rev. 632 (1972); § 13.6, infra.

10. See § 13.6, infra; P. Rohan & M. Reskin, Cooperative Housing Law & Practice § 5A.08[3] (1984).

11. While most buildings newly constructed for cooperative use are financed with fully-amortized mortgages, it is not unusual to find a balloon mortgage on a building converted from ordinary rental to co-op use. Indeed, if the interest rate on the existing mortgage is significantly below current rates at the time of conversion, it would be foolish to refinance at the time of conversion notwithstanding the balloon feature of the old loan. See Offering Statement, 72–84 Barrow Street, reprinted in 2A P. Rohan & M. Reskin, Cooperative Housing Law and Practice, at 245, 288 app. (1975).

last objective might also be achieved by the placement of a second blanket mortgage on the property without disturbing the first. Either refinancing or additional financing can result in higher monthly assessments on the members than they anticipated when they joined the cooperative. If an appropriate vote of the directors or members is forthcoming, the added assessments will be imposed on all members, whether they agree with the decision or not.[12] Thus, each member's financial future lies to some extent in the hands of his or her neighbors, a situation that some might think uncomfortable, and that is largely avoided by the condominium form of ownership.[13]

One should not assume that permanent financing is always essential to the sale of either condominiums or cooperatives. Especially in retirement developments, all-cash purchases are quite common, since many buyers have just sold larger detached houses, often at substantial gains. Retirees usually wish to reinvest these funds and find the purchase of a condominium or cooperative unit a convenient way of doing so. In addition, some luxury cooperatives operate under bylaws that require apartment purchasers to invest substantial cash, perhaps 30% to 50%, and sometimes as much as 100%.

§ 13.3 Construction Financing of Condominiums

Although the financing of condominium construction is much like subdivision financing, there are important differences.[1] The documentation of a condominium project is much more complex, its marketability more speculative (at least, from the perspective of many institutional lenders), and the risk of loss it presents in the event of failure correspondingly greater.

---

12. For example, the Standard Form Cooperative Bylaws published by the New York Attorney General provide, at Art. III, sec. 7:

> The Board of Directors shall have discretionary power to * * * determine the cash requirements of the Corporation to be paid as aforesaid by the shareholder-tenants under their respective proprietary leases. Every such determination by the Board of Directors shall be final and conclusive as to all shareholder-tenants * * *.

See P. Rohan & M. Reskin, Cooperative Housing Law and Practice § 24.67 app. (1975). Similar language is found in most proprietary leases. The decision-making power of the Board is generally very broad, and could even extend to a resolution to sell the project and distribute the proceeds to the members. See Anderson, Cooperative Apartments in Florida: A Legal Analysis, 12 U.Miami L.Rev. 13, 35 (1957).

13. But not completely. Even in a condominium, it is possible for the owners' association to levy larger-than-expected assessments to cover extravagant improvements to the recreational facilities or other common areas. Since title to common areas is held by the unit owners in tenancy in common, the association cannot mortgage them. Nonetheless, the assessments themselves are liens on the units, whether particular owners approve of the expenditures or not. In some cases, condominium bylaws may place an upper limit on assessment amounts. With respect to the inherent interdependence of cooperative apartment owners, see Howells, Economic Parity for Low-Income Cooperatives, 17 Urb. Law. 31 (1985).

§ 13.3

1. Good general discussions of condominium construction financing include K. Romney, Condominium Development Guide ch. 7 (1974); Fegan, supra § 13.2 n. 1; Pfeiler, supra § 13.2 n. 1.

Every new condominium project begins with site selection and acquisition. Developers commonly use their own capital to pay the cost of necessary land options. Before applications for institutional financing can be made, however, other costs must be incurred; surveys, engineering and market studies, and architects' fees, for example. These may be financed by use of the developer's cash or the contributions of his or her business associates, or through unsecured debt. In some cases these expenses are reimbursed out of the first draw of funds on the construction loan.

Upon exercise of the land option, the developer may be expected to pay the full cash price of the land to the seller. Often, however, the seller can be persuaded to sell on an installment basis and to accept a minimal initial cash payment. This installment indebtedness will usually be secured by a mortgage, and it will be necessary for the seller to subordinate the purchase money lien to that of the construction loan,[2] since virtually all construction lenders, as a matter of policy or the requirements of their governmental regulatory agencies, insist on first priority for the construction mortgage. Unless it is to be paid off from the proceeds of the construction loan, the land seller's subordinated mortgage (like the construction mortgage) must contain a partial release clause enabling the sale of individual units free of the lien.

When the land has been optioned and the necessary background studies completed, the developer is ready to apply for a construction loan. This submission is usually more comprehensive than would be expected in a detached-house subdivision, and the developer may seek the assistance of a mortgage loan broker in preparing and presenting it to prospective construction lenders. Prospective lenders will be particularly interested in the developer's own financial position, prior condominium experience, and reputation; they will also analyze the market demand information, architectural and engineering work, and general demographic and locational data submitted by the developer. In most cases the construction lender will make no commitment until permanent financing has been arranged for the sales of units; hence, the developer will make a similar submission of information to prospective permanent lenders, who are generally concerned with the same factors. Alternatively, the construction lender may also provide the permanent finance commitment. That commitment is not only a prerequisite to construction financing, but comprises a powerful marketing tool as well, especially if it ties the permanent lender to a fixed interest rate in a rising interest market.

A project does not become a condominium until some basic document—usually termed a master deed, declaration, or plan of unit ownership—is executed by the owners of the real estate and filed for record. This master deed describes the project, the individual units,

---

2. Subordination by vendors is discussed in Note, Purchase Money Subordination Agreements in California: An Analysis of Conditional Subordination, 45 S.Cal. L.Rev. 1109 (1972); see § 12.9, supra.

and the common areas; it assigns weights to each unit for voting and assessment purposes; it provides for a lien on the units to secure the assessments; and it may contain such covenants as a right of first refusal upon resale by a unit owner.[3] The master deed may be filed whenever the owners desire, but in many cases the construction lender will insist that filing be delayed until some fixed percentage of the units have been "presold"—that is, until prospective unit purchasers have paid earnest money deposits and signed purchase agreements. On the other hand, no conveyances by deed of units can occur until the master deed has been filed.[4] Given these constraints, the filing usually occurs sometime towards the end of the construction period.

Construction loan mortgages on condominium projects (termed "project mortgages") can be insured by the Federal Housing Administration (FHA) under section 234(d) of the National Housing Act.[5] This type of mortgage insurance coverage, which is not generally available on construction loans in detached-house subdivisions, is not particularly attractive to most developers. The principal amount of the loan may be as high as 90% of the "replacement cost" of the project;[6] in substance, this means the actual cost of land and improvements.[7] By contrast, conventional construction loans are rarely made for more that 75% or 80% of value, but "value" as calculated by conventional lenders may be as high as the total retail sale price of the units, and will generally exceed the project's cost by a substantial margin.[8] Thus, conventional construction financing may actually be for as much or more money than FHA-insured financing. In the past, having an FHA-insured construction mortgage was a necessity in order for FHA mortgage insurance to be immediately available on individual unit loans as they were sold, but this requirement has now been repealed.[9]

Unfortunately FHA-insured construction loans have numerous disadvantages. The applicable statute imposes dollar limits on the mortgage amount per unit, and in many areas effectively eliminates luxury

---

3. Some writers have questioned whether such a clause may constitute an unreasonable restraint on alienation or may violate the Rule Against Perpetuities. Neither result seems justifiable or probable. See DiLorenzo, Restraints on Alienation in a Condominium Context: An Evaluation and Theory for Decision–Making, 24 Real Prop.Prob. & Tr.J. 403 (1989); 1 (pt. 2) P. Rohan & M. Reskin, Condominium Law and Practice § 10.03 (1976). The FHA approved form of master deed does not contain a right of first refusal.

4. See 24 CFR 234.26(d)(1) (F.H.A.-insured condominium mortgages). Once the master deed of declaration has been filed, the only proper legal description of a unit or, for that matter, the entire project, is one that makes reference to the declaration. But see First Central Bank v. White, 400 N.W.2d 534 (Iowa 1987), in which a blanket construction loan mortgage was recorded after the declaration was filed, but contained only a traditional non-condominium legal description of the project. The court held the mortgage valid, noting that while the description was technically improper, the intent of the parties to impose the mortgage lien on the entire project was clear.

5. 12 U.S.C.A. § 1715. Applicable regulations are found at 24 CFR 234.1ff.

6. 12 U.S.C.A. § 1715y(e)(2).

7. 24 CFR 234.505(h).

8. See K. Romney, Condominium Development Guide § 7.04 (1974).

9. § 420, Housing and Urban–Rural Recovery Act of 1983, Pub.L.No. 98–181; see 52 Fed.Reg. 33804 (Sept.8, 1988), amending 24 CFR 234.26(a).

or even upper-middle-income projects.[10] There are severe limitations on the use of an FHA project mortgage to finance a conversion of a rental building to condominium.[11] FHA mortgage insurance premiums must be paid in addition to interest, fees, and discounts charged by the lending institution. Moreover, FHA processing of multifamily mortgage insurance applications has the reputation of being slow and cumbersome, and FHA minimum property standards with respect to some construction features may appear excessive to some developers. In light of these problems, it is not surprising that there has been relatively little construction lending under the section 234 program.

Developers of condominium projects sometimes do not complete construction. Failure to do so may result from poor planning and management of the construction work, inadequate budgeting, unanticipated increases in costs, weather problems, strikes, or weak market acceptance of the project. Abandonment will invariably constitute a default under the terms of the construction loan mortgage, and the lender may elect to foreclose. In this setting there are usually unpaid laborers, subcontractors, or suppliers who are entitled to file mechanics' liens. In addition, the prospective purchasers of units in the project will have signed contracts of sale and made down payments or earnest money deposits with the developer; some of these contracts may have been executed before construction began, and some afterward. These three groups, the construction lender, mechanics' lienors, and vendees often find themselves adverse to one another in respect to rights in the real estate.

Such problems are not unique to condominium developments; they also occur with speculative subdivisions and other types of construction. We discuss them here because condominiums have frequently been defaulted upon during construction in recent years, and because condominium statutes sometimes contain provisions which bear on these disputes. The problem of priorities as between construction lenders and mechanics' lien claimants has been discussed earlier in this book.[12] We focus here on the rights of purchase contract vendees vis-à-vis the construction lender and mechanics' lien claimants.

Priority as Between Construction Lender and Vendees

A difficult conflict may arise with respect to earnest money deposits or down payments (the terms are used here synonymously) collected from intended unit vendees before and during the construction period. If these funds, which may be very substantial, are available for current use by the developer, they may help solve serious cash shortage prob-

10. The limits have been increased on many occasions. At this writing the basic limit ranges from $30,420 for a unit with no bedrooms to $59,160 for a four-bedroom unit. These amounts can be adjusted upward for elevator-type buildings and for high-cost areas. See § 234, National Housing Act, 12 U.S.C.A. § 1715y.

11. See 12 U.S.C.A. § 1715y(k).

12. See §§ 12.4, 12.7, & 12.9 supra.

lems, but at high risk to the vendees.[13] The FHA[14] and the statutes of some states[15] require that such deposits be escrowed pending completion and transfer of title of the individual units, making them inaccessible to the developer. Such provisions are highly desirable. Where this is not the law, a problem arises in situations in which the developer has invaded the deposits and subsequently abandons the project prior to completion. The unit purchasers may well be left with only their personal rights of action against the developer, who is often insolvent. Even if the construction lender forecloses and completes construction, the original unit subscribers may have neither the right to complete their purchases by paying the remainder of the original contract price, nor the right to a return of their deposits by the lender.

This issue may be characterized as one of priority as between the purchase contracts and the construction mortgage. The contract vendee has, under the law of most states, both a right to specific performance and an equitable lien on the realty to secure the return of the down payment if the vendor fails to complete the contract.[16] The difficulty is that enforceability of these rights is constrained in two respects: first, they may be subordinate to pre-existing liens, such as the construction mortgage, if they arise after that mortgage is recorded; and second, they are not enforceable even against a subsequent mortgagee or purchaser if that party has no notice of the existence of the vendee's contract.[17] The latter constraint may not be a serious problem in most cases; seldom will a construction lender grant a loan without first asking about preconstruction sales activity, and the developer will

---

13. See Damian, Condominium Development: Representing the Developer, in Condominium Development 35, 61 (Prac. Law Inst.1971).

14. See FHA Subscription and Purchase Agreement Form No. 3279, cl. 1, reprinted in 1 P. Rohan & M. Reskin, Condominium Law and Practice § 9.04[6] (1976).

15. See, e.g., U.C.A. 4–110; Va.Code § 55–79.95 (Supp.1977); West's Fla.Stat. Ann. § 718.202 (Supp.1977) (permitting the developer to use the money to defray construction costs if the contract of sale so provides). See Note, Recent Innovations in State Condominium Legislation, 48 St. John's L.Rev. 994, 999 (1974); Note, Florida Condominiums—Developer Abuses and Security Law Implications Create a Need For a State Regulatory Agency, 25 U.Fla. L.Rev. 350, 358 (1973). The better approach is to prohibit by statute all developer use of deposit funds; the significance of contract language permitting the developer's use of deposits is unlikely to be understood by lay purchasers.

In many states, the agencies that regulate the real estate brokerage profession require earnest money received by brokers to be placed in an escrow or trust account. However, these requirements can be overridden by language in the purchase contract itself; hence, they provide no protection to condominium unit purchasers if the contract states that the earnest money will be placed in the developer's hands. See Hollbus v. Seabreeze Limited Partnership, 305 S.C. 439, 409 S.E.2d 387 (1991).

16. Gribble v. Stearman & Kaplan, Inc., 249 Md. 289, 239 A.2d 573 (1968); Brown v. Cleverly, 93 Utah 54, 70 P.2d 881 (1937). See generally Cunningham, Stoebuck & Whitman, Property §§ 10.5, 10.8 (2d ed. 1993); Annot., 43 A.L.R.2d 1384 (1954).

17. Glynn v. Marquette, 152 Cal. App.3d 277, 199 Cal.Rptr. 306 (1984); Carson v. Isabe Apartments, Inc., 20 Wash. App. 293, 579 P.2d 1027 (1978) (specific performance); Hillblom v. Ivancsits, 76 Ill. App.3d 306, 32 Ill.Dec. 172, 395 N.E.2d 119 (1979); National Indemnity Co. v. Banks, 376 F.2d 533 (5th Cir.1967); Mihranian, Inc. v. Padula, 134 N.J.Super. 557, 342 A.2d 523 (1975), affirmed 70 N.J. 252, 359 A.2d 473 (1976) (vendee's lien).

ordinarily be eager to inform the lender of the contracts that have been signed.[18]

The vendees' position is weakest if the purchase contract is signed after the construction mortgage has been recorded. In State Savings and Loan Association v. Kauaian Development Co.,[19] the Hawaii Supreme Court drew a distinction between subscription agreements entered into before and after the creation of the construction mortgage. Agreements executed after the mortgage were obviously subordinate to it, the court thought, apparently because of the constructive notice of the mortgage that the public records imparted to vendees,[20] but contracts of sale executed before the mortgage recordation had priority.[21]

---

18. See Wayne Building & Loan Co. v. Yarborough, 11 Ohio St.2d 195, 228 N.E.2d 841 (1967); Palmer v. Crews Lumber Co., Inc., 510 P.2d 269 (Okl.1973). South Carolina Fed. Sav. Bank v. San-A-Bel Corp., 307 S.C. 76, 413 S.E.2d 852 (App.1992) ("For one to have notice of an outstanding equitable interest, it is not necessary to know the identity of the third party or the extent of his interest. It is sufficient that one either knows or ought to know some third party interest exists.") These cases suggest that it is sufficient that the subsequent lender knows a contract has been executed, whether or not it is aware of the terms of the contract, the vendee's identity, or the precise amount of any down payment made.

19. 50 Hawaii 540, 445 P.2d 109 (1968).

20. The Hawaii Supreme Court revised this view of the case in State Savings & Loan Association v. Kauaian Development Co., 62 Hawaii 188, 613 P.2d 1315 (1980). Since the construction mortgage stated that it was "subject to" the condominium declaration, the court held that the mortgage was subordinate to the equitable liens of the unit purchasers who signed their contracts *after* as well as before recordation of the construction mortgage. In effect, the "subject to" language was treated as a subordination of the mortgage to the contracts of sale.

See also Palmer v. Forrest, Mackey & Associates, 251 Ga. 304, 304 S.E.2d 704 (1983) (where construction mortgage is recorded before contract of sale is executed, the contract vendee is on constructive notice of the mortgage and is subordinate to it.)

21. See also Hinsdale Federal Savings & Loan Association v. Gary-Wheaton Bank, 100 Ill.App.3d 746, 56 Ill.Dec. 558, 427 N.E.2d 963 (1981), adopting a similar position, but granting only a vendee's lien and not specific performance against the foreclosing construction lender. It is unclear why specific performance was denied. The contract was unrecorded, but the lender had actual knowledge of it. The court gave the vendees priority for all payments made before they acquired actual knowledge of the construction loan; evidently, it thought that mere recordation of the construction mortgage would not give the vendees constructive notice, once they had entered into the contract. To the same effect is Wayne Building & Loan Co. v. Yarborough, supra note 18. This conclusion is reasonable, since it would be entirely unrealistic to expect a vendee to examine the record title before making each payment under the contract; see Giorgi v. Pioneer Title Insurance Co., 85 Nev. 319, 454 P.2d 104 (1969); Cunningham, Stoebuck & Whitman, Property § 11.10 nn. 67–68 (2d ed.1993).

See also Waldorff Insurance & Bonding Co. v. Eglin National Bank., 453 So.2d 1383 (Fla.App.1984) (lender is subordinate because it had constructive notice of vendee's rights from his possession of condominium unit at the time developer executed mortgage); Caribank v. Frankel, 525 So.2d 942 (Fla.App.1988) (construction lender subordinate to equitable lien of a contract vendee of whom the lender had actual knowledge when it recorded its mortgage); Stahl v. Roulhac, 50 Md.App. 382, 438 A.2d 1366 (1982); National Indemnity Co. v. Banks, 376 F.2d 533 (5th Cir.1967); Fikes v. First Federal Savings & Loan Association, 533 P.2d 251 (Alaska 1975); Tucson Federal Savings & Loan Association v. Sundell, 106 Ariz. 137, 472 P.2d 6 (1970); Stanovsky v. Group Enterprise & Construction Co., 714 S.W.2d 836 (Mo.App.1986); Flickinger v. Glass, 222 N.Y. 404, 118 N.E. 792 (1918); South Carolina Fed. Sav. Bank v. San-A-Bel Corp., 307 S.C. 76, 413 S.E.2d 852 (App. 1992) (rejecting the lender's argument that it should have priority because of the "purchase-money" status of its construction loan). But see Nelson v. Great Northwest

However, the court observed that even prior subscription agreements could be made subordinate to the mortgage by express language of subordination, which could be placed in the purchase contract or in a separate document signed by the vendee. The court did not discuss the degree of specificity that would be necessary in such clauses, nor whether it would require that they be intelligible to or understood by the purchasers who sign them.

As a consequence of the *Kauaian* reasoning, most purchase agreements in use now probably contain subordination language.[22] A foreclosing construction lender would thus appear to be free to disregard the agreement and sell the unit to another purchaser and would have no obligation to return the deposit to the contract vendee.

However, the enforceability of such subordination clauses may be open to serious doubt. The purchaser will ordinarily be entirely unsophisticated, and is unlikely to have any concept of the significance of the clause. In addition, the clause will seldom contain details of the proposed construction financing to which the vendee is being asked to subordinate. By analogy to the cases involving so-called "automatic" subordination of purchase-money financing by land vendors to developers, it might well be argued that such subordinations by contract vendees are too vague or too unfair to enforce.[23]

Federal Savings & Loan Association, 37 Wash.App. 316, 679 P.2d 953 (1984), in which the court awarded priority to a construction deed of trust which was made and recorded *after* the execution of the contract of sale of a condominium unit. Inexplicably, the court concluded that the contract conveyed to the purchasers no interest in the realty; thus, they were denied specific performance against the lender, which had acquired title to the project by foreclosure. The case seems egregiously wrong.

In Glenview State Bank v. Shyman, 146 Ill.App.3d 136, 100 Ill.Dec. 13, 496 N.E.2d 1078 (1986), commented upon by T. Mattis, 11 So.Ill.U.L.Rev. 456 (1986), the purchaser of a unit had an oral contract of sale and took title by deed prior to the recording of the construction mortgage. However, the deed was unrecorded. The lender had no actual knowledge of the deed, but the purchaser argued that it should be held to constructive notice, since it knew that several units in the project had been presold. The court rejected this argument and gave the lender priority over the vendee's lien, at least in part on the basis that the written contracts of sale on the *other* units in the project contained subordination clauses.

22. See, e.g., Olympic Towers Purchase Agreement, reprinted in 1A P. Rohan & M. Reskin, Condominium Law and Practice, 118.17 app. (1976):

> The Purchaser agrees that all terms and provisions of this contract are and shall be subject and subordinate to the lien of any building loan mortgage heretofore or hereafter made and any advances heretofore or hereafter made thereon and any payments or expenses already made or incurred or which hereafter may be made or incurred, pursuant to the terms thereof, or incidental thereto, or to protect the security thereof, to the full extent thereof without the execution of any further legal documents by the Purchaser. This subordination shall apply whether such advances are voluntary or involuntary and whether made in accordance with the building loan schedule.

23. See Tucson Federal Savings & Loan Association v. Sundell, 106 Ariz. 137, 472 P.2d 6 (1970), refusing to enforce a rather ambiguous subordination language in a purchase contract; B.J.I. Corp. v. Larry W. Corp., 183 N.J.Super. 310, 443 A.2d 1096 (1982), construing a broad subordination clause in a purchase contract as ineffective to the extent that disbursements under the mortgage were made for purposes other than improvements to the property. See § 12.9 supra at notes 35–40; T. Mattis, Comment, 11 So.Ill.U.L.J. 456

Even a vendee who signed a purchase contract after the construction mortgage was recorded, or who has executed a valid subordination clause, might nonetheless manage to persuade a court that the vendee's lien should have priority. If the developer's default is traceable in part to the failure of the construction lender to monitor and supervise the progress of the project as its documents gave it the right to do, or if the lender negligently permitted the developer to divert loan funds away from the project, the vendee might argue that such behavior breached a duty to the vendee, and that the proper remedy is a loss of priority for the construction loan.[24] Depending on the facts, an argument against the lender's priority might also be based on estoppel. If the lender reviewed and approved the sales price schedule and the purchase agreement forms, supplied the developer with criteria for qualifying prospective purchasers in respect to income, credit worthiness, and the like, and mandated the pre-completion sale of some fixed number of units as a condition of the construction loan agreement, a court might well find the lender estopped by its extensive involvement in the vendor-vendee relationship to deny the priority of the vendee's lien.[25]

An alternative approach for the vendee might be based on an analogy to the cases that have permitted subcontractors and materials suppliers to assert an equitable lien on any undisbursed portion of the construction loan funds if the usual mechanics' lien remedies are

(1986), questioning the enforceability of a broadly-drafted subordination clause in a condominium unit sale contract.

24. See id.; § 12.10, supra, discussing various theories of lender liability. But see Pope Heating & Air Conditioning Co. v. Garrett–Bromfield Mortgage Co., 29 Colo. App. 169, 480 P.2d 602 (1971), holding a subordination agreement unconditional and binding despite diversion of construction loan funds; Forest Inc. v. Guaranty Mortgage Co., 534 S.W.2d 853 (Tenn.App. 1975) (semble); See also Falls Lumber Co. v. Heman, 114 Ohio App. 262, 181 N.E.2d 713 (1961), in which a construction lender was held liable in tort to a contract vendee for its failure to disburse construction funds in accordance with the applicable statute, thereby permitting mechanics' liens to be filed against the property; cf. Gardner Plumbing, Inc. v. Cottrill, 44 Ohio St.2d 111, 338 N.E.2d 757 (1975).

25. See § 12.9 supra. Cf. Fikes v. First Federal Savings & Loan Association, 533 P.2d 251 (Alaska 1975), holding a construction lender's lien limited to funds actually spent on construction and not diverted, as against the claim of a prior contract vendee of which the lender had knowledge; Tucson Federal Savings & Loan Association v. Sundell, 106 Ariz. 137, 472 P.2d 6 (1970) (semble) in which the court relied on the fact that the vendee had no knowledge of the construction mortgage. No cases have been found in which the estoppel argument has been raised by a junior vendee. The tendency of courts to protect contract vendees against the literal language of subordination clauses they have signed is illustrated by First Federal Savings & Loan Association v. Ott, 285 So.2d 695 (Fla.App.1973), certiorari denied 291 So.2d 10 (Fla.1974), in which the developer refinanced the original construction loan with the same lender; the court refused to enforce the subordination agreement in vendee's contract and she was permitted to take free of the refinanced mortgage. In Security National Bank v. Village Mall at Hillcrest, 85 Misc.2d 771, 382 N.Y.S.2d 882, 889 (1976), the Attorney General of New York argued that the construction lender's lien should be subordinated to the liens of contract vendees because the lender had (1) modified the construction loan agreement without recording the modification, (2) participated in a public offering of the condominium project without making the required disclosures to offerees under New York law, (3) participated in a violation of the statutory provisions allowing vendees' deposits to be used only for improvements, and (4) charged usurious interest rates. The court found that triable issues of fact were involved and denied summary judgment on the merits of these claims.

unavailing to them.[26] In equity, the contract vendee would seem to have as strong a moral claim to these funds as do those who have invested labor and materials, at least if construction has been completed without exhausting the construction loan account and the vendee's deposit has been used for construction purposes. Unfortunately, this argument may be ineffective in those jurisdictions that have codified the equitable lien concept without including contract vendees among its beneficiaries. New York, for example, has created a statutory trust consisting of the down payments of contract vendees. However, they may recover their funds after the developer's default only if they have not been used in improving the property; in addition, the usual classes of mechanics' lien claimants have first priority on the trust funds.[27] This approach seems entirely inadequate to protect the vendees, although it may be better than no protection at all.

As a matter of policy, it is entirely reasonable to impose on the construction lender a duty to return vendees' deposits in cases where the lender has played an active role in approving or supervising the developer's marketing program. The lender is far better able than the vendee to investigate the developer's solvency, experience, and reliability, and to spread the risk of the developer's default. Moreover, any construction lender wishing to avoid this risk may easily do so merely by requiring that all deposits by vendees be placed in escrow. The law should not permit developers (and construction lenders) to rely upon vendees' down payments as a means of financing construction; doing so is an indicator that the developer is dangerously underfunded, and a lender who actively countenances such a procedure should be held accountable to the vendees for their loss.[28]

Priority as Between Mechanics' Lien Claimants and Vendees

The rights of mechanics' lien claimants in condominium projects raise problems similar to, but more intricate than, claims made on subdivision lots. Even if the work was done or the materials supplied on only a single lot or unit, the matter is not simple. It is clear enough that if the vendee enters into the contract of purchase after the work

---

26. See Reitz, Construction Lenders' Liability to Contractors, Subcontractors, and Materialmen, 130 U.Pa.L.Rev. 416 (1981); § 12.6, supra.

27. New York—McKinney's Lien Law § 71–a. See Security National Bank v. Village Mall at Hillcrest, Inc., 85 Misc.2d 771, 382 N.Y.S.2d 882, 889 (1976); Glazer v. Alison Homes Corp., 62 Misc.2d 1017, 309 N.Y.S.2d 381 (1970), affirmed 36 A.D.2d 720, 320 N.Y.S.2d 715 (1971). The latter case, though sound in policy, seems to go well beyond the statutory language and permits contract vendees to assert a lien on funds that were wrongfully diverted by the developer from construction loan proceeds, although the opinion concedes that mechanics' lienors would have a superior claim to these funds.

28. In some respects the matter is similar to Connor v. Great Western Savings & Loan Association, 69 Cal.2d 850, 73 Cal. Rptr. 369, 447 P.2d 609 (1968), in which a construction lender was held liable to home purchasers for its failure to adequately supervise the construction of houses with serious structural defects. The case of diversion of vendees' downpayments seems an especially appealing one for application of the concept, since developers' marketing programs are so generally superintended by construction lenders, particularly in condominium projects. See § 12.11 supra.

has been completed and the lien filed of record, the lien will have priority and the vendee will take subject to it.[29] This means that if the developer and general contractor are unavailable for recovery, as is all too common, the unit vendee will suffer the loss unless protected by an owner's policy of title insurance.

If the vendee acquires legal title by deed to the unit or lot after the work has been done and the lien has "attached"[30] but before the lien is filed of record, he or she may be entirely innocent of any actual knowledge of the lien's attachment. A few jurisdictions, mostly in the South, protect bona fide purchasers in this situation, granting them priority over the lien.[31] Most states, however, hold the vendee's interest subject to the lien, either on the ground that even BFP's are subject to mechanics' liens[32] or that the very fact of construction activity on the land imparts notice of the potential filing of liens, and thus negates BFP status.[33] Moreover, owner's title insurance coverage is unlikely to assist the purchaser on these facts; many policies expressly exclude coverage for unfiled liens.

Suppose the vendee's contract of purchase predates the attachment of the mechanic's lien, even though the conveyance by deed occurs later. Is it arguable that the vendee's lien created by execution of the

29. Diamond Lumber, Inc. v. H.C.M.C., Ltd., 746 P.2d 76 (Colo.App.1987); United Accounts, Inc. v. Larson, 121 N.W.2d 628 (N.D.1963); Annot., 85 A.L.R. 927, 928 (1933).

30. The exact time at which priority attaches varies among jurisdictions. Many fix it as of the day the first work is done on the overall construction project, and others on the date the lien claimant first performed his work. Less popular rules attach the lien at the time the general contract or the claimant's contract is entered into or recorded, or when the notice of lien is filed of record. Under all of these rules except the last-mentioned, a lien may attach without any clear evidence of the claim appearing in the public records. The lien must usually be "perfected" by filing of record within some fixed period after the work is completed, and is then said to "relate back" to the attachment date. See R. Kratovil, Modern Mortgage Law and Practice § 214 (1972); 4 American Law of Property § 16.106F (A. J. Casner ed. 1952). See generally § 12.4 supra.

31. See, e.g., In re WWG Industries, Inc., 772 F.2d 810 (11th Cir.1985) (Georgia law); Ex parte Douthit, 480 So.2d 547 (Ala. 1985), on remand 480 So.2d 558 (Ala.Civ. App.1985) (BFP takes free of mechanics' liens on existing buildings, but is subject to liens on new buildings regardless of actual notice); Bryant v. Ellenburg, 106 Ga.App. 510, 127 S.E.2d 468 (1962); Anderson v. Streck, 190 Ga.App. 224, 378 S.E.2d 526 (1989); Ky.Rev.Stat. 376.010, construed in Walker v. Valley Plumbing Co., 370 S.W.2d 136 (Ky.1963); Mass. Gen.L.Ann. c.254, § 2, construed in J & W Wall Systems, Inc. v. Shawmut First Bank, 413 Mass. 42, 594 N.E.2d 859 (1992); Comfort–Craft Heating & Air Conditioning, Inc. v. Salamone, 19 A.D.2d 760, 241 N.Y.S.2d 581 (1963); First State Bank v. Stacey, 37 Tenn.App. 223, 261 S.W.2d 245 (1953), certiorari denied 195 Tenn. 386, 259 S.W.2d 863 (1953); Wood v. Barnes, 420 S.W.2d 425 (Tex.Civ. App.1967).

32. Schrader Iron Works, Inc. v. Lee, 26 Cal.App.3d 621, 103 Cal.Rptr. 106 (1972); State Savings & Loan Association v. Kauaian Devel. Co., 50 Hawaii 540, 445 P.2d 109, 123 (1968); Metropolitan Water Co. v. Hild, 415 P.2d 970 (Okl.1966). See generally G. Thompson, Real Property § 5218 n. 69 (1957).

33. The knowledge of work in progress may be actual or constructive. See Guaranty Pest Control, Inc. v. Commercial Investment & Development Corp., 288 Ala. 604, 264 So.2d 163 (1972); Capital Bank & Trust Co. v. Broussard Paint & Wallpaper Co., 198 So.2d 204 (La.App.1967); Clark Certified Concrete Co. v. Lindberg, 216 Md. 576, 141 A.2d 685 (1958); J. R. Meade Co. v. Forward Construction Co., 526 S.W.2d 21 (Mo.App.1975); H. Tiffany, Real Property § 1578 (1939); Annot., 50 A.L.R.3d 944 (1973).

contract has chronological, and thus legal, priority over the mechanic's lien? In Wayne Building & Loan Co. v. Yarborough,[34] the Ohio Supreme Court so held, although the vendee was given priority only to the extent of down payments made before the liens attached at the commencement of the work; the vendee had no priority as to further payments he made on the contract after work began. The decision appears to place no emphasis on whether the lien claimants had notice of the executed contract of purchase at the time they began their work, but such notice would presumably strengthen the vendee's position. Thus, in one Texas case the lien claimants were permitted priority for work done up to the time they learned of the executed contract, but not thereafter.[35] In some cases, however, the existence of the purchase contract has backfired, with the courts seeing it as clearly establishing the vendee's position as an equitable "owner," and thus a member of the class of persons whose interests are subject to mechanics' liens.[36]

As these cases suggest, the relationship of vendees' and lien claimants' rights is uncertain and confused, although the lienors have usually prevailed. The courts have vacillated between the traditional desire to protect good faith purchasers and to enhance the reliability of the public records, on the one hand, and the wish to construe the lien statutes liberally to aid lien claimants, on the other. One major defect in the system in most states lies in its failure to require potential lien claimants to record some public notice as a condition of *attachment* (rather than mere perfection) of the lien. But even a change in the law in this respect would not fully protect purchasers, since they rarely examine the public records or obtain title reports before signing purchase agreements and making deposits. In essence, the contest is between two claimants neither of whom has taken any formal step to give the world notice of his or her lien, and each of whom is at least dimly aware of the other's potential existence. On these facts it would be arbitrary to make priorities turn on which interest "attached" first, as by lien claimant's first work or the vendee's execution of a contract. Given the almost universal lack of sophisticated residential unit buyers, and the alternative methods open to lien claimants, who are generally well aware of the risks, to safeguard their interests,[37] the preferable

34. 11 Ohio St.2d 195, 228 N.E.2d 841, 849–50 (1967). See also E.E. Stump Well Drilling, Inc. v. Willis, 230 Va. 445, 338 S.E.2d 841 (1986) (mechanic's lien prevails over vendee's lien, where vendee's contract was unrecorded).

35. Stone v. Pitts, 389 S.W.2d 601 (Tex.Civ.App.1965). The lienor's knowledge of the vendee's interest may also be used to compel the lienor to include the vendee as an "owner" in the notice of lien, and failure to do so may exculpate the vendee. See F. M. Sibley Lumber Co. v. Gottesman, 314 Mich. 60, 22 N.W.2d 72 (1946); cf. Oklahoma Hardware Co. v. Townsend, 494 P.2d 326 (Okl.1972). See Annot., 48 A.L.R.3d 153 (1973).

36. Home Carpet Inc. v. Bob Antrim Homes, Inc., 210 N.W.2d 652 (Iowa 1973); Toler v. Satterthwaite, 200 Kan. 103, 434 P.2d 814 (1967).

37. Subcontractors and materials suppliers may verify the developer's credit standing, may contact the construction lender to determine whether the project is on schedule and within budget, may insist on immediate payment in cash, or may confine their business activities to developers who have payment bonds. None of these steps may be completely effective or feasible, but they place the potential lien

approach to this dilemma (short of comprehensive legislative reform) is to recognize a prior vendee's lien for all deposits paid prior to the time the purchaser learns not merely that work has been done on the land, but that delinquent payments are owed to potential lien claimants.

Assuming that a condominium unit purchaser is subject to mechanics' liens, other questions arise. If the work was done or the materials supplied for several units, the common areas, or the entire project, what interests are subjected to the lien? Most of the courts which have dealt with the issue have held that the common areas as such are not lienable.[38] Often this result follows from express language in the condominium statutes involved; the common areas have no independent legal existence apart from the units to which they are appurtenant.[39] Hence a lien claimant who has performed work only on common areas is expected to file the lien on the individual units—presumably all of them—whose owners had rights in the common facilities in question.[40] (Of course, for work done only on an individual

claimant in a considerably stronger position than contract vendees.

38. See, e.g., W. H. Dail Plumbing, Inc. v. Roger Baker & Associates, Inc., 64 N.C.App. 682, 308 S.E.2d 452 (1983), review denied 310 N.C. 152, 311 S.E.2d 296 (1984); Rainier Pacific Supply, Inc. v. Gray, 30 Wash.App. 340, 633 P.2d 1355 (1981); Country Village Heights Condominium v. Mario Bonito, Inc., 79 Misc.2d 1088, 363 N.Y.S.2d 501 (1975); Stevens Construction Corp. v. Draper Hall, Inc., 73 Wis.2d 104, 242 N.W.2d 893 (1976). But see Plateau Supply Co. v. Bison Meadows Corp., 31 Colo.App. 205, 500 P.2d 162 (1972); E. D. McGillicuddy Construction Co. v. Knoll Recreation Association, 31 Cal.App.3d 891, 107 Cal.Rptr. 899 (1973). The *Rainier Pacific* and *Stevens* cases conclude that liens on the common areas are impermissible even though the lien claimants commenced their work before the condominium declaration was recorded, and thus at a time when the building was not subject to the condominium statute.

A related problem arises if the project is a large one consisting of several buildings constructed in phases. Is a lien claimant who works on the entire project entitled to file a lien on all of the buildings, and does the time for filing the lien begin to run only when work on the last building is completed? The Arizona supreme court answered both questions affirmatively in S.K. Drywall, Inc. v. Developers Financial Group, Inc., 169 Ariz. 345, 819 P.2d 931 (1991).

Note that planned unit developments, in which the owners association holds title to the common areas, are on an entirely different footing than condominiums, and a mechanic's lien can readily be filed against such a common area for work done there at the association's request. See Pavestone v. Interlock Pavers, Inc., 771 P.2d 236 (Okl.App.1989). With respect to cooperatives, only one parcel of real estate exists, and any valid mechanics lien must exist on it. The interesting question is whether a lien can result only from work done at the behest of the cooperative corporation, or whether work done for an individual unit owner on his or her apartment can trigger a lien on the entire building. The court held that the latter had occurred in Dash Contracting Corp. v. Slater, 142 Misc.2d 512, 537 N.Y.S.2d 736 (1989).

39. FHA Model Act § 9(a). The UCA is apparently to the same effect; UCA § 3–117(c) (1980). See A. Ferber & K. Stecher, Law of Condominium § 117 (1967). There is, however, a way a mortgage can exist on the common areas: if the land in question is first mortgaged, and then added to a phased condominium as common area with the mortgagee's consent. This occurred in Sunshine Meadows Condominium Ass'n v. Bank One, 599 So.2d 1004 (Fla.App.1992). Upon default, the mortgagee argued that it should be permitted to foreclose not only on the common area in question, but also on all of the individual units that had rights to the common area. The court rejected this argument, but certified the question to the Florida supreme court.

40. See Westage Towers Associates v. ABM Air Conditioning and Refrigeration, __ A.D.2d __, 590 N.Y.S.2d 118 (1992) (notice of lien describing property merely by name of condominium project was not

unit and not on the common areas, a lien may be filed against the unit in question.)[41] A further problem for the lien claimant is raised if some of the units have been conveyed by the developer at the time the lien claimant-to-be performs the work on the common areas. The vendees of these units might argue that they cannot be held subject to the lien because they neither contracted for nor consented to the work done.[42] It is likely, however, that they would be held to have consented, or be estopped from denying their consent, if the work in question benefitted common areas in which they had rights and which they expected to use.

If work is performed on numerous units, the common areas, or the project as a whole, is a lien claimant required to apportion the lien among all of the affected units and satisfy it from each of them only on a pro rata basis? If the law does not compel this result, the claimant obviously has power to create great injustice among unit owners by "picking on" some while favoring others. This issue has risen frequently in the subdivision context, and the courts have almost uniformly held that, if the lien is susceptible to reasonable apportionment, then apportionment is required.[43] In a condominium, apportionment would seldom be difficult to calculate, since the units are even more likely to be of similar value and have similar construction than subdivision houses, and the condominium provides a "built-in" basis for apportionment. Moreover, the Uniform Condominium Act and many other

---

valid against any interest in the project); Advanced Alarm Technology, Inc. v. Pavilion Assoc., 145 A.D.2d 582, 536 N.Y.S.2d 127 (1988) (lien claimant's attempt to file "blanket lien" on entire condominium project for work done on common areas was invalid; notice of lien must describe each individual unit); Mendenhall v. Douglas L. Cooper, Inc., 239 Va. 71, 387 S.E.2d 468 (1990) (all condominium unit owners, including purchasers of units, were necessary parties to action to foreclose mechanic's lien; failure to name purchasers within time permitted for filing action to enforce lien was therefore fatal to action, which was dismissed by the court).

41. Metro Masonry, Inc. v. West 56th Street Assoc., 147 Misc.2d 565, 558 N.Y.S.2d 470 (1990) (for work done on individual unit, lien filed against entire building was improper but not fatal, since the property it described included the unit in question).

42. See, e.g., Romito Brothers Electric Construction Co. v. Frank A. Flannery, Inc., 40 Ohio St.2d 79, 320 N.E.2d 294 (1974). The New York statute permits the filing of a lien on an individual unit only if the work was requested by the owner of the unit or was for emergency repairs. See Country Village Heights Condominium v. Mario Bonito, Inc., 79 Misc.2d 1088, 363 N.Y.S.2d 501 (1975). See FHA Model Act § 9(b), imputing consent of all unit owners to any work performed on the common area if authorized by the association.

43. Apportionment of mechanics' liens was required in Meyers Plumbing & Heating Supply Co. v. Caste, 350 Pa.Super. 482, 504 A.2d 942 (1986) (townhouse development); Addington–Beaman Lumber Co. v. Lincoln Sav. & Loan Ass'n, 241 Va. 436, 403 S.E.2d 688 (1991) (supplier of lumber for townhouse development); Rosser v. Cole, 237 Va. 572, 379 S.E.2d 323 (1989) (roads in subdivision). See also West's Ann.Cal.Civ.Code § 3130; Del.Code tit. 25, § 2713.

But see Independent Trust Corp. v. Stan Miller, Inc., 796 P.2d 483 (Colo.1990), holding that apportionment could not be accomplished sufficiently readily, and was not required. The work had been done on a common area golf course, and the dispute involved only two competing owners of the course, one of whom argued for apportionment based simply on relative acreage; Northwest Fed. Sav. & Loan v. Tiffany Constr. Co., 158 Ariz. 100, 761 P.2d 174 (1988) (similar facts); Kershaw Excavating v. City Systems, Inc., 581 A.2d 1111 (Del. 1990) (apportionment not required, where work was done in site preparation before condominium declaration was recorded).

condominium statutes expressly provide that a lien on more than one unit can be satisfied and discharged by pro rata payment by each unit owner.[44] Under this language, apportionment is in effect compelled by law whether the lienor files the claim in apportioned form or not. One court has interpreted such language as applicable only when the lien is incurred by one or more individual unit owners, rather than by a developer,[45] but this construction seems strained and inequitable. Whatever the source of the lien, it should be dischargeable as to any unit when its owner pays his or her share; this seems to be the prevalent view.[46]

Pro rata apportionment of the liens among all units does not necessarily mean that all unit owners will bear equal burdens. In Hostetter v. Inland Development Corp.,[47] some units had been sold by the developer, while others remained unsold, at the time the mechanics' liens were foreclosed. The developer had violated the condominium statute by failing to place the purchasers' deposits in escrow and by failing to discharge all liens when selling the units. Hence, the court dictated an equitable foreclosure scheme, analogous to marshalling,[48] under which the units remaining in the developer's hands would be foreclosed before resort could be had to the units sold to consumers.

The creation of a condominium regime often causes confusion among those who wish to file notices of mechanics' liens. It is usually held that a notice of lien that describes the "property" by means of the original description of the land on which the condominium was built is

---

44. FHA Model Act, § 9(b); UCA § 3–117(c); Ill.Rev.Stat.–765 ILCS 605/9.1; A. Ferber & K. Stecher, Law of Condominium § 117 (1967); In re Zachman Homes, 47 B.R. 496, 518 (Bkrtcy.D.Minn.1984) (applying Minn. law); Metco, Inc. v. Moss Creek, Inc., 529 Pa. 53, 601 A.2d 802 (1992), construing Pa.Cons.Stat. § 3409(b), the Pennsylvania version of the UCA. "Pro rata" is typically taken to mean a share equal to each unit's share of common expenses, although other approaches to the question are possible; see Royal Ambassador Condominium Ass'n v. East Coast Supply Corp., 495 So.2d 932 (Fla.App.1986).

45. E.D. McGillicuddy Construction Co. v. Knoll Recreation Associates, 31 Cal. App.3d 891, 107 Cal.Rptr. 899 (1973). The court did not explain why allocation of the lien on a pro rated basis among unit owners was impractical. The opinion seemed to rely upon the fact that all purchasers had owner's title insurance coverage—a consideration which seems irrelevant and improper.

46. W. H. Dail Plumbing, Inc. v. Roger Baker & Associates Inc., 64 N.C.App. 682, 308 S.E.2d 452 (1983), review denied 310 N.C. 152, 311 S.E.2d 296 (1984); Michael Weller, Inc. v. Aetna Casualty & Surety Co., 126 Ariz. 323, 614 P.2d 865 (App.1980); Rainier Pacific Supply, Inc. v. Gray, 30 Wash.App. 340, 633 P.2d 1355 (1981); Hostetter v. Inland Development Corp., 172 Mont. 167, 561 P.2d 1323 (1977); Brunzell v. Lawyers Title Ins. Corp., 101 Nev. 395, 705 P.2d 642 (1985); United Masonry, Inc. v. Jefferson Mews, Inc., 218 Va. 360, 237 S.E.2d 171 (1977). The last case is particularly interesting, as only one-half of the 264 units had actually been constructed. The court ordered apportionment of the lien for work done on the residential structure among only the 132 units built, but apportioned the lien for work on the common-element clubhouse among all 264 units. See also Southern Colonial Mortgage Co. v. Medeiros, 347 So.2d 736 (Fla. App.1977). Plateau Supply Corp. v. Bison Meadows Corp., supra note 38, is contra, but is based on the preexisting interpretation by the Colorado courts of that mechanic's lien statute as allowing arbitrary apportionment of the lien as among the parcels covered by it.

47. 172 Mont. 167, 561 P.2d 1323 (1977).

48. See § 10.10 supra.

ineffective.[49] Similarly, a notice of lien describing the common areas is invalid, as discussed above. The units themselves must be identified in the notice. Yet courts have sometimes found ingenious ways around this requirement and sustained lien filings on the entire original parcel.[50]

Priority as Between Mechanics' Lien Claimants and the Owners Association's Assessment Lien

There are several situations in which a mechanic's lien may compete in priority with the association's lien for unpaid assessments. This may occur when the developer conveys units without paying all contractors, workers, and suppliers of materials; it may also occur when the association hires work done on the common areas or an individual unit owner contracts for work on her or his unit.

This conflict is usually resolved by reference to the jurisdiction's condominium statute. Many of the statutes, following the FHA Model Act, provide that the assessment lien is superior to all other liens except first mortgages on the units, property taxes, and governmental assessments.[51] This would appear to make mechanics' liens subor-

---

49. See Papa v. Greenwich Green, Inc., 177 Conn. 295, 416 A.2d 1196 (1979). But see FirstCentral Bank v. White, 400 N.W.2d 534 (Iowa 1987), in which the court approved an amendment to the lien filing, after the lienor had brought an action to foreclose the lien, to correct precisely this sort of error; cases cited supra note 40. See also Royal Ambassador Condominium Ass'n v. East Coast Supply Corp,. 495 So.2d 932 (Fla.App.1986) (where work is done on the common elements of only one building in a multi-building project, the lien should be filed on the units in that building, not all units in the project).

50. In Rainier Pacific Supply, Inc. v. Gray, 30 Wash.App. 340, 633 P.2d 1355 (1981), the lienors had commenced their work before the condominium declaration was filed. After it was recorded, they filed notices of lien that contained only the legal description of the land on which the condominium was located. In light of the Washington statute that made mechanics' liens relate back to the date the lienor commenced work, the court held the notices valid; the recording of the declaration, it found, automatically converted the blanket liens into proportional liens on the individual units, with no refiling necessary. A similar result was reached in Southern Colonial Mortgage Co. v. Medeiros, 347 So.2d 736 (Fla.App.1977).

See also In re Argonne Constr. Co., 10 B.R. 570 (Bkrtcy.Ill.1981), in which the court found that "owners" were entitled to a more relaxed form of mechanic's lien notice than third parties. The condominium unit purchasers (whether they contracted to buy before or after the lienor's work was done) were held to be "owners" for this purpose, and a generic description of the original real estate parcel was held sufficient to give them notice of the lien for work done on the common areas. With respect to work done on individual units, on the other hand, only purchasers who had signed sales contracts before the work was done were considered "owners," bound by the generic description. See also Metro Masonry, Inc. v. West 56th Street Assoc., 147 Misc.2d 565, 558 N.Y.S.2d 470 (1990) (notice containing description of entire parcel for work done on individual unit was incorrect procedure, but lien was nonetheless valid).

51. FHA Model Act § 9(b); A. Ferber & K. Stecher, Law of Condominium § 117 (1967). See Washington Federal Savings & Loan Association v. Schneider, 95 Misc.2d 924, 408 N.Y.S.2d 588 (1978) (under such a statute, association's lien is superior to second mortgage which was recorded before the association's notice of lien.) The UCA has a similar provision, but also gives priority to liens and encumbrances recorded before the condominium declaration; however, it grants the association's lien priority for the past six months of assessments, even as against a first mortgage. UCA § 3–116 (1980).

dinate to the association.[52] In a few states, statutes expressly grant priority to mechanics' liens.[53]

The New York statute expands the rights of mechanics' lien claimants in another fashion as well, granting them, for work done on common areas, a lien on funds collected by the owner's association.[54] This remedy was apparently thought necessary because of the impermissibility of liening the common areas directly, the difficulty of proving that unit owners requested the work done on common areas, and the cumbersomeness of apportionment of the lien among a large number of individual units. From the lienor's viewpoint this remedy is probably superior to merely filing an action to collect the debt owed. In cases in which the association itself requested the work done the procedure is reasonable, but if the work was done at the developer's request, it is difficult to see the fairness of imposing on the association the duty of repaying it.

Special Declarant Rights and Obligations in Foreclosure

When a construction lender forecloses on a condominium project in which not all units have been sold, the foreclosure sale purchaser (typically the lender itself) obviously steps into the developer's shoes as a real property owner of the unsold units. However, questions may arise concerning the extent to which the developer's *other* rights and duties, going beyond mere real estate ownership, are "inherited" by the foreclosing lender.

With respect to the developer's rights, those of greatest interest relate to the marketing program. For example, the developer, as "declarant" of the condominium, may have reserved the right to maintain a sales office and to offer prospective purchasers limited use of the common recreation facilities.[55] The developer may also have arranged the voting rights in the owners' association so as to give him

---

52. But see Security National Bank v. Village Mall at Hillcrest, 85 Misc.2d 771, 382 N.Y.S.2d 882, 896 (1976), appearing to favor the mechanics' lien claimants under such a statute, on the ground that the association's lien does not come into existence and acquire a priority date until some notice or action to enforce it is filed. This decision seems to contradict the statute. Cf. New York—McKinney's Real Prop. Law § 339–z.

The UCA expressly declares that its provisions on the priority of the assessment lien do not apply against mechanics' liens; on this point it is simply silent. UCA § 3–116(b). However, the UCA provides in general that the "association has a lien" for assessments, that recordation of the declaration is record notice and perfection of the lien, and that no further recordation of a claim of lien for assessments is required. UCA § 3.116(a), (c). From these premises, it may be reasoned that the lien's priority as against a mechanic's lien will be determined merely by the chronological order of recordation of the declaration and the "relation back" date of the mechanic's lien (typically the date work was commenced; see note 30 supra).

53. See Idaho Code § 55–1518; N.C.Gen.Stat. § 47A–22(a); Wis.Stat.Ann. 703.23(1)(a).

54. New York—McKinney's Real Prop. Law § 339–*l* (2).

55. Such rights are permitted under UCA § 2–115.

or her control for part or all of the marketing period.[56] Will such rights as these pass to the foreclosing lender?

Arguments based on covenants running with the land, or on the specific language of the construction loan mortgage, might be made to support the lender's claim to these rights. The Uniform Condominium Act clarifies the issue, stating that at the lender's request, it

> succeeds to all special declarant rights related to that real estate held by that declarant, or only to any rights reserved in the declaration * * * and held by that declarant to maintain models, sales offices and signs. The judgment or instrument conveying title shall provide for transfer of only the special declarant rights requested.[57]

Thus it appears that under the UCA the lender can pick and choose the rights which will pass to it.[58]

The other side of the coin is the lender's liability. There is obviously a possibility that, if the lender has been intimately involved in the development of the project, it will be liable for construction defects or other failures by the developer under the doctrine of Connor v. Great Western Savings and Loan Association.[59] But this sort of involvement is probably rare.[60] In its absence, courts are likely to try to achieve some sort of rough parity between the extent of the lender's assumption of benefits from the original declarant and the corresponding liabilities to be imposed on the lender.

There is little court-developed law in this area yet,[61] but the UCA formalizes the parity concept. Under the UCA, the foreclosing lender's liability depends on which of four choices it makes in assuming the declarant's rights. First, suppose the lender makes no assumption of rights; it will be held to have undertaken no corresponding liabilities (except, presumably, those relating to its own conduct after acquiring title to the unsold units.) The second choice under the UCA permits the lender to assume the declarant's rights solely for the purpose of transferring them to other persons—the buyers of the units thus

---

56. On declarant control of the executive board, see UCA § 3–103(d).

57. UCA § 3–104(c).

58. See Note, Special Declarant Rights and Obligations Following Mortgage Foreclosure on Condominium Developments, 25 Wm. & Mary L.Rev. 463 (1984), at 478 n. 103.

59. 69 Cal.2d 850, 73 Cal.Rptr. 369, 447 P.2d 609 (1968), discussed in § 12.11 supra. See Chotka v. Fidelco Growth Investors, 383 So.2d 1169 (Fla.App.1980), in which the foreclosing lender completed the construction work and finished marketing the units; the court held the lender liable for construction defects which resulted from the original developer's poor work.

60. See Roundtree Villas Assoc. v. 4701 Kings Corp., 282 S.C. 415, 321 S.E.2d 46 (1984); Riverview Condominium Corp. v. Campagna Construction Co., 406 So.2d 101 (Fla.App.1981), appeal after remand 467 So.2d 807 (1985); First Wisconsin Bank v. Roose, 348 So.2d 610 (Fla.App.1977); § 12.11, supra, at notes 11–12.

61. See Chotka v. Fidelco Growth Investors, supra note 59; Port Sewall Harbor & Tennis Club Owners Ass'n v. First Fed. Sav. & Loan Ass'n, 463 So.2d 530 (Fla.App. 1985) (foreclosing lender that markets subdivision homes is liable only for (a) its own express representations, (b) patent construction defects in the entire project, and (c) defects in the portion of the project completed by the lender).

acquired.[62] Such a lender may still exercise the control over the executive board of the association which could have been asserted by the original developer,[63] but is not liable to the unit owners except for any improper behavior in exercising those particular rights.

A third possibility is for the lender to assume the developer's rights to maintain models, offices, and signs in the project. If this is the lender's decision, its liability is limited to breaches of legal duty associated with those particular facilities, and to the duty to provide the public offering statement to customers required by the UCA.[64]

Finally, a lender which assumes all of the special declarant rights, or any rights other than those specifically mentioned above, becomes broadly liable for breaches of all declarant duties, with certain named exceptions.[65] The exceptions include liabilities associated with the misrepresentations, breaches of fiduciary duty in connection with the owner's association, and construction warranty obligations of the previous declarant, and any defaults of the previous declarant occurring after the transfer.[66] In this fashion the UCA attempts to make an even-handed allocation of liability to the original developer's successor. The UCA may well become a guideline for the courts in this area, even in states which have not adopted it by statute.[67]

§ 13.4 Financing Conversions to Condominium and Cooperative Status

Rental apartment buildings are frequently converted to condominium status. The converter may be the original landlord, or the building may be sold to an intermediary who will handle the conversion and marketing process. Often some remodeling and refurbishing of the apartments, lobby, and recreational facilities is necessary. Such facilities as the heating plant, roof, and plumbing may be replaced. Despite these expenses, the financial rewards of the conversion can be extremely attractive, since buildings often sell for as much as 33 to 40 percent more than their previous value as rental properties.[1] For landlords

---

62. UCA § 3–104(e)(4).

63. Such control is authorized (with limitations) by UCA § 3–103(d).

64. UCA § 3–104(e)(3).

65. UCA § 3–104(e)(2). See Roundtree Villas Assoc. v. 4701 Kings Corp., 282 S.C. 415, 321 S.E.2d 46 (1984) (lender liable for repairs it made negligently after it took over and marketed completed project). But see Thomas v. Reeves Southeastern Corp., 472 So.2d 493 (Fla.App.1985) (construction lender that takes title to condominium project by deed in lieu of foreclosure, and then markets the units, is not a "developer" so as to be responsible for compliance with statutory disclosure duties, such a provision of a prospectus and offering circular to potential buyers).

66. Note that if the successor owner is an "affiliate" of the original declarant, it is subject to all of the liabilities of its transferor, irrespective of the extent of its assumption of rights; UCA § 3–104(e)(1).

67. See also the discussion of Mich. Comp.Laws Ann. §§ 559.235, –237 and Or. Rev.Stat. 94.097, 94.103, in Note, supra note 58, at 482–85.

§ 13.4

1. See Jaskol, A Lender Looks at Condominium Conversions, 4 Real Estate Rev. 70 (No. 1, 1974). On efforts of converters to achieve capital gain (as distinct from ordinary income) treatment on the gain from conversions, see Rosenstein, New Tax Advantages of Condo and Co-op Conversions, 17 Real Est.Rev. 42 (No. 3, Fall 1987); Boris, Co-ops and Condominiums:

who find themselves beset with rising costs for maintenance and utilities, complaints from tenants, and the growing influence of rent control ordinances, conversion may seem an ideal way out of an uncomfortable position.[2]

At the same time, conversion is a risky business.[3] Marketing of the converted apartments may be slow, especially if numerous other buildings are being converted or new condominiums built in the same market. It is usually desirable to keep the unsold units rented, but vacancies often grow when the tenants know that the building is being converted. On the other hand, in many buildings the existing tenants cannot afford the purchase prices of the converted units, and hence are forced out of their longtime residences; they may oppose the conversion bitterly and in some jurisdictions their opposition will constitute a legal barrier.[4] Detailed discussion of these problems is beyond the scope of the present treatment, but they must be considered carefully by any lender who is asked to finance a conversion.

Occasionally an apartment building owner is able to manage a conversion without resort to new blanket financing, but this can be accomplished only if the existing mortgage lender is agreeable. If the mortgage contains a due-on-sale clause, the lender must waive it. The lender must also be willing to join in the condominium declaration, and must modify the existing mortgage documents by inserting a partial release clause, permitting the sale of individual units free of the blanket lien. Often the lender is uninterested in taking these steps, or will do so only in return for financial concessions that the converter finds unacceptable. The alternate approach for the converter is to obtain an interim loan from a different lender that will contain the necessary language, and to use its proceeds to pay off the existing loan. The attractiveness of this technique will depend on numerous factors, including the interest rate and other costs associated with the interim loan, and the prepayment penalty that may be demanded by the old lender.

Capital Gain on Conversion and Other Problems, 40 N.Y.U.Fed.Tax.Inst. 22–1 (1982); Livsey, Minimizing the Tax Consequences of Condominium Conversions and Other Real Property Development, 39 N.Y.U.Fed.Tax.Inst. 28–1 (1981); Miller, Can A Straight Condominium Conversion Produce A Capital Gain?, 54 J.Tax. 8 (Jan. 1981); Comment, Capital Gains Treatment for Gain Realized in Condominium Conversions, 47 Mo.L.Rev. 269 (1982).

2. 1 P. Rohan & M. Reskin, Condominium Law & Practice § 3A.01 (1984).

3. See Channing, Condominium Conversions: A Developer's View, 55 Fla.B.J. 85 (1981); Moss, Checklist for Successful Condominium Conversions, 5 Real Est.Rev. 116 (No. 3, 1975).

4. See, e.g., New York—McKinney's Gen.Bus.Law § 352–e et seq.; West's Fla. Stat.Ann. § 718.604–.622; 2 P. Rohan & M. Reskin, Cooperative Housing Law & Practice § 6.09 (1983) (summarizing state and local regulations throughout the nation); Comment, Displacement in Gentrifying Neighborhoods: Regulating Condominium Conversion Through Municipal Land Use Controls, 63 Bos.U.L.Rev. 955 (1983); Judson, Defining Property Rights: The Constitutionality of Protecting Tenants from Condominium Conversion, 187 Harv.Civ. Rts–Civ.Lib.L.Rev. 179 (1983); Kamer, Conversion of Rental Housing to Unit Ownership—A Noncrisis, 10 Real Est.L.J. 187 (1982).

Interim loans to finance conversions usually do not require regular principal amortization, but do require the reduction of the principal by some agreed amount for each condominium unit sold, much in the same manner as blanket construction loans on subdivisions.[5] They are usually limited to 75 or 80 percent of the property's value *as a condominium*, but if this would result in a loan approaching 100 percent of the value as a rental project, the interim lender will often require some cash investment by the converter, thus limiting the loan to, perhaps, 90 percent of the rental value. In any event, the "value" on which the loan is based will generally include the cost of the renovations that the converter plans to make. A portion of the interim loan may even be disbursed in installments as these improvements are put in place, as with a construction loan.

The interim lender is intensely concerned with the converter's cash flow projections for the conversion period. The building must generate enough cash to cover any periodic interest payments due on the interim loan as well as the usual operating, maintenance, and management costs of a rental building, and the converter's obligation to pay assessments to the new owners' association. Since a shortfall can easily result in default and foreclosure of the interim mortgage, the interim lender must be confident that it can complete the conversion successfully if necessary.

The long-term financing for units in the converted building is no different than the financing of condominium units in a newly constructed building. However, FHA loans are not available in a conversion project unless a year has elapsed since the conversion, the mortgage applicant was formerly a tenant in the building, or the conversion was sponsored by a bona fide tenants' organization.[6] Congress' apparent objective in enacting these restrictions in 1983 was to avoid encouraging conversions that would drive existing lower-income tenants out of rental housing.

Conversion of rental buildings to cooperatives is far less common than conversion to condominiums except in New York, where it is a

---

5. See Reppe, Winning Over the Condominium Lender, 5 Real Est.Rev. 104 (No. 2, 1975); Fantini, A Practical Primer for Analyzing Condominium Conversions, 34 Mortgage Banker 48 (Aug. 1973).

6. § 234(k), National Housing Act, 12 U.S.C.A. § 1715y(k). Prior to enactment of the Housing and Urban–Rural Recovery Act of 1983, Pub.L.No. 98–181, § 420, FHA was permitted to insure individual condominium unit mortgages only if the project (construction) mortgage was also FHA insured, unless the project had 11 or fewer units or more than one year had elapsed since its completion. The cited statute eliminated these restrictions; see 52 Fed. Reg. 33804 (Sept. 8, 1987). A previous rule prohibiting investor-owners from obtaining FHA loans unless they occupied at least one unit in the project under and FHA-insured mortgage was also repealed. However, FHA may not insure a mortgage on a condominium unit if approval would result in less than 80 percent of the units being occupied by mortgagors; see 24 CFR § 234.36(e)(2).

The statutory and regulatory amendments cited above also prohibit FHA insurance of a mortgage on a condominium in a project converted from rental use unless (1) the conversion is more than one year old; (2) the mortgagor is a former tenant of the rental building; or (3) the conversion was sponsored by a tenants' organization which represented a majority of the households in the rental building.

frequent and closely regulated occurrence.[7] The motivations for a cooperative conversion are much the same as have been discussed above; avoidance of rent control and high costs, and the opportunity to make a substantial profit.[8] However, the financing problems are much simpler since, absent a due-on-sale clause, the agreement of the existing lender is generally unneeded and the conversion can proceed without its participation.[9] Often the outstanding balance on the existing financing will be too low to make conversion feasible. In such cases the existing loan may be refinanced, or if its interest rate is so low that it is worth preserving, a wrap-around or second mortgage may be arranged to provide cash for refurbishing the building and to lower the required down payments of the apartment purchasers. Separate original, interim, and permanent loans are not necessarily required, however; if the existing financing on the rental building is satisfactory, there is usually no reason that it cannot be carried through the conversion period and become the permanent financing for the cooperators.

§ 13.5 Permanent Financing of Condominium Units

Permanent mortgage loans on condominium units can generally be made by institutional lenders on the same terms as loans on detached houses or other buildings. However, the permanent lender on a condominium unit must be concerned with many factors which are unimportant or nonexistent in the financing of subdivision houses.[1] Most of

---

7. See New York—McKinney's Gen. Bus.Law § 352–e (conversions in New York State generally), § 352–ee (conversions of nonresidential property), § 352–eee (conversions in municipalities of Westchester, Nassau & Rockland Counties which adopt it), and § 352–eeee (conversions in New York City.) These rules are summarized in 2 P. Rohan & M. Reskin, Cooperative Housing Law & Practice § 6.04 (1983); Comment, Examining Cooperative Conversion: An Analysis of Recent New York Legislation, 11 Ford.Urb.L.J. 1089 (1982). See Richards v. Kaskel, 32 N.Y.2d 524, 347 N.Y.S.2d 1, 300 N.E.2d 388 (1973).

8. See 2 P. Rohan & M. Reskin, supra note 6, at § 6.09[1] (1983). In Jayson Investments, Inc. v. Kemp, 746 F.Supp. 807 (N.D.Ill.1990), HUD encouraged the converter to purchase the building because its previous owner was in default on a HUD-insured mortgage loan, and absent the conversion HUD would have been obliged to take title and market the building. See also Bernstein–Baker, Cooperative Conversion: Is it Only for the Wealthy? Proposals that Promote Affordable Cooperative Housing in Philadelphia, 61 Temp. L. Rev. 393 (1988), arguing that conversion to limited-equity cooperative status can provide significant housing benefits for low and moderate income families.

9. Not necessarily so, however, if the rental project was insured under a HUD subsidized housing program. See Boston Five Cents Savings Bank v. Secretary of HUD, 768 F.2d 5 (1st Cir.1985) (conversion might constitute a "change of use" as that phrase was used in the HUD regulatory agreement). See Joselow, Cooperatives: Shared Ownership in 1985, Mortgage Banking, Nov. 1985, at 44, pointing out the advantages of preserving an existing low-interest blanket mortgage when converting a rental building to cooperative form.

§ 13.5

1. See generally Anderson & Buck, Attorneys' and Lenders' Guide to Common Interest Ownership Acts (1989); Rosenthal, Condominium and P.U.D. Projects: Steps to Approval, Mortgage Banking, May, 1984, at 57; Jackson, Attorneys for Lenders: What You Should Check in Condominium and PUD Documentations, (pts. 1 & 2) 4 Barrister 47 (Winter), 55 (Spring) (1977) [hereinafter cited as Jackson]; Waldron, Curtain May Soon Rise on Act Two of Condominium Problems, 37 Mortgage Banker 27 (Nov. 1976); Zinman, Condominium Investments and the Institutional Lender—A Review, Symposium on the Law of Condominiums, 48 St.John's L.Rev. 749 (1974).

these factors are related to the importance of the owner's association and the common areas to the success (and thus the future security value) of the project. While the discussion which follows concentrates on the permanent lender's concerns, construction lenders should also be cognizant of the factors mentioned, since they may be forced into a permanent lending role in the event of the developer's default on the construction loan or the permanent lender's refusal to honor its loan commitment. Indeed, unit purchasers themselves should be equally mindful of these problem areas, although they are often insufficiently sophisticated to realize the potential dangers.

Certain precautions are particularly significant to the permanent lender if it finances the sale of some units while other units or the common areas are still under construction or remain in the developer's hands. Obviously, the unit being financed should itself be completed. To ensure that the project will be successfully marketed as a condominium, many permanent lenders impose a "pre-sale requirement;" that is, they will refuse to close any loans until the developer has entered into binding sale contracts for some fixed percentage of the units.[2] The permanent lender will also be legitimately concerned with the developer's financial ability to complete the project, and may wish to verify that sufficient funds remain in the construction loan account for this purpose.

The payment of assessments to the association for unsold units can also pose a problem. Many statutes make no distinction between sold and unsold units, and require that assessments be collected uniformly from all.[3] This approach seems unreasonable from the developer's viewpoint, since unoccupied units obviously contribute little or nothing to certain variable costs of the association's operations; for example, they supply no users for the swimming pool, tennis courts, or equestrian trails. On the other hand, many fixed costs are independent of the number of users. A fair resolution of this problem would be to require a somewhat smaller assessment for units still owned by the developer than are paid for occupied units. While a two-level assessment system is not permitted under many statutes, the same result may be achieved if the developer pays a full assessment but is entitled to reimbursement of a portion from the other owners under a separate contract. Alternatively, the developer might pay the full assessment amounts and attempt to recover the outlays through higher sale prices for the later-sold units.[4] In any event, the permanent lender should ascertain that the developer is obligated to pay a fair share of the costs of operating the association during the marketing period and has the financial strength to do so; a default might result in deteriorating physical

---

[2]. See Vishny, Financing the Condominium, 1970 U.Ill.L.F. 181, 190.

[3]. U.C.A. § 3-115 requires that once any units have been assessed, all units (including those still owned by the developer) must be assessed under the same formula. Until that time, however, the developer is free to pay all common area expenses.

[4]. See Wolfe, How to Set Up a Homeowners Association So It Works For (Not Against) You, House & Home 74 (Sept. 1974).

facilities or a financially weakened or even insolvent association. The lender may even require a cash deposit from the developer to secure these payments.

The permanent lender must also be concerned with the developer's attempts to retain control over the association until most of the units have been sold. Often this is accomplished by creating two classes of stock, attached to unsold and sold units respectively, with the former having a greater voting power. For example, if the first class has three votes per share and the second only one vote per share, the developer can maintain effective control until the project is three-fourths sold. This degree of retention of control is probably reasonable to protect the developer against the enactment of rules or procedures that might make the project unattractive to some buyers, and thus might impair the developer's marketing program.[5] The permanent mortgagee, however, may refuse to lend if the period of developer control will extend past some given percentage of units transferred, and may also insist on the fixing of an outside date by which control must pass to the unit owners irrespective of the number of sales.

Virtually every important aspect of the association's ongoing functions concerns the permanent lender, since operational inadequacies may be reflected in diminished security value of the units. Questions on which the lender will need to be satisfied include the following: Is membership in the association automatic? Has a lien for unpaid assessments been created by proper language in the declaration or master deed? Has the association established a reasonable budget, supported by adequate assessment amounts? Is the assessment delinquency rate reasonably low? Have adequate reserves for repairs and replacements been set up, with provision that they not be used except for specified items? Has a competent management firm been hired if the project is large enough to justify it? Is the project subject to unreasonable management contracts or recreational facility leases? Is an independent annual audit made of the association's books? Has adequate blanket insurance been arranged for the common areas and exteriors of units, with provision for increased coverage to match inflation?

Many permanent lenders insist on certain types of protection in the condominium documentation. For example, the lender may want: notice from the association of default in assessments by any of its mortgagors; exemption (if the lender becomes the owner of a unit through foreclosure) from the usual clause giving the association a right of first refusal or other right to control the subsequent transfer of the unit, and from any restriction on leasing of units; notice of cancellation of any insurance policies on the project; the right to examine the association's books at reasonable times; notice of associa-

---

5. Id. at 83. A few statutes expressly limit the period of developer control; see, e.g., U.C.A. § 3–103; West's Fla.Stat.Ann. §§ 718.301 (condominiums), 719.301 (cooperatives).

tion meetings and the right to attend; notice of any substantial loss or damage to common areas; and the right to vote on, or even to veto, such major policy decisions as the hiring or firing of a management firm, amendments to the declaration or bylaws, expansion or contraction of the project, or use of hazard insurance proceeds other than for repairs.

Finally, the lender will probably wish to redraft its usual mortgage and note forms to add special provisions relating to condominiums.[6] These revisions will usually include covenants by the mortgagor to pay association assessments when due, to notify the lender of any delinquency notices received from the association, and to abide by all provisions of the condominium's declaration, bylaws, and rules. The documents may require that assessments be paid to an escrow or impound account. The mortgagor may also be required to covenant not to vote in favor of major policy changes in the project without the mortgagee's consent. Failure of the association to maintain adequate insurance coverage may be made a condition of default, and the lender may reserve the right to pay delinquent assessments and to charge them against the mortgagor's loan balance.

Authority of Lenders, Insurers, and Investors

There is little controversy concerning the power of lenders to make permanent mortgage loans on condominium units. Both federally-chartered and state-chartered institutions are generally permitted to treat them as the equivalent of single-family houses, although the lending powers of state-chartered institutions are a matter of state law and some variations exist.

The Federal Housing Administration (FHA) insures permanent mortgages on condominium units under the same general terms and conditions as mortgages on detached houses.[7]

The Veteran's Administration (VA) was first given authority to guarantee loans on condominium units in 1970, but could do so only when at least one unit in the project had been insured by FHA.[8] In 1975 this statutory limitation was dropped, and the VA now guarantees such loans regardless of prior FHA involvement.[9] VA imposes a number of requirements to protect its interests,[10] including a seventy percent presale requirement (which may be reduced in special circumstances), and limitations on reservations of rights by developers (such as

---

6. Condominium Rider, FNMA/FHLMC, Uniform Instrument; Grosser, Making the Loan Commitment, in Community Ass'n Institute, Summary of Proceedings, First Nat. Conference on Community Ass'ns 66 (1976).

7. National Housing Act § 234(c), 12 U.S.C.A. § 1715y(c); 24 CFR 234.-26(a)(1984). With respect to mortgages on units in buildings converted from rental use, see supra § 13.4 note 6.

8. Veterans Housing Act of 1970, § 3, 84 Stat. 1108 (current version at 38 U.S.C.A. § 1810(d)).

9. Veterans Housing Act of 1974, Pub.L. No. 93–569, § 3, 88 Stat. 1863 (adding 38 U.S.C.A. § 1810(a)(6) and repealing 38 U.S.C.A. § 1810(d)).

10. See 38 CFR 36.4356–.4360a, as amended, 50 Fed.Reg. 5975 (Feb. 13, 1985).

the leasing of common areas to the association and the retention of a veto over the association after unit owners obtain majority control). In addition, VA regards projects as unacceptable if they prohibit leasing of units for six months or more, or impose a right of first refusal upon resale.[11] As with FHA, the terms of the VA loan guarantee are identical to those on detached houses.[12]

Both the Federal National Mortgage Association (FNMA) and the Federal Home Loan Mortgage Corporation (FHLMC) purchase permanent mortgage loans on condominium units. The two agencies have similar, but not identical, requirements; they are too numerous and complex to be set out in detail here, but generally deal with the issues and concerns discussed earlier in this section.[13] The precise requirements depend on the nature of the project: primary residence, second home, or investor (rental) use. Among the matters covered by the FNMA and FHLMC rules are the following: the completion of common area improvements; the adequacy of reserves for repairs and replacements; the percentage of occupancy by year-round residents; the percentage of units pre-sold; the existence of reasonable provisions for transfer of control of the association from the developer to the residents; freedom for mortgagees from any rights of the association to restrict sales of units; and a power in the association to terminate management contracts by notice. This list is merely illustrative, and FNMA and FHLMC consider many other matters as well.[14]

An obvious concern to permanent lenders is the priority of the mortgage loan as against the lien of the owner's association for unpaid assessments. A large majority of the first-generation state statutes followed the FHA Model Act in providing that the lien is subordinate to any "first mortgage of record."[15] A few statutes subordinate the lien to

11. The latter requirement is imposed only on condominiums established after December 31, 1976; see 38 CFR 36.-4358(c)(6).

12. 38 CFR 36.4356.

13. See FHLMC, Sellers' and Servicers' Guide, ch. 20 (1989); FNMA, Selling Guide, Project Standards (Aug. 1, 1988).

14. The FNMA guidelines are reproduced in full and discussed in Anderson & Buck, Attorneys' and Lenders' Guide to Common Interest Ownership Acts (1989).

15. FHA Model Act § 23(a), supra § 13.1 note 2; N.Y.–McKinney's Real Prop.L. § 339–z; Va.Code § 55–79.85 (first mortgages "securing institutional lenders"). See Towne Realty, Inc. v. Edwards, 156 Wis.2d 344, 456 N.W.2d 651 (App.1990) (Wis.Stat.Ann. 703.02(12) defines "mortgage" to include a real estate installment contract vendor, and such a vendor therefore had priority over the association's lien).

The New York statute cited above has proven problematic. It states that the association's lien is prior to other liens "except all sums unpaid on a first mortgage of record." That seems clear enough, but statute also states that "upon the sale or conveyance of a unit, such unpaid common charges shall be paid out of the sale proceeds or by the grantee." See also Tex. Prop. Code Ann. § 81.201, to the same effect. In several cases associations have argued that the latter language applies to foreclosure sales, so that the mortgagee who buys at the sale must pay the delinquent assessments. In effect, this approach subordinates the mortgage to the association's lien, in seeming contradiction of the language previously quoted. Most of the New York courts considering the issue have rejected the associations' arguments and held that the mortgagee is free of any duty to pay the delinquency. See Bankers Trust Co. v. Board of Managers of Park 900 Corp., 181 A.D.2d 274, 584 N.Y.S.2d 576 (1992); Prudential Ins. Co. v. Ward, ___ Misc.2d ___, 586 N.Y.S.2d 698 (1992); Long Island Sav. Bank v. Gomez, 150 Misc.2d

all mortgages.[16] When a mortgage or lien not granted this sort of statutory priority comes into conflict with the association's lien, it is necessary to determine the latter's date for priority purposes. An argument can be made that it arises only when the applicable notice of lien is filed or served on the unit owner,[17] but the majority of jurisdictions have held instead that it relates back to the date the declaration itself was recorded creating the condominium regime.[18] Some of the statutes expressly dictate this result.[19] It seems the only sensible interpretation; otherwise, association liens would have priority against precious little.

Obviously, when a foreclosed mortgage has priority over the association's lien, the mortgagee or other purchaser at the foreclosure sale is not subject to any liability for the assessment delinquencies of the former mortgagor, and the foreclosure wipes out the association's lien as to such amounts.[20] However, the real covenant that imposes the lien

---

482, 568 N.Y.S.2d 536 (1991). See Bergman, First Mortgage vs. Condominium Common Charge Lien—In Legal and Political Battle, 64 N.Y.St.B.J. 34 (Jan.1992).

16. See, e.g.,Okl.Stat.Ann. tit.60, § 524; Utah Code Ann. 57–8–20; Brask v. Bank of St. Louis, 533 S.W.2d 223 (Mo.App. 1975).

17. See St. Paul Fed. Bank v. Wesby, 149 Ill.App.3d 1059, 103 Ill.Dec. 390, 501 N.E.2d 707 (1986), rejecting the relation-back view of the association's lien, where the declaration stated simply that the lien existed "in the event of such default." However, the court implied that express language in a declaration providing for relation back might be enforced. Board of Directors of Olde Salem Homeowners' Ass'n v. Secretary of Veterans Affairs, 226 Ill.App.3d 281, 168 Ill.Dec. 361, 589 N.E.2d 761 (1992) took the same position with respect to an association lien in a non-condominium planned unit development.

18. In re Lincoln, 30 B.R. 905 (Bkrtcy. Colo.1983); Bessemer v. Gersten, 381 So.2d 1344 (Fla.1980); Inwood North Homeowners' Ass'n v. Harris, 736 S.W.2d 632 (Tex.1987). The relation back concept can also be applied in other contexts. In Flagler Fed. Sav. & Loan Ass'n v. Crestview Towers Condominium, 595 So.2d 198 (Fla. 1992), the condominium declaration was amended after a mortgage was given on a unit. The mortgagee did not join in execution of the amendment, but was nonetheless held bound by it, on the ground that the declaration (and its provisions for amendment) were on record when the mortgage was given.

19. E.g., N.Y.–McKinney's Real Prop.L. § 339–z; N.H.Rev.Stat.Ann. 356–B:46; Uniform Condominium Act § 3–116(b). See R. Natelson, Law of Property Owners Associations § 6.3.2 (1989); Winokur, Meaner Lienor Community Associations: The "Super Priority" Lien and Related Reforms Under the Uniform Common Interest Ownership Act, 27 Wake For. L.Rev. 353, at nn.15–21 (1992).

20. FHA Model Act § 23(b), supra § 13.1 note 2. See First Federal Sav. Bank of Georgia v. Eaglewood Court Condominium Ass'n, Inc., 186 Ga.App. 605, 367 S.E.2d 876 (1988), in which the applicable statute did indeed relieve the foreclosing mortgagee from liability for (and the lien of) assessments accruing prior to foreclosure. However, the statute expressly stated that a pro rata share of the uncollectible prior assessments, being treated now as common expenses, would become the liability of the foreclosing mortgagee. The court read this provision to apply only to the unpaid base assessments, and not to such additional amounts as attorneys' fees, late charges, interest, and litigation expense associated with the unpaid assessments. It held that not even a pro rata share of these latter amounts could be imposed on the foreclosing mortgagee.

What is the precise time the foreclosing mortgagee's (or foreclosure sale purchaser's) liability for future assessments commences? In Newport Condominium Ass'n v. Talman Home Fed. Sav. & Loan Ass'n, 188 Ill.App.3d 1054, 136 Ill.Dec. 612, 545 N.E.2d 136 (1988), the mortgagee received a sheriff's certificate of sale following completion of the foreclosure. The mortgagee was entitled to exchange the certificate for a sheriff's deed after the six-month redemption period expired, but did not do so until two years after the foreclosure. The

continues to run with the land, and assessments that accrue after the mortgage foreclosure do become the liability of the foreclosure purchaser, secured by the lien.[21]

The drafters of the Uniform Condominium Act and the Uniform Common Interest Ownership Act (UCIOA) were dissatisfied with the usual statutory approach granting a full priority against the association's lien to first mortgage holders. At the same time, they recognized that to give the association unlimited priority would be extremely harsh to mortgage lenders, who might find themselves subordinate to thousands of dollars in delinquent assessments. As a compromise, they provided that the association's lien would have "super priority" even over first mortgages, but only to the extent of six months' regular expense assessments. The lien has full priority over other mortgages.[22] There are numerous questions of interpretation of the UCIOA and UCA super-priority provisions,[23] and they have received considerable opposition from lenders and secondary mortgage market investors, but they seem fundamentally sound, representing a reasonable accommodation of the lender's need to realize on its security with the association's need to collect the money necessary to maintain the project.

In an effort to avoid assessment defaults, some permanent mortgage lenders require their mortgagors to pay association assessments into an impound, reserve, or escrow account similar to those customarily maintained for taxes and insurance; the lender then remits the sums collected to the association on a regular basis. Most lenders are

court held the mortgagee's assessment liability began only when it in fact obtained the sheriff's deed. Accord, see Board of Directors of Olde Salem Homeowners' Ass'n v. Secretary of Veterans Affairs, 226 Ill.App.3d 281, 168 Ill.Dec. 361, 589 N.E.2d 761 (1992) (non-condominium planned unit development).

See also Damen Sav. and Loan Ass'n v. Johnson, 126 Ill.App.3d 940, 82 Ill.Dec. 66, 467 N.E.2d 1139 (1984) (foreclosing mortgagee has priority over association's right to take possession of unit of defaulting owner); St. Paul Fed. Bank for Sav. v. Wesby, 149 Ill.App.3d 1059, 103 Ill.Dec. 390, 501 N.E.2d 707 (1986) (association lien is subordinate to first and second mortgages, since lien only takes effect when association's assessment becomes delinquent).

21. See Chateaux Condominiums v. Daniels, 754 P.2d 425, 427 (Colo.App.1988); cases cited supra note 20. Century Park Condominium Ass'n v. Norwest Bank, 420 N.W.2d 349 (N.D.1988) may be contra. There the units foreclosed upon were unconstructed and consisted of vacant land of apparently little value; the mortgagee, after buying them at the foreclosure sale, abandoned them to a tax sale, and perhaps would have been better advised not to foreclose at all. The court held that the mortgagee would be liable for assessments accruing during the time it held title to the units only if it knew, when it took the mortgage, that unconstructed units were subject to assessment. The court did not appear to rule out the possibility of the mortgagee's having constructive notice of that fact from the recorded declaration, but remanded the case for further findings on the issue of the mortgagee's knowledge.

22. UCIOA § 3–116; UCA § 3–116. State statutes adopting this language include Alaska Stat. 34.08.470; West's Colo. Rev.Stat.Ann. § 38–33.3–316; Conn.Gen. Stat.Ann. § 47–258; D.C.Code § 45–1853; Nev.Rev.Stat. 116.3116; Pa.Cons.Stat.Ann. § 5–3101 to 5–3414; R.I.Gen.Laws § 34–36.1–1.01 to 34–36.1–4.20; Va.Code § 36B–3–116; West's Rev.Code Ann. § 64.34.-364(4). Some states adopting the UCA or UCIOA did not include the super priority feature in their statutes. See Winokur, Meaner Lienor Community Associations: The "Super Priority" Lien and Related Reforms Under the Uniform Common Interest Ownership Act, 27 Wake For.L.Rev. 353, at n.50 (1992).

23. The problems are ably analyzed in Winokur, supra note 22.

unenthusiastic about this technique, however, since it involves much more frequent payouts than are necessary for tax and insurance funds. The drafters of the UCA and UCIOA superpriority provisions expected that their adoption would stimulate lenders to begin escrowing association assessments,[24] but there is little evidence that such a movement has developed among lenders in the states enacting superpriority. Collection of assessments by the lender is a useful and desirable means of discouraging delinquencies and stabilizing the association's cash flow, but thus far relatively few lenders have considered it worth the trouble.

§ 13.6 Permanent Financing of Cooperative Units

Traditionally the only permanent financing encumbering a cooperative project was its blanket mortgage. In most respects lenders have viewed blanket mortgages as similar to loans on rental apartment buildings, although they have been concerned to some extent with the governance, internal procedures, and financial stability of cooperative corporations. Permanent blanket mortgages (as well as construction loans) on cooperative projects can be insured by FHA under section 213 of the National Housing Act.[1] Loan-to-value ratios may be as high as ninety-eight percent, a feature that makes section 213 more attractive than conventional loans, which are generally limited to eighty percent of value. While the time and complexity of FHA processing under section 213 reduce its usefulness, the program was for a time very active in those jurisdictions in which cooperatives are popular.[2]

Conventional blanket loans on co-ops are also widely available. Federal savings and loan associations are authorized by the Office of Thrift Supervision to make blanket loans on cooperatives on the same basis as on other (e.g. rental) projects.[3] OTS requires the cooperative to maintain both general operating reserves and reserves for replacements in the same amounts as are required by the FHA section 213 program.[4]

Beginning with the New York statute enacted in 1971,[5] many states have authorized institutional lenders to make loans, often called

---

24. See Wittie, Origins of the Community Association's Special Lien Priority for Unpaid Assessments Under the Uniform Acts, Multiple Ownership Acts Symposium (Community Ass'ns Inst.Research Found., Joint Editorial Bd.for Real Property Acts of the Am. Bar Ass'n & Uniform Laws Conference, 1991), at 171, 173; UCIOA § 3–116 comment. 1.

§ 13.6

1. 12 U.S.C.A. § 1715e.

2. From the initiation of the § 213 program in 1950 through 1975, project mortgages on 116,155 units were insured. The states in which use of the program was heaviest were (in order of decreasing use) California, New York, Florida, Arizona, Michigan, Illinois and New Jersey. California and New York were roughly equal in participation, and together accounted for 57 percent of the units. See U.S. Dep't of Housing and Urban Development, 1975 Statistical Yearbook 134 (1976). Participation has generally dropped off sharply in recent years.

3. 12 CFR 545.33(g)(1).

4. See 24 CFR 213.30.

5. New York—McKinney's Banking Law §§ 103(5) (banks), 235(8–a) (savings banks), 380(2–a) (savings and loan associations). These statutes have undergone a series of liberalizing amendments since their enactment in 1981. They now permit maturities and loan-to-value ratios as generous as on loans made to owner-occupants of single-family homes. See generally Goldstein, Institutional Purchase Money

"share loans," on the security of individual cooperative units.[6] Prior to this development, lack of institutional financing was a major impediment to the financial success of cooperatives. Purchasers of units were obliged to pay cash, obtain personal loans from external sources, or negotiate installment contracts or promissory notes with unit sellers to cover the the difference between the selling price of the unit and its pro rata portion of the blanket mortgage.

Institutional financing of individual co-op units was given further impetus by section 4(b) of the Emergency Home Purchase Act of 1974, which added a new subsection (n) to section 203 of the National Housing Act, authorizing FHA to insure individual unit loans.[7] Under FHA's regulations, the loan must be secured by a first lien on the corporate stock certificate and the "occupancy certificate" or proprietary lease. The loan maturity is limited to thirty years or the remaining term of the blanket mortgage, whichever is less.[8] The FHA regulations recognize that a unit purchaser is always taking, in effect, subject to the blanket mortgage; thus, a lien on the unit is economically analogous to a second mortgage. The regulations limit the share loan to no more than the normal FHA amount, less the unit's pro-rata share of the blanket mortgage.[9]

Several of the other major federal agencies involved in housing have followed FHA's example and included cooperative share loans in their programs. The Office of Thrift Supervision authorizes federally-chartered savings and loan associations to make share loans on the same basis as loans on detached housing.[10] The Veterans Administration authorizes share loans under its loan guaranty program, although it reserves the right to make project-by-project determinations of acceptability, rather than issuing detailed regulations specifying what loans will be approved.[11] The Federal National Mortgage Association [12] has a program for purchasing share loans originated by local lending institutions.[13] In the aggregate, these changes represent a vast increase in institutional borrowing opportunities over those available before the 1970s.

Financing of Cooperative Apartments, 46 St.Johns L.Rev. 632 (1972).

6. See, e.g., West's Ann.Cal.Financial Code § 7133.4; Mass.Gen.Laws Ann. c. 157B, § 1; Minn.Stat.Ann. § 47.20 subd. 3; N.J.Stat.Ann. 17:2–6.

7. 12 U.S.C.A. § 1709(n). See 24 CFR 203.43c(f). Initially, FHA could insure unit loans only in buildings that were subject to blanket mortgages insured by FHA under section 213, but this limitation was removed by § 419 of the Housing and Urban–Rural Recovery Act of 1983, Pub.L. No. 98–181, with respect to projects completed for more than one year. See 49 Fed.Reg. 40188 (Oct. 15, 1984).

8. 24 CFR 203.43c(h)(4).

9. See 24 CFR 203.43c(g).

10. 12 CFR 545.33(g)(2).

11. See 38 CFR 36.4343.

12. See FNMA, Selling Guide, Project Standards (Aug. 1, 1988), at 45–54. For a thorough description of FNMA's cooperative programs for both blanket and share loans, see Mancus, Yours, Mine, and Ours, Mortgage Banking, July 1985, at 15.

13. See also BNA Hsg. & Devel.Rptr., Aug. 27, 1984, at 273, describing a corporation, the Share Loan Service Corporation (SLSC), created to purchase share loans primarily for resale to FNMA.

Creating and Foreclosing Share Loan Security Interests

Despite the great expansion in institutional lending on cooperative apartments, there is still a surprising degree of uncertainty as to the proper method for a lender to acquire, perfect, and foreclose on a security interest in the stock and proprietary lease that represent ownership of a co-op unit. The problem stems from the fact that the cooperator holds two inseparable rights—a share of stock, which seems undeniably personal property, and a leasehold which may be viewed either as realty or personalty.[14] This dichotomy has proven troublesome in a variety of contexts: whether the federal securities laws govern cooperative apartment sales,[15] whether the usual rights and duties associated with landlord-tenant law apply,[16] and whether real estate or personal property concepts govern sales contracts[17] and distribution of decedents' estates.[18]

On the specific problem of perfection of a security interest in a cooperative apartment, the case law is helpful but not fully satisfactory. The New York courts approached the question by drawing an analogy to the cases that involve enforcement of sales contracts on cooperative apartments; those cases take the position that the principal rights of

---

14. The leasehold estate was traditionally regarded as a "chattel real," a species of personal property; see R. Cunningham, W. Stoebuck & D. Whitman, Property § 6.11 (2d ed. 1993).

15. They do not; see United Housing Foundation, Inc. v. Forman, 421 U.S. 837, 95 S.Ct. 2051, 44 L.Ed.2d 621 (1975), rehearing denied 423 U.S. 884, 96 S.Ct. 157, 46 L.Ed.2d 115 (1975).

16. Compare Linden Hill No. 1 Cooperative Corp. v. Kleiner, 124 Misc.2d 1001, 478 N.Y.S.2d 519 (1984) (statute protecting tenant ownership of pets applies to cooperatives) and Suarez v. Rivercross Tenants' Corp., 107 Misc.2d 135, 438 N.Y.S.2d 164 (1981) (implied warranty of habitability for residential tenants applies to cooperatives) with Earl W. Jimerson Housing Co. v. Butler, 97 Misc.2d 563, 412 N.Y.S.2d 560 (1978) (summary possession procedure, normally applicable to landlord-tenant relationship, does not apply to cooperatives); Kohler v. Snow Village, Inc., 16 Ohio App.3d 350, 475 N.E.2d 1298 (1984) (antidiscrimination provisions of landlord-tenant act do not apply to cooperatives). See also supra § 13.1 note 16.

17. Presten v. Sailer, 225 N.J.Super. 178, 542 A.2d 7 (1988) (contract for sale of cooperative apartment is real estate for purposes of statute of frauds); Moloney v. Weingarten, 118 A.D.2d 836, 500 N.Y.S.2d 320 (1986) (same); Weiss v. Karch, 62 N.Y.2d 849, 850, 477 N.Y.S.2d 615, 615, 466 N.E.2d 155 (1984) (sale of cooperative apartment is analogous to a sale of securities, governed by Article 2 of the Uniform Commercial Code); Friedman v. Sommer, 63 N.Y.2d 788, 481 N.Y.S.2d 326, 471 N.E.2d 139 (1984) (same); Silverman v. Alcoa Plaza Associates, 37 A.D.2d 166, 323 N.Y.S.2d 39 (1971) (U.C.C. Art. 2 governs, prohibiting forfeiture of purchaser's earnest money deposit); McManus v. McManus, 83 A.D.2d 553, 440 N.Y.S.2d 954 (1981), affirmed 55 N.Y.2d 855, 447 N.Y.S.2d 708, 432 N.E.2d 601 (1982), dismissed 55 N.Y.2d 605, 447 N.Y.S.2d 1029, 432 N.E.2d 604 (1982) (U.C.C. Art. 2 governs in determination that contract of sale is enforceable despite omission of price term.) See also Stockton v. Lucas, 482 F.2d 979 (T.E.C.A.1973) (stock and lease are personal property for purposes of federal price control legislation); Star v. 308 Owners Corp., 130 Misc.2d 732, 497 N.Y.S.2d 282, 283 (1985) (building code enforceable against cooperative unit, as holder of interest in real estate; Matter of Carton, 4 B.R. 401, 403 (Bkrtcy.Md.1980) (under Maryland law, owner's interest in cooperative apartment is real estate for purposes of attachment of judgment lien).

18. In re Jack's Estate, 126 Misc.2d 1060, 484 N.Y.S.2d 489 (1985) (cooperative apartment interest treated as personalty); In re Miller's Estate, 205 Misc. 770, 130 N.Y.S.2d 295 (1954) (same). See also Greene v. Levenhar, 24 B.R. 331 (Bkrtcy. N.Y.1982) (cooperative apartment interest is personalty, and hence cannot be held in tenancy by the entirety.)

§ 13.6   FINANCING   311

the cooperative tenant stem from the ownership of shares, and thus that the UCC controls.[19] This suggests that the UCC should govern issues relating to security interests as well. The New York Court of Appeals adopted this view in 1977 in State Tax Commission v. Shor.[20] It held that, since the cooperative apartment was not to be regarded as realty, a creditor who obtained a judgment against an apartment owner would not thereby acquire an automatic lien on the apartment. In dictum, the court asserted that a lender could perfect a security interest in the apartment merely by taking possession of the shares and the lease, in a manner analogous of the taking of a pledge of chattel paper or a promissory note.[21] The share of stock was viewed as the primary indicium of ownership, with the lease being merely ancillary. Since under UCC § 9–305, a share of stock is an "instrument," perfection could be accomplished by possession, and no filing of a financing statement would be necessary.[22] Subsequent New York state and federal court decisions confirmed this view.[23]

Lenders outside New York may well be uncomfortable with these conclusions. They may point to UCC Article 9's statement that it is inapplicable to "the creation or transfer of an interest in or lien on real estate, including a lease * * *."[24] To guard against the possibility that their interest in the proprietary lease will be held unperfected, they may wish to obtain and record a real estate mortgage on the leasehold estate, in addition to taking possession of the documents and filing under Article 9.[25] Whether all of this is necessary is simply unclear in most jurisdictions.

19. See cases cited note 17 supra.

20. 43 N.Y.2d 151, 400 N.Y.S.2d 805, 371 N.E.2d 523 (1977).

21. U.C.C. § 9–305: "A security interest in * * * goods, instruments, * * * or chattel paper may be perfected by the secured party's taking possession of the collateral." See § 5.28 supra at notes 24–42.

22. See U.C.C. § 9–302(1). Under the *Shor* case, one writer suggested that filing might still be important as a device to protect against federal tax liens and the possible bankruptcy of the cooperator; see Rifkin, Co-op Proprietary Leases, N.Y.S.B.J., June 1979, at 290; cf. Superior Financial Corp. v. Haskell, 556 F.Supp. 199 (S.D.N.Y.1983).

23. Superior Financial Corp. v. Haskell, supra note 22 (upholding priority of lender's unfiled security interest in cooperative apartment, perfected by possession of documents, against a subsequently-filed federal tax lien); Brief v. 120 Owners Corp., 157 A.D.2d 515, 549 N.Y.S.2d 706 (1990) (same, as against all subsequent liens including federal tax liens). A contrary argument can be made if one views the lease as the principal indication of ownership, with the stock as the ancillary item; a lease is plainly not an "instrument," and might be characterized as a "general intangible" under UCC § 9–106, perfection of which could be accomplished only by the filing of a financing statement. Alternatively, a security interest in the lease might simply be regarded as a real estate interest subject to perfection by recordation as a mortgage in the real property records. The New York cases cited rejected this view, but it was followed (in a transaction arising before the New Jersey legislation discussed infra at note 30) by In re McGuinness, 139 B.R. 3 (Bkrtcy.N.J. 1992), disagreeing with Presten v. Sailer, 225 N.J.Super. 178, 542 A.2d 7 (1988), at n.5. See Rifkin, Co-operative Proprietary Leases, 51 N.Y.S.B.J. 290 (1979).

24. U.C.C. § 9–104(j).

25. See P. Rohan & M. Reskin, Cooperative Housing Law & Practice § 5A.08(3) (1984). In New York, recording of a mortgage apparently gives rise to liability for the mortgage recording tax, a result to be avoided if possible.

A related question arises as to how a creditor can properly foreclose upon a security interest in a cooperative apartment. In FDIC v. Evans,[26] the secured lender, which had taken a possessory pledge of the shares and lease, conducted a nonjudicial sale to a bona fide purchaser, relying on UCC § 9–504's authorization to secured parties to dispose of collateral in a "commercially reasonable" manner. The court found this action proper, and rejected the argument of the preceding paragraph that a security interest in the proprietary lease is excluded from UCC Article 9.[27] In another case, the New York Appellate Division indicated that a judicial foreclosure under Article 9 would also be proper.[28] But a Bankruptcy Court applying Illinois law disagreed, noting that the proprietary lease was real property, so that a collateral assignment of it was not within the scope of Article 9 and would have to be foreclosed as a real estate mortgage. The court conceded that Article 9 would control a foreclosure on shares of stock alone as collateral, but concluded that it would be improper to permit the severance of the lease and stock rights in a cooperative in order to subject the stock to Article 9.[29]

Because of the bifurcated nature of cooperative apartment ownership, questions of perfection and foreclosure of security interests are not easily answered within the framework of existing law. Clarifying legislation is badly needed, and has been enacted in two of the states where many cooperatives are located. A 1988 New York statute adopted the view of prior case law that cooperative apartments are personal property, but declared that security interests in them must be perfected by the filing of an Article 9 financing statement in the local government office in which real estate mortgages are recorded.[30] New Jersey took a different approach, but with much the same ultimate result; in 1988 its legislature adopted an act that treats cooperative units as a special type of real estate, with transfers of title and perfection of security interests accomplished through recordation in the

26. No. 75–C–1947 (E.D.N.Y. Apr. 14, 1976), unreported. The opinion is reprinted in full in P. Rohan & M. Reskin, supra note 12, at § 5A.08(3) n. 32 (1984). See also Mehralian v. Riverview Tower Homeowners Ass'n, 464 N.W.2d 571 (Minn.App. 1990) (statute governing redemption following real estate mortgage foreclosure does not apply foreclosure of stock in cooperative apartment).

27. The court also rejected an argument that the sale was a violation of Due Process because it was held without a prior hearing. This is consistent with the usual attitude of the courts in reviewing power-of-sale foreclosures of real estate mortgages, see §§ 7.23–7.30 supra.

28. Fundex Capital Corp. v. Reichard, 172 A.D.2d 420, 568 N.Y.S.2d 794 (1991) (foreclosure of security interest in stock and proprietary lease is governed by UCC § 9–501(1), which authorizes the secured party to "reduce his claim to judgment, foreclose or otherwise enforce the security interest by any available judicial procedure").

29. In re McNair, 90 B.R. 912 (Bkrtcy. Ill.1988). These problems are largely resolved if the cooperative is of the type in which each owner holds a fractional share in the project as a tenant in common. Such interests are readily mortgageable and may be foreclosed upon. See Future Federal Sav. & Loan Ass'n v. Daunhauer, 687 S.W.2d 871 (Ky.App.1985).

30. McKinneys 1988 New York Laws, ch. 333, amending N.Y.—McKinney's UCC §§ 9–104, 9–304, 9–401, & 9–403. The last section mentioned declares that the filing is effective until terminated, without the need for periodic continuation statements.

county recorders' offices.[31] Such documents are recorded in the same way as real estate deeds and mortgages, and are also indexed in a master register maintained for each cooperative project.

This legislation has been extremely helpful in New York and New Jersey, but cooperatives in other states remain in a legally ambiguous position. An amendment to the UCC, adopted nationally, seems the best way to solve the problem, and the Article 9 Permanent Editorial Board has given some consideration to such an amendment, although no action on it has been taken at this writing.[32]

31. 1987 N.J.Laws, ch.381, enacting N.J.Rev.Stat. 46:8D-1 et seq. The statute has been construed to apply only to post-act cooperatives; see Drew Assoc. v. Travisano, 235 N.J.Super. 194, 561 A.2d 1177 (A.D.1989), affirmed in part, reversed in part on other grounds 122 N.J. 249, 584 A.2d 807 (1991). See also In re McGuinness, 139 B.R. 3 (Bkrtcy.N.J.1992), comparing pre-act law with the act; Meisel, A Look at the Coop Recording Act—And A Proposed Form, 122 N.J.L.J. 1130 (1988).

32. See Zinman, Report on Condominium Communities to the Advisory Group on Real Estate Related Collateral, UCC Article 9 Study Group.

§§ 13.7—14.0 are reserved for supplementary material.

Chapter 14

RESIDENTIAL FINANCING FORMS

Table of Sections

Sec.
14.1 Introduction.
14.2 FNMA/FHLMC Multistate Fixed Rate Note—Single Family.
14.3 FNMA/FHLMC Uniform Mortgage—Deed of Trust Covenants—Single Family.
14.4 FNMA/FHLMC Deed of Trust—Single Family—California.
14.5 FNMA/FHLMC Mortgage—Single Family—Kansas.
14.6 FNMA/FHLMC Mortgage With Power of Sale—Single Family—Minnesota.
14.7 FNMA/FHLMC Adjustable Rate Note.
14.8 FNMA/FHLMC Graduated Payment Note.
14.9 FNMA/FHLMC Growing Equity Note.
14.10 FNMA/FHLMC Fixed/Adjustable Rate Note.
14.11 FNMA/FHLMC Condominium Rider.
14.12 FNMA/FHLMC Uniform Instrument—1–4 Family Rider.
14.13 FHA Note and Deed of Trust—Fixed Rate Home Loan—Missouri.
14.14 FHA Adjustable Rate Note.
14.15 Department of Veterans Affairs Note and Deed of Trust—Fixed Rate Home Loan—Missouri.
14.16 FNMA/FHLMC Note, Deed of Trust and Rider—Fixed Rate Multifamily Loan—Texas.
14.17 Promissory Note, Combination Deed of Trust, Security Agreement and Fixture Filing, Assignment of Leases and Unsecured Indemnity Agreement—Multifamily Residential.

§ 14.1 Introduction

This chapter and the following one consist of real estate financing forms and commentary. The forms in this chapter are intended for long-term loans on single-family or multifamily residential property. Those in the next chapter are drafted for various commercial projects, or for the construction phase of residential projects.

The forms in this chapter are often those promulgated by the Federal National Mortgage Association (FNMA) and the Federal Home Loan Mortgage Corporation (FHLMC). Forms prepared by the Federal Housing Administration (FHA) and the Department of Veterans Affairs (DVA) are also included. We have also included a sophisticated Apartment Complex Financing Package supplied by Preston, Thorgrimson, Shidler, Gates & Ellis, a leading Seattle, Washington law firm.

These forms are widely available and might be obtained from the offices of most mortgage lending institutions. Yet we believe there is considerable value in reproducing them here. Our purpose is obviously not to supply them to readers who will use them verbatim in standard transactions. For such use, the printed versions supplied by the agencies mentioned above are more convenient. Rather, we view these forms as a sort of cafeteria of clauses from which a practitioner can gain ideas and language for use in transactions which may not fit precisely in the conventional mold. For this purpose, having the forms collected in one chapter, and coupled with our commentary, should prove a major convenience.

Of course, the drafter who uses these forms as a starting point or a source of language must work with care, making sure that he or she understands the way various terms are defined and the manner in which the concepts interact. This is especially important in respect to some of the more complex documents, such as those prepared for adjustable-rate and graduated-payment mortgages.

A word about the origin and history of these forms may be of interest. The FNMA/FHLMC forms are of relatively recent vintage. They stem from the enactment of the Emergency Home Finance Act of 1970, which created FHLMC and authorized both it and FNMA to create a secondary market in conventional mortgages. (FHMA's previous secondary market activities had all involved government-underwritten mortgages.) For a more extended discussion of both entities, see § 11.3, supra.

Both FNMA and FHLMC immediately realized that development of a conventional secondary market would be enormously impeded by the plethora of forms used throughout the nation for conventional mortgages. Unless a set of standard forms were developed, an individual review of the documents on every conventional loan submitted for purchase by FNMA or FHLMC would be necessary. Thus, in late 1970 and early 1971, FNMA and FHLMC prepared and circulated "exposure drafts" of note, mortgage, and deed of trust forms. On April 5 and 6, 1971, a public meeting was held on these drafts, with some 43 witnesses testifying. Both lending industry and consumer groups were fully represented, and there was testimony from several law professors.

Among the controversial issues were: whether impounding of tax and insurance payments should be required; whether hazard insurance claims should be applied as a matter of course to retirement of the debt; what sort of notice and grace period should be available prior to acceleration for default; whether a due-on-sale clause should be included; and the extent to which the forms should waive the borrower's homestead and marital rights. The issue of prepayment penalties was hotly debated, and ultimately resolved by language which imposed a penalty only if the loan was prepaid with the proceeds of a loan obtained from another lender—i.e., by refinancing. Although both FNMA and FHLMC dropped the prepayment penalty language entirely in 1980, the former clause remains a useful illustration of a creative drafting compromise.

Indeed, the entire process by which the FNMA/FHLMC forms were developed is exemplary of reasonable compromise. While the initial exposure drafts were quite pro-lender, the final versions gave both lenders and consumers a good deal to show for their efforts. The resulting forms have been modified in several respects since their promulgation, but most of the original language remains intact, and they are very widely employed, even by lenders who have no expectation of selling their loans to FNMA or FHLMC.

The FHA and VA forms are much older, having their inception in the 1930's and 1940's respectively. While they do not represent a public process of balancing lender and consumer interests in the manner of the FNMA/FHLMC documents, they have nonetheless stood the test of time and contain a good deal of useful language.

§ 14.2 FNMA/FHLMC Multistate Fixed Rate Note—Single Family

This Note, together with the Federal National Mortgage Association–Federal Home Loan Mortgage Corp. (FNMA/FHLMC) Uniform Mortgage and Deed of Trust Covenants considered in § 14.3 infra, constitute the core of the most pervasively used single family financing document package. Because use of these documents is required for secondary market purchase by FNMA/FHLMC, they have established a nationwide norm on numerous substantive issues, many of which are considered in Section 14.3 infra.

Two specific observations concerning the Note are appropriate. First, Section 4 affords the mortgagor the right to prepay the debt in whole or in part without a prepayment charge. See §§ 6.1–6.5 supra. Second, Section 10 of the Note restates the due-on-sale clause contained in Section 7 of the Uniform Covenants. See § 14.3 infra. In part, this duplication was probably designed to avoid the implication of the rule stated by some courts that "clauses in security instruments cannot affect notes unless they are also set forth in the note or at least incorporated by reference." Abdul–Karim v. First Federal Savings & Loan Association, 101 Ill.2d 400, 408, 78 Ill.Dec. 369, 373, 462 N.E.2d 488, 492 (1984) (due-on-sale clause in mortgage enforceable even though not contained in note, at least where no personal liability sought to be imposed); Becovic v. Harris Trust & Savings Bank, 469 N.E.2d 1379 (Ill.App.1984) (sufficient reference in note to trust deed to allow mortgagee to enforce due-on-sale clause contained in trust deed and to impose personal judgment on the maker).

NOTE

_____, 19__, _____, _____, _____.
　　　　　　　[City]　　[State]　　[Property Address]

1. BORROWER'S PROMISE TO PAY

In return for a loan that I have received, I promise to pay U.S. $_____ (this amount is called "principal"), plus interest, to the order of the Lender. The Lender is _____. I understand that the Lender may transfer this Note. The Lender or anyone who takes this Note by transfer and who is entitled to receive payments under this Note is called the "Note Holder."

2. INTEREST

Interest will be charged on unpaid principal until the full amount of principal has been paid. I will pay interest at a yearly rate of _____%.

The interest rate required by this Section 2 is the rate I will pay both before and after any default described in Section 6(B) of this Note.

3. PAYMENTS

(A) Time and Place of Payments

I will pay principal and interest by making payments every month.

I will make my monthly payments on the _____ day of each month beginning on _____, 19__. I will make these payments every month until I have paid all of the principal and interest and any other charges described below that I may owe under this Note. My monthly payments will be applied to interest before principal. If, on _____, _____, I still owe amounts under this Note, I will pay those amounts in full on that date, which is called the "maturity date."

I will make my monthly payments at _____ or at a different place if required by the Note Holder.

(B) Amount of Monthly Payments

My monthly payment will be in the amount of U.S. $_____.

4. BORROWER'S RIGHT TO PREPAY

I have the right to make payments of principal at any time before they are due. A payment of principal only is known as a "prepayment." When I make a prepayment, I will tell the Note Holder in writing that I am doing so.

I may make a full prepayment or partial prepayments without paying any prepayment charge. The Note Holder will use all of my prepayments to reduce the amount of principal that I owe under this Note. If I make a partial prepayment, there will be no changes in the due date or in the amount of my monthly payment unless the Note Holder agrees in writing to those changes.

5. LOAN CHARGES

If a law, which applies to this loan and which sets maximum loan charges, is finally interpreted so that the interest or other loan charges collected or to be collected in connection with this loan exceed the permitted limits, then: (i) any such loan charge shall be reduced by the amount necessary to reduce the charge to the permitted limit; and (ii) any sums already collected from me which exceeded permitted limits will be refunded to me. The Note Holder may choose to make this refund by reducing the principal I owe under this Note or by making a direct payment to me. If a refund reduces principal, the reduction will be treated as a partial prepayment.

6. BORROWER'S FAILURE TO PAY AS REQUIRED

(A) Late Charge for Overdue Payments

If the Note Holder has not received the full amount of any monthly payment by the end of _____ calendar days after the date it is due, I will pay a late charge to the Note Holder. The amount of the charge will be _____% of my overdue payment of principal and interest. I will pay this late charge promptly but only once on each late payment.

(B) Default

If I do not pay the full amount of each monthly payment on the date it is due, I will be in default.

(C) Notice of Default

If I am in default, the Note Holder may send me a written notice telling me that if I do not pay the overdue amount by a certain date, the Note Holder may require me to pay immediately the full amount of principal which has not been paid and all the interest that I owe on that amount. That date must be at least 30 days after the date on which the notice is delivered or mailed to me.

(D) No Waiver By Note Holder

Even if, at a time when I am in default, the Note Holder does not require me to pay immediately in full as described above, the Note Holder will still have the right to do so if I am in default at a later time.

(E) Payment of Note Holder's Costs and Expenses

If the Note Holder has required me to pay immediately in full as described above, the Note Holder will have the right to be paid back by me for all of its costs and expenses in enforcing this Note to the extent not prohibited by applicable law. Those expenses include, for example, reasonable attorneys' fees.

7. GIVING OF NOTICES

Unless applicable law requires a different method, any notice that must be given to me under this Note will be given by delivering it or by mailing it by first class mail to me at the Property Address above or at a different address if I give the Note Holder a notice of my different address.

Any notice that must be given to the Note Holder under this Note will be given by mailing it by first class mail to the Note Holder at the address stated in Section 3(A) above or at a different address if I am given a notice of that different address.

8. OBLIGATIONS OF PERSONS UNDER THIS NOTE

If more than one person signs this Note, each person is fully and personally obligated to keep all of the promises made in this Note, including the promise to pay the full amount owed. Any person who is a guarantor, surety or endorser of this Note is also obligated to do these things. Any person who takes over these obligations, including the obligations of a guarantor, surety or endorser of this Note, is also obligated to keep all of the promises made in this Note. The Note Holder may enforce its rights under this Note against each person individually or against all of us together. This means that any one of us may be required to pay all of the amounts owed under this Note.

9. WAIVERS

I and any other person who has obligations under this Note waive the rights of presentment and notice of dishonor. "Presentment" means the right to require the Note Holder to demand payment of amounts due. "Notice of dishonor" means the right to require the Note Holder to give notice to other persons that amounts due have not been paid.

10. UNIFORM SECURED NOTE

This Note is a uniform instrument with limited variations in some jurisdictions. In addition to the protections given to the Note Holder under this Note, a Mortgage, Deed of Trust or Security Deed (the "Security Instrument"), dated the same date as this Note, protects the Note Holder from possible losses which might result if I do not keep the promises which I make in this Note. That Security Instrument describes how and under what conditions I may be required to make immediate payment in full of all amounts I owe under this Note. Some of those conditions are described as follows:

Transfer of the Property or a Beneficial Interest in Borrower. If all or any part of the Property or any interest in it is sold or transferred (or if a beneficial interest in Borrower is sold or transferred and Borrower is not a natural person) without Lender's prior written consent, Lender may, at its option, require immediate payment in full of all sums secured by this Security Instrument. However, this option shall not be exercised by Lender if exercise is prohibited by federal law as of the date of this Security Instrument.

If Lender exercises this option, Lender shall give Borrower notice of acceleration. The notice shall provide a period of not less than 30 days from the date the notice is delivered or mailed within which Borrower must pay all sums secured by this Security Instrument. If Borrower fails to pay these sums prior to the expiration of this period, Lender may invoke any remedies permitted by this Security Instrument without further notice or demand on Borrower.

Witness the Hand(s) and Seal(s) of the Undersigned.

§ 14.3 FNMA/FHLMC Uniform Mortgage—Deed of Trust Covenants—Single Family

The Uniform Covenants are contained in all FNMA—FHLMC single family mortgages and deeds of trust and, consequently, serve to foster national uniformity on a variety of significant substantive mortgage law issues. The FNMA—FHLMC forms also utilize non-uniform covenants for each state to take into account local real estate security formats, substantive law requirements and foreclosure methods. Several of these state variations are included in succeeding sections in this Chapter.

The second paragraph of Paragraph 1 provides that escrow funds "are pledged as additional security for all sums secured by this security instrument." Note that this may have the unintended and undesirable effect of rendering the mortgage debt modifiable in the event mortgagor files a Chapter 13 bankruptcy proceeding. See § 8.15 supra.

Paragraph 5's disposition of hazard insurance proceeds is decidedly pro-mortgagor. Many forms afford the mortgagee the option of using insurance proceeds to pre-pay the mortgage debt or to rebuild the damaged property. See §§ 14.12, 14.14 infra. Indeed, in some jurisdictions this choice is available to the mortgagee under state law even where the mortgage is silent in this regard. See § 4.14 supra. Paragraph 5, however, requires that the insurance proceeds be used to rebuild the property if "restoration or repair is economically feasible and Lender's security is not lessened."

Paragraph 10 provides that, in the event of a partial condemnation, the mortgagee should receive that portion of the condemnation award that the mortgage debt bears to the pre-condemnation value of the mortgaged property. In the absence of such language, many courts give the entire award to the mortgagee while others permit the mortgagee to share in the award only if its security is impaired. Paragraph 10 represents a third approach and is designed to preserve for the mortgagee the pre-condemnation ratio of debt to security. See § 4.12, supra.

Paragraph 17 contains the due-on-sale provision. Unlike earlier versions of this form, it does not specifically exempt from its coverage a variety of involuntary and non-substantive transfers. However, such transfers are insulated from due-on-sale enforcement by Section 341 of the Garn–St. Germain Depository Institutions Act of 1982, which is considered at length elsewhere in this volume. See §§ 5.21–5.26, supra.

Paragraph 18 affords the mortgagor in default the right to defeat acceleration by the payment of arrearages, mortgagee's reasonable attorney's fees and related expenses at any time until 5 days prior to the foreclosure sale, if foreclosure is by power of sale, or until the entry of judgment, in the case of judicial foreclosure. While many states have arrearages legislation affording similar protections, in numerous other jurisdictions, this clause will significantly enhance the mortgagor's ability to defeat acceleration.

Paragraph 20 reflects the growing concern of mortgagees for potential liability for environmental problems on the mortgaged premises under the Comprehensive Environmental Response, Compensation, and Liability Act ("CERCLA") and similar state legislation. Note that these problems may arise prior to foreclosure if the mortgagee exercises too much control over the mortgagor's activity (although this will seldom be a problem in the single family context) and after foreclosure if the mortgagee is the sale purchaser. For consideration of the these problems, see §§ 4.47–4.51, supra.

1. Payment of Principal and Interest; Prepayment and Late Charges. Borrower shall promptly pay when due the principal of and interest on the debt evidenced by the Note and any prepayment and late charges due under the Note.

2. Funds for Taxes and Insurance. Subject to applicable law or to a written waiver by Lender, Borrower shall pay to Lender on the day monthly payments are due under the Note, until the Note is paid in full, a sum ("Funds") for: (a) yearly taxes and assessments which may attain priority over this Security Instrument as a lien on the Property; (b) yearly leasehold payments or ground rents on the Property, if any; (c) yearly hazard or property insurance premiums; (d) yearly flood insurance premiums, if any; (e) yearly mortgage insurance premiums, if any; and (f) any sums payable by Borrower to Lender, in accordance with the provisions of paragraph 8, in lieu of the payment of mortgage insurance premiums. These items are called "Escrow Items." Lender may, at any time, collect and hold Funds in an amount not to exceed the maximum amount a lender for a federally related mortgage loan may require for Borrower's escrow account under the federal Real Estate Settlement Procedures Act of 1974 as amended from time to time, 12 U.S.C.A. § 2601 et seq. ("RESPA"), unless another law that applies to the Funds sets a lesser amount. If so, Lender may, at any time, collect and hold Funds in an amount not to exceed the lesser amount. Lender may estimate the amount of Funds due on the basis of current data and reasonable estimates of expenditures of future Escrow Items or otherwise in accordance with applicable law.

The Funds shall be held in an institution whose deposits are insured by a federal agency, instrumentality, or entity (including Lender, if Lender is such an institution) or in any Federal Home Loan Bank. Lender shall apply the Funds to pay the Escrow Items. Lender may not charge Borrower for holding and applying the Funds, annually analyzing the escrow account, or verifying the Escrow Items, unless Lender pays Borrower interest on the Funds and applicable law permits Lender to make such a charge. However, Lender may require Borrower to pay a one-time charge for an independent real estate tax reporting service used by Lender in connection with this loan, unless applicable law provides otherwise. Unless an agreement is made or applicable law requires interest to be paid, Lender shall not be required to pay Borrower any interest or earnings on the Funds. Borrower and Lender may agree in writing, however, that interest shall be paid on the Funds. Lender shall give to Borrower, without charge, an annual accounting of the Funds, showing credits and debits to the Funds and the purpose for which each debit to the Funds was made. The Funds are pledged as additional security for all sums secured by this Security Instrument.

If the Funds held by Lender exceed the amounts permitted to be held by applicable law, Lender shall account to Borrower for the excess Funds in accordance with the requirements of applicable law. If the amount of the Funds held by Lender at any time is not sufficient to pay the Escrow Items when due, Lender may so notify Borrower in writing, and, in such case Borrower shall pay to Lender the amount necessary to make up the deficiency. Borrower shall make up the deficiency in no more than twelve monthly payments, at Lender's sole discretion.

Upon payment in full of all sums secured by this Security Instrument, Lender shall promptly refund to Borrower any Funds held by Lender. If, under paragraph 21, Lender shall acquire or sell the Property, Lender, prior to the acquisition or sale of the Property, shall apply any Funds held by Lender at the time of acquisition or sale as a credit against the sums secured by this Security Instrument.

3. Application of Payments. Unless applicable law provides otherwise, all payments received by Lender under paragraphs 1 and 2 shall be applied: first, to any prepayment charges due under the Note; second, to amounts payable under paragraph 2; third, to interest due; fourth, to principal due; and last, to any late charges due under the Note.

4. Charges; Liens. Borrower shall pay all taxes, assessments, charges, fines and impositions attributable to the Property which may attain priority over this Security Instrument, and leasehold payments or ground rents, if any. Borrower shall pay these obligations in the manner provided in paragraph 2, or if not paid in that manner, Borrower shall pay them on time directly to the person owed payment. Borrower shall promptly furnish to Lender all notices of amounts to be paid under this paragraph. If Borrower makes these payments directly, Borrower shall promptly furnish to Lender receipts evidencing the payments.

Borrower shall promptly discharge any lien which has priority over this Security Instrument unless Borrower: (a) agrees in writing to the payment of the obligation secured by the lien in a manner acceptable to Lender; (b) contests in good faith the lien by, or defends against enforcement of the lien in, legal proceedings which in the Lender's opinion operate to prevent the enforcement of the lien; or (c) secures from the holder of the lien an agreement satisfactory to Lender subordinating the lien to this Security Instrument. If Lender determines that any part of the Property is subject to a lien which may attain priority over this Security Instrument, Lender may give Borrower a notice identifying the lien. Borrower shall satisfy the lien or take one or more of the actions set forth above within 10 days of the giving of notice.

5. Hazard or Property Insurance. Borrower shall keep the improvements now existing or hereafter erected on the Property insured against loss by fire, hazards included within the term "extended coverage" and any other hazards, including floods or flooding, for which Lender requires insurance. This insurance shall be maintained in the amounts and for the periods that Lender requires. The insurance carrier providing the insurance shall be chosen by Borrower subject to Lender's approval which shall not be unreasonably withheld. If Borrower fails to maintain coverage described above, Lender may, at Lender's option, obtain coverage to protect Lender's rights in the Property in accordance with paragraph 7.

All insurance policies and renewals shall be acceptable to Lender and shall include a standard mortgage clause. Lender shall have the right to hold the policies and renewals. If Lender requires, Borrower shall promptly give to Lender all receipts of paid premiums and renewal notices. In the event of loss, Borrower shall give prompt notice to the insurance carrier and Lender. Lender may make proof of loss if not made promptly by Borrower.

Unless Lender and Borrower otherwise agree in writing, insurance proceeds shall be applied to restoration or repair of the Property damaged, if the restoration or repair is economically feasible and Lender's security is not lessened. If the restoration or repair is not economically feasible or Lender's security would be lessened, the insurance proceeds shall be applied to the sums secured by this Security Instrument, whether or not then due, with any excess paid to Borrower. If Borrower abandons the Property, or does not answer within 30 days a notice from Lender that the insurance carrier has offered to settle a claim, then Lender may collect the insurance proceeds. Lender may use the proceeds to repair or restore the Property or to pay sums secured by this Security Instrument, whether or not then due. The 30-day period will begin when the notice is given.

Unless Lender and Borrower otherwise agree in writing, any application of proceeds to principal shall not extend or postpone the due date of the monthly payments referred to in paragraphs 1 and 2 or change the amount of the payments. If under paragraph 21 the Property is acquired by Lender, Borrower's right to any insurance policies and proceeds resulting from damage to the Property prior to the acquisition shall pass to Lender to the extent of the sums secured by this Security Instrument immediately prior to the acquisition.

6. Occupancy, Preservation, Maintenance and Protection of the Property; Borrower's Loan Application; Leaseholds. Borrower shall occupy, establish, and use the Property as Borrower's principal residence within sixty days after the execution of this Security Instrument and shall continue to occupy the Property as Borrower's principal residence for at least one year after the date of occupancy, unless Lender otherwise agrees in writing, which consent shall not be unreasonably withheld, or unless extenuating circumstances exist which are beyond Borrower's control. Borrower shall not destroy, damage or impair the Property, allow the Property to deteriorate, or commit waste on the Property. Borrower shall be in default if any forfeiture action or proceeding, whether civil or criminal, is begun that in Lender's good faith judgment could result in forfeiture of the Property or otherwise materially impair the lien created by this Security Instrument or Lender's security interest. Borrower may cure such a default and reinstate, as provided in paragraph 18, by causing the action or proceeding to be dismissed with a ruling that, in Lender's good faith determination, precludes forfeiture of the Borrower's interest in the Property or other material impairment of the lien created by this

Security Instrument or Lender's security interest. Borrower shall also be in default if Borrower, during the loan application process, gave materially false or inaccurate information or statements to Lender (or failed to provide Lender with any material information) in connection with the loan evidenced by the Note, including, but not limited to, representations concerning Borrower's occupancy of the Property as a principal residence. If this Security Instrument is on a leasehold, Borrower shall comply with all the provisions of the lease. If Borrower acquires fee title to the Property, the leasehold and the fee title shall not merge unless Lender agrees to the merger in writing.

7. Protection of Lender's Rights in the Property. If Borrower fails to perform the covenants and agreements contained in this Security Instrument, or there is a legal proceeding that may significantly affect Lender's rights in the Property (such as a proceeding in bankruptcy, probate, for condemnation or forfeiture or to enforce laws or regulations), then Lender may do and pay for whatever is necessary to protect the value of the Property and Lender's rights in the Property. Lender's actions may include paying any sums secured by a lien which has priority over this Security Instrument, appearing in court, paying reasonable attorneys' fees and entering on the Property to make repairs. Although Lender may take action under this paragraph 7, Lender does not have to do so.

Any amounts disbursed by Lender under this paragraph 7 shall become additional debt of Borrower secured by this Security Instrument. Unless Borrower and Lender agree to other terms of payment, these amounts shall bear interest from the date of disbursement at the Note rate and shall be payable, with interest, upon notice from Lender to Borrower requesting payment.

8. Mortgage Insurance. If Lender required mortgage insurance as a condition of making the loan secured by this Security Instrument, Borrower shall pay the premiums required to maintain the mortgage insurance in effect. If, for any reason, the mortgage insurance coverage required by Lender lapses or ceases to be in effect, Borrower shall pay the premiums required to obtain coverage substantially equivalent to the mortgage insurance previously in effect, at a cost substantially equivalent to the cost to Borrower of the mortgage insurance previously in effect, from an alternate mortgage insurer approved by Lender. If substantially equivalent mortgage insurance coverage is not available, Borrower shall pay to Lender each month a sum equal to one-twelfth of the yearly mortgage insurance premium being paid by Borrower when the insurance coverage lapsed or ceased to be in effect. Lender will accept, use and retain these payments as a loss reserve in lieu of mortgage insurance. Loss reserve payments may no longer be required, at the option of Lender, if mortgage insurance coverage (in the amount and for the period that Lender requires) provided by an insurer approved by Lender again becomes available and is obtained. Borrower shall pay the premiums required to maintain mortgage insurance in effect, or to provide a loss reserve, until the requirement for mortgage insurance ends in accordance with any written agreement between Borrower and Lender or applicable law.

9. Inspection. Lender or its agent may make reasonable entries upon and inspections of the Property. Lender shall give Borrower notice at the time of or prior to an inspection specifying reasonable cause for the inspection.

10. Condemnation. The proceeds of any award or claim for damages, direct or consequential, in connection with any condemnation or other taking of any part of the Property, or for conveyance in lieu of condemnation, are hereby assigned and shall be paid to Lender.

In the event of a total taking of the Property, the proceeds shall be applied to the sums secured by this Security Instrument, whether or not then due, with any excess paid to Borrower. In the event of a partial taking of the Property in which the fair market value of the Property immediately before the taking is equal to or greater than the amount of the sums secured by this Security Instrument immediately before the taking, unless Borrower and Lender otherwise agree in writing, the sums secured by this Security Instrument shall be reduced by the amount of the proceeds multiplied by the following fraction: (a) the total amount of the sums secured immediately before the taking, divided by (b) the fair market value of the Property immediately before the taking. Any balance shall be paid to Borrower. In the event of a partial taking of the Property in which the fair market value of the Property immediately before the taking is less than the amount of the sums secured immediately before the taking, unless Borrower and Lender otherwise agree in writing or unless applicable law otherwise provides, the proceeds shall be applied to the sums secured by this Security Instrument whether or not the sums are then due.

If the Property is abandoned by Borrower, or if, after notice by Lender to Borrower that the condemnor offers to make an award or settle a claim for damages, Borrower fails to respond to Lender within 30 days after the date the notice is given, Lender is authorized to collect and apply the proceeds, at its option, either to restoration or repair of the Property or to the sums secured by this Security Instrument, whether or not then due.

Unless Lender and Borrower otherwise agree in writing, any application of proceeds to principal shall not extend or postpone the due date of the monthly payments referred to in paragraphs 1 and 2 or change the amount of such payments.

11. Borrower Not Released; Forbearance By Lender Not a Waiver. Extension of the time for payment or modification of amortization of the sums secured by this Security Instrument granted by Lender to any successor in interest of Borrower shall not operate to release the liability of the original Borrower or Borrower's successors in interest. Lender shall not be required to commence proceedings against any successor in interest or refuse to extend time for payment or otherwise modify amortization of the sums secured by this Security Instrument by reason of any demand made by the original Borrower or Borrower's successors in interest. Any forbearance by Lender in exercising any right or remedy shall not be a waiver of or preclude the exercise of any right or remedy.

12. Successors and Assigns Bound; Joint and Several Liability; Co-signers. The covenants and agreements of this Security Instrument shall bind and benefit the successors and assigns of Lender and Borrower, subject to the provisions of paragraph 17. Borrower's covenants and agreements shall be joint and several. Any Borrower who co-signs this Security Instrument but does not execute the Note: (a) is co-signing this Security Instrument only to mortgage, grant and convey that Borrower's interest in the Property under the terms of this Security Instrument; (b) is not personally obligated to pay the sums secured by this Security Instrument; and (c) agrees that Lender and any other Borrower may agree to extend, modify, forbear or make any accommodations with regard to the terms of this Security Instrument or the Note without that Borrower's consent.

13. Loan Charges. If the loan secured by this Security Instrument is subject to a law which sets maximum loan charges, and that law is finally interpreted so that the interest or other loan charges collected or to be collected in connection with the loan exceed the permitted limits, then: (a) any such loan charge shall be reduced by the amount necessary to reduce the charge to the permitted limit; and (b) any sums already collected from Borrower which exceeded permitted limits will be refunded to Borrower. Lender may choose to make this refund by reducing the principal owed under the Note or by making a direct payment to Borrower. If a refund reduces principal, the reduction will be treated as a partial prepayment without any prepayment charge under the Note.

14. Notices. Any notice to Borrower provided for in this Security Instrument shall be given by delivering it or by mailing it by first class mail unless applicable law requires use of another method. The notice shall be directed to the Property Address or any other address Borrower designates by notice to Lender. Any notice to Lender shall be given by first class mail to Lender's address stated herein or any other address Lender designates by notice to Borrower. Any notice provided for in this Security Instrument shall be deemed to have been given to Borrower or Lender when given as provided in this paragraph.

15. Governing Law; Severability. This Security Instrument shall be governed by federal law and the law of the jurisdiction in which the Property is located. In the event that any provision or clause of this Security Instrument or the Note conflicts with applicable law, such conflict shall not affect other provisions of this Security Instrument or the Note which can be given effect without the conflicting provision. To this end the provisions of this Security Instrument and the Note are declared to be severable.

16. Borrower's Copy. Borrower shall be given one conformed copy of the Note and of this Security Instrument.

17. Transfer of the Property or a Beneficial Interest in Borrower. If all or any part of the Property or any interest in it is sold or transferred (or if a beneficial interest in Borrower is sold or transferred and Borrower is not a natural person) without Lender's prior written consent, Lender may, at its option, require immediate payment in full of all sums secured by this Security Instrument. However, this option shall not be exercised by Lender if exercise is prohibited by federal law as of the date of this Security Instrument.

If Lender exercises this option, Lender shall give Borrower notice of acceleration. The notice shall provide a period of not less than 30 days from the date the notice is delivered or mailed within which Borrower must pay all sums secured by this Security Instrument. If Borrower fails to pay these sums prior to the expiration of this period, Lender may invoke any remedies permitted by this Security Instrument without further notice or demand on Borrower.

18. Borrower's Right to Reinstate. If Borrower meets certain conditions, Borrower shall have the right to have enforcement of this Security Instrument discontinued at any time prior to the earlier of: (a) 5 days (or such other period as applicable law may specify for reinstatement) before sale of the Property pursuant to any power of sale contained in this Security Instrument; or (b) entry of a judgment enforcing this Security Instrument. Those conditions are that Borrower: (a) pays Lender all sums which then would be due under this Security Instrument and the Note as if no acceleration had occurred; (b) cures any default of any other covenants or agreements; (c) pays all expenses incurred in enforcing this Security Instrument, including, but not limited to, reasonable attorneys' fees; and (d) takes such action as Lender may reasonably require to assure that the lien of this Security Instrument, Lender's rights in the Property and Borrower's obligation to pay the sums secured by this Security Instrument shall continue unchanged. Upon reinstatement by Borrower, this Security Instrument and the obligations secured hereby shall remain fully effective as if no acceleration had occurred. However, this right to reinstate shall not apply in the case of acceleration under paragraph 17.

19. Sale of Note; Change of Loan Servicer. The Note or a partial interest in the Note (together with this Security Instrument) may be sold one or more times without prior notice to Borrower. A sale may result in a change in the entity (known as the "Loan Servicer") that collects monthly payments due under the Note and this Security Instrument. There also may be one or more changes of the Loan Servicer unrelated to a sale of the Note. If there is a change of the Loan Servicer, Borrower will be given written notice of the change in accordance with paragraph 14 above and applicable law. The notice will state the name and address of the new Loan Servicer and the address to which payments should be made. The notice will also contain any other information required by applicable law.

20. Hazardous Substances. Borrower shall not cause or permit the presence, use, disposal, storage, or release of any Hazardous Substances on or in the

Property. Borrower shall not do, nor allow anyone else to do, anything affecting the Property that is in violation of any Environmental Law. The preceding two sentences shall not apply to the presence, use, or storage on the Property of small quantities of Hazardous Substances that are generally recognized to be appropriate to normal residential uses and to maintenance of the Property.

Borrower shall promptly give Lender written notice of any investigation, claim, demand, lawsuit or other action by any governmental or regulatory agency or private party involving the Property and any Hazardous Substance or Environmental Law of which Borrower has actual knowledge. If Borrower learns, or is notified by any governmental or regulatory authority, that any removal or other remediation of any Hazardous Substance affecting the Property is necessary, Borrower shall promptly take all necessary remedial actions in accordance with Environmental Law.

As used in this paragraph 20, "Hazardous Substances" are those substances defined as toxic or hazardous substances by Environmental Law and the following substances: gasoline, kerosene, other flammable or toxic petroleum products, toxic pesticides and herbicides, volatile solvents, materials containing asbestos or formaldehyde, and radioactive materials. As used in this paragraph 20, "Environmental Law" means federal laws and laws of the jurisdiction where the Property is located that relate to health, safety or environmental protection.

§ 14.4 FNMA/FHLMC Deed of Trust—Single Family—California

California, like many western and midwestern states, uses the deed of trust with power of sale as the predominant land financing instrument. While deeds of trust differ from mortgages in certain minor respects (see § 7.19, supra), most substantive mortgage law is applicable to them. Mortgages seldom are used in such states because they can be foreclosed only by judicial action.

The first sub-paragraph of Paragraph 19 is contained in the non-uniform covenants of most FNMA/FHLMC state mortgage forms. While Paragraph 18 of the Uniform Covenants affords the mortgagor the right to "deaccelerate" an already accelerated mortgage debt until 5 days before the sale (see §§ 7.7, 14.3, supra), Paragraph 19 places certain procedural restrictions on the right to accelerate itself. Under the latter provision, the mortgagee not only must afford the mortgagor written notice describing the default, but must also allow the mortgagor at least 30 days from its receipt to cure it. This requirement is more restrictive on the right to accelerate than the common law. See § 7.6, supra

The second sub-paragraph of Paragraph 19 summarizes the requirements of California law for a power of sale foreclosure. See West's Ann.Cal.Civ.Code § 2924 et seq. It is inadvisable to use such language in drafting forms for use in other states because it may be at variance with local power of sale foreclosure requirements.

Paragraph 22 gives the mortgagee the right to appoint a successor trustee. This is an important provision because, in its absence, statutes in several states authorize the appointment of the sheriff as the successor trustee. See e.g., R.S.Mo. § 443.340. This could trigger a statutorily mandated trustee's fee and possibly inject "state action" and its attendant constitutional due process problems into a subsequent power of sale foreclosure. See § 7.27, supra.

DEED OF TRUST

THIS DEED OF TRUST ("Security Instrument") is made on _____, 19__. The trustor is _____ ("Borrower"). The trustee is _____ ("Trustee"). The beneficiary is _____, which is organized and existing under the laws of _____, and whose address is _____ ("Lender"). Borrower owes Lender the principal sum of _____ Dollars (U.S. $_____). This debt is evidenced by Borrower's note dated the same date as this Security Instrument ("Note"), which provides for monthly payments, with the full debt, if not paid earlier, due and payable on _____. This Security Instrument secures to Lender: (a) the repayment of the debt evidenced by the Note, with interest, and all renewals, extensions and modifications of the Note; (b) the payment of all other sums, with interest, advanced under paragraph 7 to protect the security of this Security Instrument; and (c) the performance of Borrower's covenants and agreements under this Security Instrument and the Note. For this purpose, Borrower irrevocably grants and conveys to Trustee, in trust, with power of sale, the following described property located in _____ County, California:

which has the address of _____, _____, California _____ ("Property
　　　　　　　　　　　　　　　　　　[Street]　　[City]　　　　　　　[Zip Code]
Address");

TOGETHER WITH all the improvements now or hereafter erected on the property, and all easements, appurtenances, and fixtures now or hereafter a part of the property. All replacements and additions shall also be covered by this Security Instrument. All of the foregoing is referred to in this Security Instrument as the "Property."

BORROWER COVENANTS that Borrower is lawfully seised of the estate hereby conveyed and has the right to grant and convey the Property and that the Property is unencumbered, except for encumbrances of record. Borrower warrants and will defend generally the title to the Property against all claims and demands, subject to any encumbrances of record.

THIS SECURITY INSTRUMENT combines uniform covenants for national use and non-uniform covenants with limited variations by jurisdiction to constitute a uniform security instrument covering real property.

[*Uniform Covenants appear here. See § 14.3, supra.*]

NON–UNIFORM COVENANTS. Borrower and Lender further covenant and agree as follows:

21. Acceleration; Remedies. Lender shall give notice to Borrower prior to acceleration following Borrower's breach of any covenant or agreement in this Security Instrument (but not prior to acceleration under paragraph 17 unless applicable law provides otherwise). The notice shall specify: (a) the default; (b) the action required to cure the default; (c) a date, not less than 30 days from the date the notice is given to Borrower, by which the default must be cured; and (d) that failure to cure the default on or before the date specified in the notice may result in acceleration of the sums secured by this Security Instrument and sale of the Property. The notice shall further inform Borrower of the right to reinstate after acceleration and the right to bring a court action to assert the non-existence of a default or any other defense of Borrower to acceleration and sale. If the default is not cured on or before the date specified in the notice, Lender at its option may require immediate payment in full of all sums secured by this Security Instrument without

further demand and may invoke the power of sale and any other remedies permitted by applicable law. Lender shall be entitled to collect all expenses incurred in pursuing the remedies provided in this paragraph 21, including, but not limited to, reasonable attorneys' fees and costs of title evidence.

If Lender invokes the power of sale, Lender shall execute or cause Trustee to execute a written notice of the occurrence of an event of default and of Lender's election to cause the Property to be sold. Trustee shall cause this notice to be recorded in each county in which any part of the Property is located. Lender or Trustee shall mail copies of the notice as prescribed by applicable law to Borrower and to the other persons prescribed by applicable law. Trustee shall give public notice of sale to the persons and in the manner prescribed by applicable law. After the time required by applicable law, Trustee, without demand on Borrower, shall sell the Property at public auction to the highest bidder at the time and place and under the terms designated in the notice of sale in one or more parcels and in any order Trustee determines. Trustee may postpone sale of all or any parcel of the Property by public announcement at the time and place of any previously scheduled sale. Lender or its designee may purchase the Property at any sale.

Trustee shall deliver to the purchaser Trustee's deed conveying the Property without any covenant or warranty, expressed or implied. The recitals in the Trustee's deed shall be prima facie evidence of the truth of the statements made therein. Trustee shall apply the proceeds of the sale in the following order: (a) to all expenses of the sale, including, but not limited to, reasonable Trustee's and attorneys' fees; (b) to all sums secured by this Security Instrument; and (c) any excess to the person or persons legally entitled to it.

22. **Reconveyance.** Upon payment of all sums secured by this Security Instrument, Lender shall request Trustee to reconvey the Property and shall surrender this Security Instrument and all notes evidencing debt secured by this Security Instrument to Trustee. Trustee shall reconvey the Property without warranty and without charge to the person or persons legally entitled to it. Such person or persons shall pay any recordation costs.

23. **Substitute Trustee.** Lender, at its option, may from time to time appoint a successor trustee to any Trustee appointed hereunder by an instrument executed and acknowledged by Lender and recorded in the office of the Recorder of the county in which the Property is located. The instrument shall contain the name of the original Lender, Trustee and Borrower, the book and page where this Security Instrument is recorded and the name and address of the successor trustee. Without conveyance of the Property, the successor trustee shall succeed to all the title, powers and duties conferred upon the Trustee herein and by applicable law. This procedure for substitution of trustee shall govern to the exclusion of all other provisions for substitution.

24. **Request for Notices.** Borrower requests that copies of the notices of default and sale be sent to Borrower's address which is the Property Address.

25. **Statement of Obligation Fee.** Lender may collect a fee not to exceed the maximum amount permitted by law for furnishing the statement of obligation as provided by Section 2943 of the Civil Code of California.

26. **Riders to this Security Instrument.** If one or more riders are executed by Borrower and recorded together with this Security Instrument, the covenants and agreements of each such rider shall be incorporated into and shall amend and supplement the covenants and agreements of this Security Instrument as if the rider(s) were a part of this Security Instrument. [Check applicable box(es)]

☐ Adjustable Rate Rider
☐ Condominium Rider
☐ 1–4 Family Rider
☐ Graduated Payment Rider
☐ Planned Unit Development Rider
☐ Biweekly Payment Rider
☐ Balloon Rider
☐ Rate Improvement Rider
☐ Second Home Rider
☐ Other(s) [specify]

BY SIGNING BELOW, Borrower accepts and agrees to the terms and covenants contained in this Security Instrument and in any rider(s) executed by Borrower and recorded with it.

§ 14.5 FNMA/FHLMC Mortgage—Single Family—Kansas

Kansas, like such other states as Illinois, Iowa, Florida and New York uses the mortgage as the predominant financing device and permits only foreclosure by judicial action. Consequently, the Kansas form makes no reference to a power of sale or non-judicial foreclosure. On the other hand, it incorporates in Paragraph 19 essentially the same limits on acceleration found in its California power of sale counterpart. See § 14.4, supra.

Two other paragraphs of the Kansas non-uniform covenants are noteworthy. In Paragraph 22 the mortgagor "waives all rights of redemption to the extent allowed by law." Presumably, this waiver is intended to apply to statutory redemption as opposed to "equitable redemption" or the "equity of redemption" since any clause in the mortgage or any agreement contemporaneous with it that purports to waive the latter rights would almost surely constitute an unenforceable clog on the equity of redemption. See §§ 3.1 and 7.1, supra. In any event, courts are only slightly less hostile towards attempts to waive statutory redemption rights. See generally § 8.5, supra.

Paragraph 23 invalidates any other provision of the mortgage to the extent that it requires the mortgagor to pay mortgagee's attorney's fees. See e.g., Paragraph 18 of the Uniform Covenants, § 14.3, supra. Paragraph 23 simply reflects a Kansas statutory prohibition on mortgagee collection of attorney's fees. See Kan.Stat.Ann. 58–2312 (1983).

MORTGAGE

THIS MORTGAGE ("Security Instrument") is given on _____, 19__. The mortgagor is _____ ("Borrower"). This Security Instrument is given to _____, which is organized and existing under the laws of _____, and whose address is _____ ("Lender"). Borrower owes Lender the principal sum of _____ Dollars (U.S. $_____). This debt is evidenced by Borrower's note dated the same date as this Security Instrument ("Note"), which provides for monthly payments, with the full debt, if not paid earlier, due and payable on _____. This Security Instrument secures to Lender: (a) the repayment of the debt evidenced by the Note, with interest, and all renewals, extensions and modifications of the Note; (b) the payment of all other sums, with interest, advanced under paragraph 7 to protect the security of this Security Instrument; and (c) the performance of Borrower's covenants and agreements under this Security Instrument and the Note. For this purpose, Borrower does hereby mortgage, grant and convey to Lender the following described property located in _____ County, Kansas:

which has the address of _____, _____,
                                              [Street]   [City]
Kansas _____ ("Property Address");
        [Zip Code]

TOGETHER WITH all the improvements now or hereafter erected on the property, and all easements, appurtenances, and fixtures now or hereafter a part of the property. All replacements and additions shall also be covered by this Security Instrument. All of the foregoing is referred to in this Security Instrument as the "Property."

BORROWER COVENANTS that Borrower is lawfully seised of the estate hereby conveyed and has the right to mortgage, grant and convey the Property and that the Property is unencumbered, except for encumbrances of record. Borrower warrants and will defend generally the title to the Property against all claims and demands, subject to any encumbrances of record.

THIS SECURITY INSTRUMENT combines uniform covenants for national use and non-uniform covenants with limited variations by jurisdiction to constitute a uniform security instrument covering real property.

[*Uniform Covenants appear here. See § 14.3, supra.*]

21. Acceleration; Remedies. Lender shall give notice to Borrower prior to acceleration following Borrower's breach of any covenant or agreement in this Security Instrument (but not prior to acceleration under paragraph 17 unless applicable law provides otherwise). The notice shall specify: (a) the default; (b) the action required to cure the default; (c) a date, not less than 30 days from the date the notice is given to Borrower, by which the default must be cured; and (d) that failure to cure the default on or before the date specified in the notice may result in acceleration of the sums secured by this Security Instrument, foreclosure by judicial proceeding and sale of the Property. The notice shall further inform Borrower of the right to reinstate after acceleration and the right to assert in the foreclosure proceeding the non-existence of a default or any other defense of Borrower to acceleration and foreclosure. If the default is not cured on or before the date specified in the notice, Lender at its option may require immediate payment in full of all sums secured by this Security Instrument without further demand and may foreclose this Security Instrument by judicial proceeding. Lender shall be entitled to collect all expenses incurred in pursuing the remedies provided in this paragraph 21, including, but not limited to, costs of title evidence.

22. Release. Upon payment of all sums secured by this Security Instrument, Lender shall release this Security Instrument without charge to Borrower.

23. Waiver of Redemption. Borrower waives all rights of redemption to the extent allowed by law.

24. Attorneys' Fees. The provisions in this Security Instrument for Borrower to pay "attorneys' fees" shall be void.

25. Riders to this Security Instrument. If one or more riders are executed by Borrower and recorded together with this Security Instrument, the covenants and agreements of each such rider shall be incorporated into and shall amend and supplement the covenants and agreements of this Security Instrument as if the rider(s) were a part of this Security Instrument. [Check applicable box(es)]

☐ Adjustable Rate Rider   ☐ Rate Improvement Rider
☐ Graduated Payment Rider   ☐ 1-4 Family Rider
☐ Balloon Rider   ☐ Biweekly Payment Rider
☐ Condominium Rider   ☐ Second Home Rider
☐ Planned Unit Development Rider   ☐ Other(s) [specify]

BY SIGNING BELOW, Borrower accepts and agrees to the terms and covenants contained in this Security Instrument and in any rider(s) executed by Borrower and recorded with it.

§ 14.6 FNMA/FHLMC Mortgage With Power of Sale—Single Family—Minnesota

Minnesota uses a mortgage with power of sale as the most common land financing device. While judicial foreclosure is, of course, permissible (see Minn.Stat.Ann. § 581.01 et seq.) foreclosure is almost always by power of sale, or, as it is referred to locally, by "advertisement." See Minn.Stat.Ann. § 580.01 et seq. The power of sale is exercised by the sheriff. See Minn.Stat.Ann. § 580.06.

Paragraph 19 includes the same procedural limits on the mortgagee's right to accelerate found in both the California and Kansas FNMA/FHLMC counterparts. See §§ 14.4, 14.5, supra. However, the second subparagraph of Paragraph 19, which essentially restates the statutory notice requirement for a Minnesota power of sale foreclosure (see Minn.Stat.Ann. § 580.03), calls attention to a potential constitutional problem. The statute requires that personal notice of sale be provided only to the "person in possession." Assuming the requisite "state action" or "federal action" for purposes of the 14th or 5th amendments is present, such notice probably fails to meet minimum procedural due process requirements. See §§ 7.24, 7.27, 7.28, supra. This could prove to be a problem where the foreclosing mortgagee is a state or federal agency. See §§ 7.27, 7.28, supra. Moreover, the constitutional question may persist for even a private Minnesota mortgagee because use of the sheriff to execute the power of sale may itself supply the requisite state action. See § 7.27, supra. On the other hand, the second part of Paragraph 19 probably does no harm and, to the extent that it is constitutionally possible, constitutes a waiver by the mortgagor of his procedural due process notice rights. See § 7.26, supra.

MORTGAGE

THIS MORTGAGE ("Security Instrument") is given on _____, 19__. The mortgagor is _____. ("Borrower"). This Security Instrument is given to _____, which is organized and existing under the laws of _____, and whose address is _____ ("Lender"). Borrower owes Lender the principal sum of _____ Dollars (U.S. $_____). This debt is evidenced by Borrower's note dated the same date as this Security Instrument ("Note"), which provides for monthly payments, with the full debt, if not paid earlier, due and payable on _____ and for interest at the yearly rate of _____ percent. This Security Instrument secures to Lender: (a) the repayment of the debt evidenced by the Note, with interest, and all renewals, extensions and modifications of the Note; (b) the payment of all other sums, with interest, advanced under paragraph 7 to protect the security of this Security Instrument; and (c) the performance of Borrower's covenants and agreements under this Security Instrument and the Note. For this purpose, Borrower does hereby mortgage, grant and convey to Lender, with power of sale, the following described property located in _____ County, Minnesota:

which has the address of _____, _____,
[Street] [City]
Minnesota _____ ("Property Address");
[Zip Code]

TOGETHER WITH all the improvements now or hereafter erected on the property, and all easements, appurtenances, and fixtures now or hereafter a part of the property. All replacements and additions shall also be covered by this Security Instrument. All of the foregoing is referred to in this Security Instrument as the "Property."

BORROWER COVENANTS that Borrower is lawfully seised of the estate hereby conveyed and has the right to mortgage, grant and convey the Property and that the Property is unencumbered, except for encumbrances of record. Borrower warrants and will defend generally the title to the Property against all claims and demands, subject to any encumbrances of record.

THIS SECURITY INSTRUMENT combines uniform covenants for national use and non-uniform covenants with limited variations by jurisdiction to constitute a uniform security instrument covering real property.

[*Uniform Covenants appear here. See § 14.3, supra.*]

21. Acceleration; Remedies. Lender shall give notice to Borrower prior to acceleration following Borrower's breach of any covenant or agreement in this Security Instrument (but not prior to acceleration under paragraph 17 unless applicable law provides otherwise). The notice shall specify: (a) the default; (b) the action required to cure the default; (c) a date, not less than 30 days from the date the notice is given to Borrower, by which the default must be cured; and (d) that failure to cure the default on or before the date specified in the notice may result in acceleration of the sums secured by this Security Instrument and sale of the Property. The notice shall further inform Borrower of the right to reinstate after acceleration and the right to bring a court action to assert the non-existence of a default or any other defense of Borrower to acceleration and sale. If the default is not cured on or before the date specified in the notice, Lender at its option may require immediate payment in full of all sums secured by this Security Instrument without further demand and may invoke the power of sale and any other remedies permitted by applicable law. Lender shall be entitled to collect all expenses incurred in pursuing the remedies provided in this paragraph 21, including, but not limited to, reasonable attorneys' fees.

If Lender invokes the power of sale, Lender shall cause a copy of a notice of sale to be served upon any person in possession of the Property. Lender shall publish a notice of sale, and the Property shall be sold at public auction in the manner prescribed by applicable law. Lender or its designee may purchase the Property at any sale. The proceeds of the sale shall be applied in the following order: (a) to all expenses of the sale, including, but not limited to, reasonable attorneys' fees; (b) to all sums secured by this Security Instrument; and (c) any excess to the person or persons legally entitled to it.

22. Release. Upon payment of all sums secured by this Security Instrument, Lender shall discharge this Security Instrument without charge to Borrower. Borrower shall pay any recordation costs.

23. Waiver of Homestead. Borrower waives all right of homestead exemption in the Property.

24. Interest on Advances. The interest rate on advances made by Lender under paragraph 7 shall not exceed the maximum rate allowed by applicable law.

25. Riders to this Security Instrument. If one or more riders are executed by Borrower and recorded together with this Security Instrument, the covenants and agreements of each such rider shall be incorporated into and shall amend and supplement the covenants and agreements of this Security Instrument as if the rider(s) were a part of this Security Instrument. [Check applicable box(es)]

- [ ] Adjustable Rate Rider
- [ ] Graduated Payment Rider
- [ ] Balloon Rider
- [ ] Condominium Rider
- [ ] Planned Unit Development Rider
- [ ] Rate Improvement Rider
- [ ] 1–4 Family Rider
- [ ] Biweekly Payment Rider
- [ ] Second Home Rider
- [ ] Other(s) [specify]

BY SIGNING BELOW, Borrower accepts and agrees to the terms and covenants contained in this Security Instrument and in any rider(s) executed by Borrower and recorded with it.

§ 14.7 FNMA/FHLMC Adjustable Rate Note

The drafter of a mortgage note with an adjustable interest rate provisions must address a number of issues. Section 11.4 of this book discusses the possible variations in the structure of such note in some detail. To be specific, one major factor is the *index* itself. Another is the *frequency* of rate adjustment. In practice, these two factors are often tied together; for example, if the index is the rate on three-year U.S. Treasury securities, the adjustment frequency will typically be every three years. In addition, the documents may or may not have an *interest rate cap*—a limit above which the rate will not be raised irrespective of the movement of the index rate. Similarly, a *payment cap* may be imposed, so that monthly payments will not exceed a given amount, notwithstanding index rate fluctuations.

The particular form presented here was prepared by FNMA and FHLMC. It adopts a "one-year index"—that is, the weekly average yield on U.S. Treasury securities, adjusted to a constant maturity of one year. It contains no interest rate cap, but does employ a payment cap. The reader is cautioned that transactions which employ different parameters than these will require considerable redrafting, or the adoption of different FNMA/FHLMC forms if such are available as to fit the transaction.

The conversion of the standard fixed-rate FNMA/FHLMC forms to adjustable rate use is actually accomplished by using two documents, only one of which, the Adjustable Rate Note, is reproduced here. The other is an Adjustable Rate Rider, which is an amendment to the usual FNMA/FHLMC single-family mortgage or deed of trust. This Rider is essentially a verbatim copy of Section 4 of the Note form which is reprinted below, plus language substituting the new due-on-sale clause (which is included in Section 11 of the Note form reprinted below) for the older version of the due-on-sale clause. Thus, because virtually all of the rider's language appears in the Note form as well, we have not reprinted it in this book.

The drafting style of the Note and Rider is interesting. For the most part, they are in "plain language", with the first person pronouns

("I", "my", and the like) referring to the borrower/note-maker, and with the lender or secondary market investor being termed the "Note Holder." However, the due-on-sale clause, which technically is part of the Rider but is incorporated into the Note as Section 11, is definitely not in plain language style, and seems jarringly out of character with the rest of these documents. The content of the due-on-sale clause is discussed below.

Under this note, the adjustment frequency is annual; this is a correlative of the index, which is the rate on one-year Treasury securities. Section 2 warns the maker that the rate is adjustable, and Section 4(C) spells out the specific mechanism for computing the annual adjustments.

This note permits free prepayment, as does the fixed-rate FNMA/FHLMC note. The late charge, notice, waiver, and multiple obligor provisions are also substantially identical to those of the fixed-rate note.

The due-on-sale clause used in the FNMA/FHLMC adjustable rate instruments is quite different from that which appears in the fixed-rate instruments. It appears in Section 11 of the Note, and in the Rider it appears as an amendment to the standard fixed-rate mortgage or deed of trust. In substance, the ARM due-on-sale clause permits the borrower to forestall acceleration in the event of a sale of the property. This is done by submitting to the lender the usual information required for evaluation of a new loan; this would typically include both information on the proposed new owner—credit report, employment and income verification, and the like—and possibly an appraisal of the real estate itself. If the lender reasonably determines from this information that the transfer will not impair the security or create an unacceptable risk of default, the lender must permit the transfer to go forward.

The lender is permitted under this Section to charge a reasonable assumption fee and to require that the new owner sign an assumption agreement. There is no requirement that the lender release the previous owner from personal liability.

The rationale for this type of clause, which in effect permits the lender to accelerate only if the transfer will increase its risk to an unacceptable level, is simple. In an ARM loan, it is unnecessary for the lender to employ the due-on-sale clause as a tool for increasing the interest rate to the market level when a sale occurs, since the language of the ARM note itself has already accomplished this objective (or at least, a reasonable approximation of it) automatically. Hence, the only relevant function of the due-on-sale clause is to protect against increased risk resulting from transfer of the title.

Of course, the ARM note will not necessarily do a perfect job of keeping the loan's interest rate at market levels. The longer the interval between adjustments, the greater the possibility that the lender will be compelled to accept a lower rate for a time notwithstanding the occurrence of a sharp increase in market rates. If the ARM note includes an interest rate "cap" (as the one reproduced below does not), there is a further possibility that market rates will continue to rise after the "cap" has been reached. Thus, it would not be irrational for a lender making an ARM loan to employ a standard type of due-on-sale clause which gives the lender a nearly absolute right to accelerate, rather than the more pro-borrower sort of clause found in the FNMA/FHLMC ARM notes. In effect, FNMA and FHLMC are adopting the position that the discrepancy which can arise between loan rate and market rate is an acceptable one to them, and that they will not employ the due-on-sale clause as a means of eliminating it.

ADJUSTABLE RATE NOTE

(1 Year Treasury Index—Rate Caps)

This Note Contains Provisions Allowing for Changes in My Interest Rate and My Monthly Payment. This Note Limits the Amount My Interest Rate Can Change at Any One Time and the Maximum Rate I Must Pay.

_____, 19__, _____, _____.
　　　　　　　　[City]　　[State]　　[Property Address]

1. BORROWER'S PROMISE TO PAY

In return for a loan that I have received, I promise to pay U.S. $_____ (this amount is called "principal"), plus interest, to the order of the Lender. The Lender is _____. I understand that the Lender may transfer this Note. The Lender or anyone who takes this Note by transfer and who is entitled to receive payments under this Note is called the "Note Holder."

2. INTEREST

Interest will be charged on unpaid principal until the full amount of principal has been paid. I will pay interest at a yearly rate of _____%. The interest rate I will pay will change in accordance with Section 4 of this Note.

The interest rate required by this Section 2 and Section 4 of this Note is the rate I will pay both before and after any default described in Section 7(B) of this Note.

3. PAYMENTS

(A) Time and Place of Payments

I will pay principal and interest by making payments every month.

I will make my monthly payments on the first day of each month beginning on _____, 19__. I will make these payments every month until I have paid all of the principal and interest and any other charges described below that I may owe under this Note. My monthly payments will be applied to interest before principal. If, on _____, 20__, I still owe amounts under this Note, I will pay those amounts in full on that date, which is called the "maturity date."

I will make my monthly payments at _____ or at a different place if required by the Note Holder.

(B) Amount of My Initial Monthly Payments

Each of my initial monthly payments will be in the amount of U.S. $_____ This amount may change.

(C) Monthly Payment Changes

Changes in my monthly payment will reflect changes in the unpaid principal of my loan and in the interest rate that I must pay. The Note Holder will determine my new interest rate and the changed amount of my monthly payment in accordance with Section 4 of this Note.

4. INTEREST RATE AND MONTHLY PAYMENT CHANGES

(A) Change Dates

The interest rate I will pay may change on the first day of _____, 19__, and on that day every 12th month thereafter. Each date on which my interest rate could change is called a "Change Date."

(B) The Index

Beginning with the first Change Date, my interest rate will be based on an Index. The "Index" is the weekly average yield on United States Treasury securities adjusted to a constant maturity of 1 year, as made available by the Federal Reserve Board. The most recent Index figure available as of the date 45 days before each Change Date is called the "Current Index."

If the Index is no longer available, the Note Holder will choose a new index which is based upon comparable information. The Note Holder will give me notice of this choice.

(C) Calculation of Changes

Before each Change Date, the Note Holder will calculate my new interest rate by adding _____ percentage points (_____%) to the Current Index. The Note Holder will then round the result of this addition to the nearest one-eighth of one percentage point (0.125%). Subject to the limits stated in Section 4(D) below, this rounded amount will be my new interest rate until the next Change Date.

The Note Holder will then determine the amount of the monthly payment that would be sufficient to repay the unpaid principal that I am expected to owe at the Change Date in full on the maturity date at my new interest rate in substantially equal payments. The result of this calculation will be the new amount of my monthly payment.

(D) Limits on Interest Rate Changes

The interest rate I am required to pay at the first Change Date will not be greater than _____% or less than _____%. Thereafter, my interest rate will never be increased or decreased on any single Change Date by more than one percentage point (1.0%) from the rate of interest I have been paying for the preceding twelve months. My interest rate will never be greater than _____%.

(E) Effective Date of Changes

My new interest rate will become effective on each Change Date. I will pay the amount of my new monthly payment beginning on the first monthly payment date after the Change Date until the amount of my monthly payment changes again.

(F) Notice of Changes

The Note Holder will deliver or mail to me a notice of any changes in my interest rate and the amount of my monthly payment before the effective date of any change. The notice will include information required by law to be given me and also the title and telephone number of a person who will answer any question I may have regarding the notice.

5. BORROWER'S RIGHT TO PREPAY

I have the right to make payments of principal at any time before they are due. A payment of principal only is known as a "prepayment." When I make a prepayment, I will tell the Note Holder in writing that I am doing so.

I may make a full prepayment or partial prepayments without paying any prepayment charge. The Note Holder will use all of my prepayments to reduce the amount of principal that I owe under this Note. If I make a partial prepayment, there will be no changes in the due dates of my monthly payments unless the Note Holder agrees in writing to those changes. My partial prepayment may reduce the amount of my monthly payments after the first Change Date following my partial prepayment. However, any reduction due to my partial prepayment may be offset by an interest rate increase.

6. LOAN CHARGES

If a law, which applies to this loan and which sets maximum loan charges, is finally interpreted so that the interest or other loan charges collected or to be collected in connection with this loan exceed the permitted limits, then: (i) any such loan charge shall be reduced by the amount necessary to reduce the charge to the permitted limit; and (ii) any sums already collected from me which exceeded permitted limits will be refunded to me. The Note Holder may choose to make this refund by reducing the principal I owe under this Note or by making a direct payment to me. If a refund reduces principal, the reduction will be treated as a partial prepayment.

7. BORROWER'S FAILURE TO PAY AS REQUIRED

(A) Late Charges for Overdue Payments

If the Note Holder has not received the full amount of any monthly payment by the end of ___ calendar days after the date it is due, I will pay a late charge to the Note Holder. The amount of the charge will be _____% of my overdue payment of principal and interest. I will pay this late charge promptly but only once on each late payment.

(B) Default

If I do not pay the full amount of each monthly payment on the date it is due, I will be in default.

(C) Notice of Default

If I am in default, the Note Holder may send me a written notice telling me that if I do not pay the overdue amount by a certain date, the Note Holder may require me to pay immediately the full amount of principal which has not been paid and all the interest that I owe on that amount. That date must be at least 30 days after the date on which the notice is delivered or mailed to me.

(D) No Waiver By Note Holder

Even if, at a time when I am in default, the Note Holder does not require me to pay immediately in full as described above, the Note Holder will still have the right to do so if I am in default at a later time.

(E) Payment of Note Holder's Costs and Expenses

If the Note Holder has required me to pay immediately in full as described above, the Note Holder will have the right to be paid back by me for all of its costs and expenses in enforcing this Note to the extent not prohibited by applicable law. Those expenses include, for example, reasonable attorneys' fees.

8. GIVING OF NOTICES

Unless applicable law requires a different method, any notice that must be given to me under this Note will be given by delivering it or by mailing it by first class mail to me at the Property Address above or at a different address if I give the Note Holder a notice of my different address.

Any notice that must be given to the Note Holder under this Note will be given by mailing it by first class mail to the Note Holder at the address stated in Section 3(A) above or at a different address if I am given a notice of that different address.

9. OBLIGATIONS OF PERSONS UNDER THIS NOTE

If more than one person signs this Note, each person is fully and personally obligated to keep all of the promises made in this Note, including the promise to pay the full amount owed. Any person who is a guarantor, surety or endorser of this Note is also obligated to do these things. Any person who takes over these obligations, including the obligations of a guarantor, surety or endorser of this Note, is also obligated to keep all of the promises made in this Note. The Note Holder may enforce its rights under this Note against each person individually or against all of us together. This means that any one of us may be required to pay all of the amounts owed under this Note.

10. WAIVERS

I and any other person who has obligations under this Note waive the rights of presentment and notice of dishonor. "Presentment" means the right to require the Note Holder to demand payment of amounts due. "Notice of dishonor" means the right to require the Note Holder to give notice to other persons that amounts due have not been paid.

11. UNIFORM SECURED NOTE

This Note is a uniform instrument with limited variations in some jurisdictions. In addition to the protections given to the Note Holder under this Note, a Mortgage, Deed of Trust or Security Deed (the "Security Instrument"), dated the same date as this Note, protects the Note Holder from possible losses which might result if I do not keep the promises which I make in this Note. That Security Instrument describes how and under what conditions I may be required to make immediate payment in full of all amounts I owe under this Note. Some of those conditions are described as follows:

Transfer of the Property or a Beneficial Interest in Borrower. If all or any part of the Property or any interest in it is sold or transferred (or if a beneficial interest in Borrower is sold or transferred and Borrower is not a natural person) without Lender's prior written consent, Lender may, at its option, require immediate payment in full of all sums secured by this Security Instrument. However, this option shall not be exercised by Lender if exercise is prohibited by federal law as of the date of this Security Instrument. Lender also shall not exercise this option if: (a) Borrower causes to be submitted to Lender information required by Lender to evaluate the intended transferee as if a new loan were being made to the transferee; and (b) Lender reasonably determines that Lender's security will not be impaired by the loan assumption and that the risk of a breach of any covenant or agreement in this Security Instrument is acceptable to Lender.

To the extent permitted by applicable law, Lender may charge a reasonable fee as a condition to Lender's consent to the loan assumption. Lender may also require the transferee to sign an assumption agreement that is acceptable to Lender and that obligates the transferee to keep all the promises and agreements made in the Note and in this Security Instrument.

Borrower will continue to be obligated under the Note and this Security Instrument unless Lender releases Borrower in writing.

If Lender exercises the option to require immediate payment in full, Lender shall give Borrower notice of acceleration. The notice shall provide a period of not less than 30 days from the date the notice is delivered or mailed within which Borrower must pay all sums secured by this Security Instrument. If Borrower fails to pay these sums prior to the expiration of this period, Lender may invoke any remedies permitted by this Security Instrument without further notice or demand on Borrower.

Witness the Hand(s) and Seal(s) of the Undersigned.

§ 14.8 FNMA/FHLMC Graduated Payment Note

In concept, the Graduated Payment Mortgage (GPM) is repaid under a schedule of rising monthly payments. Payments typically increase each year for the first three, five, or ten years of the loan, and remain level thereafter. Early year payments are lower than the amount necessary to amortize the loan fully, and may be even less than the interest accruing on the principal balance. In a "pure" GPM, payments rise in the later years to levels sufficient to offset this effect, and to amortize the loan completely. For a more thorough discussion of the GPM, see Section 11.4 of this treatise.

The GPM note reproduced below combines the graduated payment feature with an adjustable interest rate; it can be described as a graduated payment adjustable rate loan, or GPARM. The frequency of the rate adjustment is three years, and the index for adjustment is the average yield on U.S. Treasury securities adjusted to a constant maturity of three years. Thus, the adjustment period and the maturity of the index securities are matched to one another, as is the common practice; see the discussion of the FNMA/FHLMC ARM note, § 14.7, supra.

In this particular GPM note, the scheduled increase in monthly payments lasts only for the first three years; see Section 5. After this time, the loan becomes, in essence, a garden-variety ARM. However, it permits the borrower to limit further payment increases to 7.5% per year, even though this may produce negative amortization (see Section 8(A)), unless the outstanding balance reaches 125% of the original balance. If this occurs, the borrower must begin making a monthly payment which will fully amortize the loan over the remaining term. See Section 6(C).

GRADUATED PAYMENT NOTE

(With Interest Rate Changes Every 3 Years)

This Note contains provisions allowing for changes in my interest rate and monthly payments.

My monthly payment will increase by 7½% each year during the first three years of this Note. My remaining monthly payments also could increase or decrease, depending on changes in my interest rate. If the provisions of this Note permit me to do so, I will be able to limit my monthly payment increases to 7½% each year.

The principal amount I must repay will be larger than the amount I originally borrowed, but not more than 125% of the original amount.

_____ 19__, _____, _____ _____.
            [City]   [State]   [Property Address]

1. BORROWER'S PROMISE TO PAY

In return for a loan that I have received, I promise to pay U.S. $_____ plus any amounts added in accordance with Section 8(A) of this Note (the total amount is called "principal"), plus interest, to the order of the Lender. The Lender is _____. I understand that the Lender may transfer this Note. The Lender or anyone who takes this Note by transfer and who is entitled to receive payments under this Note is called the "Note Holder."

2. INTEREST

(A) Interest Owed

Interest will be charged on that part of principal which has not been paid, beginning on the date I receive principal and continuing until the full amount of principal has been paid.

Beginning on the date I receive principal, I will owe interest at a yearly rate of _____%. The interest rate I will pay will change in accordance with Section 4(A) of this Note on the first day of _____, 19__ and on that day every 36th month thereafter. Each date on which my interest rate could change is called an "Interest Change Date."

(B) The Index

Beginning with the first Interest Change Date, my interest rate will be based on an Index. The "Index" is the weekly average yield on United States Treasury securities adjusted to a constant maturity of 3 years, as made available by the Federal Reserve Board. The most recent Index figure available as of the date 45 days before each Interest Change Date is called the "Current Index."

If the Index is no longer available, the Note Holder will choose a new index which is based upon comparable information. The Note Holder will give me notice of this choice.

(C) Interest After Default

The interest rate required by this Section 2 and Section 4(A) below is the rate I will pay both before and after any default described in Section 12(B) below.

3. TIME AND PLACE OF PAYMENTS

I will pay principal and interest by making payments every month. My monthly payments will be applied to interest before principal.

I will make my monthly payments on the first day of each month beginning on _____, 19__ I will make these payments every month until I have paid all the principal and interest and any other charges described below that I may owe under this Note. If, on _____, 20__, I still owe amounts under this Note, I will pay those amounts in full on that date, which is called the "maturity date."

I will make my monthly payments at _____

or at a different place if required by the Note Holder.

4. INTEREST RATE CHANGES AND FULL PAYMENT AMOUNT

(A) Calculation of New Interest Rate and Full Payment Amount

Each of my first 36 monthly payments could be less than a Full Payment Amount. A "Full Payment Amount" is the monthly amount sufficient to repay the amount I originally borrowed, or the unpaid principal balance of my loan as of an Interest Change Date, in full on the maturity date at the interest rate I am required to pay by Section 2 above or this Section 4(A) in substantially equal payments. Beginning on the date of this Note, my first Full Payment Amount will be U.S. $_____ until the first Interest Change Date.

Before each Interest Change Date, the Note Holder will determine a new Full Payment Amount for my loan. The Note Holder will first calculate my new interest rate by adding _____ percentage points (_____%) to the Current Index. The Note Holder will then round the result of this addition to the nearest one-eighth of one percentage point (0.125%). This rounded amount will be my new interest rate until the next Interest Change Date. The Note Holder will then determine the amount of the monthly payment that would be sufficient to repay the unpaid principal balance of my loan that I am expected to owe on the Interest Change Date in full on the maturity date at my new interest rate in substantially equal payments. The result of this calculation is my new Full Payment Amount.

Each new interest rate will become effective on each Interest Change Date, and each new Full Payment Amount will become effective on the first monthly payment date after the Interest Change Date.

I will pay the Full Payment Amount as my monthly payment beginning with my 37th monthly payment unless I choose to limit the amount of my monthly payment as permitted by Section 6(A) below.

5. GRADUATED MONTHLY PAYMENTS 1–36

My first 12 monthly payments will each be in the amount of U.S. $_____. On each of the first two anniversaries of the date my first monthly payment is due, I will begin paying a new monthly payment which will be equal to the amount I have been paying multiplied by the number 1.075. I will pay the new amount of my monthly payment until it changes in accordance with this Section 5 or Sections 6 or 7 below.

6. BORROWER'S RIGHT TO LIMIT AMOUNT OF REMAINING MONTHLY PAYMENTS

(A) Calculation of Graduated Monthly Payment Amount

I may choose to limit the amount of my new monthly payment following an Interest Change Date if my new interest rate would cause the monthly payment I have been paying to increase by more than seven and one-half percent (7.5%). **If I choose to limit the amount of my monthly payment, I must give the Note Holder notice that I am doing so at least 15 days before my first new monthly payment is due.** When I do so, on the first monthly payment date after the Interest Change Date I will begin paying a new monthly payment which will be equal to the amount I have been paying each month for the preceding twelve months multiplied by the number 1.075. Thereafter, on each of the first two anniversaries of the new monthly payment date, my monthly payment will again increase by an amount equal to the amount I have been paying each month for the preceding twelve months multiplied by the number 1.075.

Even if I have chosen to limit my monthly payment, Sections 6(B), 6(C) and 7 below may require me to pay a different amount.

(B) Reduced Monthly Payment Amount

My graduated monthly payment calculated under Section 6(A) above could be greater than the amount of a monthly payment which then would be sufficient to repay my unpaid principal balance in full on the maturity date at my current interest rate in substantially equal payments. If so, on the date my paying a graduated monthly payment would cause me to pay more than the lower amount, I will instead then begin paying the lower amount as my monthly payment until the next Interest Change Date.

(C) Increased Monthly Payment Amount

My paying a graduated monthly payment calculated under Section 6(A) above could cause my unpaid principal balance to exceed the limit stated in Section 8(B) below. If so, on the date that my paying a monthly payment would cause me to exceed that limit, I will instead begin paying a new monthly payment until the next Interest Change Date. The new monthly payment will be in an amount which would be sufficient to repay my then unpaid principal balance in full on the maturity date at my current interest rate in substantially equal payments.

7. FINAL MONTHLY PAYMENTS

Beginning with the first monthly payment after the last Interest Change Date, I will pay the Full Payment Amount as my monthly payment.

8. INCREASES IN THE PRINCIPAL AMOUNT TO BE PAID

(A) Additions to My Unpaid Principal Balance

My monthly payment could be less than the amount of the interest portion of a monthly payment which then would be sufficient to repay my unpaid principal balance in full on the maturity date at my current interest rate in substantially equal payments. If so, each month that the amount of my monthly payment is less than the interest portion, the Note Holder will subtract the amount of my monthly payment from the amount of the interest portion and will add the difference to my unpaid principal balance. The Note Holder will also add interest on the amount of this difference to my unpaid principal balance each month. The interest rate on the interest added to principal will be the rate required by Section 2 or 4(A) above.

(B) Limit on My Unpaid Principal Balance

My unpaid principal balance can never exceed a maximum amount equal to one hundred twenty-five percent (125%) of the principal amount I originally borrowed.

9. NOTICE OF CHANGES

The Note Holder will mail or deliver to me a notice of any changes in the amount of my monthly payment before the effective date of any change. The notice will include information required by law to be given me and also the title and telephone number of a person who will answer any question I may have regarding the notice.

10. BORROWER'S RIGHT TO PREPAY

I have the right to make payments of principal at any time before they are due. A payment of principal only is known as a "prepayment." When I make a prepayment, I will tell the Note Holder in writing that I am doing so.

I may make a full prepayment or a partial prepayment without paying any penalty. The Note Holder will use all of my prepayments to reduce the amount of principal that I owe under this Note. If I make a partial prepayment, there will be no delays in the due dates of my monthly payments unless the Note Holder agrees in writing to those delays. My partial prepayment will reduce the amount of my monthly payments after the first Change Date following my partial prepayment. However, any reduction due to my partial prepayment may be offset by an interest rate increase.

11. LOAN CHARGES

If a law, which applies to this loan and which sets maximum loan charges, is finally interpreted so that the interest or other loan charges collected or to be collected in connection with this loan exceed the permitted limits, then: (i) any such loan charge shall be reduced by the amount necessary to reduce the charge to the permitted limit; and (ii) any sums already collected from me which exceeded permitted limits will be refunded to me. The Note Holder may choose to make this refund by reducing the principal I owe under this Note or by making a direct payment to me. If a refund reduces principal, the reduction will be treated as a partial prepayment.

12. BORROWER'S FAILURE TO PAY AS REQUIRED

(A) Late Charge for Overdue Payments

If the Note Holder has not received the full amount of any of my monthly payments by the end of _____ calendar days after the date it is due, I will pay a late charge to the Note Holder. The amount of the charge will be _____% of my overdue payment of principal and interest. I will pay this late charge promptly but only once on any late payment.

(B) Default

If I do not pay the full amount of each monthly payment on the date it is due, I will be in default.

(C) Notice of Default

If I am in default, the Note Holder may send me a written notice telling me that if I do not pay the overdue amount by a certain date, the Note Holder may require me to pay immediately the full amount of principal which has not been paid and all the interest that I owe on that amount. That date must be at least 30 days after the date on which the notice is mailed or delivered to me.

(D) No Waiver By Note Holder

Even if, at a time when I am in default, the Note Holder does not require me to pay immediately in full as described above, the Note Holder will still have the right to do so if I am in default at a later time.

(E) Payment of Note Holder's Costs and Expenses

If the Note Holder has required me to pay immediately in full as described above, the Note Holder will have the right to be paid back for all of its costs and expenses in enforcing this Note to the extent not prohibited by applicable law. Those expenses include, for example, reasonable attorneys' fees.

13. GIVING OF NOTICES

Unless applicable law requires a different method, any notice that must be given to me under this Note will be given by mailing it by first class mail or delivering it to me at the Property Address above or at a different address if I give the Note Holder a notice of my different address.

Any notice that must be given to the Note Holder under this Note will be given by mailing it by first class mail to the Note Holder at the address stated in Section 3 above or at a different address if I am given a notice of that different address.

14. OBLIGATIONS OF PERSONS UNDER THIS NOTE

If more than one person signs this Note, each person is fully and personally obligated to keep all of the promises made in this Note, including the promise to pay the full amount owed. Any person who is a guarantor, surety, or endorser of this Note is also obligated to do these things. Any person who takes over these obligations, including the obligations of a guarantor, surety, or endorser of this Note, is also obligated to keep all of the promises made in this Note. The Note Holder may enforce its rights under this Note against each person individually or against all of us together. This means that any one of us may be required to pay all of the amounts owed under this Note.

15. WAIVERS

I and any other person who has obligations under this Note waive the rights of presentment and notice of dishonor. "Presentment" means the right to require the Note Holder to demand payment of amounts due. "Notice of dishonor" means the right to require the Note Holder to give notice to other persons that amounts due have not been paid.

16. THIS NOTE SECURED BY A SECURITY INSTRUMENT

In addition to the protections given to the Note Holder under this Note, a Mortgage, Deed of Trust, or Deed to Secure Debt (the "Security Instrument") with a Graduated Payment Rider, dated the same day as this Note, protects the Note Holder from possible losses which might result if I do not keep the promises which I make in this Note. That Security Instrument and Rider describe how and under what conditions I may be required to make immediate payment in full of all amounts I owe under this Note. Some of those conditions are described as follows:

> **Transfer of the Property or a Beneficial Interest in Borrower.** If all or any part of the Property or an interest therein is sold or transferred (or if a beneficial interest in Borrower is sold or transferred and Borrower is not a natural person) without Lender's prior written consent, Lender may, at Lender's option, declare all the sums secured by this Security Instrument to be immediately due and payable. However, this option shall not be exercised by Lender if exercise is not authorized by Federal law.
>
> If Lender exercises such option to accelerate, Lender shall mail Borrower notice of acceleration in accordance with paragraph 14 hereof. Such notice shall provide a period of not less than 30 days from the date the notice is mailed within which Borrower may pay the sums declared due. If Borrower fails to pay such sums prior to the expiration of such period, Lender may, without further notice or demand on Borrower, invoke any remedies permitted by paragraph 18 hereof.
>
> Notwithstanding a sale or transfer, Borrower will continue to be obligated under the Note and this Security Instrument unless Lender has released Borrower in writing."

Witness the hand(s) and seal(s) of the undersigned.

§ 14.9 FNMA/FHLMC Growing Equity Note

The Growing Equity Mortgage (or "GEM") is similar to a GPM, except that the initial monthly payments are sufficient to amortize the loan over a "normal" term, typically 30 years. In subsequent years, the monthly payments rise according to a pre-agreed schedule, and the entire additional amount of the payments is applied to reduce the principal balance. The result is a much faster reduction in principal than would be the case with level payments. Depending on the size of the annual increase in payments, the loan may thus be retired in, say, 12 to 15 years rather than the usual 30. For a more complete discussion, see § 11.4, infra.

The GEM note reproduced below provides for a stated initial monthly payment, and requires increases in this amount by some percentage each year. See Section 4(A). For example, if the initial payment were $500, and the multiplier in Section 4(A) were 1.04, the payments for the second year would be $500 × 1.04, or $520; payments for the third year would be $520 × 1.04, or $540.80; and so on. Some GEM loans allow these monthly payment increases to "plateau out" at some future point, such as the eleventh year, and to remain constant thereafter. However, the form below has no such limits, and the payments will continue to increase so long as the loan is outstanding.

Since there is no provision for adjustment of the interest rate in this note, the standard FNMA/FHLMC fixed-rate due-on-sale clause is employed; see Section 11 of the form below.

GROWING EQUITY NOTE

This Note requires an increase in the amount of my monthly payment each year.

_____, 19__, _____, _____, _____.
                           [City]   [State]   [Property Address]

1. BORROWER'S PROMISE TO PAY

In return for a loan that I have received, I promise to pay U.S. $_____ (this amount is called "principal"), plus interest, to the order of the Lender. The Lender is _____. I understand that the Lender may transfer this Note. The Lender or anyone who takes this Note by transfer and who is entitled to receive payments under this Note is called the "Note Holder."

2. INTEREST

Interest will be charged on unpaid principal until the full amount of principal has been paid. I will pay interest at a yearly rate of _____%.

The interest rate required by this Section 2 is the rate I will pay both before and after any default described in Section 7(B) of this Note.

3. TIME AND PLACE OF PAYMENTS

I will pay principal and interest by making payments every month.

I will make my monthly payments on the _____ day of each month beginning on _____, 19__. I will make these payments every month until I have paid all of the principal and interest and any other charges described below that I may owe under this Note. My monthly payments will be applied to interest before principal. If, on _____, _____, I still owe amounts under this Note, I will pay those amounts in full on that date, which is called the "maturity date."

I will make my monthly payments at _____ or at a different place if required by the Note Holder.

4. MONTHLY PAYMENT CALCULATIONS

(A) Yearly Increases

My first _____ monthly payments will each be in the amount of U.S. $_____. On the first day of _____, 19__, and on each anniversary of that date, I will begin paying a new monthly payment which will be equal to the amount I have been paying multiplied by the number 1.0__ I will pay the new amount of my monthly payment until it changes in accordance with this Section 4.

The Note Holder will give me notice of each change in the amount of my monthly payment before the effective date of any change.

(B) Effect of Increased Payments

Each of my first _____ monthly payments will be in an amount that would be sufficient to fully repay my loan in _____ years at the interest rate required by Section 2 above in substantially equal payments. Each remaining monthly payment will be greater than this amount. The Note Holder will apply the difference between these two amounts to reduce my unpaid principal balance.

5. BORROWER'S RIGHT TO PREPAY

I have the right to make payments at any time before they are due. A payment of principal only is known as a "prepayment." When I make a prepayment, I will tell the Note Holder in writing that I am doing so.

I may make a full prepayment or partial prepayments without paying any prepayment charge. The Note Holder will use all of my prepayments to reduce the amount of principal that I owe under this Note. If I make a partial prepayment, there will be no changes in the due date or in the amount of my monthly payment unless the Note Holder agrees in writing to those changes.

6. LOAN CHARGES

If a law, which applies to this loan and which sets maximum loan charges, is finally interpreted so that the interest or other loan charges collected or to be collected in connection with this loan exceed the permitted limits then: (i) any such loan charge shall be reduced by the amount necessary to reduce the charge to the permitted limit; and (ii) any sums already collected from me which exceeded permitted limits will be refunded to me. The Note Holder may choose to make this refund by reducing the principal I owe under this Note or by making a direct payment to me. If a refund reduces principal, the reduction will be treated as a partial prepayment.

7. BORROWER'S FAILURE TO PAY AS REQUIRED

(A) Late Charge for Overdue Payments

If the Note Holder has not received the full amount of any monthly payment by the end of _____ calendar days after the date it is due, I will pay a late charge to the Note Holder. The amount of the charge will be _____% of my overdue payment of principal and interest. I will pay this late charge promptly but only once on each late payment.

(B) Default

If I do not pay the full amount of each monthly payment on the date it is due, I will be in default.

(C) Notice of Default

If I am in default, the Note Holder may send me a written notice telling me that if I do not pay the overdue amount by a certain date, the Note Holder may require me to pay immediately the full amount of principal which has not been paid and all the interest that I owe on that amount. That date must be at least 30 days after the date on which the notice is delivered or mailed to me.

(D) No Waiver By Note Holder

Even if, at a time when I am in default, the Note Holder does not require me to pay immediately in full as described above, the Note Holder will still have the right to do so if I am in default at a later time.

(E) Payment of Note Holder's Costs and Expenses

If the Note Holder has required me to pay immediately in full as described above, the Note Holder will have the right to be paid back by me for all of its costs and expenses in enforcing this Note to the extent not prohibited by applicable law. Those expenses include, for example, reasonable attorneys' fees.

8. GIVING OF NOTICES

Unless applicable law requires a different method, any notice that must be given to me under this Note will be given by delivering it or by mailing it by first class mail to me at the Property Address above or at a different address if I give the Note Holder a notice of my different address.

Any notice that must be given to the Note Holder under this Note will be given by mailing it by first class mail to the Note Holder at the address stated in Section 3 above or at a different address if I am given a notice of that different address.

9. OBLIGATIONS OF PERSONS UNDER THIS NOTE

If more than one person signs this Note, each person is fully and personally obligated to keep all of the promises made in this Note, including the promise to pay the full amount owed. Any person who is a guarantor, surety or endorser of this Note is also obligated to do these things. Any person who takes over these obligations, including the obligations of a guarantor, surety or endorser of this Note, is also obligated to keep all of the promises made in this Note. The Note Holder may enforce its rights under this Note against each person individually or against all of us together. This means that any one of us may be required to pay all of the amounts owed under this Note.

10. WAIVERS

I and any other person who has obligations under this Note waive the rights of presentment and notice of dishonor. "Presentment" means the right to require the Note Holder to demand payment of amounts due. "Notice of dishonor" means the right to require the Note Holder to give notice to other persons that amounts due have not been paid.

11. UNIFORM SECURED NOTE

This Note is a uniform instrument with limited variations in some jurisdictions. In addition to the protections given to the Note Holder under this Note, a Mortgage, Deed of Trust or Security Deed (the "Security Instrument"), dated the same date as this Note, protects the Note Holder from possible losses which might result if I do not keep the promises which I make in this Note. That Security Instrument describes how and under what conditions I may be required to make immediate payment in full of all amounts I owe under this Note. Some of those conditions are described as follows:

Transfer of the Property or a Beneficial Interest in Borrower. If all or any part of the Property or any interest in it is sold or transferred (or if a beneficial interest in Borrower is sold or transferred and Borrower is not a natural person) without Lender's prior written consent, Lender may, at its option, require immediate payment in full of all sums secured by this Security Instrument. However, this option shall not be exercised by Lender if exercise is prohibited by federal law as of the date of this Security Instrument.

If Lender exercises this option, Lender shall give Borrower notice of acceleration. The notice shall provide a period of not less than 30 days from the date the notice is delivered or mailed within which Borrower must pay all sums secured by this Security Instrument. If Borrower fails to pay these sums prior to the expiration of this period, Lender may invoke any remedies permitted by this Security Instrument without further notice or demand on Borrower.

Witness the Hand(s) and Seal(s) of the Undersigned.

§ 14.10 FNMA/FHLMC Fixed/Adjustable Rate Note

This Note contains two important features. First, it provides for a period (typically three, five or seven years) when payment and interest rate remain constant. At the end of that period ("Change Date") there is one adjustment in payment amount and interest rate with the index being the weekly average yield on United States Treasury securities adjusted to a constant maturity of 10 years. The borrower's payment and interest rate will then stay the same over the remainder of the loan.

Second, the Note gives the borrower the right on dates specified in Section 5(A) to "convert" to a fixed rate evenly amortized loan. Note that the form provides for a "conversion fee" to be specified by the lender. This language would provide a helpful model for a conversion provision to be used in any type of note or financing device.

Finally, as noted earlier in § 14.7, the conversion of the standard fixed-rate FNMA/FHLMC forms to adjustable rate use is accomplished by using two documents, only one of which, the Fixed/Adjustable Rate Note, is reproduced here. The other is a Fixed/Adjustable Rate Rider (Form 3181) which is an amendment to the usual FNMA/FHLMC single-family mortgage or deed of trust. This rider is essentially a verbatim copy of Sections 4 and 5 of the Note form reprinted below. Thus, because virtually all of the Rider's language appears in the Note form as well, we have not reprinted it in this book.

FIXED/ADJUSTABLE RATE NOTE
(10 Year Treasury Index—Rate Cap—Conversion Option)

THIS NOTE PROVIDES FOR ONE CHANGE IN MY INTEREST RATE AND LIMITS THE MAXIMUM RATE I MUST PAY. THIS NOTE ALSO CONTAINS THE OPTION OF AN EARLIER CONVERSION OF MY INTEREST RATE.

_____, 19__ _____, _____
[City]   [State]

[Property Address]

1. BORROWER'S PROMISE TO PAY

In return for a loan that I have received, I promise to pay U.S. $_____ (this amount is called "principal"), plus interest, to the order of the Lender. The Lender is _____.

I understand that the Lender may transfer this Note. The Lender or anyone who takes this Note by transfer and who is entitled to receive payments under this Note is called the "Note Holder."

2. INTEREST

Interest will be charged on unpaid principal until the full amount of principal has been paid. I will pay interest at a yearly rate of _____%. The interest rate I will pay may change in accordance with Section 4 or 5 of this Note.

The interest rate required by this Section 2 and Section 4 or 5 of this Note is the rate I will pay both before and after any default described in Section 8(B) of this Note.

3. PAYMENTS

(A) Time and Place of Payments

I will pay principal and interest by making payments every month.

I will make my monthly payments on the first day of each month beginning on _____, 19__. I will make these payments every month until I have paid all of the principal and interest and any other charges described below that I may owe under this Note. My monthly payments will be applied to interest before principal. If, on _____, 20__, I still owe amounts under this Note, I will pay those amounts in full on that date, which is called the "Maturity Date."

I will make my monthly payments at _____

or at a different place if required by the Note Holder.

(B) Amount of My Initial Monthly Payments

Each of my initial monthly payments will be in the amount of U.S. $_____. This amount may change.

(C) Monthly Payment Changes

Changes in my monthly payment will reflect changes in the unpaid principal of my loan and in the interest rate that I must pay. The Note Holder will determine my new interest rate and the changed amount of my monthly payment in accordance with Section 4 or 5 of this Note.

4. ADJUSTABLE INTEREST RATE AND MONTHLY PAYMENT CHANGES

(A) Change Date

The initial fixed interest rate I will pay will change on the first day of _____, which is called the "Change Date," unless I exercise my Conversion Option in accordance with Section 5 of this Note.

(B) The Index

At the Change Date, my interest rate will be based on an Index. The "Index" is the weekly average yield on United States Treasury securities adjusted to a constant maturity of 10 years, as made available by the Federal Reserve Board. The most recent Index figure available as of the date 45 days before the Change Date is called the "Current Index."

If the Index is no longer available, the Note Holder will choose a new index that is based upon comparable information. The Note Holder will give me notice of this choice.

(C) Calculation of Change

Before the Change Date, the Note Holder will calculate my new interest rate by adding _____ percentage point(s) (_____%) to the Current Index. The Note Holder will then round the result of this addition to the nearest one-eighth of one percentage point (0.125%). Subject to the limit stated in Section 4(D) below, this rounded amount will be my new interest rate until the Maturity Date.

The Note Holder will then determine the amount of the monthly payment that would be sufficient to repay the unpaid principal that I am expected to owe at the Change Date in full on the Maturity Date at my new interest rate in substantially equal payments. The result of this calculation will be the new amount of my monthly payment.

(D) Limits on Interest Rate Change

The interest rate I am required to pay at the Change Date will not be greater than _____%, which is called the "Maximum Rate."

(E) Effective Date of Change

My new interest rate will become effective on the Change Date. I will pay the amount of my new monthly payment beginning on the first monthly payment date after the Change Date.

(F) Notice of Change

The Note Holder will deliver or mail to me a notice of any change in my interest rate and the amount of my monthly payment before the effective date of any change. The notice will include information required by law to be given me and also the title and telephone number of a person who will answer any question I may have regarding the notice.

5. FIXED INTEREST RATE CONVERSION OPTION

(A) Option to Convert to Fixed Rate

I have a Conversion Option that I can exercise unless I am in default or this Section 5(A) will not permit me to do so. The "Conversion Option" is my option to convert the interest rate I am required to pay by this Note from an initial fixed rate with one change to the new fixed rate calculated under Section 5(B) below.

The conversion can only take place on a date(s) specified by the Note Holder during the period beginning on the due date of the _____ monthly payment and ending on the due date of the _____ monthly payment. Each date on which my initial fixed interest rate can convert to the new fixed rate is called the "Conversion Date."

If I want to exercise the Conversion Option, I must first meet certain conditions. Those conditions are that: (i) I must give the Note Holder notice that I want to do so; (ii) on the Conversion Date, I must not be in default under the Note or the Security Instrument; (iii) by a date specified by the Note Holder, I must pay the Note Holder a conversion fee of U.S. $_____; and (iv) I must sign and give the Note Holder any documents the Note Holder requires to effect the conversion.

(B) Calculation of Fixed Rate

My new, fixed interest rate will be equal to the Federal National Mortgage Association's required net yield as of a date and time of day specified by the Note Holder for (i) if the original term of this Note is greater than 15 years, 30-year fixed rate first mortgages covered by applicable 60-day mandatory delivery commitments, plus five-eighths of one percentage point (0.625%), rounded to the nearest one-eighth of one percentage point (0.125%), or (ii) if the original term of this Note is 15 years or less, 15-year fixed rate first mortgages covered by applicable 60-day mandatory delivery commitments, plus five-eighths of one percentage point (0.625%), rounded to the nearest one-eighth of one percentage point (0.125%). If this required net yield cannot be determined because the applicable commitments are not available, the Note Holder will determine my interest rate by using comparable information. My new rate calculated under this Section 5(B) will not be greater than the Maximum Rate stated in Section 4(D) above.

(C) New Payment Amount and Effective Date

If I choose to exercise the Conversion Option, the Note Holder will determine the amount of the monthly payment that would be sufficient to repay the unpaid principal I am expected to owe on the Conversion Date in full on the Maturity Date at my new fixed interest rate in substantially equal payments. The result of this calculation will be the new amount of my monthly payment. Beginning with my first monthly payment after the Conversion Date, I will pay the new amount as my monthly payment until the Maturity Date.

6. BORROWER'S RIGHT TO PREPAY

I have the right to make payments of principal at any time before they are due. A payment of principal only is known as a "prepayment." When I make a prepayment, I will tell the Note Holder in writing that I am doing so.

I may make a full prepayment or partial prepayments without paying any prepayment charge. The Note Holder will use all of my prepayments to reduce the amount of principal that I owe under this Note. If I make a partial prepayment, there will be no changes in the due dates of my monthly payments unless the Note Holder agrees in writing to those changes. My partial prepayment may reduce the amount of my monthly payments after the Change Date following my partial prepayment. However, any reduction due to my partial prepayment may be offset by an interest rate increase.

7. LOAN CHARGES

If a law, which applies to this loan and which sets maximum loan charges, is finally interpreted so that the interest or other loan charges collected or to be collected in connection with this loan exceed the permitted limits, then: (i) any such loan charge shall be reduced by the amount necessary to reduce the charge to the permitted limit; and (ii) any sums already collected from me that exceeded permitted limits will be refunded to me. The Note Holder may choose to make this refund by reducing the principal I owe under this Note or by making a direct payment to me. If a refund reduces principal, the reduction will be treated as a partial prepayment.

8. BORROWER'S FAILURE TO PAY AS REQUIRED

(A) Late Charges for Overdue Payments

If the Note Holder has not received the full amount of any monthly payment by the end of _____ calendar days after the date it is due, I will pay a late charge to the Note Holder. The amount of the charge will be _____% of my overdue payment of principal and interest. I will pay this late charge promptly but only once on each late payment.

(B) Default

If I do not pay the full amount of each monthly payment on the date it is due, I will be in default.

(C) Notice of Default

If I am in default, the Note Holder may send me a written notice telling me that if I do not pay the overdue amount by a certain date, the Note Holder may require me to pay immediately the full amount of principal that has not been paid and all the interest that I owe on that amount. That date must be at least 30 days after the date on which the notice is delivered or mailed to me.

(D) No Waiver By Note Holder

Even if, at a time when I am in default, the Note Holder does not require me to pay immediately in full as described above, the Note Holder will still have the right to do so if I am in default at a later time.

(E) Payment of Note Holder's Costs and Expenses

If the Note Holder has required me to pay immediately in full as described above, the Note Holder will have the right to be paid back by me for all of its costs and expenses in enforcing this Note to the extent not prohibited by applicable law. Those expenses include, for example, reasonable attorneys' fees.

9. GIVING OF NOTICES

Unless applicable law requires a different method, any notice that must be given to me under this Note will be given by delivering it or by mailing it by first class mail to me at the Property Address above or at a different address if I give the Note Holder a notice of my different address.

Unless the Note Holder requires a different method, any notice that must be given to the Note Holder under this Note will be given by mailing it by first class mail to the Note Holder at the address stated in Section 3(A) above or at a different address if I am given a notice of that different address.

10. OBLIGATIONS OF PERSONS UNDER THIS NOTE

If more than one person signs this Note, each person is fully and personally obligated to keep all of the promises made in this Note, including the promise to pay the full amount owed. Any person who is a guarantor, surety or endorser of this Note is also obligated to do these things. Any person who takes over these obligations, including the obligations of a guarantor, surety or endorser of this Note, is also obligated to keep all of the promises made in this Note. The Note Holder may enforce its rights under this Note against each person individually or against all of us together. This means that any one of us may be required to pay all of the amounts owed under this Note.

11. WAIVERS

I and any other person who has obligations under this Note waive the rights of presentment and notice of dishonor. "Presentment" means the right to require the Note Holder to demand payment of amounts due. "Notice of dishonor" means the right to require the Note Holder to give notice to other persons that amounts due have not been paid.

12. UNIFORM SECURED NOTE

This Note is a uniform instrument with limited variations in some jurisdictions. In addition to the protections given to the Note Holder under this Note, a Mortgage, Deed of Trust or Security Deed (the "Security Instrument"), dated the same date as this Note, protects the Note Holder from possible losses that might result if I do not keep the promises which I make in this Note. That Security Instrument describes how and under what conditions I may be required to make immediate payment in full of all amounts I owe under this Note. Some of those conditions are described as follows:

Both before and after any exercise of my Conversion Option under the conditions stated in Section 5 of this Fixed/Adjustable Rate Note, Uniform Covenant 17 of the Security Instrument is described as follows:

Transfer of the Property or a Beneficial Interest in Borrower. If all or any part of the Property or any interest in it is sold or transferred (or if a beneficial interest in Borrower is sold or transferred and Borrower is not a natural person) without Lender's prior written consent, Lender may, at its option, require immediate payment in full of all sums secured by this Security Instrument. However, this option shall not be exercised by Lender if exercise is prohibited by federal law as of the date of this Security Instrument.

If Lender exercises this option, Lender shall give Borrower notice of acceleration. The notice shall provide a period of not less than 30 days from the date the notice is delivered or mailed within which Borrower must pay all sums secured by this Security Instrument. If Borrower fails to pay these sums prior to the expiration of this period, Lender may invoke any remedies permitted by this Security Instrument without further notice or demand on Borrower.

Witness the Hand(s) and Seal(s) of the Undersigned.

§ 14.11 FNMA/FHLMC Condominium Rider

Permanent mortgage loans on condominium units are usually made on much the same terms as loans on detached residential real estate. However, the condominium mortgagee confronts a variety of concerns that are unimportant or non-existent in more traditional financing contexts. Most of these concerns relate to the importance of the owners association and the common areas to the long term success of the project and, thus, to the security value of the units themselves. See § 13.5, supra. Consequently, the Condominium Rider reflects an attempt to deal with many of these special problems. A separate rider is also required in connection with planned unit development mortgage loans; however, because it is virtually identical to the Condominium Rider, we chose not to include it in this volume. See FNMA–FHLMC Multistate PUD Rider Single Family—Form 3150.

Several provisions are noteworthy. Section A obligates the mortgagor to pay promptly all dues and assessments and to abide by all provisions of the Constituent Documents (the declaration, by-laws, regulations and related documents). Section B waives the usual requirement of monthly payment by the mortgagor of $1/12$ of the annual premium for hazard insurance on the property so long as the Association maintains adequate blanket coverage. This provision reflects the fact that mortgagor's monthly association dues covers such insurance costs.

Section E places limitations on the mortgagor's voting prerogatives as a member of the owners association. For example, the mortgagee's consent is required for any vote to terminate the condominium (except after casualty loss or condemnation), any amendment of a provision in the Constituent Documents that benefits the mortgagee and any change from professional management to self-management by the owners association.

Section E also prohibits partition of a unit without the mortgagee's consent. Since partition in kind of a condominium unit is virtually impossible, this provision can only be used against partition by sale. Such a partition is already the basis for acceleration under the due-on-sale clause contained in Section 17 of the Uniform Covenants. See § 14.3 supra. To the extent that a mortgagee attempts to utilize a remedy against partition other than acceleration (such as seeking to enjoin a mortgagor from requesting it, or petitioning a court to deny it), Section E's prohibition may well be viewed as a direct restraint on alienation and, consequently, unenforceable. See Nelson and Whitman, Congressional Preemption of Mortgage Due-on-Sale Law: An Analysis of the Garn–St. Germain Act, 35 Hast.L.J. 241, 251 (1983).

CONDOMINIUM RIDER

THIS CONDOMINIUM RIDER is made this _____ day of _____, 19__ and is incorporated into and shall be deemed to amend and supplement the Mortgage, Deed of Trust or Security Deed (the "Security Instrument") of the same date given by the undersigned (the "Borrower") to secure Borrower's Note to _____ (the "Lender") of the same date and covering the Property described in the Security Instrument and located at:

[Property Address]

The Property includes a unit in, together with an undivided interest in the common elements of, a condominium project known as:

[Name of Condominium Project]

(the "Condominium Project"). If the owners association or other entity which acts for the Condominium Project (the "Owners Association") holds title to property for the benefit or use of its members or shareholders, the Property also includes Borrower's interest in the Owners Association and the uses, proceeds and benefits of Borrower's interest.

CONDOMINIUM COVENANTS. In addition to the covenants and agreements made in the Security Instrument, Borrower and Lender further covenant and agree as follows:

A. Condominium Obligations. Borrower shall perform all of Borrower's obligations under the Condominium Project's Constituent Documents. The "Constituent Documents" are the: (i) Declaration or any other document which creates the Condominium Project; (ii) by-laws; (iii) code of regulations; and (iv) other equivalent documents. Borrower shall promptly pay, when due, all dues and assessments imposed pursuant to the Constituent Documents.

B. Hazard Insurance. So long as the Owners Association maintains, with a generally accepted insurance carrier, a "master" or "blanket" policy on the

Condominium Project which is satisfactory to Lender and which provides insurance coverage in the amounts, for the periods, and against the hazards Lender requires, including fire and hazards included within the term "extended coverage," then:

(i) Lender waives the provision in Uniform Covenant 2 for the monthly payment to Lender of one-twelfth of the yearly premium installments for hazard insurance on the Property; and

(ii) Borrower's obligation under Uniform Covenant 5 to maintain hazard insurance coverage on the Property is deemed satisfied to the extent that the required coverage is provided by the Owners Association policy.

Borrower shall give Lender prompt notice of any lapse in required hazard insurance coverage.

In the event of a distribution of hazard insurance proceeds in lieu of restoration or repair following a loss to the Property, whether to the unit or to common elements, any proceeds payable to Borrower are hereby assigned and shall be paid to Lender for application to the sums secured by the Security Instrument, with any excess paid to Borrower.

C. Public Liability Insurance. Borrower shall take such actions as may be reasonable to insure that the Owners Association maintains a public liability insurance policy acceptable in form, amount, and extent of coverage to Lender.

D. Condemnation. The proceeds of any award or claim for damages, direct or consequential, payable to Borrower in connection with any condemnation or other taking of all or any part of the Property, whether of the unit or of the common elements, or for any conveyance in lieu of condemnation, are hereby assigned and shall be paid to Lender. Such proceeds shall be applied by Lender to the sums secured by the Security Instrument as provided in Uniform Covenant 10.

E. Lender's Prior Consent. Borrower shall not, except after notice to Lender and with Lender's prior written consent, either partition or subdivide the Property or consent to:

(i) the abandonment or termination of the Condominium Project, except for abandonment or termination required by law in the case of substantial destruction by fire or other casualty or in the case of a taking by condemnation or eminent domain;

(ii) any amendment to any provision of the Constituent Documents if the provision is for the express benefit of Lender;

(iii) termination of professional management and assumption of self-management of the Owners Association; or

(iv) any action which would have the effect of rendering the public liability insurance coverage maintained by the Owners Association unacceptable to Lender.

F. Remedies. If Borrower does not pay condominium dues and assessments when due, then Lender may pay them. Any amounts disbursed by Lender under this paragraph F shall become additional debt of Borrower secured by the Security Instrument. Unless Borrower and Lender agree to other terms of payment, these amounts shall bear interest from the date of disbursement at the Note rate and shall be payable, with interest, upon notice from Lender to Borrower requesting payment.

BY SIGNING BELOW, Borrower accepts and agrees to the terms and provisions contained in this Condominium Rider.

§ 14.12 FNMA/FHLMC Uniform Instrument—1–4 Family Rider

This Rider is used in conjunction with the FNMA/FHLMC Uniform Instrument where the mortgaged real estate consists of a 1–4 family dwelling. Such property usually is rental real estate. The Rider's purpose is to insure that the rental cash flow, as well as the real estate itself, stands as security for the debt. Moreover, it also seeks to increase the chances that the cash flow will continue unabated. Section C, for example, is interesting in this latter regard. Not only must the mortgagor carry the usual casualty insurance coverage, but protection against rental loss resulting from the casualty as well.

Sections E and F are aimed at enhancing the mortgagee's security interest in rents. Section E obligates the mortgagor, upon mortgagee request, to assign actual leases and security deposits to the mortgagee. Section F authorizes the mortgagee, upon mortgagor default, to collect rents from the property. This latter provision purports to be an "absolute" or "in praesenti" assignment and not one for "additional security only." The latter language to the contrary, the fact is that the assignment is for security purposes and not an outright transfer of the rents. Moreover, to the extent that the Rider is used in a jurisdiction that requires some type of affirmative action on the part of the mortgagee after default either to "perfect" or enforce (begin collection of the rents) the assignment, it is doubtful that it will be automatically enforcible. See § 4.35, supra. However, from the mortgagee's perspective, the provision can do no harm and, in some jurisdictions, may even tip the balance in favor of an automatic enforcement approach.

In Section B the mortgagor promises not to further encumber the property without mortgagee's written permission. This section at first glance seems duplicative of Section 17 of the Uniform Covenants (due-on-sale provision) in that the latter provision's prohibition of any transfer of "all or any part of the Property or an interest in it" without mortgagee's consent already encompasses a restriction on further encumbrances. More important, the Garn–St. Germain Act, which prohibits acceleration with respect to mortgages on "less than five dwelling units" based on "the creation of a lien or other encumbrance subordinate to the lender's security instrument * * * " clearly bars acceleration as a remedy for violation of the Rider language. 12 U.S.C.A. § 1701j(d) (1983). See § 5.24, supra.

Perhaps the intent of Section B was to make clear that, notwithstanding the statutory prohibition on acceleration, the mortgagee reserves the right to utilize other remedies, such as injunctive relief or damages, to enforce it. The Garn Act, after all, prohibits only acceleration as a remedy for violation of a due-on-sale clause. The foregoing interpretation, however, raises further problems. Since such non-acceleration remedies more directly burden the mortgagor's power of alienation than do their acceleration counterpart, there is a strong chance that they impose unreasonable restraints on alienation. See § 5.22, supra. On the other hand, from the mortgagee's perspective, Section B probably does no harm and may very well discourage further encumbrances by mortgagors who do not relish the prospect of litigating the restraint on alienation issue.

1-4 FAMILY RIDER

Assignment of Rents

THIS 1-4 FAMILY RIDER is made this _____ day of _____, 19__, and is incorporated into and shall be deemed to amend and supplement the Mortgage, Deed of Trust or Security Deed (the "Security Instrument") of the same date given by the undersigned (the "Borrower") to secure Borrower's Note to _____ (the "Lender") of the same date and covering the Property described in the Security Instrument and located at:

_____

[Property Address]

1-4 FAMILY COVENANTS. In addition to the covenants and agreements made in the Security Instrument, Borrower and Lender further covenant and agree as follows:

A. Additional Property Subject to the Security Instrument. In addition to the Property described in the Security Instrument, the following items are added to the Property description, and shall also constitute the Property covered by the Security Instrument: building materials, appliances and goods of every nature whatsoever now or hereafter located in, on, or used, or intended to be used in connection with the Property, including, but not limited to, those for the purposes of supplying or distributing heating, cooling, electricity, gas, water, air and light, fire prevention and extinguishing apparatus, security and access control apparatus, plumbing, bath tubs, water heaters, water closets, sinks, ranges, stoves, refrigerators, dishwashers, disposals, washers, dryers, awnings, storm windows, storm doors, screens, blinds, shades, curtains and curtain rods, attached mirrors, cabinets, panelling and attached floor coverings now or hereafter attached to the Property, all of which, including replacements and additions thereto, shall be deemed to be and remain a part of the Property covered by the Security Instrument. All of the foregoing together with the Property described in the Security Instrument (or the leasehold estate if the Security Instrument is on a leasehold) are referred to in this 1-4 Family Rider and the Security Instrument as the "Property."

B. Use of Property; Compliance With Law. Borrower shall not seek, agree to or make a change in the use of the Property or its zoning classification, unless Lender has agreed in writing to the change. Borrower shall comply with all laws, ordinances, regulations and requirements of any governmental body applicable to the Property.

C. Subordinate Liens. Except as permitted by federal law, Borrower shall not allow any lien inferior to the Security Instrument to be perfected against the Property without Lender's prior written permission.

D. Rent Loss Insurance. Borrower shall maintain insurance against rent loss in addition to the other hazards for which insurance is required by Uniform Covenant 5.

E. "Borrower's Right to Reinstate" Deleted. Uniform Covenant 18 is deleted.

F. Borrower's Occupancy. Unless Lender and Borrower otherwise agree in writing, the first sentence in Uniform Covenant 6 concerning Borrower's occupancy of the Property is deleted. All remaining covenants and agreements set forth in Uniform Covenant 6 shall remain in effect.

G. Assignment of Leases. Upon Lender's request, Borrower shall assign to Lender all leases of the Property and all security deposits made in connection with leases of the Property. Upon the assignment, Lender shall have the right to modify, extend or terminate the existing leases and to execute new leases, in

Lender's sole discretion. As used in this paragraph G, the word "lease" shall mean "sublease" if the Security Instrument is on a leasehold.

H. Assignment of Rents; Appointment of Receiver; Lender in Possession. Borrower absolutely and unconditionally assigns and transfers to Lender all the rents and revenues ("Rents") of the Property, regardless of to whom the Rents of the Property are payable. Borrower authorizes Lender or Lender's agents to collect the Rents, and agrees that each tenant of the Property shall pay the Rents to Lender or Lender's agents. However, Borrower shall receive the Rents until (i) Lender has given Borrower notice of default pursuant to paragraph 21 of the Security Instrument and (ii) Lender has given notice to the tenant(s) that the Rents are to be paid to Lender or Lender's agent. This assignment of Rents constitutes an absolute assignment and not an assignment for additional security only.

If Lender gives notice of breach to Borrower: (i) all Rents received by Borrower shall be held by Borrower as trustee for the benefit of Lender only, to be applied to the sums secured by the Security Instrument; (ii) Lender shall be entitled to collect and receive all of the Rents of the Property; (iii) Borrower agrees that each tenant of the Property shall pay all Rents due and unpaid to Lender or Lender's agents upon Lender's written demand to the tenant; (iv) unless applicable law provides otherwise, all Rents collected by Lender or Lender's agents shall be applied first to the costs of taking control of and managing the Property and collecting the Rents, including, but not limited to, attorney's fees, receiver's fees, premiums on receiver's bonds, repair and maintenance costs, insurance premiums, taxes, assessments and other charges on the Property, and then to the sums secured by the Security Instrument; (v) Lender, Lender's agents or any judicially appointed receiver shall be liable to account for only those Rents actually received; and (vi) Lender shall be entitled to have a receiver appointed to take possession of and manage the Property and collect the Rents and profits derived from the Property without any showing as to the inadequacy of the Property as security.

If the Rents of the Property are not sufficient to cover the costs of taking control of and managing the Property and of collecting the Rents any funds expended by Lender for such purposes shall become indebtedness of Borrower to Lender secured by the Security Instrument pursuant to Uniform Covenant 7.

Borrower represents and warrants that Borrower has not executed any prior assignment of the Rents and has not and will not perform any act that would prevent Lender from exercising its rights under this paragraph.

Lender, or Lender's agents or a judicially appointed receiver, shall not be required to enter upon, take control of or maintain the Property before or after giving notice of default to Borrower. However, Lender, or Lender's agents or a judicially appointed receiver, may do so at any time when a default occurs. Any application of Rents shall not cure or waive any default or invalidate any other right or remedy of Lender. This assignment of Rents of the Property shall terminate when all the sums secured by the Security Instrument are paid in full.

I. Cross-Default Provision. Borrower's default or breach under any note or agreement in which Lender has an interest shall be a breach under the Security Instrument and Lender may invoke any of the remedies permitted by the Security Instrument.

BY SIGNING BELOW, Borrower accepts and agrees to the terms and provisions contained in this 1-4 Family Rider.

§ 14.13 FHA Note and Deed of Trust—Fixed Rate Home Loan—Missouri

The following Note and Deed of Trust are used for Federal Housing Administration (FHA) insured home loans in Missouri, where the deed of trust with power of sale is the commonly used financing device.

While FHA forms are less uniform nationally than their FNMA/FHLMC counterparts, certain provisions are common to all FHA home loan transactions. For example, the Note specifically affords the mortgagor the right to prepay the debt at any time in whole or in part without a prepayment charge. Moreover, the Deed of Trust, unlike until relatively recently, contains a due-on-sale clause. However, permission for an assumption transfer will be given if the transferee is credit-worthy. Finally, it should be stressed that FHA no longer requires that the loans it insures be on its Forms, so long as the forms used contain certain specific provisions. See 54 Fed.Reg. 27596 (1989).

Paragraph 4 of the Deed of Trust, which deals with the disposition of hazard insurance proceeds, is, unlike its FNMA/FHLMC counterpart, decidedly pro-mortgagee. While the FNMA/FHLMC provision requires that insurance proceeds be used to rebuild so long as such a course of action is economically feasible and does not impair the mortgagee's security (see § 14.3, supra), under the FHA Deed of Trust language, the mortgagee has the option to eschew rebuilding in favor of prepayment of the mortgage debt. When the mortgagee opts for prepayment, the mortgagor will be faced with securing new financing in the event she chooses to rebuild.

Paragraph 7 provides that in the event of a partial condemnation of the mortgaged real estate, the award must be applied to payment of the mortgage debt. While this treatment is consistent with a significant common-law approach to this problem (see § 4.15, supra), the FNMA/FHLMC provision is more sensitive to the mortgagor's interests in that the mortgagee has the right to receive only that portion of the award that the mortgage debt bears to the pre-condemnation value of the real estate. See § 14.3, supra.

NOTE

[Property Address]

1. PARTIES

"Borrower" means each person signing at the end of this Note, and the person's successors and assigns. "Lender" means and its successors and assigns.

2. BORROWER'S PROMISE TO PAY; INTEREST

In return for a loan received from Lender, Borrower promises to pay the principal sum of _____ DOLLARS AND 00 CENTS Dollars (U.S. $ _____), plus interest, to the order of Lender. Interest will be charged on unpaid principal, from the date of disbursement of the loan proceeds by Lender, at the rate of _____ per cent (_____%) per year until the full amount of principal has been paid.

3. PROMISE TO PAY SECURED

Borrower's promise to pay is secured by a mortgage, deed of trust or similar security instrument that is dated the same date as this Note and called the "Security Instrument." That Security Instrument protects the Lender from losses which might result if Borrower defaults under this Note.

4. MANNER OF PAYMENT

(A) Time

Borrower shall make a payment of principal and interest to Lender on the first day of each month beginning on _____. Any principal and interest remaining on the first day of _____, 20__, will be due on that date, which is called the "Maturity Date."

(B) Place

Payment shall be made at, _____ or at such other place as Lender may designate in writing by notice to Borrower.

(C) Amount

Each monthly payment of principal and interest will be in the amount of $_____. This amount will be part of a larger monthly payment required by the Security Instrument, that shall be applied to principal, interest and other items in the order described in the Security Instrument.

(D) Allonge to this Note for payment adjustments

If an allonge providing for payment adjustments is executed by Borrower together with this Note, the covenants of the allonge shall be incorporated into and shall amend and supplement the covenants of this Note as if the allonge were a part of this Note. [Check applicable box]

☐ Graduated Payment Allonge   ☐ Growing Equity Allonge   ☐ Other [Specify]

5. BORROWER'S RIGHT TO PREPAY

Borrower has the right to pay the debt evidenced by this Note, in whole or in part, without charge or penalty, on the first day of any month.

6. BORROWER'S FAILURE TO PAY

(A) Late Charge for Overdue Payments

If Lender has not received the full monthly payment required by the Security Instrument, as described in Paragraph 4(C) of this Note by the end of fifteen calendar days after the payment is due, Lender may collect a late charge in the amount of _____ per cent (_____%) of the overdue amount of each payment.

(B) Default

If Borrower defaults by failing to pay in full any monthly payment, then Lender may, except as limited by regulations of the Secretary in the case of payment defaults, require immediate payment in full of the principal balance remaining due and all accrued interest. Lender may choose not to exercise this option without waiving its rights in the event of any subsequent default. In many circumstances regulations issued by the Secretary will limit Lender's rights to require immediate payment in full in the case of payment defaults. This Note does not authorize acceleration when not permitted by HUD regulations. As used in this Note, "Secretary" means the Secretary of Housing and Urban Development or his or her designee.

(C) Payment of Costs and Expenses

If Lender has required immediate payment in full, as described above, Lender may require Borrower to pay costs and expenses including reasonable and customary attorneys' fees for enforcing this Note. Such fees and costs shall bear interest from the date of disbursement at the same rate as the principal of this Note.

7. WAIVERS

Borrower and any other person who has obligations under this Note waive the rights of presentment and notice of dishonor. "Presentment" means the right to require Lender to demand payment of amounts due. "Notice of dishonor" means the right to require Lender to give notice to other persons that amounts due have not been paid.

8. GIVING OF NOTICES

Unless applicable law requires a different method, any notice that must be given to Borrower under this Note will be given by delivering it or by mailing it by first class mail to Borrower at the property address above or at a different address if Borrower has given Lender a notice of Borrower's different address.

Any notice that must be given to Lender under this Note will be given by first class mail to Lender at the address stated in Paragraph 4(B) or at a different address if Borrower is given a notice of that different address.

9. OBLIGATIONS OF PERSONS UNDER THIS NOTE

If more than one person signs this Note, each person is fully and personally obligated to keep all of the promises made in this Note, including the promise to pay the full amount owed. Any person who is a guarantor, surety or endorser of this Note is also obligated to do these things. Any person who takes over these obligations, including the obligations of a guarantor, surety or endorser of this Note, is also obligated to keep all of the promises made in this Note. Lender may enforce its rights under this Note against each person individually or against all signatories together. Any one person signing this Note may be required to pay all of the amounts owed under this Note.

BY SIGNING BELOW, Borrower accepts and agrees to the terms and covenants contained in this Note.

DEED OF TRUST

THIS DEED OF TRUST ("Security Instrument") is given on _____. The Grantor is _____ ("Borrower"). The trustee is _____ ("Trustee"). The beneficiary is _____ which is organized and existing under the laws of _____, and whose address is, _____ ("Lender"). Borrower owes Lender the principal sum of _____ _____ (U.S. $_____). This debt is evidenced by Borrower's note dated the same date as this Security Instrument ("Note"), which provides for monthly payments, with the full debt, if not paid earlier, due and payable on _____. This Security Instrument secures to Lender: (a) the repayment of the debt evidenced by the Note, with interest, and all renewals, extensions and modifications; (b) the payment of all other sums, with interest, advanced under paragraph 6 to protect the security of this Security Instrument; and (c) the performance of Borrower's covenants and agreements under this Security Instrument and the Note. For this purpose, Borrower irrevocably grants and conveys to Trustee, in trust, with power of sale, the following described property located in _____ County, Missouri:

which has the address of _____, _____,
[Street] [City]

Missouri _____ ("Property Address");
[Zip Code]

TOGETHER WITH all the improvements now or hereafter erected on the property, and all easements, rights, appurtenances, rents, royalties, mineral, oil and gas rights and profits, water rights and stock and all fixtures now or hereafter a part of the property. All replacements and additions shall also be covered by this Security Instrument. All of the foregoing is referred to in this Security Instrument as the "Property."

BORROWER COVENANTS that Borrower is lawfully seised of the estate hereby conveyed and has the right to grant and convey the Property and that the Property is unencumbered, except for encumbrances of record. Borrower warrants and will defend generally the title to the Property against all claims and demands, subject to any encumbrances of record.

1. Payment of Principal, Interest and Late Charge. Borrower shall pay when due the principal of, and interest on, the debt evidenced by the Note and late charges due under the Note.

2. Monthly Payments of Taxes, Insurance and Other Charges. Borrower shall include in each monthly payment, together with the principal and interest as set forth in the Note and any late charges, an installment of any (a) taxes and special assessments levied or to be levied against the Property, (b) leasehold payments or ground rents on the Property, and (c) premiums for insurance required by paragraph 4.

Each monthly installment for items (a), (b), and (c) shall equal one-twelfth of the annual amounts, as reasonably estimated by Lender, plus an amount sufficient to maintain an additional balance of not more than one-sixth of the estimated amounts. The full annual amount for each item shall be accumulated by Lender within a period ending one month before an item would become delinquent. Lender shall hold the amounts collected in trust to pay items (a), (b), and (c) before they become delinquent.

If at any time the total of the payments held by Lender for items (a), (b), and (c), together with the future monthly payments for such items payable to Lender prior to the due dates of such items, exceeds by more than one-sixth the estimated amount of payments required to pay such items when due, and if payments on the Note are current, then Lender shall either refund the excess over one-sixth of the estimated payments or credit the excess over one-sixth of the estimated payments to subsequent payments by Borrower, at the option of Borrower. If the total of the payments made by Borrower for item (a), (b), or (c) is insufficient to pay the item when due, then Borrower shall pay to Lender any amount necessary to make up the deficiency on or before the date the item becomes due.

As used in this Security Instrument, "Secretary" means the Secretary of Housing and Urban Development or his or her designee. In any year in which the Lender must pay a mortgage insurance premium to the Secretary, each monthly payment shall also include either: (i) an installment of the annual mortgage insurance premium to be paid by Lender to the Secretary, or (ii) a monthly charge instead of a mortgage insurance premium if this Security Instrument is held by the Secretary. Each monthly installment of the mortgage insurance premium shall be in an amount sufficient to accumulate the full annual mortgage insurance premium with Lender one month prior to the date the full annual mortgage insurance premium is due to the Secretary, or if this Security Instrument is held by the Secretary, each monthly charge shall be in an amount equal to one-twelfth of one-half percent of the outstanding principal balance due on the Note.

If Borrower tenders to Lender the full payment of all sums secured by this Security Instrument, Borrower's account shall be credited with the balance remaining for all installments for items (a), (b), and (c) and any mortgage insurance premium installment that Lender has not become obligated to pay to the Secretary, and Lender shall promptly refund any excess funds to Borrower. Immediately prior to a foreclosure sale of the Property or its acquisition by Lender, Borrower's account shall be credited with any balance remaining for all installments for items (a), (b), and (c).

3. Application of Payments. All payments under paragraphs 1 and 2 shall be applied by Lender as follows:

First to the mortgage insurance premium to be paid by Lender to the Secretary or to the monthly charge by the Secretary instead of the monthly mortgage insurance premium;

Second, to any taxes, special assessments, leasehold payments or ground rents, and fire, flood and other hazard insurance premiums, as required;

Third, to interest due under the Note;

Fourth, to amortization of the principal of the Note;

Fifth, to late charges due under the Note.

4. Fire, Flood and Other Hazard Insurance. Borrower shall insure all improvements on the Property, whether now in existence or subsequently erected, against any hazards, casualties, and contingencies, including fire, for which Lender requires insurance. This insurance shall be maintained in the amounts and for the periods that Lender requires. Borrower shall also insure all improvements on the Property, whether now in existence or subsequently erected, against loss by floods to the extent required by the Secretary. All insurance shall be carried with companies approved by Lender. The insurance policies and any renewals shall be held by Lender and shall include loss payable clauses in favor of, and in a form acceptable to, Lender.

In the event of loss, Borrower shall give Lender immediate notice by mail. Lender may make proof of loss if not made promptly by Borrower. Each insurance company concerned is hereby authorized and directed to make payment for such loss directly to Lender, instead of to Borrower and to Lender jointly. All or any part of the insurance proceeds may be applied by Lender, at its option, either (a) to the reduction of the indebtedness under the Note and this Security Instrument, first to any delinquent amounts applied in the order in paragraph 3, and then to prepayment of principal, or (b) to the restoration or repair of the damaged Property. Any application of the proceeds to the principal shall not extend or postpone the due date of the monthly payments which are referred to in paragraph 2, or change the amount of such payments. Any excess insurance proceeds over an amount required to pay all outstanding indebtedness under the Note and this Security Instrument shall be paid to the entity legally entitled thereto.

In the event of foreclosure of this Security Instrument or other transfer of title to the Property that extinguishes the indebtedness, all right, title and interest of Borrower in and to insurance policies in force shall pass to the purchaser.

5. Occupancy, Preservation, Maintenance and Protection of the Property; Borrower's Loan Application; Leaseholds. Borrower shall occupy, establish, and use the Property as Borrower's principal residence within sixty days after the execution of this Security Instrument and shall continue to occupy the Property as Borrower's principal residence for at least one year after the date of occupancy, unless the Secretary determines this requirement will cause undue hardship for Borrower, or unless extenuating circumstances exist which are beyond Borrower's control. Borrower shall notify Lenders of any extenuating circumstances. Borrower shall not commit waste or destroy, damage or substantially change the Property or allow the Property to deteriorate, reasonable wear and tear excepted. Lender may inspect the Property if the Property is vacant or abandoned or the loan is in default. Lender may take reasonable action to protect and preserve such vacant or abandoned Property. Borrower shall also be in default if Borrower, during the loan application process, gave materially false or inaccurate information or statements to Lender (or failed to provide Lender with any material information) in connection with the loan evidenced by the Note, including, but not limited to, representations concerning Borrower's occupancy of the Property as a principal residence. If this Security Instrument is on a leasehold, Borrower shall comply with the provisions of the lease. If Borrower acquires fee title to the Property, the leasehold and fee title shall not be merged unless Lender agrees to the merger in writing.

6. Charges to Borrower and Protection of Lender's Rights in the Property. Borrower shall pay all governmental or municipal charges, fines and impositions that are not included in paragraph 2. Borrower shall pay these obligations on time directly to the entity which is owed the payment. If failure to pay would adversely affect Lender's interest in the Property, upon Lender's request Borrower shall promptly furnish to Lender receipts evidencing these payments.

If Borrower fails to make these payments or the payments required by paragraph 2, or fails to perform any other covenants and agreements contained in this Security Instrument, or there is a legal proceeding that may significantly affect Lender's rights in the Property (such as a proceeding in bankruptcy, for condemnation or to enforce laws or regulations), then Lender may do and pay whatever is necessary to protect the value of the Property and Lender's rights in the Property, including payment of taxes, hazard insurance and other items mentioned in paragraph 2.

Any amounts disbursed by Lender under this paragraph shall become an additional debt of Borrower and be secured by this Security Instrument. These amounts shall bear interest from the date of disbursement, at the Note rate, and at the option of Lender, shall be immediately due and payable.

7. Condemnation. The proceeds of any award or claim for damages, direct or consequential, in connection with any condemnation or other taking of any part of the Property, or for conveyance in place of condemnation, are hereby assigned and shall be paid to Lender to the extent of the full amount of the indebtedness that remains unpaid under the Note and this Security Instrument. Lender shall apply such proceeds to the reduction of the indebtedness under the Note and this Security Instrument, first to any delinquent amounts applied in the order provided in paragraph 3, and then to prepayment of principal. Any application of the proceeds to the principal shall not extend or postpone the due date of the monthly payments, which are referred to in paragraph 2, or change the amount of such payments. Any excess proceeds over an amount required to pay all outstanding indebtedness under the Note and this Security Instrument shall be paid to the entity legally entitled thereto.

8. Fees. Lender may collect fees and charges authorized by the Secretary.

9. Grounds for Acceleration of Debt.

(a) Default. Lender may, except as limited by regulations issued by the Secretary in the case of payment defaults, require immediate payment in full of all sums secured by this Security Instrument if:

(i) Borrower defaults by failing to pay in full any monthly payment required by this Security Instrument prior to or on the due date of the next monthly payment, or

(ii) Borrower defaults by failing, for a period of thirty days, to perform any other obligations contained in this Security Instrument.

(b) Sale Without Credit Approval. Lender shall, if permitted by applicable law and with the prior approval of the Secretary, require immediate payment in full of all sums secured by this Security Instrument if:

(i) All or part of the Property, or a beneficial interest in a trust owning all or part of the Property, is sold or otherwise transferred (other than by devise or descent) by the Borrower, and

(ii) The Property is not occupied by the purchaser or grantee as his or her principal residence, or the purchaser or grantee does so occupy the Property but his or her credit has not been approved in accordance with the requirements of the Secretary.

(c) No Waiver. If circumstances occur that would permit Lender to require immediate payment in full, but Lender does not require such payments, Lender does not waive its rights with respect to subsequent events.

(d) Regulations of HUD Secretary. In many circumstances regulations issued by the Secretary will limit Lender's rights in the case of payment defaults to require immediate payment in full and foreclose if not paid. This Security Instrument does not authorize acceleration or foreclosure if not permitted by regulations of the Secretary.

(e) Mortgage Not Insured. Borrower agrees that should this Security Instrument and the Note secured thereby not be eligible for insurance under the National Housing Act within 60 days from the date hereof, Lender may, at its option and notwithstanding anything in paragraph 9, require immediate payment in full of all sums secured by this Security Instrument. A written statement of any authorized agent of the Secretary dated subsequent to 60 days from the date hereof, declining to insure this Security Instrument and the Note secured thereby, shall be deemed conclusive proof of such ineligibility. Notwithstanding the foregoing, this option may not be exercised by Lender when the unavailability of insurance is solely due to Lender's failure to remit a mortgage insurance premium to the Secretary.

10. **Reinstatement.** Borrower has a right to be reinstated if Lender has required immediate payment in full because of Borrower's failure to pay an amount due under the Note or this Security Instrument. This right applies even after foreclosure proceedings are instituted. To reinstate the Security Instrument, Borrower shall tender in a lump sum all amounts required to bring Borrower's account current including, to the extent they are obligations of Borrower under this Security Instrument, foreclosure costs and reasonable and customary attorneys' fees and expenses properly associated with the foreclosure proceeding. Upon reinstatement by Borrower, this Security instrument and the obligations that it secures shall remain in effect as if Lender had not required immediate payment in full. However, Lender is not required to permit reinstatement if: (i) Lender has accepted reinstatement after the commencement of foreclosure proceedings within two years immediately preceding the commencement of a current foreclosure proceeding, (ii) reinstatement will preclude foreclosure on different grounds in the future, or (iii) reinstatement will adversely affect the priority of the lien created by this Security Instrument.

11. **Borrower Not Released; Forbearance By Lender Not a Waiver.** Extension of the time of payment or modification of amortization of the sums secured by this Security Instrument granted by Lender to any successor in interest of Borrower shall not operate to release the liability of the original Borrower or Borrower's successor in interest. Lender shall not be required to commence proceedings against any successor in interest or refuse to extend time for payment or otherwise modify amortization of the sums secured by this Security Instrument by reason of any demand made by the original Borrower or Borrower's successors in interest. Any forbearance by Lender in exercising any right or remedy shall not be a waiver of or preclude the exercise of any right or remedy.

12. **Successors and Assigns Bound; Joint and Several Liability; Co-signers.** The covenants and agreements of this Security Instrument shall bind and benefit the successors and assigns of Lender and Borrower, subject to the provisions of paragraph 9.b. Borrower's covenants and agreements shall be joint and several. Any Borrower who co-signs this Security Instrument but does not execute the Note: (a) is co-signing this Security Instrument only to mortgage, grant and convey that Borrower's interest in the Property under the terms of this Security

Instrument; (b) is not personally obligated to pay the sums secured by this Security Instrument; and (c) agrees that Lender and any other Borrower may agree to extend, modify, forbear or make any accommodations with regard to the terms of this Security Instrument or the Note without that Borrower's consent.

13. Notices. Any notice to Borrower provided for in this Security Instrument shall be given by delivering it or by mailing it by first class mail unless applicable law requires use of another method. The notice shall be directed to the Property Address or any other address Borrower designates by notice to Lender. Any notice to Lender shall be given by first class mail to Lender's address stated herein or any address Lender designates by notice to Borrower. Any notice provided for in this Security Instrument shall be deemed to have been given to Borrower or Lender when given as provided in this paragraph.

14. Governing Law; Severability. This Security Instrument shall be governed by federal law and the law of the jurisdiction in which the Property is located. In the event that any provision or clause of this Security Instrument or the Note conflicts with applicable law, such conflict shall not affect other provisions of this Security Instrument or the Note which can be given effect without the conflicting provision. To this end the provisions of this Security Instrument and the Note are declared to be severable.

15. Borrower's Copy. Borrower shall be given one conformed copy of this Security Instrument.

16. Assignment of Rents. Borrower unconditionally assigns and transfers to Lender all the rents and revenues of the Property. Borrower authorizes Lender or Lender's agents to collect the rents and revenues and hereby directs each tenant of the Property to pay the rents to Lender or Lender's agents. However, prior to Lender's notice to Borrower of Borrower's breach of any covenant or agreement in the Security Instrument, Borrower shall collect and receive all rents and revenues of the Property as trustee for the benefit of Lender and Borrower. This assignment of rents constitutes an absolute assignment and not an assignment for additional security only.

If Lender gives notice of breach to Borrower: (a) all rents received by Borrower shall be held by Borrower as trustee for benefit of Lender only, to be applied to the sums secured by the Security Instrument; (b) Lender shall be entitled to collect and receive all of the rents of the Property; and (c) each tenant of the Property shall pay all rents due and unpaid to Lender or Lender's agent on Lender's written demand to the tenant.

Borrower has not executed any prior assignment of the rents and has not and will not perform any act that would prevent Lender from exercising its rights under this paragraph 16.

Lender shall not be required to enter upon, take control of or maintain the Property before or after giving notice of breach to Borrower. However, Lender or a judicially appointed receiver may do so at any time there is a breach. Any application of rents shall not cure or waive any default or invalidate any other right or remedy of Lender. This assignment of rents of the Property shall terminate when the debt secured by the Security Instrument is paid in full.

NON–UNIFORM COVENANTS. Borrower and Lender further covenant and agree as follows:

17. Foreclosure Procedure. If Lender requires immediate payment in full under paragraph 9, Lender may invoke the power of sale and any other remedies permitted by applicable law. Lender shall be entitled to collect all expenses incurred in pursuing the remedies provided in this paragraph 17, including, but not limited to, reasonable attorneys' fees and costs of title evidence.

If Lender invokes the power of sale, Lender or Trustee shall mail copies of a notice of sale in the manner prescribed by applicable law to Borrower and to the other persons prescribed by applicable law. Trustee shall give notice of sale by public advertisement for the time and in the manner prescribed by applicable law. Trustee, without demand on Borrower, shall sell the Property at public auction to the highest bidder for cash at the time and place and under the terms designated in the notice of sale in one or more parcels and in any order Trustee determines. Trustee may postpone sale of all or any parcel of the Property to any later time on the same date by public announcement at the time and place of any previously scheduled sale. Lender or its designee may purchase the Property at any sale.

Trustee shall deliver to the purchaser Trustee's deed conveying the Property without any covenant or warranty, expressed or implied. The recitals in the Trustee's deed shall be prima facie evidence of the truth of the statements made therein. Trustee shall apply the proceeds of the sale in the following order: (a) to all expenses of the sale, including, but not limited to, reasonable Trustee's and attorneys' fees; (b) to all sums secured by this Security Instrument; and (c) any excess to the person or persons legally entitled to it.

18. Release. Upon payment of all sums secured by this Security Instrument, Lender shall release this Security Instrument without charge to Borrower. Borrower shall pay any recordation costs.

19. Substitute Trustee. Lender, at its option, may from time to time remove Trustee and appoint a successor trustee to any Trustee appointed hereunder by an instrument recorded in the county in which this Security Instrument is recorded. Without conveyance of the Property, the successor trustee shall succeed to all the title, power and duties conferred upon Trustee herein and by applicable law.

20. Lease of the Property. Trustee hereby leases the Property to Borrower until this Security Instrument is either satisfied and released or until there is a default under the provisions of this Security Instrument. The Property is leased upon the following terms and conditions: Borrower, and every person claiming an interest in or possessing the Property or any part thereof, shall pay rent during the term of the lease in the amount of one cent per month, payable on demand, and without notice or demand shall and will surrender peaceable possession of the Property to Trustee upon default or to the purchaser of the Property at the foreclosure sale.

21. Riders to this Security Instrument. If one or more riders are executed by Borrower and recorded together with this Security Instrument, the covenants of each such rider shall be incorporated into and shall amend and supplement the covenants and agreements of this Security Instrument as if the rider(s) were a part of this Security Instrument. [Check applicable box(es)]

☐ Condominium Rider ☐ Graduated Payment Rider ☐ Other [Specify]
☐ Planned Unit Development Rider ☐ Growing Equity Rider

BY SIGNING BELOW, Borrower accepts and agrees to the terms contained in this Security Instrument and in any rider(s) executed by Borrower and recorded with it.

Witnesses:

§ 14.14 FHA Adjustable Rate Note

In this section we reproduce the Multistate "Adjustable Rate Note" which has been promulgated by the Federal Housing Administration for use under the FHA adjustable rate program. FHA ARM's were authorized by Section 443 of the Housing and Urban–Rural Recovery Act of 1983, Public Law No. 98–181. See the FHA regulations codified in 42 C.F.R. 203.49 and FHA Mortgagee Letter 84–16, July 18, 1984. For a more extended discussion of the FHA ARM program, see § 11.4, supra. An illustrative version of the standard FHA Mortgage or Deed of Trust is reproduced in § 14.13, supra.

The FHA regulations establish the rather rigid parameters of its ARM program. A one-year adjustment frequency is specified, and the pertinent index is the average weekly yield on U.S. Treasury securities adjusted to a constant maturity of one year. The loan rate may not change from its initial value by more than one percentage point in any year; nor may it change by more than 5 percentage points, either up or down, over the life of the loan. The latter limitation is termed, in the Rider, the "5% Cap."

Under the FHA's approach, monthly payments must be adjusted to account for changes in the loan rate. Neither increases in the loan maturity nor negative amortization are allowed as means of paying interest rate increases. This may be compared with the FNMA/FHLMC Adjustable Rate Note, supra § 14.7, under which negative amortization is permitted so long as the outstanding balance does not exceed 125% of its original level.

ADJUSTABLE RATE NOTE

_____, 19__, _____, _____, _____.
                [City]   [State]   [Property Address]

1. Parties

"Borrower" means each person signing at the time of this Note, and the person's successors and assigns. "Lender" means _____ and its successors and assigns.

2. Borrower's Promise to Pay; Interest

In return for a loan received from Lender, Borrower promises to pay the principal sum of DOLLARS AND 00 CENTS Dollars (U.S. $_____), plus interest, to the order of Lender. Interest will be charged on unpaid principal, from the date of disbursement of the loan proceeds by Lender, at the rate of _____ percent (_____%) per year. The interest rate may change in accordance with Paragraph 5(C) of this Note.

3. Promise to Pay Secured

Borrower's promise to pay is secured by a mortgage, deed of trust or similar security instrument that is dated the same date as this Note and called the "Security Instrument." That Security Instrument protects the Lender from losses which might result if Borrower defaults under this Note.

4. Manner of Payment

(A) Time

Borrower shall make a payment of principal and interest to Lender on the first day of each month beginning on _____. Any principal and interest remaining on the first day of _____ will be due on that date, which is called the "Maturity Date."

(B) Place

Payment shall be made at, _____ or at such other place as Lender may designate in writing by notice to Borrower.

(C) Amount

Initially, each monthly payment of principal and interest will be in the amount of $_____. This amount will be part of a larger monthly payment required by the Security Instrument that shall be applied to principal, interest and other items in the order described in the Security Instrument. This amount may change in accordance with Paragraph 5(E) of this Note.

5. Interest Rate and Monthly Payment Changes

(A) Change Date

The interest rate may change on the first day of, _____, and on that day of each succeeding year. "Change Date" means each date on which the interest rate could change.

(B) The Index

Beginning with the first Change Date, the interest rate will be based on an Index. "Index" means the weekly average yield on United States Treasury Securities adjusted to a constant maturity of one year, as made available by the Federal Reserve Board. "Current Index" means the most recent Index figure available 30 days before the Change Date. If the Index (as defined above) is no longer available, Lender will use as a new Index any index prescribed by the Secretary (as defined in paragraph 7(B)), Lender will give Borrower notice of the new Index.

(C) Calculation of Interest Rate Changes

Before each Change Date, Lender will calculate a new interest rate by adding a margin of percentage point(s) (_____%) to the Current Index and rounding the sum to the nearest one-eighth of one percentage point (0.125%). Subject to the limits stated in paragraph 5(D) of this Note, this rounded amount will be the new interest rate until the next Change Date.

(D) Limits on Interest Rate Changes

The interest rate will never increase or decrease by more than one percentage point (1.0%) on any single Change Date. The interest rate will never be more than five percentage points (5.0%) higher or lower than the initial interest rate stated in paragraph 2 of this Note.

(E) Calculation of Payment Change

If the interest rate changes on a Change Date, Lender will calculate the amount of monthly payment of principal and interest which would be necessary to repay the unpaid principal balance in full at the Maturity Date at the new interest rate through substantially equal payments. In making such calculation, Lender will use the unpaid principal balance which would be owed on the Change Date if there had been no default in payment on the Note, reduced by the amount of any prepayments to principal. The result of this calculation will be the amount of the new monthly payment of principal and interest.

(F) Notice of Changes

Lender will give notice to Borrower of any change in the interest rate and monthly payment amount. The notice must be given at least 25 days before the new monthly payment amount is due, and must set forth (i) the date of the notice, (ii) the Change Date, (iii) the old interest rate, (iv) the new interest rate, (v) the new monthly payment amount, (vi) the Current Index and the date it was published, (vii) the method of calculating the change in monthly payment amount, and (viii) any other information which may be required by law from time to time.

(G) Effective Date of Changes

A new interest rate calculated in accordance with paragraphs 5(C) and 5(D) of this Note will become effective on the Change Date. Borrower shall make a payment in the new monthly amount beginning on the first payment date which occurs at least 25 days after Lender has given Borrower the notice of changes required by paragraph 5(F) of this Note. Borrower shall have no obligation to pay any increase in the monthly payment amount calculated in accordance with paragraph 5(E) of this Note for any payment date occurring less than 25 days after Lender has given the required notice. If the monthly payment amount calculated in accordance with paragraph 5(E) of this Note decreased, but Lender failed to give timely notice of the decrease and Borrower made any monthly payment amounts exceeding the payment amount which should have been stated in a timely notice, then Borrower has the option to either (i) demand the return to Borrower of any excess payment, with interest thereon at the Note rate (a rate equal to the interest rate which should have been stated in a timely notice), or (ii) request that any excess payment, with interest thereon at the Note rate, be applied as payment of principal. Lender's obligation to return any excess payment with interest on demand is not assignable even if this Note is otherwise assigned before the demand for return is made.

6. Borrower's Right to Prepay

Borrower has the right to pay the debt evidenced by this Note, in whole or in part, without charge or penalty, on the first day of any month.

7. Borrower's Failure to Pay

(A) Late Charge for Overdue Payments

If Lender has not received the full monthly payment required by the Security Instrument, as described in Paragraph 4(C) of this Note, by the end of fifteen calendar days after the payment is due, Lender may collect a late charge in the amount of _____ percent (_____%) of the overdue amount of each payment.

(B) Default

If Borrower defaults by failing to pay in full any monthly payment, then Lender may, except as limited by regulations of the Secretary in the case of payment defaults, require immediate payment in full of the principal balance remaining due and all accrued interest. Lender may choose not to exercise this option without waiving its rights in the event of any subsequent default. This Note does not authorize acceleration when not permitted by HUD regulations. As used in this Note, "Secretary" means the Secretary of Housing and Urban Development or his or her designee.

(C) Payment of Costs and Expenses

If Lender has required immediate payment in full, as described above, Lender may require Borrower to pay costs and expenses including reasonable and customary attorneys' fees for enforcing this Note. Such fees and costs shall bear interest from the date of disbursement at the same rate as the principal of this Note.

8. Waivers

Borrower and any other person who has obligations under this Note waive the rights of presentment and notice of dishonor. "Presentment" means the right to require Lender to demand payment of amounts due. "Notice of dishonor" means the right to require Lender to give notice to other persons that amounts due have not been paid.

9. Giving of Notices

Unless applicable law requires a different method, any notice that must be given to Borrower under this Note will be given by delivering it or by mailing it by first class mail to Borrower at the property address above or at a different address if Borrower has given Lender a notice of Borrower's different address.

Any notice that must be given to Lender under this Note will be given by first class mail to Lender at the address stated in Paragraph 4(B) or at a different address if Borrower is given a notice of that different address.

10. Obligations of Persons Under This Note

If more than one person signs this Note, each person is fully and personally obligated to keep all of the promises made in this Note, including the promise to pay the full amount owed. Any person who is a guarantor, surety or endorser of this Note is also obligated to do these things. Any person who takes over these obligations, including the obligations of a guarantor, surety or endorser of this Note, is also obligated to keep all of the promises made in this Note. Lender may enforce its rights under this Note against each person individually or against all signatories together. Any one person signing this Note may be required to pay all of the amounts owed under this Note.

BY SIGNING BELOW, Borrower accepts and agrees to the terms and covenants contained in this Note.

Witnesses:

§ 14.15 Department of Veterans Affairs Note and Deed of Trust—Fixed Rate Home Loan—Missouri

The Department of Veterans Affairs (DVA) (formerly the Veterans Administration), unlike the FHA, does not require that the loans it guarantees be on its forms. Indeed, many VA loan transactions utilize FNMA/FHLMC forms with a DVA rider.

Note that DVA loans are no longer automatically assumable, as the bold, large print on both the Note and Deed of Trust so attest. An assumption will be permitted, however, if the transferee is creditworthy. Moreover, when an assumption is approved, the mortgagor will be relieved of all personal liability on the mortgage obligation. See 38 U.S.C.A. § 3714(a)(1).

DEED OF TRUST NOTE

FOR VALUE RECEIVED, the undersigned, jointly and severally, promise(s) to pay to the order of _____, Payee, the sum of _____ ($), with interest from date at the rate of _____ per centum (_____%) per annum on the unpaid balance until paid. The said principal and interest shall be payable at the office of the Payee in _____, or at such other place as the holder may designate in writing delivered or mailed to the debtor, in monthly installments of _____ ($), commencing on the first day of _____, 20__, and continuing on the first day of each month thereafter, until this note is fully paid, except that the final payment of principal and interest, if not sooner paid, shall be due and payable on the first day of _____, 20__.

Privilege is reserved to prepay at any time, without premium or fee, the entire indebtedness or any part thereof not less than the amount of one installment, or one hundred dollars ($100.00), whichever is less. Prepayment in full shall be credited on the date received. Partial prepayment, other than on an installment due date, need not be credited until the next following installment due date or thirty days after such prepayment, which ever is earlier.

If any deficiency in the payment of any installment under this note is not made good prior to the due date of the next such installment, the holder hereof may exercise the option of treating the remainder of the debt as due and collectible with interest to date of acceleration. Failure to exercise this option shall not constitute a waiver of the right to exercise it in the event of any subsequent default.

This note is secured by Deed of Trust of even date executed by the undersigned on certain property described therein and represents money actually used for the acquisition of said property or the improvements thereon.

Presentment, protest and notice are hereby waived. The undersigned also waive the benefit of any homestead or exemption right as against the debt evidenced hereby.

THIS LOAN IS NOT ASSUMABLE WITHOUT THE APPROVAL OF THE DEPARTMENT OF VETERANS AFFAIRS OR ITS AUTHORIZED AGENT.

THIS IS TO CERTIFY that this is the note described in and secured by Deed of Trust of even date herewith and in the same principal amount as herein stated to _____, Trustee(s), and secured by real estate in the County of _____, State of Missouri.

Dated this _____ day of _____.

Notary Public.

DEED OF TRUST

THIS DEED OF TRUST, made and entered into this _____ day of _____ nineteen hundred and _____ by and between _____ of the County of _____ and State of Missouri, party of the first part, hereinafter referred to as Borrower, and _____ party of the second part, hereinafter referred to as Trustee, and _____ party of the third part, hereinafter called Lender.

WITNESSETH, that the Borrower in consideration of the debt and trust hereinafter described and created, and the sum of One Dollar ($1), to him in hand paid by the Trustee, the receipt of which is hereby acknowledged, does by these presents grant, bargain and sell, convey and confirm, unto the Trustee, forever, all of the following-described property in the County of _____ and State of Missouri, to wit: together with all improvements, rights, privileges, easements an appurtenances thereto belonging, or in anywise appertaining, and the rents, issues and profits thereof, and all fixtures now or hereafter attached to or used in connection with the premises herein described, and in addition thereto the following-described household appliances, which are, and shall be deemed to be fixtures and a part of the realty, and are a portion of the security for the indebtedness herein mentioned:

TO HAVE AND TO HOLD the above-described property unto the said Trustee, forever, and possession of said premises is now delivered unto the Trustee, in trust, however for the following purposes:

WHEREAS, the Borrower on the _____ day of _____, 20__, borrowed from lender the sum of DOLLARS AND 00 CENTS Dollars ($), for which sum the Borrower has executed and delivered to the Lender his promissory note of even date, bearing interest at the rate of _____ per centum (%) per annum on the unpaid balance until paid, and payable as follows: In monthly installments of DOLLARS AND 00 CENTS Dollars ($), commencing on the first day of _____, 20__, and continuing on the first day of each month thereafter until the principal and interest are fully paid, except that, if not sooner paid, the final payment of principal and interest shall be due and payable on the first day of _____, 20__.

THIS LOAN IS NOT ASSUMABLE WITHOUT THE APPROVAL OF THE DEPARTMENT OF VETERANS AFFAIRS OR ITS AUTHORIZED AGENT.

AND WHEREAS THE BORROWER covenants with the Lender as follows:

1. The Borrower will pay the indebtedness as hereinbefore provided. Privilege is reserved to prepay at any time, without premium or fee, the entire indebtedness or any part thereof not less than the amount of one installment, or one hundred dollars ($100.00), whichever is less. Prepayment in full shall be credited on the date received. Partial prepayment, other than on an installment due date, need not be credited until the next following installment due date or thirty days after such prepayment, whichever is earlier.

2. In order more fully to protect the security of this Deed of Trust, the Borrower will pay to the Lender, as trustee, (under the terms of this trust as hereinafter stated) together with, and in addition to, the monthly payments under the terms of the note secured hereby, on the first day of each month until the said note is fully paid:

(a) A sum equal to the ground rents, if any, next due, plus the premiums that will next become due and payable on policies of fire and other hazard insurance covering the premises covered by this Deed of Trust plus taxes and assessments next due on the premises covered hereby (all estimated by the Lender, and of which the Borrower is notified) less all sums already paid therefor divided by the number of months to elapse before one month prior to the date when such ground rents, premiums, taxes and assessments will become delinquent, such sums to be held by the Lender in trust to pay said ground rents, premiums, taxes and special assessments.

(b) The aggregate of the amount payable pursuant to subparagraph (a) and those payable on the note secured hereby, shall be paid in a single payment each month, to be applied to the following items in the order stated:

(I) ground rents, taxes, special assessments, fire, and other hazard insurance premiums;

(II) interest on the indebtedness secured hereby; and

(III) amortization of the principal of said indebtedness.

Any deficiency in the amount of any such aggregate monthly payment shall, unless made good by the Borrower prior to the due date of the next such payment, constitute an event of default under this Deed of Trust. At Lender's option, Borrower will pay a "late charge" not exceeding four per cent (4%) of any installment when paid more than fifteen (15) days after the due date thereof to cover the extra expense involved in handling delinquent payments, but such "late charge" shall not be payable out of the proceeds of any sale made to satisfy the indebtedness secured hereby, unless such proceeds are sufficient to discharge the entire indebtedness and all proper costs and expenses secured hereby.

3. If the total of the payments made by the Borrower under (a) of paragraph 2 preceding shall exceed the amount of payment actually made by the lender, as trustee, for ground rents, taxes or assessments, or insurance premiums, as the case may be, such shall be credited on subsequent payments to be made by the Borrower for such items or, at the Lender's option, as trustee, shall be refunded to the Borrower. If, however, such monthly payments shall not be sufficient to pay such items when the same shall become due and payable, then the Borrower shall pay to the Lender, also trustee, any amount necessary to make up the deficiency, which notice may be given by mail. If at any time the Borrower shall tender to the Lender, in accordance with the provisions of the note secured hereby, full payment of the entire indebtedness in accordance with the terms thereof, the said Lender, as trustee, shall, in computing the amount of such indebtedness, credit to the account of the Borrower any credit balance remaining under the provisions of (a) of paragraph 2 hereof. If there shall be a default under any of the provisions of this Deed of Trust resulting in a public sale of the premises covered hereby, or if the Lender acquires the property otherwise after default, the Lender, as trustee, shall apply, at the time of the commencement of such proceedings, or at the time the property is otherwise acquired, the amount then remaining to credit of Borrower under (a) of paragraph 2 preceding as a credit on the interest accrued and unpaid and the balance to the principal then remaining unpaid on said note.

4. The lien of this instrument shall remain in full force and effect during any postponement or extensions of the time of payment of the indebtedness or any part thereof secured hereby.

5. Borrower will pay all ground rents, taxes, assessments, water rents, and other governmental or municipal charges, fines, or impositions except when payment for all such items has theretofore been made under (a) of paragraph 2 hereof, and he will promptly deliver the official receipts therefor to the Lender.

6. Borrower has a good title in fee simple (or such other estate as is stated herein) to said real estate free and clear of all encumbrances except as herein otherwise recited and will warrant and defend the same against all lawful claims and mechanics' or other liens of all persons whomsoever, has the right to execute this instrument, will execute such further assurance as may be required by the Lender, and will bear the expense of recording this instrument, releasing all former liens, and cost of title evidence and the continuation thereof when such is required by the Lender.

7. Borrower hereby assigns to the Lender any and all rents on the premises herein described during default, authorizes said Lender, by its agent, to take possession of said premises at any time there is a default in the payment of the debt hereby secured or in the performance of any obligation herein contained, and rent the same for the account of the Borrower, deduct from such rents all costs of collection and administration, and to apply the remainder of the same on the debt hereby secured.

8. Lender may perform any defaulted covenant or agreement of Borrower to such extent as Lender shall determine, and any moneys advanced by Lender for such purposes shall bear interest at the rate provided for in the principal indebtedness, shall thereupon become a part of the indebtedness secured by this instru-

ment, ratably and on a parity with all other indebtedness secured hereby, and shall be payable thirty (30) days after demand.

9. The Borrower will not remove or permit to be removed any buildings or fences from said premises without the written consent of the Lender, he will neither commit nor permit waste or trespass on or to said premises; he will maintain the buildings and improvements thereon in good repair; and will promptly satisfy and cause to be released any mechanics' liens that may hereafter be asserted against said premises.

10. Upon the request of the Lender, Borrower shall execute and deliver a supplemental note or notes for the sum or sums advanced by the Lender for the alteration, modernization, improvement, maintenance, or repair of said premises, for taxes or assessments against the same and for any other purpose authorized hereunder. Said note or notes shall be secured hereby on a parity with and as fully as if the advance evidenced thereby were included in the note first described above. Said supplemental note or notes shall bear interest at the rate provided for in the principal indebtedness and shall be payable in approximately equal monthly payments for such period as may be agreed upon by the creditor and debtor. Failing to agree on the maturity, the whole of the sum or sums so advanced shall be due and payable thirty (30) days after demand by the creditor. In no event shall the maturity extend beyond the maturity of the note first described above.

11. In the event the property conveyed by this instrument is sold under foreclosure and the proceeds are insufficient to pay the total indebtedness evidenced and secured by this instrument, the Borrower herein binds himself personally, and the Lender or its assigns will be entitled to a deficiency judgment.

12. Borrower will continuously maintain hazard insurance, of such type or types and amounts as the Lender may from time to time require, on the improvements now or hereafter on said premises, and except when payment for all such premiums has theretofore been made under (a) of paragraph 2 hereof, will pay promptly when due any premiums therefor. All insurance shall be carried in companies approved by the Lender and the policies and renewals thereof shall be held by it and have attached thereto loss payable clauses in favor of and in form acceptable to the Lender. In event of loss the Borrower will give immediate notice by mail to the Lender, who may make proof of loss if not made promptly by him, and each insurance company concerned is hereby authorized and directed to make payment for such loss directly to the Lender instead of to the Borrower and the Lender jointly, and the insurance proceeds, for any part thereof, may be applied by the Lender at its option either to the reduction of the indebtedness hereby secured or to the restoration or repair of the property damaged. In event of foreclosure of this Deed of Trust, or other transfer of title to the said premises in extinguishment of the indebtedness secured hereby, all right, title and interest of the Borrower in and to any insurance policies then in force shall pass to the purchaser or grantee.

13. If the premises, or any part thereof, be condemned under any power of eminent domain or acquired for a public use, the damages, proceeds, and the consideration for such acquisition, to the extent of the full amount of indebtedness upon this Deed of Trust, and the note secured hereby remaining unpaid, are hereby assigned by the party of the first part to the Lender and shall be paid forthwith to the Lender to be applied by it on account of the indebtedness secured hereby, whether or not due.

14. This loan is immediately due and payable upon transfer of the property securing such loan to any transferee, unless the acceptability of the assumption of the loan is established pursuant to section 1817A of chapter 37, title 38, United States Code.*

* Now 38 U.S.C.A. § 3714(a)(1).

15. *Funding Fee* A fee equal to one-half of 1 percent of the balance of this loan as of the date of transfer of the property shall be payable at the time of transfer to the loan holder or its authorized agent, as trustee for the Secretary of Veterans Affairs. If the assumer fails to pay this fee at the time of transfer, the fee shall constitute an additional debt to that already secured by this instrument, shall bear interest at the rate herein provided, and, at the option of the payee of the indebtedness hereby secured or any transferee thereof, shall be immediately due and payable. This fee is automatically waived if the assumer is exempt under the provisions of 38 U.S.C. 1829(b).

16. *Processing Charge* Upon application for approval to allow assumption of this loan, a processing fee may be charged by the loan holder or its authorized agent for determining the credit worthiness of the assumer and subsequently revising the holder's ownership records when an approved transfer is completed. The amount of this charge shall not exceed the maximum established by the Veterans' Administration for a loan to which sections 1817A of chapter 37, title 38, United States Code applies.*

17. *Indemnity Liability* If this obligation is assumed, then the assumer hereby agrees to assume all of the obligations of the Veteran under the terms of the instruments creating and securing the loan, including the obligation of the Veteran to indemnify the Veterans Administration to the extent of any claim payment arising from the guaranty or insurance of the indebtedness created by this instrument.

NOW, THEREFORE, if the Borrower shall well and truly pay, or cause to be paid unto the Lender the indebtedness secured hereby according to his obligation, and shall well and truly keep and perform all and singular the covenants and agreements hereinbefore set forth, then these presents as well as the lease hereinafter set forth shall cease and be void, and the property hereinbefore conveyed shall be released, at the cost of the Borrower, but if default be made in the payment of said indebtedness, or in the fulfillment of the several covenants and agreements hereinbefore set forth, or any of them, then the whole of said indebtedness secured hereby and interest thereon to date of foreclosure shall become due and payable and this deed shall remain in force; and said Trustee or his successor as hereinafter provided for, at the request of the legal holder of the aforesaid note, may proceed to sell the property hereinbefore conveyed, or any part thereof, at public vendue at the front door of the Court House in the City of _____ in the County of _____, and State of Missouri, to the highest bidder for cash, first giving twenty (20) days notice of the time, terms and place of sale and of the property to be sold, pursuant to and in conformity with state law and upon such sale shall execute a deed conveying the property so sold to the purchaser thereof. Said Lender shall have power successively to remove the above-mentioned Trustee or any successor Trustee, and to appoint in writing (acknowledged and recorded), a successor to such Trustee. Said Trustee shall receive the proceeds of such sale, out of which he shall pay, FIRST, the cost and expense of executing this Trust, including lawful compensation to the Trustee for his services as provided by statute, NEXT, he shall repay any money advanced for taxes, insurance, or other advances or charges with interest thereon, as above provided, NEXT, the amount unpaid on said note together with the interest accrued thereon and all overdue payments and charges provided for herein, NEXT, the Veterans Administration any sums paid by it on account of the guaranty or insurance of the indebtedness secured hereby, and the remainder, if any, shall be paid to said Borrower; PROVIDED, HOWEVER, that nothing in this instrument shall be so construed as to prevent the legal holder of said note taking every legal step and means to enforce payment of said indebtedness by court proceedings.

The Trustee hereby lets said premises to the Borrower until this instrument be satisfied and released or until default be made under the provisions hereof, upon the following terms: The Borrower, and every and all persons claiming or possessing such premises or any part thereof by, through or under him, shall pay rent therefor during said term at one cent per month, payable on demand, and shall and will surrender peaceable possession of said premises, and every part thereof to said Trustee upon default or to the purchaser thereof at foreclosure sale, without notice or demand therefor.

And the said Trustee covenants faithfully to perform and fulfill the trustees created, being liable, however, only for willful negligence or misconduct.

If the indebtedness secured hereby be guaranteed or insured under Title 38, United States Code, such Title and Regulations issued thereunder and in effect on the date hereof shall govern the rights, duties and liabilities of the parties hereto, and any provisions of this or other instruments executed in connection with said indebtedness which are inconsistent with said Title or Regulations are hereby amended to conform thereto.

The covenants herein contained shall bind, and the benefits and advantages shall inure to, the respective heirs, executors, administrators, successors or assigns of the parties hereto. Whenever used, the singular number shall include the plural, the plural the singular, the use of any gender shall be applicable to all genders and the term "Lender" shall include any payee of the indebtedness hereby secured or any transfer thereof whether by operation of law or otherwise.

IN WITNESS WHEREOF, the Borrower has hereunto act _____ hand(s) the day and year above written.

§ 14.16 FNMA/FHLMC Note, Deed of Trust and Rider—Fixed Rate Multifamily Loan—Texas

The three forms in this section comprise the essential documents for a permanent financing transaction involving a duplex, triplex, apartment house or larger multifamily project. Note that while the Note and non-uniform covenants of the Deed of Trust were designed for the purpose of complying with Texas mortgage law, the Uniform Covenants in the latter document are intended for national use and are included in all FNMA/FHLMC Multifamily mortgage or deed of trust forms. So too is the Rider to Multifamily Security Instrument. Note that the last paragraph of the Note, the fourth paragraph of the non-uniform part of the Deed of Trust and Paragraph 33 of the Uniform Covenants are intended to permit the use of these documents for construction, as well as permanent, financing.

The Note seems to be a "garden variety" multifamily debt instrument. Note that while FNMA/FHLMC single family note forms permit prepayment without charge, this is not the case in the multifamily setting. While the Note itself contains a relatively unsophisticated prepayment provision, this problem is alleviated by the prepayment language of the Rider which we consider later in this section.

The Deed of Trust Uniform Covenants contain some especially important provisions. Many are similar to the Single Family Uniform Covenants (See § 14.3 supra), but there are significant variations that reflect the fact that multifamily financing transactions deal with income producing real estate.

Paragraph 4 of the Uniform Covenants contains a covenant against further encumbrances. While the lender is probably protected in this regard by Paragraph 19, as well as Paragraph F of the Rider (due-on-sale provisions), the language of Paragraph 4 makes it exceedingly clear that both consensual and non-consensual liens may not encumber the real estate without the lender's written consent.

Paragraph 6 goes into greater detail than does its Uniform Covenants Single Family counterpart (see § 14.3 supra) in protecting the lender when the security interest is in a ground lease rather than a fee simple absolute. See also § 15.15, infra.

Paragraph 10 gives the lender broad access to the books and records of the borrower. Such a provision is crucial for a lender where the security is income-producing real estate. Thus it is understandable that a similar provision does not exist in the Single Family Uniform Covenants.

Paragraph 12 gives a broad authorization to the lender to enter into a wide variety of modification and extension agreements with the current owner of the real estate. Under the language of this provision, such agreements will not affect the liability of the original borrower and his or her subsequent grantees or the lender's priority vis á vis intervening lienors. It sweeps much more broadly than does its counterpart in the Single Family Uniform Covenants. See § 14.3, Paragraph 11, supra. For a consideration of the extent to which such mortgage language is effective, see § 5.19 supra.

Under Paragraph 16 the lender must consent to any execution, modification or termination of any lease for a term of three years or more. Since most apartment leases are for shorter periods, this provision probably does not represent a significant problem for the landlord-borrower.

Paragraph 24 purports to give the lender the sole discretion in determining the order in which any or all of the mortgaged real estate is foreclosed. Thus, the borrower, his or her successors and subsequent lienors are deemed to waive their rights under the equitable doctrine of marshalling. See §§ 10.9–10.15, supra.

Paragraph 26 purports to create an "absolute assignment" of rents. Indeed, it states that borrower and lender intend the assignment "constitutes an absolute assignment and not an assignment for additional security only." Of course, no matter how artfully drafted, an assignment *in fact* is not a "sale" of the rents to the lender and is almost always intended to create a security interest only. In any event, the main purpose is to enhance the lender's claim to the rents in the event of borrower bankruptcy. For further consideration of such "absolute" assignments and their effectiveness, see §§ 4.35, 8.17 supra. Note also that Paragraph 26 authorizes the appointment of a receiver upon any default by the borrower. Such agreements are often not enforcible, at least in the absence of statutory authorization. See § 4.35 supra.

The Rider contains several especially important provisions. First, Section A contains a highly sophisticated prepayment provision that is aimed at reimbursing lender for any *actual loss* it suffers as a result of

§ 14.16　　　　　RESIDENTIAL FINANCING FORMS　　　　　379

a prepayment. Thus, if market interest rates are sufficiently high when a prepayment occurs, no prepayment premium will be payable. On the other hand, further language makes it clear that, where the formula otherwise yields a premium due to the lender, it will be payable even when prepayment results from acceleration incident to default, casualty loss, condemnation or other "involuntary" causes. For further extensive analysis of the prepayment problem, see §§ 6.1–6.5 supra.

Note that Section B of the Rider relieves the borrower of personal liability on the mortgage obligation and, thus, makes the obligation "non-recourse." Consequently, this language must not be used if the parties intend that the borrower be personally liable. Note also that even though the borrower is exculpated from personal liability on the mortgage obligation, the language purports to make him or her liable for waste, fraud or retention of rents after receiving a notice of default. Whether this latter language will be effective may depend, in part, on the extent to which state anti-deficiency legislation, if any, limits recovery from the borrower in such settings. See § 8.3, supra.

Section D of the Rider is aimed at protecting the lender with respect to environmental problems that arise on the mortgaged real estate. Not only does the borrower covenant to refrain from creating environmental hazards and to comply with federal, state and local environmental statutes and regulations, he or she also promises to provide lender with prompt notification of any actual or threatened environmental enforcement action concerning the mortgaged real estate. For further consideration of mortgagee liability for environmental contamination of the mortgaged real estate, see §§ 4.47–4.51 supra.

Section F of the Rider, the due-on-sale provision, is similar to the language that is contained in Paragraph 19 of the Uniform Covenants. However, it makes clear that where lender consents to a transfer, it may charge a one percent transfer fee.

MULTIFAMILY NOTE

US $_____　　　　　　　　　　　　　　_____, Texas
　　　　　　　　　　　　　　　　　　　　　　　　　City

　　　　　　　　　　　　　　　　　　　　　　　　_____, 19__

　　FOR VALUE RECEIVED, the undersigned promise to pay _____, or order, the principal sum of _____ Dollars, with interest on the unpaid principal balance from the date of this Note, until paid, at the rate of _____ percent per annum. The principal and interest shall be payable at _____ in consecutive monthly installments of _____ Dollars (U.S. $_____) on the _____ day of each month beginning _____, 19__, (herein "amortization commencement date"), until the entire indebtedness evidenced hereby is fully paid, except that any remaining indebtedness, if not sooner paid, shall be due and payable on _____.

　　If any installment under this Note is not paid when due, the entire principal amount outstanding hereunder and accrued interest thereon shall at once become due and payable, at the option of the holder hereof. The holder hereof may exercise this option to accelerate during any default by the undersigned regardless of any prior forbearance. In the event of any default in the payment of this Note, and if the same is referred to an attorney at law for collection or any action at law or in equity is brought with respect hereto, the undersigned shall pay the holder hereof all expenses and costs, including, but not limited to, attorney's fees.

If any installment under this Note is not received by the holder hereof within _____ calendar days after the installment is due, the undersigned shall pay to the holder hereof a late charge of _____ percent of such installment, such late charge to be immediately due and payable without demand by the holder hereof. If any installment under this Note remains past due for _____ calendar days or more, the outstanding principal balance of this Note shall bear interest during the period in which the undersigned is in default at a rate of _____ percent per annum, or, if such increased rate of interest may not be collected from the undersigned under applicable law, then at the maximum increased rate of interest, if any, which may be collected from the undersigned under applicable law.

On and after, but not prior to _____, 19__ ("prepayment permitted date"), the undersigned may make partial prepayments of principal without charge provided that the aggregate of such prepayments does not exceed in any one loan prepayment year _____ percent of the original principal amount of this Note ("allowable prepayment"). For purposes of this paragraph, "loan prepayment year" means each twelve month period beginning with the prepayment permitted date or an anniversary date thereof. Prepayments of principal which in any loan prepayment year exceed the allowable prepayment ("excess prepayments") may be made provided that the undersigned gives the holder hereof written notice of the full amounts to be prepaid at least _____ days prior to such prepayments and provided further that the undersigned pays to the holder hereof together with each such prepayment (including prepayments occurring as a result of the acceleration by the holder hereof of the principal amount of this Note, but excluding prepayments occurring because of the application by the holder hereof of insurance or condemnation awards or proceeds pursuant to a Mortgage or Deed of Trust securing this Note) a prepayment premium. In the first [_____] * loan prepayment year(s), the prepayment premium shall be an amount equal to _____ percent of the excess prepayments. The percentage used to calculate the prepayment premium shall decline by the number _____ in the _____ loan prepayment year and in every [_____] * loan prepayment year thereafter until the percentage payable on excess prepayments is _____ percent, which percentage shall be used to calculate the prepayment premium which shall be payable on excess prepayments during the remaining term of this Note.

Prepayments shall be applied against the outstanding principal balance of this Note and shall not extend or postpone the due date of any subsequent monthly installments or change the amount of such installments, unless the holder hereof shall agree otherwise in writing. The holder hereof may require that any partial prepayments be made on the date monthly installments are due and be in the amount of that part of one or more monthly installments which would be applicable to principal.

From time to time, without affecting the obligation of the undersigned or the successors or assigns of the undersigned to pay the outstanding principal balance of this Note and observe the covenants of the undersigned contained herein, without affecting the guaranty of any person, corporation, partnership or other entity for payment of the outstanding principal balance of this Note, without giving notice to or obtaining the consent of the undersigned, the successors or assigns of the undersigned or guarantors, and without liability on the part of the holder hereof, the holder hereof may, at the option of the holder hereof, extend the time for payment of said outstanding principal balance or any part thereof, reduce the payments thereon, release anyone liable on any of said outstanding principal balance, accept a renewal of this Note, modify the terms and time of payment of

---

* *Strike through bracketed clause(s) if not completed.*

said outstanding principal balance, join in any extension or subordination agreement, release any security given herefor, take or release other or additional security, and agree in writing with the undersigned to modify the rate of interest or period of amortization of this Note or change the amount of the monthly installments payable hereunder.

Presentment, notice of dishonor, and protest are hereby waived by all makers, sureties, guarantors and endorsers hereof. This Note shall be the joint and several obligation of all makers, sureties, guarantors and endorsers, and shall be binding upon them and their successors and assigns.

The indebtedness evidenced by this Note is secured by a Mortgage or Deed of Trust dated _____, and reference is made thereto for rights as to acceleration of the indebtedness evidenced by this Note. This Note shall be governed by the law of the jurisdiction in which the Property subject to the Mortgage or Deed of Trust is located.

Prior to the commencement of amortization, the undersigned shall pay the holder hereof interest only on the outstanding principal balance of this Note at the rate of _____ percent per annum in consecutive monthly installments beginning _____, 19__, and on _____ thereafter until the amortization commencement date, at which time any remaining interest payable pursuant to this paragraph (and not paid as a part of the first monthly installment of principal and interest) shall be paid.**

MULTIFAMILY DEED OF TRUST,
ASSIGNMENT OF RENTS AND SECURITY AGREEMENT
(Security for Construction Loan Agreement)

THIS DEED OF TRUST (herein "Instrument") is made this _____ day of _____, 19__, among the Trustor/Grantor, _____, whose address is _____ (herein "Borrower"), _____ (herein "Trustee"), and the Beneficiary, _____, a _____ organized and existing under the laws of _____, whose address is _____ (herein "Lender").

BORROWER, in consideration of the indebtedness herein recited and the trust herein created, irrevocably grants, conveys and assigns to Trustee, in trust, with power of sale, [the leasehold estate pursuant to a lease (herein "ground lease") dated _____, between _____ and _____, recorded in _____ in and to *] the following described property located in _____, State of Texas:

TOGETHER with all buildings, improvements, and tenements now or hereafter erected on the property, and all heretofore or hereafter vacated alleys and streets abutting the property, and all easements, rights, appurtenances, rents (subject however to the assignment of rents to Lender herein), royalties, mineral, oil and gas rights and profits, water, water rights, and water stock appurtenant to the property, and all fixtures, machinery, equipment, engines, boilers, incinerators, building materials, appliances and goods of every nature whatsoever now or hereafter located in, or on, or used, or intended to be used in connection with the property, including, but not limited to, those for the purposes of supplying or distributing heating, cooling, electricity, gas, water, air and light; and all elevators, and related machinery and equipment, fire prevention and extinguishing apparatus, security and access control apparatus, plumbing, bath tubs, water heaters, water closets, sinks, ranges, stoves, refrigerators, dishwashers, disposals, washers, dryers, awnings, storm windows, storm doors, screens, blinds, shades, curtains and curtain rods, mirrors, cabinets, panelling, rugs, attached floor coverings, furniture, pictures, antennas, trees and plants, and _____; all of which, including replacements and additions thereto, shall be deemed to be and remain a part of the real

---

** Strike through this paragraph if not applicable.

* Delete bracketed material if not completed.

property covered by this Instrument; and all of the foregoing, together with said property (or the leasehold estate in the event this Instrument is on a leasehold) are herein referred to as the "Property".

TO SECURE TO LENDER (a) the repayment of the indebtedness evidenced by Borrower's note dated _____ (herein "Note") in the principal sum of _____ Dollars, with interest thereon, with the balance of the indebtedness, if not sooner paid, due and payable on _____, and all renewals, extensions and modifications thereof; (b) the repayment of any future advances, with interest thereon, made by Lender to Borrower pursuant to paragraph 33 hereof (herein "Future Advances"); (c) the performance of the covenants and agreements of Borrower contained in a Construction Loan Agreement between Lender and Borrower dated _____, 19__, if any, as provided in paragraph 25 hereof; (d) the payment of all other sums, with interest thereon, advanced in accordance herewith to protect the security of this Instrument; and (e) the performance of the covenants and agreements of Borrower herein contained.

Borrower covenants that Borrower is lawfully seised of the estate hereby conveyed and has the right to grant, convey and assign the Property (and, if this Instrument is on a leasehold, that the ground lease is in full force and effect without modification except as noted above and without default on the part of either lessor or lessee thereunder), that the Property is unencumbered, and that Borrower will warrant and defend generally the title to the Property against all claims and demands, subject to any easements and restrictions listed in a schedule of exceptions to coverage in any title insurance policy insuring Lender's interest in the Property.

Uniform Covenants. Borrower and Lender covenant and agree as follows:

1. PAYMENT OF PRINCIPAL AND INTEREST. Borrower shall promptly pay when due the principal of and interest on the indebtedness evidenced by the Note, any prepayment and late charges provided in the Note and all other sums secured by this Instrument.

2. FUNDS FOR TAXES, INSURANCE AND OTHER CHARGES. Subject to applicable law or to a written waiver by Lender, Borrower shall pay to Lender on the day monthly installments of principal or interest are payable under the Note (or on another day designated in writing by Lender), until the Note is paid in full, a sum (herein "Funds") equal to one-twelfth of (a) the yearly water and sewer rates and taxes and assessments which may be levied on the Property, (b) the yearly ground rents, if any, (c) the yearly premium installments for fire and other hazard insurance, rent loss insurance and such other insurance covering the Property as Lender may require pursuant to paragraph 5 hereof, (d) the yearly premium installments for mortgage insurance, if any, and (e) if this Instrument is on a leasehold, the yearly fixed rents, if any, under the ground lease, all as reasonably estimated initially and from time to time by Lender on the basis of assessments and bills and reasonable estimates thereof. Any waiver by Lender of a requirement that Borrower pay such Funds may be revoked by Lender, in Lender's sole discretion, at any time upon notice in writing to Borrower. Lender may require Borrower to pay to Lender, in advance, such other Funds for other taxes, charges, premiums, assessments and impositions in connection with Borrower or the Property which Lender shall reasonably deem necessary to protect Lender's interests (herein "Other Impositions"). Unless otherwise provided by applicable law, Lender may require Funds for Other Impositions to be paid by Borrower in a lump sum or in periodic installments, at Lender's option.

The Funds shall be held in an institution(s) the deposits or accounts of which are insured or guaranteed by a Federal or state agency (including Lender if Lender is such an institution). Lender shall apply the Funds to pay said rates, rents, taxes, assessments, insurance premiums and Other Impositions so long as Borrower is not in breach of any covenant or agreement of Borrower in this Instrument. Lender shall make no charge for so holding and applying the Funds, analyzing said account or for verifying and compiling said assessments and bills, unless Lender pays Borrower interest, earnings or profits on the Funds and applicable law permits Lender to make such a charge. Borrower and Lender may agree in writing at the time of execution of this Instrument that interest on the Funds shall be paid to Borrower, and unless such agreement is made or applicable law requires interest, earnings or profits to be paid, Lender shall not be required to pay Borrower any interest, earnings or profits on the Funds. Lender shall give to Borrower, without charge, an annual accounting of the Funds in Lender's normal format showing credits and debits to the Funds and the purpose for which each debit to the Funds was made. The Funds are pledged as additional security for the sums secured by this Instrument.

If the amount of the Funds held by Lender at the time of the annual accounting thereof shall exceed the amount deemed necessary by Lender to provide for the payment of water and sewer rates, taxes, assessments, insurance premiums, rents and Other Impositions, as they fall due, such excess shall be credited to Borrower on the next monthly installment or installments of Funds due. If at any time the amount of the Funds held by Lender shall be less than the amount deemed necessary by Lender to pay water and sewer rates, taxes, assessments, insurance premiums, rents and Other Impositions, as they fall due, Borrower shall pay to Lender any amount necessary to make up the deficiency within thirty days after notice from Lender to Borrower requesting payment thereof.

Upon Borrower's breach of any covenant or agreement of Borrower in this Instrument, Lender may apply, in any amount and in any order as Lender shall determine in Lender's sole discretion, any Funds held by Lender at the time of application (i) to pay rates, rents, taxes, assessments, insurance premiums and Other Impositions which are now or will hereafter become due, or (ii) as a credit against sums secured by this Instrument. Upon payment in full of all sums secured by this Instrument, Lender shall promptly refund to Borrower any Funds held by Lender.

3. APPLICATION OF PAYMENTS. Unless applicable law provides otherwise, all payments received by Lender from Borrower under the Note or this Instrument shall be applied by Lender in the following order of priority: (i) amounts payable to Lender by Borrower under paragraph 2 hereof; (ii) interest payable on the Note; (iii) principal of the Note; (iv) interest payable on advances made pursuant to paragraph 8 hereof; (v) principal of advances made pursuant to paragraph 8 hereof; (vi) interest payable on any Future Advance, provided that if more than one Future Advance is outstanding, Lender may apply payments received among the amounts of interest payable on the Future Advances in such order as Lender, in Lender's sole discretion, may determine; (vii) principal of any Future Advance, provided that if more than one Future Advance is outstanding, Lender may apply payments received among the principal balances of the Future Advances in such order as Lender, in Lender's sole discretion, may determine; and (viii) any other sums secured by this Instrument in such order as Lender, at Lender's option, may determine: provided, however, that Lender may, at Lender's option, apply any sums payable pursuant to paragraph 8 hereof prior to interest on and principal of the Note, but such application shall not otherwise affect the order of priority of application specified in this paragraph 3.

4. CHARGES; LIENS. Borrower shall pay all water and sewer rates, rents, taxes, assessments, premiums, and Other Impositions attributable to the Property at Lender's option in the manner provided under paragraph 2 hereof or, if not paid in such manner, by Borrower making payment, when due, directly to the payee thereof, or in such other manner as Lender may designate in writing. Borrower shall promptly furnish to Lender all notices of amounts due under this paragraph 4, and in the event Borrower shall make payment directly. Borrower shall promptly furnish to Lender receipts evidencing such payments. Borrower shall promptly discharge any lien which has, or may have, priority over or equality with, the lien of this Instrument, and Borrower shall pay, when due, the claims of all persons supplying labor or materials to or in connection with the Property. Without Lender's prior written permission, Borrower shall not allow any lien inferior to this Instrument to be perfected against the Property.

5. HAZARD INSURANCE. Borrower shall keep the improvements now existing or hereafter erected on the Property insured by carriers at all times satisfactory to Lender against loss by fire, hazards included within the term "extended coverage", rent loss and such other hazards, casualties, liabilities and contingencies as Lender (and, if this Instrument is on a leasehold, the ground lease) shall require and in such amounts and for such periods as Lender shall require. All premiums on insurance policies shall be paid, at Lender's option, in the manner provided under paragraph 2 hereof, or by Borrower making payment, when due, directly to the carrier, or in such other manner as Lender may designate in writing.

All insurance policies and renewals thereof shall be in a form acceptable to Lender and shall include a standard mortgage clause in favor of and in form acceptable to Lender. Lender shall have the right to hold the policies, and Borrower shall promptly furnish to Lender all renewal notices and all receipts of paid premiums. At least thirty days prior to the expiration date of a policy, Borrower shall deliver to Lender a renewal policy in form satisfactory to Lender. If this Instrument is on a leasehold, Borrower shall furnish Lender a duplicate of all policies, renewal notices, renewal policies and receipts of paid premiums if, by virtue of the ground lease, the originals thereof may not be supplied by Borrower to Lender.

In the event of loss, Borrower shall give immediate written notice to the insurance carrier and to Lender. Borrower hereby authorizes and empowers Lender as attorney-in-fact for Borrower to make proof of loss, to adjust and compromise any claim under insurance policies, to appear in and prosecute any action arising from such insurance policies, to collect and receive insurance proceeds, and to deduct therefrom Lender's expenses incurred in the collection of such proceeds; provided however, that nothing contained in this paragraph 5 shall require Lender to incur any expense or take any action hereunder. Borrower further authorizes Lender, at Lender's option, (a) to hold the balance of such proceeds to be used to reimburse Borrower for the cost of reconstruction or repair of the Property or (b) to apply the balance of such proceeds to the payment of the sums secured by this Instrument, whether or not then due, in the order of application set forth in paragraph 3 hereof (subject, however, to the rights of the lessor under the ground lease if this Instrument is on a leasehold).

If the insurance proceeds are held by Lender to reimburse Borrower for the cost of restoration and repair of the Property, the Property shall be restored to the equivalent of its original condition or such other condition as Lender may approve in writing. Lender may, at Lender's option, condition disbursement of said proceeds on Lender's approval of such plans and specifications of an architect satisfactory to Lender, contractor's cost estimates, architect's certificates, waivers of liens, sworn statements of mechanics and materialmen and such other evidence of costs, percentage completion of construction, application of payments, and satisfaction of liens as Lender may reasonably require. If the insurance proceeds are applied to the payment of the sums secured by this Instrument, any such application of proceeds to principal shall not extend or postpone the due dates of the monthly installments referred to in paragraphs 1 and 2 hereof or change the amounts of such installments. If the Property is sold pursuant to paragraph 27 hereof or if Lender acquires title to the Property, Lender shall have all of the right, title and interest of Borrower in and to any insurance policies and unearned premiums thereon and in and to the proceeds resulting from any damage to the Property prior to such sale or acquisition.

6. PRESERVATION AND MAINTENANCE OF PROPERTY; LEASEHOLDS. Borrower (a) shall not commit waste or permit impairment or deterioration of the Property, (b) shall not abandon the Property, (c) shall restore or repair promptly and in a good and workmanlike manner all or any part of the Property to the equivalent of its original condition, or such other condition as Lender may approve in writing, in the event of any damage, injury or loss thereto, whether or not insurance proceeds are available to cover in whole or in part the costs of such restoration or repair, (d) shall keep the Property, including improvements, fixtures, equipment, machinery and appliances thereon in good repair and shall replace fixtures, equipment, machinery and appliances on the Property when necessary to keep such items in good repair, (e) shall comply with all laws, ordinances, regulations and requirements of any governmental body applicable to the Property, (f) shall provide for professional management of the Property by a residential rental property manager satisfactory to Lender pursuant to a contract approved by Lender in writing, unless such requirement shall be waived by Lender in writing, (g) shall generally operate and maintain the Property in a manner to ensure maximum rentals, and (h) shall give notice in writing to Lender of and, unless otherwise directed in writing by Lender, appear in and defend any action or proceeding purporting to affect the Property, the security of this Instrument or the rights or powers of Lender. Neither Borrower nor any tenant or other person shall remove, demolish or alter any improvement now existing or hereafter erected on the Property or any fixture, equipment, machinery or appliance in or on the Property except when incident to the replacement of fixtures, equipment, machinery and appliances with items of like kind.

If this Instrument is on a leasehold, Borrower (i) shall comply with the provisions of the ground lease, (ii) shall give immediate written notice to Lender of any default by lessor under the ground lease or of any notice received by Borrower from such lessor of any default under the ground lease by Borrower, (iii) shall exercise any option to renew or extend the ground lease and give written confirmation thereof to Lender within thirty days after such option becomes exercisable, (iv) shall give immediate written notice to Lender of the commencement of any remedial proceedings under the ground lease by any party thereto and, if required by Lender, shall permit Lender as Borrower's attorney-in-fact to control and act for Borrower in any such remedial proceedings and (v) shall within thirty days after request by Lender obtain from the lessor under the ground lease and deliver to Lender the lessor's estoppel certificate required thereunder, if any. Borrower hereby expressly transfers and assigns to Lender the benefit of all covenants contained in the ground lease, whether or not such covenants run with the land, but Lender shall have no liability with respect to such covenants nor any other covenants contained in the ground lease.

Borrower shall not surrender the leasehold estate and interests herein conveyed nor terminate or cancel the ground lease creating said estate and interests, and Borrower shall not, without the express written consent of Lender, alter or amend said ground lease. Borrower covenants and agrees that there shall not be a merger of the ground lease, or of the leasehold estate created thereby, with the fee estate covered by the ground lease by reason of said leasehold estate or said fee estate, or any part of either, coming into common ownership, unless Lender shall consent in writing to such merger; if Borrower shall acquire such fee estate, then this Instrument shall simultaneously and without further action be spread so as to become a lien on such fee estate.

7. USE OF PROPERTY. Unless required by applicable law or unless Lender has otherwise agreed in writing, Borrower shall not allow changes in the use for which all or any part of the Property was intended at the time this Instrument was executed. Borrower shall not initiate or acquiesce in a change in the zoning classification of the Property without Lender's prior written consent.

8. PROTECTION OF LENDER'S SECURITY. If Borrower fails to perform the covenants and agreements contained in this Instrument, or if any action or proceeding is commenced which affects the Property or title thereto or the interest of Lender therein, including, but not limited to, eminent domain, insolvency, code enforcement, or arrangements or proceedings involving a bankrupt or decedent, then Lender at Lender's option may make such appearances, disburse such sums and take such action as Lender deems necessary, in its sole discretion, to protect Lender's interest, including, but not limited to, (i) disbursement of attorney's fees, (ii) entry upon the Property to make repairs, (iii) procurement of satisfactory insurance as provided in paragraph 5 hereof, and (iv) if this Instrument is on a leasehold, exercise of any option to renew or extend the ground lease on behalf of Borrower and the curing of any default of Borrower in the terms and conditions of the ground lease.

Any amounts disbursed by Lender pursuant to this paragraph 8, with interest thereon, shall become additional indebtedness of Borrower secured by this Instrument. Unless Borrower and Lender agree to other terms of payment, such amounts shall be immediately due and payable and shall bear interest from the date of disbursement at the rate stated in the Note unless collection from Borrower of interest at such rate would be contrary to applicable law, in which event such amounts shall bear interest at the highest rate which may be collected from Borrower under applicable law. Borrower hereby covenants and agrees that Lender shall be subrogated to the lien of any mortgage or other lien discharged, in whole or in part, by the indebtedness secured hereby. Nothing contained in this paragraph 8 shall require Lender to incur any expense or take any action hereunder.

9. INSPECTION. Lender may make or cause to be made reasonable entries upon and inspections of the Property.

10. BOOKS AND RECORDS. Borrower shall keep and maintain at all times at Borrower's address stated below, or such other place as Lender may approve in writing, complete and accurate books of accounts and records adequate to reflect correctly the results of the operation of the Property and copies of all written contracts, leases and other instruments which affect the Property. Such books, records, contracts, leases and other instruments shall be subject to examination and inspection at any reasonable time by Lender. Upon Lender's request, Borrower shall furnish to Lender, within one hundred and twenty days after the end of each fiscal year of Borrower, a balance sheet, a statement of income and expenses of the Property and a statement of changes in financial position, each in reasonable detail and certified by Borrower and, if Lender shall require, by an independent certified public accountant. Borrower shall furnish, together with the foregoing financial statements and at any other time upon Lender's request, a rent schedule for the Property, certified by Borrower, showing the name of each tenant, and for each tenant, the space occupied, the lease expiration date, the rent payable and the rent paid.

11. CONDEMNATION. Borrower shall promptly notify Lender of any action or proceeding relating to any condemnation or other taking, whether direct or indirect, of the Property, or part thereof, and Borrower shall appear in and prosecute any such action or proceeding unless otherwise directed by Lender in writing. Borrower authorizes Lender, at Lender's option, as attorney-in-fact for Borrower, to commence, appear in and prosecute, in Lender's or Borrower's name, any action or proceeding relating to any condemnation or other taking of the Property, whether direct or indirect, and to settle or compromise any claim in connection with such condemnation or other taking. The proceeds of any award, payment or claim for damages, direct or consequential, in connection with any condemnation or other taking, whether direct or indirect, of the Property, or part thereof, or for conveyances in lieu of condemnation, are hereby assigned to and shall be paid to lender subject, if this Instrument is on a leasehold, to the rights of lessor under the ground lease.

Borrower authorizes Lender to apply such awards, payments, proceeds or damages, after the deduction of Lender's expenses incurred in the collection of such amounts, at Lender's option, to restoration or repair of the Property or to payment of the sums secured by this Instrument, whether or not then due, in the order of application set forth in paragraph 3 hereof, with the balance, if any, to Borrower. Unless Borrower and Lender otherwise agree in writing, any application of proceeds to principal shall not extend or postpone the due date of the monthly installments referred to in paragraphs 1 and 2 hereof or change the amount of such installments. Borrower agrees to execute such further evidence of assignment of any awards, proceeds, damages or claims arising in connection with such condemnation or taking as Lender may require.

12. BORROWER AND LIEN NOT RELEASED. From time to time, Lender may, at Lender's option, without giving notice to or obtaining the consent of Borrower, Borrower's successors or assigns or of any junior lienholder or guarantors, without liability on Lender's part and notwithstanding Borrower's breach of any covenant or agreement of Borrower in this Instrument, extend the time for payment of said indebtedness or any part thereof, reduce the payments thereon, release anyone liable on any of said indebtedness, accept a renewal note or notes therefor, modify the terms and time of payment of said indebtedness, release from the lien of this Instrument any part of the Property, take or release other or additional security, reconvey any part of the Property, consent to any map or plan of the Property, consent to the granting of any easement, join in any extension or subordination agreement, and agree in writing with Borrower to modify the rate of interest or period of amortization of the Note or change the amount of the monthly installments payable thereunder. Any actions taken by Lender pursuant to the terms of this paragraph 12 shall not affect the obligation of Borrower or Borrower's successors or assigns to pay the sums secured by this Instrument and to observe the covenants of Borrower contained herein, shall not affect the guaranty of any person, corporation, partnership or other entity for payment of the indebtedness secured hereby, and shall not affect the lien or priority of lien hereof on the Property. Borrower shall pay Lender a reasonable service charge, together with such title insurance premiums and attorney's fees as may be incurred at Lender's option, for any such action if taken at Borrower's request.

13. FORBEARANCE BY LENDER NOT A WAIVER. Any forbearance by Lender in exercising any right or remedy hereunder, or otherwise afforded by applicable law, shall not be a waiver of or preclude the exercise of any right or remedy. The acceptance by Lender of payment of any sum secured by this Instrument after the due date of such payment shall not be a waiver of Lender's right to either require prompt payment when due of all other sums so secured or to declare a default for failure to make prompt payment. The procurement of insurance or the payment of taxes or other liens or charges by Lender shall not be a waiver of Lender's right to accelerate the maturity of the indebtedness secured by this Instrument, nor shall Lender's receipt of any awards, proceeds or damages under paragraphs 5 and 11 hereof operate to cure or waive Borrower's default in payment of sums secured by this Instrument.

14. ESTOPPEL CERTIFICATE. Borrower shall within ten days of a written request from Lender furnish Lender with a written statement, duly acknowledged, setting forth the sums secured by this Instrument and any right of set-off, counterclaim or other defense which exists against such sums and the obligations of this Instrument.

15. UNIFORM COMMERCIAL CODE SECURITY AGREEMENT. This Instrument is intended to be a security agreement pursuant to the Uniform Commercial Code for any of the items specified above as part of the Property which, under applicable law, may be subject to a security interest pursuant to the Uniform Commercial Code, and Borrower hereby grants Lender a security interest in said items. Borrower agrees that Lender may file this Instrument, or a reproduction thereof, in the real estate records or other appropriate index, as a financing statement for any of the items specified above as part of the Property. Any reproduction of this Instrument or of any other security agreement or financing statement shall be sufficient as a financing statement. In addition, Borrower agrees to execute and deliver to Lender, upon Lender's request, any financing statements, as well as extensions, renewals and amendments thereof, and reproductions of this Instrument in such form as Lender may require to perfect a security interest with respect to said items. Borrower shall pay all costs of filing such financing statements and any extensions, renewals, amendments and releases thereof, and shall pay all reasonable costs and expenses of any record searches for financing statements Lender may reasonably require. Without the prior written consent of Lender, Borrower shall not create or suffer to be created pursuant to the Uniform Commercial Code any other security interest in said items, including replacements and additions thereto. Upon Borrower's breach of any covenant or agreement of Borrower contained in this Instrument, including the covenants to pay when due all sums secured by this Instrument, Lender shall have the remedies of a secured party under the Uniform Commercial Code and, at Lender's option, may also invoke the remedies provided in paragraph 27 of this Instrument as to such items. In exercising any of said remedies, Lender may proceed against the items of real property and any items of personal property specified above as part of the Property separately or together and in any order whatsoever, without in any way affecting the availability of Lender's remedies under the Uniform Commercial Code or of the remedies provided in paragraph 27 of this Instrument.

16. LEASES OF THE PROPERTY. As used in this paragraph 16, the word "lease" shall mean "sublease" if this Instrument is on a leasehold. Borrower shall comply with and observe Borrower's obligations as landlord under all leases of the Property or any part thereof. Borrower will not lease any portion of the Property for non-residential use except with the prior written approval of Lender. Borrower, at Lender's request, shall furnish Lender with executed copies of all leases now existing or hereafter made of all or any part of the Property, and all leases now or hereafter entered into will be in form and substance subject to the approval of Lender. All leases of the Property shall specifically provide that such leases are subordinate to this Instrument; that the tenant attorns to Lender, such attornment to be effective upon Lender's acquisition of title to the Property; that the tenant agrees to execute such further evidences of attornment as Lender may from time to time request; that the attornment of the tenant shall not be terminated by foreclosure; and that Lender may, at Lender's option, accept or reject such attornments. Borrower shall not, without Lender's written consent, execute, modify, surrender or terminate, either orally or in writing, any lease now existing or hereafter made of all or any part of the Property providing for a term of three years or more, permit an assignment or sublease of such a lease without Lender's written consent, or request or consent to the subordination of any lease of all or any part of the Property to any lien subordinate to this Instrument. If Borrower becomes aware that any tenant proposes to do, or is doing, any act or thing which may give rise to any right of set-off against rent, Borrower shall (i) take such steps as shall be reasonably calculated to prevent the accrual of any right to a set-off against rent, (ii) notify Lender thereof and of the amount of said set-offs, and (iii) within ten days after such accrual, reimburse the tenant who shall have acquired such right to set-off or take such other steps as shall effectively discharge such set-off and as shall assure that rents thereafter due shall continue to be payable without set-off or deduction.

Upon Lender's request, Borrower shall assign to Lender, by written instrument satisfactory to Lender, all leases now existing or hereafter made of all or any part of the Property and all security deposits made by tenants in connection with such leases of the Property. Upon assignment by Borrower to Lender of any leases of the Property, Lender shall have all of the rights and powers possessed by Borrower prior to such assignment and Lender shall have the right to modify, extend or terminate such existing leases and to execute new leases, in Lender's sole discretion.

17. REMEDIES CUMULATIVE. Each remedy provided in this Instrument is distinct and cumulative to all other rights or remedies under this Instrument or afforded by law or equity, and may be exercised concurrently, independently, or successively, in any order whatsoever.

18. ACCELERATION IN CASE OF BORROWER'S INSOLVENCY. If Borrower shall voluntarily file a petition under the Federal Bankruptcy Act, as such Act may from time to time be amended, or under any similar or successor Federal statute relating to bankruptcy, insolvency, arrangements or reorganizations, or under any state bankruptcy or insolvency act, or file an answer in an involuntary proceeding admitting insolvency or inability to pay debts, or if Borrower shall fail to obtain a vacation or stay of involuntary proceedings brought for the reorganization, dissolution or liquidation of Borrower, or if Borrower shall be adjudged a bankrupt, or if a trustee or receiver shall be appointed for Borrower or Borrower's property, or if the Property shall become subject to the jurisdiction of a Federal bankruptcy court or similar state court, or if Borrower shall make an assignment for the benefit of Borrower's creditors, or if there is an attachment, execution or other judicial seizure of any portion of Borrower's assets and such seizure is not discharged within ten days, the Lender may, at Lender's option, declare all of the sums secured by this Instrument to be immediately due and payable without prior notice to Borrower, and Lender may invoke any remedies permitted by paragraph 27 of this Instrument. Any attorney's fees and other expenses incurred by Lender in connection with Borrower's bankruptcy or any of the other aforesaid events shall be additional indebtedness of Borrower secured by this Instrument pursuant to paragraph 8 hereof.

19. TRANSFERS OF THE PROPERTY OR BENEFICIAL INTERESTS IN BORROWER; ASSUMPTION. On sale or transfer of (i) all or any part of the Property, or any interest therein, or (ii) beneficial interests in Borrower (if Borrower is not a natural person or persons but is a corporation, partnership, trust or other legal entity), Lender may, at Lender's option, declare all of the sums secured by this Instrument to be immediately due and payable, and Lender may invoke any remedies permitted by paragraph 27 of this Instrument. This option shall not apply in case of

(a) transfers by devise or descent or by operation of law upon the death of a joint tenant or a partner;

(b) sales or transfers when the transferee's creditworthiness and management ability are satisfactory to Lender and the transferee has executed, prior to the sale or transfer, a written assumption agreement containing such terms as Lender may require, including, if required by Lender, an increase in the rate of interest payable under the Note;

(c) the grant of a leasehold interest in a part of the Property of three years or less (or such longer lease term as Lender may permit by prior written approval) not containing an option to purchase (except any interest in the ground lease, if this Instrument is on a leasehold);

(d) sales or transfers of beneficial interests in Borrower provided that such sales or transfers, together with any prior sales or transfers of beneficial interests in Borrower, but excluding sales or transfers under subparagraphs (a) and (b) above, do not result in more than 49% of the beneficial interests in Borrower having been sold or transferred since commencement of amortization of the Note; and

(e) sales or transfers of fixtures or any personal property pursuant to the first paragraph of paragraph 6 hereof.

20. NOTICE. Except for any notice required under applicable law to be given in another manner, (a) any notice to Borrower provided for in this Instrument or in the Note shall be given by mailing such notice by certified mail addressed to Borrower at Borrower's address stated below or at such other address as Borrower may designate by notice to Lender as provided herein, and (b) any notice to Lender shall be given by certified mail, return receipt requested, to Lender's address stated herein or to such other address as Lender may designate by notice to Borrower as provided herein. Any notice provided for in this Instrument or in the Note shall be deemed to have been given to Borrower or Lender when given in the manner designated herein.

21. SUCCESSORS AND ASSIGNS BOUND; JOINT AND SEVERAL LIABILITY; AGENTS; CAPTIONS. The covenants and agreements herein contained shall bind, and the rights hereunder shall inure to, the respective successors and assigns of Lender and Borrower, subject to the provisions of paragraph 19 hereof. All covenants and agreements of Borrower shall be joint and several. In exercising any rights hereunder or taking any actions provided for herein, Lender may act through its employees, agents or independent contractors as authorized by Lender. The captions and headings of the paragraphs of this Instrument are for convenience only and are not to be used to interpret or define the provisions hereof.

22. UNIFORM MULTIFAMILY INSTRUMENT; GOVERNING LAW; SEVERABILITY. This form of multifamily instrument combines uniform covenants for national use and non-uniform covenants with limited variations by jurisdiction to constitute a uniform security instrument covering real property and related fixtures and personal property. This Instrument shall be governed by the law of the jurisdiction in which the Property is located. In the event that any provision of this Instrument or the Note conflicts with applicable law, such conflict shall not affect other provisions of this Instrument or the Note which can be given effect without the conflicting provisions, and to this end the provisions of this Instrument and the Note are declared to be severable. In the event that any applicable law limiting the amount of interest or other charges permitted to be collected from Borrower is interpreted so that any charge provided for in this Instrument or in the Note, whether considered separately or together with other charges levied in connection with this Instrument and the Note, violates such law, and Borrower is entitled to the benefit of such law, such charge is hereby reduced to the extent necessary to eliminate such violation. The amounts, if any, previously paid to Lender in excess of the amounts payable to Lender pursuant to such charges as reduced shall be applied by Lender to reduce the principal of the indebtedness evidenced by the Note. For the purpose of determining whether any applicable law limiting the amount of interest or other charges permitted to be collected from Borrower has been violated, all indebtedness which is secured by this Instrument or evidenced by the Note and which constitutes interest, as well as all other charges levied in connection with such indebtedness which constitute interest, shall be deemed to be allocated and spread over the stated term of the Note. Unless otherwise required by applicable law, such allocation and spreading shall be effected in such a manner that the rate of interest computed thereby is uniform throughout the stated term of the Note.

23. WAIVER OF STATUTE OF LIMITATIONS. Borrower hereby waives the right to assert any statute of limitations as a bar to the enforcement of the lien of this Instrument or to any action brought to enforce the Note or any other obligation secured by this Instrument.

24. WAIVER OF MARSHALLING. Notwithstanding the existence of any other security interests in the Property held by Lender or by any other party, Lender shall have the right to determine the order in which any or all of the Property shall be subjected to the remedies provided herein. Lender shall have the right to determine the order in which any or all portions of the indebtedness secured hereby are satisfied from the proceeds realized upon the exercise of the remedies provided herein. Borrower, any party who consents to this Instrument and any party who now or hereafter acquires a security interest in the Property and who has actual or constructive notice hereof hereby waives any and all right to require the marshalling of assets in connection with the exercise of any of the remedies permitted by applicable law or provided herein.

25. CONSTRUCTION LOAN PROVISIONS. Borrower agrees to comply with the covenants and conditions of the Construction Loan Agreement, if any, which is hereby incorporated by reference in and made a part of this Instrument. All advances made by Lender pursuant to the Construction Loan Agreement shall be indebtedness of Borrower secured by this Instrument, and such advances may be obligatory as provided in the Construction Loan Agreement. All sums disbursed by Lender prior to completion of the improvements to protect the security of this Instrument up to the principal amount of the Note shall be treated as disbursements pursuant to the Construction Loan Agreement. All such sums shall bear interest from the date of disbursement at the rate stated in the Note, unless collection from Borrower of interest at such rate would be contrary to applicable law in which event such amounts shall bear interest at the highest rate which may be collected from Borrower under applicable law and shall be payable upon notice from Lender to Borrower requesting payment therefor.

From time to time as Lender deems necessary to protect Lender's interests, Borrower shall, upon request of Lender, execute and deliver to Lender, in such form as Lender shall direct, assignments of any and all rights or claims which relate to the construction of the Property and which Borrower may have against any party supplying or who has supplied labor, materials or services in connection with construction of the Property. In case of breach by Borrower of the covenants and conditions of the Construction Loan Agreement, Lender, at Lender's option, with or without entry upon the Property, (i) may invoke any of the rights or remedies provided in the Construction Loan Agreement, (ii) may accelerate the sums secured by this Instrument and invoke those remedies provided in paragraph 27 hereof, or (iii) may do both. If, after the commencement of amortization of the Note, the Note and this Instrument are sold by Lender, from and after such sale the Construction Loan Agreement shall cease to be a part of this Instrument and Borrower shall not assert any right of set-off, counterclaim or other claim or defense arising out of or in connection with the Construction Loan Agreement against the obligations of the Note and this Instrument.

26. ASSIGNMENT OF RENTS; APPOINTMENT OF RECEIVER; LENDER IN POSSESSION. As part of the consideration for the indebtedness evidenced by the Note, Borrower hereby absolutely and unconditionally assigns and transfers to Lender all the rents and revenues of the Property, including those now due, past due, or to become due by virtue of any lease or other agreement for the occupancy or use of all or any part of the Property, regardless of to whom the rents and revenues of the Property are payable. Borrower hereby authorizes Lender or Lender's agents to collect the aforesaid rents and revenues and hereby directs each tenant of the Property to pay such rents to Lender or Lender's agents; provided, however, that prior to written notice given by Lender to Borrower of the breach by Borrower of any covenant or agreement of Borrower in this Instrument, Borrower shall collect and receive all rents and revenues of the Property as trustee for the benefit of Lender and Borrower, to apply the rents and revenues so collected to the sums secured by this Instrument in the order provided in paragraph 3 hereof with the balance, so long as no such breach has occurred, to the account of Borrower, it being intended by Borrower and Lender that this assignment of rents constitutes an absolute assignment and not an assignment for additional security only. Upon delivery of written notice by Lender to Borrower of the breach by Borrower of any covenant or agreement of Borrower in this Instrument, and without the necessity of Lender entering upon and taking and maintaining full control of the Property in person, by agent or by a court-appointed receiver, Lender shall immediately be entitled to possession of all rents and revenues of the Property as specified in this paragraph 26 as the same become due and payable, including but not limited to rents then due and unpaid, and all such rents shall immediately upon delivery of such notice be held by Borrower as trustee for the benefit of Lender only; provided, however, that the written notice by Lender to Borrower of the breach by Borrower shall contain a statement that Lender exercises its rights to such rents. Borrower agrees that commencing upon delivery of such written notice of Borrower's breach by Lender to Borrower, each tenant of the Property shall make such rents payable to and pay such rents to Lender or Lender's agents on Lender's written demand to each tenant therefor, delivered to each tenant personally, by mail or by delivering such demand to each rental unit, without any liability on the part of said tenant to inquire further as to the existence of a default by Borrower.

Borrower hereby covenants that Borrower has not executed any prior assignment of said rents, that Borrower has not performed, and will not perform, any acts or has not executed, and will not execute, any instrument which would prevent Lender from exercising its rights under this paragraph 26, and that at the time of execution of this Instrument there has been no anticipation or prepayment of any of the rents of the Property for more than two months prior to the due dates of such rents. Borrower covenants that Borrower will not hereafter collect or accept payment of any rents of the Property more than two months prior to the due dates of such rents. Borrower further covenants that Borrower will execute and deliver to Lender such further assignments of rents and revenues of the Property as Lender may from time to time request.

Upon Borrower's breach of any covenant or agreement of Borrower in this Instrument, Lender may in person, by agent or by a court-appointed receiver, regardless of the adequacy of Lender's security, enter upon and take and maintain full control of the Property in order to perform all acts necessary and appropriate for the operation and maintenance thereof including, but not limited to, the execution, cancellation or modification of leases, the collection of all rents and revenues of the Property, the making of repairs to the Property and the execution or termination of contracts providing for the management or maintenance of the Property, all on such terms as are deemed best to protect the security of this Instrument. In the event Lender elects to seek the appointment of a receiver for the Property upon Borrower's breach of any covenant or agreement of Borrower in this Instrument, Borrower hereby expressly consents to the appointment of such receiver. Lender or the receiver shall be entitled to receive a reasonable fee for so managing the Property.

All rents and revenues collected subsequent to delivery of written notice by Lender to Borrower of the breach by Borrower of any covenant or agreement of Borrower in this Instrument shall be applied first to the costs, if any, of taking control of and managing the Property and collecting the rents, including, but not limited to, attorney's fees, receiver's fees, premiums on receiver's bonds, costs of repairs to the Property, premiums on insurance policies, taxes, assessments and other charges on the Property, and the costs of discharging any obligation or liability of Borrower as lessor or landlord of the Property and then to the sums secured by this Instrument. Lender or the receiver shall have access to the books and records used in the operation and maintenance of the Property and shall be liable to account only for those rents actually received. Lender shall not be liable to Borrower, anyone claiming under or through Borrower or anyone having an interest in the Property by reason of anything done or left undone by Lender under this paragraph 26.

If the rents of the Property are not sufficient to meet the costs, if any, of taking control of and managing the Property and collecting the rents, any funds expended by Lender for such purposes shall become indebtedness of Borrower to Lender secured by this Instrument pursuant to paragraph 8 hereof. Unless Lender and Borrower agree in writing to other terms of payment, such amounts shall be payable upon notice from Lender to Borrower requesting payment thereof and shall bear interest from the date of disbursement at the rate stated in the Note unless payment of interest at such rate would be contrary to applicable law, in which event such amounts shall bear interest at the highest rate which may be collected from Borrower under applicable law.

Any entering upon and taking and maintaining of control of the Property by Lender or the receiver and any application of rents as provided herein shall not cure or waive any default hereunder or invalidate any other right or remedy of Lender under applicable law or provided herein. This assignment of rents of the Property shall terminate at such time as this Instrument ceases to secure indebtedness held by Lender.

Non–Uniform Covenants. Borrower and Lender further covenant and agree as follows:

27. ACCELERATION; REMEDIES. Upon Borrower's breach of any covenant or agreement of Borrower in this Instrument, including, but not limited to, the covenants to pay when due any sums secured by this Instrument, Lender at Lender's option may declare all of the sums secured by this Instrument to be immediately due and payable without further demand and may invoke the power of sale and any other remedies permitted by applicable law or provided herein. Borrower acknowledges that the power of sale herein granted may be exercised by Lender without prior judicial hearing. Borrower has the right to bring an action to assert the non-existence of a breach or any other defense of Borrower to acceleration and sale. Lender shall be entitled to collect all costs and expenses incurred in pursuing such remedies, including, but not limited to, attorney's fees and costs of documentary evidence, abstracts and title reports.

If Lender invokes the power of sale, Lender or Trustee shall give notice of the time, place and terms of sale by posting written notice at least 21 days prior to the day of sale at the courthouse door in each of the counties in which the Property is situated. Lender shall mail a copy of the notice of sale to Borrower in the manner provided by applicable law. Trustee shall sell the Property according to the laws of Texas. Such sale shall be made at public vendue between the hours of 10 o'clock a.m. and 4 o'clock p.m. on the first Tuesday in any month. Borrower authorizes Trustee to sell the Property to the highest bidder for cash in one or more parcels and in such order as Trustee may determine. Lender or Lender's designee may purchase the Property at any sale.

Trustee shall deliver to the purchaser Trustee's deed conveying the Property so sold in fee simple with covenants of general warranty. Borrower covenants and agrees to defend generally the purchaser's title to the Property against all claims and demands. The recitals in Trustee's deed shall be prima facie evidence of the truth of the statements contained therein. Trustee shall apply the proceeds of the sale in the following order: (a) to all reasonable costs and expenses of the sale, including, but not limited to, reasonable Trustee's fees and attorney's fees and costs of title evidence; (b) to all sums secured by this Instrument in such order as Lender, in Lender's sole discretion, directs; and (c) the excess, if any, to the person or persons legally entitled thereto.

If the Property is sold pursuant to this paragraph 27, Borrower or any person holding possession of the Property through Borrower shall immediately surrender possession of the Property to the purchaser at such sale upon the purchaser's written demand. If possession is not surrendered upon the purchaser's written demand, Borrower or such person shall be a tenant at sufferance and may be removed by writ of possession or by an action for forcible entry and detainer.

28. RELEASE. Upon payment of all sums secured by this Instrument, Lender shall release this Instrument. Borrower shall pay Lender's reasonable costs incurred in releasing this Instrument.

29. SUBSTITUTE TRUSTEE. Lender at Lender's option, with or without cause, may from time to time remove Trustee and appoint a successor trustee to any Trustee appointed hereunder by an instrument recorded in the county in which this Instrument is recorded. Without conveyance of the Property, the successor trustee shall succeed to all the title, power and duties conferred upon the Trustee herein and by applicable law.

30. SUBROGATION. Any of the proceeds of the Note utilized to take up outstanding liens against all or any part of the Property have been advanced by Lender at Borrower's request and upon Borrower's representation that such amounts are due and are secured by valid liens against the Property. Lender shall be subrogated to any and all rights, superior titles, liens and equities owned or claimed by any owner or holder of any outstanding liens and debts, however remote, regardless of whether said liens or debts are acquired by Lender, by assignment or are released by the holder thereof upon payment.

31. PARTIAL INVALIDITY. In the event any portion of the sums intended to be secured by this Instrument cannot be lawfully secured hereby, payments in reduction of such sums shall be applied first to those portions not secured hereby.

32. VENDOR'S LIEN; RENEWAL AND EXTENSION. The Note secured hereby is [primarily secured by the Vendor's Lien retained in the Deed of even date herewith conveying the Property to Borrower, which Vendor's Lien has been assigned to Lender, this Instrument being additional security therefor.] * [in renewal and extension, but not in extinguishment, of that certain indebtedness described as follows:] *

33. FUTURE ADVANCES. Upon request of Borrower, Lender, at Lender's option so long as this Instrument secures indebtedness held by Lender, may make Future Advances to Borrower. Such Future Advances, with interest thereon, shall be secured by this Instrument when evidenced by promissory notes stating that said notes are secured hereby. At no time shall the principal amount of the indebtedness secured by this Instrument, not including sums advanced in accordance herewith to protect the security of this Instrument, exceed the original amount of the Note (US $_____) plus the additional sum of US $_____.

IN WITNESS WHEREOF, Borrower has executed this Instrument or has caused the same to be executed by its representatives thereunto duly authorized.

RIDER TO MULTIFAMILY INSTRUMENT

THIS RIDER TO MULTIFAMILY INSTRUMENT is made this _____ day of _____, 19__, and is incorporated into and shall be deemed to amend and supplement the Multifamily Mortgage, Deed of Trust or Deed to Secure Debt of the same date (the "Instrument") given by the undersigned (the "Borrower") to secure Borrower's Multifamily Note with Addendum to Multifamily Note of the same date (the "Note") to _____, and its successors, assigns and transferees (the "Lender"), covering the property described in the Instrument and located at:

[Property Address]

ADDITIONAL COVENANTS. In addition to the covenants and agreements made in the Instrument, Borrower and Lender further covenant and agree as follows:

A. Full Prepayment Privilege With Premium

The Note provides for a full prepayment privilege with premium as follows:

1. Yield Maintenance Period

During the first _____ *[insert "five," "seven," or "ten," as applicable]* years of the Note term beginning with the date of the Note (the "Yield Maintenance Period") and upon giving Lender 60 days prior written notice, Borrower may prepay the entire unpaid principal balance of the Note (no partial prepayments are permitted) on the Business Day before a scheduled monthly payment date by

---

* *Delete bracketed clauses as appropriate.*

paying, in addition to the entire unpaid principal balance, accrued interest and any other sums due Lender at the time of prepayment, a prepayment premium equal to:

(a) The product obtained by multiplying (1) the difference obtained by subtracting from the interest rate on the Note the yield rate on the _____% U.S. Treasury Security due _____ (the "Yield Rate"), as the Yield Rate is reported in the Wall Street Journal on the fifth Business Day preceding the date notice of prepayment is given to Lender, times (2) the present value factor calculated using the following formula

$$\frac{1 - (1 + r)^{-n}}{r}$$

[r = Yield Rate
n = the number of years, and any fraction thereof, remaining between the prepayment date and the expiration of the Yield Maintenance Period]

times (3) the entire unpaid principal balance of the Note at the time of prepayment, provided, however, that in no event shall the prepayment premium be less than 0; plus

(b) If the amount of the prepayment premium due under subparagraph (a) above is less than 1% of the entire unpaid principal balance of the Note, then an additional prepayment premium equal to 1% of the entire unpaid principal balance of the Note at the time of prepayment less any prepayment premium due under subparagraph (a) above.

In the event that no Yield Rate is published on the U.S. Treasury Security described above, then the nearest equivalent Treasury Security shall be selected at Lender's sole discretion. If the publication of such yield rates in the Wall Street Journal is discontinued, Lender shall select a security with a comparable rate and term to the U.S. Treasury Security described in subparagraph (a) above.

2. Post-Yield Maintenance Period

After the expiration of the Yield Maintenance Period and upon giving Lender 60 days prior written notice, Borrower may prepay the entire unpaid principal balance of the Note (no partial prepayments are permitted) on the Business Day before a scheduled monthly payment date by paying, in addition to the entire unpaid principal balance, accrued interest and any other sums due Lender at the time of prepayment, a prepayment premium equal to 1% of the unpaid principal balance of the Note.

3. Premium Due Whether Voluntary or Involuntary Prepayment

Borrower shall pay the prepayment premium due under this paragraph A whether the prepayment is voluntary or involuntary (in connection with Lender's acceleration of the unpaid principal balance of the Note) or the Instrument is satisfied or released by foreclosure (whether by power of sale or judicial proceeding), deed in lieu of foreclosure or by any other means. Borrower shall not pay any prepayment premium with respect to any prepayment occurring as a result of the application of insurance proceeds or condemnation awards under the Instrument.

4. Notice; Business Day

Any notice to Lender provided for in this Addendum To Multifamily Note shall be given in the manner provided in the Instrument. The term "Business Day" for purposes of this paragraph A means any day other than a Saturday or Sunday on which Lender is open for business.

B. Borrower's Exculpation

The Note also provides for Borrower's exculpation as follows:

Subject to the provisions of this paragraph B, and notwithstanding any other provision in the Note, the personal liability of Borrower, and of any general partner of Borrower, to pay the principal of and interest on the debt evidenced by the Note and any other agreement evidencing Borrower's obligations under the Note shall be limited to (1) the real and personal property described as the Property in the Instrument (the "Property"), and (2) the rents, profits, issues, products and income of the Property, including any received or collected by or on behalf of Borrower after an event of default, except to the extent that Borrower did not have the legal right, because of a bankruptcy, receivership or similar judicial proceeding, to direct the disbursement of such sums.

Except as provided in this paragraph B, Lender shall not seek (a) any judgment for a deficiency against Borrower, any general partner of Borrower, or Borrower's heirs, legal representatives, successors or assigns, in any action to enforce any right or remedy under the Instrument, or (b) any judgment on the Note except as may be necessary in any action brought under the Instrument to enforce the lien against the Property.

Borrower, and any general partner of Borrower, shall be personally liable in the amount of any loss, damage or cost resulting from (A) fraud or intentional misrepresentation by Borrower in connection with obtaining the loan evidenced by the Note, (B) insurance proceeds, condemnation awards, or other sums or payments attributable to the Property not applied in accordance with the provisions of the Instrument, except to the extent that Borrower did not have the legal right, because of a bankruptcy, receivership, or similar judicial proceeding, to direct disbursement of such sums or payments, (C) all rents, profits, issues, products and income of the Property received following any event of default under the Note or the Instrument and not applied to payment of principal and interest due under the Note (including any received or collected by or on behalf of Borrower after an event of default, except to the extent that Borrower did not have the legal right, because of a bankruptcy, receivership or similar judicial proceeding, to direct the disbursement of such sums), and payments of utilities, taxes and assessments insurance, and ground rents, if any, on the Property, as they become due or payable, or (D) Borrower's failure to pay transfer fees and charges due Lender under the Note or the Instrument in connection with any transfer of all or any part of the Property, or any interest therein, from Borrower to Borrower's transferee, or transfer of beneficial interest in Borrower (if Borrower is not a natural person or persons but is a corporation, partnership, trust or other legal entity).

No provision of this paragraph B shall (i) affect any guaranty or similar agreement executed in connection with the debt evidenced by the Note, (ii) release or reduce the debt evidenced by the Note, or (iii) impair the lien of the Instrument.

C. Fund for Replacements

In addition to Borrower's covenants and agreements under Uniform Covenant 2 ("Funds for Taxes, Insurance and Other Charges"), Borrower shall pay to Lender each month on the date monthly installments of principal and interest are payable under the Note, until the Note is paid in full, the amount of U.S. $_____ to maintain a fund for replacements with respect to the Property. This fund for replacements shall be held and, upon Borrower's breach of any covenant or agreement of Borrower in the Instrument, applied in the manner required or permitted for Funds held by Lender under Uniform Covenant 2. No disbursement from the fund for replacements shall be made without Lender's prior written consent, provided that Lender shall promptly refund to Borrower any sums held by Lender under this paragraph C upon Borrower's payment in full of all sums secured by the Instrument.

D. Environmental Hazards

In addition to Borrower's covenants and agreements under Uniform Covenant 6 of the Instrument ("Preservation and Maintenance of Property; Leaseholds"), Borrower further covenants and agrees that Borrower shall not (a) cause or permit the presence, use, generation, manufacture, production, processing, installation, release, discharge, storage (including above- and under-ground storage tanks for petroleum or petroleum products, but excluding small containers of gasoline used for maintenance equipment or similar purposes), treatment, handling, or disposal of any Hazardous Materials on, under, in or about the Property, or in any way affecting the Property or which may form the basis for any present or future claim, demand or action seeking cleanup of the Property, or the transportation of any Hazardous Materials to or from the Property, or (b) cause or exacerbate any occurrence or condition on the Property that is or may be in violation of Hazardous Materials Law. Borrower shall take all appropriate steps to secure compliance by all tenants and subtenants on the Property with Borrower's covenants and agreements in this Paragraph D.

Borrower further agrees at all times to comply fully and in a timely manner with, and to cause all employees, agents, contractors, and subcontractors of Borrower and any other persons occupying or present on the Property to so comply with, (1) any program of operations and maintenance (O & M) relating to the Property that is required by Lender with respect to one or more Hazardous Materials, and (2) all applicable federal, state, and local laws, regulations, guidelines, codes, and other legal requirements relating to the generation, use, handling, storage, treatment, transport, and disposal of any Hazardous Materials now or hereafter located or present on or under the Property.

Borrower shall promptly notify Lender in writing of: (i) any enforcement, cleanup, removal or other governmental or regulatory action, investigation, or any other proceeding instituted, completed or threatened in connection with any Hazardous Materials; (ii) any suit, cause of action, or any other claim made or threatened by any third party against Borrower or the Property relating to damage, contribution, cost recovery, compensation, loss or injury resulting from any Hazardous Materials; and (iii) Borrower's discovery of any occurrence or condition on any real property adjoining or in the vicinity of the Property that could cause all or any portion of the Property to be subject to any restrictions on the ownership, occupancy, transferability or use of the Property under Hazardous Materials Law. The provisions of the preceding sentence shall be in addition to any and all other obligations and liabilities that Borrower may have to Lender under applicable law.

The term "Hazardous Materials," for purposes of this paragraph D, includes petroleum and petroleum products (excluding a small quantity of gasoline used in maintenance equipment on the Property), flammable explosives, radioactive materials (excluding radioactive materials in smoke detectors), polychlorinated biphenyls, asbestos in any form that is or could become friable, hazardous waste, toxic or hazardous substances or other related materials whether in the form of a chemical, element, compound, solution, mixture or otherwise including, but not limited to, those materials defined as "hazardous substances," "extremely hazardous substances," "hazardous chemicals," "hazardous materials," "toxic substances," "toxic chemicals," "air pollutants," "toxic pollutants," "hazardous wastes," "extremely hazardous waste," or "restricted hazardous waste" by Hazardous Materials Law.

E. Hazard Insurance; Restoration of Property

Uniform Covenant 5 of the Instrument ("Hazard Insurance") is amended to add the following provisions at the end thereof:

Lender shall not exercise Lender's option to apply insurance proceeds to the payment of the sums secured by this Instrument if all the following conditions are met: (i) Borrower is not in breach or default of any covenant or agreement of this Instrument or the Note; (ii) Lender determines that there will be sufficient funds to restore and repair the property to a condition approved by Lender; (iii) Lender agrees in writing that the rental income of the Property, after restoration and repair of the Property to a condition approved by Lender, will be sufficient to meet all operating costs and other expenses, payments for reserves and loan repayment obligations relating to the Property; and (iv) Lender determines that restoration and repair of the Property to a condition approved by Lender will be completed within one year of the date of the loss or casualty to the Property.

F. Transfers of the Property or Beneficial Interests in Borrower; Assumption

Uniform Covenant 19 of the Instrument ("Transfers of the Property or Beneficial Interests in Borrower; Assumption") is amended to read as follows:

On sale or transfer of either (i) all or any part of the Property, or any interest therein (other than obsolete or worn personal property replaced by adequate substitutes of equal or greater value than the replaced items when new), or (ii) beneficial interests in Borrower (if Borrower is not a natural person or persons but is a corporation, partnership, trust or other legal entity), Lender may, at Lender's option, declare all sums secured by this Instrument immediately due and payable, and Lender may invoke any remedies permitted by paragraph 27 of this Instrument. Notwithstanding the foregoing, Lender shall not be entitled to declare the above-referenced sums due and payable, pursue Lender's remedies under paragraph 27 or, except as otherwise required by subparagraph (b) below, require the payment of a transfer fee in the case of:

   (a) transfers by devise or descent or by operation of law upon the death of a joint tenant or partner;

   (b) sales or transfers when the transferee's creditworthiness and management ability are satisfactory to Lender in accordance with standards customarily applied by Lender for approval of borrowers for similar properties under multifamily mortgages and when the transferee has executed, prior to the sale or transfer, a written assumption agreement containing such terms as Lender may require, including provision for processing and administration fees, and a transfer fee equal to one percent (1.0%) of the sums secured by this Instrument, provided, that such assumption agreement shall not increase the rate of interest payable under the Note or otherwise modify the payment terms thereof;

   (c) the grant of a leasehold interest in a part of the Property of three years or less (or such longer lease terms as Lender may permit by prior written approval) not containing an option to purchase (except any interest in the ground lease, if this Instrument is on a leasehold); or

   (d) sales or transfers of beneficial interests in Borrower provided that such sales or transfers, together with any prior sales or transfers of beneficial interests in Borrower, but excluding sales or transfers under subparagraphs (a) and (b) above, do not result in more than 49% of the beneficial interests in Borrower having been sold or transferred.

BY SIGNING BELOW, Borrower accepts and agrees to the agreements and covenants contained in this Rider to Multifamily Instrument.

§ 14.17 Promissory Note, Combination Deed of Trust, Security Agreement and Fixture Filing, Assignment of Leases and Unsecured Indemnity Agreement—Multifamily Residential [1]

This section contains four forms: (1) Promissory Note; (2) Deed of Trust, Security Agreement and Fixture Filing; (3) Assignment of Leases and (4) Unsecured Indemnity Agreement. Together they comprise an essential package of forms for long term financing of an apartment project. They are sophisticated and well-drafted. Note that while they were intended for use in the state of Washington, they should, with careful attention to local law, prove to be extremely valuable drafting guides in almost any jurisdiction.

The Promissory Note contains several provisions that deserve comment. Section 8 represents a highly sophisticated prepayment provision. It starts out by stating the common law rule that obligation may not be prepaid. It then spells out in detail the circumstances under which prepayment will be permitted. Note that no partial prepayments are authorized. With respect to permitted prepayments, it provides for a fee that is designed to compensate the lender only for any actual loss suffered as a result of a prepayment. In addition, Section 9 is designed to insure that the fee is also collectible when prepayment is caused by events other than a voluntary prepayment by mortgagor. These include acceleration incident to default, foreclosure, casualty loss, condemnation and other similar involuntary causes. For further extensive analysis of the law governing prepayment, see §§ 6.1–6.5 supra.

Note that Section 10 of the Promissory Note relieves the borrower of personal liability on the mortgage obligation and, consequently, makes this a "non-recourse" loan transaction. Thus, this language must be omitted if the parties intend that the borrower be personally liable. Note, in addition, that even though this section exculpates the borrower from personal liability on the mortgage obligation, it also makes it clear he or she will be personally liable for a variety of other violations of the loan documents such as fraud, waste and retention of rents after default.

The second document in this package is a combination Deed of Trust, Security Agreement and Fixture Filing. Section 1.05, the insurance provision, is especially noteworthy. It requires that borrower maintain for the lender's benefit virtually all types of insurance that the market offers. More important, in this era of environmental liability, is the language of subsection 8 requiring "environmental impairment liability coverage, nuclear reaction or radioactive contamination coverage and/or earthquake coverage, which hazards or risks at

§ 14.17
1. Form provided by Preston, Thorgrimson, Shidler, Gates & Ellis, Seattle, Washington.

the time are commonly insured against, and provided such insurance is generally available." Section 1.07 is especially clear and complete in delineating the circumstances under which insurance proceeds arising from a casualty loss will be used either to prepay the mortgage obligation or for restoration of the mortgaged premises. Further requirements concerning restoration are spelled out in Exhibit D, which is an attachment to the combination Deed of Trust, Security Agreement and Fixture Filing.

Interestingly, Section 1.09 contains a flat prohibition on conversion of the apartment complex to a condominium or cooperative. Such a conversion could seriously jeopardize the market value of the property and its cash flow and therefore seriously endanger the lender's security. This section, therefore, is highly desirable from the lender's perspective.

Section 1.10 contains an assignment of rents and profits. However, a more detailed assignment is contained in a separate document entitled "Assignment of Leases" which is considered later in this section. Section 1.10(b) requires the borrower to adhere to rigorous guidelines in leasing the apartments. These guidelines are contained in Exhibit A and specify a maximum lease term of one year and approval by lender of all lease forms. They prohibit the granting of any rights of first refusal or options to purchase any part of the mortgaged premises. They also mandate minimum rents to be charged for the apartments.

Section 1.16 contains a covenant against further encumbrances. While the lender is also protected against such subsequent liens under the due-on-sale provision (see Section 3.03), given the importance of this prohibition, it is a desirable provision.

Section 1.17 is the Deed of Trust counterpart of Section 10 of the Promissory Note. It makes the mortgage obligation "non-recourse" and should be omitted if the parties intend that the borrower be personally liable.

Section 2.02(d) authorizes the appointment of a receiver upon default "without the necessity of proving either the inadequacy of the security or the insolvency of Grantor." For a consideration of the effectiveness of such language, see § 4.35, supra.

Section 2.06 gives the lender, in the event of foreclosure, "unrestricted discretion" to determine whether the property is sold by parcel or in bulk and the order of sale. Thus, the borrower, his successors and junior lienholders waive their equitable marshalling rights. See §§ 10.9–10.15, supra.

Section 3.01 makes it clear that, to the extent that the borrower's property constitutes personalty, the Deed of Trust also operates as a UCC security agreement and, when recorded, as a fixture filing with respect to goods which are or are to become fixtures related to the real estate. This type of provision is commonly used in real estate financing transactions. See e.g., § 15.7, infra.

Section 3.03 is a due-on-sale provision. Note that in addition to the usual language in such a provision, the clause spells out carefully that it is triggered by any changes in beneficial ownership of a borrower that is a partnership or corporation. Permission is granted, however, for certain intra-family, death and estate planning transfers. For further consideration of due-on-sale clauses, see §§ 5.21–5.26, supra.

Section 3.04 requires the borrower to provide an "estoppel statement" to the lender upon its request. Such a statement's purpose is to set forth the balance owing on the loan and its status in other respects, and to do so in a manner which will bind the mortgagor. Such a statement is often used when a mortgage is sold on the secondary market to another lender or investor, and serves to assure the purchaser that the mortgage is indeed in the condition represented by the transferor.

Section 3.08 is a crucial provision in this era of environmental contamination. Not only does the borrower covenant to refrain from creating environmental hazards and to comply with federal, state and local environmental statutes and regulations, it requires the borrower to perform any remedial work that may be necessary in the future. Moreover, if the borrower fails to carry out such remedial work, the lender is authorized, but not required, to do so. Finally, the borrower becomes personally liable to the lender for any expenditures by the lender for such purposes. This is true even though the borrower has no personal liability on the mortgage obligation itself. More important protections for the lender against environmental liability are contained in a document entitled "Unsecured Indemnity Agreement" which is considered later in this section.

The third document in this package is an Assignment of Leases. It is designed to create an "absolute assignment" that is perfected upon recording. A major purpose is to enhance the lender's claim to the rents in the event borrower files a bankruptcy petition. Equally important it contains numerous covenants designed to protect the lender's security interest in leases of apartments. For further consideration of rent assignments, see §§ 4.35, 8.17, supra.

The fourth and final document in this section is the "Unsecured Indemnity Agreement." Because there is potential lender liability under CERCLA and other state and local law for environmental contamination of the mortgaged premises, a lender should be especially cautious in this regard. This agreement requires the borrower to indemnify the lender for any environmental costs that may be imposed on the lender or the property. It spells out, in substantial detail, the procedure to be followed in enforcing the indemnity. More important, the agreement "is not intended to be, nor shall it be, secured by the Deed of Trust and it is not intended to secure payment of the Note but rather is an independent obligation" of the borrower. This language is included to make it clear that even though the mortgage obligation itself may be "nonrecourse," the borrower is personally liable to the lender for any expenditures the lender incurs to remedy any environmental violations on the mortgaged real estate. For further consideration of lender liability under CERCLA and related legislation, see §§ 4.47–4.51, supra.

PROMISSORY NOTE

$_____ \hfill _____, 199__

_____, Washington

FOR VALUE RECEIVED, _____, a _____ ("Maker"), having its principal place of business at _____, promises to pay to the order of _____ ("Holder"), a _____, at its principal place of business at _____, or such other place as Holder may from time to time designate, the principal sum of _____ DOLLARS ($_____) with interest, as specified below, in lawful money of the United States of America, which shall be legal tender in payment of all debts and dues, public and private, at the time of payment.

1. Payment of Principal and Interest. Principal and interest under this promissory note (this "Note") shall be payable as follows:

(a) Interest on the principal sum evidenced by this Note, or so much thereof as has been disbursed, shall accrue from the date funds are first disbursed to Maker (the "Advance Date") at the rate of _____ percent (__%) per annum (the "Interest Rate") and shall be paid on the _____ (__) day of the calendar month next succeeding the Advance Date.

(b) Commencing on the _____ (__) day of the second (2nd) calendar month succeeding the Advance Date and on the _____ (__) day of each and every calendar month thereafter, to and including, the _____ (__) day of the _____ (__) calendar month succeeding the Advance Date, there shall be due and payable equal monthly installments of principal and interest at the Interest Rate, each in the amount of _____ Dollars ($_____), based upon an amortization period of _____ (__) months; Maker hereby acknowledges and agrees that a substantial portion of the original principal sum evidenced by this Note shall be outstanding and due on the first day of _____, 19__ (the "Maturity Date"); and

(c) On the Maturity Date, a final payment in the aggregate amount of the unpaid principal sum evidenced by this Note, all accrued and unpaid interest thereon, and all other sums evidenced by this Note or secured by the Deed of Trust (as hereinafter defined) and/or any other instrument collateral, incidental or related thereto (this Note, the Deed of Trust and any and all other documents evidencing, securing or relating to the indebtedness evidenced by this Note, and all renewals, modifications, consolidations and extensions of such documents being herein collectively referred to as the "Loan Documents"), shall become immediately due and payable in full.

Interest shall be calculated on the basis of a thirty (30) day month, and three hundred sixty (360) day year.

2. Application of Payments. All payments made hereunder shall, at the sole option of Holder, be applied to the payment of any prepayment fees, late charges and other sums due from Maker to Holder under the Loan Documents, any escrow deposits required under the Loan Documents, interest then due at the Interest Rate or at the Default Rate (as hereinafter defined), as applicable, on the unpaid principal of this Note, and the balance of said payments shall be applied in reduction of the unpaid principal sum of this Note.

3. Security. This Note is secured by that certain Deed of Trust, Security Agreement and Fixture Filing of even date herewith (the "Deed of Trust"), granted by Maker to Trustee for the benefit of Holder. Each capitalized term used herein, unless otherwise defined herein, shall have the same meaning as set forth in the

Deed of Trust. The obligations, covenants and agreements of the Deed of Trust are hereby made a part of this Note to the same extent and with the same effect as if they were fully set forth herein, and Maker does hereby agree to perform and keep each and every obligation, covenant and agreement set forth in this Note and in the other Loan Documents. This Note shall evidence, and the Deed of Trust shall secure, the indebtedness described herein, any future loans or advances that may be made to or on behalf of Maker by Holder at any time or times hereafter or under the Deed of Trust, and any other amounts required to be paid by Maker under the Loan Documents, and any such loans, advances or amounts shall be added to the indebtedness evidenced by this Note, and shall bear interest at the Interest Rate unless a greater rate is expressly provided for in this Note or the other Loan Documents.

4. Late Charge. In the event that any installment of interest, principal, principal and interest or required escrow deposits is not paid on the date due, a "late charge" of _____ (__¢) for each dollar ($1.00), or part thereof, so overdue may be charged to Maker by Holder for the purpose of defraying the expenses incident to handling such delinquent payments. This charge shall be in addition to, and not in lieu of, any other remedy Holder may have and is in addition to Holder's right to collect reasonable fees and charges of any agents or attorneys which Holder employs in connection with any Event of Default. Such late charges if not previously paid shall become part of the indebtedness evidenced hereby, and shall, at the option of Holder, be added to any succeeding monthly payment due under the Loan Documents. Failure to pay such late charges with such succeeding monthly payment shall constitute an Event of Default and such late charges shall bear interest at the Default Rate from the date due.

5. Acceleration Upon Default. It is hereby expressly agreed that upon the failure of Maker to pay any sum herein specified when due, or upon the occurrence of any other Event of Default, the unpaid principal sum evidenced by this Note, all accrued and unpaid interest thereon, and all other sums evidenced and/or secured by the Loan Documents shall, at the option of Holder, which may be exercised after the expiration of the applicable time periods set forth in Section 2.01 of the Deed of Trust, become immediately due and payable, and payment of the unpaid principal sum evidenced by this Note, all accrued and unpaid interest thereon, and all other sums evidenced or secured by the Loan Documents, may be enforced and recovered at once.

6. Interest Upon Default. Upon the occurrence of an Event of Default (including, without limitation, the failure of Maker to pay any sum herein specified when due), the unpaid principal sum evidenced by this Note, all accrued and unpaid interest thereon, and all other sums evidenced and/or secured by the Loan Documents shall bear interest at a rate per annum (the "Default Rate") equal to the lesser of: (i) the highest rate of interest permitted to be contracted for under the laws of the State, or (ii) _____ percent (__%) per annum above the Interest Rate. The Default Rate shall be in lieu of any other interest rate otherwise applicable and shall commence, without notice, immediately upon and from the occurrence of such Event of Default and shall continue until all defaults are cured and all sums then due and payable under the Loan Documents are paid in full.

7. Limitation on Interest. All agreements made by Maker relating directly or indirectly to the indebtedness evidenced by this Note and the other Loan Documents are expressly limited so that in no event or contingency whatsoever shall the amount of interest received, charged or contracted for by Holder exceed the highest lawful amount of interest permissible under the laws of the State. If, under any circumstances whatsoever, performance of any provision of this Note or the other Loan Documents, at the time performance of such provision shall be due, shall result in the highest lawful rate of interest permissible under the laws of the State being exceeded, then *ipso facto,* the amount of interest received, charged or contracted for by Holder shall be reduced to the highest lawful amount of interest permissible under the laws of the State, and if for any reason whatsoever, Holder shall ever receive, charge or contract for, as interest, an amount which would be deemed unlawful, such amount of interest deemed unlawful shall be refunded to Maker (if theretofore paid) or applied to the payment of the last maturing installment or installments of principal to be paid on this Note (whether or not due and payable) and not to the payment of interest. Without limitation of the foregoing, any amounts contracted for, charged or received under the Loan Documents relating directly or indirectly to the indebtedness evidenced by this Note, included for the purpose of determining whether the interest rate would exceed the highest lawful rate, shall be calculated, to the extent permitted by the laws of the State, by amortizing, prorating, allocating and spreading such interest over the period of the full stated term of this Note.

8. No Prepayment Privilege. The principal sum evidenced by this Note may not be prepaid, in whole or in part, at any time during the term hereof except as expressly provided in this Section 8. Maker agrees that Holder shall have no obligation to accept any prepayment of the principal sum evidenced by this Note except as expressly stated in this Section 8.

(a) *Prepayment Without Fee.* Maker may prepay the entire principal sum evidenced by this Note without a prepayment fee at any time during the _____ (__) day period immediately preceding the Maturity Date, when the indebtedness evidenced hereby may be prepaid in whole but not in part; provided that Maker gives Holder not less than _____ (__) days' prior written notice of prepayment and pays the then outstanding principal balance due on this Note together with the accrued interest thereon, and any and all other sums which may be due and payable under any of the Loan Documents.

(b) *Prepayment With Fee.* Commencing with the first month of the _____ (__) Loan Year (i.e. the first day of the _____ (__) month succeeding the Advance Date), the indebtedness evidenced hereby may be prepaid in whole but not in part on the first day of any month upon _____ (__) days' prior written notice of the intended prepayment date to the Holder and payment of the Prepayment Fee (as hereinafter defined). The "Prepayment Fee" shall be (i) the present value of all remaining payments of principal and interest, discounted at the Treasury Rate (as hereinafter defined), less (ii) the amount of principal being prepaid, but shall not be less than zero (0). The "Treasury Rate" shall be the yield on securities issued by the United States Treasury having a maturity equal to the remaining stated term of this Note, as quoted in Federal Reserve Statistical Release H.15 (519) under the heading "U.S. Government Securities–Treasury Constant Maturities" for the date most nearly two (2) weeks before the prepayment date (or a comparable rate if this is no longer published), adjusted to reflect a monthly payment interval. If the above rate is not available for a term equal to the remaining stated term of this Note as of the intended prepayment date, the Treasury Rate shall be determined by interpolating between the yields on securities of the next longer and next shorter maturity.

At the Holder's option, if Maker gives notice of intention to prepay, the entire balance of unpaid principal, accrued interest and any additional sums due under the Loan Documents shall become due and payable on the date specified in the notice of prepayment.

9. Default Prepayment Fee. Maker agrees that any tender of payment by Maker or any other party of the principal sum evidenced by this Note, other than as expressly set forth in Section 8 of this Note, shall constitute a prohibited prepayment hereunder. Maker further agrees that should: (i) any default be made in the payment of any amount due under this Note, or any other Event of Default have occurred and (ii) the maturity hereof be accelerated, then a tender of payment by Maker, or by any entity related to, or affiliated with, Maker or by anyone on behalf of Maker, of the amount necessary to satisfy all sums due under the Loan Documents (including, without limitation, any sums due on any judgment rendered in any foreclosure action, or any amounts necessary to redeem the Property) made at any time prior to, during, or after, a judicial foreclosure or a sale pursuant to the exercise of a power of sale of the Property, shall constitute an evasion of the payment terms hereof and shall be deemed to be a prohibited prepayment hereunder. Maker acknowledges that Holder has relied upon the anticipated investment return under this Note in entering into transactions with, and in making commitments to, third parties; therefore, the tender of any prohibited prepayment, shall, to the extent permitted by law, include the "Default Prepayment Fee," which term shall mean an amount equal to: (x) the present value of all remaining payments of principal and interest, discounted at the Treasury Rate (as hereinabove defined), less (y) the amount of principal being prepaid, but shall not be less than zero (0). If the above rate is not available for a term equal to the remaining stated term of this Note as of the date of such prohibited prepayment, the Treasury Rate shall be determined by interpolating between the yield on securities of the next longer and next shorter maturity. Maker agrees that the Default Prepayment Fee represents the reasonable estimate of Holder and Maker of a fair average compensation for the loss that may be sustained by Holder due to the prohibited prepayment of the indebtedness evidenced by this Note. Such Default Prepayment Fee shall be paid without prejudice to the right of Holder to collect any other amounts provided to be paid under the Loan Documents. Nothing herein contained shall constitute an agreement on the part of Holder to accept any prepayment, other than as expressly provided in Section 8 of this Note.

10. Liability of Maker. Notwithstanding anything to the contrary contained in this Note or in any of the other Loan Documents, but without in any manner releasing, impairing or otherwise affecting this Note or any of the other Loan Documents, or the validity hereof or thereof, or the lien of the Deed of Trust, upon the occurrence of an Event of Default, except as expressly set forth in this Section 10, the liability of Maker and/or the general partners of Maker, if any, to Holder for any and all such Events of Default shall be limited to and satisfied out of the Property. Notwithstanding any of the foregoing, nothing contained in this Section 10 shall be deemed to prejudice the rights of Holder to (i) proceed against any entity or person whatsoever, including Maker and the general partners of Maker, if any, with respect to the enforcement of any leases, guarantees, bonds, policies of insurance or other agreements for compliance with any of the terms, covenants and conditions of the Loan Documents; or (ii) recover damages against Maker and the general partners of Maker, if any, for fraud, breach of trust, breach of warranty, failure to maintain insurance, misrepresentation or waste; or (iii) recover any Condemnation Proceeds or Insurance Proceeds or other similar funds or payments attributable to the Property, which under the terms of the Loan Documents should have been paid to Holder; or (iv) recover any tenant security deposits, prepaid rents or other similar sums paid to or held by Maker or any other entity or person in connection with the Property; or (v) recover the Rents and Profits accruing from and after the occurrence of an Event of Default, which have not been applied to pay any portion of the indebtedness evidenced by this Note, operating and maintenance expenses of the Property, Premiums, Impositions, deposits into a reserve for replacement or other sums required by the Loan Documents; or (vi) recover damages against Maker and the general partners of Maker, if any, arising from, or in connection with, the enforcement of that certain Unsecured Indemnity Agreement of even date herewith executed by Maker and its general partners, if any, in favor of Holder; or (vii) except to the extent Holder actually receives proceeds therefor under its lender's title policy, recover from Maker or the general partners of Maker, if any, the entire indebtedness evidenced or secured by the Loan Documents, in the event of any judicial determination that the lien of the Deed of Trust is invalid; or (viii) recover from Maker and/or the general partners of Maker, if any, all amounts due and payable pursuant to Sections 3.06 and 3.10 of the Deed of Trust. Maker and the general partners of Maker, if any, shall be personally liable for Maker's obligations arising in connection with the matters set forth in the foregoing clauses (i) to (viii) inclusive.

11. Waiver by Maker. Maker and all endorsers, guarantors and sureties of this Note, and each of them, hereby waive diligence, demand, presentment for payment, notice of non-payment, protest, notice of dishonor and notice of protest, notice of intent to accelerate and notice of acceleration and specifically consent to, and waive notice of, any renewals or extensions of this Note, whether made to or in favor of Maker or any other person or persons, and hereby waive any defense by reason of extension of time for payment or other indulgence granted by Holder.

12. Exercise of Rights. No single or partial exercise by Holder, or delay or omission in the exercise by Holder, of any right or remedy under the Loan Documents shall preclude, waive or limit any other or further exercise thereof or the exercise of any other right or remedy. Holder shall at all times have the right to proceed against any portion of, or interest in, the Property in such manner as Holder may deem fit, without waiving any other rights or remedies with respect to the Property, any portion thereof, or interest therein. The release of any party under this Note shall not operate to release any other party liable hereunder or under the other Loan Documents.

13. Fees and Expenses. If this Note is placed in the hands of an attorney at law for collection by reason of default on the part of Maker, Maker hereby agrees to pay to Holder, in addition to the sums stated above, the costs and expenses of collection, including, without limitation, a reasonable sum as an attorney's fee.

14. No Modifications. This Note may not be changed, amended or modified, except in a writing expressly intended for such purpose and executed by Maker and Holder.

15. Governing Law. This Note is to be construed and enforced in all respects in accordance with the laws of the State of Washington. At the option of the Holder, the venue of any action may be laid in _____ County, Washington, or in any county where property subject to the Deed of Trust securing the indebtedness evidenced hereby is situated.

16. Construction. The words "Maker" and "Holder" shall be deemed to include the respective heirs, personal representatives, successors and assigns of each, and shall denote the singular and/or plural, and the masculine and/or feminine, and natural and/or artificial persons, whenever and wherever the context so requires. If more than one party is named as Maker, the obligation hereunder of each such party shall be deemed joint and several. The captions herein are inserted only for convenience of reference and in no way define, limit or describe the scope or intent of this Note or any particular paragraph or section hereof, or the proper construction hereof.

17. Notices. All notices, demands, requests and consents permitted or required under this Note shall be given in the manner prescribed in the Deed of Trust.

18. Time of the Essence. Time shall be of the essence in this Note with respect to all of Maker's obligations hereunder.

19. Severability. If any provision hereof should be held unenforceable or void, then such provision shall be deemed separable from the remaining provisions and shall in no way affect the validity of this Note, except that if such provision relates to the payment of any monetary sum, then, Holder may, at its option declare the indebtedness evidenced hereby immediately due and payable.

IN WITNESS WHEREOF, Maker has executed or caused this Note to be executed by its duly authorized representative(s) the day and year first above written.

DEED OF TRUST, SECURITY AGREEMENT
AND
FIXTURE FILING

This DEED OF TRUST, SECURITY AGREEMENT AND FIXTURE FILING (this "Deed of Trust") is made as of the _____ day of _____, 19__, by _____, a

§ 14.17 RESIDENTIAL FINANCING FORMS

_____, having its principal place of business at _____ as Grantor and Debtor ("Grantor") in favor of _____ ("Trustee"), whose address is _____ for the benefit of _____, a _____, having its principal place of business at _____ as Beneficiary and Secured Party ("Beneficiary").

WITNESSETH:

WHEREAS, this Deed of Trust secures: (1) the full and punctual payment of the indebtedness evidenced by that certain promissory note (the "Note") of even date with this Deed of Trust, the final payment of which is due no later than the _____ day of _____, 19__ (the "Maturity Date"), made by Grantor to the order of Beneficiary in the principal face amount of _____ DOLLARS ($_____), with interest thereon at the rates therein provided, together with any and all renewals, modifications, consolidations and extensions of the indebtedness evidenced by the Note, any and all additional advances made by Beneficiary to protect or preserve the Property (as hereinafter defined), any and all future advances as may be made by Beneficiary and any other amounts required to be paid by Grantor under any of the Loan Documents (as hereinafter defined), such indebtedness, advances and amounts being hereinafter collectively referred to as the "Secured Indebtedness," and (2) the full performance by Grantor of all of the provisions, agreements, covenants and obligations contained herein or in any of the other Loan Documents. The Note, this Deed of Trust, and any and all other documents evidencing, securing or relating to the indebtedness secured by this Deed of Trust and all renewals, modifications, consolidations, and extensions of such documents are herein collectively referred to as the "Loan Documents."

NOW, THEREFORE, IN CONSIDERATION of the sum of ONE HUNDRED DOLLARS ($100.00), in hand paid, and other good and valuable consideration, the receipt and sufficiency of which are hereby acknowledged, and in order to secure the Secured Indebtedness and other obligations of Grantor set forth in this Deed of Trust and the other Loan Documents, Grantor does hereby irrevocably bargain, sell, transfer, grant, convey, assign and warrant to:

A. Trustee, its successors and assigns, in trust, with power of sale and right of entry and possession, all of Grantor's present and future estate, right, title and interest in and to that certain real property located in the County and State (as defined in *Exhibit "A"* attached hereto and made a part hereof) and as more particularly described in *Exhibit "B"* attached hereto and made a part hereof, together with all right, title, interest and estate of Grantor, in and to all easements, rights-of-way, gaps, strips and gores of land, streets, ways, alleys, sewers, sewer rights, waters, water courses, water rights, privileges, licenses, tenements, hereditaments and appurtenances whatsoever, in any way appertaining to said real property, whether now owned or hereafter acquired by Grantor, and the reversion(s), remainder(s), possession(s), claims and demands of Grantor in and to the same, and the rights of Grantor in and to the benefits of any conditions, covenants and restrictions now or hereafter affecting said real property (collectively, the "Land"), together with all estate, right, title and interest that Grantor now has or may hereafter acquire in:

1. All things now or hereafter affixed to the Land, including all buildings, structures and improvements of every kind and description now or hereafter erected or placed thereon, any fixtures and any and all machinery, motors, elevators, boilers, equipment (including, without limitation, all equipment for the generation or distribution of air, water, heat, electricity, light, fuel or refrigeration or for ventilating or air conditioning purposes or for sanitary or drainage purposes or for the removal of dust, refuse or garbage), partitions, appliances, furniture, furnishings, building service equipment, building materials, supplies, ranges, refrigerators, cabinets, laundry equipment, hotel, kitchen and restaurant equipment, computers and software, radios, televisions, awnings, window shades, venetian blinds, drapes and drapery rods and brackets, screens, carpeting and other floor coverings, lobby furnishings, games and recreational

and swimming pool equipment, incinerators and other property of every kind and description now or hereafter placed, attached, fixed or installed in such buildings, structures, or improvements and all replacements, repairs, additions, accessions or substitutions or proceeds thereto or therefor; all of such things whether now or hereafter placed thereon being hereby declared to be real property and hereinafter collectively referred to as the "Improvements";

2. All income, rents, royalties, revenue, issues, profits, proceeds and other benefits from any and all of the Land and/or Improvements, subject, however, to the right, power and authority hereinafter conferred upon Beneficiary or reserved to Grantor to collect and apply such income, rents, royalties, revenue, issues, profits, proceeds and other benefits;

3. All deposits made with respect to the Land and/or Improvements, including, but not limited to, any security given to utility companies by Grantor, and all advance payments of insurance premiums made by Grantor with respect thereto and all claims or demands relating to such deposits, other security and/or such insurance;

4. All damages, royalties and revenue of every kind, nature and description whatsoever that Grantor may be entitled to receive, either before or after any Event of Default (as hereinafter defined), from any person or entity owning or having or hereafter acquiring a right to the oil, gas or mineral rights and reservations of the Land, with the right in Beneficiary to receive and apply the same to the Secured Indebtedness;

5. All proceeds and claims arising on account of any damage to, or Condemnation (as hereinafter defined) of, the Land and/or Improvements or any part thereof, and all causes of action and recoveries for any loss or diminution in the value of the Land and/or Improvements;

6. All licenses (including, but not limited to, any operating licenses or similar licenses), contracts, management contracts or agreements, guaranties, warranties, franchise agreements, permits, authorities or certificates required or relating the ownership, use, operation or maintenance of the Land and/or Improvements; and

7. All names under or by which the Land and/or Improvements may at any time be operated or known, and all rights to carry on business under any such names or any variant thereof, and all trademarks, trade names, patents pending and goodwill relating to the Land and/or Improvements.

TO HAVE AND TO HOLD the Real Property (as hereinafter defined), unto Trustee, its successors and assigns, in trust, for the benefit of Beneficiary, its successors and assigns, subject, however, to the terms, covenants and conditions contained herein.

All of the property described in paragraph (A) above is hereinafter collectively referred to as the "Real Property."

B. Beneficiary, its successors and assigns, as a secured party, a security interest in Grantor's interest in any portion of the Real Property which may be construed to be personal property, and in all other personal property of every kind and description, whether now existing or hereafter acquired, now or at any time hereafter attached to, erected upon, situated in or upon, forming a part of, appurtenant to, used or useful in the construction or operation of, or in connection with, or arising from the use or enjoyment of all or any portion of, or from any lease or agreement pertaining to, the Real Property, including:

1. All water rights appurtenant to the Real Property together with all pumping plants, pipes, flumes and ditches, all rights to the use of water, all rights in ditches for irrigation, all water stock, shares of stock or other evidence of ownership of any part of the Real Property that is owned by Grantor in common with others and all documents of membership in any owners' or

members' association or similar group having responsibility for managing or operating any part of the Real Property;

2. All plans and specifications prepared for construction of the Improvements and all studies, data and drawings related thereto; and all contracts and agreements of Grantor relating to the aforesaid plans and specifications or to the aforesaid studies, data and drawings, or to the construction of the Improvements;

3. All equipment, machinery, fixtures, goods, accounts, general intangibles, documents, instruments and chattel paper;

4. All substitutions and replacements of, and accessions and additions to, any of the foregoing;

5. All sales agreements, deposit receipts, escrow agreements and other ancillary documents and agreements entered into with respect to the sale to any purchasers of any part of the Real Property, together with all deposits and other proceeds of the sale thereof;

6. All money, escrow deposits, bank accounts, instruments, securities, certificates of deposit, interest accrued thereon, additional deposits thereto and all existing or future renewals, replacements and substitutions thereof, escrow agreements and other ancillary documents and agreements entered into with respect to any repair work undertaken in connection with all or any part of the Real Property; and

7. All proceeds of any of the foregoing, including, without limitation, proceeds of any voluntary or involuntary disposition or claim respecting any of the foregoing (pursuant to judgment, condemnation award or otherwise) and all goods, documents, general intangibles, chattel paper and accounts, wherever located, acquired with cash proceeds of any of the foregoing or proceeds thereof.

All of the property described in paragraph (B) above is hereinafter collectively referred to as the "Personal Property." All of the Real Property and the Personal Property is herein collectively referred to as the "Property."

PROVIDED, HOWEVER, if Grantor shall pay or cause to be paid to Beneficiary in full the Secured Indebtedness, at the times and in the manner stipulated in the Loan Documents, and shall keep, perform and observe all and singular the covenants and promises of Grantor in the Loan Documents, then this Deed of Trust and all the properties, interests and rights hereby granted, encumbered, transferred or assigned shall be released by Trustee and/or Beneficiary in accordance with the laws of the State.

GRANTOR HEREBY COVENANTS AND AGREES FOR THE BENEFIT OF BENEFICIARY AND TRUSTEE AS FOLLOWS:

ARTICLE I

COVENANTS

1.01 *Performance by Grantor.* Grantor shall pay the Secured Indebtedness to Beneficiary and shall keep and perform each and every other obligation, covenant and agreement of the Loan Documents.

1.02 *Warranty of Title.* Grantor warrants that it is lawfully seized of that portion of the Property which constitutes real property, that it holds marketable and indefeasible fee simple absolute title to same, and that it has good right and is lawfully authorized to sell, convey or encumber the Property subject only to those matters set forth in *Exhibit "C"* attached hereto and made a part hereof (the "Permitted Exceptions"). Grantor represents and warrants that the Property is not subject to any forfeiture under any state or federal law, related to any negligence, misconduct or criminal activity of Grantor. Grantor further covenants to warrant and forever defend all and singular the Property unto Beneficiary and Trustee forever from and against all persons whomsoever claiming the same or any part thereof.

1.03 *Taxes, Liens and Other Charges.* Unless sums sufficient to pay the same shall have been fully paid to Beneficiary as provided in Section 1.06 hereof, Grantor shall pay all real estate and other taxes, assessments, water and sewer charges, vault and other license or permit fees, levies, fines, penalties, interest, impositions, and other similar claims, general and special, public and private, of any kind whatsoever which may be assessed, levied, confirmed, imposed upon or arise out of or become due and payable out of, or become a lien on or against the Property or any part thereof (all of the foregoing, together with utility and refuse removal charges, being hereinafter collectively referred to as the "Imposition(s)") not later than ten (10) days before the dates on which such Impositions would become delinquent. Not later than the date when any Impositions would become delinquent, Grantor shall produce to Beneficiary official receipts of the appropriate imposing authority, or other evidence reasonably satisfactory to Beneficiary evidencing the payment thereof in full. If Grantor shall in good faith, and by proper legal action, contest any Impositions, and shall have deposited cash with Beneficiary (or as Beneficiary may direct) as a reserve for the payment thereof plus all fines, interest, penalties and costs which may become due pending the determination of such contest, in such amount as Beneficiary may require, then Grantor shall not be required to pay the same during the maintenance of said deposit and as long as such contest operates to prevent enforcement or collection of such Impositions against, or the sale or forfeiture of, the Property for non-payment thereof, and is prosecuted with due diligence and continuity, and shall not have been terminated or discontinued adversely to Grantor. Upon termination of any such proceeding or contest, Grantor shall pay the amount of such Impositions or part thereof as finally determined in such proceeding or contest. However, if monies have been deposited with Beneficiary pursuant to this Section 1.03, said funds shall be applied toward such payment and the excess, if any, shall be returned to Grantor.

1.04 *Further Taxes.* In the event of the passage, after the date of this Deed of Trust, of any law deducting from the value of the Property, for the purposes of taxation, any lien thereon or security interest therein, or changing in any way the laws now in force for the taxation of mortgages, deeds of trust and/or security agreements or debts secured by mortgages, deeds of trust and/or security agreements, or the manner of the collection of any such taxes, which has the effect of imposing payment of the whole or any portion of any taxes, assessments or other similar charges against the Property upon Beneficiary, the Secured Indebtedness shall immediately become due and payable at the option of Beneficiary; provided, however, that such election by Beneficiary shall be ineffective if prior to the due date thereof: (1) Grantor is permitted by law (including, without limitation, applicable interest rate laws) to, and actually does, pay such tax or the increased portion thereof (in addition to continuing to pay the Secured Indebtedness as and when due and payable); and (2) Grantor agrees with Beneficiary in writing to pay, or reimburse Beneficiary for the payment of any such tax or increased portion thereof when thereafter levied or assessed against the Property or any portion thereof. Any money paid by Beneficiary under this Section 1.04 shall be reimbursed to Beneficiary in accordance with Section 3.10 hereof.

1.05 *Insurance.*

(a) Grantor, at its sole cost and expense, shall at all times, unless otherwise indicated, provide, maintain and keep in force:

(1) property insurance covering the Improvements and Personal Property against loss or damage from such causes of loss as are embraced by insurance policies of the type now known as "All Risks" or "Open Perils" property insurance on a replacement cost basis with an Agreed Value Endorsement waiving co-insurance, all in an amount not less than one hundred percent (100%) of the then full replacement cost of

the Improvements (exclusive of the cost of excavations, foundations and footings below the lowest basement floor) and Personal Property, without deduction for physical depreciation thereof. Such property insurance shall include a Demolition and Increased Cost of Construction Endorsement as well as such other insurance as Beneficiary may from time to time designate to cover other risks and hazards affecting the Property;

(2) business income insurance insuring against loss of business or rental income of the Property, in an amount equal to not less than the greater of $_____ or one year's gross "business income" of the Property. "Business income" as used herein is defined as the sum of (i) the total anticipated gross income from occupancy of the Property as furnished and equipped by Grantor and (ii) the amount of all charges (such as, but not limited to, operating expenses and taxes) which are the legal obligation of tenants or occupants to Grantor pursuant to leases or other occupancy agreements, (iii) the fair rental value of any portion of the Property which is occupied by Grantor, and (iv) any other amounts payable to Grantor pursuant to leases or other occupancy agreements;

(3) flood insurance in an amount equal to the lesser of 100% of the full replacement cost of the Improvements, or the maximum amount of insurance obtainable; provided, however, that such insurance shall be required only when all or any portion of the Land is located within a 100–year flood plain or area designated as subject to flood by the Federal Emergency Management Agency or any other governmental agency, or when required by any federal, state or local law, statute, regulation or ordinance;

(4) boiler and machinery insurance insuring against loss or damage to the Property and to the major components of any heating, air conditioning, or other ventilation systems and/or such other machinery or apparatus as may be now or hereafter installed in the Improvements, in such amounts as Beneficiary may, from time to time, require;

(5) war risk insurance upon the Property as and when such insurance is obtainable from the United States of America or any agency or instrumentality thereof at a reasonable premium, in an amount not less than 100% of the then full replacement cost of the Improvements (exclusive of the cost of excavations, foundations and footings below the lowest basement floor) without deduction for physical depreciation, to the extent obtainable, and if not so obtainable, in the maximum amount obtainable;

(6) builder's risk insurance insuring against loss or damage from such causes of loss as are embraced by insurance policies of the type now known as "Builder's Risks" property insurance (written on an "all risk" or "open perils" basis), including, without limitation, fire and extended coverage, collapse of the improvements and earthquake coverage to agreed limits, all in form and substance acceptable to Beneficiary and (i) as to property then subject to Restoration (as defined in Section 1.07(b)) or any restoration accomplished in connection with a Condemnation, in an amount not less than the full replacement cost of such property, and (ii) as to any additional improvements then being constructed, in an amount not less than the completed value on a non reporting form, of the additional improvements then being constructed; provided, however, that such insurance shall be required only during any period of Restoration or any restoration accomplished in connection with a Condemnation, or any period of construction of any additional improvements;

(7) general liability insurance insuring against claims for personal injury (including, without limitation, bodily injury or death), property damage liability and such other loss or damage from such causes of loss as are

embraced by insurance policies of the type now known as "Commercial General Liability" insurance, all in an initial amount of $_____ and such other amounts as Beneficiary may require from time to time. Such insurance coverage shall be issued and maintained on an "occurrence" basis; and

(8) such other insurance and in such amounts, as may, from time to time, be required by Beneficiary against other insurable hazards or risks, including, but not limited to, environmental impairment liability coverage, nuclear reaction or radioactive contamination coverage and/or earthquake coverage, which hazards or risks at the time are commonly insured against, and provided such insurance is generally available, for property similarly situated, due regard being given to the height and type of building, its construction, use and occupancy.

(b) Except as herein expressly provided otherwise, all policies of insurance required under this Section 1.05 shall be issued by companies, and be in form, amount, and content and have an expiration date, approved by Beneficiary and as to the policies of insurance required under subparagraphs (1), (3) and (6) of Section 1.05(a), shall contain a Standard Non–Contributory Mortgagee Clause or Lender's Loss Payable Endorsement, or equivalents thereof, in form, scope and substance satisfactory to Beneficiary, in favor of Beneficiary, and as to policies of insurance required under subparagraphs (1), (2), (3), (4), (5) and (6) of Section 1.05(a), shall provide that the proceeds thereof ("Insurance Proceeds") shall be payable to Beneficiary. Any Insurance Proceeds received by Beneficiary pursuant to Section 1.05(a)(2) shall be held and applied by Beneficiary toward payment of that portion of the Secured Indebtedness then due and payable, or which will become due and payable for the period for which such Insurance Proceeds are received by Beneficiary and the remainder, if any, shall be paid to Grantor. Grantor hereby authorizes and empowers Beneficiary to settle, adjust or compromise any claims for loss, damage or destruction to the Property, regardless of whether there are Insurance Proceeds available or whether any such proceeds are sufficient in amount to fully compensate for such loss or damage. Beneficiary shall be furnished with the original or certified copy of each policy required hereunder, which policy shall provide that it shall not be modified or cancelled without thirty (30) days' prior written notice to Beneficiary. At least thirty (30) days prior to expiration of any policy required hereunder, Grantor shall furnish Beneficiary appropriate proof of issuance of a policy continuing in force the insurance covered by the policy so expiring. Grantor shall furnish Beneficiary receipts for the payment of premiums on such insurance policies or other evidence of such payment reasonably satisfactory to Beneficiary in the event that such premiums have not been paid to Beneficiary pursuant to Section 1.06 hereof. In the event that Grantor does not deposit with Beneficiary a new policy of insurance with evidence of payment of premiums thereon at least thirty (30) days prior to the expiration of any policy, then Beneficiary may, but shall not be obligated to, procure such insurance and pay the premiums therefor and any money paid by Beneficiary for such premiums shall be reimbursed to Beneficiary in accordance with Section 3.10 hereof.

(c) In the event of the foreclosure of this Deed of Trust or other transfer of the title to the Property in extinguishment, in whole or in part, of the Secured Indebtedness, all right, title and interest of Grantor in and to any insurance policy, or Premiums (as hereinafter defined) or payments in satisfaction of claims or any other rights thereunder then in force, shall pass to the purchaser or grantee. Nothing contained herein shall prevent accrual of interest as provided in the Note on any portion of the Secured Indebtedness to which the Insurance Proceeds are to be applied until such time as the Insurance Proceeds are actually received by Beneficiary and applied by Beneficiary to reduce the Secured Indebtedness.

1.06 *Escrow Deposits.* Without limiting the effect of Sections 1.03, 1.04 and 1.05 hereof, Grantor shall pay to Beneficiary monthly at the time when the monthly installment of interest, principal or principal and interest is payable, an amount equal to $\frac{1}{12}$th of what Beneficiary estimates is necessary to pay, on an annualized basis, all (1) Impositions and (2) such premiums for the insurance policies required under Section 1.05(a) hereof ("Premiums") to enable Beneficiary to pay same at least thirty (30) days before the Impositions would become delinquent and the Premiums are due, and, on demand, from time to time shall pay to Beneficiary additional sums necessary to pay the Premiums and Impositions. No amounts so paid shall be deemed to be trust funds, but may be commingled with the general funds of Beneficiary, and no interest shall be payable thereon. In the event that Grantor does not pay such sums for Premiums and Impositions, then Beneficiary may, but shall not be obligated to, pay such Premiums and Impositions and any money so paid by Beneficiary shall be reimbursed to Beneficiary in accordance with Section 3.10 hereof. If an Event of Default occurs, Beneficiary shall have the right, at its election, to apply any amounts so held under this Section 1.06 against all or any part of the Secured Indebtedness, or in payment of the Premiums or Impositions for which the amounts were deposited. Grantor will furnish to Beneficiary bills for Impositions and Premiums thirty (30) days before Impositions become delinquent and such Premiums become due. The foregoing obligations of Grantor are subject to the condition that Grantor shall not be required to pay such items unless and until (i) an Event of Default occurs or (ii) Beneficiary requests such payments, which request may be made in Beneficiary's sole discretion.

1.07 *Restoration.*

(a) After the happening of any casualty to the Property, whether or not required to be insured against under the insurance policies to be provided by Grantor hereunder, Grantor shall give prompt written notice thereof to Beneficiary generally describing the nature and cause of such casualty and the extent of the damage to or destruction of the Property.

(b) Grantor hereby assigns to Beneficiary all Insurance Proceeds which Grantor may be entitled to receive. In the event of any damage to or destruction of the Property, and provided (1) an Event of Default does not currently exist, and (2) Beneficiary has determined that (i) its security has not been impaired, and (ii) the repair, restoration and rebuilding of any portion of the Property that has been partially damaged or destroyed can be accomplished in full compliance with all Requirements (as defined in *Exhibit "A"*) to the same condition, character and general utility as nearly as possible to that existing prior to such damage or destruction and at least equal value as that existing prior to such damage or destruction (the "Restoration"), then Grantor shall commence and diligently pursue to completion the Restoration. Beneficiary shall hold and disburse the Insurance Proceeds less (x) the cost, if any, to Beneficiary of recovering such proceeds including, without limitation, attorneys' fees and expenses, adjusters' fees, and fees incurred in Beneficiary's performance of its obligations hereunder, and (y) any insurance proceeds received by Beneficiary pursuant to Section 1.05(a)(2) (the "Net Insurance Proceeds") in the manner hereinafter provided, to the Restoration. In the event that the above conditions for Restoration have not been met, Beneficiary may, at its option, apply the Net Insurance Proceeds to the reduction of the Secured Indebtedness in such order as Beneficiary may determine and Beneficiary may declare the entire Secured Indebtedness immediately due and payable. Any prepayment of the Secured Indebtedness pursuant to the provisions of this paragraph shall be without payment of the Prepayment Fee (as defined in the Note).

(c) In the event the Net Insurance Proceeds are to be used for the Restoration, Grantor shall comply with Beneficiary's Requirements For Restoration as set forth in *Exhibit "D"* attached hereto and made a part hereof. Upon Beneficiary's receipt of a final certificate of occupancy or other evidence of approval of appropriate governmental authorities for the use and occupancy of the Improvements and other evidence requested by Beneficiary that the Restoration has been completed and the costs thereof have been paid in full, and satisfactory evidence that no mechanic's or similar liens for labor, equipment or material supplied in connection with the Restoration are outstanding against the Property and provided that an Event of Default does not currently exist, Beneficiary shall pay any remaining Restoration Funds (as defined in *Exhibit "D"*) then held by Beneficiary to Grantor; provided, however, nothing contained herein shall prevent Beneficiary from applying at any time the whole or any part of the Restoration Funds to the curing of any Event of Default.

(d) In the event that Beneficiary applies all or any portion of the Restoration Funds to repay the unpaid Secured Indebtedness as provided in this Section 1.07, after payment in full of the Secured Indebtedness, any remaining Restoration Funds shall be paid to Grantor.

1.08 *Condemnation.* Should the Property or any part thereof be taken by reason of any condemnation or similar eminent domain proceeding, or a grant or conveyance in lieu thereof ("Condemnation"), Beneficiary shall be entitled to all compensation, awards and other payments or relief therefor, and shall be entitled at its option to commence, appear in and prosecute in its own name any action or proceeding or to make any compromise or settlement in connection with such Condemnation. Grantor hereby irrevocably constitutes and appoints Beneficiary as its attorney-in-fact, and such appointment is coupled with an interest, to commence, appear in and prosecute any action or proceeding or to make any compromise or settlement in connection with any such Condemnation. All such compensation, awards, damages, rights of action and proceeds (collectively, the "Condemnation Proceeds") are hereby assigned to Beneficiary, who shall, after deducting therefrom all its reasonable expenses, including attorneys' fees ("Condemnation Expenses"), apply the remaining Condemnation Proceeds to repair any damage to, and to restore the Improvements remaining on the portion of, the Property not taken in the manner provided in Section 1.07 with respect to disposition of Net Insurance Proceeds; provided, however, that at the time of application of the remaining Condemnation Proceeds: (1) there shall not exist an Event of Default; (2) Grantor shall have paid to Beneficiary all sums in excess of available Condemnation Proceeds necessary to repair any damage to and restore the Improvements remaining on the portion of the Property not taken; and (3) Beneficiary shall have determined that its security is not impaired. After restoration of the remaining Improvements, or in the event the conditions precedent for such restoration are not met, Beneficiary shall have the right, after deducting therefrom the Condemnation Expenses, to apply the balance of the Condemnation Proceeds to the Secured Indebtedness, in such manner and such order as Beneficiary in its sole discretion shall determine, without adjustment in the dollar amount of the installments due under the Note. Any prepayment of the Secured Indebtedness pursuant to the provisions of this paragraph shall be without payment of the Prepayment Fee (as defined in the Note). Nothing contained herein shall prevent the accrual of interest as provided in the Note on any portion of the Secured Indebtedness to which the Condemnation Proceeds are to be applied until such Condemnation Proceeds are actually received by Beneficiary and so applied to reduce the Secured Indebtedness.

1.09 *Care And Use Of The Property.*

(a) Grantor, at its sole cost and expense, shall keep the Property in good order, condition, and repair, and make all necessary repairs thereto, interior and exterior, structural and non-structural, ordinary and extraordinary, and foreseen and unforeseen. Grantor shall abstain from, and not permit, the commission of waste in or about the Property and shall not remove or demolish, or alter in any substantial manner, the structure or character of any Improvements without the prior written consent of Beneficiary.

(b) Grantor shall at all times comply with all present or future Requirements affecting or relating or pertaining in any way to the Property and/or the use, operation and/or the maintenance thereof, and shall furnish Beneficiary, on request, proof of such compliance. Grantor shall not use or permit the use of the Property, or any part thereof, for any illegal purpose.

(c) Beneficiary and Beneficiary's representatives and designees shall have the right, but not the duty, to enter the Property at reasonable times to inspect the same. Beneficiary shall not be liable to Grantor or any person in possession of the Property with respect to any matter arising out of such entry to the Property.

(d) Grantor shall, from time to time, if and when required by Beneficiary (1) perform a site investigation of the Property to determine the existence and levels of Hazardous Substances (as defined in *Exhibit "A"*) on the Property, (2) issue a report certifying the results of such inspection to Beneficiary, and (3) take such remedial action as may be required by Beneficiary based upon such report.

(e) Grantor shall use, or cause to be used, the Property continuously as and for first class property of its type and kind at the time of the execution of this Deed of Trust. Grantor shall not use, or permit the use of, the Property for any other use without the prior written consent of Beneficiary. To the extent the Property is used as a residential apartment complex, Grantor shall at no time file or record a Declaration of Condominium, Master Deed of Trust or any other similar document evidencing the imposition of a so-called "condominium regime" whether superior or subordinate to this Deed of Trust. Grantor shall at no time permit any part of the Property to be converted to, or operated as, a so-called "cooperative apartment house" (or on a like cooperative basis) whereby the tenants or occupants thereof participate in the ownership, management or control of any part of the Property, as tenants, stockholders or otherwise.

(f) Grantor shall not initiate or acquiesce in a change in the zoning classification of and/or restrictive covenants affecting the Property or seek any variance under existing zoning ordinances applicable to the Property or use or permit the use of the Property in such a manner which would result in such use becoming a non-conforming use under applicable zoning ordinances or other applicable laws, ordinances, rules or regulations or subject the Property to restrictive covenants without Beneficiary's prior written consent.

1.10 *Leases And Other Agreements Affecting The Property.*

(a) In order to further secure payment of the Secured Indebtedness and the observance, performance and discharge of Grantor's obligations under the Loan Documents, Grantor hereby assigns to Beneficiary all of Grantor's right, title, interest and estate in, to and under all of the leases now or hereafter affecting the Property or any part thereof and in and to all of the Rents and Profits (as defined in *Exhibit "A"*). Unless and until an Event of Default occurs, Grantor shall be entitled to collect the Rents and Profits (except as otherwise provided in this Deed of Trust) as and when they become due and payable. Beneficiary shall be liable to account only for the Rents and Profits actually received by Beneficiary pursuant to any provision of any Loan Document.

(b) Grantor shall duly and punctually perform all terms, covenants, conditions and agreements binding upon it or the Property under any lease or any other agreement or instrument of any nature whatsoever which involves or affects the Property or any part thereof. Grantor represents that it has heretofore furnished Beneficiary true and complete copies of all executed leases existing on the date of this Deed of Trust. Upon request of Beneficiary, Grantor agrees to furnish Beneficiary with executed copies of all leases hereafter entered into with respect to all or any part of the Property. Grantor shall not, without the express written consent of Beneficiary, enter into any new lease or modify, extend or renew, either orally or in writing, any lease now existing or hereafter created upon the Property, or any part thereof, unless such lease shall be in compliance with the Leasing Guidelines (as defined in *Exhibit "A"*). Grantor shall not, without the express written consent of Beneficiary, terminate or surrender any lease now existing or hereafter created upon the Property, or any part thereof, unless Grantor has entered into a new lease covering all of the leased premises to be terminated or surrendered, which new lease shall either have been approved by Beneficiary as provided herein, or shall be in compliance with the Leasing Guidelines. Grantor shall not permit an assignment or sublease of any lease now existing or hereafter created upon the Property, or any part thereof, without the express written consent of Beneficiary unless such lease shall be in compliance with the Leasing Guidelines.

(c) Each lease of any portion of the Property shall be absolutely subordinate to the lien of this Deed of Trust, but shall also contain a provision, satisfactory to Beneficiary, that in the event of the exercise of the power of sale hereunder or a sale pursuant to a judgment of foreclosure, such lease, at the sole and exclusive option of the purchaser at such sale, shall not be terminated and the tenant thereunder shall attorn to such purchaser and, if requested to do so, shall enter into a new lease for the balance of the term of such lease then remaining, upon the same terms and conditions. If Beneficiary so requests, Grantor shall cause the tenant under each or any of such leases to enter into subordination and attornment agreements with Beneficiary which are satisfactory in form, scope and substance to Beneficiary.

(d) Grantor shall not accept payment of advance rents or security deposits equal, in the aggregate, to more than two (2) months' rent.

(e) Grantor covenants and agrees that all contracts and agreements relating to the Property to pay leasing commissions, management fees or other compensation shall (1) provide that the obligation to pay such commissions, fees and other compensation will not be enforceable against any party other than the party who entered into such agreement; (2) be subordinate and inferior to the lien of this Deed of Trust; and (3) not be enforceable against Beneficiary. Grantor shall promptly furnish Beneficiary with evidence of Grantor's compliance with this paragraph upon the execution of each such contract or agreement.

1.11 *Books, Records And Accounts.* Grantor shall keep and maintain or shall cause to be kept and maintained on a calendar year basis, in accordance with generally accepted accounting principles, consistently applied, proper and accurate books, records and accounts reflecting all of the financial affairs of Grantor with respect to all items of income and expense in connection with the operation of the Property, whether such income or expense be realized by Grantor or by any other person whatsoever (excepting lessees unrelated to and unaffiliated with Grantor who have leased from Grantor portions of the Property for the purpose of occupying same). Beneficiary or its representatives or designees shall have the right from time to time at all times during normal business hours to examine, with respect to the Property, such books, records and accounts at the office of Grantor or other person maintaining such books, records and accounts and to make copies or extracts thereof as Beneficiary shall desire. Beneficiary shall also have the right to discuss Grantor's affairs, finances and accounts with representatives of Grantor, at such reasonable times as may be requested by Beneficiary. Grantor shall deliver to Beneficiary within ninety (90) days after the close of each calendar year, financial statements prepared by an independent certified public accountant satisfactory to Beneficiary, containing a balance sheet, profit and loss statements and income and expense statements with such detailed supporting schedules covering the operation of the Property as Beneficiary shall require and certified by the chief financial officer of Grantor, if Grantor is a corporation, by a general partner of Grantor, if Grantor is a partnership, or by Grantor, if Grantor is an individual. Grantor shall also furnish at such time a rent roll certified by Grantor to be correct showing each tenant, the term of the lease, the rentable area demised thereunder and the fixed annual rent, percentage rent, other charges, if any, payable thereunder, date of last rental payment, amount of security deposit, nature and amounts of defaults (if any) and such other matters as Beneficiary may require.

1.12 *Subrogation.* As additional security hereunder, Beneficiary shall be subrogated to the lien, although released of record, of any and all encumbrances paid out of the proceeds of the loan evidenced by the Note and secured by this Deed of Trust and Beneficiary, upon making such payment, shall be subrogated to all of the rights of the person, corporation or body politic receiving such payment.

1.13 *Collateral Security Instruments.* Grantor covenants and agrees that if Beneficiary at any time holds additional security for any obligations secured hereby, it may enforce the terms thereof or otherwise realize upon the same, at its option, either before or concurrently herewith or after a sale is made hereunder, and may apply the proceeds to the Secured Indebtedness in such order as Beneficiary may determine, without affecting the status of or waiving any right to exhaust all or any other security, including the security hereunder, and without waiving any breach or default or any right or power whether exercised hereunder or under any of the other Loan Documents, or contained herein or therein, or in any such other security.

1.14 *Suits and Other Acts to Protect The Property.*

(a) Grantor covenants and agrees to appear in and defend any action or proceeding purporting to affect the Property, any other security afforded by any of the Loan Documents and/or the interest of Beneficiary thereunder. Grantor shall immediately notify Beneficiary of the commencement, or receipt of notice, of any such action or proceeding or other matter or claim purporting to, or which could, affect the Property, any other security afforded by any of the Loan Documents and/or the interest of Beneficiary thereunder.

(b) Beneficiary shall have the right, at the cost and expense of Grantor, to institute and maintain such suits and proceedings and take such other action, as it may deem expedient to preserve or protect the Property, any other security afforded by any of the Loan Documents and/or Beneficiary's interest therein. Any money paid by Beneficiary under this Section 1.14(b) shall be reimbursed to Beneficiary in accordance with Section 3.10 hereof.

1.15 *Beneficiary's Right To Perform Grantor's Obligations.* Grantor agrees that, if Grantor fails to perform any act or to pay any money which Grantor is required to perform or pay under the Loan Documents, Beneficiary, at the cost and expense of Grantor and in Grantor's name or in its own name, may (but shall not be obligated to) perform or cause to be performed such act or take such action or pay any money. Any money paid by Beneficiary under this Section 1.15 shall be reimbursed to Beneficiary in accordance with Section 3.10 hereof.

1.16 *Liens and Encumbrances.* Grantor shall not, without the prior written consent of Beneficiary, create, place or suffer to be created or placed, or through any act or failure to act, allow to remain, any deed of trust, mortgage, security interest, or other lien, encumbrance or charge, or conditional sale or other title retention document, against or covering the Property, or any part thereof, other than the Permitted Exceptions and the lien for ad valorem taxes on the Property not yet delinquent, regardless of whether the same are expressly or otherwise subordinate to the lien or security interest created in this Deed of Trust, and should any of the foregoing become attached hereafter in any manner to any part of the Property, Grantor shall cause the same to be promptly discharged and released. Grantor shall own all parts of the Property and, except as expressly approved in writing by Beneficiary, shall not acquire any fixtures, equipment or other property forming a part of the Property pursuant to a lease, license, title retention document or similar agreement.

* * * OPTIONAL PROVISION

[1.17 *Liability of Grantor.* Notwithstanding anything to the contrary contained in this Deed of Trust or in any of the other Loan Documents, but without in any manner releasing, impairing or otherwise affecting the Note or any of the other Loan Documents, or the validity hereof or thereof, or the lien of this Deed of Trust, upon the occurrence of an Event of Default, except as expressly set forth in this Section 1.17, the liability of Grantor and/or the general partners of Grantor, if any, to Beneficiary for any and all such Events of Default shall be limited to and be satisfied out of the Property. Notwithstanding any of the foregoing, nothing contained in this Section 1.17 shall be deemed to prejudice the rights of Beneficiary to (1) proceed against any entity or person whatsoever, including Grantor and/or the general partners of Grantor, if any, with respect to the enforcement of any leases, guarantees, bonds, policies of insurance or other agreements for compliance with any of the terms, covenants and conditions of the Loan Documents; or (2) recover damages against Grantor and the general partners of Grantor, if any, for fraud, breach of trust, breach of warranty, misrepresentation or waste; or (3) recover any Condemnation Proceeds or Insurance Proceeds or other similar funds or payments attributable to the Property, which under the terms of the Loan Documents should have been paid to Beneficiary; or (4) recover any tenant security deposits, prepaid rents or other similar sums paid to or held by Grantor or any other entity or person in connection with the Property; or (5) recover the Rents and Profits, accruing from and after the occurrence of an Event of Default, which have not been applied to pay any portion of the Secured Indebtedness, operating and maintenance expenses of the Property, Premiums, Impositions, deposits into a reserve for replacement or other sums required by the Loan Documents; or (6) recover damages against Grantor and/or the general partners of Grantor, if any, arising from, or in connection with, the covenants, obligations, liabilities, warranties and representations contained in Section 3.08 hereof; or (7) except to the extent Beneficiary actually receives proceeds therefor under its lender's title policy, recover from Grantor and/or the general partners of Grantor, if any, the Secured Indebtedness, in the event of any judicial determination that the lien of the Deed of Trust is invalid; or (8) recover from Grantor and/or the general partners of Grantor, if any, all amounts due and payable pursuant to Sections 3.06 and 3.10 hereof. Grantor and the general partners of Grantor, if any, shall be personally liable for Grantor's obligations arising in connection with the matters set forth in the foregoing clauses (1) to (8) inclusive.]

1.18 *Management.* Grantor shall exercise the highest degree of professional competence in managing the Property and maintain the Property in a manner consistent with other first class properties within the greater _____ metropolitan area.

ARTICLE II

DEFAULTS AND REMEDIES

2.01 *Events of Default.* Any of the following shall be deemed to be a material breach of Grantor's covenants herein and shall constitute a default hereunder ("Event of Default"):

(a) The failure of Grantor to pay any installment of principal, interest or principal and interest, any required escrow deposit or any other sum required to be paid under any Loan Document, whether to Beneficiary or otherwise, when the same shall become due and payable;

(b) The failure of Grantor to perform or observe any other term, provision, covenant, condition or agreement under any Loan Document;

(c) The filing by Grantor or any general partner of Grantor of a voluntary petition or application for relief in bankruptcy or the adjudication of Grantor or any general partner of Grantor as a bankrupt or insolvent, or the filing by Grantor or any general partner of Grantor of any petition, application for relief or answer seeking or acquiescing in any reorganization, arrangement, composition, readjustment, liquidation, dissolution or similar relief for itself under any present or future federal, state or other statute, law, code or regulation relating to bankruptcy, insolvency or other relief for debtors, or the seeking or consenting to or acquiescing in the appointment of any trustee, custodian, conservator, receiver or liquidator by Grantor or any general partner of Grantor or of all or any substantial part of the Property or of any or all of the Rents and Profits thereof, or the making of any general assignment for the benefit of creditors, or the admission in writing of its inability to pay its debts generally as they become due;

(d) If any warranty, representation, certification, financial statement or other information made or furnished at any time pursuant to the terms of the Loan Documents or otherwise, by Grantor, or by any person or entity otherwise liable under any Loan Document shall be materially false or misleading or furnished with knowledge of the false nature thereof; or

(e) If Grantor shall suffer or permit the Property, or any part thereof, to be used in such manner as might tend to (1) impair Grantor's title to the Property, or any part thereof; or (2) create rights of adverse use or possession; or (3) constitute an implied dedication of the Property, or any part thereof.

2.02 *Remedies Upon Default.* Upon (1) _____ (__) days after the happening of an Event of Default described in Section 2.01(a) or (2) _____ (__) days after the date Beneficiary sends notice of an Event of Default described in Section 2.01(b) or (3) the happening of any other Event of Default, the Secured Indebtedness shall, at the option of Beneficiary, become immediately due and payable, without further notice or demand, and Beneficiary may forthwith undertake any one or more of the following:

(a) *Foreclosure.* Institute an action of foreclosure in accordance with the law of the State, or take such other action as the law may allow, at law or in equity, for the enforcement of the Loan Documents and realization on the Property or any other security afforded by the Loan Documents and, in the case of a judicial proceeding, proceed to final judgment and execution thereon for the amount of the Secured Indebtedness (as of the date of such judgment) together with all costs of suit, attorneys' fees and interest on such judgment at the maximum rate permitted by law from and after the date of such judgment until actual payment is made to Beneficiary in the full amount due Beneficiary; provided, however, if Beneficiary is the purchaser at the foreclosure sale of the Property, the foreclosure sale price (Beneficiary's final bid) shall be applied against the total amount due Beneficiary; and/or

(b) *Power of Sale.* Cause Trustee in compliance with applicable law, to sell the Property or any part of the Property at public sale or sales to the highest bidder for cash, in order to pay the Secured Indebtedness, in compliance with the requirements of the general statutes of the State relating to nonjudicial foreclosure sales in effect on the date foreclosure is commenced and to deliver to such purchaser a Trustee's deed (or Trustee's deeds) without covenant or warranty, express or implied, the recitals of such deed (or deeds) as to any matters of fact to be conclusive proof of the truthfulness thereof; and/or

(c) *Entry.* Enter into possession of the Property, lease the same, collect all Rents and Profits therefrom and, after deducting all costs of collection and administration expenses, apply the remaining Rents and Profits in such order and amounts as Beneficiary, in Beneficiary's sole discretion, may elect to the payment of Impositions, operating costs, Premiums and other charges (including, but not limited to, costs of leasing the Property and fees and costs of counsel and receivers) and to the maintenance, repair, and restoration of the Property, or on account and in reduction of the Secured Indebtedness; and/or

(d) *Receivership.* Have a receiver appointed to enter into possession of the Property, collect the Rents and Profits therefrom and apply the same as the appropriate court may direct. Beneficiary shall be entitled to the appointment of a receiver without the necessity of proving either the inadequacy of the security or the insolvency of Grantor or any other person who may be legally or equitably liable to pay any portion of the Secured Indebtedness and Grantor and each such person shall be deemed to have waived such proof and to have consented to the appointment of such receiver. Should Beneficiary or any receiver collect the Rents and Profits, the moneys so collected shall not be substituted for payment of the Secured Indebtedness nor used to cure the Event of Default.

2.03 *Application of Proceeds of Sale.* In the event of a sale of the Property pursuant to Section 2.02(a) or Section 2.02(b) hereof, the proceeds of said sale, to the extent permitted by law, shall be applied to the following, in such order as Beneficiary shall, in its sole discretion, determine: the expenses of such sale and of all proceedings in connection therewith, including attorneys' fees and expenses; Impositions, Premiums, liens, and other charges and expenses; the outstanding principal balance of the Secured Indebtedness; any accrued interest; and any other unpaid portion of the Secured Indebtedness.

2.04 *Foreclosure Sale.* In the event that this Deed of Trust is foreclosed as a mortgage and the Real Property sold at a foreclosure sale, the purchaser may, during the statutory redemption period, make such repairs or alterations on the Real Property as may be reasonably necessary for the proper operation, care, preservation, protection and insuring thereof. Any sums so paid, together with interest thereon from the time of such expenditure at an interest rate equal to the Default Rate or the maximum interest rate permitted to be paid by Grantor under applicable interest rate law, shall be added to and become a part of the amount required to be paid for redemption from such sale.

2.05 *Right of Foreclosure.* Beneficiary shall have the right, at its option, to foreclose this Deed of Trust subject to the rights of any tenant or tenants of the Real Property, and the failure to make any such tenant or tenants a party defendant to any such suit or action or to foreclose their rights will not be asserted by the Grantor as a defense in any action or suit instituted to collect the indebtedness secured hereby or any part thereof or any deficiency remaining unpaid after foreclosure and sale of the Real Property, and statute or rule of law at any time existing to the contrary notwithstanding.

2.06 *Sale of Property Pursuant to a Foreclosure.* In case of a sale pursuant to a foreclosure of this Deed of Trust, the Property, real, personal or mixed, may be sold as an entirety or in parcels, by one sale or by several sales held at one time or at different times, all as Trustee, in its unrestricted discretion, may elect, and Grantor, for and on behalf of itself and all persons claiming by, through or under Grantor, waives any and all right to have the property and estates comprising the Property marshalled upon any foreclosure sale and agrees that, upon foreclosure, the Property may be sold as an entirety and not in parcels.

ARTICLE III

GENERAL COVENANTS

3.01 *Security Agreement.*

(a) THIS DEED OF TRUST CREATES A LIEN ON THE PROPERTY, AND TO THE EXTENT THE PROPERTY IS PERSONAL PROPERTY UNDER APPLICABLE LAW, THIS DEED OF TRUST CONSTITUTES A SECURITY AGREEMENT UNDER THE WASHINGTON UNIFORM COMMERCIAL CODE

(THE "U.C.C.") AND ANY OTHER APPLICABLE LAW AND IS FILED AS A FIXTURE FILING. UPON THE OCCURRENCE OF AN EVENT OF DEFAULT, BENEFICIARY MAY, AT ITS OPTION, PURSUE ANY AND ALL RIGHTS AND REMEDIES AVAILABLE TO A SECURED PARTY WITH RESPECT TO ANY PORTION OF THE PROPERTY, AND/OR BENEFICIARY MAY, AT ITS OPTION, PROCEED AS TO ALL OR ANY PART OF THE PROPERTY IN ACCORDANCE WITH BENEFICIARY'S RIGHTS AND REMEDIES WITH RESPECT TO THE LIEN CREATED BY THIS DEED OF TRUST.

(b) The grant of a security interest to Beneficiary in the granting clause of this Deed of Trust shall not be construed to derogate from or impair the lien or provisions of or the rights of Beneficiary under this Deed of Trust with respect to any property described therein which is real property or which the parties have agreed to treat as real property. The hereby stated intention of Grantor and Beneficiary is that everything used in connection with the production of income from such real property or adapted for use thereon is, and at all times and for all purposes and in all proceedings, both legal and equitable, shall be regarded as real property, irrespective of whether or not the same is physically attached to the Land and/or Improvements.

(c) If required by Beneficiary, at any time during the term of this Deed of Trust, Grantor will execute and deliver to Beneficiary, in form satisfactory to Beneficiary, additional security agreements, financing statements and/or other instruments covering all Personal Property or fixtures of Grantor which may at any time be furnished, placed on, or annexed or made appurtenant to the Real Property or used, useful or held for use, in the operation of the Improvements.

(d) Grantor hereby irrevocably constitutes and appoints Beneficiary as its attorney-in-fact and such appointment is coupled with an interest, to execute, deliver and file with the appropriate filing officer or office such security agreements, financing statements and/or other instruments as Beneficiary may request or require in order to impose and perfect the lien and security interest created hereby more specifically on the Personal Property or any fixtures.

(e) If Grantor enters into a separate security agreement with Beneficiary relating to any of the Personal Property or fixtures, the terms of such security agreement shall govern the rights and remedies of Beneficiary after an Event of Default thereunder.

(f) It is understood and agreed that, in order to protect Beneficiary from the effect of R.C.W. 62A.9–313, as amended from time to time, in the event that Grantor intends to purchase any goods which may become fixtures attached to the Property, or any part thereof, and such goods will be subject to a purchase money security interest held by a seller or any other party:

(1) Grantor shall, before executing any security agreement or other document evidencing or perfecting such security interest, obtain the prior written approval of Beneficiary, and all requests for such written approval shall be in writing and contain the following information:

(i) a description of the fixtures to be replaced, added to, installed or substituted;

(ii) the address at which the fixtures will be replaced, added to, installed or substituted; and

(iii) the name and address of the proposed holder and proposed amount of the security interest.

Grantor's execution of any such security agreement or other document evidencing or perfecting such security interest without Beneficiary's prior written approval shall constitute an Event of Default. No consent by Beneficiary pursuant to this subparagraph shall be deemed to constitute an agreement to subordinate any right of Beneficiary in fixtures or other property covered by this Deed of Trust.

(2) If at any time Grantor fails to make any payment on an obligation secured by a purchase money security interest in the Personal Property or any fixtures, Beneficiary, at its option, may at any time pay the amount secured by such security interest. Any money paid by Beneficiary under this Subparagraph, including any expenses, costs, charges and attorney's fees incurred by Beneficiary, shall be reimbursed to Beneficiary in accordance with Section 3.10 hereof. Beneficiary shall be subrogated to the rights of the holder of any such purchase money security interest in the Personal Property.

(3) Beneficiary shall have the right to acquire by assignment from the holder of such security interest any and all contract rights, accounts receivable, negotiable or non-negotiable instruments, or other evidence of Grantor's indebtedness for such Personal Property or fixtures, and, upon acquiring such interest by assignment, shall have the right to enforce the security interest as assignee thereof, in accordance with the terms and provisions of the U.C.C. and in accordance with any other provisions of law.

(4) Whether or not Beneficiary has paid the indebtedness secured by, or taken an assignment of, such security interest, Grantor covenants to pay all sums and perform all obligations secured thereby, and if Grantor at any time shall be in default under such security agreement, it shall constitute an Event of Default.

(5) The provisions of subparagraphs (2) and (3) of this paragraph (f) shall not apply if the goods which may become fixtures are of at least equivalent value and quality as any property being replaced and if the rights of the party holding such security interest have been expressly subordinated, at no cost to Beneficiary, to the lien and security interest of this Deed of Trust in a manner satisfactory to Beneficiary, including without limitation, at the option of Beneficiary, providing to Beneficiary a satisfactory opinion of counsel to the effect that this Deed of Trust constitutes a valid and subsisting first lien on such fixtures which is not subordinate to the lien of such security interest under any applicable law, including without limitation, the provisions of R.C.W. 62A.9–313.

(g) Grantor hereby warrants, represents and covenants as follows:

(1) Grantor is and has been the sole owner of the Personal Property for at least fifteen (15) days free from any lien, security interest, encumbrance or adverse claim thereon of any kind whatsoever. Grantor will notify Beneficiary of, and will protect, defend and indemnify Beneficiary against, all claims and demands of all persons at any time claiming any rights or interest therein.

(2) The Personal Property is not used or bought and shall not be used or bought for personal, family, or household purposes, but shall be bought and used solely for the purpose of carrying on Grantor's business.

(3) The Personal Property has been located on the Land and/or Improvements for at least fifteen (15) days and will be kept on or at the Land or the Improvements and Grantor will not remove the Personal Property therefrom without the prior written consent of Beneficiary, except such portions or items of Personal Property which are consumed or worn out in ordinary usage, all of which shall be promptly replaced by Grantor with other Personal Property of value equal to or greater than the value of the replaced Personal Property when new, and except such portions or items of Personal Property temporarily stored elsewhere to facilitate refurbishing or repair thereof or of the Improvements.

(4) Grantor maintains a place of business in the State and Grantor will immediately notify Beneficiary in writing of any change in its principal place of business as set forth in the beginning of this Deed of Trust.

3.02 *No Waiver.* No single or partial exercise by Beneficiary and/or Trustee, or delay or omission in the exercise by Beneficiary and/or Trustee, of any right or remedy under the Loan Documents shall preclude, waive or limit any other or further exercise thereof or the exercise of any other right or remedy. Beneficiary shall at all times have the right to proceed against any portion of, or interest in, the Property in such manner as Beneficiary may deem fit, without waiving any other rights or remedies with respect to any other portion of the Property.

3.03 *Conveyance of Property, Change In Ownership and Composition.*

Grantor shall not cause, permit or suffer: (i) the Property, or any part thereof, or any interest therein, to be conveyed, transferred, assigned, encumbered, sold or otherwise disposed of; (ii) any conveyance, transfer, pledge or encumbrance of any interest in Grantor [including, but not limited to, any change in the percentage ownership of _____ or _____ in _____, _____, one the general partners of Grantor or any change in the percentage ownership of _____, _____, _____, or _____ in the stock of _____, a Washington _____, one of the general partners of Grantor]; or (iii) any change in the individual(s) comprising Grantor or in the partners, stockholders or beneficiaries of Grantor from those on the date hereof. The foregoing prohibitions shall not be applicable to (i) transfers of ownership as a result of the death of a natural person who is Grantor or (ii) transfers by a natural person to a spouse, son or daughter or descendant of either, a stepson or stepdaughter or descendant of either, or (iii) transfers by any natural person in connection with bona fide estate planning.

3.04 *Grantor's Estoppel.* Grantor shall, within ten (10) days after a request by Beneficiary, furnish a duly acknowledged written statement in form satisfactory to Beneficiary setting forth the amount of the Secured Indebtedness, stating either that no offsets or defenses exist against the Secured Indebtedness, or if such offsets or defenses are alleged to exist, the nature and extent thereof and such other matters as Beneficiary may reasonably request.

3.05 *Further Assurances.* Grantor shall, at the cost of Grantor, and without expense to Beneficiary and/or Trustee, do, execute, acknowledge and deliver all and every such further acts, deeds, conveyances, mortgages, deeds of trust, assignments, security agreements, financing statements, modifications, notices of assignment, transfers and assurances as Beneficiary and/or Trustee shall from time to time reasonably require, for the better assuring, conveying, assigning, transferring and confirming unto Beneficiary and/or Trustee the Property and rights hereby conveyed or assigned or intended now or hereafter so to be, or which Grantor may be or may hereafter become bound to convey or assign to Beneficiary and/or Trustee, or for carrying out the intention or facilitating the performance of the terms of this Deed of Trust or any of the other Loan Documents, or for filing, refiling, registering, reregistering, recording or rerecording this Deed of Trust. Upon any failure by Grantor to comply with the terms of this Section, Beneficiary may, at Grantor's expense, make, execute, record, file, rerecord and/or refile any and all such documents for and in the name of Grantor, and Grantor hereby irrevocably appoints Beneficiary as its attorney-in-fact so to do and such appointment is coupled with an interest.

3.06 *Fees and Expenses.* If Beneficiary becomes a party (by intervention or otherwise) to any action or proceeding affecting, directly or indirectly, Grantor, the Property or the title thereto or Beneficiary's interest under this Deed of Trust, or employs an attorney to collect any of the Secured Indebtedness or to enforce performance of the obligations, covenants and agreements of the Loan Documents, Grantor shall reimburse Beneficiary for all expenses, costs, charges and legal fees incurred by Beneficiary (including, without limitation, the fees and expenses of experts and consultants), whether or not suit be commenced, and the same shall be reimbursed to Beneficiary in accordance with Section 3.10 hereof.

3.07 *Replacement of Note.* Upon notice to Grantor of the loss, theft, destruction or mutilation of the Note, Grantor will execute and deliver, in lieu thereof, a replacement note, identical in form and substance to the Note and dated as of the date of the Note and upon such execution and delivery all references in any of the Loan Documents to the Note shall be deemed to refer to such replacement note.

3.08 *Hazardous Substances.*

(a) Grantor hereby represents, warrants, covenants and agrees to and with Beneficiary that all operations or activities upon, or any use or occupancy of the Property, or any portion thereof, by Grantor, and any tenant, subtenant or occupant of the Property, or any portion thereof, is presently and shall hereafter be in all respects in compliance with all state, federal and local laws and regulations governing or in any way relating to the generation, handling, manufacturing, treatment, storage, use, transportation, spillage, leakage, dumping, discharge or disposal (whether legal or illegal, accidental or intentional) of any Hazardous Substance; and that neither Grantor nor (to the best of Grantor's knowledge, after due inquiry) any tenant, subtenant or occupant of all or any portion of the Property, has at any time placed, suffered or permitted the presence of any such Hazardous Substances at, on, under, within or about the Property, or any portion thereof in violation of applicable law.

(b) In the event any investigation or monitoring of site conditions or any clean-up, containment, restoration, removal or other remedial work (collectively, the "Remedial Work") is required under any applicable federal, state or local law or regulation, by any judicial order, or by any governmental entity, or in order to comply with any agreement entered into because of, or in connection with, any occurrence or event described in this Section, Grantor shall perform or cause to be performed the Remedial Work in compliance with such law, regulation, order or agreement. All Remedial Work shall be performed by one or more contractors, selected by Grantor and approved in advance in writing by Beneficiary, and under the supervision of a consulting engineer, selected by Grantor and approved in advance in writing by Beneficiary. All costs and expenses of such Remedial Work shall be paid by Grantor including, without limitation, the charges of such contractor(s) and/or the consulting engineer, and Beneficiary's reasonable attorneys', architects' and/or consultants' fees and costs incurred in connection with monitoring or review of such Remedial Work. In the event Grantor shall fail to timely commence, or cause to be commenced, or fail to diligently prosecute to completion, such Remedial Work, Beneficiary may, but shall not be required to, cause such Remedial Work to be performed.

(c) No amounts which may become owing by Grantor to Beneficiary under this Section 3.08 or under any other provision of this Deed of Trust as a result of a breach of or violation of this Section 3.08 shall be secured by this Deed of Trust but such obligations shall continue in full force and effect and any breach thereunder shall constitute a default under this Deed of Trust.

3.09 *Waiver of Consequential Damages.* Grantor covenants and agrees that in no event shall Beneficiary be liable for consequential damages, whatever the nature of a failure by Beneficiary to perform its obligation(s), if any, under the Loan Documents, and Grantor hereby expressly waives all claims that it now or may hereafter have against Beneficiary for such consequential damages.

3.10 *Beneficiary Reimbursement.* Any payments made, or funds expended or advanced by Beneficiary pursuant to the provisions of any Loan Document, shall (1) become a part of the Secured Indebtedness, (2) bear interest at the Interest Rate (as such term is defined in the Note) from the date such payments are made or funds expended or advanced, (3) become due and payable by Grantor upon demand therefor by Beneficiary, and (4) bear interest at the Default Rate (as such term is defined in the Note) from the date of such demand. Failure to reimburse Beneficiary upon such demand shall constitute an Event of Default under Section 2.01(a) hereof.

3.11 *Indemnification of Trustee.* Except for gross negligence and willful misconduct, Trustee shall not be liable for any act or omission or error of judgment. Trustee may rely on any document believed by it in good faith to be genuine. All money received by Trustee shall, until used or applied as herein provided, be held in trust, but need not be segregated (except to the extent required by law), and Trustee shall not be liable for interest thereon. Grantor shall protect, indemnify and hold harmless Trustee against all liability and expenses which Trustee may incur in the performance of its duties hereunder.

3.12 *Actions by Trustee.* At any time, or from time to time, without liability therefor and without notice, upon written request of Beneficiary and presentation of this Deed of Trust and the Note for endorsement, and without affecting the personal liability of any person for payment of the Secured Indebtedness or the effect of this Deed of Trust upon the remainder of the Property, Trustee may take such actions as Beneficiary may request and which are permitted by this Deed of Trust or by applicable law.

ARTICLE IV
MISCELLANEOUS COVENANTS

4.01 *Remedies Cumulative.* No right, power or remedy conferred upon or reserved to Beneficiary and/or Trustee by any of the Loan Documents is intended to be exclusive of any other right, power or remedy, but shall be cumulative and concurrent and in addition to any other right, power and remedy given hereunder or under any of the other Loan Documents or now or hereafter existing under applicable law.

4.02 *Notices.* All notices, demands and requests given or required to be given by, pursuant to, or relating to, this Deed of Trust shall be in writing. All notices hereunder shall be deemed to have been duly given if mailed by United States registered or certified mail, with return receipt requested, postage prepaid, or by United States Express Mail or other comparable overnight courier service to the parties at the addresses set forth on *Exhibit "A"* (or at such other addresses as shall be given in writing by any party to the others) and shall be deemed complete upon receipt or refusal to accept delivery as indicated in the return receipt or in the receipt of such United States Express Mail or courier service.

4.03 *Heirs and Assigns; Terminology.*

(a) This Deed of Trust applies to, inures to the benefit of, and binds Grantor, Beneficiary and Trustee, their heirs, legatees, devisees, administrators, executors, successors and assigns. The term "Grantor" shall include both the original Grantor and any subsequent owner or owners of any of the Property. The term "Beneficiary" shall include the owner and holder of the Note, whether or not named as Beneficiary herein. The term "Trustee" shall include both the original Trustee and any subsequent successor or additional trustee(s) acting hereunder.

(b) In this Deed of Trust, whenever the context so requires, the masculine gender includes the feminine and/or neuter, and the singular number includes the plural.

4.04 *Severability.* If any provision hereof should be held unenforceable or void, then such provision shall be deemed separable from the remaining provisions and shall in no way affect the validity of this Deed of Trust except that if such provision relates to the payment of any monetary sum, then, Beneficiary may, at its option declare the Secured Indebtedness immediately due and payable.

4.05 *Applicable Law.* This Deed of Trust shall be construed and enforced in accordance with the laws of the State. At the option of the Beneficiary, the venue of any action to enforce the provisions hereof may be laid in the county of the State in which the Real Property is located.

4.06 *Captions.* The captions are inserted only as a matter of convenience and for reference, and in no way define, limit, or describe the scope or intent of this Deed of Trust, nor in any way affect this Deed of Trust.

4.07 *Time of the Essence.* Time shall be of the essence with respect to all of Grantor's obligations under this Deed of Trust and the other Loan Documents.

4.08 *No Merger.* In the event that Beneficiary should become owner of the Property, there shall be no merger of the estate created by this Deed of Trust with the fee estate in the Property.

4.09 *No Modifications.* This Deed of Trust may not be changed, amended or modified, except in a writing expressly intended for such purpose and executed by Grantor and Beneficiary.

4.10 *Non-Agricultural Use.* The Real Property which is the subject of this Deed of Trust is not used principally for agricultural or farming purposes.

4.11 **NOTICE RE ORAL COMMITMENTS. ORAL AGREEMENTS OR ORAL COMMITMENTS TO LOAN MONEY, EXTEND CREDIT, OR TO FORBEAR FROM ENFORCING REPAYMENT OF A DEBT ARE NOT ENFORCEABLE UNDER WASHINGTON LAW.**

4.12 *Counterparts.* This Deed of Trust may be executed in counterparts each of which shall constitute an original and all of which together shall constitute but one instrument.

IN WITNESS WHEREOF, Grantor has executed this Deed of Trust, or has caused this Deed of Trust to be executed by its duly authorized representative(s) as of the day and year first written above.

EXHIBIT "A"

TO DEED OF TRUST AND SECURITY AGREEMENT

I. *DEFINED TERMS*

"County" shall mean _____ County, Washington.

"Hazardous Substances" shall include without limitation:

(i) Those substances included within the definitions of "hazardous substances," "hazardous materials," "toxic substances," or "solid waste" in the Comprehensive Environmental Response Compensation and Liability Act of 1980 (42 U.S.C. § 9601 et seq.) ("CERCLA"), as amended by Superfund Amendments and Reauthorization Act of 1986 (Pub.L. 99–499, 100 Stat. 1613) ("SARA"), the Resource Conservation and Recovery Act of 1976 (42 U.S.C. § 6901 et seq.) ("RCRA"), and the Hazardous Materials Transportation Act, 49 U.S.C. § 1801 et seq., and in the regulations promulgated pursuant to said laws, all as amended;

(ii) Those substances listed in the United States Department of Transportation Table (49 CFR 172.101 and amendments thereto) or by the Environmental Protection Agency (or any successor agency) as hazardous substances (40 CFR Part 302 and amendments thereto);

(iii) Any material, waste or substance which is (A) petroleum, (B) asbestos, (C) polychlorinated biphenyls, (D) designated as a "hazardous substance" pursuant to Section 311 of the Clean Water Act, 33 U.S.C. § 1251 et seq. (33 U.S.C. § 1321) or listed pursuant to Section 307 of the Clean Water Act (33 U.S.C. § 1317); (E) flammable explosives; or (F) radioactive materials;

(iv) Those substances defined as "dangerous wastes," "hazardous wastes" or as "hazardous substances" under the Water Pollution Control Act, RCW 90.48.010 et seq., the Hazardous Waste Management Statute, RCW 70.105.010 et seq., and the Toxic Substance Control Act (Senate Bill No. 6085) RCW 70.105B.010 et seq., the Model Toxics Control Act, RCW 70.-105D.010 et seq. and the Toxic Substance Control Act, 15 U.S.C. Section 2601 et seq., and in the regulations promulgated pursuant to said laws, all as amended;

(v) Storm water discharge regulated under any federal, state or local law, ordinance or regulation relating to storm water drains, including, but not limited to, Section 402(p) of the Clean Water Act, 33 U.S.C. Section 1342 and to the regulations promulgated thereunder; and

(vi) Such other substances, materials and wastes which are or become regulated as hazardous or toxic under applicable local, state or federal law, or the United States government, or which are classified as hazardous or toxic under federal, state, or local laws or regulations.

"Leasing Guidelines" shall mean guidelines, from time to time approved in writing by Beneficiary, for the leasing of all or any part of the Property, but which in any event, unless and until further leasing guidelines are approved by Beneficiary, shall be as follows:

(a) leases must be in the form of the standard form of lease approved by Beneficiary in writing;

(b) no term of any lease or rental agreement shall exceed one (1) year;

(c) leases must not contain any rights of first refusal or options to purchase all or any portion of the property;

(d) the annual rentals under the leases, determined as if the apartments were rented on an unfurnished basis, shall not be less than $_____ and all apartments rented shall be rented on a basis so that if the apartments were one hundred percent (100%) rented, the annual rentals on an unfurnished basis would be at least $_____; and

(e) at the time of entering into any lease there must not exist an Event of Default under any of the Loan Documents.

"Rents and Profits" shall mean all and any income, rents, royalties, revenue, issues, profits, proceeds, accounts receivable and other benefits now or hereafter arising from the Property, or any part thereof.

"Requirements" shall mean all requirements relating to land and building construction, use and maintenance, including, without limitation, planning, zoning, subdivision, environmental, air quality, flood hazard, fire safety, handicapped facilities and other governmental approvals, permits, licenses and/or certificates as may be necessary from time to time to comply with any of the foregoing, and other applicable statutes, rules, orders, regulations, laws, ordinances and covenants, conditions and restrictions, which now or hereafter pertain to and/or affect the design, construction, existence, operation or use and occupancy of the Property, or any part thereof, or any business conducted therein or thereon.

"State" shall mean the State of _____, the state in which the Property is located.

II. ADDRESSES

Grantor's address:
_____
_____
_____

Beneficiary's address:

_____
_____
_____
_____

Trustee's address:

_____
_____
_____
_____

EXHIBIT "B"

TO DEED OF TRUST AND SECURITY AGREEMENT

PROPERTY DESCRIPTION

A certain tract of land situated in _____ County, Washington and more particularly described as follows:

EXHIBIT "C"

TO DEED OF TRUST AND SECURITY AGREEMENT

PERMITTED EXCEPTIONS

EXHIBIT "D"

TO DEED OF TRUST AND SECURITY AGREEMENT

REQUIREMENTS FOR RESTORATION

Unless otherwise expressly agreed in a writing signed by Beneficiary for such purpose, the Requirements For Restoration shall be as follows:

(a) In the event the Net Insurance Proceeds are to be used for the Restoration, Grantor shall, prior to the commencement of any work or services in connection with the Restoration (the "Work"), deliver or furnish to Beneficiary (i) complete plans and specifications for the Work which (A) have been approved by all governmental authorities whose approval is required, (B) bear the signed approval of an architect satisfactory to Beneficiary (the "Architect") and (C) are accompanied by Architect's signed estimate of the total estimated cost of the Work which plans and specifications shall be subject to Beneficiary's prior approval (the "Approved Plans and Specifications"); (ii) the amount of money which, as determined by Beneficiary, will be sufficient when added to the Net Insurance Proceeds, if any, to pay the entire cost of the Restoration (all such money as held by Beneficiary being herein collectively referred to as the "Restoration Funds"); (iii) copies of all permits and approvals required by law in connection with the commencement and conduct of the Work; (iv) a contract for construction executed by Grantor and a contractor satisfactory to Beneficiary (the "Contractor") in form, scope and substance satisfactory to Beneficiary (including a provision for retainage) for performance of the Work; and (v) a surety bond for and/or guarantee of payment for and completion of, the Work, which bond or guarantee shall be (A) in form, scope and substance satisfactory to Beneficiary, (B) signed by a surety or sureties, or guarantor or guarantors, as the case may be, who are acceptable to Beneficiary, and (C) in an amount not less than Architect's total estimated cost of completing the Work.

(b) Grantor shall not commence any portion of the Work, other than temporary work to protect the Property or prevent interference with business, until Grantor shall have complied with the requirements of subparagraph (a) above. After commencing the Work, Grantor shall perform or cause Contractor to perform the Work diligently and in good faith in accordance with the Approved Plans and Specifications. So long as there does not currently exist an Event of Default under any of the Loan Documents, Beneficiary shall disburse the Restoration Funds in increments to Grantor, from time to time as the Work progresses, to pay (or reimburse Grantor for) the costs of the Work, but subject to the following conditions, any of which Beneficiary may waive in its sole discretion:

(i) Architect shall be in charge of the Work;

(ii) Beneficiary shall make such payments directly or through escrow with a title company selected by Grantor and approved by Beneficiary, only upon not less than ten (10) days' prior written notice from Grantor to Beneficiary and Grantor's delivery to Beneficiary of (A) Grantor's written request for payment (a "Request for Payment") accompanied by a certificate by architect in form, scope and substance satisfactory to Beneficiary which states that all of the Work completed to that date has been done in compliance with the Approved Plans and Specifications and in accordance with all provisions of law, that the amount requested has been paid or is then due and payable and is properly a part of the cost of the Work and that when added to all sums, if any, previously paid out by Beneficiary, the requested amount does not exceed the value of the Work done to the date of such certificate; (B) evidence satisfactory to Beneficiary that there are no mechanic's or similar liens for labor or material supplied in connection with the Work to date or that any such liens have been adequately provided for to Beneficiary's satisfaction; and (C) evidence satisfactory to Beneficiary that the balance of the Restoration Funds remaining after making the payments shall be sufficient to pay the balance of the cost of the Work not completed to date (giving in such reasonable detail as Beneficiary may require an estimate of the cost of such completion). Each Request for Payment shall be accompanied by (x) waivers of liens satisfactory to Beneficiary covering that part of the Work previously paid for, if any, (y) a search prepared by a title company or by other evidence satisfactory to Beneficiary that no mechanic's liens or other liens or instruments for the retention of title in respect of any part of the Work have been filed against the Property and not discharged of record, and (z) an indorsement to Beneficiary's title policy ensuring the Beneficiary that no encumbrance exists on or affects the Property other than the Permitted Exceptions;

(iii) No lease affecting the Property immediately prior to the damage or destruction shall have been cancelled, nor contain any still exercisable right to cancel, due to such damage or destruction; and

(iv) Any Request for Payment after the Restoration has been completed shall be accompanied by a copy of any certificate or certificates required by law to render occupancy of the Improvements legal.

(c) If (i) within sixty (60) days after the occurrence of any damage or destruction to the Property requiring Restoration, Grantor fails to submit to Beneficiary and receive Beneficiary's approval of plans and specifications or fails to deposit with Beneficiary the additional amount necessary to accomplish the Restoration as provided in subparagraph (a) above, or (ii) after such plans and specifications are approved by all such governmental authorities and Beneficiary, Grantor fails to commence promptly or diligently continue to completion the Restoration, or (iii) subject to Section 1.16 hereof, Grantor becomes delinquent in payment to mechanics, materialmen or others for the costs incurred in connection with the Restoration, then, in addition to all of the rights herein set forth and after five (5) days' written notice of the non-fulfillment of one or more of the foregoing conditions, Beneficiary may apply the Restoration Funds then or thereafter held by Beneficiary to reduce the Secured Indebtedness in such order as Beneficiary may determine, and at Beneficiary's option and in its sole discretion, Beneficiary may declare the Secured Indebtedness immediately due and payable.

ASSIGNMENT OF LEASES

THIS ASSIGNMENT OF LEASES ("Assignment") dated as of _____, 19__, by _____, a _____ ("Assignor"), having its principal place of business at _____ to _____, a _____, ("Assignee"), having an address of _____, is made with reference to the following facts:

A. Assignee has loaned or will loan to Assignor the sum of $_____ evidenced by a promissory note in the original principal amount of $_____ executed by Assignor as maker in favor of Assignee as holder including any extensions, modifications or amendments thereto (the "Note"), the payment of which is secured by a Deed of Trust, Security Agreement and Fixture Filing dated as of the date hereof executed by Assignor as Grantor in favor of Assignee as Beneficiary (the "Deed of Trust"), affecting the right, title and interest of Assignor in the real property located in _____ County, Washington, more particularly described in Exhibit A attached hereto (the "Property") and Assignor's interest in the improvements situated on the Property and the right, title and interest of Assignor in the personal property, trade fixtures and equipment situated on the Property; and

B. Assignor desires to assign to Assignee all of its right, title and interest in and to all leases, including subleases thereof, whether written or oral, and all agreements for use and occupancy, now existing, which affect the Property, and any and all leases and agreements for use and occupancy hereafter arising which affect the Property and the improvements located thereon, together with any and all extensions and renewals of any leases or agreements and also together with any and all guarantees of the lessee's obligations under any leases and under any and all extensions and renewals of any leases. All of the foregoing are hereinafter collectively referred to as the "Leases".

NOW, THEREFORE, FOR VALUE RECEIVED, Assignor hereby absolutely and unconditionally grants, transfers, and assigns to Assignee all of the right, title and interest of Assignor now existing and hereafter arising in and to the Leases, and hereby gives to and confers upon Assignee the right to collect all the income, rents, royalties, revenues, issues, profits and proceeds from the Leases. Assignor irrevocably appoints Assignee its true and lawful attorney, at the option of Assignee at any time to demand, receive and enforce payment, to give receipts, releases and satisfactions and to sue, either in the name of Assignor or in the name of Assignee, for all such income, rents, royalties, revenues, issues, profits and proceeds and apply the same to the indebtedness secured by the Deed of Trust. The foregoing assignment is intended to be specific, perfected and choate upon the recording of this Deed of Trust as provided in RCW 7.28.230(3). Each capitalized term used herein, unless otherwise defined herein, shall have the same meaning as set forth in the Deed of Trust.

A. ASSIGNOR COVENANTS AND AGREES AS FOLLOWS:

1. To perform and discharge faithfully each and every obligation, covenant and agreement of the Leases by Assignor as lessor thereunder to be performed; to give prompt notice to Assignee of any notice of default on the part of Assignor with respect to the Leases received from any lessee or guarantor, if any, together with an accurate copy of any such notice; at the sole cost and expense of Assignor to enforce the performance of each and every obligation, covenant, condition and agreement of the lessees to be performed under the Leases except for non-material changes consistent with good business judgment for comparable projects in the community in which the Improvements are located; not to modify or alter in any way the terms of the Leases; not to terminate the term of the Leases and not to accept a surrender thereof (except for monetary defaults under the Leases unless required to do so by the terms of the Leases); not to consent to an assignment of the Leases or to a subletting of the Leases unless all preceding lessees remain liable for the obligations thereunder; not to anticipate the rents thereunder except to the extent specifically permitted in Section 1.10(d) of the Deed of Trust, or in any way to waive, excuse, condone or release or discharge the lessees thereunder of or from any obligation, covenant, condition or agreement by the lessees to be performed, including the obligation to pay the rental called for thereunder in the manner and at the place and time specified therein and Assignor does by these presents expressly release, relinquish and surrender unto Assignee all of Assignor's right, power and authority to modify in any way the terms or provisions of the Leases, or to terminate the term or accept a surrender thereof (except for non-material changes consistent with good business judgment for comparable projects in the community in which the Improvements are located, and except for monetary defaults under the Leases unless required to do so by the terms of the Leases), and any attempt on the part of Assignor to exercise any such right without the written authority and consent of Assignee thereto being first had and obtained shall, at the option of Assignee, be of no force or effect and shall, at the option of Assignee, constitute a breach of the terms hereof and, unless cured within the period of time provided for in the Deed of Trust, entitle Assignee to declare all sums secured by the Deed of Trust immediately due and payable and to exercise any remedies provided in the Deed of Trust and the Note.

2. At Assignor's sole cost and expense, to appear in and defend any action or proceeding arising under, growing out of or in any manner connected with the Leases or the obligations, duties or liabilities of lessor, lessee or any guarantor thereunder, and to pay all costs and expenses of Assignee, including reasonable attorneys' fees, in any such action or proceeding in which Assignee may appear.

3. That should Assignor fail to make any payment or to do any acts herein provided, then Assignee, but without obligation so to do and without notice to or demand on Assignor, and without releasing Assignor from any obligation hereof, may make or do the same in such manner and to such extent as Assignee may deem necessary, including specifically, without limiting its general powers, the right to appear in and defend any action or proceeding purporting to affect the Leases or the rights or powers of Assignee hereunder, and also the right to perform and discharge each and every obligation, covenant and agreement of Assignor as lessor contained in the Leases; and in exercising any such powers, to pay necessary costs and expenses, employ counsel and incur and pay reasonable attorneys' fees.

4. To pay immediately upon demand all sums expended by Assignee under the authority hereof, together with interest on all such sums at the Default Rate (as defined in the Note), and the same shall be added to the

indebtedness evidenced by the Note and shall be secured by the Deed of Trust.

5. Assignor shall not hire, retain or contract with any third party for property management services without the prior written approval by Assignee of such party and the terms of its contract for management services.

B. AS A MATERIAL INDUCEMENT TO THE EXECUTION AND ACCEPTANCE OF THIS ASSIGNMENT, ASSIGNOR REPRESENTS AND WARRANTS THAT:

1. Assignor has not executed any prior assignment of the Leases, or of any of them, or of its right, title and interest therein or in the rents to accrue thereunder which has not been terminated and released of record.

2. Assignor has not performed any act or executed any instrument which might prevent Assignee from operating under any of the terms and conditions hereof, or which would limit Assignee in such operations.

3. Assignor has not accepted any payment of advance rent (not including security deposits in an amount equal to or less than one month's rent) under any of the Leases for any period subsequent to the current period for which rent has already become due and payable.

4. Except as disclosed on the rent roll dated _____, 19__, there is no material default now existing under any of the Leases and no event has occurred and is continuing which would constitute an Event of Default thereunder but for the lapse of time or the requirement that notice be given thereunder.

5. Assignor has delivered to Assignee true and correct copies of all of the Leases and Assignor has not executed or granted any modification or amendment whatever of any of the Leases either orally or in writing.

6. The Leases, and each of them, are in full force and effect.

C. IT IS MUTUALLY AGREED WITH RESPECT TO EACH OF THE LEASES THAT:

1. So long as there shall exist no Event of Default as defined in the Deed of Trust or in the payment of any indebtedness secured by the Deed of Trust or any other document which evidences or secures the Note (collectively the "Loan Documents") or in the performance of any other obligation, covenant or agreement contained herein or in the Note, the Deed of Trust, or the Leases, Assignor shall have the right to receive and collect, but not prior to accrual, all rents, issues and profits from the Leases and to retain, use and enjoy the same.

2. Upon or at any time after an Event of Default hereunder or in the payment of any indebtedness secured by the Deed of Trust or the Loan Documents, or in the performance of any other obligation, term, covenant or agreement contained herein, in the Deed of Trust, the Loan Documents or in the Note, Assignee may exercise all rights and remedies contained in the Note, the Deed of Trust or the Loan Documents and without regard for the adequacy of the security for the indebtedness secured by the Deed of Trust. Assignee is authorized either in person or by agent, with or without bringing any action or proceeding, or by a receiver to be appointed by a court, to enter upon, take possession of, manage and operate the Property or any part thereof, make, enforce, modify, and accept the surrender of the Leases, or any of them, obtain and evict lessees, fix or modify rents, and do any acts which Assignee deems proper, and either with or without taking possession of the Property, in its own name sue for or otherwise collect and receive all rents, issues and profits, including those past due and unpaid (the same being hereby assigned and transferred for the benefit of Assignee), and apply the same, less costs and expenses of operation and collection, including reason-

able attorneys' fees, upon any indebtedness secured by the Deed of Trust, and in such order as Assignee may determine. The entering upon and taking possession of the Property, the collection of such rents, issues and profits and the application thereof as aforesaid, shall not cure or waive any default or waive, modify or affect notice of default under the Deed of Trust or invalidate any act done pursuant to such notice.

    3. The whole of the indebtedness evidenced by the Note shall become due upon the election by Assignee to accelerate the maturity of the indebtedness pursuant to the provisions of the Note or the Deed of Trust, or any of the Loan Documents or at the option of the Assignee, after any attempt by Assignor without the prior written consent of Assignee, to terminate any of the Leases or accept surrender thereof if such Leases required the consent or approval of Beneficiary under the Deed of Trust or, to waive or release any lessee under such Lease from the observance or performance of any material obligation on the part of the lessee to be observed or performed thereunder, or to anticipate rents under any Lease more than 30 days prior to accrual.

    4. Assignee shall not be obligated to perform or discharge, nor does it hereby undertake to perform or discharge any obligation, duty or liability under the Leases, or any of them, or under or by reason of this Agreement, and Assignor shall and does hereby agree to indemnify Assignee against and hold it harmless from any and all liability, loss or damage which it may or might incur under the Leases, or any of them, or under or by reason of this Assignment and from any and all claims and demands whatsoever which may be asserted against it by reason of any alleged obligation or undertaking on its part to perform or discharge any of the terms, covenants or agreements contained in the Leases; should Assignee incur any such liability, loss or damage under the Leases or under or by reason of this Assignment, or in defense against any such claims or demands, the amount thereof, including costs, expenses and reasonable attorneys' fees, together with interest thereon at the Default Rate (as defined in the Note), shall be secured by the Deed of Trust, and Assignor shall reimburse Assignee therefore immediately following demand, and upon failure of Assignor so to do, Assignee may declare all sums thereby secured immediately due and payable.

D. IT IS FURTHER MUTUALLY AGREED THAT:

    1. Until the Note has been paid in full, Assignor covenants to utilize its best effort to keep leased at good and sufficient rental and in compliance with the Leasing Guidelines set forth in the Deed of Trust all residential units in the improvements located thereon and, Assignor agrees, upon demand, to transfer and assign to Assignee any and all subsequent leases of the Property and the improvements located thereon upon the same or substantially the same terms and conditions as are herein contained, and to make, execute and deliver to Assignee, upon demand, any and all instruments that may be necessary or desirable therefor. The terms and provisions of this Assignment shall apply to any such subsequent lease whether or not so assigned and transferred.

    2. Assignor irrevocably authorizes and directs the lessees and any successors to the respective interest of the lessees, upon receipt of any written request of Assignee stating that an Event of Default as defined in the Deed of Trust exists in the payments due under, or in the performance of any of the terms, covenants or conditions of, the Deed of Trust, the Loan Documents or the Note, to pay to Assignee the rents due and to become due under the Leases. Assignor agrees that the lessees shall have the right to rely upon any such statement and request by Assignee, that the lessees shall pay such rents to Assignee without any obligation or right to inquire as to whether such default actually exists and notwithstanding any notice from or claim of Assignor to the contrary, and that Assignor shall have no right to claim against the lessees for any such rents so paid by the lessees to Assignee.

Upon the curing of all defaults, Assignee shall give written notice thereof to the lessees and thereafter, until the receipt of any further similar written requests of Assignee, if any, the lessees shall pay the rents to Assignor. It is understood and agreed that neither the assignment of income, rents, issues, profits and proceeds to Assignee nor the exercise by Assignee of any of its rights or remedies under this Agreement shall be deemed to make Assignee a "mortgagee-in-possession" or otherwise responsible or liable in any manner with respect to the Property or the use, occupancy, enjoyment or operation of all or any portion thereof, unless and until Assignee, in person or by agent, assumes actual possession thereof, nor shall appointment of a receiver for the Property by any court at the request of Assignee or by agreement with Assignor or the entering into possession of the Property or any part thereof by such receiver be deemed to make Assignee a "mortgagee-in-possession" or otherwise responsible or liable in any manner with respect to the Property or the use, occupancy, enjoyment or operation of all or any portion thereof.

3. At such time as a default shall occur under the Note, the Deed of Trust, this Assignment or any other instrument securing the Note, any action, suit or proceeding brought by Assignee pursuant to any of the terms hereof or of any Lease or otherwise, and any claim made by Assignee hereunder or under any Lease, may be compromised, withdrawn or otherwise dealt with by Assignee without any notice to or approval of Assignor.

4. Neither this Assignment nor any action or inaction on the part of Assignee shall constitute an assumption on the part of Assignee of any obligation or liability under any of the Leases. No action or inaction on the part of Assignor shall adversely affect or limit in any way the rights of Assignee under this Assignment or, through this Assignment, under any of the Leases.

5. Each right, power and remedy of Assignee provided for in this Assignment or now or hereafter existing at law or in equity or by statute or otherwise shall be cumulative and concurrent and shall be in addition to every other right, power or remedy provided for in this Assignment or now or hereafter existing at law or in equity or by statute or otherwise, and the exercise or beginning of the exercise by Assignee of any one or more of such rights, powers or remedies shall not preclude the simultaneous or later exercise by Assignee of all such other rights, powers or remedies. No failure or delay on the part of Assignee to exercise any such right, power or remedy shall operate as a waiver thereof.

6. Upon the payment in full of all indebtedness secured by the Deed of Trust, as evidenced by the recording of an instrument of full reconveyance of the Deed of Trust, this Assignment shall become and be void and of no effect.

7. Assignor at its expense will execute, acknowledge and deliver all such instruments and take all such action as Assignee from time to time may reasonably request for the assigning to Assignee of the rights assigned hereby and the full benefit hereof and to preserve and protect, until the termination of this Assignment as hereinabove provided, this Assignment and all of the rights, powers and remedies of Assignee provided for herein.

8. All notices, demands and requests given or required to be given by, pursuant to, or relating to, this Assignment shall be in writing. All notices hereunder shall be deemed to have been duly given if mailed by United States registered or certified mail, with return receipt requested, postage prepaid, or by United States Express Mail or other comparable overnight courier service to the parties at the addresses set forth in the opening paragraph hereof (or at such other addresses as shall be given in writing by any party to the others) and shall be deemed effective upon receipt or refusal of delivery as indicated in the return receipt or in the receipt of such United States Express Mail or courier service.

9. This Assignment or any term hereof may be changed, waived, discharged or terminated only by an instrument in writing signed by the party against which enforcement of such change, waiver, discharge or termination is sought. All the terms of this Assignment shall be binding upon the successors and assigns of Assignor and shall inure to the benefit of and be enforceable by Assignee, any successor holder of the Note and any trustee appointed for the benefit of the holder of the Note. This Assignment shall be construed and enforced in accordance with and governed by the laws of the state of Washington. The headings in this Assignment are for convenience of reference only and shall not limit or otherwise affect the meaning hereof. This Assignment may be executed in several counterparts, each of which shall be an original, but all of which shall constitute one and the same instrument.

IN WITNESS WHEREOF, this Assignment of Leases is executed as of the date hereinabove first set forth.

EXHIBIT A

A certain tract of land situated in _____ County, Washington more particularly described as follows:

UNSECURED INDEMNITY AGREEMENT

This Unsecured Indemnity Agreement (this "Agreement") is entered into as of _____, 19__ by _____, a _____ ("Indemnitor"), in favor of _____ ("Lender"), with reference to the following facts:

A. Lender has loaned or will loan to Indemnitor the sum of up to $_____ (the "Loan"), payment of which is evidenced by a promissory note of even date herewith (the "Note"), which is secured by a Deed of Trust, Security Agreement and Fixture Filing of even date herewith (the "Deed of Trust") executed by Indemnitor, as Grantor, in favor of Lender, as Beneficiary, encumbering certain real and other property more particularly described in the Deed of Trust (referred to in the Deed of Trust and herein as the "Property").

B. As a condition to making the Loan, Lender requires Indemnitor to indemnify and hold harmless Lender from any Environmental Claim, any Requirements of Environmental Law, any violation of any Environmental Permit and all Costs (as the foregoing terms are defined in Exhibit "A" hereto) relating to the Property in accordance with the terms and conditions in this Agreement. Lender would not make the Loan without this Agreement and Indemnitor acknowledges and understands that this Agreement is a material inducement for Lender's agreement to make the Loan. This Agreement is not intended to be, nor shall it be, secured by the Deed of Trust and it is not intended to secure payment of the Note but rather is an independent obligation of Indemnitor.

NOW, THEREFORE, in consideration of the sum of TEN DOLLARS ($10.00), in hand paid, and other good and valuable consideration, the receipt and sufficiency of which are hereby acknowledged, Indemnitor agrees as follows:

1. *Indemnification.*

(a) Subject to paragraph 1(c) below, Indemnitor shall protect, defend, indemnify, and hold harmless Lender, its officers, directors, shareholders, agents and employees and their respective heirs, legal representatives, successors and assigns (Lender and all such other persons and entities being referred to herein individually as an "Indemnitee" and collectively as "Indemnitees") from and against all Costs, which at any time may be imposed upon the Property, the Indemnitees, or any of them, arising out of or in connection with (i) Requirements of Environmental Law; (ii) Environmental Claims; (iii) the failure of Indemnitor, or any other party directly or indirectly connected with the Property, or affiliated with Indemnitor to obtain, maintain, or comply with any Environmental Permit; and/or (iv) the presence or existence of Hazardous Materials (as defined in Exhibit "B" hereto) at, on, about, under, within, near or in connection with the Property.

(b) In the event that any investigation, site monitoring, containment, cleanup, removal, restoration or other remedial work of any kind or nature (the "Remedial Work") is necessary or desirable under any applicable local, state or federal law or regulation, any judicial order, or by any governmental or non-governmental entity or person because of, or in connection with, the current or future presence, suspected presence, release or suspected release of Hazardous Materials in or into the air, soil, ground water, surface water or soil vapor at, on, about, under, within or near the Property (or any portion thereof), Indemnitor shall within thirty (30) days after written demand for performance thereof by any Indemnitee (or such shorter period of time as may be required under any applicable law, regulation, order or agreement), promptly commence, or cause to be commenced, and thereafter diligently prosecute to completion, all such Remedial Work. All Remedial Work shall be performed by one or more contractors, approved in advance in writing by Lender, and under the supervision of a consulting engineer approved in advance in writing by Lender. All Costs related to such Remedial Work shall be paid by Indemnitor including, without limitation, Costs incurred by any Indemnitee in connection with monitoring or review of such Remedial Work. In the event Indemnitor shall fail to promptly commence, or cause to be commenced, or fail to diligently prosecute to completion, such Remedial Work, Lender may, but shall not be required to, cause such Remedial Work to be performed and all Costs shall become an Environmental Claim hereunder.

(c) Notwithstanding anything to the contrary set forth in this Agreement, the liability of Indemnitor under this Agreement shall arise only from the matters described in paragraph 1(a) above which occur or arise (in whole or in part) prior to the complete satisfaction, assignment or reconveyance of the Deed of Trust.

(d) This Agreement, and all rights and obligations hereunder shall survive (i) surrender of the Note; (ii) satisfaction, assignment or reconveyance of the Deed of Trust and release of other security provided in connection with the Loan; (iii) foreclosure of the Deed of Trust and other security instruments in connection with the Loan; acquisition of the Property by Lender; and (iv) transfer of all of Lender's rights in the Loan and the Property.

(e) Nothing contained in this Agreement shall prevent or in any way diminish or interfere with any rights or remedies, including, without limitation, the right to contribution, which any Indemnitee may have against Indemnitor or any other party under the Comprehensive Environmental Response, Compensation and Liability Act of 1980 (codified at Title 42 U.S.C. § 9601 et seq.), as it may be amended from time to time, or any other applicable federal, state or local laws, all such rights being hereby expressly reserved.

2. *Notice of Actions.*

(a) Indemnitor shall give immediate written notice to Lender of: (i) any proceeding, inquiry, notice, or other communication by or from any governmental or non-governmental entity regarding the presence or suspected presence of any Hazardous Material at, on, about, under, within, near or in connection with the Property or any migration thereof from or to the Property; (ii) any actual or alleged violation of any Requirements of Environmental Law; (iii) all Environmental Claims; (iv) the discovery of any occurrence or condition on any real property adjoining or in the vicinity of the Property that could cause the Property or any part thereof to be subject to any environmental law restrictions on ownership, occupancy, transferability, or use, or subject the owner or any person having any interest in the Property to any liability, penalty, or disability under any Requirements of Environmental Law; and (v) the receipt of any notice or discovery of any information regarding any actual, alleged, or potential use, manufacture, production, storage, spillage, seepage, release, discharge, disposal or any other presence or existence of any Hazardous Material at, on, about, under, within, near or in connection with the Property.

(b) Immediately upon receipt of the same, Indemnitor shall deliver to Lender copies of any and all Environmental Claims, and any and all orders, notices, permits, applications, reports, and other communications, documents, and instruments pertaining to the actual, alleged, or potential presence or existence of any Hazardous Material at, on, about, under, within, near or in connection with the Property.

(c) Lender shall have the right to join and participate in, as a party if it so elects, any legal proceedings or actions in connection with the Property involving any Environmental Claim, any Hazardous Material or Requirements of Environmental Law, and Indemnitor shall reimburse Lender upon demand for all of Lender's Costs in connection therewith.

3. *Procedures Relating to Indemnification.*

(a) In any circumstance in which this Agreement applies, Lender may, but shall not be obligated to, employ its own legal counsel and consultants to investigate, prosecute, negotiate, or defend any such Environmental Claim and Lender shall have the right to compromise or settle the same without the necessity of showing actual liability therefor, with notice to but without the consent of Indemnitor. Indemnitor shall reimburse Lender, upon demand, for all Costs incurred by Lender, including the amount of all Costs of settlements entered into by Lender.

(b) Indemnitor shall not, without the prior written consent of Lender (i) settle or compromise any Environmental Claim or consent to the entry of any judgment arising out of or relating to any Environmental Claim that does not include as an unconditional term thereof the delivery by the claimant or plaintiff to Lender of (x) a full and complete written release of Lender (in form, scope and substance satisfactory to Lender in its sole discretion) from all liability in respect of such action, suit or proceeding and (y) a dismissal with prejudice of such suit, action or proceeding arising out of or relating to any Environmental Claim; or (ii) settle or compromise any Environmental Claim in any manner that may adversely affect Lender as determined by Lender in its sole discretion.

4. *Binding Effect.*

(a) This Agreement shall be binding upon the Indemnitor, its successors and permitted assigns and shall inure to the benefit of the Indemnitees and their successors and assigns, including as to Lender, without limitation, any holder of the Note and any affiliate of Lender which acquires all or part of the Property by any sale, assignment, deed in lieu of foreclosure, foreclosure under the Deed of Trust, or otherwise. The obligations of Indemnitor under this Agreement shall not be assigned without the prior written consent of Lender which consent may be given or withheld in the sole discretion of Lender.

(b) This Agreement shall run with the land described in *Exhibit C* attached hereto and constitute the binding obligation of all parties having a legal ownership interest in the Property (as distinguished from only an equitable or mortgage interest or interest of a secured creditor) at any time during the time that the Deed of Trust constitutes a lien upon the Property. All such parties shall be deemed an Indemnitor under this Agreement. This Agreement or a memorandum thereof, at Indemnitee's option, may be placed of record against the Property to impart notice of this Agreement to all parties in ownership of the Property during the term of the Deed of Trust. Upon termination of the lien of the Deed of Trust, the memorandum, but not this Agreement, shall automatically become null and void and this Agreement shall not be applicable to subsequent owners of the Property unless such subsequent owner was also an owner of the Property during the term of the Deed of Trust.

5. *Liability of Indemnitor.* The liability of Indemnitor under this Agreement shall in no way be limited or impaired by the provisions of the Note, Deed of Trust or any of the other documents evidencing or securing the Loan, or any amendment, modification, extension or renewal thereof. In addition, the liability of Indemnitor under this Agreement shall in no way be limited or impaired by any sale, assignment, or foreclosure of the Note or Deed of Trust or any sale or transfer of all or any part of the Property or any interest therein.

6. *Waiver.* Indemnitor waives any right or claim of right to cause a marshaling of the assets of Indemnitor or to cause Lender to proceed against any of the security for the Loan before proceeding under this Agreement against Indemnitor; Indemnitor agrees that any payments required to be made hereunder shall become due on demand; Indemnitor expressly waives and relinquishes all rights and remedies accorded by applicable law to indemnitors or guarantors, except any rights of subrogation that Indemnitor may have, provided that the indemnity provided for hereunder shall neither be contingent upon the existence of any such rights of subrogation nor subject to any claims or defenses whatsoever that may be asserted in connection with the enforcement or attempted enforcement of such subrogation rights, including, without limitation, any claim that such subrogation rights were abrogated by any acts or omissions of Lender.

7. *Notices.* All notices, consents, approvals, elections and other communications (collectively "Notices") hereunder shall be in writing (whether or not the other provisions of this Agreement expressly so provide) and shall be deemed to have been duly given if mailed by United States registered or certified mail, with return receipt requested, postage prepaid, or by United States Express Mail or courier service to the parties at the following addresses (or at such other addresses as shall be given in writing by any party to the others pursuant to this Section 7) and shall be deemed complete ten (10) days following receipt or refusal to accept delivery as indicated in the return receipt or in the receipt of such Express Mail or courier service:

If to Indemnitor to: _____
_____
_____

If to Lender: _____
_____
_____

8. *Attorneys' Fees.* In the event that any Indemnitee brings or otherwise becomes a party to any suit or other proceeding (including, without limitation, any administrative proceedings) with respect to the subject matter or enforce-

ment of this Agreement, such Indemnitee shall, in addition to such other relief as may be awarded, be entitled to recover from Indemnitor reasonable attorneys' fees, expenses and costs of investigation as are actually incurred (including, without limitation, attorneys' fees, expenses and costs of investigation incurred in appellate proceedings, costs incurred in establishing the right to indemnification, or in any action or participation in, or in connection with, any case or proceeding under Chapter 7, 11 or 13 of the Bankruptcy Code, 11 U.S.C. § 101 et seq., or any successor statutes).

9. *Governing Law.* This Agreement and the rights and obligations of the parties hereunder shall in all respects be governed by, and construed and enforced in accordance with, the laws of the State of Washington ("State"). Indemnitors hereby irrevocably submit to the non-exclusive jurisdiction of any State or federal court sitting in Washington over any suit, action or proceeding arising out of or relating to this Agreement, and Indemnitors hereby agree and consent that, in addition to any other methods of service of process in any such suit, action or proceeding in any State or federal court sitting in Washington, service of process may be made by certified or registered mail, return receipt requested, directed to Indemnitors at the address indicated in Section 7 hereof, and service so made shall be complete ten (10) days after the same shall have been so mailed.

10. *Successive Actions.* A separate right of action hereunder shall arise each time Lender acquires knowledge of any matter indemnified by Indemnitor under this Agreement. Separate and successive actions may be brought hereunder to enforce any of the provisions hereof at any time and from time to time. No action hereunder shall preclude any subsequent action, and Indemnitor hereby waives and covenants not to assert any defense in the nature of splitting of causes of action or merger of judgments.

11. *Partial Invalidity.* If any provision of this Agreement shall be determined to be unenforceable in any circumstances by a court of competent jurisdiction, then the balance of this Agreement shall be enforceable nonetheless, and the subject provision shall be enforceable in all other circumstances.

12. *Interest on Unpaid Amounts.* All amounts required to be paid or reimbursed to any Indemnitee hereunder shall bear interest from the date of expenditure by such Indemnitee or the date of written demand to Indemnitor hereunder, whichever is earlier, until paid to Indemnitee(s). The interest rate shall be the lesser of (a) _____ percent (__%) per annum or (b) the maximum rate then permitted for the parties to contract for under applicable law.

IN WITNESS WHEREOF, Indemnitor has executed this Agreement as of the date first set forth above.

EXHIBIT "A" TO

UNSECURED INDEMNITY AGREEMENT

Definitions. For purposes of this Agreement, the following terms shall have the following meanings:

(a) "Environmental Claim" shall include, but not be limited to, any claim, demand, action, cause of action, suit, loss, cost, damage, fine, penalty, expense, liability, judgment, proceeding, or injury, whether threatened, sought, brought, or imposed, that seeks to impose costs or liabilities for (i) noise; (ii) pollution or contamination of the air, surface water, ground water, or soil; (iii) solid, gaseous, or liquid waste generation, handling, treatment, storage, disposal, or transportation; (iv) exposure to Hazardous Materials; (v) the manufacture, processing, distribution in commerce, use, or storage of Hazardous Materials; (vi) injury to or death of any person or persons directly or indirectly connected with Hazardous Materials and directly or indirectly related to the

Property; (vii) destruction or contamination of any property directly or indirectly connected with Hazardous Materials and directly or indirectly related to the Property; or (viii) any and all penalties directly or indirectly connected with Hazardous Materials and directly or indirectly related to the Property. The term "Environmental Claim" also includes (i) the costs of removal of any and all Hazardous Materials from all or any portion of the Property, (ii) costs required to take necessary precautions to protect against the release of Hazardous Materials at, on, in, about, under, within, near or in connection with the Property in or into the air, soil, surface water, ground water, or soil vapor, any public domain, or any surrounding areas, and (iii) costs incurred to comply, in connection with all or any portion of the Property or any surrounding areas, with all applicable laws with respect to Hazardous Materials, including any such laws applicable to the work referred to in this sentence. "Environmental Claim" also means any asserted or actual breach or violation of any Requirements of Environmental Law, or any event, occurrence, or condition as a consequence of which, pursuant to any Requirements of Environmental Law, (i) Indemnitor, Lender, or any owner, occupant, or person having any interest in the Property shall be liable or suffer any disability, or (ii) the Property shall be subject to any restriction on use, ownership, transferability, or (iii) any Remedial Work shall be required.

(b) "Environmental Permit" means any permit, license, approval, or other authorization with respect to any activities, operations, or businesses conducted on or in relation to the Property under any applicable law, regulation, or other requirement of the United States or any state, municipality, or other subdivision or jurisdiction related to pollution or protection of health or the environment, or any private agreement (such as covenants, conditions and restrictions), including laws, regulations or other requirements relating to emissions, discharges, or releases or threatened releases of Hazardous Materials into ambient air, surface water, ground water, or soil, or otherwise relating to the manufacture, processing, distribution, use, generation, treatment, storage, disposal, transportation, or handling of Hazardous Materials directly or indirectly related to the Property.

(c) "Costs" shall mean all liabilities, losses, costs, damages, (including consequential damages), expenses, claims, attorneys' fees, experts' fees, consultants' fees and disbursements of any kind or of any nature whatsoever. For the purposes of this definition, such losses, costs and damages shall include, without limitation, remedial, removal, response, abatement, cleanup, legal, investigative and monitoring costs and related costs, expenses, losses, damages, penalties, fines, obligations, defenses, judgments, suits, proceedings and disbursements.

(d) "Requirements of Environmental Law" means all requirements of environmental or ecological laws or regulations or controls related to the Property, including all requirements imposed by any law, rule, order, or regulations of any federal, state, or local executive, legislative, judicial, regulatory, or administrative agency, board, or authority, or any private agreement (such as covenants, conditions and restrictions), which relate to (i) noise; (ii) pollution or protection of the air, surface water, ground water, or soil; (iii) solid, gaseous, or liquid waste generation, treatment, storage, disposal, or transportation; (iv) exposure to Hazardous Materials; or (v) regulation of the manufacture, processing, distribution and commerce, use, or storage of Hazardous Materials.

EXHIBIT "B" TO

UNSECURED INDEMNITY AGREEMENT

DEFINITION OF HAZARDOUS MATERIALS

The term "Hazardous Materials" shall include without limitation:

(i) Those substances included within the definitions of "hazardous substances," "hazardous materials," "toxic substances," or "solid waste" in the Comprehensive Environmental Response Compensation and Liability Act of 1980 (42 U.S.C. § 9601 et seq.) ("CERCLA"), as amended by Superfund Amendments and Reauthorization Act of 1986 (Pub.L. 99–499, 100 Stat. 1613) ("SARA"), the Resource Conservation and Recovery Act of 1976 (42 U.S.C. § 6901 et seq.) ("RCRA"), and the Hazardous Materials Transportation Act, 49 U.S.C. § 1801 et seq., and in the regulations promulgated pursuant to said laws, all as amended;

(ii) Those substances listed in the United States Department of Transportation Table (49 CFR 172.101 and amendments thereto) or by the Environmental Protection Agency (or any successor agency) as hazardous substances (40 CFR Part 302 and amendments thereto);

(iii) Any material, waste or substance which is (A) petroleum, (B) asbestos, (C) polychlorinated biphenyls, (D) designated as a "hazardous substance" pursuant to Section 311 of the Clean Water Act, 33 U.S.C. § 1251 et seq. (33 U.S.C. § 1321) or listed pursuant to Section 307 of the Clean Water Act (33 U.S.C. 1317); (E) flammable explosives; or (F) radioactive materials;

(iv) Those substances defined as "dangerous wastes," "hazardous wastes" or as "hazardous substances" under the Water Pollution Control Act, RCW 90.48.010 et seq., the Hazardous Waste Management Statute, RCW 70.105.010 et seq., and the Toxic Substance Control Act (Senate Bill No. 6085) RCW 70.105B.010 et seq., the Model Toxics Control Act, RCW 70.-105D.010 et seq. and the Toxic Substance Control Act, 15 U.S.C. Section 2601 et seq., and in the regulations promulgated pursuant to said laws, all as amended;

(v) Storm water discharge regulated under any federal, state or local law, ordinance or regulation relating to storm water drains, including, but not limited to, Section 402(p) of the Clean Water Act, 33 U.S.C. Section 1342 and the regulations promulgated thereunder; and

(vi) Such other substances, materials and wastes which are or become regulated as hazardous or toxic under applicable local, state or federal law, or the United States government, or which are classified as hazardous or toxic under federal, state, or local laws or regulations.

Chapter 15

COMMERCIAL FINANCING FORMS

Table of Sections

Sec.
15.1 Introduction.
15.2 Construction Loan Agreement.
15.3 ———— Condominium Development.
15.4 Subordination Agreement.
15.5 Loan Agreement With Lender Participation in Cash Flow and Appreciation.
15.6 Promissory Note—Incorporating Construction and Long-term Financing.
15.7 Combination Mortgage, Security Agreement, and Fixture Financing Statement.
15.8 Promissory Note With Lender Participation in Project Income and Appreciation.
15.9 Construction Loan Agreement—Homes in Subdivision.
15.10 Guaranty—Personally Guaranteeing Mortgage Debt.
15.11 Assignment of Leases and Rents—As Additional Security for Note and Mortgage.
15.12 Subordination, Non-disturbance and Attornment Agreement—For Lessee.
15.13 Tenant Estoppel Certificate.
15.14 Leasehold Mortgage—On Ground–Leased Income Property.
15.15 Lease Language Crucial to the Mortgageability of a Leasehold Interest.
15.16 Shopping Center Lease.

§ 15.1 Introduction

This Chapter contains forms used in a variety of complex commercial real estate financing transactions. Each is the product of a highly sophisticated real estate practice. In this connection, we are grateful to the following for their willingness to share their work product with the profession: Faegre & Benson, a leading Minneapolis law firm engaged in a large and varied commercial real estate practice; Ewing, Carter,

Smith, Gosnell, Vickers and Holerock, a Missouri law firm that is general counsel to one of the nation's largest savings and loan associations; O'Melveny & Myers, a leading Los Angeles law firm with a large and varied commercial real estate practice; the Metropolitan Life Insurance Company, one of the country's leading institutional mortgage lenders and the Rouse Company, one of the country's leading commercial real estate developers.

Several observations concerning these forms are appropriate. Many are the product of substantial negotiation and may reflect business considerations and other factors unique to the particular transaction for which they were created. Thus, they may need substantial modification for use in other contexts. Moreover, because they were often developed with a particular state's substantive law and financing methods in mind, they should be utilized only after a careful analysis of their suitability in the user's local setting. Nor should they be adopted without a close consideration of their federal and state income tax law implications. Notwithstanding the foregoing words of caution, we believe that, as the product of talented specialists, the forms will prove to be an invaluable source of drafting and structuring ideas in a variety of commercial financing settings.

§ 15.2 Construction Loan Agreement [1]

When a construction loan is made, it is customary for the parties to execute three basic documents, rather than the two (the note and the mortgage or deed of trust) which are usually employed in a long-term or non-construction loan. The third instrument is a construction loan agreement. Its purpose is to spell out in detail the lender's duties and method of disbursing the funds, the borrower/developer's obligations with respect to the funds and the construction, and other related matters.

The particular construction loan agreement set forth in this section was drafted for an income-producing project; a rental apartment building or a shopping center would be a typical example. The project was to be built on ground-leased land, with the fee owner/ground lessor joining in the mortgage, thereby "subordinating" his interest to that of the mortgagee. See Section 1.01(dd).

Article II sets out the lender's duty to disburse the loan. In addition to "hard costs"—actual materials and labor for the project—this loan contemplates the funding by the lender of certain "soft costs", such as permits, licenses, insurance premiums, and real estate taxes. Not all construction loans cover these items, and the point should be made clear in the documents. Under this loan, no funds are disbursed for land costs. Like most construction loans, this one permits capitalization, or adding to principal, of interest on the construction funds as

§ 15.2
1. Form provided by Faegre & Benson, Minneapolis, Minnesota.

they accrue. See Section 2.04. Sometimes lenders attempt to recover interest on funds before they have been disbursed, but under this agreement interest is payable only on money which has been disbursed. See Section 2.01.

As is typical, this agreement provides for a ten percent "holdback" on the "hard costs." See Section 2.02(a). This forces the developer to invest some of its own funds as the project is being built, giving it a greater incentive to avoid default and providing an additional "cushion" of value in the event of foreclosure of the construction mortgage.

Under this agreement, disbursements are to be made monthly on the basis of the cost of work performed and materials delivered to the project as of the date of the draw request. The lender is entitled to documentary evidence of the amount of work performed and materials delivered, and to a report from an Inspecting Engineer confirming that the work has indeed been done. See Section 2.02(c).

If the project appears to be "over budget" (i.e. the undisbursed funds from the construction loan are insufficient to complete the project), the lender has the right to demand a deposit by the borrower/developer of sufficient money to bring the total to the level required for completion. See Section 2.03.

One of the dilemmas in the drafting of a construction loan agreement arises from the doctrine that a mortgage securing optional advances—those made by the lender without any contractual duty to do so—lose priority as against any intervening liens of which the lender has notice when the advance in question is made. See § 12.7 supra for a detailed discussion of this doctrine. The construction lender would prefer to reserve to itself broad discretion to cease making advances if it discovers any sort of problem or irregularity in the course of construction. But if the construction loan agreement gives the lender too much discretion, the risk arises that a court will hold the advances to be optional, and thus to suffer a loss of priority. It is not easy to define precisely the line between reasonable precaution and excessive discretion on the lender's part.

Article III of this agreement contains the conditions which must be satisfied before the lender must make advances. Section 3.01 deals with the various documents which must be provided or executed. It is a useful check list for the drafter, and generally presents little risk under the optional advances doctrine mentioned in the previous paragraph. Typically, all of these documents will in fact be in order and approved by the lender before any disbursements are made; hence they raise no question of the lender's duty to advance funds.

Section 3.02 is more problematic, since it deals with events which may allow the lender to cease making advances after construction has begun. The objective of the drafter of Section 3.02 is to spell out the conditions mentioned there as objectively as possible. If the conditions lie within the lender's exclusive power or control, the advance may be considered optional. Section 3.02 does a good job in this respect.

Nevertheless, administration of a construction loan is tricky at best. For example, Section 5.01(a) requires completion of the project by the scheduled completion date. If the project is late in completion, and the lender nonetheless advances funds, it is subject to the argument that such advances were optional. Little can be done by way of drafting to forestall this problem.

The lender's right to take over the project in the event of the developer's default is granted in Section 6.02(d). If this occurs, the lender becomes a mortgagee in possession. This right is of potentially great importance, since if the lender were required to wait out a foreclosure process before acquiring possession of the project, it might suffer greatly from vandalism, damage from the elements, and the like. In some states, of course, the developer is obliged to act through a receiver rather than acquiring possession directly. The purpose of the assignments of the construction contract, the architect's contract, and the copies of drawings, specifications, and subcontracts mentioned in Section 3.01 is to permit the construction lender to complete the construction efficiently in the event that it takes possession, either before or as a consequence of foreclosure.

CONSTRUCTION LOAN AGREEMENT

This Agreement is made as of this _____ day of _____, 19__, by and between _____, a _____ (the "Borrower") and _____, (the "Lender").

In consideration of the mutual promises herein contained, the parties hereto agree as follows:

ARTICLE I

Definitions

Section 1.01 *Defined Terms.* As used in this Agreement, the following terms shall have the meanings set out respectively after each (such meanings to be equally applicable to both the singular and plural forms of the terms defined):

(a) "Advance"—An advance by the Lender to the Borrower pursuant to Article II hereof.

(b) "Agreement"—This Construction Loan Agreement by and between the Borrower and the Lender.

(c) "Architect"—_____.

(d) "Architect's Contract"—The Agreement between the Borrower and the Architect as to preparation of the Drawings and Specifications and Construction of the Project.

(e) "Assignment"—The Assignment of Rents and Leases of even date herewith, executed by the Borrower (and the Fee Owner), securing payment of the Note.

(f) "Assignment Date"—The date on which the Note and Security Documents are assigned to the Permanent Lender.

(g) "Assignment of Construction Contract"—The Assignment of Construction Contract which assigns, as additional security for repayment of the Note, the Borrower's interest in the Construction Contract.

(h) "Assignment of Architect's Contract"—The Assignment of Architect's Contract which assigns, as additional security for payment of the Note, the

Borrower's interest in the Architect's Contract and the Drawings and Specifications.

(i) "Borrower"—_____, a _____, its successors, legal representatives and assigns.

(j) "Buy and Sell Agreement"—The Buy and Sell Agreement of even date herewith, executed by the Borrower, the Permanent Lender and the Lender, pertaining to the purchase of the Note and the Security Documents by the Permanent Lender.

(k) "Commitment"—The commitment of the Lender hereunder to make Advances to the Borrower in an aggregate principal amount of up to and including $_____.

(*l*) "Commitment Termination Date"—_____, or the date of the termination of the Lender's Commitment pursuant to Section 6.02 hereof, whichever date occurs earlier.

(m) "Completion Date"—_____ (provided that if the Lender shall extend such date in writing, then the Completion Date shall be such later date), being the date of required completion of the Project.

(n) "Contractor"—Any person, including the General Contractor, who shall be engaged to work on, or to furnish materials and supplies for, the Project.

(o) "Construction Contract"—The agreement between the Borrower and the General Contractor as to construction of the Project.

(p) "Cost of Completion"—$_____, being the total amount estimated by the Borrower as necessary to complete the Project.

(q) "Disbursing Agent"—_____
_____

(r) "Disbursing Agreement"—The Disbursing Agreement of even date herewith, executed by the Lender and the Disbursing Agent, pertaining to disbursement of the Advances to the Borrower.

(s) "Draw Request"—The form, substantially in the form of Exhibit A attached hereto, which is submitted to the Lender when an Advance is requested and which is referred to in Section 2.02 hereof.

(t) "Drawings and Specifications"—The drawings and specifications prepared by the Architect and identified to this Agreement by the Architect, the Borrower and the Lender.

(u) "Equity"—$_____, being the amount the Borrower is required to invest in the Project in accordance with the provisions of Section 3.01(1).

(v) "Event of Default"—One of the events of default specified in Section 6.01 hereof.

(w) "Fee Owner"—_____, fee owner of the Real Estate and lessor under the Ground Lease.

(x) "General Contractor"—_____.

(y) "Ground Lease"—The Ground Lease of the Real Estate of even date herewith, executed by the Lessor as lessor and the Borrower as lessee.

(z) "Guarantor(s)"—_____
_____

(aa) "Guaranty(ies)"—The Guaranty(ies) of even date herewith wherein the (each) Guarantor guarantees performance of all obligations of the Borrower under the Note and the Security Documents up to the aggregate sum of $_____ (each).

(bb) "Inspecting Engineer"—_____

(cc) "Lender"—_____.

(dd) "Mortgage"—The Combination Mortgage, Security Agreement and Fixture Financing Statement of even date herewith, between the Borrower (and the Fee Owner) as Mortgagor(s) and the Lender as Mortgagee, creating a first lien on the Real Estate and a security interest in all of the personal property located thereon as security for payment of the Note.

(ee) "Note"—The Promissory Note of the Borrower in the form of Exhibit B attached hereto evidencing the Advances to be made hereunder.

(ff) "Permanent Lender"—_____.

(gg) "Permanent Loan Commitment"—The commitment of the Permanent Lender, dated _____, 19__, to purchase the Note and the Security Documents from the Lender upon completion of construction of the Project.

(hh) "Project"—_____, as described in the Drawings and Specifications, to be constructed on the Real Estate.

(ii) "Real Estate"—The land in _____ County, Minnesota, upon which the Project is to be constructed, which is more particularly described in the Mortgage.

(jj) "Security Documents"—The Mortgage, Assignment, Buy and Sell Agreement Permanent Loan Commitment, Assignment of Construction Contract and Assignment of Architect's Contract.

(kk) "Subleases"—All present and future subleases and tenancies of the Project or any portion thereof made by the Borrower under the Ground Lease as sublessor.

ARTICLE II

Commitment to Make Advances, Disbursement
Procedures and Deposit of Funds

Section 2.01 *The Advances.* The Lender agrees, on the terms and subject to the conditions hereinafter set forth, to make Advances to the Borrower from time to time during the period from the date hereof to the Commitment Termination Date in an aggregate principal amount of up to and including the maximum amount of its Commitment to pay costs actually incurred in connection with the construction of the Project, which shall include but not be limited to costs of permits, licenses, labor, supplies, materials, services, equipment, insurance premiums, real estate taxes and interest on Advances, but shall not include the cost of acquiring the Real Estate or any profit to the Borrower acting in its capacity as general contractor. The obligation of the Borrower to repay the Advances shall be evidenced by the Note dated the date of this Agreement, and containing the terms relating to maturity, interest rate, and other matters as set forth in Exhibit B. Notwithstanding any provision of the Note, interest shall be payable at the rate provided therein only on such portions of the loan proceeds as actually have been disbursed pursuant to this Agreement.

Section 2.02 *Disbursement Procedures.*

(a) Whenever the Borrower desires to borrow hereunder, which shall be no more often than monthly, the Borrower shall submit to the Lender a Draw Request, duly executed on behalf of the Borrower, setting forth the information requested therein. Each Draw Request shall be submitted on or between the 1st day and the 15th day of the month in which an Advance is requested, and shall be filed at least 7 days before the date the Advance is desired. With respect to construction items (hard costs) each Draw Request shall be limited to amounts equal to (i) the total of such costs actually incurred and paid or owing by the Borrower to the date of such Draw Request for work performed on the Project that the Lender has committed to finance pursuant to Section 2.01 hereof, plus (ii) the cost of materials and equipment not incorporated in the Project, but delivered to and suitably stored at the Project site; less, (iii) 10 percent (or such lesser holdback as authorized by the Lender) and less prior Advances. Notwithstanding anything herein to the contrary, no Advances for materials stored at the Project site will be made by the Lender unless the Borrower shall advise the Lender of its intention to so store materials prior to their delivery, and provides suitable security for such storage. With respect to all other costs (soft costs) each Draw Request shall be limited to the total of such costs incurred by the Borrower to the date of such Draw Request, less prior Advances for such costs. Each Draw Request shall constitute a representation and warranty by the Borrower that all representations and warranties set forth in Article IV are true and correct as of the date of such Draw Request.

(b) At the time of submission of each Draw Request, the Borrower shall submit to the Lender the following:

(i) A written lien waiver from each Contractor for work done and materials supplied by it which were paid for pursuant to the next preceding Draw Request.

(ii) Such other supporting evidence as may be requested by the Lender or the Disbursing Agent to substantiate all payments which are to be made out of the relevant Draw Request and/or to substantiate all payments then made with respect to the Project.

(c) If on the date an Advance is desired, the Borrower has performed all of its agreements and complied with all requirements therefor to be performed or complied with hereunder including satisfaction of all applicable conditions precedent contained in Article III hereof, and the Lender receives a current construction report from the Inspecting Engineer confirming the accuracy of the information set forth in the Draw Request, the Lender shall pay to the Disbursing Agent the amount of the requested Advance, and the Disbursing Agent will disburse such funds pursuant to and in accordance with the terms of the Disbursing Agreement. Each Advance disbursed to the Disbursing Agent shall bear interest at the rate provided in the Note from the date such Advance is so disbursed to the Disbursing Agent.

Section 2.03 *Deposit of Funds by the Borrower.* If the Lender shall at any time in good faith determine that the undisbursed amount of the Commitment is less than the amount required to pay all costs and expenses of any kind which reasonably may be anticipated in connection with the completion of the Project, and shall thereupon send written notice thereof to the Borrower specifying the amount required to be deposited by the Borrower with the Disbursing Agent to provide sufficient funds to complete the Project, the Borrower agrees that it will, within ten (10) calendar days of receipt of any such notice, deposit with the Disbursing Agent, in a non-interest bearing account, the amount of funds specified in the Lender's notice. The Borrower agrees that any such funds deposited with the Disbursing Agent may be disbursed by the Disbursing Agent, before any further disbursement of loan proceeds from the Lender, to pay any and all costs and expenses of any kind in connection with completion of the Project.

Section 2.04 *Advances Without Receipt of Draw Request.* Notwithstanding anything herein to the contrary, the Lender shall have the irrevocable right at any time and from time to time to apply funds which it agrees to advance hereunder to pay interest on the Note as and when it becomes due, and to pay any and all of the expenses referred to in Section 7.04 hereof, all without receipt of a Draw Request for funds from the Borrower.

ARTICLE III

Conditions of Advances

Section 3.01 *Condition Precedent to Initial Advance.* The obligation of the Lender to make the initial Advance shall be subject to the condition precedent that the Borrower shall be in compliance with the conditions contained in Section 3.02 and the further condition precedent that the Lender shall have received on or before the date of the initial Advance hereunder the following:

(a) The Note duly executed by the Borrower;

(b) The Mortgage duly executed, constituting a valid and perfected first lien on a good and marketable fee simple title to the Real Estate and the fixtures described in Exhibit A to the Mortgage and a security interest in the personal property described in the Mortgage;

(c) The Assignment duly executed, constituting a valid first lien on all rents derived from the Project;

(d) A financing statement, in form and substance satisfactory to the Lender, duly executed and describing the collateral as the personal property and fixtures covered by the Mortgage and the Borrower's rights under the Construction Contract and the Architect's Contract;

(e) A copy of the Drawings and Specifications, certified by the Architect and the Borrower, that are acceptable to the Lender;

(f) The Assignment of Construction Contract duly executed by the Borrower and consented to by the General Contractor;

(g) The Assignment of Architect's Contract duly executed by the Borrower and consented to by the Architect;

(h) Copies of the Construction Contract and the Architect's Contract acceptable to the Lender;

(i) Copies of the electrical, heating, masonry, plumbing, mechanical, excavation and elevator contracts relating to construction of the Project, and such other contracts relating to construction of the Project as the Lender may reasonably request, with each such contract being acceptable to the Lender, together with letters from each such contractor permitting the Lender, upon its election to complete the Project in accordance with the provisions of Section 6.02(d) hereof and to acquire the interest of the Borrower under such contracts;

(j) A sworn construction statement duly executed in form attached hereto as Exhibit _____ showing all Contractors having contracts or subcontracts for specific portions of the work on the Project and the amounts due or to become due each such Contractor, including all costs and expenses of any kind incurred and to be incurred in constructing the Project;

(k) A total project cost statement, incorporating the construction cost as shown on the sworn construction statement described in subparagraph (j) above and setting forth all the costs and expenses of any kind incurred or to be incurred in completion of the Project sworn to by the Borrower to be a true, complete and accurate account of all costs actually incurred and a reasonably accurate estimate of all costs to be incurred in the future;

(*l*) Evidence satisfactory to the Lender that the Borrower has expended not less than the amount of the required Equity in payment of costs and expenses incurred in connection with the completion of the Project which would otherwise be properly payable from an Advance, together with satisfactory lien waivers for lienable work and/or materials paid with such funds;

(m) Two copies of a recent perimeter land survey of the Real Estate, in form and substance satisfactory to the Lender, prepared at the Borrower's expense, currently certified by a licensed, registered surveyor and incorporating the legal description of the Real Estate, showing the location of all points and lines referred to in the legal description, the location of any existing improvements, the proposed location of the Project (including parking) as being within the exterior boundaries of the Real Estate and in compliance with all applicable building set-back requirements, and the location of all utilities and the location of all easements and encroachments onto or from the Real Estate that are visible on the Real Estate, known to the surveyor preparing the survey or of record, identifying easements of record by recording data, and currently certified by the surveyor that there are no such easements or encroachments upon the Real Estate except as shown on the survey;

(n) A title binder, in form and substance satisfactory to the Lender, issued by the Disbursing Agent, at the Borrower's expense, with such title binder constituting a commitment by such title company to issue a mortgagee's title policy in favor of the Lender [and the Permanent Lender] as mortgagee under the Mortgage, that will be free from all standard exceptions, including mechanics' liens and all other exceptions not previously approved by the Lender and that will insure the Mortgage to be a valid first lien on the Real Estate, subject only to such prior liens and encumbrances as are approved by the Lender, in an amount not less than the amount of the Commitment;

(o) Copies of all building permits and such other licenses and permits as may be required to construct and operate the Project; a letter from the appropriate city or county authority having jurisdiction over the Real Estate stating that the Project when constructed in accordance with the Drawings and Specifications will comply in all respects with all applicable ordinances, zoning, planned unit development subdivision, platting, environmental and land use requirements, without special variance or exception, and such other evidence as the Lender shall request to establish that the Project and the contemplated use thereof are permitted by and comply with all applicable use or other restrictions and requirements in prior conveyances, zoning ordinances, environmental laws and regulations, water shed district regulations and all other applicable laws or regulations, and have been duly approved by the municipal and other governmental authorities having jurisdiction over the Project and that all required permits for construction have been obtained;

(p) Letters from utility companies, in form satisfactory to the Lender, establishing that all utilities necessary for the construction and operation of the Project are available at the boundaries of the Real Estate, including without limitation, water, sewer, electricity, gas and telephone, and that the Borrower has the right to connect to and use such utilities to the extent required by the Project;

(q) Copies of the policy of builder's risk insurance and comprehensive general liability insurance and a certificate of the worker's compensation insurance required under Section 5.01(c) hereof, with all such insurance in full force and effect and approved by the Lender;

(r) A signed copy of a favorable opinion of counsel to the Borrower in the form attached hereto as Exhibit D;

(s) A Certificate of Good Standing issued by the State of _____ (and a certificate issued by the State of _____ that the Borrower is qualified to do business in _____); a true and correct copy of the Borrower's articles of incorporation and by-laws; a certified copy of the directors' and shareholders' resolutions authorizing the transactions contemplated by this Agreement; and a certificate of the secretary of the Borrower setting forth the true and correct signatures of the officers of the Borrower and their respective offices within the Borrower;

(t) The Guaranty(ies), duly executed by the Guarantor(s);

(u) A true and correct copy of the Borrower's Partnership Agreement certified as such by a general partner;

(v) The Buy and Sell Agreement duly executed by the Permanent Lender, the Borrower and the Lender;

(w) The Disbursing Agreement, duly executed by the Disbursing Agent and the Lender;

(x) The Ground Lease and the Subleases, in form satisfactory to the Lender and duly executed if required by the Lender, together with such subordination agreements and estoppel certificates from the parties thereto and tenants thereunder as the Lender may require; and

(y) Evidence satisfactory to the Lender establishing that the Borrower shall have satisfied, performed and complied with all of the terms and conditions of the Permanent Loan Commitment which, in the Lender's sole discretion, can reasonably be fulfilled prior to the initial Advance.

Section 3.02 *Further Conditions Precedent to All Advances.* The obligation of the Lender to make each subsequent Advance shall be subject to the condition precedent that the Borrower shall be in compliance with all conditions set forth in Section 3.01, and the further conditions precedent that on the date of such Advance:

(a) No Event of Default hereunder or event which would constitute such an Event of Default but for the requirement that notice be given or that a period of grace or time elapse, shall have occurred and be continuing and all representations and warranties made by the Borrower in Article IV shall continue to be true and correct as of the date of such Advance.

(b) No determination shall have been made by the Lender that the undisbursed amount of the Commitment is less than the amount required to pay all costs and expenses of any kind which reasonably may be anticipated in connection with the completion of the Project; or if such a determination has been made and notice thereof sent to the Borrower, the Borrower has deposited the necessary funds with the Disbursing Agent in accordance with Section 2.03 hereof.

(c) The disbursement requirements of Section 2.02 hereof and of the Disbursing Agent set forth in the Disbursing Agreement have been satisfied.

(d) If required by the Lender, the Lender shall be furnished with a statement of the Borrower and of any Contractor, in form and substance required by the Lender, setting forth the names, addresses and amounts due or to become due as well as the amounts previously paid to every Contractor, subcontractor, person, firm or corporation furnishing materials or performing labor entering into the construction of any part of the Project.

(e) The Borrower shall have provided to the Lender such evidence of compliance with all of the provisions of this Agreement as the Lender may reasonably request.

(f) No license or permit necessary for the construction of the Project shall have been revoked or the issuance thereof subjected to challenge before any court or other governmental authority having or asserting jurisdiction thereover.

Section 3.03 *Conditions Precedent to the Final Advance.* The obligation of the Lender to make the final Advance shall be subject to the condition precedent that the Borrower shall be in compliance with all conditions set forth in Sections 3.01 and 3.02 and, further, that the following conditions shall have been satisfied prior to the Completion Date:

(a) The Project, including all landscape and parking requirements, has been completed in accordance with the Drawings and Specifications and the Lender shall have received a Certificate of Completion from the General

Contractor and the Architect certifying that (i) work on the Project has been completed in accordance with the Drawings and Specifications and all labor, services, materials and supplies used in such work have been paid for and (ii) the completed Project conforms with all applicable zoning, land use planning, building and environmental laws and regulations of the governmental authorities having jurisdiction over the Project.

(b) The Lender has received satisfactory evidence that all work requiring inspection by municipal or other governmental authorities having jurisdiction has been duly inspected and approved by such authorities and by the rating or inspection organization, bureau, corporation or office having jurisdiction, and that all requisite certificates of occupancy and other approvals have been issued.

(c) The Lender shall have received a lien waiver from each Contractor for all work done and for all materials furnished by it for the Project.

(d) The Lender shall have received an "as-built" survey of the Real Estate meeting all of the requirements set forth in Section 3.01(m) and showing the location and exterior lines and egress and other improvements completed on the Real Estate and the observation of all required setbacks, that the Project as completed is entirely within the exterior boundaries of the Real Estate and any building restriction lines and does not encroach upon any easements or right-of-way, and showing such other information as the Lender may reasonably request.

(e) The Lender has received such copies of the executed Ground Lease, the Subleases, tenant subordination and estoppel letters, evidence of insurance, title insurance commitment, written approval of completion of the Project and such other documentation, confirmation or approval as is necessary to satisfy the terms and conditions of the Permanent Commitment and to effectuate the sale of the Note and the Security Documents to the Permanent Lender pursuant to the Buy and Sell Agreement.

Section 3.04 *No Waiver.* The making of any Advance prior to fulfillment of any condition thereof shall not be construed as a waiver of such condition, and the Lender reserves the right to require fulfillment of any and all such conditions prior to making any subsequent Advances.

ARTICLE IV

Representations and Warranties

Section 4.01 *Representations and Warranties.* The Borrower represents and warrants as follows:

(a) The Borrower is a _____, validly existing and in good standing under the laws of the State of _____, and has all requisite power and authority to own the Real Estate and construct the Project, and to execute and deliver and to perform all of its obligations under this Agreement, the Note and the Security Documents and the execution and delivery thereof and the carrying out of the transactions contemplated thereby will not violate, conflict with or constitute a default under the terms of the Borrower's articles of incorporation or by-laws [partnership agreement] or under any note, bond, debenture or other evidence of indebtedness or any contract, loan agreement or lease to which the Borrower is a party or by which the Real Estate is subject, or violate any law, regulation or order of the United States or the State of Minnesota or agency or political subdivision thereof, or any court order or judgment in any proceeding to which the Borrower is or was a party or by which the property of the Borrower is bound.

(b) The execution, delivery and performance by the Borrower of this Agreement, the Note and the Security Documents have been duly authorized by the Borrower.

(c) This Agreement constitutes, and the Note and the Security Documents when delivered hereunder, will constitute legal, valid and binding obligations of the Borrower, enforceable against the Borrower in accordance with their respective terms.

(d) The Borrower has all necessary licenses and permits required for construction and operation of the Project except those which cannot be obtained until completion of the Project.

(e) The Project will be constructed strictly in accordance with the Drawings and Specifications; will be constructed entirely on the Real Estate; and will not encroach upon or overhang any easement or right-of-way of land not constituting part of the Real Estate. The Project, both during construction and at the time of completion, and the contemplated use thereof, will not violate any applicable zoning or use statute, ordinance, building code, rule or regulation, or any covenant or agreement of record. The Borrower agrees that it will furnish from time to time such satisfactory evidence with respect thereto as may be required by the Lender.

(f) Any and all financial statements heretofore delivered to the Lender by the Borrower are true and correct in all respects, have been prepared in accordance with generally accepted accounting practice, and fairly present the financial conditions of the subject thereof as of the respective dates thereof. No materially adverse change has occurred in the financial conditions reflected therein since the respective dates thereof and no additional borrowings have been made by the Borrower since the date thereof other than the borrowing contemplated hereby or approved by the Lender. None of the aforesaid financial statements or any certificate or statement furnished to the Lender by or on behalf of the Borrower in connection with the transactions contemplated hereby, and none of the representations and warranties in this Agreement, contains any untrue statement of a material fact or omits to state a material fact necessary in order to make the statements contained therein or herein not misleading. To the best of the knowledge of the Borrower, there is no fact which materially adversely affects or in the future (so far as the Borrower can now foresee) may materially adversely affect the business or prospects or condition (financial or other) of the Borrower or its properties or assets, which has not been set forth herein or in a certificate or statement furnished to the Lender by the Borrower.

(g) No consent, approval, order or authorization of or registration, declaration or filing with any governmental authority is required in connection with a valid execution and delivery of this Agreement, the Note, the Security Documents or of any and all other agreements and instruments herein mentioned to which the Borrower is a party or the carrying out or performance of any of the transactions required or contemplated thereby, or, if required, such consent, approval, order or authorization shall have been obtained or such registration, declaration or filing shall have been accomplished prior to the initial Advance.

ARTICLE V

Additional Covenants of the Borrower

Section 5.01 *Affirmative Covenants.* The Borrower agrees that:

(a) The Borrower will diligently proceed with construction of the Project according to the Drawings and Specifications and in accordance with all applicable laws and ordinances, will complete the Project by the Completion Date and will use the proceeds of each of the Advances solely to pay the costs incurred in connection with the construction of the Project.

(b) The Borrower will use its best efforts to require each Contractor to comply with all rules, regulations, ordinances and laws bearing on its conduct of work on the Project.

(c) The Borrower will provide and maintain at all times during the process of building the Project (and, from time to time at the request of the Lender, furnish the Lender with proof of payment of premiums on):

(i) Builder's risk insurance, written on the so-called "Builder's Risk—Completed Value Basis", in an amount equal to 100% of the insurable value of the Project at the date of completion without a coinsurance clause, and with coverage available on the so-called "all risk", non-reporting form of policy. The Lender's interest shall be protected in accordance with a standard mortgagee's clause in form and content satisfactory to the Lender;

(ii) Comprehensive general liability insurance (including operations, contingent liability, operations of subcontractors, complete operations and contractual liability insurance) with limits acceptable to the Lender; and

(iii) Worker's compensation insurance, with statutory coverage.

The policies of insurance required pursuant to clauses (i) and (ii) above shall be in form and content satisfactory to the Lender and shall be placed with financially sound and reputable insurers licensed to transact business in the State of Minnesota. The policy of insurance referred to in clause (i) above shall contain an agreement of the insurer to give not less than thirty (30) days' advance written notice to the Lender in the event of cancellation of such policy or change affecting the coverage thereunder. Acceptance of insurance policies referred to in clauses (i) and (ii) above shall not bar the Lender from requiring additional insurance which it reasonably deems necessary.

(d) The Borrower shall maintain accurate and complete books, accounts and records pertaining to the Real Estate and the Project. The Borrower will permit the Lender, acting by and through its officers, employees and agents, to examine all books, records, contracts, plans, drawings, permits, bills and statements of account pertaining to the Project and to make extracts therefrom and copies thereof.

(e) The Borrower will furnish to the Lender within 60 days after the end of the Borrower's fiscal year, audited financial statements of the Borrower for such year setting forth in comparative form the figures for the previous fiscal year, all in reasonable detail and prepared by a certified public accountant selected by the chief financial officer of the Borrower and acceptable to the Lender, accompanied by a certificate of the Borrower that such statement is true and correct; and as soon as possible and in any event within seven days after the Borrower has obtained knowledge of the occurrence of each Event of Default or each event which with the giving of notice or lapse of time or both would constitute an Event of Default, which is continuing on the date of such statement, the statement of the chief financial officer of the Borrower setting forth details of such Event of Default or event and the action which the Borrower proposes to take with respect thereto.

(f) The Borrower will furnish to the Lender, true and correct copies of all leases of space in the Project when executed, together with such estoppel certificates and subordination agreements from the tenant under such leases as the Lender may require.

(g) The Borrower will do all things necessary or advisable to keep the Permanent Loan Commitment in full force and effect and will comply fully with all requirements and conditions contained therein in order to effectuate a sale by the Lender of the Note and the Security Documents to the Permanent Lender upon the date specified in the Buy and Sell Agreement.

Section 5.02 *Negative Covenants.* The Borrower agrees that, without the prior written consent of the Lender, it will not:

(a) Grant a security interest in the Project or any part thereof or create or permit to be created or allow to exist any mortgage, encumbrance or other lien upon the Real Estate, except those shown in the title binder referred to in paragraph (n) of Section 3.01 hereof and approved by the Lender, and except mechanics' and materialmen's liens in respect of obligations which are not due.

(b) Without the written consent of the Lender, agree or consent to any changes in the Drawings and Specifications or to any change orders or to any changes in the terms and provisions of the Construction Contract, the Architect's Contract or any of the contracts specifically identified in paragraph (i) of Section 3.01.

(c) Incorporate in the Project any materials, fixtures or property which are subject to the claims of any other person, whether pursuant to conditional sales contract, security agreement, lease, mortgage or otherwise.

(d) Except for leases in accordance with the Security Documents, lease, sell, transfer, convey, assign, or otherwise transfer all or any part of the interest of the Borrower in the Project or the Real Estate, or sell, transfer or convey a controlling interest in the Borrower.

(e) Agree or consent to any modification or amendment of the Permanent Commitment.

ARTICLE VI

Events of Default and Rights and Remedies

Section 6.01 *Events of Default.* Each of the following shall constitute an Event of Default:

(a) The Borrower shall fail to pay, when due, interest on or principal of the Note;

(b) The Borrower shall fail duly to observe or perform, any of the other terms, conditions, covenants or agreements required to be observed or performed by the Borrower hereunder, and such failure shall continue for a period of 10 calendar days after written notice of such failure has been given by the Lender to the Borrower;

(c) Any representation or warranty made by the Borrower herein or in any financial statement, certificate, report or Draw Request furnished pursuant to this Agreement, the Disbursing Agreement or the Security Documents or in order to induce the Lender to make any Advance hereunder shall prove to have been untrue in any material respect or materially misleading as of the time such representation or warranty was made;

(d) The Borrower shall be in default under or in breach of any of the covenants contained in any of the Security Documents and such default or breach shall not be cured or waived within the period or periods of grace, if any, applicable thereto;

(e) At the time any Advance is requested by the Borrower the title to the Real Estate is not reasonably satisfactory to the Lender, regardless of whether the lien, encumbrance or other question existed at the time of any prior Advance;

(f) A survey shows that the Project being constructed on the Real Estate encroaches upon any unvacated street or upon any adjoining property to an extent deemed material by the Lender;

(g) The Project is materially damaged or destroyed by fire or other casualty and the loss, in the reasonable judgment of the Lender, is not adequately covered by insurance actually collected or in the process of collection;

(h) Execution shall have been levied against the Real Estate or any other property subject to the Security Documents or any lien creditor's suit to enforce a judgment against the Real Estate or such other property shall have been brought and (in either case) shall continue unstayed and in effect for a period of more than 10 consecutive calendar days;

(i) The construction of the Project is abandoned or shall be unreasonably delayed or be discontinued for a period of 20 consecutive calendar days, in each instance for reasons other than acts of God, fire, storm, strikes, blackouts, labor difficulties, riots, inability to obtain materials, equipment or labor, governmental restrictions or any similar cause over which the Borrower is unable to exercise control;

(j) The Borrower at any time prior to the completion of the Project, shall delay construction or suffer construction to be delayed for any period of time, for any reason whatsoever, so that the completion of the Project cannot be accomplished, in the reasonable judgment of the Lender, by the Completion Date;

(k) The Lender shall have given notice to the Borrower pursuant to Section 2.03 hereof to deposit additional funds with the Disbursing Agent and the Borrower shall have failed to do so within 10 calendar days;

(*l*) The Borrower [or any of the Guarantors] shall make an assignment for the benefit of its creditors, or shall admit in writing its inability to pay its debts as they become due, or shall file or have filed against it a petition under the United States Bankruptcy Code, or shall seek or consent to or acquiesce in the appointment of any trustee, receiver or liquidator of any material part of its properties or of the Real Estate or of the Project, or shall not, within 30 days after the appointment (without its consent or acquiescence) of a trustee, receiver or liquidator of any material part of its properties or of the Real Estate or of any Project, have such appointment vacated; and

(m) The Borrower shall not be in compliance with the Permanent Loan Commitment, or the Permanent Lender shall fail to comply with any of the terms, covenants or conditions of the Permanent Loan Commitment or of the Buy and Sell Agreement, or the Permanent Commitment shall be terminated for any reason whatsoever, or, in the reasonable opinion of the Lender, the terms of the Permanent Loan Commitment or the Buy and Sell Agreement cannot be satisfied or the Note is not assigned to the Permanent Lender on or before the Assignment Date.

Section 6.02 *Rights and Remedies.* Upon the occurrence of an event which with the passage of time or the giving of notice or both would constitute an Event of Default and at any time thereafter, the Lender may by notice in writing to the Borrower, refrain from making any further Advances hereunder (but the Lender may make Advances after the occurrence of such an event or an Event of Default without thereby waiving its rights and remedies hereunder) and upon the occurrence of an Event of Default may, at its option, exercise any and all of the following rights and remedies (and any other rights and remedies available to it):

(a) The Lender may terminate the Commitment.

(b) The Lender may, by written notice to the Borrower, declare immediately due and payable all unpaid principal of and accrued interest on the Note, together with all other sums payable hereunder, and the same shall thereupon be immediately due and payable without presentment or other demand, protest, notice of dishonor or any other notice of any kind, all of which are hereby expressly waived; provided, however, that upon the filing of a petition commencing a case naming the Borrower or any Guarantor as debtor under the United States Bankruptcy Code, the principal of and all accrued interest on the Note shall be automatically due and payable without any notice to or demand on the Borrower or any other party.

(c) The Lender shall have the right, in addition to any other rights provided by law, to enforce its rights and remedies under the Security Documents.

(d) The Lender may enter upon the Real Estate and take possession thereof, together with the Project then in the course of construction, and proceed either in its own name or in the name of the Borrower, as the attorney-in-fact of the Borrower (which authority is coupled with an interest and is irrevocable by the Borrower) to complete or cause to be completed the Project, at the cost and expense of the Borrower. If the Lender elects to complete or cause to be completed the Project, it may do so according to the Drawings and Specifications or according to such changes, alterations or modifications in and to the Drawings and Specifications as the Lender may deem reasonable and appropriate; and the Lender may enforce or cancel all contracts let by the Borrower relating to construction of the Project, and/or let other contracts which in the Lender's sole judgment may seem advisable; and the Borrower shall forthwith turn over and duly assign to the Lender, as the Lender may from time to time require, contracts not already assigned to the Lender relating to construction of the Project, blueprints, shop drawings, bonds, building permits, bills and statements of accounts pertaining to the Project, whether paid or not, and any other instruments or records in the possession of the Borrower pertaining to the Project. The Borrower shall be liable under this Agreement to pay to the Lender, on demand, any amount or amounts expended by the Lender in so completing the Project, together with any costs, charges, or expenses incident thereto or resulting therefrom, all of which shall be secured by the Security Documents. In the event that a proceeding is instituted against the Borrower for recovery and reimbursement of any moneys expended by the Lender in connection with the completion of the Project, a statement of such expenditures, verified by the affidavit of an officer of the Lender, shall be prima facie evidence of the amounts so expended and of the propriety of and necessity for such expenditures; and the burden of proving to the contrary shall be upon the Borrower. The Lender shall have the right to apply any funds which it agrees to advance hereunder and any funds which the Borrower has then on deposit with the Disbursing Agent to bring about the completion of the Project and to pay the costs thereof; and if such moneys so agreed to be advanced and funds of the Borrower then on deposit with the Disbursing Agent are insufficient, in the sole judgment of the Lender, to complete the Project, the Borrower agrees to promptly deliver and pay to the Lender such sum or sums of money as the Lender may from time to time demand for the purpose of completing the Project or of paying any liability, charge or expense which may have been incurred or assumed by the Lender under or in performance of this Agreement, or for the purpose of completing the Project. It is expressly understood and agreed that in no event shall the Lender be obligated or liable in any way to complete the Project or to pay for the costs of construction thereof beyond the amount of the Commitment.

ARTICLE VII

Miscellaneous

Section 7.01 *Inspections.* The Borrower and the Architect shall be responsible for making inspections of the Project during the course of construction and shall determine to their own satisfaction that the work done or materials supplied by the Contractors to whom payment is to be made out of each Advance has been properly done or supplied in accordance with the General Contract and the other applicable contracts with the Contractors. If any work done or materials supplied by a Contractor are not satisfactory to the Borrower and/or its Architect and the same is not remedied within fifteen days of the discovery thereof, the Borrower will immediately notify the Lender in writing of such fact. It is expressly understood and agreed that the Lender and the Inspecting Engineer may conduct such inspections of the Project as either may deem necessary for the protection of the Lender's interest, and that any inspections which may be made of the Project by the Lender or the Inspecting Engineer will be made, and all certificates issued by the Inspecting Engineer will be issued, solely for the benefit and protection of the Lender, and that the Borrower will not rely thereon.

Section 7.02 *Indemnification of the Borrower.* The Borrower shall bear all loss, expense (including attorneys' fees) and damage in connection with, and agrees to indemnify and hold harmless the Lender, its agents, servants and employees from all claims, demands and judgments made or recovered against the Lender, its agents, servants and employees, because of bodily injuries, including death at any time resulting therefrom, and/or because of damages to property of the Lender or others (including loss of use) from any cause whatsoever, arising out of, incidental to, or in connection with the construction of the Project, whether or not due to any act of omission or commission, including negligence of the Borrower or any Contractor of his or their employees, servants or agents, and whether or not due to any act of omission or commission of the Lender, its employees, servants or agents. The Borrower's liability hereunder shall not be limited to the extent of insurance carried by or provided by the Borrower or subject to any exclusions from coverage in any insurance policy. The obligations of the Borrower under this Section shall survive the payment of the Note.

Section 7.03 *Additional Security Interest.* In the event any Advance is to be made for materials then being fabricated or stored, or both, for later use in the completion of the Project but which are not then stored upon the Real Estate or installed or incorporated into the Project, then such Advance shall be made only after the Borrower has given to the Lender such security instruments and insurance on such materials as the Lender may reasonably request.

Section 7.04 *Fees.* Whether or not any Advance shall be made hereunder, the Borrower agrees to pay all fees of the Disbursing Agent and Inspecting Engineer, appraisal fees, survey fees, recording fees, license and permit fees and title insurance and other insurance premiums, and agrees to reimburse the Lender upon demand for all reasonable out-of-pocket expenses actually incurred by the Lender in connection with this Agreement or in connection with the transactions contemplated by this Agreement, including, but not limited to, any and all reasonable legal expenses and attorneys' fees sustained by the Lender in the exercise of any right or remedy available to it under this Agreement or otherwise by law or equity and all reasonable fees and disbursements of counsel for the Lender for the services performed by such counsel in connection with the preparation of this Agreement and the other documents and instruments contemplated hereby.

Section 7.05 *Addresses for Notices.* All notices to be given by either party to the other hereunder shall be in writing and deemed to have been given when delivered personally or when deposited in the United States mail, registered or certified postage prepaid, addressed as follows:

(a) To the Borrower at:
_____
_____

Attention: _____

(b) To the Lender at:
_____
_____
_____

Attention: _____

or addressed to any such party at such other address as such party shall hereafter furnish by notice to the other party.

Section 7.06 *Time of Essence.* Time is of the essence in the performance of this Agreement.

Section 7.07 *Binding Effect and Assignment.* This Agreement shall be binding upon and inure to the benefit of the Borrower and the Lender and their respective successors and assigns, except that the Borrower may not transfer or assign its rights hereunder without the prior written consent of the Lender.

Section 7.08 *Waivers.* No waiver by the Lender of any default hereunder shall operate as a waiver of any other default or of the same default on a future occasion. No delay on the part of the Lender in exercising any right or remedy hereunder shall operate as a waiver thereof, nor shall any single or partial exercise of any right or remedy preclude other or future exercise thereof or the exercise of any other right or remedy.

Section 7.09 *The Lender's Remedies Cumulative.* The rights and remedies hereby specified are cumulative and not exclusive of any rights or remedies which the Lender would otherwise have.

Section 7.10 *Governing Law and Entire Agreement.* This Agreement and the Note issued hereunder shall be governed by the laws of the State of _____. This Agreement contains the entire agreement of the parties on the matters covered herein. No other agreement, statement or promise made by any party or by any employee, officer, or agent of any party that is not in writing and signed by all the parties to this Agreement shall be binding.

Section 7.11 *Counterparts.* This Agreement may be executed in any number of counterparts, each of which, when so executed and delivered, shall be an original, but such counterparts shall together constitute one and the same instrument.

Section 7.12 *Inconsistency.* In the event that any of the terms and provisions of this Agreement are inconsistent with any of the terms and provisions of the Note or Security Documents, the terms and provisions of this Agreement shall govern.

IN WITNESS WHEREOF, the parties hereto have caused this Agreement to be duly executed as of the day and year first above written.

By _____
Its _____

By _____
Its _____

§ 15.3 Construction Loan Agreement—Condominium Development [1]

This form is similar in some respects to the construction loan agreement covering income-producing property, reprinted in § 15.2 supra. But a number of differences exist, primarily flowing from the

§ 15.3
1. Form provided by Ewing, Carter, Smith, Gosnell, Vickers and Holerock, Nevada, Missouri.

fact that the property is intended to be sold at the completion of construction, rather than retained by the developer for rental to tenants. In this respect condominiums are much like detached houses in a subdivision, and this form contains much that would be equally applicable to such a development.

Perhaps the most critical element in this form is the definition of "Cash Flow" in Article 1.3. In effect, it represents the profit made by the developer from the sale of the condominium units. Under Article 5.2 the lender is entitled to 30% of the cash flow, in addition to ordinary interest at the "prime rate" under Article 5.1. Thus the lender's revenue from the loan is, in effect, dependent in part on the developer's business success. Note that the developer is entitled to reduce the cash flow by certain "borrower's fees" under Article 6, but owes certain further loan fees under Article 5.3. Under this agreement, incidentally, interest is payable monthly as it accrues. See Article 5.1. Compare the capitalization of accruing interest under the agreement in the preceding section. All of these matters are subject to individual negotiation, and the terms of this agreement should not necessarily be considered typical or standard.

Since the condominium units are to be sold to individuals, some commitment for long-term financing for these sales is essential to the development's success. In Article 11, the construction lender (which, in this case, happens to be in the business of making permanent loans as well) agrees to provide such financing at the prevailing market terms when such loans are made. Not all construction lenders wish to make such commitments, and where they do not, they will usually insist that the developer obtain a long-term financing commitment from some other institution.

The disclaimers in Article 12.3 are interesting. They represent the lender's effort to avoid any inference that it is a partner or joint venturer of the developer, or might be liable under some similar theory for defects in the physical design and construction of the project. See § 12.11, supra.

Finally, note that the developer is not personally liable for repayment of the indebtedness or the interest on it. See Article 12.13. Again, this matter is subject to negotiation, and in many similar transactions personal liability is imposed.

LOAN AGREEMENT

THIS LOAN AGREEMENT (hereinafter the "agreement") is made and entered into as of the _____ day of _____, 1982, by and between _____, (hereinafter the "Borrower") and _____, (hereinafter the "Lender").

Recitals

Borrower has applied to Lender for a loan to finance the construction of a residential-condominium project upon the real property described in Exhibit A, and to permit Borrower to recover the cost of the property upon which the same is situated, and Lender is willing to make the loan upon the terms and conditions herein set forth. In consideration of the mutual covenants and agreements herein contained, Lender and Borrower agree as follows:

ARTICLE 1

Definitions

As used in this Agreement, the following terms have the meanings as ascribed to them, respectively, below:

1.1 *The Act.* The Texas Condominium Act, Art. 1301a, V.A.T.C.S.

1.2 *Advance.* Each disbursement of a portion of the loan proceeds.

1.3 *Cash Flow.* That cash derived from the sale of units on hand from time to time in excess of that cash which, in addition to the proceeds of the loan then unadvanced and those sums which can reasonably be expected to be received from the sale of the remaining units, shall be reasonably required to pay:

(a) the cost of the property;

(b) the cost of completion of construction of the project;

(c) the cost of maintaining, advertising, marketing and selling the remaining units;

(d) all fixed interest and principal due under the loan;

(e) any and all liability under warranties to unit purchasers; and

(f) all fees payable to Borrower and Lender as hereinafter provided.

1.4 *Construction Costs.* All costs and expenses directly related to and required to fully complete the construction of the improvements in accordance with the plans, including the fees to be paid to Lender and Borrower hereunder, less, however, all rental received during the construction period.

1.5 *Deed of Trust.* The deed of trust and security agreement of even date herewith covering the property executed by Borrower and delivered to secure the note and recorded in the Real Property Records of _____ County, Texas.

1.6 *Improvements.* All of the improvements, both on the property and offsite, required for the completion and operation of the project.

1.7 *Indebtedness.* The principal and interest on all sums, amounts, payments, fees and premiums due under the note and all other indebtedness arising out of this transaction of Borrower to Lender whether or not secured by the security documents.

1.8 *Loan.* The loan to be made by Lender to Borrower pursuant to the provisions of this agreement.

1.9 *Note.* The promissory note of even date herewith in the original principal sum of _____ dollars executed by Borrower to Lender and evidencing the loan.

1.10 *Obligations.* Any and all of the covenants, promises and other obligations (other than the indebtedness) made or owing by Borrower to or due to Lender under the note or security documents.

1.11 *Permanent Loans.* All loans made by the Lender to purchasers of units for the purpose of acquiring the units from Borrower.

1.12 *Plans.* The final plans and specifications for the construction of the improvements prepared by Borrower and approved by Lender.

1.13 *Preexisting Improvements.* Those improvements situated upon the property at the time of this acquisition by Borrower.

1.14 *Prevailing Market Rate.* The effective interest rate offered on single-family residential loans to the general public by Lender at any relevant time.

1.15 *Project.* The property and the improvements and all tangible and intangible personal property owned or held by the Borrower and reasonably necessary for the operation of the project.

1.16 *Property.* That real property more particularly described in Exhibit A to this agreement.

1.17 *Property Value.* The sum of one dollar ($1.00) per square foot, being that sum which Borrower and Lender agree to be the fair market value of the property.

1.18 *Request for Advance.* The request of the Borrower for an advance, in such form as the Lender may request, specifying the sums to be advanced in respect to each unit, containing a certificate to the effect that such amounts represent payments due for services actually rendered or materials actually furnished in connection with the construction of the unit.

1.19 *Security Documents.* This agreement, the note, the deed of trust and security agreement and all other documents now or hereafter evidencing the indebtedness or securing the repayment of the indebtedness or the observance of performance of the obligations of the Borrower described herein.

1.20 *Unit.* Each individual living unit within the project and constituting an "apartment" as defined in the act.

ARTICLE 2

Loan

2.1 Subject to the strict compliance of the terms and conditions of this agreement by Borrower, and in reliance upon the representations and warranties set forth herein, Lender shall loan to Borrower an aggregate cumulative amount not to exceed _____ dollars to be used by Borrower to acquire land, construct and maintain the improvements and to advertise and sell the units.

ARTICLE 3

Advances of the Loan

3.1 *Conditions Precedent to First Advance.* The Lender shall be under no obligation to advance any amounts to the Borrower or to any other person or firm under the loan unless and until the Borrower shall have delivered to Lender:

(a) the security documents;

(b) evidence that the security documents have been filed of record in appropriate records with all filing fees paid prior to the commencement of any construction upon or delivery of materials to the property and prior to the recordation of any written contract for construction of the improvements or any affidavit of an oral agreement to furnish materials or provide services for the improvements;

(c) an interim construction binder in the amount of the note issued by the title company selected by Borrower and committing to issue a mortgagee's title insurance policy insuring that the deed of trust is a valid lien on the property, free and clear of all defects and encumbrances, except such as the Lender and its counsel shall have approved;

(d) copies of all instruments shown as exceptions on the mortgagee's title policy described above;

(e) a current survey of the property prepared and certified by a professional engineer or licensed surveyor acceptable to the Lender and the title company showing:

(i) the dimensions and total area of the property;

(ii) all easements, rights-of-way, building setback lines and lot lines;

(iii) the lines, names and widths of the streets, roads and highway abutting the property;

(iv) any encroachments upon the property and the extent thereof; and

(f) the insurance policies and endorsements thereto, and the certificates of insurance as required by Article 4 hereof, with proof of payment of premiums for such insurance;

(g) the opinion of counsel of Borrower that the loan documents have been duly authorized, executed and delivered and are legal, valid and binding instruments, enforceable against the makers thereof in accordance with their respective terms;

(h) a form of declaration designed to create a condominium regime pursuant to the act, and the form of articles of incorporation and bylaws, to be utilized in connection with the organization and operation of the council of co-owners, pursuant to the act;

The first advance shall be in an amount equal to the product of the number of square feet and decimal fraction thereof comprising the land multiplied by one dollar ($1.00).

3.2 *Conditions Precedent to Periodic Advances.* The conditions set forth in paragraph 3.1 shall be conditions to the first and all subsequent advances of the loan. In addition, advances made from and after the first advance shall be made not more frequently than monthly and only if the following conditions have been satisfied by the date of such advance:

(a) the Borrower shall have furnished Lender a schedule setting forth the estimated cost of construction of the project, the estimated cost of advertising, marketing and selling the units, the proposed sales price of the units and the estimated time of completion and sale of the units;

(b) the Borrower shall have furnished Lender a request for advance in the form described in section 1.18 hereof;

(c) the Borrower has fully complied with all of the provisions of this agreement and is entitled to the advance, it being understood that the making of any advance or part thereof when the Borrower is not so entitled will not constitute a waiver of compliance;

(d) the construction of the improvements theretofore completed having been performed in substantial compliance with the plans without any substantial departure therefrom that the Lender has not approved;

(e) the opinion of counsel of Borrower that the zoning of the property permits the construction of the improvements in accordance with the plans and that all governmental approvals, permits and consents required to permit construction of the improvements have been obtained by Borrower;

(f) the representations and warranties made in Article 7 hereof shall be true and correct and on and as of the date of the advance with the same effect as if made on such date.

3.3 *Inspection.* The Lender shall have five (5) business days after receipt of each request for advance to determine whether the amount requested should be advanced, including time to make an inspection of the improvements.

3.4 *Right to Withhold Advances.* The Lender shall not be obligated to make any advance if it receives notice that any party who has furnished materials or performed labor of any kind entering into the construction of the improvements has not been timely paid. In such event, the Lender shall not be required to resume advancement of the loan proceeds unless such party is paid or unless Borrower places in escrow with the title company sufficient funds to pay such party upon the resolution of the controversy, if any.

ARTICLE 4

Insurance

4.1 *Types of Insurance.* While the loan is outstanding, the Borrower shall maintain in full force and effect builder's all risk insurance on a completed value, non-reporting Texas multi-peril form, premiums prepaid, insuring the premises. If such insurance cannot be maintained in full force and effect following the completion of construction of the project, then such casualty insurance policy shall be duly endorsed or replaced with other insurance policies with premiums prepaid so that the premises shall be at all times insured against loss or damage by all risks, except only those excluded from coverage under the Texas multi-peril all risk insurance policy. Each of the casualty insurance policies shall name the Lender as a loss-payee and additional insured. The insurance provisions of this agreement shall control wherever in conflict with the insurance provisions of the deed of trust.

ARTICLE 5

Interest and Other Sums to be Paid Lender

5.1 *Fixed Interest.* While the loan is outstanding, it shall bear interest at the prime rate quoted by The Wall Street Journal as being the base rate on corporate loans at large U.S. money center commercial banks (but if such prime rate is specified as a range between two rates, then the lower rate specified for such range) with such rate to be adjusted on the first day of each month to that rate quoted as of the last business day of the preceding month throughout the term. Interest shall be payable monthly as it accrues from loan advances.

5.2 *Participation in Cash Flow.* In addition to the interest provided for in section 5.1 above, Lender shall be entitled to receive thirty percent (30%) of all cash flow from the project. Lender's rights to share in cash flow shall remain in effect notwithstanding the fact that any or all principal of the loan may have been theretofore paid. Borrower may retain as a reserve for contingencies ten percent (10%) of cash flow on hand, in which event Lender's share of cash flow so reserved shall be paid only at the time Borrower's share of cash flow so reserved is distributed to Borrower. Lender's share of cash flow from the project shall be distributed quarterly throughout the term of the loan.

5.3 *Lender's Loan Fees.* In addition to the interest above provided for, Borrower shall pay to Lender a commitment fee equal to one percent (1%) of sums actually advanced by Lender hereunder, such fee to be paid at time of first advance and to be based upon the maximum sums committed to be advanced hereunder with appropriate cash adjustments to be made at time of final advance. Borrower shall also pay to Lender as a management and auditing fee one percent (1%) of the gross sales price of each unit at time of the sale of such unit, subject to the provisions of section 7.1. Prior to or contemporaneously with the execution of this agreement, Borrower and Lender have entered into a loan agreement whereby Lender has lent to Borrower the sum of eight hundred forty-five thousand dollars ($845,000.00) to be used to defray the cost of the land of which the property is a part, the cost of extending streets and utilities thereto and thereon, and the cost of constructing the clubhouse, swimming pool and other common facilities to be used by the project as well as other projects to be constructed upon such land (the "development loan"). Borrower shall be entitled to credit against the first fees due under this section 5.3 for any and all loan or commitment fees paid in respect to the development loan which are attributable to the property, i.e., that portion of such loan fees bearing the same ratio to the whole as the number of units to be constructed within the project shall bear to the total number of units to be constructed within all of the projects situated on the land subject to the development loan.

5.4 *Principal Due Date and Prepayment.* The principal of the loan and all interest due under section 5.1 above shall be due and payable on the expiration of five (5) years from date hereof. Principal may be prepaid in whole or in part at any time or times without penalty and Borrower may specify to which units such prepayments are to be allocated.

ARTICLE 6

Borrower's Fees

6.1 *General Administrative Fee.* Borrower shall be entitled to receive three percent (3%) of the gross sales price of each unit at time of sale of such unit as a general administrative fee, subject to the provisions of section 7.1.

6.2 *Fee for Indirect Costs.* Borrower shall be entitled to receive a fee to cover indirect costs equal to one and one-half percent (1½%) of the sales price of each unit, one percent (1%) to be advanced from first loan advances based on the estimated sales price of each unit, and one-half percent (½%) of the sales price of each unit to be paid at closing of sale of such unit.

6.3 *Bookkeeping, etc. Fee.* Borrower shall be entitled to receive as a bookkeeping and general office overhead fee one percent (1%) of the gross sales price of each unit at time of sale of such unit.

ARTICLE 7

Limitation Upon the Payment of Certain Fees

7.1 *Limitation on Fees.* Notwithstanding anything herein to the contrary, the management and auditing fee payable to Lender, pursuant to section 5.3, and the general administrative fee payable to Borrower, pursuant to section 6.1, shall be payable, pro rata, only from cash flow (as determined in accordance with section 1.3 hereof but, of course, prior to the deduction of such fees), and any such fees not paid on due date will be accumulated, without interest, and paid from first cash flow available for such purpose.

ARTICLE 8

Guaranty of Completion

8.1 *Guaranty.* Borrower guarantees the completion of the project in substantial accordance with the plans, and shall be obligated to advance for this purpose all sums required to pay the cost of completion of the project in excess of the proceeds of the loan.

ARTICLE 9

Representations and Warranties

To induce the Lender to make the loan, Borrower represents and warrants to Lender as follows:

9.1 *Authority.* Borrower is a duly organized and validly existing joint venture, is in good standing under the laws of the State of Texas, and has full power and authority to consummate the transactions contemplated hereby. The Borrower is duly authorized and empowered to create and issue the note and to execute and deliver this agreement and all other instruments referred to or mentioned herein to which Borrower is a party and all action on its part requisite for the due creation, issuance and delivery of the note, deed of trust, this agreement and such other instruments has been duly and effectively taken.

9.2 *Plans.* The plans will have been approved by applicable governmental authorities from which approval must be obtained before construction is commenced; all construction performed on the improvements will be performed substantially in accordance with the plans without overlapping any easement affecting the property; and the anticipated use thereof complies with all applicable laws, zoning ordinances, regulations and restrictive covenants affecting the property and all requirements for such use have been satisfied.

9.3 *Financial Information.* All financial statements and related information concerning the Borrower heretofore delivered to Lender are true and correct in all respects, have been prepared in accordance with generally accepted accounting principles consistently followed and fully and accurately present the financial condition of the subject thereof as of the dates thereof and no materially adverse change has occurred in the financial conditions reflected therein since the dates thereof.

9.4 *Claims and Proceedings.* There are no actions, suits or proceedings pending, or to the knowledge of Borrower threatened, against or affecting Borrower or the property, or involving the validity of enforceability of the deed of trust or the priority of the lien thereof, at law or in equity, or before or by any governmental authority except actions, suits and proceedings fully covered by insurance or which, if adversely determined, would not substantially impair the ability of Borrower to complete the construction of the improvements by the maturity date of the note and pay when due any amounts which may become payable in respect to the note; and Borrower is not in default with respect to any order, writ, injunction, decree or demand of any court or any governmental authority; and the consummation of the transactions hereby contemplated and performance of this agreement and the deed of trust will not result in any breach of, or constitute a default under, any mortgage, deed of trust, lease, bank loan or credit agreement, partnership agreement or other instrument to which the Borrower is a party or by which Borrower may be bound or affected.

9.5 *Request for Advance.* Each request for an advance or payment of the funds requested thereby shall have the effect stated in the definition of the term "Request for Advance". All materials included in a request for advance shall have been delivered to Borrower or contractor as the case may be.

The warranties and representations in sections 9.1 through 9.5 shall be deemed to be renewed and restated by the Borrower at the time of each advance after the date hereof unless Borrower notifies Lender in writing of any change therein prior to the time of such advance.

ARTICLE 10

Covenants of the Borrower

Until the payment in full of the indebtedness to the Lender, the Borrower covenants with the Lender as follows:

10.1 *Construction.* Subject to the terms of this agreement, the Borrower shall take all action necessary or proper to cause the construction of the improvements to be prosecuted with diligence and continuity and in a good and workmanlike manner substantially in accordance with the plans.

10.2 *Inspection.* Borrower will permit Lender, or its representatives, at any reasonable time and from time to time (a) to enter upon the property to inspect the same and all materials used in the construction of the improvements or stored on the property or elsewhere, and (b) to examine and/or copy (i) the plans, shop drawings, and work details pertaining to the improvements, (ii) all of Borrower's books, records and accounts relating to work contracted for and materials ordered and received and all disbursements and accounts payable in connection with the improvements, and (iii) any certificates or reports of inspecting engineers and public officials; and Borrower shall provide proper facilities for making such inspection and/or examination.

10.3 *Payment of Costs.* Borrower will promptly pay, or cause to be paid, all construction costs incurred in connection with the improvements and all costs incurred in the advertising, marketing and sale of the units, as and when the same become due and payable, paying for the same with the proceeds of the loan advanced from time to time or from cash flow.

10.4 *Closing Costs.* The Borrower shall promptly pay all survey, recording, title, legal and other expenses paid or incurred by the Lender incident to the loan, including a reasonable fee to the Lender's attorney for preparation of the security documents and their advice to Lender with regard to closing the loan and Lender's administration thereof.

10.5 *Notice of Claims.* Borrower will promptly notify Lender of the institution of any proceedings brought against Borrower, including, but not limited to, any proceedings to assert or to enforce mechanic's, materialmen's or other liens asserted against the property.

10.6 *Conveyances and Encumbrances.* Borrower will not convey, encumber or otherwise dispose of, limit or burden the property or any portion thereof or any interest therein, in any way without the consent of Lender; nor will Borrower waive, assign or transfer any of the Borrower's rights, powers, duties or obligations under this agreement, except that Borrower may sell and convey units in the ordinary course of business and pursuant to price schedules approved by Lender without Lender's consent.

10.7 *Structural Defects.* Upon Lender's demand, Borrower will cause to be corrected any substantial departure from the plans not approved by Lender. The advance of any loan proceeds shall not constitute a waiver of the Lender's right to require compliance with this covenant with respect to any such defects or departures from the plans not theretofore discovered by, or called to the attention of the Lender.

10.8 *Disbursement of Cash Flow.* Borrower shall not distribute any portion of the cash flow to itself unless it shall distribute or shall theretofore have distributed Lender's proportionate share of such cash flow to Lender.

ARTICLE 11

Release of Liens and Commitment to Make Permanent Loans

11.1 *Release of Liens.* So long as Borrower is not in default in Borrower's obligations under the security documents, Borrower shall be entitled to the release of the security documents in respect to any unit sold by Borrower at the time of the closing of such sale upon the payment against the principal of the note of a sum equal to all sums advanced in respect to such unit less all prepayments of principal made in respect to such unit.

11.2 *Commitments for Permanent Loans.* So long as Borrower is not in default of any of Borrower's obligations under the security documents, Lender will, from time to time, at the request of Borrower, issue to contract purchasers of units, who qualify in accordance with Lender's loan underwriting standards then in effect for condominium loans, a commitment for a permanent loan on terms and conditions then being offered by Lender to qualified buyers for residential loans, provided, however, that the effective interest rate for such loan shall be the prevailing market rate with Borrower being accorded the same rights to "buy down" such loan accorded to other borrowers. The permanent mortgage may be a so-called adjustable rate mortgage, varying rate mortgage or renegotiable rate mortgage.

ARTICLE 12

General Terms and Provisions

12.1 *No Waiver.* No advance of loan proceeds hereunder shall constitute a waiver of any of the conditions to the Lender's obligations to make further advances, nor, in the event the Borrower is unable to satisfy any such condition, shall any such waiver have the effect of precluding the Lender from thereafter declaring such inability to be an event of default as hereinbefore described.

12.2 *Form of Documents.* All proceedings taken in connection with the loan as provided for herein, and all documents required or contemplated by the security documents, or otherwise, and the forms of construction contracts and policies of insurance shall be satisfactory in form, substance and coverage to the Lender, and the Lender shall have received copies (or certified copies where appropriate in the Lender's judgment) of all documents which it may request in connection herewith.

12.3 *Conditions Exclusive to the Lender.* All conditions of the obligations of the Lender to make advances hereunder are imposed solely and exclusively for the benefit of the Lender and its assigns and the Borrower. No other person shall have standing to require satisfaction of such conditions or be entitled to assume that the Lender will refuse to make advances in the absence of strict compliance with any or all of them. All of such conditions may be freely waived in whole or in part by the Lender at any time if in its sole discretion it deems it advisable to do so. The Lender has no obligations in connection with the construction of the improvements except to advance the proceeds of the loan as herein provided. The Lender shall not be liable for the performance or nonperformance or delay in performance of any contractor, subcontractor or supplier of materials or for the quality of workmanship of materials or for the failure to construct, or insure the improvements, or for the payment of any cost or expense incurred in connection therewith, or for the performance or nonperformance or delay in performance of any obligation of the Borrower to the Lender. Any inspection by the Lender of the improvements, approval of contracts or plans or other activities of a similar nature shall be only for the sole and separate benefit of the Lender and for the purpose of protecting the Lender's security and shall in no way be construed as a representation that there is compliance on the part of the owner as to its duty to independently ascertain that the improvements are being completed in accordance with the plans, and the Borrower has no right to rely on any procedures required by the Lender.

12.4 *Notices.* All notices hereunder shall be in writing and shall be deemed to have been sufficiently given or served for all purposes when presented personally or when enclosed in an envelope, addressed to the party to be notified at the address stated below (or at such other address as may have been designated by written notice), properly stamped, sealed and deposited in the United States mail, as certified mail, return receipt requested:

Lender: _____
_____
_____

Borrower: _____
_____
_____

12.5 *Waiver, Modification.* This agreement embodies the entire agreement between the parties and supersedes all prior agreements and understandings, if any, relating to the subject matter hereof. Neither this agreement nor any provision hereof may be changed, waived, discharged or terminated orally, but only by an instrument in writing signed by the party against whom enforcement of the change, waiver, discharge or termination is sought.

12.6 *Governing Law.* The security documents shall be executed in _____ County, Texas, and shall be construed in accordance with and governed by the laws of the State of Texas.

12.7 *Cumulative Remedies.* The rights and remedies of the Lender under the security documents shall be cumulative and the exercise, or partial exercise, or any such right or remedy shall not preclude the exercise of any other right or remedy.

12.8 *Binding Effect.* This agreement shall be binding upon and shall inure to the benefit of the Lender and the Borrower and their respective successors and assigns, provided that the Borrower may not assign its rights or obligations hereunder without the Lender's prior written consent.

12.9 *Survival of Agreement.* The provisions hereof shall survive the execution of all instruments herein mentioned, and shall continue in full force until the loan is paid in full.

12.10 *Counterparts.* This agreement has been executed in a number of identical counterparts, each of which for all purposes is deemed an original and all of which constitute, collectively, one agreement. In making proof of this agreement, it shall not be necessary to produce or account for more than one such counterpart.

12.11 *Conflicts.* Wherever this agreement shall conflict with the terms of the security documents, the provisions of this agreement shall control.

12.12 *Assignments.* Neither Borrower nor Lender may assign its rights hereunder.

12.13 *Personal Liability.* Notwithstanding anything herein to the contrary, Borrower shall not be personally liable for the payment of the indebtedness or the performance of any of the covenants contained in the deed of trust, the note or this agreement, and the Lender shall look solely to the security of the loan for payment thereof, save and except that Borrower shall be personally liable for the fulfillment of the guaranty set forth in section 8.1 hereof, and save and except that Borrower shall be personally liable for the payment of a portion of the indebtedness equal to that amount, if any, by which any general administrative fee received by Borrower, pursuant to section 6.1, shall exceed the management and auditing fee received by Lender, pursuant to section 5.3.

IN WITNESS WHEREOF, the parties have executed this agreement as of the day and year first above written.

15.4 Subordination Agreement [1]

Construction lenders normally insist on holding a first mortgage position on the real estate being developed. Frequently, however, the developer has acquired the property from a previous owner in a transaction in which that owner has been given a purchase-money mortgage. Hence, this seller must either be paid off or must subordinate his or her lien to the construction mortgage before the development can go forward. Sometimes this subordination is accomplished by language in the original contract or mortgage between the developer and the land vendor. But at that point, the exact terms of the construction loan are usually unknown, so it is impossible to describe it with great specificity in the subordination agreement. This may give rise to later arguments that the agreement is unenforceable because it is too vague or unfair; see § 12.9, supra, for a detailed discussion.

The subordination agreement reproduced in this section is of a different character. It is intended to be executed by the land vendor after the construction loan has been negotiated and the construction mortgage executed and recorded. The agreement can and does refer specifically to the construction mortgage, and any problems of vagueness are obviated.

---

§ 15.4

1. Form provided by Faegre & Benson, Minneapolis, Minnesota.

Note, however, that this is a lender's form. It makes no attempt to give any special protection to the land vendor. Some protections are inherent in the timing of the agreement; the land vendor has presumably satisfied himself with respect to the amount, term, and interest rate of the construction loan, the lender's reputation and character, and the general viability of the project to be built. However, a form devised with the vendor's needs in mind might well grant him additional protections. See § 12.9, supra. For example, there is no specific requirement that the construction loan funds actually be invested in labor and materials on the site. As the form in § 15.2, supra, suggests, it is fairly common for funds to be spent on "soft costs" such as fees, permits, insurance, and taxes; from the subordinated land vendor's viewpoint this may be unacceptable. There is also no provision in this form for the subordinated vendor to inspect the project as work proceeds or to examine the developer's books.

Note also the possibility that the developer and lender will amend or modify the terms of the construction loan in ways which may be very disadvantageous to the subordinated vendor. For example, they might drastically modify the physical design of the project in ways which would prolong its marketing period or make it far less marketable. They might also increase the interest rate on the construction loan or lengthen its maturity, and thereby increase the risk of default by the developer.

From the lender's viewpoint, all of this is entirely sensible; it has no desire to give the land vendor a veto power over, or indeed any right to intrude into, future negotiations between lender and developer. But a form drafted by the vendor's attorney might be very different in this regard.

The form does require that the vendor receive 30 days notice of any foreclosure, or of any deed in lieu of foreclosure which the lender proposes to accept. See paragraph 5. This will afford the vendor some opportunity to cure the default and perhaps to take over the project himself if a suitable settlement can be worked out with the construction lender. However, paragraph 5 also provides that a deed in lieu of foreclosure, given by the developer to the lender, will "wipe out" the subordinated vendor. This rather draconian result is, of course, entirely different than the usual legal consequence of a deed in lieu, which is to leave subordinate liens intact. See §§ 6.18–6.19 supra.

SUBORDINATION AGREEMENT

This Agreement is made effective as of the _____ day of _____, 19__, by and between _____ (the "Lender") and _____ (the "Undersigned").

Recitals

The Undersigned holds a certain promissory note of _____ (the "Borrower") dated _____, 19__, in the original principal amount of $_____. Said note is secured by a Mortgage on the real estate described in Exhibit A (the "Premises"), which Mortgage is dated _____, 19__, and was recorded in the office of _____ as Doc. No. _____ (the "Existing Mortgage").

Pursuant to a Construction Loan Agreement dated _____, 19__, between the Lender and the Borrower (the "Loan Agreement"), the Lender has agreed to lend up to $_____ to the Borrower to finance certain improvements to be constructed on the Premises.

The advances under the Loan Agreement will be evidenced by the Borrower's promissory note dated _____, 19__, in the principal amount of $_____ (the "Note"). The Note will be secured by a Mortgage on the Premises dated _____, 19__, which Mortgage has been recorded in the office of _____ as Doc. No. _____ (the "Construction Mortgage").

As a condition to making any advances under the Loan Agreement, the Lender has required that the lien of the Existing Mortgage be fully subordinate to the lien of the Construction Mortgage, and the Undersigned is willing to so subordinate the lien of the Existing Mortgage.

Accordingly, the Undersigned hereby agrees with the Lender as follows:

1. Regardless of the priority of the Existing Mortgage, the lien of the Existing Mortgage is hereby made and shall be fully subordinate and subject to the lien of the Construction Mortgage and to any other lien or security interest at any time hereafter acquired by the Bank in all or any portion of the Premises to secure any sums advanced or costs incurred in connection with the Loan Agreement or the Construction Mortgage, as fully as if the Construction Mortgage had been executed, delivered and recorded, and all sums secured thereby advanced, prior to the execution of the Existing Mortgage.

2. The Undersigned acknowledges receipt of a copy of the Construction Mortgage, the Note and the Loan Agreement and acknowledges that the execution and delivery thereof does not constitute a default under the Existing Mortgage.

3. Except as expressly set forth in this Agreement, the Lender shall have no obligation to the Undersigned of any kind whatsoever with respect to the Construction Mortgage, the Note or the Loan Agreement, and the Lender may exercise its rights and administer its duties under such documents in any manner it sees fit. Without limiting the generality of the foregoing, the Undersigned expressly waives notice of, or the right to consent to, any advance to be made under the Loan Agreement or the Construction Mortgage, or any waiver or modification of any provision of the Loan Agreement, Note or Construction Mortgage, or any default or exercise of any remedy under the Loan Agreement, the Note or the Construction Mortgage, and the Lender shall have no duty to the Undersigned to preserve, protect, maintain, insure, take possession of, foreclose, dispose of or otherwise realize upon the Premises.

4. If an Event of Default occurs under the Construction Mortgage, the Lender will not exercise its right to foreclose the Construction Mortgage or accept a deed to the Premises from the Borrower, without giving the Undersigned 30 days' prior written notice of its intention to do so. The notice given pursuant to this paragraph 4 shall be in addition to, not in lieu of, any notice required by statute. If, following expiration of such 30-day period, the Lender accepts a deed to the Premises from the Borrower, the Undersigned agrees that upon the recording of such deed all right, title, claim and interest of the Undersigned in or to the Premises, whether pursuant to the Existing Mortgage or otherwise, shall be automatically null and void without the need for execution or recording of any other document.

5. This Agreement shall be binding upon and inure to the benefit of the Undersigned and the Bank and their respective successors and assigns.

IN WITNESS WHEREOF, this Agreement has been executed as of the day and year first above written.

§ 15.5 Loan Agreement With Lender Participation in Cash Flow and Appreciation [1]

For the past several decades it has been common for long-term lenders on income-producing property to take, in addition to ordinary interest on the loan, a further interest or participation in the revenues generated by the project. The document reprinted below illustrates one way of accomplishing this.

The primary purpose of such a scheme is, of course, to provide an additional yield to the lender. In many states in which usury is an issue, the participation interest can be structured so as to escape the coverage of the usury statute. Thus, a relatively low rate of stated interest can be combined with a participation in revenues to produce a total return to the lender much higher than would be permissible under the interest rate alone. (That is not, however, the evident purpose of the participation in cash flow in the document below, since it specifically refers to the participation as "additional interest.") Since the value of the participation rights depends on the success of the business venture, the borrower-developer may well be willing to commit himself to a higher total cost for the loan than if the interest cost were entirely fixed; if the project does not do well financially, the developer's loan payments will be correspondingly lower.

The transaction represented below gives the lender two distinct financial rights in addition to ordinary interest. One is the right to receive the entire net cash flow from the project, defined in Paragraph 6 as including all income less the usual operating expenses, debt service on loans, and a working capital reserve of $30,000. Note that this will not necessarily produce a large sum to the lender; many rental projects operate with small, zero, or even negative cash flows, with their developers anticipating economic advantages in the form of depreciation deductions (which shelter other income) and long-term appreciation in value instead.

The other form of financial benefit given to the lender in this loan is the right to one-half of the proceeds of any sale of the property, after subtracting the expenses of sale and the balance of any loans on the property. See Paragraph 7. Thus, the loan is, in effect, a "shared appreciation loan" or "SAM". See § 11.4 for a more complete discussion of such loans. Moreover, if the sale produces less than the loan balance, Paragraph 7 makes the borrower liable for one-half of the deficiency.

In the aggregate, these benefits to the lender may seem very great by comparison with a conventional loan bearing only ordinary interest. However, the developer in this transaction is being permitted to borrow the full appraised value of the project. In effect, the lender is providing

§ 15.5

1. Form provided by Ewing, Carter, Smith, Gosnell, Vickers and Holerock, Nevada, Missouri.

the entire capital for the project, and hence is in a position to insist on major concessions in return. Every loan is different, of course, and the legal documents are necessarily governed by business considerations. Hence, this particular loan agreement may not be a fully appropriate model for other transactions.

The language defining the base on which the lender's participation in cash flow will be computed is of great importance and requires special care in drafting. Different types of projects require different approaches. A rental apartment building (as was involved in the agreement reprinted below) needs a much different definition than a retail store, an office building, or a parking lot, for example.

With shared appreciation loans, sale of the property will ordinarily trigger acceleration and repayment of the loan. See Paragraph 7. Under Paragraph 10, the lender's consent to any sale of the property is required. However, if consent is denied, the lender becomes obligated to purchase the property on the same terms as the outside offer which the developer proposed to accept.

It is also necessary, in any shared appreciation loan, to provide for repayment in the event the property is not sold by the end of the loan term—in this case, seven years. The procedure adopted in this agreement involves appraisal to determine the property's fair value. See Paragraph 8. Unlike some shared appreciation loans which have been made on single-family homes, there is no requirement in this agreement that the lender refinance the borrower upon repayment at the end of the shared appreciation loan's term.

Note the effort, in Paragraph 13, to disclaim any partnership or joint venture between lender and borrower. One objective of this language is to avoid lender liability for construction defects, injuries to tenants, or the like. See § 12.11 supra.

AGREEMENT

THIS AGREEMENT is made and entered into this _____ day of _____, 1982, by and between _____, a Texas corporation, (hereinafter the "Borrower"), and _____, (hereinafter the "Lender").

WITNESSETH:

WHEREAS, Borrower and Lender desire to enter into an agreement for the financing of _____, a proposed 80–unit apartment complex (hereinafter the "Improvements"), to be constructed upon the real property described on Exhibit "A" attached hereto and made a part hereof (hereinafter the "Land"; the Improvements and the Land being hereinafter sometimes collectively the "Property"),

NOW, THEREFORE, for and in consideration of the premises and the mutual covenants and promises contained herein:

1. Lender hereby agrees to loan Borrower _____ (hereinafter the "Loan") to be funded on or before _____, for a term of eighty-four (84) months bearing interest at _____% per annum to be paid in monthly installments, as accrued, of $_____ (hereinafter the "Amortization Payment"), with all remaining unpaid interest and principal to be finally due and payable at the maturity of said loan. All such Amortization Payments shall be due and payable on the first (1st) day of each month (hereinafter "Payment Due Date") for the preceding month. Borrower may

require funding of the loan prior to _____. Notwithstanding anything herein contained whether express or implied, if the Monthly Net Cash Flow for the month preceding the next maturing Amortization Payment is less than such Amortization Payment (such difference being hereinafter referred to the "Shortage"), then, subject to the provisions of Paragraph 2 hereof relating to additional loan proceeds to satisfy Shortages of up to an aggregate amount of $_____, in lieu of paying the Amortization Payment, Borrower shall pay the Monthly Net Cash Flow on the Payment Due Date; in which event the Payment Due Date shall be on the tenth (10th) day of the month for the preceding month so as to enable Borrower to determine the Monthly Net Cash Flow. For purposes of this Agreement, "Monthly Net Cash Flow" shall mean, on a monthly basis, all income derived from the operations of the Property of any kind whatsoever, less:

(a) reasonable and necessary operating expenses consisting of, among other things, taxes, insurance, utilities and trash removal;

(b) a management fee no greater than five percent (5%) of monthly gross rentals (including fireplaces, deposits and miscellaneous);

(c) salaries for employees directly related with the operation of the Property;

(d) necessary repairs and maintenance on the Property;

(e) capital expenditures and replacements on the Property;

(f) debt service payments on loans (for capital expenditures and operating deficits) utilized for the benefit of the Property and which loans were approved by Lender which approval Lender hereby expressly agrees not to unreasonably withhold;

(g) a reasonable working capital reserve not to exceed $_____; and

(h) legal and accounting fees.

2. Lender further agrees, from time to time prior to maturity of the Loan, to loan Borrower up to an additional _____ (hereinafter the "Shortage Loan") to fund the Shortage for a particular month or months. The proceeds of any advance of the Shortage Loan shall bear interest at the rate of _____% per annum from the date of each such advance until repaid; provided, however, the Amortization Payment shall not be adjusted, but so long as all or any part of the Shortage Loan shall be outstanding Borrower shall make payments on succeeding Payment Due Dates in the amount of the Monthly Net Cash Flow generated during the preceding month until such time as the Shortage Loan and all accrued and unpaid interest thereon is paid in full without additional interest thereon. Disbursements of the Shortage Loan shall be made by Lender immediately upon receipt by Lender of a statement by the President of Borrower of the amount of the Shortage. The note evidencing the Shortage Loan shall be substantially in the form of Exhibit B attached hereto and made a part hereof and shall be secured by the Deed of Trust substantially in the form of Exhibit C–2 attached hereto and made a part hereof.

3. Borrower warrants that upon completion of construction of the Improvements, the Property will have an appraised value of at least $_____ (same as loan amount in paragraph 1). Prior to the funding of the loan contemplated hereunder, the Borrower shall furnish to Lender an appraisal prepared by an MAI certified appraiser indicating that the Property has a value in excess of $_____. Lender acknowledges receipt and approval of the plans and specifications for the Improvements.

4. Borrower agrees to execute a promissory note (hereinafter the "Note") providing for the terms and rate as set forth in Paragraph 1 above and a deed of trust to the Land described in Exhibit "A" and the Improvements to be constructed thereon on Lender's standard commercial deed of trust form with such modifications as are necessary to carry out the additional terms and conditions of this Agreement (hereinafter the "Deed of Trust"). The Note and Deed of Trust shall be

substantially in the form of Exhibits "C–1" and "C–2" attached hereto and made a part hereof. The parties agree that the terms and conditions of this Agreement which have not been incorporated into the Note and Deed of Trust shall be in addition to the provisions thereof and shall not merge therein. Moreover, in the event of any inconsistency between the terms and conditions of this Agreement, on the one hand, and the terms and conditions of the Note, the Shortage Note and the Deed of Trust, on the other hand, then the terms and conditions of this Agreement shall in all events prevail and control. At the time of loan funding, Borrower agrees to provide Lender with a Mortgagee Policy of Title Insurance on Texas standard forms (with the usual printed exceptions) insuring the Deed of Trust to be a first lien upon the Property. Such policy shall be issued by a title insurance company acceptable to Lender and shall show fee simple title to the Property in Borrower free and clear of all liens and encumbrances other than those set forth on Exhibit "A" and other than those necessarily granted by Borrower in connection with the construction of the Improvements.

5. Borrower has upon execution of this Agreement paid Lender a commitment fee of [5% of loan amount] in consideration for Lender's agreement to make the loan in the future upon the terms and conditions set forth herein. The parties acknowledge that such fee has been earned by Lender and is nonrefundable. The parties agree that Borrower shall not be obligated to take the loan described herein in which event no part of such commitment fee shall be refunded to Borrower.

6. Commencing _____, and thereafter for the term of the Loan, Borrower agrees to pay Lender additional interest in an annual amount equal to the Net Cash Flow from the operations of the Property (hereinafter "Additional Interest"). Such Additional Interest shall be estimated and paid monthly in twelve (12) equal installments on the first day of each month commencing _____, based upon the projected cash flow as shown in Exhibit "C" attached hereto. Such adjustments as may be necessary to arrive at the correct amount of Additional Interest shall be made as soon after the end of each year as is practicable after financial records for the Property shall have been prepared; provided, however, if based upon the operations of the Property for the prior calendar year, Borrower reasonably determines that the projected cash flow for the subject calendar year will be at least ten percent (10%) more or less than the projected cash flow for such calendar year as set forth in Exhibit "C", then the projected cash flow (and the estimated monthly installments of Additional Interest based thereon for the subject calendar year) shall be increased or decreased, as the case may be, based on such determination and; provided, further, if based upon the operations of the Property for the expired portion of any calendar year the Borrower reasonably determines that the Net Cash Flow for such calendar year will be at least twenty percent (20%) more or less than the projected cash flow for such year as shown on Exhibit "C", adjusted as aforesaid, then the estimated monthly installments of the Additional Interest for the remaining unexpired portion of such calendar year shall be increased or decreased, as the case may be, based on such determination.

The sole source for the payment of the Additional Interest shall be the Net Cash Flow from the operations of the Property on a calendar year basis. Accordingly, if for any calendar year period there is no Net Cash Flow, then Lender shall receive no Additional Interest or Lender shall receive less than the full amount of the minimum projected Additional Interest, as the case may be. The parties agree that the amount of the Additional Interest to be paid to Lender shall be determined annually, as provided in this Paragraph, on a calendar year basis. For the purpose of this Agreement, "Net Cash Flow" shall mean, on a calendar year basis, all income from the operations of the Property of any kind whatsoever, less:

(a) debt service payments to the Lender other than for Additional Interest;

(b) reasonable and necessary operating expenses consisting of, among other things, taxes, insurance, utilities and trash removal;

(c) a management fee no greater than five percent (5%) of yearly gross rentals (including fireplaces, deposits and miscellaneous);

(d) salaries for employees directly related with the operation of the Property;

(e) necessary repairs and maintenance on the Property;

(f) capital expenditures and replacements on the Property;

(g) debt service payments on loans (for capital expenditures and operating deficits) utilized for the benefit of the Property and which loans were approved by Lender which approval Lender hereby expressly agrees not to unreasonably withhold;

(h) a reasonable working capital reserve not to exceed $_____; and

(i) legal and accounting fees.

7. Upon the sale, foreclosure or other disposition of the Property, one-half of the sale proceeds for the Property (hereinafter "Sale Proceeds") shall be paid to each Lender and Borrower after the payment of:

(a) fees, commissions and expenses of sale;

(b) unpaid principal and accrued interest to Lender; however, if at the time of such sale, foreclosure or other disposition there shall be outstanding all or any part of the Shortage Loan and/or there shall be a Shortage, then such outstanding balance of the Shortage Loan and/or Shortage, as the case may be, shall be reduced by the aggregate amount of any Additional Interest paid hereunder and, in addition, no accrued unpaid interest shall be paid on the Shortage Loan; and

(c) other liabilities incurred in connection with the operations of the Property which other liabilities were approved by Lender which approval Lender hereby expressly agrees not to unreasonably withhold; and

In the event Sale Proceeds are insufficient to satisfy all of the above mentioned charges, payment shall be made in the order of priority listed above. In the event of foreclosure of the Deed of Trust, the Trustee is instructed to allocate Sale Proceeds as above specified. In the event the Sale Proceeds are insufficient to repay all unpaid principal and accrued interest on the Note and all unpaid principal of the Shortage Loan, then Borrower shall be liable for fifty percent (50%) of any such deficiency. The Borrower shall have no personal liability for accrued interest on the Shortage Loan.

8. It is contemplated by the parties hereto that the Property will be sold prior to the maturity of the Note. If, however, a sale or other disposition of the Property has not been consummated within seventy-eight (78) months from the date of the Note, then the parties agree to commence the establishment of the fair market value of the Property (hereinafter "Appraised Value") in the manner hereinafter provided. If upon the maturity of the Note, the Property has still not been sold or otherwise disposed of, then, for purposes of this Agreement, the maturity of the Note shall constitute and be deemed a sale of the Property for purposes of Paragraph 7 and, in lieu of paying Lender all unpaid principal and interest due on the Note, Borrower shall pay to Lender the amount which would be receivable by Lender had the Property been sold or otherwise disposed of as provided in Paragraph 7. In connection therewith, for purposes of applying this Paragraph in conjunction with Paragraph 7, the Appraised Value shall be deemed to be the Sales Proceeds and the fees, commissions and expenses of sale referred to in Subparagraph 7(a) and shall be deemed to include the cost of an Owner Policy of Title Insurance and a six percent (6%) brokerage commission; all based on the Appraised Value.

The Appraised Value of the Property shall be established as follows:

a. By the mutual agreement of Borrowers and Lender; or

b. If Borrowers and Lender cannot mutually agree, then the Appraised Value shall be established as follows:

(i) If either Borrowers or Lender determine that at any time after the expiration of the seventy-ninth (79th) month of the term of the Note, they are unable to mutually agree upon the Appraised Value, then either may send written notice thereof to the other stating that the Appraised Value shall be established pursuant to the appraisal procedure set forth in this Paragraph and in such notice the noticing party shall designate the first appraiser ("First Appraiser").

(ii) Within fifteen days after the service of the notice referred to in the immediately preceding clause (i), the party receiving the notice shall give written notice to the party sending the notice designating the second appraiser ("Second Appraiser"). If the Second Appraiser is not so designated within or by the time above specified, then the appointment of the Second Appraiser shall be made in the same manner as hereinafter provided for the appointment of a third appraiser in a case where the First Appraiser and the Second Appraiser and the parties themselves were unable to agree upon the Third Appraiser. The First Appraiser and the Second Appraiser so designated or appointed shall meet within ten days after the Second Appraiser is appointed and if, within thirty days after the Second Appraiser is appointed, the First Appraiser and the Second Appraiser do not agree upon the Appraised Value as more fully set forth in the immediately following clause (iii), they shall themselves appoint a Third Appraiser, who shall be a competent and impartial person; and in the event of their being unable to agree upon such appointment within ten days after the time aforesaid, the Third Appraiser shall be selected by the parties themselves, if they can agree thereon within a further period of fifteen days. If the parties do not so agree, then either party, on behalf of both, may request such appointment by the Chief Judge of the U.S. District Court for the _____ District of Texas. The three Appraisers so designated or appointed shall meet within ten days after the Third Appraiser is so designated or appointed and within thirty days thereafter they shall agree upon the Appraised Value as more fully set forth in the immediately following clause (iii). In the event of the failure, refusal, or inability of an Appraiser to act, a new appraiser shall be appointed in his stead, which appointment shall be made in the same manner as hereinbefore provided for the appointment of such appraiser so failing, refusing, or being unable to act. Each Party shall pay the fees and expenses of one of the original appraisers appointed by such Party, or in whose stead, as above provided, such appraiser was appointed, and the fees and expenses of the Third Appraiser, and all other expenses, if any, shall be borne equally by all parties. Any appraiser designated to serve in accordance with the provisions of this Agreement shall be disinterested and shall be qualified to appraise real estate of the type covered by this Agreement situated in the vicinity of the Property, and shall have been actively engaged in the appraisal of real estate situated in the vicinity of the Property for a period of not less than 5 years immediately preceding his appointment.

(iii) The appraisers shall determine the Appraised Value of 100% of the Property, which shall be the fair market value of the Property at the time such appraisal is made, without reduction for liabilities encumbering the Property. Any decision joined in by two of the Appraisers shall be the decision of the Appraisers. After reaching a decision the Appraisers shall give notice thereof to Borrowers and Lender.

In the event that the Appraised Value has not been established in accordance with the above outlined procedure prior to the maturity of the Note, then Lender may instruct the trustee designated in the Deed of Trust to foreclose the same according to its terms; provided, however, if Lender shall not have taken those actions specified in this Paragraph 8 required to be taken by Lender within designated periods of time, then the maturity of the Note shall be extended by the same period of time Lender has delayed in taking such requisite actions.

9. In the event of any insured fire or other casualty loss to the Improvements, Borrower shall be entitled, at their option, to utilize any insurance proceeds paid as a result of such fire or other casualty (hereinafter the "Insurance Proceeds") to rebuild or restore the Improvements damaged or destroyed thereby. If the Insurance Proceeds exceed the total cost of rebuilding or restoring the damaged or destroyed Improvements or if Borrower elects not to rebuild or restore the Improvements so damaged or destroyed, then such excess Insurance Proceeds or the total amount thereof, as the case may be, shall, after payment of all expenses incurred in connection with obtaining such Insurance Proceeds, be applied in reduction of the then outstanding balance of the Note. If the Insurance Proceeds so applied on the Note exceed the then outstanding balance thereof, then any such excess shall be applied in the order and manner set forth in Paragraph 7 hereof. Moreover, if Borrower elects not to rebuild or restore the Improvements so damaged or destroyed and, if Borrower reasonably determines that the Improvements, or so much thereof as shall remain after such damage or destruction, cannot be operated in a profitable manner, then Borrower shall proceed to liquidate the Property as promptly as is consistent with obtaining fair value thereof. Any sums received as a result of such liquidation shall be applied in the order and manner set forth in Paragraph 7 hereof, notwithstanding that the Note may have previously been fully paid.

Any sums which may be awarded or become payable to Borrower for the condemnation of the Property, or any part thereof, for public or quasi-public use, or by virtue of private sale in lieu thereof, shall, after payment of all expenses incurred in connection with obtaining such award and all costs necessarily incurred to restore the integrity and habitability of the Improvements, be applied in reduction of the then outstanding balance of the Note. If such award so applied on the Note exceeds the then outstanding balance thereof, then any such excess shall be applied in the order and manner set forth in Paragraph 7 hereof.

If any Insurance Proceeds or any such award applied on the Note does not fully satisfy the same, then the monthly installments due and owing under the Note shall be recast to reflect such reduced outstanding principal balance.

10. The approval of Lender shall be required for the sale of the Property which approval shall not be unreasonably withheld. Notwithstanding the foregoing, if Borrower receives and desires to accept a written offer for the sale of the Property ("Offer") which Offer is not approved (whether reasonably or unreasonably) by Lender by delivery of written notice of approval to Borrower within twenty-one (21) days after Lender has received a copy of such Offer from Borrower requesting Lender's approval, then Lender, by reason of its failure to so approve the Offer, shall be obligated and hereby agrees to purchase the Property from Borrower upon the same terms, covenants, conditions and provisions for the purchase of the Property as set forth in the Offer. The purpose of this provision is not penal in nature. It has been included at the special instance and request of Lender to enable Lender to acquire Borrower's interest in the Property at such time as Borrower has received and desires to accept, an offer to sell the Property. A purchase of the Property by the Lender pursuant to this paragraph shall be considered a sale of the Property for the purposes of Paragraph 7. The request for Lender's approval shall at a minimum contain the following statement: "Your approval of the enclosed contract is being requested pursuant to Paragraph 10 of that certain Agreement between _____ and you relating to the permanent financing of [project name]." For purposes of this paragraph only and in addition to the notice provided in Paragraph 15 hereof, any notice, request or other communication to be given to Lender pursuant to this paragraph shall also be sent to: _____.

11. Borrower agrees that consideration will, from time to time, be given to the profitable conversion of the Property to a condominium regime. In this regard, either Borrower or Lender may commission a study to determine the feasibility of the same; the cost of which shall be borne by the party commissioning the same unless the parties otherwise agree. In the event Borrower and Lender decide to convert the Property to a condominium regime, Lender shall not be obligated to provide financing to individual condominium purchasers.

12. The provisions of this Agreement relating to the obligations of Borrower shall be made enforceable in part by provisions in the Deed of Trust which shall provide for acceleration of the indebtedness and foreclosure of the Property; provided, however, that in the event of foreclosure pursuant to the Deed of Trust, the provisions of Paragraph 7 relating to the distribution of Sale Proceeds shall apply.

13. The parties agree that their relationship shall be that of Borrower and Lender and not that of partners or joint venturers. Lender's sole obligations hereunder, shall be to fund the above-mentioned loans under the terms and conditions of this Agreement and, except with regard to the Shortage Loan, Lender shall not be obligated to advance any additional funds for the construction of the Improvements or the operating expenses of the Property. Borrower shall be entitled to all deductions for depreciation allowed with respect to the Improvements.

14. The Borrower acknowledges that this Agreement and the Note and Deed of Trust to be executed by the parties is personal to Borrowers and shall not be assignable without Lender's consent.

15. Any notice, request, demand, instruction or other communication to be given to either party hereunder shall be in writing, and may be personally delivered or sent by registered or certified mail and shall be deemed to be delivered on the date when sent by registered or certified mail, return receipt requested as follows:

If to Borrowers: _____
_____
_____

If to Lender: _____
_____
_____

The addresses and addressees for the purpose of the paragraph may be changed by giving notice of such change in the manner provided herein for giving notice. Unless and until such written notice is received, the last address and addressee stated herein shall be deemed to continue in effect for all purposes.

IN WITNESS WHEREOF, the parties hereto have executed this Agreement the day, month and year above written.

§ 15.6 Promissory Note—Incorporating Construction and Long-term Financing [1]

In the traditional version of construction lending, the note and mortgage will typically have a relatively short term, usually no more than two to three years. After the project is completed, the construction note will be satisfied with the proceeds of a new long-term loan,

---

§ 15.6
1. Form provided by Faegre & Benson, Minneapolis, Minnesota.

made pursuant to a long-term loan commitment issued earlier, and the construction mortgage will be released of record.

However, in many transactions today, the construction lender and its long-term counterpart utilize the same documents. Under this approach, when construction is finished the long-term lender takes an assignment of the note and mortgage which were executed at the commencement of construction. The long-term lender's obligation to do so is documented, not in a loan commitment, but rather in a "buy-sell agreement" in which it agrees to purchase the documents upon completion of the project.

Such combined documents are usually used in states with mortgage registration taxes, which typically impose a substantial levy on the face amount of all mortgages recorded. See, e.g., Kan.Stat.Ann. § 79–3101 et seq.; Minn.Stat.Ann. § 287.01 et seq.; McKinney's New York Tax Law §§ 250–267. By using combined documents, a second collection of the tax can be avoided when the "take-out" occurs. The combined documents must, of course, be acceptable to the permanent lender, and thus they will be largely in "long-term" form. The promissory note reproduced in this section, and the mortgage in the next, employ this "combination" format.

Under this note, the treatment of interest changes in important ways on the "assignment day"—the date the documents are acquired by the long-term lender. Prior to that date, interest fluctuates, and is computed as 1% in excess of the "reference rate", in essence the prime rate of the construction lender. During the construction period, interest is payable monthly, but no amortization of principal is required. After the assignment day, interest accrues at a fixed rate (13.75% in this form), and monthly installments of principal and interest are to be paid. The loan matures ten years after the assignment day.

The note states an outside date for the assignment day. If construction delays or other problems result in failure of an assignment to occur by that date, the construction lender has the right to accelerate the loan and demand full payment.

This note contains fairly typical language, including an acceleration clause and various waivers. It provides for a substantial late payment charge if a payment is delinquent for 15 days or more.

PROMISSORY NOTE

$_____.

FOR VALUE RECEIVED, _____, a _____ limited partnership, hereby promises to pay to the order of _____, a _____ corporation, at its office at _____ or at such other place as the holder hereof may from time to time in writing designate, in lawful money of the United States of America in immediately available funds, the principal sum of _____ Dollars ($_____), or so much thereof as may be advanced under the Construction Loan Agreement of even date, and to pay interest on the outstanding principal balance hereof from time to time,

(i) from the date hereof through the Assignment Day (as hereinafter defined) at a rate which is equal to one percent (1%) per annum in excess of the rate of interest from time to time publicly announced by _____ as its Reference Rate, with changes in the interest rate applicable to advances made hereunder (whether such advances are made prior to, the same day as, or subsequent to, any particular change in the Reference Rate) to become effective on the basis of a 360 day year, but charged for the actual number of days principal is unpaid; and

(ii) from and after the Assignment Day, at the rate of thirteen and three-fourths percent (13¾%) per annum.

From and after the date of this Note interest accruing on the principal balance each month through the Assignment Day shall be payable on or before the first day of the next succeeding month, commencing on the first such date immediately succeeding the date hereof, with all remaining accrued interest payable on the Assignment Day. Interest only shall be payable on the first day of the first month after the Assignment Day and thereafter the principal balance and interest thereon shall be paid together in installments as follows:

Dollars ($_____) on or before the first day of the second calendar month after the Assignment Day, and the same amount on the same day of each of the succeeding _____ months, with a final payment of the entire unpaid principal balance and all accrued interest on the tenth anniversary of the first day of the first month following the Assignment Day.

All payments and prepayments shall be credited first to accrued interest and then to principal.

This Note is secured by a Combination Mortgage, Security Agreement and Fixture Financing Statement (the "Mortgage") dated the date hereof and covering property located in _____ County, _____.

Prepayment of this Note is subject to the provisions of Article 2 of the Mortgage.

It is agreed that time is of the essence of this agreement. Upon the occurrence of any Event of Default, as defined in the Mortgage, the entire principal sum evidenced by this Note, together with all accrued and unpaid interest, shall, at the option of the holder hereof, become immediately due and payable without further notice, demand or presentment for payment, together with all costs, including all reasonable attorneys' fees incurred by the holder hereof in collecting or enforcing payment thereof, all without any relief whatever from any valuation or appraisement laws. Failure to exercise any option provided herein shall not constitute a waiver of the right to exercise the same in the event of any subsequent default.

If any payment required by this Note is not timely paid and such nonpayment continues for a period of fifteen days, the undersigned shall pay to the holder hereof an amount equal to four percent (4%) of the delinquent payment. The undersigned agrees that such payment is a reasonable charge for the costs and expenses incurred by the holder hereof in connection with a late payment.

The undersigned and all endorsers severally waive presentment, protest and demand, notice of protest, demand and of dishonor and nonpayment of this Note, and any and all lack of diligence or delays in collection or enforcement of this Note, and expressly agree that this Note, or any payment hereunder, may be extended from time to time, and expressly consent to the release of any party liable for the obligation secured by this Note, the release of any of the security of this Note, the acceptance of any other security therefor, or any other indulgence or forbearance whatsoever, all without notice to any party and without affecting the liability of the undersigned and any endorsers hereof. The acceptance by the holder of any payment hereunder which is less than payment in full of all amounts due and payable at the time of such payment shall not constitute a waiver of the right to exercise any right or remedy at that time or at any subsequent time or nullify any prior exercise of any such right or remedy without the express written consent of the holder hereof.

The term Reference Rate means the rate publicly announced by _____, from time to time as its reference rate; the Bank may lend to its customers at rates which are at, above or below the Reference Rate.

The term "Assignment Day" means the day on which the holder of this Note assigns it to _____.

In the event that the Assignment Day does not occur on or before _____, the principal balance and interest accrued thereon at the option of the holder, shall upon demand become immediately due and payable.

This Note shall be construed under and governed by the laws of the State of _____.

§ 15.7 Combination Mortgage, Security Agreement, and Fixture Financing Statement [1]

The mortgage reproduced in this section is intended to be used with the note in § 15.6 of this book. It is a "combination" document, meaning that it will be used for both construction and permanent financing, as described more fully in § 15.6, supra. See Section 46 of the mortgage below. Several other principal documents will also be executed simultaneously; they include an assignment of rents (see § 15.10 infra) and a construction loan agreement (see § 15.2 supra.)

This mortgage is designed to be used for commercial property—specifically, an office/warehouse building. Since numerous fixtures and items of equipment are covered by the mortgage in addition to the land and building, the mortgage also serves as a security agreement under Article 9 of the Uniform Commercial Code. See Section 28.

Prepayment under this mortgage is entirely restricted for the first five years, and carries a declining "premium", ranging from 5% down to 1%, in subsequent loan years. See Section 2.2.

In some respects this mortgage is similar to those used on owner-occupied residential property; this is so, for example, of the tax reserve (Section 3) and title warranty (Section 4) clauses. The provisions relating to maintenance and repairs (Section 6) are more complex than those usually found in residential mortgages, since repairs are potentially more costly and complicated. The same is true of the insurance requirements and damage provisions, set out in Sections 14 and 15, and the eminent domain provisions, found in Section 18. Section 7 reflects the fact that considerable valuable equipment is covered by the mortgage. It attempts to give the mortgagor reasonable flexibility in exchanging or disposing of equipment, while at the same time ensuring that the security value of the aggregate package of equipment is not diminished.

§ 15.7
1. Form provided by Faegre & Benson, Minneapolis, Minnesota.

Under Section 12, subordinate liens may not be placed on the property without the mortgagee's consent; in effect, this language, combined with Section 32 (the default and acceleration clause) comprises a due-on-encumbrance clause. See § 5.21 supra.

Section 20 requires the mortgagor to provide an "estoppel statement" to the mortgagee upon its request. Such a statement's purpose is to set forth the balance owing on the loan and its status in other respects, and to do so in a manner which will bind the mortgagor. Such a statement is often used when a commercial mortgage is sold on the secondary market to another lender or investor, and serves to assure the assignee that the mortgage is indeed in the condition represented by the assignor. The need for a statement of this sort is particularly obvious when the original mortgage is of the "combination" type, and contemplates assignment by the construction lender to a permanent lender when construction is complete.

It is significant that this mortgage contains no due-on-sale clause, nor any limitation on the mortgagor's right to lease or transfer the real property. Many commercial mortgages do contain such clauses. See, e.g., the leasehold mortgage reprinted in § 15.12, infra. Of course, such matters are negotiable, and the absence of such a clause in this form should not be taken as necessarily representative of all such transactions.

COMBINATION MORTGAGE, SECURITY AGREEMENT AND FIXTURE FINANCING STATEMENT

THIS COMBINATION MORTGAGE, SECURITY AGREEMENT AND FIXTURE FINANCING STATEMENT dated as of the _____ day of _____, by and between _____, a _____ limited partnership, whose address is _____ ("Mortgagor"), and _____, a _____ corporation, whose address is _____, _____ ("Mortgagee").

NOW, THEREFORE, THIS INDENTURE WITNESSETH:

TO SECURE THE PAYMENT when and as due and payable, of all indebtedness evidenced by the Note (as hereinafter defined), together with all interest thereon and all other amounts due thereunder, and to secure the payment of all indebtedness which this Mortgage or the Assignment (as hereinafter defined) by its terms secures and compliance with all of the terms hereof and of the Note and the Agreement (as hereinafter defined), Mortgagor does hereby grant, bargain, sell, mortgage, warrant, pledge, assign, transfer and convey to Mortgagee, its successors and assigns, forever, all those certain tracts or parcels of land (the "Land") situate in the County of _____, State of _____ described on Exhibit A attached hereto,

TOGETHER with all right, title and interest of Mortgagor, including any after-acquired title or reversion, in and to the beds of the ways, streets, avenues and alleys adjoining the Land; and

TOGETHER with all and singular the tenements, hereditaments, easements, appurtenances, riparian rights, other rights, liberties and privileges thereof or in any way now or hereafter appertaining to the Land, including any trade or service name or mark by which the Property (as hereinafter defined) may from time to time be known or identified, claim at law or in equity as well as any after-acquired title, franchise or license and the reversion and reversions and remainder and remainders thereof; and

TOGETHER with all rents, issues, proceeds and profits accruing and to accrue from the Property; and

TOGETHER with all Improvements and Equipment (each as hereinafter defined); and

TOGETHER with any and all after-acquired interests of Mortgagor in any of the above.

TO HAVE AND TO HOLD the same unto Mortgagee and its successors and assigns, forever.

AND Mortgagor hereby binds itself, its successors and assigns, to warrant and forever defend unto Mortgagee and its successors and assigns, the Property.

IT IS HEREBY COVENANTED by the parties hereto that the Property is to be held and applied subject to the further terms herein set forth; and Mortgagor, for itself and its successors and assigns, hereby covenants and agrees with Mortgagee as follows:

1. *Definitions.*

As used in this Mortgage, the following terms shall have the following respective meanings:

Agreement. That certain Construction Loan Agreement of even date herewith between Mortgagor as Borrower and Mortgagee as Lender, providing for construction of improvements on the Land.

Assignment. The Assignment of Leases and Rents of even date herewith between Mortgagor as assignor, and Mortgagee, as assignee, assigning rents from the Property as additional security for the Note.

Assignment Day. As defined in the Note.

Equipment. All building materials, supplies, equipment, vehicles, furniture, machinery and other personal property now or hereafter located upon or used or suitable to be used in connection with the operation, occupancy or use of the Real Estate, except for personal property and trade fixtures belonging to tenants under Leases.

Event of Default. As defined in Section 23.1.

Impositions. All taxes, assessments (including, without limitation, all assessments for public improvements or benefits, whether or not commenced or completed prior to the date hereof), water, sewer or other rents, rates and charges, excises, levies, license fees, permit fees, inspection fees and other authorization fees and other charges, in each case whether general or special, ordinary or extraordinary, or foreseen or unforeseen, of every character (including all interest and penalties thereon), which at any time may be assessed, levied, confirmed or imposed on or in respect of or be a lien upon (a) the Property or any part thereof or any rent therefrom or any estate, right or interest therein, or (b) any occupancy, use or possession of or activity conducted on the Real Estate or any part thereof, or (c) this Mortgage or the indebtedness now or hereafter secured by this Mortgage.

Improvements. All buildings, structures and other improvements now or hereafter located on the Land, and all fixtures (except Equipment) now or hereafter located in or attached to such buildings, structures and improvements.

Insurance Premiums. The premiums for the insurance required pursuant to this Mortgage.

Insurance Requirements. All terms of any insurance policy covering or applicable to the Property or any part thereof, all requirements of the issuer of any such policy, and all orders, rules, regulations and other requirements of the National Board of Fire Underwriters (or any other body exercising similar functions) applicable to or affecting the Property or any part thereof or any use or condition of the Property or any part thereof.

Leases. As defined in the Assignment.

Legal Requirements. All laws, statutes, codes, acts, ordinances, orders, judgments, decrees, injunctions, rules, regulations, permits, licenses, authorizations, directions and requirements of all governments, departments, commissions, boards, courts, authorities, agencies, officials and officers, foreseen or unforeseen, ordinary or extraordinary, which now or at any time hereafter may be applicable to the Property or any part thereof, or any of the adjoining sidewalks, or any use or condition of the Property or any part thereof, or construction thereon, or which require payments on behalf of or otherwise relate to persons from time to time employed on or occupants of the Real Estate.

Loan Year. A period of twelve consecutive calendar months commencing on the first day of the second month following the Assignment Day, as defined in the Note or any anniversary of that date.

Mortgage. This Combination Mortgage, Security Agreement and Fixture Financing Statement, as at the time amended, modified, restated, supplemented or extended.

Mortgagee. The mortgagee named herein and its successors and assigns as holder of the Note.

Mortgagor. The mortgagor named herein and its successors and assigns as Mortgagor under this Mortgage and as owners of the Real Estate.

Mortgagor's Alterations. Any change or alteration of or addition to any Improvement, and the construction, reconstruction or replacement of any Improvement, except for reconstruction or replacement in accordance with Sections 15, 16 or 18 of this Mortgage.

Note. The $_____ Promissory Note of Mortgagor of even date herewith, bearing interest prior to the Assignment Day at the rate equal to one percent (1%) per annum above the Reference Rate and from and after the Assignment Day at the rate of 13¾% per annum, with a maturity date not later than _____, as at the time amended, modified, restated or extended.

Property. The Real Estate and the Equipment, collectively.

Qualifying Rate. Prior to the Assignment Day, the lower of (a) one percent (1%) per annum above the Reference Rate and (b) the highest rate of interest permitted under _____ law with respect to the advance in question. From and after the Assignment Day, the lower of (a) 13¾ percent per annum and (b) the highest rate of interest permitted under _____ law with respect to the advance in question.

Real Estate. The Land, the Improvements and all other property referred to in the Granting Clause, except the Equipment.

Reference Rate. As defined in the Note.

Restoration. The repair, restoration or rebuilding of the Property or any part thereof following any taking, damage to or destruction of the same, as nearly as possible to its respective size, floor area, type and character immediately prior to such taking, damage or destruction, with, in the case of any restoration by Mortgagee, such alterations as may be made at Mortgagee's election, together with any temporary repairs and property protection pending completion of the work.

Taking. A taking of all or any part of the Property, or any interest therein or right accruing thereto, including, without limitation, any right of access thereto existing on the date of this Mortgage as the result of or in lieu or in anticipation of the exercise of the right of condemnation or eminent domain or a change of grade adversely affecting the Property or any part thereof.

Unavoidable Delays. Delays due to acts of God, fire, storm, strikes, blackouts, labor difficulties, enemy action, riots, inability to obtain materials, energy supplies, equipment or labor, governmental restrictions, unavoidable casualty, inclement weather, or any similar cause over which the Mortgagor is unable to exercise control if notice thereof is given to Mortgagee within 30 days of the occurrence thereof; lack of funds shall not be deemed a cause beyond the control of Mortgagor.

2. *The Note.*

2.1 *Payment.* Mortgagor will duly and punctually pay or cause the payment of:

(a) the principal of and interest on the Note in accordance with the terms thereof.

(b) all other payments required by the Note in accordance with the terms thereof, and

(c) when and as due and payable from time to time as provided herein, all other indebtedness secured hereby, together with interest at the Qualifying Rate.

2.2 *General Prepayment Restriction.* The Note may not be prepaid in whole or in part at any time prior to the end of the fifth Loan Year. Thereafter, Mortgagor shall have the right to prepay from time to time amounts of the principal balance of the Note upon payment of a prepayment premium that shall equal five percent of amounts prepaid in the sixth Loan Year and that shall decline from five percent by one percentage point in each successive Loan Year but that shall in no event be less than one percent.

2.3 *Notice of Prepayment.* In the case of each prepayment of the Note pursuant to Section 2.2, Mortgagor shall give written notice thereof to Mortgagee, not less than 30 nor more than 90 days prior to the date fixed for such prepayment, specifying such date and the aggregate principal amount to be prepaid on such date, and all prepayments must be made on regularly scheduled installment payment dates.

2.4 *Prepayment if Taking or Damage or Destruction.* If the Note is prepaid in whole or in part by reason of a Taking or damage or destruction, as hereinafter provided, such prepayment will be without premium or penalty.

2.5 *Prepayment not to Effect Subsequent Payments.* No partial prepayment, whether made voluntarily or as a result of damage, destruction, taking or otherwise, will relieve Mortgagor of its obligation to continue to make installment payments as required by the Note.

3. *Tax Reserves.*

Mortgagor shall on the date hereof deposit with Mortgagee a sum that is sufficient, when added to the monthly payments required under the next sentence hereof, to permit Mortgagee to pay installments of Impositions for the then current year, as they become due, out of amounts deposited with Mortgagee under this Section 3. Thereafter, on the first day of each and every month during the term of this Mortgage, Mortgagor shall deposit with Mortgagee a sum equal to one-twelfth of such Impositions for the then current year. All such deposits shall be received and held by Mortgagee and applied to the payment of each installment of such Impositions as the same shall become due and payable, whether or not any subsequent owner of the Property may benefit thereby, and shall not bear interest. In the event that the amount of such Impositions has not been definitely ascertained at the time when any such deposits are herein required to be made, Mortgagor shall make such deposits based upon the amount of such Impositions for the preceding year, subject to adjustment as and when the amount thereof is ascertained. If at any time when any installment of such Impositions becomes due and payable Mortgagor shall not have deposited a sum sufficient to pay the same, Mortgagor shall, within 5 days after demand, deposit with Mortgagee any deficiency, and if Mortgagor shall have deposited a sum more than sufficient to pay such installment, such excess shall be applied toward the deposits next required to be made hereunder. In the event Mortgagee at any time refunds any portion of the reserve fund, it may make the refund to whomever is represented to be the owner of the Property at the time.

   4. *Title to Property; Authority, etc.*

Mortgagor represents and warrants that it has received (and, as to Equipment hereafter acquired, will receive) good, merchantable and outright title to the Equipment, in each case subject to no lien, encumbrance or charge other than this Mortgage and has (and, as to Real Estate hereafter acquired, will have) good and marketable title in fee simple absolute to the Real Estate, subject to no lien, encumbrance or charge other than state mineral reservations and rights, this Mortgage, the Assignment, and the matters, if any, listed on Exhibit B attached hereto, and that it has good and lawful right and authority to execute the Note, the Agreement and this Mortgage and to convey the Real Estate and grant a security interest in the Equipment as provided herein. Mortgagor at its expense will warrant and defend to Mortgagee title to the Equipment and Real Estate, as the case may be, and the lien and interest of Mortgagee thereon and therein against all claims and demands, and will maintain and preserve such lien so long as the Note or any of the other indebtedness secured hereby is outstanding.

   5. *Recordation, etc.*

Mortgagor at its expense will at all times cause this Mortgage and any instruments amendatory hereof or supplemental hereto (and appropriate financing statements and continuation statements with respect thereto) to be recorded, registered and filed and to be kept recorded, registered and filed in such manner and in such places and will pay all such recording, registration, filing or other taxes, fees and other charges, and will comply with all such statutes and regulations, as may be required by law in order to establish, preserve and protect the lien of this Mortgage as a valid direct first mortgage lien of record on any property or interests now or hereafter included in the Property, validly securing all indebtedness now or hereafter secured hereunder.

   6. *Maintenance and Repairs, Shoring, Restoration, etc.*

Mortgagor at its expense will keep the Property and the adjoining sidewalks, curbs, vaults and vault space, if any, in good order and condition, subject to ordinary wear and tear and obsolescence; will promptly make all repairs, replacements and renewals thereof, whether interior or exterior, structural or non-structural, ordinary or extraordinary, foreseen or unforeseen, which are required to keep the same in good order and condition; will promptly repair or replace any worn out component of any item of Equipment with a component or components at least equal in quality and capability to the components replaced; will promptly restore the Property or any part of it which is damaged or destroyed by fire or other casualty; and, in case of a Taking, will promptly restore any Improvement or Equipment which is taken, except to the extent that such restoration is rendered impossible by reduction in area. All restoration, repairs, replacements and renewals shall be (a) equal in quality and class to the original work, (b) effected by Mortgagor with diligence (subject only to Unavoidable Delays) and in a workmanlike manner, so that as a result of their completion the fair market value immediately before such restoration, repair, replacement or renewal, (c) promptly and fully paid for by Mortgagor, and (d) made, in case the estimated cost of such restoration, repair, replacement, or renewal exceeds $50,000, only after Mortgagor shall have furnished Mortgagee a performance bond or other security satisfactory to Mortgagee. Mortgagor will do all shoring of foundations and walls of any building or other improvements or of the ground adjacent thereto and every other act necessary or appropriate for the preservation and safety of the Property by reason of or in connection with any excavation or other building operation upon the Real Estate or any adjoining property, whether or not the owner of the Property shall, by any Legal Requirement, be required to take such action or be liable for failure to do so.

7. *Removal of Equipment, etc.*

Mortgagor may, unless there is an uncured Event of Default, at its expense, abandon, scrap, salvage, dispose of or remove any item of Equipment, *provided* that (a) Mortgagor at its expense shall promptly replace such item of Equipment with another item or items of Equipment of a like nature, (b) the cost or fair market value of each such replacement, whichever is the lesser, shall be such that the aggregate thereof shall be at least equal to the fair market value of the replaced item, (c) the reasonably estimated useful life or remaining useful life of each replacement shall be at least equal to the remaining useful life of the replaced item, (d) Mortgagor shall, simultaneously therewith and without any request by Mortgagee deliver or cause to be delivered to Mortgagee all indications of title thereto and such other instruments as may be necessary or advisable in the opinion of Mortgagee to evidence Mortgagor's free, clear and unencumbered title thereto and ownership thereof, and (e) Mortgagor shall, at Mortgagor's expense, upon request of Mortgagee deliver to Mortgagee an instrument supplemental to this Mortgage, satisfactory in substance and form to Mortgagee, covering such replacement. All replacements of any item of Equipment or any part thereof shall immediately become subject to the lien of this Mortgage and constitute a part of the Equipment; provided, however, that the Mortgagor shall have none of the foregoing obligations if the item of Equipment so abandoned, scrapped, salvaged, disposed of or removed shall have become obsolete and of no value to the Property. Upon the abandonment, scrapping, salvage, disposal or removal of any item of Equipment pursuant to this Section 7, and the due subjection of the replacement thereof, if any, to the lien of this Mortgage, the lien hereof on any item of Equipment so abandoned, scrapped, salvaged, disposed of or removed shall terminate.

8. *Utility Services.*

Mortgagor will pay for all charges for all public or private utility services and all sprinkler systems and protective services at any time rendered to or in connection with or required for the proper maintenance or preservation of the Property or any part thereof, will comply with all contracts relating to any such services, and will do all other things required for the maintenance and continuance of all such services.

9. *Inspection.*

Mortgagee and its authorized representatives may enter the Real Estate or any part thereof at all reasonable times for the purpose of inspecting the Property or any part thereof. Mortgagee shall not have any duty to make any such inspection and shall not incur any liability or obligation as a result of making any such inspection.

10. *Payment of Impositions, etc.*

Subject to Sections 3 and 13, Mortgagor will pay all Impositions before the same shall become delinquent, will deliver to Mortgagee, upon request, a certificate of Mortgagor certifying to the payment of all Impositions required to be paid by this Article 10, and will furnish, without request, certified copies of official receipts or other satisfactory proof evidencing such payments.

11. *Compliance with Legal and Insurance Requirements, Instruments, etc.*

Subject to Article 13, Mortgagor at its expense will promptly observe and comply with (a) all Legal Requirements and Insurance Requirements, whether or not compliance therewith shall require structural changes in the Improvements or interfere with the use and enjoyment of the Property or any part thereof, (b) the Leases and any other instruments of record at any time in force affecting the Property or any part thereof, and (c) the Assignment.

12. *Liens, etc.*

Mortgagor will not, without the written consent of Mortgagee, directly or indirectly create or permit or suffer to be created or to remain, and will discharge, or promptly cause to be discharged, any mortgage, lien, encumbrance or charge on, pledge of, or conditional sale or other title retention agreement with respect to the Property or any part thereof (whether or not subordinate to the lien of this Mortgage) other than (a) this Mortgage, (b) liens of mechanics and materialmen, incurred in the ordinary course of business in the course of improvements permitted by this Mortgage, for sums which under the terms of the related contracts are not yet delinquent, (c) the lien of real estate taxes, installments of special assessment and personal property taxes with respect to which no penalty or interest is yet payable and (d) the Assignment.

13. *Permitted Contests.*

Mortgagor at its expense may contest, by appropriate legal proceedings conducted in good faith and with due diligence, the amount, validity or application, in whole or in part, of any Imposition or lien therefor or any Legal Requirement or the application of any instrument of record referred to in Section 12, *provided* that (a) in the case of an unpaid Imposition or lien therefor, such proceedings shall suspend the collection thereof from the Property, (b) neither the Property nor any part thereof or interest therein would be in any danger, deemed substantial by Mortgagee, of being sold, forfeited, or lost, (c) in the case of a Legal Requirement, Mortgagee would not be in any danger, deemed substantial by Mortgagee, of any civil or any criminal liability for failure to comply therewith, and (d) Mortgagor shall have furnished such security, if any, as may be required in the proceedings or requested by Mortgagee. Mortgagor shall give prompt written notice to Mortgagee of the commencement of any contest referred to in the preceding sentence.

14. *Insurance.*

14.1 *Hazard Insurance.* Mortgagor, at its sole cost and expense, shall, throughout the entire term of this Mortgage, keep the Improvements and the Equipment insured for the mutual benefit of Mortgagor and Mortgagee, as their respective interests may appear, against loss or damage by fire, windstorm, lightning, tornado, hail and such other further and additional risks as now are or hereafter may be embraced by the standard extended coverage forms or endorsements with vandalism and malicious mischief endorsement and with an all perils endorsement, in each case in their full insurable value. The term "full insurable value" as used in this Section 14.1 shall mean actual replacement cost (exclusive in the case of the Improvements of costs of excavations, foundations and footings below the ground floor), including the cost of debris removal. Whenever appropriate, while any alterations or improvements are in the course of being made, the aforesaid fire and extended coverage insurance shall be carried by Mortgagor in builder's risk form written on a completed value basis.

14.2 *Other Insurance.* Mortgagor, at its own sole cost and expense, shall, until this Mortgagor is paid in full, procure and maintain in such amounts as Mortgagee may reasonably request from time to time: (a) comprehensive general public liability insurance against claims for bodily injury, death or property damage occurring upon, in or about the Property or the elevators or escalators therein, including, among other things, coverage against so-called "occurrences"; (b) Broad Form Boiler and Machinery insurance, providing for full repair and replacement cost coverage at such times as there are pressure vessels in the Property; (c) rent and rental value insurance against the perils covered by the insurance requirement in Section 14.1 in an amount at least equal to the aggregate of (i) twelve months' gross rentals (including basic and percentage rental and all payments for taxes and occupancy and common area costs), assuming full occupancy and (ii) Impositions and Insurance Premiums for a twelve month period to the extent not included in (i) above, (if the Improvements shall be damaged or destroyed, the proceeds of such insurance shall be paid to Mortgagee and held and disbursed by Mortgagee, in payment of Impositions, Insurance Premiums, payments due on the Note and Property expenses (in such order of priority as Mortgagee may determine) from and after the date of such damage or loss until the date of completion of the restoration of the damaged or destroyed Improvements, at which time such proceeds or the balance thereof, if any, shall be paid to Mortgagor provided no Event of Default shall exist hereunder and no amounts shall be due under the Note); (d) during the entire period of making of any Mortgagor's Alterations, owner's contingent or protective liability insurance covering claims not covered by or under the terms or provisions of the above mentioned general public liability insurance policy; (e) appropriate worker's compensation insurance with respect to work on or about the Property; (f) if the Property is in a "flood plain area" as defined by the Federal Insurance Administration pursuant to Federal Flood Disaster Protection Act of 1973 (P.L. 93–234), Federal Flood Insurance in the maximum amount obtainable (but not in excess of the then principal balance of the Note) and (g) such other or different insurance and in such amounts as may be required by the Leases or as may be reasonably required by Mortgagee.

14.3 *Form of Insurance.* All insurance provided for in this Section 14(a) shall be effected under valid and enforceable policies, that are in forms issued by financially sound and responsible insurance companies authorized to do business in Minnesota which have been approved by Mortgagee and that are made payable as in this Mortgage provided; (b) shall name Mortgagee and Mortgagor as their respective interests may appear, with standard mortgagee clauses in favor of Mortgagee with loss payable (other than in the case of liability insurance) to and subject to adjustment and settlement by Mortgagee; (c) shall be acceptable to Mortgagee in form and substance, and shall to the extent obtainable, contain clauses or endorsements to the effect that: (i) no act or negligence of either Mortgagor or anyone acting for Mortgagor, which might otherwise result in a forfeiture of such insurance or any part thereof, no occupancy or use of the Property for purposes more hazardous than permitted by the terms of the policy, and no foreclosure or any other change in title to the Property or any part thereof shall in any way affect the validity or enforceability of such insurance insofar as Mortgagee is concerned, (ii) such policies shall not be changed or cancelled without at least ten (10) days' prior written notice to Mortgagee, and (iii) Mortgagee shall not be liable for any premiums thereon or subject to any assessments thereunder and (d) shall in all events be in amounts sufficient to avoid any co-insurance. Mortgagor may carry the insurance described in Sections 14.1 and 14.2 on a blanket basis under a policy covering the Property and other properties of Mortgagor, but only if such blanket coverage provides all the insurance described in Sections 14.1 and 14.2 in the amounts and on the terms there set forth and in compliance with the requirements of this Section 14.3.

14.4 *Delivery of Policies.* Mortgagor will deliver to Mortgagee the originals of all insurance policies (or satisfactory certificate of blanket coverage) with respect to the Property which Mortgagor is required to maintain or cause to be maintained pursuant to this Section 14 together with evidence as to the payment of all premiums then due thereon. A renewal policy or certificate with respect to each policy and evidence of payment of the premium for such renewal will be delivered by no later than 15 days prior to the expiration of the current policy.

14.5 *Separate Insurance.* Mortgagor shall not take out separate insurance concurrent in form or contributing in the event of loss with that required to be furnished pursuant to this Section unless losses thereunder are made payable as herein provided and the policies thereof are delivered to Mortgagee.

14.6 *Adjustment, etc.* Whether or not expressed in the policies, Mortgagee shall, if more than six months have elapsed since the occurrence of the insured event or if an Event of Default is occurring, have the right, without consent of or participation by Mortgagor to make proof of loss and compromise, settle and adjust all claims under policies maintained pursuant to this Section 14, except comprehensive general liability insurance with respect to which Mortgagee shall have none of the rights provided hereby. The insurer under any policy of insurance may conclusively rely upon a statement of Mortgagee that it is entitled to make proof of loss, settle, compromise or adjust a claim without participation by Mortgagor.

14.7 *Leases.* The maintenance by a tenant under a Lease of any insurance that meets all of the terms and requirements of Sections 14.1, 14.2, 14.3 and 14.5 shall constitute maintenance of such insurance by Mortgagor under this Section 14, and the provisions of Sections 14.4 and 14.6 shall apply to any such insurance maintained by a tenant.

15. *Damage or Destruction by Fire or Other Casualty.*

15.1 *Notice of Partial Loss.* In the event of any partial damage or loss by fire or other casualty whatsoever to the Improvements or any portion thereof, Mortgagor shall give immediate notice thereof to Mortgagee if the same equals or exceeds $10,000, and shall, if Mortgagee makes insurance proceeds available for such purpose, and regardless of the dollar amount of such damage or loss or of the adequacy of insurance proceeds, with reasonable diligence (subject to Unavoidable Delays), at Mortgagor's own sole cost and expense, complete Restoration in accordance with all applicable Legal Requirements, Insurance Requirements and Leases. If any Equipment is damaged or lost as a result of such fire or other casualty, Mortgagor shall likewise, at its own sole cost and expense, if Mortgagee makes insurance proceeds available for Restoration, repair or replace the Equipment so damaged or lost, whether or not insurance proceeds are adequate for that purpose.

15.2 *Restoration.* In the event that the Improvements or any of them shall be totally destroyed, or so substantially damaged by fire or other casualty whatsoever that the repair and restoration thereof would be impracticable, Mortgagor shall give prompt notice thereof to Mortgagee, and, if Mortgagee makes insurance proceeds available for Restoration, shall proceed with reasonable diligence (subject to Unavoidable Delays), to remove the damaged Improvement and all debris caused by the damage or destruction and thereafter complete Restoration of the replacement Improvement, and shall equip such building(s) with Equipment, all at Mortgagor's sole cost and expense, whether or not any insurance proceeds are adequate for such purpose, in accordance with all applicable Legal Requirements, Insurance Requirements and Leases. Such demolition, removal and construction shall be without cost, charge or expense of any kind to Mortgagee. Before commencing the construction of any replacement building(s), Mortgagor shall submit copies of the plans and specifications therefore to Mortgagee for its approval, which approval will not be unreasonably withheld or delayed.

15.3 *Application of Insurance Proceeds.* If by reason of any damage or destruction mentioned in Sections 15.1 and 15.2 hereof, any sums are paid under any insurance policy mentioned in Section 14 hereof (other than rent or rental value insurance policies, proceeds of which shall be distributed in accordance with Section 14.2), such sums shall be paid to Mortgagee or, at Mortgagee's option, to a disbursing agent designated by Mortgagee (Mortgagee or said agent being referred to herein as a "Depository") which, except as provided below, may apply them, in Mortgagee's absolute discretion, regardless of the adequacy of security, in any one or more of the following ways: (i) to the indebtedness secured hereby, whether or not then due and payable, in any order of priority (but without prepayment penalty); (ii) to fulfillment of such of the covenants contained herein as Mortgagee may determine; (iii) to Restoration; and, (iv) to Mortgagor. Any insurance proceeds (and interest thereon, if any) remaining after any payment to Restoration as provided in this Section may at the option of Mortgagee be applied to indebtedness secured by this Mortgage (whether or not then due and in any order of priority but without prepayment penalty) or paid to Mortgagor. If (i) no Event of Default exists at the time of payment, (ii) the damage or destruction involved will not result in the termination of any Major Lease (as defined in the Assignment), (iii) Mortgagor promptly delivers to Mortgagee letters of estoppel from each of the tenants under Major Leases unconditionally certifying, in form acceptable to Mortgagee, that its Major Lease will be in effect after Restoration is complete, (iv) the insurance proceeds do not exceed the then unpaid principal balance of the Note, and (v) the damage or destruction in question occurs prior to

_____, then the Depository shall apply such sums to Restoration in installments as restoration proceeds, subject to (a) deposit with Depository from time to time of such sums in addition to net insurance proceeds as Mortgagee may from time to time determine to be necessary to complete Restoration and (b) such conditions to advances as are contained in the Agreement (which shall, for this purpose, be deemed to apply whether or not the Assignment Day has occurred); provided, however, that Mortgagee may at its option apply any remaining funds so held, together with interest thereon, if any, to payment of indebtedness or to Restoration, in accordance with this Section, if at any time prior to the time that such funds are applied to Restoration (i) an Event of Default occurs, or (ii) Mortgagor is not diligently proceeding with Restoration or is not proceeding in accordance with applicable Legal Requirements, Insurance Requirements or Leases. Mortgagor shall promptly reimburse Mortgagee and the Depository upon demand for all charges, fees and costs (including reasonable attorneys' fees) incurred or charged by them in connection with the collection of insurance proceeds and their disbursement in accordance with this Section, and all such charges and costs, together with interest at the Qualifying Rate from and after the date of payment, shall be additional amounts secured by this Mortgage. No damage or destruction or retention of insurance proceeds as provided in this Section shall suspend any obligation to make payments pursuant to the Note or suspend the accrual of interest under the Note and the Note shall bear interest and shall be payable in accordance with its tenor. If Mortgagee applies any insurance proceeds (other than proceeds remaining after proceeds have been applied to Restoration and other than proceeds of rent or business interruption insurance) to payment of the indebtedness secured hereby, Mortgagor may, at any time within 180 days after such application, prepay the indebtedness secured hereby in full (though not in part) without penalty.

16. *Mortgagor's Alterations.*

Mortgagor may not make or permit the making of any Mortgagor's Alterations the cost of which will exceed $100,000 without Mortgagee's consent. Any Mortgagor's Alterations approved by Mortgagee (a) shall not change the general character or use of the Property, or reduce the fair market value thereof below its value immediately before such Mortgagor's Alteration, or impair the usefulness of the Land, (b) shall be effected with due diligence, in a good and workmanlike manner and in compliance with all applicable Legal Requirements, Insurance Requirements and Leases, (c) shall be promptly and fully paid for by Mortgagor, (d) shall be made, in case the estimated cost thereof exceeds $100,000, under the supervision of a qualified architect or engineer (who may be an employee of Mortgagor), pursuant to plans and specifications approved by Mortgagee and only after Mortgagor shall have furnished to Mortgagee, if requested by Mortgagee, a bond acceptable to Mortgagee, or other security satisfactory to Mortgagee, and (e) shall be constructed entirely within the boundaries of the Land. All Mortgagor's Alterations shall immediately become and remain subject to the lien of this Mortgage. Mortgagor may not remove or demolish any Improvement or any part thereof, except as provided in Sections 15.2 and 17.

17. *Use and Operation of Property.*

Mortgagor will at all times operate the Improvements as an office/warehouse facility and for manufacturing (to the extent permitted by the zoning code) and for no other purpose. Mortgagor will not use or allow the Property or any part thereof to be used or occupied for any unlawful purpose or in violation of any certificate of occupancy or other certificate permitting or affecting the use of the Property or any part thereof. Mortgagor shall not suffer any act to be done or any condition to exist on the Property or any part thereof which may, in law, constitute a nuisance, public or private, or which may make void or voidable any insurance with respect thereto. Mortgagor will not allow the Property to become unoccupied or vacant other than vacancies occurring in the ordinary course of business and shall not suffer any article to be brought upon the Land which may be dangerous unless safeguarded as required by law. After the Assignment Day Mortgagor may demolish the existing two-story warehouse building located on the Land as long as (i) no Event of Default has occurred and is continuing, (ii) Mortgagee is given not less than 30 days' notice of the commencement of demolition, and (iii) the requirements of Section 16(b), (c) and (d) of this Mortgage are met. If such building is demolished, Mortgagor shall remove all debris from the Land and shall install paved surface parking on the building site.

18. *Condemnation.*

18.1 *Mortgagor to Give Notice.* Forthwith upon receipt by Mortgagor of notice of the institution of any proceeding or negotiations for a Taking, Mortgagor shall give notice thereof to Mortgagee. Mortgagee may appear in any such proceedings and participate in any such negotiations and may be represented by counsel, and, if an Event of Default is occurring or more than six months have occurred since the Taking, Mortgagee may compromise and settle any damage claim without participation by Mortgagor. A condemning authority may conclusively rely upon Mortgagee's statement that it is entitled to compromise or settle a damage claim without participation by Mortgagor. Mortgagor, notwithstanding that Mortgagee may not be a party to any such proceeding, will promptly give to Mortgagee copies of all notices, pleadings, judgments, determinations and other papers received by Mortgagor herein. Mortgagor will not enter into any agreement permitting or consenting to the taking of the Property, or any part thereof, or providing for the conveyance thereof in lieu of condemnation, with anyone authorized to acquire the same in condemnation or by eminent domain unless Mortgagee shall first have consented thereto in writing.

18.2 *Restoration; Application of Proceeds.* In the event of a Taking, all awards payable as a result of a Taking shall be paid to Mortgagee, which may, in its absolute discretion, regardless of the adequacy of security, apply them in any one or more of the ways specified in the first sentence of Section 15.3 of this Mortgage (without prepayment penalty, in the case of application to the indebtedness secured hereby). If the Taking involves a taking of any Improvement, Mortgagor shall proceed with reasonable diligence, subject to Unavoidable Delays, and except to the extent that restoration is made impossible by reduction in area, to demolish and remove any ruins and complete Restoration of the Property in accordance with all applicable Legal Requirements, Insurance Requirements and Leases, whether or not available condemnation awards are adequate to complete Restoration. No damage or destruction or retention of awards as provided in this Section shall suspend any obligation to make payments pursuant to the Note or suspend the accrual of interest under the Note, and the Note shall bear interest and shall be payable in accordance with its tenor. Mortgagor shall promptly reimburse Mortgagee upon demand for all charges and costs (including reasonable attorneys' fees) incurred by it in collection of awards and their disbursement in accordance with this Section, and all such charges and costs, together with interest at the Qualifying Rate from and after the date of demand, shall be additional amounts secured by this Mortgage. If Mortgagee applies any condemnation awards (other than awards remaining after awards have been applied to Restoration) to the indebtedness secured hereby, Mortgagor may, at any time within 180 days after such application, prepay the indebtedness secured hereby in full (though not in part) without penalty.

18.3 *Temporary Taking.* Mortgagor shall promptly notify Mortgagee of any Taking for a temporary use or occupancy. If, but only if, any award payable to Mortgagor on account of such Taking is made in a lump sum or is paid in other than equal monthly installments, Mortgagor shall pay over such award to Mortgagee promptly upon receipt, and Mortgagee shall apply such award as provided in Section 14.2 with respect to rent or rental value insurance; provided, however, that any unapplied portion of such award held by Mortgagee when such Taking ceases or terminates, or after the indebtedness secured by this Mortgage shall have been paid in full, shall be paid to Mortgagor.

19. *Protection of Lien of Mortgage.*

If Mortgagee shall incur or expend any sums, including reasonable attorneys' fees, whether in connection with any action or proceeding or not, to sustain the lien of this Mortgage or its priority, or to protect or enforce any of Mortgagee's rights hereunder, or to recover any indebtedness hereby secured, all such sums shall become immediately due and payable by Mortgagor with interest thereon at the Qualifying Rate, and shall be secured by this Mortgage.

20. *Estoppel Certificate.*

Mortgagor agrees at any time and from time to time, upon not less than 15 days' prior notice by Mortgagee, to execute, acknowledge and deliver, without charge, to Mortgagee or to any person designated by Mortgagee, a statement in writing certifying that this Mortgage is unmodified (or if there have been modifications, identifying the same by the date thereof and specifying the nature thereof), the principal amount then secured hereby and the unpaid balance of the Note, that Mortgagor has not received any notice of default or notice of acceleration or foreclosure of this Mortgage (or if Mortgagor has received any notice, that it has been revoked, if such be the case), that no Event of Default exists hereunder (or if any such Event of Default does exist, specifying the same and stating that the same has been cured, if such be the case), that Mortgagor has no claims or offsets against Mortgagee (or if Mortgagor has any such claims, specifying the same), and the dates to which the interest and the other sums and charges payable by Mortgagor pursuant to the Note have been paid.

21. *Accounting; Financial Statements and Other Information; Equipment Records; Inspection.*

Mortgagor will prepare or cause to be prepared at its expense and deliver to Mortgagee (in such number as may reasonably be requested):

(a) As soon as practicable after the end of each fiscal year of Mortgagor, and in any event within 90 days thereafter, the financial statements of Mortgagor, including an income statement and balance sheet, all in reasonable detail and accompanied by a certificate of a general partner, which statements shall be prepared in accordance with generally accepted accounting principles consistently applied. In the event that such financial statements are not delivered by the date required, or are not prepared or certified as above required, then Mortgagee may on three days' notice to Mortgagor audit or cause to be audited the books and records of Mortgagor at Mortgagor's expense, and Mortgagor shall provide Mortgagee with access to Mortgagor's books and records so that such audit may be conducted;

(b) Immediately upon becoming aware of the existence of any condition or event which constitutes, or which after notice or lapse of time or both would constitute, an Event of Default, written notice specifying the nature and period of existence thereof and what action Mortgagor has taken, is taking or proposes to take with respect thereto; and

(c) Promptly upon request, a certificate of Mortgagor describing the items of Equipment at the time subject to this Mortgage (in making such a list, items such as office supplies may be listed generally, rather than by item).

Mortgagor at its expense will maintain, at offices on the Land or such other location as may be reasonably satisfactory to Mortgagee (i) complete and correct inventory records setting forth all items of Equipment (including, where appropriate, identification numbers) and will enter in such records all replacements and alterations of the Equipment (other than minor replacements and alterations made in the ordinary course of maintenance), including the cost of each such replacement or alteration, (ii) books of account relating to the Real Estate and (iii) the books and records of Mortgagor. Mortgagor will permit Mortgagee and its authorized representatives to inspect the Equipment and all the inventory records relating to the Equipment, and to inspect and audit the books of account relating to the Property in each case during Mortgagor's usual business hours.

22. *Subrogation—Continuing Lien.*

Mortgagee shall be subrogated for further security to the lien, although released of record, of any and all encumbrances paid out of the proceeds of the issue of the Note or otherwise paid by Mortgagee pursuant to the provisions of this Mortgage. This Mortgage creates a continuing lien to secure the full and final payment of the Note and the payments required hereunder and the performance of all other obligations imposed by this Mortgage, and hereafter arising.

23. *Event of Default; Acceleration.*

23.1 *Event of Default.* Each of the following occurrences shall constitute an event of default hereunder (herein called an "Event of Default"):

(a) If Mortgagor shall fail to pay when due any amount payable under the Note or any other indebtedness secured by this Mortgage and such failure shall continue for ten days after the due date;

(b) If Mortgagor fails duly to observe, perform or comply with any of the other provisions or terms contained in the Agreement or this Mortgage and such default shall continue for a period of thirty days after Mortgagee gives Mortgagor notice of such default;

(c) If Mortgagor or any guarantor of the Note (a "Guarantor") shall become insolvent (however evidenced) or commit any act of bankruptcy or make a general assignment for the benefit of creditors, or if any proceedings are instituted by or against Mortgagor or any Guarantor for any relief under any bankruptcy or insolvency laws, or if a receiver is appointed of, or a writ or order of attachment or garnishment is made or issued upon, or if any proceeding or procedure is commenced or any remedy supplementary to or in enforcement of a judgment is employed against or with respect to the Property (provided, that in the event of involuntary proceedings, the proceedings shall not constitute an Event of Default unless Mortgagor fails to obtain dismissal of the proceedings within 90 days after the institution thereof);

(d) If any representation or warranty made by Mortgagor in the Agreement or this Mortgage or in the Assignment, is untrue or misleading in any material respect;

(e) If there is any Event of Default as defined in the Assignment; and

(f) If the Real Estate, or any part thereof, is sold, conveyed, transferred, encumbered, or full possessory rights therein transferred, whether voluntarily, involuntarily or by operation of law, or if any general partner's interest or any controlling stock interest in Mortgagor is sold, conveyed, transferred or encumbered, whether voluntarily, involuntarily or by operation of law. This provision shall apply to each and every sale, transfer, conveyance or encumbrance regardless of whether Mortgagee has consented or waived its rights, whether by action or non-action, in connection with any previous sale, transfer, conveyance or encumbrance, whether one or more.

23.2 *Acceleration.*

23.2.1 In the event of an Event of Default specified in Section 23.1, Mortgagee may declare an Acceleration. An Acceleration is a declaration that all sums due and payable pursuant to the Note and all other indebtedness secured by this Mortgage are due and payable, and upon such declaration the same shall thereupon become immediately due and payable without presentment or other demand, protest, notice or dishonor or any other notice of any kind, all of which are hereby expressly waived.

23.2.2 An Acceleration may be waived by written waiver by Mortgagee. Such waiver shall set aside the Acceleration and thereupon the Note and the terms and provisions of this Mortgage shall remain in effect as if no Acceleration had been made.

24. *Foreclosure by Action.*

If any Event of Default shall have occurred and be continuing, Mortgagee may at any time, at its election, proceed at law or in equity or otherwise to enforce the payment of the Note in accordance with the terms hereof and thereof and to foreclose the lien of this Mortgage in one or more proceedings as against all or, to the extent permitted by law, any part of the Property, or any interest in any part thereof, and to have the same sold under the judgment or decree of a court of competent jurisdiction or proceed to take either of such actions.

25. *Power of Sale.*

If an Event of Default shall have occurred and be continuing, Mortgagee may sell, assign, transfer and deliver the whole or, from time to time to the extent permitted by law, any part of the Property or any interest in any part thereof, at public auction as required by law, the power of sale being hereby expressly conferred.

26. *Mortgagee Authorized to Apply Funds, etc.*

Notwithstanding any other provision of this Mortgage, while any Event of Default exists, any funds then held by Mortgagee in which Mortgagor has an interest (including without limitation, funds held pursuant to Sections 3, 15 and 18 of this Mortgage) may be applied at the option of Mortgagee to cure said default or in reduction of the indebtedness secured by this Mortgage.

27. *Purchase of Property by Mortgagee.*

Mortgagee may be a purchaser of the Property or of any part thereof or of any interest therein at any sale thereof, whether pursuant to foreclosure by advertisement or action, and may apply upon the purchase price the indebtedness secured hereby owing to such purchaser.

28. *Disposition of Equipment.*

Mortgagor hereby grants Mortgagee a security interest and this Mortgage Constitutes a "Security Agreement" within the meaning of and shall create a security interest under the Uniform Commercial Code, as adopted in the State of Minnesota, with respect to any personal property and fixtures which are part of the Property. Accordingly, with respect to all or any of the personal property and fixtures included within the Property, Mortgagee may, in accordance with Section 9–501(4) of the Uniform Commercial Code, as in effect in Minnesota, sell such property in the foreclosure proceedings referred to in this Mortgage with respect to the Real Estate, or may proceed with respect to all or any part of such property in accordance with Article 9 of the Uniform Commercial Code. In any disposition pursuant to said Article 9, by public or private sale, ten days notice of disposition shall be deemed commercially reasonable.

29. *Receipt a Sufficient Discharge to Purchaser.*

Upon any sale of the Property or any part thereof or any interest therein, pursuant to the terms of this Mortgage, the receipt of the officer making the sale under judicial proceedings or of Mortgagee shall be sufficient discharge to the purchaser for the purchase money, and such purchaser shall not be obliged to see to the application thereof.

30. *Waiver of Appraisement, Valuation, Marshalling, etc.*

30.1 *Waiver of Appraisement.* Mortgagor hereby waives, to the full extent it may lawfully do so, the benefit of all appraisement, valuation, stay and extension laws now or hereafter in force.

30.2 *Waiver of Guarantor Defenses, etc.* Mortgagor agrees that neither the lien of this Mortgage nor any obligation of Mortgagor will be released, impaired or subordinated by any amendment to this Mortgage or any other instrument, any release or waiver of liability, any extension of time or waiver of right or remedy as to Mortgagor or any other party or any other act or thing which, but for this provision, would so release, impair or subordinate.

31. *Application of Proceeds of Sale.*

The proceeds of any foreclosure sale of the Property or any part thereof or any interest therein, pursuant to this Mortgage, together with any other moneys at the time held by Mortgagee pursuant to this Mortgage, shall be applied in such order as Mortgagee may determine.

32. *Appointment of Receiver; Assignment of Rents.*

If an Event of Default shall have occurred and be continuing, Mortgagee shall be entitled to the appointment of a receiver for all or any part of the Property whether such receivership be incidental to a proposed sale of the Property or otherwise, and whether or not the Mortgagor is committing or permitting waste, and regardless of the adequacy of the security or the solvency of Mortgagor, and Mortgagor hereby consents to the appointment of such receiver and will not oppose any such appointment. Mortgagee may at its option advance monies to the receiver from time to time for the operation of the Property, and all such sums advanced, together with interest thereon at the Qualifying Rate, shall be immediately due and payable and secured by this Mortgage. Mortgagor hereby assigns to Mortgagee as additional security, all rents, issues and profits of the Property.

33. *Possession, Management and Income.*

If an Event of Default shall have occurred and be continuing, Mortgagee, without further notice, so far as permitted by law, may enter upon and take possession of the Property or any part thereof without judicial process, by summary proceedings, ejectment or otherwise and may remove the Mortgagor and all other persons and any and all property therefrom, and may hold, operate and manage the same and receive all earnings, income, rents, issues and proceeds accruing with respect thereto or any part thereof. Mortgagee shall be under no liability for or by reason of any such taking of possession, entry, removal or holding, operation or management.

34. *Right of Mortgagee to Perform Covenants, etc.*

If Mortgagor shall fail to make any payment or perform any act required to be made or performed hereunder or under any Lease or to release any lien affecting the Property which it is required to release by the terms of this Mortgage, Mortgagee, upon ten days notice to Mortgagor (except in the case of an emergency, when no notice is required) and without waiving or releasing any obligation or default, may (but shall be under no obligation to), if the default has not been cured within the ten day notice period (if applicable), make such payment or perform such act for the account and at the expense of Mortgagor and may enter upon the Property or any part thereof for such purpose and take all such action thereon as, in Mortgagee's opinion, may be necessary or appropriate therefor. To facilitate exercise of the foregoing rights, Mortgagor hereby irrevocably appoints Mortgagee its attorney-in-fact to exercise any and all of the foregoing rights and remedies. No such entry shall be deemed an eviction of Mortgagor. All sums so paid by Mortgagee and all costs and expenses (including, without limitation, attorneys' fees and expenses) so incurred, together with interest thereon at the Qualifying Rate from the date of payment or incurring, shall constitute additional indebtedness secured by this Mortgage and shall be paid by Mortgagor to Mortgagee on demand. Mortgagee shall not be liable for any damage resulting from any such payment or action.

35. *Remedies, etc., Cumulative.*

Each right, power and remedy of Mortgagee provided for in this Mortgage or now or hereafter existing at law or in equity or by statute or otherwise shall be cumulative and concurrent and shall be in addition to every other right, power or remedy provided for in this Mortgage or now or hereafter existing at law or in equity or by statute or other document or otherwise, and the exercise or beginning of the exercise by Mortgagee of any one or more of the rights, powers or remedies provided for in this Mortgage or now or hereafter existing at law or in equity or by statute or otherwise, or the exercise of any such right, power or remedy with respect to a part only of the Property, shall not preclude the simultaneous or later exercise by mortgagee of any or all such other rights, powers or remedies, or the simultaneous or later exercise by Mortgagee such right, power or remedy with respect to any other part of the Property.

36. *Terms Subject to Applicable Law.*

All rights, powers and remedies provided herein may be exercised only to the extent that the exercise thereof does not violate any applicable law, and are intended to be limited to the extent necessary so that they will not render this Mortgage invalid, unenforceable or not entitled to be recorded, registered or filed under any applicable law. If any term of this Mortgage or any application thereof shall be held to be invalid, illegal or unenforceable, the validity of other terms of this Mortgage or any other application of such term shall in no way be affected thereby. This Mortgage shall be governed by the laws of the State of _____.

37. *No Waiver, etc.*

No failure by Mortgagee to insist upon the strict performance of any term hereof or to exercise any right, power or remedy consequent upon a breach thereof, shall constitute a waiver of any such term or of any such breach. No breach of any provision of this Mortgage may be waived except by written waiver signed by Mortgagee and no breach of any provision requiring the payment of money may be waived except by written waiver signed by Mortgagee. No waiver of any breach shall affect or alter this Mortgage, which shall continue in full force and effect, or the rights of Mortgagee with respect to any other then existing or subsequent breach. Receipt of partial payment on the indebtedness secured by this Mortgage after a declaration of Acceleration shall not waive the Acceleration.

38. *Further Assurances.*

Mortgagor at Mortgagor's expense will execute, acknowledge and deliver all such instruments and take all such action as Mortgagee may reasonably request for the better assuring to Mortgagee of the properties and rights now or hereafter subject to the lien hereof or assigned hereunder or intended so to be.

39. *No Claims Against Mortgagee, etc.*

Nothing contained in this Mortgage shall constitute any consent or request by Mortgagee, express or implied, for the performance of any labor or services or the furnishing of any materials or other property in respect of the Property or any part thereof, nor as giving any right, power or authority to contract for or permit the performance of any labor or services or the furnishing of any materials or other property in such fashion as would permit the making of any claim against Mortgagee in respect thereof or any claim that any lien based on the performance of such labor or services or the furnishing of any such materials or other property is prior to the lien of this Mortgage.

40. *Indemnification by Mortgagor.*

Mortgagor will protect, indemnify and save harmless Mortgagee from and against all liabilities, obligations, claims, damages, penalties, causes of action, costs and expenses (including, without limitation, attorney's fees and expenses) imposed upon or incurred by or asserted against Mortgagee by reason of (a) ownership of the Property, or any interest therein, or receipt of any rent or other sum therefrom, (b) any accident, injury to or death of persons or loss of or damage to property occurring on or about the Property or any part thereof or the adjoining sidewalks, curbs, vaults and vault space, if any, (c) any use, non-use or condition of the Property or any part thereof or the adjoining sidewalks, curbs, vaults and vault space, if any, (d) any failure on the part of Mortgagor to perform or comply with any of the terms of this Mortgage, (e) performance of any labor or services or the furnishing of any materials or other property in respect of the Property or any part thereof, (f) any negligence or tortious act on the part of Mortgagor or any of its agents, contractors, sublessees, licensees or invitees, or (g) exercise by Mortgagee of any remedy provided hereunder or at law or equity; provided, however, that nothing herein shall be construed to obligate Mortgagor to protect, indemnify and save Mortgagee harmless from and against liabilities, obligations, claims, damages, penalties, causes of action, costs and expenses (including, without limitation, attorneys' fees and expenses) imposed upon or incurred by or asserted against Mortgagee by reason of the negligence of or tortious acts on the part of Mortgagee or any of its employees, agents, contractors, licensees or invitees. Any amounts payable to Mortgagee under this Section which are not paid within 10 days after written demand therefor by Mortgagee shall bear interest at the Qualifying Rate from the date of such demand, and shall be secured by this Mortgage. If any action, suit or proceeding is brought against Mortgagee by reason of any such occurrence, Mortgagor upon Mortgagee's request will at Mortgagor's expense resist and defend such action, suit or proceeding or will cause the same to be resisted and defended by counsel for the insurer of the liability or by counsel designated by Mortgagor approved by Mortgagee.

41. *Defeasance and Release, etc.*

If Mortgagor shall pay the principal of and interest on the Note in accordance with the terms thereof and all other sums payable hereunder by Mortgagor and shall comply with all the terms hereof and of the Note and the Agreement then this Mortgage shall be null and void and of no further force and effect and shall be released by Mortgagee. Upon the release of this Mortgage, Mortgagee, on the written request and at the expense of Mortgagor will execute and deliver such proper instruments of release and satisfaction as may reasonably be requested to evidence such release, and any such instrument, when duly executed by Mortgagee and duly recorded in the places where this Mortgage is recorded, shall conclusively evidence the release of this Mortgage.

42. *Notices.*

All notices, requests, demands, consents, approvals, and other communications which may be or are required to be served or given hereunder (for the purposes of this Section collectively called "Notices") shall be in writing and shall be sent by registered or certified mail, return receipt requested, postage prepaid, addressed to the party to receive such Notice at its address first above set forth, or at such other address as any party may furnish to the other party and Mortgagee in writing. Any party may, by Notice given as aforesaid, change its address for all subsequent Notices, except that no party may require Notices to it to be sent to more than two addresses. Except where otherwise expressly provided to the contrary elsewhere in this Mortgage, Notices shall be deemed given when mailed in the manner aforesaid.

43. *Warranties and Representations.*

43.1 *Partnership Existence and Power.* Mortgagor is now and at all times while this Mortgage remains in effect will be a _____ limited partnership duly created and validly existing under the laws of the State of _____, in good standing therein. Mortgagor will at all times while this Mortgage remains in effect (i) conduct continuously and operate actively its business, (ii) keep in full force and effect its limited partnership existence and comply with all the laws and regulations governing the conduct of its business, and (iii) make all such reports and pay all such franchise and other taxes and license fees and do all such other acts and things as may be lawfully required to maintain its rights, licenses and powers under the laws of the United States and of the states and jurisdictions in which it does business. The making, execution and performance by Mortgagor of this Mortgage, the Agreement, the Assignment and the Note have been duly authorized by all necessary partnership action and do not violate any provision of law or of its partnership agreement or result in the breach of or constitute a default under any indenture or other agreement or instrument to which Mortgagor is a party or by which Mortgagor or the Property may be bound or affected, and this Mortgage, the Agreement, the Assignment and the Note are valid and enforceable in accordance with their terms.

43.2 *Business Loan.* Mortgagor represents and warrants to Mortgagee that the loan evidenced by the Note and secured hereby is a business loan transacted solely for the purpose of carrying on the business of Mortgagor.

44. *Miscellaneous.*

This Mortgage may be changed, waived, discharged or terminated only by an instrument in writing signed by the party against which enforcement of such change, waiver, discharge or termination is sought. This Mortgage shall be binding upon Mortgagor and its successors and assigns, and all persons claiming under or through Mortgagor or any such successor or assign, and shall inure to the benefit of and be enforceable by Mortgagee and its successors and assigns. The headings in this Mortgage are for purposes of reference only and shall not limit or define the meaning hereof. This Mortgage may be executed in any number of counterparts, each of which shall be an original, but all of which together shall constitute one and the same instrument.

45. *Fixture Filing.*

From the date of its recording or registration, this Mortgage shall be effective as a financing statement filed as a fixture filing with respect to all goods constituting part of the Property which are or are to become fixtures related to the Real Estate. For this purpose, the following information is set forth:

(a) Name and Address of Debtor:
_____
_____
_____

(b) Name and Address of Secured Party:
_____
_____
_____

(c) This document covers goods which are or are to become fixtures.
(d) Name of Record Owner of Real Estate:
_____

46. *Construction Mortgage.*

This Mortgage secures an obligation incurred for the construction of an improvement on land and is both a construction mortgage and a permanent storage.

47. *Applicability of Agreement.*

From and after the Assignment Day the Agreement shall no longer constitute a part of or be secured by this Mortgage, and Mortgagor shall thereafter have no defenses, offsets or counterclaims with respect to its obligations hereunder arising out of the Agreement, and no such defenses, offsets or counterclaims shall be valid or effective as against the indebtedness secured hereby or as against such assignee of Mortgagee and its successors and assigns.

IN WITNESS WHEREOF, Mortgagor has caused this Mortgage to be executed as of the day and year first above written.

§ 15.8 Promissory Note with Lender Participation in Project Income and Appreciation [1]

This note is to be secured by a mortgage on a commercial rental building. It is similar to the note reprinted in § 15.6, in that it covers both a construction period and a long-term loan period thereafter. In the present transaction, however, the parties contemplate that the construction lender will continue to hold the loan after completion of the project, rather than assigning the documents to a different lender at that time. Hence the phrase "conversion date" rather than "assignment date" is used to signify the end of construction and the commencement of the long-term interest. As defined in Section 1, the conversion date must occur no later than 27 months after draws begin on the construction loan. The loan matures 17 years after the conversion date; see Section 3.4.

Since there is no assignment at the end of construction, it is not necessary in this note to provide for a change in the payment structure as of that date. Instead, the mortgagor pays (in addition to the contingent interest described below) monthly interest only for the first five years of the loan (including the construction period), and a "constant" monthly payment of 1.095% of the outstanding balance (as of the fifth anniversary of the loan) for the remainder of the 17-year term. See Section 3.2. This constant is large enough to exceed the fixed interest which accrues, and thus to produce some amortization of principal, although not enough to amortize the loan fully over the remaining term. Obviously these provisions are the result of negotiations in the particular case, and are not necessarily appropriate for other transactions.

In addition to fixed interest, this note requires payment of two forms of contingent interest. See Section 2.2. The "Cash Flow Contingent Interest" is defined as 35% of the Adjusted Income, in turn carefully defined in Section 1 as rental and other income, less operating expenses and debt service on this loan. Deductions against cash flow are allowed for equipment lease rentals, leasing commissions, and even certain capital improvements made by the mortgagor. This definition is, of course, meticulously tailored for the particular type of project involved; compare the somewhat analogous definition in the condominium project loan reprinted in § 15.3 supra. Note also the detailed record-keeping requirements of Section 4 of the note, which are designed to avoid disputes as to the amount of cash flow contingent interest due.

The other form of contingent interest is "Shared Appreciation Contingent Interest", payable at the loan's maturity or upon any earlier sale of the project, and defined in Section 2.2(b) as 35% of the amount by which the sales price exceeds the "Agreed Value"—in

§ 15.8   Minneapolis, Minnesota.
1. Form provided by Faegre & Benson,

essence, the parties' definition of the project's value at the time construction is completed. Thus, this is a Shared Appreciation Loan, or "SAM." See § 11.4 supra for a more complete discussion of such loans. If the project has not been sold by the time the note matures, the Shared Appreciation Contingent Interest is computed by reference to its then market value rather than a sale price. Section 1 describes the detailed method of determining the market value for this purpose.

Other interesting features in the note include the prepayment provisions of Section 6. It prohibits prepayment entirely for the first 12 years, and imposes a declining scale of prepayment premiums during years 13 through 17. The note is "non-recourse", with Section 8 containing the language excluding personal liability of the mortgagor. However, personal liability is triggered for any time period during which the property is encumbered by a junior mortgage.

PROMISSORY NOTE

$_____.

FOR VALUE RECEIVED, The undersigned, _____, a _____ limited partnership ("Maker"), hereby promises to pay to the order of _____, a _____ corporation, at its offices at _____ or such other place as the holder of this Note may from time to time designate, the principal sum of _____ Dollars ($_____), or so much thereof as may be advanced pursuant to the Loan Agreement (as defined below), together with interest on the unpaid principal balance hereof from the date of this Note until this Note is paid in full (and, in the event of foreclosure of the Mortgage, as defined below, until expiration of the period of redemption) at the rates set forth below. Principal and interest shall be payable in the manner and at the times set forth below.

1. *Definitions.*

As used in this Note, and in addition to other definitions herein contained, the following terms have the following respective meanings:

Adjusted Income. Gross income derived from Owner's ownership and operation of the Real Estate (computed on a cash basis) in the calendar year or partial calendar year in question from whatever source, including interest income, if any, and proceeds of business interruption and rental interruption insurance, but specifically excluding any income earned by tenants or licensees of the Real Estate, any gain arising from a sale of the Real Estate, and any management fees or leasing commissions paid to Owner, less the following:

(i) All fixed and operating expenses, foreseen and unforeseen, ordinary and extraordinary, of the Real Estate to the extent such charges are actually paid by Owner to third parties; provided, however, any charges, fees or commissions, by whatever name called, paid by Owner to Owner or any of its affiliates shall be reasonable and comparable to the amounts paid by buildings of comparable size and quality in the market area;

(ii) Rental payments under equipment lease agreements, provided, however, deductions for rental payments in excess of $5,000 annually shall be made only if the equipment lease pursuant to which such annual rental payments are made is approved by Lender;

(iii) Payments of principal and interest made pursuant to Section 3.1 or 3.2 of this Note, specifically excluding from said deduction the contingent interest payments required under Section 3.3 hereof, the payments required pursuant to Article 5 of this Note, and the final, or "balloon," principal payment payable upon maturity of this Note. Except as provided in this subparagraph (iii) and subparagraph (v), below, debt service may not be deducted;

(iv) Reasonable leasing commissions incurred in securing replacement leases in the Shell. Replacement leases for any space include all leases of such space other than the initial lease for the first tenant to occupy such space (any renewal or other lease with such first tenant shall be considered a replacement lease). For purposes of this deduction, the amount of commission allowed to be deducted in any one year shall equal the amount of leasing commissions actually paid by Owner in that year; and

(v) Deductions for the cost of capital improvements (including tenant improvements) other than Initial Improvements (as defined below) if supported by evidence satisfactory to Lender that such expenditures have been made by Owner in the calendar year in question. Initial Improvements include (a) tenant improvements made for the initial tenant of any space in the Shell, except to the extent that the cost of such improvements would have qualified as an advance of the Loan in excess of $_____$ pursuant to Section 4.02 of the Loan Agreement if said Section (other than the limitation on loan amount) had applied to it, (b) improvements made to effect the integration of the Real Estate with the adjoining _____ and (c) improvements contemplated by the Loan Agreement. Interest paid by Owner on funds borrowed to finance such capital improvements, and, to the extent provided below, interest on funds borrowed to finance Initial Improvements, may likewise be deducted provided the financing of such improvements has been approved by Lender. All capital improvements in excess of $50,000.00 shall require the approval of Lender. Lender's approval to be given in connection with this subparagraph (v) shall not be unreasonably withheld. Lender shall approve all capital improvements required by law or ordinance. Interest borrowed to finance the cost of Initial Improvements may be deducted to the extent that such interest is payable with respect to a cost which fits within the exception of clause (a) of the second sentence of this subparagraph (v). To the extent that the cost of a capital improvement is financed, such cost must be deducted over the term of the loan financing it.

The fixed and operating expenses noted above in subparagraph (i) shall not include reserves for capital improvements, depreciation, income taxes or late charges including penalty interest paid on delinquent real estate taxes. Also excluded from said expenses are loans, salary, bonuses or other payments to or for the benefit of Owner, or any principal of Owner, except for reasonable management fees and leasing commissions. If Owner or any affiliate of Owner occupies any portion of the Shell, the gross income attributed to the space so occupied shall be the greater of the payments required under the lease for such space or the fair rental value of such space.

Agreed Value. $_____.

Approved Sale. A bona fide sale of the Real Estate to which Lender shall give its written consent and a taking of all the Real Estate.

Cash Flow Contingent Interest. Interest payable pursuant to Section 2.2(a) of this Note.

Construction Loan Rate. A per annum interest rate one percentage point in excess of the publicly announced "Base Rate" of interest of _____ at its principal office in _____, as of the Initial Draw Date.

CPI. The Consumer Price Index—all Urban Consumers for the _____ Metropolitan area (1967 = 100), published by the U.S. Bureau of Labor Statistics. If such index is at any time not published, Lender shall select a reasonable substitute index. If the CPI is to be determined with respect to two dates and the base year for the CPI for such dates is different, an appropriate adjustment shall be made. The CPI as of any date shall be the CPI last published prior to the date in question.

Conversion Date. The earliest to occur of (i) the first day following the twenty-seventh monthly anniversary of the date of the Initial Draw Date, (ii) the first date on which the conditions of Section 3.04 of the Loan Agreement have been fulfilled (or waived by Lender as conditions of Loan disbursements), or (iii) the date of the first disbursement of the Loan made pursuant to Section 4.02 of the Loan Agreement.

Fixed Interest. Interest payable pursuant to Section 2.1 of this Note.

Guaranty. The Guaranty of even date herewith relating to guaranty of payment of certain amounts if Lender completes construction of the Shell.

Initial Draw Date. The date of the first disbursement of the Loan.

Lender. The initial or any subsequent holder of this Note.

Loan. The loan from Lender to Maker to be made in accordance with the Loan Agreement.

Loan Agreement. The Loan Agreement of even date herewith between Maker and Lender.

Loan Year. The first Loan Year shall commence on the Conversion Date, and successive Loan Years shall commence on successive anniversaries of the Conversion Date.

Market Value. The sum of (i) the fair market value of the Real Estate as of the date of Maturity of this Note (whether at its stated due date or at its maturity upon default resulting in acceleration of the indebtedness evidenced hereby), or as of the date of prepayment in full of this Note, whether voluntarily or involuntarily, without deduction for mortgages or any other lien, and (ii) the Taken Value. The fair market value of the Real Estate for purposes of clause (i) of this definition shall be determined in accordance with the following procedure: Either Owner or Lender (the "Valuing Party") may deliver a written notice stating the value of the Real Estate proposed by the Valuing Party. Within 20 days after receiving such notice, the other party shall give written notice of its acceptance or rejection of the Valuing Party's proposal as to such value. If within said 20 day period the other party does not give the Valuing Party written notice of rejection of the proposed value, the value proposed by the Valuing Party shall be the value of the Real Estate for purposes of clause (i) of this definition. If the value of the Real Estate is not determined as aforesaid, then, by no later than 10 days after the expiration of said 20 day period, Owner and Lender shall each select an independent M.A.I. appraiser, and, within 10 days after the selection of the second appraiser, the two appraisers shall select a third independent M.A.I. appraiser. If the two appraisers so selected are unable to agree upon the choice of a third appraiser, or if either party fails to appoint its appraiser, then the third appraiser or the second appraiser, or both, shall be appointed by the presiding judge of the District Court of _____ County, _____. Thereafter, all three appraisers shall independently appraise the fair market value of the Real Estate, based upon its then current use, and each appraiser shall submit a written report thereon to Owner and Lender within twenty days after being selected or appointed as an appraiser. The three appraisals shall be added together and divided by three and the appraisal which deviates the most from the resulting average shall be thereafter disregarded. The two remaining appraisals shall then be added together and divided by two and the resulting average shall be the value of the Real Estate. Both Owner and Lender shall be conclusively bound by the value so determined. All costs incurred by either Owner or Lender in connection with the valuation outlined above in this definition shall be paid for by Owner, secured by the Mortgage and deducted from Market Value. Notwithstanding the foregoing, if repayment of this Note is accelerated by Lender, then, in lieu of the procedure set forth above (even if such procedure is in process), Lender may select three independent M.A.I. appraisers, the fees of which will be additional sums secured by the Mortgage, and the fair market value of the Mortgaged Premises for purposes of clause (i) of this definition shall be the average of the two appraisals closest in value, or if two differ equally from the third, the average of all three. In making a determination of value, the appraisers shall ignore the Mortgage and, if there is unrestored damage from casualty or condemnation, the value of the Real Estate shall be its value immediately prior to the casualty or condemnation in question.

Mortgage. The Combination Mortgage, Security Agreement and Fixture Financing Statement of even date herewith between Maker, as mortgagor, and Lender, as mortgagee, given to secure payment of this Note.

Owner. Maker or any successor owner of the Real Estate.

Real Estate. As defined in the Mortgage.

Sales Price. The sum of (i) the gross sales price set forth in any sale or purchase agreement for an Approved Sale less, if paid, a reasonable and customary standard real estate sales commission approved by Lender, cost of a title policy, reasonable attorney's fees, escrow fees and all other customary closing costs paid by a seller of real property in _____ and (ii) the Taken Value. Any liens which survive the closing shall be included in the purchase price.

Shared Appreciation Contingent Interest. Interest payable pursuant to Section 2.2(b) of this Note.

Shell. As defined in the Loan Agreement.

Taken Value. Taken Value shall be determined as follows. Any casualty insurance proceeds and condemnation awards or proceeds of sale in lieu of condemnation relating to the Real Estate (other than proceeds or awards of any casualty or condemnation which is ignored for purposes of determining Market Value pursuant to the definition thereof) which are not applied to repair or restoration of the Real Estate shall be multiplied by a fraction the numerator of which is the CPI as of the date on which Market Value or Sales Price, as the case may be, is determined and the denominator of which is the CPI as of the date on which such proceeds or awards are paid. The Taken Value is the aggregate of all amounts determined pursuant to the immediately preceding sentence.

2. *Interest.*

2.1 Maker shall pay Fixed Interest on the outstanding principal balance of this Note (i) at the Construction Loan Rate for the period from and including the Initial Draw Date until and including the day prior to the Conversion Date, and (ii) at a rate of thirteen percent per annum for the period from and including the Conversion Date until and including the date on which this Note is paid in full; provided, however, that, if as of the Conversion Date Lender has accelerated payment of this Note or accelerates payment of this Note within three months following the Conversion Date by reason of default or right of acceleration existing on the Conversion Date, the Construction Loan Rate shall remain in effect until this Note is paid in full.

2.2 (a) Maker shall pay to Lender as contingent interest to be paid in addition to the interest described in Section 2.1 of this Note, an amount equal to thirty-five percent (35%) of Adjusted Income for (i) the period from the Conversion Date until the end of the calendar year in which it occurs, (ii) each full calendar year after the calendar year referred to in clause (i) during which this Note is outstanding, (iii) the period from the end of the last such full calendar year until the earlier of payment in full of this Note, whether by payment or prepayment (voluntary or involuntary), or foreclosure of the Mortgage, and (iv) in the event of foreclosure of the Mortgage, the period from the date of foreclosure until the date of redemption therefrom. The parties agree that, in view of the importance of having a clearly determinable interest payment in the event of redemption from foreclosure, the interest payable pursuant to this Section 2.2(a) during any period of redemption from foreclosure of the Mortgage shall not be based upon actual Adjusted Income during the period of redemption, but shall instead be an amount determined by dividing the interest payable with respect to the period referred to in clause (iii) of this Section 2.2(a) by the number of days in that period, and multiplying the result by the number of days from (but not including) the date of foreclosure sale until (and including) the date of redemption. If the Mortgage is foreclosed for installments, references in this Section to foreclosure of the Mortgage shall refer to the first foreclosure of the Mortgage, and references to redemption from foreclosure shall refer to redemption from the first foreclosure of the Mortgage.

(b) Maker shall pay to Lender, as contingent interest in addition to the interest described above in Section 2.1 and 2.2(a), (i) at the closing of an Approved Sale a sum equal to thirty-five percent (35%) of the amount, if any, by which the Sales Price derived from the sale of the Real Estate exceeds the Agreed Value, less any payment previously received by Lender pursuant to this clause (i), and (ii) upon maturity of this Note (whether at its stated due date or at its maturity upon default resulting in acceleration of the indebtedness evidenced thereby) or prepayment in full of the Note (whether voluntarily or involuntarily) a sum equal to thirty-five percent (35%) of the amount, if any, by which Market Value as of the date of acceleration, prepayment or maturity exceeds the Agreed Value, less any payment previously received by Lender (exclusive of service or other fees, if any, collected by Lender contemporaneous with the closing of an Approved Sale) pursuant to clause (i) of this Section 2.2(b).

3. *Payment of Principal and Interest.*

3.1 Maker shall pay accrued Fixed Interest on the first day of the first month following the Initial Draw Date and on the first day of the next succeeding 59 months.

3.2 On the fifth anniversary of the first day of the first month following the Initial Draw Date and on the first day of each month thereafter until and including the first day of the month in which the seventeenth anniversary of the Conversion Date occurs, Maker shall pay Lender an amount equal to 1.095 percent of the outstanding principal balance of this Note as of the fifth anniversary of the Initial Draw Date, with each payment to be applied first to accrued Fixed Interest and then to the outstanding principal balance of this Note.

3.3 Shared Appreciation Contingent Interest shall be paid at the times required by Section 2.2(b) of this Note. Cash Flow Contingent Interest shall be paid by no later than the earlier of (i) ninety days after the end of the calendar year or partial calendar year for which payment is being made, (ii) if this Note is paid in full or the Mortgage is foreclosed, the date of payment or foreclosure, or (iii) in the event of redemption from foreclosure of the Mortgage, the date of redemption.

3.4 The entire unpaid principal of this Note and all accrued interest thereon shall, if not sooner paid, be due and payable on the seventeenth anniversary of the Conversion Date.

4. *Records; Calculation of Cash Flow Contingent Interest.*

4.1 Owner shall keep full, true and accurate records of all items of income and expense from which Adjusted Income is to be determined. Such records shall be established and maintained in accordance with generally accepted accounting practices, shall be kept at the Real Estate or at an office of Owner in the _____ metropolitan area, and shall be available at all times for inspection and copying by Lender and its representatives. Owner shall comply with all reasonable directions of Lender respecting the accounting records and procedures to be adopted for the proper and accurate recording and control of all transactions affecting the determination of Adjusted Income.

4.2 By no later than the day on which a payment of Cash Flow Contingent Interest is required pursuant to Section 3.3(i) of this Note, Owner shall deliver to Lender a statement of operations prepared and audited by a certified public accountant selected by Owner and approved by Lender showing Adjusted Income for the period to which the payment relates. By no later than three days prior to the day on which a payment of Cash Flow Contingent Interest is required pursuant to Section 3.3(ii) of this Note, Owner shall deliver to Lender a statement of operations prepared by Owner and certified by the chief financial officer of Owner or the general partner of Owner showing Adjusted Income for the period to which the payment in question relates, which statement may, if necessary, include a reasonable estimate of income and expenses for the period between the date of delivery of the statement and the end of the period to which the statement relates.

4.3 Lender shall be entitled at any time and from time to time to have the accounting records and procedures affecting the determination of Adjusted Income for any period examined by an independent certified public accountant designated by Lender. If the accountant makes a determination of Adjusted Income for the period in question which discloses an underpayment of Cash Flow Contingent Interest, Owner shall immediately pay to Lender an amount equal to such underpayment. If such determination discloses an overpayment of Cash Flow Contingent Interest, Lender shall immediately pay to Owner an amount equal to such overpayment. If an audit pursuant to this Section 4.3 discloses an underpayment, Owner shall pay the cost of such audit, and such cost shall be secured by the Mortgage. If an audit pursuant to Section 4.3 discloses an overpayment, or that the initial determination by Owner was correct, Lender shall pay the cost of the audit.

4.4 The Cash Flow Contingent Interest payable with respect to any period shall be determined pursuant to the foregoing provisions of this Article 4 and the penultimate sentence of Section 2.2(a) of this Note; provided, however, that, in the event of foreclosure of the Mortgage, Lender may, at its option, elect to have Cash Flow Contingent Interest for the period (the "Foreclosure Period") from the end of the last period (the "Last Audited Period") for which Owner has delivered an audited statement in accordance with the first sentence of Section 4.2 of this Note until and including the date of foreclosure sale determined in accordance with this Section 4.4. If such election is made, the Cash Flow Contingent Interest payable with respect to the Foreclosure Period shall be an amount determined by the following formula:

$$\frac{\text{Adjusted Income in Last Audited Period}}{\text{No. of days in Last Audited Period}} \times \frac{\text{No. of days in}}{\text{Foreclosure Period}}$$

4.5 The provisions of this Article 4 shall survive payment of this Note.

5. *Default Interest and Late Charges.*

5.1 During any period in which an Event of Default, as defined in Section 7.1 of this Note, exists, and during any period of redemption from foreclosure sale of the Mortgage, Maker shall pay, as interest in addition to the interest payable in accordance with Article 2 of this Note, an amount equal to the amount by which (i) interest on the principal balance of this Note outstanding during the period in question calculated at the rate of fifteen percent per annum, exceeds (ii) Fixed Interest payable with respect to the period in question. Interest payable pursuant to this Section 5.1 prior to foreclosure sale shall be payable on the first day of each month and on the day on which the Event of Default is cured, this Note is paid in full or foreclosure sale occurs, as the case may be. Interest payable pursuant to this Section 5.1 during the period of redemption shall be payable on the date of redemption, if redemption occurs. Lender and Maker agree that the additional interest payable pursuant to this Section 5.1 is a reasonable payment for the increased risk to Lender's investment which exists by virtue of the Event of Default.

5.2 If payment of any installment required by Section 3.1 or 3.2 of this Note is not timely paid and such nonpayment continues for a period of ten (10) days, Maker shall pay Lender an amount equal to four percent of the installment in question to cover the expense involved in handling delinquent payments.

6. *Prepayment.*

This Note may not be prepaid in whole or in part either prior to the Conversion Date or during the first twelve Loan Years. Thereafter, payment in full (but not in part) of the indebtedness evidenced hereby, including all accrued interest, may be made on any date when interest becomes due and payable pursuant to Section 3.2 of this Note, if at the time of making such prepayment in full there shall also be paid, as consideration for the privilege of prepaying this indebtedness in advance of maturity, a sum equivalent to a percentage of the principal balance outstanding on such date as follows:

(a) Five percent (5%) if payment in full is made during the thirteenth (13th) Loan Year.

(b) Four percent (4%) if payment in full is made during the fourteenth (14th) Loan Year.

(c) Three percent (3%) if payment in full is made during the fifteenth (15th) Loan Year.

(d) Two percent (2%) if payment in full is made during the sixteenth (16th) Loan Year.

(e) One percent (1%) if payment in full is made during the seventeenth (17th) Loan Year.

No prepayment premium shall be required with respect to any prepayment from the proceeds of casualty, condemnation or sale in lieu thereof, but a premium shall be payable in the event the indebtedness is paid after acceleration of the indebtedness, whether such payment is made voluntarily or through foreclosure or pursuant to realization upon other security, and if such acceleration occurs prior to the thirteenth Loan Year, the premium shall be five percent.

7. *Default.*

7.1 An Event of Default as defined in the Mortgage is an Event of Default for purposes of this Note.

7.2 Upon occurrence of an Event of Default, Lender may, at its option, without notice, declare the entire unpaid principal of this Note and all accrued interest thereon to be immediately due and payable, and upon such declaration such principal and interest shall become due and payable.

8. *Non-Recourse.*

Notwithstanding the provisions of this Note, the Mortgage, the Loan Agreement or any other document, but subject to the proviso contained in this sentence, neither Maker nor any partner in Maker shall be personally liable for payment of any of the indebtedness evidenced by this Note, and Lender's sole recourse for payment of such indebtedness in the event of default shall be to pursue the security provided by the Guaranty, Mortgage, Loan Agreement and other instruments securing payment of this Note; provided, however, that Maker and its partners shall be personally liable for payment of any interest and principal which becomes payable under this Note (whether by lapse of time or acceleration) during any period in which the Real Estate is encumbered by any mortgage junior to the Mortgage which secures an obligation for which the mortgagor under said mortgage or any partner or shareholder of such mortgagor or partner of Maker is personally liable. Nothing in this Article 8 shall affect, limit or impair (i) the obligations of the parties to the Guaranty pursuant to the terms of the Guaranty, (ii) the security provided by the Mortgage, Guaranty, Loan Agreement or any other document, (iii) the right to seek monetary judgment against Maker or any Owner to the extent necessary to permit foreclosure of the Mortgage by action, or (iv) the right to seek any other judgment or determination against Maker or any other Owner, whether for equitable relief or otherwise, so long as Lender does not seek judgment for personal liability contrary to the provisions of this Article 8.

9. *Notice.*

Any notice, demand, request or other communication (a "Notice") which either Lender, Maker or Owner may be required to or may desire to give pursuant to this Note shall be in writing and given, (i) in the case of a Notice to Maker or Owner, to the party, in the manner, and at the address provided at the time for Notice to Mortgagor under the Mortgage, or (ii) in the case of a Notice to Lender, to the party, in the manner and at the address provided at the time for notice to Mortgagee under the Mortgage.

10. *Miscellaneous.*

10.1 If any provision of this Note is found by a court of law to be in violation of any applicable local, state or federal ordinance, statute, law, administrative or judicial decision, or public policy, and if such court should declare such provision of this Note to be illegal, invalid, unlawful, void or unenforceable (in whole or in part) as written, then it is the intent of the parties hereto that such provision shall be given force to the fullest possible extent that it is legal, valid and enforceable, that the remainder of this Note shall be construed as if such illegal, invalid, unlawful, void or unenforceable provision were not contained herein, and that the rights, obligations and interest of Maker and Lender under the remainder of this Note shall continue in full force and effect. All agreements herein are expressly limited so that in no contingency or event whatsoever, whether by reason of advancement of the proceeds hereof, acceleration of maturity of the unpaid principal balance hereof, or otherwise, shall the amount paid or agreed to be paid to Lender for the use, forbearance or detention of the money to be advanced hereunder exceed the highest lawful rate permissible under applicable usury laws. If, from any circumstances whatsoever, fulfillment of any provision hereof at the time performance of such provisions shall be due, shall involve transcending the limit of validity prescribed by law which a court of competent jurisdiction may deem applicable hereto, then, ipso facto, the obligation to be fulfilled shall be reduced to the limit of such validity and if from any circumstance Lender shall ever receive as interest an amount which would exceed the highest lawful rate, such amount which would be excessive interest shall be applied to the reduction of the latest maturing principal due hereunder and not to the payment of interest.

10.2 Maker agrees to pay all costs incurred by Lender in collecting any payment due under this Note, including reasonable attorneys fees, whether or not foreclosure proceedings are commenced or other remedies are pursued. All such costs shall be secured by the Mortgage.

10.3 The Maker and any endorsers, sureties, guarantors and all other persons liable for all or any part of the principal balance evidenced by this Note severally waive presentment for payment, protest and notice of non-payment. Such parties hereby consent without affecting their liability to any extension or alteration of the time or terms of payment hereof, any renewal, any release of any or all part of the security given for the payment hereof, any acceptance of additional security of any kind, and any release of, or resort to, any party liable for payment hereof. The acceptance by Lender of any payment hereunder which is less than payment in full shall not constitute a waiver of the right to exercise any right or remedy at that time or any subsequent time or nullify any acceleration or any other prior exercise of any rights or remedies.

11. *Payments and Computations.*

All payments on the indebtedness evidenced hereby, whether made voluntarily, involuntarily or by application of insurance proceeds or condemnation awards, shall be applied first to interest and then to principal, except that if any advance made by Lender under the terms of any instruments securing this Note is not repaid, any monies received, at the option of Lender, may first be applied to repay such advances, plus interest thereon, and the balance, if any, shall be applied on account of any installments then due. All computations of interest shall be made by Lender on the basis of a year of 365 days for the actual number of days occurring in the period for which such interest is payable. All payments on account of the indebtedness evidenced by this Note shall be in lawful money of the United States.

§ 15.9 Construction Loan Agreement—Homes in Subdivision [1]

This Construction Loan Agreement ("Agreement") is designed primarily for home construction in a Texas residential subdivision. The Agreement incorporates the following Exhibits:

Exhibits

A—Form of Note

B—Form of Compliance Certificate

C—Disclosures

D—Form of Master Deed of Trust and Security Agreement

E—Form of Deed of Trust and Security Agreement

F—Form of Financing Statement

G—Form of Loans to One Borrower Affidavit

H—Disbursement Schedule

I—Form of Affidavit of Commencement of Construction

J—Form of Partial Release of Lien

K—Form of Financing Statement Change (Partial Release)

L—Form of Borrower's Affidavit

M—Form of Environmental Indemnity Agreement

The types of homes which borrower is permitted to build with loan funds are limited to those homes whose plans and specifications have been approved in advance by the lender. When the borrower makes a loan request, the type of home must be identified in the Loan Request. See Sections 1.02 and 2.04 of the Agreement.

The Agreement places a limit on the total amount of advances that may be outstanding at any one time. See Section 2.01(a) of the Agreement. In addition, in order to encourage the borrower to complete the home in a timely fashion, it also limits the time for making advances with respect to the construction of a particular home. Id. Once a home financed by construction advances is completed, the

§ 15.9

1. Form provided by Ewing, Carter, Smith, Gosnell, Vickers & Hoberock, Nevada, Missouri.

Agreement provides for the lot and home to be released from the Deed of Trust. See Section 2.06(b).

Article 3 of the Agreement contains numerous representations and warranties. Two warranties are especially important. The first is found in Section 3.15 where the borrower makes representations that the borrower and its subsidiaries and its "ERISA Affiliates", as defined in the Agreement, have complied in all material respects with the Employee Retirement Income Security Act of 1974. The penalties on a borrower who has obligations to make payments under a plan and has failed to do so can be substantial. These penalties and fines together with any determinations that the borrower must fund any payment shortfalls can have a significant financial impact on the borrower and its ability to pay its other obligations, including those related to the Agreement. See also Section 5.12, which limits the borrower in taking on new obligations under ERISA.

The second important warranty deals with environmental concerns. See Section 3.24. The borrower warrants that neither the property which serves as security for the loan nor the operations conducted on the property violate any environmental laws. Environmental laws are defined to mean any and all laws, statutes, ordinances, rules, regulations, orders or determinations of any governmental authority. These include, but are not limited to, the Clean Air Act, the Comprehensive Environmental Response Compensation and Liability Act of 1980 ("CERCLA"), as amended, the Federal Water Pollution Contract Act, and other measures specified in Section 1.02(1). The foregoing warranty is buttressed by further negative covenants and warranties concerning environmental matters contained in Section 5.18 of the Agreement and Section 11 of the Deed of Trust and Security Agreement. See Exhibit E. Finally, the Agreement requires the execution by borrower of a detailed and carefully drafted Indemnity Agreement in which the borrower agrees to indemnify and hold harmless lender, its officers and affiliates with respect to any environmental damages it may incur with respect to the mortgaged real estate and borrower's operations on it. See Exhibit M. "Environmental Damages" are broadly defined in Section 7(b) of Exhibit M. For a detailed consideration of the lender's liability for environmental matters, see §§ 4.47–4.51, supra.

The Agreement requires the borrower to execute a Promissory Note. See Exhibit A. The Note sets the maximum amount which may be advanced under the terms of the Agreement. It is a future advances Note secured by a future advances deed of trust.

Because of the expense of recording, the Agreement provides for Master Deed of Trust and Security Agreement. See Exhibit D. A lender who anticipates that from time to time deeds of trust may be entered into for lender's benefit by various borrowers can elect to record Exhibit D. This latter form incorporates standard terms governing all of lender's loans to borrowers on real estate in a specific county.

Each individual Deed of Trust and Security Agreement (Exhibit E) executed by a particular borrower incorporates by reference the terms of Exhibit D. The individual Deed of Trust and Security Agreement (Exhibit E) can also provide for various additional provisions and modifications not contained in the Master (Exhibit D).

LOAN AGREEMENT

THIS LOAN AGREEMENT is made and entered into as of the _____ day of [_____], 1992, between [_____], INC., a Texas corporation with principal offices at [_____], [_____], Texas [_____] (the *"Borrower"*); and _____ (the *"Lender"*).

ARTICLE 1

GENERAL TERMS

Section 1.01 *Terms Defined Above.* As used in this Agreement, the terms *"Borrower"* and *"Lender"* shall have the meanings indicated above.

Section 1.02 *Certain Definitions.* As used in this Agreement, the following terms shall have the following meanings, unless the context otherwise requires:

"Advance" means any advance of loan proceeds made pursuant to Section 2.01.

"Affiliate" shall mean, as to any Person, any other Person which directly or indirectly controls, or is under common control with, or is controlled by, such Person and, if such Person is an individual, any member of the immediate family (including parents, spouse and children) of such individual and any trust whose principal beneficiary is such individual or one or more members of such immediate family and any Person who is controlled by any such member or trust. As used in this definition, *"control"* (including, with correlative meanings, *"controlled by"* and *"under common control with"*) shall mean possession, directly or indirectly, of power to direct or cause the direction of management or policies (whether through ownership of securities or partnership or other ownership interest, by contract or otherwise).

"Agreement" shall mean this Loan Agreement, as the same may from time to time be amended or supplemented.

"Appraisal" shall mean, with respect to each Home, a current, fair market value appraisal in form and substance satisfactory to the Lender prepared by an independent appraiser satisfactory to the Lender which appraises on a "completed value" basis the Home to be constructed on a specified Lot in an Approved Subdivision, which appraisal will designate a fair market value attributable to the applicable Lot and which is prepared based on written instructions from Lender.

"Appraised Value" shall mean (a) with respect to each Lot and Home, to be constructed thereon, the fair market value of such Lot and Home, upon one hundred percent (100%) completion of all construction thereof in accordance with the Plans and Specifications for such Home plus Lot Value for such Lot, all as determined by the Appraisal; provided that such fair market value reflected in such Appraisal may be adjusted by the Lender in its reasonable discretion, and (b) with respect to a Lot on which a Home is to be constructed, the fair market value attributable to such Lot in the Appraisal.

"Approved Subdivision" shall mean a Developed Subdivision in which the Lender shall have approved in writing the acquisition of Lots and the construction of Homes thereon. Factors to be considered by the Lender in determining whether or not to approve such Developed Subdivision shall include, but shall not be limited to, the following:

(a) the sales history of Homes in such subdivision constructed by the Borrower;

(b) the sales history of Homes in such subdivision constructed by a Person other than the Borrower;

(c) the location of the subdivision;

(d) the price range of the Homes being sold in the subdivision and the market concept of such Homes; and

(e) community demographic concentrations.

If the Lender determines in its sole discretion, reasonably exercised, that factors have changed such that a subdivision no longer qualifies as an Approved Subdivision, then upon written notice to the Borrower, such subdivision shall no longer qualify as an Approved Subdivision. Upon correction of such factors to the Lender's satisfaction, such subdivision may again qualify as an Approved Subdivision.

"Borrower's Deposit" shall have the meaning assigned such term in Section 4.13.

"Business Day" shall mean a day other than a Saturday, Sunday or legal holiday for savings and loan associations under the laws of the State of Texas.

"Change Order" shall mean a change order evidencing and instructing a change to the Plans and Specifications for a given Home.

"Code" shall mean the Internal Revenue Code of 1986, as amended, and any successor statute.

"Commitment" shall mean the obligation of the Lender to make loans to the Borrower under Subsection 2.01(a) up to the maximum amount therein stated.

"Construction Costs Schedule" shall mean a schedule in form and substance satisfactory to the Lender showing, for each Home to be constructed in an Approved Subdivision under the Construction Facility, the budgeted construction costs for each such Home.

"Construction Facility" shall mean the loan facility provided for in Subsection 2.01(a).

"Construction Facility Advance" shall mean an advance by the Lender to the Borrower under Subsection 2.01(a), which advance may be an Initial Advance, Interim Advance or Final Advance.

"Current Assets" shall mean the sum of cash, certificates of deposit, ordinary trade accounts receivable (excluding any amount due from any officer, employee, director, shareholder or any Affiliate of any of the foregoing Related Person), earnest money and other operating deposits, operating prepaid costs, including but not limited to prepaid insurance, prepaid rent, prepaid sales draws, inventory (including model homes) at lower of cost or net realizable value and improved lots. With the exception of the assets described above, all other assets included as "Current Assets" must satisfy the definition of current assets according to GAAP. In general, current assets according to GAAP are those resources reasonably expected to be realized in cash, sold or consumed during the normal operating cycle of a business. In the event of a dispute relative to the carrying value of said Current Assets, including but not limited to inventory and accounts receivable, or the classification of an asset as a Current Asset, the determination thereof by an independent Certified Public Accountant chosen by Borrower and acceptable to Lender shall be controlling.

"Current Liabilities" shall include all indebtedness normally held as due within one (1) year (exclusive of Subordinate Debt, if any), and any unsubordi-

nated debt due any officer, employee, shareholder, director, or Related Person.

"*Debt*" shall mean, for any Person, without duplication: (i) all indebtedness of such Person for borrowed money or for the deferred purchase price of Property or services for which such Person is liable, contingently or otherwise, as obligor, guarantor or otherwise, or in respect of which such Person otherwise assures a creditor against loss; and (ii) all obligations under leases which shall have been, or should have been, in accordance with GAAP in effect on the date of this Agreement, recorded as capital leases in respect of which such Person is liable, contingently or otherwise, as obligor, guarantor or otherwise, or in respect of which obligations such Person otherwise assures a creditor against loss.

"*Default*" shall mean the occurrence of any of the events specified in Section 6.01, whether or not any requirement for notice or lapse of time or other condition precedent has been satisfied.

"*Developed Subdivision*" shall mean a residential subdivision of real property located in one or more Valid Counties and which has been developed to a stage acceptable to the Lender. In determining whether such subdivision is developed to an acceptable stage, the Lender will consider, among other things, the following:

(a) such subdivision must be a platted subdivision pursuant to a recorded subdivision plat that has been approved by all necessary Governmental Authorities;

(b) whether the improvements shown on the subdivision plat for such subdivision are completed in accordance with all requirements of all necessary Governmental Authorities, including, but not limited to, all roads;

(c) whether the roads shown on the subdivision plat for such subdivision are properly dedicated to the public and accepted for public maintenance by the applicable Governmental Authorities;

(d) whether the common area amenities for such subdivision are completed;

(e) whether the improvements and systems necessary to provide adequate utility service and drainage to all residential lots located within such subdivision are completed in accordance with all requirements of all applicable Governmental Authorities and extend utility service and drainage to the boundaries of all residential lots in such subdivision, such utility service to include water, electrical, gas, telephone, and sanitary and storm sewer service;

(f) whether the providers of utility service to such subdivision have adequate capacity and treatment facilities to service the subdivision and have committed to provide adequate service to such subdivision;

(g) whether any part of such subdivision is contaminated with hazardous substances or solid wastes and whether such subdivision is located near any Property which is so contaminated (in order to allow the Lender to make such determination, the Borrower will provide the Lender with any information which Borrower has received with respect to environmental matters);

(h) whether the subdivision is restricted and, if applicable, zoned to limit use to detached single family residences, and whether there is in place a recorded set of restrictive covenants acceptable to the Lender covering such subdivision and pursuant to which adequate provisions are made for a homeowners' association, architectural integrity, and maintenance assessments;

(i) whether such subdivision is located within the 100-year flood plain or any other area that is flood prone;

(j) whether such subdivision is located upon a geological fault; and

(k) whether such subdivision is located on, over or within one mile of any underground storage facilities used for injected natural or processed gas or other liquid hydrocarbons or petroleum products.

(*l*) the total of all tax rates imposed by all applicable taxing authorities against Property located within such subdivision.

If the Lender determines in its sole discretion, reasonably exercised, that factors have changed such that a subdivision no longer qualifies as a Developed Subdivision, then upon written notice to the Borrower, such subdivision shall no longer qualify as a Developed Subdivision. Upon correction of such factors to the Lender's satisfaction, such subdivision may again qualify as a Developed Subdivision.

"*Drawdown Termination Date*" shall mean that date which is [_____] ([_____]) months from the date of the last Initial Advance made on or prior to the Initial Advance Period Termination Date.

"*Environmental Laws*" shall mean any and all laws, statutes, ordinances, rules, regulations, orders, or determinations of any Governmental Authority pertaining to health or the environment applicable to the Borrower, any Subsidiary, or any of their Properties in effect in any and all jurisdictions in which the Borrower or the Subsidiaries are conducting or at any time have conducted business, or where any Property of the Borrower or the Subsidiaries is located, or where any hazardous substances generated by or disposed of by the Borrower or the Subsidiaries are located, including but not limited to the Clean Air Act, as amended, the Comprehensive Environmental Response, Compensation, and Liability Act of 1980, as amended by the Superfund Amendments and Reauthorization Act of 1986 ("*CERCLA*"), as amended, the Federal Water Pollution Control Act, as amended, the Occupational Safety and Health Act of 1970, as amended, the Resource Conservation and Recovery Act of 1976, as amended by the Used Oil Recycling Act of 1980, the Solid Waste Disposal Act Amendments of 1980, and the Hazardous and Solid Waste Amendments of 1984 ("*RCRA*"), as amended, the Safe Drinking Water Act, as amended, the Toxic Substances Control Act, as amended, the Hazardous Materials Transportation Act, as amended, the Texas Water Code, the Texas Solid Waste Disposal Act, and other environmental conservation or protection laws. The terms "*hazardous substance*", "*release*" and "*threatened release*" shall have the meanings specified in CERCLA, and the terms "*solid waste*" and "*disposal*" (or "*disposed*") shall have the meanings specified in RCRA; provided, however, that (i) in the event either CERCLA or RCRA is amended so as to broaden the meaning of any term defined thereby, such broader meaning shall apply hereunder subsequent to the effective date of such amendment, (ii) to the extent the laws of the state in which any Property of the Borrower or any Subsidiary is located establish a meaning for "*hazardous substance*", "*release*", "*threatened release*", "*solid waste*" or "*disposal*" which is broader than that specified in either CERCLA or RCRA, such broader meaning shall apply, and (iii) the terms "*hazardous substance*" and "*solid waste*" shall include all oil and gas exploration and production wastes that may present an endangerment to public health or welfare or the environment, even if such wastes are specifically exempt from classification as hazardous substances or solid wastes pursuant to CERCLA or RCRA or the state analogues to those statutes.

"*ERISA*" shall mean the Employee Retirement Income Security Act of 1974, as amended, and any successor statute.

"*ERISA Affiliate*" shall mean each trade or business (whether or not incorporated) which together with the Borrower or a Subsidiary would be deemed to be a "single employer" within the meaning of Section 4001(b)(1) of ERISA or subsections (b), (c), (m) or (*o*) of Section 414 of the Code.

"*Event of Default*" shall mean the occurrence of any of the events specified in Section 6.01, provided that any requirement for notice or lapse of time or any other condition precedent has been satisfied.

"*Excepted Liens*" shall mean Liens (i) for ad valorem taxes, assessments, or other governmental charges or levies not yet due or which are being contested in good faith by appropriate action; (ii) in connection with workmen's compensation, unemployment insurance or other social security, old age pension or public liability obligations; (iii) vendors', carriers', warehousemen's, repairmen's, mechanics', workmen's, materialmen's, construction or other like Liens arising by operation of law in the ordinary course of business or incident to the construction or improvement of any Property in respect of obligations permitted under the terms of this Agreement which are (x) in all cases subordinate to the Liens created by the Security Interest, and (y) not yet due or which are being contested in good faith by appropriate proceedings by or on behalf of the Borrower or any Subsidiary in accordance with the procedures and requirements set forth in Section 4.14; and (iv) customary Liens in any Approved Subdivision, including customary restrictive covenants and utility easements, which do not and will not unreasonably interfere with the construction, operation, maintenance and sale of Homes.

"*Final Advance*" shall mean, for each Lot and the Home constructed thereon, the last advance of loan proceeds to be made in connection therewith and which advance is made at such time as the Percentage of Completion for such Lot and Home is one hundred percent (100%).

"*Financial Statements*" shall mean the consolidated and/or consolidating financial statements of the Borrower, its Subsidiaries, and Guarantor described or referred to in Section 3.06.

"*Financing Statement*" shall mean a UCC-1 Financing Statement naming the Borrower as debtor and the Lender as secured party in the form of the Financing Statement attached as Exhibit F, with such changes thereto as the Lender shall deem necessary, perfecting a first priority security interest in any and all personal Property and general intangibles now or hereafter located on, used in connection with, or related to the Lot or Lots and Home or Homes covered thereby.

"*GAAP*" shall mean generally accepted accounting principles.

"*Governmental Authority*" shall mean the United States of America, the State of Texas, the state, county, city and political subdivisions in which any Property of the Borrower or any Subsidiary is located or which exercises jurisdiction over any such Property, and any agency, department, commission, board, bureau, homeowners association, utility district, flood control district, improvement district, or similar district, court, grand jury or instrumentality or any of them which exercises jurisdiction over any such Property.

"*Governmental Requirement*" shall mean any law, statute, code, ordinance, order, rule, regulation, judgment, decree, injunction, franchise, permit, certificate, license, authorization, or other direction or requirement (including but not limited to any of the foregoing which relate to zoning and planning standards or controls, environmental standards or controls, energy regulations and occupational, safety and health standards or controls) of any Governmental Authority.

"*Guarantor*" shall mean [_____].

"*Guaranty Agreement*" shall mean those certain Guaranty Agreement executed by the Guarantors.

"*Highest Lawful Rate*" shall mean the maximum nonusurious interest rate, if any, that at any time or from time to time may be contracted for, taken, reserved, charged or received on the Note or on other Indebtedness, as the case may be, under the law of the State of Texas (or the law of any other jurisdiction whose laws may be mandatorily applicable notwithstanding other provisions of this Agreement), or law of the United States of America applicable to the Lender and the Transactions which would permit the Lender to contract for, charge, take, reserve or receive a greater amount of interest than under Texas (or such other jurisdiction's) law.

"*Home*" shall mean a detached single family residential structure and related amenities.

"*Indebtedness*" shall mean any and all amounts owing or to be owing by the Borrower to the Lender in connection with the Note or any Security Instrument, including this Agreement, and all other liabilities of the Borrower to the Lender from time to time existing, whether in connection with this or other transactions.

"*Initial Advance*" shall mean, for each Lot and the Home to be constructed thereon and financed under the Construction Facility, the initial advance of loan proceeds made in connection therewith.

"*Initial Advance Period Termination Date*" shall mean [_____].

"*Initial Counties*" shall mean the counties in which the Master Deed of Trust shall initially be recorded.

"*Inventory Status Report*" shall mean a monthly report with respect to the Lots acquired and the completion status of each Home under construction by Borrower (whether or not financed by Lender) properly completed by the Borrower and in form and substance satisfactory to the Lender.

"*Lien*" shall mean any interest in Property securing an obligation owed to, or a claim by, a Person other than the owner of the Property, whether such interest is based on the common law, statute or contract, and including but not limited to the lien or security interest arising from a mortgage, encumbrance, pledge, security agreement, conditional sale or trust receipt or a lease, consignment or bailment for security purposes. The term "*Lien*" shall include reservations, exceptions, encroachments, easements, rights of way, covenants, conditions, restrictions, leases and other title exceptions and encumbrances affecting Property. For the purposes of this Agreement, the Borrower or any Subsidiary shall be deemed to be the owner of any Property which it has acquired or holds subject to a conditional sale agreement, financing lease or other arrangement pursuant to which title to the Property has been retained by or vested in some other Person for security purposes.

"*Loan Request*" shall mean a request for an Advance pursuant to Section 2.01 duly and properly executed by an authorized officer of the Borrower which shall be in a form satisfactory to Lender.

"*Loan Value*" shall mean, with respect to each Lot and Home to be constructed thereon, the lesser of (i) the sum of the construction costs shown in the Construction Costs Schedule delivered to Lender with respect to such Home, which schedule shall in all cases include the lesser of (a) the cost of the Lot to Borrower as set forth in the purchase contract, or (b) the Appraised Value of the Lot as set forth in the Appraisal, or (ii) [_____] percent ([_____]%) of the Appraised Value of such Lot and Home, or (iii) if a Home is a Sold Home, [_____] percent ([_____]) of the contract price.

"*Lot*" shall mean an unimproved (but fully developed) single family residential lot located in an Approved Subdivision.

"*Margin Percentage*" shall mean the percent per annum which is expressly enumerated in Section 2.02 (before or after maturity, as appropriate) to be added to the Prime Rate to determine (except as may be limited by applicable law) the interest rate on the Note.

"*Master Deed of Trust*" shall mean the Master Form of Deed of Trust and Security Agreement Recorded by Farm & Homes Savings Association attached as Exhibit D.

"*Material Adverse Effect*" shall mean as to the Borrower, any material and adverse effect on (i) the assets, liabilities, financial condition, business or operations of the Borrower and its Subsidiaries, taken as a whole, from those reflected in the Financial Statements or from the facts represented or warranted in this Agreement or any other Security Instrument, or (ii) the ability of the Borrower and its Subsidiaries, taken as a whole, to carry out their business as at the date of this Agreement or as proposed at the date of this Agreement to be conducted or meet the Borrower's obligations under the Note, this Agreement, or the other Security Instruments on a timely basis.

"*Model Home*" shall mean any Home owned by the Borrower or any Affiliate of the Borrower which has been fully completed, decorated and furnished to be used as a model for display to prospective purchasers of Homes built by the Borrower in the particular Approved Subdivision in which such "Model Home" is located.

"*Mortgage*" shall mean a Deed of Trust and Security Agreement in the form of the Deed of Trust and Security Agreement attached as Exhibit E, with such changes thereto as the Lender shall deem reasonably necessary, securing the payment of any and all Indebtedness and creating in favor of the Lender a valid and enforceable first priority Lien on and security interest in the Lot or Lots described therein and any and all interests of the Borrower in any improvements, personal Property, and general intangibles now or hereafter located on, used in connection with, or related to such Lot or Lots.

"*Note*" shall mean the promissory note of the Borrower described in Subsection 2.01(a) and being in the form of note attached as Exhibit A, together with any and all renewals, extensions for any period, increases or rearrangements thereof.

"*Percentage of Completion*" shall mean, with respect to each Lot and Home as of any time of determination (which determination shall be made by the Lender in its sole discretion), the percentage of completion determined in accordance with the disbursement schedule attached hereto as Exhibit H.

"*Percentage of Completion Value*" shall mean, for each Home to be constructed at any time and from time to time, the result of (i) the Loan Value of such Lot and Home to be constructed as defined in subpart (a) of the definition of "Loan Value" minus the Advance made for the Lot upon which the Home is to be constructed multiplied by (ii) the Percentage of Completion of such Home as of such time.

"*Permitted Expenses*" shall mean, for any fiscal year of the Borrower, all costs and expenses incurred by the Borrower during such year in the ordinary course of the Borrower's business, including but not limited to (i) payroll, (ii) business income, and other taxes and real and personal property taxes and assessments, and fees and expenses, (iii) insurance premiums, (iv) all other costs and expenses, including capital expenditures, required to be made by the Borrower in the ordinary course of business, and (v) payments during such fiscal year into reserve funds and accounts for future costs, expenses and payments referred to in clauses (i)-(iv) above, in accordance with prudent business practices. Permitted Expenses shall in no event include any dividends or any other payments or distributions of any nature to any venturer or partner.

"*Person*" shall mean any individual, corporation, partnership, joint venture, association, joint stock company, trust, unincorporated organization, government or any agency or political subdivision thereof, or any other form of entity.

"*Plan*" shall mean any employee pension benefit plan, as defined in Section 3(2) of ERISA.

"*Plans and Specifications*" shall mean, for each Home, the Borrower's construction plans detailing the plans and specifications, and containing architectural drawings specifying the type and style of such Home.

"*Prime Rate*" shall mean the rate of interest established by Texas Commerce Bank, Houston, Texas ("Texas Commerce") from time to time as its "prime rate." Such rate is set by Texas Commerce as a general reference rate of interest, taking into account such factors as Texas Commerce may deem appropriate, it being understood that many of Texas Commerce's commercial or other loans are priced in relation to such rate, that it is not necessarily the lowest or best rate actually charged to any customer and that Texas Commerce may make various commercial or other loans at rates of interest having no relationship to such rate.

"*Property*" shall mean any interest in any kind of property or asset, whether real, personal or mixed, or tangible or intangible.

"*Release Price*" shall mean, as to any Lot and Home, 100% of all amounts advanced by Lender with respect thereto, plus all accrued and unpaid interest thereon.

"*Reserved Commitment*" shall mean, for each Lot and Home being financed under the Construction Facility, the difference at any time and from time to time between (i) the Loan Value thereof less (ii) the principal amount with respect to such Lot and Home previously advanced by the Lender, in its sole discretion, for the acquisition and construction of such Lot and Home.

"*Security Instruments*" shall mean this Agreement, the Master Deed of Trust, each Mortgage, each Financing Statement, and any and all other agreements or instruments now or hereafter executed and delivered by the Borrower, any Subsidiary or any other Person (other than participation or similar agreements between the Lender and any other bank or creditor with respect to any Indebtedness pursuant to this Agreement) in connection with, or as security for the payment or performance of, the Note or this Agreement, as such agreements may be amended or supplemented from time to time.

"*Sold Home*" shall mean a Home with respect to which a Person, other than the Borrower or any Affiliate of the Borrower, has executed a valid and enforceable contract for the purchase thereof (a copy of which shall have been provided to Lender), provided that upon the recision or cancellation of any such contract for any reason, the Home shall no longer be a Sold Home.

"*Subsidiary*" shall mean any corporation of which more than fifty percent (50%) of the issued and outstanding securities having ordinary voting power for the election of directors is owned or controlled, directly or indirectly, by the Borrower and/or one or more of its subsidiaries.

"*Title Binder*" shall mean a paid Mortgagee Title Policy Binder on Interim Construction Loan issued by the Title Insurer and otherwise satisfactory to the Lender.

"*Title Insurer*" shall mean a title insurance company or companies satisfactory to the Lender.

"*Title Policy*" shall mean a paid Mortgagee Policy of Title Insurance issued by a Title Insurer and otherwise satisfactory to the Lender.

"*Transactions*" shall mean the transactions provided for in and contemplated by this Agreement, the other Security Instruments and the Note.

"*Type of Home*" shall mean each of the various types or styles of homes being constructed by the Borrower, the Plans and Specifications of which have been approved by the Lender and shall be referenced as between Lender and

Borrower by a name or number to be agreed upon that describes each such Type of Home. Each such Type of Home shall be identified in Loan Requests (or schedules thereto) by use of such name or number, together with the street address and name of subdivision.

"*Valid County*" shall mean any of the Initial Counties or any other county in the State of Texas in which the Master Deed of Trust has been properly filed and recorded.

"*Working Capital*" shall mean the excess of Current Assets over Current Liabilities.

Section 1.03 *Accounting Principles.* Where the character or amount of any asset or liability or item of income or expense is required to be determined or any consolidation or other accounting computation is required to be made for the purposes of this Agreement, it shall be done in accordance with GAAP applied on a basis consistent with those reflected by the Financial Statements, except where such principles are inconsistent with the requirements of this Agreement.

ARTICLE 2
AMOUNT AND TERMS OF LOANS

Section 2.01 *The Loans and Commitment.* Subject to the terms and conditions and relying on the representations and warranties contained in this Agreement, the Lender agrees to make the following loans to the Borrower:

(a) Construction Facility Advances—From the date of this Agreement through the Drawdown Termination Date, the Lender will make Advances to the Borrower from time to time on any Business Day in such amounts as the Borrower may request up to the maximum amount hereinafter stated, subject to the limitations set forth herein, and the Borrower may make borrowings, prepayments (as permitted or required in Sections 2.06 and 2.07) and reborrowings in respect thereof; provided, however, that the sum of the aggregate principal amount of all such Advances at any one time outstanding plus the aggregate amount, at such time, of the Reserved Commitments shall not exceed $[_____]. To evidence the loans made by the Lender pursuant to this Subsection, the Borrower will issue, execute and deliver the Note dated as of the date of its issuance in the amount of the Commitment. No Construction Facility Advances shall be made to finance the construction of a Home after the date which is [_____] ([_____]) months from the date of the Initial Advance relating to such Home and the Lot upon which it is being constructed, or, in the event of an extension of the due date for the Release Price for such Lot and Home pursuant to Section 2.01(b)(2), after the date which is [_____] ([_____]) months from the date of the Initial Advance relating to such Home and the Lot upon which it is being constructed. No Initial Advance shall be made after the Initial Advance Period Termination Date.

(b) Payment of Construction Facility Advances—

(1) Interest on the Note shall be payable monthly, on the first day of each month, as it accrues on the principal amount from time to time outstanding, at the rate provided in Section 2.02, commencing on [_____], 1992.

(2) The Release Price for any Lot and Home shall be due and payable in full, regardless of whether such Lot and Home has been sold, on or before the date which is [_____] ([_____]) months from the date on which the Initial Advance relating to such Lot and Home was made (for each such Lot and Home, the "Initial Due Date"). Notwithstanding the foregoing, if Lender by written notice prior to an Initial Due Date offers to extend such date and if Borrower does not repay the Release Price for such Lot and Home on or before such Initial Due Date, the Initial Due Date shall be automatically extended for an additional three

(3) months, and Borrower shall pay to Lender an extension fee equal to one-quarter of one percent (0.25%) of the Loan Value for such Lot and Home within ten (10) Business Days after the Initial Due Date. In the event of such an extension the "Drawdown Termination Date with respect to such Lot and Home shall also be extended for an additional three (3) month period.

(c) Certain Limitations On Amounts—The Advance made to purchase the Lot shall not exceed the lesser of (x) one hundred percent (100%) of the Appraised Value of such Lot or (y) one hundred percent (100%) of the cost of such Lot. The aggregate Advances related to any Home being constructed shall not, at any time, exceed the Percentage of Completion Value of such Home. The aggregate Advances related to any Lot and Home shall not be in excess of the lesser of (x) [_____] percent ([_____]%) of the Appraised Value of such Lot and Home being constructed or (y) [_____] percent ([_____]%) of the contract price for such Home, if Borrower has a signed contract from a third party purchaser to purchase such Home. No Construction Facility Advance shall be made with respect to any Lot and Home in excess of [_____] Thousand and No/100 Dollars ($[_____])) without the prior written approval of Lender.

Section 2.02 *Interest Rate.* The Note shall bear interest on the outstanding principal balance thereof from the date thereof until maturity at a varying rate per annum which is one and one-half percent (1.50%) per annum above the Prime Rate, but in no event to exceed the Highest Lawful Rate. Past due principal and interest in respect of the Note shall bear interest at a varying rate per annum which is five percent (5%) per annum above the Prime Rate, but in no event to exceed the Highest Lawful Rate. Adjustments in the varying interest rate shall be made on the same day as each change in the Prime Rate and, to the extent allowed by law, on the effective date of any change in the Highest Lawful Rate.

Section 2.03 *Origination Fee.* For the period from the date hereof through the Drawdown Termination Date, the Borrower agrees to pay an origination fee in connection with each Home equal to [_____] percent ([_____]%) of the Reserved Commitment related to such Home. The Borrower shall have the right at any time, on at least five (5) Business Days' prior notice, to terminate permanently the Commitment. Any such termination of the Commitment shall be accompanied by payment in full of all amounts outstanding under the Construction Facility, together with accrued but unpaid interest thereon.

Section 2.04 *Loan Procedures and Amounts of Advances.* During any given month, the Borrower may request with respect to each Home under construction funding of Construction Facility Advances by submitting to the Lender one or more Loan Requests at least five (5) Business Days prior to the date each such Advance is requested to be funded. No Advance with respect to any Home shall be funded sooner than five days after the last Advance related to such Home. All conditions precedent for any Construction Facility Advance shall have been satisfied, prior to delivery of the Loan Request for such Advance and no Construction Facility Advance (whether initial, interim or final) shall be made unless all conditions precedent to such Advance have been satisfied. Each Construction Facility Advance shall be made at the office of the Lender and shall be funded prior to 3:00 p.m., Houston time, on the day so requested in immediately available funds in the amount so requested.

Section 2.05 *Computation.* All payments of interest shall be computed on the per annum basis of a year of 360 days and for the actual number of days (including the first day but excluding the last day) elapsed unless such calculation would result in a usurious rate, in which case interest shall be calculated on the per annum basis of a year of 365 or 366 days, as the case may be.

Section 2.06 *Voluntary Prepayments; Partial Releases.*

(a) Voluntary Prepayments. The Borrower may at its option prepay the principal amount of the Note outstanding hereunder at any time in whole or from time to time in part without premium or penalty, upon giving the Lender prior notice of the aggregate principal amount to be prepaid, together with accrued interest thereon to the date of prepayment; provided, that a prepayment pursuant to Subsection 2.06(b) shall not constitute a prepayment pursuant to this Subsection 2.06(a).

(b) Partial Releases. Provided that no Default or Event of Default has occurred and is continuing, the Lender agrees to release from any Mortgage Lien the Lender may have thereon, individual Lots and the Homes being constructed thereon that are financed by Construction Facility Advances upon payment by the Borrower to the Lender of the "Release Price. Upon payment by the Borrower of the appropriate Release Price as provided in this Subsection, the Lender will prepare and execute a partial release of Lien and a UCC-3 partial release substantially in the form of Exhibits K and L, respectively. Upon the payment of the Release Price, the Reserved Commitment attributable to the Lot and Home being released shall no longer be reserved but shall again become part of the available Commitment.

Section 2.07 *Mandatory Prepayments.* If at any time the outstanding principal balance under the Note attributable to such Lot and Home exceeds the Percentage of Completion Value of any Lot and Home, then the Borrower shall forthwith prepay the amount of such excess for application towards reduction of the outstanding principal balance of the Note. If the Borrower exercises its option in Subsection 2.03 to terminate the Commitment, then the Borrower shall forthwith prepay the outstanding principal balance under the Note. Each prepayment made pursuant to this Section shall be without premium or penalty, and shall be made together with the payment of accrued interest on the amount prepaid.

Section 2.08 *Inspections.* The Borrower shall submit to the Lender a Loan request covering each Home for which funding is requested. The Lender will at its option inspect such Homes for which a Loan request has been received for purposes of evaluating the Percentage of Completion of each such Home. Based upon the Lender's inspection and evaluation, the Lender in its reasonable discretion shall fund the incremental Percentage of Completion Value determined by Lender in its reasonable discretion at such time for each Lot and Home financed under the Construction Facility for which a Loan Request has been received.

Section 2.09 *Payment Procedure.* All payments and prepayments made by the Borrower under the Note or this Agreement shall be made to the Lender at its offices described above in immediately available funds before 2:00 p.m., Houston time, on the date that such payment is required to be made. Any payment received and accepted by the Lender after such time shall be considered for all purposes (including the calculation of interest, to the extent permitted by law) as having been made on the Lender's next following Business Day.

Section 2.10 *Business Days.* If the date for any loan payment or prepayment or commitment fee payment hereunder falls on a day which is not a Business Day, then for all purposes of the Note and this Agreement the same shall be deemed to have fallen on the next following Business Day, and such extension of time shall in such case be included in the computation of payments of interest.

Section 2.11 *Changes in Subdivision Status.* If the Lender determines that any Approved Subdivision or Developed Subdivision no longer qualifies as such, the Lender shall (subject to all other terms and conditions hereof) continue to provide financing under the Construction Facility for Lots and Homes located in such subdivision with respect to which Initial Advances were made prior to such change in status, but Lender shall not be required to make any further Initial Advances with respect to Lots and/or Homes in such subdivision.

ARTICLE 3
REPRESENTATIONS AND WARRANTIES

In order to induce the Lender to enter into this Agreement, the Borrower makes the representations and warranties to the Lender (which representations and warranties will survive the delivery of the Note and the making of the loan or loans thereunder) set forth below:

Section 3.01 *Existence.* The Borrower is a corporation duly organized, legally existing and in good standing under the laws of the State of Texas.

Section 3.02 *Power and Authorization.* The Borrower is duly authorized and empowered to create and issue the Note; and the Borrower is duly authorized and empowered to execute, deliver and perform the Security Instruments, including this Agreement, to which it is a party; and all corporate action on the Borrower's part requisite for the due creation and issuance of the Note and for the due execution, delivery and performance of the Security Instruments, including this Agreement, to which the Borrower is a party has been duly and effectively taken.

Section 3.03 *Binding Obligations.* The Borrower represents and warrants to the Lender that this Agreement does, and the Note and other Security Instruments to which the Borrower is a party upon their creation, issuance, execution and delivery will, constitute valid and binding obligations of the Borrower enforceable in accordance with their terms, except as such enforceability may be limited by bankruptcy laws.

Section 3.04 *No Legal Bar or Resultant Lien.* The Borrower represents and warrants to the Lender that the Note and the Security Instruments, including this Agreement, to which the Borrower or any Subsidiary is a party and the compliance with and performance by the Borrower or any Subsidiary of the terms thereof do not and will not violate any provision of the articles of incorporation, bylaws, or partnership agreement of Borrower or any Subsidiary, or any contract, agreement, instrument or Governmental Requirement presently in effect to which the Borrower or any Subsidiary is subject, or will result in the creation or imposition of any Lien upon any Properties of the Borrower or any Subsidiary other than those permitted by this Agreement, except where such violation does not and will not have a Material Adverse Effect.

Section 3.05 *No Consent.* The Borrower represents and warrants to the Lender that except as disclosed in Exhibit C, the Borrower's and each Subsidiary's execution, delivery and performance of the Note and the Security Instruments, including this Agreement, to which the Borrower and each Subsidiary respectively are parties do not require the consent or approval of any venturer, partner, or of any stockholder of or partner in any of the venturers or partners, or of any other Person which has not been obtained, including but not limited to any regulatory authority or governmental body of the United States of America or any state thereof or any political subdivision of the United States of America or any state thereof, except where the failure to obtain such consent or approval would not have a Material Adverse Effect.

Section 3.06 *Financial Condition.* The Borrower represents and warrants to the Lender that the financial statements of the Borrower for the period ending [_____] (including any related schedules or notes) which have been delivered to the Lender have been prepared in accordance with generally accepted accounting principles, consistently applied, and present fairly the financial condition and changes in financial position of the Borrower as at the date or dates and for the period or periods stated and that no change has since occurred in the condition, financial or otherwise, of the Borrower which would have a Material Adverse Effect, except as disclosed in Exhibit C.

Section 3.07 *Investments and Guaranties.* The Borrower represents and warrants to the Lender that, at the date of this Agreement, neither the Borrower nor any Subsidiary has made investments in, advances to or guaranties of the obligations of any Person, except as reflected in the Financial Statements or disclosed to the Lender in Exhibit C and except as otherwise permitted by this Agreement.

Section 3.08 *Liabilities; Litigation.* The Borrower represents and warrants to the Lender that except for liabilities incurred in the normal course of business, neither the Borrower nor any Subsidiary has any material (individually or in the aggregate) liabilities, direct or contingent, except as disclosed or referred to in the Financial Statements or as disclosed to the Lender in Exhibit C and that, except as disclosed to the Lender in Exhibit C, at the date of this Agreement there is no litigation, legal, administrative or arbitral proceeding, investigation or other action of any nature pending or, to the knowledge of the Borrower, threatened against or affecting the Borrower or any Subsidiary which (A) challenges the validity of this Agreement, the Note or any of the other Security Instruments or (B) involves the possibility of any judgment or liability not fully covered by insurance, and which would have a Material Adverse Effect.

Section 3.09 *Taxes; Governmental Charges.* The Borrower represents and warrants to the Lender that the Borrower and its Subsidiaries have filed all tax returns and reports required to be filed and have paid all taxes, assessments, fees, and other governmental charges levied upon any of them or upon any of their respective Properties or income which are due and payable, including interest and penalties, or have provided adequate reserves for the payment thereof.

Section 3.10 *Titles, Etc.* The Borrower represents and warrants to the Lender that the Borrower and its Subsidiaries have good title to their respective material (individually or in the aggregate) Properties, free and clear of all Liens except (i) Liens referred to in the Financial Statements, (ii) Liens disclosed to the Lender in Exhibit C, (iii) Liens and minor irregularities in title which do not interfere with the occupation, use, or enjoyment by the Borrower or any Subsidiary of any of their respective Properties in the normal course of business as presently conducted or impair the value thereof for such business, except where such interference or impairment do not have a Material Adverse Effect, (iv) Liens otherwise permitted or contemplated by this Agreement or the other Security Instruments, or (v) Excepted Liens.

Section 3.11 *Defaults.* The Borrower represents and warrants to the Lender that neither the Borrower nor any Subsidiary is in default nor has any event or circumstance occurred which, but for the passage of time or the giving of notice, or both, would constitute a default under any material loan or credit agreement, indenture, mortgage, deed of trust, security agreement or other agreement or instrument evidencing or pertaining to any Debt of the Borrower or any Subsidiary, or under any material agreement or other instrument to which the Borrower or any Subsidiary is a party or by which the Borrower or any Subsidiary is bound, except as disclosed to the Lender in Exhibit C, and that no Default hereunder has occurred and is continuing.

Section 3.12 *Casualties; Taking of Properties.* The Borrower represents and warrants to the Lender that since the date of the Financial Statements, neither the business nor the Properties of the Borrower and the Subsidiaries, taken as a whole, have been materially and adversely affected by any cause or event.

Section 3.13 *Use of Proceeds; Margin Stock.* The Borrower represents and warrants to the Lender that (i) the proceeds of each Construction Facility Advance will be used solely to pay for the cost of the acquisition of Lots located in an Approved Subdivision and the cost of new construction of Homes on each such Lot; and (ii) none of such proceeds will be used for the purpose of purchasing or carrying any "*margin stock*" as defined in Regulation U of the Board of Governors of the Federal Reserve System (12 C.F.R. Part 221), or for the purpose of reducing or retiring any indebtedness which was originally incurred to purchase or carry a margin stock or for any other purpose which might constitute this transaction a "*purpose credit*" within the meaning of such Regulation U. The Borrower represents and warrants to the Lender that neither the Borrower nor any Subsidiary is engaged principally, or as one of its important activities, in the business of extending credit for the purpose of purchasing or carrying margin stocks and that neither the Borrower nor any Subsidiary, nor any Person acting on behalf of the Borrower or any Subsidiary, has taken or will take any action which might cause the Note or any of the Security Instruments, including this Agreement, to violate Regulation U or any other regulation of the Board of Governors of the Federal Reserve System or to violate Section 7 of the Securities Exchange Act of 1934 or any rule or regulation thereunder, in each case as now in effect or as the same may hereinafter be in effect.

Section 3.14 *Compliance with the Law.* The Borrower represents and warrants to the Lender that neither the Borrower nor any Subsidiary (i) is in violation of any Governmental Requirement or (ii) has failed to obtain any license, permit, franchise or other governmental authorization necessary to the ownership of any of their respective Properties or the conduct of their respective business, which violation or failure would have (in the event such violation or failure were asserted by any Person through appropriate action) a Material Adverse Effect.

Section 3.15 *ERISA.* The Borrower represents and warrants to the Lender that:

(a) The Borrower, each Subsidiary, and each ERISA Affiliate have complied in all material respects with ERISA and, where applicable, the Code regarding each Plan.

(b) Each Plan is and has been maintained in substantial compliance with ERISA and, where applicable, the Code.

(c) No act, omission or transaction has occurred which could result in imposition on the Borrower, any Subsidiary or any ERISA Affiliate (whether directly or indirectly) of (i) either a civil penalty assessed pursuant to subsections (c), (i) or (*l*) of Section 502 of ERISA or tax imposed pursuant to Section 4975 of the Code or (ii) breach of fiduciary duty liability damages under Section 409 of ERISA.

(d) Full payment has been made when due of all amounts which the Borrower, the Subsidiaries, and any ERISA Affiliate is required under the terms of each Plan or applicable law to have paid as contributions to such Plan as of the date hereof.

(e) Neither the Borrower, any Subsidiary nor any ERISA Affiliate sponsors, maintains or contributes to an employee welfare benefit plan, as defined in Section 3(1) of ERISA, including but not limited to any such plan maintained to provide benefits to former employees of such entities, that may not be terminated by the Borrower, any Subsidiary or any ERISA Affiliate in its sole discretion at any time without incurring liability in excess of $250,000.

(f) Neither the Borrower, the Subsidiaries, nor any ERISA Affiliate sponsors, maintains, or contributes to, or has at any time in the six-year period preceding the date of this Agreement sponsored, maintained or contributed to, any employee pension benefit plan, as defined in Section 3(2) of ERISA, that is subject to Title IV of ERISA (including, without limitation, any multiemployer plan as defined in Section 3(37) or 4001(a)(3) of ERISA).

Section 3.16 *Location of the Borrower.* The Borrower represents and warrants to the Lender that the Borrower's principal place of business and chief executive offices are located at the address stated in the first paragraph of this Agreement.

Section 3.17 *Utility Services.* The Borrower represents and warrants to the Lender that all utility services necessary for the construction of the Homes on all Lots mortgaged to the Lender and the operation thereof for their intended purpose are available (or will be available prior to the completion of construction of the applicable Home) at the boundaries of each such Lot, including water supply, storm and sanitary sewer facilities, gas, electric, and telephone facilities. All roads necessary for the full utilization of such Homes for their intended purposes have been completed substantially (or will be completed substantially prior to the completion of construction of the applicable Home or Homes) in accordance with all regulations and specifications of applicable Governmental Authorities and accepted for maintenance by the county or city in which they are located.

Section 3.18 *Geological Fault.* The Borrower represents and warrants to the Lender that to the best of Borrower's knowledge, no part of any Lot mortgaged to the Lender is situated upon a geological fault.

Section 3.19 *No Underground Storage Facilities.* The Borrower represents and warrants to the Lender that to the best of Borrower's knowledge no part of any Lot or other real property mortgaged to the Lender nor any Approved Subdivision is located on, over or within one mile of any underground storage facilities used for injected natural or processed gas or other liquid hydrocarbons or petroleum products.

Section 3.20 *No Material Misstatements.* The Borrower represents and warrants to the Lender that no information, exhibit or report furnished to the Lender by the Borrower or any Subsidiary in connection with the negotiation of this Agreement contained any material misstatement of fact or omitted to state a material fact or any fact necessary to make the statement contained therein not misleading.

Section 3.21 *Investment Company Act.* The Borrower represents and warrants to the Lender that neither the Borrower nor any Subsidiary is an *"investment company"* or a company *"controlled"* by an *"investment company"*, within the meaning of the Investment Company Act of 1940, as amended.

Section 3.22 *Public Utility Holding Company Act.* The Borrower represents and warrants to the Lender that neither the Borrower nor any Subsidiary is a *"holding company"*, or a *"subsidiary company"* of a *"holding company"*, or an *"affiliate"* of a *"holding company"* or of a *"subsidiary company"* of a *"holding company"*, or a *"public utility"* within the meaning of the Public Utility Holding Company Act of 1935, as amended.

Section 3.23 *Subsidiaries.* The Borrower represents and warrants to the Lender that the Borrower has no Subsidiaries, except [_____].

Section 3.24 *Environmental Matters.* The Borrower represents to the Lender that:

(a) Neither any Property of the Borrower or the Subsidiaries nor the operations conducted thereon violate any order or requirement of any court or Governmental Authority or any Environmental Law;

(b) There are no conditions existing on any Property of the Borrower or the Subsidiaries or resulting from operations conducted thereon that could give rise to or result in the imposition of remedial obligations under Environmental Laws other than conditions that customarily exist in the homebuilding business that are not material and are remediable without significant cost or any liability;

(c) Except as disclosed to the Lender in Exhibit C, without limitation of clause (a) above, no Property of the Borrower or the Subsidiaries, nor the operations currently conducted thereon or by any prior owner or operator of such Property or operation, are in violation of or subject to any existing, pending, or threatened action, suit, investigation, inquiry, or proceeding by or before any court or Governmental Authority or to any remedial obligations under Environmental Laws;

(d) All notices, permits, licenses or similar authorizations, if any, required to be obtained or filed in connection with the operation or use of any and all Property of the Borrower and the Subsidiaries, including but not limited to past or present treatment, storage, disposal, or release of a hazardous substance or solid waste into the environment, have been duly obtained or filed, and the Borrower and the Subsidiaries are in compliance with the terms and conditions of any such notice, permit, license or similar authorization;

(e) All hazardous substances or solid waste generated at any Property of the Borrower and the Subsidiaries have during the term of Borrower's ownership and to Borrower's knowledge in the past been transported only by carriers maintaining valid permits under RCRA and any other Environmental Law and only at treatment, storage and disposal facilities maintaining valid permits under RCRA and any other Environmental Law, which carriers and facilities have been and are operating in compliance with such permits and are not the subject of any existing, pending or threatened action, investigation or inquiry by any Governmental Authority in connection with any Environmental Law;

(f) The Borrower and the Subsidiaries have taken all reasonable and prudent steps necessary to determine and have determined that no hazardous substances or solid waste have been disposed of or otherwise released and there has been no threatened release of any hazardous substances on or to any Property of the Borrower or the Subsidiaries except in compliance with Environmental Laws, and that there are no storage tanks or other containers on or under the Property of the Borrower or the Subsidiaries from which hazardous substances or other contaminants may be released into the surrounding environment; and

(g) The Borrower and the Subsidiaries have no material contingent liability in connection with any release or threatened release of any hazardous substance or solid waste into the environment.

Section 3.25 *Solvency.* The Borrower is solvent, is generally paying its debts as they become due, and has no outstanding liens, suits, garnishments, bankruptcies or court actions which could render it insolvent.

ARTICLE 4

AFFIRMATIVE COVENANTS

The Borrower will at all times comply with the covenants contained in this Article 4, from the date hereof and for so long as any part of the Indebtedness or the Commitment is outstanding.

Section 4.01 *Financial Statements and Reports.* The Borrower will promptly furnish to the Lender from time to time upon request such information regarding the business and affairs and financial condition of the Borrower and the Subsidiaries as the Lender may reasonably request, and the Borrower will furnish to the Lender:

(a) Annual Reports. Promptly after becoming available and in any event within ninety (90) days after the close of each fiscal year of the Borrower the consolidated (or, where appropriate, combined) and consolidating balance sheets of the Borrower and its Subsidiaries, as of the end of such year (compiled by an independent certified public accountant), the consolidated (or, where appropriate, combined) and consolidating statements of profit and loss of the Borrower and its Subsidiaries, respectively, for such year (compiled by an independent certified public accountant), and the consolidated (or, where appropriate, combined) and consolidating statements of reconciliation of capital accounts of the Borrower and its Subsidiaries, respectively, for such year (compiled by an independent certified public accountant), and the consolidated (or, where appropriate, combined) and consolidating statement of changes in financial position (cash flow statements) of the Borrower and its Subsidiaries, respectively, for such year (compiled by an independent certified public accountant) and notes to the financial statements, all as compiled by an independent certified public accountant, which reports shall be accompanied by the related report of an independent certified public accountant acceptable to Lender, which report shall be to the effect that such statements have been prepared in accordance with GAAP consistently followed throughout the period indicated except for such changes in such principles with which the independent public accountants shall have concurred;

(b) *Monthly Financial Reports.* Promptly after becoming available and in any event within twenty-five (25) days after the end of each month in each fiscal year of the Borrower, the consolidated (or, where appropriate, combined) and consolidating balance sheets of the Borrower and its Subsidiaries as at the end of such month, and the consolidated (or, where appropriate, combined) and consolidating statements of profit and loss of the Borrower and its Subsidiaries for such month and for the period from the beginning of the fiscal year to the end of such month, certified by the principal financial officer of the Borrower to have been prepared in accordance with GAAP consistently followed throughout the period indicated except to the extent stated therein, subject to normal changes resulting from year-end adjustment;

(c) Other Reports—

(i) Within ten (10) days following the end of each calendar month, an Inventory Status Report and a sales report by Approved Subdivision with respect to all Lots and Homes financed under the Construction Facility indicating (A) sales (whether or not the Home sold was financed by Lender) since the last monthly report, (B) as to completed Homes (whether or not the Home was financed by Lender), whether or not they are subject to a contract for sale, (C) as to Homes under construction (whether or not financed by Lender), whether or not they are Sold Homes, and (D) such other information as the Lender may reasonably request; and

(ii) As soon as available, and in any event within ninety (90) days after the end of each fiscal year of the Borrower, a statement of contingent liabilities of the Borrower; and

(iii) As soon as available, and in any event within one hundred twenty (120) days after the end of each fiscal year of the Borrower, a copy of the 1991 Federal Income Tax Return of the Borrower; and

(iv) As soon as available, a copy of the 1991 Federal Income Tax Return of the Guarantors; and

(v) Quarter-Annual Financial Reports of Guarantors—Promptly after becoming available and in any event within twenty-five (25) days after the end of each calendar quarter in each fiscal year of the Borrower, the consolidated (or, where appropriate, combined) and consolidating balance sheets of the Guarantors as at the end of such quarter, and the consolidated (or, where appropriate, combined) and consolidating statements of profit and loss of the Guarantors for such quarter and for the period from the beginning of the fiscal year to the end of such quarter,

(vi) As soon as available, a copy of the 1992 annual business plan and cash flow projections of the Borrower; and

(d) Satisfaction of Conditions Precedent—Promptly upon request by the Lender, the Borrower shall provide the Lender with such documents, reports or other evidence as the Lender may reasonably request evidencing the satisfaction by the Borrower of the conditions precedent set forth in Article 7, including, but not limited to, environmental site assessments.

Section 4.02 *Quarter-Annual Certificates of Compliance.* Concurrently with the furnishing of the quarter-annual financial statements pursuant to Subsection 4.01(a), the Borrower will furnish or cause to be furnished to the Lender a certificate signed by the principal financial officer of the Borrower (i) stating that a review of the activities of the Borrower and the Subsidiaries has been made under his supervision with a view to determining whether the Borrower and the Subsidiaries have fulfilled all of their obligations under this Agreement, the other Security Instruments and the Note; (ii) stating that the Borrower and the Subsidiaries have fulfilled their obligations under such instruments and that all representations made herein continue to be true and correct in all material respects (or specifying the nature of any change), or if there shall be a Default or Event of Default, specifying the nature and status thereof and the Borrower's proposed response thereto; (iii) demonstrating in reasonable detail compliance (including but not limited to showing all calculations) as at the end of such fiscal year with Sections 5.14, 5.15, and 5.16, and with such other provisions hereof as the Lender may reasonably request; and (iv) containing or accompanied by such financial or other details, information and material as the Lender may reasonably request to evidence such compliance.

Section 4.03 *Taxes and Other Liens.* The Borrower will pay and discharge promptly all material taxes, assessments and governmental charges or levies imposed upon the Borrower or any Subsidiary or upon the income or any Property of the Borrower or any Subsidiary as well as all material claims of any kind (including claims for labor, materials, supplies and rent) which, if unpaid, might become a Lien upon any or all of the Property of the Borrower or any Subsidiary; provided, however, that neither the Borrower nor any Subsidiary shall be required to pay any such tax, assessment, charge, levy or claim if the amount, applicability or validity thereof shall currently be contested in good faith by appropriate proceedings diligently conducted by or on behalf of the Borrower or such Subsidiary, and if the Borrower or such Subsidiary shall have set up reserves therefor adequate under GAAP.

Section 4.04 *Maintenance.* The Borrower will and will cause each Subsidiary to (i) maintain its joint venture, partnership or corporate, as the case may be, existence, rights and franchises and (ii) observe and comply with all Governmental Requirements.

Section 4.05 *Further Assurances.* The Borrower will and will cause each Subsidiary to cure promptly any defects in the creation and issuance of the Note and the execution and delivery of the Security Instruments, including this Agreement. The Borrower at its expense will promptly execute and deliver to the Lender upon request all such other and further documents, agreements and instruments (or cause any of the Subsidiaries to take such action) in compliance with or accomplishment of the covenants and agreements of the Borrower or any of the Subsidiaries in the Security Instruments, including this Agreement, or to further evidence and more fully describe the collateral intended as security for the Note, or to correct any omissions in the Security Instruments, or more fully to state the security obligations set out herein or in any of the Security Instruments, or to perfect, protect or preserve any Liens created pursuant to any of the Security Instruments, or to make any recordings, to file any notices, or obtain any consents, all as may be reasonably necessary or appropriate in connection therewith.

Section 4.06 *Costs and Expenses.* The Borrower will pay all reasonable legal fees incurred by the Lender in connection with the administration of this Agreement and any and all other Security Instruments contemplated hereby (including any amendments hereto or thereto or consents or waivers hereunder or thereunder) and will also pay all other fees, charges or taxes for the recording or filing of the Security Instruments. The Borrower will also pay all reasonable out-of-pocket expenses of the Lender in connection with the administration of this Agreement and the other Security Instruments including, but not limited to, fees charged by the Lender's independent or internal inspectors (provided that such fees for internal inspectors shall not exceed the fees the Lender would have paid its independent inspectors for substantially similar work), attorneys' fees, appraisal fees, title endorsement premiums and premiums for any conversion of a Title Binder to a Title Policy. The Borrower will, upon request, promptly reimburse the Lender for all amounts reasonably expended, advanced or incurred by the Lender to satisfy any obligation of the Borrower under this Agreement or any other Security

Instrument, or to collect the Note, or to enforce the rights of the Lender under this Agreement or any other Security Instrument, which amounts will include all court costs, attorneys' fees (including but not limited to trial, appeal or other proceedings), fees of auditors and accountants, and investigation expenses reasonably incurred by the Lender in connection with any such matters, together with interest at the post-maturity rate specified in Section 2.02 on each such amount from the date three (3) days after written demand or request by the Lender for reimbursement until the date of reimbursement to the Lender. The Borrower will pay at the time of execution of this Agreement, or when due, or at the option of the Lender at any time or times hereafter specified by the Lender, all costs and expenses required by the terms of this Agreement, the Note, or the Security Instruments, and including but not limited to:

(a) All survey and continuations of survey costs and expenses, including the cost of a survey;

(b) All premiums for Title Binders, Title Policies and other insurance policies;

(c) All architects and engineers; and

(d) All other reasonable costs and expenses payable to third parties incurred by the Lender in connection with the consummation of the transactions contemplated by this Agreement.

Section 4.07 *Insurance.* The Borrower and the Subsidiaries now maintain and will continue to maintain, with financially sound and reputable insurers, insurance with respect to their respective Properties and business against such liabilities, casualties, risks and contingencies and in such types and amounts as is customary in the case of Persons engaged in the same or similar businesses and similarly situated, including but not limited to public liability insurance in the minimum amount of $2,000,000, workmen's compensation insurance up to the statutory limits, an umbrella policy in the minimum amount of $2,000,000, completed value fire and extended coverage insurance, and, with respect to all Property mortgaged to the Lender, flood insurance for each Lot if located within the 100-year flood plain, builder's risk insurance in the amount at any time of one hundred percent (100%) of the Percentage of Completion Value for each of the Homes financed under the Construction Facility, together with such other insurance as the Lender may require covering the associated Lot and the Home to be constructed thereon, all in amounts approved by the Lender, such insurance to be written in form and with companies approved by the Lender with loss made payable to the Lender pursuant to the Texas standard mortgagee clause, without contribution, and the Borrower shall have delivered the corresponding certificates of insurance to the Lender with evidence of payment of premiums thereon. Such policy shall provide, by way of riders, endorsements or otherwise, that the insurance provided thereby shall not be terminated, reduced or otherwise limited regardless of any breach of the representations and agreements set forth therein and that no such policy shall be cancelled, endorsed or amended to any extent unless the issuer thereof shall have first given the Lender at least thirty (30) days' prior written notice. Upon request of the Lender, the Borrower will furnish or cause to be furnished to the Lender from time to time (i) a summary of the insurance coverage of the Borrower and the Subsidiaries in form and substance satisfactory to the Lender and if requested will furnish the Lender copies of the applicable policies and (ii) a copy of any Completion Status Report provided by the Borrower to any insurance company. In the case of any fire, accident or other casualty causing loss or damage to any Properties of the Borrower securing the payment of the Indebtedness, the proceeds of such policies shall be used either (i) to repair or replace such damaged Property, or (ii) to prepay the Indebtedness, such election to be made by the Lender.

Section 4.08 *Right of Inspection.* The Borrower will permit and will cause each Subsidiary to permit any officer, employee or agent of the Lender to visit and inspect any of the Properties of the Borrower or any Subsidiary, examine the Borrower's or any Subsidiary's books of record and accounts, take copies and extracts therefrom, and discuss the affairs, finances and accounts of the Borrower or any Subsidiary with the Borrower's or such Subsidiary's officers, accountants and auditors, all at such reasonable times and as often as the Lender may desire.

Section 4.09 *Notice of Certain Events.* The Borrower shall promptly notify the Lender if the Borrower obtains knowledge of the occurrence of (i) any event which constitutes a Default, together with a detailed statement by a responsible officer of the Borrower of the steps being taken to cure the effect of such Default; or (ii) the receipt of any notice from, or the taking of any other action by, the holder of any promissory note, debenture, or other evidence of indebtedness of the Borrower or any Subsidiary or of any security (as defined in the Securities Act of 1933, as amended) of the Borrower or any Subsidiary with respect to a claimed default, together with a detailed statement by a responsible officer of the Borrower specifying the notice given or other action taken by such holder and the nature of the claimed default and what action the Borrower or such Subsidiary is taking or proposes to take with respect thereto; or (iii) any legal, judicial or regulatory proceedings affecting the Borrower or any Subsidiary or any of the Properties of the Borrower or any Subsidiary and involving an amount in controversy equal to $25,000 or more individually; or (iv) any dispute between the Borrower or any Subsidiary and any governmental or regulatory body or any other Person which, if adversely determined, would have a Material Adverse Effect; or (v) any event or condition having a Material Adverse Effect.

Section 4.10 *Affiliates.* All transactions between the Borrower or any Subsidiary and any Affiliate of the Borrower or any Subsidiary shall be arms length transactions undertaken in good faith and in the ordinary course of business, unless approved by the Lender in its reasonable discretion, but the foregoing shall not limit or prohibit payments by the Subsidiaries to the Borrower.

Section 4.11 *Notices by Governmental Authority, Fire and Casualty Losses, Etc.* The Borrower will timely comply with and promptly furnish to the Lender true and complete copies of any official notice or claim by any Governmental Authority pertaining to any Lot mortgaged to the Lender or any Home to be constructed thereon. The Borrower will promptly notify the Lender of any fire or casualty or any notice of taking or eminent domain action or proceeding affecting any such Lot or Home. In the event any such Lot or Home is taken in an eminent domain action or proceeding, the condemnation proceeds resulting from such action or proceeding shall be paid to the Lender to be applied as a prepayment of the Indebtedness.

Section 4.12 *Application of Construction Facility Advances.* The Borrower will disburse all Construction Facility Advances for payment of costs of labor, material, and services supplied for the construction of Homes on the associated Lot and other costs and expenses incident to such Lot and the construction of the Homes thereon.

Section 4.13 *Required Deposit by Borrower.* If the Lender determines at any time that the unadvanced portion of the construction costs for any given Lot and Home mortgaged to the Lender will be insufficient for payment in full of:

(a) The remaining unpaid cost of labor, materials and services required for the completion of the Home being constructed thereon; and

(b) Any other costs and expenses required to be paid in connection with the completion of construction of such Home in accordance with any Governmental Requirements; then the Borrower will, on request of the Lender, promptly deposit with the Lender any sum or sums over and above the unadvanced portion of the construction costs allocated to such Lot and Home necessary to complete such Home (the *"Borrower's Deposit"*). The Lender shall not be required to pay interest on such Borrower's Deposit. The Lender may advance all or a portion of the Borrower's Deposit prior to making any additional Construction Facility Advance with respect to such Lot and Home. The Borrower will promptly notify the Lender in writing if and when the costs of the completion of construction of any Homes on a Lot mortgaged to the Lender exceed (or appear likely to exceed) by more than $10,000 the unadvanced portion of the related construction costs.

Section 4.14 *Payment of Claims.* The Borrower shall promptly pay or cause to be paid when due all costs and expenses incurred in connection with all Lots mortgaged to the Lender and the construction of the Homes thereon, and the Borrower shall keep such Lots free and clear of any mechanic's Liens, Liens other than Excepted Liens, charges, or claims other than the Lien of the Mortgage and other Liens approved in writing by the Lender, whether inferior or superior to the Mortgage. A discharge of any Mortgage and taking of a new Mortgage in substitution thereof shall not release or diminish this obligation. Notwithstanding anything to the contrary contained in this Agreement, the Borrower may contest (i) the validity or amount of any claim of any contractor, consultant, architect, or other Person providing labor, materials, or services with respect to any Lot mortgaged to the Lender or the construction of the Home thereon, (ii) any tax or special assessment levied by any Governmental Authority, or (iii) the enforcement of or compliance with any Governmental Requirements, and any such contest on the part of the Borrower shall not be a Default hereunder provided that during the pendency of any such contest the Borrower shall furnish to the Lender and the Title Insurer an indemnity bond with a corporate surety satisfactory to the Lender and the Title Insurer or other security acceptable to them in an amount equal to one hundred fifty percent (150%) of such claim or tax, and provided further that the Borrower shall pay any amount finally adjudged by a court of competent jurisdiction to be due, with all costs, interest, and penalties thereon before such judgment creates a Lien on such Lot or the Home to be constructed thereon.

Section 4.15 *Appraisals.* The Borrower shall allow the Lender's appraiser access to its Properties and records and shall cooperate in any other reasonable manner in allowing such Appraisal to be prepared and completed on a timely basis.

Section 4.16 *Plans and Specifications; Change Orders; Construction Costs Schedule.* Prior to commencement of construction, Borrower shall furnish Lender for review and approval copies of the Plans and Specifications for each Home to be constructed under the Construction Facility, together with a Construction Costs Schedule related thereto. The Borrower will construct each Home in substantial compliance with the Plans and Specifications. Any change or changes to the Plans and Specifications for any Home resulting in a decrease in the construction costs of such Home or which exceed in the aggregate five percent (5%) of the total construction costs of such Home shall be disclosed to the Lender by providing the Lender with all Change Orders instructing and evidencing such changes.

Section 4.17 *Sold Homes; Lot Purchase.* Upon request of the Lender, Borrower shall furnish to Lender the name, telephone number and loan officer of any mortgage lender issuing a permanent loan covering any Sold Home, and Borrower shall request that said permanent lender cooperate with Lender in providing evidence of loan status of the permanent loan covering any Sold Home. In addition, upon request of Lender, the Borrower shall provide a copy of any loan approval issued by said permanent lender. Borrower shall furnish to Lender a copy of the purchase contract or other evidence satisfactory to Lender with respect to the cost of each Lot financed under the Construction Facility. Prior to commencement of construction, Lender shall obtain at Borrower's expense, the Appraisal.

Section 4.18 *Title Policies.* If, for any reason and notwithstanding any other provision of this Agreement to the contrary, a Title Binder is within two (2) weeks of its expiration date or if a material defect in title to the Property covered thereby becomes known, the Borrower shall cause the Title Insurer that issued such Title

Binder to convert such Title Binder to a Title Policy and shall pay all premiums therefor.

Section 4.19 *Commencement of Construction; Continuation of Construction.* Prior to the recordation of any Mortgage, no construction contract shall have been recorded with respect to each Lot to be covered thereby, no work of any kind (including but not limited to the destruction or removal of any existing improvements, site work, clearing, grubbing, draining, or fencing of each such Lot by the Borrower or its agents) shall have commenced or shall have been performed on any such Lot, no equipment or material shall have been delivered to or upon any such Lot for any purpose whatsoever, no contract (or memorandum or affidavit thereof) for the supplying of labor, materials or services for the construction of the improvements thereto shall have been recorded by any Person in the mechanic's lien or other appropriate records in the county where any such Lot is located, and no specially fabricated materials or equipment shall have been ordered or received. Construction shall be commenced within 30 days after a Construction Facility Advance has been made to finance the acquisition of the Lot on which a Home is to be constructed. Borrower shall not cease construction of any Home for more than 15 days without the consent of Lender.

Section 4.20 *List of Subcontractors, etc.* Borrower will, if requested, make available to the Lender, or its representatives within a reasonable period after such request is made, counterparts and/or conditional assignments of any and all construction contracts, bills of sale, statements, conveyances, receipted vouchers or agreements of any nature under which the Borrower claims title to any materials or supplies used or to be used in the construction of the Home.

Section 4.21 *Correction of Defects.* Borrower will, upon demand of the Lender, correct any structural defect in any Home or any material departure from the Plans and Specifications not accepted by the Lender.

Section 4.22 *Foundation Survey.* Borrower will, if requested by Lender, furnish to the Lender, immediately after the pouring of each concrete slab, street and curbstone within the Lot, the completion of each foundation and the completion of the Home, a survey certified to by a licensed engineer acceptable to the Lender showing all of same and that the location thereof is entirely within the property lines of the Lot and does not encroach upon, breach or violate any building line, easement or similar restriction.

ARTICLE 5

NEGATIVE COVENANTS

The Borrower will at all times comply with the covenants contained in this Article 5, from the date hereof and for so long as any part of the Indebtedness or the Commitment is outstanding.

Section 5.01 *Debt.* Neither the Borrower nor any Subsidiary will incur, create, assume or suffer to exist any Debt, or any Debt which would arise under commitments to lend, in excess of the maximum aggregate amount of $[_____] incurred after the date hereof for the purpose of acquiring Lots for the purpose of the construction (primarily by the Borrower) of Homes thereon (provided, however, that the maximum amount of Debt pursuant to this Subsection together with the amount of investments outstanding at any time pursuant to Subsection 5.03(f) shall not exceed $[_____]).

Section 5.02 *Liens.* Neither the Borrower nor any Subsidiary will create, incur, assume or permit to exist any Lien on any of its Properties (now owned or hereafter acquired), except:

    (a) Liens securing the payment of any Indebtedness;

    (b) Excepted Liens;

    (c) Liens disclosed in Exhibit C;

(d) Liens securing Debt described in Subsections 5.01(c) and (d); and

(e) Non-consensual statutory, administrative or judicial Liens that are not material either individually or in the aggregate.

Section 5.03 *Investments, Loans and Advances.* Neither the Borrower nor any Subsidiary will make or permit to remain outstanding any loans or advances to or investments in any Person, except that the foregoing restriction shall not apply to:

(a) Investments, loans or advances, the material details of which have been set forth in the Financial Statements or are disclosed to the Lender in Exhibit C;

(b) Investments in direct obligations of the United States of America or any agency thereof;

(c) Investments in certificates of deposit of maturities less than one year, issued by commercial banks in the United States of America having capital and surplus in excess of $50,000,000;

(d) Investments in commercial paper of maturities less than one year if at the time of purchase such paper is rated in either of the two highest rating categories of Standard & Poors Corporation, Moody's Investors Service, Inc., or any other rating agency satisfactory to the Lender;

(e) Routine loans or advances to employees made in the ordinary course of business not to exceed the aggregate amount, for the Borrower and all Subsidiaries combined, of ten percent (10%) of the retained earnings of the Borrower in any one year; and

(f) Investments for the purpose of acquiring real Property to develop into Lots (and for such development) for the purpose of the construction (primarily by the Borrower) of Homes thereon in the maximum amount of $250,000.00 (provided, however, that the maximum amount of investments pursuant to this Subsection together with the amount of Debt outstanding at any time pursuant to Subsection 5.01(c) shall not exceed $250,000.00.

Section 5.04 *Distributions, Payments, Issuance of Stock, Etc. by the Borrower.* The Borrower will not make any distributions, returns of capital, payments of fees or salary or other payments of any nature whatsoever, except the Borrower may make payments for Permitted Expenses, provided such payment does not cause Borrower to breach any other covenant of this Agreement. Borrower shall not sell and shall not permit any Subsidiary to issue, sell or otherwise dispose of any shares of its capital stock or other securities or rights, warrants or options to purchase, or acquire any shares or securities or issue any class of capital stock if the effect thereof would be to cause Borrower to breach any other covenant of this Agreement.

Section 5.05 *Sales and Leasebacks.* Neither the Borrower nor any Subsidiary will enter into any arrangement, directly or indirectly, with any Person whereby the Borrower or any Subsidiary shall sell or transfer any Property, whether now owned or hereafter acquired, and whereby the Borrower or any Subsidiary shall then or thereafter rent or lease as lessee such Property or any part thereof or other Property which the Borrower or any Subsidiary intends to use for substantially the same purpose or purposes as the Property sold or transferred.

Section 5.06 *Nature of Business.* Neither the Borrower nor any Subsidiary will engage in any business other than the home building business or in the acquisition of real Property and the development of such Property into Lots for the purpose of the construction of Homes thereon primarily by the Borrower.

Section 5.07 *Speculative Home Limitations.* At no time will the total number of Homes (whether or not financed by the Lender) completed or under construction by the Borrower or any Subsidiary which are not Sold Homes exceed [_____]

percent ([_____]%) of the total number of Homes (whether or not financed by the Lender) completed or under construction by the Borrower or any Subsidiary. At no time will the Advances under the Note related to Homes financed by the Lender, which are completed or under construction by the Borrower or any Subsidiary, and which are not Sold Homes, together with the aggregated Reserved Commitments related to such Homes, exceed [_____] percent ([_____]%) of the total of Advances and Reserved Commitments under the Construction Facility.

Section 5.08 *Construction Starts and New Lot Purchases.* The Borrower will not undertake any construction start on any Home to be financed under the Construction Facility unless it has first granted to the Lender a first lien Mortgage on all of the Borrower's right, title, and interest in the Lot associated with such Home as security for any and all Indebtedness. The Borrower will not undertake any construction start on any Home financed under the Construction Facility for which Lender has not approved the Plans and Specifications or for which Lender has not received an Appraisal. The Borrower will not undertake construction of any Home which is not a Sold Home in any Approved Subdivision in which Borrower has more than [_____] ([_____]) Homes completed or under construction (whether or not financed by Lender) which are not Sold Homes. The Borrower will not finance construction of any Model Home under the Construction Facility.

Section 5.09 *Restrictions and Annexation.* Neither the Borrower nor any Subsidiary will impose any restrictive covenants or encumbrances upon any Lot mortgaged to the Lender or the Home to be constructed thereon, or execute or file any subdivision plat or effect the annexation of all or part of any such Lot to any city or other political unit without the prior written consent of the Lender.

Section 5.10 *Mergers, Stock of Borrower.* (a) The Borrower will not merge or consolidate with or sell, assign, lease or otherwise dispose of (whether in one transaction or in a series of transactions) all or substantially all of its Properties (whether now owned or hereafter acquired) to any Person. (b) Borrower will not permit any Subsidiary to take any of the actions set forth in (a) if such action would have a Material Adverse effect on Borrower. Neither Borrower nor Guarantors will permit or suffer to exist any transaction or circumstance whereby Guarantors shall cease to own at least 51% of the issued and outstanding shares of capital stock of Borrower.

Section 5.11 *Proceeds of Note.* The Borrower will not permit the proceeds of the Note to be used for any purpose other than those permitted by Section 3.13.

Section 5.12 *ERISA.* The Borrower and the Subsidiaries will not at any time:

(a) Engage in, or permit any ERISA Affiliate to engage in, any transaction in connection with which the Borrower, any Subsidiary or any ERISA Affiliate could be subjected to either a civil penalty assessed pursuant to subsections (c), (i) or (*l*) of Section 502 of ERISA or a tax imposed by Section 4975 of the Code;

(b) Fail to make, or permit any ERISA Affiliate to fail to make, full payment when due of all amounts which, under the provisions of any Plan, agreement relating thereto or applicable law, the Borrower, a Subsidiary or any ERISA Affiliate is required to pay as contributions thereto;

(c) Contribute to or assume an obligation to contribute to, or permit any ERISA Affiliate to contribute to or assume an obligation to contribute to, any employee pension benefit plan, as defined in Section 3(2) of ERISA, that is subject to Title IV of ERISA (including, without limitation, any multiemployer plan as defined in Section 3(37) of 4001(a)(3) of ERISA);

(d) Acquire, or permit any ERISA Affiliate to acquire, an interest in any Person that causes such Person to become an ERISA Affiliate with respect to the Borrower or any Subsidiary or with respect to any ERISA Affiliate of the Borrower or any Subsidiary if such Person sponsors, maintains or contributes to, or at any time in the six-year period preceding such acquisition has sponsored, maintained, or contributed to, any employee pension benefit plan, as defined in Section 3(2) of ERISA, that is subject to Title IV or ERISA (including, without limitation, any multiemployer plan as defined in Section 3(37) of 4001(a)(3) or ERISA); or

(e) Contribute to or assume an obligation to contribute to, or permit any ERISA Affiliate to contribute to or assume an obligation to contribute to, any employee welfare benefit plan, as defined in section 3(1) of ERISA, including but not limited to any such plan maintained to provide benefits to former employees of such entities, that may not be terminated by such entities in their sole discretion at any time without liability in excess of $250,000.

Section 5.13 *Sale or Discount of Receivables.* Neither the Borrower nor any Subsidiary will discount or sell with recourse, or sell for less than the greater of the face or market value thereof, any of its notes receivable or accounts receivable.

Section 5.14 *Net Worth.* The Borrower will not permit its consolidated net worth to be less than $[_____] at any time.

Section 5.15 *Ratio of Total Liabilities to Tangible Net Worth.* The Borrower will not permit its ratio of (i) consolidated total liabilities (including contingent liabilities) to (ii) consolidated tangible net worth to be greater than [_____] to 1 at any time. As used in this Section, *"consolidated tangible net worth"* shall mean the sum of preferred stock (if any), par value of common stock (if any), capital in excess of par value of common stock, and retained earnings less treasury stock (if any), less good will, cost in excess of net assets acquired and all other assets as are properly classified as intangible assets, all as determined on a consolidated basis.

Section 5.16 *Ratio of Advances to Percentage of Completion Values.* The Borrower will not permit the ratio of the aggregate principal amount of all Construction Facility Advances at any time outstanding to the aggregate Percentage of Completion Values, at such time, of all Lots and Homes financed under the Construction Facility to be greater than 0.75 to 1.

Section 5.17 *Ratio of Current Assets to Current Liabilities, Working Capital.* The Borrower will not permit its ratio of (i) Current Assets as that term is defined herein to (ii) Current Liabilities as that term is defined herein (herein the "Current Ratio") to be less than [_____] to 1.0 at any time during the term of the Construction Facility. The Borrower will not permit its Working Capital to be less than $[_____] during the term of the Construction Facility.

Section 5.18 *Environmental Matters.* Neither the Borrower nor any Subsidiary will cause or permit any Property of any such party to be in violation of, or do anything or permit anything to be done which will subject any such Property to, any remedial obligations under any Environmental Laws, assuming disclosure to the applicable Governmental Authority of all relevant facts, conditions and circumstances, if any, pertaining to such Property, and the Borrower and the Subsidiaries will promptly notify the Lender in writing of any existing, pending or threatened action or investigation by any Governmental Authority in connection with any Environmental Laws. The Borrower and the Subsidiaries will establish and implement such procedures as may be necessary to continuously determine and assure that they fully comply with these covenants. Neither the Borrower nor any Subsidiary will use any Property owned by any such party in a manner which will result in (i) violation of any order or requirement of any court or Governmental Authority or any Environmental Law, (ii) the disposal of any solid waste on or to any such Property or as a result of operation conducted on such Property in quantities or locations that would require remedial action under any Environmental Laws, (iii) a release of a hazardous substance on or to any such Property in a quantity equal to or exceeding that quantity which requires reporting pursuant to Section 103 of CERCLA, or (iv) the release of any hazardous substance on or to any such

Property so as to pose an imminent and substantial endangerment to public health or welfare or the environment. The Borrower and the Subsidiaries covenant and agree to keep or cause all Property owned by them to be kept free of any hazardous waste or contaminants and to remove the same (or if removal is prohibited by law, to take whatever action is required by law) promptly upon discovery at its sole expense. Without limitation of the Lender's rights to declare a default hereunder and to exercise all remedies available by reason thereof, if the Borrower fails to comply with or perform any of the foregoing covenants and obligations, the Lender may (without any obligation, express or implied) remove any hazardous substance or solid waste from such Property (or if removal is prohibited by law, take whatever action is required by law) and the cost of the removal or such other action shall be a demand obligation owing by the Borrower to the Lender (which obligation the Borrower hereby promises to pay) pursuant to this Agreement and shall be subject to and covered by the provisions of Sections 4.14 and 8.09. The Borrower grants to the Lender and its agents, employees, contractors and consultants access to such Property and the license (which is coupled with an interest and irrevocable while this Agreement is in effect) to remove the hazardous substance or solid waste (or if removal is prohibited by law, to take whatever action is required by law) and agrees to indemnify and save the Lender harmless from all costs and expenses involved therewith, other than costs or expenses resulting from the Lender's gross negligence or willful misconduct. Upon the Lender's reasonable request, at any time and from time to time during the existence of this Agreement, the Borrower will provide at the Borrower's sole expense an inspection or audit of such Property from an engineering or consulting firm approved by the Lender, indicating the presence or absence of hazardous substances and solid wastes on such Property. If the Borrower fails to provide same after twenty (20) days' notice, the Lender may order same, and the Borrower grants to the Lender and its employees, agents, contractors and consultants access to such Property and a license (which is coupled with an interest and irrevocable while this Agreement is in effect) to perform inspections and tests, including but not limited to the taking of soil borings and groundwater samples. The cost of such inspections and tests shall be a demand obligation owing by the Borrower (which the Borrower hereby promises to pay) to the Lender pursuant to this Agreement and shall be subject to and covered by the provisions of Sections 4.14 and 8.09.

Section 5.19 *Flood Plain.* No part of any Lot mortgaged to the Lender will lie within the 100-year flood plain or any area that has been designated by the Secretary of Housing and Urban Development as an area having special flood hazards or, if it does, the community in which such Lot is located shall have been approved for flood insurance under the National Flood Insurance Program and flood insurance shall be available for such Lot under such program.

Section 5.20 *Geological Fault.* No part of any Lot upon which the Lender shall be granted a Lien shall be situated upon a geological fault.

Section 5.21 *Underground Storage Facilities.* No part of any Lot or other real property upon which the Lender shall be granted a Lien nor shall any part of any Approved Subdivision be situated on, over or within one mile of any underground storage facilities used for injected natural gas or processed gas or other liquid hydrocarbons or petroleum products.

ARTICLE 6

EVENTS OF DEFAULT

Section 6.01 *Events.* Any of the following events shall be considered an "*Event of Default*" as that term is used herein:

(a) Payments. Default is made in the payment when due of any installment of principal or interest on the Note or other Indebtedness; or

(b) Representations and Warranties. Any representation or warranty by the Borrower or any Subsidiary or other Person herein or in any other Security Instrument, or in any certificate, request, or other document furnished pursuant to or under this Agreement or any other Security Instrument proves to have been incorrect in any material respect as of the date when made or deemed made; or

(c) Affirmative Covenants. Default is made in the due observance or performance by the Borrower of any of the covenants or agreements contained in Article 4, and such default continues unremedied for a period of thirty (30) days after the earlier of (i) notice thereof being given by the Lender to the Borrower, or (ii) such default otherwise becoming known to the Borrower]; or

(d) Negative Covenants. Default is made in the due observance or performance by the Borrower of any of the covenants or agreements contained in Article 5; or

(e) Other Security Instrument Obligations. Default is made in the due observance or performance by the Borrower or any Subsidiary or other Person of any of the other covenants or agreements contained in any Security Instrument other than this Agreement, and such default continues unremedied beyond the expiration of any applicable grace period which may be expressly allowed under such Security Instrument; or

(f) Involuntary Bankruptcy or Other Proceedings. An involuntary case or other proceeding shall be commenced against the Borrower which seeks liquidation, reorganization or other relief with respect to it or its debts or other liabilities under any bankruptcy, insolvency or other similar law now or hereafter in effect or seeking the appointment of a trustee, receiver, liquidator, custodian or other similar official of it or any substantial part of its Property, and such involuntary case or other proceeding shall remain undismissed or unstayed for a period of thirty (30) days, or an order for relief against the Borrower shall be entered in any such case under the Federal Bankruptcy Code; or

(g) Voluntary Petitions, Etc. The Borrower shall commence a voluntary case or other proceeding seeking liquidation, reorganization or other relief with respect to itself or its debts or other liabilities under any bankruptcy, insolvency or other similar law now or hereafter in effect or seeking the appointment of a trustee, receiver, liquidator, custodian or other similar official of it or any substantial part of its Property, or shall consent to any such relief or to the appointment of or taking possession by any such official in an involuntary case or other proceeding commenced against it, or shall make a general assignment for the benefit of creditors, or shall fail generally to, or shall admit in writing its inability to pay its debts generally as they become due, or shall take any corporate or partnership action to authorize or effect any of the foregoing; or

(h) Discontinuance of Business. The Borrower discontinues its homebuilding business; or

(i) Winding Up Business, Etc. The Borrower shall take any action to or shall otherwise begin the process of winding up its business or affairs, or dissolving, liquidating, or terminating; or

(j) Default on Other Debt. Any Debt of the Borrower which exceeds the aggregate amount of $[_____] is not paid when due (or within any grace period applicable thereto) or as a result of the occurrence of any default or event of default (howsoever described and whether or not involving culpability on the part of any Person), or any Debt of Borrower is declared to be or otherwise become due and payable prior to its specified maturity and is not paid within five (5) days of the due date thereof; or

(k) Undischarged Judgments. The Borrower shall fail within thirty (30) days to pay, bond or otherwise discharge any judgment or order for the payment of money in excess of $50,000 that is not otherwise being satisfied in accordance with its terms and is not stayed on appeal or otherwise being appropriately contested in good faith; or

(*l*) Subsidiary. Any Subsidiary takes, suffers or permits to exist any of the events or conditions referred to in Subsections 6.01(f), (g), (i), (j) or (k); or

(m) [_____] (or another person reasonably acceptable to Lender who is appointed within thirty (30) days of the event specified herein) does any of the following:

(i) dies, becomes disabled or permits to exist as to such Person any of the events or conditions referred to in Subsections 6.01(f) or (g) (unless a replacement for said parties has been appointed that is acceptable to Lender);

(ii) ceases to be chief executive officer and majority stockholder of Borrower;

(iii) ceases to be President of the Borrower and in charge of the day-to-day operations of the Borrower; or

(iv) engages in any homebuilding business other than under the Borrower or any Subsidiary (and in the case of a Subsidiary, only as expressly allowed herein); or

(n) Guarantors shall cease to own at least 51% of the issued and outstanding capital stock of Borrower; or

(*o*) Security Instruments. Any Mortgage or Financing Statement after delivery thereof shall for any reason, except to the extent permitted by the terms thereof, cease to be in full force and effect and valid, binding and enforceable in accordance with its terms, or cease to create a valid and perfected Lien of the priority required thereby on any of the collateral purported to be covered thereby and the Borrower fails to fully remedy or cure the same within fifteen (15) days after the Lender gives notice thereof to the Borrower, or the Borrower shall so state in writing; or

(p) Title. The Borrower's title to any Lot mortgaged to the Lender is not reasonably satisfactory to the Lender, regardless of whether the Lien, encumbrance or question existed at the time of a prior Construction Facility Advance with respect to such Lot or the Home constructed thereon, and such objection is not remedied or cured within fifteen (15) days after the Lender gives notice thereof to the Borrower; or

(q) Any Affidavit of Commencement of Construction is filed with respect to any Lot or Home which specifies a date of commencement which is prior to the date the Mortgage covering such Lot or Home was recorded; or

(r) There shall not have occurred any change in "control" of Borrower. "Control" as used in this Section 6.01(r) shall mean (possession, directly or indirectly, of power to direct or cause the direction of management or policies of Borrower whether through ownership of securities or other ownership interest, by contract or otherwise.

With respect to the events specified in Paragraph 6.01(m)(i), (ii) or (iii), the Borrower may present Lender a contingency plan specifying Borrower's intention (and proposed officers) in the case of an occurrence of the events specified in said paragraph, and, when approved by Lender, said plan shall constitute compliance with the provisions of this paragraph as to the specified events.

Section 6.02 *Remedies.* Upon the occurrence of any Event of Default described in Subsection 6.01(f) or (g), or in Subsection 6.01(1) or (m) to the extent that such Subsections refer to Subsection 6.01(f) or (g), the Commitment and other lending obligations, if any, of the Lender hereunder shall immediately terminate, and the entire principal amount of all Indebtedness then outstanding together with interest then accrued thereon shall become immediately due and payable, all without written notice and without presentment, demand, notice of intent to accelerate, notice of acceleration, protest, notice of protest or dishonor or any other notice of default of any kind, all of which are hereby expressly waived by the Borrower and its Subsidiaries. Upon the occurrence and at any time during the continuance of any other Event of Default specified in Section 6.01, the Lender may by written notice to the Borrower (i) declare the entire principal amount of all Indebtedness then outstanding together with interest then accrued thereon to be immediately due and payable without presentment, demand, protest, notice of protest or dishonor or other notice of default of any kind, all of which are hereby expressly waived by the Borrower and its Subsidiaries and/or (ii) terminate the Commitment and other lending obligations, if any, of the Lender hereunder, unless and until the Lender shall reinstate same in writing and (iii) exercise any and all rights and remedies provided Lender under the Security Instruments. In addition to the foregoing, upon the occurrence and during the continuance of any Event of Default, the Lender shall have the right, but not the obligation, in its own name or in the name of the Borrower, to enter into possession of the Lots mortgaged to the Lender and the Homes being or to be constructed thereon, to perform all work and labor necessary to complete such Homes, and to employ watchmen and other safeguards to protect such Lots and Homes. Upon the occurrence and continuance of an Event of Default, the Lender may take any one or more of the following actions and the Borrower hereby constitutes and appoints the Lender as the true and lawful attorney-in-fact of the Borrower, with full power of substitution, and in the name of the Borrower, if the Lender elects to do so, and hereby empowers the Lender and/or said attorney or attorneys to:

(a) Use such sums as are necessary, including any proceeds of any Construction Facility Advance and the Borrower's Deposits, and employ such architects, engineers, contractors, subcontractors, agents and inspectors, as may be required for the purpose of completing the construction of the Homes financed under the Construction Facility substantially in accordance with the Governmental Requirements and the Plans and Specifications;

(b) Execute all applications and certificates in the name of the Borrower which may be required for completion of construction of the Homes financed under the Construction Facility;

(c) Pay, settle, or compromise all existing bills and claims which may be Liens against the Homes financed under the Construction Facility or as may be necessary for the completion of the job, or clearance of title;

(d) Endorse the name of the Borrower on any checks or drafts representing proceeds of the insurance policies, or other checks or instruments payable to the Borrower with respect to such Lots and Homes to be constructed thereon and financed under the Construction Facility;

(e) Execute all applications and certificates in the name of the Borrower which may be required by any of the contract documents;

(f) Employ at the expense of the Borrower a watchman or such other security agency as the Lender may choose to protect the Homes financed under the Construction Facility, building materials and equipment from depreciation or injury;

(g) Do any and every act with respect to the construction of the Homes financed under the Construction Facility which the Borrower may do; and

(h) Prosecute or defend any action or proceeding incident to the construction of the Homes financed under the Construction Facility as the Lender deems necessary.

All sums so expended by the Lender hereunder shall be deemed to be advanced to the Borrower and secured by the Mortgages even if in excess of the amount of the Loan Value of the related Lots and Homes, and the total thereof shall be due and payable from the Borrower to the Lender pursuant to the terms of the Note. The power-of-attorney granted hereby is a power coupled with an interest and is irrevocable. The Lender shall have no obligation to undertake any of the foregoing actions, and if the Lender should do so, it shall have no liability to the Borrower for the sufficiency or adequacy of any such action.

Notwithstanding the preceding paragraph, if an Event of Default described in Subsection 6.01(b), (c), (d), (*o*), or (p) arises with respect to a particular Lot in connection with a violation or breach of or default under Section 3.17, 3.18, 3.19, 4.11, 4.12, 4.13, 4.18, 4.19, 5.09, 5.19, 5.20 or 5.21, or, as to Properties in which the Lender has been granted a Mortgage Lien, Section 3.10, then in any such instance the Lender shall not be entitled to exercise its rights and remedies arising from such Event of Default unless it has first given the Borrower five (5) days' notice of such Event of Default and the Borrower has failed during such period to prepay the entire Release Price, together with accrued interest, for such Lot and the Home being constructed thereon with respect to which such Event of Default arose. After the expiration of such five (5) day period and the Borrower's failure to so prepay, the Lender shall be fully entitled to exercise all its rights and remedies arising from such Event of Default. This paragraph shall in no way restrict, limit or impair the Lender's rights and remedies arising from the occurrence of Events of Default other than those Events of Default relating to those Sections of Articles 3, 4, and 5 which are specifically listed above with respect to particular Lots and Homes.

Section 6.03 *Right of Set-off.* Upon the occurrence and during the continuance of any Event of Default, the Lender is hereby authorized at any time and from time to time, without notice to the Borrower (any such notice being expressly waived by the Borrower), to set-off and apply any and all deposits (general or special, time or demand, provisional or final) at any time held and other indebtedness at any time owing by the Lender to or for the credit or the account of the Borrower against any and all of the Indebtedness of the Borrower, irrespective of whether or not the Lender shall have made any demand under this Agreement or the Note and although such obligations may be unmatured. The Lender agrees promptly to notify the Borrower after any such set-off and application, provided that the failure to give such notice shall not affect the validity of such set-off and application. The rights of the Lender under this Section are in addition to other rights and remedies (including but not limited to other rights of set-off) which the Lender may have.

ARTICLE 7

CONDITIONS OF LENDING

The obligations of the Lender to make the Advances pursuant to this Agreement are subject to the conditions precedent stated in this Article 7.

Section 7.01 *First Advance.* The obligation of the Lender to make the first Advance under this Agreement is subject to the following conditions precedent, wherein each document to be delivered to the Lender shall be in form and substance satisfactory to it and at Borrower's cost and expense:

(a) Closing. The Borrower shall have delivered to the Lender (unless waived by the Lender) at least three (3) Business Days' advance written notice of the closing date, which shall be a Business Day not later than 30 days from the date of this Agreement, for the delivery of all instruments, certificates and opinions referred to in this Section not theretofore delivered (except as to the Compliance Certificate, which is to be delivered at the time provided in Subsection 7.01(c) hereof).

(b) Note. The Borrower shall have duly and validly issued, executed and delivered the Note to the Lender.

(c) Compliance Certificate. The Lender shall have received a Compliance Certificate substantially in the form of Exhibit B hereto, which shall be true and correct and dated as of the date of the funding of the first Advance.

(d) Certificates. The Lender shall have received a certificate signed by the Secretary of Borrower certifying (i) the names, titles, and true signatures of the officers of Borrower authorized to sign this Agreement, the Note, the Security Instruments and the other documents or certificates to be delivered pursuant thereto, and (ii) the resolutions of the Board of Directors of Borrower authorizing, among other things, this Agreement and all transactions contemplated hereby, together with all affidavits and documents evidencing other necessary partnership or corporate action with respect to any thereof.

(e) Corporate Documents. The Lender shall have received a copy, certified as true by an appropriate officer of the Borrower of the articles of incorporation and bylaws of Borrower.

(f) Opinion of Borrower's Counsel. The Lender shall have received from counsel for the Borrower and its Subsidiaries, a favorable written opinion as to (i) the matters contained in Sections 3.01 through 3.05, 3.21 and 3.22; (ii) such counsel's knowledge of pending or threatened material litigation or governmental or regulatory proceedings against the Borrower or any Subsidiary; and (iii) such other matters incident to the formation of the Borrower or the transactions herein contemplated as the Lender may reasonably request.

(g) Recordings. The Master Deed of Trust shall have been duly delivered to the appropriate offices of each Initial County for filing or recording, and the Lender shall have received confirmations of receipt thereof from the appropriate filing or recording offices.

(h) Loans to One Borrower Affidavit. The Borrower and each Guarantor, if any, shall have executed and delivered to the Lender a Loans to One Borrower Affidavit in the form of Exhibit G hereto.

(i) Environmental Indemnity Agreement. The Lender shall have received an Environmental Indemnity Agreement executed by Borrower in the form of Exhibit [_____] hereto.

(j) Other. The Lender shall have received such other documents as it may reasonably have requested at any time at or prior to the closing referred to in Subsection 7.01(a).

Section 7.02 *Construction Facility Advances.*

(a) Each Construction Facility Advance. The obligation of the Lender to make each Construction Facility Advance (whether initial, interim or final) is subject, in addition to the conditions precedent set forth in Section 7.01, to the following further conditions precedent:

(i) Loan Request. The Lender shall have received the appropriate Loan Request satisfactory to the Lender.

(ii) Work Completed. All work on each Lot and Home financed under the Construction Facility that is required to have been completed for such Lot and Home to satisfy the requirements for the Percentage of Completion set forth in the most current Inventory Status Report for such Lot and Home shall have been completed and performed in a good and workmanlike manner, all materials and fixtures usually installed and furnished at such stage of construction shall have been furnished and installed, and all construction materials and fixtures shall have been incorporated in the Homes on such Lots, all substantially in accordance with the Plans and Specifications.

(iii) Inspection. At the Lender's option, the Lender shall have inspected the Lots and Homes financed under the Construction Facility, either by its personnel or through inspectors acceptable to the Lender, and shall have made a determination that the Percentage of Completion of each of such Homes is as reflected in the most current Completion Facility Status Report and shall have approved the progress of such construction.

(iv) No Default. The fact that immediately after such Advance, no Default shall have occurred and be continuing.

(v) Representations and Warranties. The fact that the representations and warranties of the Borrower and each Subsidiary contained in this Agreement or any other Security Instrument (other than those representations and warranties which are by their terms limited to the date of the agreement in which they are initially made) are true and correct in all material respects on and as of the date of such Advance.

(vi) No Material Adverse Change. There shall have occurred, in the sole opinion of the Lender, no change, either in any case or in the aggregate, in the condition, financial or otherwise, of the Borrower or any Subsidiary or with respect to the Borrower's or any Subsidiary's Properties from the facts represented in any Security Instrument, including this Agreement, which would have a Material Adverse Effect.

(vii) Title Update. Upon request by the Lender, the Borrower shall obtain from the appropriate Title Insurer a title report showing that since the date of issuance of the applicable Title Binder, there are no liens affecting the Property covered by such Title Binder other than those expressly listed in such Title Binder.

(viii) Other. The Lender shall have received such other documents as it may reasonably have requested at any time or prior to funding such Advance and all fees then due and payable hereunder shall have been paid.

Each borrowing hereunder shall be deemed to be a representation and warranty by the Borrower on the date of such borrowing as to the facts specified in Subsections 7.02(a)(iv) and (v).

(b) Initial Advance. The obligation of the Lender to make each Initial Advance is subject to the following further conditions precedent:

(i) Mortgage and Financing Statement. A Mortgage and Financing Statement covering the Lots identified in the Loan Request shall have been executed by the Borrower; the Mortgage shall have been duly delivered to the appropriate offices of the appropriate Valid County or Counties for filing or recording, and the Lender shall have received confirmations of receipt thereof from the appropriate filing or recording offices; and the Financing Statement shall have been delivered to the Office of the Texas Secretary of State for filing, and the Lender shall have received confirmation of the receipt thereof from the Office of the Texas Secretary of State.

(ii) Title Binder. The Lender shall have received a paid Title Binder dated the date of the Initial Advance in the amount of the Appraised Value of the associated Lots and the Homes to be constructed thereon. The Title Binder shall (x) show fee simple title vested in the Borrower to the associated Lots, (y) bind the Title Insurer to insure the Lien of the Mortgage on such Lots in favor of the Lender to be a valid first and prior Lien free and clear of all defects or encumbrances other than Excepted Liens and except as the Lender shall approve in writing, and (z) contain no survey exceptions not theretofore approved by the Lender in writing, and the status of the title to the Lots shown therein shall otherwise be satisfactory to the Lender. It is hereby expressly agreed and understood that the recordation of a Mortgage subject to specific title exceptions and the acceptance of a Title Binder shall not mean or indicate that the Lender has approved the status of the title to the Lots as shown in such Title Binder or otherwise. The Lender has the right to require that the Borrower remove or cure any and all impediments, whether of record or otherwise, which affect the development, construction, leasing, sale or operation of such Lots or the Homes to be constructed thereon.

(iii) Plat of Approved Subdivision, Etc. The Lender shall have received and approved (x) a copy of the plat of the Approved Subdivision, which shall be entirely located in the State of Texas, in which the associated Lots are located, identifying the location of each such Lot, and (y) evidence satisfactory to the Lender that the subdivision in which the associated Lots are located is an Approved Subdivision as defined herein in all respects.

(iv) Plans and Specifications, Etc. The Lender shall have received and approved (x) Plans and Specifications for each Home to be constructed on the associated Lots; (y) a Construction Cost Schedule showing the budgeted construction costs for each Home; and (z) all governmental and non-governmental approvals required for the construction of Homes on the associated Lots.

(v) No Construction Started. The Borrower shall provide the Lender with satisfactory evidence that no construction was started on any associated Lot prior to the recording of the Mortgage granting the Lender a Lien in such Lot.

(vi) Number of Lots. Each Loan Request for an Initial Advance shall be associated with a minimum of one (1) Lot (unless the Lender shall agree otherwise).

(vii) Appraisal. The Lender shall have obtained at Borrower's expense, for each Home that the Borrower desires to finance under the Construction Facility, an Appraisal which shall be dated not more than thirty (30) days prior to the date of such Initial Advance for such Home.

(viii) Other. Upon request by the Lender, the Borrower shall furnish to the Lender, each in form and substance satisfactory to the Lender, indemnity bonds and waivers of liens or claims on the Lots and Homes being financed by the Construction Facility as well as any construction contracts, other documents or invoices related thereto.

(ix) Advance Delivery. Any document, instrument, commitment, or other writing or written evidence required to be provided pursuant to Subsection 7.02(b)(i) through (viii) shall have been furnished to the Lender at least fifteen (15) Business Days prior to the date upon which the Lender is to fund the applicable Initial Advance pursuant to Section 2.04. Additionally, the legal description of the Lots and Homes associated with the applicable Initial Advance shall be furnished at least fifteen (15) days prior to the date upon which the Lender is to fund such Initial Advance.

(x) Commencement of Construction. Borrower shall execute and deliver to Lender an Affidavit of Commencement of Construction in substantially the form attached hereto as Exhibit I and specifying a date of commencement of construction which is later than the date the Mortgage relating to the respective Lot was recorded.

(xi) Site Plan. Borrower shall deliver to Lender a site plan showing the location of the Home on the respective Lot.

(xii) Borrower's Affidavit. Borrower shall execute and deliver to Lender a Borrower's Affidavit in the form of Exhibit L hereto.

In the event Borrower complies with the terms of this Section 7.02 and Lender is satisfied that all terms of this Agreement have been duly satisfied with respect to a particular loan request, the Lender shall make an Initial Advance with respect to the Lots described in the Loan Request. In addition, the Lender may, at the time of such Initial Advance, make such additional Interim Advances as may be appropriate pursuant to the terms of this Agreement.

(c) *Special Procedure*

(i) It is contemplated that the Borrower may request Initial Advances (and subsequent Interim Advances) on Property which has become subject to a Mortgage and Financing Statement as well as the subject of a Title Binder prior to the submission of a Loan Request covering the Property. In such event, Lender will only make an Initial Advance with respect to such Loan Request if Borrower has satisfied all other conditions to an Initial Advance in this Agreement, including, without limitation, Subsections 7.02(a) and (b).

(ii) In the event the Loan Request fails to comply with all of the provisions hereof, the Lender shall execute a Partial Release of lien as provided in Exhibit [_____] hereof and shall execute a Financing Statement Change upon the form specified in Exhibit [_____] hereof and the Lender shall be under no obligation to make an Initial Advance (or any other advance whatsoever) with respect to such Loan Request.

(d) Final Advance. The obligation of the Lender to make each Final Advance is subject to the following further conditions precedent:

(i) Completion of Construction. All Homes subject to the request for a Final Advance shall have been completed in substantial compliance with the Plans and Specifications, as verified by the Lender through inspection either by its personnel or through inspectors acceptable to the Lender, and that all requirements for the Percentage of Completion of any such Home to be deemed to be one hundred percent (100%), as provided in the Disbursement Schedule applicable to such Home, shall have been fully complied with to the satisfaction of the Lender.

(ii) Governmental Requirements. The Lender shall have received evidence satisfactory to it that all Governmental Requirements and non-governmental requirements regarding the construction and completion of each such Home have been satisfied.

(iii) No Mechanic's Liens. The Lender shall have received evidence satisfactory to it that all actual construction costs for each such Home have been paid in full, or that such payment has been adequately provided for, and that no mechanic's or materialmen's liens or other encumbrances have been filed and remain in effect against all or any part of such Lots.

ARTICLE 8

MISCELLANEOUS

Section 8.01 *Notices.* Any notice required or permitted to be given under or in connection with this Agreement, the other Security Instruments (except as may otherwise be expressly required therein) or the Note shall be in writing and shall be mailed by first class or express mail, postage prepaid, or sent by telex, telegram, telecopy or other similar form of rapid transmission confirmed by mailing (by first class or express mail, postage prepaid) written confirmation at substantially the same time as such rapid transmission, or personally delivered to an officer of the receiving party. All such communications shall be mailed, sent or delivered,

(a) if to the Borrower, to its address shown at the beginning of this Agreement, or to such other address or to such individual's or department's attention as it may have furnished the Lender in writing; or

(b) if to the Lender, to its address shown at the beginning of this Agreement, or to such other address or to such individual's or department's attention as it may have furnished the Borrower in writing.

Any communication so addressed and mailed shall be deemed to be given within 48 hours of when so mailed, except that Loan Requests or communications related to Loan Requests shall not be effective until actually received by the Lender; any notice so sent by rapid transmission shall be deemed to be given when receipt of such transmission is acknowledged; and any communication so delivered in person shall be deemed to be given when receipted for by, or actually received by, an authorized officer of the Borrower or the Lender, as the case may be.

Section 8.02 *Amendments and Waivers.* Any provision of this Agreement, the other Security Instruments or the Note may be amended or waived if, but only if, such amendment or waiver is in writing and is signed by the Borrower (and/or any other Person which is a party to any Security Instrument being amended or with respect to which a waiver is being obtained) and the Lender.

Section 8.03 *Invalidity.* In the event that any one or more of the provisions contained in the Note, this Agreement or in any other Security Instrument shall, for any reason, be held invalid, illegal or unenforceable in any respect, such invalidity, illegality or unenforceability shall not affect any other provision of the Note, this Agreement or any other Security Instrument.

Section 8.04 *Survival of Agreements.* All representations and warranties of the Borrower herein or in the other Security Instruments, and all covenants and agreements herein not fully performed before the effective date or dates of this Agreement and of the other Security Instruments, shall survive such date or dates.

Section 8.05 *Successors and Assigns.* The Note, this Agreement and any other Security Instrument shall be binding upon and enure to the benefit of and be enforceable by the respective successors and assigns of the parties hereto. The Borrower shall not, however, have the right to assign its rights under this Agreement or any interest herein without the prior written consent of the Lender. The Lender may sell participations in the Note or other Indebtedness of the Borrower incurred or to be incurred pursuant to this Agreement to other Lenders without notice to or the consent of Borrower. In the event that the Lender sells participations in the Note or other Indebtedness of the Borrower incurred or to be incurred pursuant to this Agreement to other lenders, each of such other lenders shall have the right to set off against such Indebtedness and similar rights or Liens to the same extent as may be available to the Lender.

Section 8.06 *Renewal, Extension or Rearrangement.* All provisions of this Agreement and of any other Security Instruments relating to the Note or other Indebtedness shall apply with equal force and effect to each and all promissory notes hereinafter executed which in whole or in part represent a renewal, extension for any period, increase or rearrangement of any part of the Indebtedness originally represented by the Note or of any part of such other Indebtedness.

Section 8.07 *Waivers.* No course of dealing on the part of the Lender, its officers, employees, consultants or agents, including but not limited to any course of dealing whereby the Lender does not require complete compliance with the terms, provisions and conditions hereof, nor any failure or delay by the Lender with respect to exercising any right, power or privilege of the Lender under the Note, this Agreement or any other Security Instrument shall operate as a waiver thereof, except as otherwise provided in Section 8.02 and, without limiting the foregoing, the Lender may at any time require complete compliance with any and all terms, provisions and conditions hereof.

Section 8.08 *No Liability of Lender.* The Lender shall have no liability, obligation or responsibility whatsoever with respect to the construction of any Home except to make Advances hereunder upon the terms and conditions herein stated in the Lender's sole function as lender, and the only consideration passing from the Lender to the Borrower is the loan proceeds in accordance with and subject to the terms and conditions of this Agreement. The Lender shall not be obligated to inspect any Lot mortgaged to the Lender or for the construction of a Home thereon. The Lender shall have the right from time to time to waive any of the terms of this Agreement without prejudice to its right to require strict compliance in the future, and no Person shall be a third party beneficiary of this Agreement or be entitled to require or rely upon the Lender's enforcement of this Agreement. The Borrower has selected all architects, engineers, contractors, subcontractors, materialmen, as well as all others furnishing services or materials to the construction of such Homes, and the Lender has, and shall have, no responsibility whatsoever for them or any other party or for their performance or default or for the quality of their materials or workmanship or for any failure to construct, complete, protect, or insure such Homes, or for the payment of costs of labor, materials, or services supplied for the construction of such Homes, or for the performance of any obligation of the Borrower whatsoever. Nothing, including but not limited to any disbursement of loan proceeds or acceptance hereunder of any document or instrument, shall be construed as a representation or warranty, express or implied, to any party by the Lender. Approval by Lender of the Plans and Specifications shall be deemed to be strictly limited to consent by Lender to the Home being constructed in accordance therewith and shall not be deemed to imply any warranty, representation, or approval by Lender that the Home, if so constructed, will be structurally sound, will comply with all Governmental Requirements, will be fit for any particular purpose, or will have a market value of any particular magnitude.

Section 8.09 *Indemnities.* The Borrower hereby agrees to indemnify the Lender, its officers, directors, employees, representatives, agents and Affiliates from, hold each of them harmless against, and promptly upon demand pay or reimburse each of them for, any and all claims, demands, and causes of action, loss, damage, liabilities, costs and expenses (including attorneys' fees and court costs) of any and every kind or character, known or unknown, fixed or contingent, incurred by the Lender or asserted by any Person, including but not limited to employees of the Borrower, any contractor constructing the Homes and the employees of any such contractor, any tenant of the Borrower, any subtenant or concessionaire of such tenant, and the employees and business or other invitees or trespassers of any such tenant, subtenant or concessionaire arising, (i) from or out of the construction, use, occupancy, or possession of the Homes, and (ii) out of or in any way related to (A) the breach of any representation or warranty as set forth herein regarding environmental matters, (B) the failure of the Borrower or any Subsidiary to perform any obligation herein required to be performed pursuant to Environmental Laws, or (C) any act, omission, event or circumstance pertaining to environmental matters that is associated with the ownership, construction, occupancy, operation, use and/or maintenance of any Property of the Borrower, regardless of whether the act, omission, event or circumstance constituted a violation of any Environmental Laws at the time of its existence or occurrence. The foregoing indemnity shall apply with respect to matters caused by or arising out of the negligence of the Lender but shall not apply with respect to matters caused by or arising out of the gross negligence or willful misconduct of the Lender. The provisions of this Section shall survive the final payment of all Indebtedness and the termination of this Agreement and shall continue thereafter in full force and effect.

Section 8.10 *Cumulative Rights.* All rights and remedies of the Lender under the Note, this Agreement and each other Security Instrument shall be cumulative, and the exercise or partial exercise of any such right or remedy shall not preclude the exercise of any other right or remedy.

Section 8.11 *Singular and Plural.* Words used herein in the singular, where the context so permits, shall be deemed to include the plural and vice versa. The definitions of words in the singular herein shall apply to such words when used in the plural where the context so permits and vice versa.

Section 8.12 *Construction.* This Agreement is, and the Note will be, a contract made under and shall be construed in accordance with and governed by the laws of the United States of America and the State of Texas, as such laws are now in effect and, with respect to usury laws, if any, applicable to the Lender and to the extent allowed thereby, as such laws may hereafter be in effect which allow a higher maximum nonusurious interest rate than such laws now allow. Tex.Rev. Civ.Stat.Ann. art. 5069, ch. 15 (which regulates certain revolving credit loan accounts and revolving triparty accounts) shall not apply to this Agreement or the Note.

Section 8.13 *Interest.* The real property covered by each Mortgage is "residential real property", and the Advances are or will be secured by a first lien on residential real property within the meaning of Part A, Title V of the Depository Institutions Deregulation and Monetary Control Act of 1980, as amended (the "*Act*"), and the regulations promulgated thereunder. If, for any reason, the provisions of Part A, Title V of the Act shall be found not to exempt any and all interest and other charges contracted for, charged, taken, received or reserved in connection with the Advances from any limitations otherwise applicable, then the provisions of the immediately following paragraph shall apply, but otherwise the immediately following paragraph shall be inapplicable.

It is the intention of the parties hereto to conform strictly to usury laws applicable to the Lender and the Transactions. Accordingly, if the Transactions would be usurious under applicable law, then, notwithstanding anything to the contrary in the Note, this Agreement or in any other Security Instrument or agreement entered into in connection with the Transactions or as security for the Note, it is agreed as follows: (i) the aggregate of all consideration which constitutes interest under applicable law that is contracted for, taken, reserved, charged or received under the Note, this Agreement or under any of such other Security Instruments or agreements or otherwise in connection with the Transactions shall under no circumstances exceed the maximum amount allowed by such applicable law, and any excess shall be cancelled automatically and if theretofore paid shall be credited by the Lender on the principal amount of the Indebtedness (or, to the extent that the principal amount of the Indebtedness shall have been or would thereby be paid in full, refunded by the Lender to the Borrower); (ii) in the event that the maturity of the Note is accelerated for any reason, or in the event of any required or permitted prepayment, then such consideration that constitutes interest under applicable law may never include more than the maximum amount allowed by such applicable law; and (iii) excess interest, if any, provided for in this Agreement or otherwise in connection with the Transactions shall be cancelled automatically and, if theretofore paid, shall be credited by the Lender on the principal amount of the Indebtedness (or, to the extent that the principal amount of the Indebtedness shall have been or would thereby be paid in full, refunded by the Lender to the Borrower). The right to accelerate the maturity of the Note does not include the right to accelerate any interest which has not otherwise accrued on the date of such acceleration, and the Lender does not intend to collect any unearned interest in the event of acceleration. All sums paid or agreed to be paid to the Lender for the use, forbearance or detention of sums included in the Indebtedness shall, to the extent permitted by applicable law, be amortized, prorated, allocated and spread throughout the full term of the Note until payment in full so that the rate or amount of interest on account of the Indebtedness does not exceed the applicable usury ceiling, if any. As used in this Section, the term "*applicable law*" shall mean the law of the State of Texas (or the law of any other jurisdiction whose laws may be mandatorily applicable notwithstanding other provisions of this Agreement), or law of the United States of America applicable to the Lender and the Transactions which would permit the Lender to contract for, charge, take, reserve or receive a greater amount of interest than under Texas (or such other jurisdiction's) law. To the extent that Article 5069–1.04 of the Texas Revised Civil Statutes is relevant to the Lender for the purpose of determining the Highest Lawful Rate, the Lender hereby elects to determine the applicable rate ceiling under such Article by the indicated (weekly) rate ceiling from time to time in effect, subject to the Lender's right subsequently to change such method in accordance with applicable law. In no event shall the provisions of Tex.Rev.Civ.Stat. art. 5069–2.01 through 5069–8.06 or 5069–15.01 through 5069–15.11 be applicable to this Agreement or the Note.

If at any time the sum of the Margin Percentage plus the Prime Rate exceeds the Highest Lawful Rate, the rate of interest to accrue on the Note shall be limited to the Highest Lawful Rate, but any subsequent reductions in the Prime Rate shall not reduce the interest to accrue on the Note below the Highest Lawful Rate until the total amount of interest accrued on the Note equals the amount of interest which would have accrued if a varying rate per annum equal to the sum of the Margin Percentage plus the Prime Rate had at all times been in effect. If at maturity or final payment of the Note the total amount of interest paid or accrued on the Note under the foregoing provisions is less than the total amount of interest which would have been paid or accrued if a varying rate per annum equal to the sum of the Margin Percentage plus the Prime Rate had at all times been in effect, then the Borrower agrees, to the fullest extent permitted by law, to pay to the Lender an amount equal to the difference between (a) the lesser of (i) the amount of interest which would have been paid or accrued on the Note if the Highest Lawful Rate had at all times been in effect or (ii) the amount of interest which would have been paid or accrued on the Note if a varying rate per annum equal to the sum of the Margin Percentage plus the Prime Rate had at all times been in effect, and (b) the amount of interest paid or accrued in accordance with the other provisions of the Note.

Section 8.14 *References.* The words "herein," "hereof," "hereunder" and other words of similar import when used in this Agreement refer to this Agreement as a whole, and not to any particular article, section or subsection. Any reference herein to an Article, Section or Subsection shall be deemed to refer to the applicable Article, Section or Subsection of this Agreement unless otherwise stated herein. Any reference herein to an exhibit shall be deemed to refer to the applicable exhibit attached hereto unless otherwise stated herein.

Section 8.15 *Taxes, etc.* Any taxes (excluding income taxes) payable or ruled payable by federal or state authority in respect of the Note, this Agreement or the other Security Instruments shall be paid by the Borrower, together with interest and penalties, if any.

Section 8.16 *Governmental Regulation.* Anything contained in this Agreement to the contrary notwithstanding, the Lender shall not be obligated to extend credit to the Borrower in an amount in violation of any limitation or prohibition provided by any applicable statute or regulation.

Section 8.17 *Exhibits.* The exhibits attached to this Agreement are incorporated herein and shall be considered a part of this Agreement for the purposes stated herein, except that in the event of any conflict between any of the provisions of such exhibits and the provisions of this Agreement, the provisions of this Agreement shall prevail.

Section 8.18 *Titles of Articles, Sections and Subsections.* All titles or headings to articles, sections, subsections or other divisions of this Agreement or the exhibits hereto are only for the convenience of the parties and shall not be construed to have any effect or meaning with respect to the other content of such articles, sections, subsections or other divisions, such other content being controlling as to the agreement between the parties hereto.

Section 8.19 *Satisfaction Requirement.* If any agreement, certificate, instrument or other writing, or any action taken or to be taken, is by the terms of this

Agreement required to be satisfactory to any party, the determination of such satisfaction shall be made by such party in its sole and exclusive judgment exercised in good faith.

Section 8.20 *Entire Agreement.* **THIS WRITTEN AGREEMENT, THE NOTE, AND THE SECURITY INSTRUMENTS REPRESENT THE FINAL AGREEMENT BETWEEN THE PARTIES AND MAY NOT BE CONTRADICTED BY EVIDENCE OF PRIOR, CONTEMPORANEOUS OR SUBSEQUENT ORAL AGREEMENTS OF THE PARTIES. THERE ARE NO UNWRITTEN ORAL AGREEMENTS BETWEEN THE PARTIES.**

IN WITNESS WHEREOF, the parties hereto have caused this instrument to be duly executed as of the date first above written.

BORROWER

LENDER:

EXHIBIT A

FORM OF
CONSTRUCTION FACILITY NOTE

$[_____],000   _____, Texas   [_____], 1992

[_____], a Texas corporation with principal offices at [_____] (the "*Borrower*"), for value received, promises and agrees to pay on or before [_____], or such earlier time as provided in the Loan Agreement hereinafter mentioned, to the order of _____ (the "*Lender*") in coin or currency of the United States of America which at the time of payment is legal tender for the payment of public and private debts, the principal sum of [_____] MILLION AND NO/100 DOLLARS ($[_____],000,000), or so much thereof as may be advanced pursuant to the Loan Agreement hereinafter mentioned.

All capitalized terms which are used but not defined in this Note shall have the same meanings as in the Loan Agreement dated as of [_____], among the Borrower and the Lender (such Loan Agreement, together with all amendments or supplements thereto, being the "*Loan Agreement*").

In addition to the principal sum referred to in the first paragraph of this Note, the Borrower also agrees to pay interest on all amounts hereof so advanced and remaining from time to time unpaid hereon from the date hereof until maturity at a varying rate per annum which is one and one-half percent (1.50%) per annum above the Prime Rate, but in no event to exceed the Highest Lawful Rate. Past due principal and interest shall bear interest at a varying rate per annum which is five percent (5%) per annum above the Prime Rate, but in no event to exceed the Highest Lawful Rate. Adjustments in the varying interest rate shall be made on the same day as each change announced in the Prime Rate and, to the extent allowed by law, on the effective date of any change in the Highest Lawful Rate.

Accrued interest is due and payable monthly, the first such payment being due and payable on [_____] 1, 1992, and the remaining payments being due and payable on the first day of each and every succeeding month thereafter and at the maturity of this Note.

Each payment and prepayment made by the Borrower under this Note shall be made in immediately available funds before 2:00 p.m., _____ time, on the date that such payment or prepayment is required to be made. Any payment or prepayment received and accepted by the Bank after such time shall be considered for all purposes (including the calculation of interest, to the extent permitted by law) as having been made on the Bank's next following Business Day.

If the date for any payment or prepayment hereunder falls on a day which is not a Business Day, then for all purposes of this note the same shall be deemed to have fallen on the next following Business Day, and such extension of time shall in such case be included in the computation of payments of interest.

The Borrower and any and each co-maker, guarantor, accommodation party, endorser or other Person liable for the payment or collection of this Note expressly waive demand and presentment for payment, notice of nonpayment, notice of intent to accelerate, notice of acceleration, protest, notice of protest, notice of dishonor, bringing of suit, and diligence in taking any action to collect amounts called for hereunder and in the handling of Property at any time existing as security in connection herewith, and shall be directly and primarily liable for the payment of all sums owing and to be owing hereon, regardless of and without any notice, diligence, act or omission as or with respect to the collection of any amount called for hereunder or in connection with any Lien at any time had or existing as security for any amount called for hereunder.

This Note is issued pursuant to and is entitled to the benefits of the Loan Agreement. Reference is made to the Loan Agreement for provisions for the acceleration of the maturity hereof on the occurrence of certain events specified therein, for interest rate computations in the event that the otherwise agreed rate is at any time limited by the Highest Lawful Rate, for the reimbursement of attorneys' fees or other costs of collection or enforcement, and for all other pertinent purposes. It is contemplated that by reason of prepayment hereon there may be times when no Indebtedness is owning hereunder; but notwithstanding such occurrences, this Note shall remain valid and shall be in full force and effect as to loans made pursuant to the Loan Agreement subsequent to each occurrence.

This Note has been made and issued and is payable in the State of Texas and shall be governed by the laws of the United States of America and the State of Texas as such laws are now in effect and, with respect to usury laws, if any, applicable to the Lender and to the extent allowed thereby, as such laws may hereafter be in effect which allow a higher maximum nonusurious interest rate than such laws now allow. Tex.Rev.Civ.Stat.Ann. art. 5069, Ch. 15 (which regulates certain revolving triparty accounts) shall not apply to this Note.

[_____], a Texas corporation

By: _____
[_____]
President

EXHIBIT B

FORM OF
COMPLIANCE CERTIFICATE

The undersigned hereby certifies that he is the _____ of [_____], a Texas corporation (the "*Borrower*"), and that as such he is authorized to execute this certificate on behalf of the Borrower. With reference to the Loan Agreement dated as of [_____], 1992 (together with all amendments or supplements thereto being the "*Agreement*") between the Borrower and _____ (the "*Lender*"), the undersigned further certifies, represents and warrants as follows (each capitalized term used herein having the same meaning given to it in the Agreement unless otherwise specified):

(a) The representations and warranties of the Borrower contained in the Agreement and otherwise made in writing by or on behalf of the Borrower pursuant to the Agreement were true and correct when made, and are repeated at and as of the time of delivery hereof and are true and correct at and as of the time of delivery hereof.

(b) The Borrower has performed and complied with all agreements and conditions contained in the Agreement required to be performed or complied with by it prior to or at the time of delivery hereof.

(c) Neither the Borrower nor any Subsidiary has incurred any material liabilities, direct or contingent, since [_____], except as disclosed or referred to in the Financial Statements or as set forth in Exhibit C to the Agreement.

(d) Since [_____], no change has occurred, either in any case or in the aggregate, in the condition, financial or otherwise, of the Borrower or any Subsidiary which would have a Material Adverse Effect, except as disclosed in Exhibit C to the Loan Agreement.

(e) There exists, and, after giving effect to the loan or loans with respect to which this certificate is being delivered, will exist, no Default under the Agreement or any event or circumstance which constitutes, or with notice or passage of time (or both) would constitute, an event of default under any loan or credit agreement, indenture, mortgage deed of trust, security agreement or other agreement or other instrument evidencing or pertaining to any Debt of the Borrower or any Subsidiary, or under any material agreement or instrument to which the Borrower or any Subsidiary is a party or by which the Borrower or any Subsidiary is bound.

(f) The following is a true and accurate statement of actual figures as compared to the figures required by Article 5 of the Agreement for the calendar [quarter] [year] ending _____, 19__:

    (i) Section 5.14—Net Worth:
        Required: $[_____]   Actual: $_____

    (ii) Section 5.15—Ratio of Total Liabilities to Tangible Net Worth:
        Required: [_____] to 1   Actual: _____ to 1

    (iii) Section 5.17—Ratio of Current Assets to Current Liabilities:
        Required: [_____] to 1   Actual: _____ to 1

    (iv) Section 5.17—Working Capital:
        Required: $[_____]   Actual: _____

EXECUTED AND DELIVERED this _____ day of _____, 19__.

[_____], a Texas corporation

By: _____
[_____]
President

EXHIBIT C

DISCLOSURES

The following constitute all disclosures required to be made by the Borrower in accordance with the following Sections of the Loan Agreement dated as of [_____], 1992 (the "*Agreement*"):

Section 3.06: Consents or approvals required:

Section 3.07: Material adverse changes occurred since December 31, 1990:

Section 3.08: Investments, advances and guaranties other than as reflected in the Financial Statements:

Section 3.09: Material liabilities and litigation or actions other than those disclosed or referred to in the Financial Statements:

Sections 3.11 and 5.02(b): Liens other than those referred to in the Financial Statements and other than Excepted Liens:

Section 3.12: Defaults under the Agreement or other instruments:

Section 3.25: Property or operations in violation of Environmental Laws:

Section 5.03(a): Investments, loans or advances other than as set forth in the Financial Statements:

[_____], a Texas corporation

By: _____
[_____]
President

ATTENTION: COUNTY CLERK—THIS INSTRUMENT COVERS GOODS THAT ARE OR ARE TO BECOME FIXTURES ON THE REAL PROPERTY DESCRIBED HEREIN AND IS TO BE FILED FOR RECORD IN THE RECORDS WHERE MORTGAGES ON REAL ESTATE ARE RECORDED. ADDITIONALLY, THIS INSTRUMENT SHOULD BE APPROPRIATELY INDEXED, NOT ONLY AS A MORTGAGE, BUT ALSO AS A FINANCING STATEMENT COVERING GOODS THAT ARE OR ARE TO BECOME FIXTURES ON THE REAL PROPERTY DESCRIBED HEREIN. THE MAILING ADDRESSES OF THE GRANTOR (DEBTOR) AND BENEFICIARY (SECURED PARTY) ARE SET FORTH IN THIS INSTRUMENT.

EXHIBIT D
MASTER FORM OF
DEED OF TRUST AND SECURITY AGREEMENT

This **MASTER FORM OF DEED OF TRUST AND SECURITY AGREEMENT** (hereinafter referred to as the "Master Form Deed of Trust") is recorded by and for the use and benefit of _____ (together with the subsequent holder or holders, from time to time, of the Note (as defined in Paragraph 1.1(*l*) hereinbelow, the "Beneficiary"):

WITNESSETH:

It is anticipated that from time to time a Deed of Trust and Security Agreement (each a "Deed of Trust and Security Agreement") shall be entered into for the benefit of the Beneficiary pursuant to which the Grantor named in such Deed of Trust and Security Agreement will **BARGAIN, GRANT, SELL, ASSIGN, MORTGAGE, TRANSFER and CONVEY** unto the Trustee named in such Deed of Trust and Security Agreement, and his successors and substitutes in trust thereunder, for the use and benefit of the Beneficiary, an interest in certain real and personal property described in each such Deed of Trust and Security Agreement (such description of real and personal property may incorporate provisions of this Master Form Deed of Trust by reference).

It is intended that each Deed of Trust and Security Agreement will incorporate by reference various provisions of this Master Form Deed of Trust, and it is intended that such provisions shall be effective in each Deed of Trust and Security Agreement as if set forth therein originally and in full. Any capitalized terms used in the language incorporated into each such Deed of Trust and Security Agreement shall have the meaning assigned such term in such Deed of Trust and Security Agreement.

ARTICLE 1
DEFINITIONS

1.1 *Definitions.* As used herein, the following terms shall have the following meanings:

(a) *Buildings:* Any and all buildings, covered garages, utility sheds, workrooms, air conditioning towers, open parking areas and other improvements, and any and all additions, alterations, betterments or appurtenances thereto, now or at any time hereafter situated, placed or constructed upon the Land (as defined in Paragraph 1.1(h) hereinbelow) or any part thereof.

(b) *Event of Default:* Any happening or occurrence described in Article 6 hereinbelow.

(c) *Fixtures:* All materials, supplies, equipment, machinery, apparatus and other items now or hereafter acquired by Grantor and now or hereafter attached or affixed to, installed in or used in connection with (temporarily or permanently) any of the Buildings or the Land, including but not limited to any and all partitions, dynamos, window screens and shades, drapes, rugs and other floor coverings, awnings, motors, engines, boilers, furnaces, pipes, plumbing, cleaning, call and sprinkler systems, fire extinguishing apparatus and equipment, water tanks, swimming pools, heating, ventilating, plumbing, laundry, incinerating, air conditioning and air cooling equipment and systems, gas and electric machinery, appurtenances and equipment, disposals, dishwashers, refrigerators and ranges, counter-top units, appliances, recreational equipment and facilities of all kinds, and water, gas, electrical, storm and sanitary sewer facilities and all other utilities whether or not situated in easements, together with all accessions, replacements, betterments and substitutions for any of the foregoing and the proceeds thereof.

(d) *Governmental Authority:* Any and all courts, boards, agencies, departments, commissions, offices or authorities of any nature whatsoever for any governmental unit (federal, state, county, district, municipal, city or otherwise) whether now or hereafter in existence.

(e) *Grantor:* The Grantor shall be defined in each Deed of Trust and Security Agreement and shall include any and all subsequent owners of the Mortgaged Property (as defined in Paragraph 1.1(k) hereinbelow) or any part thereof.

(f) *Impositions:* All real estate and personal property taxes; water, gas, sewer, electricity and other utility rates and charges; charges for any easement, license or agreement maintained for the benefit of the Mortgaged Property; and all other taxes, charges and assessments and any interest, costs or penalties with respect thereto, general and special, ordinary and extraordinary, foreseen and unforeseen, of any kind and nature whatsoever which at any time prior to or after the execution hereof may be assessed, levied or imposed upon the Mortgaged Property or the Rents (as defined in Paragraph 1.1(q) hereinbelow) or the ownership, use, occupancy or enjoyment thereof.

(g) *Indebtedness:* Each Deed of Trust and Security Agreement shall describe the Indebtedness secured thereby.

(h) *Land:* The real estate or interest therein described in Exhibit A attached to each Deed of Trust and Security Agreement, all Buildings and Fixtures, and all rights, titles and interests appurtenant thereto.

(i) *Leases:* Any and all leases, subleases, licenses, concessions or other agreements (written or verbal, now or hereafter in effect) which grant a possessory interest in and to, or the right to use, the Mortgaged Property, and all other agreements, such as utility contracts, maintenance agreements and service contracts, which in any way relate to the use, occupancy, operation, maintenance, enjoyment or ownership of the Mortgaged Property, including without limitation, the leases (if any), save and except any and all leases, subleases or other agreements pursuant to which Grantor is granted a possessory interest in the Land.

(j) *Legal Requirements:* (i) any and all present and future judicial decisions, statutes, rulings, rules, regulations, permits, certificates or ordinances of any Governmental Authority in any way applicable to Grantor or the Mortgaged Property, including the ownership, use, occupancy, possession, operation, maintenance, alteration, repair or reconstruction thereof; (ii) if Grantor is not an individual, Grantor's presently or subsequently effective Bylaws and Articles or Certificate of Incorporation or Partnership, Limited Partnership, Joint Venture, Trust or other form of business association agreement; (iii) any and all Leases; and (iv) any and all leases, restrictive covenants and other contracts (written or oral) of any nature to which Grantor is or may be bound, including without limitation, any lease or other contract pursuant to which Grantor is granted a possessory interest in the Land.

(k) *Mortgaged Property:* The Land, Buildings, Fixtures, Personalty (as defined in Paragraph 1.1(*o*) hereinbelow) and Rents, together with:

(i) all rights, privileges, tenements, hereditaments, rights-of-way, easements, appendages and appurtenances in anywise appertaining thereto, and all right, title and interest of Grantor in and to any streets, ways, alleys, strips or gores of land adjoining the Land or any part thereof;

(ii) all betterments, additions, alterations, appurtenances, substitutions, replacements and revisions thereof and thereto and all reversions and remainders therein;

(iii) all of Grantor's right, title and interest in and to any awards, remuneration, settlements or compensation heretofore made or hereafter to be made by any Governmental Authority pertaining to the Land, Buildings, Fixtures or Personalty, including those for any vacation of, or change of grade in, any streets affecting the Land or the Buildings;

(iv) all of Grantor's general intangibles of any kind whether now existing or hereafter arising in connection with the Land, Buildings, Fixtures, Personalty and Rents, including but not limited to all contract rights, plans and specifications relating to the construction of improvements on the Land, and all rights now or hereafter existing in and to all security agreements, leases, and other contracts securing or otherwise relating to any such general intangibles; and

(v) any and all other security and collateral of any nature whatsoever, now or hereafter given for the repayment of the Indebtedness or the performance and discharge of the Obligations.

As used in this Deed of Trust, the term "Mortgaged Property" shall be expressly defined as meaning all or, where the context permits or requires, any portion of the above, and all or, where the context permits or requires, any interest therein.

(*l*) *Note:* Each Deed of Trust and Security Agreement shall describe the Note(s) secured thereby.

(m) *Obligations:* Any and all of the covenants, warranties, representations and other obligations (other than to repay the Indebtedness) made or undertaken by Grantor, or others to Beneficiary, Trustee or others as set forth in the Security Instruments or any lease, sublease or other agreement pursuant to which Grantor is granted a possessory interest in the Land.

(n) *Permitted Encumbrances:* The outstanding liens, easements, building lines, restrictions, security interests and other matters (if any) as reflected on Exhibit B attached to each Deed of Trust and Security Agreement or otherwise listed in a Mortgagee Title Policy Binder on Interim Construction Loan or a Mortgagee Policy of Title Insurance covering the Premises to the extent same are valid and subsisting, in full force and effect and do, in fact, cover or affect the Land described in Exhibit A attached to each Deed of Trust and Security

Agreement, and the lien and security interests created by the Security Instruments.

(o) *Personalty:* All of the right, title and interest of Grantor in and to all furniture, furnishings, equipment, machinery, goods, general intangibles, money, insurance proceeds, accounts, contract rights, inventory, all refundable, returnable or reimbursable fees, deposits or other funds or evidences of credit or indebtedness deposited by or on behalf of Grantor with any governmental agencies, boards, corporations, providers of utility services, public or private, including specifically but without limitation, all refundable, returnable or reimbursable tap fees, utility deposits, commitment fees and development costs, and all other personal property (other than the Fixtures) of any kind or character as defined in and subject to the provisions of the Texas Business and Commerce Code (Article 9—Secured Transactions), which are now or hereafter located or to be located upon, within or about the Land and the Buildings, or which are or may be used in or related to the planning, development, financing or operation of the Mortgaged Property, together with all accessories, replacements and substitutions thereto or therefor and the proceeds thereof.

(p) *Plans:* Any and all plans, specifications and other technical descriptions prepared for construction of any improvements on the Land, including any Building.

(q) *Rents:* All of the rents, revenues, income, proceeds, profits, security and other types of deposits, and other benefits paid or payable by parties to the Leases other than Grantor for using, leasing, licensing, possessing, operating from, residing in, selling or otherwise enjoying the Mortgaged Property.

(r) *Security Instruments:* This Deed of Trust, any loan agreement executed by Grantor as borrower in connection with the Indebtedness, including the Note, and any and all other instruments executed by Grantor or any other person in connection with or as security for the payment or performance of the Note or such loan agreement, as such agreements or instruments may be modified, amended, or supplemented from time to time.

(s) *Trustee:* That certain Trustee named in each Deed of Trust and Security Agreement or such Trustee's successor or substitute duly appointed in accordance with the provisions of Paragraph 10.3 hereof.

ARTICLE 2

GRANT

2.1 *Grant.* To secure the full and timely payment of the Indebtedness and the full and timely performance and discharge of the Obligations, Grantor has GRANTED, BARGAINED, SOLD and CONVEYED, and by these presents does GRANT, BARGAIN, SELL and CONVEY, unto Trustee the Mortgaged Property, subject, however, to the Permitted Encumbrances, TO HAVE AND TO HOLD the Mortgaged Property unto Trustee, forever, and Grantor does hereby bind itself, its successors and assigns to WARRANT AND FOREVER DEFEND the title to the Mortgaged Property unto Trustee against every person whomsoever lawfully claiming or to claim the same or any part thereof, subject to the enforceable claims, if any, of third parties in connection with the Permitted Encumbrances; provided, however, that if Grantor shall pay (or cause to be paid) the Indebtedness as and when the same shall become due and payable and shall perform and discharge (or cause to be performed and discharged) the Obligations on or before the date same are to be performed and discharged, then in that case only the liens, security interests, estates and rights granted by the Security Instruments shall terminate and be released by Beneficiary at Grantor's expense; otherwise same shall remain in full force and effect. A certificate or statement from Beneficiary confirming that the Indebtedness has not been paid in full or that the Obligations have not been fully performed and discharged shall be sufficient evidence thereof for the purposes of reliance by third parties on that fact.

ARTICLE 3
WARRANTIES AND REPRESENTATIONS

Grantor hereby unconditionally warrants and represents to Beneficiary as follows:

3.1 *Organization and Power.* Grantor (a) is a corporation, general partnership, limited partnership, joint venture, trust, or other type of business association, as the case may be, duly organized, validly existing and in good standing under the laws of the State of its formation or existence, and has complied with all conditions prerequisite to its doing business in the State where the Land is situated and (b) has all requisite power and all governmental certificates of authority, licenses, permits, qualifications and documentation to own, lease and operate its properties and to carry on its business as now being, and as proposed to be, conducted.

3.2 *Validity of Loan Instruments.* The execution, delivery and performance by Grantor of the Security Instruments, and the borrowing evidenced by the Note, (a) if Grantor is a corporation, general partnership, limited partnership, joint venture, trust or other type of business association, as the case may be, are within Grantor's powers and have been duly authorized by Grantor's Board of Directors, shareholders, partners, venturers, trustees or other necessary parties, and all other requisite action for such authorization has been taken; (b) have received all (if any) requisite prior governmental approval in order to be legally binding and enforceable in accordance with the terms thereof; and (c) will not violate, be in conflict with, result in a breach of or constitute (with due notice or lapse of time, or both) a default under, any Legal Requirement or result in the creation or imposition of any lien, charge or encumbrance of any nature whatsoever upon any of Grantor's property or assets, except as contemplated by the provisions of the Security Instruments. The Security Instruments constitute the legal, valid and binding obligations of Grantor, and others obligated under the terms of the Security Instruments, in accordance with their respective terms.

3.3 *Information.* All information, reports, papers and data given to Beneficiary with respect to Grantor or others obligated under the terms of the Security Instruments or with respect to the Mortgaged Property are accurate, complete and correct in all material respects and do not omit any fact, the inclusion of which is necessary to prevent the facts contained therein from being materially misleading.

3.4 *Title to Mortgaged Property and Lien of This Instrument.* Grantor has good and indefeasible title to the Land and Buildings in fee simple, and good and marketable title to the Fixtures and Personalty, free and clear of any liens, charges, encumbrances, security interests and adverse claims whatsoever except the Permitted Encumbrances. This Deed of Trust constitutes a valid, and subsisting first lien deed of trust on the Land, the Buildings and the Fixtures and a valid, subsisting, first security interest in and to, and a valid first assignment of, the Personalty, Plans, Leases and Rents, all in accordance with the terms hereof. The Land and Buildings are not Grantor's homestead or residence (or the homestead or residence of any of Grantor's partners or shareholders, if applicable), and are not and will not be claimed, used, occupied or enjoyed by Grantor (or such partners or shareholders) as such.

3.5 *Taxes and Other Payments.* Grantor has filed all federal, state, county, municipal and city income and other tax returns required to have been filed by Grantor and has paid all taxes which have become due pursuant to such returns or pursuant to any assessments received by Grantor, and Grantor does not know of any basis for any additional assessment in respect of any such taxes.

3.6 *Litigation.* Except as heretofore disclosed in writing by Grantor to Beneficiary, there are no actions, suits or proceedings pending, or to the knowledge of Grantor threatened, against or affecting the Grantor or the Mortgaged Property, or involving the validity or enforceability of this Deed of Trust or the priority of the liens and security interests created by the Security Instruments, and no event has occurred (including specifically Grantor's execution of the Security Instruments and its consummation of the loan represented thereby) which will violate, be in conflict with, result in the breach of, or constitute (with due notice or lapse of time, or both) a default under, any Legal Requirement or result in the creation or imposition of any lien, charge or encumbrance of any nature whatsoever upon any of Grantor's property other than the liens and security interests created by the Security Instruments.

ARTICLE 4
AFFIRMATIVE COVENANTS

Grantor hereby unconditionally covenants and agrees with Beneficiary as follows:

4.1 *Payment and Performance.* Grantor will pay the Indebtedness as and when called for in the Security Instruments and on or before the due dates thereof, and will perform all of the Obligations in full and on or before the dates same are to be performed.

4.2 *Existence.* Grantor will preserve and keep in full force and effect its existence, rights, franchises and trade names.

4.3 *Compliance with Legal Requirements.* Grantor will promptly and faithfully comply with, conform to and obey all present and future Legal Requirements whether or not same shall necessitate structural changes in, improvements to or interfere with the use or enjoyment of, the Mortgaged Property.

4.4 *First Lien Status:* Grantor will protect the first lien and security interest status of this Deed of Trust and will not, without the prior written consent of Beneficiary, create, place, or permit to be created or placed, or otherwise mortgage, hypothecate or encumber the Mortgaged Property with, any other lien or security interest of any nature whatsoever (statutory, constitutional or contractual) regardless of whether same is allegedly or expressly inferior to the lien and security interest created by this Deed of Trust, and, if any such lien or security interest is asserted against the Mortgaged Property, Grantor will promptly, at its own cost and expense, (a) pay the underlying claim in full or take such other action so as to cause same to be released and (b) within five (5) days from the date such lien or security interest is so asserted, give Beneficiary notice of such lien or security interest; provided, however, that Grantor may contest such claim in accordance with the provisions of Paragraph 11.22 hereof. Such notice shall specify who is asserting such lien or security interest and shall detail the origin and nature of the underlying claim giving rise to such asserted lien or security interest.

4.5 *Payment of Impositions.* Grantor will duly pay and discharge, or cause to be paid and discharged, the Impositions not later than the due date thereof, or the day any fine, penalty, interest or cost may be added thereto or imposed, or the day any lien may be filed, for the non-payment thereof (if such day is used to determine the due date of the respective item); provided, however, that Grantor may, if permitted by law and if such installment payment would not create or permit the filing of a lien against the Mortgaged Property, pay the Impositions in installments whether or not interest shall accrue on the unpaid balance of such Impositions. In addition, Grantor will duly pay and discharge, or cause to be paid and discharged, not later than the due date thereof, or the date any fine, penalty, interest or cost may be added thereto or imposed, or the day any lien may be filed, for the non-payment thereof (if such day is used to determine the due date of the respective item), all taxes, assessments and charges of every nature and to whomever assessed that may now or hereafter be levied or assessed upon this Deed of Trust, upon the lien or estate hereby created, or upon the Indebtedness, subject, however, to the provisions of Paragraph 11.10 hereof. In the event of the passage after the date of this Deed of Trust of any law of the State of Texas changing in any way the laws for the taxation of deeds of trust or debts and the interest thereon secured by deeds of trust for state or local purposes, or the manner of the collection of any such taxation, so as to adversely affect this Deed of Trust, the Beneficiary shall have the right to give sixty (60) days' written notice to the Grantor requiring the payment of the Indebtedness, and if such notice be given the Indebtedness shall become due, payable and collectible at the expiration of said sixty (60) day period, subject, however, to the provisions of Paragraph 11.10 hereof. Grantor may also contest such Impositions in accordance with the provisions of Paragraph 11.22 hereof.

4.6 *Repair.* Grantor will keep the Mortgaged Property in first-class order and condition and will make all repairs, replacements, renewals, additions, betterments, improvements and alterations thereof and thereto, interior and exterior, structural and non-structural, ordinary and extraordinary, foreseen and unforeseen, which are necessary or reasonably appropriate to keep same in such order and condition. Grantor will also use its best efforts to prevent any act or occurrence which might impair the value or usefulness of the Mortgaged Property for its intended usage as set forth in the Plans or elsewhere in the Security Instruments. In instances where repairs, replacements, renewals, additions, betterments, improvements or alterations are required in and to the Mortgaged Property on an emergency basis to prevent loss, damage, waste or destruction thereof, Grantor shall proceed to construct same, or cause same to be constructed, notwithstanding anything to the contrary contained in Paragraph 5.2 hereinbelow; provided, however, that in instances where such emergency measures are to be taken, Grantor will notify Beneficiary in writing of the commencement of same and the measures to be taken and, when same are completed, the completion date and the measures actually taken.

4.7 *Insurance.* Grantor will obtain and maintain, or cause to be obtained and maintained, insurance upon and relating to the Mortgaged Property insuring against personal injury and death, loss by fire and such other hazards, casualties and contingencies (including business interruption insurance covering loss of Rents, flood insurance and Builder's all risk coverage) as are normally and usually covered by extended coverage policies in effect where the Land is located and such other risks as may be reasonably specified by Beneficiary, from time to time, all in such amounts and with such insurers of recognized responsibility as are acceptable to Beneficiary. Each insurance policy issued in connection therewith shall provide by way of endorsements, riders or otherwise that (a) proceeds will be payable to Beneficiary as its interest may appear, all amounts recoverable under any such policy being hereby assigned to Beneficiary; (b) the coverage of Beneficiary shall not be terminated, reduced or affected in any manner regardless of any breach or violation by Grantor of any warranties, declarations or conditions in such policy; (c) no such insurance policy shall be cancelled, endorsed, altered or reissued to effect a change in coverage for any reason and to any extent whatsoever unless such insurer shall have first given Beneficiary thirty (30) days prior written notice thereof; and (d) Beneficiary may, but shall not be obligated to, make premium payments to prevent any cancellation, endorsement, alteration or reissuance and such payments shall be accepted by the insurer to prevent same. Beneficiary shall be furnished with the original of each such initial policy (or endorsement thereto), or an original certificate of insurance for such policy or endorsement, coincident with the execution of this Deed of Trust and the original of each renewal policy not less than fifteen (15) days prior to the expiration of the initial or each succeeding renewal policy together with receipts or other evidence that the premiums thereon have been paid. Grantor shall furnish to Beneficiary, upon request, but at least annually, a statement certified by Grantor or a duly authorized officer or partner of Grantor of the amounts of insurance maintained in compliance with this Paragraph 4.7, of the risks covered by such insurance and of the insurance company or companies which carry such insurance. In the event of a loss, the amount collected under each such insurance policy shall, at the option of Beneficiary, be used in any one or more of the following ways: (w) applied upon the Indebtedness, whether such Indebtedness then be matured or unmatured; (x) used to perform or discharge any of the Obligations; (y) used for the restoration, repair or replacement of the Mortgaged Property; or (z) released to Grantor. Beneficiary is hereby irrevocably appointed by Grantor as attorney-in-fact (coupled with an interest) of Grantor to (i) assign any insurance policy in the event of the foreclosure of this Deed of Trust or other extinguishment of the Indebtedness, and (ii) endorse any check made payable to Grantor (or to Grantor and any other person, including without limitation Beneficiary) representing amounts payable under or other proceeds from any insurance policies maintained with respect to the Mortgaged Property. Beneficiary shall not be obligated to collect, and shall not be liable for failure to collect, any such amounts or proceeds.

4.8 *Application of Proceeds.* If the proceeds of the insurance described in Paragraph 4.7 hereinabove are to be used for restoration, repair or replacement (hereinafter referred to as the "Work") of the Mortgaged Property, such proceeds shall be paid out by Beneficiary from time to time to Grantor (or, at the option of Beneficiary, jointly to Grantor and the persons furnishing labor and/or material incident to such Work or directly to such persons) as the Work progresses, subject to the following conditions: (a) an architect or engineer, approved by Beneficiary, shall be retained by Grantor (at Grantor's expense) and charged with the supervision of the Work and Grantor shall have prepared, submitted to Beneficiary and secured Beneficiary's written approval (such approval not to be unreasonably withheld) of the plans and specifications for such Work; (b) each request for payment by Grantor shall be made on ten (10) days' prior written notice to Beneficiary and shall be accompanied by a certificate to be made by the architect or engineer supervising the Work and by Grantor or an executive officer of Grantor, stating, among such other matters as may be reasonably required by Beneficiary, that: (i) all of the Work completed has been done in compliance with the approved plans and specifications; (ii) the sum requested is justly required to reimburse Grantor for payments by Grantor to, or is justly due to, the contractor, subcontractors, materialmen, laborers, engineers, architects or other persons rendering services or materials for the Work (giving a brief description of such services and materials); (iii) when added to all sums previously paid out by Grantor, the sum requested does not exceed the value of the Work done to the date of such certificate; and (iv) the amount of insurance proceeds remaining in the hands of Beneficiary will be sufficient upon completion of the Work to pay for the same in full (giving in such reasonable detail as Beneficiary may require an estimate of the cost of such completion); (c) each request shall be accompanied by waivers of lien satisfactory in form and substance to Beneficiary covering that part of the Work for which payment or reimbursement is being requested and by a search prepared by a title company or licensed abstracter or by other evidence satisfactory to Beneficiary that there has not been filed with respect to the Mortgaged Property any mechanic's lien or other lien, affidavit or instrument asserting any lien or any lien rights with respect to the Mortgaged Property; (d) there has not occurred any Event of Default since the hazard, casualty or contingency giving rise to payment of the insurance proceeds; (e) in the case of the request for the final disbursement, such request is accompanied by a copy of any Certificate of Occupancy or other certificate required by any Legal Requirement to render occupancy of the damaged portion of the Mortgaged Property lawful; and (f) if, in Beneficiary's reasonable judgment, the amount of such insurance proceeds will not be sufficient to complete the Work (which determination may be made prior to or during the performance of the Work), Grantor shall deposit with Beneficiary, immediately upon a request therefor, an amount of money which when added to such insurance proceeds will be sufficient, in Beneficiary's reasonable judgment, to complete the Work. If, upon completion of the Work, any portion of the insurance proceeds has not been disbursed to Grantor (or one or more of the other aforesaid persons), Beneficiary may, at Beneficiary's option, disburse such balance to Grantor or apply such balance toward the payment of the Indebtedness. Nothing herein shall be interpreted to prohibit Beneficiary from applying at any time the whole or any part of such insurance proceeds to the curing of any Event of Default.

4.9 *Restoration Following Casualty.* If any act or occurrence of any kind or nature, ordinary or extraordinary, foreseen or unforeseen (including any casualty for which insurance was not obtained or obtainable), shall result in damage to or loss or destruction of the Mortgaged Property, Grantor will give notice thereof to Beneficiary and, if so instructed by Beneficiary will promptly, at Grantor's sole cost and expense and regardless of whether the insurance proceeds (if any) shall be sufficient or available for the purpose, commence and continue diligently to completion to restore, repair, replace and rebuild the Mortgaged Property as nearly as possible to its value, condition and character immediately prior to such damage, loss or destruction.

4.10 *Performance of Leases:* Grantor covenants: (a) duly and punctually to perform and comply with any and all representations, warranties, covenants and agreements expressed as binding upon it under each of the Leases, (b) not to do or permit to be done anything to impair the security of any of the Leases, (c) except for tenant deposits, not to collect any of the Rent more than thirty (30) days in advance of the time when the same becomes due under the terms of such Leases, (d) not to discount any future accruing Rent, (e) to maintain each of the Leases in full force and effect during the full term thereof (except as otherwise provided in (g) below), (f) to appear in and defend any action or proceeding arising under or in any manner connected with any of the Leases or the representations, warranties, covenants and agreements of it or the other party or parties thereto, (g) not to amend, modify, or terminate any of the Leases or accept a surrender of the leased premises thereunder in any respect or enter into any new Leases without the prior written consent of Beneficiary, (h) not to assign or grant a security interest in and to any of the Leases to any party other than Beneficiary without the prior written consent of Beneficiary, (i) at the request of Beneficiary, to collaterally assign and transfer to Beneficiary any specific Leases (said collateral assignment to be in form and substance satisfactory to Beneficiary), but no such assignment shall be construed as a consent by Beneficiary to any Lease so assigned, or to impose upon Beneficiary any obligation with respect thereto, (j) at the request of Beneficiary, to execute and deliver all such further assurances and assignments in and to the Mortgaged Property as Beneficiary shall from time to time reasonably require, and (k) to deliver to Beneficiary executed counterparts of all Leases regardless of whether such Leases were or are executed before or after the date hereof.

4.11 *Inspection.* Grantor will permit Trustee and Beneficiary, and their agents, representatives and employees, to inspect the Mortgaged Property at all reasonable times.

4.12 *Hold Harmless.* Grantor will defend, at its own cost and expense, and hold Beneficiary harmless from, any action, proceeding or claim affecting the Mortgaged Property or the Security Instruments, or resulting from or arising out of the failure of Grantor to perform or discharge the Obligations or otherwise to comply with the provisions of the Security Instruments, and all costs and expenses incurred by Beneficiary in protecting its interests hereunder in such an event (including all court costs and attorneys' fees) shall be borne by Grantor.

4.13 *Books and Records.* Grantor will maintain full and accurate books of account and other records reflecting the results of its operations of the Mortgaged Property, and will furnish or cause to be furnished to Beneficiary, such financial data as Beneficiary shall reasonably request with respect to the ownership, maintenance, use and operation of the Mortgaged Property, and Beneficiary shall have the right, at reasonable times and upon reasonable notice, to audit, examine and make copies or extracts of Grantor's books of account and records relating to the Mortgaged Property, all of which shall be maintained and made available to

Beneficiary and Beneficiary's representatives for such purpose on the Mortgaged Property or at such other location as Beneficiary may approve.

4.14 *Maintenance of Rights of Way, Easements, and Licenses.* Grantor will maintain, preserve and renew all rights of way, easements, grants, privileges, licenses and franchises reasonably necessary for the use of the Mortgaged Property from time to time and will not, without the prior consent of Beneficiary, initiate, join in or consent to any private restrictive covenant or other public or private restriction as to the use of the Mortgaged Property. Grantor shall, however, comply with all restrictive covenants which may at any time affect the Mortgaged Property, zoning ordinances and other public or private restrictions as to the use of the Mortgaged Property.

ARTICLE 5
NEGATIVE COVENANTS

Grantor hereby covenants and agrees with Beneficiary that, until the entire Indebtedness shall have been paid in full and all of the Obligations shall have been fully performed and discharged:

5.1 *Use Violations.* Grantor will not use, maintain, operate or occupy, or allow the use, maintenance, operation or occupancy of, the Mortgaged Property in any manner which (a) violates any Legal Requirement, (b) may be dangerous unless safeguarded as required by law, (c) constitutes a public or private nuisance or (d) makes void, voidable or cancellable, or increases the premium of, any insurance then in force with respect thereto.

5.2 *Alterations.* Grantor will not commit or permit any waste of the Mortgaged Property and will not (subject to the provisions of Paragraphs 4.6 and 4.9 hereinabove), without the prior written consent of Beneficiary make or permit to be made any alterations or additions to the Mortgaged Property of a material nature.

5.3 *Replacement of Fixtures and Personalty.* Grantor will not, without the prior written consent of Beneficiary, permit any of the Fixtures or Personalty to be removed at any time from the Land or Buildings unless the removed item is removed temporarily for maintenance and repair or, if removed permanently, is replaced by an article of equal suitability and value, owned by Grantor, free and clear of any lien or security interest except such as may be first approved in writing by Beneficiary.

ARTICLE 6
EVENTS OF DEFAULT

The term "Event of Default", as used herein, shall mean the occurrence or happening, at any time and from time to time, of any one or more of the following:

6.1 *Payment of Indebtedness.* If Grantor shall fail, refuse or neglect to pay, in full, any installment or portion of the Indebtedness as and when the same shall become due and payable, whether at the due date thereof stipulated in the Security Instruments, or at a date fixed for prepayment, or by acceleration or otherwise, and such failure, refusal or neglect has not been cured within any applicable grace period set forth in the Security Instruments or instruments evidencing the Indebtedness; provided, further, that such installment or portion of the indebtedness not paid when due shall bear interest at the Default Rate pursuant to the Note from the date same is due until the date same is paid in full, without the necessity of any such notice and without any grace period.

6.2 *Foreclosure of Other Liens.* If the holder of any lien or security interest on the Mortgaged Property (without hereby implying Beneficiary's consent to the existence, placing, creating or permitting of any such lien or security interest) institutes foreclosure or other proceedings for the enforcement of its remedies thereunder.

6.3 *Default Under Other Security Instruments.* If any Event of Default occurs and is continuing under any other Security Instrument.

6.4 *Further Encumbrance.* If Grantor, without the prior written consent of Beneficiary, creates, places or permits to be created or placed, or through any act or failure to act, acquiesces in the placing of, or allows to remain, any mortgage, pledge, lien (statutory, constitutional or contractual), security interest, encumbrance or charge on, or conditional sale or other title retention agreement, regardless of whether same is expressly subordinate to the liens of the Security Instruments, with respect to, the Mortgaged Property, the Leases, the Plans or the Rents, other than the Permitted Encumbrances.

ARTICLE 7
DEFAULT AND FORECLOSURE

7.1 *Remedies.* If an Event of Default shall occur, Beneficiary may, subject to the provisions of Paragraph 7.9 hereinbelow, at Beneficiary's election and by or through Trustee or otherwise, exercise any or all of the following rights, remedies and recourses:

(a) *Acceleration:* Declare the Principal Balance (defined hereby as meaning the then unpaid principal balance on the Note), the accrued interest and any other accrued but unpaid portion of the Indebtedness to be immediately due and payable, without further notice, presentment, protest, demand or action of any nature whatsoever (each of which hereby is expressly waived by Grantor), whereupon the same shall become immediately due and payable.

(b) *Entry Upon Mortgaged Property:* Enter upon the Mortgaged Property and take exclusive possession thereof and of all books, records and accounts relating thereto. If Grantor remains in possession of all or any part of the Mortgaged Property after an Event of Default and without Beneficiary's prior written consent thereto, Grantor shall be deemed to be a tenant at will or sufferance of Beneficiary, and Beneficiary may invoke any and all legal remedies to dispossess Grantor, including specifically one or more actions for forcible entry and detainer, trespass to try title and writ of restitution. Nothing contained in the foregoing sentence shall, however, be construed to impose any greater obligation or any prerequisites to acquiring possession of the Mortgaged Property after an Event of Default than would have existed in the absence of such sentence.

(c) *Operation of Mortgaged Property:* Hold, lease, manage, operate or otherwise use or permit the use of the Mortgaged Property, either itself or by other persons, firms or entities, in such manner, for such time and upon such other terms as Beneficiary may deem to be prudent and reasonable under the circumstances (making such repairs, alterations, additions and improvements thereto and taking any and all other action with reference thereto, from time to time, as Beneficiary shall deem necessary or desirable), and apply all Rents and other amounts collected by Trustee or Beneficiary in connection therewith in accordance with the provisions of Paragraph 7.8 hereinbelow.

(d) *Foreclosure and Sale:* Sell or offer for sale the Mortgaged Property (i) in such portions, order and parcels as Beneficiary may determine, with or without having first taken possession of same, to the highest bidder for cash at public auction at the county courthouse of any county in which any of the Land to be sold is situated, in the area in such courthouse designated for real property foreclosure sales in accordance with applicable law (or in the absence of any such designation, in the area set forth in the notice of sale hereinafter described), on the first Tuesday of any month between the hours of 10:00 A.M. and 4:00 P.M. (commencing no earlier than such time as may be designated in the hereinafter described notice of sale), after giving legally adequate notice of the time, place and terms of sale and that portion of the Mortgaged Property to be sold, by (1) posting or causing to be posted written or printed notices thereof for at least 21 consecutive days prior to the date of said sale at the county courthouse door of each county in which the Land is situated, (2) filing or causing to be filed a copy of such notice in the office of the county clerk of each county in which the Land is situated at least 21 days preceding the date of such sale, and (3) at least 21 days preceding the date of such sale, serving written notice (by the Beneficiary or any person chosen by the Beneficiary) of such proposed sale by certified mail on each debtor obligated to pay the indebtedness evidenced by the Note according to the records of Beneficiary; service of such notice to each debtor to be completed upon deposit of the notice, enclosed in a postpaid wrapper, properly addressed to each debtor at the most recent address as shown by the records of Beneficiary, in a post office or official depository under the care and custody of the United States Postal Service (it being expressly understood that the affidavit of any person having knowledge of the facts to the effect that such service was completed shall be prima facie evidence of the fact of such service), or (ii) accomplishing all or any of the aforesaid in such manner as permitted or required by Section 51.002 of the Property Code of the State of Texas relating to the sale of real estate or by Chapter 9 of the Texas Business and Commerce Code relating to the sale of collateral after default by a debtor (as said section and chapter now exist or as may be hereafter amended), or by any other present or subsequent articles or enactments relating to same; provided, however, that nothing contained in this Paragraph 7.1(d) shall be construed so as to limit in any way Trustee's rights to sell the Mortgaged Property, or any portion thereof, by private sale if, and to the extent that, such private sale is permitted under the laws of the State of Texas or by public or private sale after entry of a judgment by any court of competent jurisdiction ordering same. At any such sale (i) whether made under the power herein contained, the aforesaid Property Code Section 51.002, the Texas Business and Commerce Code or any other legal enactment, or by virtue of any judicial proceedings or any other legal right, remedy or recourse, it shall not be necessary for Trustee to have physically present, or to have constructive possession of, the Mortgaged Property (Grantor hereby covenanting and agreeing to deliver to Trustee any portion of the Mortgaged Property not actually or constructively possessed by Trustee immediately upon demand by Trustee) and the title to and right of possession of any such property shall pass to the purchaser thereof as completely as if the same had been actually present and delivered to purchaser at such sale, (ii) each instrument of conveyance executed by Trustee shall contain a general warranty of title, binding upon Grantor and its successors and assigns, (iii) each and every recital contained in any instrument of conveyance made by Trustee shall be prima facie evidence of the truth and accuracy of the matters recited therein, including, without limitation, nonpayment of the Indebtedness, advertisement and conduct of such sale in the manner provided herein and otherwise by law and appointment of any successor Trustee hereunder, (iv) any and all prerequisites to the validity thereof shall be conclusively presumed to have been performed, (v) the receipt of Trustee or of such other party or officer making the sale shall be a sufficient discharge to the purchaser or purchasers for its purchase money and no such purchaser or purchasers, or its assigns or personal representatives, shall thereafter be obligated to see to the application of such purchase money, or be in any way answerable for any loss, misapplication or non-application thereof, (vi) to the fullest extent permitted by law, Grantor shall be completely and irrevocably divested of all of its right, title, interest, claim and demand whatsoever, either at law or in equity, in and to the property sold and such sale shall be a perpetual bar both at law and in equity against Grantor, and against any and all other persons claiming or to claim the property sold or any part thereof, by, through or under Grantor, and (vii) to the extent and under such circumstances as are permitted by law, Beneficiary may be a purchaser at any such sale, and shall have the right, after paying or accounting for all costs of said sale or sales, to credit the amount of the bid upon the amount of the Indebtedness (in the order of priority set forth in Paragraph 7.8 hereof) in lieu of cash payment.

(e) *Trustee or Receiver:* Make application to a court of competent jurisdiction as a matter of strict right and without notice to Grantor or regard to the adequacy of the Mortgaged Property for the repayment of the Indebtedness or the solvency of any person or entity liable for the repayment of the Indebtedness, for appointment of a receiver of the Mortgaged Property and Grantor does hereby irrevocably consent to such appointment. Any such receiver shall have all the usual powers and duties of receivers in similar cases, including the full power to rent, maintain and otherwise operate the Mortgaged Property upon such terms as may be approved by the court, and shall apply such Rents in accordance with the provisions of Paragraph 7.8 hereinbelow. The right to the appointment of a receiver shall apply regardless of whether Beneficiary has commenced procedures for the foreclosure of the liens and security interests created herein, or has commenced any other legal proceedings to enforce payment of the Indebtedness or performance or discharge of the Obligations, and shall also apply upon the actual or threatened waste to any part of the Mortgaged Property.

(f) *Foreclosure for Installments:* Beneficiary shall also have the option to proceed with foreclosure in satisfaction of any installments of the Indebtedness which have not been paid when due either through the courts or by directing the Trustee or his successors in trust to proceed with foreclosure in satisfaction of the matured but unpaid portion of the Indebtedness as if under a full foreclosure, conducting the sale as herein provided and without declaring the entire Principal Balance and accrued interest due; such sale may be made subject to the unmatured portion of the Indebtedness, and any such sale shall not in any manner affect the unmatured portion of the Indebtedness, but as to such unmatured portion of the Indebtedness this Deed of Trust shall remain in full force and effect just as though no sale had been made hereunder. It is further agreed that several sales may be made hereunder without exhausting the right of sale for any unmatured part of the Indebtedness, it being the purpose hereof to provide for a foreclosure and sale of the security for any matured portion of the Indebtedness without exhausting the power to foreclose and sell the Mortgaged Property for any subsequently maturing portion of the Indebtedness.

(g) *Other:* Exercise any and all other rights, remedies and recourses granted under the Security Instruments or now or hereafter existing in equity, at law, by virtue of statute or otherwise.

7.2 *Separate Sales.* The Mortgaged Property may be sold in one or more parcels and in such manner and order as Trustee, in his sole discretion, may elect, it being expressly understood and agreed that the right of sale arising out of any Event of Default shall not be exhausted by any one or more sales but other and successive sales may be made until all of the Mortgaged Property has been sold or until the Indebtedness has been fully satisfied.

7.3 *Remedies Cumulative, Concurrent and Non–Exclusive.* Beneficiary shall have all rights, remedies and recourses granted in the Security Instruments and available at law or equity (including specifically those granted by the Uniform Commercial Code in effect and applicable to the Mortgaged Property, the Leases, the Plans, or any portion thereof), and same (a) shall be cumulative and concurrent; (b) may be pursued separately, successively or concurrently against Grantor or others obligated under the Note, or against the Mortgaged Property, or against any one or more of them, at the sole discretion of Beneficiary; (c) may be exercised as often as occasion therefor shall arise, it being agreed by Grantor that the exercise or failure to exercise any of same shall in no event be construed as a waiver or release thereof or of any other right, remedy or recourse; and (d) are intended to be, and shall be, nonexclusive.

7.4 *No Conditions Precedent to Exercise of Remedies.* Neither Grantor nor any other person hereafter obligated for payment of all or any part of the Indebtedness or fulfillment of all or any of the Obligations shall be relieved of such obligation by reason of (a) the failure of Trustee to comply with any request of Grantor or any other person so obligated to foreclose the lien of this Deed of Trust or to enforce any provisions of the other Security Instruments; (b) the release, regardless of consideration, of the Mortgaged Property or any portion thereof or the addition of any other property to the Mortgaged Property; (c) any agreement or stipulation between any subsequent owner of the Mortgaged Property and Beneficiary extending, renewing, rearranging or in any other way modifying the terms of the Security Instruments without first having obtained the consent of, given notice to or paid any consideration to Grantor or such other person, and in such event Grantor and all such other persons shall continue to be liable to make payment according to the terms of any such extension or modification agreement unless expressly released and discharged in writing by Beneficiary; or (d) by any other act or occurrence save and except the complete payment of the Indebtedness and the complete fulfillment of all of the Obligations.

7.5 *Release of and Resort to Collateral.* Pursuant to the terms of any of the Security Instruments, Beneficiary may release, regardless of consideration, any part of the Mortgaged Property without, as to the remainder, in any way impairing, affecting, subordinating or releasing the lien or security interest created in or evidenced by the Security Instruments or their stature as a first and prior lien and security interest in and to the Mortgaged Property, and without in any way releasing or diminishing the liability of any person or entity liable for the repayment of the Indebtedness or the performance of the Obligations. For payment of the Indebtedness, Beneficiary may resort to any other security therefor held by Beneficiary or Trustee in such order and manner as Beneficiary may elect.

7.6 *Waiver of Redemption, Notice and Marshalling of Assets.* To the fullest extent permitted by law, Grantor hereby irrevocably and unconditionally waives and releases (a) all benefits that might accrue to Grantor by virtue of any present or future moratorium law or other law exempting the Mortgaged Property from attachment, levy or sale on execution or providing for any appraisement, valuation, stay of execution, exemption from civil process, redemption or extension of time for payment; (b) all notices of any Event of Default (except as may be expressly provided for in Article 6 or 7 hereof) or of Beneficiary's intention to accelerate maturity of the Indebtedness or of Trustee's election to exercise or his actual exercise of any right, remedy or recourse provided for under the Security Instruments; and (c) any right to a marshalling of assets or a sale in inverse order of alienation.

7.7 *Discontinuance of Proceedings.* In case Beneficiary shall have proceeded to invoke any right, remedy or recourse permitted under the Security Instruments and shall thereafter elect to discontinue or abandon same for any reason, Beneficiary shall have the unqualified right so to do and, in such an event, Grantor and Beneficiary shall be restored to their former positions with respect to the Indebtedness, the Obligations, the Security Instruments, the Mortgaged Property and otherwise, and the rights, remedies, recourses and powers of Beneficiary shall continue as if same had never been invoked.

7.8 *Application of Proceeds.* The proceeds of any sale of, and the Rents and other amounts generated by the holding, leasing, operating or other use of, the Mortgaged Property, the Leases or the Plans shall be applied by Trustee or Beneficiary (or the receiver, if one is appointed) to the extent that funds are so available therefrom in the following order of priority:

(a) first, to that portion of the Indebtedness then remaining unpaid (including without limitation principal and interest and the reasonable costs and expenses of taking possession of the Mortgaged Property and of holding, managing, operating, using, leasing, repairing, improving and selling the same, including by way of illustration but not by way of limitation any one or more of the following to the extent Beneficiary deems appropriate: (i) trustees' and receivers' fees, (ii) court costs, (iii) attorneys', brokers', managers', accountants' and appraisers' fees and expenses, (iv) costs of advertisement and (v) the payment of any and all Impositions, liens, security interests or other rights, titles or interests equal or superior to the lien and security interest of this Deed of Trust [except those to which the Mortgaged Property has been or will be sold subject to and without in any way implying Beneficiary's prior consent to the creation thereof]) as to which Grantor is not fully personally liable, it being agreed that the application of such proceeds shall be in such a manner as not to extinguish or reduce Grantor's personal liability until all the Indebtedness as to which Grantor is not personally liable has been paid in full;

(b) second, to the payment of that portion of the Indebtedness as to which Grantor is fully liable;

(c) third, to the extent permitted by law, to the extent funds are available therefor out of the sale proceeds or the Rents and, to the extent known by Beneficiary, to the payment of any indebtedness or obligations secured by a subordinate deed of trust on or security interest in the Mortgaged Property; and

(d) fourth, to Grantor.

7.9 *Acceleration Following Certain Events.* Notwithstanding anything to the contrary contained in or inferable from any provision hereof, upon the occurrence of an Event of Default as defined in Paragraph 6.4 hereinabove, the Principal Balance, the unpaid accrued interest under the Note and any other accrued but unpaid portion of the Indebtedness shall be automatically and immediately due and payable in full without the necessity of any action on the part of Trustee or Beneficiary.

7.10 *Occupancy After Foreclosure.* The purchaser at any foreclosure sale pursuant to Paragraph 7.1(d) shall become the legal owner of the Mortgaged Property. All occupants of the Mortgaged Property or any part thereof shall become tenants at sufferance of the purchaser at the foreclosure sale and shall deliver possession thereof immediately to the purchaser upon demand. It shall not be necessary for the purchaser at said sale to bring any action for possession of the Mortgaged Property other than the statutory action of forcible detainer in any Justice Court having jurisdiction over the Mortgaged Property.

ARTICLE 8

CONDEMNATION

8.1 *General.* Immediately upon Grantor's obtaining knowledge of the institution of any proceeding for the condemnation of the Mortgaged Property, Grantor shall notify Trustee and Beneficiary of such fact. Grantor shall then, if requested by Beneficiary, file or defend its claim thereunder and prosecute same with due diligence to its final disposition and shall cause any awards or settlements to be paid over to Beneficiary for disposition pursuant to the terms of this Deed of Trust. Grantor may be the nominal party in such proceeding, but Beneficiary shall be entitled to participate in and to control same and to be represented therein by counsel of its own choice, and Grantor will deliver, or cause to be delivered, to Beneficiary such instruments as may be requested by it from time to time to permit such participation. If the Mortgaged Property is taken or diminished in value (including without limitation by any change or changes of grade of any streets affecting the Land and Buildings), or if a consent settlement is entered, by or under threat of such proceeding, the award or settlement payable to Grantor by virtue of its interest in the Mortgaged Property shall be, and by these presents is, assigned, transferred and set over unto Beneficiary to be held by it, in trust, subject to the lien and security interest of this Deed of Trust, and may, at the Beneficiary's election, be used in any one or more of the following ways: (a) apply the same or any part thereof upon the Indebtedness, whether such Indebtedness then be matured or unmatured; (b) use the same or any part thereof to perform or discharge the Obligations; (c) use the same or any part thereof to restore, repair or replace the Mortgaged Property to a condition satisfactory to the Beneficiary (with the disbursement of such funds being made in accordance with the procedures established in Paragraph 4.8 hereof); or (d) release the same to Grantor. Beneficiary is empowered to collect and receive the proceeds of any condemnation award or settlement; Grantor hereby irrevocably appoints Beneficiary as Grantor's attorney-in-fact (coupled with an interest) to collect and receive such proceeds. Beneficiary shall not be obligated to collect, and shall not be liable for failure to collect, any such proceeds.

ARTICLE 9
SECURITY AGREEMENT

9.1 *Security Interest.* This Deed of Trust shall be construed as a deed of trust on real property and it shall also constitute and serve as (a) a "Security Agreement" on personal property within the meaning of, and shall constitute, until the grant of this Deed of Trust shall terminate as provided in Article 2 hereinabove, a first and prior security interest under, the Uniform Commercial Code (being Chapter 9 of the Texas Business and Commerce Code, as to property within the scope thereof and situated in the State of Texas) with respect to the Personalty, Fixtures, Plans, Leases, and Rents and (b) as an "Assignment of Rents and Leases" of the Rents, and Leases. To this end, Grantor has GRANTED, BARGAINED, CONVEYED, ASSIGNED, TRANSFERRED and SET OVER, and by these presents does GRANT, BARGAIN, CONVEY, ASSIGN, TRANSFER and SET OVER, unto Trustee and unto Beneficiary a first and prior security interest and all of Grantor's right, title and interest in, to and under the Personalty, Fixtures, Plans, Leases, and Rents to secure the full and timely payment of the Indebtedness and the full and timely performance and discharge of the Obligations.

9.2 *Financing Statements.* Grantor hereby agrees with Beneficiary to execute and deliver to Beneficiary, in form and substance satisfactory to Beneficiary, such "Financing Statements" and such further assurances as Beneficiary may, from time to time, consider reasonably necessary to create, perfect, and preserve Beneficiary's security interest herein granted, and Beneficiary may cause such statements and assurances to be recorded and filed, at such times and places as may be required or permitted by law to so create, perfect and preserve such security interest.

9.3 *Uniform Commercial Code Remedies.* Beneficiary and/or Trustee shall have all the rights, remedies and recourses with respect to the Personalty, Fixtures, Plans, Leases, and Rents afforded to it by the aforesaid Uniform Commercial Code (being Chapter 9 of the Texas Business and Commerce Code, as to property within the scope thereof and situated in the State of Texas) in addition to, and not in limitation of, the other rights, remedies and recourses afforded by the Security Instruments.

9.4 *No Obligation of Trustee or Beneficiary.* The assignment and security interest herein granted shall not be deemed or construed to constitute Trustee or Beneficiary as a trustee in possession of the Mortgaged Property, to obligate Trustee or Beneficiary to lease the Mortgaged Property or attempt to do same, or to take any action, incur any expense or perform or discharge any obligation, duty or liability whatsoever under any of the Leases or otherwise.

9.5 *Payment of Rents to Grantor Until Default.* Unless and until an Event of Default occurs, Grantor shall be entitled to collect the Rents as and when, but not before, they become due and payable. Grantor hereby agrees with Beneficiary that the other parties under the Leases may, upon notice from Trustee or

Beneficiary of the occurrence of an Event of Default, thereafter pay direct to Beneficiary the Rents due and to become due under the Leases and attorn all other obligations thereunder directly to Beneficiary without any obligation on their part to determine whether an Event of Default does in fact exist. Additionally, Grantor hereby constitutes and appoints Beneficiary its true and lawful attorney-in-fact with full power of substitution to collect Rents and other sums due and to become due under the Leases and to endorse, either in the name of Grantor or in the name of Beneficiary, any check made payable to Grantor or any assumed business name of Grantor representing Rents and other sums due and to become due under the Leases. Any such Rent and other sums shall be applied in accordance with the Security Instruments. It is understood and agreed that this power is coupled with an interest which cannot be revoked.

9.6 *Fixture Filing.* This Deed of Trust shall constitute a "fixture filing" for all purposes of Chapter 9 of the Texas Business and Commerce Code. All or part of the Mortgaged Property are or are to become fixtures; information concerning the security interest herein granted may be obtained at the addresses set forth on the first page hereof. The address of the Secured Party (Beneficiary) is the address set forth in the opening recitals hereinabove and the address of the Debtor (Grantor) is the address set forth in the opening recital of this Deed of Trust.

9.7 *Remedies.* If an Event of Default shall occur, Beneficiary may elect, in addition to exercising any and all other rights, remedies and recourses set forth in Article 7 or referred to in Paragraph 9.3 hereinabove, to collect and receive all of the Rents and to proceed in the manner set forth in Section 9.501(d) of Chapter 9 of the Texas Business and Commerce Code relating to the procedure to be followed when a Security Agreement covers both real and personal property. Except as otherwise set forth in this Paragraph 9.7, at any foreclosure and sale as described in Paragraph 7.1(d) hereinabove, it shall be deemed that the Trustee proceeded under such Section 9.501(d) and that such sale passed title to all of the Mortgaged Property and other property described herein to the purchaser thereat, including without limitation, the Personalty, Plans, Leases and Rents. Beneficiary, acting by and through the Trustee or any other representative, may elect either prior to or at such sale not to proceed under such Section 9.501(d) by notifying Grantor of the manner in which Beneficiary intends to proceed with regard to the Personalty, Plans, Leases and Rents.

9.8 *Hold Harmless.* Beneficiary shall not be obligated to perform or discharge, nor does it hereby undertake to perform or discharge, any obligation, duty or liability under the Leases or under or by reason of this Deed of Trust, and Grantor shall and does hereby agree to indemnify Beneficiary for and to hold Beneficiary harmless from any and all liability, loss, or damage which it may or might incur under any of the Leases or by reason of this Deed of Trust and from any and all claims and demands whatsoever which may be asserted against it by reason of any alleged obligations or undertakings on its part to perform or discharge any of the terms, covenants, or agreements contained in any of the Leases. Should Beneficiary incur any such liability, loss or damage under any of the Leases or under or by reason of this Deed of Trust or in the defense of any such claims or demands, the amount thereof, including all costs, expenses and reasonable attorneys' fees, shall be secured hereby, and Grantor shall reimburse Beneficiary therefor immediately upon demand.

ARTICLE 10
CONCERNING THE TRUSTEE

10.1 *No Liability.* Trustee shall not be liable for any error of judgment or act done by Trustee in good faith, or be otherwise responsible or accountable under any circumstances whatsoever, except for Trustee's negligence or bad faith. Trustee shall not be personally liable in case of entry by him, or anyone entering by virtue of the powers herein granted him, upon the Mortgaged Property for debts contracted or liability or damages incurred in the management or operation of the

Mortgaged Property. Trustee shall have the right to rely on any instrument, document or signature authorizing or supporting any action taken or proposed to be taken by him hereunder, believed by him in good faith to be genuine. Trustee shall be entitled to reimbursement for reasonable expenses incurred by him in the performance of his duties hereunder (including without limitation any amounts payable to attorneys, accountants, engineers or others selected by Trustee to aid Trustee in the performance of his duties hereunder) and to reasonable compensation for such of his services hereunder as shall be rendered. Grantor will, from time to time, pay the compensation due to Trustee hereunder and reimburse Trustee for, and save him harmless against, any and all liability and expenses which may be incurred by him in the performance of his duties. Grantor hereby absolutely ratifies and confirms any and all acts that Trustee or any successor or substitute Trustee may lawfully do by virtue of this Deed of Trust.

10.2 *Retention of Moneys.* All moneys received by Trustee shall, until used or applied as herein provided, be held in trust for the purposes for which they were received, but need not be segregated in any manner from any other moneys (except to the extent required by law), and Trustee shall be under no liability for interest on any moneys received by him hereunder.

10.3 *Successor Trustees.* Trustee may resign by the giving of notice of such resignation in writing to Beneficiary. If Trustee shall die, resign or become disqualified from acting in the execution of this trust or shall fail or refuse to execute the same when requested by Beneficiary so to do, or if, for any reason, with or without cause, Beneficiary shall prefer to appoint a substitute trustee to act instead of the aforenamed Trustee, Beneficiary shall have full power to appoint a substitute trustee and, if preferred, several substitute trustees in succession who shall succeed to all the estate, rights, powers and duties of the aforenamed Trustee. Such appointment may be executed by any authorized officer or agent of Beneficiary and such appointment shall be conclusively presumed to be executed with authority and shall be valid and sufficient without proof of any action by the Board of Directors or any superior officer of the Beneficiary.

10.4 *Succession Instruments.* Any new Trustee appointed pursuant to any of the provisions hereof shall, without any further act, deed or conveyance, become vested with all the estates, properties, rights, powers and trusts of his predecessor in the rights hereunder with like effect as if originally named as Trustee herein; but nevertheless, upon the written request of Beneficiary or of the successor Trustee, the Trustee ceasing to act shall execute and deliver an instrument transferring to such successor Trustee, upon the trusts herein expressed, all the estates, properties, rights, powers and trusts of the Trustee so ceasing to act, and shall duly assign, transfer and deliver any of the property and moneys held by such Trustee to the successor Trustee so appointed in his place.

10.5 *No Required Action.* Trustee shall not be required to take any action toward the execution and enforcement of the trust hereby created or to institute, appear in or defend any action, suit or other proceeding in connection therewith where in his opinion such action will be likely to involve him in expense or liability, unless requested so to do by a written instrument signed by Beneficiary and, if Trustee so requests, unless Trustee is tendered security and indemnity satisfactory to him against any and all costs, expenses and liabilities arising therefrom. Trustee shall not be responsible for the execution, acknowledgment or validity of the Security Instruments, or for the proper authorization thereof, or for the sufficiency of the lien and security interest purported to be created hereby, and makes no representation in respect thereof or in respect of the rights, remedies and recourses of Beneficiary.

ARTICLE 11

MISCELLANEOUS

11.1 *Performance at Grantor's Expense.* The cost and expense of performing or complying with any and all of the Obligations shall be borne solely by

Grantor, and no portion of such cost and expense shall be, in any way or to any extent, credited against any installment on or portion of the Indebtedness.

11.2 *Survival of Obligations.* Each and all of the Obligations shall survive the execution and delivery of the Security Instruments, and the consummation of the loan called for therein and shall continue in full force and effect until the Indebtedness shall have been paid in full.

11.3 *Further Assurances.* Grantor, upon the request of Trustee or Beneficiary, will execute, acknowledge, deliver and record and/or file such further instruments and do such further acts as may be necessary, desirable or proper to carry out more effectively the purposes of the Security Instruments and to subject to the liens and security interests thereof any property intended by the terms thereof to be covered thereby, including specifically, but without limitation, any renewals, additions, substitutions, replacements, betterments, or appurtenances to the then Mortgaged Property.

11.4 *Recording and Filing.* Grantor will cause the Security Instruments and all amendments and supplements thereto and substitutions therefor to be recorded, filed, re-recorded and refiled in such manner and in such places as Trustee or Beneficiary shall reasonably request, and will pay all such recording, filing, re-recording and refiling taxes, fees and other charges.

11.5 *Notices.* All notices or other communications required or permitted to be given pursuant to this Deed of Trust shall be in writing and shall be considered as properly given if mailed by first class United States Mail, postage prepaid, registered or certified with return receipt requested, or by delivering same in person to the intended addressee or by prepaid telegram. Notice so mailed shall be effective upon the expiration of three business days after its deposit. Notice given in any other manner shall be effective only if and when received by the addressee. For purposes of notice, the addresses of Beneficiary and Grantor shall be as set forth in the opening recitals hereinabove, respectively; provided, however, that either party shall have the right to change its address for notice hereunder to any other location within the continental United States by the giving of thirty (30) days' notice to the other party in the manner set forth hereinabove. Notices to Beneficiary shall include a copy sent or delivered to Mr. Milton Feder at 3 Riverway, Suite 730, Houston, Texas 77056.

11.6 *No Waiver.* Any failure by Trustee or Beneficiary to insist, or any election by Trustee or Beneficiary not to insist, upon strict performance by Grantor of any of the terms, provisions or conditions of the Security Instruments shall not be deemed to be a waiver of same or of any other terms, provisions or conditions thereof and Trustee or Beneficiary shall have the right at any time or times thereafter to insist upon strict performance by Grantor of any and all of such terms, provisions and conditions.

11.7 *Beneficiary's Right to Perform the Obligations.* If Grantor shall fail, refuse or neglect to make any payment or perform any act required by the Security Instruments, then at any time thereafter, and without notice to or demand upon Grantor and without waiving or releasing any other right, remedy or recourse Beneficiary may have because of same, Beneficiary may (but shall not be obligated to) make such payment or perform such act for the account of and at the expense of Grantor, and shall have the right to enter upon or in the Land and Buildings for such purpose and to take all such action thereon and with respect to the Mortgaged Property as it may deem necessary or appropriate. If Beneficiary shall elect to pay any Imposition or other sums due with reference to the Mortgaged Property, Beneficiary may do so in reliance on any bill, statement or assessment procured from the appropriate Governmental Authority or other issuer thereof without inquiring into the accuracy or validity thereof. Similarly, in making any payments to protect the security intended to be created by the Security Instruments, Beneficiary shall not be bound to inquire into the validity of any apparent or threatened adverse title, lien, encumbrance, claim or charge before making an advance for the purpose of preventing or removing the same. Grantor shall indemnify Beneficiary for all losses, expenses, damage, claims and causes of action, including reasonable attorneys' fees, incurred or accruing by reason of any acts performed by Beneficiary pursuant to the provisions of this Paragraph 11.7 or by reason of any other provision in the Security Instruments. All sums paid by Beneficiary pursuant to this Paragraph 11.7, and all other sums expended by Beneficiary to which it shall be entitled to be indemnified, together with interest thereon at the default rate or post-maturity rate of interest provided for in the Note from the date of such payment or expenditure, shall constitute additions to the Indebtedness, shall be secured by the Security Instruments and shall be paid by Grantor to Beneficiary upon demand.

11.8 *Covenants Running with the Land.* All Obligations contained in the Security Instruments are intended by the parties to be, and shall be construed as, covenants running with the Mortgaged Property.

11.9 *Successors and Assigns.* All of the terms of the Security Instruments shall apply to, be binding upon and inure to the benefit of the parties thereto, their respective successors, assigns, heirs and legal representatives, and all other persons claiming by, through or under them.

11.10 *Severability and Compliance With Usury Law.* The Security Instruments are intended to be performed in accordance with, and only to the extent permitted by, all applicable Legal Requirements. If any provision of any of the Security Instruments or the application thereof to any person or circumstance shall, for any reason and to any extent, be invalid or unenforceable, neither the remainder of the instrument in which such provision is contained, nor the application of such provision to other persons or circumstances, nor the other instruments referred to hereinabove, shall be affected thereby, but rather shall be enforceable to the greatest extent permitted by law. The Land and Buildings are "residential real property" and the extensions of credit (collectively, the "Loan") evidenced by the Note is secured by a first lien on residential real property within the meaning of Part A, Title V of the Depository Institutions Deregulation and Monetary Control Act of 1980, as amended (the "Act"), and the regulations promulgated thereunder. If, for any reason, the provisions of Part A, Title V of the Act shall be found not to exempt any and all interest and other charges contracted for, charged, taken, received or reserved in connection with the Loan from any limitation otherwise applicable, then the following provisions of this Paragraph shall apply, but otherwise the following provisions of this Paragraph shall be inapplicable. It is expressly stipulated and agreed to be the intent of Grantor and Beneficiary at all times to comply with the applicable Texas law governing the maximum rate or amount of interest payable on or in connection with the Indebtedness (or applicable United States federal law to the extent that it permits Beneficiary to contract for, charge, take, reserve or receive a greater amount of interest than under Texas law). If the applicable law is ever judicially interpreted so as to render usurious any amount called for under the Security Instruments, or contracted for, charged, taken, reserved or received with respect to the Loan, or if acceleration of the maturity of the Indebtedness or if any prepayment by Grantor results in Grantor having paid any interest in excess of that permitted by law, then it is Grantor's and Beneficiary's express intent that all excess amounts theretofore collected by Beneficiary be credited on the principal balance of the Note (or, if the Note has been or would thereby be paid in full, refunded to Grantor), and the provisions of the Security Instruments immediately be deemed reformed and the amounts thereafter collectible thereunder reduced, without the necessity of the execution of any new document, so as to comply with the applicable law, but so as to permit the recovery of the fullest amount otherwise called for hereunder and thereunder. The right to accelerate maturity of Indebtedness does not include the right to accelerate any interest which has not otherwise accrued on the date of such acceleration, and Beneficiary does not intend to collect any unearned interest in the event of acceleration. All sums paid or agreed to be paid to Beneficiary for the use, forbearance or detention of the Indebtedness shall, to the extent permitted by applicable law, be amortized, prorated, allocated and spread throughout the full term of the Indebtedness until payment in full so that the rate or amount of interest on account of the Indebtedness does not exceed the applicable usury ceiling.

11.11 *Entire Agreement and Modification.* The Security Instruments contain the entire agreements between the parties relating to the subject matter hereof and thereof and all prior agreements relative thereto which are not contained herein or therein are terminated. The Security Instruments may not be amended, revised, waived, discharged, released or terminated orally but only by a written instrument or instruments executed by the party against which enforcement of the amendment, revision, waiver, discharge, release or termination is asserted. Any alleged amendment, revision, waiver, discharge, release or termination which is not so documented shall not be effective as to any party.

11.12 *Counterparts.* This Deed of Trust may be executed in any number of counterparts, each of which shall be an original but all of which together shall constitute but one instrument.

11.13 *Applicable Law.* This Deed of Trust, the Note and the other Security Instruments shall be deemed to be contracts made under and shall be construed in accordance with and governed by and construed in accordance with the laws of the State of Texas and the federal laws of the United States of America, if applicable.

11.14 *Subrogation.* If any or all of the proceeds of the Note have been used to extinguish, extend or renew any indebtedness heretofore existing against the Mortgaged Property, then, to the extent of such funds so used, the Indebtedness and this Deed of Trust shall be subrogated to all of the rights, claims, liens, titles and interests (herein collectively called the "Prior Liens") heretofore existing against the Mortgaged Property to secure the indebtedness so extinguished, extended or renewed and the Prior Liens, if any, are not waived but rather are continued in full force and effect in favor of Beneficiary and are merged with the lien and security interest created herein as cumulative security for the repayment of the Indebtedness and the satisfaction of the Obligations.

11.15 *No Partnership.* Nothing contained in the Security Instruments is intended to, or shall be construed as, creating to any extent and in any manner whatsoever, any partnership, joint venture, or association between Grantor, Trustee and Beneficiary, or in any way make Beneficiary or Trustee co-principals with Grantor with reference to the Mortgaged Property, and any inferences to the contrary are hereby expressly negated.

11.16 *Tax and Insurance Escrow.* In order to implement the provisions of Paragraphs 4.5 and 4.7 hereinabove, Grantor shall pay to Beneficiary monthly, annually, or as otherwise directed by Beneficiary, an amount ("Escrowed Sums") equal to the sum of (a) the annual Impositions (estimated wherever necessary) to become due for the tax year during which such payment is so directed and (b) the insurance premiums for the same year for those insurance policies as are required hereunder. If Beneficiary determines that any amounts theretofore paid by Grantor are insufficient for the payment in full of such Impositions and insurance premiums, Beneficiary shall notify Grantor of the increased amounts required to provide a sufficient fund, whereupon Grantor shall pay to Beneficiary within thirty (30) days thereafter the additional amount as stated in Beneficiary's notice. The Escrowed Sums may be held by Beneficiary in non-interest bearing accounts and may be commingled with Beneficiary's other funds. Upon assignment of this Deed of Trust, Beneficiary shall have the right to pay over the balance of the Escrowed Sums then in its possession to its assignee whereupon the Beneficiary and its Trustee shall then become completely released from all liability with respect thereto. Upon full payment of the Indebtedness or at such earlier time as Beneficiary may elect, the balance of the Escrowed Sums in its possession shall be paid over to Grantor (whether the person identified in the introductory paragraph of this Deed of Trust or the then owner of the Mortgaged Property) and no other party (including prior owners of the Mortgaged Property) shall have any right or claim thereto. If no Event of Default shall have occurred and be continuing hereunder, the escrowed sums shall, at the option of Beneficiary, be repaid to Grantor in sufficient time to allow Grantor to satisfy Grantor's obligations under the Security Instruments to pay the Impositions and the required insurance premiums or be paid directly to the Governmental Authority and the insurance company entitled thereto. In an Event of Default shall have occurred and be continuing hereunder, however, Beneficiary shall have the additional option of crediting the full amount of the escrowed sums against the Indebtedness. Beneficiary is not obligated to render the Mortgaged Property to taxing authorities or to attempt to obtain any adjustments to the assessed valuation or the amount of taxes, insurance premiums or Impositions with respect to the Mortgaged Property. Notwithstanding anything to the contrary contained in this Paragraph 11.16 or elsewhere in this Deed of Trust, Beneficiary hereby reserves the right to waive the payment by Grantor to Beneficiary of the Escrowed Sums, and, in the event Beneficiary does so waive such payment, it shall be without prejudice to Beneficiary's rights to insist, at any subsequent time or times, that such payments be made in accordance herewith.

11.17 *Headings.* The Article, Paragraph and Subparagraph entitlements hereof are inserted for convenience of reference only and shall in no way alter, modify or define, or be used in construing, the text of such Articles, Paragraphs or Subparagraphs.

11.18 *Gender.* Each gender used herein shall include and apply to all genders, including the neuter.

11.19 *Agents.* Any right, remedy, privilege, duty or action available to or to be performed by Beneficiary under the Security Instruments may, if and to the extent determined by Beneficiary, be exercised or performed by any agent, attorney, correspondent or other representative of Beneficiary.

11.20 *Disposition of Mortgaged Property, Leases, or Beneficial Interest in Grantor.* Upon the sale, exchange, assignment, conveyance or other disposition (herein collectively called "Disposition") of all or any portion of the Mortgaged Property (or any interest therein), or of all or any part of the beneficial ownership interest in Grantor, an Event of Default shall be deemed to have occurred and Beneficiary may, at Beneficiary's option, enforce any and all of Beneficiary's rights, remedies and recourses available upon the occurrence of an Event of Default; provided, however, Beneficiary shall not enforce such rights, remedies and recourses if Beneficiary consents in writing to the Disposition in question. It is expressly agreed that in connection with determining whether to grant or withhold such consent to each such Disposition, Beneficiary may, *inter alia,* (a) consider (based upon Beneficiary's then current criteria for approving borrowers for mortgage loans similar to the Loan) the financial strength and experience of the party to whom such Disposition will be made and its management ability with respect to the Mortgaged Property, (b) consider whether or not the security for payment of the Indebtedness and the performance of the Obligations, or Beneficiary's ability to enforce its rights, remedies and recourses with respect to such security, will be impaired in any way by the proposed Disposition, (c) require as a condition to granting such consent, an increase in the rate of interest payable under the Note (subject to the provisions of Paragraph 11.10 hereof), (d) require that Beneficiary be reimbursed for all costs and expenses incurred by Beneficiary in investigating the financial strength, experience and management ability of the party to whom such Disposition will be made and in determining whether Beneficiary's security will be impaired by the proposed Disposition, (e) require the payment to Beneficiary of a transfer fee to cover the cost of documenting the Disposition in its records on the date of closing of such Disposition, (subject to the provisions of Paragraph 11.10 hereof), (f) require the payment of its reasonable attorney's fees in connection with such Disposition, (g) require the express assumption of payment of the Indebtedness and performance of the Obligations by the party to whom such Disposition will be made (with or without the release of Grantor from liability for such Indebtedness and Obligations), (h) require the execution of assumption agreements, modification agreements, supplemental security documents and financing statements satisfactory in form and substance to Beneficiary, (i) require endorsements (to the extent available under applicable law) to any existing mortgagee title insurance policies insuring Beneficiary's liens and security interests covering the Mortgaged Property or new mortgagee title policies, (j) require additional security for the payment of the Indebtedness and performance of the Obligations, and (k) shorten the stated term of the Note or otherwise rearrange the payment terms of the Note.

11.21 *Credit Reports.* Grantor hereby authorizes Beneficiary to obtain from time to time credit reports through reputable credit reporting agencies relating to Grantor and any of the partners in Grantor.

11.22 *Right of Contest.* Provided that no Event of Default then remains uncured, Grantor shall have the right to contest in good faith and by appropriate proceedings any Impositions, claim, demand, levy, tax or assessment by a third party, the existence of which would otherwise be an Event of Default hereunder. Any such contests shall be prosecuted diligently and in a manner not prejudicial to Beneficiary or the rights of Beneficiary hereunder. Upon demand by Beneficiary, and as a condition to Grantor's rights under this Paragraph 11.22, Grantor shall deposit funds with Beneficiary or obtain a bond in form and substance and with an issuing company satisfactory to Beneficiary in an amount sufficient to cover any amounts which may be owing in the event the contest may be unsuccessful, including interest, penalties, attorneys' fees and court costs. Grantor shall make such deposit or obtain such bond, as the case may be, within five (5) days after demand therefor; and, if made by payment of funds to Beneficiary, the amount so deposited shall be disbursed in accordance with the resolution of the contest either to Grantor or the adverse claimant. In no event may Grantor delay the payment of any taxes or other sums beyond the date on which the Mortgaged Property could be sold due to non-payment. Furthermore, Beneficiary shall have the right, pursuant to Paragraph 11.7 hereof, to pay any such Impositions, claims, demands, levies, taxes or assessments to prevent the sale of the Mortgaged Property.

11.23 *Construction Mortgage.* This Deed of Trust is a "construction mortgage" within the meaning of Sections 9.105(a)(1) and 9.313(a)(3) of the Uniform Commercial Code—Secured Transactions of the State of Texas. This instrument secures an obligation for the construction of an improvement on land, including the acquisition of the land.

11.24 *Environmental Matters.*

(a) Beneficiary shall have the right, at any time so long as any part of the Note shall remain unpaid, to inspect the Mortgaged Property or any part thereof during reasonable hours and upon reasonable notice to Grantor to determine if any environmental hazard is present or is threatening to be created which will impair the value of the Mortgaged Property. Beneficiary may conduct any test or investigation, or collect any samples of materials from on, about, or under the Mortgaged Property necessary to determine whether such hazards might exist so long as it uses reasonable efforts not to interfere with Grantor's use of Mortgaged Property. If an environmental hazard (whether existing prior to the date hereof or coming into existence after the date hereof) which is likely to damage collateral value of the Mortgaged Property, and Grantor does not remove or cure the risk which threatens to impair value of the Mortgaged Property within a reasonable period of time, such failure shall be an Event of Default under the terms of this Deed of Trust.

(b) So long as any part of the Note remains unpaid, Grantor shall not allow any activity to be conducted on the Mortgaged Property or any use to be made of the Mortgaged Property which presents a high risk of environmental contamination, including but not limited to:

(1) Chemical manufacturing or storage;

(2) Operation of any hazardous waste handling or recycling facility; and

(3) Underground storage of petroleum products.

(c) The use of the Mortgaged Property for any of the uses prohibited in Paragraph 11.24(c) above shall be deemed an Event of Default under the terms of this Deed of Trust.

[End of Document]

ATTENTION: COUNTY CLERK—THIS INSTRUMENT COVERS GOODS THAT ARE OR ARE TO BECOME FIXTURES ON THE REAL PROPERTY DESCRIBED HEREIN AND IS TO BE FILED FOR RECORD IN THE RECORDS WHERE DEEDS OF TRUST ON REAL ESTATE ARE RECORDED. ADDITIONALLY, THIS INSTRUMENT SHOULD BE APPROPRIATELY INDEXED, NOT ONLY AS A DEED OF TRUST, BUT ALSO AS A FINANCING STATEMENT COVERING GOODS THAT ARE OR ARE TO BECOME FIXTURES ON THE REAL PROPERTY DESCRIBED HEREIN. THE MAILING ADDRESSES OF THE GRANTOR (DEBTOR) AND BENEFICIARY (SECURED PARTY) ARE SET FORTH IN THIS INSTRUMENT. GRANTOR IS THE RECORD OWNER OF THE PROPERTY DESCRIBED HEREIN.

EXHIBIT E
FORM OF
DEED OF TRUST AND SECURITY AGREEMENT

THE STATE OF TEXAS)
)
COUNTY OF _____)

THIS DEED OF TRUST AND SECURITY AGREEMENT (this "*Deed of Trust*") made and entered into as of the _____ day of _____, 19__ by [_____], a Texas corporation, whose address for notice hereunder is [_____] (the "*Grantor*"), for the use and benefit of _____ (the "*Beneficiary*");

WITNESSETH:

In consideration of the sum of Ten Dollars ($10.00) and other valuable consideration in hand paid by the Beneficiary to the Grantor, and in consideration of the debts and agreements hereinafter mentioned, the receipt and sufficiency of all of which are hereby acknowledged, the Grantor by these presents does hereby **BARGAIN, GRANT, SELL, ASSIGN, MORTGAGE, TRANSFER and CONVEY** unto _____ (the "*Trustee*"), and his successors and substitutes in trust hereunder, for the use and benefit of the Beneficiary, the following described or referenced real and personal property, rights, titles, interests and estates (collectively the "*Mortgaged Property*"), to-wit:

1. The property set forth and described on Exhibit "A" attached hereto and made a part hereof (the "*Land*"), together with all buildings and other improvements thereon and hereafter placed thereon.

2. The definition of Mortgaged Property contained in Paragraph 1.1(k) of the Master Deed of Trust (defined in Section II hereof) is hereby incorporated by reference in its entirety as if such paragraph were fully set forth herein.

3. All of the Grantor's rights, titles and interests in and to the Plans and Specifications (as defined in the Loan Agreement hereinafter defined) for the Type of Home or Types of Home (as defined in the Loan Agreement) being constructed on the Land.

TO HAVE AND TO HOLD the Mortgaged Property unto the Trustee and to his successors and assigns forever to secure the payment of the Indebtedness (hereinafter defined) and to secure the performance of the Obligations (other than payment of the Indebtedness) of the Grantor.

I.

This Deed of Trust is executed and delivered by the Grantor to secure and enforce the payment and performance of all of the indebtedness, covenants and obligations of the Grantor described or referred to in that certain Loan Agreement dated as of [_____], 1992, among the Grantor, as the borrower, and the Beneficiary, as the lender, as now in effect and as may hereafter be amended and supplemented from time to time (the "*Loan Agreement*"), including but not limited to:

(a) that certain promissory note dated [_____], 1992, in the principal amount of $[_____],000,000 executed by the Grantor and payable to the order of the Beneficiary with final maturity on or before [_____], 1993, and bearing interest, containing acceleration of maturity and attorneys' fees and collection clauses, all as specified therein, together with all renewals, rearrangements, extensions and modifications thereof and increases thereto;

(b) any sums which may be advanced or paid by the Beneficiary or the Trustee under the terms hereof on account of the failure of the Grantor to comply with the covenants or agreements of the Grantor contained herein or in the Loan Agreement or in any instrument or agreement referred to therein; and

(c) all other indebtedness of the Grantor arising pursuant to the provisions of this Deed of Trust or of any other instrument executed in connection with or as security for the aforesaid promissory notes and any additional loans made by the Beneficiary to the Grantor pursuant to the Loan Agreement or the Security Instruments described therein (it being contemplated that the Beneficiary may lend additional sums to the Grantor from time to time, but shall not be obligated to do so, and the Grantor hereby agrees that any such additional loans shall be secured by this Deed of Trust).

The term "*Indebtedness*" as used herein shall mean and include said promissory notes and all other indebtedness and obligations described, referred to or mentioned in this Section I.

II.

1. Except as hereinafter set forth, the Grantor hereby agrees that all of the provisions of Articles 1, 2, 3, 4, 6, 7, 8, 9, 10, and 11 of the Master Form of Deed of Trust and Security Agreement Recorded by the Beneficiary (the "*Master Deed of Trust*"), filed for record in the Real Property Records as follows:

County	Date Filed	Instrument No.	Volume	Page	Film Code No.

are hereby incorporated herein by reference as if such representations, warranties, covenants and other provisions set forth in the Master Deed of Trust were fully made in this Deed of Trust and apply to the Mortgaged Property herein described as if they were set forth in this Deed of Trust; and all other provisions of the

Master Deed of Trust not specifically incorporated by reference in this Deed of Trust are not incorporated herein and not made a part hereof.

2. Grantor shall be entitled to receive partial releases from the liens created hereunder upon the following terms and conditions:

(a) Payment of all amounts advanced by Beneficiary with respect to the Lot and Home to be released, together with accrued interest thereon and all other amounts incurred by Beneficiary in connection therewith and not previously reimbursed by Grantor;

(b) No default shall exist under the Security Instruments;

(c) Grantor shall pay any and all reasonable expenses, including reasonable attorney's fees, incurred by Beneficiary in connection with such release;

(d) Every such payment shall be credited upon fees due and unpaid or upon the Note as to principal or accrued interest at the sole discretion of Beneficiary;

(e) Any such payment shall not release Grantor from the payment of the Note according to its terms and conditions, and no such payment or partial release shall in anywise impair or affect the validity, priority or standing of such lien as to the remainder of the Mortgaged Property, regardless of who may own the same, or any part thereof, or the order of its alienation or acquisition; and

(f) The right of Grantor to partial releases shall be exercised by written request to Beneficiary accompanied by recordable partial releases, in form and substance satisfactory to Grantor describing the portion of the Mortgaged Property that Grantor desires to have released. Each such request shall be delivered to Beneficiary a reasonable period of time prior to the date on which Grantor desires to have the partial release executed and delivered.

3. Section 7.1(a) of the Master Deed of Trust is amended for purposes of this Deed of Trust to read as follows:

(a) *Acceleration:* Declare the Principal Balance (defined hereby as meaning the then unpaid principal balance on the Note), the accrued interest, and any other accrued but unpaid portion of the Indebtedness to be immediately due and payable, without notice except as provided in the Loan Agreement, present, protest, demand, or action of any nature whatsoever, each of which is hereby expressly waived by Grantor, whereupon the same shall become immediately due and payable.

4. Section 7.6 of the Master Deed of Trust is amended for purposes of this Deed of Trust to read as follows:

7.6 *Waiver of Redemption, Notice and Marshalling of Assets.* To the fullest extent permitted by law, Grantor hereby irrevocably and unconditionally waives and releases (a) all benefits that might accrue to Grantor by virtue of any present or future moratorium law or other law exempting the Mortgaged Property from attachment, levy or sale on execution or providing for any appraisement, valuation, stay of execution, exemption from civil process, redemption or extension of time for payment; (b) except as set forth in the Loan Agreement, all notices of any Event of Default (except as may be expressly provided for in Article 6 or 7 hereof) of Trustee's election to exercise or his actual exercise of any right, remedy or recourse provided for under the Security Instruments; and (c) any right to a marshalling of assets or a sale in inverse order of alienation.

5. The reference to Section 6.4 contained in Section 7.9 of the Master Deed of Trust is hereby amended for purposes of this Deed of Trust to refer to Section 6.2.

6. Section 11.16 set forth in the Master Deed of Trust is hereby deleted for purposes of this Deed of Trust.

7. The last sentence in Section 11.5 of the Master Deed of Trust is hereby deleted for purposes of this Deed of Trust.

8. Paragraph 1.1(*o*) of the Master Deed of Trust is amended to read as follows:

(*o*) *Personalty:* All of the right, title and interest of Grantor in and to all furniture, furnishings, equipment, machinery, goods, money, insurance proceeds, accounts, contract rights, inventory, all refundable, returnable or reimbursable fees, deposits or other funds or evidences of credit or indebtedness deposited by or on behalf of Grantor with any governmental agencies, boards, corporations, providers of utility services, public or private, including specifically but without limitation, all refundable, returnable or reimbursable tap fees, utility deposits, commitment fees and development costs, and all other personal property (other than the Fixtures) of any kind or character as defined in and subject to the provisions of the Texas Business and Commerce Code (Article 9—Secured Transactions), which are now or hereafter located or to be located upon, within or about the Land and the Buildings, or which are or may be used in or related to the planning, development, financing or operation of the Mortgaged Property, together with all accessories, replacements and substitutions thereto or therefor and the proceeds thereof.

9. Article 4 of the Master Deed of Trust is amended to add new Paragraph 4.15 as follows:

4.15 *Compliance with Anti-Forfeiture Laws.* Grantor will not commit, permit, or suffer to exist any act or omission affording the federal government or any state or local government the right of forfeiture as against the Mortgaged Property or any part thereof or any money paid in performance of Grantor's obligations under the Note or under any of the Security Documents. In furtherance thereof, Grantor hereby agrees to indemnify Beneficiary and Trustee and agrees to defend and hold Beneficiary and Trustee harmless from and against any loss, damage or injury by reason of the breach of the covenants and agreements set forth in this Paragraph 4.15. Without limiting the generality of the foregoing, the filing of formal charges for the commencement of proceedings against Grantor, or against all of any part of the Mortgaged Property under any federal or state law for which forfeiture of the Mortgaged Property or any part thereof or of any monies paid in the performance of Grantor's obligations under the Security Documents is a potential result shall, at the election of the Beneficiary, constitute an Event of Default hereunder without notice or opportunity to cure.

10. Paragraph 11.24 of the Master Deed of Trust is hereby deleted for purposes of this Deed of Trust.

11. The Master Deed of Trust is amended to add a new Article 12 to read as follows:

ARTICLE 12

HAZARDOUS MATERIALS

12.1 *Definitions.* Grantor, Beneficiary and Trustee agree that, for purposes of this Article 12 only, the following terms shall have the meaning herein specified:

(a) "*Governmental Authority*" shall mean the United States, the state, the county, the city, or any other political subdivision in which the Mortgaged Property is located, and any other political subdivision, agency, or instrumentality exercising jurisdiction over Grantor or the Mortgaged Property.

(b) "*Environmental Laws*" shall mean all laws, ordinances, orders, interpretations, rules and regulations of any Governmental Authority applicable to

Grantor or the Mortgaged Property relating to human health or the environment, including, without limitation, RCRA and CERCLA (as hereinafter defined), the Toxic Substances Control Act, 15 U.S.C. Section 2601 et seq., the Hazardous Materials Transportation Act, 49 U.S.C. Section 1801 et seq., the Clean Water Act, 33 U.S.C. Section 1251 et seq., the Clean Air Act, 42 U.S.C. Section 7401 et seq., the Texas Solid Waste Disposal Act, V.A.T.S. Article 4477-7, all as now or hereafter amended, as well as any common law or any other rule of law of any Governmental Authority applicable to the Grantor or the Mortgaged Property and relating to human health or the environment.

(c) *"Hazardous Materials"* shall mean any of the following: (i) any "hazardous waste" as defined by the Resource Conservation and Recovery Act of 1976 (42 U.S.C. Section 6901 et seq.), as amended from time to time, and regulations promulgated thereunder ("RCRA"); (ii) any "hazardous substance", "pollutant" or "contaminant", as defined by the Comprehensive Environmental Response, Compensation and Liability Act of 1980 (42 U.S.C. Section 9601 et seq.), as amended from time to time, and regulations promulgated thereunder ("CERCLA"); (iii) asbestos (whether or not friable) and asbestos-containing materials; (iv) any volatile organic compounds, including oil and petroleum products; (v) any substances which because of their quantitative concentration, chemical, radioactive, flammable, explosive, infectious or other characteristics, constitute or may reasonably be expected to constitute or contribute to a danger or hazard to public health, safety or welfare or to the environment, including, without limitation, any polychlorinated biphenyls (PCBs), toxic metals, etchants, pickling and plating wastes, explosives, reactive metals and compounds, pesticides, herbicides, radon gas, urea formaldehyde foam insulation and chemical, biological and radioactive wastes; (vi) any other substance the presence of which on the Mortgaged Property is prohibited by any Environmental Laws; and (vii) any other substance which by any Environmental Laws requires special handling or notification of any federal, state or local governmental entity in its collection, storage, treatment, or disposal.

(d) *"Hazardous Materials Contamination"* shall mean the contamination (whether presently existing or hereafter occurring) of the Buildings, facilities, soil, groundwater, air or other elements on or of the Mortgaged Property by Hazardous Materials, or the contamination of the buildings, facilities, soil, groundwater, air or other elements on or of any other property as a result of Hazardous Materials at any time (whether before or after the date of this Deed of Trust) emanating from the Mortgaged Property.

12.2 *Grantor's Warranties.* Grantor hereby represents and warrants that:

(a) Grantor has performed reasonable investigations, studies and tests as to any possible environmental contamination, remedial obligation, liabilities or problems with respect to the Land and such investigations, studies and tests have disclosed no Hazardous Materials or violations of Environmental Laws.

(b) To the best of Grantor's knowledge, there have been no releases of Hazardous Materials either at, upon, under or within the Land, and no Hazardous Materials have migrated to the Land from neighboring properties.

(c) No Hazardous Materials are located on or have been stored, processed or disposed of on, or released or discharged from (including discharges to groundwater), the Land or any other adjoining property currently owned or operated by Grantor or any affiliate of Grantor, and no above or underground storage tanks exist on the Land.

(d) Grantor has not received notice from any Governmental Authority or other occupant or from any other person with respect to any release of Hazardous Materials at, upon, under or within the Land, and to the best of Grantor's knowledge no investigation, administrative order, consent order and agreement, litigation or settlement with respect to Hazardous Materials or Hazardous Materials Contamination is proposed, threatened, anticipated or in existence with respect to the Land. The Land is not currently on, and to Grantor's knowledge, after diligent investigation and inquiry, has never been on, any federal or state "Superfund" or "Superlien" list.

(e) To the best of Grantor's knowledge, there is no asbestos or asbestos-containing materials, PCBs, radon gas, or urea formaldehyde foam insulation at or within the Land.

(f) Grantor possesses all permits, licenses, registrations, and similar authorizations required to operate the Mortgaged Property under Environmental Laws, and the Mortgaged Property and all operations conducted thereon are currently in compliance with all Environmental Laws.

12.3 *Grantor's Covenants.* Grantor hereby covenants and agrees as follows:

(a) Grantor has not been, is not, and will not become involved in operations at the Land which could lead to the imposition on Grantor or any subsequent owner of the Land of liability under any Environmental Laws.

(b) Grantor will strictly comply with all Environmental Laws, and will notify Beneficiary of the presence of or any release of Hazardous Materials at, upon, under or within the Land, or of the receipt by Grantor of any notice from any Governmental Authority or from any tenant or other occupant or from any other person with respect to any alleged such release or presence, promptly upon discovery of such release or presence or receipt of such notice, and will send to Beneficiary copies of all results of tests of underground storage tanks at the Land. Without limiting the generality of the foregoing, Grantor will give to Beneficiary prompt notice of the commencement of any litigation or threat of litigation relating to any alleged release of any Hazardous Materials at, upon, under or within the Land. Grantor will deliver to Beneficiary any documentation or records Beneficiary may reasonably request and which are susceptible of being obtained by Grantor without undue cost or expense and without the necessity for initiating legal proceedings to obtain the same in connection with all such notices, inquiries, and communications, and shall endeavor to advise Beneficiary of any subsequent developments.

(c) Grantor shall, at its own cost and expense, take all actions as shall be necessary or advisable for the clean-up of the Land or any other property currently, previously or subsequently owned or operated by Grantor or any affiliate of Grantor, including all removal, containment and remedial action in accordance with all applicable Environmental Laws (and in all events in a manner satisfactory to Beneficiary), and shall further pay or cause to be paid at no expense to Beneficiary all clean-up, administrative, and enforcement costs of all Governmental Authorities or the parties protected by Environmental Laws which may be asserted against the Land or any other property previously or subsequently owned or operated by Grantor or any affiliate of Grantor, the owner or operator thereof or a lienholder secured thereby. All costs (including, without limitation, those costs described above), damages, liabilities, losses, claims, expenses (including, without limitation, attorneys' fees and disbursements) which are incurred by Beneficiary, without the requirement that Beneficiary wait for the ultimate outcome of any litigation, claim or other proceeding, shall be paid by Grantor to Beneficiary within ten (10) days after notice to Grantor from Beneficiary itemizing the amounts incurred to the effective date of such notice, with interest thereon from the date of payment by Beneficiary at the default or post-maturity rate of interest provided for in the Note. Until such amounts shall be paid by Grantor, they shall be added to and become a part of the Indebtedness secured hereby.

12.4 *Site Assessments.* Beneficiary (by its officers, employees and agents) at any time and from time to time, either prior to or after the occurrence of an

Event of Default, may contract for the services of persons (the "Site Reviewers") to perform environmental site assessments ("Site Assessments") on the Mortgaged Property for the purpose of determining whether there exists on the Mortgaged Property any environmental condition which could reasonably be expected to result in any liability, cost or expense to the owner, occupier or operator of such Mortgaged Property arising under any Environmental Laws. The Site Assessments may be performed at any time or times, upon reasonable notice, and under reasonable conditions established by Grantor (including, without limitation, those designed to prevent unreasonable interference with use of the Mortgaged Property) which do not impede the performance of the Site Assessments. The Site Reviewers are hereby authorized to enter upon the Mortgaged Property for such purposes. The Site Reviewers are further authorized to perform both above and below ground testing for environmental damage or the presence of Hazardous Materials on the Mortgaged Property and such other tests on the Mortgaged Property as may be necessary to conduct the Site Assessments in the reasonable opinion of the Site Reviewers. Grantor will supply to the Site Reviewers such historical and operational information regarding the Mortgaged Property as may be reasonably requested by the Site Reviewers to facilitate the Site Assessments and will make available for meetings with the Site Reviewers appropriate personnel having knowledge of such matters. On request, Beneficiary shall make the results of such Site Assessments fully available to Grantor, which (prior to an Event of Default) may at its election participate under reasonable procedures in the direction to such Site Assessments and the description of tasks of the Site Reviewers. The cost of performing such Site Assessments shall be paid by Grantor to Beneficiary within ten (10) days after notice to Grantor from Beneficiary itemizing the amounts incurred to the effective date of such notice, with interest thereon from the date of payment by Beneficiary at the default or post-maturity rate of interest provided for in the Note. Until such amounts shall be paid by Grantor, they shall be added to and become a part of the indebtedness secured hereby.

12.5 *Indemnification.* Grantor shall defend, indemnify and hold harmless Beneficiary and Trustee from any and all liabilities (including strict liability), actions, demands, penalties, losses, costs or expenses (including, without limitation, attorneys' fees and expenses, and remedial costs), suits, costs of any settlement or judgment and claims of any and every kind whatsoever which may now or in the future (whether before or after the release of this Deed of Trust) be paid, incurred or suffered by or asserted against Beneficiary or Trustee by any person or entity or Governmental Authority for, with respect to, or as a direct or indirect result of, the presence on or under, or the escape, seepage, leakage, spillage, discharge, emission or release from the Mortgaged Property of any Hazardous Materials or any Hazardous Materials Contamination or arise out of or result from the environmental condition of the Mortgaged Property or the applicability of any Environmental Laws relating to Hazardous Materials (including, without limitation, CERCLA or any federal, state or local so-called "Superfund" or "Superlien" laws, statute, law, ordinance, code, rule, regulation, order or decree), regardless of whether or not caused by or within the control of Grantor, Beneficiary or Trustee all in accordance with the terms of that certain Indemnity Agreement executed by Grantor of even date herewith the "Indemnification Agreement"). The indemnification obligations and other covenants, warranties and representations contained in this Article 12 are in addition to, and not in lieu of, the indemnification obligations and other covenants, warranties and representations contained in the Indemnification Agreement. The representations, covenants, warranties and indemnifications contained in this Article 12 shall survive the foreclosure or release of this Deed of Trust.

12.6 *Cure of Violations of Environmental Laws.* If Grantor fails to comply with the requirements of any Environmental Laws, Beneficiary shall have the right (but not the obligation) prior or subsequent to an Event of Default, to give such notices or cause such work to be performed at, upon, under or within the Land, or to take any and all other actions as Beneficiary deems necessary, to cure said failure of compliance. All amounts paid or incurred by Beneficiary in the exercise of any such rights shall be paid by Grantor to Beneficiary within ten (10) days after notice to Grantor from Beneficiary itemizing the amounts incurred to the effective date of such notice, with interest thereon from the date of payment by Beneficiary at the default or post-maturity rate of interest provided for in the Note. Until such amounts shall be paid by Grantor, they shall be added to and become a part of the Indebtedness secured hereby.

12. This Deed of Trust is executed subject to the matters set forth in Exhibit "B" hereto (the "Permitted Encumbrances").

13. This Deed of Trust shall constitute a "fixture filing" for all purposes of Chapter 9 of the Texas Business and Commerce Code. All or part of the Mortgaged Property are or are to become fixtures; information concerning the security interest herein granted may be obtained at the addresses set forth on the first page hereof. The address of the Secured Party (Beneficiary) is the address set forth in the opening recitals hereinabove and the address of the Debtor (Grantor) is the address set forth in the opening recitals of this Deed of Trust. Grantor is the record owner of the Property covered hereby.

The Grantor hereby acknowledges receipt of a copy of the Master Deed of Trust upon the execution and delivery of this Deed of Trust.

WITNESS THE EXECUTION HEREOF as of the date first above written.

GRANTOR:

[_____], a Texas corporation

By: _____
[_____]
President

EXHIBIT "A"
[Description of Land]
EXHIBIT "B"
[Permitted Encumbrances]

EXHIBIT F

FORM OF FINANCING STATEMENT

This Financing Statement is presented to a Filing Officer in the Office of the Secretary of State of the State of Texas for filing pursuant to the Texas Uniform Commercial Code.

1. The name and address of the *Debtor* is:
2. The name and address of the *Secured Party* is:
3. This Financing Statement covers the following *Collateral:*

All of Debtor's rights, titles and interests in and to the following described real and personal property, rights, titles, interests and estates, to-wit:

(a) The property set forth and described on Exhibit "A" attached hereto and made a part hereof (the "*Premises*"), together with all buildings and other improvements thereon and hereafter placed thereon.

(b) All building material, machinery, apparatus, equipment, fittings, fixtures, and personal property of every kind and nature whatsoever, now in, part of, affixed to, delivered to or used in connection with the buildings and improvements on the Premises, or hereafter acquired by the Debtor and hereafter placed in, affixed to, delivered to, or used in connection with such buildings and improvements or any buildings hereafter constructed or placed upon the Premises or any part thereof, including, but without limiting the generality of the foregoing, all engines, furnaces, boilers, stokers, pumps, heaters, tanks, dynamos, transformers, motors, generators, fans, blowers, vents, switchboards, electrical equipment, heating, plumbing, lifting and ventilating apparatus, air-cooling and air-conditioning apparatus, water, gas and electrical fixtures, elevators, mail conveyors, escalators, drapes, carpets, shades, awnings, screens, radiators, partitions, ducts, shafts, pipes, conduits, lines, and facilities of whatsoever nature for air, gas, water, steam, electricity, waste sewerage, and for other utilities, services and uses, compressors, vacuum cleaning systems, call systems, fire prevention and extinguishing apparatus, kitchen equipment, cafeteria equipment and recreational equipment, all of which to the extent permitted by law are hereby understood and agreed to be part and parcel of the Premises and improvements thereon and appropriated to the use and operation of the Premises and said improvements, and whether affixed or annexed or not, excluding, however, readily movable trade fixtures not used or acquired for use in connection with the operation of any such building or any part thereof, readily movable office furniture, furnishings and equipment not so used or acquired for use, and consumable supplies, whether or not affixed or annexed, that have been or that may hereafter be placed in any building constructed upon the Premises or any part thereof.

(c) All reversions and remainders in the property hereinbefore described or referred to.

(d) All and singular the tenements, hereditaments, privileges, easements, franchises, rights, appendages and appurtenances now or hereafter belonging or in anywise appertaining unto the Premises, including all interests in the streets adjacent thereto.

(e) All the rents, issues, profits, revenues, and other income of the property described in this item 3, and all the estate, right, title and interest of every nature whatsoever of the Debtor, now owned or hereafter acquired, in and to the same and every part and parcel thereof.

(f) All of Debtor's general intangibles of any kind, whether now existing or hereafter arising in connection with all of the property described in this item 3, including but not limited to all contract rights and plans and specifications relating to the construction of improvements on the Premises; all chattel papers, documents and instruments relating to such general intangibles; and all rights now or hereafter existing in and to all security agreements, leases and other contracts securing or otherwise relating to any such general intangibles or any such chattel papers, documents and instruments.

(g) The proceeds and products of all of the property described in this item 3.

DEBTOR:

[_____], a Texas corporation

By: _____
[_____]
President

EXHIBIT G

FORM OF
LOANS TO ONE BORROWER AFFIDAVIT

The undersigned and, if the undersigned be more than one, each of the undersigned (collectively the "Borrower") executes this Loans to One Borrower Affidavit as of the _____ day of March, 1992, in favor of _____ (the "Lender").

I.
DEFINED TERMS

1. As used in this Loans to One Borrower Affidavit, the following terms shall have the following meanings:

   a. "Borrower's Loan" shall mean the loan being made or to be made by the Lender to the Borrower in connection with which this Loans to One Borrower Affidavit is being executed.

   b. "Control" shall mean the power, directly or indirectly, acting individually or in concert, to exercise a controlling influence over the management or policies of a Person, or to vote ten percent or more of any class of voting securities of a Person, or to control the election of a majority of the directors, trustees or other Persons exercising similar functions of a Person.

   c. "Outstanding Loan" shall mean (i) any direct or indirect advance of funds (including obligations of makers and endorsers arising from the discounting of commercial paper) to a Person on the basis of any obligation of that Person to repay the funds, or repayable from specific property pledged by or on behalf of a Person; (ii) funds a creditor has an obligation to advance under a written commitment to lend, unless the loan is subject to a legally binding overline purchase commitment of another Person; (iii) credit extended in the form of finance leases; (iv) potential liabilities under standby letters of credit, lines of credit, and guarantees or suretyship obligations, and other similar obligations; and (v) investments in commercial paper and corporate debt obligations.

   d. "Owner" shall mean, for any Borrower that is a trust, syndicate, partnership or corporation, any beneficiary of such Borrower, any member of such Borrower, any general partner of such Borrower, any limited partner of such Borrower owning an interest of ten percent or more, or any record or beneficial stockholder of such Borrower owning ten percent or more of the capital stock of such Borrower.

   e. "Person" shall mean an individual, sole proprietorship, partnership, joint venture, association, trust, estate, business trust, corporation, non-profit corporation, financial institution, sovereign government or any agency, instrumentality or political subdivision thereof, or any similar entity or organization.

   f. "Related Person" shall mean:

   i. nominees of the Borrower;

   ii. all Persons of which the Borrower is a nominee;

   iii. all Persons of which Borrower is a beneficiary or a member;

   iv. all Persons of which the Borrower is a general partner;

   v. all Persons in which the Borrower is a limited partner and in which the Borrower owns an interest of ten percent or more (based upon the value of the Borrower's contribution);

   vi. all Persons in which the Borrower is a record or beneficial stockholder owning ten percent or more of such Person's capital stock;

vii. any Person that, directly or indirectly, owns or Controls, or is owned or Controlled by the Borrower or is under common Control with the Borrower;

viii. any Person that, directly or indirectly, owns or Controls or is owned or Controlled by any Person that is: a nominee of the Borrower; a limited partner owning an interest of ten percent or more in or a general partner of the Borrower (if the Borrower is a partnership); the beneficiary of the Borrower (if the Borrower is a trust); a member of the Borrower (if the Borrower is a syndicate);

ix. any Person directly benefitting from the Borrower's Loan;

x. if the Borrower is acquiring a business enterprise with one or more Persons of which the Borrower and such Persons will in the aggregate own 50% or more of the capital stock or voting securities, such Persons shall be included as a "Related Person";

xi. if the Borrower and one or more Persons obtain loans or extensions of credit for which the expected source of repayment is the same, such Persons shall be included as a "Related Person" to the extent of such loans or extensions of credit;

xii. if the Borrower is a trust, syndicate, partnership or corporation, the term "Related Person" shall also include all trusts, syndicates, partnerships, and corporations of which any Owner is a beneficiary, member, general partner, limited partner owning an interest of ten percent or more, or record or beneficial stockholder holding ten percent or more of the capital stock; and

xiii. if the proceeds of the Borrower's Loan are being used to purchase an interest in a partnership, joint venture or association, the term "Related Person" shall include the other members of such partnership, joint venture or association to the extent that such other members have Outstanding Loans from the Lender for the same purpose.

II.

BORROWER'S CERTIFICATE

2. In consideration of the Lender's agreement to make Borrower's Loan, the Borrower hereby certifies and represents to the Lender that:

a. The Borrower has full power and authority to execute this Loans to One Borrower Affidavit;

b. The Borrower is the obligor or guarantor on the Borrower's Loan;

c. No person other than the Borrower is an obligor or guarantor on the Borrower's Loan, except as identified on Exhibit "A" hereto, which is made a part hereof for all purposes; and

d. Except for the Borrower's Loan and any other Outstanding Loans identified on Exhibit "A" hereto, neither the Borrower nor any Related Person has any Outstanding Loans payable to the Lender or any service corporation or operating subsidiary of Lender.

EXECUTED AS OF the date first written above.

BORROWER:

[_____], a Texas corporation

By: _____
[_____]
President

[acknowledgement]

EXHIBIT "A"

1. Other obligors or guarantors on the Borrower's Loan:

2. Other Outstanding Loans to the Borrower and Related Persons:

EXHIBIT H

FORM OF
DISBURSEMENT SCHEDULE

[To be provided by Lender]

EXHIBIT I

FORM OF
AFFIDAVIT OF COMMENCEMENT OF CONSTRUCTION

THE STATE OF TEXAS)
)
COUNTY OF _____)

Before me, the undersigned authority, on this day personally appeared _____, _____ of [_____], a Texas corporation (hereinafter called "Affiant"), personally known to me to be the person whose name is subscribed below and who, after being by me first duly sworn, upon his oath deposes and says:

1. [_____] is the owner of the property described in Exhibit "A" attached hereto which has been mortgaged to _____ to secure a construction loan for the construction of a single family dwelling on said property.

2. The date on which construction commenced with respect to such dwelling was _____, 19__.

[_____], a Texas corporation

By: _____
[_____]
President

SUBSCRIBED AND SWORN TO BEFORE ME this _____ day of _____, 19__.

_____
Notary Public in and for
The State of TEXAS

EXHIBIT J

FORM OF
PARTIAL RELEASE OF LIEN

THE STATE OF TEXAS)
)
COUNTY OF _____)

1. For valuable consideration paid to the undersigned, the receipt of which is hereby acknowledged, the undersigned hereby releases and discharges all of the rights, titles, interests and liens held by the undersigned that were created and exist under the following described instrument heretofore executed for the benefit of the undersigned:

Deed of Trust and Security Agreement dated _____, 19__, executed by [_____], filed for record in the Office of the County Clerk of _____ County, Texas on _____, 19__ and recorded in Volume _____, Page _____ of the Real Property Records of _____ County, Texas;

INSOFAR AND ONLY INSOFAR AS SUCH RIGHTS, TITLES, INTERESTS AND LIENS PERTAIN TO THE PROPERTY SET FORTH AND DESCRIBED ON EXHIBIT "A" ATTACHED HERETO.

2. It is expressly understood and agreed that this is a partial release and shall in no way release, affect or impair the undersigned's rights, titles, interests and liens against any other property described in and covered by the above described instrument.

3. Reference is hereby made to the above described instrument and the recordation thereof for all purposes in connection herewith.

EXECUTED this _____ day of _____, 19__.

By: _____
Name:
Title:

[acknowledgement]

EXHIBIT K

FORM OF
FINANCING STATEMENT CHANGE

This Financing Statement is presented to a Filing Officer in the Office of the Secretary of State of the State of Texas for filing pursuant to the Uniform Commercial Code.

1. The name and address of the *Debtor* is:

2. The name and address of the *Secured Party* is:

3. This Financing Statement Change refers to original Financing Statement No. _____, filed _____, 19__.

4. PARTIAL RELEASE: The Secured Party releases the following collateral which is described in the Financing Statement bearing the file number shown above:

All of the rights, titles and interests in and to such collateral INSOFAR AND ONLY INSOFAR as such collateral pertains to the property set forth on Exhibit "A" attached hereto.

SECURED PARTY:

By: _____
Name:
Title:

EXHIBIT L

FORM OF
BORROWER'S AFFIDAVIT

THE STATE OF TEXAS)
)   KNOW ALL MEN BY THESE PRESENTS
COUNTY OF HARRIS   )

BEFORE ME, the undersigned notary public, on this day personally appeared _____, known to me to be the person whose name is subscribed hereto, and who after being by me first duly sworn according to law, upon oath, deposed and said:

"1. He is the _____ of [_____], a Texas corporation (hereinafter called "Borrower").

2. That he has full power and authority in the name and on behalf of Borrower to:

(a) obtain credit, with security, from Lender, hereinbelow defined, in the principal sum of $[_____], and upon such terms as may seem advisable;

(b) execute the note in aggregate amount of $[_____], drafts, guarantees, or give agreements of any type as evidence thereof;

(c) pledge, assign, mortgage, hypothecate, and execute Deeds of Trust upon and/or Security Agreements covering property of the Borrower as security for any or all obligations, now or hereafter existing, of the Borrower as pertains to the above described obligations;

(d) accept or direct delivery from or to Lender of any property of Borrower at any time held by Lender, and direct the disposition of the proceeds of any obligation of the Borrower to Lender; all such instruments hereinabove referred to be in such form and to contain such terms and conditions as may be approved by Borrower, such approval to be conclusively evidenced by Borrower's execution thereof.

3. That Borrower is the owner of, or is using loan proceeds provided by Lender to purchase, the real property in _____ County, Texas described in Exhibit "A" attached hereto (herein called the "Property").

4. That as of the date hereof, the only party in possession with respect to the Property is Borrower and there are no agreements which would prohibit Borrower from consummating the loan described herein.

5. That as of the date hereof, except as previously disclosed to Lender, there are no unpaid bills for labor or materials, or for either of them, incident to any improvements upon the Property, nor are there any materials previously delivered to the Property which could give rise to lien claims of any kind against the Property or improvements, if any, situated thereon, which would be superior or prior to the liens or security interest granted to Lender.

6. That as of the date hereof, no construction contract of any kind between Borrower and any contractor for the construction of any improvements upon the Property has been recorded and no work has commenced upon and no materials have been delivered to the Property for use in connection with any proposed improvements to be constructed on the Property. Borrower hereby agrees that any liens and rights or claims of liens owned, claimed, or held by Borrower against the Property by reason of labor and services performed and equipment, materials and rentals furnished by Borrower to or for the Property as of the date hereof shall be subordinate and inferior to the lien granted in favor of Lender, its successors and assigns as security for the loans described herein and any renewals and extensions thereof. In

the event of a foreclosure of the liens and security interests created or to be created under or by virtue of the Construction Deed of Trust and Security Agreement executed of even date herewith and any renewals or extensions thereof, in whole or in part, then such foreclosure shall operate to cut off, extinguish and otherwise terminate all such liens, rights and other interests of every kind and nature whatsoever that the Borrower may now or hereinafter have in and to the Property and all improvements now or hereafter constructed or situated thereon.

7. That as of the date hereof, except as previously disclosed to Lender, no leases, either written or oral, have been entered into affecting the Property or any portion thereof.

8. That there are no judgments against [_____], a Texas corporation, in any court remaining unpaid; that there are no material suits pending against [_____], a Texas corporation in any court; that there are no liens or claims that might become liens upon the Property except the following:

_____
_____:

9. That the extension of credit in the transaction described herein is solely for business, investment or commercial purpose other than agricultural purposes, to-wit: acquisition of real property and construction of improvements thereon for residential use; and to his knowledge the transaction is specifically exempt under Section 226.3(a) of Regulation Z issued by the Board of Governors of the Federal Reserve System and under Title I (Truth in Lending Act) and Title V (General Provisions) of the Consumer Credit Protection Act, and that no disclosures are required to be given under such regulations and Federal laws in connection with said transaction, and that Lender is making said loan without giving Borrower the disclosures that may otherwise be required under such law and regulations.

10. That Borrower is solvent.

11. That this Affidavit has been for the purposes of inducing Lender to make a $[_____] loan to [_____], a Texas corporation with full knowledge and intent that Lender shall rely upon the recitals herein contained when entering into such loan transaction, and that but for this instrument and the recital of such facts herein contained and the truth thereof, Lender would not take such action.

12. That this Affidavit is made on behalf of and for the benefit of Borrower."

Executed this _____ day of _____, 19__.

Name:
Affiant:

[acknowledgement]

EXHIBIT M

FORM OF
ENVIRONMENTAL INDEMNITY AGREEMENT

[_____], a Texas corporation, ("Borrower") executes this Agreement as a condition to, and to induce _____ ("Lender") to make a loan (the "Loan") to Borrower evidenced or to be evidenced by that certain Construction Facility Note ("Note") of even date herewith made by Borrower payable to the order of Lender in the original principal amount of _____, which loan is secured or to be secured by a Deed of Trust and Security Agreement (the "Mortgage") of even date herewith from Borrower to _____, Trustee, encumbering certain real and personal property as therein described (collectively, the "Property") including the land described in Exhibit A which is attached hereto and made a part hereof. The term "Loan Documents" as used herein shall mean the Note, Mortgage, that certain Loan Agreement executed by Borrower and Lender of even date herewith and the Security Instruments as defined in the Loan Agreement and Mortgage. This Agreement is one of the Loan Documents.

1. *Definitions.* As used in this Agreement:

(a) "Environmental Claim" means an investigative, enforcement, cleanup, removal, containment, remedial or other private or governmental or regulatory action at any time threatened, instituted or completed against Borrower or against or with respect to the Property or any use or activity on the Property pursuant to any applicable Environmental Requirement, and any claim at any time threatened or made by any person against Borrower or against or with respect to the Property or any use or activity on the Property, relating to damage, contribution, cost recovery, compensation, loss or injury resulting from or in any way arising in connection with any Hazardous Material or any Environmental Law.

(b) "Environmental Requirement" means any Environmental Law, agreement or restriction (including but not limited to any condition or requirement imposed by any insurance or surety company), as the same now exists or may be changed or amended or come into effect in the future, which pertains to health, safety, or the environment, including but not limited to ground or air or water or noise pollution, contamination, and underground or aboveground tanks.

(c) "Hazardous Material" means any substance, whether solid, liquid or gaseous: (i) which is listed, defined or regulated as a "hazardous substance", "hazardous waste" or "solid waste", or otherwise classified as hazardous or toxic, in or pursuant to any Environmental Requirement; or (ii) which is or contains asbestos, radon, any polycholorinated biphenyl, urea formaldehyde foam insulation, explosive or radioactive material, or motor fuel or other petroleum hydrocarbons; or (iii) which causes or poses a threat to cause a contamination or nuisance on the property or any adjacent property or a hazard to the environment or to the health or safety of persons on or about Property.

(d) "Environmental Law" means any federal, state or local law, statute, ordinance, code, rule, regulation, license, authorization, decision, order, injunction or decree, which pertains to health, safety or environment (including but not limited to ground or air or water or noise pollution or contamination, underground or aboveground tanks) and shall include without limitation, the Comprehensive Environmental Response, Compensation and Liability Act of 1980, as amended ("CERCLA"), the Resource Conservation and Recovery Act of 1976, as amended ("RCRA"), the Texas Water Code and the Texas Solid Waste Disposal Act or any other state lien or state superlien or environmental statutes.

(e) "National Priorities List" ("NPL") means the U.S. Environmental Protection Agency's ("EPA") list of sites that are priorities for cleanup actions among the known releases or threatened releases of hazardous substances, pollutants, or contaminants throughout the United States.

(f) "CERCLA Information System" ("CERCLIS") means EPA is inventory of sites that potentially require cleanup. CERCLIS includes all sites identified by EPA as candidates for inclusion on the NPL.

(g) "On" or "on", when used with respect to the Property or any property adjacent to the Property, means "on, in, under, above or about".

2. *Representations and Warranties.* Borrower, after due inquiry and investigation, represents and warrants to Lender, without regard to whether Lender has or hereafter obtains any knowledge or report of the environmental condition of the Property, as follows:

(a) During the period of Borrower's ownership of the Property, the Property has not been used for industrial or manufacturing purposes, for landfill, dumping or other waste disposal activities or operations, for generation, storage, use, sale, treatment, processing, recycling or disposal of any Hazardous Material, for underground or aboveground storage tanks, or for any other use that would give rise to the release of any Hazardous Material on, under or about the Property; and to the best of Borrower's knowledge after inquiry in accordance with good commercial or customary practices, no such use of the Property occurred at any time prior to the period of Borrower's ownership of the Property, nor did any such use on any adjacent property occur during or at any time prior to the period of Borrower's ownership of the Property;

(b) There is no Hazardous Material, storage tank (or similar vessel) whether underground or otherwise, sump or well currently on the Property;

(c) Borrower has received no notice and has no knowledge of any Environmental Claim regarding the Property or any adjacent property;

(d) The present conditions, uses and activities on the Property do not violate any Environmental Requirement and the use of the Property which Borrower (and each tenant and subtenant, if any) makes and intends to make of the Property complies and will comply with all applicable Environmental Requirements; and neither Borrower, nor to Borrower's knowledge, any tenant, has obtained or is required to obtain any permit or other authorization to construct, occupy, operate or use any of the Property by reason of any Environmental Requirement; and

(e) The Property is not currently on, and to the best of Borrower's knowledge after inquiry in accordance with good commercial or customary practices, has never been on, any federal or state "superfund" or "superlien" list, including but not limited to CERCLIS, the NPL or other list pursuant to CERCLA or other laws.

3. *Violations.* Borrower will not cause, commit, permit or allow to continue any violation of any Environmental Requirement by Borrower or by or with respect to the Property or any use or activity on the Property, or the attachment of any environmental lien to the Property. Borrower will not place, install, dispose of or release, or cause, permit, or allow the placing, installation, disposal or release of, any Hazardous Material or storage tank (or similar vessel) on the Property.

4. *Notice to Lender.* Borrower shall promptly deliver to Lender a copy of each report pertaining to the Property or to Borrower prepared by or on behalf of Borrower pursuant to any Environmental Law. Borrower shall promptly advise Lender in writing of any Environmental Claim or of the discovery of any Hazardous Material on the Property, as soon as Borrower first obtains knowledge thereof, including a full description of the nature and extent of the Environmental Claim and/or Hazardous Material and all relevant circumstances.

5. *Site Assessments and Information.* If Lender shall ever have reason to believe that any Hazardous Material affects the Property, or if any Environmental Claim is made or threatened, or if a default shall have occurred under the Loan Documents, Borrower will at its expense provide to Lender from time to time, in each case within 30 days of Lender's request, a report (including all drafts thereof) of an environmental assessment of the Property made after the date of Lender's request and of such scope (including but not limited to the taking of soil borings and air and groundwater samples and other above and below ground testing) as Lender may request and by a consulting firm acceptable to Lender. Borrower will cooperate with each consulting firm making any such assessment and will supply

to the consulting firm, from time to time and promptly on request, all information available to Borrower to facilitate the completion of the assessment and report. Lender may cause any such assessment to be made at Borrower's expense and risk if Borrower fails to comply punctually with such agreement to do so, and Lender and its designees are hereby granted access to the Property at any time or times, upon reasonable notice, and a license which is coupled with an interest and irrevocable, to make such environmental assessments. Lender may disclose to interested parties any information Lender ever has about the environmental condition or compliance of the Property.

6. *Remedial Actions.*

(a) If any Hazardous Material is discovered on the Property at any time and regardless of the cause, Borrower shall (i) promptly at Borrower's sole risk and expense remove, treat, and dispose of the Hazardous Material in compliance with all applicable Environmental Requirements and solely under Borrower's name (or if removal is prohibited by any Environmental Requirement, take whatever action is required by any Environmental Requirement), in addition to taking such other action as is necessary to have the full use and benefit of the Property as contemplated by the Loan Documents, and provide Lender with satisfactory evidence thereof, and (ii) if requested by Lender, provide to Lender within 30 days of Lender's request a bond, letter of credit or other financial assurance evidencing to Lender's satisfaction that all necessary funds are readily available to pay the costs and expenses of the actions required by clause (i) preceding and to discharge any assessments or liens established against the Property as a result of the presence of the Hazardous Material on the Property.

(b) Lender may, but shall never be obligated to, remove or cause the removal of any Hazardous Material from the Property (or if removal is prohibited by any Environmental Requirement, take or cause the taking of such other action as is required by any Environmental Requirement) if Borrower fails to do so promptly upon discovery (without limitation of Lender's rights to declare a default under any of the Loan Documents and exercise all rights and remedies available by reason thereof); and Lender and its designees are hereby granted access to the Property at any time or times, upon reasonable notice, and a license which is coupled with an interest and irrevocable, to remove or cause such removal or to take or cause the taking of any such other action. All costs, including, without limitation, those costs set forth above, damages, liabilities, losses, claims, expenses (including attorneys' fees and disbursements) which are incurred by Lender, as the result of Borrower's failure to comply with the provisions of this Section 6, shall be paid by Borrower to Lender as incurred upon demand by Lender.

7. *Indemnity.*

(a) Borrower hereby agrees to protect, indemnify and hold Lender, the Trustee under the Mortgage (the "Trustee"), the directors, officers, partners, employees and agents of Lender and/or Trustee, respectively, and any persons or entities owned or controlled by, owning or controlling, or under common control or affiliated with Lender and/or Trustee, and their successors and assigns and participants in the Loan (each an "Indemnified Party") harmless from and against, and reimburse them on demand for, any and all Environmental Damages (as hereinafter defined). Without limitation, the foregoing indemnity shall apply to each Indemnified Party with respect to Environmental Damages which in whole or in part are caused by or arise out of the negligence of such (and/or any other) Indemnified Party. Borrower understands and agrees that its liability to the aforementioned Indemnified Parties shall arise upon the earlier to occur of (i) discovery of any Hazardous Material on, under or about the Property or (ii) the institution of any Environmental Claim, and not upon the realization of loss or damage. If a court of competent jurisdiction determines that the subject of the indemnification was caused by or arose out of the gross negligence or willful misconduct of a particular Indemnified Party, Borrower is entitled to reimbursement from that Indemnified Party for any amount paid by Borrower to that Party arising out of the same subject matter and paid as a result of this Agreement. However, there shall be no such reimbursement to Borrower if the gross negligence or willful misconduct consisted of the Indemnified Party's assistance to, or encouragement of, Borrower in violating Environmental Requirements.

(b) As used in this Agreement, the term "Environmental Damages" means all claims, demands, liabilities (including strict liability), losses, damages (including consequential damages), causes of action, judgments, penalties, fines, costs and expenses (including fees, cost and expenses of attorneys, consultants, contractors, experts and laboratories), of any and every kind or character, contingent or otherwise, matured or unmatured, known or unknown, foreseeable or unforeseeable, made, incurred, suffered, or brought at any time and from time to time and arising in whole or in part from:

(1) The presence of any Hazardous Material on the Property, or any escape, seepage, leakage, spillage, emission, release, discharge or disposal of any Hazardous Material on the Property, or the migration or release or threatened migration or release of any Hazardous Material to, from or through the Property, at any time on or before the first anniversary after the Release Date (as hereinafter defined); or

(2) any act, omission, event or circumstance existing or occurring in connection with the handling, treatment, containment, removal, storage, decontamination, cleanup, transport or disposal of any Hazardous Material which is at any time on or before the first anniversary after the Release Date present on the Property; or

(3) the breach of any representation, warranty, covenant or agreement contained in this Agreement; or

(4) any violation on or before the first anniversary after the Release Date, of any Environmental Requirement in effect on or before the first anniversary after the Release Date, regardless of whether any act, omission, event or circumstance giving rise to the violation constituted a violation at the time of the occurrence or inception of such act, omission, event or circumstance; or

(5) any Environmental Claim, or the filing of an imposition of any environmental lien against the Property, because of, resulting from, in connection with, or arising out of the matters referred to in clauses (1) through (4) preceding; or

(6) any claim that an Indemnified Party encouraged or assisted Borrower in violating any Environmental Requirements described in clause (4) preceding; or

(7) the enforcement of this Agreement or the assertion by Borrower of any defense to its obligations hereunder (except the successful defense of actual performance not subject to further appeal);

and regardless of whether any of the foregoing was caused by Borrower or Borrower's tenant or subtenant, or a prior owner of the Property or its tenant or subtenant, or any third party, including but not limited to: (i) injury or damage to any person, property or natural resource occurring upon or off of the Property, including but not limited to the cost of demolition and rebuilding of any improvements on real property, and (ii) the investigation or remediation of any such Hazardous Material or violation of Environmental Requirement, including but not limited to the preparation of any feasibility studies or reports and the performance of any cleanup, remediation, removal, response, abatement, containment, closure, restoration, monitoring or similar work required by any Environmental Requirement or necessary to make full use and benefit of the Property as contemplated by the Loan Documents (including any of the same in connection with any foreclosure action or transfer in lieu thereof), and all liability to pay or indemnify any person or governmental authority for costs expended in connection with any of the foregoing; and (iii) the investigation and defense of any claim, whether or not such claim is ultimately defeated, and the settlement of any claim or judgment.

(c) As used in this Agreement, the term "Release Date" means the earlier of the following two dates: (i) the date on which the indebtedness and obligations secured by the Mortgage have been paid and performed in full and the Mortgage has been released, or (ii) the date on which the lien of the Mortgage is fully and finally foreclosed or a conveyance by deed in lieu of such foreclosure is fully and finally effective; provided that, if such payment, performance, release, foreclosure or conveyance is challenged, in bankruptcy proceedings or otherwise, the Release Date shall be deemed not to have occurred until such challenge is rejected, dismissed or withdrawn with prejudice.

(d) Notwithstanding anything to the contrary contained above:

(1) The Indemnified Partie(s) shall not be required to give the Borrower notice of any Environmental Damage until 30 days after the Indemnified Partie(s) receives written notice of that Environmental Damage. Even if the Indemnified Partie(s) fails to give Borrower timely notice of that Environmental Damage or otherwise defaults in its obligation under this Agreement, the Indemnified Partie(s) shall retain the right to defend and control the settlement of the Environmental Damages. The Borrower's sole remedy for such a default by the Indemnified Partie(s) shall be to offset against the indemnification liability otherwise payable by the Borrower to the Indemnified Partie(s) the amount of damages actually suffered by the Borrower as a result of the late notice or other default by the Indemnified Partie(s) under this Agreement.

(2) The Borrower shall have no right to defend or control the settlement of any Environmental Damage unless each of the following conditions is satisfied: (i) The Environmental Damage seeks only monetary damages and does not seek any injunction or other equitable relief against the Indemnified Partie(s); (ii) The Borrower unconditionally acknowledges in writing, in a notice of election to contest or defend the Environmental Damage given to the Indemnified Partie(s) within 10 days after the Indemnified Partie(s) gives the Borrower notice of the Environmental Damage, that the Borrower is jointly and severally obligated to indemnify the Indemnified Partie(s) in full with respect to the Environmental Damage, irrespective of any limitation of liability that may be contained elsewhere in the Agreement; (iii) The Borrower is not then in default in any of their other obligations to the Indemnified Partie(s) under the Loan Documents; (iv) The counsel chosen by the Borrower to defend the Environmental Damage is reasonably satisfactory to the Indemnified Partie(s); and (v) The Borrower furnishes the Indemnified Partie(s) with a letter of credit, surety bond, or similar security in form and substance reasonably satisfactory to the Indemnified Partie(s) in an amount sufficient to secure the Borrower's potential indemnity liability to the Indemnified Partie(s) in the full amount of the Environmental Damage.

(3) If the Borrower elects to defend against an Environmental Damage, the Indemnified Partie(s) shall, at its own expense, be entitled to participate in (but not control) the defense of, and receive copies of all pleadings and other papers in connection with, that Environmental Damage. If the Borrower does not—or is not entitled to—elect to defend an Environmental Damage in conformity with the requirements hereof, the

Indemnified Partie(s) shall be entitled to defend or settle (or both) that Environmental Damage on such terms as the Indemnified Partie(s) in its sole discretion, deems appropriate, and the obligation of the Borrower to indemnify the Indemnified Partie(s) for that Environmental Damage shall be satisfied in the manner provided for in this Agreement.

(4) The Indemnified Partie(s) will permit the Borrower to control the settlement of an Environmental Damage only if: (i) The terms of the settlement require not more than the payment of money—that is, the settlement does not require the Indemnified Partie(s) to admit any wrongdoing or take or refrain from taking any action; (ii) The full amount of the monetary settlement will be paid by the Borrower; and (iii) The Indemnified Partie(s) receives, as part of the settlement, a legally binding and enforceable unconditional satisfaction or release, which is in form and substance reasonably satisfactory to the Indemnified Partie(s), providing that the Environmental Damage and any claimed liability of the Indemnified Partie(s) with respect to its being fully satisfied because of the settlement and that the Indemnified Partie(s) is being released from any and all obligations or liabilities it may have with respect to the Environmental Damage.

8. *Consideration; Survival; Secured Indebtedness; Cumulative Rights.* Borrower acknowledges that Lender has relied and will rely on the representations, warranties, covenants and agreements herein in closing and funding the Loan and that the execution and delivery of this Agreement is an essential condition but for which Lender would not close or fund the Loan. The representations, warranties, covenants and agreements in this Agreement: (i) shall be binding upon Borrower and Borrower's successors, assigns and legal representatives and shall inure to the benefit of Lender and its successors, assigns and legal representatives and participants in the Loan; and (ii) shall not terminate on the Release Date or upon the release, foreclosure or other termination of the Mortgage, but will survive the Release Date, the payment in full of the indebtedness secured by the Mortgage, foreclosure of the Mortgage or conveyance in lieu of foreclosure, the release or termination of the Mortgage and any and all of the other Loan Documents, any investigation by or on behalf of Lender, and any bankruptcy or other debtor relief proceeding, and any other event whatsoever. Any amount to be paid under this Agreement by Borrower to Lender and/or Trustee shall be a demand obligation owing by Borrower (which Borrower hereby promises to pay) to Lender and/or Trustee and shall be a part of the indebtedness secured by the Mortgage. Lender's rights under this Agreement shall be in addition to all rights of Lender under the Loan Documents, and payments by Borrower under this Agreement shall not reduce Borrower's obligations and liabilities under any of the Loan Documents. The liability of Borrower under this Agreement shall not be limited or impaired in any way by any provision in the Loan Documents limiting Borrower's liability or Lender's recourse or rights to a deficiency judgment, or by any change, extension, release, inaccuracy, breach or failure to perform by any party under the Loan Documents, Borrower's liability hereunder being direct and primary and not as a guarantor or surety. Nothing in this Agreement or in any other Loan Document shall limit or impair any rights or remedies of Lender and/or Trustee against Borrower or any third party under any Environmental Requirement or otherwise at law or in equity, including without limitation any rights of contribution or indemnification.

9. *No Waiver.* No delay or omission by Lender to exercise any right under this Agreement shall impair any such right nor shall it be construed to be a waiver thereof. No waiver of any single breach or default under this Agreement shall be deemed a waiver of any other breach or default. Any waiver, consent or approval under this Agreement must be in writing to be effective.

10. *Notices.* All notices, requests, consents, demands and other communications required or which any party desires to give hereunder shall be in writing and

shall be deemed sufficiently given or furnished if delivered by personal delivery, by telegram, telex, or facsimile, by expedited delivery service with proof of delivery, or by registered or certified United States mail, postage prepaid, at the addresses specified at the end of this Agreement (unless changed by similar notice in writing given by the particular party whose address is to be changed). Any such notice or communication shall be deemed to have been given either at the time of personal delivery or, in the case of delivery service or mail, as of the date of first attempted delivery at the address and in the manner provided herein, or, in the case of telegram, telex or facsimile, upon receipt. Notwithstanding the foregoing, no notice of change of address shall be effective except upon receipt. This Section shall not be construed in any way to affect or impair any waiver of notice or demand provided in any Loan Document or to require giving of notice or demand to or upon any person in any situation or for any reason.

11. *Invalid Provisions.* A determination that any provision of this Agreement is unenforceable or invalid shall not affect the enforceability or validity of any other provision and the determination that the application of any provision of this Agreement to any person or circumstance is illegal or unenforceable shall not affect the enforceability or validity of such provision as it may apply to other persons or circumstances.

12. *Construction.* Whenever in this Agreement the singular number is used, the same shall include plural where appropriate, and vice versa, and words of any gender in this Agreement shall include each other gender where appropriate. The headings in this Agreement are for convenience only and shall be disregarded in the interpretation hereof.

13. *Applicable Law.* This Agreement is performable in Harris County, Texas, and the laws of the State of Texas and applicable United States federal law shall govern the rights and duties of the parties hereto and the validity, construction, enforcement and interpretation hereof.

14. *Execution; Modification.* This Agreement: (i) has been executed in a number of identical counterparts, each of which shall be deemed an original for all purposes and all of which constitute, collectively, one agreement, but, in making proof of this Agreement, it shall not be necessary to produce or account for more than one such counterpart, and (ii) may be amended only by an instrument in writing intended for that purpose executed jointly by an authorized representative of each party hereto.

Executed and dated as of the _____ day of _____, 1992.

BORROWER: [_____], a Texas corporation

By: _____
[_____]   President

LENDER:

By: _____

§ 15.10 Guaranty—Personally Guaranteeing Mortgage Debt [1]

This form provides for a personal guaranty of a partnership debt by its general partners. State anti-deficiency legislation may in some

§ 15.10
1. Form provided by Faegre & Benson, Minneapolis, Minnesota.

instances prove to be a substantial obstacle to recovering personal judgments against guarantors. While there is a general judicial predisposition to deny guarantors the protection of anti-deficiency legislation, generalization in this area is hazardous. Cases often turn on specific and sometimes unique language of a particular statute as well as its policy objectives. Indeed, courts have had more than their share of difficulty in dealing with partner-guarantors in the anti-deficiency context. Consequently, close attention to local law in this regard is especially important. See § 8.3 supra.

GUARANTY

THIS AGREEMENT, made as of _____, 19__, by and between _____ (hereinafter referred to as "Guarantors") and _____, a _____ corporation ("Lender").

WITNESSETH:

WHEREAS, Lender has agreed upon certain conditions to make a loan to _____ (the "Borrower") in the amount of One Million Three Hundred Thousand Dollars ($1,300,000) (the "Loan") evidenced by a Promissory Note (the "Note") and to be secured by a Combination Mortgage, Security Agreement and Fixture Financing Statement (the "Mortgage") and an Assignment of Leases and Rents (the "Assignment") on the property described in said Mortgage (the "Mortgaged Property"); and

WHEREAS, Guarantors are each a general partner of Borrower; and

WHEREAS, in order to induce Lender to make said Loan, and accept the Note, the Mortgage and the Assignment, Borrower has agreed to procure and deliver, and Guarantors have agreed to give, this Guaranty; and

WHEREAS, Lender has refused to make said Loan or to accept the Note, the Mortgage or the Assignment unless this Guaranty is executed by Guarantors and delivered to Lender;

NOW, THEREFORE, in consideration of the premises, Guarantors hereby covenant and agree with Lender as follows:

1. Guarantors hereby jointly and severally absolutely and unconditionally guarantee to Lender, its successors and assigns, the full and prompt payment when due of all indebtedness and other sums now or hereafter payable pursuant to the terms of the Note, the Mortgage, and the Assignment and the full and prompt performance of all obligations of Borrower under the Note, the Mortgage and the Assignment.

2. Upon such terms and at such times as it deems best and without notice to Guarantors, Lender may alter, compromise, accelerate, extend or change the time or manner for the payment of any indebtedness or the performance of any obligation hereby guaranteed, increase or reduce the rate of interest, release Borrower, by acceptance of a deed in lieu of foreclosure or otherwise, as to all or any portion of the indebtedness and obligations hereby guaranteed, release, substitute or add any one or more guarantors or endorsers, accept additional or substituted security therefor, or release or subordinate any security therefor. No exercise or non-exercise by Lender of any right hereby given it, no dealing by Lender with Borrower or either Guarantor or any other person, no change, impairment or suspension or any right or remedy of Lender, and no other act or thing which but for this provision could act as a release of the liabilities of Guarantors hereunder shall in any way affect any of the obligations of Guarantors hereunder or give Guarantors any recourse against Lender.

3. Guarantors hereby waive and agree not to assert or take advantage of (a) any right to require Lender to proceed against Borrower or any other person or to

proceed against or exhaust any security held by it at any time or to pursue any other remedy in its power before proceeding against Guarantors; (b) the defense of the statute of limitations in any action hereunder or for the collection of any indebtedness or the performance of any obligation hereby guaranteed; (c) any defense that may arise by reason of the incapacity, lack of authority, death or disability of, Borrower or either of the Guarantors or any other person or the failure of Lender to file or enforce a claim against the estate (either in administration, bankruptcy or any other proceeding) of Borrower or either of the Guarantors or any other person or by reason of the invalidity or unenforceability in whole or in part of any instrument referred to herein, or by reason of any anti-deficiency law; (d) demand, protest and notice of any other kind, or (e) any defense based upon an election of remedies (including, if available, an election of remedies to proceed by non-judicial foreclosure) by Lender which destroys or otherwise impairs the subrogation rights of Guarantors or the rights of Guarantors to proceed against Borrower for reimbursement, or both.

4. (a) Any indebtedness of Borrower to the Guarantors now or hereafter existing together with any interest thereon shall be, and such indebtedness is hereby, deferred, postponed and subordinated to the indebtedness of Borrower to Lender under the Note, the Mortgage and the Assignment. Guarantors hereby waive (i) all rights of subrogation to any collateral for the indebtedness secured hereby and all rights against Borrower, whether under the Mortgage or the Assignment or otherwise, until the indebtedness secured by this Guaranty shall have been fully paid and the obligations secured hereby fully performed, and (ii) all rights of subrogation against Borrower with respect to any deficiency which is subject to any anti-deficiency law or document to the extent such right of subrogation would defeat Lender's right to deficiency against Guarantors.

(b) Any lien or charge on the Mortgaged Property, including any personal property located thereon, and all rights therein and thereto, and on the revenue and income to be realized therefrom, which Guarantors may have or obtain as security for any loans, advances or costs in connection with the Mortgaged Property shall be, and such lien or charge hereby is, subordinated to the indebtedness of Borrower to Lender under the Note and to the lien of the Mortgage.

5. Guarantors will file all claims against Borrower in any bankruptcy or other proceeding in which the filing of claims is required by law upon any indebtedness of Borrower to Guarantors and will assign to Lender all rights of the Guarantors thereunder. If Guarantors do not file any such claim, Lender, as attorney-in-fact for Guarantors, is hereby authorized to do so in the name of Guarantors or, in Lender's discretion, to assign the claim and to cause proof of claim to be filed in the name of Lender or Lender's nominee. In all such cases, whether in administration, bankruptcy or otherwise, the person or persons authorized to pay such claim shall pay Lender the full amount thereof and, to the full extent necessary for that purpose, Guarantors hereby assign to Lender all of Guarantors' right to any such payments or distributions to which Guarantors would otherwise be entitled.

6. The amount of liability of Guarantors and all rights, powers and remedies of Lender hereunder and under any other agreement now or at any time hereafter in force between Lender and Guarantors relating to any indebtedness of Borrower to Lender shall be cumulative and not alternative and such rights, powers and remedies shall be in addition to all rights, powers and remedies given to Lender by law.

7. The agreements, obligations, warranties and representations of Guarantors hereunder are joint and several and are independent of the obligations of Borrower and, in the event of any default hereunder, a separate action or actions may be brought and prosecuted against Guarantors whether or not Borrower is joined therein or a separate action or actions is brought against Borrower. Lender may maintain successive actions for other defaults. Its rights hereunder shall not be exhausted by its exercise of any of its rights or remedies or by any such action

or by any number of successive actions until and unless all indebtedness and obligations hereby guaranteed have been paid and fully performed. All references herein to "Guarantors" shall refer to the undersigned individually as well as collectively.

8. Should any one or more provisions of this Guaranty be determined to be illegal or unenforceable, all other provisions nevertheless shall be effective.

9. The Guaranty shall inure to the benefit of Lender, its successors and assigns, including the assignees of any indebtedness hereby guaranteed, and shall bind the heirs, executors, administrators, successors and assigns of the undersigned. This Guaranty is assignable by Lender with respect to all or any portion of the indebtedness hereby guaranteed, and when so assigned, Guarantors shall be liable to the assignees under this Guaranty without in any manner affecting the liability of Guarantors hereunder with respect to any indebtedness retained by Lender.

10. No provision of this Guaranty or right of Lender hereunder can be waived nor can Guarantors be released from Guarantors' obligations hereunder except by a writing duly executed by an authorized officer of Lender.

11. This Guaranty shall be governed by and construed in accordance with the laws of the State of _____. Except as provided in any other written agreement now or at any time hereafter in force between Lender and the undersigned, this Guaranty shall constitute the entire agreement of the undersigned with Lender with respect to the subject matter hereof, and no representation, understanding, promise or condition concerning the subject matter hereof shall be binding upon Lender unless expressed herein.

12. If it becomes necessary for Lender to employ counsel to enforce the obligations of Guarantors hereunder, Guarantors agree to pay reasonable attorneys' fees and expenses in connection therewith.

13. If at any time payment or payments received by Lender from or on behalf of Borrower are insufficient to pay all indebtedness then subject to this Guaranty and all other indebtedness ("Other Indebtedness") of Borrower to Lender then due and owing, such payment or payments shall, for purposes of applying this Guaranty, be applied to the Other Indebtedness, notwithstanding payment instructions to the contrary, unless Lender otherwise elects.

14. Guarantors shall remain liable hereunder notwithstanding discharge or release of Borrower by bankruptcy or insolvency laws. If any payment to Lender is set aside in bankruptcy or by reason of any other provision of law, this Guaranty shall reattach as to the indebtedness payment which has been set aside.

IN WITNESS WHEREOF, the Guarantors have caused this Guaranty to be executed as of the date first above written.

§ 15.11 Assignment of Leases and Rents—As Additional Security for Note and Mortgage

While mortgagees routinely include a general assignment of rents provision in the mortgage, most also require the mortgagee to execute a separate assignment of rents agreement. This is done for a variety of reasons. First, a separate agreement, unlike the boilerplate mortgage clause, establishes that the mortgagor gave the issue careful consideration and thus emphasizes that an assignment or rents was actually intended. In addition, it enables the parties, to a greater degree than in the mortgage itself, to spell out the rights and liabilities of the parties under it. Finally, as we noted earlier in this treatise, (see §§ 4.35, 8.17, supra) state law concerning perfection and enforceability of rental assignments varies significantly and is in significant disarray. Ideally, every mortgagee desires to have its assignment treated as both perfected and enforceable from the date of recording. If this is accomplished, the rents will be treated as "cash collateral" or, better yet, not even property of the estate, if the mortgagor subsequently files a bankruptcy petition. In order to accomplish this, mortgagees frequently use language to make the assignment as "absolute" as humanly possible. For further consideration of this issue, see §§ 4.35, 8.17 supra.

We have included here two assignment forms. The first was developed for use in Minnesota and the second, for California. Several sections of these forms are noteworthy. Not infrequently, a financially precarious mortgagor-lessor will agree to substantial lease modifications, rental reduction and other "sweetheart" deals in return for substantial rental prepayment. Sections 5 and 18 of the Minnesota form and Section 8 of the California counterpart are specifically aimed at discouraging such practices. Note also, when mortgagor defaults and the mortgagee notifies tenants to pay the rent to it under the assignment, the latter, because of fears of potential double liability, are often reluctant to redirect the rental payments. Section 13 of the Minnesota form and Section 6 of the California agreement are expressly aimed at protecting tenants who comply with mortgagee instructions from incurring liability to the mortgagor-lessor for doing so. For further consideration of the California form, see Geiger and Frobes, Lenders and Leases, 7 Cal.Real Prop.J. 1 (No. 4, Fall, 1989).

ASSIGNMENT OF LEASES AND RENTS [1]

THIS ASSIGNMENT is made this _____ day of _____, 19__, between _____, assignors and _____, Minnesota corporation, Assignee.

RECITALS

Assignors have made and delivered to the Assignee their Promissory Note of even date herewith (the "Note").

The Assignee, as a condition of purchasing the Note and making the loan evidenced by the Note, has required this Assignment as additional security for the Note.

NOW, THEREFORE, THIS INDENTURE WITNESSETH:

1. *Definitions.*

As used in this Assignment, and in addition to other definitions herein contained, the following terms have the following respective meanings:

Assignee. _____ and its successors from time to time as holder of the Note.

Assignment. This Assignment of Leases and Rents.

Assignors. All of the individuals above named except for _____ and any of their successors and assigns from time to time as owners of the Mortgaged Property. _____ joins herein solely for purposes of binding her marital interest in the Rents and Leases and of consenting to, but not being liable under, the terms and provisions hereof. All references herein to Assignors shall refer to each of said individuals collectively and individually.

---

1. Form provided by Faegre & Benson, Minneapolis, Minnesota.

Event of Default. As defined in the Mortgage.

Improvements. As defined in the Mortgage.

Land. The parcel of real estate described on Exhibit A attached hereto and hereby made a part hereof.

Leases. Any and all leases of real or personal property constituting all or any part of the Mortgaged Property, any tenancy with respect to the Mortgaged Property or any part thereof, whether or not in writing, any license or concession agreement and any other agreement, by whatever name called, involving a transfer or creation of possessory rights or rights of use in the Mortgaged Property or any part thereof without transfer of title, and any and all guaranties of any of the foregoing.

Mortgage. The Combination Mortgage, Security Agreement and Fixture Financing Statement of even date herewith, between the Assignors, as mortgagors, and the Assignee, as mortgagee, encumbering the Land and other property therein described as security for payment of the Note and certain other indebtedness.

Mortgaged Property. As defined in the Mortgage.

Qualifying Rate. As defined in the Mortgage.

Rents. (a) All rents, issues, income and profits now or hereafter payable to the Assignors with respect to the Mortgaged Property or any part thereof, including without limitation all amounts (whether or not designated as rent) payable under or by reason of any Lease, including without limitation amounts so payable on account of maintenance, repairs, insurance, taxes, common area or other charges, whether similar or dissimilar, and all security deposits and other amounts paid by tenants with respect to Leases, whether in consideration of surrender or cancellation or otherwise, any amounts payable under any guaranty of any Lease and any amounts payable in bankruptcy of any tenant, and (b) all insurance proceeds and insurance premium refunds, condemnation awards, tax refunds and abatements, damage awards and other payments of any kind due or payable or to become due or payable to the Assignors with respect to the Mortgaged Property.

2. *Assignment of Leases and Rents.*

The Assignors hereby grant, transfer and assign to the Assignee all of the right, title and interest of the Assignors in and to (i) any and all present and future Leases, and (ii) all Rents, for the purpose of securing:

(a) Payment of all indebtedness evidenced by the Note and all other sums secured by the Mortgage or this Assignment; and

(b) Performance and discharge of each and every obligation, covenant and agreement of the Assignors contained herein and in the Mortgage.

3. *Warranty of Title.*

The Assignors warrant and covenant that they are and will remain the absolute owner of the Rents and Leases free and clear of all liens and encumbrances other than the lien granted herein; that they have not heretofore assigned or otherwise encumbered and will not hereafter assign or otherwise encumber their interest in any of the Rents or Leases to any person; that they have the right under applicable law, under the Leases, and otherwise to execute and deliver this Assignment and keep and perform all of their obligations hereunder; and that they will warrant and defend the Leases and Rents against all adverse claims, whether now existing or hereafter arising.

4. *Performance of Leases.*

The Assignors will faithfully abide by, perform and discharge each and every obligation, covenant and agreement which they become liable to observe or perform under the Leases, and, at their sole cost and expense, will enforce or secure the performance of each and every obligation, covenant, condition and agreement to be performed by the tenant under each Lease. The Assignors will give prompt written notice to the Assignee of any notice of default on the part of the Assignors with respect to any Lease received from the tenant thereunder, and will also at their sole cost and expense, appear in and defend any action or proceeding arising under, growing out of or in any manner connected with any Lease or the obligations, duties or liabilities of the Assignors or any tenant thereunder.

5. *Collection of Rents.*

The Assignors will not collect or accept any Rents for more than one month in advance.

6. *Protecting the Security of This Assignment.*

Should the Assignors fail to perform or observe any covenant or agreement contained in this Assignment, then the Assignee, but without obligation to do so and without releasing the Assignors from any obligation hereunder, may make or do the same in such manner and to such extent as the Assignee may deem appropriate to protect the security hereof, including, specifically, without limiting its general powers, the right to appear in and defend any action or proceeding purporting to affect the security hereof or the rights or powers of the Assignee, and also the right to perform and discharge each and every obligation, covenant and agreement of the Assignors contained in the Leases and in exercising any such powers to pay necessary costs and expenses, employ counsel and pay reasonable attorneys' fees. The Assignors will pay immediately upon demand all sums expended by the Assignee under the authority of this Assignment and all sums, if any, which the Assignee may advance to any receiver of the Mortgaged Property, together with interest thereon at the Qualifying Rate and the same shall be added to said indebtedness and shall be secured hereby and by the Mortgage.

7. *Present Assignment.*

This Assignment shall constitute a perfected, absolute and present assignment, provided that the Assignors shall have the right to collect, but not prior to accrual, all of the Rents, and to retain, use and enjoy the same unless and until an Event of Default shall occur or the Assignors shall have breached any warranty or covenant in this Assignment. Any Rents which accrue prior to an Event of Default but are paid thereafter shall be paid to the Assignee.

8. *Survival of Obligation to Comply With Mortgage and This Assignment.*

This Assignment is given as security in addition to the Mortgage. The Assignors covenant and agree to observe and comply with all terms and conditions contained in the Mortgage and in this Assignment and to preclude any Event of Default from occurring under the Mortgage. All of the Assignors' obligations under the Mortgage and this Assignment shall survive foreclosure of the Mortgage and the Assignors covenant and agree to observe and comply with all terms and conditions of the Mortgage and this Assignment and to preclude any Event of Default from occurring under the Mortgage throughout any period of redemption after foreclosure of the Mortgage.

9. *Default, Remedies.*

Upon the occurrence of any Event of Default or upon the breach of any warranty or covenant in this Assignment, the Assignee may, at its option, at any time:

(a) in the name, place and stead of the Assignors and without becoming a mortgagee in possession (i) enter upon, manage and operate the Mortgaged Property or retain the services of one or more independent contractors to manage and operate all or any part of the Mortgaged Property; (ii) make, enforce, modify and accept surrender of the Leases; (iii) obtain or evict tenants, collect, sue for, fix or modify the Rents and enforce all rights of the

Assignors under the Leases; and (iv) perform any and all other acts that may be necessary or proper to protect the security of this Assignment;

(b) without regard to waste, adequacy of the security or solvency of the Assignors, apply for, and the Assignors hereby consent to, the appointment of a receiver of the Mortgaged Property, whether or not foreclosure proceedings have been commenced under the Mortgage and if such proceedings have been commenced, whether or not a foreclosure sale has occurred;

(c) with or without exercising the rights set forth in subparagraph (a) above, give or require the Assignors to give, notice to any or all tenants under the Lease authorizing and directing the tenants to pay all Rents under the Leases directly to the Assignee.

The exercise of any of the foregoing rights or remedies and the application of the Rents, pursuant to Article 10, shall not cure or waive any Event of Default (or notice of default) under the Mortgage or invalidate any act done pursuant to such notice.

10. *Application of Rents.*

All Rents collected by the Assignee or the receiver each month shall be applied as follows:

(a) to payment of all reasonable fees of the receiver approved by the court;

(b) to payment of all tenant security deposits then owing to tenants under any of the Leases pursuant to the provisions of Minn.Stat. § 504.20;

(c) to payment of all prior or current real estate taxes and special assessments with respect to the Mortgaged Property, or if the Mortgage requires periodic escrow payments for such taxes and assessments, to the escrow payments then due;

(d) to payment of all premiums then due for the insurance required by the provisions of the Mortgage, or if the Mortgage requires periodic escrow payments for such premiums, to the escrow payments then due;

(e) to payment of expenses incurred for normal maintenance of the Mortgaged Property;

(f) if received prior to any foreclosure sale of the Mortgaged Property, to the Assignee for payment of the indebtedness secured by the Mortgage or this Assignment, but no such payment made after acceleration of the indebtedness shall affect such acceleration;

(g) if received during or with respect to the period of redemption after a foreclosure sale of the Mortgaged Property:

(1) if the purchaser at the foreclosure sale is not the Assignee, first to the Assignee to the extent of any deficiency of the sale proceeds to repay the indebtedness secured by the Mortgage or this Assignment, second to the purchaser as a credit to the redemption price, but if the Mortgaged Property is not redeemed, then to the purchaser of the Mortgaged Property;

(2) if the purchaser at the foreclosure sale is the Assignee, to the Assignee to the extent of any deficiency of the sale proceeds to repay the indebtedness secured by the Mortgage or this Assignment and the balance to be retained by the Assignee as a credit to the redemption price, but if the Mortgaged Property is not redeemed, then to the Assignee, whether or not any such deficiency exists.

The rights and powers of the Assignee under this Assignment and the application of Rents under this Article 10 shall continue until expiration of the redemption period from any foreclosure sale, whether or not any deficiency remains after a foreclosure sale.

11. *No Liability for Assignee.*

The Assignee shall not be obligated to perform or discharge, nor does it hereby undertake to perform or discharge, any obligation, duty or liability of the Assignors under the Leases. This Assignment shall not operate to place upon the Assignee responsibility for the control, care, management or repair of the Mortgaged Property or for the carrying out of any of the terms and conditions of the Leases. The Assignee shall not be responsible or liable for any waste committed on the Mortgaged Property, for any dangerous or defective condition of the Mortgaged Property, for any negligence in the management, upkeep, repair or control of said Mortgaged Property or for any negligence in the management, upkeep, repair or control of said Mortgaged Property or for failure to collect the Rents.

12. *Assignors' Indemnification.*

The Assignors shall and do hereby agree to indemnify and to hold the Assignee harmless of and from any and all claims, demands, liability, loss or damage (including all costs, expenses, and reasonable attorney's fees incurred in the defense thereof) asserted against, imposed on or incurred by the Assignee in connection with or as a result of this Assignment or the exercise of any rights or remedies under this Assignment or under the Leases or by reason of any alleged obligations or undertakings of the Assignee to perform or discharge any of the terms, covenants or agreements contained in the Leases; provided, however, that nothing herein shall be construed to obligate the Assignors to indemnify and hold the Assignee harmless from and against any and all claims, demands, liability, loss or damage (including all costs, expenses and reasonable attorney's fees incurred in the defense thereof) enacted against, imposed on or incurred by the Assignee by reason of the negligence or tortious acts on the part of the Assignee or any of its employees, agents, contractors, licensees or invitees. Should the Assignee incur any such liability, the amount thereof, together with interest thereon at the Qualifying Rate, shall be secured hereby and by the Mortgage and the Assignors shall reimburse the Assignee therefor immediately upon demand.

13. *Authorization to Tenants.*

The tenants under the Leases are hereby irrevocably authorized and directed whenever there shall exist an uncured Event of Default, to pay to the Assignee all sums due under the Leases, and the Assignors hereby consent and direct that said sums shall be paid to the Assignee, and to the extent such sums are paid to the Assignee, the Assignors agree that the tenants shall have no further liability to Assignors for the same. The signature of the Assignee alone shall be sufficient for the exercise of any rights under this Assignment and the receipt of the Assignee alone for any sums received shall be a full discharge and release therefor to any such tenant or occupant of the Mortgaged Property.

14. *Satisfaction.*

Upon the payment in full of all indebtedness secured hereby as evidenced by the recorded satisfaction of the Mortgage executed by the Assignee, this Assignment shall, without the need for any further satisfaction or release, become null and void and be of no further effect.

15. *Power of Attorney.*

The Assignors irrevocably constitute and appoint the Assignee their true and lawful attorney in their name and stead: (a) to collect any and all Rents; (b) to use such measures, legal or equitable, as in its discretion may be deemed necessary or appropriate to enforce the payment of Rents and/or any security given in connection therewith; (c) to secure and maintain the use and/or possession of the Mortgaged Property; (d) to fill any and all vacancies and to make, enforce and cancel Leases; (e) to order, purchase, cancel, modify, amend and/or in any and all ways control and deal with any and all policies of insurance of any and all kinds now or hereafter on or in connection with the whole or any part of the Mortgaged Property at its discretion and to adjust any loss or damage thereunder and/or to bring suit at law or in equity therefor and to execute and/or render any and all instruments deemed by the Assignee to be necessary or appropriate in connection therewith; (f) to adjust, bring suit at law or in equity for, settle or otherwise deal with any taking of any or all of the Mortgaged Property for public purposes as aforesaid or any claim for real or alleged harm or damage as aforesaid and to execute and/or render any and all instruments deemed by the Assignee to be necessary or appropriate in connection therewith, and (g) to adjust, settle or otherwise deal with any abatements and to execute and/or render any and all instruments deemed by the Assignee to be necessary or appropriate in connection therewith; hereby granting full power and authority to the Assignee to use and apply the Rents to the payment of taxes, assessments and charges of any nature whatsoever that may be levied or assessed in connection with the Mortgaged Property, to the payment of premiums on such policies of insurance on or in connection with the whole or any part of the Mortgaged Property as may be deemed advisable by the Assignee, to the payment of any and all indebtedness, liability or interest of the Mortgaged Property, whether now existing or hereafter to exist, to the purchase of and/or the payment for such personal property as may be deemed necessary or advisable by the Assignee, to the payment of all expenses in the care and management of the Mortgaged Property, including such repairs, alterations, additions and/or improvements to the Mortgaged Property or any part thereof as may be deemed necessary or advisable by the Assignee, to the payment of attorneys' fees, court costs, labor, charges and/or expenses incurred in connection with any and all things which the Assignee may do or cause to be done by virtue hereof and to the payment of such interest on the indebtedness or on any of the foregoing, if any, as may be deemed necessary or advisable by the Assignee; also hereby granting to the Assignee and providing for such compensation as may be deemed advisable by the Assignee, and for the performance or execution of any or all of these presents, to constitute, appoint, authorize and in its place and stead put and substitute one attorney or more for the Assignors and as their attorney or attorneys, and/or the same at its pleasure again to revoke, and to do, execute, perform and finish for the Assignors and in their name all and singular those things which shall be necessary or advisable or which said attorney or its substitute or substitutes shall deem necessary or advisable in and about, for, touching or concerning these presents or the Mortgaged Property or any of them as thoroughly, amply and fully as the Assignors could do concerning the same, being personally present, and whatsoever said attorney or its substitute or substitutes shall do or cause to be done in, about or concerning these presents or Mortgaged Property or any part of any of them the Assignors hereby ratify and confirm; and also hereby granting to the Assignee full power and authority to exercise at any and all times each and every right, privilege and power herein granted, without notice to the Assignors. This Power of Attorney and the rights and power conferred hereby shall be effective only if there shall exist an uncured Event of Default.

16. *Assignee Not a Mortgagee in Possession.*

Nothing herein contained and no actions taken pursuant to this Assignment shall be construed as constituting the Assignee a mortgagee in possession.

17. *Specific Assignment of Leases.*

The Assignors will transfer and assign to the Assignee upon written notice by the Assignee, any and all specific Leases that the Assignee requests. Such transfer and assignment by the Assignors shall be upon the same or substantially the same terms and conditions as are herein contained, and the Assignors will properly file or record such assignments, at the Assignors' expense, if requested by the Assignee.

18. *No Amendment, Termination, Etc., of Leases.*

The Assignors will not without the Assignee's prior written consent (i) enter into any Lease, (ii) modify or in any manner alter the terms of any Lease, (iii) terminate or accept a surrender of the term of any Lease, either with or without cause or (iv) waive, condone or in any manner release or discharge any tenant under any Lease from the obligations, covenants, conditions or agreements of the tenant under its Lease, including the obligation to pay rent and other charges at the times and in the manner provided therein. The Assignors do hereby release, relinquish and surrender unto the Assignee, all of the Assignors' right, power and authority to do any of the foregoing, and any attempt to do any of the foregoing without the assignee's prior written consent shall be null and void and of no force and effect. The provisions of this Article 18 shall apply at all times while the Mortgage remains in effect, and shall also apply during any period of redemption from foreclosure of the Mortgage.

19. *Unenforceable Provisions Severable.*

All rights, powers and remedies provided herein may be exercised only to the extent that the exercise thereof does not violate any applicable law, and are intended to be limited to the extent necessary so that they will not render this Assignment invalid, unenforceable or not entitled to be recorded, registered or filed under any applicable law. If any term of this Assignment shall be held to be invalid, illegal or unenforceable, the validity of other terms hereof shall in no way be affected thereby. It is the intention of the parties hereto, however, that this Assignment shall confer upon the Assignee the fullest rights, remedies and benefits available pursuant to Chapter 202, Minnesota Laws of 1977.

20. *Successors and Assigns.*

The covenants and agreements herein contained shall bind, and the rights hereunder shall inure to the respective successors and assigns of the Assignors and the Assignee, including any purchaser at a foreclosure sale.

21. *Captions; Amendments; Notices.*

The captions and headings of the Articles of this Assignment are for convenience only and shall not be used to interpret or define the provisions of this Assignment. This Assignment can be amended only in writing signed by the Assignors and the Assignee. Any notice from the Assignee to the Assignors under this Assignment shall be deemed to have been given when given by the Assignee in accordance with the requirements for notice to the Assignors under the Mortgage.

22. *Counterparts.*

This Assignment may be executed in any number of counterparts, each of which shall be an original but all of which shall constitute one instrument.

23. *Waiver of Guarantor Defenses, etc.*

The Assignors agree that neither the security of this Assignment nor any obligation of the Assignors under the Mortgage will be released, impaired or subordinated by any amendment to this Assignment or any other instrument, any extension of time or waiver of right or remedy as to the Assignors or any other party or any other act or remedy as to the Assignors or any other party or any other act or thing which, but for this provision, would so release, impair or subordinate. This Assignment shall be in all respects valid and enforceable, securing all payments under the Note and all other indebtedness secured by the Mortgage and this Assignment, regardless of whether the Note has been validly authorized, executed and delivered or is legal, valid or enforceable.

IN WITNESS WHEREOF, the Assignors have caused this Assignment to be made as of the day and year first above written.

ASSIGNMENT OF RENTS AND LEASES [1]

THIS ASSIGNMENT OF RENTS AND LEASES (the "Assignment") is made as of this _____ day of _____, 19__, by _____, a _____ ("Assignor"), whose address is _____, _____, a _____ ("Assignee"), whose address is _____.

RECITALS

A. Assignor is the present owner of the real property described in Exhibit A attached hereto (the "Premises") together with the Improvements now existing or to be constructed thereon. The Premises and the Improvements are herein referred to collectively as the "Project."

B. Assignee has agreed to make a loan (the "Loan") to Assignor in the original principal sum of _____ Dollars ($_____) pursuant to that certain Loan Agreement between Assignor and Assignee of even date herewith (the "Loan Agreement").

C. Pursuant to the Loan Agreement, and in order to induce Assignee to make the Loan to Assignor, Assignor has agreed to execute this Assignment.

NOW, THEREFORE, with reference to the foregoing Recitals and in reliance thereon and for good and valuable consideration, the receipt of which is hereby acknowledged, Assignor agrees as follows:

1. *Definitions.* All initially capitalized terms used herein which are defined in the Loan Agreement shall have the same meaning herein unless the context otherwise requires.

2. *Assignment.* Assignor hereby absolutely and irrevocably grants, sells, assigns, transfers and sets over to Assignee all of the rents, issues, profits, royalties, income and other benefits (collectively, the "Rents") derived from any lease, sublease, license, franchise, concession or other agreement (collectively, the "Leases") now existing or hereafter created and affecting all of any portion of the Project or the use or occupancy thereof; together with all of Assignor's right, title and interest in the Leases, including all modifications, amendments, extensions and renewals of the Leases and all rights and privileges incident thereto; together with all security deposits, guaranties and other security now or hereafter held by Assignor as security for the performance of the obligations of the tenants thereunder.

This Assignment of Rents is intended by Assignor and Assignee to create and shall be construed to create an absolute assignment to Assignee of all of Assignor's right, title and interest in the Rents and in the Leases and shall not be deemed to create a security interest therein for the payment of any indebtedness or the performance of any obligations of Assignor under the Loan Agreement. Assignor and Assignee further agree that, during the term of this Assignment, the Rents shall not constitute property of Assignor (or of any estate of Assignor) within the meaning of 11 U.S.C. § 541, as amended from time to time. By its acceptance of this Assignment and so long as an Event of Default shall not have occurred and be continuing under the Loan Agreement, Assignee hereby grants to Assignor a revocable license to enforce the Leases, to collect the Rents, to apply the Rents to the payment of the costs and expenses incurred in connection with the development, construction, operation, maintenance, repair and restoration of the Project and to any indebtedness secured thereby and to distribute the balance, if any, to Assignor as may be permitted by the terms of the Loan Agreement.

3. *Revocation of License.* Upon the occurrence of an Event of Default and at any time thereafter during the continuance thereof, Assignee shall have the right to revoke the license granted to Assignor hereby by giving written notice of such

---

1. Form provided by O'Melveny & Myers, Los Angeles, California.

revocation to Assignor. Upon such revocation, Assignor shall promptly deliver to Assignee all Rents then held by Assignor and Assignee shall thereafter be entitled to enforce the Leases, to collect and receive, without deduction or offset, all Rents payable thereunder, including but not limited to, all Rents which were accrued and unpaid as of the date of such revocation and to apply such Rents as provided in Paragraph 7 hereof.

4. *Appointment of Assignor as Agent for Assignee.* Upon such revocation, Assignee may, at its option, appoint Assignor to act as agent for Assignee for the purpose of (i) managing and operating the Project and paying all expenses incurred in connection therewith and approved by Assignee; (ii) enforcing the provisions of the Leases; and (iii) collecting all Rents due thereunder. If Assignee so elects, Assignee shall give written notice thereof to Assignor and Assignor agrees to act as agent of Assignee for the purpose or purposes specified in such notice. Assignor shall promptly comply with all instructions and directions from Assignee with respect thereto. Assignor shall not be entitled to any management fee, commission or other compensation unless expressly agreed to in writing by Assignee. All Rents collected by Assignor as agent for Assignee pursuant to this Paragraph 4 shall be immediately deposited in an insured account in the name of Assignee in a bank or other financial institution designated by Assignee. All Rents collected by Assignor and all amounts deposited in such account, including interest thereon, shall be the property of Assignee and Assignor shall not be entitled to withdraw any amount from such account without the prior written consent of Assignee. The agency hereby created shall be solely for the purpose of implementing the provisions of this Assignment and collecting the Rents due Assignee hereunder. Nothing contained herein shall place upon Assignee the responsibility for the management, control, operation, repair, maintenance or restoration of the Project nor shall Assignee be liable under or be deemed to have assumed Assignor's obligations with respect to the Leases. Assignee may, at any time, terminate the agency relationship with Assignor by written notice to Assignor.

5. *Collection by Assignee.* Upon the occurrence of an Event of Default and at any time thereafter during the continuance thereof, Assignee shall have the right, in addition to the rights granted pursuant to Paragraph 4 hereof, to collect all or any portion of the Rents assigned hereby directly or through a court-appointed receiver. Such right may be exercised and shall include the following:

    (a) The right to notify the tenant or tenants under the Leases in accordance with the provisions of Paragraph 6 hereof and, with or without taking possession of the Project, to demand that all Rents under such Leases thereafter be paid to Assignee;

    (b) The right to enter into possession of the Project, to assume control with respect to and to pay all expenses incurred in connection with the development, construction, operation, maintenance, repair or restoration of the Project, to enforce all Leases and to collect all Rents due thereunder, to apply all Rents received by Assignee as provided in Paragraph 7 hereof, to amend, modify, extend, renew and terminate any or all Leases, to execute new Leases and to do all other acts which Assignee shall determine, in its sole discretion, to be necessary or desirable to carry out the purposes of this Assignment; and

    (c) The right to specifically enforce the provisions of this Assignment and, if Assignee shall so elect, to obtain the appointment of a receiver pursuant to and in accordance with the provisions of Section _____ of the Deed of Trust.

6. *Protection of Tenants.* Assignor and Assignee agree that all tenants under the Leases shall be bound by and required to comply with the provisions of this Assignment. In connection therewith, Assignor and Assignee further agree as follows:

    (a) If requested by Assignee, Assignor shall (i) notify each tenant under any Lease now affecting all or any portion of the Project of the existence of this Assignment and the rights and obligations of Assignor and Assignee hereunder, (ii) provide each tenant with a copy of this Assignment; and (iii) obtain such tenant's agreement to be bound by and comply with the provisions hereof;

(b) All Leases hereafter executed with respect to the Project or any portion thereof shall contain a reference to this Assignment and shall state that such tenant shall be bound by and shall comply with the provisions hereof;

(c) Upon the occurrence of an Event of Default and at any time thereafter during the continuance thereof, Assignee may, at its option, send any tenant a notice pursuant to Paragraph 5 hereof to the effect that: (i) an Event of Default has occurred and that Assignee has revoked Assignor's license to collect the Rents; (ii) Assignee has elected to exercise its rights under this Assignment; and (iii) such tenant is thereby directed to thereafter make all payments of Rent and to perform all obligations under its Lease to or for the benefit of Assignee or as Assignee shall direct;

(d) Upon receipt of any such notice from Assignee, each tenant is hereby instructed by Assignor and Assignee to comply with the provisions of such notice, to make all payments of Rent and to perform all obligations under the Lease to and for the benefit of Assignee or as Assignee shall direct. Such notice and direction shall remain effective until the first to occur of: (i) the receipt by tenant of a subsequent notice from Assignee to the effect that such Event of Default has been cured or that Assignee has appointed Assignor to act as agent for Assignee pursuant to Paragraph 4 hereof; (ii) the appointment of a receiver pursuant to Paragraph 5 hereof, in which event such tenant shall thereafter make payments of Rent and perform all obligations under the Leases as may be directed by such receiver; or (iii) the issuance of an order of a court of competent jurisdiction terminating this Assignment or otherwise directing such tenant to pay Rent and perform obligations in a manner inconsistent with said notice;

(e) Each tenant shall be entitled to rely upon any notice from Assignee and shall be protected with respect to any payment of Rent made pursuant to such notice, irrespective of whether a dispute exists between Assignor and Assignee with respect to the existence of an Event of Default or the rights of Assignee hereunder;

(f) Each tenant who receives a notice from Assignee pursuant to this Assignment shall not be required to investigate or determine the validity or accuracy of such notice or the validity or enforceability of this Assignment. Assignor hereby agrees to indemnify, defend and hold such tenant harmless from and against any and all loss, claims, damage or liability arising from or related to any payment of Rent or performance of obligations under any Lease by such tenant made in good faith in reliance on and pursuant to such notice;

(g) The payment of Rent to Assignee pursuant to any such notice and the performance of obligations under any Lease to or for the benefit of Assignee shall not cause Assignee to assume or be bound by the provisions of such Lease including but not limited to the duty to return any security deposit to the tenant under such Lease unless and to the extent such security deposit was paid to Assignee by Assignor; and

(h) The provisions of this Paragraph 6 are expressly made for the benefit of and shall be binding on and enforceable by each tenant under any Lease now or hereafter affecting all or any portion of the Project.

7. *Application of Rents; Security Deposits.* All Rents received by Assignee pursuant to this Assignment shall be applied by Assignee, in its sole discretion, to any of the following:

(a) the costs and expenses of collection, including, without limitation, reasonable attorneys' fees;

(b) the costs and expenses incurred in connection with the development, construction, operation, maintenance, repair or restoration of the Project;

(c) the establishment of reasonable reserves for working capital and for anticipated or projected costs and expenses, including, without limitation, capital improvements which may be necessary or desirable or required by law; and

(d) the payment of any indebtedness then owing by Assignor to Assignee.

In connection therewith, Assignor further agrees that all Rents received by Assignee from any tenant may be allocated first, if Assignee so elects, to the payment of all current obligations of such tenant under its Lease and not to amounts which may be accrued and unpaid as of the date of revocation of Assignor's license to collect such Rents. Assignee may, but shall have no obligation to, pursue any tenant for the payment of Rent which may be due under its Lease with respect to any period prior to the exercise of Assignee's rights under this Assignment or which may become due thereafter. Assignee shall not be liable to any tenant for the payment or return of any security deposit under any Lease unless and to the extent that such security deposit has been paid to and received by Assignee and Assignor agrees to indemnify, defend and hold Assignee harmless from and against any and all loss, claims, damage or liability arising out of any claim by a tenant with respect thereto. Assignor further agrees that the collection of Rents by Assignee and the application of such Rents by Assignee to the costs, expenses and obligations referred to in this Paragraph 7 shall not cure or waive any default or Event of Default or invalidate any act (including, but not limited to, any sale of all or any portion of the Project of any property now or hereafter securing the Loan) done in response to or as a result of such default or Event of Default or pursuant to any notice of default or notice of sale issued pursuant to any Loan Document.

8. *Covenants of Assignor.* Assignor agrees as follows:

(a) Assignor will not enter into any Lease of all or any portion of the Project except in accordance with the provisions of the Loan Agreement;

(b) Assignor will not accept any advance rent in excess of one month from any tenant or enter into any agreement whereby rent is abated or reduced in each case without the prior written consent of Assignee;

(c) Assignor will not amend, modify or terminate any Lease or accept the surrender of any space thereunder or permit the assignment or subletting of any space thereunder without the prior written consent of Assignee except as may be permitted by the Loan Agreement;

(d) Assignor shall provide Assignee with true, correct and complete copies of all Leases together with such other information relating to the Leases or to the tenants thereunder as Assignee shall reasonably request;

(e) Assignor shall not lease any space in the Project to or for the benefit of any affiliate of Assignor without the prior written consent of Assignee;

(f) Upon request of Assignee, Assignor shall make available to Assignee all books, records, financial statements and other information relating to the Lease of the Project, the collection of all Rents and the disposition and disbursement thereof; and

(g) Assignor shall promptly notify Assignee and shall send to Assignee copies of any notice or correspondence given or received by Assignor relating to any default by Assignor or by any tenant under any Lease or any event which, if not promptly cured, may become a default thereunder.

9. *Priority of Assignment; Further Assurances.* Assignor hereby represents and warrants that the Assignment of Rents hereby granted is a first priority assignment and that no other assignments of all or any portion of the Rents or the Leases exist or remain outstanding. Assignor agrees to take such action and to execute, deliver and record such documents as may be reasonably necessary to evidence such assignment, to establish the priority thereof and to carry out the intent and purpose hereof. If requested by Assignee, Assignor shall execute a specific assignment of any Lease now or hereafter affecting all or any portion of the Project and shall cause the tenant or tenants thereunder to execute, deliver and record a Subordination, Nondisturbance and Attornment Agreement, in form and substance reasonably satisfactory to Assignee.

10. *Successors and Assigns.* The provisions of this Assignment shall be binding upon Assignor, its legal representatives, successors or assigns and shall be for the benefit of Assignee, its successors and assigns.

11. *Remedies Cumulative.* The rights granted Assignee under this Assignment or any other Loan Document or allowed it by law or in equity shall be cumulative and may be exercised at any time and from time to time. No failure on the part of Assignee to exercise, and no delay in exercising, any right shall be construed or deemed to be a waiver thereof, nor shall any single or partial exercise by Assignee of any right preclude any other or future exercise thereof or the exercise of any other right.

12. *Assignee Not Responsible for Assignor's Obligations.* Nothing contained herein shall operate or be construed to obligate Assignee to perform any of the terms, covenants and conditions contained in any Lease or otherwise to impose any obligation upon Assignee with respect to any Lease including, but not limited to, any obligation arising out of any covenant of quiet enjoyment therein contained in the event the lessee under any such Lease shall have been joined as a party defendant in any action to foreclose and the estate of such lessee shall have been thereby terminated. Prior to actual entry into and taking possession of the Project by Assignee, this Assignment shall not operate to place upon Assignee any responsibility for the operation, control, care, management or repair of the Project or any portion thereof, and the execution of this Assignment by Assignor shall constitute conclusive evidence that all responsibility for the operation, control, care, management and repair of the Project is and shall be that of Assignor, prior to such actual entry and taking of possession.

13. *Termination of Assignment.* A full and complete release and reconveyance of the Deed of Trust shall operate as a full and complete release of all of Assignee's rights and interest hereunder. Upon the recordation of such release and reconveyance, this Assignment shall thereafter be void and of no further effect.

14. *Notices.* All notices, requests and demands to be made hereunder to the parties hereto shall be in writing and shall be given pursuant to Section _____ of the Loan Agreement.

15. *Governing Law.* This Assignment shall be governed by and construed in accordance with the laws of the State of California.

16. *Counterparts.* This Assignment may be executed in any number of counterparts each of which shall be deemed an original and all of which shall constitute one and the same instrument with the same effect as if all parties had signed the same signature page. Any signature page of this Assignment may be detached from any counterpart of this Assignment and reattached to any other counterpart of this Assignment identical in form hereto but having attached to it one or more additional signature pages.

17. *Severability.* If any term of this Assignment, or the application thereof to any person or circumstance, shall, to any extent, be invalid or unenforceable, the remainder of this Assignment, or the application of such term to persons or

circumstances other than those as to which it is invalid or unenforceable, shall not be affected thereby, and each term of this Assignment shall be valid and enforceable to the fullest extent permitted by law.

18. *Amendments.* This Assignment may not be amended, modified or changed nor shall any waiver of any provision hereof be effective, except only by an instrument in writing and signed by the party against whom enforcement of any such amendment, modification change, or waiver is sought.

IN WITNESS WHEREOF, Assignor has caused this Assignment to be executed by its _____ hereunto duly authorized as of the date first above written.

§ 15.12 Subordination, Nondisturbance, and Attornment Agreement—For Lessee

Subordination agreements are often used to adjust the priorities between commercial tenants and the mortgagee of the real estate, whether the construction lender or its long-term counterpart. Absent such an adjustment, priorities will be governed by the recording acts and related common law principles. If under these rules the lease is senior to the mortgage, foreclosure of the latter will not affect the validity of the lease. Both the lessee and the foreclosure sale purchaser will each retain those rights and obligations under the lease that touch and concern the land. If the lease is junior to the mortgage and the lessee is effectively made a party to the foreclosure proceeding, the lease and, with it, the lessee's rights and obligations under it, will be destroyed.

Generalizations about the priority preferences of the parties in commercial lease settings can be hazardous. One would assume that a major shopping center tenant normally desires protection against a foreclosure wiping out its lease rights, especially if the lease is favorable from the tenant's perspective. On the other hand, it is not inconceivable that a tenant, given the choice, would prefer subordinate status. He or she may reason that if foreclosure occurs, it will probably be because the shopping center proves to be economically unsuccessful. Under such circumstances, the tenant might be only too pleased to be "off the hook" on the lease. For its part, the mortgagee typically wants senior status vis a vis the lessees because if foreclosure occurs, it wants to have the option of compelling a renegotiation of the leases of those it desires to retain as tenants. After all, it is perhaps equally plausible that a future foreclosure will be more attributable to lease terms that were unfavorable to the lessor rather than to the economic nonviability of the shopping center.

There are two forms reprinted below. The first was developed for use in Minnesota and the second for California. The former was designed for shopping center construction financing, while the latter was created with long-term financing of commercial real estate in mind. First, note that both forms afford the mortgagee seniority over the lessee. However, the lessee then acquires the protection of a "nondisturbance" clause. Under this provision the mortgagee, as a potential foreclosure purchaser and successor in interest of the lessor, agrees to recognize lessee's rights under the lease. Note that the California form purports to bind any non-mortgagee foreclosure purchaser as well in this regard. Finally, the lessee, by attorning, agrees to be bound under the terms of the lease to any foreclosure purchaser (only a mortgagee purchaser under the Minnesota form) even though, as the junior party, a foreclosure would otherwise terminate his or her leasehold obligations.

One might reasonably ask why a mortgagee who is willing to accept a non-disturbance provision should not also be willing to allow the the lessee to retain seniority. Consider, in this regard, the following analysis:

> "Even if a prior lease is economically beneficial, the lender may still find it wise to obtain a [Subordination, Non-disturbance and Attornment Agreement] ("Attornment Agreement") for several reasons. First, an Attornment Agreement puts the tenant and lender in direct privity of contract, thus giving the lender the right to make demands directly on the tenant (such as the demand to pay rent directly to the lender after default and to obtain the lender's consent to any modification of the lease). Second, the Attornment Agreement provides the lender with a specific covenant from the tenant that, after foreclosure, the tenant will perform for the benefit of the lender upon demand to do so. Third, to the extent there are conflicting provisions in the lease and deed of trust regarding insurance proceeds and the like, the Attornment Agreement provides a vehicle for addressing and, hopefully, resolving those conflicts. Fourth, the Attornment Agreement can clarify and, from the lender's perspective, limit, the lender's obligation to construct tenant improvements. Finally, the Attornment Agreement can limit the tenant's recourse, in the event of the lender/landlord's breach, to specified assets of the lender, such as the lender's interest in the real property of which the leased premises are a part."

Geiger and Frobes, 7 Cal.Real Prop.J. 1, 15 (No. 4, Fall, 1989).

SUBORDINATION, NON-DISTURBANCE AND ATTORNMENT AGREEMENT *

THIS AGREEMENT is made this _____ day of _____, 19__, by and between _____ a _____ corporation whose address is _____ (the "Tenant") and _____, _____ ("Mortgagee").

Recitals

_____ (the "Landlord") is the fee owner of the real estate described in Exhibit A attached hereto and made a part hereof (the "Real Estate") and has entered into a Construction Loan Agreement with the Mortgagee dated _____, 19__ pursuant to which the Mortgagee has agreed to lend up to the sum of $_____ to the Landlord to finance construction of a shopping center on the Real Estate.

* Form provided by Faegre & Benson, Minneapolis, Minnesota.

Said construction loan is secured by a Mortgage, covering the Real Estate dated _____, 19__ (the "Mortgage"). The Mortgage was recorded in the office of the County Recorder in and for _____ County, _____ on _____, 19__ as document no. _____.

The Tenant is the lessee of a portion of the shopping center to be constructed on the Real Estate pursuant to a Lease between it and the Landlord dated _____, 19__ (the "Lease").

The Mortgagee has required the execution of this Agreement as a condition precedent to making its advances under the aforesaid Construction Loan Agreement.

Accordingly, the parties hereby agree as follows:

1. *Subordination.* Except as otherwise provided in paragraphs 2 and 3 of this Agreement, the Lease, and all rights of the Tenant under the Lease and to the Real Estate, including without limitation any option to purchase or otherwise acquire title to the Real Estate, are hereby subjected and subordinated, and shall remain in all respects and for all purposes subject and subordinate, to the lien of the Mortgage, and to the rights and interest of the Mortgagee and its successors and assigns, as fully and with the same effect as if the Mortgage had been duly executed, acknowledged and recorded, and the indebtedness secured thereby had been fully disbursed prior to the execution of the Lease or possession of the Real Estate by Tenant, or its predecessors in interest.

2. *Mortgagee Not to Disturb Tenant.* At any time that the Mortgage shall be in effect, Mortgagee agrees that so long as the Tenant is not in default (beyond any period given the Tenant under the Lease to cure such default) in the payment of rent or additional rent or in the performance of any of the terms, covenants or conditions of the Lease on the Tenant's part to be performed, the Mortgagee will not join the Tenant as a party defendant in any action or proceeding foreclosing the Mortgage unless required to foreclose the Mortgage and then only for such purpose and not for the purpose of terminating the Lease, and further, that the Tenant's possession of the Real Estate and the Tenant's rights and privileges under the Lease, or any extensions or renewals thereof which may be effected in accordance with the Lease, shall not be diminished or interfered with by the Mortgagee and the Tenant's occupancy of the Real Estate shall not be disturbed by the Mortgagee.

3. *Tenant to Attorn to Mortgagee.* If the interest of the Landlord shall be transferred to and owned by the Mortgagee by reason of foreclosure of the Mortgage or other proceedings brought by it in lieu of or pursuant to a foreclosure, or in any other manner, and the Mortgagee succeeds to the interest of the Landlord under the Lease, the Tenant shall be bound to the Mortgagee under all of the terms, covenants and conditions of the Lease for the balance of the term thereof remaining and any extensions or renewals thereof which may be effected in accordance with any option therefor in the Lease, with the same force and effect as if the Mortgagee were originally the landlord under the Lease, and the Tenant does hereby attorn to the Mortgagee as its Landlord, such attornment to be automatically effective immediately upon the Mortgagee's succeeding to the interest of the Landlord under the Lease without the execution of any further instruments on the part of any of the parties hereto. The respective rights and obligations of the Tenant and the Mortgagee upon such attornment, to the extent of the then remaining balance of the term of the Lease and any such extensions and renewals hereto, shall be and are the same as now set forth in the Lease, the terms of which are hereby fully incorporated herein by reference and made a part of this Agreement.

4. *Mortgagee Not Bound by Certain Acts of Landlord.* If the Mortgagee shall succeed to the interest of the Landlord under the Lease, the Mortgagee shall not be liable for any act or omission of Landlord; nor subject to any offsets or

defenses which the Tenant might have against the Landlord; nor bound by any rent or additional rent which the Tenant might have paid for more than the then current installment; nor bound by any amendment or modification of the Lease made without the Mortgagee's consent.

5. *Successors and Assigns.* This Agreement and each and every covenant, agreement and other provision hereof shall be binding upon the parties hereto and their successors and assigns, including without limitation each and every holder of the Lease or any other person having an interest therein and shall inure to the benefit of the Mortgagee, and its successors and assigns.

6. *Choice of Law.* This Agreement is made and executed under and in all respects is to be governed and construed by the laws of the State of _____.

7. *Captions and Headings.* The captions and headings of the various sections of this Agreement are for convenience only and are not to be construed as confining or limiting in any way the scope or intent of the provisions hereof. Whenever the context requires or permits, the singular shall include the plural, the plural shall include the singular.

8. *Notices.* Any notices which any party hereto may desire or may be required to give to any other party shall be in writing and the mailing thereof by certified mail, or equivalent, to the addresses as set forth above, or to such other places and party hereto may be notice in writing designate shall constitute service of notice hereunder.

```
_____
Tenant

By _____
Its _____


_____
(Mortgagee)

By _____
Its _____
```

SUBORDINATION, NONDISTURBANCE AND ATTORNMENT AGREEMENT [1]

NOTICE: THIS SUBORDINATION, NONDISTURBANCE AND ATTORNMENT AGREEMENT RESULTS IN THE LEASEHOLD ESTATE IN THE PROPERTY BECOMING SUBJECT TO AND OF LOWER PRIORITY THAN THE LIEN OF SOME OTHER OR LATER SECURITY INSTRUMENT. THIS SUBORDINATION, NONDISTURBANCE AND ATTORNMENT AGREEMENT (the "Agreement") is made as of _____, 19__, by and among _____,
a _____
("Landlord"), _____,
a _____
("Tenant"), and _____,
a _____
("Lender").

§ 15.12

1. Form provided by O'Melveny & Myers, Los Angeles, California.

RECITALS

A. Landlord is the owner of certain land (the "Land") located in the City of _____, County of _____, State of California, known as _____, and more particularly described in *Exhibit A* attached hereto and by this reference made a part hereof. As used herein, the term "Property" shall refer to the Land together with all improvements located thereon.

B. Pursuant to the terms of that certain Loan Agreement of even date herewith by and between Landlord and Lender (the "Loan Agreement"), Lender has agreed to make a loan to Landlord in the principal amount of _____ Dollars ($_____) (the "Loan"), which Loan is evidenced by that certain Secured Promissory Note of even date herewith, in the original principal amount of the Loan, and executed by Landlord in favor of Lender (the "Note"). The Note is secured, *inter alia,* by that certain Deed of Trust, Financing Statement and Fixture Filing (with Assignment of Rents) of even date herewith executed by Landlord, as trustor, to _____, as trustee, for the benefit of Lender, as beneficiary (the "Deed of Trust"), and by that certain Assignment of Rents, Leases, Income and Profits of even date herewith, executed by Landlord, as assignor, for the benefit of Lender, as assignee (the "Assignment of Rents"). The Loan Agreement, the Note, the Deed of Trust, the Assignment of Rents and all other documents and instruments evidencing or securing the Loan shall hereinafter be collectively referred to as the "Security Documents."

C. The Deed of Trust and the Assignment of Rents are to be recorded concurrently herewith and, upon recordation, will constitute a lien on the Property.

D. Tenant and Landlord entered into that certain lease (the "Lease") dated _____, 19__, pursuant to which Landlord leased to Tenant a portion of the improvements located on the Land and more particularly described in the Lease (the "Premises").

E. Tenant has obligated itself under the terms of the Lease to execute any document necessary or appropriate to subordinate the Lease to the Security Documents.

NOW, THEREFORE, in consideration of the foregoing recitals, which are, by this reference, incorporated herein, and for other valuable consideration, the receipt and sufficiency of which are hereby acknowledged, the parties hereto hereby covenant and agree as follows:

1. The Security Documents (and each of them) and all supplements, amendments, and modifications thereto and all renewals, placements or extensions thereof, shall unconditionally be and remain at all times a lien or charge on the Property prior and superior to the Lease, to the leasehold estate created thereby and to all rights and privileges of Tenant thereunder. The Lease, the leasehold estate created thereby, together with all rights and privileges of Tenant thereunder, are hereby unconditionally subjected, and made subordinate, to the lien or charge of the Security Documents (and each of them) in favor of Lender. Tenant declares, agrees and acknowledges that in making disbursements pursuant to the Loan Documents (as defined in the Deed of Trust), Lender is under no obligation or duty to, nor has Lender represented that it will, see to the application of such proceeds by the person or persons to whom Lender disburses such proceeds, and any application or use of such proceeds for purposes other than those provided for in such agreement or agreements shall not defeat the subordination herein made in whole or in part.

2. So long as Tenant is not in default in performance of the terms, provisions and conditions contained in the Lease, and so long as Tenant observes the provisions of Paragraph 4 of this Agreement:

    (a) Tenant shall not be named or joined in any foreclosure, trustee's sale or other proceeding to enforce the Deed of Trust unless such joinder be required by law in order to perfect such foreclosure, trustee's sale or other proceeding;

(b) enforcement of the Deed of Trust shall not terminate the Lease or disturb Tenant in the possession and use of the Premises; and

(c) the leasehold estate granted by the Lease shall not be affected in any manner by any foreclosure, trustee's sale or other proceeding instituted or action taken under or in connection with the Deed of Trust or the Assignment of Rents or in case Lender takes possession of the Premises pursuant to any provision of the Deed of Trust, except that a transferee (including, but not limited to, Lender) of the interest of Landlord as a result of such foreclosure, trustee's sale or other proceeding and such transferee's successors and assigns (such transferee, its successors and assigns, including, but not limited to, Lender, being hereinafter referred to as "Purchaser") shall not:

(i) be liable for any damages or other relief attributable to any act or omission of any prior landlord under the Lease (including, without limitation, Landlord);

(ii) be liable for any damages or other relief attributable to any latent or patent defects in construction with respect to the Premises;

(iii) be liable for any consequential damages attributable to any act or omission of Purchaser;

(iv) be liable for any damages or other relief attributable to any breach by Purchaser or any prior landlord under the Lease of any representation or warranty contained in the Lease;

(v) be subject to any offsets or defenses not specifically provided for in the Lease and which Tenant may have against any prior landlord under the Lease; and

(vi) be bound by any prepayment by Tenant of more than one month's installment of rent or for any security deposit not actually delivered to Purchaser, or by any modification of or amendment to the Lease, unless such prepayment, amendment or modification shall have been approved in writing by Lender or by any subsequent beneficiary under the Deed of Trust.

3. If the interest of Landlord under the Lease shall be transferred by reason of any foreclosure, trustee's sale or other proceeding for enforcement of the Deed of Trust or by deed in lieu thereof, and if Tenant is not in default under the Lease, Purchaser shall be bound to Tenant, and Tenant shall be bound to Purchaser, under all of the terms, covenants and conditions of the Lease (except as provided in Paragraph 2 hereof) for the balance of the term thereof, and any extensions or renewals thereof which may be effected in accordance with any option therefor in the Lease, with the same force and effect as if Purchaser were the original landlord under the Lease. Tenant does hereby attorn to Purchaser, including Lender if it be Purchaser, as the landlord under the Lease, said attornment to be effective and self-operative without the execution of any further instruments upon Purchaser's succeeding to the interest of the landlord under the Lease; provided, however, that Tenant waives any right to exercise any purchase option contained in the Lease in the event of any transfer to Purchaser.

4. In the event of default by Landlord in its performance of the terms, provisions and conditions of the Note or of any Security Document, Tenant agrees to recognize the assignment of the Lease made by Landlord to Lender pursuant to the Assignment of Rents and shall pay to Lender, as assignee, the rents under the Lease, but only those which are due or which come due to Landlord under the terms of the Lease at or after the time Lender gives Tenant notice that Landlord is in default under the terms of the Note or Security Documents. Such payments of

rents to Lender by Tenant by reason of said assignment and of Landlord's default shall continue until the first to occur of the following:

    (a) No further rent is due or payable under the Lease;

    (b) Lender gives Tenant notice that the default of Landlord under the Note or Security Documents has been cured and instructs Tenant that the rents shall thereafter be payable to Landlord; or

    (c) The lien of the Deed of Trust has been foreclosed and Purchaser gives Tenant notice of such foreclosure. Purchaser shall thereupon succeed to the interests of Landlord under the Lease as provided in Paragraphs 2 and 3 hereof, after which time the rents and other benefits of Landlord under the Lease shall be payable to Purchaser as the owner thereof.

    5. In complying with the provisions of Paragraph 4 hereof, Tenant shall be entitled to rely solely upon the notices given by Lender which are referred to in Paragraph 4 hereof and Landlord agrees to indemnify and hold Tenant harmless from and against any and all loss, claim, damage or liability arising out of Tenant's compliance with such notice. Tenant shall be entitled to full credit under the Lease for any rents paid to Lender in accordance with the provisions of Paragraph 4 hereof to the same extent as if such rents were paid directly to Landlord. Any dispute between Lender (or other Purchaser) and Landlord as to the existence or continuance of a default by Landlord under the terms of the Note or Security Documents, or with respect to the extent or nature of such default, or with respect to foreclosure of the Deed of Trust by Lender, shall be dealt with and adjusted solely between Lender (or other Purchaser) and Landlord, and Tenant shall not be made a party thereto (unless required by law).

    6. Nothing in this Agreement shall be deemed to be or construed to be an agreement by Lender to perform any covenant of the Landlord as landlord under the Lease unless and until it obtains title to the Premises by power of sale or judicial foreclosure or deed in lieu thereof or obtains possession of the Premises pursuant to the terms of the Deed of Trust.

    7. Tenant agrees that during the term of the Lease, without Lender's prior written consent, Tenant will not:

    (a) pay any rent or additional rent more than one month in advance to any landlord (including, but not limited to, Landlord); or

    (b) cancel, terminate or surrender, except at the normal expiration of the Lease term, the Lease or enter into any agreement, amendment or modification of the Lease.

    8. Landlord, Tenant and Lender agree that unless Lender shall otherwise consent in writing, Landlord's estate in and to the Property and the leasehold estate created by the Lease shall not merge but shall remain separate and distinct, notwithstanding the union of said estates either in Landlord or Tenant or any third party by purchase, assignment or otherwise.

    9. Tenant, from and after the date hereof, shall send a copy of any notice of default or similar statement under the Lease to Lender at the same time such notice or statement is sent to the Landlord under the Lease. Such notices shall be delivered to Lender in the manner and at the addresses set forth in *Paragraph 17* hereof.

    10. Anything herein or in the Lease to the contrary notwithstanding, in the event that any Purchaser shall acquire title to the Property, Purchaser shall have no obligation, nor incur any liability, beyond the then interest, if any, of Purchaser in the Property and Tenant shall look exclusively to such interest of Purchaser, if any, in the Property for the payment and discharge of any obligations imposed upon Purchaser hereunder or under the Lease, and Purchaser is hereby released and relieved of any other liability hereunder and under the Lease. As regards such Purchaser, Tenant shall look solely to the estate or interest owned by Purchaser in

the Property and Tenant will not collect or attempt to collect any such judgment out of any other assets of Purchaser. By executing this Agreement, Landlord specifically acknowledges and agrees that nothing contained in this *Paragraph 10* shall impair, limit, affect, lessen, abrogate or otherwise modify the obligations of Landlord to Tenant under the Lease.

11. Tenant and Landlord each hereby certify that as of the date hereof there are no known defaults (or events which with the giving of notice or the passage of time or both could give rise to a default) on the part of the other party under the Lease, that the Lease is a complete statement of the agreement of the parties thereto with respect to the leasing of the Premises, that the Lease is in full force and effect, and that all conditions to the effectiveness or continuing effectiveness thereof required to be satisfied as of the date hereof have been satisfied.

12. This Agreement shall be the whole and only agreement with regard to the subjection and subordination of the Lease and the leasehold estate created thereby, together with all rights and privileges of Tenant thereunder, to the lien or charge of the Security Documents (and each of them) and shall supersede and cancel, but only insofar as would affect the priority between the Lease and the Security Documents (and each of them), any prior agreements as to such subjection or subordination, including, but not limited to, those provisions contained in the Lease which provide for the subjection or subordination of the Lease and the leasehold estate created thereby to a deed or deeds of trust or to a mortgage or mortgages.

13. This Agreement may be executed in any number of counterparts, each of which when so executed and delivered shall be deemed to be an original and all of which counterparts taken together shall constitute but one and the same instrument. Signature and acknowledgment pages may be detached from the counterparts and attached to a single copy of this Agreement to form one document, which may be recorded.

14. This Agreement may not be modified orally or in any manner other than by an agreement in writing signed by the parties hereto or their respective successors in interest. This Agreement shall inure to the benefit of and be binding upon the parties hereto and their respective successors and assigns.

15. In the event any legal action or proceeding is commenced to interpret or enforce the terms of, or obligations arising out of, this Agreement, or to recover damages for the breach thereof, the party prevailing in any such action or proceeding shall be entitled to recover from the non-prevailing party all reasonable attorneys' fees, costs and expenses incurred by the prevailing party.

16. The interpretation, validity and enforcement of this Agreement shall be governed by and construed under the laws of the State of California.

17. All notices and other communications provided for herein shall be in writing and shall be given by hand or sent by registered or certified mail, postage prepaid, addressed as follows:

To Lender: _____
_____
_____
_____
Attention: _____

To Landlord: _____
_____
_____
_____
Attention: _____

To Tenant: _____
_____

_____
_____
Attention: _____

Each party may change its address by notice to each of the other parties as provided herein. Notices, if sent by mail, shall be deemed given on the fifth day following the deposit in United States mail, and, if delivered by hand, shall be deemed given when delivered.

IN WITNESS WHEREOF, the parties have executed this Agreement as of the date first above written.

NOTICE: THIS AGREEMENT CONTAINS A PROVISION WHICH ALLOWS THE PERSON OBLIGATED ON YOUR LEASE TO OBTAIN A LOAN, A PORTION OF WHICH MAY BE EXPENDED FOR PURPOSES OTHER THAN IMPROVEMENT OF THE PROPERTY.

§ 15.13 Tenant Estoppel Certificate [1]

In determining whether to underwrite a loan, it is crucial that the lender be able to obtain an accurate assessment of the income that is or will be generated by the real estate. This is an especially important concern in the nonrecourse loan setting where the lender is looking almost entirely to the real estate and its income stream to support a decision to make a loan. Thus, a close examination of the borrower's leases and the execution of estoppel certificates by the lessees, in which they confirm certain facts concerning those leases, are extremely important to the underwriting process. The following represents a valuable enumeration of the elements such statements should contain:

> "The length and complexity of an estoppel certificate will vary depending on the size of the transaction, the importance of a particular lease and the bargaining power of the tenant. Nevertheless, there are certain facts that the lender will want the tenant to confirm: (1) the amount of the rent, the fact that it is payable without offset or deduction, that all rent due as of the date of the estoppel has been paid, and that no rental payments have been made more than 30 days prior to the date on which such rental is due; (2) the term of the lease; (3) provisions for free rent or rental adjustments; (4) the description of the space covered by the lease; (5) the existence (or nonexistence) of extension, expansion or purchase options, or rights of first refusal; (6) the existence (or nonexistence) of any defaults by the landlord or the tenant and of any events which, with notice or the passage of time, could give rise to any such default; (7) that there are no oral or written agreements between the landlord and tenant relating to the tenant's occupancy other than the lease; and (8) that the lease has not been amended or modified other than as described in the estoppel certificate. In addition, if the lease required the landlord to

§ 15.13   Myers, Los Angeles, California.
1. Form provided by O'Melveny &

complete tenant improvements, the lender will want to verify that the tenant has accepted its space as satisfactory and complete."

Geiger and Frobes, Lenders and Leases, 7 Cal.Real Prop.J. 1, 3 (No. 4, Fall, 1989). The estoppel certificate should also disclose whether any material disputes exist between the borrower and the tenant. Id.

Equally important, the estoppel certificate is executed to provide the lender with the ability to assert equitable estoppel when a subsequent tenant claim concerning the lease is contradicted by the estoppel certificate. The doctrine is designed to prevent a person from "asserting one set of facts against another person if he or she intentionally led the other person to believe that a different set of facts was true *and* the other person acted, to his or her detriment, in reliance on the truth of the facts as represented." Id. at 4.

The form in this section was developed for use in California. However, since the issues it covers are seldom state specific, it should supply valuable drafting ideas in most jurisdictions.

TENANT ESTOPPEL CERTIFICATE

BUILDING: _____

To: [Name of Lender] (the "Lender")

THIS IS TO CERTIFY THAT AS OF _____, 19__:

1. The undersigned is the present owner and holder of the tenant's interest under that certain agreement of lease dated _____, modified by the agreements, if any, attached hereto pursuant to paragraph 2(a) below (the lease, as so modified, being hereinafter referred to as the "Lease"), by and between _____ (the "Landlord") or the Landlord's predecessor in interest named in paragraph 2(b) below, and _____, as tenant, covering those certain premises designated as the floors or portions thereof specified in paragraph 2(c) below (the "Premises") in the building (the "Building") which has an address of _____, _____, and which is part of the development commonly known as _____.

2. (a) A true, correct and complete copy of the Lease (including all amendments and supplements thereto and modifications thereof) as attached hereto.

(b) The original landlord under the Lease was _____.

(c) The Premises covered by the Lease is for Suite # _____. (If applicable: In addition, pursuant to the terms of the Lease, the undersigned has the right to use or rent _____ unassigned parking spaces near the Building or in the garage portion of the Building during the term of the Lease.)

(d) The term of the Lease has commenced and will expire on _____, subject to any renewal or cancellation rights specified in the Lease. The undersigned does not have any option or right to renew or cancel the Lease, nor to lease additional space in the Premises, or to use any parking other than that specified in paragraph 2(c) above, nor to purchase any part of the Premises, except in each case as specified in the Lease.

(e) The annual minimum rent currently payable pursuant to the Lease is at the rate of $_____ and has been paid through _____, 19__. If applicable: The annual percentage rent currently payable pursuant to the Lease is at the rate of _____ and has been paid through _____, 19__.

(f) If applicable: Additional rent for (i) operating, maintenance and/or repair expenses, (ii) property taxes, (iii) consumer price index cost of living adjustments and (iv) percentage of gross sales adjustments (i.e., adjustments made based on underpayments of percentage point) is payable pursuant to the Lease and has been paid in accordance with Landlord's rendered bills through _____. The base year amounts for the additional rent items are as follows: (i) operating, maintenance and/or repair expenses $_____, (ii) property taxes $_____, and (iii) consumer price index _____ (please indicate base year CPI level).

(g) Landlord currently holds a security deposit in the amount of $_____ which is to be applied by Landlord or returned to the undersigned in accordance with the terms of the Lease. The undersigned acknowledges and agrees that Lender shall have no responsibility or liability for any security deposit, except to the extent such security deposit has been actually received by Lender.

3. (a) The Lease constitutes the entire agreement between the undersigned and Landlord with respect to the Premises, has not been modified, changed, altered or amended, and is in full force and effect.

(b) To the best knowledge of the undersigned, no party to the Lease is in default thereunder.

(c) To the best knowledge of the undersigned, no event has occurred which, with the giving of notice or passage of time, or both, would constitute such a default. The interest of the undersigned in the Lease has not been assigned or encumbered. The undersigned is not entitled to any credit against any rent or other charge or rent concession under the Lease except as set forth in the Lease. No rental payments have been made more than one month in advance.

4. All contributions required to be paid by Landlord to date for improvements to the Premises have been paid in full and all of Landlord's obligations with respect to tenant improvements have been fully performed. The undersigned has accepted the Premises, subject to no conditions other than those set forth in the Lease.

5. There are no actions, whether voluntary or otherwise, pending against the undersigned or any guarantor of the undersigned's obligations under the Lease pursuant to the bankruptcy or insolvency laws of the United States or any state thereof.

6. The undersigned represents and warrants that it has not used, generated, released, discharged, stored or disposed of any hazardous waste, toxic substances or related materials (collectively, "Hazardous Materials") on, under, in or about the Premises, or transported any Hazardous Materials to or from the Premises, other than Hazardous Materials used in the ordinary and commercially reasonable course of the undersigned's business in compliance with all applicable laws. The term "Hazardous Materials" shall mean (a) any "hazardous substance" as such term is presently defined in Section 101(14) of the Comprehensive Environmental Response, Compensation, and Liability Act of 1980, as amended (42 U.S.C. § 9601 et seq.) and any regulations promulgated thereunder ("CERCLA"); (b) any additional substances or materials which are hereafter incorporated in or added to the definition of "hazardous substance" for purposes of CERCLA; and (c) any additional substances or materials which are now or hereafter defined as "hazardous substances," "hazardous waste," "toxic substances" or "toxic waste" under any other federal law or under any state, county, municipal or other law applicable to the Premises or under any regulations promulgated pursuant thereto.

7. The undersigned hereby acknowledges that Landlord intends to encumber the Building with a deed of trust in favor of Lender. The undersigned further acknowledges the right of Landlord, Lender and any and all of Landlord's present and future lenders to rely upon the statements and representations of the undersigned contained in this Certificate and further acknowledges that any loan secured by any such deed of trust or further deeds of trust will be made and entered into in material reliance on this Certificate.

Tenant: _____
By: _____
Title: _____

§ 15.14 Leasehold Mortgage—On Ground–Leased Income Property [1]

Mortgages on the security of a ground lease typically involve substantial income producing projects. The ground lease is often made to the developer by a long-time owner of the land or a land speculator who has previously purchased it from such an owner. On the other hand, sometimes a pension fund or other institutional investor will purchase land with an advance commitment to lease it to a developer. The term of the ground lease must be at least as long as the term of the permanent mortgage loan which the developer will use to finance the improvements; typical terms range from 30 to 99 years. The lease usually provides that the improvements built by the developer will remain his or her property until termination of the lease, at which time they will revert to the ground lessor. Almost invariably ground leases are "net" leases, in the sense that the lessee is obligated to pay taxes, insurance, maintenance costs, and all other expenses related to the property.

Economically, the ground lease is viewed by the developer as a substitute for purchase money financing of the land. It is true that a purchase would give the developer title in perpetuity, while the lease gives him possession for only a limited (although long) time; but this difference is relatively unimportant to the developer, since the present value of the reversion is very small at the time he enters into the lease.

From the developer's viewpoint, the ground lease has several attractions as a land acquisition vehicle. He will own and take depreciation deductions on the improvements. The ground rent he pays to the lessor will be fully deductible; by contrast, if he purchased the land with a purchase-money mortgage, a portion of his payments would be non-deductible amortization. Aside from a modest security deposit, the ground lease usually requires no front-end cash investment by the developer. If the ground lessor is willing to "subordinate" to the construction and permanent loans which the developer will obtain (technically, to subject the fee interest to those mortgages), the developer will often be able to obtain significantly greater leverage than if land purchase were necessary.

From the mortgagee's perspective, lending on the security of a leasehold portends greater risk than a comparable loan on a fee simple absolute. Because the mortgagee's security exists only so long as the mortgagor's leasehold is in good standing, lenders need be especially

§ 15.14
1. Form provided by the Metropolitan Life Insurance Company.

scrupulous to insure that provisions of both the mortgage and the ground lease eliminate or substantially reduce the risk of lease termination. This section focuses on the mortgage, while the next deals with ground lease provisions that are crucial to the protection of the mortgagee's security.

The mortgage form provided in this section is not only highly sophisticated, it is also especially meticulous in protecting the mortgagee's interests. First and foremost, it affords the mortgagee maximum authority and flexibility to insure that the mortgagor complies with the terms of the ground lease. In the event the mortgagor fails in this regard, the mortgagee is authorized to take whatever steps are necessary to cure any ground lease defaults and to prevent its termination. Among other things, the mortgage authorizes the mortgagee to cure mortgagor defaults under the ground lease (Section 5(b)), requires the mortgagor to supply the mortgagee with prompt notification of lessor default (Section 5(f)), prohibits the mortgagor from terminating or surrendering its leasehold or consenting to modification of it without the approval of the mortgagee (Section 5(c)), and affords the mortgagee the right to exercise ground lease renewal options upon mortgagor's failure to do so (Section 5(i)). Moreover, because the value of a leasehold as security depends on the strength of the space leases (subleases), the mortgagee typically reserves the right to disapprove them. Here the mortgagee retains this right as to most non-residential space leases. See Section 14(a). In addition, the mortgage confers on the mortgagee substantial control over language contained in space leases. This is to insure that the mortgagee has the right to keep such leases in good standing whatever misfortune may befall the mortgagor-tenant. For example, the mortgage specifies that space leases must contain language obligating their lessees to attorn to any successor in interest of the mortgagor-tenant. See Section 14(c). This enables a foreclosure sale purchaser, whether the mortgagee or a third party, to keep alive space leases that otherwise would be destroyed by foreclosure of the leasehold mortgage.

The due-on-sale protection afforded the mortgagee is both complex and thorough. Not only does it contain the usual language covering the transfer of all or any part of the mortgaged property or any interest therein, it also encompasses a multitude of more subtle changes in the structure of the mortgagor. See Sections 33(c) and 33(d). For example, it covers changes in the numbers and financial stake of the partners of the mortgagor (where the mortgagor is a partnership), reduction in stock ownership (where the mortgagor is a corporation) and the death or incapacity of those who have a significant ownership interest in the mortgagor. Interestingly, the occurrence of such events do not afford the mortgagee the right to accelerate the entire mortgage debt, but rather simply the prerogative to demand prepayment of 35% of it.

The foregoing provisions may not be governed by the Garn–St. Germain Act. That Act preempts state law only with respect to due-on-sale clauses that "authorize a lender, at its option, to declare due and payable sums secured by the lender's security instrument if all or any part of the property, or an interest therein * * * is sold or transferred without the lender's prior written consent." 12 U.S.C.A. § 1701j-3(a)(1). See § 5.24 supra. Many of the transactions encompassed by the language of the form may not involve a transfer of an "interest" in the mortgaged property. In any event, the language will probably be enforceable under state law. First, since the provisions arose in the context of a highly sophisticated commercial transaction and were obviously the product of substantial bargaining, courts will be more favorably disposed toward enforcement than would be the case in the usual residential mortgage setting. More important, all courts enforce due-on-sale clauses when they are being relied upon to protect the mortgagee's security rather than simply to increase its portfolio interest rate return. See generally, § 5.22 supra. Here the provisions are largely aimed at protecting the mortgagee's security by discouraging key persons from reducing their stake in the enterprise. Moreover, the mortgagee's remedy calls not for the acceleration of the entire mortgage debt but only for prepayment of 35% of it. It is surely reasonable for a lender to have the option to reduce its stake in a project when key parties reduce or readjust theirs.

In Section 30 the mortgagee waives the right to proceed against the mortgagor or any of its partners or principals personally on the mortgage debt, whether by a suit on the debt itself or by seeking a deficiency judgment after foreclosure. This creates a "non-recourse" mortgage loan transaction. Such mortgages are valid even though they secure a debt on which there is no personal liability. See § 2.1 supra.

LEASEHOLD MORTGAGE

THIS MORTGAGE (this "Mortgage"), dated _____ between _____ a limited partnership having its principal office at _____ (the "Mortgagor") and _____ having its principal office at _____ (the "Mortgagee").

WITNESSETH, that to secure (a) the payment of an indebtedness of the Mortgagor to the Mortgagee in the sum of $_____ with interest thereon according to a certain note dated _____ ("Note I"), (b) the payment of an indebtedness of the Mortgagor to the Mortgagee in the sum of $_____ with interest thereon according to a certain note dated _____ ("Note II"; Note I and Note II being herein collectively called the "Notes", and all of the terms of the Notes and all of the covenants, conditions and agreements contained therein being hereby made a part of this Mortgage as fully as if the same were set forth herein in their entirety), (c) the payment of other moneys secured hereby and (d) the performance of the covenants and _____ agreements contained herein, in the Notes and in a certain Building Loan Agreement dated _____ between the Mortgagor and the Mortgagee (the "Building Loan Agreement") (which Building Loan Agreement shall be deemed to be of no further force and effect from and after the Advance Date (as defined in paragraph 33 hereof)), the Mortgagor does hereby grant, bargain, sell, convey, warrant, assign, transfer, mortgage, pledge and set over unto the Mortgagee and its successors and assigns, all the following property (the "Mortgaged Property"):

(a) All right, title and interest of the Mortgagor in and to a certain ground lease, dated as of _____ between _____ as landlord, and _____ as tenant, recorded in the Office of the _____ and assigned to the Mortgagor by instrument dated _____ and recorded in the aforesaid Office on _____ in _____ at page _____ and modified in its entirety by an Agreement Restating Lease, dated _____ between the _____ as landlord, and the Mortgagor, as tenant, recorded in the aforesaid Office on _____ in _____, at page _____, and the leasehold estate created thereby (the "Ground Lease"), affecting the lands and premises known as _____ and _____ and more particularly described in Exhibit A hereto (the "Premises");

(b) All and singular the tenements, hereditaments, easements, rights of way and appurtenances belonging or in anywise appertaining to the Premises, and all of the estate, right, title, interest, claim or demand whatsoever of the Mortgagor therein and in the streets, ways and areas adjacent thereto;

(c) The leasehold estate now owned or hereafter acquired by the Mortgagor under the Ground Lease in and to any and all buildings, structures and improvements now or at any time hereafter erected, constructed or situated upon the Premises or any part thereof, and in and to all apparatus, equipment and fixtures now or hereafter attached to or used or procured for use in connection with the operation or maintenance of any such building, structure or other improvement, whether as a hotel, apartment house, or otherwise, including, but without limiting the generality of the foregoing, all engines, furnaces, boilers, stokers, pumps, heaters, tanks, dynamos, motors, generators, switchboards, electrical equipment, television and radio systems, heating, plumbing, lifting and ventilating apparatus, air-cooling and air conditioning apparatus, gas and electric fixtures, elevators, escalators, fittings, and machinery and all other equipment of every kind and description used or procured for use in the operation of any and all such buildings, structures and improvements (except apparatus, equipment and fixtures belonging to tenants or occupants of particular suites, stores or offices in the Premises and consumable supplies) (collectively, the "Improvements");

(d) The leasehold estate now owned or hereafter acquired by the Mortgagor in and to any and all sidewalks and alleys, and all strips and gores of land, adjacent to or used in connection with the Premises;

(e) All right, title and interest of the Mortgagor, now owned or hereafter acquired, in and to all of the furniture, furnishings, beds, bedsprings, mattresses, bureaus, chiffoniers, chairs, chests, desks, bookcases, tables, rugs, carpets, curtains, draperies, hangings, decorations, pictures, divans, couches, glassware, silverware, tableware, linens, towels, bedding, blankets, china, ornaments, bric-a-brac, kitchen equipment and utensils, bars, bar fixtures, uniforms, safes, cash registers, accounting and duplicating machines, communication equipment, vaults, washtubs, sinks, stoves, ranges, radios, television sets, laundry machines, iceboxes, refrigerators, awnings, screens, window shades, venetian blinds, statuary, lamps, mirrors and all other appliances, fittings, furniture, furnishings and hotel equipment of every kind now or hereafter situated in, or used in the operation of, the rooms, halls, lounges, offices, lobbies, lavatories, basements, cellars, vaults and other portions of any building, structure or other improvement now or hereafter erected, constructed or situated on the Premises, together with any and all replacements thereof and additions thereto (collectively, the "Furnishings and Fixtures");

(f) All right, title and interest of the Mortgagor, if any, in and to (i) all modifications, extensions and renewals of the Ground Lease and in and to all rights to renew or extend the term thereof; and (ii) all other options, credits, security, deposits, privileges and rights granted and demised to the Mortgagor, under the Ground Lease;

(g) All right, title and interest of the Mortgagor in and to any and all present and future Space Leases (as defined in paragraph 14(a) hereof) in any and all buildings now or hereafter erected upon the premises demised under the Ground Lease, and the rents, issues and profits payable thereunder, subject, however, to the right upon the part of the Mortgagor, so long as no Default (as defined in paragraph 15 hereof), shall exist, to collect and use the rents, issues and profits payable under such Space Leases; together with all the right or privilege of the Mortgagor, without the prior consent of the Mortgagee, (i) to terminate, cancel, modify, or amend the Ground Lease, (ii) to accept prepayment of more than one periodic installment of rent or other consideration payable under any present or future Space Leases, except as permitted pursuant to paragraph 14 hereof, (iii) to accept a surrender of any Major Non-Residential Space Lease (as defined in paragraph 14 hereof) and (iv) to modify, abridge or terminate any Major Non-Residential Space Lease;

(h) All the reversion or reversions, remainder and remainders, rents, revenues, issues, income and profits of the Premises and the Improvements, all of which are hereby assigned to the Mortgagee, subject, however, to the right of the Mortgagor to receive and use the same until a Default shall have occurred and be continuing;

(i) All right, title and interest of the Mortgagor, now owned or hereafter acquired, in and to all materials, equipment, fixtures and appurtenances (together with all photographs, catalogues, lists and specifications relating thereto) used in connection with the restoration work required under the Declaration (as defined in paragraph 6(b)(vii) hereof) as set forth in Exhibit E thereto; and

(j) All proceeds of the insurance required to be maintained under paragraph 6 and all awards heretofore or hereafter made to the Mortgagor with respect to any part of the Premises and the Improvements as the result of the exercise of the power of eminent domain, including any awards for changes of the grades of streets, or as the result of any other damage to the Premises and the Improvements for which compensation shall be given by any governmental authority, all of which are hereby assigned to the Mortgagee who is hereby authorized to collect and receive the proceeds thereof and to give proper receipts and acquittances therefor, and to apply the same in accordance with the provisions hereof (to the extent not prohibited by or inconsistent with the terms of the Ground Lease).

TO HAVE AND TO HOLD the Mortgaged Property unto the Mortgagee, its successors and assigns, forever.

PROVIDED ALWAYS, that if the Mortgagor, its successors and assigns, shall pay in full the principal of and interest on the Notes in accordance with their respective terms and all other sums becoming due and payable hereunder, and abides by and complies with each and every covenant and condition set forth herein, in the Notes and in the Building Loan Agreement, then this Mortgage and the estate hereby granted shall cease, terminate and become void, and, in such event, if requested by the Mortgagor or required by law, the Mortgagee shall execute and deliver to the Mortgagor an instrument in form for recording reconveying to the Mortgagor the estate hereby granted.

AND the Mortgagor covenants with the Mortgagee as follows:

1. The Mortgagor shall pay the indebtedness as in the Notes and herein provided and shall abide by and comply with each and every covenant and condition set forth in the Notes and the Building Loan Agreement.

2. The Mortgagor warrants that (i) it is lawfully seized and possessed of an indefeasible leasehold estate in the Premises and the Improvements, subject to no mortgage, lien, charge or encumbrance, except those matters listed as exceptions to title in the title policy insuring the lien of this Mortgage, (ii) it has full power and lawful authority to grant, bargain, sell, convey, assign, transfer and mortgage the Mortgaged Property and (iii) the Ground Lease is a valid and subsisting lease of the Premises for the term therein set forth, is in full force and effect, has not been

modified and no defaults by the lessor or the lessee exist thereunder. The Mortgagor shall forever warrant and defend the title to the Mortgaged Property against the claims and demands of all persons whomsoever.

3. (a) The Mortgagor shall execute, acknowledge and deliver, from time to time, such further instruments as the Mortgagee may require to accomplish the purposes of this Mortgage.

(b) The Mortgagor, immediately upon the execution and delivery of this Mortgage, and thereafter from time to time, shall cause this Mortgage, any mortgage supplemental hereto and each instrument of further assurance to be filed, registered or recorded and refiled, reregistered or rerecorded in such manner and in such places as may be required by any present or future law in order to publish notice of and perfect the lien of this Mortgage upon the Mortgaged Property.

(c) The Mortgagor shall pay all filing, registration and recording fees, all refiling, reregistration and rerecording fees, and all expenses incident to the execution and acknowledgment of this Mortgage, any mortgage supplemental hereto and any instrument of further assurance, and all federal, state, county and municipal taxes, duties, imposts, assessments and charges arising out of or in connection with the execution and delivery of this Mortgage or any mortgage supplemental hereto or any instruments of further assurance.

4. The Mortgagor shall not create or suffer to be created any mortgage, lien, charge or encumbrance upon the Mortgaged Property prior to, on a parity with or subordinate to the lien of this Mortgage (or any pledge or other encumbrance on the stock or partnership interests of the Mortgagor) without the prior consent of the Mortgagee, except (i) a subordinate mortgage or mortgages held by _____ (or persons related to and/or entities owned and/or controlled by _____) or a Controlled Entity (as defined in paragraph 33 hereof) in any amount, and (ii) an arm's-length, bona fide second subordinate mortgage (to provide for constant payments on account of principal and interest thereof at an annual rate not in excess of 11% of the original principal amount thereof) held by persons or entities other than _____ (or persons related to _____ and/or entities owned and/or controlled by _____) or a Controlled Entity in an aggregate principal amount at any time not exceeding $8,000,000; provided, however, that each such subordinate mortgage shall provide that (x) a default thereunder shall be deemed a default under this Mortgage, (y) notices of default thereunder shall be served upon the Mortgagee and (z) any assignment of rents thereunder shall be expressly subordinate to the assignment of rents contained in this Mortgage and no tenant occupying space in the Improvements shall be joined as a defendant in any foreclosure proceedings thereunder without the prior written consent of the Mortgagee. In the case of any subordinate mortgage held by _____ (or persons related to _____ and/or entities owned and/or controlled by _____) or a Controlled Entity, the Mortgagor shall cause an assignment thereof to be made to the Mortgagee as additional security for the indebtedness secured hereby, which assignment shall be made on the date of the execution and delivery of said mortgage.

5. (a) The Mortgagor shall (i) promptly perform and observe all of the terms, covenants and conditions required to be performed and observed by the lessee under the Ground Lease and do all things necessary to preserve and to keep unimpaired its rights thereunder, (ii) promptly notify the Mortgagee of any default by the Mortgagor under the Ground Lease in the performance of any of the terms, covenants or conditions on the part of the Mortgagor to be performed or observed thereunder or of the giving of any notice by the lessor under the Ground Lease to the Mortgagor of such lessor's intention to end the term thereof and (iii) promptly cause a copy of each such notice given by the lessor under the Ground Lease to the Mortgagor to be delivered to the Mortgagee.

(b) If the Mortgagor shall fail promptly to perform or observe any of the terms, covenants or conditions required to be performed by it under the Ground Lease, including, without limitation, payment of all basic rent and additional rent due thereunder, the Mortgagee may take such action as is appropriate to cause such terms, covenants or conditions to be promptly performed or observed on behalf of the Mortgagor but no such action by the Mortgagee shall release the Mortgagor from any default under this Mortgage. Upon receipt by the Mortgagee from the lessor under the Ground Lease of any notice of default by the Mortgagor thereunder, the Mortgagee may rely thereon and take any action as aforesaid to cure such default even though the existence of such default or the nature thereof be questioned or denied by the Mortgagor or by any party on behalf of the Mortgagor.

(c) The Mortgagor shall not surrender its leasehold estate and interests under the Ground Lease, nor terminate or cancel the Ground Lease, and the Mortgagor shall not modify, change, supplement, alter or amend the Ground Lease either orally or in writing, and the Mortgagor does hereby expressly release, relinquish and surrender unto the Mortgagee all its right, power and authority to modify, change, supplement, alter or amend the provisions of the Ground Lease in any way, and any attempt on the part of the Mortgagor to exercise any such right without the consent of the Mortgagee shall be null and void.

(d) No release or forbearance of any of the Mortgagor's obligations under the Ground Lease, pursuant to the Ground Lease or otherwise, shall release the Mortgagor from any of its obligations under this Mortgage.

(e) The fee title to the properties demised by the Ground Lease and the leasehold estate shall not merge, but shall always remain separate and distinct, notwithstanding the union of the aforesaid estates either in the lessor or the lessee under the Ground Lease or in a third party by purchase or otherwise.

(f) The Mortgagor shall enforce the obligations of the lessor under the Ground Lease to the end that the Mortgagor may enjoy all of the rights granted to it under the Ground Lease, and will promptly notify the Mortgagee of any default by the lessor, or by the Mortgagor as lessee, in the performance or observance of any of the terms, covenants and conditions on the part of the lessor or the Mortgagor, as the case may be, to be performed or observed under the Ground Lease and the Mortgagor will promptly advise the Mortgagee of the occurrence of any of the events of default enumerated in Article 19 of the Ground Lease and of the giving of any notice by the lessor to the Mortgagor of any default by the Mortgagor, as such lessee, in the performance or observance of any of the terms, covenants or conditions of the Ground Lease on the part of the Mortgagor to be performed or observed and will deliver to the Mortgagee a true copy of each such notice. If, pursuant to the Ground Lease, the lessor shall deliver to the Mortgagee a copy of any notice of default given to the Mortgagor, as lessee under the Ground Lease, such notice shall constitute full authority and protection to the Mortgagee for any action taken or omitted to be taken by the Mortgagee, in good faith in reliance thereon. If the Mortgagor shall have notified the Mortgagee that there is a bona fide dispute between the Mortgagor and the lessor under the Ground Lease as to the existence of any default referred to in any such copy of notice of default delivered to the Mortgagee, the Mortgagee shall not take any action pursuant to the foregoing sentence which would prejudice the rights of the Mortgagor in the event of any such dispute, unless, in the judgment of the Mortgagee, the lien of the Mortgage on the Mortgaged Premises, or any part thereof, would, by reason of such forbearance, be in imminent danger of being forfeited, lost or subordinated.

(g) The Mortgagor shall give the Mortgagee prompt notice of the commencement of any arbitration or appraisal proceeding under and pursuant to the provisions of the Ground Lease. The Mortgagee shall have the right to intervene and participate in any such proceeding and the Mortgagor shall confer with the Mortgagee and its attorneys and experts and cooperate with them to the extent which the Mortgagee deems reasonably necessary for the protection of the Mortgagee. Upon the request of the Mortgagee, the Mortgagor will exercise all rights of arbitration conferred upon it by the Ground Lease. If at any time such proceeding shall be commenced, the Mortgagor shall be in default in the performance of observance of any covenant, condition or other requirement of the Ground Lease, or of the Mortgage, on the part of the Mortgagor to be performed or observed, the Mortgagee shall have, and is hereby granted, the sole and exclusive right to designate and appoint on behalf of the Mortgagor the arbitrator or arbitrators, or appraiser, in such proceeding.

(h) The Mortgagor shall use its best efforts to obtain from the lessor under the Ground Lease and deliver to the Mortgagee, within 20 days after demand from the Mortgagee, a statement in writing certifying that the Ground Lease is unmodified and in full force and effect and the dates to which the ground rent and other charges, if any, have been paid in advance, and stating whether or not, to the best knowledge of the signer of such certificate, the Mortgagor is in default in the performance of any covenant, agreement or condition contained in the Ground Lease, and, if so, specifying each such default of which the signer may have knowledge.

(i) The Mortgagor shall, at least six months prior to the last day upon which the Mortgagor, as lessee under the Ground Lease, may validly exercise any option to renew or extend the term of the Ground Lease, (i) exercise such option in such manner as will cause the term of the Ground Lease to be effectively renewed or extended for the period provided by such option and (ii) give immediate notice thereof to the Mortgagee; it being expressly understood that in the event of the failure of the Mortgagor so to do, the Mortgagee shall have, and is hereby granted, the irrevocable right to exercise any such option, either in its own name and behalf, or in the name and behalf of the Mortgagor, as the Mortgagee shall in its sole discretion determine; provided, however, that if the Mortgagor shall pay the indebtedness hereby secured at least six months prior to the last day upon which the Mortgagor may validly exercise any option to renew or extend the term of the Ground Lease, the Mortgagor shall not be obliged to exercise any such option of renewal or extension, nor will the Mortgagee have any right to exercise any such option. In the event of damage by fire or other casualty to the Mortgaged Premises during the last three years of the term granted under the Ground Lease, or any renewal thereof, the Mortgagor will not exercise the election granted to it pursuant to the provisions of the Ground Lease to terminate the same without the consent of the Mortgagee.

(j) The Mortgagor shall promptly notify the Mortgagee of any change, made pursuant to the provisions of Ground Lease, in the ground rent payable by the lessee under the Ground Lease, and in the event that any proceeds of insurance on any part of the Mortgaged Premises, or any proceeds of any award for the taking by eminent domain of any part of the Mortgaged Premises, shall be deposited with any person pursuant to the requirements of the Ground Lease, the Mortgagor shall promptly notify the Mortgagee of the name and address of the person with whom such proceeds have been deposited and of the amount so deposited.

6. (a) The Mortgagor shall keep the Improvements continuously insured for the benefit of the Mortgagee against loss or damage by fire and against such other hazards (including without limitation, by the types of insurance set forth in paragraph 6(b)) as the Mortgagee shall from time to time require. All such insurance at

all times shall be in an insurance company or companies and on terms acceptable to the Mortgagee, with loss, if any, payable to the Mortgagee as its interest may appear, pursuant to the _____ Standard Mortgage Non–Contributory mortgagee clause. Forthwith upon the issuance of such policies, the Mortgagor shall deliver the same and all renewals thereof to the Mortgagee and shall also deliver to the Mortgagee receipts for the premiums paid thereon. All policies furnished the Mortgagee shall become its property in the event the Mortgagee becomes the owner of the Mortgaged Property by foreclosure or otherwise. To the extent permitted by the Ground Lease, the Mortgagee is hereby authorized and empowered, at its option, to adjust or compromise any loss under any insurance policies on the Mortgaged Property, and to collect and receive the proceeds from any such policy or policies. To the extent permitted by the Ground Lease, each insurance company is hereby authorized and directed to make payment for all such losses directly to the Mortgagee, instead of to the Mortgagor and the Mortgagee jointly.

(b) The Mortgagor shall deliver to the Mortgagee original and fully paid insurance policies with respect to the following:

(i) Fire, lightning and extended coverage insurance (including, without limitation, riot and civil commotion, vandalism, malicious mischief and such other insurable hazards as in good insurance practice are insured against for hotels, hotel-service apartments and office buildings of similar character and location as the Improvements) insuring against loss of or damage to the Improvements. The amount of such insurance shall be not less than the greater of (x) the amount of the indebtedness secured hereby, (y) 90% of the full replacement cost of the Improvements, or (z) an amount sufficient to prevent the Mortgagor and the Mortgagee from becoming co-insurers within the terms of the applicable policies. The term "full replacement cost" means the actual replacement cost of the Improvements (exclusive of the cost of excavations, foundations and footings below the lowest basement floor of the parking garage comprising a part of the Improvements, and without deduction for depreciation). Each insurance policy required to be maintained pursuant to this subparagraph (i) shall contain a replacement cost endorsement, and may provide for a $250,000 deductible provision in respect of structures and a $50,000 deductible provision in respect of furnishings. Notwithstanding the foregoing, if the insurance company agrees to delete the co-insurance clause and include the "agreed value endorsement" in the policy, the amount of insurance shall be the greater of (i) 90% of the full replacement cost as determined by the insurance company and agreed to by Mortgagee or (ii) 111% of the then amount of the indebtedness secured hereby, but in no event shall the amount of insurance cause the Mortgagor to become a co-insurer within the terms of the applicable policies.

(ii) War risk insurance, when and to the extent obtainable from the United States of America or an agency thereof, in an amount not less than the amount of the insurance required to be maintained under subparagraph (b)(i) above, except that if said amount is not obtainable, then such war risk insurance shall be procured in the maximum amount obtainable.

(iii) Boiler and machinery insurance in an amount not less than $5,000,000 or such greater amount as the Mortgagee may require covering physical damage to the Improvements from explosion of boilers, pressure vessels, pressure piping and all major components of any centralized heating or air-conditioning or cooling system and such additional equipment as the Mortgagee may at any time require.

(iv) Business interruption insurance against loss of income by reason of any hazard covered under the insurance required under subparagraphs (i), (ii) and (iii) of this paragraph 6(b), in an amount sufficient to avoid any co-insurance penalty, but in any event in an amount not less than 85% of the annual gross receipts of the Mortgaged Property. All proceeds of such insurance in the event of loss recovery thereunder shall be paid to the Mortgagee and if this Mortgage is not in default shall be held and applied by the Mortgagee to the extent of such loss recovery to the payment of interest and amortization under the Notes, Impositions (as defined in paragraph 7 hereof) and all obligations under this Mortgage until satisfactory completion of restoration of the Improvements has been effected, at which time, provided the Mortgagor is not in default hereunder, the balance of the loss recovery, if any, shall be paid over to the Mortgagor.

(v) Comprehensive general liability insurance (including protective liability coverage on operations of independent contractors engaged in construction, blanket contractual liability insurance, garage liability, innkeeper's liability, products liability and elevator liability) on an "occurrence" basis against claims for "personal injury" liability, including, without limitation, bodily injury, death or property damage liability occurring on, in or about the Premises and the Improvements and on, in or about the adjoining sidewalks, streets, areas and passageways, such insurance to afford minimum protection of not less than $_____ in the event of personal injury to any number of persons or of damage to property arising out of one occurrence.

(vi) Insurance on Furniture and Fixtures against loss or damage by fire and other hazards presently included in so-called "extended coverage" and against vandalism and malicious mischief in the amount of at least $_____ but in any event in such amount as would preclude the Mortgagor from being a co-insurer.

(vii) To the extent not covered by the other subsections of this paragraph 6(b), such insurance as may be required to be obtained and maintained under either (i) the Declaration by _____ and _____ dated _____ and recorded in _____ as modified by agreement dated _____ and recorded in the _____ and by agreement dated _____ and recorded in _____ in _____ (the "Declaration"); or (ii) Special Permit _____ of the Planning Commission of _____.

(viii) Such other insurance with respect to the Improvements or any replacements or substitutions therefor in such amounts as may from time to time be required by the Mortgagee which at the time under good insurance practice are commonly insured against in the case of premises, similarly situated, due regard being given to the height and type of the Improvements, their construction, location, use and occupancy, or any replacements or substitutions therefor.

(c) In the event that all or any portion of the Improvements are damaged or destroyed, the Mortgagor shall give the Mortgagee prompt notice thereof and shall restore or rebuild the same promptly and with all reasonable speed so that the Improvements when restored or rebuilt shall be at least equal in material, quality and value to the Improvements immediately prior to such damage or destruction. In the event such damage or destruction shall be equal to less than 1% of the then Insurable Value (as defined in the Ground Lease) of the Improvements, the proceeds of insurance policies shall be paid to the Mortgagor to be applied to the payment of the cost of restoration, repairs, replacement, rebuilding or alterations, and any balance may be retained by the Mortgagor. The Mortgagor shall, in the event of such damage or destruction equal to 1% or more of the then Insurable Value, promptly furnish to the Mortgagee detailed plans and specifications for the restoration and rebuilding of the damaged or destroyed portion of the Improvements and shall not proceed with such restoration and rebuilding without in all cases having secured the Mortgagee's prior approval. In the event of damage or destruction equal to 1% or more but less than 5% of the then Insurable Value of the Improvements, the proceeds of insurance policies, less the actual cost, fees and expenses, if any, incurred in connection with adjustment of the loss, shall be paid to and applied by the Mortgagee to the payment of the cost of restoration, repairs, replacement, rebuilding or alterations, and shall be paid out from time to time as such restoration progresses upon the Mortgagor's request which shall be accompanied by (i) a certificate signed by the architect in charge of the restoration (who shall be selected by the Mortgagor and approved by the Mortgagee) dated not more than 30 days prior to such request, setting forth the following: (w) that the full deductible amount contained in the insurance policies under which proceeds have been disbursed has been theretofore applied by the Mortgagor to the cost of restoration or rebuilding of the damaged or destroyed portion of the Improvements; (x) that the sum then requested either has been paid by the Mortgagor or is justly due to contractors, sub-contractors, materialmen, engineers, architects or other persons who have rendered services or furnished materials for the restoration therein specified, and giving the names and addresses of such persons and a brief description of such services and materials and the several amounts so paid or due to each of said persons in respect thereof, and stating that no part of such expenditures has been or is being made the basis, in any previous or then pending request, for the withdrawal of insurance proceeds, or has been made out of the proceeds of insurance, and that the sum then requested does not exceed the value of the services and materials described in the certificate; (y) that except for the amount, if any, stated (pursuant to the foregoing clause (i)(x)) in such certificate to be due for services or materials, there is no outstanding indebtedness known to the persons signing such certificate, after due inquiry, which is then due for labor, wages, materials, supplies or services in connection with such restoration which, if unpaid, might become the basis of a vendor's, mechanic's, laborer's or materialman's statutory or similar lien upon such restoration or upon the Mortgaged Property or any part thereof or upon the Mortgagor's interest therein; and (z) that the cost, as estimated by the persons signing such certificate, of the restoration required to be done subsequent to the date of such certificate in order to complete the same, does not exceed the insurance proceeds remaining in the hands of the Mortgagee; and (ii) an opinion of counsel or other evidence reasonably satisfactory to the Mortgagee to the effect that there has not been filed with respect to the Mortgaged Property or any part thereof or upon the Mortgagor's interest therein any vendor's, mechanic's, laborer's, materialman's or other lien which has not been discharged of record, except such as will be discharged by payment of the amount then requested. Upon compliance with the foregoing provisions, the Mortgagee shall, out of such insurance money, pay or cause to be paid to the Mortgagor or the persons named (pursuant to the foregoing clause (i)(x)) in such certificate the respective amounts stated therein to have been paid by the Mortgagor or to be due to them, as the case may be. Any such proceeds held by the Mortgagee shall be so held without payment or allowance of interest. In the event the insurance proceeds held by the Mortgagee are not sufficient to pay the cost of such restoration, the Mortgagor shall pay on demand to the Mortgagee the amount of any such deficiency to be used in payment of the cost of restoration. Upon compliance with the foregoing provisions, the Mortgagee shall remit to the Mortgagor any insurance proceeds in excess of the amount actually used for restoration or replacement. In the event of damage or destruction equal to more than 5% of the then Insurable Value of the Improvements, the net insurance proceeds shall be paid to and applied by the Depositary (as defined in the Ground Lease) in the manner set forth in the Ground Lease to the restoration, repair or replacement of the Improvements (with any insurance proceeds in excess of the amount actually used for restoration or replacement to be remitted to the Mortgagor), provided that all plans and specifications (together with any supplements or amendments thereto) for such restoration, repair or replacement of the Improvements shall be subject to the prior approval of the Mortgagee as to form and substance.

7. (a) To the extent not otherwise provided in subparagraph (b) of this paragraph 7, the Mortgagor shall pay, before any fine, penalty, interest or cost attaches thereto, all taxes, assessments, water and sewer rates, and all other governmental charges or levies now or hereafter assessed or levied against any part of the Mortgaged Property or upon the lien or estate of this Mortgage therein (collectively, "Impositions"), as well as all claims for labor, materials or supplies which, if unpaid, might by law become a prior lien thereon, and within 10 days after request by the Mortgagee will exhibit receipts showing payment of any of the foregoing; provided, however, that if by law any such impositions may be paid in installments (whether or not interest shall accrue on the unpaid balance thereof), the Mortgagor may pay the same in installments (together with accrued interest on the unpaid balance thereof) as the same respectively become due, before any fine, penalty, interest or cost attaches thereto; and provided, further, that if the Mortgagor contests the validity or amount of any such Imposition or claim in good faith and by appropriate proceedings and provides to the Mortgagee security in such amount and in such form as the Mortgagee may require to assure the discharge thereof, the Mortgagor may defer payment thereof during the pendency of such contest.

(b) After the Advance Date (as defined in the Notes) and until the indebtedness secured hereby shall be paid in full, the Mortgagor shall deposit with the Mortgagee in an escrow account on the first day of each month (i) such amount as in the discretion of the Mortgagee will enable the Mortgagee to pay at least 30 days before the same would become delinquent all taxes and assessments and (ii) if requested by the Mortgagee, such amounts as will enable the Mortgagee to pay at least 30 days before the same would become delinquent all water charges and sewer rents and at least 30 days before the same are due all premiums on fire and extended coverage insurance policies. Such amounts shall be held in escrow by the Mortgagee, without interest, solely for the account of the Mortgagor and shall in no event be applied to the payment of the principal of or interest on the Notes or other sums secured thereby, but shall be applied to the payment of Impositions and insurance premiums on or before the respective dates on which the same would become delinquent or due. If one month prior to the delinquency date of any Imposition or the due date of any insurance premium, the amount then on deposit shall be insufficient for the payment thereof in full, the Mortgagor shall, within 10 days after demand, deposit the amount of the deficiency with the Mortgagee. Nothing herein contained shall be deemed to affect any right or remedy of the Mortgagee under any provision of this Mortgage or of any statute or rule of law to pay any such Imposition or insurance premium, to the extent the foregoing escrow account is insufficient for the purpose, and to add the amount so paid, together with interest at the maximum rate permitted by law, to the indebtedness secured hereby.

8. (a) Any parties or entities operating all or a part of the Improvements (excluding, however, tenants of portions but not the whole of the commercial space located within the Improvements, but including, specifically, the hotel which forms a part of the Improvements) shall operate and manage the same under a management agreement satisfactory in form and substance to the Mortgagee. All such agreements and any and all payments due said parties or entities under the management agreement shall be subordinate to all payments due under the Notes and this Mortgage and the Mortgagee shall have the right to require repayment to it of any payments made in violation of this provision. All laws, regulations and ordinances regarding the payment of persons engaged in the operation of the Improvements shall be complied with. None of the facilities usually provided by a first-class hotel shall be leased for operation by others without consent of Mortgagee, with the exception of the parking, newsstand and checking facilities.

(b) The Mortgagor shall not permit the Improvements to be removed, demolished or materially altered; shall maintain the Mortgaged Property in good repair, working order and condition, except for reasonable wear and use; and shall restore, replace or rebuild the Improvements or any part thereof now or hereafter damaged or destroyed by any casualty or other cause (whether or not insured against or insurable) or affected by any taking by way of the exercise of the power of eminent domain.

(c) The Mortgagor shall at all times maintain, or cause to be kept and maintained, the Improvements, the Furnishings and Fixtures and all other improvements and property now or at any time hereafter erected or situated upon, or constituting any portion of, the Mortgaged Premises, and the sidewalks, vaults and curbs abutting the same, in good order and condition, and in a usable, rentable and tenantable condition and state of repair, and in a manner which is wholly in keeping with a first class hotel of the finest character, and will make or cause to be made, as and when the same shall for any reason become necessary, all structural and non-structural, exterior and interior, ordinary and extraordinary, foreseen and unforeseen, repairs, renewals and replacements necessary to that end.

(d) The Mortgagor shall furnish services to the guests and other lawful occupants and users of the Mortgaged Premises, (including the various public rooms and other hotel facilities), which, as to the nature, character, quality and quantity thereof, shall be of a standard wholly appropriate for a first class hotel. To the extent not prohibited by or inconsistent with the terms of the Ground Lease, the Mortgagor shall have the right, at any time and from time to time, to remove and dispose of portions of the Improvements and of the Furnishings and Fixtures which shall have become obsolete or unfit for use, or which shall be no longer useful or necessary in the operation of the Mortgaged Premises; provided that the Mortgagor shall promptly replace with other improvements or furnishings and fixtures, not necessarily of the same character but of a value at least equal to that of those disposed of, and free of superior title, liens and claims, any such Improvements or Furnishings and Fixtures so removed or disposed of; and provided, further, that if and to the extent that technological advances shall have rendered the replacement thereof unnecessary in the proper operation and maintenance of the Mortgaged Premises, the replacement of any such Improvement or Furnishings and Fixtures so removed or disposed of shall not be required.

(e) In addition to any other rights of inspection and examination hereunder, the Mortgagee shall have the right, once each year, at reasonable times and on reasonable advance notice to the Mortgagor, to inspect the Mortgaged Property and examine the books and records of the Mortgagor for the purpose of preparing (i) a list of any Improvements removed or disposed of and the replacements thereof, if any, during the previous fiscal year and (ii) a list of all Furnishings and Fixtures acquired by the Mortgagor and installed in the Premises during such year either as replacements of or as additions to any Furnishings and Fixtures, and within 20 days after demand therefor made at any time by the Mortgagee, the Mortgagor will execute and deliver to the Mortgagee, in recordable form and otherwise in form and substance satisfactory to the Mortgagee, a supplemental mortgage, or such other security instrument of similar legal effect as the Mortgagee shall reasonably require, covering such replacements of and additions to the Improvements and the Furnishings and Fixtures and will pay the fees, including reasonable counsel fees, for the preparation and recording of any such supplemental mortgage or other security instrument.

9. The Mortgagor shall comply with all laws, ordinances, orders, rules and regulations of all federal, state, county and municipal governments and of the appropriate departments, commissions, boards and officers thereof, and the orders, rules and regulations of the Board of Fire Underwriters or any other body hereafter constituted exercising similar functions, which at any time are applicable to the Mortgaged Property. The Mortgagor shall at all times cause the Mortgaged Property to be operated in such a manner so that the same shall continue to

qualify for tax abatement under Chapter _____ of the Administrative Code of _____ for the maximum period for which such tax abatement is available.

10. The Mortgagor shall not initiate, join in or consent to any change in any private restrictive covenant, zoning ordinance or other public or private restrictions limiting or defining the uses which may be made of the Premises and the Improvements or any part thereof.

11. The Mortgagor, within 5 days upon request in person or within 10 days upon request by mail, shall furnish the Mortgagee a written statement, duly acknowledged, of the amount due on this Mortgage and whether any offsets or defenses exist against the indebtedness secured hereby.

12. If the Mortgagor shall fail to (a) perform and observe any of the terms, covenants or conditions required to be performed by it under the Ground Lease, including, without limitation, payment of all basic rent and additional rent thereunder, (b) effect the insurance required by paragraph 6, (c) make the payments required by paragraph 7 or (d) perform or observe any of its other covenants or agreements hereunder, the Mortgagee may, after 10 days' notice (except in emergencies) and so long as a Default shall have occurred and not been cured, effect, pay or perform or observe the same. All sums, including reasonable attorneys' fees, so expended by the Mortgagee or expended to sustain the lien of this Mortgage or its priority, or to protect or enforce any of the Mortgagee's rights hereunder, or to recover any indebtedness hereby secured, shall be a lien on the Mortgaged Property, shall be deemed secured by this Mortgage and shall be paid by the Mortgagor within 5 days after demand, with interest at the maximum rate permitted by law. In any action or proceeding to foreclose this Mortgage, or to recover or collect the indebtedness secured hereby, the provisions of law respecting the recovery of costs, disbursements and allowances shall prevail unaffected by this covenant.

13. (a) In the event that the Ground Lease shall be wholly terminated as a result of any condemnation proceeding, the Mortgagee shall be entitled to and shall receive, and the Mortgagor hereby assigns to the Mortgagee, the total of all awards made or allowed with respect to all right, title and interest of the Mortgagor in and to the Mortgaged Premises or the portion or portions thereof taken or affected by such condemnation proceeding (the "Mortgagor's Award"); provided, however, that to the extent that the Mortgagor's Award, when received by the Mortgagee, shall exceed the amount required to satisfy in full the then total indebtedness secured hereby, the Mortgagee shall pay over to the Mortgagor the amount of such excess.

(b) In the event of the condemnation or taking of a portion of the Mortgaged Premises (other than a taking for a temporary use or occupancy), which shall not result in a termination of the Ground Lease, the Mortgagor shall forthwith proceed with the restoration of the remaining portion of the Mortgaged Premises in accordance with the provisions of the Ground Lease and, subject to the provisions of the Ground Lease with respect thereto, the Mortgagee shall receive, and the Mortgagor hereby assigns to the Mortgagee, all award moneys for such condemnation or taking which the lessor is required to apply and make available to the Mortgagor pursuant to the provisions of the Ground Lease, and, until the occurrence of Default hereunder, the Mortgagee shall hold and apply the same in accordance with the applicable provisions of the Ground Lease; provided, however, that any unexpended balance of such moneys remaining after such application shall, at the option of the Mortgagee, be applied toward the payment of unpaid installments of the then outstanding principal sum secured hereby in the inverse order in which such installments shall become due and payable.

(c) The Mortgagor shall not enter into any agreement for the taking of the Mortgaged Premises, or any part thereof, with anyone authorized to acquire the same by condemnation, unless the Mortgagee shall have consented thereto or the agreement (to which the Mortgagee shall be a party) shall provide for the payment in full of the then outstanding indebtedness secured hereby.

14. (a) With respect to any leases of a portion of the space in the Improvements (collectively, "Space Leases"): (a) the Mortgagor shall (i) furnish the Mortgagee a photostatic copy of each Space Lease promptly after its execution and (ii) from time to time furnish to the Mortgagee, within 15 days after demand therefor, a written statement containing the names of the lessees, the expiration dates thereof, the spaces occupied and the rents payable, together with a photostatic copy of each Space Lease not previously furnished to the Mortgagee; and (b) the Mortgagor shall not (i) assign the rents therefrom to anyone other than the Mortgagee unless such assignment shall, by its terms, be expressly subject and subordinate to the assignment of rents, revenues, issues, income and profits herein contained, (ii) except for security deposits, accept a prepayment of rent thereunder beyond one month in advance, or (iii) with respect to non-residential Space Leases (each of which to be subject to the approval of the Mortgagee prior to the execution thereof and the Mortgagee shall use its best efforts to answer promptly all requests by the Mortgagor for approvals) having an original term of more than seven years (or having an original term of less than seven years, but containing renewal options which, if exercised, would extend the total term thereof beyond seven years) and having an annual rental of more than $_____ (collectively, "Major Non-Residential Space Leases"), consent to the cancellation or surrender of the same or modify the same so as to shorten the term, decrease the rent, accelerate the payment of rent or change the term of any renewal option. Within 90 days after the end of each fiscal year of the Mortgagor, the Mortgagor shall furnish to the Mortgagee a certificate of its managing partner or chief executive officer to the effect that the Mortgagor has at all times during the prior fiscal year complied in every respect with the covenants contained in this paragraph 14(a).

(b) Each Space Lease (except (i) residential Space Leases for terms of less than five (5) years and (ii) "net" Space Leases of portions of the Mortgaged Property requiring the tenant thereunder to pay all taxes and operating expenses applicable to its portion) shall contain provisions requiring the tenant to pay additional rent for increases in taxes and operating expenses of the Mortgaged Property and/or in the cost of living, or graduated rents in lieu thereof. The Mortgagor shall have the right to determine which type of clause shall be contained in each such Space Lease. The Mortgagor shall not be deemed in default of this paragraph 14(b) if Space Leases for less than an aggregate of 20% of the rentable area of the Mortgaged Property (exclusive of the area covered by Space Leases described in clauses (i) and (ii) above) do not have such provisions. Proof of compliance with the provisions of this paragraph 14(b) shall be furnished by the Mortgagor to the Mortgagee once each year during the term of this Mortgage.

(c) Each Space Lease shall, by its terms, provide in substance:

(i) that in the event of any act or omission by the Mortgagor which would give the lessee under such Space Lease the right to terminate such Space Lease, such lessee shall not exercise such right unless and until (y) it has given written notice of such act or omission to the Mortgagee and (z) a reasonable period for remedying such act or omission shall have elapsed following the giving of such notice;

(ii) that the lessee under such Space Lease shall, upon the execution and delivery of a new lease in substitution for the Ground Lease, attorn to the tenant under such new lease and recognize such tenant as the lessor under such Space Lease as though such Space Lease had continued to full force and effect;

(iii) that in the event the Mortgagee or any person claiming by, through or under the Mortgagee becomes the tenant under the Ground Lease, the lessee will attorn to and recognize the Mortgagee or any such person as the lessor with respect to such Space Lease; and

(iv) that it is subject and subordinate to this Mortgage.

(d) The Mortgagor shall promptly perform and observe all the terms, covenants and conditions required to be performed and observed by the Mortgagor under each Space Lease and shall do all things necessary to preserve and to keep unimpaired its rights under each Space Lease. The Mortgagor shall promptly notify the Mortgagee of the receipt of any notice from any lessee under any Space Lease claiming that the Mortgagor is in default in the performance or observance of any of the terms, covenants or conditions thereof to be performed or observed by the Mortgagor and shall promptly deliver to the Mortgagee a copy of each such notice.

(e) Promptly after the execution and delivery hereof, the Mortgagor will cause the lessee under each Space Lease to be duly notified in writing, by registered or certified mail, of the subjection of the Mortgagor's interest, as lessor, in and to such Space Lease to the lien of the Mortgage. The Mortgagor shall use its best efforts to obtain from each lessee under each Space Lease to whom such notice is sent an acknowledgment of receipt of such notice, and shall promptly deliver to the Mortgagee the original or a photostatic copy of each such acknowledgment received by the Mortgagor.

(f) Within 90 days after the expiration of the first fiscal year and of each subsequent fiscal year, the Mortgagor shall furnish to the Mortgagee a statement dated not more than 30 days prior to the furnishing thereof and certified as true and correct by a principal executive officer of the Mortgagor:

(i) setting forth the names of all lessees under Space Leases then in force, a description of the space demised to and the annual rent currently payable by each of them;

(ii) stating which, if any, of all Space Leases then in force are in default as to payment of rent and the extent of each such default and which, if any, of the Major Non-Residential Space Leases then in force have been amended since the date of the last such statement (or since the date hereof, in the case of the first such statement) and describing the nature of each such amendment; and

(iii) stating that the Mortgagor has, to the extent required by subsection (e) of this paragraph 14, given to the lessee under each Space Lease the notice required by said subsection (e).

Each such statement shall, to the extent not theretofore furnished to the Mortgagee, be accompanied by copies of each such Space Lease and of each amendment thereto.

(g) From time to time, upon demand of the Mortgagee, the Mortgagor shall execute and deliver to the Mortgagee instruments in form and substance satisfactory to the Mortgagee assigning specific Space Leases to the Mortgagee further to secure the indebtedness secured by this Mortgage.

(h) The Mortgagor shall cause any agreement to pay leasing commissions in respect to Space Leases to provide that the obligation to pay such commissions shall not be enforceable by any party except against the party who entered into such agreement and shall by its terms be subject and subordinate to this Mortgage. Upon request therefor, the Mortgagor shall furnish appropriate evidence of its compliance with the foregoing covenant.

15. If any one of the following events of default (a "Default") shall occur and shall not have been remedied:

a. The Mortgagor shall default in the payment when due of any installment of the principal of or interest on the Notes;

b. The Mortgagor shall default in the prepayment of the Notes when the same is required in accordance with the provisions of Section 5.B thereof;

c. Any representation or warranty made by the Mortgagor in this Mortgage, the Building Loan Agreement or any other mortgages or deeds of trust affecting the Mortgaged Property to which the Mortgagor is a party or if any certificate or notice furnished by the Mortgagor hereunder or thereunder proves incorrect in any material respect, or if the Mortgagor defaults in the performance of any agreements contained in this Mortgage (other than a default in the payment or prepayment when due of any principal of or interest on the Notes), the Building Loan Agreement or any other mortgages or deeds of trust affecting the Mortgaged Property to which the Mortgagor is a party and such default continues unremedied for ten (10) days after notice;

d. The Mortgagor shall engage in any trade or business other than the ownership, operation and management of the Mortgaged Property or shall change the managing agent of the Mortgaged Property without the prior consent of the Mortgagee;

e. Default shall be made in the performance or observance of any of the covenants or agreements contained in (i) the Ground Lease on the part of the lessee thereunder to be performed or observed, or (ii) any sublease covering any part of the Mortgaged Property on the part of the landlord thereunder to be performed or observed;

f. The Mortgagor shall (1) apply for or consent to the appointment of a receiver, trustee or liquidator of itself or of all or a substantial part of its assets, (2) be unable, or admit in writing its inability to pay its debts as they mature, (3) make a general assignment for the benefit of creditors, (4) be adjudicated a bankrupt or insolvent or (5) file a voluntary petition in bankruptcy or a petition or an answer seeking reorganization or an arrangement with creditors to take advantage of any insolvency law or an answer admitting the material allegations of a petition filed against it in any bankruptcy, reorganization or insolvency proceeding, or action shall be taken by it for the purpose of effecting any of the foregoing; or

g. An order, judgment or decree shall be entered, without the application, approval or consent of the Mortgagor, by any court of competent jurisdiction, approving a petition seeking reorganization of the Mortgagor or appointing a receiver, trustee or liquidator of the Mortgagor or of all or a substantial part of its assets, and such order, judgment or decree shall continue unstayed and in effect for any period of ninety (90) consecutive days;

thereupon, the Mortgagee may declare the entire unpaid principal amount of and accrued interest on the Notes and all other sums secured hereby to be immediately due and payable from the Mortgagor whereupon the same shall become immediately due and payable without presentment, demand, notice of dishonor or protest thereof, all of which are hereby expressly waived.

16. If a Default shall occur and shall not have been remedied, the Mortgagee may, to the extent permitted by law:

(a) enter and take possession of the Mortgaged Property or any part thereof, exclude the Mortgagor and all persons claiming under the Mortgagor whose claims are junior to the lien of this Mortgage wholly or partly therefrom, and use, operate, manage and control the same either in the name of the Mortgagor or otherwise as the Mortgagee shall deem best, and upon such entry, from time to time at the expense of the Mortgagor, make all such repairs, replacements, alterations, additions or improvements to the Mortgaged Property or any part thereof as the Mortgagee may deem proper, and, whether or not the Mortgagee has so entered and taken possession of the Mortgaged Property or any part thereof, collect and receive all the rents, revenues, issues, income and profits thereof and apply the same, to the extent permitted by law, to the payment of all expenses which the Mortgagee may be authorized to make under the provisions of this Mortgage, the remainder to be applied to the payment of the principal of and interest on the Notes until the same shall have been repaid in full; and

(b) personally or, to the extent permitted by law, by agents, with or without entry, if the Mortgagee shall deem it advisable:

(i) sell the Mortgaged Property to the highest bidder at public auction at a sale or sales held at such place and time and upon such notice or otherwise in such manner as may be required by law, or in the absence of any such requirement, as the Mortgagee may deem appropriate and from time to time adjourn such sale by announcement at the time and place specified for such sale or for such adjourned sale or sales without further notice, except such as may be required by law; or

(ii) proceed to protect and enforce its rights under this Mortgage by suit for specific performance of any covenant herein contained, or in aid of the execution of any power herein granted, or for the foreclosure of this Mortgage and the sale of the Mortgaged Property under the judgment or decree of a court of competent jurisdiction, or for the enforcement of any other right as the Mortgagee shall deem most effectual for such purpose.

17. In any action to foreclose this Mortgage, the Mortgagee, to the extent permitted by law, shall be entitled as a matter of right to the appointment of a receiver of the Mortgaged Property and of the rents, revenues, issues, income and profits thereof, without notice or demand, and without regard to the adequacy of the security for the indebtedness secured hereby or the solvency of the Mortgagor.

18. The Mortgagor, in the event of any Default, shall pay monthly in advance to the Mortgagee, or to any receiver appointed at the request of the Mortgagee to collect the rents, revenues, issues, income and profits of the Mortgaged Property, the fair and reasonable rental value for the use and occupancy of the Mortgaged Property or of such part thereof as may be in the possession of the Mortgagor. Upon default in the payment thereof, the Mortgagor shall vacate and surrender possession of the Mortgaged Property to the Mortgagee or such receiver, and upon a failure so to do may be evicted by summary proceedings.

19. In any sale under any provision of this Mortgage or pursuant to any judgment or decree of court, the Mortgaged Property, to the extent permitted by law, may be sold in one or more parcels or as an entirety and in such order as the Mortgagee may elect, without regard to the right of the Mortgagor or any person claiming under it, to the marshalling of assets. The purchaser at such sale shall take title to the Mortgaged Property so sold free and discharged of the estate of the Mortgagor therein, the purchaser being hereby discharged from all liability to see to the application of the purchase money. Any person, including the Mortgagee, may purchase at any such sale.

20. The proceeds of any sale made either under the power of sale hereby given or under a judgment, order or decree made in any action to foreclose or to enforce this Mortgage shall be applied:

(a) first to the payment of (i) all costs and expenses of such sale, including reasonable attorneys' fees in the court of original jurisdiction and in any appellate proceedings, and (ii) all charges, expenses and advances incurred or made by the Mortgagee in order to protect the lien of this Mortgage or the security afforded thereby;

(b) then to the payment of the principal and accrued interest on the Notes;

any surplus remaining to be paid to the Mortgagor or to whosoever may be lawfully entitled to receive the same.

21. The Mortgagee shall have the right from time to time to sue for any sums required to be paid by the Mortgagor under the terms of this Mortgage as the same become due, without regard to whether or not the principal sum secured hereby or any other sums secured by this Mortgage shall be, or have become, due and without prejudice to the right of the Mortgagee thereafter to bring any action or proceeding of foreclosure or any other action upon the occurrence of any Default existing at the time such earlier action was commenced.

22. The Mortgagor hereby waives, to the full extent permitted by law, (i) any and all rights and equities of redemption from sale under the power of sale created under this Mortgage or from sale under any order or decree of foreclosure of this Mortgage and all notice or notices of seizure and (ii) the benefit of any appraisement, marshalling, valuation, stay or extension law now or hereafter in force.

23. No failure to exercise, nor any delay in exercising any power or right hereunder by the Mortgagee shall operate as a waiver thereof, nor shall any single or partial exercise by the Mortgagee of any right hereunder preclude any other or further exercise thereof or the exercise of any other right. The remedies provided herein are cumulative and not exclusive of any remedies provided by law.

24. The Mortgagee may at any time or from time to time renew or extend this Mortgage, or alter or modify the same in any way, or waive any of the terms, covenants or conditions hereof in whole or in part and may release any portion of the Mortgaged Property or any other security, and grant such extensions and indulgences in relation to the indebtedness secured hereby as the Mortgagee may determine without the consent of any junior lienor or encumbrancer and without any obligation to give notice of any kind thereto and without in any manner affecting the priority or the lien hereof on any part of the Mortgaged Property.

25. All notices, demands, consents, requests, approvals or other communications (collectively, "notices") which are permitted or required to be given by either party to the other hereunder shall be in writing. All notices shall be deemed to be properly given if delivered or mailed registered or certified mail, return receipt requested, addressed to the parties hereto at their respective addresses set forth above, c/o in the case of the Mortgagee, _____ and c/o in the case of the Mortgagor, _____. Either party may by notice to the other designate a new address to which all notices shall thereafter be delivered or mailed.

26. This Mortgage cannot be modified, changed or discharged except by an agreement in writing, duly acknowledged in form for recording, signed by the party against whom enforcement of such modification, change or discharge is sought.

27. This Mortgage shall be construed and enforced in accordance with the laws of the State of _____.

28. The Mortgagor shall, in compliance with Section 13 of the Lien Law, receive the advances secured hereby and shall hold the right to receive such advances as a trust fund to be applied first for the purpose of paying the cost of the improvement to the Premises and the Improvements and shall apply the same first to the payment of the cost of such improvement before using any part of the total of the same for any other purpose.

29. In the event of the passage after the date of this Mortgage of any law of the State of _____ deducting from the value of land for the purposes of taxation any lien thereon, or changing in any way the laws for the taxation of mortgages or debts secured by mortgages for state or local purposes, or the manner of the collection of any such taxes, so as to affect this Mortgage, the holder of this Mortgage and of the indebtedness secured hereby shall have the right to give 90 days' notice to the then owner of the Mortgaged Premises requiring the payment of said indebtedness. If such notice be given, the said indebtedness shall become due, payable and collectible at the expiration of said 90 days.

30. Notwithstanding anything to the contrary in this Mortgage, the Notes, the Building Loan Agreement or in any other instrument given as security for the

indebtedness secured hereby, in the event of the maturity of said indebtedness, or any part thereof, by acceleration or passage of time, or in the event of a default under this Mortgage, the Building Loan Agreement or under any other instrument given as security for said indebtedness, or a breach of any warranties or covenants contained in this Mortgage, the Building Loan Agreement or in any other instrument given as security for said indebtedness: (i) the Mortgagee shall not seek any judgment for a deficiency or money judgment against the Mortgagor (or any partner or principal thereof, disclosed or undisclosed), its successors or assigns, in connection with any action to foreclose this Mortgage, any action brought on the Notes or any action brought under this Mortgage, the Building Loan Agreement or any other instrument given as security for said indebtedness; and (ii) the Mortgagee shall not seek any judgment on the Notes except as a part of judicial proceedings to foreclose this Mortgage, and in the event any suit is brought on the Notes, or concerning said indebtedness as a part of judicial proceedings to foreclose this Mortgage, any judgment obtained in such suit will by its terms constitute a lien on, and will be enforced only against the Mortgaged Property or any other property conveyed by any other instrument given as security for said indebtedness (together with the income therefrom, any funds held by the Mortgagee pursuant to this Mortgage, the Notes or the Building Loan Agreement, insurance and condemnation proceeds, and escrow and security deposits) and not against any other assets or property of the Mortgagor (or any partner or principal thereof, disclosed or undisclosed), its successors or assigns. Nothing contained in this paragraph shall be deemed to constitute a release or impairment of the indebtedness secured hereby, or the lien of this Mortgage on the Mortgaged Property, or shall preclude the Mortgagee from foreclosing this Mortgage in case of any Default, from enforcing any of the other rights of the Mortgagee hereunder, except as expressly prohibited by this paragraph, or from enforcing any of the rights of the Mortgagee against any other person or entity at any time liable (under any guaranty, bond, policy of insurance or otherwise) for the payment of the indebtedness secured hereby or for the performance of any of the terms, covenants and conditions contained herein, in the Notes, in the Building Loan Agreement or in any other instrument given as security for the payment of said indebtedness.

31. The term "Accounts Receivable" shall mean any right of the Mortgagor arising from the operation of the Improvements to payment for goods sold or leased or for services rendered, whether or not yet earned by performance, not evidenced by an instrument of chattel paper, including, without limiting the generality of the foregoing, (i) all accounts arising from the operation of the hotel comprising a part of the Improvements and (ii) all rights to payment from any consumer credit/charge card organization or entity (such as or similar to the organization or entities which sponsor and administer the American Express Card, the Bankamericard or Visa, the Carte Blanche Card and the Master Charge Card). Accounts Receivable shall include those now existing or hereafter created, substitutions therefor, proceeds thereof (whether cash or non-cash, movable or immovable, tangible or intangible) received upon the sale, exchange, transfer, collection or other disposition or substitution thereof and any and all of the foregoing and proceeds therefrom.

The Accounts Receivable are assigned to the Mortgagee as collateral security for the indebtedness secured hereby effective upon Mortgagor's default, but such Accounts Receivable shall be re-assigned by the Mortgagee to the Mortgagor upon payment by the Mortgagor of all accounts payable relating to goods and services supplied to the Mortgaged Property and employees' compensation including all accrued pension, welfare and other benefits when the same become due or upon payment by the Mortgagor to the Mortgagee of the aggregate amount of all such obligations.

32. With respect to the Mortgaged Property and the Mortgagor's operations thereon (i) the Mortgagor shall keep proper books of record and account in accordance with sound accounting practice, which shall reflect and disclose in

reasonable detail the Net Operating Income (as defined in the Notes) and the Gross Annual Room Income (as defined in the Notes), (ii) the Mortgagee shall have the right to examine and audit the books of account and the records of the Mortgagor and the statements furnished by the Mortgagor pursuant to this paragraph (which books, records and statements, and the data used as a basis for their preparation, shall be kept and preserved for at least five years) and to discuss the affairs, finances and accounts of the Mortgagor and to be informed as to the same by the Mortgagor's managing partner or chief executive officer, all at such reasonable times and intervals as the Mortgagee may desire, and the Mortgagor shall furnish to the Mortgagee convenient facilities for the examination and audit of such books, records, statements and data, (iii) the Mortgagor shall furnish to the Mortgagor within 90 days after the end of each Fiscal Year (as defined in the Notes) a balance sheet and copies of the statement of income and expense of the Mortgagor for such Fiscal Year resulting from the operation of the Mortgaged Property, in reasonable detail and stating in comparative form the figures as of the end of and for the previous Fiscal Year, with each such statement showing separately and in reasonable detail the Net Operating Income on an accrual basis and with a reconciliation of the Gross Annual Room Income to the income shown on said statement and to be certified by independent certified public accountants of recognized standing satisfactory to Mortgagee, such statement to be prepared in accordance with the Uniform System of Accounts for Hotels and accompanied by all supporting schedules covering the operation of the Mortgaged Property; and, with such financial statements for each Fiscal Year, the Mortgagor shall furnish to the Mortgagee a written statement of such accountants that in making the examination necessary for their certification of such financial statements they have obtained no knowledge of any default by the Mortgagor hereunder or under the Notes or, if such accountants shall have obtained knowledge of any such default, they shall disclose in such statement such default or defaults and the nature thereof.

33. (a) The Mortgagor shall have no right to prepay the Notes at any time during the period from the date hereof to and including the date of assignment of this Mortgage (the "Advance Date") to _____.

(b) the Mortgagor shall have the right to prepay the entire principal amount of the Notes (but not a part thereof) together with all Basic Interest (as defined therein) and Contingent Interest (as defined therein) accrued thereon to the date of such prepayment, on the first day of any month commencing with the first day of the first month of the thirteenth Loan Year (as defined in the Notes), but not prior to said day, upon payment of a prepayment premium equal to three percent (3%) of the principal amount of the Notes so prepaid if such prepayment occurs in the thirteenth Loan Year, declining one percent (1%) in each succeeding Loan Year thereafter with no premium payable at maturity; *provided, however,* the Mortgagor having given such notice of intention to prepay, the principal amount of the Notes shall, at the option of the Mortgagee, become due and payable on the date specified together with the premium as aforesaid.

(c) In the event that:

(i) The Mortgagor shall divest itself, voluntarily or involuntarily; of all or any part of the Mortgaged Property or of any interest therein except for a transfer to a Controlled Entity (as defined in this paragraph 33);

(ii) If the Mortgagor is a joint venture or a partnership, the sole managing joint venturer or sole managing partner, as the case may be, shall cease to be _____ (or, in the event of his death or judicial incompetence, his wife, one of his executors, one of his testamentary trustees or one of his legal representatives or successors by will or operation of law) or a Controlled Entity;

(iii) If the Mortgagor is a partnership, there shall at any time be more than ten general partners and twenty limited partners (the identity of each of whom shall be disclosed to the Mortgagee upon admission as a partner), or any limited partner shall at any time fail to be the holder of an investment in the Mortgagor of at least $1,000,000;

(iv) If the Mortgagor is a corporation, the sole director (or if there is more than one director, the chairman of the board) shall cease to be _____ (or, in the event of his death or judicial incompetence, his wife, one of his executors, one of his testamentary trustees or one of his legal representatives or successors by will or by operation of law);

(v) _____ (or, in the event of his death or judicial incompetence, his wife, his estate, his testamentary trustees, his legal representatives or successors by will or operation of law) or a Controlled Entity, or any combination thereof, shall fail to maintain an investment in the Mortgagor in an aggregate amount (inclusive of subordinate loans permitted to be made by _____ or a Controlled Entity under subparagraph (i) of paragraph 4 of this Mortgage) equal to at least (i) $5,000,000 if $25,000,000 or less is invested in the Mortgagor, and (ii) 25% of any investment in excess of $25,000,000 until the date the Mortgagor shall have had Net Operating Income (except that for purposes of this paragraph 33(c)(v), Net Operating Income shall be computed without deduction for the payments of principal and interest on the second subordinate mortgage permitted under subparagraph (ii) of this Mortgage) of at least $4,000,000 for two consecutive Fiscal Years (the "Required Investment") (it being expressly understood that from and after said date the provisions of this paragraph 33(c)(v), as they apply herein and in the definition of Controlled Entity below, shall be of no further force or effect); or

(vi) _____ or a Controlled Entity shall cease to manage the Mortgaged Property;

thereupon, upon demand of the Mortgagee, the Mortgagor shall prepay the Notes (without prepayment premium and in the inverse order of maturity) in an amount equal to 35% of the then remaining principal balance thereof.

(d) In the event that _____ shall die or become judicially incompetent and the Net Operating Income of the Mortgaged Property for the Fiscal Year ending immediately prior to the Fiscal Year in which such death or judicial incompetence occurred shall have been less than $1,000,000, or shall at any time thereafter be less than $1,000,000 for a Fiscal Year, the Mortgagee may at its option serve notice upon the Mortgagor to replace the current managing agent of the Mortgaged Property, which notice shall contain the names of three (3) management firms satisfactory to the Mortgagee. Within thirty days after the service of said notice, the Mortgagor shall either:

(i) replace the then managing agent of the Mortgaged Property with one of the management firms named in the Mortgagee's notice;

(ii) prepay (without prepayment premium and in the inverse order of maturity) the Notes in an amount equal to 35% of the then remaining principal balance thereof;

(iii) prepay (without prepayment premium) the entire remaining unpaid principal balance of the Notes together with all Basic Interest and Contingent Interest accrued thereon to the date of such prepayment; or

(iv) if _____ death or judicial incompetence shall have occurred at any time during the period commencing on the Advance Date and ending on the last day of the third Loan Year, furnish to the Mortgagee an unconditional irrevocable letter of credit on the account of the Mortgagor, a Controlled Entity, _____ wife, his estate, his testamentary trustees, his legal representatives or successors by will or by operation of law, in form or substance satisfactory to the Mortgagee and drawn on a bank approved by the Mortgagee, as security for and in an amount equal to the aggregate amount of the installments of the principal of the Notes and Basic Interest due and payable in respect of the period commencing on the date of such death or judicial incompetence and ending on the last day of the third Loan Year.

(e) At any time upon the request of the Mortgagee, the Mortgagor shall promptly submit to the Mortgagee evidence satisfactory to it in respect of the Mortgagor's compliance with the requirements of this paragraph 33, including, without limitation, true copies of the Mortgagor's partnership agreements and amendments thereof.

For purposes of this Mortgage, the term "Controlled Entity" means any one of the following:

>   (i) a corporation (a "Parent Corporation") in which _____ (or, in the event of his death or judicial incompetence, his wife, his estate, his testamentary trustees, his legal representatives or successors by will or operation of law (or any combination thereof) owns both an investment at least equal to the Required Investment and at least 90% of the voting stock;
>
>   (ii) a corporation (a "Subsidiary Corporation") in which a Parent Corporation owns both an investment at least equal to the Required Investment and at least 90% of the voting stock;
>
>   (iii) a corporation (an "Affiliated Corporation") in which a Parent Corporation or a Subsidiary Corporation owns both an investment at least equal to the Required Investment and 100% of the voting stock; or
>
>   (iv) a joint venture, general partnership or a limited partnership in which _____ (or, in the event of his death or judicial incompetence, his wife, his estate, his testamentary trustees, his legal representatives or successors by will or operation of law (or any combination thereof)), a Parent Corporation, a Subsidiary Corporation or an Affiliated Corporation, or any combination thereof, owns both an investment at least equal to the Required Investment and at least 51% of the voting rights (in the case of a general partnership) or at least 51% of the general partnership interests (in the case of a limited partnership).

34. The covenants contained in this Mortgage shall run with the land and shall bind the Mortgagor, its successors and assigns, and all subsequent encumbrancers, tenants and subtenants of the Mortgaged Property and shall inure to the benefit of the Mortgagee, its successors and assigns.

IN WITNESS WHEREOF, this Mortgage has been duly executed by the Mortgagor the day and year first above written.

THE _____ COMPANY

By _____
A General Partner

By /s/ _____
President

[*Seal*]

§ 15.15 Lease Language Crucial to the Mortgageability of a Leasehold Interest [1]

As we emphasized in the preceding section, lending on the security of a leasehold entails greater risks than a comparable loan on a fee interest. These risks, of course, can be obviated if the landlord is willing to join in the mortgage or otherwise subordinate his fee interest to the mortgage. Absent such a willingness, however, the leasehold mortgagee is confronted not only with the usual risks associated with lending on a fee, but also by a variety of concerns unique to the leasehold mortgage context. We have chosen here not to duplicate an entire ground lease, but rather only those provisions that address the foregoing concerns and are crucial to the lender's security.

It is crucial that the tenant-mortgagor have the right to assign the leasehold without the landlord's consent. This ensures that a foreclosure purchaser, whether the mortgagee or a third party, will be able to acquire the mortgagor's interest and also enables a mortgagee to take a deed in lieu of foreclosure. Section 18.01 affords the tenant the right to assign freely after the construction of the new building contemplated by the parties has been completed. Any assignee is required to assume the lease and thus will become personally liable under it. Because any assignee comes into privity of estate with the landlord, it will, in any event, become personally liable with respect to those lease covenants that touch and concern the leased premises. Moreover, while an express assumption would normally continue assignee liability after a reassignment, this will not be the case here because, under Section 18.01, an assignee will be released from personal liability upon reassignment.

As one commentator has stressed, "the leasehold mortgagee is in effect a third party to the principal lease, a tenant once removed." Committee on Leases, Ground Leases and Their Financing, 4 Real Prop.Prob. & Trust J. 437, 445 (1969). Thus, the mortgagee especially needs protection against lease modification or voluntary surrender of the leasehold by the tenant. In this connection, Section 18.02 prohibits lease modifications without mortgagee consent. In the same subsection, landlord agrees not to accept a voluntary surrender by tenant.

Another essential concern of the mortgagee is that a default by the tenant-mortgagor will result in the termination of the leasehold and, with it, the destruction of the mortgagee's security. Thus, the lease must provide that the mortgagee will receive notice of any lease default and, if the tenant fails to cure it, the mortgagee will be afforded an ample period in which to do so. Section 19.02(b) not only requires that the mortgagee be provided with written notice of any tenant default, it also specifies that "the mortgagee shall have and be subrogated to any and all rights of the tenant with respect to the curing of any default

---

§ 15.15

1. Form language provided by the Metropolitan Life Insurance Company.

hereunder by the tenant . . ." Moreover, even if the landlord becomes entitled to serve a notice of termination, it must also be served on the leasehold mortgagee and the latter will have an additional ten days to cure the default. See Section 18.02(c)(1).

Even if the lease actually terminates, Section 18.02(c)(2) requires the landlord to enter into a new lease with the leasehold mortgagee on the same terms and conditions as the original lease. The mortgagee must, however, make the request for a new lease within 40 days after the termination notice and cure any of the tenant's past rental obligations and "perform * * * all other [lease] covenants and conditions * * * to the extent that tenant shall have failed to perform and observe the same." Similar rights are also afforded to a sub-lessee of the entire premises and its mortgagee, if any. See Section 18.02(e). Moreover, additional rights are afforded the senior Institutional Mortgagee (there apparently was more than one mortgagee in the transaction for which this language was used). Under Section 18.02(c)(3), the Institutional Mortgagee is entitled at any time within the foregoing 40 day period to postpone the lease termination date for such period of time as may be necessary for the Institutional Mortgagee using "reasonable diligence" to foreclose its Leasehold Mortgage or otherwise to acquire the Tenant's interest in the lease and to cure any default [under the default and remedy section of the lease]." In the event more than one leasehold mortgagee asserts its right to a new lease, "priority shall be given * * * to any Leasehold Mortgagee making such request in the order of the priority of the lien of such Mortgage, then to the sublessee making such request and then to any subleasehold mortgagee making such a request in the order of priority of the lien of such mortgagee." Section 18.02(f).

A leasehold mortgage can also be jeopardized by certain non-default related inaction by the tenant. Suppose, for example, the tenant simply fails to exercise its option to renew the lease. Section 18.02(g) gives the mortgagee the right to receive notice from the landlord in the event the tenant fails to exercise its renewal option and, for 30 days thereafter, to exercise the option itself.

The provisions governing the landlord's control over subletting by the tenant-mortgagor are complicated and reflect a variety of considerations and dynamics unique to the transaction for which they were designed. See Section 18.04 and especially the first paragraph thereof. They envisage both a subletting of the whole of the demised premises and leases from either the tenant or a sub-tenant to space lessees. Whether landlord consent for subletting is required, as well as the criteria to be applied in considering a consent decision, depend on a variety of factors, including whether the sublease is of all or a part of the demised premises and whether the new construction contemplated by the parties has been completed.

Normally, if the leasehold is terminated, either because of tenant default under the ground lease or foreclosure of the leasehold mortgage (assuming the mortgage is senior to the sublease), it will also terminate the sub-tenant's interest. It is possible by utilizing language in the sublease to make it survive such a ground lease termination. Clauses in both the mortgage (see Section 14(c) of the mortgage in § 15.12 supra) and the ground lease will often specify attornment language to be included in sub-leases. The attornment provisions required by Section 18.04 are highly detailed, reflecting the complexity of the underlying transaction.

ASSIGNMENT, SUBLETTING AND MORTGAGING

18.01. Prior to completion of the new building described in Section 9.01, Tenant shall not assign this lease without the prior consent of Landlord, except for assignments to a permitted assignee. The permitted assignees are: _____ (or upon his death or judicial declaration of incapacity, his legal representatives or his successors by will or operation of law), any corporation in which _____ (or his legal representatives or successors as aforesaid) owns, directly or indirectly, without restriction, at least 51% of the voting shares, or any partnership in which _____ (or his legal representatives or successors as aforesaid or any such corporation) is a general partner and holds at least 51% of the management rights. After completion of that new building, without prior consent of Landlord, this lease may be assigned on one or more occasions to any person, firm or corporation. In any circumstances, no assignment shall be valid unless there shall be delivered to Landlord in due form for recording, within ten days after the date of the assignment (a) a duplicate original of the instrument of assignment, and (b) an instrument of assumption by the transferee of all of the Tenant's obligations under this lease, including without limitation any unperformed obligations which have accrued at the date of the assumption. The compliance by Tenant with the provisions of the preceding sentence as to any invalid assignment made before the completion of the new building under Article 9 shall not operate to validate such premature assignment. Upon any assignment of this lease conforming to the terms hereof, but not otherwise, the assignor shall be released from the performance of all obligations on the part of Tenant to be performed under this lease except any obligation to hold and apply moneys held by the assignor at the date of the assignment, the disposition whereof is governed by the terms of this lease. Without limiting any of the foregoing but in addition thereto, any assignment in contravention of the terms hereof is void, but this shall not impair any remedy of Landlord because of Tenant having engaged in an act prohibited by the terms hereof.

18.02. (a) Tenant shall have the right, without the consent of Landlord, to make a mortgage or mortgages on this lease and the leasehold estate hereby created to any persons, firms or corporations. Any such mortgage may be increased by additional mortgages and agreements consolidating the liens. Subject to Section 18.05, as to any such permitted Leasehold Mortgage, Landlord consents to a provision therein for an assignment of rents to the holder thereof, effective upon any default, and to a provision therein that the holder thereof in any action to foreclose the same shall be entitled to the appointment of a receiver. No Leasehold Mortgage shall be binding upon Landlord in the enforcement of Landlord's rights and remedies under this lease or under any law, unless and until either an executed counterpart or a certified or photostatic copy of the original thereof and of the original note or bond which such Leasehold Mortgage was given to secure shall have been delivered to Landlord, notwithstanding any other form of notice, actual or constructive. For the benefit of any such Leasehold Mortgagee who shall have become entitled to notice as hereinafter provided in this Article, Landlord agrees, subject, nevertheless, to all the terms, covenants, agreements, provisions, conditions and limitations contained in this lease, not to accept a voluntary surrender of this lease at any time during which such Mortgage shall remain a lien. It is further understood and agreed that such Leasehold Mortgagee will not be bound by any modification of this lease unless such modification is made with the prior written consent of such Leasehold Mortgagee and no sale of the demised premises or any portion thereof to Tenant shall terminate this lease by merger or otherwise so long as any Leasehold Mortgage exists with respect to the portion of the demised premises so sold.

(b) Any notice or demand which, under the terms of this lease, or under any statute, must or may be given or made by Landlord to Tenant, if so requested by a Leasehold Mortgagee who shall have duly registered with the Landlord its name and address, shall also be delivered to that Leasehold Mortgagee at its registered address (or if two Institutional Lenders shall hold interests in the First Leasehold Mortgage, both Institutional Lenders at their registered addresses). In the event of any such registration, no default predicated on the giving of any notice shall be deemed complete unless like notice of such default shall have been given to and received by that Leasehold Mortgagee and the time specified in such notice for the bringing of such default into existence shall have expired. Any such Leasehold Mortgagee shall have and be subrogated to any and all rights of the Tenant with respect to the curing of any default hereunder by the Tenant; but Landlord shall not be obligated to accept performance and compliance by the Leasehold Mortgagee if, at the time of the curing of the default, Landlord shall not be furnished with evidence reasonably satisfactory to Landlord of the interest in this lease claimed by the Leasehold Mortgagee tendering the performance or compliance. Without impairing the generality of the foregoing right of subrogation, it is particularly agreed that any such Leasehold Mortgagee shall have the following rights: (a) to exercise any renewal option within thirty (30) days after the Tenant's time to do so has expired, of which fact Landlord shall give such Leasehold Mortgagee prompt written notice, and (b) to appoint wherever required under this lease, an appraiser or arbitrator in case the Tenant shall fail to make any such appointment after written notice from the Landlord as provided in this lease and, for this purpose, that Leasehold Mortgagee shall have an additional period of thirty (30) days to make such appointment, and the appraiser or arbitrator so appointed shall thereupon be recognized in all respects as if he had been appointed by the Tenant. A Fee Mortgagee, in the event of failure of Landlord to appoint an arbitrator or appraiser, shall likewise be entitled to an additional period of thirty (30) days within which to appoint an arbitrator or appraiser who shall thereupon be recognized in all respects as if he had been appointed by Landlord.

(c)(1) Landlord agrees that if Landlord shall become entitled to serve a notice of termination of lease under Section 19.02 by reason of any default of Tenant under subdivision (a) of Section 19.01 hereof not cured within the applicable grace period, Landlord will, before service of such notice, give to each Leasehold Mortgagee who shall have duly registered its name and address a further notice that a specified default remains and that Landlord is entitled to serve such termination notice, and that Leasehold Mortgagee shall have the right to remedy such default within ten (10) days of giving of such notice.

(2) If, by reason of any default by Tenant, either this lease or any renewal thereof shall be terminated at the election of the Landlord prior to the stated expiration thereof, Landlord will enter into a new lease of the demised premises with a Leasehold Mortgagee for the remainder of the term, effective as of the date of such termination, at the rent and additional rent and upon the terms, provisions, covenants and agreements herein contained, modified or enlarged to reflect any changes in governmental regulations, codes, orders, ordinances and laws affecting the demised premises or their use or any changes in the physical or title conditions thereof as the same may exist at the time of delivery of the new lease, subject, however, to the rights, if any, of any parties then in possession of any part of the demised premises provided (a) that Leasehold Mortgagee shall make written request upon Landlord for such new lease within forty (40) days after the date of such termination and such written request is accompanied by payment to the Landlord of all sums then due to Landlord under this lease, which the Landlord has

specified as due in any notice to that Leasehold Mortgagee given as provided in accordance with the provisions of Article 19, as well as any additional installments of rent, or additional rent, which would have become due between the giving of such notice and the date of such request but for the termination of this lease; (b) that Leasehold Mortgagee shall pay to Landlord at the time of the execution and delivery of said new lease, any and all sums which would at the time of the execution and delivery thereof be due under this lease but for such termination (whether or not specified in any notice) and in addition thereto any reasonable expenses, including legal and attorney's fees, to which Landlord shall have been subjected by reason of such default; and (c) that Leasehold Mortgagee shall, on or before execution and delivery of such new lease, by instrument in writing, duly executed and acknowledged, agree that promptly following delivery of possession of the demised premises to the Leasehold Mortgagee it will perform and observe all other covenants and conditions herein contained on Tenant's part to be performed and observed to the extent that Tenant shall have failed to perform and observe the same. In order to facilitate performance by the Leasehold Mortgagee of the provisions of the foregoing, Landlord agrees that upon request of the Leasehold Mortgagee, it will advise the Leasehold Mortgagee of the exact amount of the sums required to be paid. But nothing herein contained shall be deemed to impose any obligation on the part of the Landlord to deliver physical possession of the demised premises to the Leasehold Mortgagee, but Landlord agrees that Landlord will, at the sole cost and expense of that Leasehold Mortgagee, cooperate in the prosecution of summary proceedings to evict the then defaulting Tenant.

(3) If Landlord should elect to terminate this lease by reason of a default as set forth in Subdivisions (b), (c) and (d) of Section 19.01 of this lease, the then first Institutional Leasehold Mortgagee (but no other Leasehold Mortgagee) shall not only have and be subrogated to any and all rights of Tenant with respect to curing of any default but shall also have the right within forty (40) days from the receipt of such notice to postpone and extend the specified date for the termination of this lease as fixed by the Landlord in a notice given pursuant to said Article 19, for such period or periods as may be necessary for that Leasehold Mortgagee with the exercise of reasonable diligence to foreclose its Leasehold Mortgage or otherwise to acquire the Tenant's interest in the lease and to cure any default under Subdivision (b) of Section 19.01, provided that Leasehold Mortgagee, prior to the specified date for the termination of this lease fixed by the Landlord as aforesaid, shall (a) notify the Landlord of its election to proceed promptly to foreclose its Leasehold Mortgage or otherwise to acquire the Tenant's interest in the lease, (b) pay to Landlord all sums then due to the Landlord under this lease which the Landlord has specified as due in any notice to the Leasehold Mortgagee given as provided aforesaid, and (c) deliver to the Landlord an instrument in writing duly executed and acknowledged wherein the Leasehold Mortgage agrees that (i) if delivery of possession of the premises shall be made to the Leasehold Mortgagee, or its nominee, or to anyone claiming by, through or under the Leasehold Mortgagee, pursuant to any foreclosure proceedings or otherwise, the Leasehold Mortgagee shall, promptly following such delivery of possession, perform and observe, or cause its nominee or anyone claiming by, through or under the Leasehold Mortgagee, to perform and observe, as the case may be, all the other covenants and conditions herein contained on Tenant's part to be performed and observed to the extent that Tenant shall have failed to perform and observe the same to the date of delivery of possession as aforesaid, and (ii) if pursuant to any assignment of rents theretofore made by the Tenant to the Leasehold Mortgagee, any subrents are collected by the Leasehold Mortgagee during the pendency of the foreclosure or other proceedings to acquire Tenant's interest in the lease, such subrents shall be held in trust by the Leasehold Mortgagee for application first to the performance of Tenant's obligations under this lease and further provided that the Leasehold Mortgagee shall diligently prosecute the foreclosure of its Leasehold Mortgage or other means to acquire the Tenant's interest in the lease and shall pay to Landlord all sums due to the Landlord under this lease as the same become

due and payable. If the Tenant in default under the provisions of Subdivisions (c) and (d) of said Section 19.01 shall be duly removed from possession, then and in such event, the default under Subdivisions (c) and (d) of Section 19.01 shall not be deemed in effect.

(4) If an Institutional Leasehold Mortgagee holding the mortgage made for the initial permanent financing of the new building referred to in Section 9.01 (the "Initial Permanent Mortgage") shall be in ownership of the lease or possession of the premises after _____ as the result of the acquisition of a new lease pursuant to Section 18.02(c), foreclosure proceedings or assignment of the lease in lieu of foreclosure or as mortgagee in possession, then such Leasehold Mortgagee (or its nominee) shall be required to pay the increase in the net rent, if any, pursuant to Section 2.01(c) payable for any calendar year only to the extent of the excess, if any, of the cash receipts from the operation of the premises for such calendar year over the sum of (x) the operating expenses (including the net rent of $1,000,000 and real estate taxes) actually paid in such calendar year and (y) an amount equal to the sum of the monthly fixed installments of principal and interest which were payable under that Leasehold Mortgage in the calendar year preceding the acquisition of title or possession (but not exceeding the aggregate fixed installments payable in each year in respect of the Initial Permanent Mortgage as originally made or as increased in accordance with the terms of the original commitment for the Initial Permanent Mortgage (the "Initial Loan Commitment")), each calendar year being treated separately, with no carryover of any increase not so paid to any subsequent year. The benefits of the preceding sentence shall not be available if that Institutional Leasehold Mortgagee shall hold, or have held immediately prior to the beginning of any proceeding resulting in the acquisition of title or possession, an interest in any indebtedness secured by a lien on the interest of the Tenant under the lease other than (x) the indebtedness initially secured by the Initial Permanent Mortgage or as increased from time to time by advances made under the terms of the Initial Permanent Mortgage as originally made or by advances made in accordance with the Initial Loan Commitment and (y) a subordinate mortgage or mortgages, if any, which is held by that Institutional Leasehold Mortgagee solely as collateral security in accordance with the Initial Loan Commitment for the payment of the indebtedness initially secured by the Initial Permanent Mortgage as increased from time to time by advances made under the terms of the Initial Permanent Mortgage as originally made or by advances made in accordance with the Initial Loan Commitment and shall terminate on the earlier of _____ or the assignment of the interest of the Tenant under the lease, or the subletting of the entire premises, by that Leasehold Mortgagee or its nominee.

(5) The provisions of this paragraph (c) shall be deemed to be exclusively for the benefit of the Leasehold Mortgagees and shall not inure to the benefit of the Tenant and the exercise by a Leasehold Mortgagee of any of its rights under this paragraph (c) shall not affect the validity of any notice of termination or impair the enforceability of the conditional limitation provided in Article 19. The provisions of subparagraphs (3) and (4) of this paragraph (c) shall be solely for the benefit of the first Institutional Leasehold Mortgagee (or Mortgagees) and only to the extent provided in those subparagraphs.

(d) No other party, including a Leasehold Mortgagee or the nominee of such Leasehold Mortgagee, shall be entitled to become the owner of, or acquire any interest in this lease pursuant to a judgment of foreclosure and sale, unless such party, such Leasehold Mortgagee or the nominee of such Leasehold Mortgagee shall first have delivered to Landlord an assumption agreement, dated as of the date of such foreclosure sale and executed in recordable form, wherein and whereby such party, such Leasehold Mortgagee or the nominee of such Leasehold Mortgagee assumes this lease by covenanting and agreeing on behalf of such party, such Leasehold Mortgagee or the nominee of such Leasehold Mortgagee, the legal representatives, the successors and assigns thereof, to keep, observe or perform all of the terms, covenants, agreements, provisions, conditions and limitations of this lease on Tenant's part to be kept, observed or performed. Such party or such Leasehold Mortgagee or the nominee of such Leasehold Mortgagee, in connection with any assignment of this lease, shall, upon satisfying fully all the conditions and complying fully with all the applicable requirements of this Article, be released from any and all liabilities and obligations as Tenant under this lease.

(e) In case of the termination of this lease by reason of the happening of a default, the provisions, requirements and conditions of this Article applicable to Leasehold Mortgagees with reference to the securing of a new lease from Landlord shall also be applicable to the sublessee under a sublease of the whole of the demised premises and to a mortgagee holding a mortgage on the subleasehold interest of sublessee (including a trustee under any trust indenture under which that sublease shall have been mortgaged), provided, however, that any such sublessee and any such subleasehold mortgagee, before any default shall have occurred under this lease, shall have given written notice to the Landlord, specifying the name and address of such sublessee or such subleasehold mortgagee and the sublease is in full force and effect and free from a default at the time of such termination, and the default under this lease causing the termination thereof shall not have resulted, directly or indirectly, from any acts or omissions of such sublessee or such subleasehold mortgagee. Such qualified sublessee or such qualified subleasehold mortgagee shall, after compliance with all the provisions, conditions and requirements applicable, as aforesaid, to any Leasehold Mortgagee, be entitled to a new lease from Landlord to be dated as of the date of any such termination for the balance of the term of this lease including covenants with respect to any remaining renewals, which new lease shall include the same subject clause and the same terms, covenants, agreements, provisions, conditions and limitations as are required to be inserted by the provisions of this Article.

(f) In the event that more than one request for a new lease shall have been received by Landlord within the forty (40) day period specified in this Article, priority shall be given (regardless of the order in which requests shall be made or received) to any Leasehold Mortgagee making such request in the order of the priority of the lien of such Mortgagee, then to the sublessee making such request and then to any subleasehold mortgagee making such a request in the order of the priority of the lien of such mortgagee. It shall be a condition of the effectiveness of any request by the sublessee to Landlord for a new lease that a copy of such request be sent by the sublessee at the same time to any Leasehold Mortgagee which shall have given written notice to the sublessee specifying the name and address of such Leasehold Mortgagee; and the sublessee shall furnish to Landlord, together with such request for a new lease, proof, by affidavit, of the sending of such notice to the Leasehold Mortgagee, and Landlord shall be entitled to rely upon such affidavit.

(g) In the event that Tenant shall fail to exercise its option to renew any term of this lease within the period prescribed in this lease Landlord shall give prompt written notice of that fact to any Leasehold Mortgagee who shall have become entitled to notice as provided in this lease, at the address last furnished to Landlord and, provided this lease shall be in full force and effect, such Leasehold Mortgagee may, within thirty (30) days thereafter, exercise said option to renew by requesting in writing that a new lease, in form and substance as hereinafter mentioned, be made either to itself or to its nominee covering the applicable renewal period. Pursuant thereto Landlord shall, subject to the conditions set forth in the following paragraph, at such Leasehold Mortgagee's sole cost and expense, including the cost and expense for preparation, printing, execution, delivery, and recording, and reasonable attorneys' fees, execute with and deliver to, such Leasehold Mortgagee or its nominee, as the case may be, not later than fifteen (15) days prior to the commencement of such renewal term, a new lease of the demised premises for the renewal term in question at the rent, and upon and subject to the same terms, agreements, conditions and limitations, including any remaining renewal option or options, as provided in this lease, but, without weakening the full force and effect of the provisions and conditions of the following paragraph, such new lease shall also include such additional terms, agreements, conditions and limitations as Landlord shall deem necessary to secure the timely discharge of all liabilities and the timely performance of all obligations of the next preceding Tenant which shall have accrued or which shall have originated prior to the execution and delivery of such new lease.

(h) Any exercise of option in respect of a renewal term, and the renewal term created by such exercise of option, shall cease to be of any force or effect if, prior to the date upon which such renewal term would otherwise commence the term of this lease shall have been terminated as provided in Article 19; provided, however, that if a Leasehold Mortgagee shall have exercised the renewal option referred to above, or the Tenant shall have exercised a renewal option pursuant to this lease and, within the last two years of the then current term, this lease shall have terminated and the Leasehold Mortgagee shall have become entitled to a new lease, the exercise of such option shall continue in full force and effect and the right to a renewal or a new lease arising out of such option shall inure to the benefit of the Leasehold Mortgagee; and if a sublessee of the entire demised premises shall have become entitled to a new lease pursuant to the provisions of this lease, the exercise of such option shall continue in full force and effect and the right to a renewal or a new lease arising out of such option shall inure to the benefit of the sublessee of the entire demised premises subject to the priority provisions in paragraph (f).

(i) If at any time during the term of this lease, a Leasehold Mortgagee or its nominee shall become a partner of Tenant or shall otherwise participate in the ownership of the leasehold estate created by this lease and shall give to Landlord notice of its status as such partner or participant and the address to which notices to it should be addressed, Landlord shall give to such Leasehold Mortgagee or its designated nominee notice of any default hereunder concerning which Landlord shall have given notice of default to Tenant as herein provided.

18.03. The demised premises have been let subject to, among other things, the leases which (or memoranda of which) are recorded in _____ as amended to date. Tenant agrees to perform or observe all of the obligations of the Landlord to be performed or to be observed under those leases and to indemnify and hold harmless Landlord from any claim, loss or liability arising from or in connection with those leases, provided, if any successor Tenant is an Institutional Leasehold Mortgagee, the assumption and indemnity shall only be applicable from and after the date on which the Institutional Leasehold Mortgagee shall become the Tenant.

18.04. So long as _____ is the Landlord, Tenant shall not sublet the whole or any portions of the buildings in the _____ area (whether or not any other part of the demised premises is included in the subletting) without Landlord's prior consent. The foregoing sentence shall not apply to a sublease of the entire demised premises. Prior to the completion of the new building under Article 9 hereof, Tenant may not lease (except to existing tenants) or grant any license or tenancy or right of possession or use of any part of the structures presently located on the demised premises outside the _____ area without Landlord's prior written consent, which consent shall not be unreasonably withheld, due regard being had to the diligent compliance by Tenant with its obligations under Article 9. In respect to the period to begin with the completion of construction of the new building, Tenant may sublet the whole or any portions of the new building without Landlord's consent, subject to the first sentence of this Section and the provisions hereinafter set forth, which if not observed render the subletting void, but without thereby impairing any remedy of Landlord because of Tenant having engaged in an act prohibited by the terms hereof. Tenant on demand will furnish Landlord with copies of all subleases.

Each sublease of the whole of the demised premises hereafter made for a term to begin on or after the completion of construction of the building under Article 9 must in each instance contain provisions substantially as follows:

"Tenant covenants and agrees that, if by reason of a default upon the part of Landlord who is the tenant under the Underlying Lease covering the demised premises, to wit, Agreement Restating Lease _____ as landlord, _____ as tenant, covering the demised premises, recorded in the office of the Register _____, in the performance of any of the terms or provisions of such Underlying Lease or if for any other reason of any nature whatsoever such Underlying Lease and the leasehold estate of the tenant thereunder are terminated by summary dispossess proceeding or otherwise, Tenant, at the request in writing of the then landlord under such Underlying Lease, shall attorn to and recognize such landlord as Tenant's landlord under this lease. Tenant covenants and agrees to execute and deliver, at any time and from time to time, upon the request of the landlord under such Underlying Lease, any instrument which may be necessary or appropriate to evidence such attornment. Tenant further waives the provisions of any statute or rule of law now or hereafter in effect which may terminate this lease or give or purport to give Tenant any right of election to terminate this lease or to surrender possession of the premises demised hereby in the event such Underlying Lease terminates or in the event any such proceeding is brought by the landlord under such Underlying Lease, if such landlord shall have requested in writing that Tenant attorn, as aforesaid, and in that circumstance Tenant agrees that this lease shall not be affected in any way whatsoever by any such proceeding or termination."

If this lease and the leasehold estate of Tenant hereunder are terminated by summary dispossess proceeding or otherwise, Landlord shall accept attornment by the Tenant under any sublease of the whole of the demised premises in force and effect at the date of termination of this lease, if such sublease shall have been first approved in writing by Landlord which approval shall not be unreasonably withheld, or if no such sublease of the whole of the demised premises shall be then in force and effect Landlord shall accept attornment by space tenants under space leases if such space leases shall have been first approved in writing by Landlord, which approval shall not be unreasonably withheld. Without limiting that which would constitute reasonable grounds for Landlord's withholding of approval, it is agreed that it shall not be deemed unreasonable for the Landlord to refuse to give its consent to a sublease of the whole of the demised premises if the rental reserved by that sublease is less than the net rent reserved by this lease or to any space lease if the rental reserved by such sublease shall be less than the fair market rental in respect to the premises therein demised at the time of the execution of such sublease, taking into account the term of such sublease and possible graduations in rental during such term. In no circumstance shall Landlord be required to give its approval if such sublease: (a) calls for the granting of a concession in rent at any time except during the first sixty days of the term of such sublease or allows the prepayment of rent beyond the current month for which rent is due and payable except the prepayment of rental for the first month of the term or (b) would impose upon the Landlord any obligation to make alterations to the premises demised under the sublease or to pay the sublessee for alterations made by it.

Each lease of space in the demised premises hereafter made by Tenant, as Landlord, for a term to begin on or after the completion of construction of the new building under Article 9, shall in each instance contain a provision substantially as follows:

"Tenant covenants and agrees that this lease shall not terminate upon the termination of the Underlying Lease, to wit, Agreement Restating Lease _____ between _____ as landlord, and _____ as tenant, recorded in the office of the Register _____ if for any reason of any nature whatsoever such

Underlying Lease and the leasehold estate of the tenant thereunder are terminated by summary dispossess proceeding or otherwise, Tenant at the request in writing of the then landlord under such Underlying Lease shall attorn to said landlord, and in that circumstance this lease shall not be affected in any way whatsoever by any such proceeding or termination and this lease shall continue in full force and effect in accordance with its terms."

Each lease of space in the demised premises hereafter made by any subtenant of the whole of the demised premises, as Landlord, for a term to begin on or after the completion of construction of the new building under Article 9 shall in each instance contain a provision substantially to the following effect:

The space tenant covenants and agrees that the space lease shall not terminate upon the termination of a sublease of the whole of the demised premises, if for any reason of any nature whatsoever such sublease is terminated by a summary dispossess proceeding or otherwise, or if such sublease is terminated through foreclosure proceedings brought by the holder of any mortgage to which such sublease is subject and subordinate (regardless of whether or not such termination of such sublease or such foreclosure proceedings occurs: (i) prior to the termination of the Underlying Lease, to wit Agreement Restating Lease _____ as Landlord, and _____ as Tenant, _____ (ii) simultaneously with the termination of such Underlying Lease, or (iii) subsequent to the termination of such Underlying Lease and the attornment by the Tenant under such sublease to the Landlord under such Underlying Lease or the purchaser in such foreclosure proceedings, as the case may be, and the acceptance of such attornment by the Landlord under such Underlying Lease or the purchaser in such foreclosure proceedings, as the case may be), unless the Landlord under such sublease or the holder of such mortgage, as the case may be, shall have named the space Tenant as a party in any such dispossess proceeding or such foreclosure proceedings, and the naming of the space Tenant as a party in such dispossess proceeding or such foreclosure proceedings by the Landlord under such sublease or the holder of such mortgage, as the case may be, shall not be contrary to the terms and provisions of any agreement binding upon the Landlord under such sublease or the holder of such mortgage, as the case may be; and in the event of termination of such sublease resulting from any such dispossess proceeding without the space Tenant having been made a party therein, the space tenant shall attorn to the Landlord under such sublease, the then Landlord under such Underlying Lease (if such Landlord shall have requested such attornment in writing), or the purchaser in such foreclosure proceedings, as the case may be, and the space lease shall not be affected in any way whatsoever by any such proceeding or termination and the space lease shall continue in full force and effect in accordance with its terms.

18.05. Tenant hereby assigns to Landlord all rents due or to become due from any present or future subtenant, provided that so long as Tenant is not in default hereunder, Tenant shall have the right to collect and receive such rents for its own uses and purposes. This assignment shall be subject to the rights of any Leasehold Mortgagee under a similar assignment of rents, provided that the Leasehold Mortgagee shall have exercised its rights under Section 18.02(c) to remedy the default of Tenant under Article 19 and shall have made all payments required by Section 18.02(c) to be made to the Landlord and be otherwise diligently performing the conditions of that Section. The effective date of Landlord's right to collect rents shall be the date of the happening of a default under Article 19 of this lease. Thereupon, Landlord shall apply any net amount collected by it from subtenants to the rent or additional rent due under this lease. No collection of rent by Landlord from an assignee of this lease or from a subtenant shall constitute a waiver of any of the provisions of this Article or an acceptance of the assignee or subtenant as a tenant or a release of Tenant from performance by Tenant of its obligations under this lease. Tenant, without the prior consent of Landlord in writing, will not directly or indirectly collect or accept any payment of subrent under

§ 15.16   COMMERCIAL FINANCING FORMS   657

any sublease more than six months in advance of the date when the same shall become due.

§ 15.16 Shopping Center Lease [1]

Reprinted below is a highly sophisticated shopping center lease. It is clearly "pro-landlord" and is aimed at use in a large retail shopping center. For some large tenants with significant bargaining strength, it may represent merely the beginning point in lease negotiations. This form is also advantageous to a landlord's long-term lender, who, of course, has a crucial interest in both the quality of borrower's tenants, the cash flow of the center and the terms of its leases.

Section 4.4 contains an affirmative covenant to operate the leased premises during hours specified by the landlord. This language is important in that, in its absence, a tenant may sometimes decide to cease operating and simply pay the landlord the minimum fixed rent ("Annual basic rental"). Courts will specifically enforce such covenants provided they do not view possible supervision of performance to be a major judicial burden. Compare Dover Shopping Center, Inc. v. Cushman's Sons, Inc., 63 N.J.Super. 384, 164 A.2d 785 (1960) (affirming a mandatory injunction compelling bakery tenant to operate) with Madison Plaza, Inc. v. Shapira Corp., 387 N.E.2d 483 (Ind.App.1979) (affirming denial, on supervision grounds, of request for injunction to compel tenant to operate a department store) and M. Leo Storch Limited Partnership v. Erol's, Inc., 95 Md.App. 253, 620 A.2d 408 (1993) (affirming denial on supervision grounds of request for interlocutory injunction to compel tenant to reopen and operate a video store). In any event, Section 4.4 contains a liquidated damages clause which may be a suitable remedy irrespective of the availability of injunctive relief.

Since this is a "percentage lease" in which rent, in large measure, is determined by tenant's gross sales, the presence of a well-drafted definition of "gross sales" is crucial. Section 5.5 is both all-inclusive and tightly drafted. Suppose, for example, the tenant takes an order by telephone on the leased premises, but the customer picks up and pays for the item at another of tenant's locations. Section 5.5 clearly treats this as part of the gross sales from the leased premises. The second paragraph carefully delineates exceptions from the definition such as customer refunds and the sale of tenant's fixtures. Section 5.7 is designed to give landlord broad rights to inspect tenant's sales receipts and other records to make sure that tenant is not concealing sales activity on the leased premises.

Tenant is required by this form to pay real estate taxes attributable to its leased area. Since taxes are, in all likelihood assessed on the entire center, a formula is needed to arrive at the tenant's share of the

§ 15.16

1. Form provided by the Rouse Company, Columbia, Maryland and Richard R. Goldberg, its Associate General Counsel. All rights reserved.

landlord's tax bill. This percentage is determined by dividing the tenant's floor area by the landlord's floor area.

Landlords must be concerned about environmental contamination that may result from the operations of some tenants. Section 8.6 not only requires tenant to comply with all environmental laws and to keep landlord informed of enforcement actions against it, landlord has the right to require at least annually, at tenant's expense, an environmental audit of the leased premises by an independent expert. Section 13.1 requires tenant to indemnify landlord with respect to any liability it incurs for hazardous substances that are used on the leased premises.

Section 10.4 makes it clear that tenant is to be responsible for its share of landlord's operating costs in connection with operating the common areas of the shopping center. This percentage is determined by dividing the tenant's floor area by the landlord's leased floor area. Section 10.5 contains a highly inclusive and well-drafted definition of "landlord's operating costs."

Section 13.1 broadly requires the tenant to indemnify landlord for any liability that it may incur arising from tenant's occupation and use of the leased premises. Section 13.3 requires tenant and any contractor who performs work on the leased premises to maintain a wide variety of liability insurance. Moreover, as to comprehensive commercial liability policies, landlord must be named as an additional insured. Tenant is also liable to pay as additional rent, its proportionate share of casualty and other insurance that landlord carries on the building. This percentage is determined by dividing the tenant's floor area by landlord's floor area. Finally, tenant's rent will be increased to the extent that its activities on the leased premises cause premiums on insurance that landlord carries to rise.

A significant provision of any commercial lease deals with what transpires after a casualty loss. If a casualty loss does not render the leased premises wholly or partially untenantable, landlord is obligated to repair the damage and there is no rental abatement. Where the damage causes the leased premises to be wholly or partially untenantable, landlord will make the needed repairs, but rents will be abated proportionately. Where the premises are rendered wholly untenantable, there is insufficient insurance, the premises are damaged during the last three years of the lease term or if 50% or more of the landlord's floor area is damaged, landlord has the option to terminate the lease.

Note that if the leased premises are taken, in whole or in part, by eminent domain, the condemnation award, under Section 15.2 belongs to the landlord. Thus, even though the lease may be economically favorable to the tenant, the latter will not be able to capture any "bonus value" out of the condemnation award.

The form has a well-drafted (from landlord's perspective) provision governing transfer of the tenant's interest. See Sections 16.1–16.3. Not only does the lease prohibit assignment or subletting without landlord's consent, it also provides that consent may be withheld in landlord's "sole and absolute discretion." This latter language is designed to avoid a judicial determination that consent may only be withheld on reasonable grounds. See R. Cunningham, W. Stoebuck and D. Whitman, The Law of Property, § 6.71 (2d Ed.1993). The lease then identifies ten conditions which landlord may impose in the event it consents to transfer. Note also that since "no-transfer" provisions are restraints on alienation, they will be narrowly construed against any restraint. Therefore this form wisely makes it clear that changes in beneficial ownership of a tenant that is a corporation or partnership constitute impermissible transfers and are grounds for termination of the lease.

When a tenant under a percentage lease defaults, damages are extremely difficult to ascertain since a determination of future gross sales are, at best, problematic and, at worst, highly speculative. Thus, the inclusion of a well-drafted liquidated damages provision is especially important. Section 17.3 of this lease form provides that if "termination shall take place after the expiration of two or more Rental Years, then, for purposes of computing Liquidated Damages, the Annual Percentage Rental payable with respect to each Rental Year following termination * * * shall be conclusively presumed to be equal to the average Annual Percentage Rental payable with respect to each complete Rental Year preceding termination." By using past performance to measure future gross sales, this provision reaches a reasonable solution to an otherwise difficult problem.

Section 17.4 spells out in great detail the landlord's remedies in the event the tenant files a bankruptcy petition. This situation is governed by Section 365 of the Bankruptcy Code. See 11 U.S.C.A. § 365. Of particular concern to the landlord is whether the trustee or debtor-in-possession will "assume" or "reject" the lease under the foregoing section and, if assumption occurs, whether there will be a transfer of the tenant's interest. For further analysis of this problem, see D. Epstein, S. Nickles and J. White, Bankruptcy §§ 5-2—5.23 (1993).

Section 18.1 provides that unless a mortgagee elects otherwise, this lease will automatically be subordinate to any mortgage or other security instrument on the landlord's interest. Thus, in the event of foreclosure of such a mortgage or security interest, the tenant's interest will be destroyed. On the other hand, Section 18.2 gives the mortgagee, upon its election, the right to treat the lease as senior to the mortgage. Moreover, Section 18.3 requires the tenant to attorn to any successor in interest to the landlord. Given the fact that mortgagee's decision to be either senior or junior to mortgagor's tenant is often a difficult one, the provisions of this lease give mortgagee maximum flexibility in this regard. Consequently, they should be viewed favorably by any potential mortgage lender to the landlord. We consider these issues elsewhere in this Chapter. See §§ 15.12–15.13 supra.

Frequently, a tenant will be operating at other locations in the geographic area. This has the potential of reducing the percentage rentals payable to the landlord for the leased premises. As a result, leases frequently contain a "radius" provision that prohibits the tenant and its beneficial owners from operating at any other location within a defined restricted area in competition with the business conducted on the leased premises. Section 20.1 of this lease form provides for such a restriction.

Section 20.2 requires the tenant, upon landlord's request, to provide estoppel certificates to landlord's mortgagees. Note that we consider the contents of such certificates and why mortgagees find it in their interest to demand them elsewhere in this Chapter. See § 15.13, supra.

LEASE AGREEMENT

THIS LEASE AGREEMENT ("Lease") dated _____ by and between _____ ("Landlord"), and _____ ("Tenant").

WITNESSETH:

THAT FOR AND IN CONSIDERATION of the sum of One Dollar ($1.00) and the mutual covenants herein contained, the parties hereto do hereby covenant and agree as follows:

ARTICLE I

DEFINITIONS AND ATTACHMENTS

Section 1.1 *Certain Defined Terms.*

As used herein, the term:

A. "Shopping Center Area" means that certain parcel of land owned, leased or controlled by Landlord situate in the _____, as more particularly described in Schedule "A-1", and upon the opening for business with the public, any such property used for expansion or addition.

B. "Shopping Center" means the Shopping Center Area and the adjacent parcel or parcels of land not owned, leased or controlled by Landlord but which are operated as an integral part of the shopping center known as _____; and, upon the opening for business with the public, any such property used for expansion or addition.

C. "Landlord's Building" means the structure or portions of a structure constructed or to be constructed by Landlord in the Shopping Center Area intended to be leased to retail tenants in the location shown on Schedule "A", as the same may be altered, reduced, expanded or replaced from time to time.

D. "Premises" means Tenant's portion of Landlord's Building shown on Schedule "A" having the following Area:

E. "Outside Commencement Date" means _____.

"Termination Date" means _____.

F. "Permitted Use" means the sale at retail of _____.

G. "Annual Basic Rental" means an amount equal to the product of the following figure multiplied by Tenant's Floor Area (subject to adjustment as provided in Section 5.1.): $_____.

H. "Annual Percentage Rental" means a sum equal to one percent (1%) of the amount by which annual Gross Sales exceed the product of $100.00

(the "Breakpoint") multiplied by Tenant's Floor Area (subject to adjustment as provided in Section 5.1.); provided, however, that if, during the first or last Rental Year in the Term, the Premises are not open for business with the general public for twelve (12) full calendar months, the Breakpoint shall be adjusted for any such Rental Year by multiplying the Breakpoint specified above by a fraction, the numerator of which shall be the actual number of full calendar months in such Rental Year during which the Premises were open for business with the general public, and the denominator of which shall be twelve (12).

I. "Advance Rental" means the sum of $_____. See Section 5.9.

J. "HVAC Equipment Contribution Rate" means the sum of $_____. See Schedule "F".

K. "Mall Heating, Ventilating and Air-Conditioning Equipment Contribution Rate" is included in HVAC Equipment Contribution Rate in Section 1.1.J.

L. "Merchants' Association Contribution Rate" means the sum of $_____. See Article XI. "xx" means the sum of $_____. See Article XI.

M. "Sprinkler Contribution Rate" means the sum of $_____ See Section 12.3.

N. "Trash Removal Service Charge". See Section 8.4.

O. "Water and Sewer Charge". See Schedule E.

P. "Tenant Notice Address" means _____.

Q. "Tenant Trade Name" means _____ which Tenant represents it is entitled to use pursuant to all applicable laws.

R. "Store Hours" means _____.

S. "Restriction Area" means _____.

T. "Landlord's Floor Area" means the aggregate number of square feet of Landlord's leasable floor area in Landlord's Building (exclusive of Anchor Stores and exclusive of any building not structurally connected to the enclosed mall or not having an opening into the enclosed mall) which, with respect to any such floor area which has been leased to any rent-paying tenant, shall be determined in accordance with the provisions of any lease applicable thereto and which, with respect to any such floor area not so leased, shall consist of all such leasable floor area in Landlord's Building designed for the exclusive use and occupancy of rent-paying tenants, which shall exclude Common Areas, storage areas leased separately from retail areas, mezzanine areas and areas used for Landlord's management and promotion offices.

U. "Tenant's Floor Area" means the number of square feet contained in that portion of Landlord's Floor Area constituting the Premises which shall be measured (a) with respect to the front and rear width thereof, from the exterior face of the adjacent exterior or corridor wall or, if none, from the center of the demising partition, to the opposite exterior face of the adjacent exterior or corridor wall or, if none, to the center of the opposite demising partition, and (b) with respect to the depth thereof, from the front lease line to the exterior face of the rear exterior wall, or corridor wall, or, if neither, to the center of the rear demising partition; and in no case shall there be any deduction for columns or other structural elements within any tenant's premises.

V. "Common Areas" means those areas and facilities which may be furnished by Landlord or others in or near the Shopping Center Area for the non-exclusive general common use of tenants, Anchor Stores and other occupants of the Shopping Center, their officers, agents, employees and customers, including (without limitation) parking areas, access areas (other than public streets), employee parking areas, truckways, driveways, loading docks and areas, delivery passageways, package pick-up stations, sidewalks, interior and exterior pedestrian walkways and pedestrian bridges, malls, promenades, mezzanines, roofs, sprinklers, plazas, courts, ramps, common seating areas, landscaped and planted areas, retaining walls, balconies, stairways, escalators, elevators, bus stops, first-aid stations, sewage treatment facilities (if any) lighting facilities, comfort stations or rest rooms, civic center, meeting rooms, and other similar areas, facilities or improvements.

W. "Default Rate" means an annual rate of interest equal to the lesser of (i) the maximum rate of interest for which Tenant may lawfully contract in the State in which the Shopping Center is situate, or (ii) eighteen percent (18%).

X. "Anchor Store" means any department or specialty store which either (i) occupies a floor area in excess of 50,000 square feet in the Shopping Center, or (ii) is designated an Anchor Store in a notice to that effect given by Landlord to Tenant.

Y. "Landlord's Leased Floor Area" means the monthly average of the aggregate number of square feet contained in those portions of Landlord's Floor Area leased to tenants (including the Premises) as of the first day of each calendar month during the billing period in question, but not less than eighty-five percent (85%) of Landlord's Floor Area.

Section 1.2 *Additional Defined Terms.*

The following additional terms are defined in the Sections of this Lease noted below:

Term	Section
"Additional Rental"	5.1
"Annual Merchants' Association Contribution"	11.2
"Association"	11.1
"Association Year"	11.4
"Casualty"	14.1
"Commencement Date"	3.1
"Consumer Price Index"	11.2
"Electricity Component"	Schedule E (if applicable)
"Electricity Factor"	Schedule E (if applicable)
"Event of Default"	17.1
"Expansion Opening Contribution"	11.2
"First Association Year"	11.4
"Fiscal Year"	Schedule F (if applicable)
"Gross Sales"	5.5
"Hazardous Substance"	8.6
"HVAC Equipment Contribution"	Schedule F (if applicable)
"HVAC Factor"	Schedule F (if applicable)
"Landlord's Operating Costs"	10.5
"Liquidated Damages"	17.3
"Mortgage"	18.2
"Mortgagee"	18.2
"Release"	8.6
"Rental"	5.1
"Rental Year"	5.4
"Taxes"	6.1
"Tax Year"	6.3
"Tenant's Electrical Installation"	Schedule E (if applicable)
"Tenant's HVAC Charge"	Schedule F (if applicable)
"Tenant's V/CW Charge"	Schedule F (if applicable)
"Term"	3.1
"Termination Damages"	17.3
"Umpire"	Schedule E (if applicable)

Term	Section
"V/CW Equipment Contribution"	Schedule F (if applicable)
"V/CW Factor"	Schedule F (if applicable)

Section 1.3 *Attachments.*

The following documents are attached hereto, and such documents, as well as all drawings and documents prepared pursuant thereto, shall be deemed to be a part hereof:

Schedule "A"	—	Drawing of Shopping Center Area including Landlord's Building and Tenant's Premises
Schedule "A–1"	—	Legal Description of Shopping Center
Schedule "A–2"	—	Additional Legal Description of Shopping Center (if applicable)
Schedule "B"	—	None
Schedule "C"	—	None
Schedule "D"	—	None
Schedule "E"	—	Utility Consumption and Payment Schedule
Schedule "F"	—	Tenant Heating, Ventilating and Air–Conditioning Schedule or V/CW Schedule (if applicable)

ARTICLE II
PREMISES

Section 2.1 *Demise.*

Landlord hereby leases to Tenant, and Tenant hereby rents from Landlord, the Premises having the Floor Area as set forth in clause D of Section 1.1 hereof, which Landlord and Tenant hereby conclusively agree represents Tenant's Floor Area for all purposes of this Lease.

Landlord warrants that it and no other person or corporation has the right to lease the Premises hereby demised, and that so long as Tenant is not in default hereunder, Tenant shall have peaceful and quiet use and possession of the Premises, subject to any Mortgage, and all matters of record or other agreements to which this Lease is or may hereafter be subordinated.

Notwithstanding anything to the contrary contained herein, the Premises have been inspected by Tenant who shall be deemed to have accepted the same as existing as of the date Landlord delivers the Premises to Tenant for completion of all work required of it.

ARTICLE III
TERM

Section 3.1 *Term.*

The term of this Lease (the "Term") shall commence on that date (the "Commencement Date") which shall be the earlier to occur of (a) the Outside Commencement Date or (b) the opening by Tenant of its business in the Premises, and shall terminate on the Termination Date. Landlord and Tenant agree, upon demand of the other, to execute a declaration setting forth the Commencement Date as soon as the Commencement Date has been determined.

Section 3.2 *Termination.*

This Lease shall terminate on the Termination Date, without the necessity of any notice from either Landlord or Tenant to terminate the same, and Tenant hereby waives notice to vacate or quit the Premises and agrees that Landlord shall be entitled to the benefit of all provisions of law respecting the summary recovery of possession of the Premises from a tenant holding over to the same extent as if statutory notice had been given. Tenant hereby agrees that if it fails to surrender the Premises at the end of the Term, or any renewal thereof, Tenant will be liable to Landlord for any and all damages which Landlord shall suffer by reason thereof, and Tenant will indemnify Landlord against all claims and demands made by any succeeding tenants against Landlord, founded upon delay by Landlord in delivering possession of the Premises to such succeeding tenant. For the period of three (3) months prior to the expiration of the Term, Landlord shall have the right to display on the exterior of the Premises a "For Rent" sign (not to exceed one foot by one foot in size) and during such period Landlord may show the Premises and all parts thereof to prospective tenants during normal business hours.

Section 3.3 *Holding Over.*

If Tenant shall be in possession of the Premises after the expiration of the Term, in the absence of any agreement extending the Term, the tenancy under this Lease shall become one from month to month, terminable by either party on thirty (30) days' prior notice, and shall be subject to all of the terms and conditions of this Lease as though the Term had been extended from month to month, except that (i) the Annual Basic Rental payable hereunder for each month during said holdover period shall be equal to twice the monthly installment of Annual Basic Rental payable during the last month of the Term, (ii) the installments of Annual Percentage Rental payable hereunder for each such month shall be equal to one-twelfth (1/12th) of the average Annual Percentage Rental payable hereunder for the last three (3) Rental Years of the Term, or if the Term is less than three (3) Rental Years, then such installments shall be equal to one-twelfth (1/12th) of the Annual Percentage Rental payable hereunder for the last complete Rental Year preceding expiration of the Term, and (iii) all Additional Rental payable hereunder shall be prorated for each month during such holdover period.

ARTICLE IV
USE

Section 4.1 *Prompt Occupancy and Use.*

Tenant shall occupy the Premises upon commencement of the Term and thereafter will continuously use the Premises for the Permitted Use and for no other purpose whatsoever.

Section 4.2 *Storage and Office Areas.*

Tenant shall use only such minor portions of the Premises for storage and office purposes as are reasonably required therefor.

Section 4.3 *Tenant Trade Name.*

Unless otherwise approved by Landlord, Tenant shall conduct business in the Premises only in the Tenant Trade Name.

Section 4.4 *Store Hours.*

Tenant shall cause its business to be conducted and operated in good faith and in such manner as shall assure the transaction of a maximum volume of business in and at the Premises. Tenant covenants and agrees that the Premises shall remain open for business at least during the Store Hours or such other hours as shall be seasonally adjusted by Landlord. If Tenant shall fail to cause its business to be operated during the hours required by the preceding sentence, or as otherwise required by Landlord, in addition to any other remedy available to Landlord under this Lease, Tenant shall pay to Landlord, as liquidated damages for such breach, a sum equal to One Hundred Dollars ($100.00) for each hour or portion thereof during which Tenant shall fail to so operate.

If Tenant shall request Landlord's approval of the opening of the Premises for business for periods exceeding those designated above and Landlord shall approve such request, Tenant shall pay for any additional costs incurred by Landlord in connection with Tenant's opening the Premises for business during such additional hours, including but not limited to, a proportionate share of any additional amounts of Landlord's Operating Costs, additional costs of heating, ventilating and air-conditioning the Premises, and additional utilities furnished to the Premises by Landlord.

ARTICLE V
RENTAL

Section 5.1 *Rentals Payable.*

Tenant covenants and agrees to pay to Landlord as rental ("Rental") for the Premises, the following:

    (a) the Annual Basic Rental specified in clause G of Section 1.1; plus

    (b) the Annual Percentage Rental specified in clause H of Section 1.1; plus

    (c) all additional sums, charges or amounts of whatever nature to be paid by Tenant to Landlord in accordance with the provisions of this Lease, whether or not such sums, charges or amounts are referred to as additional rental (collectively referred to as "Additional Rental");

provided, however, that the Annual Basic Rental and the minimum amount of Gross Sales utilized in the computation of Annual Percentage Rental shall be adjusted proportionately for any Rental Year of more or less than twelve (12) calendar months.

Section 5.2 *Annual Basic Rental.*

Annual Basic Rental shall be payable in equal monthly installments in advance on the first day of each full calendar month during the Term, the first such payment to include also any prorated Annual Basic Rental for the period from the date of the commencement of the Term to the first day of the first full calendar month in the Term.

Section 5.3 *Annual Percentage Rental.*

Annual Percentage Rental shall be determined and payable monthly on or before the fifteenth (15th) day following the close of each full calendar month during the Term, based on Gross Sales for the preceding calendar month. Monthly payments of Annual Percentage Rental shall be calculated by (a) dividing the product specified in clause H of Section 1.1 by twelve (12); (b) subtracting the quotient thus obtained from the amount of Gross Sales for the month in question, and (c) multiplying the difference thus obtained (if greater than zero) by the percentage specified in clause H of Section 1.1. The first monthly payment of Annual Percentage Rental due hereunder shall include prorated Annual Percentage Rental based on Gross Sales from the Commencement Date through the last day of the month immediately prior to the first full calendar month in the Term. As soon as practicable after the end of each Rental Year, the Annual Percentage Rental paid or payable for such Rental Year shall be adjusted between Landlord and Tenant, and each party hereby agrees to pay to the other, on demand, the amount of any excess or deficiency in Annual Percentage Rental paid by Tenant to Landlord during the preceding Rental Year as may be necessary to effect adjustment to the agreed Annual Percentage Rental.

Section 5.4 *"Rental Year" Defined.*

The first "Rental Year" shall commence on the first day of the Term and shall end at the close of the twelfth full calendar month following the commencement of the Term; thereafter each Rental Year shall consist of successive periods of twelve calendar months. Any portion of the Term remaining at the end of the last full Rental Year shall constitute the final Rental Year and all Rental shall be apportioned therefor.

Section 5.5 *"Gross Sales" Defined.*

"Gross Sales" means the actual sales prices or rentals of all goods, wares and merchandise sold, leased, licensed or delivered and the actual charges for all services performed by Tenant or by any subtenant, licensee or concessionaire in, at, from, or arising out of the use of the Premises, whether for wholesale, retail, cash, credit, trade-in or otherwise, without reserve or deduction for inability or failure to collect. Gross Sales shall include, without limitation, sales and services (a) where the orders therefor originate in, at, from, or arising out of the use of the Premises, whether delivery or performance is made from the Premises or from some other place, (b) made or performed by mail, telephone, or telegraph orders, (c) made or performed by means of mechanical or other vending devices in the Premises, or (d) which Tenant or any subtenant, licensee, concessionaire or other person in the normal and customary course of its business would credit or attribute to its operations in any part of the Premises. Any deposit not refunded shall be included in Gross Sales. Each installment or credit sale shall be treated as a sale for the full price in the month during which such sale is made, regardless of whether or when Tenant receives payment therefor. No franchise, occupancy or capital stock tax and no income or similar tax based on income or profits shall be deducted from Gross Sales.

The following shall not be included in Gross Sales: (i) any exchange of merchandise between stores of Tenant where such exchange is made solely for the convenient operation of Tenant's business and not for the purpose of consummating a sale made in, at or from the Premises, or for the purpose of depriving Landlord of the benefit of a sale which would otherwise be made in or at the Premises, (ii) returns to shippers or manufacturers, (iii) cash or credit refunds to customers on transactions (not to exceed the actual selling price of the item returned) otherwise included in Gross Sales, (iv) sales of trade fixtures, machinery and equipment after use thereof in the conduct of Tenant's business, (v) amounts collected and paid by Tenant to any government for any sales or excise tax, and (vi) the amount of any discount on sales to employees.

Section 5.6 *Statements of Gross Sales.*

Tenant shall deliver to Landlord: (a) within ten (10) days after the close of each calendar month of the Term, a written report signed by Tenant or by an authorized officer or agent of Tenant, showing the Gross Sales made in the preceding calendar month and (b) within sixty (60) days after the close of each Rental Year, a statement of Gross Sales for the preceding Rental Year which shall conform to and be in accordance with generally accepted accounting principles and Section 5.5. The annual statement shall be accompanied by the signed certificate of an independent Certified Public Accountant stating specifically that (i) he has examined the report of Gross Sales for the preceding Rental Year, (ii) his examination included such tests of Tenant's books and records as he considered necessary or appropriate under the circumstances, (iii) such report presents fairly the Gross Sales of the preceding Rental Year, and (iv) the said Gross Sales conform with and are computed in compliance with the definition of Gross Sales contained in Section 5.5 hereof. If Tenant shall fail to deliver such annual statement and certificate to Landlord within said sixty (60) day period, Landlord shall have the right thereafter to employ an independent Certified Public Accountant to examine such books and records, including without limitation all records required by Section 5.7, as may be necessary to certify the amount of Tenant's Gross Sales for such Rental Year, and Tenant shall pay to Landlord the cost thereof as Additional Rental.

If such audit shall disclose that Tenant's records, in the opinion of such independent Certified Public Accountant, are inadequate to disclose such Gross Sales, Landlord shall be entitled to collect, as Additional Rental, an equitable sum determined by such independent Certified Public Accountant but not exceeding fifty percent (50%) of the Annual Basic Rental payable by Tenant during the period in question.

Section 5.7 *Tenant's Records.*

For the purpose of permitting verification by Landlord of any amounts due as Rental, Tenant will (i) cause the business upon the Premises to be operated so that a duplicate sales slip, invoice or nonresettable cash register receipt, serially numbered, or such other device for recording sales as Landlord approves, shall be issued with each sale or transaction, whether for cash, credit or exchange, and (ii) preserve for at least three (3) years, and during the Term shall keep at the Tenant Notice Address or the Premises, a general ledger, required receipts and disbursement journals and such sales records and other supporting documentation, together with original or duplicate books and records, which shall disclose all information required to determine Tenant's Gross Sales and which shall conform to and be in accordance with generally accepted accounting principles. At any time or from time to time after advance notice to Tenant, Landlord or any Mortgagee, their agents and accountants, shall have the right during business hours to make any examination or audit of such books and records which Landlord or such Mortgagee may desire. If such audit shall disclose a liability in any Rental Year for Rental in excess of the Rental theretofore paid by Tenant for such period, Tenant shall promptly pay such liability. Should any such liability for Rental equal or exceed three percent (3%) of Annual Percentage Rental previously paid for such Rental Year, or if such audit shall disclose that Tenant has underreported Gross Sales by five percent (5%) or more during any Rental Year, (a) Tenant shall promptly pay the cost of audit and interest at the Default Rate on all additional Annual Percentage Rental then payable, accounting from the date such additional Annual Percentage Rental was due and payable, and (b) an Event of Default shall be deemed to exist unless, within ten (10) days after Landlord shall have given Tenant notice of such liability, Tenant shall furnish Landlord with evidence satisfactorily demonstrating to Landlord that such liability for additional Annual Percentage Rental was the result of good faith error on Tenant's part. If such audit shall disclose that Tenant's records, in Landlord's opinion, are inadequate to accurately reflect Tenant's Gross Sales, Landlord shall have the right to retain a consultant to prepare and establish a proper recording system for the determination of Tenant's Gross Sales and Tenant agrees that it shall use the system, books and records prescribed by such consultant for such purpose. Tenant shall pay to Landlord, as Additional Rental, the fees and expenses of such consultant.

Section 5.8 *Payment of Rental.*

Tenant shall pay all Rental when due and payable, without any setoff, deduction or prior demand therefor whatsoever. Except as provided herein, Tenant shall not pay any Rental earlier than one (1) month in advance of the date on which it is due. If Tenant shall fail to pay any Rental within seven (7) days after the same is due, Tenant shall be obligated to pay a late payment charge equal to the greater of One Hundred Dollars ($100.00) or ten percent (10%) of any Rental payment not paid when due to reimburse Landlord for its additional administrative costs. In addition, any Rental which is not paid within seven (7) days after the same is due shall bear interest at the Default Rate from the first day due until paid. Any Additional Rental which shall become due shall be payable, unless otherwise provided herein, with the next installment of Annual Basic Rental. Rental and statements required of Tenant shall be paid and delivered to Landlord at the management office of Landlord in the Shopping Center Area during normal business hours, or at such other place as Landlord may from time to time designate in a notice to Tenant. Any payment by Tenant or acceptance by Landlord of a lesser amount than shall be due from Tenant to Landlord shall be treated as a payment on account. The acceptance by Landlord of a check for a lesser amount with an endorsement or statement thereon, or upon any letter accompanying such check, that such lesser amount is payment in full, shall be given no effect, and Landlord may accept such check without prejudice to any other rights or remedies which Landlord may have against Tenant.

Section 5.9 *Advance Rental.*

Upon execution of this Lease by Tenant, Tenant shall pay to Landlord the Advance Rental, the same to be held as security for the performance by Tenant of all obligations imposed under this Lease which Tenant is required to perform prior to the commencement of the Term. If Tenant shall faithfully perform all such obligations, then the Advance Rental shall be applied, pro tanto, by Landlord against the Rental first becoming due hereunder. Otherwise, Landlord shall be entitled to apply the Advance Rental, pro tanto, against any damages which it may sustain by reason of Tenant's failure to perform its obligations under this Lease, but such application shall not preclude Landlord from recovering greater damages if the same can be established.

Section 5.10 *Future Expansion.*

In the event that during the Term (i) additional Anchor Stores are constructed in the Shopping Center and Landlord's Floor Area is not diminished by more than [10,000] square feet as a result thereof, or (ii) one or more expansions of Landlord's Building, each involving the addition of at least 50,000 square feet of Landlord's Floor Area, are constructed, then, upon the opening for business of each such additional Anchor Store or expansion of Landlord's Building, the Annual Basic Rental shall be increased by ten percent (10%) for each such Anchor Store or expansion opening and the Breakpoint shall be increased by a like percentage.

ARTICLE VI
TAXES

Section 6.1 *Tenant to Pay Proportionate Share of Taxes.*

Tenant shall pay in each Tax Year during the Term, as Additional Rental, a proportionate share of all amounts payable by Landlord with respect to real estate taxes, ad valorem taxes and assessments, general and special, taxes on real estate rental receipts, taxes on Landlord's gross receipts, or any other tax imposed upon or levied against real estate, or upon owners of real estate as such rather than persons generally, extraordinary as well as ordinary, foreseeable and unforeseeable, including taxes imposed on leasehold improvements which are assessed against Landlord, payable with respect to or allocable to the Shopping Center Area, including all land, Landlord's Building and all other buildings and improvements situated thereon, together with the reasonable cost (including fees of attorneys, consultants and appraisers) of any negotiation, contest or appeal pursued by Landlord in an effort to reduce any such tax, assessment or charge, and all of Landlord's reasonable administrative costs in relation to the foregoing, all of the above being collectively referred to herein as "Taxes." Tenant's proportionate share of Taxes shall be computed by multiplying the amount of such Taxes (less any contributions by Anchor Stores) by a fraction, the numerator of which shall be Tenant's Floor Area and the denominator of which shall be Landlord's Floor Area. For the Tax Year in which the Term commences or terminates, the provisions of this Section shall apply, but Tenant's liability for its proportionate share of any Taxes for such year shall be subject to a pro rata adjustment based upon the number of days of such Tax Year falling within the Term.

Section 6.2 *Payment of Proportionate Share of Taxes.*

Tenant's proportionate share of Taxes shall be paid by Tenant in monthly installments in such amounts as are estimated and billed for each Tax Year during the Term by Landlord, each such installment being due on the first day of each calendar month. At any time during a Tax Year, Landlord may reestimate Tenant's proportionate share of Taxes and thereafter adjust Tenant's monthly installments payable during the Tax Year to reflect more accurately Tenant's proportionate share of Taxes. Within one hundred twenty (120) days after Landlord's receipt of tax bills for each Tax Year, or such reasonable (in Landlord's determination) time thereafter, Landlord will notify Tenant of the amount of Taxes for the Tax Year in question and the amount of Tenant's proportionate share thereof. Any overpayment or deficiency in Tenant's payment of its proportionate share of Taxes for each Tax Year shall be adjusted between Landlord and Tenant, and Landlord and Tenant hereby agree that Tenant shall pay Landlord or Landlord shall credit to Tenant's account (or, if such adjustment is at the end of the Term, Landlord shall pay Tenant), as the case may be, within fifteen (15) days of the aforesaid notice to Tenant, such amounts as may be necessary to effect such adjustment. Failure of Landlord to provide such notice within the time prescribed shall not relieve Tenant of its obligations hereunder. Notwithstanding the foregoing, if Landlord is required under law to pay Taxes in advance, Tenant agrees to pay Landlord, upon commencement of the Term of this Lease, an amount equal to Tenant's share of Taxes for the entire Tax Year in which the Term of this Lease commences, and in such event, at the termination of this Lease, Tenant shall be entitled to a refund of Taxes paid which are attributable to a period after this Lease expires.

Section 6.3   *"Tax Year" Defined.*

The term "Tax Year" means each twelve (12) month period (deemed, for the purpose of this Section, to have 365 days) established as the real estate tax year by the taxing authorities having lawful jurisdiction over the Shopping Center Area.

Section 6.4   *Taxes on Rental.*

In addition to Tenant's proportionate share of Taxes, Tenant shall pay to the appropriate agency any sales, excise and other taxes (not including, however, Landlord's income taxes) levied, imposed or assessed by the State in which the Shopping Center is situate or any political subdivision thereof or other taxing authority upon any Rental payable hereunder. Tenant shall also pay, prior to the time the same shall become delinquent or payable with penalty, all taxes imposed on its inventory, furniture, trade fixtures, apparatus, equipment, leasehold improvements installed by Tenant or by Landlord on behalf of Tenant (except to the extent such leasehold improvements shall be covered by Taxes referred to in Section 6.1), and any other property of Tenant. Landlord may require that Tenant's leasehold improvements be separately assessed by the taxing authority.

ARTICLE VII

IMPROVEMENTS

Section 7.1   *Tenant's Improvements.*

Tenant agrees, at its sole cost and expense, to remodel the interior and exterior of the Premises in accordance with approved plans and specifications, using new and quality materials and equipment. Plans and specifications for all improvements, including the type of materials to be used by Tenant in the Premises, must be set forth in detail and submitted to Landlord for approval immediately upon execution of this Lease. Tenant agrees to commence remodeling of the Premises promptly upon approval by Landlord of such plans and specifications. All such remodeling must be completed prior to commencement of the Term.

For the purpose of performing its obligations hereunder and for the purpose of installing its fixtures and other equipment, Tenant will be permitted to enter the Premises not less than thirty (30) days prior to the commencement of the Term, on condition that (i) Tenant's activities are conducted in such a manner so as not to unreasonably interfere with Landlord's shopping center activities, and (ii) Tenant shall, at its own expense, remove from the Premises and from the Shopping Center Area in its entirety all trash which may accumulate in connection with Tenant's activities. It is understood and agreed that during said thirty (30) day period, Tenant shall perform all duties and obligations imposed by this Lease, saving and excepting only the obligation to pay Rental (other than any Additional Rental due Landlord by reason of Tenant's failure to perform any of its obligations hereunder).

Section 7.2   *Effect of Opening for Business.*

By opening the Premises for business, Tenant shall be deemed to have (a) accepted the Premises, (b) acknowledged that the same are in the condition called for hereunder, and (c) agreed that the obligations of Landlord imposed hereunder have been fully performed.

Section 7.3 *Mechanic's Liens.*

No work performed by Tenant pursuant to this Lease, whether in the nature of erection, construction, alteration or repair, shall be deemed to be for the immediate use and benefit of Landlord so that no mechanic's or other lien shall be allowed against the estate of Landlord by reason of any consent given by Landlord to Tenant to improve the Premises. Tenant shall place such contractual provisions as Landlord may request in all contracts and subcontracts for Tenant's improvements assuring Landlord that no mechanic's liens will be asserted against Landlord's interest in the Premises or the property of which the Premises are a part. Said contracts and subcontracts shall provide, among other things, the following: That notwithstanding anything in said contracts or subcontracts to the contrary, Tenant's contractors, subcontractors, suppliers and materialmen (hereinafter collectively referred to as "Contractors") will perform the work and/or furnish the required materials on the sole credit of Tenant; that no lien for labor or materials will be filed or claimed by the Contractors against Landlord's interest in the Premises or the property of which the Premises are a part; that the Contractors will immediately discharge any such lien filed by any of the Contractor's suppliers, laborers, materialmen or subcontractors; and that the Contractors will indemnify and save Landlord harmless from any and all costs and expenses, including reasonable attorneys' fees, suffered or incurred as a result of any such lien against Landlord's interest that may be filed or claimed in connection with or arising out of work undertaken by the Contractors. Tenant shall pay promptly all persons furnishing labor or materials with respect to any work performed by Tenant or its Contractors on or about the Premises. If any mechanic's or other liens shall at any time be filed against the Premises or the property of which the Premises are a part by reason of work, labor, services or materials performed or furnished, or alleged to have been performed or furnished, to Tenant or to anyone holding the Premises through or under Tenant, and regardless of whether any such lien is asserted against the interest of Landlord or Tenant, Tenant shall forthwith cause the same to be discharged of record or bonded to the satisfaction of Landlord. If Tenant shall fail to cause such lien forthwith to be so discharged or bonded after being notified of the filing thereof, then, in addition to any other right or remedy of Landlord, Landlord may bond or discharge the same by paying the amount claimed to be due, and the amount so paid by Landlord, including reasonable attorneys' fees incurred by Landlord either in defending against such lien or in procuring the bonding or discharge of such lien, together with interest thereon at the Default Rate, shall be due and payable by Tenant to Landlord as Additional Rental.

Section 7.4 *Tenant's Leasehold Improvements and Trade Fixtures.*

All leasehold improvements (as distinguished from trade fixtures and apparatus) installed in the Premises at any time, whether by or on behalf of Tenant or by or on behalf of Landlord, shall not be removed from the Premises at any time, unless such removal is consented to in advance by Landlord; and at the expiration of this Lease (either on the Termination Date or upon such earlier termination as provided in this Lease), all such leasehold improvements shall be deemed to be part of the Premises, shall not be removed by Tenant when it vacates the Premises, and title thereto shall vest solely in Landlord without payment of any nature to Tenant.

All trade fixtures and apparatus (as distinguished from leasehold improvements) owned by Tenant and installed in the Premises shall remain the property of Tenant and shall be removable at any time, including upon the expiration of the Term; provided Tenant shall not at such time be in default of any terms or covenants of this Lease, and provided further, that Tenant shall repair any damage to the Premises caused by the removal of said trade fixtures and apparatus and shall restore the Premises to substantially the same condition as existed prior to the installation of said trade fixtures and apparatus.

To protect Landlord in the event Tenant defaults hereunder, Tenant hereby grants to Landlord a security interest in all goods, inventory, equipment, trade fixtures, and all personal property belonging to Tenant which are or may be put into the Premises during the Term and all proceeds of the foregoing. Said security interest shall secure all amounts to be paid by Tenant to Landlord hereunder, including all costs of collection and other costs specified in Sections 17.2 and 17.3 hereof, and any other indebtedness of Tenant to Landlord. Tenant agrees to sign any financing statement or security agreement requested by Landlord in order to perfect such security interest. The lien granted hereunder shall be in addition to any Landlord's lien that may now or at any time hereafter be provided by law.

ARTICLE VIII OPERATIONS

Section 8.1 *Operations by Tenant.*

In regard to the use and occupancy of the Premises, Tenant will at its expense: (a) keep the inside and outside of all glass in the doors and windows of the Premises clean; (b) keep all exterior store surfaces of the Premises clean; (c) replace promptly any cracked or broken glass of the Premises with glass of like color, grade and quality; (d) maintain the Premises in a clean, orderly and sanitary condition and free of insects, rodents, vermin and other pests; (e) keep any garbage, trash, rubbish or other refuse in rat-proof containers within the interior of the Premises until removed; (f) deposit such garbage, trash, rubbish and refuse, on a daily basis, in designated receptacles provided by Landlord; (g) keep all mechanical apparatus free of vibration and noise which may be transmitted beyond the Premises; (h) comply with all laws, ordinances, rules and regulations of governmental authorities and all reasonable recommendations of Landlord's casualty insurer(s) and other applicable insurance rating organization now or hereafter in effect; (i) light the show windows of the Premises and exterior signs and turn the same off to the extent required by Landlord; (j) keep in the Premises and maintain in good working order one (1) or more type 2A10BC dry chemical fire extinguisher(s); (k) comply with and observe all rules and regulations established by Landlord from time to time which apply generally to all retail tenants in the Shopping Center Area; (l) maintain sufficient and seasonal inventory and have sufficient number of personnel to maximize sales volume in the Premises; and (m) conduct its business in all respects in a dignified manner in accordance with high standards of store operation consistent with the quality of operation of the Shopping Center Area as determined by Landlord and provide an appropriate mercantile quality comparable with the entire Shopping Center.

In regard to the use and occupancy of the Premises and the Common Areas, Tenant will not: (n) place or maintain any merchandise, signage, trash, refuse or other articles in any vestibule or entry of the Premises, on the footwalks or corridors adjacent thereto or elsewhere on the exterior of the Premises, nor obstruct any driveway, corridor, footwalk, parking area, mall or any other Common Areas; (*o*) use or permit the use of any objectionable advertising medium such as, without limitation, loudspeakers, phonographs, public address systems, sound amplifiers, reception of radio or television broadcasts within the Shopping Center, which is in any manner audible or visible outside of the Premises; (p) permit undue accumulations of or burn garbage, trash, rubbish or other refuse within or without the Premises; (q) cause or permit objectionable odors (in Landlord's opinion) to emanate or to be dispelled from the Premises; (r) solicit business in any Common Areas; (s) distribute handbills or other advertising matter in any Common Areas (including placing any of the same in or upon any automobiles parked in the parking areas); (t) permit the parking of vehicles so as to interfere with the use of any driveway, corridor, footwalk, parking area, mall or other Common Areas; (u) receive or ship articles of any kind outside the designated loading areas for the Premises; (v) use the mall, corridor or any other Common Areas adjacent to the

Premises for the sale or display of any merchandise or for any other business, occupation or undertaking; (w) conduct or permit to be conducted any auction, fictitious fire sale, going out of business sale, bankruptcy sale (unless directed by court order), or other similar type sale in or connected with the Premises (but this provision shall not restrict the absolute freedom of Tenant in determining its own selling prices, nor shall it preclude the conduct of periodic seasonal, promotional or clearance sales); (x) use or permit the use of any portion of the Premises in a manner which will be in violation of law, or for any activity of a type which is not generally considered appropriate for regional shopping centers conducted in accordance with good and generally accepted standards of operation; (y) place a load upon any floor which exceeds the floor load which the floor was designed to carry; (z) operate its heating or air-conditioning in such a manner as to drain heat or air-conditioning from the Common Areas or from the premises of any other tenant or other occupant of the Shopping Center; or (aa) use the Premises for any unlawful or illegal business, use or purpose, or for any business, use or purpose which is immoral or disreputable (including without limitation "adult entertainment establishments" and "adult bookstores"), or which is hazardous, or in such manner as to constitute a nuisance of any kind (public or private), or for any purpose or in any way in violation of the certificates of occupancy (or other similar approvals of applicable governmental authorities).

Tenant acknowledges that it is Landlord's intent that the Shopping Center Area be operated in a manner which is consistent with the highest standards of decency and morals prevailing in the community which it serves. Toward that end, Tenant agrees that it will not sell, distribute, display or offer for sale any item which, in Landlord's good faith judgment, is inconsistent with the quality of operation of the Shopping Center Area or may tend to injure or detract from the moral character or image of the Shopping Center Area within such community. Without limiting the generality of the foregoing, Tenant will not sell, distribute, display or offer for sale (i) any roach clip, water pipe, bong, coke spoon, cigarette papers, hypodermic syringe or other paraphernalia commonly used in the use or ingestion of illicit drugs, (ii) any pornographic, lewd, suggestive, or "adult" newspaper, book, magazine, film, picture, recording, representation or merchandise of any kind, or (iii) any handgun.

Section 8.2 *Signs and Advertising.*

Tenant will not place or suffer to be placed or maintained on the exterior of the Premises, or any part of the interior visible from the exterior thereof, any sign, banner, advertising matter or any other thing of any kind (including, without limitation, any hand-lettered advertising), and will not place or maintain any decoration, letter or advertising matter on the glass of any window or door of the Premises without first obtaining Landlord's approval. Tenant will, at its sole cost and expense, maintain such sign, banner, decoration, lettering, advertising matter or other thing as may be permitted hereunder in good condition and repair at all times.

Section 8.3 *Painting and Displays by Tenant.*

Tenant will not paint or decorate any part of the exterior of the Premises, or any part of the interior of the Premises visible from the exterior thereof, without first obtaining Landlord's approval. Tenant will install and maintain at all times, subject to the other provisions of this Section, displays of merchandise in the show windows (if any) of the Premises. All articles, and the arrangement, style, color and general appearance thereof, in the interior of the Premises including, without limitation, window displays, advertising matter, signs, merchandise and store fixtures, shall be in keeping with the character and standards of the improvements within the Shopping Center, as determined by Landlord. Landlord reserves the right to require Tenant to correct any non-conformity.

Section 8.4 *Trash Removal Service.*

At its option, Landlord may furnish (or authorize others to furnish) a service for the removal of trash from receptacles designated by Landlord for the daily deposit by Tenant of its garbage, trash, rubbish or other refuse, and, if it shall do so, then in each Rental Year, at Landlord's election, Tenant shall either (i) reimburse Landlord monthly, as Additional Rental, for all costs incurred by Landlord in furnishing such service, or (ii) pay Landlord the Trash Removal Service Charge, if any, set forth in clause N of Section 1.1 in twelve (12) equal monthly installments, subject to adjustments reflecting any increase in Landlord's cost and expense in furnishing such trash removal service, or (iii) pay directly such person, firm or corporation authorized by Landlord to provide such trash removal service; provided, however, that all amounts which Tenant is obligated to pay to Landlord pursuant to clause (i) or (ii) above shall not exceed the amounts which Tenant would otherwise be obligated to pay directly to the same independent contractor utilized by Landlord for the removal of Tenant's trash, if Tenant were dealing with such contractor at arm's length for trash removal services for the Premises.

Section 8.5 *Permitted Use Disclaimer.*

Nothing contained in this Lease shall be construed to indicate any intent or attempt on the part of Landlord to restrict the price or prices at which Tenant may sell any goods or services permitted to be sold at or from the Premises pursuant to this Lease.

Section 8.6 *Hazardous Substances.*

Tenant shall not use or allow the Premises to be used for the Release, storage, use, treatment, disposal or other handling of any Hazardous Substance, without the prior consent of Landlord. The term "Release" shall have the same meaning as is ascribed to it in the Comprehensive Environmental Response, Compensation and Liability Act, 42 U.S.C. § 9601 *et seq.,* as amended, ("CERCLA"). The term "Hazardous Substance" means (i) any substance defined as a "hazardous substance" under CERCLA, (ii) petroleum, petroleum products, natural gas, natural gas liquids, liquefied natural gas, and synthetic gas, and (iii) any other substance or material deemed to be hazardous, dangerous, toxic, or a pollutant under any federal, state or local law, code, ordinance or regulation.

Tenant shall: (a) give prior notice to Landlord of any activity or operation to be conducted by Tenant at the Premises which involves the Release, use, handling, generation, treatment, storage, or disposal of any Hazardous Substance ("Tenant's Hazardous Substance Activity"), (b) comply with all federal, state, and local laws, codes, ordinances, regulations, permits and licensing conditions governing the Release, discharge, emission, or disposal of any Hazardous Substance and prescribing methods for or other limitations on storing, handling, or otherwise managing Hazardous Substances, (c) at its own expense, promptly contain and remediate any Release of Hazardous Substances arising from or related to Tenant's Hazardous Substance Activity in the Premises, Landlord's Building, the Shopping Center, the Shopping Center Area or the environment and remediate and pay for any resultant damage to property, persons, and/or the environment, (d) give prompt notice to Landlord, and all appropriate regulatory authorities, of any Release of any Hazardous Substance in the Premises, Landlord's Building, the Shopping Center, the Shopping Center Area or the environment arising from or related to Tenant's Hazardous Substance Activity, which Release is not made pursuant to and in conformance with the terms of any permit or license duly issued by appropriate governmental authorities, any such notice to include a description of measures taken or proposed to be taken by Tenant to contain and remediate the Release and resultant damage to property, persons, or the environment, (e) at Landlord's request, which shall not be more frequent than once per calendar year, retain an independent engineer or other qualified consultant or expert acceptable to Landlord, to conduct, at Tenant's expense, an environmental audit of the Premises and immediate surrounding areas, and the scope of work to be performed by such engineer, consultant, or expert shall be approved in advance by Landlord, and all of the engineer's, consultant's, or expert's work product shall be made available to Landlord, (f) at Landlord's request from time to time, execute affidavits, representations and the like concerning Tenant's best knowledge and belief regarding the presence of Hazardous Substances in the Premises, (g) reimburse to Landlord, upon demand, the reasonable cost of any testing for the purpose of ascertaining if there has been any Release of Hazardous Substances in the Premises, if such testing is required by any governmental agency or Landlord's Mortgagee, (h) upon expiration or termination of this Lease, surrender the Premises to Landlord free from the presence and contamination of any Hazardous Substance.

ARTICLE IX
REPAIRS AND ALTERATIONS

Section 9.1 *Repairs To Be Made By Landlord.*

Landlord, at its expense, will make, or cause to be made structural repairs to exterior walls, structural columns, roof penetrations and structural floors which collectively enclose the Premises (excluding, however, all doors, door frames, storefronts, windows and glass); provided Tenant shall give Landlord notice of the necessity for such repairs.

Section 9.2 *Repairs To Be Made By Tenant.*

All repairs to the Premises or any installations, equipment or facilities therein, other than those repairs required to be made by Landlord pursuant to Sections 9.1, 12.3 or Section 14.1, shall be made by Tenant at its expense. Without limiting the generality of the foregoing, Tenant will keep the interior of the Premises, together with all electrical, plumbing and other mechanical installations therein and (if and to the extent provided in Schedule F) the heating, ventilating and air-conditioning system installed by Tenant in the Premises, in good order and repair and will make all replacements from time to time required thereto at its expense. Tenant will surrender the Premises at the expiration of the Term or at such other time as it may vacate the Premises in as good condition as when received, excepting depreciation caused by ordinary wear and tear, damage by Casualty, unavoidable accident or Act of God. Tenant will not overload the electrical wiring serving the Premises or within the Premises, and will install at its expense, subject to the provisions of Section 9.4, any additional electrical wiring which may be required in connection with Tenant's apparatus. Any damage or injury sustained by any person because of mechanical, electrical, plumbing or any other equipment or installations, whose maintenance and repair shall be the responsibility of Tenant, shall be paid for by Tenant, and Tenant hereby agrees to indemnify and hold Landlord harmless from and against all claims, actions, damages and liability in connection therewith, including, but not limited to attorneys' and other professional fees, and any other cost which Landlord might reasonably incur.

Section 9.3 *Damage to Premises.*

Tenant will repair promptly at its expense any damage to the Premises and, upon demand, shall reimburse Landlord (as Additional Rental) for the cost of the repair of any damage elsewhere in the Shopping Center, caused by or arising from the installation or removal of property in or from the Premises, regardless of fault or by whom such damage shall be caused (unless caused by Landlord, its agents, employees or contractors). If Tenant shall fail to commence such repairs within five (5) days after notice to do so from Landlord, Landlord may make or cause the same to be made and Tenant agrees to pay to Landlord promptly upon Landlord's demand, as Additional Rental, the cost thereof with interest thereon at the Default Rate until paid.

Section 9.4 *Alterations by Tenant.*

Tenant will not make any alterations, renovations, improvements or other installations in, on or to any part of the Premises (including, without limitation, any alterations of the storefront, signs, structural alterations, or any cutting or drilling into any part of the Premises or any securing of any fixture, apparatus, or equipment of any kind to any part of the Premises) unless and until Tenant shall have caused plans and specifications therefor to have been prepared, at Tenant's expense, by an architect or other duly qualified person and shall have obtained Landlord's approval thereof. If such approval is granted, Tenant shall cause the work described in such plans and specifications to be performed, at its expense, promptly, efficiently, competently and in a good and workmanlike manner by duly qualified and licensed persons or entities, using first grade materials, without interference with or disruption to the operations of tenants or other occupants of the Shopping Center. All such work shall comply with all applicable codes, rules, regulations and ordinances.

Section 9.5 *Changes and Additions to Shopping Center.*

Landlord reserves the right at any time and from time to time to (a) make or permit changes or revisions in the plan for the Shopping Center or the Shopping Center Area including additions to, subtractions from, rearrangements of, alterations of, modifications of, or supplements to, the building areas, walkways, driveways, parking areas, or other Common Areas, (b) construct improvements in Landlord's Building and the Shopping Center Area and to make alterations thereof or additions thereto and to build additional stories on or in any such building(s) and build adjoining same, including (without limitation) kiosks, pushcarts and other displays in the Common Areas, and (c) make or permit changes or revisions in the Shopping Center or the Shopping Center Area, including additions thereto, and to convey portions of the Shopping Center Area to others for the purpose of constructing thereon other buildings or improvements, including additions thereto and alterations thereof; provided, however, that no such changes, rearrangements or other construction shall reduce the parking areas below the number of parking spaces required by law.

Section 9.6 *Roof and Walls.*

Landlord shall have the exclusive right to use all or any part of the roof of the Premises for any purpose; to erect additional stories or other structures over all or any part of the Premises; to erect in connection with the construction thereof temporary scaffolds and other aids to construction on the exterior of the Premises, provided that access to the Premises shall not be denied; and to install, maintain, use, repair and replace within the Premises pipes, ducts, conduits, wires and all other mechanical equipment serving other parts of the Shopping Center Area, the same to be in locations within the Premises as will not unreasonably deny Tenant's use thereof. Landlord may make any use it desires of the side or rear walls of the Premises or other structural elements of the Premises (including, without limitation, free-standing columns and footings for all columns), provided that such use shall not encroach on the interior of the Premises unless (i) all work carried on by Landlord with respect to such encroachment shall be done during hours when the Premises are not open for business and otherwise shall be carried out in such a manner as not to unreasonably interfere with Tenant's operations in the Premises, (ii) Landlord, at its expense, shall provide any security services to the Premises required by such work, and (iii) Landlord, at its expense, shall repair all damage to the Premises resulting from such work.

ARTICLE X

COMMON AREAS

Section 10.1 *Use of Common Areas.*

Landlord grants to Tenant and its agents, employees and customers a non-exclusive license to use the Common Areas in common with others during the Term, subject to the exclusive control and management thereof at all times by Landlord or others and subject, further, to the rights of Landlord set forth in Sections 9.5 and 10.2.

Section 10.2 *Management and Operation of Common Areas.*

Landlord will operate and maintain, or will cause to be operated and maintained, the Common Areas in a manner deemed by Landlord to be reasonable and appropriate and in the best interests of the Shopping Center. Landlord will have the right (i) to establish, modify and enforce reasonable rules and regulations with respect to the Common Areas; (ii) to enter into, modify and terminate easement and other agreements pertaining to the use and maintenance of the Common Areas; (iii) to enforce parking charges (by operation of meters or otherwise) with appropriate provisions for free parking ticket validation by tenants; (iv) to close all or any portion of the Common Areas to such extent as may, in the opinion of Landlord, be necessary to prevent a dedication thereof or the accrual of any rights to any person or to the public therein; (v) to close temporarily any or all portions of the Common Areas; (vi) to discourage non-customer parking; and (vii) to do and perform such other acts in and to said areas and improvements as, in the exercise of good business judgment, Landlord shall determine to be advisable.

Section 10.3 *Employee Parking Areas.*

Tenant and its employees shall park their cars only in such areas designated for that purpose by Landlord. Upon request by Landlord, Tenant shall furnish Landlord with State automobile license numbers assigned to Tenant's car or cars and cars used by its employees and shall thereafter notify Landlord of any changes in such information within five (5) days after such changes occur. If Tenant or its employees shall fail to park their cars in the designated parking areas, then, without limiting any other remedy which Landlord may pursue in the event of Tenant's default, Landlord, after giving notice to Tenant, shall have the right to charge Tenant, as Additional Rental, the sum of Ten Dollars ($10.00) per day per car parked in violation of the provisions of this Section. Tenant shall notify its employees in writing of the provisions of this Section.

Section 10.4 *Tenant to Share Expense of Common Areas.*

Tenant will pay Landlord, as Additional Rental, a proportionate share of Landlord's Operating Costs which shall be computed by multiplying Landlord's Operating Costs (less any contribution to such costs and expenses made by the owner or operator of any Anchor Store in the Shopping Center) by a fraction, the numerator of which is Tenant's Floor Area and the denominator of which is Landlord's Leased Floor Area. Such proportionate share shall be paid by Tenant in monthly installments in such amounts as are estimated and billed by Landlord at the beginning of each twelve (12) month period commencing and ending on dates designated by Landlord, each installment being due on the first day of each calendar month. At any time during any such twelve (12) month period, Landlord may reestimate Tenant's proportionate share of Landlord's Operating Costs and thereafter adjust Tenant's monthly installments payable during such twelve (12) month period to reflect more accurately Tenant's proportionate share of Landlord's Operating Costs. Within one hundred twenty (120) days (or such additional time thereafter as is reasonable under the circumstances) after the end of each such twelve (12) month period, Landlord shall deliver to Tenant a statement of Landlord's Operating Costs for such twelve (12) month period and the monthly installments paid or payable shall be adjusted between Landlord and Tenant, and Tenant shall pay Landlord or Landlord shall credit Tenant's account (or, if such adjustment is at the end of the Term, Landlord shall pay Tenant), as the case may be, within fifteen (15) days of receipt of such statement, such amounts as may be necessary to effect such adjustment. Upon reasonable notice, Landlord shall make available for Tenant's inspection (which inspection shall be at Tenant's sole cost and expense) at Landlord's office, during normal business hours, Landlord's records relating to Landlord's Operating Costs for such preceding twelve (12) month period. Failure of Landlord to provide the statement called for hereunder within the time prescribed shall not relieve Tenant from its obligations hereunder.

Section 10.5 *"Landlord's Operating Costs" Defined.*

The term "Landlord's Operating Costs" means all costs and expenses incurred by or on behalf of Landlord in operating, managing, insuring, securing and maintaining the Common Areas pursuant to Section 10.2. "Landlord's Operating Costs" includes, but is not limited to, all costs and expenses of operating, maintaining, repairing, lighting, signing, cleaning, painting, striping, policing and security of the Common Areas (including the cost of uniforms, equipment and employment taxes); alarm and life safety systems; insurance, including, without limitation, liability insurance for personal injury, death and property damage, all-risks casualty insurance (including coverage against fire, flood, theft or other casualties), worker's compensation insurance or similar insurance covering personnel, fidelity bonds for personnel, insurance against liability for assault and battery, defamation and claims of false arrest occurring on and about the Common Areas, plate glass insurance for glass exclusively serving the Common Areas; the costs and expenses of maintenance of all exterior glass; maintenance of sprinkler systems; removal of water, snow, ice, trash and debris; regulation of traffic; surcharges levied upon or assessed against parking spaces or areas by governmental or quasi-governmental authorities, payments toward mass transit or car pooling facilities or otherwise as required by governmental or quasi-governmental authorities; costs and expenses in connection with maintaining federal, state or local governmental ambient air and environmental standards; the cost of all materials, supplies and services purchased or hired therefor; operation of public toilets; installing and renting of signs; fire protection; maintenance, repair and replacement of utility systems serving the Common Areas, including, but not limited to, water, sanitary sewer and storm water lines and other utility lines, pipes and conduits; costs and expenses of maintaining and operating sewage treatment facilities, if any; costs and expenses of inspecting and depreciation of machinery and equipment used in the operation and maintenance of the Common Areas and personal property taxes and other charges (including, but not limited to, financing, leasing or rental costs) incurred in connection with such equipment; costs and expenses of the coordination and use of truck docks and loading facilities; costs and expenses of repair or replacement of awnings, paving, curbs, walkways, landscaping, drainage, pipes, ducts, conduits and similar items, plate glass, lighting facilities, floor coverings, and the roof; costs and expenses of planting, replanting, replacing and displaying flowers, shrubbery and planters; costs and expenses incurred in the purchase or rental of music program services and loudspeaker systems, including furnishing electricity therefor; costs of providing light and power to the Common Areas; costs of providing energy to heat, ventilate and air-condition the Common Areas and the operation, maintenance, and repair of equipment required therefor (including, without limitation, the costs of energy management systems serving the Shopping Center Area); cost of water services, if any, furnished by Landlord for the non-exclusive use of all tenants; parcel pick-up and delivery services; and administrative costs attributable to the Common Areas for on-site personnel and an overhead cost equal to fifteen percent (15%) of the total costs and expenses of operating and maintaining the Common Areas. Landlord may elect to amortize any of the foregoing costs and expenses over a useful life determined in accordance with generally accepted accounting principles.

Section 10.6 *Mall Heating, Ventilating and Air-Conditioning Equipment Contribution Rate.*

In each Rental Year, Tenant shall pay Landlord annually (in twelve (12) equal monthly installments together with the Annual Basic Rental), as Additional Rental, an amount (the "Mall Heating, Ventilating and Air-Conditioning Equipment Contribution") determined by multiplying the Mall Heating, Ventilating and Air-Conditioning Equipment Contribution Rate by Tenant's Floor Area.

Section 10.7 *Renovation or Expansion of Common Areas.*

If, during the Term, the Common Areas, or any part thereof, are expanded or renovated to the extent that Landlord's Improvement Costs incurred in connection therewith exceed a sum equal to Twenty Dollars ($20.00) per square foot of

Landlord's Floor Area, the Annual Basic Rental and the dollar amount set forth in clause H of Section 1.1 each shall be increased by ten percent (10%) thereof for each such expansion or renovation effective as of the date on which Landlord delivers to Tenant a notice that Landlord has incurred such costs. The term "Landlord's Improvement Costs" means all direct and indirect costs and expenses incurred by Landlord and properly allocated to the construction and development of capital improvements to the Common Areas, but not including any cost or expense included in Landlord's Operating Costs. Upon reasonable notice, Landlord shall make available for Tenant's inspection (which inspection shall be at Tenant's sole cost and expense) at Landlord's office, during normal business hours, Landlord's records relating to Landlord's Improvement Costs as to which any such notice shall have been delivered.

ARTICLE XI
MERCHANTS' ASSOCIATION

Section 11.1 *Merchants' Association.*

Tenant agrees to maintain a membership in any merchants' association, if and when established by Landlord (the "Association"), and for the purpose of creating and maintaining a fund for the general promotion and welfare of the Shopping Center as a whole, agrees to pay to the Association or its agent the amounts specified in Section 11.2 regardless of whether Tenant shall remain a member of the Association during the Term. Notwithstanding anything to the contrary which may be contained in this Lease, or in any Article of Incorporation, Corporate Charter or By-Laws of the Association, Tenant covenants and agrees that Landlord may in its sole discretion elect to provide the Association with any or all of the following, and Tenant further expressly authorizes the Association to reimburse Landlord for providing: (i) the services of a marketing manager and all staff deemed necessary by Landlord to carry out effectively the promotion and public relations objectives of the Association; (ii) such reasonable space as may be necessary to carry out the functions of the marketing manager and his or her staff; and (iii) such office equipment, supplies, telephones and other related costs as may be deemed necessary by Landlord to service fully the marketing manager and his or her staff. The Association may appoint Landlord as its agent for the collection of the Association contributions with the right, joint and several, to collect and enforce on behalf of the Association all debts owing by Tenant to the Association. The Association shall have the benefit of Tenant's obligations under this Article XI and shall be entitled to enforce such obligations directly.

Section 11.2 *Tenant's Contribution to Merchants' Association.*

Tenant shall make the following contributions to the Association:

(a) In the First Association Year Tenant shall pay to the Association on the first day of each calendar month an amount determined by (i) multiplying the Merchants' Association Contribution Rate set forth in Section 1.1.L. by Tenant's Floor Area, and (ii) dividing the product thus obtained by twelve (12). In each subsequent Association Year, Tenant shall pay to the Association an amount (the "Annual Merchants' Association Contribution") determined by multiplying the Merchants' Association Contribution Rate, adjusted as provided below, by Tenant's Floor Area. The Annual Merchants' Association Contribution shall be paid by Tenant in twelve (12) equal monthly installments, in advance, on the first day of each calendar month. The Annual Merchants' Association Contribution shall be adjusted annually, as of the first day of each Association Year during the Term, in the same proportion as the Consumer Price Index for All Urban Consumers (U.S. City Average) published by the Bureau of Labor Statistics of the United States Department of Labor (the "Consumer Price Index") most recently reported as of such adjustment date bears to the Consumer Price Index reported for the first full calendar month of the Term, all such adjustments to be apportioned for fractional years.

If during the Term the Consumer Price Index is changed or discontinued, Landlord shall choose a comparable index, formula or other means of measurement of the relative purchasing power of the dollar and such substitute index, formula or other means shall be utilized in place of the Consumer Price Index as if it had been originally designated in this Lease.

In addition to the adjustment for the Consumer Price Index, the Annual Merchants' Association Contribution may be increased at any time during the Term by a vote of tenants (exclusive of Anchor Stores and Landlord) occupying more than fifty percent (50%) of Landlord's Floor Area.

(b) If the Shopping Center shall be expanded by adding floor area equal to more than ten percent (10%) of Landlord's Floor Area contained in the Shopping Center as of the date of this Lease, Tenant shall pay to said Association a one time charge for each such expansion (the "Expansion Opening Contribution") determined by (i) multiplying Tenant's Floor Area by the average rate per square foot of all contributions which tenants in the expansion area shall become obligated pursuant to their respective leases to make to the Association with respect to promotion and advertising of the opening of such expansion for business, and (ii) dividing the product thus obtained by two (2).

Section 11.3 *Landlord's Contribution to Merchants' Association.*

Landlord shall contribute to the Association for the First Association Year and for each subsequent Association Year, an amount equal to one-fifth (⅕) of the aggregate contributions made by the other contributors to the Association for each such period.

Section 11.4 *"First Association Year" and "Association Year" Defined.*

"First Association Year" means the period commencing on the first day of the Term and terminating on the second succeeding December 31. "Association Year" means each successive period of twelve (12) months commencing with January 1.

Section 11.5 *Advertising.*

During each Rental Year, Tenant shall advertise its business at the Premises either (i) by expending an amount equal to a minimum of three percent (3%) of Tenant's annual Gross Sales for such period in recognized regional print or electronic advertising media, or (ii) by participating in twelve (12) cooperative advertising units per year sponsored by the Association. Each advertisement shall specify Tenant's business located at the Premises. If Tenant elects to advertise pursuant to clause (i) hereof, Tenant shall preserve original or duplicate books and records at Tenant's Notice Address which shall disclose all information required to determine Tenant's advertising expenditures. Upon advance notice, Landlord, its agents and accountants, shall have the right to audit such books and records. If the audit discloses noncompliance by Tenant for any Rental Year in question, Tenant, in addition to the remedies contained in this Lease, shall pay to Landlord a sum equal to Landlord's cost of the audit, which sum shall be deemed to be Additional Rental, plus as liquidated damages, a sum equal to the amount by which Tenant's expenditures for advertising as required by clause (i) above shall be less than three percent (3%) of Tenant's annual Gross Sales.

Tenant shall, within ten (10) days after the beginning of each Rental Year, notify Landlord of its election to advertise its business either under clause (i) or (ii) above. If Tenant elects to advertise under clause (ii), Tenant may not withdraw such election until the following Rental Year; however, if Tenant elects clause (i), Tenant shall have the right at any time during the Rental Year to change such election to clause (ii).

ARTICLE XII

UTILITIES

Section 12.1 *Water, Electricity, Telephone and Sanitary Sewer.*

Landlord will provide, or cause to be provided, at points in or near the Premises the facilities necessary to enable Tenant to obtain for the Premises water, electricity, telephone and sanitary sewer service. Schedule E sets forth those utilities for which service shall be provided to the Premises by Landlord, if any, as well as the manner in which charges for their consumption shall be determined and paid by Tenant. Unless otherwise provided in Schedule E, Landlord shall not be responsible for providing any utility service to the Premises, nor for providing meters or other devices for the measurement of utilities supplied to the Premises, and Tenant shall arrange for the furnishing to the Premises of such utility services as it may require, as well as for the installation of all such meters or other devices. Tenant shall be solely responsible for and shall promptly pay, as and when the same become due and payable, all charges for water, sewer, electricity, gas, telephone and any other utility used or consumed in the Premises and supplied by a public utility or public authority or any other person, firm or corporation, including Landlord, supplying the same.

If Schedule E does not provide that Landlord will supply electricity to the Premises, Landlord shall have the option, exercisable at any time and from time to time during the Term, to supply electricity to the Premises. If Landlord shall elect to supply electricity to the Premises, Tenant will purchase its requirements for such service tendered by Landlord, and Tenant will pay Landlord, within ten (10) days after mailing by Landlord to Tenant of statements therefor, at the applicable rates determined by Landlord from time to time which Landlord agrees shall not be in excess of the public utility rates for the same service, if applicable. If Landlord so elects to supply electricity, Tenant shall execute and deliver to Landlord, within ten (10) days after request therefor, any documentation reasonably required by Landlord to effect such change in the method of furnishing of electricity.

Landlord, in its sole discretion, shall have the right, from time to time, to alter the method and source of supply to the Premises of electricity or any other utility, and Tenant agrees to execute and deliver to Landlord such documentation as may be required to effect such alteration, provided, however, that Tenant shall not be required to bear any portion of the cost of such alteration or to incur any additional financial obligation as a result of such alteration, other than as provided in Schedule E.

Tenant shall not at any time overburden or exceed the capacity of the mains, feeders, ducts, conduits, or other facilities by which such utilities are supplied to, distributed in or serve the Premises. If Tenant desires to install any equipment which shall require additional utility facilities or utility facilities of a greater capacity than the facilities provided by Landlord, such installation shall be subject to Landlord's prior approval of Tenant's plans and specifications therefor. If such installation is approved by Landlord and if Landlord provides such additional facilities to accommodate Tenant's installation, Tenant agrees to pay Landlord, on demand, the cost for providing such additional utility facilities or utility facilities of greater capacity.

Section 12.2 *Heating, Ventilating and Air-Conditioning.*

Schedule F entitled "Tenant Heating, Ventilating and Air-Conditioning" specifies the obligations of Landlord and Tenant (other than those obligations set forth in Article X) regarding the heating, ventilating, and air-conditioning equipment and system serving the Premises or the Shopping Center Area and the energy required to operate the heating, ventilating and air-conditioning equipment serving the Premises. Tenant covenants and agrees to pay to Landlord, as Additional Rental and in the same manner as Annual Basic Rental is payable, all charges as the same may be adjusted from time to time, and as more particularly set forth in said Schedule F.

Landlord, in its sole discretion, shall have the right, from time to time, to alter the heating, ventilating and air-conditioning systems and equipment serving the Shopping Center, or any part thereof, and Tenant agrees to execute and deliver to Landlord such documentation as may be required to effect such alteration; provided, however, that Tenant shall not be required to bear any portion of the cost of such alteration or to incur any additional financial obligation as a result of such alteration.

Section 12.3 *Fire Protection Sprinkler System.*

Landlord shall provide, install, repair and maintain, or cause to be provided, installed, repaired and maintained, a fire protection sprinkler system in the Premises, which system shall remain the property of Landlord. Tenant shall pay Landlord, as Additional Rental, for providing such fire protection sprinkler system, an annual amount determined by multiplying the Sprinkler Contribution Rate by Tenant's Floor Area, said annual sum to be payable in twelve (12) equal monthly installments, in advance on the first day of each calendar month. Any modifications or additions to the existing sprinkler system, whether required as a result of the improvements to be made to the Premises pursuant to Section 7.1 or requested by Tenant after commencement of the Term, shall be made by Landlord at Tenant's cost and expense (after agreement between Landlord and Tenant on a price for such work) or, at Landlord's election, shall be made by Tenant (at its cost and expense), provided Tenant utilizes a licensed contractor approved by Landlord for such purpose.

Section 12.4 *Discontinuances and Interruptions of Utility Services.*

Landlord reserves the right to cut off and discontinue, upon notice to Tenant, furnishing any heating, ventilation, air-conditioning or other utility services furnished by Landlord at any time when Tenant has failed to pay when due any amount (whether as Rental or otherwise) due under this Lease. Landlord shall not be liable for any damages resulting from or arising out of any such discontinuance and the same shall not constitute a termination of this Lease or an eviction of Tenant. Landlord shall not be liable to Tenant in damages or otherwise (i) if any utility shall become unavailable from any public utility company, public authority or any other person or entity (including Landlord) supplying or distributing such utility, or (ii) for any interruption in any utility service (including, without limitation, any heating, ventilation, air-conditioning or sprinkler) caused by the making of any necessary repairs or improvements or by any cause beyond Landlord's reasonable control, and the same shall not constitute a termination of this Lease or an eviction of Tenant.

ARTICLE XIII

INDEMNITY AND INSURANCE

Section 13.1 *Indemnities.*

To the extent permitted by law, Tenant shall and does hereby indemnify Landlord and agrees to save it harmless and, at Landlord's option, defend it from and against any and all claims, actions, damages, liabilities and expenses (including attorneys' and other professional fees) judgments, settlement payments, and fines paid, incurred or suffered by Landlord in connection with loss of life, personal injury and/or damage to property or the environment suffered by third parties arising from or out of the occupancy or use by Tenant of the Premises or any part thereof or any other part of the Shopping Center, occasioned wholly or in part by any act or omission of Tenant, its officers, agents, contractors, employees or invitees, or arising, directly or indirectly, wholly or in part, from any conduct, activity, act, omission, or operation involving the use, handling, generation, treatment storage, disposal, other management or Release of any Hazardous Substance in, from or to the Premises, whether or not Tenant may have acted negligently with respect to such Hazardous Substance. Tenant's obligations pursuant to this Section shall survive any termination of this Lease with respect to any act, omission or occurrence which took place prior to such termination.

To the extent permitted by law, Landlord shall and does hereby indemnify Tenant and agrees to save it harmless from and against any and all claims, actions, damages, liabilities and expenses (including attorneys' and other professional fees) in connection with loss of life, personal injury and/or damage to property suffered by third parties arising from or out of the use of any portion of the Common Areas by Landlord, occasioned wholly or in part by any act or omission of Landlord, its officers, agents, contractors or employees.

Section 13.2 *Landlord Not Responsible for Acts of Others.*

Landlord shall not be responsible or liable to Tenant, or to those claiming by, through or under Tenant, for any loss or damage which may be occasioned by or through the acts or omissions of persons occupying space adjoining the Premises or any part of the premises adjacent to or connecting with the Premises or any other part of the Shopping Center, or otherwise, or for any loss or damage resulting to Tenant, or those claiming by, through or under Tenant, or its or their property, from the breaking, bursting, stoppage or leaking of electrical cable and wires, or water, gas, sewer or steam pipes. To the maximum extent permitted by law, Tenant agrees to use and occupy the Premises, and to use such other portions of the Shopping Center as Tenant is herein given the right to use, at Tenant's own risk.

Section 13.3 *Tenant's Insurance.*

At all times after the execution of this Lease, Tenant will carry and maintain, at its expense, a non-deductible:

(a) commercial (comprehensive) liability insurance policy, including (but not limited to) insurance against assumed or contractual liability under this Lease, with respect to liability arising out of the ownership, use, occupancy or maintenance of the Premises and all areas appurtenant thereto, to afford protection with respect to personal injury, death or property damage of not less than Two Million Dollars ($2,000,000) per occurrence combined single limit/Four Million Dollars ($4,000,000) general aggregate (but not less than $2,000,000 per location aggregate); and

(b) all-risks property and casualty insurance policy, including theft coverage, written at replacement cost value and with replacement cost endorsement, covering all of Tenant's personal property in the Premises (including, without limitation, inventory, trade fixtures, floor coverings, furniture and other property removable by Tenant under the provisions of this Lease) and all leasehold improvements installed in the Premises by or on behalf of Tenant; and

(c) comprehensive boiler and machinery equipment policy, including electrical apparatus, if applicable; and

(d) if and to the extent required by law, worker's compensation insurance policy, or similar insurance in form and amounts required by law.

Section 13.4 *Tenant's Contractor's Insurance.*

Tenant shall require any contractor of Tenant performing work on the Premises to carry and maintain, at no expense to Landlord, a non-deductible:

(a) commercial (comprehensive) liability insurance policy, including (but not limited to) contractor's liability coverage, contractual liability coverage, completed operations coverage, broad form property damage endorsement and contractor's protective liability coverage, to afford protection, with respect to personal injury, death or property damage of not less than Three Million

Dollars ($3,000,000) per occurrence combined single limit/Five Million Dollars ($5,000,000) general aggregate (but not less than $3,000,000 per location aggregate);

(b) comprehensive automobile liability insurance policy with limits for each occurrence of not less than One Million Dollars ($1,000,000) with respect to personal injury or death and Five Hundred Thousand Dollars ($500,000) with respect to property damage; and

(c) worker's compensation insurance policy or similar insurance in form and amounts required by law.

Section 13.5 *Policy Requirements.*

The company or companies writing any insurance which Tenant is required to carry and maintain or cause to be carried or maintained pursuant to Sections 13.3 and 13.4, as well as the form of such insurance, shall at all times be subject to Landlord's approval and any such company or companies shall be licensed to do business in the State in which the Shopping Center is located. Comprehensive commercial liability and all-risks property and casualty insurance policies evidencing such insurance shall, with respect to comprehensive commercial liability policies, name Landlord and/or its designee(s) as additional insured and, with respect to all-risks property and casualty insurance policies, name Landlord and/or its designee(s) as loss payee, shall be primary and non-contributory, and shall also contain a provision by which the insurer agrees that such policy shall not be cancelled, materially changed or not renewed without at least thirty (30) days' advance notice to Landlord, Attention: Risk Manager, by certified mail, return receipt requested, or to such other party or address as may be designated by Landlord or its designee. Each such policy, or a certificate thereof, shall be deposited with Landlord by Tenant promptly upon commencement of Tenant's obligation to procure the same. If Tenant shall fail to perform any of its obligations under Sections 13.3, 13.4 or 13.5, Landlord may perform the same and the cost of same shall be deemed Additional Rental and shall be payable upon Landlord's demand.

Section 13.6 *Increase in Insurance Premiums.*

Tenant will not do or suffer to be done, or keep or suffer to be kept, anything in, upon or about the Premises which will violate Landlord's policies of hazard or liability insurance or which will prevent Landlord from procuring such policies in companies acceptable to Landlord. If anything done, omitted to be done or suffered by Tenant to be kept in, upon or about the Premises shall cause the rate of fire or other insurance on the Premises or on other property of Landlord or of others within the Shopping Center to be increased beyond the minimum rate from time to time applicable to the Premises or to any such property for the use or uses made thereof, Tenant will pay, as Additional Rental, the amount of any such increase upon Landlord's demand.

Section 13.7 *Waiver of Right of Recovery.*

Except as provided in Section 8.6, neither Landlord nor Tenant shall be liable to the other or to any insurance company (by way of subrogation or otherwise) insuring the other party for any loss or damage to any building, structure or other tangible property, or any resulting loss of income, or losses under worker's compensation laws and benefits, even though such loss or damage might have been occasioned by the negligence of such party, its agents or employees. The provisions of this Section 13.7 shall not limit the indemnification for liability to third parties pursuant to Section 13.1.

Section 13.8 *Tenant to Pay Proportionate Share of Insurance Costs.*

Tenant will pay Landlord, as Additional Rental, a proportionate share of Landlord's cost of maintaining all insurance with respect to Landlord's Building (other than the Common Areas) including, without limitation, all-risks property and casualty insurance and rent insurance. Such insurance may be carried at the discretion of Landlord in such amounts and companies as Landlord shall determine.

Tenant's proportionate share of such costs shall be computed by multiplying Landlord's insurance costs by a fraction, the numerator of which shall be Tenant's Floor Area and the denominator of which shall be Landlord's Floor Area. Such proportionate share shall be paid by Tenant in monthly installments in such amounts as are estimated and billed by Landlord during each twelve (12) month period commencing and ending on dates designated by Landlord, each installment being due on the first day of each calendar month. At any time during any such twelve (12) month period, Landlord may reestimate Tenant's proportionate share of Landlord's insurance costs and thereafter adjust Tenant's monthly installments payable during such twelve (12) month period to reflect more accurately Tenant's proportionate share of such costs. Within one hundred twenty (120) days (or such additional time thereafter as is reasonable under the circumstances) after the end of each such twelve (12) month period, Landlord shall deliver to Tenant a statement of such insurance costs for such twelve (12) month period and the installments paid or payable shall be adjusted between Landlord and Tenant, and Tenant shall pay Landlord or Landlord shall credit to Tenant's account (or, if such adjustment is at the end of the Term) Landlord shall pay Tenant, as the case may be, within fifteen (15) days of receipt of such statement, such amounts as may be necessary to effect such adjustment. Upon reasonable notice, Landlord shall make available for Tenant's inspection at Landlord's office, during normal business hours, Landlord's records relating to such insurance costs for such preceding twelve (12) month period. Failure of Landlord to provide the statement called for hereunder within the time prescribed shall not relieve Tenant of its obligations hereunder.

ARTICLE XIV
DAMAGE AND DESTRUCTION

Section 14.1 *Landlord's Obligation to Repair and Reconstruct.*

If the Premises shall be damaged by fire, the elements, accident or other casualty (any of such causes being referred to herein as a "Casualty"), but the Premises shall not be thereby rendered wholly or partially untenantable, Landlord shall promptly cause such damage to be repaired and there shall be no abatement of Rental. If, as the result of Casualty, the Premises shall be rendered wholly or partially untenantable, then, subject to the provisions of Section 14.2, Landlord shall cause such damage to be repaired and all Rental (other than any Additional Rental due Landlord by reason of Tenant's failure to perform any of its obligations hereunder) shall be abated proportionately as to the portion of the Premises rendered untenantable during the period of such untenantability, and, in addition, during such period of untenantability, the Breakpoint shall also be proportionately reduced by an amount equal to the amount obtained by multiplying the Breakpoint by a fraction, the numerator of which shall be the length of time the Premises are closed and the denominator of which shall be the length of the Rental Year(s) in question. All such repairs shall be made at the expense of Landlord; provided, however, that Landlord shall not be liable for interruption to Tenant's business or for damage to or replacement or repair of Tenant's personal property (including, without limitation, inventory, trade fixtures, floor coverings, furniture and other property removable by Tenant under the provisions of this Lease) or to any leasehold improvements installed in the Premises by or on behalf of Tenant, all of which damage, replacement or repair shall be undertaken and completed by Tenant promptly.

Section 14.2 *Landlord's Option to Terminate Lease.*

If the Premises are (a) rendered wholly untenantable, or (b) damaged as a result of any cause which is not covered by Landlord's insurance or (c) damaged or destroyed in whole or in part during the last three (3) years of the Term, or if Landlord's Building is damaged to the extent of fifty percent (50%) or more of Landlord's Floor Area, then, in any of such events, Landlord may elect to terminate this Lease by giving to Tenant notice of such election within ninety (90) days after the occurrence of such event. If such notice is given, the rights and obligations of the parties shall cease as of the date of such notice, and Rental (other than any Additional Rental due Landlord by reason of Tenant's failure to perform any of its obligations hereunder) shall be adjusted as of the date of such termination.

Section 14.3 *Demolition of Landlord's Building.*

If Landlord's Building shall be so substantially damaged that it is reasonably necessary, in Landlord's sole judgment, to demolish same for the purpose of reconstruction, Landlord may demolish the same, in which event the Rental shall be abated to the same extent as if the Premises were rendered untenantable by a Casualty.

Section 14.4 *Insurance Proceeds.*

If Landlord does not elect to terminate this Lease pursuant to Section 14.2, Landlord shall, subject to the prior rights of any Mortgagee, disburse and apply any insurance proceeds received by Landlord to the restoration and rebuilding of Landlord's Building in accordance with Section 14.1 hereof. All insurance proceeds payable with respect to the Premises (excluding proceeds payable to Tenant pursuant to Section 13.3) shall belong to and shall be payable to Landlord.

ARTICLE XV
CONDEMNATION

Section 15.1 *Effect of Taking.*

If the whole or any part of the Premises shall be taken under the power of eminent domain, this Lease shall terminate as to the part so taken on the date Tenant is required to yield possession thereof to the condemning authority. Landlord shall make, or cause to be made, such repairs and alterations as may be necessary in order to restore the part not taken to useful condition and all Rental (other than any Additional Rental due Landlord by reason of Tenant's failure to perform any of its obligations hereunder) shall be reduced in the same proportion as the portion of the floor area of the Premises so taken bears to Tenant's Floor Area. If the aforementioned taking renders the remainder of the Premises unsuitable for the Permitted Use, either party may terminate this Lease as of the date when Tenant is required to yield possession by giving notice to that effect within thirty (30) days after such date. If twenty percent (20%) or more of Landlord's Floor Area is taken as aforesaid, or if parking spaces in the Shopping Center are so taken thereby reducing the number of parking spaces to less than the number required by law and Landlord does not deem it reasonably feasible to replace such parking spaces with other parking spaces on the portion of the Shopping Center not taken, then Landlord may elect to terminate this Lease as of the date on which possession thereof is required to be yielded to the condemning authority, by giving notice of such election within ninety (90) days after such date. If any notice of termination is given pursuant to this Section, this Lease and the rights and obligations of the parties hereunder shall cease as of the date of such notice and Rental (other than any Additional Rental due Landlord by reason of Tenant's failure to perform any of its obligations hereunder) shall be adjusted as of the date of such termination.

Section 15.2 *Condemnation Awards.*

All compensation awarded for any taking of the Premises, Landlord's Building, the Shopping Center Area, or any interest in any of the same, shall belong to and be the property of Landlord, Tenant hereby assigning to Landlord all rights with respect thereto; provided, however, nothing contained herein shall prevent Tenant from applying for reimbursement from the condemning authority (if permitted by law) for moving expenses, or the expense of removal of Tenant's trade fixtures, or loss of Tenant's business good will, but only if such action shall not reduce the amount of the award or other compensation otherwise recoverable from the condemning authority by Landlord or the owner of the fee simple estate in the Shopping Center Area.

ARTICLE XVI

ASSIGNMENTS AND SUBLETTING

Section 16.1 *Landlord's Consent Required.*

(a) Except as provided in Section 17.4 with respect to assignment of this Lease following Tenant's bankruptcy, Tenant will not assign this Lease, in whole or in part, nor sublet all or any part of the Premises, nor license concessions or lease departments therein, nor pledge or encumber by mortgage or other instruments its interest in this Lease (each individually and collectively referred to in this Section as a "transfer") without first obtaining the consent of Landlord, which consent Landlord may withhold in its sole and absolute discretion. This prohibition includes, without limitation, any subletting or assignment which would otherwise occur by operation of law, merger, consolidation, reorganization, transfer or other change of Tenant's corporate, partnership or proprietary structure. Any transfer to or by a receiver or trustee in any federal or state bankruptcy, insolvency, or similar proceeding shall be subject to, and in accordance with, the provisions of Section 17.4. Consent by Landlord to any transfer shall not constitute a waiver of the requirement for such consent to any subsequent transfer.

(b) Subject to the provisions of Section 17.4 respecting assignment of this Lease following Tenant's bankruptcy and assumption of this Lease by Tenant or its trustee, it is expressly understood and agreed that Landlord may, in its sole and absolute discretion, withhold its consent to any transfer of this Lease or of all or any part of the Premises. The parties recognize that this Lease and the Premises are unique, and that this Lease and the Premises derive value from the remainder of Landlord's Building and the Shopping Center Area as a whole, and that the nature and character of the operations within and management of the Premises are important to the success of Landlord's Building and the Shopping Center Area. Accordingly, and without limiting the generality of the foregoing, Landlord may condition its consent to any transfer upon satisfaction of all or any of the following conditions:

(i) the net assets of the assignee, licensee, sublessee or other transferee or permittee (collectively "transferee") immediately prior to the transfer shall not be less than the greater of the net assets of Tenant immediately prior to the transfer or the net assets of Tenant at the time of the signing of this Lease;

(ii) such transfer shall not adversely affect the quality and type of business operation which Tenant has conducted theretofore;

(iii) such transferee shall possess qualifications for the Tenant business substantially equivalent to those of Tenant and shall have demonstrated recognized experience in successfully operating such a business, including, without limitation, experience in successfully operating a similar quality business in first-class shopping centers;

(iv) such transferee shall continue to operate the business conducted in the Premises under the same Tenant Trade Name, in the same manner as Tenant and pursuant to all of the provisions of this Lease;

(v) such transferee shall assume in writing, in a form acceptable to Landlord, all of Tenant's obligations hereunder and Tenant shall provide Landlord with a copy of such assumption/transfer document;

(vi) Tenant shall pay to Landlord a transfer fee of One Thousand Dollars ($1,000.00) prior to the effective date of the transfer in order to reimburse Landlord for all of its internal costs and expenses incurred with respect to the transfer, including, without limitation, costs incurred in connection with the review of financial materials, meetings with representatives of transferor and/or transferee and preparation, review, approval and execution of the required transfer documentation, and, in addition, Tenant shall reimburse Landlord for any out-of-pocket costs and expenses incurred with respect to such transfer;

(vii) as of the effective date of the transfer and continuing throughout the remainder of the Term, the Annual Basic Rental shall be the greater of (A) the Annual Basic Rental set forth in Section 1.1.G hereof, or (B) the sum of all Annual Basic Rental and all Annual Percentage Rental payable by Tenant during the twelve calendar months preceding the transfer;

(viii) Tenant to which the Premises were initially leased shall continue to remain liable under this Lease for the performance of all terms, including, but not limited to, payment of Rental due under this Lease;

(ix) Tenant's guarantor, if any, shall continue to remain liable under the terms of the Guaranty of this Lease and, if Landlord deems it necessary, such guarantor shall execute such documents necessary to insure the continuation of its guaranty;

(x) Landlord shall receive upon execution of its consent the full unamortized amount of any construction or other allowances given to the original Tenant under this Lease, any due but unpaid Rental, and an amount equal to fifteen percent (15%) of any and all consideration paid or agreed to be paid, directly or indirectly, to Tenant for such transfer or for the sale of Tenant's business in connection with which any such transfer is made; and

(xi) each of Landlord's Mortgagees shall have consented in writing to such transfer.

Section 16.2 *Transfer of Corporate Shares.*

If Tenant is a corporation (other than a corporation the outstanding voting stock of which is listed on a "national securities exchange," as defined in the Securities Exchange Act of 1934) and if at any time after execution of this Lease any part or all of the corporate shares shall be transferred by sale, assignment, bequest, inheritance, operation of law or other disposition (including, but not limited to, such a transfer to or by a receiver or trustee in federal or state bankruptcy, insolvency, or other proceedings) so as to result in a change in the present control of said corporation by the person(s) now owning a majority of said corporate shares, Tenant shall give Landlord notice of such event within fifteen (15) days of the date of such transfer. If any such transfer is made (and regardless of whether Tenant has given notice of same), Landlord may elect to terminate this Lease at any time thereafter by giving Tenant notice of such election, in which event this Lease and the rights and obligations of the parties hereunder shall cease as of a date set forth in such notice which date shall not be less than sixty (60) days after the date of such notice. In the event of any such termination, all Rental (other than any Additional Rental due Landlord by reason of Tenant's failure to perform any of its obligations hereunder) shall be adjusted as of the date of such termination.

Section 16.3 *Transfer of Partnership Interests.*

If Tenant is a general or limited partnership and if at any time after execution of this Lease any part or all of the interests in the capital or profits of such partnership or any voting or other interests therein shall be transferred by sale, assignment, bequest, inheritance, operation of law or other disposition (including, but not limited to, such a transfer to or by a receiver or trustee in federal or state bankruptcy, insolvency or other proceedings, and also including, but not limited to, any adjustment in such partnership interests) so as to result in a change in the present control of said partnership by the person or persons now having control of same, Tenant shall give Landlord notice of such event within fifteen (15) days of the date of such transfer. If any such transfer is made (and regardless of whether Tenant has given notice of same), Landlord may elect to terminate this Lease at any time thereafter by giving Tenant notice of such election, in which event this Lease and the rights and obligations of the parties hereunder shall cease as of a date set forth in such notice which date shall be not less than sixty (60) days after the date of such notice. In the event of any such termination, all Rental (other than any Additional Rental due Landlord by reason of Tenant's failure to perform any of its obligations hereunder) shall be adjusted as of the date of such termination.

Section 16.4 *Acceptance of Rent from Transferee.*

The acceptance by Landlord of the payment of Rental following any assignment or other transfer prohibited by this Article shall not be deemed to be a consent by Landlord to any such assignment or other transfer nor shall the same be deemed to be a waiver of any right or remedy of Landlord hereunder.

Section 16.5 *Additional Provisions Respecting Transfers.*

Without limiting Landlord's right to withhold its consent to any transfer by Tenant, and regardless of whether Landlord shall have consented to any such transfer, neither Tenant nor any other person having an interest in the possession, use or occupancy of the Premises or any part thereof shall enter into any lease, sublease, license, concession, assignment or other transfer or agreement for possession, use or occupancy of all or any portion of the Premises which provides for rental or other payment for such use, occupancy or utilization based, in whole or in part, on the net income or profits derived by any person or entity from the space so leased, used or occupied, and any such purported lease, sublease, license, concession, assignment or other transfer or agreement shall be absolutely void and ineffective as a conveyance of any right or interest in the possession, use or occupancy of all or any part of the Premises. There shall be no deduction from the rental payable under any sublease or other transfer nor from the amount thereof passed on to any person or entity, for any expenses or costs related in any way to the subleasing or transfer of such space.

If Tenant shall make or suffer any such transfer without first obtaining any consent of Landlord required by Section 16.1, any and all amounts received as a result of such transfer shall be the property of Landlord to the extent the same (determined on a square foot basis) is greater than the Annual Basic Rental (on a square foot basis) payable under this Lease, it being the parties' intent that any profit resulting from such transfer shall belong to Landlord, but the same shall not be deemed to be a consent by Landlord to any such transfer or a waiver of any right or remedy of Landlord hereunder.

ARTICLE XVII
DEFAULT

Section 17.1 *"Event of Default" Defined.*

Any one or more of the following events shall constitute an "Event of Default":

(a) The sale of Tenant's interest in the Premises under attachment, execution or similar legal process, or if Tenant is adjudicated as bankrupt or insolvent under any state bankruptcy or insolvency law or an order for relief is entered against Tenant under the Federal Bankruptcy Code and such adjudication or order is not vacated within ten (10) days.

(b) The commencement of a case under any chapter of the Federal Bankruptcy Code by or against Tenant or any guarantor of Tenant's obligations hereunder, or the filing of a voluntary or involuntary petition proposing the adjudication of Tenant or any such guarantor as bankrupt or insolvent, or the reorganization of Tenant or any such guarantor, or an arrangement by Tenant or any such guarantor with its creditors, unless the petition is filed or case commenced by a party other than Tenant or any such guarantor and is withdrawn or dismissed within thirty (30) days after the date of its filing.

(c) The admission in writing by Tenant or any such guarantor of its inability to pay its debts when due;

(d) The appointment of a receiver or trustee for the business or property of Tenant or any such guarantor, unless such appointment shall be vacated within ten (10) days of its entry.

(e) The making by Tenant or any such guarantor of an assignment for the benefit of its creditors, or if in any other manner Tenant's interest in this Lease shall pass to another by operation of law.

(f) The failure of Tenant to pay any Rental or other sum of money within seven (7) days after the same is due hereunder.

(g) Default by Tenant in the performance or observance of any covenant or agreement of this Lease (other than a default involving the payment of money), which default is not cured within ten (10) days after the giving of notice thereof by Landlord, unless such default is of such nature that it cannot be cured within such ten (10) day period, in which case no Event of Default shall occur so long as Tenant shall commence the curing of the default within such ten (10) day period and shall thereafter diligently prosecute the curing of same; provided, however, if Tenant shall default in the performance of any such covenant or agreement of this Lease two (2) or more times in any twelve (12) month period, then notwithstanding that each of such defaults shall have been cured by Tenant, any further similar default shall be deemed an Event of Default without the ability for cure.

(h) The vacation or abandonment of the Premises by Tenant at any time following delivery of possession of the Premises to Tenant.

(i) The occurrence of any other event described as constituting an "Event of Default" elsewhere in this Lease.

Section 17.2 *Remedies.*

Upon the occurrence of an Event of Default, Landlord, without notice to Tenant in any instance (except where expressly provided for below or by applicable law) may do any one or more of the following:

(a) With or without judicial process, enter the Premises and take possession of any and all goods, inventory, equipment, fixtures and all other personal property of Tenant, which is or may be put into the Premises during the Term, whether exempt or not from sale under execution or attachment (it being agreed that said property shall at all times be bound with a lien in favor of Landlord and shall be chargeable for all Rental and for the fulfillment of the other covenants and agreements herein contained), and Landlord may sell all or any part thereof at public or private sale. Tenant agrees that five (5) days prior notice of any public or private sale shall constitute reasonable notice. The proceeds of any such sale shall be applied, first, to the payment of all costs and expenses of conducting the sale or caring for or storing said property (including reasonable attorneys' fees); second, toward the payment of any indebtedness, including (without limitation) indebtedness for Rental, which may be or may become due from Tenant to Landlord; and third, to pay Tenant, on demand, any surplus remaining after all indebtedness of Tenant to Landlord has been fully paid;

(b) Perform, on behalf and at the expense of Tenant, any obligation of Tenant under this Lease which Tenant has failed to perform and of which Landlord shall have given Tenant notice, the cost of which performance by

Landlord, together with interest thereon at the Default Rate from the date of such expenditure, shall be deemed Additional Rental and shall be payable by Tenant to Landlord upon demand. Notwithstanding the provisions of this clause (b) and regardless of whether an Event of Default shall have occurred, Landlord may exercise the remedy described in this clause (b) without any notice to Tenant if Landlord, in its good faith judgment, believes it would be materially injured by failure to take rapid action or if the unperformed obligation of Tenant constitutes an emergency;

(c) Elect to terminate this Lease and the tenancy created hereby by giving notice of such election to Tenant, and reenter the Premises, without the necessity of legal proceedings, and remove Tenant and all other persons and property from the Premises, and may store such property in a public warehouse or elsewhere at the cost of and for the account of Tenant without resort to legal process and without Landlord being deemed guilty of trespass or becoming liable for any loss or damage occasioned thereby; or

(d) Exercise any other legal or equitable right or remedy which it may have.

Any costs and expenses incurred by Landlord (including, without limitation, reasonable attorneys' fees) in enforcing any of its rights or remedies under this Lease shall be deemed to be Additional Rental and shall be repaid to Landlord by Tenant upon demand.

Section 17.3 *Damages.*

If this Lease is terminated by Landlord pursuant to Section 17.2, Tenant nevertheless shall remain liable for (a) any Rental and damages which may be due or sustained prior to such termination, all reasonable costs, fees and expenses including, but not limited to, reasonable attorneys' fees, costs and expenses incurred by Landlord in pursuit of its remedies hereunder, or in renting the Premises to others from time to time (all such Rental, damages, costs, fees and expenses being referred to herein as "Termination Damages"), and (b) additional damages (the "Liquidated Damages"), which, at the election of Landlord, shall be either:

(i) an amount equal to the Rental which, but for termination of this Lease, would have become due during the remainder of the Term, less the amount of Rental, if any, which Landlord shall receive during such period from others to whom the Premises may be rented (other than any Additional Rental received by Landlord as a result of any failure of such other person to perform any of its obligations to Landlord), in which case such Liquidated Damages shall be computed and payable in monthly installments, in advance, on the first day of each calendar month following termination of the Lease and continuing until the date on which the Term would have expired but for such termination, and any suit or action brought to collect any such Liquidated Damages for any month shall not in any manner prejudice the right of Landlord to collect any Liquidated Damages for any subsequent month by a similar proceeding; or

(ii) an amount equal to the present worth (as of the date of such termination) of Rental which, but for termination of this Lease, would have become due during the remainder of the Term, less the fair rental value of the Premises, as determined by an independent real estate appraiser named by Landlord, in which case such Liquidated Damages shall be payable to Landlord in one lump sum on demand and shall bear interest at the Default Rate until paid. For purposes of this clause (ii), "present worth" shall be computed by discounting such amount to present worth at a discount rate equal to one percentage point above the discount rate then in effect at the Federal Reserve Bank nearest to the location of the Shopping Center.

If such termination shall take place after the expiration of two or more Rental Years, then, for purposes of computing the Liquidated Damages, the Annual Percentage Rental payable with respect to each Rental Year following termination (including the Rental Year in which such termination shall take place) shall be conclusively presumed to be equal to the average Annual Percentage Rental payable with respect to each complete Rental Year preceding termination. If such termination shall take place before the expiration of two Rental Years, then, for purposes of computing the Liquidated Damages, the Annual Percentage Rental payable with respect to each Rental Year following termination (including the Rental Year in which such termination shall take place) shall be conclusively presumed to be equal to twelve (12) times the average monthly payment of Annual Percentage Rental due prior to such termination, or if no Annual Percentage Rental shall have been payable during such period, then the Annual Percentage Rental for each year of the unexpired Term shall be conclusively presumed to be a sum equal to twenty-five percent (25%) of the Annual Basic Rental due and payable during such unexpired Term. Termination Damages shall be due and payable immediately upon demand by Landlord following any termination of this Lease pursuant to Section 17.2. Liquidated Damages shall be due and payable at the times set forth herein.

If this Lease is terminated pursuant to Section 17.2, Landlord may relet the Premises or any part thereof, alone or together with other premises, for such term or terms (which may be greater or less than the period which otherwise would have constituted the balance of the Term) and on such terms and conditions (which may include concessions or free rent and alterations of the Premises) as Landlord, in its sole discretion, may determine, but Landlord shall not be liable for, nor shall Tenant's obligations hereunder be diminished by reason of, any failure by Landlord to relet the Premises or any failure by Landlord to collect any rent due upon such reletting.

Nothing contained in this Lease shall limit or prejudice the right of Landlord to prove for and obtain, in proceedings for the termination of this Lease by reason of bankruptcy or insolvency, an amount equal to the maximum allowed by any statute or rule of law in effect at the time when, and governing the proceedings in which, the damages are to be proved, whether or not the amount be greater, equal to, or less than the amount of the loss or damages referred to above. The failure or refusal of Landlord to relet the Premises or any part or parts thereof shall not release or affect Tenant's liability for damages.

Section 17.4 *Remedies in Event of Bankruptcy or Other Proceeding.*

(a) Anything contained herein to the contrary notwithstanding, if termination of this Lease shall be stayed by order of any court having jurisdiction over any proceeding described in paragraph (b) of Section 17.1, or by federal or state statute, then, following the expiration of any such stay, or if Tenant or Tenant as debtor-in-possession or the trustee appointed in any such proceeding (being collectively referred to as "Tenant" only for the purposes of this Section 17.4) shall fail to assume Tenant's obligations under this Lease within the period prescribed therefor by law or within fifteen (15) days after entry of the order for relief or as may be allowed by the court, or if Tenant shall fail to provide adequate protection of Landlord's right, title and interest in and to the Premises or adequate assurance of the complete and continuous future performance of Tenant's obligations under this Lease, Landlord, to the extent permitted by law or by leave of the court having jurisdiction over such proceeding, shall have the right, at its election, to terminate this Lease on fifteen (15) days' notice to Tenant and upon the expiration of said fifteen (15) day period this Lease shall cease and expire as aforesaid and Tenant shall immediately quit and surrender the Premises as aforesaid. Upon the termination of this Lease as provided above, Landlord, without notice, may re-enter and repossess the Premises using such force for that purpose as may be necessary without being liable to indictment, prosecution or damages therefor and may dispossess Tenant by summary proceedings or otherwise.

(b) For the purposes of the preceding paragraph (a), adequate protection of Landlord's right, title and interest in and to the Premises, and adequate assurance of the complete and continuous future performance of Tenant's obligations under this Lease, shall include, without limitation, the following requirements:

(i) that Tenant comply with all of its obligations under this Lease;

(ii) that Tenant pay to Landlord, on the first day of each month occurring subsequent to the entry of such order, or the effective date of such stay, a sum equal to the amount by which the Premises diminished in value during the immediately preceding monthly period, but, in no event, an amount which is less than the aggregate Rental payable for such monthly period;

(iii) that Tenant continue to use the Premises in the manner originally required by this Lease;

(iv) that Landlord be permitted to supervise the performance of Tenant's obligations under this Lease;

(v) that Tenant pay to Landlord within fifteen (15) days after entry of such order or the effective date of such stay, as partial adequate protection against future diminution in value of the Premises and adequate assurance of the complete and continuous future performance of Tenant's obligations under this Lease, an additional security deposit in an amount acceptable to Landlord;

(vi) that Tenant has and will continue to have unencumbered assets after the payment of all secured obligations and administrative expenses to assure Landlord that sufficient funds will be available to fulfill the obligations of Tenant under this Lease;

(vii) that if Tenant assumes this Lease and proposes to assign the same (pursuant to Title 11 U.S.C. § 365, or as the same may be amended) to any person who shall have made a bona fide offer to accept an assignment of this Lease on terms acceptable to such court having competent jurisdiction over Tenant's estate, then notice of such proposed assignment, setting forth (x) the name and address of such person, (y) all of the terms and conditions of such offer, and (z) the adequate assurance to be provided Landlord to assure such person's future performance under this Lease, including, without limitation, the assurances referred to in Title 11 U.S.C. § 365(b)(3), as it may be amended, shall be given to Landlord by Tenant no later than fifteen (15) days after receipt by Tenant of such offer, but in any event no later than thirty (30) days prior to the date that Tenant shall make application to such court for authority and approval to enter into such assignment and assumption, and Landlord shall thereupon have the prior right and option, to be exercised by notice to Tenant given at any time prior to the effective date of such proposed assignment, to accept, or to cause Landlord's designee to accept, an assignment of this Lease upon the same terms and conditions and for the same consideration, if any, as the bona fide offer made by such person less any brokerage commissions which may be payable out of the consideration to be paid by such person for the assignment of this Lease; and

(viii) that if Tenant assumes this Lease and proposes to assign the same, and Landlord does not exercise its option pursuant to paragraph (vii) of this Section 17.4, Tenant hereby agrees that:

(A) such assignee shall have a net worth not less than the net worth of Tenant as of the Commencement Date, or such Tenant's obligations under this Lease shall be unconditionally guaranteed by a person having a net worth equal to Tenant's net worth as of the Commencement Date;

(B) such assignee shall not use the Premises except subject to all the restrictions contained in this Lease;

(C) such assignee shall assume in writing all of the terms, covenants and conditions of this Lease including, without limitation, all of such terms, covenants and conditions respecting the Permitted Use and payment of Rental, and such assignee shall provide Landlord with assurances satisfactory to Landlord that it has the experience in operating stores having the same or substantially similar uses as the Permitted Use, in first-class shopping centers, sufficient to enable it so to comply with the terms, covenants and conditions of this Lease and successfully operate the Premises for the Permitted Use;

(D) such assignee shall indemnify Landlord against, and pay to Landlord the amount of, any payments which Landlord may be obligated to make to any Mortgagee by virtue of such assignment;

(E) such assignee shall pay to Landlord an amount equal to the unamortized portion of any construction allowance made to Tenant; and

(F) if such assignee makes any payment to Tenant, or for Tenant's account, for the right to assume this Lease (including, without limitation, any lump sum payment, installment payment or payment in the nature of rent over and above the Rental payable under this Lease), Tenant shall pay over to Landlord one-half of any such payment, less any amount paid to Landlord pursuant to clause (E) above on account of any construction allowance.

ARTICLE XVIII
SUBORDINATION AND ATTORNMENT

Section 18.1 *Subordination.*

Unless a Mortgagee (as hereinafter defined) shall otherwise elect as provided in Section 18.2, Tenant's rights under this Lease are and shall remain subject and subordinate to the operation and effect of

(a) any lease of land only or of land and buildings in a sale-leaseback or lease-subleaseback transaction involving the Premises or Landlord's interest therein, or

(b) any mortgage, deed of trust or other security instrument constituting a lien upon the Premises or Landlord's interest therein,

whether the same shall be in existence at the date hereof or created hereafter, any such lease, mortgage, deed of trust or other security instrument being referred to herein as a "Mortgage", and the party or parties having the benefit of the same, whether as lessor, mortgagee, trustee or noteholder, being referred to herein as a "Mortgagee". Tenant's acknowledgment and agreement of subordination provided for in this Section are self-operative and no further instrument of subordination shall be required; however, Tenant shall execute such further assurances thereof as shall be requisite or as may be requested from time to time by Landlord or any Mortgagee.

Section 18.2 *Mortgagee's Unilateral Subordination.*

If a Mortgagee shall so elect by notice to Tenant or by the recording of a unilateral declaration of subordination, this Lease and Tenant's rights hereunder shall be superior and prior in right to the Mortgage of which such Mortgagee has the benefit, with the same force and effect as if this Lease had been executed, delivered and recorded prior to the execution, delivery and recording of such Mortgage, subject, nevertheless, to such conditions as may be set forth in any such notice or declaration.

Section 18.3 *Attornment.*

If any person shall succeed to all or part of Landlord's interest in the Premises, whether by purchase, foreclosure, deed in lieu of foreclosure, power of sale, termination of lease or otherwise, and if so requested or required by such successor in interest, Tenant shall attorn to such successor in interest and shall execute such agreement in confirmation of such attornment as such successor in interest shall reasonably request.

ARTICLE XIX

NOTICES

Section 19.1 *Sending of Notices.*

Any notice, request, demand, approval or consent given or required to be given under this Lease shall be in writing and shall be deemed to have been given as follows:

(i) if intended for Landlord, on the third day following the day on which the same shall have been mailed by United States registered or certified mail or express mail, return receipt requested, with all postage charges prepaid, addressed to Landlord, Attention: _____ with a copy to Landlord's management office in the Shopping Center except that payment of Rental and sales reports shall be delivered to Landlord's management office in the Shopping Center; and

(ii) if intended for Tenant, upon the earlier to occur of the following:

(a) the third day following the day on which the same shall have been mailed by United States registered or certified mail or express mail, return receipt requested, with all postal charges prepaid, addressed to Tenant at the Tenant Notice Address, or

(b) actual receipt at the Tenant Notice Address, and in the event more than one copy of such notice shall have been sent or delivered to Tenant, the first actually received shall control for the purposes of this clause (b).

Either party may, at any time, change its address for the above purposes by sending a notice to the other party stating the change and setting forth the new address.

Section 19.2 *Notice to Mortgagees.*

If any Mortgagee shall notify Tenant that it is the holder of a Mortgage affecting the Premises, no notice, request or demand thereafter sent by Tenant to Landlord shall be effective unless and until a copy of the same shall also be sent to such Mortgagee in the manner prescribed in Section 19.1 and to such address as such Mortgagee shall designate.

ARTICLE XX

MISCELLANEOUS

Section 20.1 *Radius Restriction.*

Tenant agrees that Tenant (and if Tenant is a corporation or partnership, its officers, directors, stockholders, any affiliates or partners) shall not, directly or indirectly, operate, manage or have any interest in any other store or business (unless in operation on the date of this Lease) which is similar to or in competition with the Permitted Use on the commencement date of this Lease and for the Term of this Lease within the Restriction Area. Without limiting any of Landlord's remedies under this Lease, in the event Tenant operates, manages or has any interest in a store or business violating the provisions of this Section, then, at Landlord's option, Landlord may by notice to Tenant require Tenant to include the gross sales of such other store or business in the Gross Sales of the Premises for the purposes of calculating Annual Percentage Rental under this Lease.

Section 20.2 *Estoppel Certificates.*

At any time and from time to time, within ten (10) days after Landlord shall request the same, Tenant will execute, acknowledge and deliver to Landlord and to such Mortgagee or other party as may be designated by Landlord, a certificate in an acceptable form with respect to the matters required by such party and such other matters relating to this Lease or the status of performance of obligations of the parties hereunder as may be reasonably requested by Landlord. If Tenant fails to provide such certificate within ten (10) days after request by Landlord, Tenant shall be deemed to have approved the contents of any such certificate submitted to Tenant by Landlord and Landlord is hereby authorized to so certify.

Section 20.3 *Inspections and Access by Landlord.*

Tenant will permit Landlord, its agents, employees and contractors to enter all parts of the Premises during Tenant's business hours to inspect the same and to enforce or carry out any provision of this Lease, including, without limitation, any access necessary for the making of any repairs which are Landlord's obligation hereunder; provided, however, that, in the event of an emergency, Landlord may enter the Premises for such purposes at any time, upon such notice to Tenant, if any, as shall be feasible under the circumstances.

Section 20.4 *Memorandum of Lease.*

Neither this Lease nor a short form or memorandum thereof shall be recorded in the public records.

Section 20.5 *Remedies Cumulative.*

No reference to any specific right or remedy shall preclude Landlord from exercising any other right or from having any other remedy or from maintaining any action to which it may otherwise be entitled at law or in equity. No failure by Landlord to insist upon the strict performance of any agreement, term, covenant or condition hereof, or to exercise any right or remedy consequent upon a breach thereof, and no acceptance of full or partial rent during the continuance of any such breach, shall constitute a waiver of any such breach, agreement, term, covenant or condition. No waiver by Landlord of any breach by Tenant under this Lease or of any breach by any other tenant under any other lease of any portion of the Shopping Center shall affect or alter this Lease in any way whatsoever.

Section 20.6 *Successors and Assigns.*

This Lease and the covenants and conditions herein contained shall inure to the benefit of and be binding upon Landlord, its successors and assigns, and shall be binding upon Tenant, its successors and assigns and shall inure to the benefit of Tenant and only such assigns and subtenants of Tenant to whom the assignment of this Lease or the subletting of the Premises by Tenant has been consented to by Landlord as provided in this Lease. Upon any sale or other transfer by Landlord of its interest in the Premises and in this Lease, and the assumption by Landlord's transferee of the obligations of Landlord hereunder, Landlord shall be relieved of any obligations under this Lease accruing thereafter.

Section 20.7 *Compliance with Laws and Regulations.*

Tenant, at its sole cost and expense, shall comply, and shall cause the Premises to comply with (a) all federal, state, regional, county, municipal and other governmental statutes, laws, rules, orders, regulations and ordinances affecting any part of the Premises, or the use thereof, including, but not limited to, those which require the making of any structural, unforeseen or extraordinary changes, whether or not any such statutes, laws, rules, orders, regulations or ordinances which may be hereafter enacted involve a change of policy on the part of the governmental body enacting the same, and (b) all rules, orders and regulations of the National Fire Protection Association, Landlord's casualty insurer(s) and other applicable insurance rating organizations or other bodies exercising similar functions in connection with the prevention of fire or the correction of hazardous conditions which apply to the Premises.

Section 20.8 *Captions and Headings.*

The table of contents and the Article and Section captions and headings are for convenience of reference only and in no way shall be used to construe or modify the provisions set forth in this Lease.

Section 20.9 *Joint and Several Liability.*

If two or more individuals, corporations, partnerships or other business associations (or any combination of two or more thereof) shall sign this Lease as Tenant, the liability of each such individual, corporation, partnership or other business association to pay rent and perform all other obligations hereunder shall be deemed to be joint and several and all notices, payments and agreements given or made by, with or to any one of such individuals, corporations, partnerships or other business associations shall be deemed to have been given or made by, with or to all of them. In like manner, if Tenant shall be a partnership or other business association, the members of which are, by virtue of statute or federal law, subject to personal liability, the liability of each such member shall be joint and several.

Section 20.10 *Broker's Commission.*

Each of the parties represents and warrants that there are no claims for brokerage commissions or finders' fees in connection with the execution of this Lease, and agrees to indemnify the other against, and hold it harmless from, all liability arising from any such claim including, without limitation, the cost of counsel fees in connection therewith.

Section 20.11 *No Discrimination.*

It is intended that the Shopping Center shall be developed so that all prospective tenants thereof, and all customers, employees, licensees and invitees of all tenants shall have the opportunity to obtain all the goods, services, accommodations, advantages, facilities and privileges of the Shopping Center without discrimination because of race, creed, color, sex, age, national origin or ancestry. To that end, Tenant shall not discriminate in the conduct and operation of its business in the Premises against any person or group of persons because of the race, creed, color, sex, age, national origin or ancestry of such person or group of persons.

Section 20.12 *No Joint Venture.*

Any intention to create a joint venture or partnership relation between the parties hereto is hereby expressly disclaimed. The provisions of this Lease in regard to the payment by Tenant and the acceptance by Landlord of a percentage of Gross Sales of Tenant and others is a reservation for rent for the use of the Premises.

Section 20.13 *No Option.*

The submission of this Lease for examination does not constitute a reservation of or option for the Premises, and this Lease shall become effective only upon execution and delivery thereof by both parties. Execution by signature of an authorized officer of Landlord or any corporate entity acting on behalf of Landlord shall be effective only upon attestation thereof and the affixation of the seal of such corporation by a corporate Secretary or Assistant Secretary of Landlord.

Section 20.14 *No Modification.*

This writing is intended by the parties as a final expression of their agreement and as a complete and exclusive statement of the terms thereof, all negotiations, considerations and representations between the parties having been incorporated herein. No course of prior dealings between the parties or their officers, employees, agents or affiliates shall be relevant or admissible to supplement, explain or vary any of the terms of this Lease. Acceptance of, or acquiescence in, a course of performance rendered under this or any prior agreement between the parties or their affiliates shall not be relevant or admissible to determine the meaning of any of the terms of this Lease. No representations, understandings or agreements have been made or relied upon in the making of this Lease other than those specifically set forth herein. This Lease can be modified only by a writing signed by the party against whom the modification is enforceable.

Section 20.15 *Severability.*

If any portion of any term or provision of this Lease, or the application thereof to any person or circumstances shall, to any extent, be invalid or unenforceable, the remainder of this Lease, or the application of such term or provision to persons or circumstances other than those as to which it is held invalid or unenforceable, shall not be affected thereby, and each term and provision of this Lease shall be valid and be enforced to the fullest extent permitted by law.

Section 20.16 *Third Party Beneficiary.*

Nothing contained in this Lease shall be construed so as to confer upon any other party the rights of a third party beneficiary except rights contained herein for the benefit of a Mortgagee.

Section 20.17 *Corporate Tenants.*

If Tenant is a corporation, the persons executing this Lease on behalf of Tenant hereby covenant and warrant that: Tenant is a duly constituted corporation qualified to do business in the State in which the Shopping Center is located; all Tenant's franchises and corporate taxes have been paid to date; all future forms, reports, fees and other documents necessary for Tenant to comply with applicable laws will be filed by Tenant when due; and such persons are duly authorized by the board of directors of such corporation to execute and deliver this Lease on behalf of the corporation.

Section 20.18 *Applicable Law.*

This Lease and the rights and obligations of the parties hereunder shall be construed in accordance with the laws of the State in which the Shopping Center is located.

Section 20.19 *Performance of Landlord's Obligations by Mortgagee.*

Tenant shall accept performance of any of Landlord's obligations hereunder by any Mortgagee of Landlord.

Section 20.20 *Waiver of Certain Rights.*

Landlord and Tenant hereby mutually waive any and all rights which either may have to request a jury trial in any action, proceeding or counterclaim (except for those involving personal injury or property damage) arising out of this Lease or Tenant's occupancy of or right to occupy the Premises.

Tenant further agrees that in the event Landlord commences any summary proceeding for non-payment of rent or possession of the Premises, Tenant will not interpose and hereby waives all right to interpose any counterclaim of whatever nature in any such proceeding. Tenant further waives any right to remove said summary proceeding to any other court or to consolidate said summary proceeding with any other action, whether brought prior or subsequent to the summary proceeding.

Section 20.21 *Limitation on Right of Recovery Against Landlord.*

Tenant acknowledges and agrees that the liability of Landlord under this Lease shall be limited to its interest in the Shopping Center Area and any judgments rendered against Landlord shall be satisfied solely out of the proceeds of sale of its interest in the Shopping Center Area. No personal judgment shall lie against Landlord upon extinguishment of its rights in the Shopping Center Area and any judgment so rendered shall not give rise to any right of execution or levy against Landlord's assets. The provisions hereof shall inure to Landlord's successors and assigns including any Mortgagee. The foregoing provisions are not intended to relieve Landlord from the performance of any of Landlord's obligations under this Lease, but only to limit the personal liability of Landlord in case of recovery of a judgment against Landlord; nor shall the foregoing be deemed to limit Tenant's rights to obtain injunctive relief or specific performance or to avail itself of any other right or remedy which may be awarded Tenant by law or under this Lease.

If Tenant claims or asserts that Landlord has violated or failed to perform a covenant of Landlord not to unreasonably withhold or delay Landlord's consent or approval, Tenant's sole remedy shall be an action for specific performance, declaratory judgment or injunction and in no event shall Tenant be entitled to any money damages for a breach of such covenant and in no event shall Tenant claim or assert any claim for any money damages in any action or by way of set off, defense or counterclaim and Tenant hereby specifically waives the right to any money damages or other remedies.

Section 20.22 *Survival.*

All representations, warranties, covenants, conditions and agreements contained herein which either are expressed as surviving the expiration or termination of this Lease or, by their nature, are to be performed or observed, in whole or in part, after the termination or expiration of this Lease, including (without limitation) the obligations of Tenant pursuant to Sections 8.6 and 13.1, shall survive the termination or expiration of this Lease.

Section 20.23 *Relocation of Premises.*

In the event of an expansion, renovation or remerchandising of the Shopping Center in the vicinity of the Premises, Landlord may elect, by giving notice of such election to Tenant, to require Tenant to surrender possession of all or such portion of the Premises and for such period of time (including the remainder of the Term) as Landlord, in its sole discretion, shall deem to be required for such purposes. Such election shall be exercised not more than once during the Term, except that if any such notice of election shall be withdrawn by Landlord, the same shall be deemed not to have been given. Landlord's notice of the exercise of such election shall designate (i) the portion of the Premises required for such purposes, (ii) the period of time during which such surrender shall be required, and (iii) the date by which possession of same shall be surrendered by Tenant, which date shall not be earlier than ninety (90) days after the date on which such notice is given.

If Tenant shall be required to surrender possession of all or a portion of the Premises for a period of time which is less than the remainder of the Term, Rental shall abate as to such portion or all of the Premises required to be surrendered, such abatement to be effective beginning as of the date Tenant is required to surrender such possession and continuing until the date on which Landlord redelivers possession to Tenant. For purposes of determining the extent of such abatement of Rental, Tenant's Floor Area hereunder shall be deemed to be reduced during the abatement period by the number of square feet contained in the portion of the Premises of which possession is required to be surrendered.

If Tenant shall be required to surrender possession of a portion of the Premises for the entire remainder of the Term, this Lease shall terminate as to such portion as of the date on which Tenant is required to surrender possession thereof to Landlord and all Rental shall be proportionately reduced. For purposes of determining the extent of such reduction of Rental, Tenant's Floor Area hereunder shall be deemed to be reduced as of the date of such termination by the number of square feet contained in the portion of the Premises of which possession is required to be surrendered.

If Tenant shall be required to surrender possession of a portion of the Premises, Landlord shall (a) provide any permanent or temporary barriers required by the nature of Landlord's use of such portion, which barriers shall be constructed in such a manner so as to not materially interfere with Tenant's business operations in the Premises; and (b) make such alterations as may be necessary in order to restore the remainder of the Premises to useful condition.

If Tenant shall be required to surrender possession of a portion of the Premises and the remainder of the Premises shall be rendered unsuitable for the Permitted Use, or if Tenant shall be required to surrender possession of the entire Premises, Landlord shall have the further right and option to cause Tenant to relocate its business, within ninety (90) days after notice to do so, to another location within the Shopping Center Area, comparable in size and location to the Premises, mutually agreed upon by Landlord and Tenant. Within sixty (60) days after any such notice shall be given, Landlord and Tenant shall execute and deliver an amendment to this Lease which shall substitute a description of the premises to which Tenant is to be relocated for the description of the Premises contained herein and shall modify Tenant's Floor Area accordingly; otherwise all of the terms and conditions of this Lease shall be applicable to Tenant's occupancy of the new premises.

If Landlord and Tenant cannot agree on a new location within such sixty (60) days after notice of the exercise by Landlord of its relocation option described in the preceding paragraph, then Landlord may elect to withdraw its notice requiring Tenant to relocate its business, in which event Tenant shall remain in possession of the Premises and this Lease shall remain in full force and effect. If Landlord shall not elect to withdraw its notice requiring Tenant to relocate its business, the Term shall terminate on the ninetieth (90th) day after such notice, in which event Landlord agrees to pay to Tenant, provided Tenant is not in default under this Lease, and, provided Tenant shall have furnished Landlord with the statement referred to in the last sentence of this paragraph, an amount equivalent to the unamortized value of Tenant's leasehold improvements which were installed in the Premises at Tenant's sole cost and expense. Said amortization shall be determined on the straight-line depreciation method allowed by the Internal Revenue Code of 1986 (as amended) assuming a depreciation period commencing with the placement in service of such leasehold improvements and ending on the date of expiration of the Term determined pursuant to Section 3.1. Payment of the amount equivalent to the unamortized value of Tenant's leasehold improvements will be made to Tenant within thirty (30) days after Tenant shall have vacated the Premises in accordance with the terms of this Lease, provided that Landlord shall have the right to deduct therefrom any amounts due Landlord from Tenant pursuant to this Lease. For purposes of this Section, "Tenant's leasehold improvements" shall include partitioning, electrical wiring, plumbing (other than plumbing fixtures), painting, wallpaper, storefront and other permanent improvements installed, affixed or attached in or to the Premises, but shall not include (x) Tenant's inventory or stock in trade, (y) such trade fixtures, electrical fixtures, equipment or apparatus as are removable by Tenant at the expiration of the Term pursuant to Section 7.4, or (z) Landlord's fixtures or other improvements installed by or at the expense of Landlord. In order for Tenant to be entitled to payment of the unamortized value of its leasehold improvement as set forth in this paragraph, Tenant shall, within sixty (60) days after commencement of the Term, furnish to Landlord a statement, signed by an independent certified public accountant, setting out in detail the cost of Tenant's leasehold improvements.

If this Lease shall be terminated as to any portion or all of the Premises pursuant to this Section, the rights and obligations of the parties hereunder shall cease as of the date specified herein and Rental (other than any Additional Rental due Landlord by reason of Tenant's failure to perform any of its obligations hereunder) shall be adjusted as of the date of such termination. No further documentation shall be required to effect the termination of this Lease, but each party agrees that, upon the request of the other party to do so, it shall execute, acknowledge and deliver an appropriate instrument evidencing such termination prepared by or at the expense of the party requesting the same.

IN WITNESS WHEREOF, the parties hereto intending to be legally bound hereby have executed this Lease under their respective hands and seals as of the day and year first above written.

ATTEST: _____, Landlord

_____ By:_____(SEAL)
Assistant Secretary   Vice–President

(CORPORATE SEAL)

ATTEST: _____, Tenant

_____ By:_____(SEAL)
Secretary   President

(CORPORATE SEAL)

If Tenant is a corporation, the authorized officers must sign on behalf of the corporation, and by doing so such officers make the covenants and warranties contained in Section 20.17 hereof. The Lease must be executed for Tenant, if a corporation, by the president or vice-president and be attested by the secretary or the assistant secretary, unless the by-laws or a resolution of the board of directors shall provide that other officers are authorized to execute the Lease, in which event, a certified copy of the by-laws or resolution, as the case may be, must be furnished. Tenant's corporate seal must be affixed.

THIS ACKNOWLEDGMENT OF MEMBERSHIP AGREEMENT, _____ dated _____, by _____, a Maryland corporation (hereinafter called "Member").
_____ The undersigned member hereby acknowledges that in satisfaction of certain conditions pertaining to the maintenance of a membership in good standing in the Merchants' Association in a Lease Agreement between Member and _____, made on _____, Member elects to join the _____, and acknowledges the obligation of membership, including the payment of dues to the Association in the amounts set forth in the Lease as they may be increased from time to time, and grants to that Association and Landlord the right, joint and several, to collect and enforce on behalf of the Association all debts owing by Member to the Association pursuant to valid action taken by the Association, and the right to do all acts necessary to carry out the provisions hereof.

IN WITNESS WHEREOF, Member, intending to be legally bound, has set its hand and seal as of the day and year first above written.

ATTEST: XX, Member

_____ By:_____(SEAL)
Secretary   President

(CORPORATE SEAL)

SCHEDULE "E"

UTILITY CONSUMPTION AND PAYMENT SCHEDULE

ANNEXED TO and forming part of the Lease dated _____ by and between _____ ("Landlord") and _____, a Maryland corporation, t/a _____ ("Tenant").

Section 12.1. of the above mentioned Lease Agreement provides for the inclusion of this Schedule as the basis for the determination of electricity used by Tenant in the Premises and the payment therefore.

Landlord will provide and maintain the necessary conduits to bring electricity to the Premises. Tenant shall pay all charges for electricity used by it and supplied by Landlord, public utility or public authority, or any other person, firm or corporation.

Landlord shall have the option to supply electricity to the Premises. If Landlord shall elect to supply electricity to the Premises, Tenant will pay all charges for its requirements for such service tendered by Landlord, and Tenant will pay Landlord within ten (10) days after mailing by Landlord to Tenant of statements therefor at the applicable rates determined by Landlord from time to time which Landlord agrees shall be reasonable and not in excess of the public utility rates for the same service, if applicable, but in no event less than Landlord's actual cost.

If Landlord so elects to supply electricity, Tenant shall execute and deliver to Landlord, within ten (10) days after request therefor, any documentation reasonably required by Landlord to effect such change in the method of furnishing of electricity.

Landlord shall provide water and sewer service to the Premises. Tenant shall pay all charges for water and sewer used by it and supplied by Landlord, a public utility or public authority, or any other person, firm or corporation. In addition to the foregoing, at Landlord's option, Tenant shall pay to Landlord, as Additional Rental, the annual Water and Sewer Charge set forth in clause O of Section 1.1, which annual sum shall be paid in twelve (12) equal monthly installments in advance on the first day of each calendar month during the Term, the first such payment to include also any prorated Water and Sewer Charge for the period from the date of the commencement of the Term to the first day of the first full calendar month in the Term.

If the foregoing correctly sets forth our agreement, kindly sign and date this Schedule where indicated below.

XX, Landlord

By:_____   DATE_____
    Vice–President

XX, Tenant

By:_____   DATE_____
    President

SCHEDULE "F"

TENANT HEATING, VENTILATING AND AIR-CONDITIONING SCHEDULE

ANNEXED TO and forming part of the Lease dated _____ by and between _____ ("Landlord") and _____, a Maryland corporation, t/a _____ ("Tenant")

Section 12.2 of the above mentioned Lease provides for the inclusion of this Schedule as the basis for establishing the obligations of Landlord and Tenant with regard to the heating, ventilating and air-conditioning equipment and system servicing the Premises and the cost of energy used to provide heating, ventilating and air-conditioning to the Premises.

A. *HVAC System:*

Landlord and/or others have heretofore installed heating, ventilating, and air-conditioning equipment and system serving the Premises and Landlord's Building. Landlord shall maintain, repair and operate such system at its expense, but subject to the payment by Tenant of the charges provided for herein.

B. *Tenant's HVAC Charge:*

In each calendar month of Landlord's fiscal year (the "Fiscal Year"), Tenant shall pay Landlord, as Additional Rental, Tenant's proportionate share of (i) the cost of energy used in heating, ventilating and air-conditioning the Premises and (ii) the cost of maintenance, repair and operation of such equipment and system as installed or owned by Landlord ("Tenant's HVAC Charge") which shall be determined as follows:

> (a) Landlord shall cause a heating, ventilating and air-conditioning consultant designated by Landlord to review such data and information regarding the mechanical capacity of said equipment and system as such consultant shall deem relevant and, based on such data and information, such consultant shall assign to Tenant an "HVAC Factor" which shall fairly represent the relationship between (x) the mechanical capacity of the equipment and system which is required for heating, ventilating and air-conditioning the Premises and (y) the total mechanical capacity of such equipment and system which is available for heating, ventilating and air-conditioning Landlord's Floor Area; and

> (b) In each Fiscal Year, the actual cost to Landlord of such energy, operation, maintenance and repair as is attributable by Landlord to the heating, ventilating and air-conditioning of Landlord's Floor Area, together with costs and fees of Landlord's consultant in recalculating HVAC Factors of Tenant and other tenants of Landlord's Building from time to time, shall be multiplied by a fraction, the numerator of which is Tenant's HVAC Factor and the denominator of which is the total of all HVAC Factors assigned to Landlord's Leased Floor Area. The product thus obtained shall be the Tenant's HVAC Charge for such Fiscal Year.

Tenant's HVAC Charge for each calendar month shall be paid by Tenant in such amounts as are estimated and billed by Landlord, each such charge being estimated and billed as of the first day of each Fiscal Year. At any time during each Fiscal Year, Landlord may reestimate Tenant's HVAC Charge and adjust Tenant's monthly installments payable during such Fiscal Year to reflect more accurately Tenant's HVAC Charge. Within one hundred twenty (120) days after the termination of each Fiscal Year, Landlord will send Tenant a notice which shall:

> (c) set forth the amount of Tenant's HVAC Charge based upon Landlord's energy bills and maintenance, repair and operation costs for such Fiscal Year; and

> (d) state that the aggregate of all tenant HVAC Charges paid or payable by all tenants of leased portions of Landlord's Floor Area with respect to such Fiscal Year, as adjusted, does not exceed the actual cost to Landlord of such energy, operation, maintenance and repair as is attributable by Landlord to the heating, ventilating and air-conditioning of Landlord's Floor Area, together with fees and costs of Landlord's consultant in recalculating HVAC Factors of Tenant and other tenants of Landlord's Building from time to time.

Tenant's HVAC Charge paid for such Fiscal Year shall be adjusted between Landlord and Tenant, the parties hereby agreeing that Tenant shall pay Landlord or Landlord shall credit to Tenant's account (or, if such adjustment is at the end of the Term, Landlord shall pay Tenant), as the case may be, within fifteen (15) days of such notification to Tenant, the amounts necessary to effect such adjustment. Failure of Landlord to provide the notification called for hereunder within the time prescribed shall not relieve Tenant of its obligations hereunder.

C. *HVAC Equipment:*

In each Rental Year, Tenant shall pay Landlord annually (in twelve (12) equal monthly installments together with the Annual Basic Rental), as Additional Rental, an amount (the "HVAC Equipment Contribution") determined by multiplying the HVAC Equipment Contribution Rate by Tenant's Floor Area.

If the foregoing correctly sets forth our agreement, kindly sign and date this Schedule where indicated below.

_____, Landlord

By:_____ DATE_____
  Vice–President

_____, Tenant

By:_____ DATE_____
  President

RIDER TO LEASE

THIS RIDER is annexed to and forms part of the Lease dated _____, between _____, as Landlord, and _____, a Maryland corporation, t/a _____, as Tenant

The printed part of the Lease is hereby modified and supplemented as follows. Wherever there is any conflict between this Rider and the Lease, the provisions of this Rider are paramount and the Lease shall be construed accordingly.

IN WITNESS WHEREOF, the parties hereto intending to be legally bound hereby have executed this Lease under their respective hands as of the day and year first above written.

ATTEST: _____, Landlord

                                       By:_____(SEAL)
_____   Vice–President
  Assistant Secretary

(CORPORATE SEAL)

ATTEST: _____, Tenant

                                       By:_____(SEAL)
_____   President
  Secretary

(CORPORATE SEAL)

NOTICE OF LEASE MODIFICATIONS

Please be advised that those Sections of the Lease between _____ and _____ listed below have been modified and/or supplemented by the Rider to Lease found immediately following the signature page of the Lease. It is therefore imperative that the Lease and Rider be read simultaneously. Wherever there is any conflict between the Rider and the Lease, the provisions of the Rider are paramount and the Lease shall be construed accordingly.

Appendix

REAL ESTATE FINANCE LAW RESEARCH ON WESTLAW®

Analysis

1. Introduction
2. Real Estate Finance and Property Law Databases
3. Menu–Driven WESTLAW: EZ ACCESS®
4. Retrieving a Document with a Citation: Find and Jump
   - 4.1 Find
   - 4.2 Jump
5. Natural Language Searching: WIN™—WESTLAW is Natural™
   - 5.1 Natural Language Searching
   - 5.2 Concept Ranking
   - 5.3 Browsing a Natural Language Search Result
   - 5.4 Modifying Your Natural Language Search
6. Terms and Connectors Searching
   - 6.1 Terms
   - 6.2 Alternative Terms
   - 6.3 Connectors
   - 6.4 Restricting Your Search by Field
   - 6.5 Restricting Your Search by Date
7. Verifying Your Research with Citators
   - 7.1 Insta–Cite®
   - 7.2 Shepard's® Citations
   - 7.3 Shepard's PreView®
   - 7.4 Quick*Cite*™
   - 7.5 WESTLAW As a Citator
   - 7.6 Selected Citator Commands
8. Research Examples
   - 8.1 Retrieving Law Review Articles
   - 8.2 Retrieving Statutes
   - 8.3 Retrieving Federal and State Cases in One Search
   - 8.4 Retrieving Continuing Legal Education Materials
   - 8.5 Using Citator Services
   - 8.6 Retrieving Multistate Property Cases
   - 8.7 Following Recent Developments

Section 1. Introduction

Nelson and Whitman's *Real Estate Finance Law,* 2d edition, provides a strong base for analyzing even the most complex real estate finance law problem. Whether your research requires examination of case law, statutes, administrative materials or expert commentary, West books and WESTLAW® are excellent sources.

WESTLAW expands your library by giving you access to decisions from federal and state courts as well as the *Restatement of the Law of Property,* and texts and periodicals such as *The Law of Distressed Real Estate* (Clark Boardman), *Hofstra Property Law Journal* and the *Real Property, Probate and Trust Journal.* To help keep you up-to-date with decisions affecting real estate finance and other property law issues, WESTLAW provides a topical highlights database for real property. With WESTLAW, you have unparalleled legal research resources at your fingertips.

Additional Resources

If you have not used WESTLAW or have questions not covered in this appendix, see the *WESTLAW Reference Manual* or call the West Reference Attorneys at **1–800–REF–ATTY (1–800–733–2889).** The West Reference Attorneys are trained, licensed attorneys available throughout the work day and on weekends to assist you with your WESTLAW or West book research questions.

Section 2. Real Estate Finance and Property Law Databases

Each database on WESTLAW is assigned an abbreviation called an *identifier,* which you use to access the database. You can find identifiers for all databases in the online WESTLAW Directory and in the *WESTLAW Database List.* When you need to know more detailed information about a database, use Scope. Scope contains coverage information, related databases and valuable search tips. To use Scope from the WESTLAW Directory, type **sc** and the database or service identifier, e.g., **sc allfeds.**

The following chart lists WESTLAW databases that contain real estate finance and property law information. Because new information is continually being added to WESTLAW, you should check the Welcome to WESTLAW screen and the WESTLAW Directory for new database information.

REAL ESTATE FINANCE AND PROPERTY LAW DATABASES ON WESTLAW

Description	Database Identifier	Coverage
FEDERAL DATABASES		
Case Law		
Combined Federal Cases	ALLFEDS	From 1945*
U.S. Supreme Court	SCT	From 1945*
U.S. Courts of Appeals	CTA	From 1945*
Individual Courts of Appeals	CTA1–CTA11 CTAF CTADC	Varies
U.S. District Courts	DCT	Varies

Description	Database Identifier	Coverage
(includes cases reported in West's® *Federal Rules Decisions*®		
Statutes and Regulations		
United States Public Laws (current)	US–PL	Current
United States Public Laws (historical)**	US–PLYY	Starts 1989
United States Code Annotated®	USCA	Current
Legislative History—U.S. Code	LH	From 1948
Federal Register	FR	1980–present
Code of Federal Regulations	CFR	Current
COMBINED FEDERAL AND STATE CASE LAW DATABASES		
Case law including all United States Supreme Court decisions, all decisions of the circuit,*** all the bankruptcy and district court decisions for each state within the circuit, all decisions of the Judicial Panel on Multidistrict Litigation, and all state court decisions from each state within the circuit	CTAX–ALL	Varies
Case law including all of the contents of a state's**** state case law database, all of the bankruptcy and district court decisions from that state, all decisions of the Judicial Panel on Multidistrict Litigation, all the decisions from the circuit which the state is in, and all United States Supreme Court decisions	XX–CS–ALL	Varies
STATE DATABASES		
Case Law—Real Property		

Description	Database Identifier	Coverage
Multistate Real Property Cases (Case law from all 50 states and the District of Columbia)	MRP–CS	Varies
Individual State Cases ****	XXRP–CS	Varies
Statutes		
State Statutes—Annotated Statutes from all 50 states, the District of Columbia, Puerto Rico and the Virgin Islands, including annotations from all jurisdictions except Nebraska	ST–ANN–ALL	Varies by state
State Statutes—Unannotated Statutes from all 50 states, the District of Columbia, Puerto Rico and the Virgin Islands	STAT–ALL	Varies by state
Individual State Statutes—Annotated ****	XX–ST–ANN	Varies by state
Individual State Statutes—Unannotated ****	XX–ST	Varies by state
Multistate Legislative Services from all 50 states, the District of Columbia, Puerto Rico and the Virgin Islands	LEGIS–ALL	Varies by state
Individual State Legislative Service ****	XX–LEGIS	Varies by state
Individual State Statutes General Indexes **** General index references for the statutes and constitutions of all available states, the District of Columbia and the Virgin Islands	XX–ST–IDX	Varies by state
SPECIALIZED MATERIALS		
Clark Boardman—Law of Distressed Real Estate	CB–DRE	Current
Restatement of the Law—Property	REST–PROP	Current
Tax Management Portfolios—Real Estate Series	TM–RE	Varies

Description	Database Identifier	Coverage
Tax Management Real Estate Journal	TM–REJ	1987
WESTLAW Topical Highlights—Real Property	WTH–RP	Current data
West's Legal Directory—Real Property	WLD–RP	Current data
TEXTS & PERIODICALS		
The Journal of Real Estate Taxation	WGL–JRETAX	Winter 1985
Law Reviews, Texts & Bar Journals	RP–TP	Varies by publication
PLI Real Estate Law and Practice Course Handbook Series	PLI–REAL	From September 1984
Real Estate Law Report	WGL–RELR	April 1990
All Law Reviews, Texts & Bar Journals	TP–ALL	Varies
Texts and Treatises	TEXTS	Varies
PUBLIC RECORDS DATABASES		
Prentice Hall Public Records—California Notice of Default Data	PH–CADFLT	February 1986

* Cases dated before 1945 are contained in databases whose identifiers end with the suffix –OLD. For example, the identifier for the U.S. Supreme Court Cases—Before 1945 database is SCT–OLD. Coverage for federal databases whose identifiers end with the suffix –OLD is from 1789–1944. Coverage for the ALLSTATES–OLD database varies by state.
** YY is the last two digits of a year, e.g., 90 for 1990.
*** X is the circuit number or DC.
**** XX is the two-letter postal abbreviation for a state or DC.

Section 3. Menu–Driven WESTLAW: EZ ACCESS®

EZ ACCESS is West Publishing Company's menu-driven research system. It is ideal for new or infrequent WESTLAW users because it requires no experience or training on WESTLAW.

To access EZ ACCESS, type **ez**. The EZ ACCESS main menu will be displayed. Whenever you are unsure of the next step, or if the choice you want is not listed, simply type **ez**; additional choices will be displayed. Once you retrieve documents with EZ ACCESS, use standard WESTLAW commands to browse your documents. For more information on browsing documents, see the *WESTLAW Reference Manual* or the *WESTLAW User Guide*.

Section 4. Retrieving a Document with a Citation: Find and Jump

4.1 Find

Find is a WESTLAW service that allows you to retrieve a document by entering its citation. Find allows you to retrieve documents from anywhere in WESTLAW without accessing or changing databases or losing your search result. Find is available for many documents, including case law (federal and state), state statutes, the *United States Code Annotated,* the *Code of Federal Regulations,* the *Federal Register,* federal rules, state and federal public laws, and texts and periodicals such as PLI materials and selected law reviews.

To use Find, type **fi** followed by the document citation. Below is a list of examples:

To Find This Document	Type
Metfirst Financial Co. v. Price, 1993 WL 115506 (7th Cir.1993)	**fi 1993 wl 115506**
Gray v. Bowers, 332 N.W.2d 323 (Iowa 1983)	**fi 332 nw2d 323**
Alaska Statutes § 34.20.070	**fi ak st s 34.20.070**
12 U.S.C.A. § 3701	**fi 12 usca 3701**
57 *Federal Register* 29491	**fi 57 fr 29491**
24 *Code of Federal Regulations* § 27.2 *	**fi 24 cfr 27.2**
United States Public Law 103–3*	**fi us pl 103–3**

4.2 Jump

Retrieving Cited References: While viewing a case online, use Jump to automatically retrieve a cited case or section of the *United States Code Annotated.* Use your mouse to select the Jump marker (> or ▶) displayed before the citation, or press the **Tab** key until the cursor reaches the desired location, then press **Enter.** The cited document will be displayed.

Between Headnotes and Text: In West-reported cases, you can also use Jump to move between the headnotes and the corresponding text in an opinion. Simply select the Jump marker (> or ▶) next to a headnote number to move to the corresponding text in an opinion. From an opinion, select the > or ▶ at the beginning of a segment of text to return to the corresponding headnote. If a segment of text relates to several headnotes, Jump will return you to the first headnote in the string. For example, if the text relates to headnotes [3], [4] or [5], Jump will return you to headnote 3.

Headnote to Key Number Service: You can jump directly from a headnote in a West-reported case to the Key Number service. The Key Number service provides the complete topic and key number outline used by West's editors to classify headnotes to specific topics and key numbers. To jump from a headnote to the Key Number service, select a Jump marker at the beginning of any line of the classification hierarchy of a headnote. You will go directly to the point in the Key Number service where the line you selected is displayed. WESTLAW will display your selection in context so that you can determine additional key numbers that may be related to your research project.

---

* To retrieve historical versions of the C.F.R. or public laws using a citation, access the appropriate database and search for your terms in the citation field.

Within the Key Number Service: You can jump from one level of the Key Number service to another. Just select the Jump marker preceding the line for which you would like to see the next level.

Section 5. Natural Language Searching: WIN™—WESTLAW is Natural™

Overview: WIN (WESTLAW is Natural) is a Natural Language search method on WESTLAW. With WIN, you can retrieve documents by simply describing your issue in plain English. If you are a relatively new user, Natural Language searching makes it easier to retrieve cases on point. If you are an experienced user, Natural Language increases your research proficiency by giving you a valuable alternative search method.

When you enter a Natural Language description, WESTLAW automatically identifies legal phrases, removes common words and generates variations of terms in your description. WESTLAW then searches for the legal phrases and other concepts in your description. Concepts may include significant terms, phrases, legal citations or topic and key numbers. Based on the frequency with which each concept occurs in the database and in each document, WESTLAW retrieves the 20 documents that most closely match your description, beginning with the document most likely to match.

5.1 Natural Language Searching

To use Natural Language searching, access the database containing documents relevant to your issue, such as the Multistate Real Property Cases database (MRP–CS). If your current search method is Terms and Connectors, type **nat** to change to the Natural Language method and display the Enter Description screen. Then enter a Natural Language description such as

> **is inadequacy of price sufficient to invalidate a mortgage foreclosure sale**

5.2 Concept Ranking

WESTLAW displays the 20 documents that most closely match your description, beginning with the document most likely to match. To change the maximum number of documents retrieved with a Natural Language search, access the Options Directory by typing **opt.** Select the *Set the number of documents retrieved for Natural Language search* feature by typing its corresponding number and pressing **Enter.** Then follow the on-screen instructions to designate the number (from 1 to 100) of documents retrieved.

5.3 Browsing a Natural Language Search Result

Best Mode: Best mode allows you to see the best portion (the portion that most closely matches your description) of each document retrieved by a Natural Language search. To see the best portion, type **b.**

Standard Browsing Commands: You can also browse your Natural Language search result using standard WESTLAW browsing commands, such as citations list (L), Locate (Loc), page mode (P) and term mode (T). When you browse your Natural Language search result in term mode, the five portions of each document that are most likely to match your description are displayed.

5.4 Modifying Your Natural Language Search

Restrictions: You can add restrictions, such as court, date, added date, attorney and judge, to a Natural Language search. Note: Restrictions available may vary depending on the database that you have selected.

To add restrictions before you run your description, type **res** at the Enter Description screen and press **Enter.** Enter your restriction(s) on the displayed Restrictions screen. To move from one entry field to the next, press the **Tab** key. Then press **Enter** to return to the Enter Description screen and type your description.

To add restrictions after you have run your description, type **res** from your search result and press **Enter.** Then enter your restrictions on the displayed Restrictions screen.

Legal Phrases: WESTLAW automatically identifies many legal phrases or terms of art in your Natural Language description and puts them in quotation marks for you. To identify additional phrases yourself, place quotation marks around the terms you want to identify as a phrase when you type your description. Suppose you are performing legal research to determine whether the statutory right of redemption can be waived. To identify the phrase *statutory right of redemption,* place the phrase in quotation marks when you type your description:

can the "statutory right of redemption" be waived

Alternative Terms: The WESTLAW thesaurus provides a list of concepts you can add to your description. To add terms from the thesaurus after you have run a description, type **thes** from your search result and press **Enter.** WESTLAW will display a screen showing the concepts in your original description that have related concepts. To view a list of related concepts for a concept listed, type the concept number. To add one or more of these concepts to your description as alternative terms, type their corresponding numbers.

To add your own alternative terms to your description, add the alternative terms following the concepts to which they relate. Enclose the alternative term in parentheses ( ). For example, using the description from § 5.1, you could type

is inadequacy of price sufficient to invalidate (nullify void vitiate) a mortgage foreclosure sale

Section 6. Terms and Connectors Searching

Overview: With standard Terms and Connectors searching, you enter a query, which consists of key terms from your research issue and connectors specifying the relationship between these terms.

Terms and Connectors searching is useful when you want to retrieve a document for which you have specific information, such as the title or the citation. Terms and Connectors searching is also useful when you want to retrieve documents relating to a specific issue. To change from Natural Language searching to Terms and Connectors searching, type **tc** at the Enter Description screen.

6.1 Terms

Plurals and Possessives: Plurals are automatically retrieved when you enter the singular form of a term. This is true for both regular and irregular plurals (e.g., **child** retrieves *children*). If you enter the plural form of a term, you will not retrieve the singular form.

If you enter the non-possessive form of a term, WESTLAW automatically retrieves the possessive form as well. However, if you enter the possessive form, only the possessive form is retrieved.

Automatic Equivalencies: Some terms have alternative forms or equivalencies; for example, *5* and *five* are equivalent terms. WESTLAW automatically retrieves equivalent terms. The *WESTLAW Reference Manual* contains a list of equivalent terms.

Compound Words and Acronyms: When a compound word is one of your search terms, use a hyphen to retrieve all forms of the word. For example, the term *good-will* retrieves *good-will, goodwill* and *good will*.

When using an acronym as a search term, place a period after each of the letters in the acronym to retrieve any of its forms. For example, the term **f.m.v.** (fair market value) retrieves *fmv, f.m.v., f m v* and *f. m. v.*

Root Expander and Universal Character: When you use the Terms and Connectors search method, placing a root expander (!) at the end of a root term generates all other terms with that root. For example, adding the ! symbol to the root *foreclos* in the query

                foreclos! /s sale

instructs WESTLAW to retrieve such words as *foreclose, foreclosed, foreclosure* and *foreclosing*.

The universal character (*) stands for one character and can be inserted in the middle or at the end of a term. For example, the term

                subrogat***

will retrieve *subrogating* and *subrogation*. But adding only two asterisks to the root *jur* in the query

jur**

instructs WESTLAW to retrieve all forms of the root with up to two additional characters. Terms like *jury* or *juror* are retrieved by this query. However, terms with more than two letters following the root, such as *jurisdiction,* are not retrieved. Plurals are always retrieved, even if more than two letters follow the root.

Phrase Searching: To search for a phrase, place it within quotation marks. For example, to search for discussions of the title theory as it relates to mortgages, type **"title theory" /s mortgage.** When you are using the Terms and Connectors search method, you should use phrase searching only if you are certain that the phrase will not appear in any other form.

6.2 Alternative Terms

After selecting the terms for your query, consider which alternative terms are necessary. For example, if you are searching for the term *contract,* you might also want to search for the term *agreement.* You should consider both synonyms and antonyms as alternative terms.

You can also use the WESTLAW thesaurus to add alternative terms to your query. To add terms from the thesaurus to your query, type **thes** from your search result and press **Enter.** A screen listing the terms in your query that have related terms in the thesaurus will be displayed. To view a list of related terms for any of the terms listed, type the term number. To add one or more of these terms to your query as alternative terms, type their corresponding numbers.

6.3 Connectors

After selecting terms and alternative terms for your query, use connectors to specify the relationship that should exist between search terms in your retrieved documents. The connectors you can use are described below:

Use:	To retrieve documents with:	Example:
& (and)	both terms	**condominium & financ!**
or (space)	either term or both terms	**lessee tenant**
/p	search terms in the same paragraph	**"power of sale" /p deficiency**
/s	search terms in the same sentence	**necessary /s party**
+s	one search term preceding the other within the same sentence, especially useful when searching in the title field (ti) where both parties have the same name	**junior +s mortgagee**

/n	search terms within "n" terms of each other (where "n" is a number)	**trust /3 deed**
+n	one search term preceding the other by "n" terms (where "n" is a number), especially useful when searching in the citation field (ci)	**dragnet +2 clause**

Use:	To exclude documents with:	Example:
% (but not)	search terms following the % symbol	**accelerat! /3 clause % to(56)**

6.4 Restricting Your Search by Field

Overview: Documents in each WESTLAW database consist of several segments, or fields. One field may contain the citation, another the title, another the synopsis, and so forth. Not all databases contain the same fields. Also, depending on the database, fields of the same name may contain different types of information.

To retrieve only those documents containing your search terms in a specified field, restrict your search by field. To view the fields and field content for a specific database, see Scope or type **f** while in the database. Note that in some databases, not every field is available for every document.

To retrieve only those documents containing your search terms in a specific field, restrict your search to that field. To restrict your search to a specific field, type the field name or abbreviation followed by your search terms enclosed in parentheses. For example, to retrieve a case in the Pennsylvania Cases database (PA-CS) entitled *Bankers Trust Co. v. Foust,* search for your terms in the title field:

ti("banker trust" & foust)

The fields discussed below are available in WESTLAW databases you might use for real estate finance law research.

Digest and Synopsis Fields: The digest (di) and synopsis (sy) fields, provided in case law databases by West Publishing Company's editors, summarize the main points of a case. The synopsis field contains a brief description of a case. The digest field contains the topic, headnote, court and title fields and includes the complete hierarchy of concepts used to classify the point of law, including the West digest topic name and number and the key number. Restricting your search to these fields limits your result to cases in which your terms are related to a major issue in the case.

Consider restricting your search to one or both of these fields if
• you are searching for common terms or terms with more than one meaning, and you need to narrow your search; or

• you cannot narrow your search by moving to a smaller database.

For example, to retrieve cases that discuss the duty of a mortgagee-in-possession to maintain and repair premises, access the Multistate Real Property Cases database (MRP–CS) and type the following query:

> sy,di(mortgagee-in-possession   /p   duty responsibl   /p   repair! maintain!)

Headnote Field: The headnote field is a part of the digest field, but does not contain the topic number, hierarchical classification information, key number or the title. The headnote field contains only the one-sentence summary of the point of law and any supporting statutory citations given by the author of the opinion. A headnote field restriction is useful when you are searching for specific statutory sections or rule numbers. For example, to retrieve headnotes that cite 12 U.S.C.A. § 1717, type the following query:

> he(12 +5 1717)

Topic Field: The topic field is also a part of the digest field. It contains hierarchical classification information, including the West digest topic name and number and the key number. You should restrict your search to the topic field in a case law database if

- a digest field search retrieves too many documents; or
- you want to retrieve cases with digest paragraphs classified under more than one topic.

For example, the topic *Mortgages* has the topic number 266. To retrieve Iowa cases that discuss the circumstances under which a court will consider parol or extrinsic evidence to show that a warranty deed was intended as a mortgage, access the Iowa Real Property Cases database (IARP–CS) and type a query like the following:

> to(266) /p parol extrinsic

To retrieve West headnotes classified under more than one topic and key number, search for your terms in the topic field. For example, to search for cases discussing the validity of acceleration clauses in real estate contracts, which could be classified under a variety of topics, access the Multistate Real Property Cases database (MRP–CS) and type a query like the following:

> to(contracts) /p accelerat! /3 clause provision /p valid! enforc!

For a complete list of West Digest topics and their corresponding topic numbers, access the Key Number service; type **key**.

Be aware that slip opinions and cases from topical services do not contain the digest, headnote or topic fields.

Prelim and Caption Fields: When searching in a database containing statutes, rules or regulations, restrict your search to the prelim and caption fields to retrieve documents in which your terms are important enough to appear in a section name or heading. For example, to retrieve Florida statutes discussing foreclosure of mortgages, access the Florida Statutes Annotated database (FL–ST–ANN) and type the following:

                pr,ca(foreclos! /p mortgage)

6.5 Restricting Your Search by Date

You can instruct WESTLAW to retrieve documents *decided* or *issued* before, after, or on a specified date, as well as within a range of dates. The following are examples of queries that contain date restrictions:

            da(aft 1986) & "deficiency judgment"
            da(1990) & "bona fide purchaser"
            da(3/1/93) & fixture /5 attach!

You can also instruct WESTLAW to retrieve documents *added to a database* on or after a specified date, as well as within a range of dates. The following are examples of queries that contain added date restrictions:

            ad(aft 1-1-92) & purchase /3 money /3 mortgage
            ad(aft 2-1-92 & bef 3-1-92) & "escrow account"

Section 7. Verifying Your Research with Citators

Overview: WESTLAW contains four citator services to assist you in checking the validity of cases you intend to rely on. These four citator services—Insta–Cite®, Shepard's® Citations, Shepard's PreView®, and Quick*Cite*™—help you perform many valuable research tasks, saving you hours of manual research. Sections 7.1 through 7.4 and 7.6 provide further information on these services.

WESTLAW also contains Shepard's Citations for federal statutes; Shepard's Citations for state statutes are being added on a state by state basis.

For citations not covered by the citator services, including persuasive secondary authority such as restatements, treatises and law review articles, use a technique called WESTLAW as a citator to retrieve cases that cite your authority (see Section 7.5).

7.1 Insta–Cite

Insta–Cite is West Publishing Company's case history and citation verification service. It is the most current case history service available. Use Insta–Cite to see whether your case is good law. Insta–Cite provides the following types of information about a citation:

Direct History. In addition to reversals and affirmances, Insta-Cite gives you the complete reported history of a litigated matter including any related cases. Insta-Cite provides the direct history of federal cases from 1754 and state cases from 1879. Related references (cases related to the litigation) are provided from 1983 to date. Direct case history is available within 24–36 hours of receipt of a case at West Publishing.

Negative Indirect History. Insta-Cite lists subsequent cases that may have a substantial negative impact on your case, including cases overruling your case or calling it into question. Cases affected by decisions from 1972 to date will be displayed on Insta-Cite. To retrieve negative indirect history prior to 1972, use Shepard's Citations (discussed in Section 7.2).

Secondary Source References. Insta-Cite also provides references to secondary sources that cite your case. These secondary sources currently include the legal encyclopedia *Corpus Juris Secundum*®.

Parallel Citations. Insta-Cite provides parallel citations for cases, including citations to *U.S. Law Week* and many topical reporters.

Citation Verification. Insta-Cite confirms that you have the correct volume and page number for a case, as well as the correct spelling of proper names. Citation verification information is available from 1754 for federal cases and from 1879 for state cases.

7.2 Shepard's Citations

For case law, Shepard's provides a comprehensive list of cases and publications that have cited a particular case. Shepard's also includes explanatory analysis to indicate how the citing cases have treated the case, e.g., "followed," "explained."

Shepard's Citations for statutes provides a comprehensive list of cases citing a particular statute, as well as information on subsequent legislative action.

7.3 Shepard's PreView

Shepard's PreView gives you a preview of citing references for case law from West's National Reporter System® that will appear in Shepard's Citations. Depending on the citation, Shepard's PreView provides citing information days, weeks or even months before the same information appears in Shepard's online. Use Shepard's PreView to update your Shepard's results.

7.4 Quick*Cite*

Quick*Cite* is a citator service that enables you to automatically retrieve the most recent citing cases on WESTLAW, including slip opinions.

There is a four- to six-week gap between a citing case's availability on WESTLAW and its listing in Shepard's PreView. This gap occurs because cases go through an editorial process at West Publishing Company before they are added to Shepard's PreView. To retrieve the most recent citing cases, therefore, you need to search case law databases on WESTLAW for references to your case.

QuickCite formulates a query using the title, the case citation(s) and an added date restriction. QuickCite then accesses the appropriate database, either ALLSTATES or ALLFEDS, and runs the query for you. QuickCite also allows you to tailor the query to your specific research needs; you can choose a different date range or select another database.

QuickCite is designed to retrieve documents that cite cases. To retrieve citing references to other documents, such as law review articles, use WESTLAW as a citator (see below).

7.5 WESTLAW As a Citator

Using WESTLAW as a citator, you can search for documents citing a specific statute, regulation, rule, agency decision or other authority. For example, to retrieve documents citing Wash.Rev.Code § 61.12.060, access the Washington Real Property Cases database (WARP–CS), select Terms and Connectors as your search method, and type a query like the following:

> 61.12.060

If the citation is not a unique term, add descriptive terms. For example, to retrieve cases citing Tex.Prop.Code Ann. § 52.001 concerning judgment liens, access the Texas Real Property Cases database (TXRP–CS) and type a Terms and Connectors query like the following:

> 52.001 /p lien

7.6 Selected Citator Commands

The following are some of the commands that can be used in the citator services. For a complete list, see the *WESTLAW User Guide* or the *WESTLAW Reference Manual.*

Command: *Definition:*

ic xxx or **ic** — Retrieves an Insta–Cite result when followed by a case citation (where xxx is the citation), or when entered from a displayed case, Shepard's result or Shepard's PreView result.

sh xxx or **sh** — Retrieves a Shepard's result when followed by a case or statute citation (where xxx is the citation), or when entered from a displayed case or statute, Insta–Cite result or Shepard's PreView result.

sp xxx or **sp** — Retrieves a Shepard's PreView result when followed by a case citation (where xxx is the citation), or when entered from a displayed case, Insta–Cite result or Shepard's result.

qc xxx or **qc** — Retrieves a QuickCite result when followed by a case citation (where xxx is the citation), or when entered

Command:	Definition:
	from a displayed case, Insta–Cite result, Shepard's result or Shepard's PreView result.
sc	Retrieves the scope of coverage for a specific service when you are viewing a result from that service.
sc xx	Retrieves the scope of coverage (where xx is the citator service), e.g., **sc ic**.
sh sc xxx	Retrieves the scope of coverage for a specific publication in Shepard's, where xxx is the publication abbreviation (e.g., **sh sc f2d**).
xx pubs	Retrieves a list of publications available in the citator service and their abbreviations (where xx is the citator service abbreviation).
xx cmds	Retrieves a list of commands in the citator service (where xx is the citator service abbreviation).
sh analysis	Retrieves a list of Shepard's analysis codes, e.g., *extended, revised,* etc.
sh courts	Retrieves a list of courts and their abbreviations used in Shepard's Citations.
loc	Automatically restricts an Insta–Cite, Shepard's or Shepard's PreView result to selected categories.
loc auto	Restricts all subsequent Insta–Cite, Shepard's or Shepard's PreView results to selected categories.
xloc	Cancels a Locate request.
xloc auto	Cancels a Locate Auto request.

Section 8. Research Examples

8.1 Retrieving Law Review Articles

Recent law review articles are often the best place to begin researching a legal issue because law review articles serve as 1) an excellent introduction to a new topic or review for a stale one, providing terminology to help in query formulation; 2) a finding tool for pertinent primary authority, such as cases and statutes; and 3) in some instances, persuasive secondary authority.

For example, suppose a colleague refers you to a law review article by Frank S. Alexander, *Federal Intervention in Real Estate Finance: Preemption and Federal Common Law,* 71 N.C.L.Rev. 293 (1993). How can you retrieve the article on WESTLAW?

Solution

- If you know the citation, access the North Carolina Law Review database (NCLR). Using the Terms and Connectors search method, search for terms from the citation in the citation field (ci):

    ci(71 +5 293)

- If you know the title of an article, but not which journal it appears in, access the Real Property—Law Reviews, Texts and Bar Journals database (RP–TP). Using the Terms and Connectors search method, search for key terms from the title in the title field (ti):

ti(intervention & "real estate finance")

8.2 Retrieving Statutes

You need to retrieve Arizona statutes concerning deeds of trust.

Solution

- Access the Arizona Statutes—Annotated database (AZ–ST–ANN). Search for your terms in the prelim (pr) and caption (ca) fields:

pr,ca(deed /5 trust)

- When you know the citation for a specific section of a statute, use Find to retrieve the statute. (Note: For more information on Find, see Section 4.1 of this appendix.) For example, to retrieve Ariz.Rev. Stat.Ann. § 33–809, type

fi az st s 33–809

- To look at surrounding statutory sections, use the Documents in Sequence command. To retrieve the section preceding § 33–809, type **d–**. To retrieve the section immediately following § 33–809, type **d+**.
- To see whether a statute has been amended or repealed, use the Update service. Simply type **update** while viewing the statute to display any editorially enhanced sessions law available on WESTLAW that amend or repeal the statute.

> Remember that because slip copy versions of laws are added to WESTLAW before they contain full editorial enhancements, they are not retrieved with Update. To retrieve slip copy versions of laws, access the United States Public Laws database by typing **db us-pl** (or access the appropriate state legislative service database by typing **db xx-legis**, where xx is the state's two-letter postal abbreviation) and then type **ci(slip)** and descriptive terms, e.g., **ci(slip) & [terms]**. Slip copy documents are replaced by the editorially enhanced versions within a few working days.
> Update also does not retrieve legislation that enacts a new statute or covers a topic that will not be incorporated into the statutes. To retrieve this legislation, access US–PL (or access the appropriate state legislative service database) and enter a query containing terms that describe the new legislation.

8.3 Retrieving Federal and State Cases in One Search

One of your firm's clients is a large lender located in the Midwest that needs to know whether a provision in a mortgage that prohibits prepayment is valid and enforceable. How can you use WESTLAW to retrieve applicable case law from both federal and state courts?

Solution

- Access the appropriate CTAX–ALL databases (where X stands for the circuit number or DC). These databases contain all United States Supreme Court decisions, all decisions of that circuit, all the bankruptcy and district court decisions for each of the states within that circuit, and all of the state court decisions from each state within that circuit. To access the Seventh Circuit Federal and State Cases database type **db cta7–all**; then enter a Natural Language description like the following:

is a clause in a mortgage prohibiting prepayment valid and enforceable

8.4 Retrieving Continuing Legal Education Materials

You have been retained to represent a buyer of a new home at a real estate closing. As part of your preparation, you want to retrieve articles that can give you background information on what to expect.

Solution

- The PLI–REAL database contains selected documents from the PLI Real Estate Law and Practice Course Handbook Series of continuing legal education materials published by the Practising Law Institute (PLI). To access the database type **db pli-real**. To change your search method to Terms and Connectors, if necessary, type **tc** and search for key terms in the title field (ti):

ti(closing)

8.5 Using Citator Services

One of the cases you plan to cite in a brief is *Fidelity Savings & Loan Assn. v. de la Cuesta*, 102 S.Ct. 3014 (1982), an important decision concerning due-on-sale clauses in mortgages. You want to see whether this case is still good law and whether other cases have cited this case.

Solution

- Use Insta–Cite to retrieve the direct history and negative indirect history of *de la Cuesta*. While viewing the case, type **ic**.
- You want to Shepardize® *de la Cuesta*. Type **sh**.

  Limit your Shepard's result to decisions containing a reference to a specific headnote, such as headnote 4. Type **loc 4**.
- Check Shepard's PreView for more current cases citing *de la Cuesta*. Type **sp**.
- Check Quick*Cite* for the most current cases citing *de la Cuesta*. Type **qc** and follow the on-screen instructions.

8.6 Retrieving Multistate Property Cases

You need to review cases from a variety of jurisdictions that discuss the rights of a junior mortgagee to rents collected by a receiver.

Solution

- The Multistate Real Property Cases database (MRP–CS) contains decisions selected for relevance to the topic of real property from the state courts of all 50 states and the District of Columbia. Type **db mrp-cs** to access the database and type a Natural Language description like the following:

    is a junior (second) mortgagee (lien-holder) entitled to rents (profits) collected by a receiver

- If you prefer to use Terms and Connectors searching, type **tc** to change your search method and search for your terms in the digest field (di) and the synopsis field (sy) as follows:

    sy,di(junior second +s mortgagee lien-holder /p entitl! /p rent profit /p receiver!)

8.7 Following Recent Developments

As the new associate in the firm, you are expected to keep up on and summarize recent legal developments in the area of real estate finance law. How can you do this efficiently?

Solution

- One of the easiest ways to stay abreast of recent developments in real property law is by accessing the WESTLAW Topical Highlights—Real Property database (WTH–RP). The WTH–RP database summarizes recent legal developments, including court decisions, legislation and materials released by administrative agencies.

    To access the database, type **db wth-rp**. You will automatically retrieve a list of documents added to the database in the last two weeks.

- To read a summary of a document listed, type its corresponding number.

- You can also search this database by typing **s** to display the Enter Query screen. At the Enter Query screen, type your query. For example, to retrieve references discussing escrow agents, type a query like the following:

    "escrow agent"

*

Table of Cases

A

AAA Elec. & Neon Service, Inc. v. R-Design Co.—§ **12.4, n. 21.**
Aalfs Wall Paper & Paint Co. v. Bowker—§ **12.5, n. 3.**
Aaron v. Kent—§ **7.17, n. 6, 8, 13.**
Abacus Mortg. Ins. Co. v. Whitewood Hills Development Corp.—§ **7.10, n. 1, 3.**
Abberton v. Stephens—§ **3.8, n. 17.**
Abbot v. Stevens—§ **6.2, n. 9.**
Abbott v. Godfroy's Heirs—§ **7.12, n. 18.**
Abdelhaq v. Pflug—§ **8.15, n. 41.**
Abdul-Karim v. First Federal Sav. and Loan Ass'n of Champaign—§ **14.2.**
Abraham v. Fioramonte—§ **5.24, n. 23.**
Abrahams v. Berkowitz—§ **4.43, n. 12.**
Abramoff, In re—§ **5.22, n. 40;** § **6.5, n. 3;** § **6.2, n. 7;** § **6.1, n. 10.**
Abrams v. Crocker-Citizens Nat. Bank—§ **4.18, n. 9.**
Abrams v. Federal Deposit Ins. Corp.—§ **11.7, n. 33.**
Abramson v. Lakewood Bank and Trust Co.—§ **8.17, n. 61.**
Abrego v. United Peoples Federal Sav. and Loan Ass'n—§ **5.22, n. 19;** § **7.7, n. 25.**
Ace Contracting Co., a Div. of Cell-San Const. Co., Inc. v. Garfield & Arma Associates—§ **12.4, n. 19.**
Acevedo, In re—§ **8.15, n. 35, 41.**
Ackerman v. Hunsicker—§ **12.7, n. 4.**
Ackerson v. Lodi Branch R. Co.—§ **4.27, n. 17.**
Adair v. Carden—§ **5.1 n. 4;** § **5.8, n. 11, 13.**
Adams v. B & D, Inc.—§ **12.4, n. 35.**
Adams v. Boyd—§ **7.21, n. 85.**
Adams v. George—§ **5.4, n. 3;** § **5.8, n. 9;** § **9.8;** § **9.8, n. 28.**
Adams v. Gwinnett Commercial Bank—§ **7.21, n. 9.**
Adams v. Hill—§ **9.1, n. 18.**
Adams v. Holden—§ **7.5, n. 15.**
Adams v. Madison Realty & Development, Inc., 937 F.2d 845—§ **5.29, n. 39;** § **11.7, n. 35.**
Adams v. Madison Realty & Development, Inc., 853 F.2d 163—§ **5.28, n. 6.**
Adams v. Sayre—§ **4.32, n. 6.**
Adams v. Sims—§ **4.44, n. 14.**
Adams v. Southern California First Nat. Bank—§ **7.27, n. 14.**
Adams v. Walker—§ **11.7, n. 11.**
Addington-Beaman Lumber Co., Inc. v. Lincoln Sav. and Loan Ass'n—§ **13.3, n. 43.**
Adirondack Trust Co. v. Snyder—§ **7.31, n. 1, 3.**
Adkinson v. Nyberg—§ **7.8, n. 1, 10.**
Adkison v. Hannah—§ **7.22, n. 35.**
Adler v. Newell—§ **5.34, n. 42.**
Admiral Builders Sav. and Loan Ass'n v. South River Landing, Inc.—§ **6.6, n. 31;** § **12.1, n. 30.**
Adolphsen, In re—§ **3.33, n. 24, 25, 26.**
Advanced Alarm Technology, Inc. v. Pavilion Associates—§ **13.3, n. 40.**
Advantage Bank, Commonwealth v.—§ **4.47, n. 1.**
A.E. Pennebaker Co., Inc. v. Fuller—§ **5.28, n. 35.**
Aetna Cas. and Sur. Co. v. Buck—§ **12.4, n. 37.**
Aetna Cas. and Sur. Co. v. United States—§ **12.4, n. 41;** § **12.6, n. 23.**
Aetna Cas. & Sur. Co. v. Valdosta Federal Sav. & Loan Ass'n—§ **9.1, n. 4, 6.**
Aetna Ins. Co. v. Maryland Cast Stone Co.—§ **12.2, n. 39.**
Aetna Ins. Co. of Hartford, Conn. v. Baker—§ **4.13, n. 8.**
Aetna Life Ins. Co. v. Broecker—§ **4.35, n. 3, 51.**
Aetna Life Ins. Co. v. McElvain, 363 N.W.2d 186—§ **4.35, n. 15.**
Aetna Life Ins. Co. v. McElvain, 717 P.2d 1081—§ **12.9, n. 6.**
Aetna Life Ins. Co. v. Satterlee—§ **8.5, n. 14, 15.**
Aetna Life Ins. Co. v. Slack—§ **7.16, n. 20, 21.**
Aetna Life Ins. Co. of Hartford, Conn. v. Maxwell—§ **5.12, n. 1, 3, 9.**
A. F. C., Inc. v. Brockett—§ **10.3, n. 5.**
Affronti v. Bodine—§ **6.6, n. 1.**
Aggs v. Shackelford County—§ **4.4, n. 26.**
Agri Export Co-op. v. Universal Sav. Ass'n—§ **11.7, n. 16, 36.**
Agrownautics, Inc., In re—§ **10.2, n. 12.**
A. G. Sharp Lumber Co. v. Manus Homes, Inc.—§ **12.1, n. 2.**
Aguilar v. Bocci—§ **6.11, n. 40.**
Aguirre, In re—§ **8.15, n. 39.**
Ahlers, In re—§ **8.14;** § **8.14, n. 82.**
Aiello v. Aiello—§ **10.3, n. 6.**

TABLE OF CASES

Airline Commerce Bank v. Commercial Cred. Corp.—§ 12.8, n. 10.
Air One, Inc., In re—§ 10.2, n. 11.
Air Temperature, Inc. v. Morris—§ 12.2, n. 32.
Aitchison v. Bank of America—§ 4.2, n. 16.
A.J. Lane & Co., Inc., In re—§ 6.2, n. 24.
Ajootian, In re—§ 11.7, n. 19.
Akamine and Sons, Limited v. American Sec. Bank—§ 12.8, n. 10.
Akeley v. Miller—§ 7.15, n. 7, 11.
Akron Sav. & Loan Co. v. Ronson Homes, Inc.—§ 12.7, n. 11.
Aladdin Heating Corp. v. Trustees of Central States—§ 6.15, n. 1, 2; § 6.17, n. 5, 10; § 6.19, n. 10.
Alamosa Nat. Bank v. San Luis Valley Grain Growers, Inc.—§ 9.7, n. 3.
Alaska Cascade Financial Services, Inc. v. Doors Northwest, Inc.—§ 12.4, n. 10.
Alaska Statebank v. Fairco—§ 7.22, n. 45.
Albany Sav. Bank, F.S.B v. Novak—§ 6.6, n. 36; § 7.3, n. 5.
Albertina Realty Co. v. Rosbro Realty Corporation—§ 7.6, n. 15.
Albright v. Allday—§ 5.19, n. 38.
Albuquerque Nat. Bank v. Albuquerque Ranch Estates, Inc.—§ 3.27, n. 5.
Alda Commercial Corp., In re—§ 5.35, n. 44, 52.
Aldape v. Lubcke—§ 3.30, n. 13, 16.
Alden Hotel Co. v. Kanin—§ 6.15, n. 1; § 6.17, n. 9.
Aldrich v. Cooper—§ 10.9, n. 4; § 10.13, n. 12.
Alexandria Associates, Ltd. v. Mitchell Co.—§ 11.7, n. 37.
Alexandria Sav. Inst. v. Thomas—§ 12.7, n. 16.
Alf Holding Corporation v. American Stove Co.—§ 9.6, n. 6.
All American Holding Corp. v. Elgin State Bank—§ 10.9, n. 7.
Allen, In re—§ 8.15, n. 50, 52.
Allen, Matter of—§ 8.15, n. 24.
Allen v. McGaughey—§ 8.6, n. 16.
Allen v. Martin—§ 7.17, n. 4.
Allen v. Shepherd—§ 6.11, n. 21.
Allen v. Stainback—§ 2.4, n. 2.
Allen v. Wilson—§ 5.24, n. 34.
Allendale Furniture Co., Inc. v. Carolina Commercial Bank—§ 7.6, n. 13.
Allgood v. Spearman—§ 5.4, n. 1; § 5.8, n. 5; § 5.11, n. 6.
Allison v. Allison—§ 7.17, n. 12.
Allison v. Armstrong—§ 4.44, n. 11, 13.
Allison v. Home Sav. Ass'n of Kansas City—§ 12.11, n. 12.
Allison v. Liberty Sav.—§ 4.19, n. 33.
Allstate Financial Corp. v. Westfield Serv. Mgt. Co.—§ 10.9, n. 7.
All State Plumbing, Inc. v. Mutual Sec. Life Ins. Co.—§ 12.6, n. 44.
Alois v. Waldman—§ 12.3, n. 28.
Aloma Square, Inc., In re—§ 4.35, n. 25.
Alsop, In re—§ 8.17; § 8.17, n. 18, 21.
Alston v. Bitely—§ 10.14, n. 11; § 12.7, n. 37.
Altabet v. Monroe Methodist Church—§ 6.17, n. 10.
Althausen v. Kohn—§ 4.35, n. 51.
Althouse v. Provident Mut. Building-Loan Ass'n—§ 12.7, n. 35.
Altus Bank v. State Farm Fire and Cas. Co.—§ 4.16, n. 7.
Alvord v. Spring Valley Gold Co.—§ 5.11, n. 5.
Amberboy v. Societe de Banque Privee—§ 5.29, n. 6.
Amco Trust, Inc. v. Naylor—§ 4.20, n. 2.
Amelco Window Corp. v. Federal Ins. Co.—§ 12.2, n. 31.
American Bancshares Mortg. Co., Inc. v. Empire Home Loans, Inc.—§ 12.3, n. 48.
American Bldg. & Loan Ass'n. v. Farmers' Ins. Co.—§ 4.14, n. 10.
American Brake Shoe & Foundry Co. v. New York Rys. Co.—§ 4.39, n. 8.
American Century Mortg. Investors v. Unionamerica Mortg. and Equity Trust—§ 12.9, n. 32.
American Federal Sav. and Loan Ass'n v. Orenstein—§ 12.9, n. 23.
American Federal Sav. and Loan Ass'n of Madison v. Mid-America Service Corp.—§ 6.5, n. 2.
American Federal Sav. & Loan Ass'n of Tacoma v. McCaffrey—§ 8.1, n. 3.
American Fidelity Fire Ins. Co. v. Construcciones Werl, Inc.—§ 12.2, n. 40.
American Fletcher Mortg. Co., Inc. v. First American Inv. Corp.—§ 12.3, n. 6.
American Freehold Land Mortg. Co. of London v. Pollard—§ 4.29, n. 1; § 4.30, n. 1.
American Freehold Land Mortg. Co. of London, Ltd. v. Turner—§ 4.20, n. 2.
American Fuel & Power Co., In re—§ 8.18, n. 5.
American Future Systems, Inc., United States v.—§ 11.5, n. 18.
American Institute of Real Estate Appraisers of Nat. Ass'n of Realtors, United States v.—§ 11.5, n. 3, 10.
American Inv. Co. v. Farrar—§ 4.34, n. 19.
American Laundry Machinery Co. v. Larson—§ 9.6, n. 9.
American Loan & Trust Co. v. Toledo, C. & S. R. Co.—§ 4.10, n. 9.
American Mariner Industries, Inc., In re—§ 8.14; § 8.14, n. 15; § 8.16; § 8.16, n. 13.
American Medical Services, Inc. v. Mutual Federal Sav. & Loan Ass'n—§ 4.34, n. 14, 15.
American Metals Corp., In re—§ 6.2, n. 24.
American Metropolitan Mortg., Inc. v. Maricone—§ 5.32, n. 25, 26.
American Mini-Storage, Marietta Blvd., Ltd. v. Investguard, Ltd.—§ 6.6, n. 36.

TABLE OF CASES

American Nat. Bank v. Northwestern Mut. Life Ins. Co.—§ 4.34, n. 18.
American Nat. Bank and Trust Co. of Chicago, United States v., 595 F.Supp. 324—§ 7.7, n. 39.
American Nat. Bank and Trust Co. of Chicago, United States v., 573 F.Supp. 1317—§ 4.33, n. 1, 7.
American Nat. Bank and Trust Co. of Chicago, United States v., 443 F.Supp. 167—§ 7.7, n. 38.
American Nat. Bank of Jacksonville v. International Harvester Credit Corp.—§ 9.3, n. 5.
American Nat. Bank of Jacksonville v. Norris—§ 12.1, n. 26.
American Nat. Bank of Jacksonville, United States v.—§ 12.8, n. 15.
American Nat. Bank & Trust Co., United States v.—§ 8.18, n. 35, 36.
American Nat. Bank & Trust of New Jersey v. Leonard—§ 4.18, n. 9.
American Sav. Bank & Trust Co. v. Helgesen—§ 5.31, n. 13.
American Sav. & Loan Ass'n v. Leeds—§ 4.9, n. 5.
American Seating Co. v. Philadelphia—§ 12.4, n. 35.
American Sec. & Trust Co. v. John J. Juliano, Inc.—§ 5.33, n. 5, 13, 33.
American Transit Mix Co. v. Weber—§ 12.4, n. 38, 39.
American Trucking Ass'ns, United States v.—§ 5.24, n. 58.
American Trust Co v. England—§ 4.24, n. 24.
American Trust Co. v. North Belleville Quarry Co.—§ 4.7, n. 3.
American Waterworks Co. of Illinois v. Farmers' Loan & Trust Co.—§ 5.17, n. 6.
Amerson, In re—§ 8.15, n. 39.
Ames v. Miller—§ 5.34, n. 17.
Ames v. Pardue—§ 7.21, n. 29.
AMI Operating Partners Ltd. Partnership v. JAD Enterprises, Inc.—§ 12.4, n. 18; § 12.5, n. 40.
A.M.R. Enterprises, Inc. v. United Postal Sav. Ass'n—§ 12.3, n. 44.
Amsterdam Sav. Bank v. Amsterdam Pharmaceutical Development Corp.—§ 8.1, n. 10.
Anchor Concrete Co. v. Victor Sav. & Loan Ass'n—§ 12.4, n. 42.
Anderman v. 1395 E. 52nd St. Realty Corp.—§ 7.31, n. 9.
Anderson, In re, 88 B.R. 877—§ 8.16, n. 17.
Anderson, In re, 50 B.R. 728—§ 8.18, n. 53.
Anderson, In re, 36 B.R. 120—§ 8.19, n. 9.
Anderson, In re, 16 B.R. 697—§ 8.15, n. 40.
Anderson v. Anderson, 266 A.2d 56—§ 7.21, n. 2.
Anderson v. Anderson, 84 N.W. 112—§ 3.24, n. 2, 7.
Anderson v. Beneficial Mortg. Corp.—§ 12.3, n. 1.
Anderson v. Breezy Point Estates—§ 12.4, n. 14.
Anderson v. Brinkerhoff—§ 3.29, n. 1.
Anderson v. Foothill Industrial Bank—§ 5.30, n. 15.
Anderson v. Heart Federal Sav.—§ 2.4, n. 15.
Anderson v. Lee—§ 2.1, n. 5; § 2.3, n. 9.
Anderson v. Reed—§ 2.2, n. 8.
Anderson v. Robbins—§ 4.22, n. 7, 9, 17, 18.
Anderson v. Sharp—§ 5.35, n. 15.
Anderson v. Streck—§ 12.4, n. 29; § 13.3, n. 31.
Anderson v. Taylor—§ 12.4, n. 21.
Anderson Oaks (Phase I) Ltd. Partnership v. Anderson Mill Oaks, Ltd.—§ 7.22, n. 10.
Andreasen v. Hansen—§ 12.3, n. 28.
Andrews v. Fleet Real Estate Funding Corp.—§ 6.8, n. 4.
Andrews v. Robertson—§ 5.3, n. 2.
Andrews v. Townshend—§ 5.28, n. 23.
Angel, United States v.—§ 4.11, n. 10, 11; § 7.6, n. 5.
Anglo–Californian Bank v. Cerf—§ 3.8, n. 1; § 3.15, n. 20; § 3.16, n. 6.
Anglo–Californian Bank v. Field—§ 4.24, n. 14; § 4.27, n. 5; § 4.28, n. 11.
Anson v. Anson—§ 4.45, n. 8.
Anspec Co., Inc. v. Johnson Controls, Inc.—§ 4.47, n. 7.
Anthony, In re—§ 3.37, n. 11.
Antioch Foundation, United States v.—§ 7.7, n. 42.
A-1 Door & Materials Co. v. Fresno Guarantee Sav. & Loan Ass'n—§ 12.6, n. 6.
Apex Siding & Roofing Co. v. First Federal Sav. & Loan Ass'n of Shawnee—§ 12.7, n. 42.
Appeal of (see name of party)
Apple Tree Partners, L.P., In re—§ 8.14, n. 67.
Application of (see name of party)
Araserv, Inc. v. Bay State Harness Horse Racing & Breeding Ass'n, Inc.—§ 4.1, n. 18.
Archer–Daniels–Midland Co. v. Paull—§ 12.3, n. 41, 43.
Architectonics, Inc. v. Salem–American Ventures, Inc.—§ 12.6, n. 42, 45.
Argall v. Pitts—§ 4.38, n. 3.
Argonaut Ins. Co. v. C & S Bank of Tifton—§ 12.2, n. 44.
Argonne Const. Co., Inc., In re—§ 13.3, n. 50.
Arkansas Supply, Inc. v. Young—§ 3.35, n. 1.
Arkansas Teacher Retirement System v. Coronado Properties, Ltd.—§ 4.16, n. 7.
Arlington Heights, Village of v. Metropolitan Housing Development Corp.—§ 11.5, n. 18.

TABLE OF CASES

Armand's Engineering, Inc. v. Town & Country Club, Inc.—§ 7.14, n. 3; § 7.31, n. 12, 13.
Armetta v. Clevetrust Realty Investors—§ 12.10, n. 34; § 12.11, n. 12.
Armistead v. Bishop—§ 4.24, n. 14.
Armour & Co. v. Western Const. Co.—§ 12.4, n. 6.
Armsey v. Channel Associates, Inc.—§ 4.16, n. 12; § 9.8, n. 3, 6.
Armstead, In re—§ 11.2, n. 30.
Armstrong v. Armstrong—§ 5.29, n. 15.
Armstrong v. Isbell—§ 5.28, n. 28, 31.
Armstrong v. Resolution Trust Corp.—§ 11.7, n. 28.
Army Nat. Bank v. Equity Developers, Inc.—§ 5.28, n. 35.
Arnold v. Broad—§ 4.4, n. 26.
Arnold v. Gebhardt—§ 8.6, n. 10, 11.
Arnold v. Haberstock—§ 7.15, n. 1.
Arnold v. Howard—§ 5.3, n. 2.
Arnold, United States v.—§ 8.16, n. 27.
Arnolds Management Corp. v. Eischen—§ 7.22, n. 17.
Aronoff v. Western Federal Sav. & Loan Ass'n—§ 6.2, n. 16.
Arrington v. Becker—§ 5.4, n. 5.
Arrington v. Liscom—§ 7.5, n. 8, 18.
Arthur v. Burkich—§ 6.1, n. 2; § 6.2, n. 3.
Arthurs Travel Center, Inc. v. Alten—§ 6.16, n. 6.
Artz v. Yeager—§ 5.34, n. 17.
Asbell v. Marshall Bldg. & Loan Ass'n—§ 5.19, n. 21.
A & S Distributing Co. v. Nall-Tucker, Inc.—§ 9.4, n. 6.
Ashburn Bank v. Reinhardt—§ 6.16, n. 6; § 6.17, n. 8; § 12.8, n. 17.
Ashford Apartments Ltd. Partnership, In re—§ 4.35, n. 40.
Ashkenazy Enterprises, Inc., In re—§ 4.35, n. 41.
Ashland Oil, Inc. v. Sonford Products Corp.—§ 4.49, n. 7, 10, 16.
Ashley, State ex rel. v. Circuit Court of Milwaukee County—§ 7.12, n. 24.
Askew v. Sanders—§ 7.5, n. 4, 5.
Aslan, In re—§ 8.19, n. 9.
Aspen Homes, Inc., In re—§ 12.6, n. 8, 10.
Assets Realization Co. v. Clark—§ 5.33, n. 8, 10, 21.
Associated Schools, Inc. v. Dade County—§ 6.3, n. 16.
Associates Discount Corp. v. Gomes—§ 9.1, n. 4, 10, 12, 13, 14.
Associates Nat. Mortg. Corp. v. Farmers Ins. Exchange—§ 4.16, n. 7.
Associates Realty Credit Ltd. v. Brune—§ 10.13, n. 2.
Association Center Ltd. Partnership, In re—§ 8.18, n. 54.
Association of Relatives and Friends of AIDS Patients (A.F.A.P.S.) v. Regulations and Permits Admin. or Administracion de Reglamentos y Permisos (A.R.P.E.)—§ 11.5, n. 18.
Astor v. Hoyt—§ 4.26, n. 6.
Astor v. Turner—§ 4.40, n. 1.
Atco Const. & Development Corp. v. Beneficial Sav. Bank, F.S.B.—§ 4.34, n. 10.
Atherton v. Toney—§ 6.16, n. 27.
Atlantic Bank v. Farmers' Mut. Fire Ins. Ass'n—§ 4.14, n. 7.
Atlantic Coast Line R. Co. v. Rutledge—§ 4.4, n. 12.
Atlantic Mortg. Corp., In re—§ 5.27, n. 10; § 5.28, n. 30, 40; § 5.35, n. 43.
Atlantic Trust Co. v. Dana—§ 4.43, n. 9.
Audsley v. Allen—§ 5.28, n. 6; § 5.29, n. 11, 14.
Auernheimer v. Metzen, 783 P.2d 1027—§ 3.29, n. 1, 3.
Auernheimer v. Metzen, 780 P.2d 796—§ 5.26, n. 5.
August Tobler, Inc. v. Goolsby—§ 7.7, n. 7.
Augustus Court Associates, In re—§ 8.14, n. 28.
Aultman v. United Bank of Crawford—§ 10.2, n. 1.
Aultman & Taylor Co. v. Meade—§ 7.21, n. 39.
Ausherman, In re—§ 8.14, n. 11.
Aust v. Rosenbaum—§ 7.4, n. 4.
Austin v. Atlas Subsidiaries of Miss., Inc.—§ 5.29, n. 27; § 5.31, n. 4.
Austin v. Austin—§ 2.2, n. 10
Austin, United States v.—§ 12.3; § 12.3, n. 54.
Automatic Heating & Equipment Co., United States v.—§ 12.8, n. 9.
Auto-Plaza, Inc. v. Central Bank of Alabama, N. A.—§ 6.9, n. 32.
A.V.A. Const. Corp. v. Palmetto Land Clearing, Inc.—§ 12.4, n. 19.
Avco Financial Services Loan, Inc. v. Hale—§ 7.13, n. 9.
Averall v. Wade—§ 10.9, n. 4.
Averill v. Taylor—§ 10.8, n. 5.
Avery, In re—§ 9.7, n. 3, 25.
Avret, In re—§ 8.15, n. 70.
Aycock Bros. Lumber Co. v. First Nat. Bank of Dothan—§ 3.29, n. 18.
Ayers v. Philadelphia Housing Authority—§ 11.6, n. 63, 83.
Ayrault v. Murphy—§ 7.13, n. 22.
A-Z Servicenter, Inc. v. Segall—§ 7.7, n. 7.
Aztec Co., In re—§ 8.14, n. 62.
Aztec Properties, Inc. v. Union Planters Nat. Bank of Memphis—§ 11.4, n. 95.

B

Baber v. Hanie—§ 5.6, n. 6.
Back v. Union Life Ins. Co.—§ 12.9, n. 28.
Bacon v. Bowdoin—§ 7.2, n. 11.
Bacon v. Van Schoonhoven—§ 5.34, n. 13, 17.

TABLE OF CASES

Badger State Agri-Credit & Realty, Inc. v. Lubahn—§ 12.8, n. 7.
Bailey v. Barranca—§ 8.8, n. 18.
Bailey v. Call—§ 12.4, n. 36.
Bailey v. First Federal Sav. & Loan Ass'n of Ottawa—§ 5.23, n. 7.
Bailey v. Inman—§ 5.19, n. 8, 12.
Bailey v. Lilly—§ 3.29, n. 1.
Bailey v. Mills—§ 5.29, n. 8.
Bailey v. Pioneer Federal Sav. & Loan Ass'n—§ 7.20, n. 15.
Bailey v. St. Louis Union Trust Co.—§ 3.3, n. 2.
Bailey Mortg. Co. v. Gobble-Fite Lumber Co., Inc.—§ 12.4, n. 21.
Baily v. Smith—§ 5.31, n. 14.
Baird v. Baird—§ 2.1, n. 4.
Baird v. Chamberlain—§ 4.44, n. 6.
Baird v. Fischer—§ 4.45, n. 5, 8, 15.
Baker v. Aalberg—§ 4.31, n. 1.
Baker v. Baker—§ 10.5, n. 7.
Baker v. Citizens State Bank of St. Louis Park—§ 2.3, n. 2, 17, 19.
Baker v. F & F Inv. Co.—§ 5.32, n. 26; § 11.5, n. 2.
Baker v. Gardner—§ 8.3, n. 28.
Baker v. Gavitt—§ 6.6, n. 12.
Baker v. Jacobson—§ 3.1, n. 37.
Baker v. Loves Park Sav. and Loan Ass'n—§ 5.22, n. 14, 16.
Baker v. Surman—§ 12.11, n. 37.
Baker v. Taggart—§ 3.8, n. 10; § 3.18, n. 3.
Baker v. Varney—§ 4.35, n. 3.
Bakker v. Empire Sav., Bldg. and Loan Ass'n—§ 5.24, n. 118.
Baksa, In re—§ 8.15, n. 65.
Balance Ltd., Inc. v. Short—§ 7.31, n. 11.
Balboa Ins. Co. v. Bank of Boston Connecticut—§ 12.2, n. 44.
Baldi v. Chicago Title & Trust Co.—§ 7.12, n. 6; § 7.15, n. 11, 15, 18.
Baldin, In re—§ 8.13, n. 11.
Baldridge v. Morgan—§ 12.5, n. 3, 4.
Balducci v. Eberly—§ 7.6, n. 19.
Baldwin v. Bright Mortg. Co.—§ 12.10, n. 34.
Baldwin v. McDonald—§ 3.18, n. 6.
Baldwin v. Walker—§ 4.21, n. 5.
Baldwin-Bellmore Federal Sav. & Loan Ass'n v. Stellato—§ 7.12, n. 26.
Baldwin Locomotive Works v. Edward Hines Lumber Co.—§ 12.4, n. 16.
Bale v. Wright—§ 5.33, n. 17.
Balen v. Lewis—§ 10.15, n. 2.
Ballengee v. New Mexico Federal Sav. and Loan Ass'n—§ 5.28, n. 6.
Ballentyne v. Smith—§ 7.16, n. 29.
Balme v. Wambaugh—§ 6.7, n. 26.
Baltimore Life Ins. Co. v. Harn—§ 5.22, n. 19; § 5.24, n. 87.
Baltimore Markets v. Real Estate-Land Title & Trust Co.—§ 4.21, n. 9.
BA Mortg. Co., Inc. v. Unisal Development, Inc.—§ 12.3, n. 4.

Banco Espanol de Credito v. Security Pacific Nat. Bank—§ 5.35, n. 26.
Banco Espanol De Credito v. Security Pacific Nat. Bank—§ 5.35, n. 26.
Ban-Co Inv. Co. v. Loveless—§ 12.9, n. 28; § 12.10, n. 60.
Banco Totta e Acores v. Fleet Nat. Bank—§ 5.35, n. 19.
B and P Development v. Walker—§ 12.5, n. 18, 19, 25.
Bangs v. Farm Credit Bank of Columbia—§ 7.7, n. 52.
Bank v. Crumley—§ 12.9, n. 6.
Bankers Federal Sav. and Loan Ass'n v. House—§ 7.16, n. 26.
Bankers Life Co. v. Denton—§ 7.7, n. 30, 31.
Bankers' Mortg. Co. of Topeka v. O'Donovan—§ 7.10, n. 17.
Bankers Mortg. Corp. v. Jacobs—§ 5.4, n. 1.
Bankers Trust Co. v. Board of Managers of Park 900 Condominium—§ 13.5, n. 15.
Bankers Trust Co. v. El Paso Pre-Cast Co.—§ 12.5, n. 18, 19, 25.
Bankers Trust New York Corp. v. Renting Office, Inc.—§ 2.1, n. 5.
Bankier v. First Federal Sav. & Loan Ass'n of Champaign—§ 6.1, n. 10.
Bank of Alameda County v. Hering—§ 5.11, n. 5.
Bank of America v. Daily—§ 8.3; § 8.3, n. 60.
Bank of America v. Kaiser Steel Corp.—§ 10.2, n. 12.
Bank of America Nat. Ass'n v. Dames—§ 7.8, n. 10.
Bank of America Nat. Trust and Sav. Ass'n v. Denver Hotel Ass'n Ltd. Partnership—§ 4.35, n. 5.
Bank of America Nat. Trust & Sav. Ass'n v. Bank of Amador County—§ 4.25, n. 3.
Bank of America Nat. Trust & Savings Ass'n v. Reidy—§ 7.16, n. 12.
Bank of Babylon v. Zaffuto Const. Co., Inc.—§ 5.29, n. 14.
Bank of Barron v. Gieseke—§ 12.7, n. 11.
Bank of Boston Connecticut v. Platz—§ 6.6, n. 36; § 7.3, n. 5.
Bank of California Nat. Ass'n v. Leone—§ 5.28, n. 40.
Bank of Commerce v. Waddell—§ 9.7, n. 19.
Bank of Commerce of Evansville v. First Nat. Bank of Evansville—§ 10.13, n. 7, 19.
Bank of Commonwealth v. Bevan—§ 8.17, n. 4.
Bank of Ephraim v. Davis—§ 12.8, n. 4.
Bank of Hawaii v. Horwoth—§ 3.36, n. 14.
Bank of Hemet v. United States—§ 8.3; § 8.3, n. 120.
Bank of Honolulu, N.A. v. Anderson—§ 7.6, n. 8.

TABLE OF CASES

Bank of Italy Nat. Trust & Sav. Ass'n v. Bentley—§ 1.6; § 1.6, n. 1; § 6.1, n. 32; § 6.11, n. 32; § 8.2, n. 3, 11, 12.
Bank of Kansas v. Nelson Music Co., Inc.—§ 12.8, n. 7.
Bank of Kirkwood Plaza v. Mueller—§ 8.3, n. 45, 47.
Bank of Lafayette v. Giles—§ 6.7, n. 4.
Bank of Manhattan Trust Co. v. 571 Park Ave. Corporation—§ 4.42, n. 14, 21.
Bank of Montgomery County's Appeal—§ 12.7, n. 16.
Bank of New South Wales v. O'Connor—§ 6.7, n. 4.
Bank of N. M. v. Rice—§ 12.3, n. 45.
Bank of Oak Grove v. Wilmot State Bank—§ 2.4, n. 5.
Bank of Ogdensburgh v. Arnold—§ 4.34, n. 2, 4.
Bank of Powell v. Peoples Bank—§ 6.17, n. 10.
Bank of Santa Fe v. Garcia—§ 3.36, n. 3, 4.
Bank of Searcy v. Kroh—§ 9.4, n. 14; § 12.8, n. 9.
Bank of Seoul and Trust Co. v. Marcione—§ 7.21, n. 6.
Bank of Stamford v. Alaimo—§ 7.18, n. 3.
Bank of Woodson v. Hibbitts—§ 12.8, n. 15.
Bank One Texas, N.A. v. A.J. Warehouse, Inc.—§ 5.35, n. 1.
Banks–Miller Supply Co. v. Smallridge—§ 7.31, n. 2; § 7.32, n. 7; § 10.13, n. 6.
Bank USA v. Sill—§ 5.6, n. 13; § 5.19, n. 45; § 5.24, n. 131.
Banner, In re—§ 4.43, n. 9.
Banta v. Vreeland—§ 10.6, n. 5.
Bantuelle v. Williams—§ 3.18, n. 2, 3; § 3.17, n. 8.
Barbano v. Central-Hudson Steamboat Co—§ 9.4, n. 14.
Barber v. Federal Land Bank of Houston—§ 5.17, n. 5.
Barbieri v. Ramelli—§ 8.2, n. 4, 6.
Barbin v. Moore—§ 10.14, n. 11.
Barbizon Plaza, In re—§ 4.38, n. 20.
Barbour v. Handlos Real Estate and Bldg. Corp.—§ 5.29, n. 17; § 5.34, n. 33.
Barclays Bank of California v. Superior Court for City and County of San Francisco—§ 4.34, n. 22; § 4.35, n. 3, 5, 6, 49.
Barclay's Bank of New York, N.A. v. Smitty's Ranch, Inc.—§ 7.6, n. 3.
Bardwell v. Mann—§ 12.5, n. 3.
Bargioni v. Hill—§ 8.3, n. 33, 83.
Barker's Inc. v. B.D.J. Development Co.—§ 12.4, n. 24.
Barkhausen v. Continental Illinois Nat. Bank & T. Co.—§ 5.4, n. 5.
Barkis v. Scott—§ 3.29; § 3.29, n. 23.
Barnaby v. Boardman—§ 8.3, n. 28.
Barnard v. First Nat. Bank of Okaloosa County—§ 8.3, n. 18.
Barnard v. Jennison—§ 3.9, n. 3.

Barnard v. Paterson—§ 4.29, n. 3, 10; § 4.30, n. 2, 5.
Barnard v. Wilson—§ 4.44, n. 15.
Barnard-Curtiss Co. v. United States—§ 12.2, n. 20.
Barnard-Curtiss Co. v. United States for Use and Benefit of D.W. Falls Const. Co.—§ 12.2, n. 20.
Barnes, In re—§ 8.15, n. 72.
Barnes v. Hampton—§ 10.2, n. 1.
Barnes v. Mott—§ 5.7, n. 3; § 10.7, n. 12.
Barnes v. Racster—§ 10.13, n. 12, 18.
Barnes v. Ward—§ 7.10, n. 9.
Barnett v. Nelson—§ 4.28, n. 9; § 4.29, n. 9; § 4.31, n. 2.
Barnett & Jackson v. McMillan—§ 6.16, n. 24, 26.
Barnhart v. Edwards—§ 12.7, n. 11.
Barr v. Granahan—§ 3.2, n. 1, 8; § 3.3, n. 1.
Barr v. Van Alstine—§ 7.3, n. 8.
Barrera v. Security Bldg. & Inv. Corp.—§ 3.30, n. 12; § 7.27; § 7.27, n. 2, 6, 11, 13, 20, 31, 32.
Barrett v. Commonwealth Federal Sav. and Loan Ass'n—§ 8.17, n. 40.
Barrett v. Millikan—§ 12.5, n. 3, 5.
Barringer v. Loder—§ 5.34, n. 42.
Barrows v. Jackson—§ 7.27, n. 26.
Barry v. Dow—§ 4.30, n. 7.
Barry v. Hamburg-Bremen Fire Ins. Co.—§ 3.10, n. 2.
Barry v. Harlow—§ 4.30, n. 7.
Barry v. Raskov—§ 12.11, n. 30.
Barry Properties, Inc. v. Fick Bros. Roofing Co.—§ 12.4, n. 5; § 12.5; § 12.5, n. 18, 20, 32.
Barson v. Mulligan—§ 4.24, n. 6.
Bart v. Streuli—§ 4.11, n. 8.
Bartels v. Fowler—§ 4.41, n. 11.
Barter v. Wheeler—§ 4.26, n. 1.
Barth v. Ely—§ 8.2, n. 4.
Barthell v. Syverson.—§ 4.29, n. 3.
Bartholf v. Bensley—§ 5.33, n. 5.
Bartlett Bank & Trust Co. v. McJunkins—§ 7.7, n. 21.
Bartley v. Karas—§ 3.29, n. 27.
Bartley v. Pikeville Nat. Bank & Trust Co.—§ 10.9, n. 3, 7; § 10.10, n. 11; § 10.14, n. 4.
Bartmess v. Bourassa—§ 2.1, n. 26.
Barton v. Anderson—§ 7.14, n. 16.
Bartz v. Paff—§ 3.36, n. 4.
Basile v. Erhal Holding Corp.—§ 3.1, n. 10.
Bass v. Boston Five Cent Sav. Bank—§ 4.19, n. 6.
Basse v. Gallegger—§ 7.6, n. 15.
Bateman v. Grand Rapids & I. R. Co.—§ 8.1, n. 2.
Bateman v. Kellogg—§ 7.16, n. 9.
Bates v. Humboldt County—§ 4.5, n. 9; § 4.4, n. 13.
Bates v. Ruddick—§ 10.10, n. 11, 12.
Bates v. Schuelke—§ 7.16, n. 15.
Batty v. Snook—§ 3.3, n. 5.

Bauermeister v. McDonald—§ 3.36, n. 10.
Baumgard v. Bowman—§ 4.28, n. 8; § 4.29, n. 2.
Baumgarten v. Bubolz—§ 8.3, n. 6.
Bautz v. Adams—§ 5.33, n. 11.
Baxter v. Pritchard—§ 3.10, n. 3.
Baxter v. Redevco, Inc.—§ 5.33, n. 7; § 6.16, n. 27, 28.
Bay v. Williams—§ 5.18, n. 14.
Bayer v. Hoagland—§ 4.2, n. 16.
Bayles v. Husted—§ 10.8, n. 5.
Bay Metro Glass Co., Inc., In re—§ 10.9, n. 7.
Bay Minette Production Credit Ass'n v. Federal Land Bank of New Orleans—§ 6.17, n. 8; § 6.19, n. 10.
Baypoint Mortg. v. Crest Premium Real Estate Investments Retirement Trust—§ 6.9; § 6.9, n. 31.
BBT, In re—§ 8.14, n. 10.
BCW Assoc. Ltd. v. Occidental Chemical Corp.—§ 4.47, n. 15.
Beach v. Cooke—§ 7.4, n. 4.
Beach v. Waite—§ 5.9, n. 8.
Beacham v. Gurney—§ 6.17, n. 7, 14.
Beacon Distributors, Inc., In re—§ 10.9, n. 7; § 10.11, n. 3.
Beacon Federal Sav. and Loan Ass'n v. Panoramic Enterprises, Inc.—§ 5.5, n. 1; § 5.6, n. 1; § 5.11, n. 6.
Beacon Terrace Mut. Homes, Inc., United States v.—§ 7.7, n. 39.
Beal v. First Federal Sav. and Loan Ass'n of Madison—§ 11.6, n. 29.
Beals v. Cryer—§ 3.33, n. 14.
Bean v. Walker—§ 3.29; § 3.29, n. 64; § 5.21, n. 27; § 5.24, n. 35.
Beardsley v. Empire Trust Co.—§ 10.15, n. 8.
Bearss v. Ford—§ 3.8, n. 12.
Beaudet v. Saleh—§ 12.4, n. 36.
Beaver v. Ledbetter—§ 5.5, n. 1, 6.
Beaver Falls Building & Loan Ass'n v. Allemania Fire Ins. Co.—§ 4.14, n. 10.
Beaver Flume & Lumber Co. v. Eccles—§ 4.10, n. 7.
Beck v. Sheldon—§ 2.1, n. 4.
Becker v. Hopper—§ 12.4, n. 18.
Becker v. McCrea—§ 7.5, n. 8.
Beckman v. Ward—§ 5.34, n. 12.
Beckwith v. Seborn—§ 4.45, n. 1, 3.
Becovic v. Harris Trust & Sav. Bank—§ 14.2.
Bedian v. Cohn—§ 2.1, n. 9.
Bedortha v. Sunridge Land Co., Inc.—§ 3.36, n. 10.
Beebe v. Wisconsin Mortg. Loan Co.—§ 3.10, n. 3.
Beeler v. American Trust Co.—§ 3.19, n. 17.
Beelman v. Beelman—§ 3.8, n. 1; § 3.5, n. 3.
Begelfer v. Najarian—§ 6.9, n. 14, 21.
Behr, In re—§ 8.13, n. 1.
Bein v. Mueson Realty Corp.—§ 4.40, n. 4.

Beitel v. Dobbin—§ 4.44, n. 4.
Beitelspacher v. Winther—§ 3.29, n. 32.
Bekins Bar V Ranch v. Huth—§ 7.22, n. 1.
Belanger, United States v.—§ 11.6, n. 47.
Belbridge Prop. Trust, Re—§ 4.43, n. 5.
Belcher v. Belcher—§ 10.7, n. 10.
Belgrano v. Finkelstein—§ 8.3, n. 18.
Belknap v. Gleason—§ 6.11, n. 16.
Belknap Sav. Bank of Laconia, N.H. v. Lamar Land & Canal Co.—§ 12.9, n. 1.
Bell v. Bell—§ 3.15, n. 19.
Bell v. First Columbus Nat. Bank—§ 4.4, n. 19.
Bell v. Fleming's Ex'rs—§ 2.4, n. 4.
Bell v. Tollefsen—§ 12.4, n. 35.
Bellah v. First Nat. Bank of Hereford—§ 7.21, n. 29, 30.
Bellamy v. Federal Home Loan Mortgage—§ 8.15, n. 70.
Belland v. O.K. Lumber Co., Inc.—§ 9.1, n. 4, 27, 28.
Bell Bakeries, Inc. v. Jefferson Standard Life Ins. Co.—§ 6.2, n. 7; § 6.3, n. 1.
Belleville Sav. Bank v. Reis—§ 6.16, n. 17.
Bell Federal Sav. and Loan Ass'n of Bellevue v. Laura Lanes, Inc.—§ 7.6, n. 8.
Bellingham First Federal Sav. and Loan Ass'n v. Garrison—§ 5.22, n. 31.
Bell & Murphy and Associates, Inc. v. Interfirst Bank Gateway, N.A.—§ 5.29, n. 33; § 11.7, n. 23.
Belloc v. Rogers—§ 7.11, n. 2.
Bellon v. Malnar—§ 3.29, n. 32, 41.
Bellows Falls Trust Co. v. Gibbs—§ 12.8, n. 15.
Belmont v. Coman—§ 5.7, n. 4; § 5.8, n. 9.
Belote v. McLaughlin—§ 8.1, n. 2.
Bement v. Ohio Valley Banking & Trust Co.—§ 6.13, n. 6.
Benedict v. Griffith—§ 6.12, n. 18.
Benedict v. Mortimer—§ 7.10, n. 14.
Beneficial Standard Life Ins. Co. v. Trinity Nat. Bank—§ 4.16, n. 7.
Benham v. Rowe—§ 4.30, n. 5.
Benjamin Franklin Federal Sav. & Loan Ass'n v. Parker—§ 5.26, n. 6.
Bennett v. Bates—§ 5.17, n. 5.
Bennett v. Harrison—§ 3.15, n. 19; § 3.24, n. 6.
Bennett Const. Co., Inc. v. Allen Gardens, Inc.—§ 12.6, n. 37.
Benson, State ex rel. Bickford v.—§ 4.29, n. 2.
Benton v. Patel—§ 7.6, n. 4, 18.
Berenato v. Bell Sav. and Loan Ass'n—§ 6.3, n. 3.
Berg v. Liberty Federal Sav. and Loan Ass'n—§ 5.1, n. 4; § 5.3, n. 4; § 8.1, n. 2.
Berge, In re—§ 8.17, n. 12, 14.
Berger v. Baist—§ 5.34, n. 35.
Bergin v. Robbins—§ 4.43, n. 8.
Bergkamp v. New York Guardian Mortgagee Corp.—§ 4.19, n. 33.
Bergsoe Metal Corp., In re—§ 4.48; § 4.48, n. 6.

Bering v. Republic Bank of San Antonio—§ 7.21, n. 14.
Berk & Berk, United States v.—§ 4.35, n. 9.
Berkley Multi-Units, Inc., Matter of—§ 8.13, n. 13.
Berkshire Life Ins. Co. v. Hutchings—§ 5.18, n. 17.
Berks Title Ins. Co. v. Haendiges—§ 12.3, n. 4.
Berlin v. Dassel—§ 2.1, n. 19.
Berliner Handels-Und Frankfurter Bank v. East Texas Steel Facilities, Inc.—§ 10.2, n. 12.
Bermes v. Kelley—§ 4.43, n. 5.
Bermes v. Sylling—§ 5.1, n. 1.
Bernhardt v. Lymburner—§ 10.13, n. 30.
Bernheim v. Pessou—§ 2.1, n. 4.
Beronio v. Ventura County Lumber Co.—§ 7.14, n. 15.
Berry v. Government Nat. Mortg. Ass'n—§ 7.22, n. 17.
Bertelsen, In re—§ 8.19, n. 9.
Bessemer v. Gersten—§ 13.5, n. 18.
Best Fertilizers of Arizona, Inc. v. Burns, 571 P.2d 675—§ 5.27, n. 7.
Best Fertilizers of Arizona, Inc. v. Burns, 570 P.2d 179—§ 5.9; § 5.9, n. 9; § 5.28, n. 1; § 10.2, n. 9.
Bethesda Air Rights Ltd. Partnership, In re—§ 4.35, n. 25.
Beth–June, Inc. v. Wil-Avon Merchandise Mart, Inc.—§ 6.1, n. 7.
Bethlehem v. Annis—§ 2.2, n. 1, 8, 12.
Betts v. Brown—§ 5.10, n. 3.
Betz v. Heebner—§ 5.27, n. 12.
Betz v. Verner—§ 4.5, n. 9; § 4.6; § 4.6, n. 1, 2.
Bevins v. Peoples Bank & Trust Co.—§ 4.35, n. 31, 33.
B.F. Avery & Sons' Plow Co. v. Kennerly—§ 4.39, n. 12.
BFP, In re—§ 8.17; § 8.17, n. 34.
B.F. Saul Real Estate Inv. Trust v. McGovern—§ 12.3, n. 15, 19, 26.
Bichel Optical Laboratories, Inc. v. Marquette Nat. Bank of Minneapolis—§ 7.27, n. 14.
Bickford, State ex rel. v. Benson—§ 4.29, n. 2.
Bickford v. United States—§ 8.8, n. 13.
Biddel v. Brizzolara—§ 5.18, n. 6.
Biddle v. National Old Line Ins. Co.—§ 7.21, n. 39.
Biddle v. Pugh—§ 6.13, n. 3.
Biersdorff v. Brumfield—§ 12.7, n. 37.
Big Apple Supermarkets, Inc. v. Corkdale Realty, Inc.—§ 7.2, n. 8.
Bigelow v. Cassedy—§ 7.14, n. 11.
Bigelow v. Willson—§ 7.2, n. 14.
Big Land Inv. Corp. v. Lomas & Nettleton Financial Corp.—§ 9.4, n. 15; § 12.10, n. 35.
Bigoness v. Hibbard—§ 7.12, n. 19.
Big Sespe Oil Co. v. Cochran—§ 8.5, n. 10.

Big S Trucking Co., Inc. v. Gervais Favrot, Inc.—§ 12.4, n. 14.
Bill Nay & Sons Excavating v. Neeley Const. Co.—§ 3.35, n. 1; § 3.36, n. 3.
Bill Stremmel Motors, Inc. v. IDS Leasing Corp.—§ 12.11, n. 11.
Bindseil v. Liberty Trust Co—§ 8.18, n. 6.
Bingaman, State ex rel. v. Valley Sav. & Loan Ass'n—§ 5.22, n. 13, 19.
Binns v. Baumgartner—§ 5.13, n. 8.
Birch River Boom & Lumber Co. v. Glendon Boom & Lumber Co.—§ 10.13, n. 9.
Birkenfeld v. Cocalis—§ 2.1, n. 9.
Bishop v. Pecsok—§ 11.5, n. 21.
Bisno v. Sax—§ 7.6, n. 7; § 7.7, n. 10.
Biswell v. Gladney—§ 10.10, n. 8.
Bittner v. McGrath—§ 5.32, n. 17.
B. J. I. Corp. v. Larry W. Corp.—§ 12.9, n. 28, 44; § 12.10, n. 32, 58; § 13.3, n. 23, 24.
B Kuppenheimer & Co. v. Mornin—§ 3.38, n. 5.
Black, In re—§ 9.7, n. 3.
Black v. Krauss—§ 5.4, n. 1; § 5.11, n. 6.
Black v. Reno—§ 7.8, n. 4.
Black v. Sullivan—§ 2.4, n. 15; § 5.28, n. 40; § 5.30, n. 10.
Black v. Suydam—§ 10.9, n. 21.
Black Jack, Missouri, City of, United States v.—§ 11.5, n. 17.
Blackmar v. Sharp—§ 12.7, n. 11.
Blackmon v. Patel—§ 5.3, n. 4.
Blackstone Valley Nat. Bank v. Hanson—§ 4.25, n. 9.
Blackwood v. Sakwinski—§ 6.16, n. 15.
Blades v. Ossenfort—§ 7.21, n. 6; § 7.22, n. 17.
Blank v. Michael—§ 5.19, n. 12.
Blankenship v. Boyle—§ 6.11, n. 10.
Blanton v. Federal Deposit Ins. Corp.—§ 12.9, n. 6.
Blass v. Terry—§ 5.5, n. 5.
Blaylock v. Dollar Inns of America, Inc.—§ 10.6, n. 3, 11.
Blazey v. Delius—§ 7.8, n. 4; § 7.16, n. 22.
Blessett v. Turcotte—§ 5.28, n. 16.
Blitz v. Marino—§ 5.24, n. 54.
B.L. Nelson and Associates, Inc. v. Sunbelt Sav., FSB—§ 5.29, n. 33.
Bloch v. Budish—§ 5.14, n. 2.
Block v. Neal—§ 12.11; § 12.11, n. 44.
Block v. Tobin—§ 7.21, n. 84; § 7.22, n. 45, 46.
Blockley v. Fowler—§ 7.21, n. 50.
Blodgett v. Martsch—§ 7.21, n. 59.
Blondell v. Beam—§ 3.32, n. 21.
Bloomer v. Henderson—§ 5.32, n. 25, 26.
Bloomington HH Investors, Ltd. Partnership, In re—§ 8.14, n. 27.
Blossom v. Milwaukee & C. R. Co.—§ 7.16, n. 1, 4; § 7.17, n. 1, 3.
Blue Spot, Inc. v. Rakower—§ 12.4, n. 23.
Blumenthal v. Concrete Constructors Co. of Albuquerque, Inc.—§ 3.6, n. 1.
Blumenthal v. Jassoy—§ 5.33, n. 20.

Blumenthal v. Serota—§ 5.19, n. 5.
Blunt v. Norris—§ 5.34, n. 30, 48.
Board of Directors of Olde Salem Homeowners' Ass'n v. Secretary of Veterans Affairs—§ 13.5, n. 17, 20.
Board of Ed. of Chillicothe City School Dist. v. Sever-Williams Co.—§ 12.2, n. 12.
Board of Ed. of City of Bayonne v. Kolman—§ 10.5, n. 12.
Board of Trustees of General Retirement System of City of Detroit v. Ren-Cen Indoor Tennis & Racquet Club—§ 6.16, n. 17.
Boatmen's Bank of Jefferson County v. Community Interiors, Inc.—§ 7.21, n. 1, 74.
Boatmen's Bank of Pulaski County v. Wilson—§ 7.21, n. 75.
Bock v. Bank of Bellevue—§ 2.1, n. 2; § 2.3, n. 19.
Bode v. Tannehill—§ 10.10, n. 18.
Boden Min. Corp., In re—§ 9.7, n. 3, 20.
Bodwell Granite Co. v. Lane—§ 2.2, n. 13.
Boedeker v. Jordan—§ 7.31, n. 6.
Bogart v. George K. Porter Co.—§ 5.17, n. 5, 6; § 6.13, n. 10.
Bogert v. Striker—§ 6.6, n. 2.
Boggs v. Fowler—§ 7.17, n. 10, 12.
Bohm v. Forum Resorts, Inc.—§ 11.7, n. 26.
Bohn Sash & Door Co. v. Case—§ 6.17, n. 13.
Bohra v. Montgomery—§ 7.31, n. 12.
Boies v. Benham—§ 9.2, n. 10.
Boise Cascade Corp. v. Stephens—§ 12.4, n. 47.
Boise Jr. College Dist. v. Mattefs Const. Co.—§ 12.2, n. 15.
Boley v. Daniel—§ 10.5, n. 5.
Boley v. Principi—§ 11.6, n. 72.
Bolivar Reorganized School Dist. No. 1, Polk County v. American Sur. Co. of N.Y.—§ 12.2, n. 13.
Bolles v. Beach—§ 5.7, n. 6, 8.
Bolles v. Duff—§ 7.4, n. 12.
Bolln v. La Prele Live Stock Co.—§ 5.6, n. 1; § 6.17, n. 6.
Bond, In re—§ 4.3, n. 1.
Bond, United States v.—§ 4.31, n. 12.
Bonithron v. Hockmore—§ 4.30, n. 3.
Bonner, In re—§ 12.8, n. 7.
Bonner Bldg. Supply, Inc. v. Standard Forest Products, Inc.—§ 12.4, n. 22.
Bonuchi v. United States—§ 12.11, n. 44.
Booker v. Booker—§ 10.14, n. 13.
Boorum v. Tucker—§ 7.17, n. 8; § 9.1, n. 23.
Booth, In re—§ 3.33, n. 24, 25, 26; § 8.19, n. 7, 9.
Booth v. Landau—§ 3.17, n. 8.
Boothe v. Henrietta Egleston Hosp. for Children, Inc.—§ 8.10, n. 28.
Boqut v. Coburn—§ 7.3, n. 8.
Borden v. Graves—§ 7.8, n. 5.

Border City Sav. and Loan Ass'n v. First American Title Ins. Co. of Mid-America—§ 5.35; § 5.35, n. 56.
Borg, In re—§ 8.16, n. 22.
Borgess Inv. Co. v. Vette—§ 5.31, n. 13.
Borgonovo v. Henderson—§ 5.29, n. 8.
Boris v. Heyd—§ 3.33, n. 6.
Boromei, In re—§ 8.15, n. 40.
Bor-Son Bldg. Corp. v. Heller—§ 12.6, n. 23.
Bosteder, Matter of—§ 8.15, n. 39.
Boston & Berlin Transp. Co., United States v.—§ 10.8, n. 2.
Boston Five Cents Sav. Bank v. Secretary of HUD—§ 13.4, n. 9.
Boston Trade Bank v. Kuzon—§ 10.6, n. 3, 13.
Bostwick v. McEvoy—§ 4.2, n. 16.
Boteler v. Leber—§ 4.42, n. 5.
Bottenfield v. Wood—§ 3.16, n. 2.
Bottomly v. Kabachnick—§ 7.20, n. 2.
Boucher v. Eastern Sav. Bank—§ 12.3, n. 9.
Boucofski v. Jacobsen—§ 6.12, n. 16.
Bowden v. Bridgman—§ 4.4, n. 22.
Bowen v. Bankers' Life Co.—§ 7.22, n. 39.
Bowen v. Brockenbrough—§ 10.14, n. 11.
Bowen v. Danna—§ 7.7, n. 25.
Bowen v. Kicklighter—§ 12.8, n. 14.
Bower v. Stein—§ 7.7, n. 2.
Bowers v. Norton—§ 10.14, n. 8.
Bowman v. Poole—§ 6.7, n. 2, 9, 22.
Bown v. Loveland—§ 3.6, n. 1; § 3.7, n. 2; § 3.8, n. 1; § 5.30, n. 15.
Boyce v. Hughes—§ 7.21, n. 47.
Boyd v. Brabham—§ 6.6, n. 2.
Boyd v. Lefrak Organization—§ 11.5, n. 17.
Boyd v. Life Ins. Co. of Southwest—§ 6.2, n. 7, 11.
Boyd & Lovesee Lumber Co. v. Modular Marketing Corp.—§ 12.6, n. 21.
Boyer v. Keller—§ 12.5, n. 3, 6.
Boykin v. First State Bank of Comanche—§ 10.14, n. 11, 15.
Boyle v. Sweeney—§ 8.3, n. 102.
Bradbury v. Davenport—§ 3.1, n. 3.
Bradfield v. Hale—§ 4.3, n. 2; § 6.11, n. 14.
Bradford v. Thompson—§ 7.20, n. 3.
Bradford Realty Corporation v. Beetz—§ 7.10, n. 2.
Bradler v. Craig—§ 12.11, n. 11.
Bradley v. Apel—§ 3.29, n. 1.
Bradley v. Bryan—§ 9.1, n. 9.
Bradley v. George—§ 7.3, n. 9.
Bradley v. Merrill, 40 A. 132—§ 4.30, n. 7; § 4.29, n. 31.
Bradley v. Merrill, 34 A. 160—§ 4.29, n. 22.
Bradley v. Norris—§ 7.5, n. 1, 6, 15, 16, 19, 20, 23.
Bradley v. Parkhurst—§ 7.14, n. 14.
Bradley v. Snyder—§ 4.29, n. 21.
Bradshaw, In re—§ 8.15, n. 50, 52.
Bradshaw v. Farnsworth—§ 2.3, n. 9.
Bradstreet v. Gill—§ 5.1, n. 4; § 5.3, n. 3.
Brady v. Waldron—§ 4.10, n. 4.

TABLE OF CASES

Braidwood v. Harmon—§ 5.28, n. 3.
Brainard v. Cooper—§ 7.15, n. 2.
Brainerd Nat. Bank, Petition of—§ 8.7, n. 5.
Branch Banking & Trust Co. v. Home Federal Sav. & Loan Ass'n of Eastern North Carolina—§ 6.17, n. 10, 12.
Brandenstein v. Johnson—§ 6.12, n. 6, 14.
Brandt v. Thompson—§ 3.10, n. 2.
Branecky v. Seaman—§ 12.4, n. 14.
Branning v. Morgan Guar. Trust Co. of New York—§ 12.1, n. 23.
Brant v. Lincoln Nat. Life Ins. Co. of Fort Wayne—§ 7.16, n. 5.
Brask v. Bank of St. Louis—§ 13.5, n. 16.
Brassey v. New York & N. E. R. Co.—§ 4.10, n. 9.
Braun v. Crew—§ 5.19, n. 22.
Braunstein v. Trottier—§ 3.27, n. 3, 5; § 5.24, n. 35.
Brayton & Lawbaugh v. Monarch Lumber Co.—§ 4.29, n. 2.
Breaux Bridge Bank & Trust Co. v. Simon—§ 11.7, n. 41.
Bredenberg v. Landrum—§ 4.2, n. 5.
Bremen Bank and Trust Co. of St. Louis v. Muskopf—§ 5.29, n. 2; § 5.28, n. 6; § 5.34, n. 15.
Brenner v. Neu—§ 5.34, n. 9.
Brent v. Staveris Development Corp.—§ 7.17, n. 3.
Brewer v. Maurer—§ 5.15, n. 14.
Brewer v. Myers—§ 12.3, n. 28.
Brewer, Estate of v. Iota Delta Chapter—§ 3.35, n. 2, 4.
Briarwood Towers 85th Co. v. Guterman—§ 12.7, n. 13.
Brice v. Griffin—§ 5.3, n. 2; § 5.8, n. 5; § 5.10, n. 6.
Brickle v. Leach—§ 3.8, n. 12.
Bricks Unlimited, Inc. v. Agee—§ 5.29, n. 17; § 5.34, n. 33.
Bridgewater Roller Mills Co v. Receivers of Baltimore Building & Loan Ass'n—§ 10.15, n. 2.
Bridgewater Roller-Mills Co. v. Strough—§ 10.15, n. 2.
Bridgkort Racquet Club, Inc. v. University Bank—§ 12.3, n. 40.
Brief v. 120 Owners Corp.—§ 13.6, n. 23.
Briggs, In re—§ 8.15, n. 35.
Briggs Transp. Co., In re—§ 8.14, n. 16.
Brimie v. Benson—§ 3.11, n. 6.
Brimwood Homes Inc. v. Knudsen Builders Supply Co.—§ 12.4, n. 47.
Brindisi, Estate of v. State Farm Ins. Co.—§ 4.16, n. 3.
Brinton v. Davidson—§ 5.6, n. 6.
Briscoe v. Power—§ 10.11, n. 15.
Bristol Associates, Inc., In re—§ 5.28, n. 34.
Bristol Lumber Co. v. Dery—§ 7.13, n. 22.
Britton, In re—§ 8.15, n. 24.
Britton v. Roth—§ 5.8, n. 7.
Broad and Locust Associates v. Locust-Broad Realty Co.—§ 7.22, n. 8.

Broad & Market Nat. Bank of Newark v. Larsen—§ 4.34, n. 6.
Brock v. Adams—§ 5.31, n. 17.
Brock v. First South Sav. Ass'n in Receivership—§ 9.1, n. 17.
Brockington v. Lynch—§ 3.3, n. 6.
Brockton Sav. Bank v. Shapiro—§ 5.19, n. 53.
Brockton Savings Bank v. Shapiro—§ 5.6, n. 1; § 5.19, n. 53.
Brockway v. McClun—§ 7.12, n. 14.
Brogdon v. Exterior Design—§ 11.7, n. 35.
Brokmeyer, In re—§ 8.14, n. 9.
Bronaugh v. Burley Tobacco Co.—§ 10.10, n. 11; § 10.13, n. 15, 19.
Brooklyn Bank v. Barnaby—§ 6.13, n. 1.
Brooks v. Benham—§ 10.15, n. 3, 6.
Brooks v. Dalrymple—§ 2.1, n. 17.
Brooks v. Owen—§ 2.1, n. 5; § 2.3, n. 9.
Brooks v. Resolution Trust Corp.—§ 10.6, n. 3.
Brooks v. Rice—§ 6.17, n. 11.
Brooks v. Sullivan—§ 3.32, n. 27.
Brooks v. Valley Nat. Bank—§ 4.18, n. 9, 23, 29, 41.
Brose, In re—§ 8.18, n. 5.
Brosseau v. Lowy—§ 5.7, n. 13.
Brost v. L.A.N.D., Inc.—§ 7.5, n. 4; § 7.12, n. 17.
Broughton v. Mt. Healthy Flying Service, Inc.—§ 10.15, n. 1; § 10.9, n. 3; § 10.10, n. 6; § 10.9, n. 13.
Brown, In re, 126 B.R. 481—§ 8.17, n. 40.
Brown, In re, 104 B.R. 609—§ 8.17, n. 33.
Brown v. Avemco Inv. Corp.—§ 7.7, n. 22, 24.
Brown v. Bellamy—§ 10.3, n. 11.
Brown v. Berry—§ 4.31, n. 12; § 7.5, n. 12.
Brown v. Blydenburgh—§ 5.33, n. 10.
Brown v. Cleverly—§ 13.3, n. 16.
Brown v. Cohn—§ 7.13, n. 15.
Brown v. Cole, 768 S.W.2d 549—§ 3.6, n. 1; § 3.7, n. 2; § 3.8, n. 1.
Brown v. Cole, 14 L.J. (N.S.) Ch. 167—§ 6.1; § 6.1, n. 1.
Brown v. Commissioner—§ 2.1, n. 17.
Brown v. Coriell—§ 7.3, n. 4.
Brown v. Cram—§ 4.1, n. 6.
Brown v. Critchfield—§ 4.4, n. 10; § 4.5, n. 9.
Brown v. Crookston Agr. Ass'n—§ 7.31, n. 6.
Brown v. Daniel—§ 4.29, n. 1.
Brown v. Eckhardt—§ 7.21, n. 54.
Brown v. Financial Sav.—§ 2.1, n. 12; § 6.6, n. 36; § 7.3, n. 5.
Brown v. First Nat. Bank in Lenox—§ 8.19, n. 9.
Brown v. Gerber—§ 8.10, n. 21.
Brown v. Gilmor's Ex'rs—§ 7.17, n. 13.
Brown v. Hoover—§ 2.1, n. 15.
Brown v. Jensen—§ 8.3; § 8.3, n. 85.
Brown v. Loeb—§ 4.1, n. 6, § 4.24, n. 2.
Brown v. Lynn, 392 F.Supp. 559—§ 7.7, n. 28.

TABLE OF CASES

Brown v. Lynn, 385 F.Supp. 986—§ **7.7, n. 28.**
Brown v. Mifflin—§ **2.3, n. 23.**
Brown v. Muetzel—§ **4.34, n. 11.**
Brown v. Nickle—§ **3.18, n. 6.**
Brown v. Simons—§ **4.31, n. 11**; § **4.45, n. 1**; § **10.9, n. 6**; § **10.10, n. 5, 15**; § **10.15, n. 5.**
Brown v. South Boston Sav. Bank—§ **4.28, n. 4**; § **4.29, n. 9**; § **5.7, n. 4.**
Brown v. Stead—§ **6.17, n. 6.**
Brown v. Storey—§ **4.22, n. 24.**
Brown v. Turner—§ **5.19, n. 38.**
Brown v. Tuttle—§ **11.2, n. 17.**
Brown Co. v. Superior Court, County of San Bernardino Appellate Dept.—§ **12.5, n. 30.**
Browne v. San Luis Obispo Nat. Bank—§ **3.38**; § **3.38, n. 14.**
Brown-Marx Associates, Ltd. v. Emigrant Sav. Bank—§ **12.3, n. 10.**
Brown to Use of Par Bond & Mortgage Co. v. Aiken—§ **4.22, n. 2.**
Brown Wholesale Elec. Co. v. Beztak of Scottsdale, Inc.—§ **12.4, n. 43.**
Bruce Const. Corporation v. Federal Realty Corporation—§ **12.4, n. 46.**
Bruckman v. Breitenbush Hot Springs, Inc.—§ **2.1, n. 4.**
Brunsoman v. Scarlett—§ **8.3, n. 36.**
Brunswick Nursing & Convalescent Center, Inc. v. Great Am. Ins. Co.—§ **12.2, n. 28.**
Brunzell v. Lawyers Title Ins. Corp.—§ **13.3, n. 46.**
Bryan v. Brasius—§ **4.24, n. 15.**
Bryan v. Easton Tire Co.—§ **5.27, n. 7.**
Bryant, In re—§ **6.9, n. 14, 21.**
Bryant v. Ellenburg—§ **13.3, n. 31.**
Bryant v. Erskine—§ **2.2, n. 9, 11, 12.**
Bryant v. Jefferson Federal Sav. and Loan Ass'n—§ **3.30, n. 12**; § **7.27, n. 2, 11.**
Bryant v. Young—§ **3.13, n. 4.**
Bryson v. Newtown Real Estate & Development Corp.—§ **10.9, n. 11**; § **10.13, n. 16.**
Bryson Properties, XVIII, In re—§ **8.14, n. 86, 88.**
Buchanan v. Brentwood Federal Sav. and Loan Ass'n—§ **4.17, n. 11**; § **4.18**; § **4.18, n. 4, 9**; § **4.19, n. 6.**
Buchanan v. Century Federal Sav. and Loan Ass'n of Pittsburgh—§ **4.18, n. 5.**
Buchanan v. Century Federal Sav. & Loan Ass'n—§ **4.18, n. 9.**
Buchert, In re—§ **8.19, n. 9.**
Buckman v. Bragaw—§ **7.21, n. 85.**
Budget Realty, Inc. v. Hunter—§ **8.3**; § **8.3, n. 84, 94.**
Buehler v. McCormick—§ **5.31, n. 13.**
Buehner Block Co. v. UWC Associates—§ **12.3, n. 7.**
Buel v. Austin—§ **7.16, n. 34.**
Buell v. Underwood—§ **5.28, n. 23.**
Buell Rlty. Note Col. Tr. v. Central Oak Invest. Co.—§ **4.12, n. 5, 7, 11.**

Buettel v. Harmount—§ **4.29, n. 7.**
Buffalo County v. Richards—§ **2.3, n. 13, 14.**
Buford v. Smith—§ **7.8, n. 5.**
Bugden v. Bignold—§ **10.13, n. 12.**
Builders Affiliates, Inc. v. North River Ins. Co.—§ **4.16, n. 13.**
Builders Supply Co. of Hattiesburg v. Pine Belt Sav. & Loan Ass'n—§ **7.31, n. 2.**
Building 62 Ltd. Partnership, In re—§ **8.14, n. 27.**
Bulger v. Wilderman—§ **4.22, n. 13.**
Bullington v. Mize—§ **8.3, n. 8.**
Bullock v. Bishop—§ **7.21, n. 17.**
Bulson v. Moffatt—§ **4.24, n. 1.**
Bundles, Matter of—§ **8.17**; § **8.17, n. 37.**
Bunge Corp. v. St. Louis Terminal Field Warehouse Co.—§ **10.4, n. 2.**
Burchard v. Roberts—§ **4.45, n. 6.**
Burchett v. Allied Concord Financial Corp.—§ **5.31, n. 3.**
Burden v. Thayer—§ **4.20, n. 3**; § **4.21, n. 5.**
Burdick v. Wentworth—§ **3.10, n. 3.**
Burgess v. Shiplet—§ **3.27, n. 5.**
Burgoon v. Lavezzo—§ **10.1, n. 7**; § **10.5, n. 2**; § **10.6, n. 11**; § **10.7, n. 1, 9, 10, 12.**
Burke, In re—§ **8.12, n. 14.**
Burke v. Willard—§ **4.22, n. 5, 22.**
Burkons v. Ticor Title Ins. Co. of California—§ **12.10, n. 32.**
Burks v. Verschuur—§ **6.1, n. 7.**
Burley v. Pike—§ **4.6, n. 3.**
Burman and Wieher v. Holzkamper—§ **12.6, n. 43.**
Burnett v. Manufacturer's Hanover Trust Co.—§ **7.22, n. 32, 35.**
Burnett v. Wright—§ **2.4, n. 2, 7.**
Burns, In re—§ **8.12, n. 13.**
Burns v. Hiatt—§ **4.24, n. 1, 13.**
Burns v. Williams—§ **4.29, n. 7, 15.**
Burr v. Beckler—§ **2.1, n. 4.**
Burrill v. First Nat. Bank of Shawnee Mission, N.A.—§ **7.20, n. 16.**
Burriss v. Owen—§ **2.4, n. 9.**
Burroughs v. Burroughs—§ **3.6, n. 1**; § **3.8, n. 9, 18.**
Burroughs v. Ellis—§ **7.8, n. 10.**
Burroughs v. Garner—§ **6.6, n. 9.**
Burrow v. Timmsen—§ **12.9, n. 17.**
Burton-Lingo Co. v. Patton—§ **4.14, n. 7.**
Burt's Spirit Shop, Inc. v. Ridgway—§ **2.4, n. 2.**
Busconi, In re—§ **8.14, n. 11, 28.**
Bush v. Cooper—§ **2.1, n. 15.**
Bush v. Cushman—§ **5.32, n. 3.**
Bush v. Lathrop—§ **5.32, n. 11.**
Bustop Shelters of Louisville, Inc. v. Classic Homes, Inc.—§ **8.14, n. 36, 37, 42.**
Butler v. HUD—§ **11.2, n. 30.**
Butler v. Michel—§ **3.32, n. 26.**
Butler v. Taylor—§ **10.8, n. 7.**
Butler, United States v.—§ **11.3, n. 29.**

Butler v. Wilkinson—§ 3.35, n. 1; § 3.36, n. 3, 5.
Butner v. United States—§ 8.18; § 8.18, n. 7.
Butter v. Melrose Sav. Bank—§ 7.6, n. 14.
Butterfield v. Lane—§ 4.44, n. 2.
Butts v. Atlanta Federal Sav. & Loan Ass'n—§ 12.11, n. 8, 9, 12.
Butts v. Peacock—§ 3.13, n. 1.
B.W. Alpha, Inc., In re—§ 8.14, n. 76.
Byler v. Great American Ins. Co.—§ 12.2, n. 32.
Byles v. Kellogg—§ 10.2, n. 6.
Byrne v. Carson—§ 7.21, n. 52.
Byrom v. Chapin—§ 4.4, n. 5.

C

Cabana, Inc. v. Eastern Air Control, Inc.—§ 12.4, n. 35; § 12.5, n. 39.
Cabbage v. Citizens Bank—§ 2.4, n. 2, 7.
Cabot, Cabot & Forbes Land Trust v. First National Bank of Fort Walton Beach—§ 12.8, n. 12.
Cacavalle v. Lombardi—§ 5.19, n. 17.
Cadd v. Snell—§ 8.6, n. 28.
Cady v. Barnes—§ 10.7, n. 6.
Cagle, Inc. v. Sammons—§ 10.1, n. 7; § 10.3, n. 1; § 10.4, n. 2; § 10.5, n. 10.
Cain & Bultman, Inc. v. Miss Sam, Inc.—§ 3.37, n. 1.
Caito v. United California Bank—§ 7.15, n. 20.
Cake v. Mohun—§ 4.41, n. 7.
Calder v. Richardson—§ 5.10, n. 21.
Calfo v. D.C. Stewart Co.—§ 5.29, n. 3.
California Bank v. Stimson—§ 8.2, n. 5; § 8.3, n. 36.
California Federal Bank v. Matreyek—§ 6.6, n. 24.
California Housing Finance Agency v. Elliott—§ 12.11, n. 20.
California Housing Securities, Inc. v. United States—§ 11.7, n. 3.
California Joint Stock Land Bank of San Francisco v. Gore—§ 7.16, n. 33.
California Title Ins. & Trust Co. v. Kuchenbeiser—§ 5.33, n. 13.
Calkins v. Copley—§ 5.7, n. 4.
Calkins v. Isbell—§ 7.5, n. 17.
Call v. Jeremiah—§ 8.6, n. 29.
Call v. LaBrie—§ 3.29; § 3.29, n. 66.
Call v. Thunderbird Mortgage Co.—§ 8.6, n. 19, 25.
Callaizakis v. Astor Development Co.—§ 12.11, n. 11.
Calumet River Ry. Co. v. Brown—§ 4.12, n. 3, 13, 20.
Calverley v. Gunstream—§ 7.22, n. 26.
Calvo v. Davies—§ 5.19, n. 6, 53.
Cal-West Nat. Bank v. Superior Court (Phillips)—§ 12.6, n. 21.

Cambridge Acceptance Corp. v. Hockstein—§ 12.7, n. 60; § 12.10; § 12.10, n. 10, 40.
Cambridge Mortg. Corp., In re—§ 5.35, n. 43.
Cambridge Sav. Bank v. Cronin—§ 7.21, n. 53.
Camden v. Mayhew—§ 7.17, n. 7.
Camden Trust Co. v. Handle—§ 4.4, n. 4; § 4.5, n. 4; § 4.11, n. 4.
Cameron v. Ah Quong—§ 4.24, n. 12.
Cameron v. Churchill Mortg. Corp.—§ 12.9, n. 2.
Cameron–Schroth–Cameron Co. v. Geseke—§ 12.5, n. 3.
Caminetti v. United States—§ 5.24, n. 58.
Campanella v. Ranier Nat. Bank—§ 12.9, n. 5.
Campbell v. Dearborn—§ 3.9, n. 2.
Campbell v. Freeman—§ 3.20, n. 2, 3; § 3.21, n. 2, 4.
Campbell v. Warren—§ 5.27, n. 12.
Campbell v. Werner—§ 7.6, n. 1.
Campbell v. West—§ 7.7, n. 4.
Campbell Inns, Inc. v. Banholzer, Turnure & Co., Inc.—§ 12.9, n. 24.
Campbell Leasing, Inc. v. Federal Deposit Ins. Corp.—§ 5.29, n. 32.
Cambell v. Tompkins—§ 2.1, n. 17; § 2.3, n. 1.
Canada Mort. & Housing Corp. v. Hong Kong Bank of Canada—§ 5.26, n. 7.
Canal Nat. Bank v. Becker—§ 12.8, n. 10.
Candlewick Lake Ass'n, Inc., Petition of—§ 4.45, n. 8.
Canfield v. Shear—§ 5.8, n. 4, 5.
Cannefax v. Clement—§ 3.36, n. 14, 15.
Cannon v. McDaniel & Jackson—§ 5.35, n. 15.
Canterbury Court, Inc. v. Rosenberg—§ 3.32, n. 16.
Cantor v. Union Mut. Life Ins. Co.—§ 10.8, n. 1.
Capac State Sav. Bank v. McKnight—§ 5.18, n. 6.
Caperonis Estate, In re—§ 5.27, n. 7.
Capital Bank & Trust Co. v. Broussard Paint & Wallpaper Co.—§ 13.3, n. 33.
Capital Holding Corp. v. Octagon Development Co.—§ 12.3, n. 30.
Capital Investors Co. v. Devers—§ 5.32, n. 22.
Capital Investors Co. v. Executors of Estate of Morrison—§ 5.32; § 5.32, n. 6, 21.
Capital Lumber Co. v. Saunders—§ 3.13, n. 6.
Capitol Federal Sav. and Loan Ass'n, Inc. v. Glenwood Manor, Inc.—§ 5.21, n. 33; § 5.22, n. 16.
Capitol Nat. Bank v. Holmes—§ 10.7, n. 2.
Capitol Sav. & Loan Ass'n v. First Financial Sav. & Loan Ass'n—§ 5.35, n. 5, 12.
Caplinger v. Patty—§ 10.9, n. 14.
Capocasa v. First Nat. Bank of Stevens Point—§ 12.8, n. 16.

TABLE OF CASES

Capps, Appeal of—§ 8.15, n. 77.
Cardwell v. Virginia State Ins. Co.—§ 7.2, n. 14, 19.
Cargill v. Thompson—§ 4.26, n. 7.
Caribank v. Frankel—§ 12.9, n. 41; § 13.3, n. 21.
Carl A. Morse, Inc. (Diesel Const., Division) v. Rentar Indus. Development Corp.—§ 12.5; § 12.5, n. 19, 25, 26.
Carley Capital Group, In re, 128 B.R. 652—§ 4.35, n. 13.
Carley Capital Group, In re, 119 B.R. 646—§ 10.2, n. 12.
Carl H. Peterson Co. v. Zero Estates—§ 9.4, n. 9; § 10.6, n. 7, 14.
Carlin Trading Corp. v. Bennett—§ 4.40, n. 3.
Carlsberg Resources Corp. v. Cambria Sav. and Loan Ass'n—§ 12.10, n. 7.
Carlson-Grefe Const., Inc. v. Rosemount Condominium Group Partnership—§ 12.4, n. 27.
Carnahan v. Lloyd—§ 6.13, n. 10.
Carnahan v. Tousey—§ 5.15, n. 1; § 5.18, n. 4, 17.
Carnegie Bank v. Shalleck—§ 5.31, n. 4; § 5.29, n. 6; § 5.31, n. 13.
Caro v. Wollenberg—§ 4.24, n. 12.
Carolina Builders Corp. v. Howard-Veasey Homes, Inc.—§ 12.4, n. 35; § 12.9, n. 2.
Carolina Housing & Mortg. Corp. v. Orange Hill A. M. E. Church—§ 5.32, n. 17.
Carolina Housing & Mortg. Corp. v. Reynolds—§ 5.31, n. 13.
Carollo v. Financial Federal Sav. and Loan Ass'n—§ 6.4, n. 19.
Carondelet Sav. & Loan Ass'n v. Boyer—§ 8.1, n. 12.
Carondelet Sav. & Loan Ass'n v. Citizens Sav. & Loan Ass'n—§ 5.35, n. 5.
Carpenter v. Koons—§ 10.3, n. 8; § 10.10, n. 5, 15.
Carpenter v. Lewis—§ 3.11, n. 4.
Carpenter v. Longan—§ 5.27, n. 5; § 5.31, n. 13.
Carpenter v. Plagge—§ 7.4, n. 12.
Carpenter v. Smith—§ 3.32, n. 8, 14.
Carpenter v. Suffolk Franklin Sav. Bank, 346 N.E.2d 892—§ 4.18, n. 6, 22, 24, 35.
Carpenter v. Suffolk Franklin Sav. Bank (Carpenter I), 291 N.E.2d 609—§ 4.18; § 4.18, n. 2.
Carpenter v. Walker—§ 9.6, n. 3.
Carpenter v. Winn—§ 6.1, n. 2.
Carpenter & Carpenter, Inc. v. Kingham—§ 3.19, n. 9.
Carr, In re, 52 B.R. 250—§ 8.13, n. 32.
Carr, In re, 34 B.R. 653—§ 8.17, n. 12.
Carr v. Carr—§ 3.9, n. 1; § 3.24, n. 8.
Carr v. Dorenkamper—§ 5.28, n. 12.
Carr v. Nodvin—§ 5.15, n. 19.
Carroll v. Edmondson—§ 4.4, n. 14; § 4.5, n. 9.
Carroll v. Miller—§ 9.8; § 9.8, n. 14.
Carroll v. Tomlinson—§ 4.28, n. 3.

Carrollton-Farmers Branch Independent School Dist. v. Federal Deposit Ins. Corp.—§ 11.7, n. 44.
Carrols Equities Corp. v. Villnave—§ 12.2, n. 19.
Carson v. Isabel Apartments, Inc.—§ 13.3, n. 17.
Carson Redevelopment Agency v. Adam—§ 4.12, n. 1, 8.
Carter v. Bennett—§ 5.28, n. 15.
Carter v. Derwinski—§ 11.6; § 11.6, n. 67, 76.
Carter v. Holahan—§ 5.10, n. 18.
Carter v. McMillan—§ 4.29, n. 8.
Carter v. Rich—§ 3.33, n. 4.
Carter v. Simpson Estate Co.—§ 3.18, n. 1.
Carter v. South Texas Lumber Co.—§ 5.33, n. 5.
Carteret Sav. and Loan Ass'n, F.A. v. Davis—§ 8.5, n. 9; § 8.8, n. 3.
Carteret Sav. Bank, FA v. OTS—§ 11.1, n. 8.
Carteret Sav. Bank, P.A. v. Compton, Luther & Sons, Inc.—§ 11.7, n. 10.
Carteret Sav. & Loan Ass'n, F.A. v. Davis—§ 7.2, n. 7.
Carton, Matter of—§ 13.6, n. 17.
Cartwright v. American Sav. & Loan Ass'n—§ 11.5, n. 28.
Caruso v. Great Western Sav.—§ 4.16, n. 7.
Caruthers v. Humphrey—§ 6.6, n. 15; § 6.7, n. 9.
Carver, In re—§ 8.13, n. 33; § 8.17, n. 4.
Cary v. Metropolitan Life Ins. Co.—§ 7.8, n. 10.
Casa Grande, Inc. v. Minnesota Mut. Life Ins. Co.—§ 5.24, n. 9, 87.
Casassa v. Smith—§ 4.22, n. 19.
Casbeer, In re—§ 8.18, n. 53.
Cascade Sec. Bank v. Butler—§ 3.36, n. 3, 5, 6; § 3.37; § 3.37, n. 5.
Case v. Egan—§ 5.15, n. 7.
Case v. Los Angeles Lumber Products Co.—§ 8.14, n. 81.
Casey v. Travelers Ins. Co.—§ 6.6, n. 31; § 12.1, n. 30.
Cash v. United States—§ 12.11, n. 47.
Cashway Concrete & Materials v. Sanner Contracting Co.—§ 12.4, n. 11.
Cason v. Chambers—§ 6.12, n. 5, 6.
Cason v. United States—§ 12.11, n. 39.
Casselman's Adm'x v. Gordon & Lightfoot—§ 5.15, n. 13.
Cassem v. Heustis—§ 7.5, n. 4.
Casserly v. Witherbee—§ 7.4, n. 4, 5, 6.
Cassidy v. Bonitatibus—§ 5.3, n. 2; § 5.4, n. 1; § 5.6, n. 1.
Caster, In re—§ 8.15, n. 56.
Castillian Apartments, Inc., In re—§ 7.32; § 7.32, n. 2.
Castleglen, Inc. v. Commonwealth Sav. Ass'n—§ 11.7, n. 1, 10.
Castleman Const. Co. v. Pennington—§ 10.6, n. 2, 4, 5.
Castle Rock Industrial Bank v. S.O.A.W. Enterprises, Inc.—§ 3.37, n. 11; § 5.35, n. 47.

738 TABLE OF CASES

Cast Stone Co v. McGown—§ 5.29, n. 15.
Cates v. White—§ 2.4, n. 11.
Catlin v. Mills—§ 4.31, n. 17.
Catterlin v. Armstrong—§ 7.15, n. 10, 13.
Caudle v. First Federal Sav. and Loan Ass'n of Sylacauga—§ 7.5, n. 4.
Caufman v. Sayre—§ 7.8, n. 4.
Caulder v. Lewis—§ 7.7, n. 2.
Cavalier Homes of Georgia, Inc., In re—§ 10.1, n. 16.
C.A. Warren Co. v. San Francisco Sav. Union—§ 4.2, n. 16.
Cawley v. Kelley—§ 2.1, n. 5; § 2.3, n. 9.
C & B Oil Co., Inc., In re—§ 10.9, n. 7.
CBS Real Estate of Cedar Rapids, Inc. v. Harper—§ 2.3, n. 13.
C & C Tile and Carpet Co., Inc. v. Aday—§ 12.4, n. 37.
C & D Investments v. Beaudoin—§ 2.3, n. 1.
Cedar v. W. E. Roche Fruit Co.—§ 12.7, n. 33.
Cedar Avenue Building etc. v. McLaughlin—§ 4.4, n. 20.
Cedar Vale Co-op Exchange, Inc. v. Allen Utilities, Inc.—§ 12.2, n. 33.
Cedarwood Associates, L. T. D. v. Trammell—§ 3.3, n. 1.
Cedrone v. Warwick Federal Sav. and Loan Ass'n—§ 7.21, n. 2.
Celeste Court Apartments, Inc., Matter of—§ 8.14, n. 45.
Cely v. DeConcini, McDonald, Brammer, Yetwin & Lacy, P.C.—§ 5.3, n. 2.
Centennial Square, Ltd. v. Resolution Trust Co.—§ 6.16, n. 17.
Centex Homes Corp. v. Boag—§ 3.32, n. 6; § 12.3, n. 35.
Central Bank, N.A. v. Baldwin—§ 12.11; § 12.11, n. 5.
Central Federal Sav. and Loan Ass'n of Nassau County, People v.—§ 12.3, n. 20.
Central Holding Co. v. Bushman—§ 5.17, n. 4, 7.
Central Life Ins. Co. of Illinois v. Thompson—§ 5.6, n. 6.
Central Nat. Bank of Greencastle v. Shoup—§ 5.22, n. 19; § 5.24; § 5.24, n. 132.
Central Penn Nat. Bank v. Stonebridge Ltd.—§ 8.2, n. 1.
Central Pennsylvania Sav. Ass'n v. Carpenters of Pennsylvania, Inc., 463 A.2d 414—§ 12.7, n. 33.
Central Pennsylvania Sav. Ass'n v. Carpenters of Pennsylvania, Inc., 444 A.2d 755—§ 12.7, n. 29, 37.
Central Production Credit Ass'n v. Page—§ 12.8, n. 17.
Central Production Credit Ass'n v. Reed—§ 12.7, n. 11.
Central Republic Trust Co. v. 33 South Wabash Building Corp.—§ 4.39, n. 14.
Central Trust Co. of Illinois v. Stepanek—§ 5.34, n. 14.

Central Trust Co. of New York v. Chattanooga R. & C. R. Co.—§ 4.43, n. 3.
Central Trust Co of New York v. Kneeland—§ 9.3, n. 6.
Central Wisconsin Trust Co. v. Swenson—§ 4.31, n. 10.
Centrust Mortg. Corp. v. PMI Mortg. Ins. Co.—§ 11.2, n. 58.
Century Enterprises, Inc. v. Butler—§ 7.15, n. 33, 37.
Century Federal Sav. and Loan Ass'n v. Madorsky—§ 6.2, n. 20.
Century Federal Sav. and Loan Ass'n of Bridgeton v. Van Glahn—§ 5.21, n. 33.
Century Federal Sav. and Loan Ass'n of Ormond Beach, United States v.—§ 7.32, n. 8.
Century Inv. Fund VIII Ltd. Partnership, Matter of—§ 4.35, n. 31, 32.
Century Park Condominium Ass'n v. Norwest Bank Bismarck, Nat. Ass'n—§ 13.5, n. 21.
Century Sav. Ass'n of Kansas v. C. Michael Franke & Co., Inc.—§ 5.21, n. 33.
Certified Mortg. Corp., Matter of—§ 8.14, n. 21.
Chace v. Johnson—§ 3.29; § 3.29, n. 42.
Chace v. Morse—§ 7.5, n. 4, 5.
Chadbourn v. Johnston—§ 7.12, n. 18.
Chain O'Mines v. Williamson—§ 3.36, n. 10.
Chamberlain v. Forbes—§ 4.44, n. 3.
Chambers, In re—§ 8.15, n. 45.
Chambers v. Goodwin—§ 3.1, n. 21.
Champion v. Hinkle—§ 7.17, n. 17.
Champlain Valley Fed. Sav. & Loan Ass'n of Plattsburgh v. Ladue—§ 10.14, n. 4.
Champlin v. Foster—§ 7.14, n. 5.
Chanango Bank v. Cox—§ 4.7, n. 3.
Chancellor Kent in Mills v. Dennis—§ 7.11, n. 2.
Chancellor of New Jersey v. Towell—§ 10.11, n. 1, 4.
Chandler v. Cleveland Sav. and Loan Ass'n—§ 7.22, n. 40.
Chapa v. Herbster—§ 7.6, n. 3.
Chapel State Theatre Co. v. Hooper—§ 12.5, n. 3, 7.
Chapin v. Freeland—§ 6.11, n. 3.
Chapin v. Wright—§ 7.5, n. 18.
Chapman v. Cooney—§ 4.28, n. 4, 6.
Chapman v. Nation—§ 7.6, n. 3.
Chapple v. Mahon—§ 3.1, n. 18.
Charles Const. Co., Inc. v. Leisure Resources, Inc.—§ 10.13, n. 1, 2; § 10.15, n. 3.
Charles F. Curry Co. v. Goodman—§ 8.8, n. 2.
Charles White Co., Inc. v. Percy Galbreath & Sons, Inc.—§ 10.9, n. 14.
Charmicor v. Deaner—§ 7.27, n. 2.
Charter Bank v. Eckert—§ 5.4, n. 5.
Charter Federal Sav. and Loan Ass'n v. OTS—§ 11.1, n. 5.
Charter Mortg. Co. v. Gray—§ 12.11, n. 8.

TABLE OF CASES

Charter Nat. Bank—Houston v. Stevens—§ 7.22, n. 35, 40, 41, 42.
Chase Manhattan Bank v. S/D Enterprises, Inc.—§ 12.6, n. 28, 33.
Chase Manhattan Bank, N. A. v. Gems-By-Gordon, Inc.—§ 3.38, n. 16.
Chase Manhattan Bank, N. A. v. Turabo Shopping Center, Inc.—§ 4.34, n. 11, 12.
Chase Nat. Bank v. Sweezy—§ 9.1, n. 14.
Chase Nat. Bank v. Tover—§ 3.17, n. 3.
Chateaux Condominiums v. Daniels—§ 13.5, n. 21.
Chatham-Phenix Nat. Bank & Trust Co. v. Hotel Park-Central—§ 4.41, n. 9.
Chaudoin v. Claypool—§ 7.13, n. 21.
Chauncy Street Assoc. Ltd. Partnership, In re—§ 8.14, n. 10.
Chears Floor & Screen Co. v. Gidden—§ 12.5, n. 3.
Chena Lumber & Light Co. v. Laymon—§ 5.6, n. 1.
Cherry v. Amoco Oil Co.—§ 11.5, n. 18.
Chesser v. Chesser—§ 2.3, n. 9.
Chester Heights Associates, United States v.—§ 12.10, n. 11, 13; § 12.6, n. 29.
Chestnut Corp. v. Bankers Bond & Mortg. Co.—§ 6.3; § 6.3, n. 12.
Cheswick v. Weaver—§ 10.6, n. 2.
Cheves v. First Nat. Bank—§ 3.36, n. 7.
Chew v. Hyman—§ 7.2, n. 6; § 7.12, n. 18.
Chicago v. Gage—§ 4.12, n. 3.
Chicago, City of v. Sullivan Machinery Co.—§ 4.2, n. 16.
Chicago City Bank & Trust Co. v. Walgreen Co.—§ 4.39, n. 1.
Chicago Lumber Co. v. Newcomb—§ 12.5, n. 3.
Chicago, R. I. & P. Ry. Co. v. Fleming—§ 8.14, n. 111.
Chicago Title and Trust Co. v. First Arlington Nat. Bank—§ 12.10, n. 13.
Chicago Title Ins. Co. v. Lawrence Investments, Inc.—§ 10.6, n. 1.
Chicago Title Ins. Co. v. Sherred Village Associates—§ 11.6; § 11.6, n. 79, 94; § 12.4, n. 32.
Chicago Title & Trust Co. v. McDowell—§ 4.39, n. 7.
Chicago Title & Trust Co. v. Prendergast—§ 7.8, n. 10.
Child v. Child—§ 3.7, n. 2.
Childers v. Parker's, Inc.—§ 8.3, n. 25.
Childs v. Childs—§ 7.15, n. 2.
Childs v. Smith—§ 4.31, n. 14.
Chilivis v. Tumlin Woods Realty Associates, Inc.—§ 5.21, n. 19; § 5.22, n. 29.
Chillingworth, State v.—§ 12.5, n. 3.
Chilton v. Brooks—§ 5.19, n. 21.
Chimento, In re—§ 3.35, n. 1.
Chittick v. Thompson Hill Development Corporation—§ 5.34, n. 13.
Choate, Hall & Stewart v. SCA Services, Inc.—§ 5.12, n. 1.
Chotka v. Fidelco Growth Investors—§ 13.3, n. 59.

Chrisman v. Daniel—§ 10.5, n. 10.
Chrisman v. Hough—§ 4.45, n. 8.
Christensen v. Idaho Land Developers, Inc.—§ 12.4, n. 35.
Christian, Matter of—§ 8.15, n. 35.
Christiansen v. Philcent Corp.—§ 12.11, n. 11.
Christ Protestant Episcopal Church v. Mack—§ 7.15, n. 3.
Christy v. Campbell—§ 3.10, n. 2.
Christy v. Guild—§ 3.29, n. 4.
Chromy v. Midwest Federal Sav. & Loan Ass'n of Minneapolis—§ 4.35, n. 4.
Chrysler First Financial Services Corp., Ex parte—§ 4.16, n. 11.
Cinque v. Buschlen—§ 3.6, n. 2.
Circle v. Jim Walter Homes, Inc., 654 F.2d 688—§ 5.30, n. 19.
Circle v. Jim Walter Homes, Inc., 535 F.2d 583—§ 5.30, n. 7.
Circuit Court of Milwaukee County, State ex rel. Ashley v.—§ 7.12, n. 24.
C.I.T. Financial Services v. Premier Corp.—§ 9.7, n. 3, 19.
Citibank (Mid-Hudson), N.A. v. Rohdie—§ 8.3, n. 41.
Citibank Mortg. Corp. v. Carteret Sav. Bank, F.A.—§ 9.1, n. 4.
Citibank, N.A. v. Covenant Ins. Co.—§ 8.1, n. 3.
Citibank, N.A. v. Nyland (CF8) Ltd.—§ 7.7, n. 6.
Citibank, N.A. v. Oxford Properties & Finance Ltd.—§ 7.12, n. 6; § 7.15, n. 7.
Citibank Nevada, N.A. v. Wood—§ 7.31, n. 3.
Citicorp Mortg., Inc. v. Pessin—§ 7.10, n. 14, 18; § 7.15, n. 27.
Citicorp Sav. of Illinois, F.A. v. Occhipinti—§ 4.34, n. 6.
Citizens and Southern Nat. Bank of South Carolina v. Smith—§ 9.4, n. 10; § 12.9, n. 6, 37; § 12.10, n. 28.
Citizens Bank, Drumright v. Satcher—§ 7.12, n. 18.
Citizens Bank of Edina v. West Quincy Auto Auction, Inc.—§ 7.20, n. 8; § 7.21, n. 64.
Citizens Bank of Sheboygan v. Rose—§ 7.16, n. 18.
Citizens Bank & Trust Co. of Washington v. Gibson, 490 N.E.2d 728—§ 12.8, n. 15.
Citizens Bank & Trust Co. of Washington v. Gibson, 463 N.E.2d 276—§ 12.8, n. 15.
Citizens Federal Sav. & Loan Ass'n v. Andrews—§ 12.8, n. 18.
Citizens' Mercantile Co. v. Easom—§ 10.7, n. 3.
Citizens Nat. Bank v. Coates—§ 12.8, n. 18.
Citizens Nat. Bank of Quitman v. Brazil—§ 5.31, n. 4.
Citizens Sav. Bank v. Guaranty Loan Co.—§ 4.31, n. 14.

TABLE OF CASES

Citizens' Sav. Bank v. Kock.—§ 12.7, n. 11.
Citizens Sav. Bank, F.S.B. v. Verex Assur., Inc.—§ 11.2, n. 58.
Citizens Sec. Bank of Bixby v. Courtney—§ 6.17, n. 8; § 6.19, n. 10.
Citizens' State Bank of Ralston v. Petersen—§ 6.16, n. 17.
Citizens State Bank of Tulsa v. Pittsburg County Broadcasting Co.—§ 10.5, n. 4.
Citrowske, In re—§ 8.16, n. 23, 24.
Citrus State Bank v. McKendrick—§ 8.3, n. 125.
City and County of (see name of city)
City Bank of Portage v. Plank—§ 5.33, n. 9; § 5.34, n. 13.
City Centre One Associates v. Teachers Ins. and Annuity Ass'n of America—§ 12.3, n. 34.
City Consumer Services, Inc. v. Peters—§ 8.2, n. 6.
City Federal Sav. and Loan Ass'n v. Jacobs—§ 4.1, n. 20, 22.
City Federal Savings and Loan Association v. Crowley—§ 11.6, n. 21, 23.
City Mortg. Inv. Club v. Beh—§ 5.12, n. 2.
City Nat. Bank v. F.D.I.C.—§ 5.35, n. 22.
City of (see name of city)
City Sav. Bank of Bridgeport v. Dessoff—§ 7.6, n. 8.
C.J. Richard Lumber Co., Inc. v. Melancon—§ 12.5, n. 25.
Clack v. RICO Exploration Co.—§ 5.6, n. 1.
Claflin v. South Carolina R. Co.—§ 12.7, n. 6.
Claise v. Bernardi—§ 5.10, n. 13.
Clambey v. Copland—§ 3.10, n. 2.
Clark, In re—§ 4.2, n. 2; § 8.14, n. 48; § 8.15, n. 35, 41.
Clark v. Baker—§ 4.44, n. 2.
Clark v. Equitable Life Assur. Soc. of United States—§ 7.6, n. 19.
Clark v. General Elec. Co.—§ 12.4, n. 27.
Clark v. Grant—§ 6.12, n. 4.
Clark v. Grover—§ 12.11, n. 12, 43.
Clark v. Hannafeldt—§ 7.5, n. 6.
Clark v. Henderson—§ 5.7, n. 15.
Clark v. Howard—§ 12.7, n. 11.
Clark v. Jackson—§ 6.16, n. 10.
Clark v. Kraker—§ 7.16, n. 18; § 10.15, n. 7.
Clark v. Lachenmeier—§ 5.24, n. 87.
Clark v. Morris—§ 3.11, n. 7.
Clark v. Munroe—§ 9.1, n. 10.
Clark v. Paddock—§ 8.2, n. 4.
Clark v. Reyburn—§ 7.4, n. 11; § 7.12, n. 22.
Clark Certified Concrete Co. v. Lindberg—§ 13.3, n. 33.
Clarke v. Cordis—§ 7.12, n. 20.
Clarke v. Cowan—§ 10.15, n. 2.
Clarke v. Curtis—§ 4.22, n. 16.
Clarke v. Selben Apartments—§ 3.13, n. 1.
Clark-Robinson Corp. v. Jet Enterprises, Inc.—§ 7.6, n. 8.

Clark Technical Associates, Ltd., In re—§ 8.14, n. 25.
Clary v. Owen—§ 9.6, n. 1, 2.
Classic Enterprises, Inc. v. Continental Mortg. Investors—§ 7.21, n. 28.
Clawson v. Munson—§ 3.1, n. 37.
Clay v. Tyson—§ 5.6, n. 1.
Clayton v. Crossroads Equipment Co.—§ 7.7, n. 21.
Clayton v. Fort Worth State Bank of Fort Worth, Tex—§ 5.10, n. 2.
Clearfield Trust Co. v. United States—§ 11.6; § 11.6, n. 48.
Clement v. Ireland—§ 7.17, n. 12.
Clement v. Willett—§ 5.4, n. 8; § 5.15, n. 14.
Clements v. Fleet Finance, Inc.—§ 6.16, n. 15.
Clementz v. M. T. Jones Lumber Co.—§ 2.4, n. 2.
Clemons v. Elder—§ 3.14, n. 2.
Clermont v. Secured Inv. Corp.—§ 6.9; § 6.9, n. 1, 5.
Cleve v. Adams—§ 10.14, n. 6.
Cleveland v. Cleveland—§ 7.21, n. 46.
Cleveland v. Detroit Trust Co.—§ 4.26, n. 7.
CLIC & Co. v. Goldfarb—§ 5.27, n. 1.
Cliff's Ridge Skiing Corp., In re—§ 12.9, n. 2.
Clift v. Williams—§ 6.12, n. 21.
Cline v. Robbins—§ 7.4, n. 12.
Clinton Capital Corp. v. Straeb—§ 6.3, n. 5.
Clinton County v. Cox—§ 6.11, n. 24.
Clinton Loan Ass'n v. Merritt—§ 5.33, n. 10.
Clinton, Town of v. Town of Westbrook—§ 6.6, n. 10.
Cloud v. Jacksonville National Bank.—§ 5.34, n. 33.
Clover Square Associates v. Northwestern Mut. Life Ins. Co.—§ 5.22, n. 42; § 6.2, n. 3.
Clovis Nat. Bank v. Harmon—§ 12.8, n. 6, 9.
Clowes v. Dickenson—§ 10.9, n. 4; § 10.10, n. 5.
Club Associates, In re—§ 5.28, n. 24.
Clute v. Emmerich—§ 10.7, n. 13.
Coast Bank v. Minderhout—§ 3.38; § 3.38, n. 9.
Coast Cent. Credit Union v. Superior Court (Lee)—§ 12.7, n. 36.
Coastland Corp. v. Third Nat. Mortg. Co.—§ 12.3, n. 42, 44.
Coatings Mfrs., Inc. v. DPI, Inc.—§ 12.6, n. 4.
Cobb v. Osman—§ 10.3, n. 1; § 10.11, n. 1; § 10.4, n. 2; § 10.9, n. 23.
Cobe v. Lovan—§ 7.20, n. 4.
Coburn v. Bartholomew—§ 8.2, n. 4.
Coburn v. Coburn—§ 8.10, n. 26.
Coca-Cola Bottling Works (Thomas) Inc. v. Hazard Coca-Cola Bottling Works, Inc.—§ 12.3, n. 28.

Cochran v. Deposit Guar. Nat. Bank—§ 12.8, n. 20.
Cochran v. Goodell—§ 7.14, n. 5.
Cock v. Bailey—§ 6.16, n. 9.
Cocklereece v. Moran—§ 12.3, n. 60.
Cockrell v. Houston Packing Co.—§ 4.26, n. 6.
Cockrell v. Republic Mortg. Ins. Co.—§ 11.7, n. 23.
Codman v. Deland—§ 5.19, n. 33.
Codrington v. Johnstone—§ 4.38, n. 16.
Coffey, In re—§ 8.15, n. 51.
Coffey v. Hunt—§ 4.21, n. 5.
Coffey v. Lawman—§ 5.35, n. 50.
Coffin v. Parker—§ 7.3, n. 2.
Coffman, In re—§ 8.19, n. 9, 13.
Coggins v. Mimms—§ 3.34, n. 4.
Cohen, In re—§ 8.13, n. 1.
Cohen v. Thomas & Son Transfer Line, Inc.—§ 12.9, n. 40.
Cohn v. Bridgeport Plumbing Supply Co.—§ 3.3, n. 5.
Cohn v. Cohn—§ 7.5, n. 9, 23.
Cohn v. Middle Road Riverhead Development Corp.—§ 7.7, n. 7.
Cohn v. Plass—§ 4.3, n. 1, 3.
Coke Lumber & Mfg. Co. v. First Nat. Bank in Dallas—§ 12.6, n. 28; § 12.7, n. 23.
Coker v. Whitlock—§ 4.10, n. 4.
Colandrea, In re—§ 3.13, n. 1.
Colburn v. Mid-State Homes, Inc.—§ 5.31, n. 3.
Cole, In re, 89 B.R. 433—§ 8.17, n. 51.
Cole, In re, 81 B.R. 326—§ 8.17, n. 15, 17.
Cole v. Hotz—§ 9.8, n. 23; § 10.1, n. 1.
Cole v. Morris—§ 10.1, n. 5.
Colegrove, In re—§ 8.15, n. 77.
Cole Mfg. Co. v. Falls—§ 12.5, n. 3.
Colin v. Fidelity Standard Mortg. Corp.—§ 5.35, n. 43.
Collateral Inv. Co. v. Pilgrim—§ 10.5, n. 2; § 10.6, n. 3.
Collective Federal Sav. & Loan Ass'n v. Toland—§ 7.1, n. 1.
Collingwood v. Brown—§ 7.13, n. 7.
Collins v. Drake—§ 5.33, n. 35.
Collins v. Gregg—§ 7.4, n. 10.
Collins v. Home Savings & Loan Ass'n—§ 12.9, n. 3, 37; § 12.10; § 12.10, n. 19.
Collins v. Nagel—§ 7.7, n. 7.
Collins v. Rea—§ 4.10, n. 4.
Collins v. Riggs—§ 7.15, n. 2.
Collins v. Union Federal Sav. & Loan Ass'n—§ 6.10, n. 6.
Colman v. Packard—§ 2.2, n. 14.
Colonial Bank v. Marine Bank, N.A.—§ 12.7, n. 37.
Colonial Mortg. Service Co. v. Southard—§ 12.7, n. 14.
Colonial & United States Mortg. Co. v. Flemington—§ 6.12, n. 6.
Colonial & United States Mortg. Co. v. Northwest Thresher Co.—§ 6.12, n. 21.

Colonial Villas, Inc. v. Title Ins. Co. of Minnesota—§ 12.9, n. 2; § 12.10, n. 33.
Colorado Nat. Bank of Denver v. F. E. Biegert Co., Inc., of Denver—§ 12.9, n. 7.
Colorado Sav. Bank v. Bales—§ 5.15, n. 5.
Colpetzer v. Trinity Church—§ 12.5, n. 3, 7.
Colter Realty v. Primer Realty Corporation—§ 4.42, n. 6, 14, 21.
Columbia Bank for Cooperatives v. Lee—§ 10.13, n. 2.
Columbus Club v. Simons—§ 12.3, n. 48.
Columbus Park Corp. v. Department of Housing Preservation and Development of City of New York—§ 6.4, n. 31.
Columbus Production Credit Ass'n v. Weeks—§ 11.4, n. 61.
Colwell v. Warner—§ 7.2, n. 20.
Comanche Ice & Fuel Co. v. Binder & Hillery—§ 7.13, n. 12.
Comet Development Corp. v. Prudential Ins. Co. of America—§ 12.10, n. 34.
ComFed Sav. Bank v. Newtown Commons Plaza Assoc.—§ 4.27, n. 9, 10; § 4.29, n. 17, 20; § 4.30, n. 1.
Comfort-Craft Heating & Air Conditioning, Inc. v. Salamone—§ 13.3, n. 31.
Commerce Financial v. Markwest Corp.—§ 12.3, n. 47.
Commerce Sav. Lincoln, Inc. v. Robinson—§ 9.1, n. 4, 6, 13; § 9.4, n. 4, 14.
Commerce Union Bank v. Davis—§ 5.20, n. 5.
Commerce Union Bank v. May—§ 5.20, n. 5; § 5.19, n. 42.
Commercial Bank v. Readd—§ 12.7, n. 23.
Commercial Bank v. Rockovits—§ 2.4, n. 2; § 12.7, n. 7, 11.
Commercial Bank v. Stafford—§ 9.2, n. 3; § 12.9, n. 7.
Commercial Casualty Ins. Co. v. Roman—§ 5.19, n. 24, 26.
Commercial Credit Co. v. Childs—§ 5.29; § 5.29, n. 21.
Commercial Credit Corp. v. Orange County Mach. Works—§ 12.11, n. 22.
Commercial Credit Corporation v. Gould—§ 9.6, n. 3.
Commercial Factors of Denver v. Clarke & Waggener—§ 2.4, n. 2.
Commercial Federal Sav. and Loan Ass'n v. ABA Corp.—§ 7.17, n. 1.
Commercial Federal Sav. and Loan Ass'n v. Grabenstein—§ 9.4, n. 4, 5.
Commercial Investments, Ltd., In re—§ 12.6, n. 33; § 12.7, n. 42.
Commercial Laundries, Inc. v. Golf Course Towers Associates—§ 7.12, n. 31.
Commercial Products Corp. v. Briegel—§ 5.27, n. 7.
Commercial Standard Ins. Co. v. American Emp. Ins. Co.—§ 10.4, n. 3.

TABLE OF CASES

Commercial Standard Ins. Co. v. Bank of America—§ 12.10; § 12.10, n. 48.
Commonwealth v. ———— (see opposing party)
Commonwealth Land Title Co. v. Kornbluth (Contreras)—§ 10.9, n. 3; § 10.10, n. 13.
Commonwealth Mortg. Assur. Co. v. Superior Court (Sampson)—§ 11.2, n. 52.
Commonwealth Mortg. Co. v. De Waltoff—§ 4.39, n. 19.
Commonwealth Mortg. Corp. v. First Nationwide Bank—§ 5.35, n. 20.
Commonwealth of (see name of Commonwealth)
Community Bank v. Jones—§ 10.9, n. 7.
Community Bank of Homestead v. Barnett Bank of the Keys—§ 9.7, n. 3.
Community Federal Sav. and Loan Ass'n of Palm Beaches v. Orman—§ 7.7, n. 7.
Community Federal Savings and Loan Association of Independence, Mo. v. Fields—§ 11.6, n. 22.
Community Title Co. v. Crow—§ 12.9, n. 2.
Community Title Co. v. Roosevelt Federal Sav. & Loan Ass'n—§ 11.6, n. 19.
Compton v. Jesup—§ 4.24, n. 14.
Comstock v. Drohan—§ 5.10, n. 8, 14.
Comstock & Davis, Inc. v. G.D.S. & Associates—§ 12.4, n. 23.
Conaty v. Guaranty Loan Co.—§ 4.31, n. 14.
Concept Management, Ltd. v. Carpenter—§ 9.8, n. 5.
Concepts, Inc. v. First Sec. Realty Services, Inc.—§ 7.20, n. 15.
Con Co, Inc. v. Wilson Acres Apartments, Ltd.—§ 12.4, n. 41.
Concord Mill Ltd. Partnership, In re—§ 4.35, n. 31.
Conference Center Ltd. v. TRC—The Research Corp. of New England—§ 4.1, n. 16.
Conference of Federal Sav. & Loan Associations v. Stein, 604 F.2d 1256—§ 11.5, n. 43.
Conference of Federal Sav. and Loan Associations v. Stein, 495 F.Supp. 12—§ 5.23, n. 18.
Conference of State Bank Sup'rs v. Conover—§ 11.4, n. 60; § 11.6, n. 29.
Congregational Church Bldg. Soc. v. Scandinavian Free Church of Tacoma—§ 5.32, n. 26.
Congregation Kehal Adath Jeshurun M'yassy v. Universal Bldg. & Const. Co.—§ 3.24, n. 11.
Conley v. Downing—§ 3.28, n. 11.
Conley v. Sharpe—§ 2.2, n. 8.
Conneaut Bldg. & Loan Co. v. Felch—§ 10.9, n. 18; § 10.13, n. 16.
Connecticut v. Doehr—§ 7.25, n. 12.

Connecticut General Life Ins. Co. v. Dredge—§ 12.9, n. 29.
Connecticut Mut. Life Ins. Co. v. Bulte—§ 4.45, n. 8, 10, 11, 14; § 4.46, n. 24.
Connecticut Mut. Life Ins. Co. v. Carter—§ 7.16, n. 26.
Connecticut Mut. Life Ins. Co. v. Scammon—§ 4.13, n. 2.
Connecticut Mut. Life Ins. Co. v. Talbot—§ 5.33, n. 21.
Connecticut Nat. Bank v. Esposito—§ 2.4, n. 2.
Connecticut Sav. Bank v. Burger—§ 7.10, n. 3.
Connell v. Kaukauna etc. Co.—§ 4.12, n. 3.
Connelly v. Derwinski—§ 11.2, n. 44; § 11.6, n. 65.
Conner v. Coggins—§ 6.14, n. 6, 7.
Conner v. First Nat. Bank and Trust Co. of Rockford—§ 5.22, n. 35.
Connolly v. Plaza Cards and Gifts—§ 4.38, n. 4.
Connolly Development, Inc. v. Superior Court of Merced County—§ 12.5; § 12.5, n. 19, 28; § 12.6; § 12.6, n. 14, 17.
Connor v. Great Western Sav. & Loan Ass'n—§ 12.11; § 12.11, n. 1; § 13.3; § 13.3, n. 28, 59.
Conrad v. Harrison—§ 10.13, n. 10.
Conroy v. Aniskoff—§ 8.9, n. 19.
Conshohocken Federal Sav. and Loan Ass'n v. Period and Country Homes, Inc.—§ 12.9, n. 4; § 12.10, n. 7, 33.
Consolidated Am. Life Ins. Co. v. Covington—§ 12.3, n. 41.
Consolidated Capital Income Trust v. Colter, Inc.—§ 8.18, n. 53.
Consolidated Capital Properties, II, Ltd. v. National Bank of North America—§ 5.22, n. 19; § 5.24, n. 87.
Consolidated Loans, Inc. v. Smith—§ 6.9, n. 18.
Consolidated Nat. Bank of Tucson v. Van Slyke—§ 6.12, n. 9, 20.
Constable Plaza Associates, L.P., In re—§ 4.35, n. 31.
Constitution Bank and Trust Co. v. Robinson—§ 7.10, n. 3.
Construction Machinery of Arkansas v. Roberts—§ 6.15, n. 2; § 6.17, n. 13.
Consumers Sav. Bank v. Coven—§ 5.7, n. 11.
Continental Bank v. Barclay Riding Academy, Inc.—§ 2.3, n. 1, 17, 19.
Continental Country Club, Inc., In re—§ 12.8, n. 7, 12.
Continental Federal Sav. and Loan Ass'n v. Fetter—§ 5.22, n. 13.
Continental Mut. Sav. Bank v. Elliott—§ 5.20, n. 2.
Continental Nat. Bank & Trust Co. v. Reynolds—§ 5.19, n. 8.
Continental Oil Co. of Texas v. Graham—§ 10.9, n. 16.

TABLE OF CASES 743

Continental Resources Corp., In re—§ 12.8, n. 10.
Continental Supply Co. v. Marshall—§ 10.-15, n. 4.
Continental Title & Trust Co. v. Devlin—§ 6.16, n. 16.
Conway v. Alexander—§ 2.1, n. 6; § 3.8, n. 10; § 3.15, n. 14.
Conway v. Andrews—§ 7.21, n. 25; § 10.10, n. 4.
Conway v. Yadon—§ 5.35, n. 9, 11.
Conway Sav. Bank v. Vinick—§ 5.3, n. 3.
Conwell v. Clifford—§ 2.3, n. 9.
Cook v. American States Ins. Co.—§ 5.19, n. 33; § 10.14, n. 4.
Cook v. Bartholomew—§ 2.2, n. 1, 10.
Cook v. Carlson—§ 12.4, n. 12, 25; § 12.5, n. 19, 25.
Cook v. Citizens Sav. and Loan Ass'n—§ 12.10, n. 44.
Cook v. Curtis—§ 4.24, n. 2.
Cook v. McFarland—§ 3.1, n. 1; § 8.5, n. 13.
Cook v. Merrifield—§ 3.29, n. 18.
Cook v. Metal Building Products, Inc.—§ 12.4, n. 42.
Cook v. Ottawa University—§ 4.29, n. 15.
Cook v. Prindle—§ 6.12, n. 20.
Cook v. Union Trust Co.—§ 6.12, n. 18.
Cookes v. Culbertson—§ 4.29, n. 22.
Cooklin v. Cooklin—§ 2.1, n. 17.
Cooley v. Fredinburg—§ 11.7, n. 45.
Cooley v. Murray—§ 10.11, n. 9.
Coomes v. Frey—§ 7.17, n. 17.
Coon v. Shry—§ 2.1, n. 4, 17.
Cooper, Matter of—§ 8.15, n. 39.
Cooper v. Bane—§ 5.14, n. 8.
Cooper v. Bigly—§ 10.10, n. 9.
Cooper v. Cooper—§ 6.6, n. 9.
Cooper v. Davis—§ 4.5, n. 9; § 4.6, n. 5; § 4.7, n. 4.
Cooper v. Deseret Federal Sav. and Loan Ass'n—§ 5.24, n. 118.
Cooper v. Harvey—§ 5.28, n. 18.
Cooper v. Maurer—§ 8.5, n. 9; § 8.6, n. 28.
Cooper v. Peak—§ 7.3, n. 8.
Cooperatieve Centrale Raiffeisen-Boerenleenbank B.A. v. Bailey—§ 5.29, n. 7.
Coors of North Mississippi, Inc., In re—§ 10.9, n. 7.
Coplan Pipe & Supply Co. v. Ben-Frieda Corp.—§ 5.31, n. 18.
Copp v. Sands Point Marina, Inc.—§ 8.1, n. 1.
Copper, United States v.—§ 11.6, n. 76.
Coppola v. Housing Inv. Corp. of Florida—§ 8.3, n. 21.
Coraci v. Noack—§ 5.22, n. 37.
Coral Gables Federal Sav. and Loan Ass'n v. Whitewater Enterprises, Inc.—§ 8.3, n. 18.
Corbett, In re—§ 8.17, n. 17.
Cordell v. Regan—§ 12.6, n. 12.
Core v. Bell—§ 4.10, n. 8.
Core v. Strickler—§ 7.17, n. 12.
Corey, In re—§ 3.19, n. 9.

Corey v. Roberts—§ 3.8, n. 1; § 3.19, n. 3.
Corkrell v. Poe—§ 5.15, n. 14.
Cornelison v. Kornbluth—§ 4.5, n. 3; § 11.6, n. 58.
Corning v. Burton—§ 5.15, n. 1.
Corning v. Smith—§ 7.14, n. 14.
Corning Bank v. Bank of Rector—§ 9.7, n. 19.
Cornish v. Woolverton—§ 5.33, n. 21.
Cornwell v. Bank of America Nat. Trust and Sav. Ass'n—§ 6.7, n. 1.
Coronet Capital Co., In re—§ 5.35, n. 47.
Cortelyeu v. Hathaway—§ 4.34, n. 2, 6.
Cory v. Santa Ynez Land & Imp. Co.—§ 4.24, n. 1; § 7.5, n. 12, 23.
Cosby v. Buchanan—§ 3.4, n. 4, 10.
Costa v. Neimon—§ 12.11, n. 30.
Costa v. Sardinha—§ 10.11, n. 4.
Costanzo v. Ganguly—§ 8.3, n. 93.
Cote, In re—§ 8.14, n. 21, 23.
Cottle v. Wright—§ 4.4, n. 21, 22, 23.
Cottman Co. v. Continental Trust Co.—§ 4.15, n. 6.
Cotton v. Carlisle—§ 4.8, n. 1.
Cotton, Trustee v. Graham—§ 2.1, n. 4, 17.
Cottrell v. Purchase—§ 3.4, n. 3.
Cottrell v. Shepherd—§ 6.13, n. 2.
Coulter v. Blieden—§ 7.16, n. 9.
Country Village Heights Condominium (Group I) v. Mario Bonito, Inc.—§ 13.3, n. 38, 42.
County of (see name of county)
Coursey v. Fairchild—§ 3.1, n. 1, 30.
Courson v. Atkinson & Griffin, Inc.—§ 12.7, n. 23.
Courtright Cattle Co. v. Dolsen Co.—§ 9.7, n. 3, 22.
Courts v. Winston—§ 3.8, n. 16.
Coventry Commons Associates, In re—§ 4.35, n. 25.
Coventry Commons Associates, Matter of—§ 8.18, n. 42.
Covington v. Pritchett—§ 3.32, n. 26.
Cowart, In re—§ 8.15, n. 5.
Cowles v. Marble—§ 6.7, n. 12.
Cowles v. Zlaket—§ 3.18, n. 2, 3.
Cowley v. Shields—§ 3.1, n. 4.
Cox, In re, 68 B.R. 788—§ 3.35, n. 4.
Cox, In re, 57 B.R. 290—§ 12.8, n. 10.
Cox v. First Nat. Bank of Aitkin—§ 6.15, n. 2; § 6.17, n. 5.
Cox v. Helenius—§ 7.21, n. 59, 75.
Cox v. Townsend—§ 7.16, n. 23.
Cox v. Wheeler—§ 7.8, n. 6.
Cox v. Wooten Brothers Farms, Inc.—§ 10.2, n. 4; § 10.4, n. 1.
C.P.C. Development Co. No. 5, In re—§ 11.7, n. 36.
Cracco v. Cox—§ 6.11, n. 18.
Crahan v. Chittenden—§ 4.3, n. 3.
Craig v. Kansas City Terminal Ry. Co.—§ 4.8, n. 2.
Crain v. McGoon—§ 6.7, n. 4, 16, 24, 25.
Crain, United States v.—§ 11.6, n. 56, 60.
Crane v. Turner—§ 5.34, n. 29.

Crane Co. v. Fine—§ 12.6, n. 22.
Cranesville Block Co., Inc. v. Pentagon Const. Co., Inc.—§ 5.31, n. 3.
Cranston v. Crane—§ 6.7, n. 8.
Crawford, In re—§ 7.1, n. 1, 3.
Crawford v. Edwards—§ 5.13, n. 1.
Crawford v. Nimmons—§ 5.17, n. 3, 4.
Crawford v. Taylor, Richards & Burden—§ 7.5, n. 15.
Creamer Industries, Inc., United States v.—§ 3.33, n. 30.
Credit Bureau Corp. v. Beckstead—§ 10.6, n. 8.
Credit Finance, Inc. v. Bateman—§ 3.35, n. 2.
Credithrift, Inc. v. Knowles—§ 12.9, n. 6.
Crescent Beach Co. of Florida v. Conzelman—§ 7.32, n. 4.
Crescent Beach Inn, Inc., In re—§ 8.14, n. 20.
Crescent Lumber Co. v. Larson—§ 8.2, n. 4.
Cresco Realty Co. v. Clark—§ 7.6, n. 7.
Crest Sav. and Loan Ass'n v. Mason—§ 6.8, n. 5.
Cretella, In re—§ 8.15, n. 43.
Cretex Companies, Inc. v. Construction Leaders, Inc.—§ 12.2, n. 31.
Crichton v. Himlie Properties—§ 3.37, n. 11.
Crippen v. Morrison—§ 4.2, n. 14.
Criswell v. McKnight—§ 4.31, n. 14.
Crockett v. First Federal Sav. and Loan Ass'n of Charlotte—§ 5.22, n. 14.
Croft v. Jensen—§ 3.29, n. 21.
Crofts v. Johnson—§ 4.31, n. 10.
Crone v. Stinde—§ 5.15, n. 14.
Cronin v. Hazleteine—§ 7.15, n. 10, 12.
Cronkhite v. Kemp—§ 11.2, n. 30.
Cross v. Federal Nat. Mortg. Ass'n—§ 7.7, n. 28, 33.
Cross v. Robinson—§ 6.6, n. 8.
Cross Companies, Inc. v. Citizens Mortg. Inv. Trust—§ 4.24, n. 6; § 4.35, n. 46, 47; § 8.4, n. 6; § 8.6, n. 14.
Crossland Mortg. Corp. v. Frankel—§ 7.16, n. 29.
Crossland Sav. Bank FSB v. Constant—§ 5.28, n. 6.
Crossland Sav., FSB v. LoGuidice–Chatwal Real Estate Investments Co.—§ 4.35, n. 7.
Crouse, In re—§ 8.15, n. 89.
Crow v. Heath—§ 8.1, n. 12.
Crowder v. Scott State Bank of Bethany—§ 8.5, n. 6; § 8.7, n. 11.
Crowe v. Malba Land Co.—§ 5.17, n. 8.
Crowell v. Currier—§ 5.18, n. 6.
Crowell v. Hospital of St. Barnabas—§ 5.13, n. 1.
Crowley Bros. Inc. v. Ward—§ 12.4, n. 36.
Crown Iron Works Co. v. Melin—§ 8.7, n. 13.
Crum v. AVCO Financial Services of Indianapolis, Inc.—§ 12.10, n. 33.

Crum v. United States Fidelity and Guar. Co.—§ 2.3, n. 13.
Crutchfield v. Johnson & Latimer—§ 9.4, n. 10.
Crystal Ice Co. of Columbia, Inc. v. First Colonial Corp.—§ 9.2, n. 7.
CSS Corp. v. Sheriff of Chester County—§ 7.17, n. 11.
C.T.W. Co., Inc. v. Rivergrove Apartments, Inc.—§ 6.6, n. 2; § 10.3, n. 3.
Cucumber Creek Development, Inc., In re—§ 8.13, n. 31; § 8.17, n. 4, 5.
Culbertson State Bank of Culbertson, Mont. v. Dahl—§ 5.33, n. 6.
Culligan Corp. v. Transamerica Ins. Co.—§ 12.2, n. 35.
Cullum v. Erwin—§ 5.35, n. 8.
Culp v. Western Loan & Building Co.—§ 12.3, n. 42.
Culpepper v. Aston—§ 10.9, n. 8.
Cumberland Lumber Co. v. First and Farmers Bank of Somerset, Inc.—§ 7.13, n. 9.
Cumming v. Cumming—§ 10.9, n. 6.
Cumps v. Kiyo—§ 6.6, n. 2, 3.
CUNA Mortg. v. Aafedt—§ 6.6, n. 36.
Cuna Mut. Ins. Soc. v. Dominguez—§ 12.3, n. 49.
Cunningham, In re—§ 5.12, n. 2.
Cunningham v. Hawkins—§ 7.5, n. 15.
Cunningham v. Williams—§ 6.11, n. 31.
Curlee v. Morris—§ 5.6, n. 1.
Curry v. SBA—§ 11.6, n. 84.
Curry v. Tucker—§ 3.27, n. 5; § 3.29, n. 11.
Curry, United States v.—§ 11.6, n. 69.
Curtin v. Krohn—§ 4.2, n. 16.
Curtis v. Curtis—§ 4.31, n. 2.
Curtis v. Cutler—§ 7.8, n. 3.
Curtis v. Holee—§ 6.13, n. 7, 13, 16.
Curtis v. Moore—§ 5.34, n. 17.

D

Dad's Properties, Inc. v. Lucas—§ 7.7, n. 3.
D'Agostino v. Wheel Inn, Inc.—§ 8.3, n. 41.
D.A. Hill Co. v. Clevetrust Realty Investors—§ 12.6, n. 25, 27.
Dahlke v. Doering—§ 8.14, n. 108; § 8.16, n. 28.
Dail v. Campbell—§ 5.5, n. 1; § 5.15, n. 5.
Dailey, United States v.—§ 9.1, n. 4, 6, 25, 27.
Daily v. Mid–America Bank and Trust Co. of Carbondale—§ 12.4, n. 21.
Dairy Farm Leasing Co., United States v.—§ 8.7, n. 6.
Dairyland Financial Corp. v. Federal Intermediate Credit Bank of St. Paul—§ 5.27, n. 1; § 5.28, n. 3.
Daiwa Bank, Ltd. v. La Salle Nat. Trust, N.A.—§ 7.3, n. 4.
Dakota Bank and Trust Co. of Fargo v. Funfar—§ 5.10, n. 4.

TABLE OF CASES

Dakota Loan & Trust Co. v. Parmalee—§ 4.6, n. 5.
Dale v. Pushor—§ 3.28, n. 11.
Dallam v. Hedrick—§ 3.27, n. 5.
Dallas v. Dallas—§ 6.7, n. 1.
Dallas Bldg. Material, Inc. v. Rose—§ 12.4, n. 19.
Dallasta, In re—§ 8.14, n. 20.
Dalton v. Brown—§ 7.2, n. 7.
Dalton v. First Nat. Bank of Grayson—§ 12.8, n. 10.
Daly v. Maitland—§ 3.1, n. 37, 38.
Daly v. New York & G.L. Ry. Co.—§ 9.3, n. 10.
Damascus Milk Company v. Morriss—§ 8.6, n. 22, 23.
Damen Sav. and Loan Ass'n v. Johnson—§ 13.5, n. 20.
Damiano v. Bergen County Land Co.—§ 5.19, n. 42.
Damm v. Damm—§ 10.3, n. 9.
Danbury v. Robinson—§ 5.32, n. 8.
Danforth v. Gautreau—§ 4.44, n. 11.
Danforth v. Lindsey—§ 8.6, n. 28.
Daniel v. Coker—§ 4.24, n. 14.
Daniels v. Army Nat. Bank—§ 12.11, n. 25.
Daniels v. Big Horn Federal Sav. and Loan Ass'n—§ 12.10; § 12.10, n. 57.
Daniels v. Hart—§ 4.26, n. 1.
Daniels v. Johnson, 61 P. 1107—§ 6.13, n. 4, 5, 16.
Daniels v. Johnson, 24 Mich. 430—§ 3.19, n. 9.
Dansby, United States v.—§ 11.6, n. 75, 94.
Danvers Sav. Bank v. Hammer—§ 7.21, n. 8, 53; § 7.22, n. 24, 35; § 8.1, n. 11.
Darby's Estate, In re—§ 10.12, n. 3.
Darling, In re—§ 8.13, n. 18.
Darr v. First Federal Sav. & Loan Ass'n of Detroit—§ 5.24, n. 67.
Darrough v. Herbert Kraft Company Bank—§ 10.7, n. 12.
Dart v. Western Sav. & Loan Ass'n—§ 4.34, n. 10, 14; § 4.35, n. 3.
Dart and Bogue Co., Inc. v. Slosberg—§ 2.4, n. 2, 11.
Dash Contracting Corp. v. Slater—§ 13.3, n. 38.
Daubenspeck v. Platt—§ 7.4, n. 4.
Daugharthy v. Monritt Associates—§ 5.6, n. 1; § 5.8, n. 5; § 9.8; § 9.8, n. 11.
Daugherty v. Diment—§ 5.26, n. 8.
Daugherty Associates v. Silmon—§ 8.5, n. 11.
Daugherty Cattle Co. v. General Const. Co.—§ 3.27, n. 5.
Dauphin Deposit Bank and Trust Co. v. Tenny—§ 7.18, n. 3.
Dave Kolb Grading, Inc. v. Lieberman Corp.—§ 12.4, n. 33; § 12.6, n. 25; § 12.7, n. 22, 42.
Davenport v. Unicapital Corp.—§ 5.31, n. 11.
Davey v. Nessan—§ 5.8, n. 9.

David v. Sun Federal Sav. & Loan Ass'n, 461 So.2d 93—§ 7.6, n. 1.
David v. Sun Federal Sav. and Loan Ass'n, 429 So.2d 1277—§ 7.7, n. 7.
Davidoff, In re—§ 8.15, n. 70.
Davidson v. Click—§ 9.1, n. 11, 23, 26.
Davidson v. D.H. Hansen Ranch, Inc.—§ 7.31, n. 2.
David Stevenson Brewing Co. v. Iba—§ 5.32, n. 1.
Davie v. Sheffield—§ 7.21, n. 8, 9.
Davin v. Isman—§ 5.28, n. 4.
Davis, In re, 989 F.2d 208—§ 8.15, n. 51, 59.
Davis, In re, 16 B.R. 473—§ 8.15, n. 35.
Davis, In re, 15 B.R. 22—§ 8.15, n. 35, 40.
Davis v. Alton, Jacksonville & Pacific Railway Co.—§ 4.10, n. 9.
Davis v. Ashburn—§ 6.7, n. 6.
Davis v. Bechstein—§ 5.32, n. 17.
Davis v. Boyajian, Inc.—§ 7.12, n. 34.
Davis v. Davis, 196 N.W.2d 473—§ 7.7, n. 13.
Davis v. Davis, 127 P. 1051—§ 5.17, n. 3, 5.
Davis v. Davis, 6 So. 908—§ 3.35, n. 1.
Davis v. First Interstate Bank of Idaho, N.A.—§ 12.3, n. 47.
Davis v. German American Insurance Co.—§ 4.14, n. 10.
Davis v. Huntsville Production Credit Ass'n—§ 7.31, n. 12.
Davis v. Johnson—§ 10.6, n. 3, 13.
Davis v. National Homes Acceptance Corp.—§ 5.1, n. 4.
Davis v. Nevada Nat. Bank—§ 12.11; § 12.11, n. 24, 25.
Davis v. Romney—§ 12.11, n. 37.
Davis v. Small Business Inv. Co. of Houston—§ 12.3, n. 44.
Davis, United States v.—§ 11.2, n. 45; § 11.6, n. 72.
Davis v. Vecaro Development Corp.—§ 5.26, n. 5.
Davis Oil Co. v. Mills—§ 7.24, n. 18, 22.
Dawson v. Danbury Bank—§ 7.14, n. 9.
Dawson v. Overmyer—§ 7.2, n. 1, 21; § 7.4, n. 2.
Dayton v. Rice—§ 4.31, n. 8; § 4.44, n. 11.
Deadman v. Yantis—§ 7.5, n. 4.
Deal v. Christenbury—§ 2.1, n. 2.
Dealers Elec. Supply v. United States Fidelity & Guaranty Co.—§ 12.2, n. 31.
Dean v. Smith—§ 3.8, n. 1; § 3.19, n. 3.
Dean v. Walker—§ 5.15, n. 14.
Dearle v. Hall—§ 5.34, n. 24.
Deaver v. Deaver—§ 5.7, n. 6, 8.
De Bartlett v. De Wilson—§ 3.15, n. 18.
Debnam v. Watkins—§ 6.7, n. 8.
DeBry v. Valley Mortg. Co.—§ 12.11, n. 12.
Dechow v. Sko-Fed Credit—§ 6.4, n. 14.
Decker v. Decker—§ 6.6, n. 2, 14.
Decker v. Patton—§ 7.15, n. 1.
Decorah State Bank v. Zidlicky—§ 12.8, n. 10.
Dedes v. Strickland—§ 10.6, n. 14.

Deep v. Rose—§ 7.20, n. 1, 7.
DeKalb County v. United Family Life Ins. Co.—§ 6.3, n. 16.
Delacroix v. Stanley—§ 7.12, n. 14.
DeLaigle v. Federal Land Bank of Columbia—§ 7.28, n. 11, 12.
Delaney's, Inc. v. Pritchard—§ 6.11, n. 12.
Delano v. Bennett—§ 5.28, n. 13.
Delano v. Smith—§ 4.4, n. 4.
Delaplaine v. Hitchcock—§ 4.2, n. 12.
Delaware etc. Telephone Co. v. Elvins—§ 4.9, n. 3, 6.
De Leon v. Rhines—§ 5.15, n. 6; § 5.19, n. 7, 21.
De Lotto v. Zipper—§ 5.19, n. 5.
Delta Sav. & Loan Ass'n, Inc. v. I.R.S.—§ 8.4, n. 16.
Demarest v. Wynkoop—§ 5.27, n. 9.
DeMers, In re—§ 8.15, n. 41.
Demeter v. Wilcox—§ 9.1, n. 19, 20.
Demharter v. First Fed. Sav. & Loan Ass'n of Pittsburgh—§ 12.6, n. 28.
Deming Nat. Bank v. Walraven—§ 7.15, n. 23.
Dempsey v. McGowan—§ 12.7, n. 25, 27.
De Nichols v. Saunders—§ 4.21, n. 10.
Dennett v. Codman—§ 7.4, n. 10.
Dennis v. McEntyre Mercantile Co.—§ 6.16, n. 2.
Dennis v. Rotter—§ 5.31, n. 14.
Dennison v. Jack—§ 7.27, n. 2.
Dent, In re—§ 8.15, n. 61.
Dent v. Pickens—§ 7.13, n. 11.
Denton v. Ontario County Nat. Bank—§ 7.15, n. 27, 29.
Department of Banking and Finance of State of Neb. v. Davis—§ 5.33, n. 13; § 5.34, n. 12.
Department of Transp. v. New Century Engineering and Development Corp.—§ 4.12, n. 1.
Department of Transp., People ex rel. v. Redwood Baseline, Ltd.—§ 4.12, n. 1, 8.
De Penning v. Bedell—§ 2.1, n. 4.
Depew v. Colton—§ 6.12, n. 1.
Depner Architects and Planners, Inc. v. Nevada Nat. Bank—§ 12.4, n. 22.
Depon v. Shawye—§ 6.7, n. 2.
Deposit Guar. Bank v. Hall—§ 11.7, n. 7.
Derenco, Inc. v. Benjamin Franklin Federal Sav. and Loan Ass'n—§ 4.18, n. 21; § 11.6, n. 4.
De Roberts v. Stiles—§ 10.7, n. 6.
Derrico, In re—§ 2.1, n. 17.
Desert Gold Mining Co., United States v.—§ 5.32, n. 26.
Desiderio v. Iadonisi—§ 4.39, n. 7; § 6.6, n. 9.
Desloge v. Ranger—§ 3.8, n. 14.
Desmond v. F.D.I.C.—§ 5.29, n. 6, 32; § 11.7, n. 32, 35.
Desser v. Schatz—§ 6.6, n. 1.
Destin Sav. Bank v. Summerhouse of FWB, Inc.—§ 5.24, n. 16, 118.

Detroit Properties Corporation v. Detroit Hotel Co.—§ 4.43, n. 5.
Detroit Trust Co. v. Hart—§ 7.16, n. 26.
Deuster v. McCamus—§ 10.15, n. 5.
Developer's Mortg. Co. v. TransOhio Sav. Bank—§ 5.35, n. 26.
Development, Inc., In re—§ 8.14, n. 10, 13, 20, 26, 27.
Devlin v. Collier—§ 5.28, n. 13, 15.
De Voe v. Rundle—§ 6.12, n. 5, 14.
Dewsnup v. Timm—§ 8.13; § 8.13, n. 5, 9.
Dexter v. Arnold, 7 Fed.Cas. 606—§ 7.5, n. 13.
Dexter v. Arnold, 7 Fed.Cas. 597—§ 4.29, n. 6, 8.
Dey v. Dunham—§ 3.14, n. 2.
Dezell v. King—§ 6.2, n. 7.
D & F Const. Inc., Matter of—§ 8.14, n. 77.
D. H. Overmyer Co., Inc. of Ohio v. Frick Co.—§ 3.30, n. 10; § 7.26; § 7.26, n. 1.
Dial v. Reynolds—§ 7.14, n. 14.
Diamond Intern. Corp. v. Bristol County Builders Corp.—§ 12.6, n. 4.
Diamond Lumber, Inc. v. H.C.M.C., Ltd.—§ 13.3, n. 29.
Dickason v. Williams—§ 6.16, n. 11.
Dicken v. Simpson—§ 4.27, n. 16.
Dickens v. First American Title Ins. Co. of Arizona—§ 12.9, n. 34.
Dickinson v. Oliver—§ 3.4, n. 7.
Dick & Reuteman Co. v. Jem Realty Co.—§ 4.2, n. 21.
Dicus v. Ripley County Bank, Osgood, Indiana 47037—§ 12.8, n. 5.
Di Diego v. Zarro—§ 8.1, n. 6.
Dieckman v. Walser—§ 5.6, n. 1; § 10.11, n. 6.
Dieckmann v. Walser—§ 10.11, n. 15.
Dieffenbach v. Attorney General of Vermont—§ 7.10; § 7.10, n. 6.
Dill v. Zielke—§ 3.29, n. 8.
Dillard & Coffin Co. v. Smith—§ 7.13, n. 11.
Dillman, Petition of—§ 4.12, n. 2.
Dillon v. Legg—§ 12.10, n. 49.
Dills v. Jasper—§ 7.17, n. 6.
Dimatteo v. North Tonawanda Auto Wash, Inc.—§ 7.7, n. 10.
Dimeo v. Ellenstein—§ 7.3, n. 10.
Dime Sav. Bank of New York v. Dooley—§ 7.6, n. 8.
Dime Sav. Bank of New York, FSB v. Roberts—§ 12.9, n. 1.
Dimmitt v. Johnson—§ 5.8, n. 6.
Dinniny v. Gavin—§ 6.11, n. 2.
Dinsmore, In re—§ 8.15, n. 54, 70.
Dirks v. Cornwell—§ 3.30, n. 16; § 3.35, n. 4.
Dismuke, United States v.—§ 11.6, n. 77.
Disrud v. Arnold—§ 4.16, n. 3.
Diversified, Inc. v. Walker—§ 7.20, n. 3.
Diversified Mortg. Investors v. Gepada, Inc.—§ 12.4, n. 27.
Divine Homes, Inc. v. Gulf Power Co.—§ 12.6, n. 44.

Dixie Heating and Cooling Co., Inc. v. Bank of Gadsden—§ 12.4, n. 24.
Dixieland Realty Co. v. Wysor—§ 4.44, n. 1; § 10.13, n. 1.
Dixon v. Clark—§ 6.7, n. 3.
Dixon v. Clayville—§ 5.35, n. 15.
Dixon v. Morgan—§ 10.7, n. 2.
Dixon v. Windsor—§ 5.34, n. 4.
Dixon v. Wright—§ 3.19, n. 5.
D & M Development Co. v. Sherwood & Roberts, Inc.—§ 12.3, n. 27.
D & N Elec., Inc. v. Underground Festival, Inc.—§ 12.4, n. 35.
D. Nelsen & Sons, Inc. v. General Am. Development Corp.—§ 5.32, n. 15.
Dobbs v. Bowling—§ 10.5, n. 8.
Dobbs v. Kellogg—§ 3.10, n. 2.
Dobkin v. Landsberg—§ 5.8, n. 2.
Dodd v. Harper—§ 2.1, n. 5.
Dodds v. Spring—§ 10.2, n. 5.
Doe v. Pott—§ 1.2, n. 7.
Doe d. Parsley v. Day—§ 4.1, n. 8.
Doe d. Roby v. Maisey—§ 4.1, n. 7.
D'Oench, Duhme & Co. v. F.D.I.C.—§ 5.29; § 5.29, n. 37; § 11.7; § 11.7, n. 9.
Dolan v. Borregard—§ 10.3, n. 2.
Dolese v. Bellows–Claude Neon Co.—§ 4.39, n. 19; § 7.12, n. 31, 34.
Dollar Dry Dock Bank v. Piping Rock Builders, Inc.—§ 8.1, n. 3.
Dolphin v. Aylward—§ 10.14, n. 1.
Domard v. Fisher & Burke, Inc.—§ 5.27, n. 6; § 5.28, n. 9, 21.
Domeyer v. O'Connell—§ 5.35, n. 7, 11.
Dominex, Inc. v. Key—§ 7.1, n. 4, 6.
Dominion Financial Corp. v. 275 Washington St. Corp.—§ 10.3, n. 7.
Donahue v. LeVesque—§ 6.4, n. 10.
Donaldson v. Sellmer—§ 3.29; § 3.29, n. 59.
Don Anderson Enterprises, Inc. v. Entertainment Enterprises, Inc.—§ 7.7, n. 25.
Donlon & Miller Manuf'g Co. v. Cannella—§ 4.38, n. 20.
Donnybrook Bldg. Supply Co., Inc. v. Alaska Nat. Bank of North—§ 12.6, n. 8, 20.
Dorff v. Bornstein—§ 4.44, n. 2, 7; § 7.15, n. 3.
Dorn v. Robinson—§ 7.7, n. 4.
Dorothy Edwards Realtors, Inc. v. McAdams—§ 5.3, n. 2; § 9.4, n. 14; § 12.9, n. 24, 42.
Dorr v. Dudderar—§ 4.5, n. 7; § 4.6, n. 3.
Dorsey Elec. Supply Co., In re—§ 12.8, n. 10.
Doss, In re—§ 8.15, n. 72.
Dotto v. Ciamboli—§ 5.33, n. 17, 18.
Dougherty v. McColgan, Md.—§ 4.29, n. 22.
Douglas v. United States—§ 12.3, n. 3, 19.
Douglas County State Bank v. Steele—§ 10.14, n. 8.
Douglas Northwest, Inc. v. Bill O'Brien & Sons Const., Inc.—§ 12.4, n. 11.
Douglass v. Bishop—§ 7.2, n. 13; § 7.3, n. 2.
Douglass v. Moody—§ 3.19, n. 1.

Douthit, Ex parte—§ 13.3, n. 31.
Dover Lumber Co. v. Case—§ 2.2, n. 1.
Dover Mobile Estates v. Fiber Form Products, Inc.—§ 4.22, n. 3; § 4.23, n. 3, 4; § 7.12, n. 5; § 12.9, n. 47, 50, 56.
Dover Shopping Center, Inc. v. Cushman's Sons, Inc.—§ 15.16.
Downey State Bank v. Major–Blakeney Corp.—§ 7.1, n. 3.
Downs v. Ziegler—§ 3.7, n. 8; § 3.17, n. 5; § 3.18, n. 2, 6; § 3.19; § 3.19, n. 3, 15, 17, 19; § 5.16, n. 1.
Downstate Nat. Bank v. Elmore—§ 7.15, n. 7.
Dozier v. Farrior—§ 7.16, n. 22.
Dozier v. Mitchell—§ 4.29, n. 9, 26, 33.
Drach v. Hornig—§ 7.16, n. 34.
Drake v. Drake—§ 2.2, n. 8.
Drake v. Morris Plan Co. of California—§ 12.11, n. 11.
Drannek Realty Co. v. Nathan Frank, Inc.—§ 8.1, n. 12.
Draper v. American Funding Ltd.—§ 6.4, n. 10, 13, 14.
Dreckshage v. Community Federal Sav. and Loan Ass'n—§ 12.9, n. 12.
Drew v. Anderson, Clayton & Co.—§ 6.17, n. 6.
Drew Associates of N.J., L.P. v. Travisano—§ 13.6, n. 31.
Drexler v. Commercial Sav Bank—§ 10.9, n. 21.
Drey v. Doyle—§ 3.33, n. 13; § 5.25, n. 5.
Drilling Service Co. v. Baebler—§ 12.4, n. 33.
Drimmel, In re—§ 8.14, n. 87.
Driscoll, In re—§ 8.15, n. 5.
Drobnick v. Western Federal Sav. & Loan Ass'n of Denver—§ 12.10, n. 7.
Drury v. Holden—§ 5.7, n. 4; § 5.8, n. 5; § 10.2, n. 5, 7.
D.T. McCall & Sons v. Seagraves—§ 12.4, n. 21.
Duck v. Wells Fargo Bank—§ 10.9, n. 8.
Dudley, In re—§ 8.15, n. 5; § 8.17, n. 11, 15.
Duff v. Randall—§ 7.13, n. 3.
Dugan v. First Nat. Bank in Wichita—§ 12.9, n. 2.
Dugan v. Grzybowski—§ 6.1, n. 2; § 6.6, n. 18.
Duke v. Kilpatrick—§ 10.7, n. 10.
Duncan, In re—§ 2.4, n. 2, 5.
Duncan v. Essary—§ 3.21, n. 2.
Dundee Naval Stores Co. v. McDowell—§ 4.39, n. 19; § 7.2, n. 11; § 7.12, n. 31.
Dunfee v. Waite—§ 7.6, n. 7.
Dunham v. Ware Sav. Bank—§ 5.22, n. 14; § 5.24, n. 118.
Dunklee v. Adams—§ 2.2, n. 9.
Dunkley v. Van Buren—§ 8.1, n. 4.
Dunlap v. Hinkle—§ 12.4, n. 35.
Dunlap v. Wilson—§ 7.2, n. 4.
Dunlop v. James—§ 4.31, n. 18.
Dunn v. Barry—§ 7.7, n. 2.

Dunn v. Midwestern Indem., Mid-American Fire and Cas. Co.—§ 11.5, n. 3.
Dunning v. Leavitt—§ 5.17, n. 15.
Dunson v. Stockton, Whatley, Davin & Co.—§ 12.9, n. 43; § 12.10, n. 8; § 12.11; § 12.11, n. 6.
DuPage Lumber and Home Imp. Center Co., Inc. v. Georgia-Pacific Corp.—§ 10.9, n. 7.
Duparquet Huot & Moneuse Co. v. Evans—§ 4.41, n. 16.
Dupnik v. United States—§ 11.6, n. 62.
Durant Const., Inc. v. Gourley—§ 12.4, n. 42.
Durham v. First Guaranty Bank of Hammond—§ 12.8, n. 9.
Durling v. Gould—§ 12.4, n. 4.
Durrett v. Washington Nat. Ins. Co.—§ 8.17; § 8.17, n. 8.
Dusenbery v. Bidwell—§ 4.45, n. 1.
Dutcher v. Hobby—§ 5.28, n. 17.
Duty v. Graham—§ 6.11, n. 21.
Duvall v. Laws, Swain, & Murdoch, P.A.—§ 3.18, n. 3.
Duvall-Percival Trust Co v. Jenkins—§ 5.13, n. 8; § 5.15, n. 14.
D. W. Jaquays & Co. v. First Sec. Bank—§ 10.1, n. 2.
Dye v. Lewis—§ 7.12, n. 5, 8.
Dye v. Lincoln Rochester Trust Co.—§ 12.9, n. 1.
Dyer v. Shurtleff—§ 7.21, n. 50.

E

Eakin v. Shultz—§ 5.15, n. 5.
Eardley v. Greenberg—§ 7.22, n. 17.
Earl, In re—§ 9.4, n. 4.
Earl W. Jimerson Housing Co., Inc. v. Butler—§ 13.6, n. 16.
Earnshaw v. First Federal Sav. & Loan Ass'n of Lowell—§ 12.7, n. 13.
Earp v. Boothe—§ 3.18, n. 10.
East Bay Ltd. Partnership v. American General Life & Acc. Ins. Co.—§ 5.22, n. 42; § 6.1, n. 11.
Eastern Idaho Production Credit Ass'n v. Placerton, Inc.—§ 8.2, n. 4.
Eastern Illinois Trust and Sav. Bank v. Vickery—§ 8.1, n. 2.
Eastern Nat. Bank v. Glendale Federal Sav. and Loan Ass'n—§ 10.6, n. 4.
East Grand Forks Federal Sav. & Loan Ass'n v. Mueller—§ 4.35, n. 15.
East India Co. v. Atkyns—§ 3.1, n. 4.
Eastman v. Batchelder—§ 2.2, n. 12.
Easton v. Littooy—§ 6.7, n. 19.
Eblen v. Major's Adm'r—§ 4.31, n. 14.
Eck v. Swennenson—§ 4.45, n. 6.
Eckley v. Bonded Adjustment Co.—§ 3.36, n. 8.
Eckman v. Centennial Sav. Bank—§ 12.11, n. 8.

Economy Sav. & Loan Co. v. Hollington—§ 3.29, n. 4.
Edd Helms Elec. Contracting, Inc. v. Barnett Bank of South Florida, N.A.—§ 12.6, n. 33.
Edenfield v. Trust Co. Mortg.—§ 6.6, n. 23.
Edgar v. Edgar—§ 7.8, n. 5.
Edgerton v. Young—§ 5.34, n. 17.
Edgewater Motel, Inc., In re—§ 8.14, n. 67.
Ed Hackstaff Concrete, Inc. v. Powder Ridge Condominium 'A' Owners' Ass'n, Inc.—§ 12.4, n. 11.
Edler v. Hasche—§ 4.4, n. 22.
E. D. McGillicuddy Const. Co., Inc. v. Knoll Recreation Ass'n, Inc.—§ 13.3, n. 38, 45.
Edmonds v. Augustyn—§ 5.27, n. 3.
Edrington v. Harper—§ 3.4, n. 7.
Edwards, In re—§ 8.15, n. 40.
Edwards v. Columbia, S. C., Teachers Federal Credit Union—§ 10.2, n. 2.
Edwards v. Smith—§ 7.7, n. 3.
Edwards v. Wall—§ 3.8, n. 12.
E. E. E., Inc. v. Hanson—§ 2.3, n. 13.
E.E. Stump Well Drilling, Inc. v. Willis—§ 13.3, n. 34.
E.F. Hutton Mortg. Corp. v. Equitable Bank, N.A.—§ 5.27, n. 3.
E.F. Hutton Mortg. Corp. v. Pappas—§ 5.27, n. 3.
Egan v. Engeman—§ 6.16, n. 8.
Eggensperger v. Lanpher—§ 4.29, n. 3.
Eggert v. Beyer—§ 5.33, n. 7.
Ehle v. Brown—§ 7.13, n. 3.
E. H. Ogden Lumber Co. v. Busse—§ 4.4, n. 12, 18, 20.
Ehring, In re—§ 8.17; § 8.17, n. 33, 76.
Eichorn v. Lunn—§ 6.6, n. 32; § 12.1, n. 31.
E. I. C., Inc. v. M & O Enterprises—§ 5.28, n. 40.
Eilermann, In re Estate of—§ 3.37, n. 7.
Eisen v. Kostakos—§ 4.27, n. 12; § 4.31, n. 9, 12; § 4.32, n. 1; § 7.6, n. 3, 19.
Eisenhut v. Steadman—§ 12.4, n. 21.
E. Landau Industries, Inc. v. 385 McLean Corp.—§ 5.28, n. 40.
Eldred v. Hart—§ 6.2, n. 12.
Eldridge v. Eldridge—§ 7.10, n. 14, 18.
Eldridge v. Wright—§ 8.7, n. 8.
Eldriedge v. Hoefer—§ 4.28, n. 4.
Electric City Concrete Co., Inc. v. Phillips—§ 12.4, n. 20.
Electric M & R, Inc. v. Banco Popular de Puerto Rico—§ 12.9, n. 36.
Electric Supply Co. of Durham, Inc. v. Swain Elec. Co., Inc.—§ 12.4, n. 19.
Elkins v. Edwards—§ 6.11, n. 16.
Ellickson v. Dull—§ 5.4, n. 1; § 5.11, n. 6; § 10.10, n. 6.
Elliott v. Brady—§ 4.27, n. 16.
Elliott v. Denver Joint Stock Land Bank of Denver—§ 5.12, n. 2.
Elliott v. Sackett—§ 5.5, n. 6.
Elliott, State ex rel. v. Holliday—§ 7.16, n. 1.

TABLE OF CASES

Ellis v. Butterfield—§ 3.27, n. 5; § 3.29, n. 70; § 3.32, n. 3.
Ellis v. Glover & Hobson, Limited—§ 4.4, n. 5.
Ellis v. Harrison—§ 5.14, n. 8.
Ellis v. Kristofersen—§ 5.18, n. 15.
Ellis v. Powell—§ 7.16, n. 12.
Ellis, United States v.—§ 11.6; § 11.6, n. 59.
Ellsworth v. Homemakers Finance Service, Inc.—§ 5.9, n. 8.
Ellzey, United States v.—§ 12.3, n. 19.
Elmendorf-Anthony Co. v. Dunn—§ 12.7, n. 35.
Elmora & West End Bldg. & Loan Ass'n v. Dancy—§ 10.5, n. 9.
Eloff v. Riesch—§ 10.3, n. 5.
El Paso v. Simmons—§ 4.19, n. 25.
El Paso Development Co. v. Berryman—§ 7.22, n. 3, 8.
Elsey v. People's Bank of Bardwell—§ 5.19, n. 38.
Elson Development Co. v. Arizona Sav. & Loan Ass'n.—§ 3.1, n. 1; § 8.5, n. 14, 15.
Embree Const. Group, Inc. v. Rafcor, Inc.—§ 12.6, n. 25.
Emerson v. Knight—§ 2.2, n. 2.
Emerson v. Murray—§ 3.4, n. 9.
Emigrant, etc., Savings Bank v. Goldman—§ 7.14, n. 10.
Emmons v. Brown—§ 12.11, n. 39.
Emmons v. Lake States Ins. Co.—§ 4.16, n. 7.
Emory v. Keighan—§ 6.11, n. 19.
Empire Trust Co. v. Heinze—§ 6.11, n. 2.
Emporia State Bank & Trust Co. v. Mounkes—§ 12.8, n. 1, 10.
Engels v. Valdesuso—§ 8.5, n. 9.
Engle v. Haines—§ 10.11, n. 14.
Engle v. Hall—§ 6.7, n. 20.
Engleman Transp. Co. v. Longwell—§ 4.28, n. 8, 10.
English v. Fischer—§ 4.15, n. 2.
Ennis v. Finanz Und Kommerz-Union Etabl.—§ 6.17, n. 10; § 6.19, n. 10.
Ennis v. Smith—§ 4.7, n. 3.
Enos v. Anderson—§ 5.6, n. 1, 4.
Enos v. Sanger—§ 5.15, n. 14.
Ensign v. Batterson—§ 4.29, n. 23.
Ensign v. Colburn—§ 4.7, n. 5.
Ensign Financial Corp. v. Federal Deposit Ins. Corp.—§ 11.1, n. 8.
ENT Federal Credit Union v. Chrysler First Financial Services Corp.—§ 9.7, n. 20.
Epic Associates, 80-XX v. Wasatch Bank—§ 12.1, n. 31.
Epperson v. Cappellino—§ 10.11, n. 4.
Epstein v. Enterprise Leasing Corp.—§ 8.3, n. 129.
Equitable Bldg. & Loan Ass'n v. King—§ 2.4, n. 2.
Equitable Development Corp., In re—§ 3.37, n. 10.
Equitable Development Corp., Matter of—§ 3.37, n. 11.

Equitable Life Assur. Soc. of United States v. Bostwick—§ 5.8, n. 9.
Equitable Mortg. Resources, Inc. v. Carter—§ 12.10, n. 34.
Equitable Securities Co. v. Talbert—§ 9.1, n. 14.
Equitable Trust Co. v. Imbesi—§ 3.38, n. 16.
Equity Associates v. Society for Sav.—§ 12.3, n. 36.
Equity Sav. and Loan Ass'n v. Chicago Title Ins. Co.—§ 10.6, n. 9.
Erickson v. First Nat. Bank of Minneapolis—§ 3.35, n. 11; § 3.37, n. 1.
Erickson v. Kendall—§ 5.33, n. 33.
Erickson v. Rocco—§ 4.11, n. 14; § 7.22, n. 1, 11.
Erie County Savings Bank v. Schuster—§ 7.14, n. 16.
Ernest v. Carter—§ 3.29, n. 18, 73.
Ernst v. McChesney—§ 6.17, n. 6.
Errett v. Wheeler—§ 6.17, n. 7, 14.
Erskine v. Townsend—§ 3.4, n. 4, 7.
Erwin v. Brooke—§ 10.1, n. 17.
Esplendido Apartments v. Metropolitan Condominium Ass'n of Arizona II—§ 5.3, n. 2; § 5.4, n. 9; § 5.26, n. 7.
Essex Cleaning Contractors, Inc. v. Amato—§ 4.26, n. 2.
Essex Sav. Bank v. Leeker—§ 12.10, n. 47, 57.
Estate of (see name of party)
Etchin, In re—§ 8.15, n. 72.
Eurovest Ltd. v. 13290 Biscayne Island Terrace Corp.—§ 9.4, n. 10.
Evans, In re—§ 8.15, n. 35, 95.
Evans v. Abney—§ 7.27, n. 26.
Evans v. Atkins—§ 7.10, n. 18.
Evans v. Elliot—§ 4.22, n. 14, 24.
Evans v. Evans—§ 3.7, n. 2.
Evans v. Faircloth-Byrd Mercantile Co.—§ 5.17, n. 13.
Evans v. First Federal Sav. Bank of Indiana—§ 11.5, n. 5, 18.
Evans v. Newton—§ 7.27, n. 17.
Evans v. Sperry—§ 5.10, n. 8.
Evans v. Thompson—§ 3.8, n. 16.
Everett Credit Union v. Allied Ambulance Services, Inc.—§ 12.8, n. 7.
Evergreen Bank v. D & P Justin's, Inc.—§ 8.3, n. 7.
Evergreen Ventures, In re—§ 4.4, n. 29.
Ewing v. Bay Minette Land Co.—§ 10.11, n. 4.
Ewing v. Mytinger & Casselberry, Inc.—§ 4.36, n. 8.
Excelsior Insurance Co. v. Royal Insurance Co.—§ 4.13, n. 4, 8, 9.
Exchange Bank, Milledgeville v. Hill—§ 7.22, n. 7.
Exchange Bank & Trust Co. v. Lone Star Life Ins. Co.—§ 12.3, n. 38.
Exchange Corp. v. Kuntz—§ 3.29, n. 20.
Exchange Sav. & Loan Ass'n v. Monocrete Pty. Ltd.—§ 12.6, n. 5.

Exchange Trust Co. v. Ireton—§ 5.17, n. 5.
Executive Hills Home Builders, Inc. v. Whitley—§ 5.24, n. 54.
Ex parte (see name of party)
ExtraOrdinary Learning and Educational Complex/Minneapolis Communiversity, Inc. v. New Bethel Baptist Church—§ 3.28, n. 11.
Eyde Bros. Development Co. v. Equitable Life Assur. Soc. of United States—§ 6.1, n. 10; § 6.2, n. 19; § 6.3, n. 3, 9; § 6.5, n. 3.
Eyster v. Hatheway—§ 9.1, n. 12.

F

Fagan v. People's Sav. & Loan Ass'n—§ 7.32, n. 1.
Fair v. Brown—§ 4.45, n. 12.
Fairbank v. Cudworth—§ 4.10, n. 4.
Fairchild v. Gray—§ 4.41, n. 6.
Faires, In re—§ 8.14, n. 20, 21.
Fairfax v. Dime Sav. Bank of Williamsburg—§ 4.13, n. 20, 22.
Fairfield Financial Group, Inc. v. Gawerc—§ 7.7, n. 3.
Fairhaven Sav. Bank v. Callahan—§ 8.1, n. 13.
Fairmont Associates v. Fairmont Estates—§ 7.7, n. 10.
Faith Cathedral Church of God in Christ v. Booker T. Washington Ins. Co., Inc.—§ 7.27, n. 2.
Falcon Holdings, Ltd. v. Isaacson—§ 12.4, n. 34.
Falls Lumber Co. v. Heman—§ 12.10, n. 8, 51; § 13.3, n. 24.
Familian Corp. v. Imperial Bank—§ 12.6, n. 7.
Fandel, Inc. v. First of Denver Mortg. Investors—§ 12.9, n. 27; § 12.10, n. 7, 17.
F. & H. Investment Co. v. Sackman-Gilliland Corp.—§ 7.22, n. 1.
F & M Enterprises, Inc., In re, 58 B.R. 436—§ 3.18, n. 4.
F & M Enterprises, Inc., In re, 34 B.R. 211—§ 3.18, n. 2.
Fannin Inv. & Development Co. v. Neuhaus—§ 5.34, n. 9.
Fara Mfg. Co., Inc. v. First Federal Sav. and Loan Ass'n of Miami—§ 8.3, n. 18.
Farm Credit Bank of Spokane v. Fauth—§ 7.7, n. 52.
Farm Credit Bank of Spokane v. Parsons—§ 7.7, n. 52.
Farm Credit Bank of St. Paul v. Kohnen—§ 7.19, n. 4.
Farm Credit Bank of St. Paul v. Rub—§ 7.16, n. 19.
Farmers and Mechanics Bank v. Arbucci—§ 7.10, n. 3.
Farmers and Merchants Bank v. Riede—§ 9.4, n. 4.
Farmers' Bank of Kentucky v. Peter—§ 7.17, n. 13.
Farmers Fire Insurance & Loan Co. v. Edwards—§ 6.6, n 8; § 6.7, n. 7.
Farmers' Loan & Trust Co. v. Meridian Waterworks Co—§ 4.10, n. 9.

Farmers' & Merchants' State Bank of Tripp v. Tasche—§ 5.19, n. 38.
Farmers Nat. Bank of Cherokee v. De Fever—§ 12.8, n. 9.
Farmers Production Credit Ass'n v. McFarland—§ 8.6, n. 19, 28.
Farmers Trust and Sav. Bank v. Manning, 359 N.W.2d 461—§ 8.5, n. 13.
Farmers Trust and Sav. Bank v. Manning, 311 N.W.2d 285—§ 12.8, n. 15.
Farmers Trust Co. v. Bomberger—§ 9.2, n. 11.
Farmers Union Trading Co. v. Wiggins—§ 3.3, n. 2.
Farrell v. Lewis—§ 5.28, n. 14.
Farrier, In re—§ 9.7, n. 3, 19.
Farver v. DeKalb County Farm Bureau, Co-op Credit Union—§ 4.35, n. 7.
Faulkner County Bank & Trust Co. v. Vail—§ 9.1, n. 14.
Faure v. Winans—§ 4.31, n. 2.
Faxon v. All Persons—§ 4.24, n. 14; § 6.11, n. 19, 26.
Fay Corp. v. Bat Holdings I, Inc.—§ 11.4, n. 95.
Fazio v. Alan Sinton, Limited, 59 B.R. 312—§ 8.13, n. 1.
Fazio v. Alan Sinton, Limited, 41 B.R. 865—§ 12.8, n. 6.
FBS Financial, Inc. v. CleveTrust Realty Investors—§ 12.3, n. 60.
FCX, Inc. v. Long Meadow Farms, Inc.—§ 3.36, n. 7.
F.D.I.C. v. Hy Kom Development Co.—§ 8.3, n. 19.
F.D.I.C. v. Myers—§ 7.21, n. 1, 61.
F.D.I.C. v. Payne—§ 5.29, n. 35.
F.D.I.C. v. Sather—§ 11.7, n. 11, 14, 42.
F.D.I.C. v. Schwarzer—§ 8.3, n. 7.
F.D.I.C. v. Verex Assur., Inc.—§ 11.2, n. 58.
Fears v. Albea—§ 10.8, n. 5.
Febbraro v. Febbraro—§ 4.35, n. 7.
Fecteau v. Fries—§ 9.1, n. 16, § 9.2, n. 8.
Federal Deposit Ins. Corp. v. Aetna Cas. & Sur. Co.—§ 5.29, n. 38.
Federal Deposit Ins. Corp. v. Bennett—§ 11.7, n. 45.
Federal Deposit Ins. Corp. v. Bertling—§ 11.7, n. 28.
Federal Deposit Ins. Corp. v. Bracero & Rivera, Inc.—§ 5.28, n. 6.
Federal Deposit Ins. Corp. v. Briarwood Holding Corp.—§ 4.43, n. 6.
Federal Deposit Ins. Corp. v. Byrne—§ 5.31, n. 8; § 11.7, n. 38.
Federal Deposit Ins. Corp. v. Caledonia Inv. Corp.—§ 5.29, n. 34; § 11.7, n. 43.
Federal Deposit Ins. Corp. v. Caporale—§ 11.7, n. 35.
Federal Deposit Ins. Corp. v. Circle Bar Ranch, Inc.—§ 8.3, n. 19.
Federal Deposit Ins. Corp. v. Connecticut Nat. Bank—§ 12.3, n. 6, 9.
Federal Deposit Ins. Corp. v. Engel—§ 11.7, n. 10.

Federal Deposit Ins. Corp. v. Forte, 535 N.Y.S.2d 75—§ 8.3, n. 6.
Federal Deposit Ins. Corp. v. Forte, 463 N.Y.S.2d 844—§ 5.28, n. 41.
Federal Deposit Ins. Corp. v. Friedland—§ 11.7, n. 19.
Federal Deposit Ins. Corp. v. Gettysburg Corp.—§ 11.7, n. 35.
Federal Deposit Ins. Corp. v. Hamilton—§ 11.7, n. 14, 25.
Federal Deposit Ins. Corp. v. Harrison—§ 11.7, n. 38.
Federal Deposit Ins. Corp. v. International Property Management, Inc.—§ 4.35, n. 14.
Federal Deposit Ins. Corp. v. Key Biscayne Development Ass'n—§ 12.6, n. 33; § 12.7, n. 42.
Federal Deposit Ins. Corp. v. Kratz—§ 5.31, n. 4.
Federal Deposit Ins. Corp. v. Laguarta—§ 11.7, n. 14.
Federal Deposit Ins. Corp. v. La Rambla Shopping Center, Inc.—§ 11.7, n. 18.
Federal Deposit Ins. Corp. v. Manatt, 922 F.2d 486—§ 11.7, n. 20.
Federal Deposit Ins. Corp. v. Manatt, 688 F.Supp. 1327—§ 5.31, n. 8.
Federal Deposit Ins. Corp. v. McClanahan—§ 11.7; § 11.7, n. 35, 39.
Federal Deposit Ins. Corp. v. McCullough—§ 11.7, n. 10, 29.
Federal Deposit Ins. Corp. v. Meo—§ 11.7, n. 36.
Federal Deposit Ins. Corp. v. Merchants Nat. Bank of Mobile—§ 5.29, n. 31.
Federal Deposit Ins. Corp. v. Meyer—§ 5.29, n. 36, 40; § 5.31, n. 2; § 11.7, n. 35.
Federal Deposit Ins. Corp. v. Morrison—§ 7.24; § 7.24, n. 8, 14; § 7.28, n. 1, 4; § 7.30, n. 2.
Federal Deposit Ins. Corp. v. Mr. "T'S", Inc.—§ 11.7, n. 14.
Federal Deposit Ins. Corp. v. Municipality of Ponce—§ 11.7, n. 36.
Federal Deposit Ins. Corp. v. Newhart—§ 5.29, n. 33.
Federal Deposit Ins. Corp. v. Orrill—§ 5.29, n. 34; § 11.7, n. 10.
Federal Deposit Ins. Corp. v. Percival—§ 5.29, n. 35; § 11.7, n. 37.
Federal Deposit Ins. Corp. v. Republicbank, Lubbock, N.A., Lubbock, Tex.—§ 12.9, n. 2.
Federal Deposit Ins. Corp. v. Sarvis—§ 11.7, n. 29.
Federal Deposit Ins. Corp. v. Shain, Schaffer & Rafanello—§ 11.7, n. 44.
Federal Deposit Ins. Corp. v. Sumner—§ 6.6, n. 27.
Federal Deposit Ins. Corp. v. Sumner Financial Corp.—§ 5.24, n. 57.
Federal Deposit Ins. Corp. v. Texas Country Living, Inc.—§ 11.7, n. 30.

Federal Deposit Ins. Corp. v. Thomson—§ 11.7, n. 45.
Federal Deposit Ins. Corp. v. Turner—§ 5.31, n. 5.
Federal Deposit Ins. Corp. v. Virginia Crossings Partnership—§ 11.7, n. 18, 28.
Federal Deposit Ins. Corp. v. Waldron—§ 11.7, n. 20.
Federal Deposit Ins. Corp. v. Wisenbaker—§ 5.29, n. 33.
Federal Deposit Ins. Corp. v. Wood—§ 5.29, n. 31, 40; § 11.7, n. 43.
Federal Deposit Ins. Corp. v. W.R. Grace & Co.—§ 12.3, n. 7.
Federal Deposit Ins. Corp. v. Wright—§ 11.7, n. 19.
Federal Farm Mortgage Corporation v. Ganser—§ 4.34, n. 16.
Federal Farm Mortgage Corporation v. Larson—§ 4.44, n. 3.
Federal Home Loan Mortg. Corp. v. Spark Tarrytown, Inc.—§ 4.36, n. 1.
Federal Home Loan Mortg. Corp. v. Superior Court (Gillespie)—§ 11.6, n. 93.
Federal Home Loan Mortg. Corp. v. Taylor—§ 6.9, n. 31; § 7.7, n. 10, 11.
Federal Land Bank Ass'n of Tyler v. Sloane—§ 12.3, n. 1.
Federal Land Bank of Baltimore v. Joynes—§ 10.5, n. 5; § 10.6, n. 6.
Federal Land Bank of Columbia v. Bank of Lenox—§ 4.44, n. 6.
Federal Land Bank of Columbia v. Brooks—§ 4.31, n. 17.
Federal Land Bank of Columbia v. Jones—§ 4.5, n. 6.
Federal Land Bank of Columbia v. Lackey—§ 7.24, n. 8.
Federal Land Bank of Columbia v. Saint Clair Lumber Co.—§ 4.5, n. 9.
Federal Land Bank of Columbia v. Wood—§ 7.21, n. 28.
Federal Land Bank of Louisville v. Taggart—§ 5.19, n. 50.
Federal Land Bank of New Orleans v. Corinth Bank & Trust Co.—§ 5.34, n. 12.
Federal Land Bank of New Orleans v. Davis—§ 4.6, n. 6.
Federal Land Bank of New Orleans v. Newsom—§ 10.3, n. 5.
Federal Land Bank of Spokane v. Snider—§ 8.4, n. 6.
Federal Land Bank of Springfield v. Smith—§ 10.7, n. 2.
Federal Land Bank of Wichita v. Bott—§ 8.3, n. 1.
Federal Land Bank of Wichita v. Brown—§ 8.7, n. 1.
Federal Land Bank of Wichita v. Colorado Nat. Bank of Denver—§ 6.17, n. 10.
Federal Land Bank of Wichita v. Cummings—§ 6.6, n. 36.
Federal Land Bank of Wichita v. Ferguson—§ 11.6, n. 79.

Federal Land Bank of Wichita v. Story—§ 8.3, n. 1.
Federal Nat. Mortg. Ass'n v. Carrington—§ 5.6, n. 1; § 5.11, n. 6.
Federal Nat. Mortg. Ass'n v. Cobb—§ 7.7, n. 4.
Federal Nat. Mortg. Ass'n v. Dacon Bolingbrook Associates Ltd. Partnership—§ 8.18, n. 53.
Federal Nat. Mortg. Ass'n v. Gregory—§ 5.31, n. 4.
Federal Nat. Mortg. Ass'n v. Howlett—§ 3.30, n. 12; § 7.27; § 7.27, n. 2, 5, 11, 13, 14, 21, 27.
Federal Nat. Mortg. Ass'n v. Moore—§ 7.7, n. 31.
Federal Nat. Mortg. Ass'n v. Prior—§ 7.7, n. 32.
Federal Nat. Mortg. Ass'n v. Rathgens—§ 11.2, n. 30.
Federal Nat. Mortg. Ass'n v. Ricks—§ 7.7, n. 28, 33.
Federal Nat. Mortg. Ass'n v. Scott—§ 7.28, n. 14.
Federal Nat. Mortg. Ass'n v. Walter—§ 7.7, n. 4.
Federal Sav. and Loan Ins. Corp. v. Cribbs—§ 11.7, n. 43.
Federal Sav. and Loan Ins. Corp. v. Gemini Management—§ 11.7, n. 14.
Federal Sav. and Loan Ins. Corp. v. Kidwell—§ 11.6, n. 23.
Federal Sav. and Loan Ins. Corp. v. Locke—§ 11.7, n. 28.
Federal Sav. and Loan Ins. Corp. v. Mackie—§ 5.29, n. 33, 34.
Federal Sav. and Loan Ins. Corp. v. Murray—§ 5.29, n. 30; § 11.7, n. 10, 25, 39, 43.
Federal Sav. and Loan Ins. Corp. v. T.F. Stone–Liberty Land Associates—§ 11.7, n. 30, 37.
Federal Sav. and Loan Ins. Corp. v. Treaster—§ 8.6, n. 12.
Federal Sav. and Loan Ins. Corp. v. Two Rivers Associates, Inc.—§ 11.7, n. 25.
Federal Sav. & Loan Ins. Corp. v. Gordy—§ 11.7, n. 35.
Federal Sav. & Loan Ins. Corp. v. Provo Excelsior Ltd.—§ 12.3, n. 61.
Federal Title & Mortg. Guaranty Co. v. Lowenstein—§ 7.16, n. 33.
Federal Trust Co. v. East Hartford Fire Dist.—§ 4.12, n. 3.
Federal Union Life Ins. Co. v. Deitsch—§ 10.5, n. 5.
Feigenbaum v. Hizsnay—§ 5.19, n. 23.
Feimster, Matter of—§ 8.15, n. 91.
Feldman v. Kings Highway Sav. Bank—§ 6.1, n. 6.
Feldman v. M. J. Associates—§ 8.6, n. 19.
Feldman v. Rucker—§ 7.21, n. 85, 86.
Felin Associates, Inc. v. Rogers—§ 5.28, n. 4; § 5.33, n. 4, 5, 7.
Felton v. West—§ 8.2, n. 2.

Fendley v. Smith—§ 7.14, n. 3.
Fenton v. Torrey—§ 7.21, n. 39.
Fenwick–Schafer v. Sterling Homes Corp.—§ 11.5, n. 8.
Ferguson, In re—§ 12.8, n. 6.
Ferguson v. Boyd—§ 3.10, n. 3; § 3.4, n. 5; § 4.29, n. 24; § 7.5, n. 1.
Ferguson v. Cloon—§ 7.15, n. 3; § 7.17, n. 17.
Ferguson v. Mueller—§ 12.7, n. 11.
Ferreira v. Yared—§ 6.3, n. 3, 4; § 6.4, n. 9.
Ferrell v. Pierce—§ 11.2, n. 29.
Ferris v. Prudence Realization Corporation—§ 5.35, n. 15.
Ferris v Wilcox—§ 3.3, n. 2.
Ferry v. Fisk—§ 6.16, n. 14.
Fetes v. O'Laughlin—§ 2.4, n. 2.
Fiacre v. Chapman—§ 4.46, n. 3, 11, 20.
Fibkins v. Fibkins—§ 12.6, n. 42.
Fidelity and Cas. Co. of New York v. Central Bank of Birmingham—§ 12.2, n. 45.
Fidelity Bankers Life Ins. Co. v. Williams—§ 4.35, n. 14; § 8.18, n. 5.
Fidelity Bond & Mortg. Co. v. Paul—§ 4.23, n. 6.
Fidelity Capital Corp., United States v.—§ 2.3, n. 14.
Fidelity & Casualty Co. of New York v. Massachusetts Mut. Life Ins. Co.—§ 10.9, n. 2; § 10.13, n. 3, 7.
Fidelity & Deposit Co. v. Oliver—§ 2.2, n. 2.
Fidelity Federal Sav. and Loan Ass'n v. de la Cuesta—§ 5.21, n. 14; § 5.23; § 5.23, n. 9, 20; § 5.24, n. 86, 120; § 11.6; § 11.6, n. 27, 37.
Fidelity Federal Savings and Loan Association v. Grieme—§ 5.21, n. 33.
Fidelity Financial Corp. v. Federal Home Loan Bank of San Francisco—§ 11.3, n. 40.
Fidelity Mortg. Co. v. Mahon—§ 4.43, n. 13.
Fidelity Mortg. Investors v. Camelia Builders, Inc.—§ 8.14, n. 113.
Fidelity Mut. Sav. Bank v. Mark—§ 6.6, n. 2; § 8.5, n. 11; § 8.6, n. 15.
Fidelity Nat. Title Ins. Co. v. Department of the Treasury—§ 10.6, n. 3.
Fidelity Sav. Ass'n of Kansas v. Witt—§ 5.9, n. 8; § 6.17, n. 8; § 6.19, n. 10; § 12.7, n. 23.
Fidelity Title Service v. Ball Homes, Inc.—§ 5.33, n. 35.
Fidelity Trust Co. v. BVD Associates—§ 5.26, n. 5.
Fidelity Trust Co. v. Gardiner—§ 5.32, n. 3, 17.
Fidelity Trust Co. v. Hoboken etc. R. Co.—§ 4.10, n. 4.
Fidelity Trust Co. v. Irick—§ 7.10, n. 3.
Fidelity Trust Co. v. Orr—§ 5.35, n. 15.
Fidelity Trust Co. v. Saginaw Hotels Co.—§ 4.29, n. 8, 9; § 4.41, n. 8.

TABLE OF CASES

Fidelity Trust Co. v. Wayne County—§ 5.24, n. 23.
Fidelity Union Trust Co. v. Pasternack—§ 7.16, n. 34.
Field v. Thistle—§ 5.18, n. 4.
Fields v. Danehower—§ 8.6, n. 16.
Fienhold v. Babcock—§ 7.17, n. 7.
Fierst v. Commonwealth Land Title Ins. Co.—§ 12.9, n. 1.
Fikes v. First Federal Sav. and Loan Ass'n of Anchorage—§ 12.10; § 12.10, n. 35; § 12.7, n. 60; § 13.3, n. 21, 25.
Filippi v. McMartin—§ 12.2, n. 35.
Filippini v. Trobock—§ 6.12, n. 18.
Fillion v. David Silvers Co.—§ 6.7, n. 1; § 7.22, n. 17.
Finance Co. of America v. Heller—§ 5.3, n. 8; § 5.10, n. 2; § 10.2, n. 2.
Finance Co. of America v. United States Fidelity & Guaranty Co.—§ 12.2, n. 44.
Finance Inv. Co. (Bermuda) Ltd. v. Gossweiler—§ 7.1, n. 1, 2.
Financial Acceptance Corp. v. Garvey—§ 9.4, n. 4; § 12.8, n. 10.
Financial Center Associates of East Meadow, L.P., In re—§ 4.35, n. 27, 31; § 6.2, n. 27.
Financial Credit Corp. v. Williams—§ 5.29, n. 12, 20.
Financial Federal Sav. and Loan Ass'n v. Burleigh House, Inc.—§ 12.3, n. 27.
Financial Federal Sav. and Loan Ass'n of Dade County v. Continental Enterprises, Inc.—§ 12.3, n. 41.
Fincher v. Miles Homes, Inc.—§ 3.35, n. 1, 2, 10.
Findlay v. Hosmer—§ 6.16, n. 10.
Finest Investments v. Security Trust Co. of Rochester—§ 12.9, n. 28.
Finger v. McCaughey—§ 3.1, n. 14.
Finlayson v. Crooks—§ 12.4, n. 31.
Finlayson v. Peterson—§ 4.45, n. 9.
Finley, In re—§ 8.19, n. 9.
Finley v. Chain—§ 4.4, n. 29.
Finley v. Erickson—§ 4.24, n. 1.
Finlon v. Clark—§ 3.10, n. 1.
Finzer v. Peter—§ 5.9, n. 5; § 5.10, n. 8, 15; § 5.15, n. 1.
Fireman's Fund Ins. Co. v. Grover (In re Woodson Co.)—§ 5.35, n. 47, 54.
Fireman's Fund Ins. Co. v. Rogers—§ 5.15, n. 2.
Fireman's Fund Mortg. Corp. v. Allstate Ins. Co.—§ 4.16, n. 11.
Fireman's Fund Mortg. Corp. v. Zollicoffer—§ 4.24, n. 10.
Firemen's Ins. Co. v. New York—§ 12.2, n. 47.
First v. Byrne—§ 12.8, n. 7, 9, 15.
First Alabama Bank of Birmingham v. Hartford Acc. & Indem. Co., Inc.—§ 12.2, n. 44.
First Am. Title Ins. & Trust Co. v. Cook—§ 6.9, n. 4.

First Arlington Nat. Bank v. Stathis—§ 5.20, n. 7.
First Bank of Wakeeney v. Peoples State Bank—§ 5.35, n. 5.
Firstbank Shinnston v. West Virginia Ins. Co.—§ 4.13, n. 4; § 4.14, n. 10.
First Bank & Trust v. Novak—§ 5.22, n. 35, 36.
First Barnstable Corp., In re—§ 8.13, n. 22.
First Capital Life Ins. Co. v. Schneider, Inc.—§ 4.51, n. 3.
FirstCentral Bank v. White—§ 13.3, n. 4, 49.
First Citizens Federal Sav. and Loan Ass'n v. Worthen Bank and Trust Co., N.A.—§ 5.35; § 5.35, n. 24, 26.
First City Federal Sav. Bank v. Bhogaonker—§ 5.29, n. 6.
First Commercial Title, Inc. v. Holmes—§ 5.22, n. 14.
First Connecticut Small Business Inv. Co. v. Arba, Inc.—§ 12.9; § 12.9, n. 30; § 12.10, n. 7.
First Connecticut Small Business Inv. Co. v. Ruark—§ 8.14, n. 20; § 8.15, n. 89.
First Family Mortg. Corp. of Florida v. Lubliner—§ 12.11, n. 8.
First Federal Sav. and Loan Ass'n v. Twin City Sav. Bank, FSB—§ 5.35, n. 20, 27.
First Federal Sav. and Loan Ass'n, Chickasha, Okl. v. Nath—§ 7.15, n. 23.
First Federal Sav. and Loan Ass'n of Alexandria v. Botello—§ 5.21, n. 33.
First Federal Sav. and Loan Ass'n of Chicago v. Walker—§ 7.7, n. 18.
First Federal Sav. and Loan Ass'n of Englewood v. Lockwood—§ 5.22, n. 31; § 5.23, n. 8; § 5.24, n. 87.
First Federal Sav. and Loan Ass'n of Gary v. Arena—§ 5.19, n. 9, 45, 46, 49, 51.
First Federal Sav. and Loan Ass'n of Gary v. Stone—§ 4.15, n. 4; § 7.6, n. 7, 13.
First Federal Sav. and Loan Ass'n of Harrison, Ark. v. Myrick—§ 5.24, n. 87.
First Federal Sav. and Loan Ass'n of Miami v. Mortgage Corp. of South—§ 12.3, n. 60.
First Federal Sav. and Loan Ass'n of Palm Beaches v. Sailboat Key, Inc.—§ 12.3, n. 19.
First Federal Sav. and Loan Ass'n of Phoenix v. Lehman—§ 8.3; § 8.3, n. 82, 141.
First Federal Sav. and Loan Ass'n of Rochester v. Brown—§ 7.31, n. 1.
First Federal Sav. and Loan Ass'n of Rochester v. Capalongo—§ 6.11, n. 12.
First Federal Sav. and Loan Ass'n of Winter Haven v. Quigley—§ 5.23, n. 16; § 5.24, n. 87.
First Federal Sav. Bank v. Hart—§ 12.11, n. 11.
First Federal Sav. Bank v. Tazzia—§ 5.29, n. 14.

First Federal Sav. Bank of Georgia v. Eaglewood Court Condominium Ass'n, Inc.—§ 13.5, n. 20.
First Federal Sav. & Loan Ass'n of Akron v. Cheton & Rabe—§ 7.7, n. 7.
First Federal Sav. & Loan Ass'n of Bowling Green v. Savage—§ 4.13, n. 19.
First Federal Sav. & Loan Ass'n of Chicago v. Connelly—§ 12.4, n. 21.
First Federal Sav. & Loan Ass'n of Coffeyville v. Moulds—§ 4.34, n. 13.
First Federal Sav. & Loan Ass'n of Martin County v. Ott—§ 13.3, n. 25.
First Federal Sav. & Loan Ass'n of Rochester v. Green-Acres Bldg. Corp.—§ 12.7, n. 29.
First Federal Sav. & Loan Ass'n of Salt Lake City v. Gump & Ayers Real Estate, Inc.—§ 5.29, n. 3.
First Federal Sav. & Loan Ass'n of Toledo v. Perry's Landing, Inc.—§ 5.22, n. 10.
First Federal Sav. & Loan Ass'n of Warner Robbins v. Standard Bldg. Associates, Ltd.—§ 8.17, n. 13, 17, 77.
First Federal Sav. of Arkansas, F.A. v. City Nat. Bank of Ft. Smith, Ark.—§ 4.35, n. 13, 14.
First Fed. Sav. and Loan Ass'n of Boston v. Greenwald—§ 11.6, n. 26.
First Financial Federal Sav. & Loan Ass'n v. E.F. Hutton Mortg. Corp.—§ 5.35, n. 19, 26.
First Funding Corp. v. Birge—§ 12.9, n. 1.
First Gibraltar Bank, FSB v. Morales—§ 11.4, n. 106.
First Hawaiian Bank v. Alexander—§ 11.6, n. 23.
Firstier Mortg. Co. v. Investors Mortg. Ins. Co.—§ 11.2, n. 58.
First Illinois Nat. Bank v. Hans—§ 3.1, n. 9; § 3.9, n. 4.
First Indiana Federal Sav. Bank v. F.D.I.C.—§ 5.35, n. 45, 58; § 11.7, n. 7.
First Indiana Federal Sav. Bank v. Hartle—§ 5.4, n. 7; § 5.11, n. 6; § 8.1, n. 2.
First Indiana Federal Sav. Bank v. Maryland Development Co., Inc.—§ 6.5, n. 2.
First Interstate Bank of Arizona, N.A. v. Tatum and Bell Center Associates—§ 8.3, n. 48.
First Interstate Bank of California v. H.C.T.—§ 10.9, n. 7.
First Interstate Bank of Fargo, N.A. v. Larson—§ 8.3, n. 52.
First Interstate Bank of Idaho v. SBA—§ 11.6, n. 84.
First Interstate Bank of Kalispell, N.A. v. Wann—§ 8.3, n. 22.
First Interstate Bank of Nevada v. Shields—§ 8.3, n. 48.
First Interstate Bank of Washington, N.A. v. Nelco Enterprises, Inc.—§ 5.3, n. 2; § 5.4, n. 3; § 5.7, n. 17; § 5.10, n. 5.
First Maryland Financial Services Corp. v. District-Realty Title Ins. Corp.—§ 5.29, n. 18, 19; § 5.34, n. 33.

First Mississippi Bank of Commerce v. Latch—§ 12.3, n. 44.
First Mustang State Bank v. Garland Bloodworth, Inc.—§ 3.33, n. 9.
First Nat. Bank v. Larson—§ 3.37, n. 12; § 5.27, n. 5; § 5.28, n. 24, 35, 40; § 5.33, n. 4, 21.
First Nat. Bank v. Springfield Fire & Marine Ins. Co.—§ 4.14, n. 9, 18.
First Nat. Bank & Trust Co. v. Hager Oil Co.—§ 4.6, n. 3.
First Nat. Bank & Trust Co. v. Lygrisse—§ 12.8, n. 9, 12.
First Nat. Bank & Trust Co. of Ardmore v. Worthley—§ 12.7, n. 26.
First Nat. Bank in Alamogordo v. Cape—§ 3.27, n. 5; § 3.32, n. 2.
First Nat. Bank in Bozeman v. Powell—§ 10.14, n. 14.
First Nat. Bank in Creston v. Smith—§ 12.4, n. 43.
First Nat. Bank in Dallas v. Rozelle—§ 12.8, n. 6, 10.
First Nat. Bank of Atwood v. Drew—§ 5.17, n. 9.
First Nat. Bank of Auburn v. Manser—§ 12.7, n. 11.
First Nat. Bank of Benson v. Gallagher—§ 2.1, n. 9.
First Nat Bank of Boston v. Proctor—§ 10.13, n. 19.
First Nat. Bank of Cape Cod v. North Adams Hoosac Sav. Bank—§ 5.29, n. 17.
First Nat. Bank of Chicago v. Gordon—§ 4.38, n. 9; § 4.39, n. 5, 9, 10; § 4.42, n. 16.
First Nat. Bank of Chicago v. Paris—§ 5.34, n. 16.
First Nat. Bank of Crestview, United States v.—§ 12.7, n. 32.
First Nat. Bank of David City v. Spelts—§ 3.10, n. 3.
First Nat. Bank of Duluth v. National Liberty Ins. Co. of America—§ 4.14, n. 5.
First Nat. Bank of Florida v. Ashmead—§ 3.4, n. 10.
First Nat. Bank of Gadsden v. Sproull—§ 4.4, n. 5.
First Nat. Bank of Guntersville v. Bain—§ 12.7, n. 7.
First Nat. Bank of Jackson v. Huff—§ 10.1, n. 5.
First Nat. Bank of Joliet v. Illinois Steel Co.—§ 4.34, n. 6.
First Nat. Bank of Lincoln v. Brown—§ 5.24, n. 118.
First Nat. Bank of Logansport v. Logan Mfg. Co., Inc.—§ 12.3, n. 1.
First Nat. Bank of Maryland v. Philadelphia Nat. Bank—§ 6.2, n. 19.
First Nat. Bank of Mobile v. Gilbert Imported Hardwoods, Inc.—§ 4.1, n. 16.
First Nat. Bank of Okmulgee v. Matlock—§ 4.26, n. 2.
First Nat. Bank of Omaha v. First Cadco Corp.—§ 10.9, n. 14.
First Nat. Bank of Plattsmouth v. Tighe—§ 3.10, n. 3.

TABLE OF CASES

First Nat. Bank of Rapid City v. McCarthy—§ 4.45, n. 3.
First Nat. Bank of Springfield v. Equitable Life Assur. Soc. of United States—§ 6.5, n. 2.
First Nat. Bank of St. Paul v. McHasco Electric, Inc.—§ 12.2, n. 45.
First Nat. Bank of Union City v. Leslie—§ 7.12, n. 22; § 7.13, n. 1, 2.
First Nat. Bank of Van Hook v. Zook—§ 12.7, n. 33.
First Nat. Bank of Vicksburg v. Caruthers—§ 5.22, n. 14; § 5.24, n. 87.
First Nat. City Bank v. Phoenix Mut. Life Ins. Co.—§ 10.14, n. 11.
First Nat. City Bank v. Tara Realty Corp.—§ 12.8, n. 1.
First Nat. City Bank v. United States, 548 F.2d 928—§ 10.1, n. 1.
First Nat. City Bank v. United States, 537 F.2d 426—§ 10.4, n. 2.
First Nat. Entertainment Corp. v. Brumlik—§ 5.31, n. 7.
First Nat. Fidelity Corp. v. Perry—§ 8.15, n. 40.
First National Bank of Atlanta v. Blum—§ 7.6, n. 3.
First National Bank of Madison v. Kolbeck—§ 6.11, n. 20.
First National Mortgage Company v. Arkmo Lumber & Supply Company—§ 12.3, n. 18.
First Nat. State Bank of N. J. v. Carlyle House, Inc.—§ 12.6, n. 28; § 12.7, n. 20, 42.
First Nat. State Bank of New Jersey v. Commonwealth Federal Sav. and Loan Ass'n of Norristown—§ 12.3, n. 9, 51.
First RepublicBank Fort Worth, N.A. v. Norglass, Inc.—§ 11.7, n. 37.
First Sav. and Loan Ass'n of Bureau County v. Kern—§ 6.8, n. 3.
First Sav. Bank & Trust Co. of Albuquerque, N. M. v. Stuppi—§ 4.43, n. 9.
First Sec. Bank of Idaho v. Rogers—§ 3.36, n. 10, 11.
First Sec. Bank of Idaho, N.A. v. Gaige—§ 8.3, n. 45, 47.
First Sec. Bank of Utah v. Shiew—§ 12.8, n. 10.
First Sec. Bank of Utah, N.A. v. Banberry Crossing—§ 7.21, n. 61.
First Sec. Bank of Utah N.A. v. Banberry Development Corp.—§ 10.6, n. 1.
First Sec. Bank of Utah, N.A. v. Felger—§ 8.2, n. 8.
First Southern Federal Sav. and Loan Ass'n of Mobile v. Britton—§ 5.22, n. 21.
FirstSouth, F.A. v. LaSalle Nat. Bank—§ 12.4, n. 32.

First State Bank v. Stacey—§ 13.3, n. 31.
First State Bank of Binford v. Arneson—§ 6.16, n. 3.
First State Bank of Cooperstown v. Ihringer—§ 8.2, n. 10; § 8.3, n. 10.
First State Bank of Franklin County v. Ford—§ 6.6, n. 33.
First State Bank of Wheatland v. American Nat. Bank—§ 5.35, n. 26.
First Texas Sav. Ass'n v. Comprop Inv. Properties Ltd.—§ 11.7, n. 36.
First Valley Bank v. First Sav. and Loan Ass'n of Cent. Indiana—§ 5.28, n. 1.
First Vermont Bank & Trust Co. v. Kalomiris—§ 10.1, n. 1; § 10.2, n. 2; § 10.5, n. 1.
First Vermont Bank & Trust Co. v. Village of Poultney—§ 12.2, n. 43.
First Wisconsin Nat. Bank of Milwaukee v. Federal Land Bank of St. Paul—§ 9.7, n. 23.
First Wisconsin Nat. Bank of Milwaukee v. Roose—§ 13.3, n. 60.
First Wisconsin Nat. Bank of Oshkosh v. KSW Investments, Inc.—§ 7.16, n. 36.
First Wisconsin Trust Co. v. Rosen—§ 7.31, n. 12; § 10.9, n. 7.
First Wisconsin Trust Co. v. Schroud—§ 2.4, n. 16.
Fischer v. Spierling—§ 6.16, n. 15.
Fischer-Flack, Inc. v. Churchfield—§ 12.4, n. 37.
Fisel v. Yoder—§ 3.29; § 3.29, n. 58.
Fish v. Glover—§ 5.9, n. 17.
Fisher, In re—§ 8.15, n. 35.
Fisher v. Koper—§ 3.6, n. 1.
Fisher v. Norman Apartments, Colorado Nat. Bank of Denver—§ 4.24, n. 10; § 4.35, n. 17.
Fisk v. Potter—§ 5.32, n. 25.
Fiske v. Tolman—§ 5.8, n. 9.
Fitch v. Applegate—§ 6.17, n. 11.
Fitch v. Miller—§ 3.4, n. 8; § 7.5, n. 15.
Fitcher v. Griffiths—§ 10.3, n. 4; § 10.8, n. 8.
Fitzgerald v. Cleland, 650 F.2d 360—§ 7.25, n. 18.
Fitzgerald v. Cleland, 498 F.Supp. 341—§ 7.10, n. 11; § 7.24, n. 27, 31; § 7.25, n. 23; § 7.28, n. 30.
Fitzgerald v. Flanagan—§ 6.13, n. 2, 7, 16; § 7.12, n. 14.
500 Ygnacio Associates, Ltd., In re—§ 8.3, n. 68.
5000 Skelly Corp., In re—§ 12.7, n. 42.
Flack v. Boland—§ 6.11, n. 35.
Flack v. McClure—§ 3.8, n. 9, 15, 18.
Flagg v. Sun Inv. & Loan Corp.—§ 8.11, n. 7.
Flagg Bros., Inc. v. Brooks—§ 7.27; § 7.27, n. 22; § 12.5, n. 2.

Flagler Federal Sav. and Loan Ass'n of Miami v. Crestview Towers Condominium Ass'n, Inc.—§ 13.5, n. 18.
Flagship State Bank of Jacksonville v. Drew Equipment Co.—§ 8.3, n. 19.
Flake v. High Point Perpetual Bldg. & Loan Ass'n—§ 7.32, n. 11.
Flamingo Drift Fishing, Inc. v. Nix—§ 12.11, n. 11.
Flanagan v. Germania, F.A.—§ 11.6; § 11.6, n. 44.
Flanders v. Aumack—§ 8.6, n. 30.
Flanders v. Hall—§ 7.4, n. 12.
Flanders v. Lamphear—§ 2.2, n. 12, 14.
Fleeman, Matter of—§ 8.13, n. 11.
Fleet Bank of Maine v. Zimelman—§ 4.35, n. 5.
Fleet Factors Corp., United States v.—§ 4.48; § 4.48, n. 3, 5.
Fleet Mortg. Corp. v. Stevenson—§ 9.1, n. 4, 25, 28.
Fleet Real Estate Funding Corp. v. Frampton—§ 6.7, n. 1.
Fleetwood v. Med Center Bank—§ 10.5, n. 5.
Fleming v. First American Bank & Trust Co.—§ 12.8, n. 10.
Fletcher v. Bass River Sav. Bank—§ 4.29, n. 11.
Fletcher v. Carpenter—§ 5.28, n. 22.
Flexter v. Woomer—§ 2.4, n. 2, 11.
Flickinger v. Glass—§ 13.3, n. 21.
Flint v. Howard—§ 10.13, n. 12.
Flint v. Winter Harbor Land Co.—§ 5.6, n. 1.
Flintkote Co. v. Presley of Northern California—§ 12.6, n. 10.
Flora Bank & Trust v. Czyzewski—§ 6.16, n. 6.
Floral Park Development Co., United States v.—§ 8.18, n. 35, 36.
Florea v. Iowa State Ins. Co.—§ 4.13, n. 3.
Florida Land Inv. Co. v. Williams—§ 4.44, n. 2.
Florida Nat. Bank of Miami v. Bankatlantic—§ 6.3, n. 10.
Florida Reinvestment Corp. v. Cypress Sav. Ass'n—§ 4.35, n. 5.
Floyer v. Lavington—§ 3.1, n. 3.
Fluge, In re—§ 4.35, n. 25, 26.
Fluke Capital & Management Services Co. v. Richmond—§ 5.8, n. 9; § 10.2, n. 1.
Flynn v. Holmes—§ 3.10, n. 2; § 4.2, n. 17.
Flynn v. Kenrick—§ 5.3, n. 2; § 5.8, n. 9.
Flynn v. Lowrance—§ 4.39, n. 13.
F. M. Sibley Lumber Co. v. Gottesman—§ 13.3, n. 35.
Fogg v. Providence Lumber Co.—§ 7.13, n. 11.
Folk v. United States—§ 4.34, n. 9.
Foote v. City of Pontiac—§ 7.24, n. 19.
Foote v. Sprague—§ 3.1, n. 37.
Foothill Indus. Bank v. Mikkelson—§ 6.9, n. 33.
Foothills Holding Corp. v. Tulsa Rig, Reel & Mfg. Co.—§ 8.1, n. 2.
Forbes v. Thorpe—§ 5.14, n. 2.
Ford v. Manufacturers Hanover Mortg. Corp.—§ 4.15, n. 13.
Ford, United States v.—§ 7.24, n. 27; § 7.25; § 7.25, n. 23, 25; § 7.28, n. 1.
Ford v. Washington Nat. Bldg. & Loan Inv. Ass'n—§ 5.17, n. 10.
Ford v. Waxman—§ 7.6, n. 3.
Foreclosure of a Deed of Trust Given by Bill M. Taylor, In re—§ 5.21, n. 33.
Foreclosure of Ruepp, Matter of—§ 5.24, n. 54.
Foreman v. Foreman—§ 3.24, n. 14.
Foremost Guar. Corp. v. Meritor Sav. Bank—§ 11.2, n. 58.
Foremost Ins. Co. v. Allstate Ins. Co.—§ 4.14, n. 11.
Forester, In re—§ 10.3, n. 3; § 10.13, n. 2, 14.
Forest Inc. of Knoxville v. Guaranty Mortg. Co., Inc.—§ 12.10, n. 7, 11, 34; § 13.3, n. 24.
Forman, In re—§ 4.12, n. 4.
Fort v. Colby—§ 4.29, n. 18.
Forthman v. Deters—§ 6.16, n. 3.
Fortier v. Fortier—§ 10.2, n. 7.
Fortner Enterprises, Inc. v. United States Steel Corp.—§ 12.11, n. 3.
Fortune v. Superior Court In and For Maricopa County—§ 12.4, n. 14.
Forty-Four Hundred East Broadway Co. v. 4400 East Broadway—§ 5.24, n. 35; § 8.5, n. 5; § 8.6, n. 4, 7.
Fosdick v. Van Husan—§ 7.4, n. 12.
Foskett, In re—§ 9.7, n. 49.
Foss v. Dullam—§ 5.34, n. 13.
Foster, Matter of—§ 8.15, n. 54, 55.
Foster v. Augustanna College & Theological Seminary of Rock Island, Ill.—§ 5.34, n. 34.
Foster v. Carson—§ 5.33, n. 4, 19.
Foster v. Maryland State Sav. and Loan Ass'n—§ 4.19, n. 6.
Foster v. Trowbridge, 46 N.W. 350—§ 7.14, n. 5, 8.
Foster v. Trowbridge, 40 N.W. 255—§ 5.28, n. 23.
Foster v. Van Reed—§ 4.13, n. 4, 9, 16.
Foster Lumber Co. v. Harlan County Bank—§ 9.1, n. 12.
Foster Lumber Co., Inc. v. Weston Constructors, Inc.—§ 6.7, n. 2.
Fouche v. Delk—§ 6.16, n. 24.
Foulk, Matter of—§ 8.15, n. 8.
Founders Bank and Trust Co. v. Upsher—§ 8.3, n. 46.
Fountain, Matter of—§ 8.17, n. 73.
495 Corp. v. New Jersey Ins. Underwriting Ass'n, 430 A.2d 203—§ 4.16, n. 3.

TABLE OF CASES

495 Corp. v. New Jersey Ins. Underwriting Ass'n, 413 A.2d 630—§ 4.13, n. 1.
499 W. Warren Street Associates, Ltd. Partnership, In re—§ 8.18, n. 42.
Four Seasons Developers, Inc. v. Security Federal Sav. & Loan Ass'n—§ 12.7, n. 37.
Four Strong Winds, Inc. v. Lyngholm—§ 4.33, n. 2.
Fourth Nat. Bank, Appeal of—§ 5.35, n. 15.
Fourth Nat. Bank in Wichita v. Hill—§ 5.3, n. 2; § 6.13, n. 4.
Fowler, In re—§ 9.4, n. 10.
Fowler v. Johnson, 6 N.W. 486—§ 7.8, n. 6.
Fowler v. Johnson, 3 N.W. 986—§ 7.8, n. 6.
Fowler v. Lilly—§ 7.12, n. 13.
Fox, In re—§ 8.19, n. 9.
Fox, Matter of—§ 6.16, n. 4.
Fox v. Federated Dept. Stores, Inc.—§ 6.9, n. 22.
Fox v. Peck Iron and Metal Co., Inc.—§ 3.18, n. 3.
Fox & Carskadon Financial Corp. v. San Francisco Federal Sav. and Loan Ass'n—§ 12.11, n. 11, 28.
FPCI RE-HAB 01 v. E & G Investments, Ltd.—§ 9.8; § 9.8, n. 4.
Frady v. Ivester—§ 7.5, n. 11.
Frago v. Sage—§ 10.3, n. 3; § 10.4, n. 8.
Frame v. Boatmen's Bank of Concord Village—§ 5.35, n. 1; § 12.3, n. 1.
Framingham Trust Co. v. Gould-National Batteries, Inc.—§ 12.2, n. 42.
Francis, United States v.—§ 12.6, n. 42.
Frank, In re—§ 8.17, n. 14.
Franklin, In re—§ 8.3, n. 139, 145.
Franklin v. Commissioner—§ 5.35, n. 40.
Franklin v. Community Federal Sav. and Loan Ass'n—§ 9.3, n. 3.
Franklin v. Spencer—§ 8.6, n. 19.
Franklin Sav. Ass'n v. Reese—§ 7.22, n. 8.
Frank Maio General Contractor, Inc. v. Consolidated Elec. Supply, Inc.—§ 12.4, n. 43.
Franzen v. G. R. Kinney Co.—§ 4.42, n. 18.
Frazee v. Inslee—§ 6.17, n. 14.
Frazer v. Couthy Land Co.—§ 3.1, n. 3.
Frazier v. Neilsen & Co.—§ 8.2, n. 11.
Fred v. Pacific Indem. Co.—§ 4.14, n. 1, 10.
Freda v. Commercial Trust Co. of New Jersey—§ 6.11, n. 12.
Fred Miller Brewing Co. v. Manasse—§ 5.34, n. 42.
Freeborn, In re—§ 3.37; § 3.37, n. 1, 2, 3.
Freedland v. Greco—§ 8.3, n. 35.
Freedlander, Inc., In re—§ 8.13, n. 22.
Freedman v. Rector, Wardens & Vestrymen of St. Mathias Parish—§ 3.29; § 3.29, n. 46.
Freedom Sav. and Loan Ass'n, Inc. v. LaMonte—§ 5.21, n. 33.
Freel, United States v.—§ 12.2, n. 27.
Freeman v. Auld—§ 5.17, n. 5, 6.
Freeman v. Lind—§ 7.6, n. 3.
Freichnecht v. Meyer—§ 4.29, n. 21.

Freidus, United States v.—§ 11.6, n. 76.
Fremming Const. Co. v. Security Sav. & Loan Ass'n—§ 12.3, n. 1.
Fremont Joint Stock Land Bank of Fremont, Neb., v. Foster—§ 7.8, n. 10.
French v. Boese—§ 3.6, n. 1; § 3.7, n. 2.
French v. Grand Beach Co.—§ 10.8, n. 6.
French v. May—§ 10.2, n. 2.
Frey, In re—§ 8.15, n. 35.
Frick Co. v. Ketels—§ 10.14, n. 11.
Fridley v. Munson—§ 3.36, n. 3, 8.
Friedman v. Gerax Realty Associates—§ 4.36, n. 9, 10.
Friedman v. Sommer—§ 13.6, n. 17.
Friedman v. Zuckerman—§ 5.8, n. 7.
Fries v. Clearview Gardens Sixth Corporation—§ 9.3, n. 1.
Friese, In re—§ 3.38, n. 16.
Frio Investments, Inc. v. 4M-IRC/Rohde—§ 4.4, n. 14, 15.
Froidevaux v. Jordan—§ 3.4, n. 7.
Frontier Properties, Inc., In re—§ 8.19, n. 9.
Frost v. Beekman—§ 7.4, n. 7.
Frost v. Johnson—§ 6.13, n. 2.
Frothingham v. McKusick—§ 4.5, n. 6.
Fry v. Ausman—§ 5.15, n. 7.
Fry v. D. H. Overmyer Co., Inc.—§ 3.7, n. 2; § 3.18, n. 1, 3; § 3.19, n. 1.
Ft. Dodge Bldg. & Loan Ass'n v. Scott—§ 6.17, n. 13.
Fuentes v. Shevin—§ 3.30, n. 10; § 4.36; § 4.36, n. 3; § 7.25; § 7.25, n. 2; § 7.26, n. 4, 5; § 12.5; § 12.5, n. 2, 13.
Fugate v. Rice—§ 3.27, n. 5.
Fukunaga v. Fukunaga—§ 3.6, n. 1.
Fuller v. Devolld—§ 5.7, n. 4.
Fuller v. Langum—§ 7.31, n. 6.
Fuller-Warren Co. v. Harter—§ 9.6, n. 6.
Fulmer v. Goldfarb—§ 5.17, n. 17.
Fundex Capital Corp. v. Reichard—§ 13.6, n. 28.
Future Federal Sav. and Loan Ass'n v. Daunhauer—§ 13.6, n. 29.
F. W. Eversley & Co., Inc. v. East New York Non-Profit HDFC, Inc.—§ 5.30, n. 11; § 12.6, n. 28.
Fye v. Cox—§ 5.3, n. 2.

G

Gabbert v. Schwartz—§ 5.31, n. 13.
Gabel v. Drewrys Limited, U.S.A., Inc.—§ 2.3, n. 23.
Gaff v. Federal Deposit Ins. Corp.—§ 11.6, n. 19.
Gaffney v. Downey Sav. and Loan Ass'n—§ 6.7, n. 1.
Gage v. Perry—§ 7.12, n. 2; § 7.14, n. 14.
Gaim Development Corp., In re—§ 8.14, n. 10.
Gaines, In re—§ 8.17, n. 17.
Gainesville Nat. Bank v. Martin—§ 4.13, n. 9, 10.

Gainesville Oil & Gas Co., Inc. v. Farm Credit Bank of Texas—§ 7.22, n. 24.
Gainey v. Anderson—§ 6.17, n. 14.
Gainey v. Gainey—§ 8.10, n. 26.
Gaither v. Tolson—§ 3.1, n. 37.
Gajewski v. Bratcher—§ 3.15, n. 5.
Gale v. Tuolumne County Water Co.—§ 7.13, n. 12.
Galladora v. Richter—§ 3.28, n. 7.
Gallegos v. Gulf Coast Inv. Corp.—§ 5.31, n. 3.
Galleria Towers, Inc. v. Crump Warren & Sommer, Inc.—§ 4.35, n. 29.
Galvin, In re—§ 4.35, n. 14.
Gammel v. Goode—§ 7.3, n. 11.
Gamut v. Gregg—§ 7.10, n. 16.
Ganbaum v. Rockwood Realty Corp.—§ 4.2, n. 18.
Gancedo Lumber Co., Inc. v. Flagship First Nat. Bank of Miami Beach—§ 12.7, n. 42.
Gandrud v. Bremer—§ 6.7, n. 4.
Gandrud v. Hansen—§ 4.24, n. 10; § 4.25, n. 2; § 4.27, n. 15.
Ganz v. Clark—§ 4.22, n. 19; § 4.39, n. 12.
Garbish v. Malvern Federal Sav. and Loan Ass'n—§ 12.10, n. 47, 51.
Garcia v. Atmajian—§ 12.9, n. 40.
Gardner v. Buckeye Savings & Loan Co.—§ 6.6, n. 10.
Gardner v. Cohn—§ 2.4, n. 2.
Gardner v. Gardner—§ 7.13, n. 16.
Gardner v. Heartt—§ 4.4, n. 17; § 4.5, n. 13, 14.
Gardner v. Leck—§ 12.4, n. 31.
Gardner & Meeks Co. v. New York Cent. & H. R. R. Co.—§ 12.5, n. 3.
Gardner Plumbing, Inc. v. Cottrill—§ 12.10, n. 51; § 13.3, n. 24.
Gargan v. Grimes—§ 7.14, n. 5.
Garner, In re—§ 8.14, n. 45.
Garner v. Tri-State Development Co.—§ 3.30, n. 5, 10; § 7.25; § 7.25, n. 3, 14, 21; § 7.27, n. 6.
Garnett State Sav. Bank v. Tush—§ 12.8, n. 10.
Garnsey v. Rogers—§ 5.16, n. 1.
Garretson Inv. Co. of San Diego v. Arndt—§ 2.1, n. 4.
Garrett v. Coastal Financial Management Co., Inc.—§ 11.7, n. 27, 37.
Garrett v. Coast and Southern Federal Sav. and Loan Ass'n—§ 6.8, n. 2; § 6.9; § 6.9, n. 1, 9.
Garrett v. Cobb—§ 6.7, n. 8.
Garrett v. Commonwealth Mortg. Corp. of America—§ 11.7, n. 11.
Garrett v. Fernauld—§ 5.33, n. 6, 9.
Garrett Tire Center, Inc. v. Herbaugh—§ 9.1, n. 4, 6.
Garris v. A & M Forest Consultants, Inc.—§ 7.2, n. 13.
Garris v. Federal Land Bank of Jackson—§ 7.21, n. 25, 27.
Garrity v. Rural Mut. Ins. Co.—§ 10.1, n. 4.

Garrow v. Brooks—§ 4.9, n. 1, 5.
Gartside v. Outley—§ 4.22, n. 12.
Gaskell v. Viquesney—§ 4.27, n. 15.
Gaskill v. Sine—§ 10.15, n. 5.
Gaslight Village, Inc., In re—§ 8.18, n. 19.
Gas Reclamation, Inc. Securities Litigation, In re—§ 5.32, n. 4.
Gassert v. Bogk—§ 3.4, n. 11.
Gate City Federal Sav. and Loan Ass'n v. Dalton—§ 5.24, n. 131.
Gates v. Crocker-Anglo Nat. Bank—§ 12.8, n. 16.
Gates, State v.—§ 12.3, n. 61.
Gatter v. Nimmo—§ 7.7, n. 29.
Gatx Tank Erection Corp. v. Tesoro Petroleum Corp.—§ 7.15, n. 7, 10, 12, 23.
Gaumer v. Hartford-Carlisle Sav. Bank—§ 10.14, n. 9.
Gautney v. Gautney—§ 12.9, n. 3.
Gay v. Broder—§ 12.11, n. 39.
Gaynor v. Blewett—§ 4.42, n. 17, 19, 24.
G. B. Seely's Son, Inc. v. Fulton-Edison, Inc.—§ 7.2, n. 8; § 10.3, n. 7.
G. Credit Co. v. Mid-West Development, Inc.—§ 12.10, n. 59.
Gee v. Eberle—§ 12.6, n. 28.
Geffen v. Paletz—§ 5.28, n. 20.
Geiser v. Permacrete, Inc.—§ 12.4, n. 30.
Geishaker v. Pancoast—§ 7.13, n. 1, 2.
Gellert, In re—§ 8.15, n. 89.
Gelof v. First Nat. Bank of Frankford—§ 7.11, n. 1.
Gelwicks, In re—§ 8.18, n. 53.
Gemini at Dadeland, Ltd., Matter of—§ 8.14, n. 75.
Gem Valley Ranches, Inc. v. Small—§ 7.17, n. 17.
General Acrylics v. United States Fidelity and Guaranty Co.—§ 12.2, n. 46.
General Bank, F.S.B. v. Westbrooke Pointe, Inc.—§ 7.31, n. 2, 3.
General Builders Supply Co. v. Arlington Co-op. Bank—§ 7.32, n. 7; § 10.15, n. 1.
Generale Bank, New York Branch v. Choudhury—§ 5.32, n. 4.
General Elec. Co. v. Levine—§ 5.16, n. 2.
General Elec. Credit Corp. v. Air Flow Industries, Inc.—§ 5.27, n. 6.
General Electric Supply Co. v. Southern New England Telephone Co.—§ 12.5, n. 34.
General Glass Corp. v. Mast Const. Co.—§ 2.4, n. 2; § 7.11, n. 3.
General G.M.C. Sales, Inc. v. Passarella—§ 4.14, n. 10; § 4.15, n. 2.
General Industries, Inc., In re—§ 8.17, n. 40.
General Motors Acceptance Corp. v. Uresti—§ 6.3, n. 3.
Genesis Engineering Co., Inc. v. Hueser—§ 12.4, n. 33; § 12.7, n. 42.
Geneva Ltd. Partners v. Kemp—§ 7.7, n. 42; § 7.19, n. 20.
George v. Andrews—§ 5.19, n. 21.
George v. Butler—§ 6.12, n. 10.

TABLE OF CASES

George v. Cone—§ 7.16, n. 26; § 7.17, n. 2.
George A.Z. Johnson, Jr., Inc. v. Barnhill—§ 12.4, n. 14.
George H. Nutman, Inc. v. Aetna Business Credit, Inc.—§ 6.3, n. 1, 3.
George W. Hyde Building & Loan Ass'n No. 3, In re—§ 4.27, n. 15.
Georgia Casualty Co. v. O'Donnell—§ 7.10, n. 16.
Georgia Farm Bureau Mut. Ins. Co. v. Brewer—§ 4.16, n. 7, 11.
Georgia R. Bank & Trust Co. v. McCullough—§ 12.8, n. 14.
Georgia R. R. Bank and Trust Co. v. Doolittle—§ 5.29, n. 9.
Gerard C. Wallace Co., Inc. v. Simpson Land Co.—§ 12.4, n. 42.
Gerdine v. Menage—§ 5.7, n. 4.
Gerhardt v. Ellis—§ 7.4, n. 4.
Germania Life Ins. Co. v. Casey—§ 5.19, n. 11.
Gerrish v. Black—§ 4.28, n. 1, 2.
Gevertz v. Gevertz—§ 6.11, n. 12.
G.G.C. Co. v. First Nat. Bank of St. Paul—§ 4.35, n. 48.
G. Herndt & Bros. v. Porterfield—§ 6.12, n. 5, 23.
G.H. Swope Bldg. Corp. v. Horton—§ 12.3, n. 28.
Gianguzzi, In re—§ 8.15, n. 39.
Gibbs v. Cruikshank—§ 4.1, n. 8.
Gibbs v. Didier—§ 4.26, n. 5.
Gibbs v. Hartford Acc. & Indem. Co.—§ 12.2, n. 25.
Gibbs v. Johnson—§ 6.17, n. 8.
Gibbs v. Tally—§ 12.4, n. 18.
Gibbs v. Titelman—§ 7.27, n. 14.
Giberson v. First Federal Sav. and Loan Ass'n of Waterloo—§ 4.15, n. 8.
Gibraltar Financial Corp. v. Lumbermens Mut. Cas. Co.—§ 4.14, n. 11.
Gibson v. Crehore—§ 7.3, n. 3, 8; § 10.3, n. 4.
Gibson v. Green's Adm'r—§ 8.1, n. 2.
Gibson v. Hough—§ 3.10, n. 3.
Gibson v. Johnson—§ 6.11, n. 40.
Gibson v. Lambeth—§ 7.21, n. 85.
Giffen Industries of Jacksonville, Inc. v. Southeastern Associates, Inc.—§ 12.6, n. 38.
Gifford v. Corrigan, 22 N.E. 756—§ 5.18, n. 5, 15.
Gifford v. Corrigan, 11 N.E. 498—§ 5.18, n. 10.
Gilbert v. Cherry—§ 7.22, n. 45.
Gilbert v. Lusk—§ 7.21, n. 1.
Gilchrist v. Gough—§ 2.4, n. 9.
Gilcrist v. Wright—§ 5.33, n. 21.
Gill v. Mission Sav. & Loan Ass'n—§ 12.10, n. 7, 17.
Gilliam v. McCormack—§ 10.13, n. 17.
Gilliam v. McLemore—§ 5.19, n. 33.
Gillis v. Bonelli-Adams Co.—§ 5.14, n. 2.
Gillis v. Martin—§ 4.29, n. 21.

Gilman v. Federal Deposit Ins. Corp.—§ 5.29, n. 34.
Gilman v. Forgione—§ 7.3, n. 10.
Gilman v. Wills—§ 4.1, n. 6.
Gilmer v. Powell—§ 5.7, n. 11.
Gilpin v. Brooks—§ 4.29, n. 19.
Ginther-Davis Center, Ltd. v. Houston Nat. Bank—§ 7.22, n. 12.
Giorgi v. Pioneer Title Ins. Co.—§ 5.33, n. 19; § 13.3, n. 21.
Gish, United States v.—§ 11.6, n. 56, 63.
Givins v. Carroll—§ 7.15, n. 2.
Glacier Campground v. Wild Rivers, Inc.—§ 3.32, n. 5, 9, 25.
Gladding v. Warner—§ 4.32, n. 6.
Glade Springs, Inc., In re—§ 10.2, n. 11.
Glass v. Hieronymus—§ 3.19, n. 9.
Glazer v. Alison Homes Corp.—§ 13.3, n. 27.
Glendale Federal Sav. and Loan Ass'n v. Fox—§ 5.23, n. 7.
Glendale Federal Sav. and Loan Ass'n v. Guadagnino—§ 7.2, n. 14.
Glendale Federal Savings and Loan Ass'n v. Marina View Heights Development, Inc.—§ 8.3, n. 139.
Glen Ellyn Sav. and Loan Ass'n v. Tsoumas—§ 11.5, n. 43; § 11.6, n. 2.
Glen Johnson, Inc. v. Resolution Trust Corp.—§ 11.7, n. 26.
Glenn, In re—§ 8.13, n. 33; § 8.15, n. 41, 43; § 8.17, n. 4.
Glenn v. Hollums—§ 7.16, n. 9.
Glenview State Bank v. Shyman—§ 13.3, n. 21.
Glenville and 110 Corp. v. Tortora—§ 7.16, n. 26, 28.
Glidden v. Municipal Authority of Tacoma—§ 7.21, n. 89, 94.
Glines v. Theo. R. Appel Realty Co.—§ 7.22, n. 13, 14.
Global Industries, Inc. v. Harris—§ 3.30, n. 12; § 7.27, n. 2, 28.
Global Realty Corp. v. Charles Kannel Corp.—§ 10.8, n. 5.
Glover v. Marine Bank of Beaver Dam—§ 4.2, n. 2.
Gluskin v. Atlantic Sav. and Loan Ass'n—§ 12.10, n. 28.
G. L. Wilson Bldg. Co. v. Leatherwood—§ 12.6, n. 28.
Glynn v. Marquette—§ 13.3, n. 17.
GMAC Mortgage Corp., People v.—§ 4.19, n. 35.
GMAC Mortg. Corp. of Pa. v. Stapleton—§ 4.19, n. 35.
Goddard v. Clarke—§ 4.43, n. 5.
Godfrey v. Chadwell—§ 7.15, n. 1.
Godwin v. Gerling—§ 8.10, n. 24.
Goebel v. Iffla—§ 7.14, n. 15.
Goetz v. Selsor—§ 5.27, n. 5; § 5.29, n. 16, 24; § 5.31, n. 13; § 5.33, n. 36.
Goff v. Graham—§ 3.29, n. 60.
Goff v. Price—§ 2.4, n. 2.

TABLE OF CASES

Goldberg, United States v.—§ 5.33, n. 18; § 5.34, n. 4.
Goldberg v. Xorco, Ltd.—§ 5.29, n. 5.
Golden Acres, Inc., United States v.—§ 7.7, n. 40.
Golden Forest Properties, Inc. v. Columbia Sav. and Loan Ass'n—§ 6.3, n. 5.
Golden Plan of California, Inc., In re—§ 5.35, n. 44, 47.
Gold Key Properties, Inc., In re—§ 3.37, n. 11.
Goldman v. Connecticut General Life Ins. Co.—§ 12.3, n. 25, 29.
Goldome Realty Credit Corp. v. Harwick—§ 6.6, n. 27.
Goldstein v. Lincoln Sav. Bank—§ 12.3, n. 36.
Goldwater v. Hibernia Sav. & Loan Soc.—§ 6.11, n. 26.
Gonzales v. Gem Properties, Inc.—§ 7.22, n. 39, 45.
Gonzales v. Tama—§ 7.6, n. 2; § 7.8, n. 2.
Gonzales County Sav. & Loan Assoc. v. Freeman—§ 12.3, n. 20.
Goodbar & Co. v. Bloom—§ 3.18, n. 6.
Gooden, In re—§ 8.15, n. 35, 45.
Goodenow v. Ewer—§ 7.12, n. 12.
Gooding v. Shea—§ 4.4, n. 6; § 4.9, n. 2.
Goodman v. Commissioner—§ 3.34, n. 20, 21.
Goodman v. Pate Const., Inc.—§ 12.11, n. 8.
Goodrich v. Commissioners, Atchison County—§ 4.12, n. 16.
Goodyear v. Goodyear—§ 10.7, n. 3, 4, 10.
Goodyear v. Mack—§ 8.3, n. 82.
Goodyear Shoe-Mach. Co. v. Selz, Schwab & Co.—§ 3.1, n. 12.
Gordon v. Krellman—§ 4.29, n. 7, 11, 20, 29.
Gordon v. Ware Savings Bank—§ 4.13, n. 6, 17; § 4.14, n. 14.
Gordon Finance Co. v. Chambliss—§ 6.9, n. 17.
Goss v. Trinity Sav. & Loan Ass'n—§ 5.29, n. 6.
Gosselin v. Better Homes, Inc.—§ 12.7, n. 11.
Goswami v. Metropolitan Sav. and Loan Ass'n—§ 7.22, n. 17.
Gotta, In re—§ 8.18, n. 3, 23, 54.
Gottlieb v. City of New York—§ 5.28, n. 15.
Gottlieb v. McArdle—§ 7.21, n. 4.
Gottschalk v. Jungmann—§ 5.9, n. 18.
Gottschamer v. August, Thompson, Sherr, Clark & Shafer, P.C.—§ 8.1, n. 2.
Goudreau v. Standard Federal Sav. & Loan Ass'n—§ 4.19, n. 28.
Gould, In re—§ 4.35, n. 14.
Gould v. Maine Farmers' Mut. Fire Ins. Co.—§ 4.13, n. 9.
Gould v. McKillip—§ 3.3, n. 2; § 7.5, n. 15.
Gourley v. Wollam—§ 6.19, n. 10.
Government Nat. Mortg. Ass'n v. Screen—§ 7.7, n. 33.
Governor's Island, In re—§ 5.28, n. 6.

Gower v. Winchester—§ 7.5, n. 22.
Graf v. Hope Bldg. Corporation—§ 7.7, n. 7.
Graffam v. Burgess—§ 7.16, n. 26.
Graham, Matter of—§ 8.15, n. 54.
Graham v. Durnbaugh—§ 5.10, n. 9.
Graham v. Fireman's Insurance Co.—§ 4.14, n. 13.
Graham v. Graham—§ 3.11, n. 1.
Graham v. Linden—§ 7.3, n. 1.
Graham v. Mullins—§ 3.17, n. 2.
Graham v. Oliver—§ 7.20, n. 2, 4, 5, 6, 16.
Graham v. Stoneham—§ 3.32, n. 26.
Gramatan Co., Limited v. D'Amico—§ 5.31, n. 9, 13.
Granada Wines, Inc. v. New England Teamsters and Trucking Industry Pension Fund—§ 8.14, n. 98.
Grand Island Hotel Corp. v. Second Island Development Co.—§ 5.25, n. 4.
Grand Prairie Sav. and Loan Ass'n, Stuttgart v. Worthen Bank and Trust Co., N.A.—§ 5.35, n. 26.
Grand Tower Manufacturing & Transportation Co. v. Ullman—§ 4.26, n. 1.
Grangers' Mut. Fire Ins. Co. of Frederick County v. Farmers' Nat. Bank of Annapolis—§ 4.14, n. 17.
Granite Computer Leasing Corp. v. Travelers Indem. Co.—§ 12.2, n. 17.
Grannis-Blair Audit Co. v. Maddux—§ 4.35, n. 15.
Grant v. Burr—§ 6.11, n. 19, 35.
Grant v. Oten—§ 2.1, n. 19.
Grattan v. Wiggins—§ 7.5, n. 8.
Gray v. Bankers Trust Co. of Albany, N.A.—§ 7.18, n. 4.
Gray v. Bowers—§ 3.32, n. 31.
Gray v. Case—§ 4.12, n. 22.
Gray v. Fraser—§ 3.19, n. 3.
Gray v. H. M. Loud & Sons Lumber Co.—§ 10.10, n. 18.
Graybeal v. American Sav. & Loan Ass'n—§ 4.19, n. 6.
Graydon v. Colonial Bank-Gulf Coast Region—§ 12.9, n. 3.
Great American First Sav. Bank v. Bayside Developers—§ 8.3, n. 65.
Great American Ins. Co. v. United States—§ 12.2, n. 42.
Great Cobar, Limited, In re—§ 4.39, n. 8.
Greater Atlantic and Pacific Inv. Group, Inc., In re—§ 4.35, n. 41.
Greater Houston Bank v. Conte—§ 7.22, n. 1, 6.
Greater Southwest Office Park, Ltd. v. Texas Commerce Bank Nat. Ass'n—§ 7.21, n. 1.
Great Lakes Mortg. Corp. v. Collymore—§ 7.10, n. 9.
Great Northern Sav. Co. v. Ingarra—§ 5.24, n. 118.
Great Southwest Fire Ins. Co. v. DeWitt—§ 6.6, n. 24.
Great Southwest Life Ins. Co. v. Frazier—§ 11.6, n. 65.

Great Western Bank v. Sierra Woods Group—§ 8.14, n. 67.
Great Western Sav. Bank v. George W. Easley Co., J.V.—§ 12.10, n. 8.
Great-West Life Assur. Co. v. Raintree Inn—§ 4.35, n. 14, 41.
Green v. Dixon—§ 4.29, n. 21, 23; § 7.3, n. 3.
Green v. Kemp—§ 4.1, n. 6.
Green v. Lamb—§ 4.30, n. 3.
Green v. Ramage Et Al—§ 10.13, n. 9, 11, 16.
Green v. Thornton—§ 4.27, n. 13.
Green v. Wescott—§ 4.32, n. 3.
Greenberg v. Service Business Forms Industries, Inc.—§ 7.7, n. 25.
Greene v. Levenhar—§ 13.6, n. 18.
Greenhouse Patio Apartments v. Aetna Life Ins. Co.—§ 6.3, n. 2.
Greenleaf v. Grounder—§ 2.2, n. 13.
Greenwich Sav Bank v. Samotas—§ 4.38, n. 5.
Greer v. Turner—§ 6.7, n. 8.
Gregg v. Williamson—§ 5.28, n. 14, 23.
Gregory v. Arms—§ 5.6, n. 1.
Gregory v. Savage—§ 5.34, n. 17.
Greiner v. Wilke—§ 3.37, n. 12; § 5.28, n. 28, 29, 40.
Grella v. Berry—§ 7.22, n. 12.
Grellet v. Heilshorn—§ 6.17, n. 11.
Grenada Ready-Mix Concrete, Inc. v. Watkins—§ 12.9, n. 28; § 12.10, n. 7, 33, 34.
Gresham v. Ware—§ 4.29, n. 31.
Grether v. Nick, 215 N.W. 571—§ 4.42; § 4.42, n. 22, 24.
Grether v. Nick, 213 N.W. 304—§ 4.34, n. 6.
Greve v. Coffin—§ 5.28, n. 16.
Grevemeyer v. Southern Mutual Fire Insurance Co.—§ 4.13, n. 4.
Greystone III Joint Venture, In re—§ 8.14, n. 61.
Greystone III Joint Venture, Matter of—§ 8.14; § 8.14, n. 86, 93, 102, 103.
Gribble v. Mauerhan—§ 5.29, n. 11; § 5.31, n. 13.
Gribble v. Stearman & Kaplan, Inc.—§ 7.31, n. 15; § 7.32, n. 7; § 10.10, n. 1; § 13.3, n. 16.
Grider v. Mutual Federal Sav. & Loan Ass'n—§ 12.7, n. 38.
Griesbaum v. Baum—§ 7.10, n. 9.
Griffin v. Federal Land Bank of Wichita—§ 7.7, n. 51.
Griffin v. New Jersey Oil Co.—§ 2.4, n. 8; § 12.7, n. 10.
Griffin v. Reis—§ 7.8, n. 4.
Griffin Wellpoint Corp. v. Engelhardt, Inc.—§ 5.19, n. 54.
Griffiths v. Sears—§ 5.32, n. 3.
Griggs v. Duke Power Co.—§ 11.5; § 11.5, n. 14.
Grigsby v. Miller—§ 4.12, n. 19.
Grinnell Fire Protection Systems Co., Inc. v. American Sav. and Loan Ass'n—§ 12.5, n. 29.
Grise v. White—§ 10.9, n. 16.
Grissom, Matter of—§ 8.17, n. 40.
Grissom, United States v.—§ 12.3, n. 18.
Grizaffi, In re—§ 12.8, n. 10.
Grombone v. Krekel—§ 3.27, n. 5; § 3.29, n. 70.
Grooms v. Williams—§ 12.9, n. 23.
Groover v. Peters—§ 5.33, n. 5.
Grout v. Stewart—§ 3.23, n. 2.
Grove v. Great Northern Loan Co.—§ 5.17, n. 10.
Growth Equities Corp. v. Freed—§ 5.29, n. 4.
Grubb v. Delathauwer—§ 3.20, n. 3.
Grubbs v. Houston First American Sav. Ass'n—§ 8.15, n. 18, 21, 22, 35, 39.
Grundy Nat. Bank v. Tandem Min. Corp.—§ 8.14, n. 16.
Gruskin v. Fisher—§ 3.32, n. 33.
G.R.W. Engineers, Inc. v. Elam—§ 10.5, n. 5.
Guam Hakubotan, Inc. v. Furusawa Inv. Corp.—§ 3.3, n. 6.
Guarantee Bank v. Magness Const. Co.—§ 2.3, n. 16; § 12.9, n. 6.
Guarantee Elec. Co. v. Big Rivers Elec. Corp.—§ 12.6, n. 20.
Guarantee Safe & Trust Deposit Co. v. Jenkins—§ 7.16, n. 22.
Guaranty Mortg. Co. of Nashville v. Seitz—§ 12.10, n. 46.
Guaranty Mortg. & Ins. Co. v. Harris—§ 5.32, n. 9, 28.
Guaranty Pest Control, Inc. v. Commercial Inv. & Development Corp.—§ 13.3, n. 33.
Guaranty Sav. and Loan Ass'n v. Ultimate Sav. Bank, F.S.B.—§ 5.35, n. 25, 45.
Guardian Depositors Corporation of Detroit v. Savage—§ 6.11, n. 2.
Guardian Depositors Corporation of Detroit v. Wagner—§ 6.13, n. 3.
Guardian Sav. & Loan Ass'n v. Reserve Ins. Co.—§ 4.16, n. 3.
Guay v. Brotherhood Building Ass'n—§ 7.22, n. 36.
Guernsey v. Kendall—§ 10.2, n. 7.
Guerra v. Mutual Federal Sav. & Loan Ass'n—§ 7.16, n. 27.
Guidarelli v. Lazaretti—§ 3.30, n. 5; § 7.25, n. 3.
Guidice v. BFG Electroplating and Mfg. Co., Inc.—§ 4.48, n. 9.
Guild Mortg. Co. v. Heller—§ 8.3, n. 139.
Guilmette v. Peoples Savings Bank—§ 12.8, n. 9.
Guin & Hunt, Inc. v. Hughes Supply, Inc.—§ 12.2, n. 35.
Guleserian v. Fields—§ 9.4, n. 4, 10.
Gulf Petroleum, S.A. v. Collazo—§ 3.33, n. 19.
Gulley v. Macy—§ 3.14, n. 1.

Gunter v. Hutcheson—§ 5.29, n. 28; § 11.7, n. 43.
Gunther v. White—§ 5.22, n. 14.
Gustafson v. Koehler—§ 5.7, n. 11; § 5.10, n. 10, 11, 12.
Guttenberg Sav. and Loan Ass'n v. Rivera—§ 4.3, n. 1; § 4.22, n. 2.
Gutzi Associates v. Switzer—§ 6.2, n. 3; § 9.8, n. 24.
Gwinn, Inc., State ex rel. v. Superior Court—§ 4.2, n. 18.
Gyles v. Hall—§ 6.7, n. 4.

H

Haas v. Teets—§ 2.4, n. 2.
Hacohn v. F.D.M.B., Inc.—§ 6.6, n. 32.
Haddon Haciendas Co., United States v.—§ 11.6, n. 57.
Hadley v. Schow—§ 9.4, n. 5.
Hadlock v. Benjamin Drainage Dist.—§ 4.45, n. 6.
Hafford v. Smith—§ 5.5, n. 1.
Hagan v. Gardner—§ 7.12, n. 6.
Hagan v. Walker—§ 7.14, n. 10.
Hagen v. Butler—§ 12.9, n. 3.
Hagen v. Silva—§ 5.33, n. 33.
Hagendorfer v. Marlette—§ 8.14, n. 9.
Hager v. Astorg—§ 7.13, n. 7.
Hagerstown, City of v. Groh—§ 4.22, n. 2.
Haggerty v. Brower—§ 3.8, n. 13.
Haile v. Amarillo Nat. Bank—§ 5.4, n. 2.
Haines v. Beach—§ 7.10, n. 15; § 7.15, n. 1.
Haines v. Thomson—§ 3.4, n. 11.
Halbert v. Turner—§ 4.29, n. 3, 27, 30.
Halbert's Lumber, Inc. v. Lucky Stores, Inc.—§ 12.4, n. 42.
Halderman v. Woodward—§ 2.1, n. 4.
Hall v. Davis—§ 2.3, n. 9.
Hall v. Federal Deposit Ins. Corp.—§ 11.7, n. 10, 25.
Hall v. Hall—§ 4.2, n. 18.
Hall v. Livesay—§ 3.8, n. 4.
Hall v. Morgan—§ 10.11, n. 15.
Hall v. O'Brien—§ 5.28, n. 3.
Hall v. O'Connell—§ 3.10, n. 3; § 3.21, n. 3.
Hall v. Owen County State Bank—§ 5.30, n. 15.
Hall v. Savill—§ 4.2, n. 17.
Hall v. Westcott—§ 4.45, n. 1, 12.
Hall Colttree Associates, In re—§ 4.35, n. 25, 27.
Hall's Miscellaneous Ironworks, Inc. v. All Southern Inv. Co., Inc.—§ 12.6, n. 33, 45.
Ham v. Flowers—§ 7.5, n. 8.
Hamilton, Matter of—§ 8.15, n. 39.
Hamilton v. Browning—§ 5.28, n. 21.
Hamilton v. Dobbs—§ 10.8, n. 7.
Hamilton v. Griffin—§ 4.8, n. 2.
Hamilton v. Rhodes—§ 12.7, n. 33.
Hamilton Co. v. Rosen—§ 5.5, n. 4.

Hamilton Inv. Trust v. Escambia Developers, Inc.—§ 8.3, n. 18.
Hamlett, In re—§ 9.8, n. 33.
Hamlin v. Parsons—§ 4.6, n. 6.
Hammelburger v. Foursome Inn Corp.—§ 5.32, n. 3, 4.
Hamner v. Rock Mountain Lake, Inc.—§ 3.27, n. 5.
Hampe v. Manke—§ 5.19, n. 39.
Hampshire Nat. Bank v. Calkins—§ 2.4, n. 2.
Hampton Farmers Co-op. Co. v. Fehd—§ 3.28, n. 6.
Hamre v. United States—§ 12.11, n. 45.
Han v. United States—§ 10.6, n. 3.
Hand v. Pelham Banking Co.—§ 12.9, n. 46, 47.
Hand Trading Co. v. Daniels—§ 9.1, n. 6, 13.
Handy v. Gordon—§ 12.9; § 12.9, n. 17; § 12.10, n. 29.
Handy v. Rogers—§ 7.21, n. 1.
Handzel v. Bassi—§ 5.22, n. 37.
Hankins v. Administrator of Veterans Affairs—§ 7.21, n. 23.
Hannan v. Hannan—§ 2.3, n. 9.
Hanneman v. Olson—§ 3.13, n. 5.
Hansen, In re—§ 10.9, n. 7.
Hansen, In re Estate of—§ 10.13, n. 2; § 10.14, n. 8.
Hansen v. Branner—§ 6.12, n. 1.
Hansen v. Kohler—§ 3.6, n. 1.
Hansom v. Derby—§ 4.29, n. 1.
Hanson v. Acceptance Finance Co.—§ 6.2, n. 7.
Hanson v. First Bank of South Dakota, N.A.—§ 8.14, n. 99.
Hanson v. Neal—§ 7.21, n. 16, 42.
Hanson v. Spear—§ 8.3, n. 22.
Harada v. Ellis—§ 7.13, n. 16.
Harambee Uhuru School, Inc. v. Kemp—§ 11.5, n. 40.
Harbel Oil Company v. Steele—§ 5.24, n. 23.
Harbert's Case—§ 10.9, n. 4.
Harbour Town Associates, Ltd., In re—§ 8.18, n. 54.
Harden v. Akridge—§ 12.11, n. 12.
Hardin, In re—§ 8.15, n. 35.
Hardin Const. Group, Inc. v. Carlisle Const. Co.—§ 12.4, n. 14.
Harding v. Garber—§ 4.29, n. 2.
Harding v. Home Inv. & Sav. Co.—§ 6.6, n. 16.
Hare v. Headley—§ 4.14, n. 19.
Hare v. Murphy—§ 5.15, n. 14.
Hargrove, United States v.—§ 11.6, n. 59.
Harlan, In re—§ 8.15, n. 39.
Harlem Savings Bank v. Cooper—§ 4.2, n. 9.
Harms v. Sprague—§ 4.2, n. 1.
Harner v. Schecter—§ 12.4, n. 35.
Harnish v. Peele—§ 3.20, n. 6.
Harpe v. Stone—§ 6.7, n. 1.
Harper v. Edwards—§ 2.4, n. 1.

TABLE OF CASES 763

Harper v. Ely—§ 4.30, n. 1, 2.
Harper v. Federal Land Bank of Spokane—§ 7.7, n. 51.
Harper v. Union Sav. Ass'n—§ 11.5, n. 3.
Harper's Appeal—§ 4.29, n. 21.
Har-Rich Realty Corp. v. America Consumer Industries, Inc.—§ 7.7, n. 5.
Harrington v. Butte & Superior Copper Co.—§ 3.11, n. 1.
Harrington v. Harrington—§ 10.1, n. 8; § 10.3, n. 1.
Harrington v. Taylor—§ 10.13, n. 14.
Harris, In re—§ 8.15, n. 39.
Harris v. Foster—§ 4.22, n. 22.
Harris v. Haynes—§ 4.5, n. 6.
Harris v. Jex—§ 6.7, n. 22.
Harris v. Kemp—§ 3.6, n. 1; § 3.7, n. 2; § 3.8, n. 9, 11.
Harris v. Lesster—§ 4.43, n. 10.
Harris v. Mills—§ 6.11, n. 2, 16.
Harrison v. Galilee Baptist Church—§ 5.32, n. 3.
Harrison v. Guerin—§ 10.12, n. 4.
Harrison v. Otto G. Heinzeroth Mortg. Co.—§ 11.5, n. 27.
Harron v. Du Bois—§ 10.13, n. 9, 10, 19.
Harstad, In re—§ 8.3, n. 51.
Hart, In re—§ 8.15, n. 70.
Hart v. Bingman—§ 4.35, n. 11.
Hart v. Chalker—§ 2.4, n. 2.
Hart v. Randolph—§ 3.8, n. 17.
Hartford Federal Sav. and Loan Ass'n v. Tucker—§ 4.36, n. 10; § 7.10, n. 2, 3.
Hartford Fire Ins. Co. v. Associates Capital Corp.—§ 4.14, n. 1.
Hartford Fire Ins. Co. v. Merrimack Mut. Fire Ins. Co.—§ 4.14, n. 10.
Hartford Life Ins. Co. v. Randall—§ 6.2, n. 3.
Hartley v. Harrison—§ 5.17, n. 7.
Hartman v. Anderson—§ 6.7, n. 1.
Hartman Paving, Inc., In re—§ 8.14, n. 6.
Hartshorn v. Chaddock—§ 4.4, n. 20.
Hartshorn v. Hubbard—§ 4.1, n. 10.
Harvey v. Lowry—§ 5.3, n. 8; § 5.10, n. 9, 17.
Harwood v. Underwood—§ 7.2, n. 21.
Hasquet v. Big West Oil Co.—§ 6.6, n. 17.
Hasselman v. McKernan—§ 7.2, n. 14.
Hastings v. Perry—§ 4.10, n. 4.
Hastings v. Westchester Fire Insurance Co.—§ 4.14, n. 18.
Hastings v. Wise—§ 9.4, n. 11.
Hatch v. Collins—§ 7.21, n. 61, 70.
Hatch v. Security-First Nat. Bank of Los Angeles—§ 8.3, n. 74.
Hatcher v. Chancey—§ 7.8, n. 6.
Hatcher v. Rose—§ 6.1, n. 4.
Hatley v. Johnston—§ 5.11, n. 6.
Haueter v. Rancich—§ 10.9, n. 3.
Haug v. Haug—§ 3.6.
Haugen v. Western Federal Sav. & Loan Ass'n of Denver—§ 11.6, n. 27.
Havana Nat. Bank v. Wiemer—§ 3.6, n. 1; § 3.7, n. 2.

Haven Federal Sav. and Loan Ass'n v. Carl—§ 5.23, n. 18.
Havighorst v. Bowen—§ 5.34, n. 14.
Hawke v. Milliken—§ 3.18, n. 6.
Hawkeye Bank & Trust Co. v. Michel—§ 12.8, n. 12.
Hawkeye Bank & Trust N.A., of Centerville-Seymour v. Milburn—§ 7.1, n. 2; § 8.4, n. 11.
Hawley v. Bibb—§ 5.31, n. 13.
Hawley v. Levee—§ 5.28, n. 15.
Hawn v. Malone—§ 5.8, n. 4, 7.
Hayden v. Huff.—§ 10.7, n. 12.
Hayes, In re—§ 8.3, n. 10; § 8.13, n. 10.
Hayes v. Dickenson—§ 4.43, n. 4.
Hayes v. First Nat. Bank of Memphis—§ 6.9, n. 4, 13.
Haynes v. Blackwell—§ 3.6, n. 6.
Haynsworth v. Bischoff—§ 5.32, n. 30.
Hays v. Christiansen, 209 N.W. 609—§ 4.28, n. 4; § 4.31, n. 1, 12.
Hays v. Christiansen, 181 N.W. 379—§ 4.29, n. 20, 29.
Hays v. Peck—§ 5.7, n. 6, 8.
Hays, United States v.—§ 5.20, n. 11; § 5.19, n. 54.
Hayward v. Cain—§ 7.2, n. 7.
Hayward v. Chase—§ 6.7, n. 20.
Hazeltine v. Granger—§ 4.35, n. 3.
Hazifotis v. Citizens Federal Sav. and Loan Ass'n—§ 5.3, n. 5.
Hazle v. Bondy—§ 10.2, n. 4.
H. B. Deal Const. Co. v. Labor Discount Center, Inc.—§ 12.7, n. 42.
Headley v. Stewart—§ 3.11, n. 1; § 4.29, n. 23, 30, 34.
Heaney v. Riddle—§ 5.8, n. 1.
Heartline Farms, Inc. v. Daly—§ 8.19, n. 9.
Heart of Atlanta Motel, Inc. v. United States—§ 5.24, n. 12.
Heath v. Dodson—§ 3.36, n. 10.
Heath v. Haile—§ 4.4, n. 10, 22, 23.
Heaton v. Grant Lodge No. 335, I. O. O. F.—§ 4.23, n. 3.
Hebrew Home for Orphans and Aged of Hudson County, New Jersey v. Freund—§ 5.28, n. 3.
Hector, Inc. v. United Sav. and Loan Ass'n—§ 6.6, n. 19, 23.
Hedrick v. Bigby—§ 8.8, n. 17.
Hefner v. Northwestern Mut. Life Ins. Co.—§ 7.14, n. 12, 16.
Heggen Const. Co., Inc. v. Turalba—§ 5.5, n. 4; § 5.4, n. 6.
Heid v. Vreeland—§ 5.8, n. 6.
Heide v. Mading King County Enterprises, Inc.—§ 3.37, n. 11.
Heider v. Dietz—§ 3.36, n. 10.
Heighe v. Sale of Real Estate—§ 10.8, n. 8.
Heins v. Byers—§ 5.10, n. 13.
Heintz v. Klebba—§ 5.34, n. 12, 13.
Heirs of Stover v. Heirs of Bounds—§ 3.1, n. 3.
Heisel v. Cunningham—§ 3.32, n. 19.

Helbling Brothers, Inc. v. Turner—§ 8.3, n. 22.
Hellenschmidt, In re—§ 8.18, n. 19.
Heller v. Amawalk Nursery—§ 4.41, n. 12.
Heller v. Gate City Bldg. & Loan Ass'n—§ 12.7, n. 32.
Heller v. Gerry—§ 4.11, n. 8.
Heller Financial v. Insurance Co. of North America—§ 6.6, n. 26; § 10.3, n. 10.
Hembree v. Mid-America Federal S. & L. Assn.—§ 7.12, n. 31.
Hemmerle v. First Federal Sav. and Loan Ass'n of Desoto County—§ 12.7, n. 9.
Hemphill's Estate, In re—§ 4.30, n. 4.
Hempstead Bank v. Babcock—§ 5.30, n. 23.
Hemsing, In re—§ 8.15, n. 50.
Henderson v. Guest—§ 6.1, n. 2.
Henderson v. Security Mortg. & Finance Co.—§ 3.18, n. 8.
Hendricks v. Brooks—§ 6.13, n. 6, 9.
Hendricks v. Hess—§ 6.6, n. 14.
Hendricks v. Webster—§ 12.7, n. 11.
Hendrickson v. Farmers' Bank & Trust Co.—§ 12.8, n. 10.
Hendrie v. Hendrie—§ 2.1, n. 5.
Henke, In re—§ 8.19, n. 9.
Henke v. First Southern Properties, Inc.—§ 7.20, n. 1.
Hennessey v. Bell—§ 6.6, n. 36.
Hennessey v. Rafferty—§ 3.4, n. 12.
Henniges v. Johnson—§ 5.34, n. 9.
Henningsen v. United States Fidelity & Guaranty Co—§ 12.2, n. 18, 40.
Henry v. Tupper—§ 2.2, n. 9.
Henry & Coatsworth Co. v. Fisherdick, Administrator—§ 12.4, n. 31.
Henry-Luqueer Properties, Inc., In re—§ 8.17, n. 40.
Henshaw, Ward & Co. v. Wells—§ 4.39, n. 3.
Henslee v. Madison Guar. Sav. and Loan Ass'n—§ 12.3, n. 20.
Hentges v. P.H. Feely & Son, Inc.—§ 3.33, n. 9, 12.
Hepperly v. Bosch—§ 3.32, n. 26, 29.
Herberman v. Bergstrom—§ 10.6, n. 1.
Herd v. Tuohy—§ 5.19, n. 33.
Hergenreter v. Sommers—§ 3.21, n. 2.
Heritage Bank, N.A. v. Ruh—§ 7.7, n. 32, 33.
Herman, United States v.—§ 10.13, n. 2.
Hernandez, In re—§ 8.15, n. 59.
Hernandez v. Leiva—§ 5.1, n. 4.
Hernandez v. Westoak Realty & Inv., Inc.—§ 6.6, n. 19.
Herrin v. Abbe—§ 5.6, n. 1; § 5.7, n. 11.
Herrmann v. Cabinet Land Co.—§ 4.24, n. 13.
Herrmann v. Churchill—§ 3.9, n. 5; § 7.10, n. 12; § 7.15, n. 31.
Herron v. Millers Nat. Ins. Co.—§ 3.10, n. 2.
Hervey v. Krost—§ 8.5, n. 7.
Hess v. Hess—§ 7.12, n. 21.

Hess v. State Bank of Goldendale—§ 6.12, n. 10, 20.
Heuisler v. Nickum—§ 9.1, n. 8.
Hewitt, In re—§ 8.14, n. 46, 49.
H & H Operations, Inc. v. West Georgia Nat. Bank of Carrollton—§ 5.20, n. 8.
Hibernia Nat. Bank v. Federal Deposit Ins. Corp.—§ 5.35, n. 4.
Hibernia Sav. & Loan Soc. v. Thornton—§ 8.2, n. 6.
Hickey v. Polachek—§ 12.4, n. 30.
Hicklin v. Marco—§ 4.29, n. 21, 23.
Hicks v. Bridges—§ 3.21, n. 2.
Hicks v. Resolution Trust Corp.—§ 11.5, n. 36, 40.
Hicks v. Sullivan—§ 5.7, n. 5.
Hickson Lumber Co. v. Gay Lumber Co.—§ 9.1, n. 14; § 9.3, n. 5, 14.
Hidalgo v. Surety Savings and Loan Association—§ 5.31, n. 3.
Hidalgo v. Surety Sav. & Loan Ass'n—§ 5.31, n. 7.
Hidalgo Properties, Inc. v. Wachovia Mortg. Co.—§ 12.3, n. 15, 19.
Hidden v. Jordan—§ 4.29, n. 7.
Hieber v. Florida Nat. Bank—§ 10.7, n. 10.
Higbee v. Aetna Bldg. & Loan Ass'n—§ 5.17, n. 7.
Higby v. Hooper—§ 12.4, n. 41.
Highland Fed. Sav & Loan, People v.—§ 11.6, n. 46.
High Point Bank v. Morgan-Schultheiss Inc.—§ 3.18, n. 8.
Hightower v. Bailey—§ 12.4, n. 18; § 12.5, n. 3.
Higman v. Humes—§ 7.4, n. 4.
Hildrith v. Walker—§ 5.10, n. 5.
Hill v. Edwards—§ 3.4, n. 7.
Hill v. Farmers' & Mechnics' Nat. Bank—§ 7.21, n. 24.
Hill v. Favour—§ 5.28, n. 21.
Hill v. Hall—§ 6.16, n. 21.
Hill v. Hill—§ 9.1, n. 6.
Hill v. Hoeldtke—§ 5.18, n. 15.
Hill v. Howell—§ 10.15, n. 5.
Hill v. International Indemnity Co.—§ 4.14, n. 2.
Hill v. Townley—§ 4.31, n. 14, 17.
Hillblom v. Ivancsits—§ 12.9, n. 40; § 13.3, n. 17.
Hilton v. Bissell—§ 4.44, n. 1.
HIMC Inv. Co. v. Siciliano—§ 5.29, n. 17.
Himes v. Cameron County Const. Corp.—§ 12.2, n. 45.
Himes v. Schiro—§ 6.6, n. 19.
Himmelmann v. Fitzpatrick—§ 6.7, n. 11.
Hinck v. Cohn—§ 4.22, n. 13.
Hinckley v. Eggers—§ 5.29, n. 3, 5.
Hinckley Estate Co. v. Gurry—§ 5.15, n. 6.
Hinds v. Ballou—§ 5.28, n. 12.
Hinds v. Mooers—§ 5.35, n. 17.
Hines, In re—§ 8.15, n. 54, 55.
Hines v. Wells—§ 3.29, n. 32.
Hinners v. Birkevaag—§ 7.10, n. 18.

TABLE OF CASES

Hinsdale Federal Sav. & Loan Ass'n v. Gary-Wheaton Bank—§ 13.3, n. 21.
Hirsch v. Northwestern Mut. Life Ins. Co.—§ 4.27, n. 15.
Hirsh v. Arnold—§ 4.29, n. 5.
H & L Land Co. v. Warner—§ 3.29; § 3.29, n. 12.
Ho v. Presbyterian Church of Laurelhurst—§ 3.28, n. 7.
Hobaica, In re—§ 8.15, n. 49.
Hochevar v. Maryland Cas. Co.—§ 12.2, n. 28.
Hodges v. Hodges—§ 3.18, n. 2, 8.
Hodson v. Treat—§ 7.13, n. 3.
Hoelting Enterprises v. Trailridge Investors, L.P.—§ 4.35, n. 25.
Hoeppner, In re—§ 3.37, n. 11.
Hoer v. Wurdack—§ 7.21, n. 28.
Hoffman v. Harrington—§ 7.5, n. 4.
Hoffman v. Key Federal Sav. and Loan Ass'n—§ 12.1, n. 28.
Hoffman v. Kleinjan—§ 9.1, n. 16.
Hoffman v. McCracken—§ 7.21, n. 43.
Hoffman v. Semet—§ 3.29; § 3.36, n. 5; § 3.29, n. 16.
Hoffman, United States v.—§ 5.27, n. 7; § 6.6, n. 2.
Hofheimer v. Booker—§ 5.6, n. 6.
Hofmeister v. Hunter—§ 3.8, n. 1.
Hogan v. Jaques—§ 3.11, n. 2.
Hogan v. Weeks—§ 3.33, n. 9.
Hogg v. Longstreth—§ 4.31, n. 16.
Hogsett v. Ellis—§ 4.2, n. 14.
Hoiden v. Kohout—§ 5.33, n. 33.
Holbrook v. Finney—§ 9.1, n. 18.
Holcomb v. Webley—§ 6.11, n. 2.
Holden Land & Live Stock Co. v. Interstate Trading Co.—§ 3.3, n. 4, 5.
Holevas v. Mills—§ 9.8; § 9.8, n. 13.
Holf v. Creamer—§ 2.4, n. 7.
Holiday Acres No. 3 v. Midwest Federal Sav. and Loan Ass'n of Minneapolis—§ 5.23, n. 8.
Holiday Associates Ltd. Partnership, Matter of—§ 8.14, n. 54.
Holiday Inns, Inc. v. Susher-Schaefer Inv. Co.—§ 12.8, n. 15.
Holiday Interval, Inc., In re, 94 B.R. 594—§ 5.29, n. 3.
Holiday Intervals, Inc., In re, 931 F.2d 500—§ 3.37, n. 13, 14, 15.
Holiday Mart, Inc., In re—§ 6.9, n. 21, 27.
Holland v. Citizens' Sav. Bank—§ 10.8, n. 7.
Holland Jones Co. v. Smith—§ 9.1, n. 13.
Holland Mortg. and Inv. Corp. v. Bone—§ 12.11, n. 8, 27.
Hollbus v. Seabreeze Ltd. Partnership—§ 13.3, n. 15.
Hollenbeck v. Donell—§ 4.34, n. 4.
Hollenbeck v. Woodford—§ 2.4, n. 11.
Hollenbeck-Bush Planing Mill Co. v. Amweg—§ 12.5, n. 3, 5.
Holles v. Wyse—§ 3.1, n. 12.

Holliday, State ex rel. Elliott v.—§ 7.16, n. 1.
Holliger v. Bates—§ 7.13, n. 1.
Hollingsworth v. Campbell—§ 7.4, n. 12.
Hollinrake, Matter of—§ 4.35, n. 13, 24.
Holly Hill Acres, Ltd. v. Charter Bank of Gainesville—§ 5.29, n. 4.
Hollywood Lumber Co. v. Love—§ 4.2, n. 16.
Holman v. Bailey—§ 6.6, n. 3, 10.
Holman v. Hansen—§ 3.32, n. 7.
Holman v. Mason City Auto Co.—§ 3.7, n. 8; § 3.8, n. 1; § 3.18, n. 6.
Holman v. Toten—§ 7.13, n. 7.
Holmberg v. Hardee—§ 3.8, n. 1.
Holmes v. Bybee—§ 7.15, n. 1.
Holmes v. Gravenhorst—§ 4.40; § 4.40, n. 2; § 4.39, n. 6.
Holmes v. Grant—§ 3.4, n. 7.
Holmes Case—§ 4.41.
Holsclaw v. Catalina Sav. & Loan Ass'n—§ 5.33, n. 33.
Holsonback v. First State Bank of Albertville—§ 5.29, n. 3.
Holt v. Citizens Central Bank—§ 7.21, n. 2.
Holt v. Queen City Loan & Inv., Inc.—§ 5.31, n. 7.
Home Bldg. Corp. v. Ventura Corp.—§ 12.5, n. 19.
Home Building & Loan Ass'n v. Blaisdell—§ 8.3, n. 2.
Home Carpet Inc. v. Bob Antrim Homes, Inc.—§ 13.3, n. 36.
Home Federal Sav. and Loan Ass'n v. Dooley's of Tucson, Inc.—§ 4.13, n. 20, 21.
Home Federal Sav. & Loan Ass'n v. DePass—§ 12.10, n. 45.
Home Federal Sav. & Loan Ass'n of Palm Beach v. English—§ 5.24, n. 87.
Home Life Ins. Co. v. American Nat. Bank and Trust Co.—§ 4.35, n. 7.
Home Life Ins. Co. v. Elwell—§ 6.13, n. 2.
Home Mortg. Bank v. Ryan—§ 11.1, n. 5.
Home Owners' Loan Corp. v. Guaranty Title Trust Co.—§ 4.44, n. 1.
Home Owners' Loan Corp. v. Joseph—§ 4.31, n. 14.
Home Owners' Loan Corporation v. Collins—§ 6.17, n. 15; § 10.5, n. 5.
Home Owners' Loan Corporation v. Humphrey—§ 9.1, n. 9.
Home Owners' Loan Corporation v. Washington—§ 6.7, n. 4.
Home Owners' Loan Corporation v. Wood—§ 7.16, n. 33.
Home Owners' Loan Corporation of Washington, D. C., v. Dougherty—§ 10.5, n. 5.
Homer Nat. Bank v. Namie—§ 8.12, n. 14.
Homer Nat. Bank v. Tri-District Development Corp.—§ 12.3, n. 6.
Home Sav. Ass'n of Kansas City, F.A. v. State Bank of Woodstock—§ 12.10, n. 13, 33.

Home Sav. Bank of Upstate New York v. Baer Properties, Ltd.—§ 5.22, n. 25; § 5.24, n. 40.
Home Savings & Loan Ass'n v. Sullivan—§ 12.7, n. 14.
Home Sav. of America, F.A. v. Van Cleave Development Co., Inc.—§ 7.22, n. 10, 11, 12.
Home Sec. Corp. v. Gentry—§ 5.29, n. 24.
Home State Bank v. Johnson—§ 12.7, n. 8.
Homestead Sav. v. Darmiento—§ 7.21, n. 94; § 7.27, n. 2, 11, 31.
Home Unity Sav. and Loan Ass'n to Use of Kallish v. Balmos—§ 10.15, n. 6.
Honey v. Henry's Franchise Leasing Corp. of America—§ 3.29; § 3.29, n. 48.
Honore v. Lamar Insurance Co.—§ 4.13, n. 9, 15.
Hood v. Young—§ 5.7, n. 11.
Hood Oil Co. v. Moss—§ 7.21, n. 11.
Hool v. Rydholm—§ 9.8, n. 32.
Hooper v. Bail—§ 6.6, n. 9.
Hooper v. Capitol Life Ins. Co.—§ 10.11, n. 15.
Hooper v. Henry—§ 5.7, n. 3; § 10.2, n. 6.
Hopkins v. Warner—§ 5.4, n. 5; § 5.11, n. 5; § 5.13, n. 1.
Hopkins Mfg. Co. v. Ketterer—§ 6.7, n. 22.
Hopkinson v. Rolt—§ 12.7, n. 13.
Hopler v. Cutler—§ 9.1, n. 9.
Hoppe v. Phoenix Homes, Inc.—§ 10.1, n. 9.
Hopper v. Smyser—§ 3.8, n. 12; § 5.7, n. 4.
Hoppin v. Doty—§ 7.10, n. 15.
Hopping v. Baldridge—§ 3.2, n. 1.
Horicon State Bank v. Kant Lumber Co., Inc.—§ 7.17, n. 13.
Horizon Bank, N.A. v. Sigrist—§ 9.3, n. 11.
Horn v. Keteltas—§ 3.8, n. 9.
Horne v. Payne—§ 6.6, n. 32.
Hoskin v. Woodward—§ 4.4, n. 7.
Hostetter v. Inland Development Corp. of Montana—§ 13.3; § 13.3, n. 46, 47.
Hotel St. James Co., In re—§ 4.43, n. 4; § 8.18, n. 5.
Hougland, In re, 886 F.2d 1182—§ 8.15, n. 70.
Hougland, In re, 93 B.R. 718—§ 8.15, n. 59.
Houle v. Guilbeault—§ 4.5, n. 8.
House v. Carr—§ 6.11, n. 19.
House v. Scott—§ 12.7, n. 36.
House of Carpets, Inc. v. Mortgage Inv. Co.—§ 12.7, n. 11, 13.
Housing Mortgage Corporation v. Allied Construction—§ 12.7, n. 14, 29.
Housing Study Group v. Kemp—§ 11.2, n. 68.
Houston v. National Mut. Bldg. & Loan Ass'n—§ 7.5, n. 1.
Houston & B. V. Ry. Co. v. Hughes.—§ 4.10, n. 9.
Houston Lumber Co. v. Skaggs—§ 9.4, n. 2, 4, 7, 8.
Howard v. Bar Bell Land & Cattle Co.—§ 3.29, n. 32.

Howard v. Burns, 116 N.E. 703—§ 10.2, n. 3.
Howard v. Burns, 201 Ill.App. 579—§ 4.35, n. 49.
Howard v. Clark, 48 A. 656—§ 4.29, n. 30, 34.
Howard v. Clark, 45 A. 1042—§ 6.17, n. 12.
Howard v. Harris—§ 3.1, n. 7.
Howard v. Robbins, 63 N.E. 530—§ 5.3, n. 1; § 5.5, n. 7; § 5.7, n. 1; § 5.9, n. 4, 7.
Howard v. Robbins, 73 N.Y.S. 172—§ 5.4, n. 3.
Howard v. Shaw—§ 5.34, n. 17.
Howard v. Steen—§ 3.7, n. 2; § 3.8, n. 9.
Howe v. City Title Ins. Co.—§ 7.22, n. 37, 38.
Howell v. Baker—§ 7.12, n. 15.
Howell v. Butler—§ 2.3, n. 19.
Howell v. Continental Credit Corp.—§ 11.7, n. 36.
Howell v. Leavitt—§ 4.24, n. 19.
Howser v. Cruikshank—§ 7.2, n. 13; § 10.-12, n. 4.
Howze v. Dew—§ 4.45, n. 1.
Hoy v. Bramhall—§ 10.11, n. 15.
Hoyle v. Dickinson—§ 12.9, n. 12.
Hoyos Precsas, Matter of—§ 8.15, n. 5.
Hubard & Appleby v. Thacker—§ 5.18, n. 8.
Hubbard, In re, 89 B.R. 920—§ 10.7, n. 10.
Hubbard, In re, 23 B.R. 671—§ 8.15, n. 41.
Hubbard v. Ascutney Milldam Co.—§ 7.2, n. 12.
Hubbell v. Avenue Inv. Co.—§ 4.35, n. 3.
Hubbell v. Moulson—§ 4.27, n. 4, 11, 13.
Hubbell v. Sibley—§ 4.2, n. 10; § 7.4, n. 1.
Huckabee Auto Co., Matter of—§ 8.14, n. 55, 56.
Huckins v. Straw—§ 4.8, n. 1.
Huddleston v. Texas Commerce Bank–Dallas, N.A.—§ 8.12, n. 13.
Huderson, In re—§ 11.2, n. 30.
Hudkins v. Crim—§ 7.4, n. 4.
Hudnit v. Nash—§ 7.14, n. 1.
Hudson v. Dismukes—§ 10.2, n. 4; § 10.7, n. 12.
Hudson Bros. Com'n Co. v. Glencoe Sand & Gravel Co.—§ 6.7, n. 17.
Huff v. Farwell—§ 10.10, n. 11.
Huggins v. Dement—§ 3.30, n. 10; § 7.27, n. 1; § 7.26, n. 7.
Hughes v. Edwards—§ 3.9, n. 4.
Hughes v. Frisbye—§ 7.8, n. 10.
Hughes v. Holt—§ 12.11, n. 29.
Hughes v. Riggs—§ 7.16, n. 22.
Hughes v. Thweatt—§ 2.3, n. 9.
Hughes v. Tyler—§ 5.19, n. 38; § 5.20, n. 5.
Hughes v. Williams—§ 4.29, n. 6.
Hughes Co. v. Callahan—§ 10.5, n. 5.
Huguley v. Hall—§ 3.29, n. 12.
Huitink v. Thompson—§ 5.34, n. 15.
Hulbert v. Clark—§ 6.11, n. 18.
Hulinsky v. Parriott—§ 12.4, n. 30.
Hull, Matter of—§ 12.6, n. 5.

TABLE OF CASES

Hull v. Alaska Federal Sav. & Loan Ass'n of Juneau—§ 8.3, n. 22.
Hulm, In re, 738 F.2d 323—§ 8.17, n. 10, 11.
Hulm, In re, 45 B.R. 523—§ 8.17, n. 17.
Hulseman v. Dirks Land Co.—§ 4.2, n. 21.
Hulsman v. Deal—§ 3.10, n. 2.
Humble v. Curtis—§ 5.32, n. 5.
Humble Oil & Refining Co. v. Doerr—§ 3.2, n. 1, 2.
Hummell v. Republic Federal Sav. & Loan—§ 7.22, n. 8.
Hummer v. R. C. Huffman Const. Co.—§ 4.4, n. 26.
Humphries v. Fitzpatrick—§ 10.13, n. 19.
Humrich v. Dalzell—§ 4.28, n. 6.
Hungate v. Hetzer—§ 7.13, n. 12.
Hunt v. Gorenberg—§ 5.19, n. 6, 56.
Hunt v. Manville—§ 5.19, n. 6.
Hunt v. Townsend—§ 10.13, n. 7.
Hunter v. Bane—§ 3.8, n. 1.
Hunter v. Dennis—§ 7.2, n. 6.
Hunter's Estate, In re—§ 5.19, n. 38.
Huntingburg Production Credit Ass'n v. Griese—§ 2.3, n. 2, 15, 19; § 9.1, n. 6, 21.
Huntington v. Kneeland—§ 12.7, n. 11.
Huntington, N.Y., Town of v. Huntington Branch, N.A.A.C.P.—§ 11.5, n. 18.
Hurlburt v. Chrisman—§ 7.5, n. 9.
Hurley v. Estes and others—§ 6.11, n. 35.
Hurricane Resort Co., In re—§ 5.28, n. 21.
Hursey v. Hursey—§ 9.1, n. 4.
Hurst v. Flynn–Harris–Bullard Co.—§ 12.7, n. 23.
Hurst v. Merrifield—§ 5.15, n. 1.
Hurt, In re—§ 8.15, n. 41.
Huscheon v. Huscheon—§ 3.9, n. 3.
Hussey v. Hill—§ 6.16, n. 21.
Hussey v. Ragsdale—§ 5.3, n. 2; § 5.8, n. 9.
Hussman, In re—§ 8.15, n. 72.
Huston v. Lewis—§ 8.6, n. 9.
Huston v. Seeley—§ 7.2, n. 22.
Hutchins v. King—§ 4.7, n. 5.
Hutchison v. Bristol Court Properties, Ltd.—§ 7.22, n. 11.
Hutchison v. Page—§ 3.13, n. 6.
Hux v. Raben—§ 12.9, n. 23.
Huzzey v. Heffernan—§ 4.44, n. 3.
Hyatt v. Maryland Federal Sav. and Loan Ass'n—§ 12.9, n. 24, 28; § 12.10, n. 7, 58, 59, 60.
Hyde Park Thomson–Houston Light Co. v. Brown—§ 10.9, n. 17, 18.
Hyde Wholesale Dry Goods Co. v. Edwards—§ 5.4, n. 3.
Hyland's Estate v. Foote's Estate—§ 5.3, n. 2.
Hyman v. Hauff—§ 2.2, n. 3; § 12.7, n. 33.
Hynson, In re—§ 8.15, n. 50.

I

Idaco Lumber Co. v. Northwestern Sav. & Loan Ass'n—§ 12.6, n. 13.
Idaho First Nat. Bank v. Wells—§ 12.7, n. 14, 37.
Ideal Realty Co. v. Reese—§ 12.9, n. 24.
I.E. Associates v. Safeco Title Ins. Co., 216 Cal.Rptr. 438—§ 7.21, n. 62.
I.E. Associates v. Safeco Title Ins. Co., 204 Cal.Rptr. 340—§ 7.21, n. 62.
Iglehart v. Crane & Wesson—§ 10.9, n. 6; 10.10, n. 15; § 10.15, n. 2, 5.
Illini Federal Sav. and Loan Ass'n v. Doering—§ 8.1, n. 4.
Illinois Housing Development Authority v. LaSalle Nat. Bank—§ 8.5, n. 19.
Illinois Nat. Bank of Springfield v. Gwinn—§ 8.8, n. 15.
Illinois State Bank of Quincy, Ill. v. Yates—§ 5.28, n. 6; § 9.8, n. 23.
Illinois Trust Co. of Paris v. Bibo—§ 3.4, n. 8.
Imboden v. Hunter—§ 7.21, n. 50.
Imperial Coronado Partners, Ltd., In re—§ 6.2, n. 22, 24.
Imperial Fire Insurance Co. v. Bull—§ 4.13, n. 16; § 4.14, n. 7.
Imperial–Yuma Production Credit Ass'n v. Nussbaumer—§ 7.31, n. 3.
Income Realty & Mortg., Inc. v. Columbia Sav. and Loan Ass'n—§ 5.21, n. 32, 33; § 5.22, n. 14, 15.
Indemnity Ins. Co. of North America v. Lane Contracting Corp.—§ 10.4, n. 2.
Independence Federal Sav. and Loan Ass'n v. Davis—§ 5.24, n. 87.
Independence Village, Inc., In re—§ 3.19, n. 23.
Independent Trust Corp. v. Stan Miller, Inc.—§ 13.3, n. 43.
Indiana Inv. Co. v. Evens—§ 7.15, n. 26.
Indiana Mortg. and Realty Investors v. Peacock Const. Co.—§ 12.6, n. 45.
Indianapolis Morris Plan Corp. v. Karlen—§ 5.19, n. 50; § 5.20, n. 5.
Industrial Indem. Co. v. Anderson—§ 5.29, n. 13; § 5.31, n. 10.
Industrial Supply Corp. v. Bricker—§ 12.7, n. 11.
Ingell v. Fay—§ 4.4, n. 1.
Ingersoll v. Sawyer—§ 7.2, n. 19.
Ingersoll v. Somers Land Co.—§ 10.13, n. 7, 10, 19.
Ingersoll–Rand Financial Corp. v. Anderson—§ 5.31, n. 5.
Ingold v. Phoenix Assur. Co.—§ 6.7, n. 1.
Ingram v. Smith—§ 7.4, n. 12.
Inland Finance Co. v. Home Ins. Co.—§ 4.14, n. 2.
Inland Real Estate Corp. v. Oak Park Trust and Sav. Bank—§ 5.29, n. 3, 5; § 5.32, n. 17.
Inman v. Wearing—§ 7.4, n. 12.
Innoncente v. Guisti—§ 6.13, n. 1.
In re (see name of party)
Insley v. Webb—§ 5.19, n. 33.
Insurance Co. of North America v. Martin—§ 4.14, n. 8.

Interfirst Bank Dallas, N.A. v. United States Fidelity and Guar. Co.—§ 12.2, n. 44.
International Minerals and Min. Corp. v. Citicorp North America, Inc.—§ 12.3, n. 1.
International Paper Co. v. Priscilla Co.—§ 4.39, n. 1.
International State Bank v. Bray—§ 5.32, n. 30.
International Tel. & Tel. Corp. v. Envirco Services, Inc.—§ 12.6, n. 7.
Interstate Production Credit Ass'n v. MacHugh—§ 7.7, n. 51.
Inversiones Inmobiliarias Internacionales de Orlando Sociedad Anomina v. Barnett Bank of Cent. Florida, N.A.—§ 12.10, n. 13, 16, 51.
Investment Sales Diversified, Inc., In re—§ 5.35, n. 43.
Investment Service Co. v. Smither—§ 12.3, n. 48.
Investors Sav. & Loan Ass'n v. Ganz—§ 5.21, n. 16.
Investors Syndicate v. Smith—§ 4.2, n. 18; § 4.34, n. 19.
Inwood North Homeowners' Ass'n, Inc. v. Harris—§ 13.5, n. 18.
Iowa County Board of Supervisors v. Mineral Point R. Co.—§ 7.12, n. 2, 3, 6, 22, 24; § 7.14, n. 9.
Iowa Nat. Mut. Ins. Co. of Cedar Rapids, Iowa v. Central Mortg. & Inv. Co. of Colorado Springs—§ 5.4, n. 7.
IPI Liberty Village Associates, In re—§ 8.17, n. 14.
Irby, United States v.—§ 11.6, n. 78.
Ireland v. United States Mortg. & Trust Co.—§ 4.25, n. 5.
Irving Independent School Dist. v. Packard Properties, Ltd.—§ 11.7, n. 44.
Irwin v. Grogan-Cole—§ 5.17, n. 5.
Irwin Concrete, Inc. v. Sun Coast Properties, Inc.—§ 12.6, n. 25; § 12.7, n. 27.
Isaak v. Idaho First Nat. Bank—§ 2.3, n. 9.
Isam Mitchell & Co. v. Norwach—§ 7.2, n. 7.
Iser v. Herbert Mark Bldg. Corporation—§ 12.8, n. 9.
Island Financial, Inc. v. Ballman—§ 7.24, n. 19, 22, 23, 25; § 7.27, n. 2.
Island Pond Nat. Bank v. Lacroix—§ 5.28, n. 14.
ITT Diversified Credit Corp. v. First City Capital Corp.—§ 12.9, n. 7.
ITT Indus. Credit Co. v. Regan—§ 9.3, n. 2.
Ives v. Stone—§ 3.4, n. 7; § 3.14, n. 2.
Ivey, In re—§ 8.15, n. 66.
Ivory, In re—§ 8.15, n. 45.
Ivrey v. Karr—§ 7.21, n. 85.
Ivy Properties, Inc., In re—§ 5.28, n. 9, 34.

J

Jack Green's Fashions for Men-Big & Tall, Inc., In re—§ 10.9, n. 7.

Jack's Estate, In re—§ 13.6, n. 18.
Jackson, In re, 136 B.R. 797—§ 8.15, n. 59.
Jackson, In re, 76 B.R. 597—§ 8.17, n. 15.
Jackson v. Austin—§ 9.1, n. 9.
Jackson v. Blankenship—§ 7.21, n. 50.
Jackson v. Brandon Realty Co.—§ 4.5, n. 15.
Jackson v. Condict—§ 10.12, n. 1.
Jackson v. Klein—§ 7.20, n. 14; § 7.21, n. 67.
Jackson v. Lodge—§ 3.10, n. 2.
Jackson v. Lynch—§ 3.1, n. 5.
Jackson v. Maxwell—§ 3.21, n. 3.
Jackson v. Metropolitan Edison Co.—§ 7.27; § 7.27, n. 29; § 7.28; § 7.28, n. 19.
Jackson v. Reid—§ 9.2, n. 2.
Jackson v. Stickney—§ 5.34, n. 14, 22.
Jackson v. Weaver—§ 7.2, n. 7.
Jackson County Federal Sav. and Loan Ass'n v. Urban Planning, Inc.—§ 12.1, n. 29.
Jackson County Federal Sav. & Loan Ass'n v. Maduff Mortg. Corp.—§ 5.28, n. 40.
Jackson ex dem. Hendricks v. Andrews—§ 7.13, n. 14.
Jackson Investment Corp. v. Pittsfield Products, Inc.—§ 7.20, n. 12.
Jackson & Scherer, Inc. v. Washburn—§ 9.4, n. 4.
Jacobie v. Mickle—§ 7.14, n. 7.
Jacobs v. City Nat. Bank of Fort Smith, Smith—§ 12.8, n. 17.
Jacobs v. Phillippi—§ 3.27, n. 5.
Jacobsen v. Conlon—§ 12.6, n. 44.
Jacobsen v. Nieboer—§ 4.44, n. 2.
Jacobson v. First Nat. Bank of Bloomingdale—§ 12.3, n. 49.
Jacobson v. General Finance Corp.—§ 6.4, n. 14.
Jacobson v. McClanahan—§ 7.6, n. 15.
Jacobson v. Swan—§ 3.29, n. 33, 41.
Jaffe-Spindler Co. v. Genesco, Inc.—§ 4.4, n. 5.
Jager v. Vollinger—§ 5.5, n. 1; § 5.8, n. 9.
Jaggar v. Plunkett—§ 4.24, n. 13, 17.
Jahnke v. Palomar Financial Corp.—§ 3.29, n. 1.
Jala Corp. v. Berkeley Sav. & Loan Ass'n of Newark—§ 6.3, n. 16.
Jamaica House, Inc., In re—§ 8.14, n. 9, 11, 28.
Jamaica Sav. Bank v. Lefkowitz—§ 4.19; § 4.19, n. 19.
James v. Brainard-Jackson & Co.—§ 7.12, n. 15.
James v. Ragin—§ 3.18, n. 5, 8; § 3.19, n. 2.
James v. Van Horn—§ 12.4, n. 26.
James B. Sheehan Bldg. & Loan Ass'n v. Scanlon—§ 6.16, n. 5, 6.
James Wilson Associates, Matter of—§ 8.14, n. 76.
Jamieson v. Bruce—§ 4.1, n. 6.
Janke v. Chace—§ 10.9, n. 7.
Janus Properties, Inc. v. First Florida Bank, N.A.—§ 6.17, n. 10.

TABLE OF CASES

Jarchow v. Transamerica Title Ins. Co.—§ 7.22, n. 44.
Jardine, In re—§ 8.16, n. 9.
Jarrett v. Holland—§ 7.13, n. 15.
Jarvis v. Woodruff—§ 7.5, n. 6.
Jason v. Eyres—§ 3.1, n. 3.
Jasper State Bank v. Braswell—§ 4.24, n. 1, 12.
Jayson Investments, Inc. v. Kemp—§ 13.4, n. 8.
J & B Schoenfeld Fur Merchants, Inc. v. Kilbourne & Donohue, Inc.—§ 5.29, n. 14.
Jeferne, Inc. v. Capanegro—§ 7.6, n. 7, 13.
Jeffers, Matter of—§ 8.18, n. 19.
Jeffers v. Pease—§ 4.5, n. 6.
Jefferson Federal Sav. and Loan Ass'n v. Berks Title Ins. Co.—§ 7.31, n. 12.
Jeffery v. Seven Seventeen Corp.—§ 7.6, n. 3, 18.
Jeffrey Towers, Inc. v. Straus—§ 2.2, n. 3.
Jeffries v. Georgia Residential Finance Authority—§ 7.28, n. 31.
Jehle v. Brooks—§ 4.31, n. 1.
Jelic v. Sears Mortg. Corp.—§ 7.31, n. 1.
Jeminson v. Montgomery Real Estate & Co., 240 N.W.2d 205—§ 12.11; § 12.11, n. 14.
Jeminson v. Montgomery Real Estate & Co., 210 N.W.2d 10—§ 5.29, n. 27; § 12.11, n. 14.
Jenkins, In re, 36 B.R. 788—§ 8.14, n. 11, 28.
Jenkins, In re, 14 B.R. 748—§ 8.15, n. 40.
Jenkins, In re, 13 B.R. 721—§ 8.18, n. 19.
Jenkins v. Eldredge—§ 3.15, n. 8.
Jenkins v. Moyse—§ 8.5, n. 20.
Jenkins v. Thyer—§ 7.5, n. 13; § 7.6, n. 3, 8, 18.
Jenkins v. Wise—§ 3.29; § 3.29, n. 9, 32; § 5.21, n. 25.
Jenks v. Hart Cedar & Lumber Co.—§ 4.9, n. 2.
Jenks v. Shaw—§ 5.34, n. 17.
Jensen v. Dalton—§ 3.29, n. 51.
Jensen v. Duke—§ 4.44, n. 6.
Jensen v. Schreck—§ 3.28, n. 8; § 3.30, n. 13.
Jensen v. Turnage—§ 11.2, n. 43, 45.
Jerome v. McCarter—§ 7.14, n. 1, 8.
Jersey City Medical Center, In re—§ 8.14, n. 99.
Jesco, Inc. v. Home Life Ins. Co.—§ 12.4, n. 29.
Jessee v. First Nat. Bank of Atlanta—§ 10.1, n. 16.
Jesz v. Geigle—§ 3.32, n. 16.
Jewett v. Hamlin—§ 8.1, n. 2.
J. G. Plumbing Service, Inc. v. Coastal Mortg. Co.—§ 12.6, n. 28, 38.
J.H. Dowling, Inc. v. First Federal Sav. and Loan Ass'n of Perry—§ 9.3, n. 5.
J. H. Magill Lumber Co. v. Lane-White Lumber Co.—§ 5.3, n. 2.

J. H. Morris, Inc. v. Indian Hills, Inc.—§ 7.21, n. 24, 25, 27.
J. I. Case Co. v. Borak—§ 12.3, n. 56.
J. I. Kislak Mortg. Corp. of Del. v. William Matthews Builder, Inc.—§ 12.7; § 12.7, n. 14, 26.
Jim Walter Homes, Inc. v. Bowling—§ 12.4, n. 28.
Jinkins v. Chambers—§ 7.21, n. 6.
JLJ, Inc., In re—§ 5.28, n. 4.
J. M. Realty Inv. Corp. v. Stern—§ 9.8, n. 6.
J. N. A. Realty Corp. v. Cross Bay Chelsea, Inc.—§ 7.7, n. 10.
Jo Ann Homes at Bellmore, Inc. v. Dworetz—§ 2.1, n. 5.
John Deere Plow Co. of Moline v. Tuinstra—§ 5.10, n. 5.
John Hancock Mut. Life Ins. Co. v. Bruening Farms Corp.—§ 11.6, n. 69.
John Hancock Mutual Life Ins. Co., United States v.—§ 8.4, n. 17, 18.
John McMenamy Inv. & Real Estate Co. v. Dawley—§ 4.43, n. 10.
Johns v. Church—§ 2.4, n. 9.
Johns v. Moore—§ 4.27, n. 2; § 4.28, n. 1; § 4.31, n. 12.
Johns-Manville Corp., In re—§ 8.14, n. 61.
Johnson, Ex parte—§ 9.2, n. 10.
Johnson, In re—§ 8.15, n. 45.
Johnson v. Bratton—§ 4.6, n. 6.
Johnson v. Cherry—§ 3.8, n. 5, 6, 9; § 3.18, n. 9; § 3.19, n. 7, 9.
Johnson v. Clark—§ 4.44, n. 6.
Johnson v. Cornett—§ 5.28, n. 15.
Johnson v. Donnell—§ 7.10, n. 9.
Johnson v. Elmen—§ 5.7, n. 6, 8.
Johnson v. First Nat. Bank of Montevideo, Minn.—§ 8.13, n. 33; § 8.17, n. 3, 4.
Johnson v. Fugate—§ 9.1, n. 17.
Johnson v. Hosford—§ 4.30, n. 1.
Johnson v. Howe—§ 5.33, n. 5.
Johnson v. HUD—§ 6.4; § 6.4, n. 29.
Johnson v. Jefferson Standard Life Ins. Co.—§ 7.16, n. 30.
Johnson v. Johnson—§ 6.12, n. 20, 21.
Johnson v. LaPorte Bank & Trust Co.—§ 4.34, n. 21.
Johnson v. Lowman—§ 6.11, n. 16.
Johnson v. Masterson—§ 5.31, n. 16.
Johnson v. Maxwell—§ 3.32, n. 13.
Johnson v. Midland Bank and Trust Co.—§ 6.7, n. 1; § 12.8, n. 9, 13.
Johnson v. National Bank of Commerce—§ 3.18, n. 9.
Johnson v. Rutoskey—§ 3.29, n. 58.
Johnson v. Sherman—§ 4.26, n. 7.
Johnson v. Smith—§ 8.6, n. 8.
Johnson v. Sowell—§ 5.9, n. 3; § 5.32, n. 13.
Johnson v. Tootle—§ 10.7, n. 2.
Johnson v. United States Dept. of Agriculture—§ 7.24, n. 27; § 7.25, n. 3, 30; § 7.26, n. 14; § 7.28, n. 1; § 11.6, n. 83.
Johnson v. Zink—§ 5.3, n. 1, 8; § 5.9, n. 3, 7; § 10.2, n. 3; § 10.8, n. 4.

TABLE OF CASES

Johnson, Wilson and Dillon, In re—§ 8.18, n. 53.
John Spry Lumber Co. v. Sault Sav. Bank, Loan & Trust Co.—§ 12.5, n. 3.
John Stepp, Inc. v. First Federal Sav. and Loan Ass'n of Miami—§ 7.2, n. 2.
Johnston v. Farmers and Merchants Bank—§ 2.1, n. 4.
Johnstone v. Mills, 22 B.R. 753—§ 5.28, n. 28, 29; § 5.29, n. 4; § 5.33, n. 3, 7.
Johnstone v. Mills, 20 B.R. 259—§ 5.34, n. 30; § 5.35, n. 32, 43, 45, 46, 50.
Johnston & Stewart v. Riddle—§ 4.38, n. 3.
John Wagner Associates v. Hercules, Inc.—§ 12.4, n. 10.
Jones, In re, 152 B.R. 155—§ 8.15, n. 70.
Jones, In re, 20 B.R. 988—§ 8.17, n. 11.
Jones v. Alfred H. Mayer Co.—§ 11.5; § 11.5, n. 1.
Jones v. American Coin Portfolios, Inc.—§ 6.6, n. 28.
Jones v. Approved Bancredit Corp.—§ 5.29, n. 26.
Jones v. Bates—§ 5.10, n. 7.
Jones v. Black—§ 4.45, n. 3.
Jones v. Brinson—§ 3.6, n. 4; § 3.18, n. 7.
Jones v. Burr—§ 3.32, n. 10.
Jones v. Garcia—§ 7.22, n. 3.
Jones v. Great Southern Fireproof Hotel Co.—§ 12.4, n. 2, 18; § 12.5, n. 3, 6.
Jones v. Kingsey—§ 4.44, n. 6.
Jones v. Parker—§ 9.1, n. 12.
Jones v. Rhodes—§ 5.9, n. 3.
Jones v. Sacramento Sav. & Loan Ass'n—§ 12.9, n. 37.
Jones v. Third Nat. Bank of Sedalia—§ 3.13, n. 1.
Jones v. Titus—§ 5.28, n. 9.
Jones v. Turnage—§ 11.6, n. 65.
Jones v. United Sav. and Loan Ass'n—§ 5.32, n. 15.
Jones v. Williams—§ 7.16, n. 4.
Jordan, In re—§ 6.9, n. 21, 30.
Jorgensen v. Endicott Trust Co.—§ 7.13, n. 11; § 7.15, n. 23; § 7.17, n. 9, 12.
Joseph v. Donovan, 171 A. 24—§ 9.1, n. 13.
Joseph v. Donovan, 157 A. 638—§ 3.36, n. 5.
Joseph v. Lake Michigan Mortg. Co.—§ 12.3, n. 19.
Josephs, In re—§ 8.15, n. 41.
Joslyn v. Parlin—§ 2.2, n. 10.
Joyce v. Dauntz—§ 10.7, n. 7.
Joyce v. Hawtof—§ 5.19, n. 16.
J. R. Meade Co. v. Forward Const. Co.—§ 13.3, n. 33.
Judd v. First Federal Sav. and Loan Ass'n of Indianapolis—§ 4.18, n. 9, 13, 41.
Judkins v. Woodman—§ 4.4, n. 1.
Justice v. Arab Lumber and Supply, Inc.—§ 12.4, n. 19.
Justice v. Valley Nat. Bank—§ 8.15, n. 41, § 8.16, n. 31.
J & W Wall Systems, Inc. v. Shawmut First Bank & Trust Co.—§ 12.4, n. 29; § 13.3, n. 31.

K

Kable v. Mitchell—§ 7.17, n. 3.
Kaczmarczyk, In re—§ 8.15, n. 72.
Kadish v. Kallof—§ 2.3, n. 19.
Kahn v. McConnell—§ 10.7, n. 13.
Kaiman Realty, Inc. v. Carmichael—§ 3.29, n. 11.
Kaiser v. Idleman—§ 6.12, n. 20.
Kaiser Industries Corp. v. Taylor—§ 3.38; § 3.38, n. 12.
Kal-Cen Corp. v. Beztak Properties, Inc.—§ 5.27, n. 1.
Kalen v. Gelderman—§ 5.34, n. 9.
Kallenbach v. Lake Publications, Inc.—§ 3.32, n. 16.
Kamaole Resort Twenty-One v. Ficke Hawaiian Investments, Inc.—§ 12.8, n. 9.
KAM, Inc. v. White—§ 5.4, n. 5.
Kangas, In re—§ 8.17, n. 13.
Kankakee Federal Sav. and Loan Ass'n v. Mueller—§ 7.31, n. 3.
Kansas City Journal-Post Co, In re—§ 9.3, n. 4.
Kansas City Mortg. Co. v. Crowell—§ 5.34, n. 9.
Kansas Mortg. Co. v. Weyerhaeuser—§ 12.4, n. 26.
Kansas Sav. and Loan Ass'n v. Rich Eckel Const. Co., Inc.—§ 5.17, n. 5.
Kansas State Bank in Holton v. Citizens Bank of Windsor—§ 5.35, n. 20, 26.
Kanters v. Kotick—§ 12.2, n. 24.
Kaplan v. Ruffin—§ 7.14, n. 12; § 7.31, n. 2.
Karas v. Wasserman—§ 7.7, n. 10.
Kardon v. National Gypsum Co.—§ 12.3, n. 56.
Karim v. Werner—§ 5.24, n. 33.
Karoutas v. HomeFed Bank—§ 7.21, n. 87.
Kartheiser v. Hawkins—§ 3.1, n. 11; § 3.6, n. 1; § 3.7, n. 2.
Kasal v. F.D.I.C.—§ 11.7; § 11.7, n. 40.
Kaski v. First Federal Sav. and Loan Ass'n of Madison—§ 11.6; § 11.6, n. 30.
Kass v. Weber—§ 8.3, n. 139.
Kassuba, Matter of—§ 3.18, n. 5.
Kaston v. Storey—§ 8.5, n. 10.
Katzenbach v. McClung—§ 5.24, n. 12, 14.
Kaufman v. Bernstein—§ 5.33, n. 1.
Kawauchi v. Tabata—§ 3.17, n. 8.
Kaw Valley State Bank & Trust Co. v. Riddle—§ 5.29, n. 25.
Kay v. Wood—§ 3.29, n. 34, 41.
Kaylor v. Kelsey—§ 4.24, n. 15.

TABLE OF CASES

Kayser-Roth Corp., Inc., United States v.—§ 4.47, n. 8.
Kearney Hotel Partners, In re—§ 4.35, n. 41.
Keech v. Hall—§ 4.22, n. 1, 2.
Keeler v. Richards Storage Corporation—§ 5.6, n. 1.
Keeline v. Clark—§ 4.32, n. 3.
Keese v. Parnell—§ 6.7, n. 10.
Keesee v. Fetzek—§ 3.32, n. 34.
Keil's Estate, In re—§ 10.3, n. 2.
Keith v. Day—§ 4.22, n. 21.
Keith v. El-Kareh—§ 11.4, n. 39.
Keith, County of v. Fuller—§ 2.1, n. 1.
Keithley v. Wood—§ 3.17, n. 3.
Keith, Mack, Lewis & Allison v. Boraks—§ 2.1, n. 5; § 5.29, n. 13.
Keith Young & Sons Const. Co. v. Victor Senior Citizens Housing, Inc.—§ 12.5, n. 19.
Keller v. Ashford—§ 5.5, n. 1; § 5.13, n. 1; § 5.19, n. 16, 21.
Kelleran v. Brown—§ 3.4, n. 8, 9.
Kelley v. Boettcher—§ 7.5, n. 5.
Kelley ex rel. Michigan Natural Resources Com'n v. Tiscornia—§ 4.49, n. 7.
Kelley/Lehr & Associates, Inc. v. O'Brien—§ 4.2, n. 1.
Kellogg v. Smith—§ 5.33, n. 10.
Kellogg Bros. Lumber Co. v. Mularkey—§ 9.4, n. 4, 7.
Kelly, In re—§ 8.15, n. 59.
Kelly v. Central Hanover Bank & Trust Co—§ 3.38, n. 7.
Kelly v. Hannan—§ 12.4, n. 35.
Kelly v. Hurt—§ 7.5, n. 1.
Kelly v. Johnson—§ 12.5; § 12.5, n. 3, 9.
Kelly v. Martin—§ 6.6, n. 10.
Kelly v. Middlesex Title Guarantee & Trust Co.—§ 5.35, n. 17.
Kelly v. Roberts—§ 4.2, n. 21.
Kelsey v. Welch—§ 7.12, n. 18.
Kelso v. Norton—§ 4.24, n. 1.
Kemp v. Thurmond—§ 12.7, n. 13.
Kemp v. Zions First Nat. Bank—§ 9.2, n. 2.
Kendrick v. Davis—§ 3.35, n. 1, 2, 4, 11.
Kenly v. Miracle Properties—§ 3.30, n. 12; § 7.27, n. 2.
Kennebec, Inc. v. Bank of the West—§ 7.27, n. 2.
Kennebec Sav. Bank v. Chandler—§ 8.3, n. 14.
Kennebunk Sav. Bank v. West—§ 2.1, n. 2.
Kennedy v. Betts—§ 12.10, n. 7.
Kennedy v. Columbia Lumber and Mfg. Co., Inc.—§ 12.11, n. 32.
Kenneth D. Collins Agency v. Hagerott—§ 12.4, n. 14.
Kennon v. Camp—§ 7.20, n. 12.
Kensington Court Associates v. Gullo—§ 6.6, n. 31.
Kent v. Pipia—§ 7.6, n. 7.
Kent v. Rhomberg—§ 5.19, n. 8, 50.
Kent v. Walter E. Heller & Co.—§ 12.3, n. 48.

Kent Farm Co. v. Hills—§ 7.7, n. 37.
Keokuk State Bank v. Eckley—§ 3.29, n. 1; § 3.28, n. 9, 11.
Kernochan v. New York Bowery Fire Ins. Co.—§ 4.13, n. 8, 16.
Kernohan v. Manss—§ 5.27, n. 6.
Kern Valley Bank v. Koehn—§ 6.11, n. 22.
Kerr v. Erickson—§ 4.44, n. 6.
Kerr v. Gilmore—§ 3.18, n. 6.
Kerr v. Miller—§ 8.6, n. 30.
Kerr Land & Livestock, Inc. v. Glaus—§ 6.19, n. 5.
Kerschensteiner v. Northern Michigan Land Co.—§ 7.4, n. 11.
Kerse v. Miller—§ 7.3, n. 7.
Kershaw Excavating Co. v. City Systems, Inc.—§ 13.3, n. 43.
Kerwin-White, In re—§ 8.16, n. 28.
Kessler, In re—§ 8.15, n. 56.
Kessler v. Liberty Ins. Bank—§ 2.3, n. 19.
Kessler v. Tarrats—§ 5.6, n. 8.
Ketchum, Konkel, Barrett, Nickel & Austin v. Heritage Mountain Development Co.—§ 12.4, n. 25, 27.
Key v. Gregory—§ 3.29, n. 8.
Key West Wharf & Coal Co. v. Porter—§ 5.17, n. 6.
Kham & Nate's Shoes No. 2, Inc. v. First Bank of Whiting—§ 8.14, n. 86.
Kidd's Estate, In re—§ 4.35, n. 21.
Kiefer v. Fortune Federal Sav. and Loan Ass'n—§ 5.24, n. 40.
Kilpatrick v. Germania Life Ins. Co.—§ 6.3, n. 1.
Kimball v. Lockwood & Smith—§ 4.22, n. 4, 7, 10, 15.
Kimbell Foods, Inc., United States v.—§ 11.6; § 11.6, n. 51.
Kincaid v. Alderson—§ 5.10, n. 3.
Kincaid v. Landing Development Corp.—§ 12.11, n. 5.
Kinee v. Abraham Lincoln Federal Sav. and Loan Ass'n—§ 4.19, n. 6.
King v. Crone—§ 3.8, n. 17.
King v. First Nat. Bank of Fairbanks—§ 8.8, n. 13.
King v. Housatonic R. Co.—§ 4.21, n. 5, 7.
King v. King—§ 3.1, n. 1; § 8.5, n. 13.
King v. Smith—§ 4.10, n. 4.
King v. State Mutual Fire Insurance Co.—§ 4.13, n. 9.
King v. Whitely—§ 5.7, n. 4.
King v. Zagorski—§ 8.8, n. 18.
King County Trust Co. v. Derx—§ 5.9, n. 17.
Kinkead v. Peet—§ 4.29, n. 15.
Kinna v. Smith—§ 5.27, n. 11.
Kinner v. World Sav. and Loan Ass'n—§ 12.7, n. 29.
Kinney v. Heuring—§ 5.2, n. 5.
Kinnison v. Guaranty Liquidating Corp.—§ 4.2, n. 21; § 4.35, n. 15.
Kipf v. United States—§ 12.11, n. 41.
Kircher v. Schalk—§ 4.6, n. 5.
Kirk, In re—§ 12.7, n. 14, 37.

TABLE OF CASES

Kirk v. United States—§ 12.11, n. 44.
Kirk v. Welch—§ 5.10, n. 8.
Kirker v. Wylie—§ 5.10, n. 15.
Kirkham v. Dupont—§ 7.2, n. 14.
Kirklevington Associates, Ltd. v. Kirklevington North Associates, Ltd.—§ 8.6, n. 28.
Kitchell v. Mudgett—§ 10.7, n. 6, 10.
Kitchen v. Herring—§ 12.3, n. 35.
Kittermaster v. Brossard—§ 3.1, n. 37.
Kittle v. Sand Mountain Bank—§ 2.1, n. 2.
Kitzer v. Kitzer—§ 2.3, n. 21.
Kjar v. Brimley—§ 3.17, n. 8; § 3.19, n. 3.
Kjerulf, In re—§ 8.16, n. 3.
Klapworth v. Dressler—§ 5.13, n. 1.
Klein, In re—§ 8.15, n. 59.
Kleven v. Brunner—§ 7.12, n. 31.
Kline v. McGuckin—§ 3.4, n. 12; § 3.13, n. 7; § 3.14, n. 2.
Kling v. Ghilarducci—§ 4.2, n. 1; § 7.17, n. 17.
Klinke v. Samuels—§ 8.3, n. 50.
Kloepping v. Stellmacher—§ 7.16, n. 12.
Kloos v. Jacobson—§ 12.5, n. 19.
Kloster-Madsen, Inc. v. Tafi's, Inc.—§ 12.4, n. 25.
Klotz v. Klotz—§ 10.6, n. 1.
Kluge v. Fugazy—§ 5.28, n. 21.
K.M. Young & Associates, Inc. v. Cieslik—§ 3.29, n. 11, 32.
Knapp v. Victory Corp.—§ 4.13, n. 11, 12.
Knauss v. Miles Homes, Inc.—§ 3.35, n. 8.
Kneeland v. Moore—§ 6.16, n. 3; § 6.17, n. 6.
Kneen v. Halin—§ 9.1, n. 9, 11.
Knepper v. Monticello State Bank—§ 8.3, n. 1.
Knevel, In re—§ 5.1, n. 4.
Knickerbocker v. McKindley Coal & Mining Co.—§ 4.41, n. 7.
Knickerbocker Ice Co. v. Benson—§ 4.26, n. 2.
Knickerbocker Oil Corporation v. Richfield Oil Corporation of New York—§ 4.39, n. 23.
Knight v. Hilton—§ 4.24, n. 1; § 7.5, n. 8.
Knight Const. Co., Inc. v. Barnett Mortg. Trust—§ 12.6, n. 26.
Knollenberg v. Nixon—§ 6.7, n. 24.
Knott v. Shepherdstown Manuf'g Co.—§ 3.38, n. 5.
Knowlton v. Walker—§ 7.5, n. 1.
Knox v. Farmers' State Bank of Merkel—§ 6.6, n. 17.
Koch, In re—§ 8.16, n. 27.
Koch v. Kiron State Bank of Kiron—§ 4.45, n. 6.
Kocher, In re—§ 8.16, n. 18.
Koehler v. Pioneer Am. Ins. Co.—§ 7.21, n. 15.
Koehm v. Kuhn—§ 6.6, n. 19.
Koenig v. Van Reken—§ 3.8, n. 5, 6; § 3.19, n. 7, 9, 14.
Koerner v. Willamette Iron Works—§ 7.10, n. 18; § 7.15, n. 27.

Kohler v. Gilbert—§ 3.7, n. 2; § 3.20, n. 3.
Kohler v. Snow Village, Inc.—§ 13.6, n. 16.
Kohn v. Beggi—§ 5.19, n. 8.
Kollen v. Sooy—§ 5.10, n. 15.
Konoff v. Lantini—§ 5.10, n. 5; § 10.2, n. 2; § 10.14, n. 4.
Kooistra v. Gibford—§ 4.38, n. 6.
Koopmans, In re—§ 8.14, n. 20.
Kopper v. Dyer—§ 7.4, n. 4, 6.
Kortright v. Cady—§ 6.6, n. 15; § 6.7, n. 9, 15.
Kosloff v. Castle—§ 3.29, n. 27, 28.
Kottcamp v. Fleet Real Estate Funding Corp.—§ 7.27, n. 2, 38.
Kouros v. Sewell—§ 7.21, n. 1, 7.
Kozan v. Levin—§ 5.7, n. 16, § 5.16, n. 3.
Kramer v. Relgov Realty Co.—§ 8.3, n. 50.
Kramer v. Trustees of Farmers' and Mechanics' Bank of Steubenville—§ 12.7, n. 10.
Kranz v. Centropolis Crusher, Inc.—§ 12.4, n. 33; § 12.7, n. 22.
Kratz, In re—§ 8.19, n. 9.
Kraus v. Hartung, 162 A. 724—§ 7.14, n. 6, 8.
Krause v. Hartung, 155 A. 621—§ 7.14, n. 1, 9.
Kreiensieck v. Cook—§ 3.6, n. 1; § 3.8, n. 9; § 3.11, n. 1.
Kremer v. Rule—§ 7.16, n. 34.
Kremser v. Tonokaboni—§ 2.1, n. 19.
Krentz v. Johnson—§ 3.29, n. 1.
Kreshek v. Sperling—§ 4.15; § 4.15, n. 9.
Kreutz v. Wolff—§ 5.29, n. 27.
Krick v. Zemel—§ 7.12, n. 27.
Kristal, In re—§ 8.3, n. 59.
Krochta v. Green—§ 7.12, n. 31.
Kroh Bros. Development Co., In re, 101 B.R. 114—§ 5.28, n. 6.
Kroh Bros. Development Co., In re, 88 B.R. 997—§ 6.2, n. 6, 22, 26.
Krone v. Goff—§ 4.11, n. 7, 10, 12.
Kronisch v. Howard Sav. Inst.—§ 4.18, n. 9, 11, 27, 28.
Krutz v. Gardner—§ 7.5, n. 22.
K & S Partnership v. Continental Bank, N.A.—§ 5.35, n. 28.
Kudokas v. Balkus—§ 3.29, n. 51.
Kuhn v. National Bank of Holton—§ 10.7, n. 3, 4.
Kuhn v. Shreeve—§ 6.11, n. 34, 45.
Kuhn Const. Co., Inc., In re—§ 8.18, n. 19.
Kuhne v. Gau—§ 2.1, n. 4, 17.
Kupiec v. Republic Federal Savings & Loan Ass'n—§ 11.6, n. 21.
Kurth Ranch, In re—§ 4.35, n. 31; § 8.18, n. 54.
Kurtz v. Ripley County State Bank—§ 7.21, n. 1.
KVR Realties, Inc. v. Treasure Star, Inc.—§ 12.9, n. 56.
Kyner v. Clark—§ 5.10, n. 6.

Kynerd v. United States Dept. of Housing and Urban Development—§ 12.11, n. 45.

L

Laber v. Minassian—§ 7.6, n. 5.
Labor Discount Center, Inc. v. State Bank & Trust Co. of Wellston—§ 12.3, n. 1.
La Boutique of Beauty Academy, Inc. v. Meloy—§ 7.7, n. 3.
La Brada, In re—§ 8.15, n. 39.
Lacentra Trucking Inc. v. Flagler Federal Sav. and Loan Ass'n of Miami—§ 12.4, n. 27.
Lackawanna Trust & Safe Deposit Co. v. Gomeringer—§ 10.2, n. 5; § 10.7, n. 6; § 10.8, n. 6.
Laclede Inv. Corp. v. Kaiser—§ 2.1, n. 9.
Lacy, In re—§ 3.32, n. 26, 30.
Ladd v. Parmer—§ 4.29, n. 26, 30.
Ladner, Matter of—§ 12.8, n. 15, 17.
Ladner v. Hogue Lumber & Supply Co.—§ 12.9, n. 7.
Ladue v. Detroit etc. Co.—§ 2.1, n. 1; § 4.2, n. 14; § 12.7, n. 16, 39.
LaFarge Fire Insurance Co. v. Bell—§ 10.10, n. 18; § 10.13, n. 24.
LaGrange Federal Sav. and Loan Ass'n v. Rock River Corp.—§ 5.11, n. 2.
Laguna, In re—§ 8.15, n. 77.
Lahaina-Maui Corp. v. Tau Tet Hew—§ 12.9, n. 23.
Laidley v. Aikin—§ 9.1, n. 6, 24.
Laight v. Idaho First Nat. Bank—§ 12.10, n. 8, 47.
La Jolla Mortg. Fund v. Rancho El Cajon Associates—§ 8.14, n. 10, 20.
Lake Geneva, City of v. States Imp. Co.—§ 12.2, n. 11.
Lake Hillsdale Estates, Inc. v. Galloway—§ 7.21, n. 8.
Lakeshore Apartments of Ft. Oglethorpe, II, Ltd., In re—§ 8.14, n. 27.
Lake Townsend Aviation, Inc., Matter of—§ 6.13, n. 6, 16.
Lake View Trust & Sav. Bank v. Filmore Const. Co., Inc.—§ 12.2, n. 17.
Lakhaney v. Anzelone—§ 5.29, n. 2.
Lally, In re—§ 8.17, n. 3.
Lamb v. Montague—§ 5.9, n. 7; § 10.8, n. 7.
Lamb v. Tucker—§ 5.6, n. 1; § 5.7, n. 11.
Lambert v. Barker—§ 5.28, n. 6; § 5.33, n. 6, 10, 13, 27.
Lambert v. Superior Court (MacEwen)—§ 12.5, n. 30.
Lamberth, Estate of v. Commissioner—§ 3.34, n. 16.
Lamka v. Donnelly—§ 5.8, n. 5, 7.
Lammey v. Producers Livestock Credit Corp.—§ 12.8, n. 6.
Lamoille County Sav. Bank & Trust Co. v. Belden—§ 10.7, n. 9; § 12.7, n. 11.
Lamont v. Cheshire—§ 7.13, n. 20.

Lamont v. Evjen—§ 3.32, n. 12.
Lampert Yards, Inc. v. Thompson-Wetterling Const. & Realty, Inc.—§ 6.17, n. 2, 10; § 6.19, n. 10; § 12.10, n. 11, 34.
Lamprey v. Nudd—§ 5.28, n. 18.
Lamson & Co. v. Abrams—§ 4.21, n. 8.
Lancaster Sec. Inv. Corp. v. Kessler—§ 7.21, n. 62.
Land, In re—§ 8.15, n. 40.
Landas Fertilizer Co. v. Hargreaves—§ 12.4, n. 35.
Land Associates, Inc. v. Becker—§ 5.24, n. 37; § 7.1, n. 7; § 7.2, n. 15; § 7.13, n. 9, 18; § 7.15, n. 34.
Landau v. Western Pennsylvania Nat. Bank—§ 4.27, n. 15; § 4.28, n. 4; § 4.29, n. 4; § 4.32, n. 1; § 12.9, n. 51.
Land Finance Corporation v. Giorgio—§ 4.31, n. 5.
Landis to Use of Security Savings & Trust Co. v. Robacker—§ 5.34, n. 17.
Landmark Bank v. Ciaravino—§ 2.1, n. 2; § 6.6, n. 34; § 10.6, n. 2, 7, 10.
Landmark Financial Services v. Hall—§ 8.15, n. 72, 77.
Landmark KCI Bank v. Marshall—§ 5.19, n. 33.
Landmark Land Co., Inc. v. Sprague—§ 5.28, n. 4, 40.
Landmark Park & Associates, United States v.—§ 8.18, n. 24, 35, 36; § 11.6, n. 85.
Land Title Bank & Trust Co. v. Schenck—§ 5.35, n. 7.
Lane, In re—§ 8.14, n. 9.
Langan v. Iverson—§ 5.6, n. 1.
Langdon v. Paul—§ 4.4, n. 4; § 4.6, n. 3.
Langel v. Moore, 168 N.E. 57—§ 10.13, n. 19.
Langel v. Moore, 164 N.E. 118—§ 10.13, n. 15.
Langenes v. Bullinger—§ 3.32, n. 26.
Langerman v. Puritan Dining Room Co.—§ 12.7, n. 11.
Langeveld v. L.R.Z.H. Corp.—§ 10.2, n. 1.
Langley v. F.D.I.C.—§ 5.29, n. 31; § 11.7, n. 21.
Lanier v. Mandeville Mills—§ 6.7, n. 19.
Lanier v. Romm—§ 6.7, n. 1.
Lansing v. Goelet—§ 7.11, n. 2; § 8.1, n. 4.
Lantana Motel, In re—§ 12.9, n. 46, 47.
Lapaglia, In re—§ 8.15, n. 24.
Lapis Enterprises, Inc. v. International Blimpie Corp.—§ 5.32, n. 16.
La Plant v. Beechley—§ 7.6, n. 8.
Lapp, In re—§ 8.15, n. 54.
Larsen, In re—§ 3.29, n. 32.
Larsen v. United Federal Sav. and Loan Ass'n of Des Moines—§ 12.11, n. 30.
Larson v. Orfield—§ 4.34, n. 14.
La Sala v. American Sav. & Loan Ass'n—§ 5.22, n. 29.
Lassen v. Vance—§ 9.1, n. 12.
Last v. Winkel—§ 4.43, n. 2.

TABLE OF CASES

Las Vegas Ranch Club v. Bank of Nevada—§ 6.6, n. 32.
Lathrop v. Bell Federal Sav. and Loan Ass'n—§ 4.18, n. 9.
La Throp v. Bell Federal Sav. & Loan Ass'n—§ 4.18, n. 10, 23.
Laub v. Warren Guarantee Title & Mortgage Co.—§ 7.16, n. 5, 11.
Laudman v. Ingram—§ 5.7, n. 6, 9.
Laufman v. Oakley Bldg. & Loan Co.—§ 11.5; § 11.5, n. 27.
Laughlin v. Walters—§ 7.24, n. 27; § 7.25, n. 18.
Laurence J. Rich & Associates v. First Interstate Mortg. Co. of Colorado—§ 12.4, n. 14.
Lavenson v. Standard Soap Co.—§ 4.4, n. 22.
Laventall v. Pomerantz—§ 4.46; § 4.46, n. 2.
Law v. Edgecliff Realty Co.—§ 7.7, n. 7.
Law v. United States—§ 7.24, n. 8; § 7.26, n. 8; § 3.30, n. 4, 10.
Lawrence v. Cornell—§ 7.17, n. 13.
Lawrence v. DuBois—§ 3.19, n. 9.
Lawrence v. Knap—§ 5.27, n. 11.
Lawrence v. Murphy—§ 5.28, n. 18.
Lawson v. Estate of Slaybaugh—§ 5.28, n. 22.
Lawson v. Smith—§ 3.30, n. 12; § 7.27, n. 2.
Lawson, People v.—§ 8.3, n. 130.
Lawson Pressed Brick & Tile Co. v. Ross-Kellar Triple Pressure Brick Mach. Co.—§ 9.6, n. 6.
Lawyers Mortgage Co., Matter of—§ 5.35, n. 15.
Lawyers Title & Guaranty Co., In re—§ 5.35, n. 15.
Lawyers' Title & Guaranty Co. v. Claren—§ 4.46, n. 13.
Lawyers' Title Guaranty Fund v. Sanders—§ 10.1, n. 8.
Lawyers Title Ins. Corp. v. Edmar Const. Co., Inc.—§ 10.4, n. 1, 4.
Laylin v. Knox—§ 2.3, n. 9.
Lazarus v. Caesar—§ 7.21, n. 36.
Lazzareschi Inv. Co. v. San Francisco Federal Sav. & Loan Ass'n—§ 6.1, n. 8; § 6.2; § 6.2, n. 13.
L.B. Nelson Corp. of Tucson v. Western American Financial Corp.—§ 12.8, n. 10.
Leach v. Hall—§ 10.3, n. 9.
Leben v. Nassau Sav. and Loan Ass'n—§ 12.3, n. 52.
Leche v. Ponca City Production Credit Ass'n—§ 12.7, n. 12, 37.
Le Doux v. Dettmering—§ 4.13, n. 9, 15.
Lee v. Evans—§ 3.15, n. 5, 15.
Lee v. Lee—§ 7.21, n. 73.
Lee v. Mercantile First Nat. Bank of Doniphan—§ 10.14, n. 8.
Lee v. Navarro Sav. Ass'n—§ 12.3, n. 60.
Lee v. Newman—§ 5.6, n. 1.
Lee v. O'Leary—§ 5.4, n. 3.
Leeds v. Gifford—§ 4.27, n. 18.
Leedy v. Ellsworth Const. Co.—§ 5.31, n. 3.

LeFevre, State ex rel. v. Stubbs—§ 5.1, n. 4; § 5.3, n. 4, 8.
Legg v. Allen—§ 3.29, n. 1.
Lehner v. United States—§ 7.24, n. 27.
Leininger v. Merchants & Farmers Bank, Macon—§ 7.27, n. 2, 11.
Leipert v. R. C. Williams & Co.—§ 3.33, n. 30.
Leisure Villa Investors v. Life & Cas. Ins. Co. of Tennessee—§ 5.4, n. 1, 7; § 5.11, n. 6.
Leland v. Morrison—§ 7.5, n. 15.
Lemanski, Matter of—§ 5.28, n. 12.
LeMay, United States v.—§ 10.13, n. 2.
Lemon v. Nicolai—§ 5.22, n. 36.
Lemons & Associates, Inc., In re—§ 5.35, n. 47, 54.
Lenexa State Bank & Trust Co. v. Dixon—§ 7.12, n. 26; § 7.15, n. 7, 10, 14.
Lennartz v. Quilty—§ 5.34, n. 22.
Lenske v. Steinberg—§ 7.10, n. 12.
Lentz v. Stoflet—§ 10.1, n. 9.
Lentz Plumbing Co. v. Fee—§ 12.4, n. 35.
Leonard v. Brazosport Bank of Texas—§ 10.5, n. 3.
Leonard v. Pell—§ 7.5, n. 24; § 7.32, n. 11.
Leslie v. Smith—§ 7.10, n. 18.
Leslie , Inc. v. Solomon—§ 7.22, n. 17.
Lester v. Resolution Trust Corp.—§ 12.3, n. 40.
Lester v. United States—§ 8.8, n. 14.
Lett v. Grummer—§ 3.28, n. 10.
Levenson v. Barnett Bank of Miami—§ 12.3, n. 19, 26.
Levin v. Carney—§ 4.3, n. 1.
Leviston v. Swan—§ 7.16, n. 9.
Lewis v. Frank Love Limited—§ 3.2, n. 1.
Lewis v. Kirk—§ 5.34, n. 13.
Lewis v. Nangle—§ 7.2, n. 6.
Lewis v. Wells—§ 3.8, n. 15.
Leyden v. Lawrence—§ 4.13, n. 9.
L.H. & A. Realty Co., Inc., In re—§ 8.13, n. 32.
LHD Realty Corp., In re—§ 6.3, n. 2, 4, 9.
Libbey v. Tufts—§ 10.10, n. 2.
Libel v. Pierce—§ 3.9, n. 5.
Liberty Bank v. Talman Home Mortg. Corp.—§ 5.35, n. 6.
Liberty Loan Corp. of Illinois v. FNMA—§ 6.6, n. 19.
Liberty Mut. Ins. Co. v. Davis—§ 10.1, n. 1.
Liberty Mut. Ins. Co. v. Thunderbird Bank—§ 10.8, n. 1.
Liberty Nat. Bank & Trust Co. of Oklahoma City v. Kaibab Industries, Inc.—§ 12.6, n. 28; § 12.7, n. 14, 42.
Liberty Parts Warehouse, Inc. v. Marshall County Bank & Trust—§ 9.1, n. 4, 13.
Lichtstern v. Forehand—§ 5.9, n. 17.
Lichty v. Whitney—§ 6.7, n. 3.
Licursi v. Sweeney—§ 6.16, n. 19.
Lido Intern., Inc. v. Lambeth—§ 6.7, n. 1.
Lieberman, etc. v. Knight—§ 4.4, n. 14.

TABLE OF CASES

Lieberman Music Co. v. Hagen—§ 10.9, n. 14.
Life Ins. Co. of Virginia v. Hocroft Associates—§ 4.35, n. 5.
Life Sav. and Loan Ass'n v. Bryant—§ 3.33, n. 12; § 5.3, n. 2; § 12.9, n. 6, 43.
Lifgren v. Yeutter—§ 6.4, n. 28.
Light v. Equitable Mortg. Resources, Inc.—§ 12.10, n. 14.
Light v. Federal Land Bank of St. Louis—§ 7.8, n. 10.
Lillienstern v. First Nat. Bank—§ 2.1, n. 5.
Lillo v. Thee—§ 2.3, n. 1.
Lilly v. Palmer—§ 6.16, n. 12, 27.
Linbrook Realty Corporation v. Rogers—§ 5.9, n. 5; § 5.10, n. 11.
Lincoln, In re—§ 13.5, n. 18.
Lincoln Federal S. & L. Ass'n v. Platt Homes, Inc.—§ 12.7, n. 39.
Lincoln First Bank v. Bank of New York—§ 2.3, n. 1; § 5.32, n. 17, 26.
Lincoln First Bank, N.A. v. Spaulding Bakeries Inc.—§ 10.9, n. 14.
Lincoln Mortg. Investors v. Cook—§ 3.1, n. 29, 31, 33.
Lincoln Nat. Life Ins. Co. v. NCR Corp.—§ 12.3, n. 27, 31.
Lincor Contractors, Ltd. v. Hyskell—§ 12.3, n. 41.
Lindberg v. Thomas—§ 3.10, n. 3.
Lindell Trust Co. v. Lieberman—§ 8.1, n. 4.
Linden Hill No. 1 Co-op. Corp. v. Kleiner—§ 13.6, n. 16.
Lindsay, In re—§ 8.17, n. 33, 40.
Lindsey v. Delano—§ 7.4, n. 11.
Lindsey v. Meyer—§ 8.6, n. 21.
Lindy v. Lynn—§ 5.30, n. 11.
Lineham v. Southern New England Production Ass'n—§ 6.6, n. 19, 27; § 10.9, n. 7.
Linsker v. Savings of America—§ 12.3, n. 1.
Linville v. Bell—§ 4.2, n. 12.
Liona Corp., N.V., In re—§ 8.14, n. 10.
Lippold v. White—§ 7.21, n. 1.
Lipps v. First American Service Corp.—§ 5.21, n. 33.
Liskey v. Snyder—§ 4.28, n. 9; § 4.29, n. 21, 23.
Littke, In re—§ 8.12, n. 13, 14.
Little v. CFS Service Corp.—§ 7.20, n. 7.
Little v. United Investors Corp.—§ 10.13, n. 1.
Little Earth of United Tribes, Inc. v. United States Dept. of Housing and Urban Development—§ 4.34, n. 11, 15.
Littleton, In re—§ 8.17, n. 40.
Littleton, Matter of—§ 8.17, n. 17.
Littleton's Case—§ 1.2, n. 5.
Livesey v. Brown—§ 3.4, n. 12; § 3.14, n. 2.
Lloyd v. Cannon—§ 8.3, n. 19.
Lloyd v. Chicago Title Ins. Co.—§ 5.34, n. 9.
Lloyd Corp., Limited v. Tanner—§ 7.27, n. 18.

Lloyd's of London v. Fidelity Securities Corp.—§ 6.6, n. 13.
Local Acceptance Co. v. Kinkade—§ 5.29, n. 19.
Lockard v. Hendrickson—§ 7.10, n. 18.
Locke v. Aetna Acceptance Corp.—§ 5.32, n. 15.
Locke v. Caldwell—§ 7.5, n. 15.
Locke v. Homer—§ 5.10, n. 11, 13.
Lockett v. Western Assur. Co.—§ 4.13, n. 4.
Lockhart Co. v. B.F.K., Ltd.—§ 3.35, n. 2.
Lockhart Co. v. Equitable Realty, Inc.—§ 8.2, n. 7.
Loder v. Hatfield—§ 5.17, n. 8.
Loeb v. Tinkler—§ 7.10, n. 18.
Lofsky v. Maujer—§ 4.38, n. 16.
Logan Ranch, Karg Partnership v. Farm Credit Bank of Omaha—§ 7.7, n. 51.
Lomanto v. Bank of America Nat. Trust & Sav. Ass'n—§ 12.8, n. 16.
Lomas Mortg. USA v. Wiese—§ 8.15, n. 70.
Lombard v. Louisiana—§ 7.27, n. 26.
London Bank & Trust Co. v. American Fidelity Bank & Trust Co.—§ 6.17, n. 5.
Long v. Richards—§ 7.2, n. 14.
Long v. Smith—§ 3.27, n. 5.
Long v. Superior Court (Rickert)—§ 8.3, n. 102.
Long v. Wade.—§ 4.22, n. 4.
Long v. Zirkle—§ 6.6, n. 25.
Longdock Mills & Elevator v. Alpen—§ 4.43, n. 5.
Long & Foster Real Estate, Inc. v. Clay—§ 12.9, n. 38.
Long Island Bond & Mortgage Guarantee Co. v. Brown—§ 4.35, n. 32.
Long Island Sav. Bank, F.S.B. v. Gomez—§ 13.5, n. 15.
Long Island Sav. Bank of Centereach, F.S.B. v. Jean Valiquette, M.D., P.C.—§ 7.16, n. 28.
Loomis v. Knox—§ 7.2, n. 4, 17.
Looney v. Farmers Home Admin.—§ 3.29, n. 62.
Looper v. Madison Guar. Sav. & Loan Ass'n—§ 7.16, n. 29, 30.
Loosemore v. Radford—§ 5.10, n. 13.
Loosley, United States v.—§ 8.6, n. 8, 9.
Lord v. Morris and Goodman—§ 6.12, n. 9, 13.
Lord Mansfield v. Hamilton—§ 4.39, n. 3.
Loring M. Hewen Co., Inc. v. Malter—§ 4.39, n. 23.
Lortz v. Swartfager—§ 2.3, n. 19.
Los Quatros, Inc. v. State Farm Life Ins. Co.—§ 5.24, n. 103; § 6.4, n. 11.
Lotterer v. Leon—§ 7.10, n. 18.
Loudermilk v. Citizens Bank of Mooresville—§ 12.8, n. 15.
Louisiana Nat. Bank of Baton Rouge v. Belello—§ 10.6, n. 1.
Louisville Title Co.'s Receiver v. Crab Orchard Banking Co.—§ 5.35, n. 15.
Loveland v. Clark—§ 7.21, n. 24.

Lovell v. One Bancorp—§ 11.1, n. 5.
Loveridge v. Shurtz—§ 5.28, n. 23.
Loving v. Ponderosa Systems, Inc.—§ 4.15, n. 2.
Lowe v. Massachusetts Mut. Life Ins. Co.—§ 12.3, n. 25, 26.
Lowell, In re—§ 2.3, n. 19.
Lowell v. Doe—§ 4.41, n. 8.
Lowry v. Northwestern Sav. & Loan Ass'n—§ 6.7, n. 1; § 7.6, n. 13, 16.
Lozano, Matter of—§ 8.15, n. 5.
LTV Federal Credit Union v. UMIC Government Securities, Inc.—§ 12.3, n. 60.
Lucas v. Jones—§ 5.24, n. 9.
Lucas v. Skinner—§ 7.5, n. 4.
Luchesi v. Capitol Loan & Finance Co.—§ 6.2, n. 9.
Lucier v. Marsales—§ 4.22, n. 22.
Luckinbill v. United States Through Farmers Home Admin.—§ 12.11, n. 45.
Ludwig v. Scott—§ 6.11, n. 11.
Lueben, United States v.—§ 12.3, n. 7.
Lugar v. Edmondson Oil Co., Inc.—§ 7.27; § 7.27, n. 36.
Lumber Exchange Ltd. Partnership, In re—§ 8.14, n. 87.
Lumsden v. Manson—§ 7.4, n. 3.
Lund v. Lund—§ 3.4, n. 1, 4, 8.
Lundberg v. Northwestern Nat. Bank of Minneapolis—§ 6.11, n. 18.
Lundgren v. National Bank of Alaska—§ 12.8, n. 9, 10, 13.
Lundquist v. Nelson—§ 5.19, n. 38, 41.
Lunn Woods v. Lowery—§ 7.6, n. 3.
Lupis v. Peoples Mortg. Co.—§ 11.3, n. 45.
Lusk v. Krejci—§ 6.11, n. 9.
Lustenberger v. Hutchinson—§ 7.20, n. 5.
Luther P. Stephens Inv. Co. v. Berry Schools—§ 4.25, n. 3.
Lutton v. Rodd—§ 6.7, n. 4.
Lydon v. Campbell—§ 6.16, n. 24; § 10.2, n. 5.
Lyman v. Lyman—§ 10.15, n. 7.
Lynch v. Harrer.—§ 4.39, n. 23.
Lynch v. Ryan—§ 4.29, n. 7, 18, 28, 32; § 4.30, n. 2; § 4.31, n. 5.
Lynn Five Cents Sav. Bank v. Portnoy—§ 5.19, n. 41.
Lyon, In re—§ 8.15, n. 41.
Lyon v. Sandford—§ 7.2, n. 14.
Lyons v. National Savings Bank of City of Albany—§ 6.2, n. 9.
Lyons Sav. and Loan Ass'n v. Federal Home Loan Bank Bd.—§ 11.6, n. 20.
Lyons Sav. and Loan Ass'n v. Geode Co.—§ 5.29, n. 3.

M

Mabry v. Abbott—§ 7.21, n. 14.
MacArthur v. North Palm Beach Utilities, Inc.—§ 3.2, n. 1.
Macauley v. Smith—§ 3.8, n. 16; § 3.11, n. 1.
Mace v. Norwood—§ 3.1, n. 1; § 8.5, n. 14, 15.
MacFadden v. Walker—§ 3.29; § 3.29, n. 25.
MacFarlane v. Thompson—§ 4.29, n. 11, 20, 25.
MacIntyre v. Hark—§ 6.1, n. 3.
Mack v. Beeland Bros. Mercantile Co.—§ 4.22, n. 14.
Mack v. Patchin—§ 4.39, n. 12.
Mack v. Shafer—§ 10.9, n. 9.
Mackenna v. Fidelity Trust Co. of Buffalo—§ 7.3, n. 4, 8; § 7.2, n. 10; § 7.15, n. 1.
MacKenzie, United States v.—§ 11.6, n. 54.
Mackey v. Nationwide Ins. Companies—§ 11.5, n. 3.
MacLeod v. Moran—§ 4.2, n. 16.
MacNeil Bros. Co. v. Cambridge Sav. Bank—§ 4.30, n. 7; § 4.31, n. 7; § 4.32, n. 4, 6.
Macon–Atlanta State Bank v. Gall—§ 7.20, n. 16.
Maddox v. Wright—§ 2.4, n. 15.
Madigan, In re—§ 8.3, n. 57.
Madison, In re—§ 11.2, n. 30.
Madison Avenue Baptist Church v. Baptist Church in Oliver St.—§ 4.27, n. 3.
Madison Hotel Associates, Matter of—§ 8.14, n. 47.
Madison Plaza, Inc. v. Shapira Corp.—§ 15.16.
Madrid, In re, 725 F.2d 1197—§ 8.17; § 8.17, n. 10, 26, 29.
Madrid, In re, 21 B.R. 424—§ 8.17, n. 28.
Madrid, In re, 10 B.R. 795—§ 8.17, n. 27.
Madsen v. Prudential Federal Sav. and Loan Ass'n, 558 P.2d 1337—§ 4.18; § 4.18, n. 36.
Madsen v. Prudential Federal Savings & Loan Association, Memo Decision 3—§ 4.18, n. 39.
Magers, In re—§ 12.8, n. 13.
Magill v. Hinsdale—§ 4.22, n. 9, 13.
Maglione v. BancBoston Mortg. Corp.—§ 4.1, n. 12, 16.
Magna Development Co. v. Reed—§ 12.9, n. 17.
Magney v. Lincoln Mut. Sav. Bank—§ 5.22, n. 14, 19.
Magnus v. Morrison—§ 6.7, n. 4.
Magoun v. Fireman's Fund Ins. Co.—§ 4.14, n. 10.
Mahaffy v. Faris—§ 7.5, n. 4.
Maher v. Lanfrom—§ 5.7, n. 3.
Mahoney v. Bostwick—§ 4.29, n. 22; § 7.3, n. 4.
Mahoney v. Furches—§ 6.1, n. 4; § 6.2, n. 4.
Maier v. Thorman—§ 5.19, n. 53.
Main, In re—§ 8.13, n. 20.
Main Bank of Chicago v. Baker—§ 5.20, n. 5.
Majestic Motel Associates, In re—§ 4.35, n. 41.
Major Funding Corp., In re—§ 5.28, n. 28.

… TABLE OF CASES

Major Lumber Co., Inc. v. G & B Remodeling, Inc.—§ 12.4, n. 22.
Makeel v. Hotchkiss—§ 4.41, n. 8.
Malani v. Clapp—§ 12.9; § 12.9, n. 20.
Malcolm v. Lavinson—§ 5.3, n. 2.
Mall v. Johnson—§ 7.31, n. 1.
Mallalieu v. Wickham—§ 4.27, n. 15.
Mallory v. La Crosse Abattoir Co.—§ 12.5, n. 3.
Malone v. Roy—§ 4.29, n. 12, 22.
Malone v. United States—§ 10.2, n. 2.
Malouff v. Midland Federal Sav. and Loan Ass'n—§ 5.24, n. 118.
Malsberger v. Parsons—§ 2.1, n. 2.
Mancha, In re—§ 3.31, n. 1.
Manget Foundation, Inc. v. White—§ 5.6, n. 1.
Manilla Anchor Brewing Co. v. Raw Silk Trading Co.—§ 5.9, n. 6.
Mankato First Nat. Bank v. Pope—§ 5.27, n. 12.
Mann v. Bugbee—§ 5.19, n. 37.
Mann v. Jummel—§ 5.34, n. 22.
Man Ngok Tam v. Hoi Hong K. Luk—§ 9.8, n. 30.
Manos v. Degen—§ 12.6, n. 9.
Manson v. Reed—§ 8.3, n. 139, 140.
Mansura State Bank v. Southwest Nat. Bank, Hibernia Nat. Bank—§ 5.35, n. 5.
Mantz v. Mantz—§ 8.8, n. 9.
Manufacturers & Traders Trust Co. v. First Nat. Bank—§ 2.3, n. 23.
Manufacturers and Traders Trust Co. v. Miner Homes, Inc.—§ 10.15, n. 5.
Manufacturers & Traders Trust Co. v. Murphy—§ 5.31, n. 6.
Manufacturers Hanover Mortg. Corp. v. Snell—§ 7.7, n. 32.
Manufacturers Hanover Trust Co. v. 400 Garden City Associates—§ 8.1, n. 3.
Manufacturers Life Ins. Co. v. Patterson—§ 4.36, n. 12.
Maple Hill Apartment v. Pierce—§ 12.11, n. 45.
Marble Sav. Bank v. Mesarvey—§ 5.15, n. 14.
Marcon v. First Federal Sav. and Loan Ass'n—§ 3.7, n. 7; § 4.1, n. 22.
Marcus Garvey Square, Inc. v. Winston Burnett Const. Co. of California, Inc.—§ 12.6, n. 23.
Maresca v. Allen—§ 7.10, n. 1.
Margiewicz v. Terco Properties of Miami Beach, Inc.—§ 5.27, n. 6; § 5.28, n. 4.
Marianna Lime Products Co. v. McKay—§ 5.14, n. 8.
Mariash v. Bastianich—§ 7.7, n. 4.
Marin v. Knox—§ 9.1, n. 18.
Marine Bank Appleton v. Hietpas, Inc.—§ 12.7, n. 23.
Marine Midland Bank, N.A. v. Cafferty—§ 12.10, n. 34.
Marine Midland Bank, N.A. v. CES/Compu-Tech, Inc.—§ 5.32, n. 4.

Marine Midland Bank, N.A. v. Charmant Travel Lodge, Inc.—§ 8.1, n. 10.
Marine Midland Bank, N.A. v. Virginia Woods, Ltd.—§ 8.1, n. 1.
Mariners Sav. & Loan Ass'n v. Neil—§ 8.3, n. 45.
Marine View Sav. and Loan Ass'n v. Andrulonis—§ 10.8, n. 7.
Markantonis v. Madlan Realty Corporation—§ 4.39, n. 19, 23.
Markey, In re—§ 8.12, n. 14.
Markham v. Smith—§ 10.9, n. 22; § 10.11, n. 15.
Markman v. Russell State Bank—§ 10.13, n. 1.
Marks v. Baum Bldg. Co.—§ 4.46, n. 3.
Marks v. Tucumcari—§ 3.36, n. 14, 15.
Mark Twain Kansas City Bank v. Cates—§ 12.8, n. 10, 21.
Mark Twain Kansas City Bank v. Kroh Bros. Development Co.—§ 12.4, n. 14.
Markus v. Chicago Title & Trust Co.—§ 6.11, n. 16.
Marley v. Consolidated Mortg. Co.—§ 6.2, n. 7.
Marling v. Jones—§ 5.34, n. 13.
Marling v. Milwaukee Realty Co.—§ 5.34, n. 9.
Marple v. Wyoming Production Credit Ass'n—§ 3.1, n. 10, 11.
Marra v. Stocker—§ 5.24, n. 54.
Marriott v. Harris—§ 5.29, n. 3.
Marsh v. Home Federal Sav. and Loan Ass'n—§ 4.18, n. 9, 15.
Marsh v. National Bank of Commerce of El Dorado—§ 10.9, n. 7.
Marsh v. Pike—§ 5.3, n. 8; § 5.10, n. 7.
Marsh v. State of Alabama—§ 7.27; § 7.27, n. 16.
Marsh v. Stover—§ 5.34, n. 22.
Marshall, Matter of—§ 8.17, n. 13.
Marshall v. Davies—§ 5.9, n. 17.
Marston v. Marston—§ 6.16, n. 10.
Marston v. Williams—§ 3.14, n. 2.
Martin v. Alter—§ 4.2, n. 16.
Martin v. Baxter—§ 5.22, n. 36.
Martin v. Block—§ 12.11, n. 44, 50.
Martin v. C. Aultman & Co.—§ 10.7, n. 5.
Martin v. First Nat. Bank of Opelika—§ 9.1, n. 12; § 12.8, n. 15.
Martin v. Hickenlooper—§ 10.1, n. 9, 10, 13; § 10.4, n. 5; § 10.5, n. 2, 5, 10; § 10.6, n. 5.
Martin v. McNeely—§ 7.21, n. 50.
Martin v. Peoples Mut. Sav. and Loan Ass'n—§ 5.22, n. 12, 14.
Martin v. Raleigh State Bank—§ 4.44, n. 3, 6.
Martin v. Ratcliff—§ 4.29, n. 21; § 7.4, n. 12.
Martin v. Sprague—§ 8.5, n. 3.
Martin v. Uvalde Sav. and Loan Ass'n—§ 6.6, n. 36.

TABLE OF CASES

Martinez v. Continental Enterprises—§ 4.2, n. 3, 16, 18; § 4.24, n. 5; § 6.11, n. 21.
Martinez v. Martinez—§ 3.27, n. 6.
Martinson, In re, 731 F.2d 543—§ 8.17, n. 3.
Martinson, In re, 26 B.R. 648—§ 8.17, n. 3.
Martorano v. Spicola—§ 4.35, n. 52.
Martyn v. First Federal Sav. & Loan Ass'n—§ 4.2, n. 3; § 12.3, n. 1.
Martynes and Associates, No. 1 by Martynes v. Devonshire Square Apartments—§ 10.2, n. 4; § 10.3, n. 1.
Marvin v. Stemen—§ 3.32, n. 32.
Maryland v. Wirtz—§ 5.24, n. 15.
Maryland Bank & Trust Co., United States v.—§ 4.48; § 4.48, n. 8.
Maryville Sav. & Loan Corp., In re—§ 5.28, n. 34, 40.
Mascarel v. Raffour—§ 7.8, n. 3.
Masgai v. Masgai—§ 5.8, n. 1.
Mason v. Lenderoth—§ 4.23, n. 2.
Mason v. Western Mortg. Loan Corp.—§ 12.10, n. 8.
Mason & Dixon Lines, Inc. v. First Nat. Bank of Boston—§ 5.35, n. 1, 5.
Massachusetts Mut. Life Ins. Co. v. Avon Associates, Inc.—§ 4.36, n. 12.
Massachusetts Mut. Life Ins. Co. v. Transgrow Realty Corp.—§ 7.7, n. 3.
Massari v. Girardi—§ 4.30, n. 8.
Massey v. National Homeowners Sales Service Corp. of Atlanta—§ 7.22, n. 17, 20.
Masters v. Templeton—§ 7.14, n. 10, 14.
Masterson v. Roberts—§ 12.5, n. 3.
Matter of (see name of party)
Matthew v. Wallwyn—§ 5.32, n. 2.
Matthews v. Saleen—§ 5.20, n. 5, 11.
Matthews v. Sheehan—§ 3.18, n. 5.
Matz v. Arick—§ 12.7, n. 11.
Matzke v. Block—§ 7.28, n. 1.
Maulding v. Sims—§ 6.16, n. 17.
Maurer v. Arab Petroleum Corp.—§ 10.11, n. 14.
Mayer v. Middlemiss—§ 6.7, n. 4.
Mayer v. Myers—§ 7.6, n. 8.
Mayes v. Robinson—§ 5.31, n. 13.
Maynard v. Hunt—§ 6.7, n. 6.
Mays v. Tharpe & Brooks, Inc.—§ 8.10, n. 28.
May's Estate, In re—§ 5.3, n. 3.
McArthur v. Franklin, 16 Ohio St. 193—§ 7.12, n. 19.
McArthur v. Franklin, 15 Ohio St. 485—§ 7.12, n. 19.
McArthur v. Martin—§ 10.14, n. 8.
McBain v. Santa Clara Sav. & Loan Ass'n—§ 12.6, n. 31, 38.
MCB Ltd. v. McGowan—§ 12.9, n. 23.
McBride v. Comley—§ 4.43, n. 13.
Mccabe v. Farnsworth—§ 6.16, n. 2.
McCae Management Corp. v. Merchants Nat. Bank and Trust Co. of Indianapolis—§ 6.1, n. 2.
McCamant v. Roberts—§ 5.28, n. 16.

McCampbell v. Mason—§ 7.12, n. 20.
McCann, In re, 140 B.R. 926—§ 8.18, n. 42.
McCann, In re, 27 B.R. 678—§ 8.15, n. 41.
McCannon v. Marston—§ 5.25, n. 4.
McCarthy v. Bank—§ 9.7, n. 22.
McCarthy v. Louisiana Timeshare Venture—§ 6.3, n. 3.
McCarty v. Mellinkoff—§ 6.2, n. 7.
McCausland v. Bankers Life Ins. Co. of Nebraska—§ 5.22, n. 40; § 5.24, n. 25; § 6.1, n. 10; § 6.5, n. 2.
Mcclellan v. Coffin—§ 6.7, n. 12.
McClellan Realty Corp. v. Institutional Investors Trust—§ 5.29, n. 14.
McClintic-Marshall Co. v. Scandinavian-American Bldg. Co.—§ 10.14, n. 3.
McClintock, In re—§ 8.16, n. 9; § 8.17, n. 56.
McClory v. Ricks—§ 4.24, n. 6.
McClure v. Delguzzi—§ 8.3, n. 7.
McClure v. First Nat. Bank of Lubbock, Tex.—§ 12.3, n. 60.
McClure v. Smith—§ 3.13, n. 5.
McConnell v. Gentry—§ 3.23, n. 2.
McCormick v. Bauer—§ 5.34, n. 17.
McCormick v. Johnson—§ 5.6, n. 2.
McCorristin v. Salmon Signs—§ 4.5, n. 5.
McCourt v. Peppard—§ 2.1, n. 4.
McCown v. Nicks—§ 5.18, n. 6.
McCoy v. Wynn—§ 10.15, n. 5.
McCraney v. Morris—§ 6.17, n. 5, 15, 17.
McCreery, In re—§ 8.15, n. 41.
McCulloch v. Maryland—§ 11.6, n. 1.
McCullough v. F.D.I.C.—§ 11.7, n. 27.
McCumber v. Gilman—§ 4.29, n. 21.
McCurdy v. Clark—§ 7.8, n. 10.
McCutchen, In re—§ 4.35, n. 25, 26.
McDaniel v. Sprick—§ 7.20, n. 18; § 7.21, n. 42.
McDaniels v. Colvin—§ 2.2, n. 2; § 12.7, n. 5, 11.
McDermott v. Burke—§ 4.23, n. 5; § 4.39, n. 19; § 7.12, n. 31.
McDonald v. Duckworth—§ 4.44, n. 7.
McDonald v. Lingle—§ 4.28, n. 6.
McDonald v. Magirl—§ 6.16, n. 17.
McDonough v. O'Niel—§ 3.20, n. 6.
McDougal v. Downey—§ 7.8, n. 10.
McDowell v. St. Paul Fire & Marine Ins. Co.—§ 4.14, n. 4.
McEnroe v. Morgan—§ 3.27, n. 5; § 3.29, n. 70; § 3.31, n. 1.
McFarland v. Christoff—§ 6.7, n. 2.
McFarland v. Melson—§ 5.5, n. 2; § 5.7, n. 12, 14, 17; § 5.8, n. 9.
McGill v. Biggs—§ 3.7, n. 2; § 3.8; § 3.8, n. 1, 17, 19.
McGinty v. Dennehy—§ 5.10, n. 18.
McGlaun v. Southwest Georgia Production Credit Ass'n—§ 12.8, n. 17.
McGough v. Sweetzer—§ 7.3, n. 3.
McGovern Plaza Joint Venture v. First of Denver Mortg. Investors—§ 12.3; § 12.3, n. 59.

TABLE OF CASES

McGraw v. Premium Finance Co. of Missouri—§ 7.15, n. 10, 11, 18, 26.
McGuinness, In re—§ 13.6, n. 23, 30.
McGuire v. Halloran—§ 4.29, n. 18.
McHenry v. Cooper—§ 7.2, n. 20.
McHugh v. Church—§ 7.21, n. 29, 59.
McIlroy Bank & Trust Fayetteville v. Federal Land Bank of St. Louis—§ 9.5, n. 2; § 9.7, n. 25, 26.
McInnis v. Cooper Communities, Inc.—§ 5.24, n. 11; § 11.6, n. 10.
McKay v. Farmers and Stockmens Bank of Clayton—§ 7.7, n. 21.
McKee v. First Nat. Bank of Brighton—§ 12.3, n. 1, 7; § 12.9, n. 21.
McKelvey v. Creevey—§ 4.5, n. 9; § 4.6, n. 5.
McKeon, In re—§ 8.15, n. 40.
McKinley v. Hinnant—§ 3.18, n. 2, 8.
McKinney, In re—§ 8.16, n. 29.
McKnight v. Board of Directors—§ 12.11, n. 34.
McKnight v. United States—§ 8.1, n. 4.
McLain v. Real Estate Bd. of New Orleans, Inc.—§ 5.24, n. 12.
McLain, United States v.—§ 5.4, n. 7.
McLaughlin v. Acom—§ 4.45, n. 3.
McLaughlin v. Estate of Curtis—§ 10.3, n. 8.
McLaughlin and Ryland v. Hart—§ 10.14, n. 8.
McLaughlin Elec. Supply v. American Empire Ins. Co.—§ 12.2, n. 28.
McLeod v. Building & Loan Ass'n of Jackson—§ 5.6, n. 6.
McManus v. McManus—§ 13.6, n. 17.
McMillan v. Richards—§ 4.2, n. 15; § 6.6, n. 14.
McMillan v. United Mortg. Co.—§ 8.2, n. 11.
McMillen Feed Mills, Inc., of South Carolina v. Mayer—§ 12.7, n. 37.
McMullin v. Shimmin—§ 12.3, n. 28.
McMurry v. Mercer—§ 3.18, n. 1; § 3.19, n. 16.
McMurtry v. Bowers—§ 5.32, n. 8, 26.
McNair, In re—§ 13.6, n. 29.
McNeal v. Moberly—§ 7.12, n. 14.
McPherson v. Purdue—§ 7.21, n. 87.
McQueen v. Whetstone—§ 7.2, n. 12.
McReynolds v. Munns—§ 7.14, n. 4, 6.
McSorley, In re—§ 8.15, n. 41.
McSorley v. Larissa—§ 4.29, n. 21.
McVay, In re—§ 8.15, n. 55.
McVay v. Western Plains Service Corp.—§ 5.35, n. 26.
McVeigh v. Mirabito—§ 5.8, n. 9.
M.D. Marinich, Inc. v. Michigan Nat. Bank—§ 12.4, n. 24.
Meader v. Farmers' Mut. Fire Relief Ass'n—§ 4.13, n. 8.
Meadow Brook Nat. Bank v. Recile—§ 12.3, n. 20.
Meadowlands Nat. Bank v. Court Development, Inc.—§ 10.11, n. 12.
Means v. United Fidelity Life Ins. Co.—§ 10.5, n. 2, 5.
Mecham v. United Bank of Ariz.—§ 5.31, n. 7.
Mechanics' Bank, In re—§ 3.14, n. 2.
Medford Trust Co. v. Priggen Steel Garage Co.—§ 9.6, n. 3.
Medina, Village of v. Title Guar. & Sur. Co. of Scranton, PA.—§ 12.2, n. 23.
Med O Farm, Inc., United States v.—§ 5.22, n. 25; § 11.6, n. 86.
Medovoi v. American Savings and Loan Association—§ 5.25, n. 7.
Meehan v. Forrester—§ 3.11, n. 1, 10.
Mehralian v. Riverview Tower Homeowners Ass'n, Inc.—§ 13.6, n. 26.
Meigs v. McFarlan—§ 7.4, n. 12.
Meisler v. Republic of Texas Sav. Ass'n—§ 5.22, n. 40; § 6.5, n. 3.
Meister v. J. Meister, Inc.—§ 12.4, n. 31.
Meldola v. Furlong—§ 5.19, n. 7, 26.
Melendy v. Keen—§ 5.32, n. 3.
Mellish v. Robertson—§ 7.5, n. 1.
Mellon Bank, N.A. v. Aetna Business Credit, Inc.—§ 12.3, n. 11.
Mellon Bank, N.A. v. Barclays American/Business Credit, Inc.—§ 10.1, n. 7.
Meltzer v. Wendell-West—§ 3.37, n. 4.
Mendenhall v. Douglas L. Cooper, Inc.—§ 13.3, n. 40.
Mendez v. Rosenbaum—§ 7.1, n. 1.
Mennonite Bd. of Missions v. Adams—§ 3.30, n. 4; § 4.12, n. 17; § 7.24; § 7.24, n. 4, 7, 20.
Menzel v. Hinton—§ 6.11, n. 19.
Mercado v. Calumet Federal Sav. & Loan Ass'n—§ 5.25, n. 7; § 5.26, n. 5.
Mercantile Collection Bureau v. Roach—§ 9.1, n. 9.
Mercantil Intercontinental, Inc. v. Generalbank—§ 12.9, n. 37.
Mercer v. Daoran Corp.—§ 12.8, n. 9.
Mercer v. Jaffe, Snider, Raitt and Heuer, P.C.—§ 5.35, n. 26; § 11.3, n. 29.
Merchants Bank v. Economic Enterprises, Inc.—§ 10.2, n. 12.
Merchants Bank of Rugby v. Haman—§ 3.35, n. 1.
Merchants' Bank & Trust Co. of Winston-Salem v. Watson—§ 7.14, n. 12.
Merchants' Nat. Bank of Crookston v. Stanton—§ 10.14, n. 15.
Merchants' Nat. Bank of Fargo v. Miller—§ 4.44, n. 3, 6.
Merchants' Nat. Bank of Omaha v. McDonald—§ 7.13, n. 13.
Merchants Nat. Bank & Trust Co. v. Professional Constructors, Inc.—§ 12.6, n. 26.
Merchants' State Bank of Fargo v. Tufts—§ 12.7, n. 10.
Merchants Trust Co. v. Davis—§ 5.34, n. 17.
Mergener v. Fuhr—§ 9.4, n. 14.
Merriam v. Goss—§ 4.29, n. 30.

Merriam v. Miles—§ 5.19, n. 33.
Merriam v. Wimpfheimer—§ 8.17, n. 9.
Merrick Sponsor Corp., United States v.—§ 8.1, n. 9.
Merrill v. Hurley—§ 5.34, n. 9, 14.
Merrills v. Swift—§ 2.2, n. 2.
Merrimack Valley Oil Co., Inc., In re—§ 8.14, n. 55.
Merriman v. Moore—§ 5.15, n. 14.
Merritt v. Bartholick—§ 5.28, n. 15.
Merritt v. Hosmer—§ 7.2, n. 12; § 7.3, n. 3.
Mershon v. Castree—§ 4.3, n. 3.
Mesiavech v. Newman—§ 7.13, n. 1; § 7.10, n. 18; § 7.15, n. 27, 29.
Metco, Inc. v. Moss Creek, Inc.—§ 13.3, n. 44.
Metr. Amal. Ests, Re—§ 4.43, n. 5.
Metro Masonry, Inc. v. West 56th Street Associates—§ 13.3, n. 41, 50.
Metropolitan Federal Bank of Iowa v. A.J. Allen Mechanical Contractors, Inc.—§ 12.4, n. 30.
Metropolitan Life Ins. Co. v. Childs Co.—§ 4.20, n. 3; § 4.38, n. 2; § 4.39, n. 19, 22; § 7.12, n. 31, 33.
Metropolitan Life Ins. Co. v. Coleman—§ 7.21, n. 19.
Metropolitan Life Ins. Co. v. First Sec. Bank of Idaho—§ 10.4, n. 6.
Metropolitan Life Ins. Co. v. Foote—§ 7.16, n. 18, 19.
Metropolitan Life Ins. Co. v. Guy—§ 5.34, n. 12.
Metropolitan Life Ins. Co. v. Jash Lap Realty Corp.—§ 4.43, n. 2.
Metropolitan Life Ins. Co. v. La Mansion Hotels & Resorts, Ltd.—§ 7.22, n. 1, 8, 12.
Metropolitan Sav. and Loan Ass'n v. Nabours—§ 5.22, n. 40; § 6.5, n. 2.
Metropolitan Water Co. v. Hild—§ 13.3, n. 32.
Metter Banking Co. v. Millen Lumber & Supply Co., Inc.—§ 5.35, n. 21.
Metzger v. Nova Realty Co.—§ 5.19, n. 53.
Meyer v. Berlandi—§ 12.5; § 12.5, n. 3, 10.
Meyer v. Hansen—§ 4.4, n. 19.
Meyer v. United States—§ 10.9, n. 8; § 10.14, n. 11.
Meyers v. Beverly Hills Federal Sav. and Loan Ass'n—§ 11.6, n. 19, 25.
Meyers v. Guarantee Sav. and Loan Ass'n—§ 12.11, n. 8.
Meyers v. Home Sav. and Loan Ass'n—§ 6.2; § 6.2, n. 14, 16.
Meyers Plumbing and Heating Supply Co. v. Caste—§ 13.3, n. 43.
M. F. Kemper Const. Co. v. City of Los Angeles—§ 12.2, n. 14.
MGIC Financial Corp. v. H. A. Briggs Co.—§ 5.19; § 5.19, n. 61; § 10.2, n. 4.
Miami Mortg. & Guaranty Co. v. Drawdy—§ 7.8, n. 10.

Miami Oil Co. v. Florida Discount Corporation—§ 5.35, n. 8.
Michael Weller, Inc. v. Aetna Cas. & Sur. Co.—§ 13.3, n. 46.
Michigan Air Line Ry. Co. v. Barnes—§ 4.12, n. 19.
Michigan Ins. Co. v. Brown—§ 6.11, n. 18.
Michigan Protection and Advocacy Service, Inc. v. Babin—§ 5.24, n. 13.
Michigan Sav. and Loan League v. Francis—§ 11.5, n. 43.
Michigan Trust Co. v. Cody—§ 7.16, n. 33.
Michigan Trust Co. v. Dutmers—§ 7.16, n. 33.
Michigan Trust Co. v. Lansing Lumber Co.—§ 4.2, n. 21.
Michigan Wineries, Inc. v. Johnson—§ 5.17, n. 5.
Mickelson v. Anderson—§ 7.10, n. 16.
Mickie v. McGehee—§ 6.6, n. 17.
Mickle v. Gould—§ 10.11, n. 14.
Mickles v. Dillaye—§ 4.29, n. 23, 30.
Mickles v. Townsend—§ 4.2, n. 10.
Mid–City Hotel Associates, In re—§ 4.35, n. 41.
Mid–Continent Cas. Co. v. First Nat. Bank & Trust Co. of Chickasha—§ 12.2, n. 18.
Middlebrook–Anderson Co. v. Southwest Sav. & Loan Ass'n—§ 12.10; § 12.10, n. 15, 25.
Middlemist v. Mosier—§ 7.7, n. 10.
Mid Kansas Federal Sav. and Loan Ass'n of Wichita v. Dynamic Development Corp.—§ 6.16, n. 17, 19.
Midland Mortg. Co. v. Sanders England Investments—§ 12.4, n. 14.
Midlantic Nat. Bank v. Sourlis—§ 4.35, n. 25; § 8.18, n. 46, 47.
Mid–State Homes, Inc. v. Jackson—§ 6.7, n. 1.
Mid–State Inv. Corp. v. O'Steen—§ 3.29, n. 12.
Midtaune v. Burns—§ 5.16, n. 2.
Midwest Sav. Ass'n v. Riversbend Associates Partnership—§ 11.6, n. 49.
Midyett v. Rennat Properties, Inc.—§ 9.8, n. 6.
Mihalko, In re—§ 12.9, n. 2.
Mihoover v. Walker—§ 8.6, n. 19.
Mihranian, Inc. v. Padula—§ 13.3, n. 17.
Mikolaitis, United States v.—§ 11.6, n. 83.
Mikole Developers, Inc., In re—§ 8.14, n. 26.
Milbrandt v. Huber—§ 3.35, n. 1.
Miles v. Perpetual Sav. & Loan Co.—§ 12.11, n. 26.
Miles v. Stehle—§ 7.10, n. 14, 18; § 7.15, n. 29.
Miles Homes Div. of Insilco Corp. v. First State Bank of Joplin—§ 9.8, n. 22.
Miles Homes, Inc., of Illinois v. Mintjal—§ 3.29, n. 1.
Mill Ass'n, Inc., United States v.—§ 12.6, n. 31.

TABLE OF CASES

Miller, In re, 133 B.R. 882—§ 4.35, n. 25, 27.
Miller, In re, 53 B.R. 100—§ 8.15, n. 49.
Miller v. American Exp. Co.—§ 11.5, n. 18.
Miller v. American Wonderlands, Inc.—§ 3.28, n. 11.
Miller v. Berry—§ 5.28, n. 21.
Miller v. Citizens Sav. & Loan Ass'n—§ 12.6, n. 38; § 12.9; § 12.9, n. 26, 28, 36; § 12.10; § 12.10, n. 23.
Miller v. Cote—§ 5.22, n. 33.
Miller v. Curry—§ 4.29, n. 7, 21.
Miller v. Davis—§ 7.10, n. 9.
Miller v. Deering—§ 7.22, n. 2.
Miller v. Diversified Loan Service Co.—§ 5.29, n. 16, 22; § 5.31, n. 3; § 6.11, n. 12.
Miller v. First Nat. Bank of Englewood—§ 4.45, n. 8.
Miller v. Frederick's Brewing Co.—§ 5.28, n. 9.
Miller v. Hartwood Apartments, Ltd.—§ 7.28, n. 31.
Miller v. Jeff Davis Apartments, Ltd. II—§ 9.8; § 9.8, n. 15.
Miller v. Jones—§ 7.6, n. 13.
Miller v. Kendrick—§ 7.16, n. 22.
Miller v. Kyle—§ 3.1, n. 37.
Miller v. Lincoln—§ 4.28, n. 3.
Miller v. Little—§ 6.16, n. 10, 14; § 8.7, n. 13.
Miller v. Miller—§ 3.21, n. 1; § 3.22, n. 5; § 3.25, n. 4.
Miller v. Mountain View Sav. & Loan Ass'n—§ 12.6, n. 15.
Miller v. Pacific First Federal Savings & Loan Ass'n—§ 5.21, n. 22; § 5.22, n. 30.
Miller v. Peter, 150 N.W. 554—§ 4.28, n. 9.
Miller v. Peter, 122 N.W. 780—§ 3.9, n. 3.
Miller v. Roach—§ 5.6, n. 1.
Miller v. Safeco Title Ins. Co.—§ 12.2, n. 9.
Miller v. Trudgeon—§ 7.16, n. 18.
Miller v. Uhrick—§ 7.7, n. 3.
Miller v. Van Kampen—§ 4.15, n. 6.
Miller v. Ward—§ 4.29, n. 6, 14, 19, 29; § 4.31, n. 3.
Miller v. Wines—§ 12.9, n. 2.
Miller's Estate, In re—§ 13.6, n. 18.
Millers Mut. Fire Ins. Co. of Tex. v. Farmers Elevator Mut. Ins. Co.—§ 10.1, n. 14.
Millett v. Blake—§ 7.2, n. 7.
Milligan v. Gilmore Meyer Inc.—§ 5.29, n. 36.
Milligan's Appeal—§ 10.13, n. 30.
Mills, In re, 40 B.R. 72—§ 10.9, n. 15, 16, 19.
Mills, In re, 39 B.R. 564—§ 12.8, n. 12.
Mills v. Darling—§ 3.4, n. 7.
Mills v. Hamilton—§ 4.23, n. 2.
Mills v. Heaton—§ 4.23, n. 2.
Mills v. Kelley—§ 10.12, n. 1.
Mills v. Mutual Building & Loan Ass'n—§ 7.21, n. 50, 51, 60, 70, 78.
Mills v. Nashua Federal Sav. and Loan Ass'n—§ 5.22, n. 14, 25; § 9.8, n. 10.

Mills v. Pope—§ 4.6, n. 6.
Mills v. United Counties Bank—§ 5.8, n. 13.
Milmo Nat. Bank v. Rich—§ 7.15, n. 1.
Milstein v. Security Pac. Nat. Bank—§ 4.12, n. 10.
Milwaukee Mechanics' Ins. Co. v. Ramsey—§ 4.14, n. 7.
Milwaukee Western Bank v. Cedars of Cedar Rapids, Inc.—§ 7.18, n. 4; § 8.6, n. 14.
Mindlin v. Davis—§ 9.8, n. 33.
Miner v. Beekman—§ 4.29, n. 23; § 7.5, n. 2.
Minick, In re—§ 8.15, n. 39.
Ministers Life & Cas. Union v. Franklin Park Towers Corp.—§ 2.1, n. 8, 17; § 3.19, n. 1.
Minnesota Building & Loan Ass'n v. Murphy—§ 4.34, n. 12.
Minnesota Kicks, Inc., In re—§ 10.2, n. 11.
Mirabile, United States v.—§ 4.48, n. 4.
Missouri, K. & T. Trust Co. v. Richardson—§ 7.14, n. 8.
Mitchell v. Bickford—§ 6.11, n. 40.
Mitchell v. Oliver—§ 6.6, n. 19, 23.
Mitchell v. Roberts—§ 6.7, n. 26.
Mitchell v. Trustees of United States Mut. Real Estate Inv. Trust—§ 9.8, n. 21.
Mitchell v. W. T. Grant Co.—§ 4.36; § 4.36, n. 5; § 7.25; § 7.25, n. 8; § 12.5; § 12.5, n. 2, 15, 16.
Mixon v. Burleson—§ 8.5, n. 11.
M. Leo Storch Ltd. Partnership v. Erol's, Inc.—§ 15.16.
Mobile Components, Inc. v. Layon—§ 12.5, n. 19.
Mobley v. Brundidge Banking Co., Inc.—§ 10.9, n. 3.
Modesto Lumber Co. v. Wylde—§ 12.10; § 12.10, n. 8.
Modlin v. Atlantic Fire Ins. Co.—§ 3.10, n. 2.
Moeller v. Good Hope Farms—§ 3.32, n. 16.
Moffet v. Farwell—§ 6.17, n. 11.
Moffett v. Parker—§ 5.32, n. 8, 26.
Mohler v. Buena Vista Bank and Trust Co.—§ 12.8, n. 15.
Mollerup v. Storage Systems Intern.—§ 7.1, n. 3; § 8.6, n. 11.
Moloney v. Weingarten—§ 13.6, n. 17.
Monaghan v. May—§ 7.16, n. 33.
Moncrieff v. Hare—§ 4.34, n. 19; § 4.35, n. 3.
Monegan v. Pacific Nat. Bank of Washington—§ 10.9, n. 19.
Monese v. Struve—§ 7.10, n. 18; § 7.15, n. 1.
Monforton, In re—§ 8.13, n. 33.
Monica Road Associates, In re—§ 8.14, n. 27.
Monolith Portland Cement Co. v. Tendler—§ 7.21, n. 84.
Monroe County Housing Corp., Inc., In re—§ 12.6, n. 25, 28.

TABLE OF CASES

Monroe Park, In re—§ 8.14, n. 45.
Monroe Park v. Metropolitan Life Ins. Co.—§ 7.11, n. 1.
Monro–King etc., Corporation v. 9 Avenue–31 Street Corporation—§ 4.39, n. 15; § 4.22, n. 22.
Monte Enterprises, Inc. v. Kavanaugh—§ 4.4, n. 10, 14.
Monterey S.P. Partnership v. W.L. Bangham, Inc.—§ 6.6, n. 19; § 7.21, n. 61, 70.
Montgomery v. Chadwick—§ 4.29, n. 23, 33.
Montgomery, State ex rel. v. Superior Court of Kittitas County—§ 4.24, n. 13.
Moody v. United States—§ 12.11, n. 47.
Mooney v. Byrne—§ 2.1, n. 17; § 3.11, n. 1, 5; § 5.28, n. 12.
Moore v. Beasom—§ 7.2, n. 17.
Moore v. Cable—§ 4.29, n. 15; § 4.30, n. 2.
Moore v. Great Western Sav. and Loan Ass'n—§ 4.19, n. 3, 4, 5, 6.
Moore v. Hall—§ 8.6, n. 26.
Moore v. Hamilton—§ 7.21, n. 26.
Moore v. Kime—§ 6.1, n. 2.
Moore v. Lewis—§ 5.3, n. 5; § 5.27, n. 6.
Moore v. Linville—§ 3.10, n. 3.
Moore v. Lomas Mortg. USA—§ 6.8, n. 4.
Moore v. Moore—§ 7.22, n. 28.
Moore v. Moran—§ 4.6, n. 4.
Moore v. Norman—§ 6.6, n. 8; § 6.7, n. 7.
Moore v. Parkerson—§ 7.22, n. 3.
Moore v. Penney—§ 8.7, n. 13.
Moore v. Shurtleff—§ 10.11, n. 3, 14.
Moore v. Simonson—§ 10.3, n. 9.
Moore v. Titman—§ 4.45, n. 1.
Moore Bros. Oil Co., Inc. v. Dean—§ 2.3, n. 16.
Moore–Mansfield Const. Co. v. Indianapolis, N.C. & T. Ry. Co.—§ 12.4, n. 5.
Moore's Guardian v. Williamson's Ex'r—§ 4.29, n. 30.
Moose Lodge No. 107 v. Irvis—§ 7.27, n. 29.
Moran v. Gardemeyer—§ 12.8, n. 13.
Moran v. Holman—§ 3.29, n. 32.
Moran v. Pittsburgh, C. & St. L. R. Co.—§ 4.22, n. 14.
More v. United States—§ 7.15, n. 11, 15, 18; § 11.6, n. 74.
Moreland v. Marwich, Ltd.—§ 8.6, n. 11.
Morello v. Metzenbaum—§ 8.3, n. 36, 37.
Morgan, Ex parte—§ 1.2, n. 4.
Morgan v. Farmington Coal & Coke Co.—§ 5.31, n. 13.
Morgan v. Glendy—§ 7.21, n. 66.
Morgan v. South Milwaukee Lake View Co.—§ 5.7, n. 13.
Morgan v. Walbridge—§ 4.29, n. 23.
Morgan v. Willman—§ 4.12, n. 3, 19.
Morgen–Oswood & Associates, Inc. of Florida v. Continental Mortg. Investors—§ 12.6, n. 28.
Moriarty v. Ashworth—§ 4.10, n. 6.
Moring v. Dickerson—§ 9.1, n. 20.
Morris v. Budlong—§ 4.28, n. 11; § 4.29, n. 23.

Morris v. Davis—§ 4.38, n. 5.
Morris v. Mix—§ 5.15, n. 5.
Morris v. Sykes—§ 3.29, n. 32, 41.
Morris v. Twichell—§ 10.7, n. 5.
Morris v. Way—§ 4.2, n. 16.
Morris v. Woodside—§ 5.24, n. 40.
Morris Communications NC, Inc., In re—§ 8.17, n. 40.
Morrison v. Buckner—§ 4.34, n. 1.
Morrisse v. Inglis—§ 7.17, n. 5.
Morrocco v. Felton—§ 12.11; § 12.11, n. 16.
Morrow v. H.E.B., Inc.—§ 7.22, n. 35.
Morrow v. Stanley—§ 5.34, n. 30, 47.
Morrow v. Turney's Adm'r—§ 4.32, n. 3.
Morse v. City Federal Sav. and Loan Ass'n—§ 5.4, n. 3; § 5.5, n. 1.
Morse v. Mutual Fed. Sav. & Loan Ass'n of Whitman—§ 7.22, n. 47.
Morsemere Federal Sav. & Loan Ass'n v. Nicolaou—§ 7.31, n. 1.
Morse Tool, Inc., In re—§ 6.2, n. 22.
Morstain v. Kircher—§ 5.18, n. 4, 18.
MortgageAmerica Corp. v. American Nat. Bank of Austin—§ 11.3, n. 26.
Mortgage Associates, Inc. v. Monona Shores, Inc.—§ 12.6, n. 39.
Mortgage Commission Realty Corporation v. Columbia Heights Garage Corporation—§ 7.15, n. 23.
Mortgage Funding, Inc., In re—§ 5.35, n. 43.
Mortgage Guarantee Co. v. Chotiner—§ 5.19, n. 22, § 5.20, n. 2.
Mortgage Guarantee Co. v. Hammond Lumber Co.—§ 12.7, n. 29.
Morton v. Allen—§ 3.19, n. 3.
Morton v. Rifai—§ 6.16, n. 6.
Morvay v. Drake—§ 2.1, n. 4.
Moseley v. Lathan—§ 7.7, n. 4.
Mosely v. Marshall—§ 10.3, n. 5.
Moser Paper Co. v. North Shore Pub. Co.—§ 10.9, n. 7.
Moshier v. Norton—§ 4.28, n. 9; § 4.29, n. 7, 9.
Moss v. Gallimore—§ 4.21, n. 1.
Moss v. McDonald—§ 5.19, n. 52; § 5.20, n. 5, 11.
Moss v. Robertson—§ 7.32, n. 1.
Motel Enterprises, Inc. v. Nobani—§ 7.12, n. 5.
Motes v. Roberson—§ 10.8, n. 5.
Motor Equipment Co. v. Winters—§ 7.12, n. 26.
Mott v. Clark—§ 5.32, n. 7, 26.
Mott v. German Hosp.—§ 5.34, n. 29.
Moulton v. Cornish—§ 7.15, n. 25.
Mountain Village Co., United States v.—§ 4.35, n. 9; § 4.36, n. 12; § 11.6, n. 49.
Mount Pleasant Ltd. Partnership, In re—§ 8.18, n. 43.
Mowry v. Mowry—§ 5.10, n. 7.
Mox v. Jordan—§ 5.29, n. 19.
Mozingo v. North Carolina Nat. Bank—§ 2.1, n. 19; § 5.31, n. 6.

Mr. U Inc. v. Mobil Oil Corp.—§ 6.6, n. 19; § 6.7, n. 1, 2.
M.S. Foundations, Inc. v. Perma-Crete Bldg. Systems, Inc.—§ 12.7, n. 23.
Mueller v. Novelty Dye Works—§ 3.36, n. 14, 15.
Mueller v. Simmons—§ 7.21, n. 1, 21.
Muhlig v. Fiske—§ 5.7, n. 15.
Muir, In re—§ 10.9, n. 7.
Muir v. Berkshire—§ 5.28, n. 17.
Muir v. Jones—§ 9.6, n. 6.
Mulkey v. Reitman—§ 7.27, n. 10.
Mullane v. Central Hanover Bank & Trust Co.—§ 3.30; § 3.30, n. 3; § 4.36; § 4.36, n. 2; § 7.24; § 7.24, n. 3.
Mullin v. Claremont Realty Co.—§ 5.15, n. 14.
Multi-Group III Ltd. Partnership, In re—§ 8.18, n. 54, 55.
Mundy v. Monroe—§ 4.2, n. 14.
Munger v. Moore—§ 7.22, n. 35, 37, 38.
Munger v. T. J. Beard & Bros.—§ 7.13, n. 20.
Municipal Sav. & Loan Corp. v. Fiorentino—§ 8.3, n. 18.
Munn v. American General Inv. Corp.—§ 4.19, n. 6.
Munro v. Barton—§ 7.5, n. 1, 8.
Munsey Trust Co., United States v.—§ 12.2, n. 47.
Munson v. Munson—§ 6.6, n. 2.
Munzenrieder Corp., In re—§ 10.2, n. 12; § 10.4, n. 2.
Murdock v. Clarke—§ 3.9, n. 3.
Murdock Acceptance Corp. v. Jones—§ 12.8, n. 10.
Murel Holding Corp., In re—§ 8.14; § 8.14, n. 71.
Murello Const. Co. v. Citizens Home Sav. Co.—§ 11.4, n. 52, 61.
Murphy v. Barnard—§ 5.34, n. 29, 35.
Murphy v. Colonial Federal Sav. & Loan Ass'n—§ 11.6, n. 19, 21.
Murphy v. Farwell—§ 7.15, n. 3, 22.
Murphy v. Financial Development Corp.—§ 7.21, n. 5, 55; § 7.22, n. 36; § 8.8, n. 7.
Murphy v. New Hampshire Sav. Bank—§ 7.4, n. 11.
Murphy v. Zuigaro—§ 6.16, n. 5.
Murray v. Marshall—§ 5.3, n. 8; § 5.19, n. 5, 24.
Murray v. O'Brien—§ 6.7, n. 12.
Murray First Thrift & Loan Co. v. Stevenson—§ 5.22, n. 35, 37.
Murry v. Western American Mortg. Co.—§ 12.11, n. 12.
Mursor Builders, Inc. v. Crown Mountain Apartment Associates—§ 12.6, n. 25, 32.
Murtin v. Walker—§ 4.39, n. 8.
Muss v. Bergman—§ 4.41, n. 2.
Musser v. First Nat. Bank of Corinth—§ 6.12, n. 4.
Mustard v. Sugar Valley Lakes—§ 3.32, n. 12.

Mutual Aid Building & Loan Co. v. Gashe—§ 9.1, n. 8.
Mutual Ben. Life Ins. Co. v. Frantz Klodt & Son—§ 4.2, n. 3; § 4.24, n. 5; § 4.34, n. 11; § 4.35, n. 51.
Mutual Ben. Life Ins. Co. v. Lindley—§ 5.19, n. 26, 27.
Mutual Bldg. and Loan Ass'n v. Collins—§ 3.36, n. 3, 4, 8, 9.
Mutual Federal S & L Ass'n v. Wisconsin Wire Works—§ 5.21, n. 33.
Mutual Fire Ins. Co. of Harford County v. Dilworth—§ 4.14, n. 20.
Mutual Life Ins. Co. of New York v. Grissett—§ 10.6, n. 3.
Mutual Life Ins. Co. of New York v. Hilander—§ 6.3, n. 2; § 6.7, n. 1.
Mutual Life Ins. Co. of New York v. J. H. C. Corporation—§ 5.19, n. 16, 53, 54.
Mutual Life Ins. Co. of New York v. Newell—§ 4.31, n. 16.
Mutual Life Ins. Co. of New York v. Rothschild—§ 5.19, n. 8, 50.
Mutual Security Financing v. Unite—§ 5.12, n. 1.
M. Vickers, Ltd., In re—§ 4.35, n. 41.
Myer v. Hart—§ 6.7, n. 19.
Myers v. Bank of Prattville—§ 5.31, n. 4.
Myers-Macomber Engineers v. M. L. W. Const. Corp.—§ 4.24, n. 6; § 4.27, n. 6, 9, 10, 19.

N

N.A.A.C.P. v. American Family Mut. Ins. Co.—§ 11.5, n. 3, 8, 18.
Namer, United States v.—§ 12.3, n. 60.
Napue v. Gor-Mey West Inc.—§ 6.7, n. 1.
Nash, In re—§ 5.28, n. 6; § 5.29, n. 14, 25.
Nash v. Preston—§ 1.2, n. 2; § 9.1, n. 18.
Nassar v. Utah Mortg. & Loan Corp.—§ 4.14, n. 2, 10.
Nassau Savings & Loan Ass'n v. Ormond—§ 8.8, n. 11.
Nassau Trust Co. v. Montrose Concrete Products Corp.—§ 7.7, n. 6.
National American Bank v. Southcoast Contr., Inc.—§ 12.2, n. 25.
National Bank v. Tennessee etc.—§ 4.2, n. 16.
National Bank of Eastern Ark. v. Blankenship—§ 12.8, n. 9.
National Bank of Washington v. Equity Investors, 546 P.2d 440—§ 4.45, n. 6; § 7.16, n. 35.
National Bank of Washington v. Equity Investors, 506 P.2d 20—§ 12.7; § 12.7, n. 14, 24; § 12.10, n. 7.
National Bank of Waterloo v. Moeller—§ 12.9, n. 6.
National City Bank of Chicago v. Wagner—§ 2.3, n. 3.
National Credit Union Admin. Bd. v. Metzler—§ 5.33, n. 7.

National Credit Union Admin. Bd. v. Regine—§ 11.7, n. 10.
National Indem. Co. v. Banks—§ 13.3, n. 17, 21.
National Inv. Co. v. Nordin—§ 6.16, n. 11.
National Life Ins. Co. v. Cady—§ 7.22, n. 1, 3.
National Life Ins. Co. v. Silverman—§ 7.21, n. 15; § 7.22, n. 40, 43.
National Loan & Inv. Co. of Detroit, Mich. v. Stone—§ 5.17, n. 8.
National Lumber Co. v. Advance Development Corp.—§ 12.7, n. 13, 27.
National Mortg. Co. v. Williams—§ 7.22, n. 45.
National Mortg. Corp. v. American Title Ins. Co.—§ 12.9, n. 38.
National Mortg. Equity Corp. Mortg. Pool Certificates Securities Litigation, In re—§ 11.3, n. 29.
National Mut. Bldg. & Loan Ass'n v. Retzman—§ 5.17, n. 8.
National Park Bank of New York v. Koehler—§ 5.19, n. 54.
National Reserve Life Ins. Co. v. Kemp—§ 7.16, n. 4.
National Sav. Bank of Albany v. Hartmann—§ 6.7, n. 1.
National Sav. Bank of City of Albany v. Fermac Corporation—§ 5.9, n. 18.
National Sav. Bank of District of Columbia v. Creswell—§ 10.9, n. 4; § 10.10, n. 5.
National Sec. Fire & Cas. Co. v. Mazzara—§ 5.34, n. 33.
National Service Lines, Inc., In re—§ 10.2, n. 11.
National State Bank, Elizabeth, N. J. v. Long—§ 11.5, n. 43.
National Sur. Co. v. Walker—§ 4.45, n. 1.
National Sur. Corp. v. State Nat. Bank of Frankfort—§ 12.2, n. 45.
Navarro v. United States—§ 12.11, n. 41, 48.
Nazar v. Southern—§ 5.28, n. 28; § 5.34, n. 30.
Nazro v. Ware—§ 2.4, n. 7.
NCNB Texas Nat. Bank v. Sterling Projects, Inc.—§ 4.35, n. 24.
Neal v. Bradley—§ 5.32, n. 13; § 5.33, n. 5; § 5.34, n. 23.
Nebraska State Bank v. Pedersen—§ 9.4, n. 4.
Needles v. Keys—§ 3.28, n. 6.
Neff v. Elder—§ 10.7, n. 10.
Neises v. Solomon State Bank—§ 4.14, n. 10.
Neiswanger v. McClellan—§ 5.6, n. 1.
Nelson, In re—§ 7.20, n. 7.
Nelson v. Bowen—§ 4.25, n. 7.
Nelson v. First Nat. Bank of Jewell—§ 7.13, n. 1.
Nelson v. Great Northwest Federal Sav. and Loan Ass'n—§ 13.3, n. 21.
Nelson v. Loder—§ 6.7, n. 12, 23, 24.
Nelson v. Nelson—§ 3.24, n. 7.

Nelson v. Pinegar—§ 4.10, n. 3.
Nelson v. Robinson—§ 3.29; § 3.29, n. 19.
Nelson v. Stoker—§ 9.1, n. 4, 13, 27.
Nelson-American Developers, Ltd. v. Enco Engineering Corp.—§ 12.5, n. 19.
Nemec v. Rollo—§ 3.32, n. 22, 26, 27.
Nemeti, In re—§ 8.17, n. 59.
Nerwal Realty Corporation v. 9 AVENUE-31 Street Corporation—§ 4.42, n. 9.
Nettles v. First Nat. Bank of Birmingham—§ 4.25, n. 4.
Neustadt, United States v.—§ 12.11, n. 39.
Nevada Land & Mortg. Co. v. Hidden Wells Ranch, Inc.—§ 8.2, n. 11, 12.
Nevada Nat. Bank v. Snyder—§ 12.4, n. 14.
Neves v. Wright—§ 3.33, n. 4, 6.
Nevis v. Fidelity New York, F.A.—§ 12.10, n. 33.
New Amsterdam Cas. Co. v. Bettes—§ 12.2, n. 37, 38.
Newark, City of v. Sue Corp.—§ 4.26, n. 1.
New Bank of New England, N.A. v. Toronto-Dominion Bank—§ 5.35, n. 5.
Newby v. Fox—§ 10.13, n. 10, 20, 21, 22; § 10.14, n. 1.
New Castle County, United States v.—§ 4.48, n. 4.
Newcomb v. Bascomb—§ 3.1, n. 6.
Newcomb v. Bonham—§ 3.1, n. 3.
New Connecticut Bank & Trust Co., N.A. v. Stadium Management Corp.—§ 5.29, n. 35, 40; § 11.7, n. 31, 34.
Newdigate Colliery, Limited, In re,—§ 4.39, n. 8.
New England Loan & Trust Co. v. Browne—§ 7.21, n. 91.
New England Loan & Trust Co. v. Stephens—§ 10.11, n. 14.
New England Mortgage Realty Co. v. Rossini—§ 10.9, n. 22.
New Haven Bank v. Jackson—§ 10.9, n. 22.
New Haven Sav. Bank v. Atwater—§ 4.31, n. 16.
New Home Federal Sav. and Loan Ass'n v. Trunk—§ 5.21, n. 33.
New Jersey Bldg., Loan & Inv. Co. v. Bachelor—§ 9.1, n. 21.
New Jersey Mortg. & Inv. Corp. v. Calvetti—§ 5.29, n. 14.
New Jersey Nat. Bank & Trust Co. v. Morris—§ 4.35, n. 15.
New Jersey Title Guarantee & Trust Co. v. Cone—§ 4.43, n. 8.
New Maine Nat. Bank v. Seydler—§ 11.7, n. 23, 33.
Newman v. American Nat. Bank—§ 8.6, n. 19, 20.
Newman v. Chapman—§ 7.13, n. 15.
New Mexico Bank & Trust Co. v. Lucas Bros.—§ 12.8, n. 4.
New Order Building & Loan Ass'n v. 222 Chancellor Avenue, Inc.—§ 4.21, n. 7; § 4.38, n. 19.
New Orleans & Ohio R. Co., United States v.—§ 9.1, n. 14.

TABLE OF CASES

Newport Condominium Ass'n v. Talman Home Federal Sav. and Loan Ass'n of Chicago—§ 13.5, n. 20.
Newport etc. Co. v. Douglass—§ 4.43, n. 9.
New South Bldg. & Loan Ass'n v. Reed—§ 10.15, n. 5.
Newton v. Fay—§ 3.15, n. 8.
Newton v. Mckay—§ 4.2, n. 14.
Newton v. Uniwest Financial Corp.—§ 11.7, n. 27, 35.
Newton County Bank, Louin Branch Office v. Jones—§ 12.8, n. 15.
New Way Bldg. Co. v. Mortimer Taft Bldg. Corporation—§ 4.38, n. 16.
New York and Suburban Federal Sav. and Loan Ass'n v. Sanderman—§ 4.27, n. 9, 10.
New York Cas. Co. v. Sinclair Refining Co.—§ 10.1, n. 5.
New York City Community Preservation Corp. v. Michelin Associates—§ 4.42, n. 17.
New York Guardian Mortgagee Corp. v. Olexa—§ 7.7, n. 7.
New York Investors Mut. Group, Inc., In re—§ 3.33; § 3.33, n. 17.
New York Life Ins. Co. v. Aitkin—§ 5.18, n. 5, 15.
New York Life Ins. Co. v. Bremer Towers—§ 4.35, n. 25.
New York Life Ins. Co. v. Fulton Development Corporation—§ 4.21, n. 6; § 4.38, n. 18; § 4.43, n. 5.
New York Life Ins. Co. v. Simplex Products Corporation—§ 7.12, n. 34.
New York & Suburban Federal Sav & Loan Ass'n v. Fi-Pen Realty Co.—§ 12.7, n. 29.
Niagara Fire Ins. Co. v. Scammon—§ 4.13, n. 7.
Nibbi Bros., Inc. v. Brannan Street Investors—§ 12.6, n. 21, 28.
Nicholas McPickolus Realty Corp. v. Jamaica Plain Co-op. Bank—§ 7.21, n. 44.
Nichols, In re—§ 5.28, n. 28, 30.
Nichols v. Ann Arbor Federal Sav. and Loan Ass'n—§ 5.22, n. 19.
Nichols v. Baxter—§ 4.13, n. 12.
Nichols v. Evans—§ 7.6, n. 19.
Nickel v. Brown—§ 5.34, n. 6.
Nickerman v. Ryan—§ 8.3; § 8.3, n. 103.
Niehaus v. Niehaus—§ 6.12, n. 1.
Nielsen, In re—§ 8.16, n. 22.
Nigh v. Hickman—§ 3.29; § 3.29, n. 8.
Nikole, Inc. v. Klinger—§ 3.33, n. 7.
Nilson v. Sarment—§ 6.6, n. 14.
Nippel v. Hammond—§ 3.1, n. 1.
Nissen v. Sabin—§ 5.7, n. 16.
Nitkey v. Ward—§ 3.18, n. 3, 5; § 3.19, n. 1, 3.
Nixon v. Haslett—§ 5.32, n. 3.
Noakes and Co. Limited v. Rice—§ 3.1, n. 2, 39.
Nobelman v. American Sav. Bank—§ 8.15, n. 74.

Noble v. Brooks—§ 4.21, n. 5.
Noble v. Watkins—§ 5.28, n. 16.
Noble County Bank v. Waterhouse—§ 2.1, n. 4.
Nobleman, Matter of—§ 8.15; § 8.15, n. 72, 73.
Noelker v. Wehmeyer—§ 6.19, n. 5.
Nolte v. Smith—§ 12.4, n. 14.
North American Cold Storage Co. v. Chicago—§ 4.36, n. 8.
North Coast Ry. Co. v. Hess—§ 4.12, n. 19.
North Community Bank v. Northwest Nat. Bank of Chicago—§ 5.24, n. 40, 87.
Northeast Sav., F.A. v. Bailey—§ 5.5, n. 1.
Northeast Sav., F.A. v. Rodriguez—§ 5.3, n. 2; § 12.11, n. 28.
Northeast Sav., F.A. v. Sennett—§ 5.17, n. 5.
North End Bank & Trust Co. v. Mandell—§ 7.10, n. 2.
North End Savings Bank v. Snow—§ 5.3, n. 1; § 5.19, n. 23.
Northern Acres, Inc., In re—§ 3.37, n. 11.
Northern Illinois Development Corp., In re—§ 3.29, n. 1.
Northern Pac. R. Co. v. Boyd—§ 8.14, n. 79.
Northern Trust Co. v. F.D.I.C.—§ 5.35, n. 24.
Northgate Terrace Apartments, Ltd., In re—§ 8.14, n. 27.
North Georgia Finishing, Inc. v. Di-Chem, Inc.—§ 7.25; § 7.25, n. 10; § 12.5; § 12.5, n. 2, 14, 16, 17.
Northlake Concrete Products, Inc. v. Wylie—§ 12.4, n. 10.
Northland Pine Co. v. Northern Insulating Co.—§ 8.7, n. 13.
North Park Bank of Commerce v. Nichols—§ 12.8, n. 6.
North Point Patio Offices Venture v. United Ben. Life Ins. Co.—§ 5.22, n. 19.
Northport Marina Associates, In re, 136 B.R. 911—§ 4.35, n. 40.
Northport Marina Associates, In re, 136 B.R. 903—§ 8.14, n. 27.
Northrip v. Federal Nat. Mortg. Ass'n—§ 3.30, n. 5, 11, 12; § 7.25, n. 3, 19; § 7.26, n. 9; § 7.27, n. 2, 6, 11, 12, 13, 21, 35; § 7.28; § 7.28, n. 14, 18, 20, 23.
North River Construction Co., In re—§ 10.5, n. 12.
Northside Bldg. & Inv. Co. v. Finance Co. of America—§ 5.33, n. 13, 33.
North Star Apartments v. Goppert Bank & Trust Co.—§ 7.7, n. 4.
Northup v. Reese—§ 5.34, n. 9.
Northwest Commons, Inc., In re—§ 4.35, n. 25, 26; § 8.18, n. 43.
Northwestern Mut. Life Ins. Co., Application of—§ 4.34, n. 21.
Northwestern Mut. Life Ins. Co. v. Butler—§ 3.1, n. 37.

Northwestern Mut. Life Ins. Co. v. Nebraska Land Corp.—§ 7.31, n. 11.
Northwestern Nat. Bank v. Sloan—§ 10.2, n. 7.
Northwestern Nat. Ins. Co. v. Maggio—§ 5.29, n. 11, 16.
Northwestern Nat. Ins. Co. v. Mildenberger—§ 4.16, n. 7, 8.
Northwestern State Bank v. Hanks—§ 3.9, n. 5; § 3.10, n. 3.
Northwestern Trust Co. v. Ryan—§ 7.10, n. 18.
Northwest Federal Sav. & Loan v. Tiffany Const. Co.—§ 13.3, n. 43.
Northwest Land and Inv., Inc. v. New West Federal Sav. and Loan Ass'n—§ 11.7, n. 22, 36.
Northwest Land & Inv., Inc. v. New West Federal Sav. and Loan Ass'n—§ 12.3, n. 47.
Norton v. Palmer—§ 6.11, n. 16.
Norwest Bank Indiana, N.A. v. Friedline—§ 4.51, n. 4.
Norwest Bank Nebraska, Nat. Ass'n v. Kizzier—§ 6.6, n. 34.
Norwest Bank Worthington v. Ahlers—§ 8.14, n. 83.
Norwich Fire Insurance Co. v. Boomer—§ 4.13, n. 9.
Norwood v. De Hart—§ 5.15, n.5.
Novus Equities Corp. v. EM-TY Partnership—§ 3.32, n. 28.
Noyes v. Hall—§ 7.13, n. 3.
Nusor, In re—§ 5.29, n. 16.
Nussear v. Hazard—§ 5.33, n. 23.
Nutting v. Bradford Nat. Bank—§ 12.8, n. 12.
Nutz v. Shepherd—§ 5.4, n. 1; § 5.5, n. 3, 4; § 5.7, n. 16.
Nye v. Swan—§ 7.4, n. 4.
Nygaard v. Anderson—§ 3.32, n. 2.
Nymark v. Heart Federal Sav. & Loan Ass'n—§ 12.11, n. 29.

O

Oakes v. Michigan Oil Co.—§ 12.9, n. 46, 47.
Oak Glen R-Vee, In re—§ 8.18, n. 19.
Oakland Bank of Sav. v. California Pressed Brick Co.—§ 9.6, n. 6.
Oaks v. Weingartner—§ 2.4, n. 2.
Oaks Fire Co. v. Herbert—§ 6.11, n. 45.
Obermeier v. Bennett—§ 5.22, n. 35.
O'Boskey v. First Federal Sav. & Loan Ass'n of Boise—§ 5.22, n. 19.
O'Briant v. Lee, 200 S.E. 865—§ 3.19, n. 3.
O'Briant v. Lee, 195 S.E. 15—§ 3.19, n. 16.
Occi Co., United States v.—§ 7.7, n. 41.
Occidental Sav. and Loan Ass'n v. Venco Partnership—§ 5.22, n. 12, 14.
Ocean County Nat. Bank v. J. Edwin Ellor & Sons—§ 10.15, n. 2.
Oceanview/Virginia Beach Real Estate Associates, In re—§ 4.35, n. 41.
O'Connell v. Dockendorff—§ 5.21, n. 22; § 5.22, n. 30, 32; § 5.24, n. 27.
O'Connor v. Richmond Sav. & Loan Ass'n—§ 6.9, n. 2.
Odell v. Buck—§ 4.6, n. 4.
Odell v. Hoyt—§ 7.6, n. 8.
Odell v. Montross—§ 3.3, n. 2; § 7.4, n. 12.
O'Donnell, In re—§ 4.22, n. 19.
Oellerich v. First Federal Sav. and Loan Ass'n of Augusta—§ 5.19, n. 45.
Officer v. American Eagle Fire Ins. Co.—§ 4.14, n. 5.
Official Limited Partners 1981 Equidyne Properties, I v. Credit Alliance Corp.—§ 9.8, n. 29.
O'Gasapian v. Danielson—§ 5.34, n. 30.
Ogden v. Gibraltar Sav. Ass'n—§ 7.6, n. 10, 11.
Ogle v. Koerner—§ 8.7, n. 11.
Oglesby v. South Georgia Grocery Co.—§ 5.17, n. 2.
Ohio Mutual Savings & Loan Co. v. Public Construction Co.—§ 4.35, n. 49.
Ohio Realty Investment Corp. v. Southern Bank of West Palm Beach—§ 7.16, n. 16.
Ohmer v. Boyer—§ 5.9, n. 6.
Oklahoma Hardware Co. v. Townsend—§ 13.3, n. 35.
Okura & Co. (America), Inc. v. Careau Group—§ 4.35, n. 6.
Olathe Bank v. Mann—§ 8.3, n. 6.
Olds Bros. Lumber Co. v. Marley—§ 12.9, n. 4.
Old Stone Capital Corp. v. John Hoene Implement Corp.—§ 12.9, n. 21.
Old Stone Mortgage and Realty Trust v. New Georgia Plumbing, Inc.—§ 12.9, n. 7.
Old West End Ass'n v. Buckeye Federal Sav. & Loan—§ 11.5, n. 28.
Olean v. Treglia—§ 5.22, n. 14.
Oliver v. Bledsoe—§ 5.28, n. 42.
Oliver v. Resolution Trust Corp.—§ 11.7, n. 14, 37.
Olsen v. Financial Federal Sav. and Loan Ass'n—§ 11.6, n. 26.
Olshan Lumber Co. v. Bullard—§ 5.33, n. 2.
Olympic Federal v. Witney Development Co., Inc.—§ 4.1, n. 17.
Omaha Nat. Bank v. Continental Western Corp.—§ 10.13, n. 16.
O'Maley v. Pugliese—§ 5.33, n. 4.
OMNE Partners II, In re—§ 3.18, n. 3.
OMP v. Security Pacific Business Finance, Inc., 716 F.Supp. 251—§ 8.3, n. 12.
OMP v. Security Pacific Business Finance, Inc., 716 F.Supp. 239—§ 12.3, n. 1.
Onderdonk v. Gray—§ 4.32, n. 1.
One Fourth Street North, Ltd., In re—§ 4.35, n. 25.
163rd Street Mini Storage, Inc., In re—§ 4.35, n. 25, 26.

TABLE OF CASES

O'Neil v. General Sec. Corp.—§ 8.2, n. 10; § 8.3, n. 57; § 10.13, n. 2.
O'Neill Production Credit Ass'n v. Mitchell—§ 2.3, n. 21; § 3.35, n. 1, 11; § 12.8, n. 6, 15.
1934 Realty Corporation, In re—§ 5.35, n. 15.
1300 Lafayette East, United States v.—§ 5.27, n. 1.
1301 Connecticut Ave. Associates, In re—§ 4.35, n. 24.
Ontiveros v. MBank Houston, N.A.—§ 4.20, n. 2; § 4.23, n. 3.
Onyx Refining Co. v. Evans Production Corp.—§ 4.6, n. 4.
Opdyke v. Bartles—§ 7.2, n. 22.
Opelika Mfg. Corp., In re—§ 3.19, n. 23.
Oran v. Canada Life Assur. Co.—§ 12.3, n. 19.
Orange County Teachers Credit Union v. Peppard—§ 3.38; § 3.38, n. 13.
Oransky, In re—§ 10.9, n. 14.
Ordway v. Downey—§ 5.7, n. 11, 12.
Oregon Mortg. Co. v. Leavenworth Securities Corporation—§ 4.45, n. 8.
Original Vienna Bakery Co. v. Heissler—§ 4.10, n. 10.
Orlando v. Berns—§ 3.18, n. 2; § 3.19, n. 10.
Orlando Tennis World Development Co., Inc., In re—§ 8.14, n. 46.
Orloff v. Metropolitan Trust Co. of California—§ 5.18, n. 5.
Orloff v. Petak—§ 7.15, n. 10, 15.
Orr v. Bennett—§ 4.2, n. 18.
Orr v. Broad—§ 4.23, n. 2.
Orr v. Hadley—§ 4.8, n. 1.
Orrego v. HUD—§ 6.4, n. 30.
Ortega, Snead, Dixon & Hanna v. Gennitti—§ 5.17, n. 5.
Ortegel v. ITT Thorp Corp.—§ 6.4, n. 14.
Osage Oil & Refining Co. v. Mulber Oil Co.—§ 7.14, n. 1.
Osborn v. Aetna Life and Casualty Company—§ 5.19, n. 11.
Osborne v. Cabell—§ 5.14, n. 10; § 5.15, n. 5.
Osborne v. Heyward—§ 5.9, n. 18.
Osborne's Estate, In re—§ 6.11, n. 45.
Osipowicz v. Furland—§ 3.19, n. 11.
Ottaviano, Matter of—§ 8.15, n. 5.
Ott Hardware Co. v. Yost—§ 12.4, n. 35.
Outlook/Century, Ltd., In re—§ 8.14, n. 87.
Overland Park Sav. and Loan Ass'n v. Braden—§ 7.13, n. 11.
Owen, Matter of—§ 2.1, n. 2.
Owens, In re—§ 8.13, n. 31; § 8.17, n. 3, 4, 5.
Owens v. Grimes—§ 7.22, n. 40, 41, 42.
Owens v. Idaho First Nat. Bank—§ 6.7, n. 1.
Owens–Corning Fiberglas Corp. v. Texas Commerce Bank Nat. Ass'n—§ 12.10, n. 33.

Oxford House, Inc. v. Township of Cherry Hill—§ 11.5, n. 18.
Ozark Production Credit Ass'n v. Walden—§ 7.21, n. 75.

P

Pacheco v. Heussler—§ 4.13, n. 19.
Pachter v. Woodman—§ 7.22, n. 17.
Pacific Coast Engineering Co. v. Detroit Fidelity & Surety Co.—§ 12.2, n. 25.
Pacific Development Co. v. Stewart—§ 3.29, n. 5.
Pacific First Federal Sav. and Loan Ass'n v. Lindberg—§ 5.17, n. 5.
Pacific Hide & Fur Depot, Inc., United States v.—§ 4.47, n. 13.
Pacific Loan Management Corp. v. Superior Court (Armstrong)—§ 7.31, n. 3.
Pacific Northwest Packing Co v. Allen—§ 4.41, n. 7.
Pacific States Savings & Loan Co. v. North American Bond & Mortgage Co.—§ 4.2, n. 16.
Pacific States Sav., Loan & Bldg. Co. v. Dubois—§ 12.4, n. 31.
Pacific Trust Co. TTEE v. Fidelity Federal Sav. & Loan Ass'n—§ 6.1, n. 9; § 6.3, n. 5, 8.
Packard Properties, Ltd., In re—§ 10.9, n. 1.
Packer v. Rochester etc., Railway Co.—§ 4.2, n. 10.
Padgett v. Haston—§ 12.8, n. 17.
Page v. Clark—§ 3.16, n. 2.
Page v. Hinchee—§ 5.7, n. 16.
Page v. Robinson—§ 4.4, n. 2, 7.
Pain v. Packard—§ 5.9; § 5.9, n. 15.
Paine v. Woods—§ 4.9, n. 2.
Pajaro Dunes Rental Agency, Inc., In re—§ 8.2, n. 10; § 8.3, n. 56.
Palcar Real Estate Co. v. Commissioner—§ 8.5, n. 20.
Palm v. Schilling—§ 8.3, n. 35, 37.
Palmer v. Crews Lumber Co., Inc.—§ 13.3, n. 18.
Palmer v. Forrest, Mackey and Associates, Inc.—§ 12.4, n. 23; § 13.3, n. 20.
Palmer v. Guaranty Trust Co. of New York—§ 7.14, n. 6.
Palmer v. Lundy—§ 3.7, n. 1; § 3.8, n. 1.
Palmer v. Uhl—§ 6.6, n. 9.
Palmer First Nat. Bank v. Rinker Materials Corp.—§ 12.7, n. 42.
Palmeri v. Allen—§ 3.38, n. 5.
Palmer River Realty, Inc., In re—§ 8.14, n. 10, 21.
Palmieri v. New York Preparatory School—§ 4.38, n. 16.
Panama Timber Co., Inc. v. Barsanti—§ 3.28, n. 22.
Panas, In re—§ 4.3, n. 1; § 4.24, n. 10.

Pancake v. Cauffman—§ 3.8, n. 12; § 3.11, n. 1.
Panko v. Pan American Federal Sav. and Loan Assn.—§ 5.23, n. 8.
Pankow Const. Co. v. Advance Mortg. Corp.—§ 10.9, n. 16; § 12.6, n. 21.
Pannell v. Continental Can Co., Inc.—§ 8.8, n. 18.
Papa v. Greenwich Green, Inc.—§ 13.3, n. 49.
Papamechail v. Holyoke Mut. Ins. Co.—§ 5.5, n. 3; § 5.12, n. 2; § 5.14, n. 2.
Paradise Land and Cattle Co. v. McWilliams Enterprises, Inc.—§ 8.3, n. 51.
Paramount Bldg. & Loan Ass'n of City of Newark v. Sacks—§ 4.35, n. 18; § 4.38, n. 12, 14, 18, 19; § 4.43, n. 10.
Pardee v. Van Anken—§ 7.15, n. 16; § 10.8, n. 1.
Parise v. Citizens Nat. Bank—§ 3.29, n. 18, 73.
Parish v. Gilmanton—§ 4.12, n. 16.
Park v. United States—§ 12.11, n. 44.
Park at Dash Point L.P., In re—§ 4.35, n. 25, 27; § 8.18, n. 42, 46, 48.
Parker v. Columbia Bank—§ 12.10, n. 34.
Parker v. Sheldon—§ 7.22, n. 40.
Parkinson v. Hanbury—§ 4.28, n. 11.
Parkman v. Welch—§ 10.15, n. 6.
Park North Partners, Ltd., In re, 80 B.R. 551—§ 8.17, n. 73.
Park North Partners, Ltd., In re, 72 B.R. 79—§ 9.8, n. 8.
Parks v. Mulledy—§ 3.18, n. 3.
Park Tuscon Investors Ltd. Partnership v. Ali—§ 11.7, n. 35.
Park Valley Corp. v. Bagley—§ 3.29; § 3.29, n. 39; § 3.32, n. 2.
Parlette v. Equitable Farm Mortg. Ass'n—§ 5.8, n. 5.
Parlier v. Miller—§ 5.6, n. 1.
Parmer v. Parmer—§ 3.1, n. 1.
Paro v. Biondo—§ 12.4, n. 11.
Parr v. Reiner—§ 2.1, n. 2.
Parsons v. Lender Service, Inc.—§ 9.7, n. 23.
Parsons v. Noggle—§ 7.5, n. 23.
Parsons v. Welles—§ 6.6, n. 10.
Partridge v. Hemenway—§ 4.6, n. 6.
Pasadena Associates v. Connor—§ 12.3, n. 43.
Pastor v. Lafayette Bldg. Ass'n—§ 12.9, n. 29; § 12.10, n. 32.
Pastos, United States v.—§ 11.6; § 11.6, n. 62.
Patterson v. Cappon—§ 5.7, n. 5.
Patterson v. Federal Deposit Ins. Corp.—§ 11.7, n. 35.
Patterson v. Miller—§ 7.21, n. 24.
Pattison v. Pattison—§ 3.6.
Patton v. Beecher—§ 3.16, n. 8.
Patton v. First Federal Sav. and Loan Ass'n of Phoenix—§ 5.24, n. 87.
Paul v. Kitt—§ 3.29, n. 1.
Paul Rochester Inv. Co. v. United States—§ 12.8, n. 10, 15.
Paulsen v. Jensen—§ 8.6, n. 28.

Paulson v. Lisowy—§ 3.32, n. 22.
Pavestone v. Interlock Pavers, Inc.—§ 13.3, n. 38.
Pawtucket Inst. for Sav. v. Gagnon—§ 2.2, n. 1, 3, 4, 5; § 2.4, n. 1.
Payne v. Avery—§ 10.13, n. 30.
Payne v. Foster—§ 10.8, n. 5.
Payne v. Morey—§ 3.11, n. 4.
Payne v. Snyder—§ 4.4, n. 10, 14.
Payne & Haddock, Inc., In re—§ 10.9, n. 1, 14.
P & C Const. Co. v. American Diversified/Wells Park II—§ 12.4, n. 46.
PCH Associates, In re—§ 3.19, n. 24.
Peabody v. Roberts—§ 7.14, n. 12; § 7.15, n. 10, 12, 13.
Peace v. Bullock—§ 8.8, n. 15.
Peacock v. Farmers and Merchants Bank—§ 5.19, n. 40.
Pearce v. Hall—§ 2.4, n. 2.
Pearll v. Williams—§ 12.8, n. 12.
Pearlman v. National Bank of New York City—§ 12.9, n. 21.
Pearlman v. Reliance Ins. Co.—§ 12.2, n. 40.
Pearmain v. Massachusetts Hospital Life Ins. Co.—§ 4.46, n. 11.
Pearson, In re—§ 8.15, n. 40.
Pearson v. Bailey—§ 10.11, n. 16.
Pee Dee State Bank v. Prosser—§ 10.2, n. 5; § 10.6, n. 3, 11.
Peerless Const. Co., Inc. v. Mancini—§ 3.7, n. 3.
Pelican Homestead and Sav. Ass'n v. Campbell—§ 11.7, n. 30.
Pelican Homestead and Sav. Ass'n v. Security First Nat. Bank—§ 10.6, n. 2.
Pellerito v. Weber—§ 5.22, n. 36.
Pendleton v. Elliott—§ 4.13, n. 15, 16.
Pennamco, Inc. v. Nardo Management Co., Inc.—§ 7.11, n. 1.
Penn Central Transp. Co., In re—§ 8.14, n. 107.
Penn Cent. Transp. Co., In re—§ 10.10, n. 1, 6.
Penn Mut. Life Ins. Co. v. Katz—§ 4.2, n. 21.
Penn Packing Co., In re—§ 8.13, n. 21; § 8.17, n. 65.
Penn's Ad. v. Tolleson—§ 7.16, n. 4.
Pennsylvania, Dept. of Highways, Com. of, United States v.—§ 10.1, n. 2.
Penn York Mfg., Inc., In re—§ 8.14, n. 9.
Pentad Joint Venture v. First Nat. Bank of La Grange—§ 7.21, n. 83.
Penthouse Intern., Ltd. v. Dominion Federal Sav. & Loan Ass'n—§ 12.3, n. 9.
People v. _____ (see opposing party)
People ex rel. v. _____ (see opposing party and relator)
Peoples Bank and Trust Co. and Bank of Mississippi v. L & T Developers, Inc.—§ 12.7, n. 60; § 12.10, n. 32, 45.
People's Bank of Wilkesbarre v. Columbia Collieries Co.—§ 7.13, n. 11.

Peoples Federal Sav. and Loan Ass'n of East Chicago, Ind. v. Willsey—§ 5.21, n. 33.
Peoples Nat. Bank of Greenville v. Upchurch—§ 6.7, n. 10.
Peoples-Pittsburgh Trust Co. v. Henshaw—§ 4.22, n. 6.
People's Sav. Bank in Providence v. Champlin Lumber Co.—§ 12.7, n. 39.
Peoples Sav. Bank of New York v. D & P Realty Corp.—§ 7.12, n. 13.
People's Trust Co. of Binghamton v. Goodell—§ 4.38, n. 20.
Peoples Trust & Sav. Bank v. Humphrey—§ 12.3, n. 1.
Peppard Realty Co. v. Emdon—§ 3.24, n. 14.
Percy Galbreath & Son, Inc. v. Watkins—§ 12.7, n. 14.
Perdido Bay Country Club Estates, Inc., In re—§ 8.17, n. 12.
Perez v. United States—§ 5.24, n. 12, 14, 15.
Perine v. Dunn—§ 7.4, n. 11, 12.
Perkins v. Brown—§ 5.4, n. 6; § 5.5, n. 2.
Perkins v. Coombs—§ 12.9, n. 2.
Perkins v. Factory Point Nat. Bank—§ 6.7, n. 1.
Perkins v. Trinity Realty Co.—§ 2.1, n. 4; § 2.3, n. 3, 6.
Perkins' Lessee v. Dibble—§ 6.6, n. 11.
Perpetual Federal Sav. and Loan Ass'n v. Willingham—§ 3.38, n. 16.
Perre v. Castro—§ 6.7, n. 11.
Perretta v. St. Paul Fire & Marine Ins. Co.—§ 4.14, n. 20.
Perry v. Carr—§ 7.4, n. 6.
Perry v. Island Sav. and Loan Ass'n—§ 5.24, n. 87.
Perry v. Miller—§ 2.3, n. 3.
Perry v. Sindermann—§ 7.25, n. 20.
Perry v. Virginia Mortg. and Inv. Co., Inc.—§ 7.21, n. 65, 75.
Person v. Leathers—§ 7.16, n. 18.
Peshine v. Ord—§ 7.5, n. 23.
Peter v. Finzer—§ 5.20, n. 2.
Peter Fuller Enterprises, Inc. v. Manchester Sav. Bank—§ 6.1, n. 2.
Peterman-Donnelly Engineers & Contractors Corp. v. First Nat. Bank of Ariz., Phoenix—§ 10.6, n. 2, 9.
Peters v. Jamestown Bridge Co.—§ 5.28, n. 15.
Petersen v. Hartell—§ 3.29; § 3.29, n. 29, 47, 53.
Petersen v. Ridenour—§ 3.29, n. 1.
Peterson v. Brent Banking Co.—§ 10.14, n. 1.
Peterson v. John J. Reilly, Inc.—§ 5.28, n. 7.
Peterson v. Kansas City Life Ins. Co.—§ 7.22, n. 28, 29.
Peterson Bank v. Langendorf—§ 2.1, n. 2; § 12.7, n. 9.
Peterson Development Co., Inc. v. Torrey Pines Bank—§ 12.3, n. 1.

Petition of (see name of party)
Petrillo v. Pelham Bay Park Land Co.—§ 12.4, n. 36.
Pettengill v. Evans—§ 4.4, n. 7.
Pettibone v. Griswold—§ 2.4, n. 1.
Pettingill v. Hubbell—§ 7.15, n. 29.
Pettit v. Louis—§ 4.24, n. 12.
Pettus v. Gault—§ 5.27, n. 11.
Petz v. Estate of Petz—§ 3.35, n. 1.
Peugh v. Davis—§ 3.3, n. 2; § 6.19, n. 5.
Peyton v. Ayres—§ 7.8, n. 6.
Pezzimenti v. L.R. Cirou—§ 7.6, n. 4.
Phyfe v. Riley—§ 4.2, n. 10; § 4.24, n. 19.
Pfeifer v. W. B. Worthen Co.—§ 5.19, n. 21.
Pfleiderer, In re—§ 8.15, n. 45.
Phelps v. Sage—§ 6.6, n. 8.
Philadelphia Penn Worsted Company, In re—§ 3.33, n. 19.
Philco Finance Co. v. Patton—§ 5.20, n. 5.
Phillippi, In re—§ 5.35, n. 15.
Phillips v. Atlantic Bank & Trust Co.—§ 7.21, n. 1.
Phillips v. Hagart—§ 8.5, n. 10.
Phillips v. Latham—§ 5.28, n. 7; § 7.20, n. 1; § 7.22, n. 17, 44.
Phillips v. Leavitt—§ 7.2, n. 19.
Phillips v. Nay—§ 3.29, n. 61.
Phillips v. Phillips—§ 3.20, n. 5; § 3.21, n. 5.
Phillips v. Plymale—§ 5.19, n. 49.
Phinney v. Levine, 381 A.2d 735—§ 6.11, n. 12, 30.
Phinney v. Levine, 359 A.2d 636—§ 6.11, n. 13, 28, 29.
Phoenix Mut. Life Ins. Co. v. Legris—§ 8.6, n. 8, 13.
Phoenix Trust Co. v. Garner—§ 5.19, n. 7.
Photomagic Industries, Inc. v. Broward Bank—§ 10.4, n. 2, 11.
Piea Realty Co. v. Papuzynski—§ 9.4, n. 4.
Piedmont Associates v. Cigna Property & Cas. Ins. Co.—§ 8.14, n. 87.
Pierce v. Grimley—§ 4.24, n. 13.
Pierce v. Kneeland—§ 3.1, n. 37.
Pierce v. Parrish—§ 3.22, n. 1, 3.
Pierce v. Pierce—§ 8.17, n. 9.
Pierce v. Robinson—§ 3.6, n. 1; § 3.15; § 3.15, n. 7, 12.
Pierce v. Yochum—§ 3.29, n. 1.
Pierce County v. King—§ 3.37, n. 7.
Pierre v. United States—§ 12.11, n. 45.
Pike v. Tuttle—§ 12.7, n. 37.
Pima County v. INA/Oldfather 4.7 Acres Trust No. 2292—§ 4.12, n. 10.
Pindus v. Newmat Leasing Corp.—§ 7.31, n. 10, 11.
Pine v. Pittman—§ 8.5, n. 5; § 8.6, n. 4.
Pineda v. PMI Mortg. Ins. Co.—§ 11.2, n. 52.
Pine Lake Village Apartment Co., In re—§ 8.14, n. 98.
Pine Lawn Bank and Trust Co. v. M. H. & H., Inc.—§ 4.2, n. 1.

Pinellas County v. Clearwater Federal Sav. & Loan Ass'n—§ 4.44, n. 7; § 9.1, n. 4, 6, 14.
Pines v. Novick—§ 4.31, n. 8; § 4.44, n. 12.
Pink v. Thomas—§ 5.35, n. 15.
Pinnell v. Boyd—§ 5.17, n. 4.
Pinney v. Merchants' Nat. Bank of Defiance—§ 7.13, n. 3.
Pinnix v. Maryland Casualty Co.—§ 5.17, n. 13.
Pintor v. Ong—§ 6.6, n. 19, 22.
Pioneer Annuity Life Ins. Co. v. National Equity Life Ins. Co.—§ 2.3, n. 1; § 2.4, n. 2.
Pioneer Enterprises, Inc. v. Goodnight—§ 5.34, n. 8.
Pioneer Federal Sav. and Loan Ass'n v. Reeder—§ 5.21, n. 33; § 5.24, n. 40.
Pioneer Lumber & Supply Co. v. First-Merchants Nat. Bank—§ 2.1, n. 2; § 2.4, n. 1.
Pioneer Plumbing Supply Co. v. Southwest Sav. & Loan Ass'n.—§ 12.6, n. 34.
Pioneer Sav. & Trust, F.A. v. Ben-Shoshan—§ 5.7, n. 16.
Pipkin v. Thomas & Hill, Inc.—§ 12.3, n. 41, 42.
Pipola v. Chicco—§ 10.6, n. 2.
Pitrolo v. Community Bank—§ 2.1, n. 2.
Pittsburgh-Duquesne Development Co., In re—§ 8.18, n. 6.
Pizer v. Herzig, 106 N.Y.S. 370—§ 4.35, n. 52.
Pizer v. Herzig, 105 N.Y.S. 38—§ 7.6, n. 15.
Pizzullo, In re—§ 8.15, n. 95.
Plain v. Roth—§ 10.14, n. 10.
Planters' Lumber Co. v. Griffin Chapel M.E. Church—§ 12.7, n. 29.
Planvest Equity Income Partners IV, In re—§ 6.3, n. 1.
Plateau Supply Co. v. Bison Meadows Corp.—§ 13.3, n. 38.
Platte Valley Bank of North Bend v. Kracl—§ 10.9, n. 11, 14; § 10.13, n. 15.
Pletcher v. Albrecht—§ 5.33, n. 24.
Plumbing Connections, Inc. v. Kostelnik—§ 12.10, n. 52.
Plummer v. Ilse—§ 3.1, n. 11.
Poco-Grande Investments v. C & S Family Credit, Inc.—§ 2.4, n. 12.
Poe v. Dixon—§ 5.10, n. 5.
Pogue, In re—§ 8.19, n. 9.
Polish Nat. Alliance of Brooklyn, U.S.A. v. White Eagle Hall Co., Inc.—§ 7.2, n. 5; § 7.12, n. 6, 12, 17, 26; § 7.13, n. 22; § 7.15, n. 8.
Pollak v. Millsap—§ 3.25, n. 1, 3; § 3.1, n. 11.
Pollard v. Harlow—§ 7.16, n. 9; § 8.5, n. 9.
Pollock v. Maison—§ 6.6, n. 12.
Pollock v. Pesapane—§ 7.32, n. 11; § 7.5, n. 24.
Polo Club Apartments Associates Ltd. Partnership, In re—§ 4.35, n. 25.
Polokoff v. Vebb—§ 3.7, n. 1.

Polytherm Industries, Inc., In re—§ 8.14, n. 55.
Pongetti v. Bankers Trust Sav. and Loan Ass'n—§ 10.9, n. 7; § 10.15, n. 5; § 12.8, n. 14.
Poole v. Johnson—§ 4.29, n. 21, 34.
Poole v. Kelsey—§ 10.7, n. 4.
Pope v. Biggs—§ 4.22, n. 24.
Pope Heating & Air Conditioning Co. v. Garrett-Bromfield Mortg. Co.—§ 13.3, n. 24.
Pope & Slocum v. Jacobus—§ 5.28, n. 21.
Porras v. Petroplex Sav. Ass'n—§ 11.7, n. 23.
Porter, In re—§ 8.15, n. 39.
Porter v. Corbin—§ 4.45, n. 6.
Porter v. Smith—§ 3.32, n. 26, 33.
Portland Mortgage Co. v. Creditors Protective Ass'n—§ 7.15, n. 22, 37.
Port Sewall Harbor and Tennis Club Owners Ass'n, Inc. v. First Federal Sav. and Loan Ass'n of Martin County—§ 12.11, n. 33; § 13.3, n. 61.
Post v. Door—§ 4.43, n. 5.
Postal Sav. & Loan Ass'n v. Freel—§ 7.7, n. 4.
Post Bros. Const. Co. v. Yoder—§ 12.4, n. 43.
Poston v. Bowen—§ 3.6, n. 4; § 3.18, n. 7.
Potter v. United States—§ 10.6, n. 3.
Potter Material Service, Inc., In re—§ 8.14, n. 81.
Potwin State Bank v. J. B. Houston & Son Lumber Co.—§ 12.7, n. 11, 13.
Poulos Inv., Inc. v. Mountainwest Sav. and Loan Ass'n—§ 12.7, n. 14, 33.
Powell, Ex parte—§ 6.16, n. 10.
Powell v. Phenix Federal Sav. & Loan Ass'n—§ 5.22, n. 25.
Powell v. Woodbury—§ 7.4, n. 6.
Power Bldg. & Loan Ass'n v. Ajax Fire Ins. Co.—§ 4.16, n. 1.
Powers v. Pense—§ 9.1, n. 12.
Poweshiek County v. Dennison—§ 7.8, n. 5.
Poydan, Inc. v. Agia Kiriaki, Inc.—§ 7.6, n. 1; § 7.7, n. 7.
Poynot v. J & T Developments, Inc.—§ 5.19, n. 39.
Poyzer v. Amenia Seed and Grain Co.—§ 12.9, n. 2.
Prahmcoll Properties v. Sanford—§ 5.4, n. 5.
Prairie State Nat Bank of Chicago v. United States—§ 12.2; § 12.2, n. 40.
Pratt v. Buckley—§ 5.9, n. 8.
Pratt v. Conway—§ 5.19, n. 5.
Pratt v. Pratt—§ 3.9, n. 3; § 3.10, n. 2, 3, 5; § 6.11, n. 22.
Preferred Sav. and Loan Ass'n, Inc. v. Royal Garden Resort, Inc.—§ 12.4, n. 21.
Preiss v. Campbell—§ 7.22, n. 5.
President and Directors of Manhattan Co. v. Mosler Safe Co.—§ 4.4, n. 12, 26.
Presidential Realty Corp. v. Bridgewood Realty Investors—§ 4.43, n. 10.

Presten v. Sailer—§ 13.6, n. 17, 23.
Preston v. First Bank of Marietta—§ 11.4, n. 61.
Prestridge v. Lazar—§ 10.7, n. 10.
Prewitt v. Wortham—§ 6.11, n. 21.
Price v. Geller—§ 6.6, n. 2.
Price v. Northern Bond & Mortgage Co.—§ 5.34, n. 28, 30, 31.
Price v. Perrie—§ 3.1, n. 3.
Price v. Rea—§ 6.16, n. 27.
Price v. Salisbury—§ 4.45, n. 3.
Prichard Plaza Associates Ltd. Partnership, In re—§ 4.35, n. 13; § 8.18, n. 54.
Prideaux v. Des Moines Joint-Stock Land Bank—§ 7.8, n. 3.
Priess v. Buchsbaum—§ 5.19, n. 37.
Prigal v. Kearn—§ 5.19, n. 33.
Prima Co, In re—§ 8.14, n. 112.
Prime Motor Inns, Inc., In re—§ 4.35, n. 41.
Prince v. Neal-Millard Co.—§ 12.4, n. 17; § 12.5, n. 3.
Prince George's County v. McMahon—§ 9.8, n. 34.
Prince Hall Village, Inc., United States v.—§ 7.7, n. 42.
Pritchett v. Mitchell—§ 5.17, n. 12.
Production Credit Ass'n of Mandan v. Henderson—§ 7.16, n. 19.
Production Credit Ass'n of Southern New Mexico v. Williamson—§ 7.24, n. 27.
Professional Development Corp., In re—§ 8.14, n. 87.
Professional Equities, Inc. v. Commissioner—§ 3.34, n. 18; § 9.8, n. 37.
Protective Equity Trust #83, Ltd. v. Bybee—§ 12.9, n. 34, 37; § 12.10, n. 17.
Protestant Episcopal Church of the Diocese of Georgia v. E. E. Lowe Co.—§ 9.1, n. 6, 18, 24.
Provencal v. Michel Const., Inc.—§ 12.11, n. 39.
Providence Institution for Savings v. Sims—§ 10.6, n. 1, 4.
Provident Federal Sav. and Loan Ass'n v. Idaho Land Developers, Inc.—§ 12.9, n. 24; § 12.10, n. 33.
Provident Inst. for Sav. in Town of Boston v. Merrill—§ 6.13, n. 2.
Provident Loan Trust Co. v. Marks—§ 7.14, n. 14.
Prudence Co. v. 160 West Seventy-Third St. Corporation—§ 4.39, n. 24; § 4.42, n. 17, 20.
Prudence Co. v. Sussman—§ 7.8, n. 10.
Prudence Realization Corp. v. Ferris—§ 5.35, n. 18.
Prudence Realization Corporation v. Geist—§ 5.35, n. 17, 18.
Prudential Ins. Co. of America v. Bull Market, Inc.—§ 12.9, n. 46, 47.
Prudential Ins. Co. of America v. Clybourn Realty Co.—§ 5.15, n. 14.
Prudential Ins. Co. of America v. Executive Estates, Inc.—§ 12.10, n. 8, 47, 51.
Prudential Ins. Co. of America v. Liberdar Holding Corp.—§ 4.35, n. 20; § 4.43, n. 12.
Prudential Ins. Co. of America v. Nuernberger—§ 9.4, n. 14.
Prudential Ins. Co. of America v. Spencer's Kenosha Bowl Inc.—§ 4.4, n. 14, 29, 32, 33; § 4.5, n. 2; § 4.11, n. 2, 3.
Prudential Ins. Co. of America v. Ward—§ 13.5, n. 15.
Prudential Sav. and Loan Ass'n v. Nadler—§ 5.1, n. 4; § 10.11, n. 2.
Prunty v. Bank of America—§ 8.3; § 8.3, n. 22, 97.
Public Bank of New York v. London—§ 4.40, n. 1.
Public Park, In re—§ 4.12, n. 4.
Pugh v. Richmond—§ 7.21, n. 2, 20.
Pulleyblank v. Cape—§ 8.1, n. 4.
Pulse v. North American Land Title Co. of Montana—§ 9.2, n. 10.
Purcell v. Gann—§ 7.2, n. 4.
Purcell v. Thornton—§ 4.29, n. 24; § 7.5, n. 1.
Purdy v. Coar—§ 5.17, n. 8.
Purdy v. Huntington—§ 5.34, n. 17.
Pustejovsky v. K. J. Z. T. Lodge—§ 5.35, n. 16.
Puyallup Valley Bank v. Mosby—§ 5.19, n. 39, 65.
Puziss v. Geddes—§ 3.32, n. 5.

Q

Quail Ridge Associates v. Chemical Bank—§ 12.1, n. 29.
Quality Inns Intern. Inc. v. Booth, Fish, Simpson, Harrison and Hall—§ 9.8, n. 2.
Quazzo v. Quazzo—§ 2.1, n. 17.
Queen City Sav. & Loan Ass'n v. Mannhalt—§ 7.21, n. 19.
Queen's Court Apartments, Inc., United States v.—§ 4.35, n. 9; § 11.6, n. 49.
Quinn, In re—§ 8.17, n. 77.
Quinn Plumbing Co. v. New Miami Shores Corporation—§ 7.3, n. 7, 8; § 7.10, n. 18; § 7.15, n. 1, 2.

R

Rabbit v. First National Bank—§ 7.10, n. 9.
Raby, In re—§ 8.19, n. 9.
Radunich v. Basso—§ 12.10, n. 47.
Ragan v. Standard Scale Co.—§ 10.7, n. 10.
Raggio v. Palmtag—§ 4.24, n. 12.
Rainer v. Security Bank & Trust Co.—§ 12.8, n. 17.
Rainer Mortg. v. Silverwood Ltd.—§ 8.3, n. 6, 81.
Rainier Pac. Supply, Inc. v. Gray—§ 13.3, n. 38, 46, 50.

Rains v. Mann—§ 7.8, n. 3.
Rake v. Wade—§ 8.15, n. 86.
Rakestraw v. Dozier Associates, Inc.—§ 5.24, n. 118; § 5.25, n. 2.
Raleigh & C. R. Co. v. Baltimore Nat. Bank—§ 7.16, n. 26; § 7.17, n. 9.
Ram Co., Inc. v. Estate of Kobbeman—§ 2.4, n. 16; § 12.8, n. 9.
Ramirez, In re—§ 8.15, n. 54.
Ramsey v. Hutchinson—§ 6.13, n. 3.
Ramsey v. Peoples Trust and Sav. Bank—§ 12.4, n. 42.
Rancourt, In re—§ 4.35, n. 25, 27.
Randall v. Home Loan & Investment Co.—§ 6.9; § 6.9, n. 3, 16.
Randall v. Norton—§ 5.25, n. 1, 10.
Randall v. Riel—§ 3.29, n. 32; § 5.21, n. 23.
Randolph Nat. Bank v. Vail—§ 5.30, n. 1.
Ranier v. Mount Sterling Nat. Bank—§ 12.9, n. 29.
Rank v. Nimmo—§ 7.7, n. 29; § 7.28, n. 30.
Ranken v. East and West India Docks Co., etc.—§ 1.2, n. 8.
Rankin v. First Nat. Bank—§ 2.3, n. 13.
Rankin County Bank v. McKinion—§ 8.1, n. 9.
Rankin-Whitham State Bank v. Mulcahey—§ 4.38, n. 5; § 4.39, n. 3.
Rapps v. Gottlieb—§ 5.32, n. 17.
Rasdall's Adm'rs v. Rasdall—§ 3.15, n. 10; § 3.16, n. 9, 11.
Ratner v. Miami Beach First Nat. Bank—§ 6.11, n. 12.
Ratto v. Sims (In re Lendvest Mortg., Inc.)—§ 5.28, n. 28; § 5.35, n. 47.
Rau v. Cavenaugh—§ 7.24, n. 8; § 7.26; § 7.26, n. 8, 13; § 7.28, n. 1; § 7.30, n. 2.
Rauscher Pierce Refsnes, Inc. v. Federal Deposit Ins. Corp.—§ 11.7, n. 38.
Ravnaas v. Andrich—§ 3.3, n. 6.
Ray v. Adams—§ 9.1, n. 19.
Ray v. Alabama Cent. Credit Union—§ 6.16, n. 10.
Ray v. Donohew—§ 10.1, n. 4, 16; § 10.2, n. 1.
Rayford v. Louisiana Sav. Ass'n—§ 5.24, n. 87.
Raymond L. Sabbag, Inc. v. Federal Deposit Ins. Corp.—§ 11.7, n. 32.
Raynor v. United States—§ 12.11, n. 8, 43.
Ray Thomas Enterprises v. Fox—§ 12.9, n. 8.
R.B. Thompson, Jr. Lumber Co. v. Windsor Development Corp.—§ 12.7, n. 39.
R. C. Mahon Co. v. Hedrich Const. Co., Inc.—§ 12.2, n. 32.
RDC, Inc. v. Brookleigh Builders, Inc. by Burns—§ 12.4, n. 22.
Read v. Cambridge—§ 4.12, n. 16.
Ready v. Koebke—§ 5.17, n. 12.
Real Estate–Land Title & Trust Co. v. Homer Building & Loan Ass'n—§ 4.27, n. 7.
Rebel v. National City Bank of Evansville—§ 9.4, n. 4, 14.

Rebel Mfg. and Marketing Corp., In re—§ 9.3, n. 11.
Rechnitzer v. Boyd—§ 5.28, n. 30; § 5.35, n. 47.
Rector of Christ Protestant Episcopal Church v. Mack—§ 7.12, n. 27; § 7.17, n. 17.
Red Cedar Const. Co., Inc., In re—§ 12.9, n. 2.
Reddell v. Jasper Federal Sav. & Loan Ass'n—§ 7.22, n. 35.
Redding v. Stockton, Whatley, Davin & Co.—§ 7.12, n. 29.
Redhead v. Skidmore Land Credit Co.—§ 5.8, n. 9.
Redic v. Mechanics & Farmers Bank—§ 4.31, n. 10.
Redmond v. Merrill Lynch Relocation Management, Inc.—§ 7.6, n. 7.
Redmond v. Ninth Federal Sav & Loan Ass'n of New York City—§ 6.2, n. 12.
Redwood Baseline, Ltd., People ex rel. Department of Transp. v.—§ 4.12, n. 1, 8.
Reed, Appeal of—§ 12.7, n. 6.
Reed v. Bartlett—§ 4.22, n. 9.
Reed v. Paul—§ 5.10, n. 15.
Reeder v. Longo—§ 12.9, n. 16.
Reedy v. Camfield—§ 7.12, n. 18.
Rees v. Craighead Inv. Co.—§ 10.4, n. 2.
Reese v. AMF-Whitely—§ 10.1, n. 4.
Reese v. First Missouri Bank and Trust Co. of Creve Coeur—§ 7.22, n. 48.
Reeves, In re—§ 8.15, n. 54.
Reeves v. Cordes—§ 5.19, n. 5, 33.
Regan v. Williams—§ 6.13, n. 2.
Regional Inv. Co. v. Willis—§ 8.1; § 8.1, n. 12, 16.
Rehberger v. Wegener—§ 4.40, n. 1.
Reid v. Whisenant—§ 10.11, n. 1, 2, 10.
Reilly v. Firestone Tire and Rubber Co.—§ 7.12, n. 29.
Reilly v. Lucraft—§ 5.10, n. 15.
Reilly v. Mayer—§ 10.13, n. 10.
Reimer v. Newell—§ 4.45, n. 3.
Reiserer v. Foothill Thrift and Loan—§ 7.22, n. 1, 9, 10, 11.
Reisig v. Resolution Trust Corp.—§ 11.7, n. 36.
Reisterstown Lumber Co. v. Royer—§ 12.4, n. 22.
Reitenbaugh v. Ludwick—§ 3.4, n. 10.
Reitman v. Mulkey—§ 7.27; § 7.27, n. 9.
Reitz, In re—§ 8.16, n. 24.
Reliance Equities, Inc., In re—§ 5.28, n. 28.
Reliance Ins. Co. v. Brown—§ 2.1, n. 2.
Rembert v. Ellis—§ 5.27, n. 11.
Renard v. Allen—§ 3.32, n. 5.
Renard v. Brown and Brown—§ 7.15, n. 3.
Rennich, In re—§ 8.16, n. 15.
Rent America, Inc. v. Amarillo Nat. Bank—§ 11.4, n. 61.
Republic Bank & Trust Co. of Tulsa v. Bohmar Minerals, Inc.—§ 12.4, n. 24.
Republic Financial Corp. v. Mize—§ 3.19, n. 9.

Republic Nat. Life Ins. Co. v. Lorraine Realty Corp.—§ 7.31, n. 2; § 12.9; § 12.9, n. 33.
Republic Nat. Life Ins. Co. v. Marquette Bank & Trust Co. of Rochester—§ 12.9, n. 45.
Resident Advisory Bd. v. Rizzo—§ 11.5, n. 18.
Resnick, In re—§ 12.8, n. 12.
Resolution Trust Corp. v. Associated Inv. Group—§ 11.7, n. 43.
Resolution Trust Corp. v. Camp—§ 11.7, n. 10.
Resolution Trust Corp. v. Dubois—§ 11.7, n. 18, 25.
Resolution Trust Corp. v. Heights of Texas, FSB—§ 5.35, n. 11, 58.
Resolution Trust Corp. v. Liberty Homes, Inc.—§ 11.7, n. 34.
Resolution Trust Corp. v. Maldonado—§ 11.7, n. 28.
Resolution Trust Corp. v. McCrory—§ 11.7, n. 16.
Resolution Trust Corp. v. Minassian—§ 6.4, n. 2; § 6.2, n. 7.
Resolution Trust Corp. v. Niagara Asset Corp.—§ 12.9, n. 6.
Resolution Trust Corp. v. Oaks Apartments Joint Venture—§ 5.29, n. 33.
Resolution Trust Corp. v. 1601 Partners, Ltd.—§ 5.29, n. 4, 35; § 11.7, n. 37.
Resolution Trust Corp. v. Ruggiero—§ 5.29, n. 36; § 5.31, n. 2; § 11.7, n. 35.
Resolution Trust Corp. v. Toler—§ 11.7, n. 14.
Resolution Trust Corp. v. 12A Associates—§ 2.1, n. 9; § 6.9, n. 21.
Resolution Trust Corp. v. Urban Redevelopment Authority of Pittsburgh—§ 11.2, n. 58.
Resolution Trust Corp. by Federal Deposit Ins. Corp. v. Crow—§ 11.7, n. 20.
Rettig v. Arlington Heights Federal Sav. and Loan Ass'n—§ 11.6, n. 23.
Rex Smith Propane, Inc. v. National Bank of Commerce—§ 5.35, n. 30.
Reynolds v. London & Lancashire Fire Ins. Co.—§ 4.16, n. 1.
Reynolds v. Ramos—§ 5.32, n. 16.
R. F. C. v. Smith—§ 5.35, n. 15, 16.
Rhinelander v. Richards—§ 4.35, n. 49.
Rhoades, In re—§ 8.15, n. 91, 93, 94.
Rhoades v. Parker—§ 2.2, n. 14.
Ribs Auto Sales, Inc., In re—§ 8.14, n. 87.
Ricard v. Equitable Life Assur. Soc. of the United States—§ 3.29, n. 73.
Rice, In re, 133 B.R. 722—§ 8.13, n. 11.
Rice, In re, 42 B.R. 838—§ 8.17, n. 1.
Rice v. Campisi—§ 7.7, n. 10.
Rice v. First Federal Sav. & Loan Ass'n of Lake County—§ 12.11, n. 8.
Rice v. Rice—§ 2.1, n. 9.
Rice v. St. Paul & P. R. Co.—§ 4.2, n. 21.
Rice v. Winters—§ 6.17, n. 13.
Rice v. Wood—§ 3.18, n. 2, 5; § 3.19, n. 9.

Richard, In re—§ 8.17, n. 16.
Richards, In re—§ 8.15, n. 70.
Richards v. Cowles—§ 10.13, n. 15.
Richards v. Kaskel—§ 13.4, n. 7.
Richardson, In re, 48 B.R. 141—§ 6.16, n. 20.
Richardson, In re, 23 B.R. 434—§ 8.17, n. 13, 16.
Richardson v. Baker—§ 5.17, n. 12.
Richardson v. Hockenhull—§ 6.17, n. 11.
Richards Trust Co. v. Rhomberg—§ 5.34, n. 42.
Richman v. Security Sav. and Loan Ass'n—§ 4.18, n. 9.
Rich Supply House, Inc., In re—§ 10.9, n. 7.
Rickel v. Energy Systems Holdings, Ltd.—§ 3.32, n. 8, 12, 13.
Ricker v. United States—§ 7.10, n. 11; § 7.24; § 7.24, n. 8, 9, 28; § 7.25; § 7.25, n. 3, 6; § 7.26; § 7.26, n. 8, 9, 10; § 7.28, n. 1; § 7.29; § 7.29, n. 3, 5; § 7.30, n. 2, 4, 5, 10.
Riddle v. Lushing—§ 8.3, n. 52.
Ridgeview Const. Co., Inc. v. American Nat. Bank and Trust Co. of Chicago—§ 12.4, n. 39.
Ridgewood Utilities Corp. v. King—§ 3.34, n. 5.
Ridley v. Ridley—§ 2.2, n. 10.
Riebe v. Budget Financial Corp.—§ 5.28, n. 40.
Riedle v. Peterson—§ 5.10, n. 10.
Rife v. Woolfolk—§ 7.21, n. 2, 3.
Riggs v. Kellner—§ 6.15, n. 2; § 6.17, n. 5, 10.
Riggs Nat. Bank of Washington, D.C. v. Wines—§ 12.9, n. 6.
Riley Bldg. Supplies, Inc. v. First Citizens Nat. Bank—§ 12.10, n. 44.
Rinaldo v. Holdeen—§ 12.7, n. 11.
Ring v. First Interstate Mortg., Inc.—§ 11.5, n. 26.
Ringling Joint Venture II v. Huntington Nat. Bank—§ 3.3, n. 6.
Ringo v. Woodruff—§ 4.46, n. 3.
Rinkel v. Lubke—§ 3.7, n. 5.
Rinker Materials Corp. v. Palmer First Nat. Bank & Trust Co. of Sarasota—§ 12.6, n. 28.
Rippe, In re—§ 8.15, n. 35.
Risken v. Clayman—§ 3.32, n. 31; § 4.13, n. 4.
Risse v. Thompson—§ 3.32, n. 29.
Rist v. Andersen—§ 8.6, n. 32.
Ritz v. Karstenson—§ 5.29, n. 27.
Rivera Rivera, United States v.—§ 5.4, n. 1; § 5.3, n. 4.
Riveredge Associates v. Metropolitan Life Ins. Co.—§ 6.1, n. 2; § 6.2, n. 3.
Rivers v. Rice—§ 12.9, n. 24.
Riverside Apartment Corporation v. Capitol Const. Co.—§ 10.13, n. 7.
Riverside Nat. Bank v. Manolakis—§ 8.3, n. 46.

Riverside Nursing Home, Matter of—§ 4.35, n. 31.
Riverside Park Realty Co. v. Federal Deposit Ins. Corp.—§ 11.7, n. 36.
Riverview Condominium Corp. v. Campagna Const. Co.—§ 13.3, n. 60.
Rives v. Mincks Hotel Co.—§ 4.2, n. 18.
Riviera Inn of Wallingford, Inc., In re—§ 8.14, n. 10.
R. K. Cooper Const. Co. v. Fulton—§ 8.3, n. 17.
R. L. Sweet Lumber Co. v. E. L. Lane, Inc.—§ 4.2, n. 1.
R. M. Shoemaker Co. v. Southeastern Pennsylvania Economic Development Corp.—§ 12.6, n. 26.
Roa v. Miller—§ 5.29, n. 3.
Roach, Matter of—§ 8.15, n. 35, 40.
Robar v. Ellingson—§ 6.19, n. 1, 5.
Robbins v. Larson—§ 5.33, n. 21.
Robbins v. Wilson Creek State Bank—§ 5.35, n. 12.
Robert C. Roy Agency, Inc. v. Sun First Nat. Bank of Palm Beach—§ 12.8, n. 9.
Robert R. Wisdom Oil Co., Inc. v. Gatewood—§ 7.21, n. 1.
Roberts v. Cameron–Brown Co., 556 F.2d 356—§ 7.7, n. 38; § 7.27, n. 21; § 7.28, n. 29.
Roberts v. Cameron–Brown Co., 410 F.Supp. 988—§ 7.24, n. 8; § 7.25, n. 15; § 7.28; § 7.28, n. 24.
Roberts v. Cameron-Brown Co.—§ 7.7, n. 28; § 7.24, n. 8; § 7.25, n. 15; § 7.27, n. 21; § 7.28; § 7.28, n. 24, 29.
Roberts v. Fleming—§ 4.29, n. 12, 23.
Roberts v. Harkins—§ 12.9, n. 25; § 12.10, n. 7.
Roberts v. Littlefield—§ 7.5, n. 6.
Roberts v. Morin—§ 3.35, n. 2.
Roberts v. State Bd. of Dental Examiners—§ 7.21, n. 73.
Robertson v. Cilia—§ 4.1, n. 5.
Robertson v. United States Live Stock Co.—§ 5.32, n. 26.
Robeson, Appeal of—§ 10.13, n. 7.
Robinson v. Builders Supply & Lumber Co.—§ 3.7, n. 2; § 3.8, n. 1, 5, 6, 9, 18.
Robinson v. Durston—§ 3.17, n. 8, 9; § 3.18, n. 2; § 3.19, n. 3, 7.
Robinson v. Fife—§ 7.3, n. 8.
Robinson v. Miller—§ 7.6, n. 8.
Robinson v. Ryan—§ 7.15, n. 2, 4.
Robinson v. Smith—§ 4.24, n. 8.
Robinson v. Williams—§ 12.7, n. 4.
Robson v. O'Toole, 214 P. 278—§ 5.10, n. 14.
Robson v. O'Toole, 187 P. 110—§ 5.15, n. 1.
Roby v. Maisey—§ 4.1, n. 6.
Rochester Lumber Co. v. Dygert—§ 12.7, n. 37.
Rockaway Park Series Corporation v. Hollis Automotive Corporation—§ 7.7, n. 10.

Rockford Life Ins. Co. v. Department of Revenue—§ 11.6, n. 93.
Rockhill v. United States—§ 12.9, n. 14; § 12.10, n. 13, 33.
Rock Island Bank v. Anderson—§ 9.7, n. 19.
Rock River Lumber Corp. v. Universal Mortg. Corp. of Wisconsin—§ 10.1, n. 4, 9, 10; § 10.3, n. 3; § 10.5, n. 3; § 10.6, n. 8.
Rockwell Intern. Corp. v. IU Intern. Corp.—§ 4.48, n. 4.
Rocky Mountain Tool & Mach. Co. v. Tecon Corp.—§ 12.2, n. 26.
Roden v. Walker—§ 6.11, n. 12.
Rodgers v. Rainier Nat. Bank—§ 6.1, n. 10; § 6.3, n. 3, 9.
Rodgers v. Seattle-First Nat. Bank—§ 5.33, n. 3, 10, 33.
Rodney v. Arizona Bank—§ 5.27, n. 7; § 5.28, n. 28, 30.
Roffinella v. Sherinian—§ 8.3, n. 102.
Rogers v. Barnes—§ 7.22, n. 40.
Rogers v. Challis—§ 12.3, n. 48.
Rogers v. Davis—§ 3.8, n. 12; § 3.19, n. 9.
Rogers v. First Tennessee Bank Nat. Ass'n—§ 12.8, n. 10.
Rogers v. Gosnell—§ 5.18, n. 16.
Rogers v. Houston—§ 7.10, n. 15.
Rogers v. Meyers—§ 10.14, n. 1.
Rogers v. Wheeler—§ 4.6, n. 1.
Rogers v. Williamsburgh Sav. Bank—§ 6.4, n. 11.
Rohrer v. Deatherage—§ 4.22, n. 22; § 4.38, n. 5; § 4.39, n. 3; § 4.42, n. 15.
Roll v. Smalley—§ 7.14, n. 5.
Rollins v. Bravos—§ 4.16, n. 7.
Romak Iron Works v. Prudential Ins. Co. of America—§ 12.6, n. 7.
Romito Bros. Elec. Const. Co. v. Frank A. Flannery, Inc.—§ 13.3, n. 42.
Ron Pair Enterprises, Inc., United States v.—§ 8.15; § 8.15, n. 84.
Roosevelt Hotel Corporation v. Williams—§ 4.22, n. 12; § 7.12, n. 30.
Roosevelt Sav. Bank v. A.V.R. Realty Corp.—§ 5.25, n. 7.
Roosevelt Sav. Bank v. Goldberg—§ 7.31, n. 1.
Ropfogel v. Enegren—§ 8.4, n. 6.
Rorie, In re—§ 8.15, n. 89.
Rose v. Lurton Co.—§ 9.3, n. 5.
Rose v. Rein—§ 5.34, n. 30.
Roseleaf Corporation v. Chierighino—§ 8.2, n. 6; § 8.3; § 8.3, n. 118.
Rosemont, Village of v. Maywood-Proviso State Bank—§ 6.3, n. 16.
Rosenbaum v. Funcannon—§ 4.16, n. 7, 9.
Rosenberg v. General Realty Service—§ 7.3, n. 10, 11.
Rosenberg v. Rolling Inn, Inc.—§ 5.6, n. 3.
Rosenberg v. Smidt—§ 7.20, n. 2, 14, 17.
Rosenthal v. Le May—§ 3.8, n. 1.

TABLE OF CASES

Roskamp Manley Associates, Inc. v. Davin Development and Inv. Corp.—§ 12.9, n. 17, 38.
Ross v. Boardman—§ 7.10, n. 18.
Ross v. Continental Mortg. Investors—§ 12.10, n. 11, 34.
Ross v. Leavitt—§ 7.5, n. 1.
Ross v. Title Guarantee & Trust Co.—§ 5.34, n. 34.
Rosselot v. Heimbrock—§ 7.6, n. 7.
Rosser v. Cole—§ 13.3, n. 43.
Rossi, United States v.—§ 11.6; § 11.6, n. 64.
Rossiter v. Merriman—§ 8.1, n. 2.
Ross Realty Co. v. First Citizens Bank & Trust Co.—§ 2.1, n. 14; § 8.3, n. 28.
Ross v. Johnson—§ 5.33, n. 17.
Roth, In re—§ 5.19, n. 33, 37.
Rothschild v. Title Guarantee & Trust Co.—§ 5.32, n. 3.
Rott v. Connecticut General Life Ins. Co.—§ 7.18, n. 4.
Rotta v. Hawk—§ 12.4, n. 14.
Roundhouse Const. Corp. v. Telesco Masons Supplies Co., Inc.—§ 12.5; § 12.5, n. 20, 31.
Roundtree Villas Ass'n, Inc. v. 4701 Kings Corp.—§ 12.11, n. 32; § 13.3, n. 60, 65.
Roven v. Miller—§ 12.9, n. 17.
Rowan v. Sharps' Rifle Mfg. Co.—§ 12.7, n. 33.
Rowe v. Small Business Admin.—§ 5.34, n. 4.
Rowell v. Jewett—§ 2.2, n. 9.
Rowland v. Christian—§ 12.10, n. 50.
Royal Ambassador Condominium Ass'n, Inc. v. East Coast Supply Corp.—§ 13.3, n. 44, 49.
Royal Bank of Canada v. Clarke—§ 9.2, n. 2; § 9.1, n. 4.
Roystone Co. v. Darling—§ 12.4, n. 18.
Rubin v. Centerbanc Federal Sav. & Loan Ass'n—§ 5.26, n. 6.
Rubin v. Los Angeles Federal Sav. and Loan Ass'n—§ 5.24, n. 118.
Rubin v. Pioneer Federal Sav. & Loan Ass'n—§ 12.3, n. 41, 42.
Rubottom, In re—§ 8.15, n. 52.
Rucker v. State Exchange Bank—§ 5.28, n. 29, 34; § 5.33, n. 17, 21.
Ruckman v. Astor—§ 4.27, n. 16.
Rude, In re—§ 12.8, n. 12.
Rudisill v. Buckner—§ 4.29, n. 26.
Rudnitski v. Seely—§ 3.32, n. 29.
Rudolph v. First Southern Federal Sav. & Loan Ass'n—§ 12.11; § 12.11, n. 9.
Ruebeck, In re—§ 8.17, n. 33.
Rugg v. Record—§ 7.3, n. 10.
Ruggiero v. United States—§ 12.2, n. 14.
Ruggles v. Barton—§ 5.28, n. 12, 14.
Ruidoso State Bank v. Castle—§ 12.8, n. 9.
Runnemede Owners, Inc. v. Crest Mortg. Corp.—§ 12.3, n. 1.
Ruocco v. Brinker—§ 12.5, n. 19, 25.
Ruohs v. Traders' Fire Ins. Co.—§ 5.6, n. 1.

Rupp v. Earl H. Cline & Sons, Inc.—§ 12.4, n. 27.
Rusch v. Kauker—§ 3.33, n. 4.
Rusher v. Bunker—§ 10.6, n. 3, 4.
Russell v. Allen—§ 4.21, n. 5; § 4.22, n. 6.
Russell v. Ely—§ 4.24, n. 8.
Russell v. Pistor—§ 6.16, n. 13, 24.
Russell v. Richards—§ 3.27, n. 5.
Russell v. Roberts—§ 8.3, n. 37.
Russell v. Russell—§ 4.38, n. 16.
Russell v. Smithies—§ 4.29, n. 9.
Russell v. Southard—§ 3.15, n. 14; § 3.18, n. 5, 10.
Russo v. Wolbers—§ 3.1, n. 2; § 3.3, n. 1; § 8.5, n. 16, 17.
Rust v. Johnson—§ 11.6; § 11.6, n. 91.
Rustic Hills Shopping Plaza, Inc. v. Columbia Sav. and Loan Ass'n—§ 5.21, n. 33.
Ruther v. Thomas—§ 5.4, n. 1.
Ruyter v. Wickes—§ 7.14, n. 9.
Ruzyc to Use of Bumbaugh v. Brown.—§ 5.10, n. 11.
Ryan, In re—§ 8.3, n. 11; § 8.13, n. 11.
Ryan v. Adamson—§ 4.13, n. 7.
Ryan v. Bloom—§ 8.10, n. 13.
Ryan v. Dox—§ 3.24, n. 11.
Ryer v. Gass—§ 10.7, n. 12.
Ryan v. Kolterman—§ 3.32, n. 12, 16, 20.
Ryan v. Weiner—§ 3.6, n. 1.
Ryder v. Bank of Hickory Hills—§ 7.6, n. 9; § 7.7, n. 6.
Ryer v. Morrison—§ 7.4, n. 9.
Rzepiennik v. United States Home Corp.—§ 12.11, n. 8.

S

Sabiston's Adm'r v. Otis Elevator Co.—§ 4.26, n. 1.
SAC Const. Co., Inc. v. Eagle Nat. Bank of Miami—§ 10.9, n. 7.
Sacramento Bank v. Alcorn—§ 4.2, n. 16.
Sacramento Bank v. Murphy—§ 6.11, n. 35.
Sacramento Mansion, Ltd., In re—§ 4.35, n. 41.
Sacramento Sav. and Loan Ass'n v. Superior Court for Sacramento County—§ 6.2, n. 18.
Sadd v. Heim—§ 12.7, n. 10.
Sadow v. Poskin Realty Corp.—§ 7.31, n. 1, 8, 10, 11.
Safari, Inc. v. Verdoorn—§ 3.29, n. 32.
Safeco Ins. Co. of America v. State—§ 12.2, n. 47.
Safe-Deposit & Trust Co. v. Wickhem—§ 4.45, n. 8.
Safety Federal Sav. and Loan Ass'n v. Thurston—§ 2.3, n. 1, 19.
Sage, United States v.—§ 7.31, n. 12.
Sager v. Rebdor Realty Corporation—§ 4.39, n. 16; § 4.42, n. 10.
Sager v. Tupper—§ 10.13, n. 10.

Saint Peter's School, In re—§ 8.14, n. 20, 45.
Sale City Peanut & Mill. Co. v. Planters & Citizens Bank—§ 7.22, n. 47.
Salem v. Salem—§ 2.3, n. 23.
Salem Plaza Associates, In re—§ 4.35, n. 25.
Salemy v. Diab—§ 5.29, n. 11.
Saline State Bank v. Mahloch—§ 4.35, n. 31; § 8.18, n. 53.
Salt v. Marquess of Northampton—§ 3.1, n. 3, 8, 12.
Salter v. Ulrich—§ 8.2, n. 9; § 8.3, n. 36, 37.
Samuel v. Jarrah Timber & W.P. Corp., Limited—§ 3.1, n. 15.
Samuelson v. Promontory Inv. Corp.—§ 12.9, n. 21.
Sanborn, McDuffee Co. v. Keefe—§ 10.13, n. 7, 10.
Sanders v. Hicks—§ 5.22, n. 14; § 5.24, n. 87.
Sanders v. John Nuveen & Co., Inc.—§ 12.3, n. 60.
Sanders v. Lackey—§ 10.2, n. 2; § 10.9, n. 23; § 10.11, n. 1, 12; § 10.14, n. 4.
Sanders v. Ovard—§ 8.2, n. 6.
Sanders v. Reed—§ 4.5, n. 6, 11; § 4.9, n. 2.
Sanders v. Wilson—§ 4.28, n. 9.
Sanderson v. Price—§ 4.3, n. 3.
Sanderson v. Turner—§ 5.8, n. 5; § 5.10, n. 11.
Sandler v. Green—§ 6.7, n. 6.
Sandmann v. Old Delancey Bldg. & Loan Ass'n—§ 6.11, n. 45.
Sandon v. Hooper—§ 4.29, n. 1, 13.
Sandusky v. First Nat. Bank of Sikeston—§ 11.2, n. 52.
Sandwich Manuf'g Co. v. Zellmer—§ 4.44, n. 3.
Sandy Ridge Oil Co., Inc., In re—§ 8.13, n. 11; § 8.14, n. 6.
Sanford v. Bergin—§ 6.11, n. 26.
Sanford v. Hill—§ 10.9, n. 4.
Sanford v. Lichtenberger—§ 4.31, n. 1.
San Francisco, City and County of v. Lawton—§ 7.12, n. 5; § 7.14, n. 14.
San Jose Safe Deposit Bank of Sav. v. Bank of Madera—§ 6.11, n. 26.
San Jose Water Co. v. Lyndon—§ 8.5, n. 7.
Santa Clara Land Title Co. v. Nowack & Associates, Inc.—§ 12.4, n. 42.
Santa Cruz Rock Pavement Co. v. Lyons—§ 12.5, n. 3.
Santopadre v. Pelican Homestead & Sav. Ass'n—§ 11.7, n. 7.
Saporita v. Delco Corp.—§ 5.30, n. 23.
Sargent v. Hamblin—§ 3.17, n. 11; § 3.18, n. 3.
Sarmiento v. Stockton, Whatley, Davin & Co.—§ 9.1, n. 6, 13.
SAS Partnership v. Schafer—§ 3.32, n. 5.
Sauber, In re—§ 8.15, n. 72.
Saunders v. Dunn—§ 2.1, n. 5; § 2.3, n. 9.
Saunders v. Frost—§ 4.31, n. 2.
Saunders v. Stradley—§ 7.6, n. 1, 3, 18.
Sautter v. Frick—§ 6.16, n. 15.
Savarese v. Ohio Farmers' Ins. Co.—§ 4.13, n. 4; § 4.14, n. 10, 15; § 4.15, n. 2.
Savarese v. Schoner—§ 7.7, n. 10, 12.
Savers Federal Sav. and Loan Ass'n of Little Rock v. First Federal Sav. and Loan Ass'n of Harrison—§ 5.35, n. 6.
Savers Federal Sav. & Loan Ass'n v. Reetz—§ 8.1, n. 5.
Savers Federal Sav. & Loan Ass'n v. Sandcastle Beach Joint Venture—§ 8.3, n. 21.
Savings Bank of Rockland County v. F.D.I.C.—§ 5.35, n. 47, 52, 54.
Savings Bank of Southern California v. Thornton—§ 5.16, n. 1.
Savings Investment & Trust Co. of East Orange v. United Realty & Mortgage Co.—§ 10.11, n. 15.
Savings & Loan Soc. v. Burnett—§ 12.7, n. 10.
Savoy v. White—§ 11.7, n. 10.
Sawyer v. Marco Island Development Corp.—§ 3.29; § 3.29, n. 43.
Sayre Village Manor, In re—§ 3.33, n. 15.
Sazant v. Foremost Investments, N.V.—§ 4.35, n. 3, 4.
S.B.D., Inc. v. Sai Mahen, Inc.—§ 3.29, n. 62.
Scaling v. First Nat. Bank—§ 4.4, n. 5.
Scania Ins. Co. v. Johnson—§ 4.14, n. 5.
Scanlan, In re—§ 8.19, n. 9.
Scappaticci v. Southwest Sav. and Loan Ass'n—§ 5.24, n. 87.
Scarfo v. Peever—§ 7.7, n. 4.
Scarry v. Eldridge—§ 7.12, n. 16.
SCD Chemical Distributors, Inc. v. Maintenance Research Laboratory, Inc.—§ 10.-13, n. 2.
Schaad v. Robinson—§ 10.15, n. 5.
Schack v. McKey—§ 4.10, n. 10.
Schalk v. Kingsley—§ 4.4, n. 14.
Schanawerk v. Hobrecht—§ 7.21, n. 21.
Scharaga v. Schwartzberg—§ 7.12, n. 5.
Schaumburg Hotel Owner Ltd. Partnership, In re—§ 6.2, n. 25.
Schenck v. Kelley—§ 4.45, n. 1.
Scherer v. Bang—§ 4.29, n. 5.
Scherrer Const. Co., Inc. v. Burlington Memorial Hospital—§ 12.2, n. 21.
Schiele v. First Nat. Bank of Linton, 436 N.W.2d 248—§ 8.3, n. 6, 10.
Schiele v. First Nat. Bank of Linton, 404 N.W.2d 479—§ 5.28, n. 40.
Schifferstein v. Allison—§ 6.11, n. 24.
Schley v. Fryer—§ 5.5, n. 1.
Schmidt, In re—§ 8.13, n. 33, 34.
Schmidt v. Barclay—§ 3.7, n. 1.
Schmitz v. Grudzinski—§ 12.7, n. 11.
Schmucker v. Sibert—§ 6.11, n. 24; § 6.12, n. 5, 21; § 6.13, n. 5, 9, 14, 16.
Schneberger v. Wheeler—§ 5.29, n. 25, 27.
Schneider v. Ampliflo Corp.—§ 12.9, n. 28.

TABLE OF CASES

Schneider v. Ferrigno—§ 5.14, n. 6; § 5.15, n. 12.
Schneider v. United States—§ 12.11, n. 39, 44.
Schnitzer v. State Farm Life Ins. Co.—§ 6.4, n. 5, 17.
Schoch v. Birdsall—§ 9.2, n. 8.
Scholnick, United States v.—§ 11.6; § 11.6, n. 70.
Scholtz v. Yastrzemski—§ 2.3, n. 25.
Schoolcraft v. Ross—§ 4.15; § 4.15, n. 6, 7.
Schrack v. Shriner—§ 10.15, n. 5.
Schrader Iron Works, Inc. v. Lee—§ 13.3, n. 32.
Schram v. Coyne—§ 5.4, n. 8.
Schreiber v. Carey—§ 7.8, n. 6.
Schroeder v. City of New York—§ 7.24, n. 6.
Schuck v. Gerlach—§ 7.2, n. 14.
Schuetz v. Schuetz—§ 4.29, n. 13.
Schulte v. Benton Sav. and Loan Ass'n—§ 5.24, n. 87.
Schulte v. Franklin—§ 3.17, n. 8.
Schultz v. Beulah Land Farm and Racing Stables, Inc.—§ 6.6, n. 2.
Schultz v. Cities Service Oil Co.—§ 4.44, n. 7.
Schultz v. Schultz—§ 3.6, n. 1; § 3.7, n. 4; § 3.15, n. 17.
Schultz v. Stevens—§ 5.24, n. 54.
Schultz v. Weaver—§ 5.15, n. 22.
Schwartz v. Federated Realty Group, Inc.—§ 12.3, n. 18.
Schwegmann Bank & Trust Co. of Jefferson v. Falkenberg—§ 5.29, n. 27.
Schwegmann Bank & Trust Co. of Jefferson v. Simmons—§ 5.29, n. 14.
Schweiker v. McClure—§ 7.25, n. 31.
Scott, In re—§ 8.15, n. 89.
Scott v. Farmers' Loan & Trust Co.—§ 4.41, n. 2.
Scott v. First Investment Corp.—§ 12.11, n. 39, 41.
Scott v. Paisley—§ 7.24; § 7.24, n. 1.
Scott v. Scott—§ 8.6, n. 19.
Scott v. Wharton—§ 5.15, n. 10.
Scott, Carhart & Co. v. Warren and Spicer—§ 9.1, n. 13, 18.
Scott & Wimbrow, Inc. v. Calwell—§ 7.14, n. 1.
Scranes, Inc., In re—§ 12.8, n. 1.
Scribner v. Malinowski—§ 5.7, n. 1.
S/D Enterprises, Inc. v. Chase Manhattan Bank—§ 8.3, n. 19, 20.
Seaboard All-Florida Ry. v. Leavitt—§ 4.12, n. 20.
Seaboard Citizens Nat. Bank of Norfolk, United States v.—§ 12.7, n. 31.
Seabury v. Hemley—§ 5.28, n. 23.
Seaman v. Bisbee—§ 4.8, n. 1.
Searle v. Chapman—§ 10.14, n. 13.
Searle v. Sawyer—§ 4.4, n. 1, 2; § 4.5, n. 8; § 4.6, n. 3.
Searles v. Kelley, Simmons & Co.—§ 4.44, n. 5.

Sears v. Dixon—§ 3.4, n. 4, 7, 10.
Sears v. Riemersma—§ 6.6, n. 31; § 12.1, n. 30.
Sears, Roebuck & Co. v. Bay Bank & Trust Co.—§ 9.7, n. 3.
Sears, Roebuck & Co. v. Camp—§ 7.10, n. 14, 18; § 7.15, n. 27.
Sease v. John Smith Grain Co., Inc.—§ 2.4, n. 2.
Seasons, Inc. v. Atwell—§ 7.16, n. 7; § 10.9, n. 3; § 10.10, n. 6, 10.
Seatrain Lines, Inc., In re—§ 3.19, n. 23.
Seattle-First Nat. Bank v. F.D.I.C.—§ 5.35, n. 23.
Seattle First Nat. Bank, N.A. v. Siebol—§ 12.3, n. 1.
Seaver v. Ransom—§ 5.11, n. 5.
Sebastian v. Floyd—§ 3.29; § 3.29, n. 67; § 5.21, n. 25, 27.
Second Baptist Church of Reno v. First Nat. Bank of Nevada—§ 8.2, n. 12.
Second Nat. Bank of New Haven v. Dyer—§ 5.27, n. 8; § 5.34, n. 30, 48.
Second Nat. Bank of North Miami v. G. M. T. Properties, Inc.—§ 5.28, n. 6.
Second Nat. Bank of Warren v. Boyle—§ 12.7, n. 16; § 12.8, n. 13.
SECOR Bank, Federal Sav. Bank v. Dunlap—§ 8.15, n. 58.
Securities and Exchange Com'n v. W. J. Howey Co.—§ 12.3, n. 57.
Security and Inv. Corp. of the Palm Beaches v. Droege—§ 12.7, n. 60; § 12.10, n. 47.
Security Bank v. Chiapuzio—§ 3.37, n. 11.
Security Bank v. First Nat. Bank—§ 12.8, n. 10.
Security Bank and Trust Co. v. Pocono Web Press, Inc.—§ 12.4, n. 25.
Security Bank & Trust Co. v. Bogard—§ 12.3, n. 18.
Security Co-op. Bank of Brockton v. Holland Furnace Co.—§ 9.6, n. 9.
Security Federal Sav. and Loan Ass'n of Albuquerque v. Federal Sav. and Loan Ins. Corp.—§ 11.1, n. 8.
Security Federal Sav. Bank of Florida v. OTS—§ 11.1, n. 8.
Security First Federal Sav. & Loan Ass'n v. Chamberlain—§ 5.24, n. 87.
Security First Federal Sav. & Loan Ass'n v. Jarchin—§ 5.24, n. 87.
Security Indus. Bank, United States v.—§ 5.24, n. 41.
Security Loan & Trust Co. v. Mattern—§ 2.4, n. 2.
Security Mortg. Co. v. Delfs—§ 5.34, n. 34.
Security Mortg. Co. v. Harrison—§ 4.45, n. 7.
Security Mortg. Co. v. Herron—§ 4.45, n. 7.
Security Nat. Bank v. Village Mall at Hillcrest, Inc., 382 N.Y.S.2d 882—§ 13.3, n. 25, 27, 52.

Security Nat. Bank v. Village Mall at Hillcrest, Inc., 361 N.Y.S.2d 977—§ 4.36, n. 9, 12.
Security Pacific Mortg. and Real Estate Services, Inc. v. Republic of Philippines—§ 12.6, n. 43.
Security Pacific Nat. Bank v. Chess—§ 5.28, n. 6.
Security Pacific Nat. Bank v. Wozab—§ 8.3; § 8.3, n. 62, 64.
Security Sav. and Loan Ass'n v. OTS, 960 F.2d 1318—§ 11.1, n. 8.
Security Sav. and Loan Ass'n v. OTS, 761 F.Supp. 1277—§ 11.1, n. 8.
Security Sav. and Loan Ass'n v. Fenton—§ 7.21, n. 1.
Security Sav. Bank of Cedar Rapids v. King—§ 7.16, n. 18; § 10.14, n. 3.
Security Sav. & Trust Co. v. Loewenberg—§ 3.14, n. 2.
Security State Bank v. Taylor—§ 4.36, n. 10.
Security Trust Co. of Rochester v. Graney—§ 12.7, n. 37.
Security Trust Co. of Rochester v. Miller—§ 7.31, n. 1.
Security Trust Federal Sav. & Loan Ass'n v. Gill Sav. Ass'n—§ 12.9, n. 6.
Sedlak v. Duda—§ 4.28, n. 12; § 4.29, n. 22.
Seekright v. Moore—§ 9.1, n. 10.
Seiberling v. Tipton—§ 6.17, n. 12.
Seidel, In re—§ 8.15, n. 37.
Seieroe v. First Nat. Bank of Kearney—§ 2.1, n. 9.
Selective Builders, Inc. v. Hudson City Sav. Bank—§ 12.3, n. 37, 51, 53.
Selik v. Goldman Realty Co.—§ 3.19, n. 3.
Selma Sash, Door & Blind Factory v. Stoddard—§ 12.4, n. 18; § 12.5; § 12.5, n. 3, 11.
Semble, Brown v. Bement—§ 3.4, n. 7.
Semmes Nurseries, Inc. v. McDade—§ 7.16, n. 20, 21.
Senior Care Properties, Inc., In re—§ 8.14, n. 9.
Sennett v. Taylor—§ 5.33, n. 18.
Sennhenn, In re—§ 8.19, n. 9.
Sens v. Slavia, Inc.—§ 7.31, n. 3, 11.
Sensor Systems, Inc., In re—§ 10.2, n. 11.
Serafini, United States v.—§ 4.47, n. 14.
Seven Lakes Inv. Group, Inc. v. Crowe—§ 5.19, n. 11.
Seventeenth & Locust STS Corporation v. Montcalm Corporation—§ 5.4, n. 8.
Seward v. New York Life Ins. Co.—§ 5.3, n. 8; § 5.9, n. 3.
Sewer Viewer, Inc. v. Shawnee Sunset Developers, Inc.—§ 12.4, n. 19.
Seymour, In re—§ 8.19, n. 9.
Seymour v. McKinstry—§ 5.32, n. 25.
S.F. Drake Hotel Associates, In re—§ 4.35, n. 41.
Shackley v. Homer—§ 7.12, n. 20.
Shaddix v. National Surety Co.—§ 12.9, n. 7.

Shade v. Wheatcraft Industries, Inc.—§ 9.2, n. 2; § 12.4, n. 29.
Shadman v. O'Brien—§ 3.9, n. 4.
Shaefer v. Chambers—§ 4.28, n. 1, 7, 9; § 4.29, n. 5.
Shaffer, In re—§ 8.15, n. 52.
Shaikh v. Burwell—§ 7.14, n. 12; § 7.31, n. 12.
Shankle Equipment Co., Inc. v. Liberty Nat. Bank & Trust Co. of Oklahoma City—§ 12.10, n. 34.
Shapiro v. Family Bank of Hallandale—§ 5.28, n. 4.
Sharp v. Machry—§ 12.1, n. 26.
Shattuck v. Bascom—§ 3.10, n. 2.
Shaw v. Dawson—§ 3.33, n. 24, 25, 26; § 8.19, n. 5, 9, 11.
Shaw v. G. B. Beaumont Co.—§ 4.30, n. 2.
Shayne v. Burke—§ 8.8, n. 9.
Shea v. First Federal Sav. and Loan Ass'n of New Haven—§ 11.6; § 11.6, n. 42.
Shea v. H.S. Pickrell Co., Inc.—§ 12.11, n. 28.
Sheaffer v. Baeringer—§ 5.24, n. 21.
Shea Realty, Inc., In re—§ 8.17, n. 4.
Shearer v. Allied Live Oak Bank—§ 7.20, n. 7.
Shedoudy v. Beverly Surgical Supply Co.—§ 10.9, n. 7.
Shell v. Strong—§ 6.11, n. 9.
Shelley v. Cody—§ 4.29, n. 22.
Shelley v. Kraemer—§ 7.27; § 7.27, n. 25.
Shellnut v. Shellnut—§ 4.29, n. 18.
Shelton, In re—§ 9.7, n. 1, 3.
Shepard v. Barrett—§ 7.10, n. 18, 19.
Shepard v. Jones—§ 4.29, n. 20.
Shepard v. Vincent—§ 4.45, n. 6.
Shepcaro, In re—§ 8.14, n. 87.
Shepherd v. Derwinski—§ 11.6, n. 65.
Shepherd v. May—§ 5.3, n. 2.
Shepherd v. Pepper—§ 4.34, n. 14; § 7.14, n. 13.
Shepherd v. Robinson—§ 8.3; § 8.3, n. 101.
Sherburne v. Strawn—§ 7.13, n. 13.
Shervold v. Schmidt—§ 3.29, n. 1.
Sherwood v. City of La Fayette—§ 4.12, n. 21.
Shewmaker v. Yankey—§ 10.13, n. 19.
Shields, In re—§ 8.17, n. 66.
Shields v. Lozear—§ 4.3, n. 3; § 6.7, n. 5, 6.
Shillaber v. Robinson—§ 3.11, n. 10.
Shimer, United States v.—§ 11.2, n. 44; § 11.6, n. 89.
Shindledecker v. Savage—§ 3.35, n. 1, 2, 4.
Shine Laundry, Inc. v. Washington Loan & Banking Co.—§ 5.19, n. 37.
Shingler v. Coastal Plain Production Credit Ass'n—§ 7.21, n. 49.
Shipley v. First Federal Sav. & Loan Ass'n of Delaware—§ 11.5, n. 3.
Shipp Corp., Inc. v. Charpilloz—§ 7.2, n. 14, 15; § 7.16, n. 26, 27.
Shippen v. Kimball—§ 7.13, n. 3.

TABLE OF CASES

Shirey v. All Night and Day Bank—§ 3.10, n. 2.
Shirley v. State Nat. Bank of Connecticut—§ 7.27, n. 14.
Shirras v. Caig—§ 2.4, n. 7; § 12.7, n. 10.
Shoemaker v. Commonwealth Bank—§ 4.31, n. 11.
Shoemaker v. Minkler—§ 5.33, n. 11.
Shore Haven Motor Inn, Inc., In re—§ 4.35, n. 41.
Shores v. Rabon—§ 4.16, n. 3, 4.
Short v. A. H. Still Inv. Corp.—§ 7.7, n. 3.
Shreiner v. Farmers' Trust Co of Lancaster—§ 7.16, n. 9.
Shuler v. Resolution Trust Corp.—§ 11.7, n. 22.
Shull, In re—§ 10.13, n. 7.
Shultis v. Woodstock Land Development Associates—§ 9.4, n. 14.
Shumate v. McLendon—§ 3.10, n. 3.
Shumway v. Horizon Credit Corp.—§ 7.6, n. 11.
Shuput v. Lauer—§ 7.18, n. 3.
Shuster, In re—§ 3.37, n. 11.
Shutze v. Creditthrift of America, Inc.—§ 12.7, n. 23, 59.
Sibell v. Weeks—§ 7.10, n. 15.
Sibley v. Baker—§ 10.13, n. 7.
Sidenberg v. Ely—§ 4.46, n. 8.
Siegel v. American Sav. & Loan Ass'n—§ 11.6; § 11.6, n. 45.
Sierra-Bay Federal Land Bank Ass'n v. Superior Court (Ciabattari)—§ 7.7, n. 51.
Sigler v. Phares—§ 8.6, n. 29, 32.
Signet Corp. v. Interbank Financial Services, Inc.—§ 5.31, n. 2.
Silas v. Robinson—§ 3.6, n. 1; § 3.7, n. 2; § 3.8, n. 9.
Silliman v. Gammage—§ 6.17, n. 12.
Silver v. Rochester Sav. Bank—§ 5.22, n. 21.
Silverdale Hotel Associates v. Lomas & Nettleton Co.—§ 12.3, n. 1, 39.
Silverman v. Alcoa Plaza Associates—§ 13.6, n. 17.
Silverman v. Gossett—§ 12.5, n. 19, 25.
Silverman v. State—§ 4.12, n. 1; § 6.3, n. 16.
Silver Spring Development Corp. v. Guertler—§ 7.21, n. 12.
Silver Spring Title Co. v. Chadwick—§ 5.33, n. 6, 33.
Silver Waters Corp. v. Murphy—§ 12.7, n. 45.
Simanovich v. Wood—§ 5.7, n. 5.
Simon v. Superior Court (Bank of America, NT & SA)—§ 8.3, n. 110, 114.
Simonetti, In re—§ 8.12, n. 14, 15.
Simon Home Builders, Inc. v. Pailoor—§ 3.32, n. 5.
Simonson v. Lauck—§ 10.8, n. 5.
Simonton v. Gray—§ 7.3, n. 8.
Simpson v. Castle—§ 8.6, n. 29.
Simpson v. Cleland—§ 7.7, n. 29.

Simpson v. Del Hoyo—§ 5.32, n. 5, 26.
Simpson v. Ennis—§ 10.2, n. 4.
Simpson v. Harris—§ 5.6, n. 1.
Simpson v. North Carolina Local Government Employees' Retirement System—§ 8.3, n. 27.
Sims, In re—§ 8.17, n. 39.
Sims v. McFadden—§ 10.14, n. 11.
Sims v. Sims—§ 3.6, n. 1; § 3.8, n. 9, 11.
Sims v. Smith—§ 7.15, n. 11, 18; § 11.6, n. 74.
Sindlinger v. Paul—§ 7.6, n. 7.
Singer-Fleischaker Royalty Co. v. Whisenhunt—§ 5.19, n. 22.
Singleton v. Scott—§ 7.21, n. 24.
Sisk v. Rapuano—§ 4.14, n. 6.
Siuslaw Valley Bank, Inc. v. Christopher H. Canfield Associates, Oreg., Ltd.—§ 8.1, n. 2.
604 Columbus Ave. Realty Trust, In re—§ 5.29, n. 32.
Sixty St. Francis Street, Inc. v. American Sav. and Loan Ass'n of Brazoria County—§ 5.34, n. 12.
Skach v. Sykora—§ 8.6, n. 9.
Skaneateles Sav. Bank v. Herold—§ 9.4, n. 4, 10, 14.
Skauge v. Mountain States Tel. & Tel. Co.—§ 10.1, n. 6, 8.
S.K. Drywall, Inc. v. Developers Financial Group, Inc.—§ 13.3, n. 38.
Skeels v. Blanchard—§ 3.3, n. 2.
Skeen v. Glenn Justice Mortgage Co., Inc.—§ 7.21, n. 54.
Skendzel v. Marshall—§ 3.29; § 3.29, n. 55; § 5.21, n. 27.
Skerlec v. Wells Fargo Bank, Nat. Ass'n—§ 12.11, n. 11.
Skinner v. Cen-Pen Corp.—§ 9.8, n. 33.
Skorpios Properties, Ltd. v. Waage—§ 6.6, n. 17, 18, 20.
Skousen v. L.J. Development Co., Inc.—§ 8.6, n. 19.
Skubal v. Meeker—§ 3.28, n. 9.
Skyler Ridge, In re—§ 6.2, n. 22, 26; § 6.9, n. 29.
Skyles v. Burge—§ 6.4, n. 6.
Slate v. Marion—§ 9.1, n. 4, 6, 18, 25.
Slaughter v. Jefferson Federal Sav. and Loan Ass'n, 538 F.2d 397—§ 5.29, n. 27.
Slaughter v. Jefferson Federal Sav. & Loan Ass'n, 361 F.Supp. 590—§ 5.29, n. 19.
SLC Ltd. V, In re, 152 B.R. 755—§ 4.35, n. 13, 25.
SLC Ltd. V, In re, 137 B.R. 847—§ 8.14, n. 87.
Slevin Container Corp. v. Provident Federal Sav. and Loan Ass'n of Peoria—§ 6.5, n. 2.
Slingerland v. Sherer—§ 6.11, n. 18.
Sloan v. Klein—§ 5.10, n. 10.
Sloane v. Lucas—§ 7.4, n. 12.
Slodov v. United States—§ 9.1, n. 28.
S. Lotman & Son, Inc. v. Southeastern Financial Corp.—§ 10.9, n. 14.

Slusky v. Coley—§ 5.22, n. 14.
Small v. South Norwalk Sav. Bank—§ 12.11, n. 27.
Smart v. Tower Land and Inv. Co.—§ 4.46, n. 3.
Smiddy v. Grafton—§ 6.1, n. 2.
Smith, In re, 43 B.R. 313—§ 8.15, n. 43; § 8.17, n. 4.
Smith, In re, 24 B.R. 19—§ 8.17, n. 13, 16.
Smith, In re, 19 B.R. 592—§ 8.15, n. 35, 41.
Smith, Matter of—§ 8.15, n. 49, 50.
Smith v. Austin—§ 7.2, n. 1, 22; § 7.4, n. 2.
Smith v. Bailey—§ 7.4, n. 12.
Smith v. Berry—§ 3.8, n. 15.
Smith v. Bush—§ 6.12, n. 10, 20, 21.
Smith v. Citizens & Southern Financial Corp.—§ 7.21, n. 45.
Smith v. Credico Indus. Loan Co.—§ 7.21, n. 70.
Smith v. Dinsmoor—§ 10.7, n. 2, 10.
Smith v. Feltner—§ 10.7, n. 3.
Smith v. Fried—§ 3.7, n. 7; § 4.47, n. 1.
Smith v. Frontier Federal Sav. and Loan Ass'n—§ 5.21, n. 33; § 5.24, n. 67.
Smith v. General Investments, Inc.—§ 5.4, n. 1; § 5.7, n. 16; § 5.11, n. 6.
Smith v. General Mortg. Corp.—§ 4.16, n. 7.
Smith v. Goodwin—§ 4.5, n. 6.
Smith v. Grilk—§ 4.35, n. 15.
Smith v. Haertel—§ 2.1, n. 4; § 2.4, n. 2.
Smith v. Haley—§ 7.21, n. 74.
Smith v. Jarman—§ 5.33, n. 6.
Smith v. Kibbe—§ 5.18, n. 15.
Smith v. Landy—§ 7.7, n. 3.
Smith v. Mangels—§ 5.3, n. 8, § 5.10, n. 2.
Smith v. McCullough—§ 4.41, n. 2.
Smith v. Moore—§ 4.4, n. 2, 7.
Smith v. MRCC Partnership—§ 3.27, n. 5.
Smith v. Newbaur—§ 12.5, n. 3.
Smith v. Olney Federal Savings and Loan Ass'n—§ 10.11, n. 2.
Smith v. Player—§ 3.8, n. 9, 11, 17; § 3.11, n. 1.
Smith v. Potter—§ 3.6, n. 2.
Smith v. Shattls—§ 3.3, n. 1.
Smith v. Shaver—§ 8.5, n. 11.
Smith v. Shay—§ 7.15, n. 3.
Smith v. Shepard—§ 4.22, n. 9.
Smith v. Simpson—§ 7.3, n. 3.
Smith v. Smith, 135 A. 25—§ 3.1, n. 39; § 3.2, n. 1.
Smith v. Smith, 45 So. 168—§ 3.15, n. 17.
Smith v. Smith, 15 N.H. 55—§ 5.28, n. 13.
Smith v. Sprague—§ 10.5, n. 7.
Smith v. Stringer—§ 4.29, n. 1.
Smith v. Swendsen—§ 3.17, n. 3.
Smith v. Union State Bank—§ 12.8, n. 6.
Smith v. Varney—§ 7.2, n. 3, 19; § 7.12, n. 14.
Smith v. Vincent—§ 6.6, n. 8.
Smith by Coe v. Piluso—§ 7.6, n. 12.

Smith & Lowe Const. Co. v. Herrera—§ 12.2, n. 14.
Smyth v. Munroe—§ 5.32, n. 3.
Snapwoods Apartments of Dekalb County, Ltd., In re—§ 8.14, n. 27.
Snead Const. Corp. v. First Federal Sav. and Loan Ass'n of Orlando—§ 12.7, n. 45.
Sniadach v. Family Finance Corp. of Bay View—§ 7.25; § 7.25, n. 1; § 12.5; § 12.5, n. 1, 12.
Snow v. Western Sav. & Loan Ass'n—§ 5.22, n. 19.
Snyder v. Crawford—§ 10.15, n. 5.
Snyder v. Griswold—§ 3.4, n. 11.
Snyder v. New Hampshire Sav. Bank—§ 7.19, n. 4.
Snyder v. Parker—§ 3.10, n. 2.
Sobel v. Mutual Development, Inc.—§ 5.28, n. 23.
Societe Generale v. Charles & Company Acquisition, Inc.—§ 9.4, n. 14.
Society Bank & Trust Co. v. Zigterman—§ 7.14, n. 1, 3.
Society of Friends v. Haines—§ 5.6, n. 1; § 5.7, n. 2.
Soderlund, In re—§ 8.15, n. 24.
Sofias v. Bank of America Nat. Trust and Sav. Ass'n—§ 12.6, n. 21, 26.
Solecki v. United States—§ 4.47, n. 1.
Soles v. Sheppard—§ 7.15, n. 20.
Soloff v. Dollahite—§ 5.29, n. 17.
Solondz Bros. Lumber Co. v. Piperato—§ 12.4, n. 39.
Soltis v. Liles—§ 3.29, n. 1.
Somero, In re—§ 4.35, n. 14.
Somers v. Avant—§ 5.15, n. 19.
Somersworth Sav. Bank v. Roberts—§ 2.4, n. 2.
Sonny Arnold, Inc. v. Sentry Sav. Ass'n—§ 5.22, n. 12, 14.
Sooner Federal Sav. and Loan Ass'n v. Oklahoma Cent. Credit Union—§ 5.3, n. 2.
Soper v. Guernsey—§ 2.2, n. 8.
Sorenson v. Olson—§ 3.7, n. 2.
Sosebee v. Atha—§ 5.32, n. 17.
Southampton Wholesale Food Terminal, Inc. v. Providence Produce Warehouse Company—§ 12.3, n. 49.
South Carolina Federal Sav. Bank v. San-A-Bel Corp.—§ 13.3, n. 18, 21.
South Carolina Ins. Co. v. Kohn—§ 5.5, n. 1; § 5.15, n. 5, 12.
South Carolina Nat. Bank v. Halter—§ 5.27, n. 7.
South Central Dist. of Pentecostal Church of God of America, Inc. v. Bruce-Rogers Co.—§ 12.5, n. 19.
Southern Bank of Lauderdale County v. I.R.S.—§ 7.19, n. 6.
Southern Colonial Mortg. Co., Inc. v. Medeiros—§ 13.3, n. 46, 50.
Southern Floridabanc Federal Sav. and Loan Ass'n v. Buscemi—§ 12.9, n. 3.

TABLE OF CASES

Southern Gardens, Inc., In re—§ 8.18, n. 19, 53.
Southern Indus. Banking Corp., In re—§ 5.35, n. 45.
Southern Life Ins. Co. v. Pollard Appliance Co.—§ 12.7, n. 36; § 12.10, n. 46.
Southern Oregon Mortg., Inc., In re—§ 5.28, n. 28.
Southern Realty & Utilities Corp. v. Belmont Mortg. Corp.—§ 7.16, n. 29.
Southern Steel Co. v. Hobbs Const. & Development, Inc.—§ 12.2, n. 34.
Southern Trust & Mortgage Co. v. Daniel—§ 7.21, n. 54, 76.
South Fork Canal Co. v. Gordon—§ 12.4, n. 2.
South Park Commissioners v. Todd—§ 4.12, n. 21, 22.
South Sanpitch Co. v. Pack—§ 5.34; § 5.34, n. 50; § 6.6, n. 18.
Southwestern Electrical Co. v. Hughes—§ 12.4, n. 46.
Southwest National Bank v. Southworth—§ 3.37, n. 11.
Southwest Paving Co. v. Stone Hills—§ 12.4, n. 21.
Southwest State Bank v. Quinn—§ 8.5, n. 11.
Southwest Title Ins. Co. v. Northland Bldg. Corp.—§ 12.8; § 12.8, n. 24.
Southwest Title & Trust Co. v. Norman Lumber Co.—§ 10.4, n. 1, 6; § 10.5, n. 4.
Southwick v. Spevak—§ 3.24, n. 11.
Sovereign Group 1985-27, Ltd., In re—§ 8.14, n. 87.
Sowell v. Federal Reserve Bank of Dallas, Tex—§ 10.14, n. 3.
Sowers v. Federal Deposit Ins. Corp.—§ 12.8, n. 10.
Spangler v. Memel—§ 8.3; § 8.3, n. 90.
Spangler v. Yarborough—§ 2.2, n. 8.
Spanish Lake Associates, In re—§ 8.14, n. 67.
Sparkman v. Gove—§ 5.5, n. 1.
Sparks v. Farmers Federal Sav. and Loan Ass'n—§ 12.3, n. 40.
Spaziani v. Millar—§ 12.10, n. 27.
Spears, United States v.—§ 11.6, n. 83.
Speck, In re—§ 8.19, n. 9.
Speck v. Federal Land Bank of Omaha—§ 7.7, n. 51.
Spect v. Spect—§ 4.24, n. 1, 12; § 4.27, n. 8.
Speers Sand & Clay Works v. American Trust Co.—§ 7.16, n. 26.
Spellman v. Dixon—§ 12.9, n. 16.
Spencer v. Harford's Executors—§ 6.16, n. 10.
Spencer v. Spencer—§ 5.19, n. 24.
Spencer and Miller v. Lee et als.—§ 7.21, n. 66.
Sperry, In re—§ 8.13, n. 12.
Sperry v. Butler—§ 4.46, n. 15.

Spickes Bros. Painting Contractors, Inc. v. Worthen Bank & Trust Co., N.A.—§ 12.10, n. 55.
Spielman-Fond, Inc. v. Hanson's, Inc.—§ 12.5; § 12.5, n. 18, 19, 22.
Spillman v. Spillman—§ 6.1, n. 4.
Spires v. Edgar—§ 7.21, n. 59, 63.
Spires v. Lawless—§ 7.6, n. 13; § 7.22, n. 31.
Spokane Manuf'g & Lumber Co. v. McChesney—§ 12.5, n. 3.
Spokane Savings & Loan Soc. v. Liliopoulos—§ 7.12, n. 6.
Sprague v. Martin—§ 8.7, n. 13.
Sprague v. Smith—§ 4.26, n. 1.
Spring Const. Co., Inc. v. Harris, 562 F.2d 933—§ 12.6, n. 35.
Spring Constr. Co., Inc. v. Harris, 614 F.2d 374—§ 12.6, n. 28.
Spring Creek Investments of Dallas, N.V., Inc., In re—§ 8.13, n. 11.
Springer Corp. v. Kirkeby-Natus—§ 7.3, n. 3; § 7.15, n. 1, 7, 11.
Springfield Fire & Marine Insurance Co. v. Allen—§ 4.14, n. 17.
Springfield Institution for Savings v. Worcester Federal Savings & Loan Ass'n—§ 11.6, n. 20.
Spring Garden Foliage, Inc., Matter of—§ 8.14, n. 21, 22.
Springham v. Kordek—§ 10.4, n. 3.
Spruill v. Ballard—§ 7.21, n. 59.
Spurlock v. Fayette Federal Sav. & Loan Ass'n—§ 12.10, n. 57.
S.P. Wragge v. Denham—§ 4.29, n. 6, 9.
S.S. Silberblatt, Inc. v. East Harlem Pilot Block-Bldg. 1 Housing Development Fund Co., Inc.—§ 12.6, n. 25, 40.
Staats v. Praegitzer—§ 3.29, n. 1, 3.
Stadium Apartments, Inc., United States v.—§ 11.6, n. 52, 53.
Staff Mortg. & Inv. Corp., Matter of—§ 5.28, n. 35.
Stafford Metal Works, Inc. v. Cook Paint & Varnish Co.—§ 10.1, n. 1.
Stagecrafters Club, Inc. v. District of Columbia Division of American Legion—§ 5.24, n. 21.
Stahl v. Roulhac—§ 7.31, n. 17; § 13.3, n. 21.
Stalcup, In re Estate of—§ 8.1, n. 12.
Stalcup v. Easterly—§ 5.10, n. 3.
Staley Farms, Inc. v. Rueter—§ 3.30; § 3.30, n. 13, 14.
Stallings v. Erwin—§ 4.45, n. 6.
Stamer v. Nisbitt—§ 4.39, n. 8.
Stamnes v. Milwaukee & St. L. Ry. Co.—§ 4.12, n. 19, 20.
Standard Bldg. Associates, Ltd., In re—§ 8.14, n. 9.
Standard Conveyor Co., In re—§ 4.35, n. 13.
Standard Fire Ins. Co. v. Fuller—§ 2.1, n. 4.

Standard Sur. & Cas. Co. of New York v. Standard Acc. Ins. Co.—§ 10.1, n. 17.
Stanford v. Aulick—§ 10.2, n. 2.
Stanish v. Polish Roman Catholic Union of America—§ 12.3, n. 44.
Stanley v. Ames—§ 5.20, n. 11.
Stanley v. Veterans Administration—§ 12.11, n. 37.
Stanley Station Associates, L.P., In re—§ 4.35, n. 13, 31.
Stannard v. Marboe—§ 3.35, n. 1, 2, 3.
Stanovsky v. Group Enterprise & Const. Co., Inc.—§ 13.3, n. 21.
Stansberry v. McDowell—§ 7.22, n. 40.
Stansell v. Roberts—§ 9.1, n. 8.
Stantons v. Thompson—§ 6.17, n. 7, 11; § 10.7, n. 7.
Staples, In re—§ 8.17, n. 33.
Staples v. Barret—§ 3.11, n. 6.
Stapleton v. Rathbun—§ 2.1, n. 17.
Star v. 308 Owners Corp.—§ 13.6, n. 17.
Starbird v. Cranston—§ 5.18, n. 14.
Starek v. TKW, Inc.—§ 12.4, n. 29.
Starfish Condominium Ass'n v. Yorkridge Service Corp., Inc.—§ 12.11, n. 5.
Stark v. Bauer Cooperage Co.—§ 3.25, n. 2.
Starkman v. Sigmond—§ 4.14, n. 10; § 4.15, n. 6; § 6.3, n. 15.
Starr v. Bruce Farley Corp.—§ 5.28, n. 30, 31, 40.
Starr v. Mooslin—§ 12.9, n. 38.
Stastny v. Pease—§ 10.7, n. 5, 10.
State v. _____ (see opposing party)
State Bank of Albany v. Fioravanti—§ 12.8, n. 17, 18.
State Bank of Geneva v. Sorenson—§ 2.3, n. 19.
State Bank of Hardinsburg v. Brown—§ 7.16, n. 9.
State Bank of Hartland v. Arndt—§ 10.14, n. 14.
State Bank of Lehi v. Woolsey—§ 7.7, n. 22.
State ex rel. v. _____ (see opposing party and relator)
State Life Ins. Co. v. Freeman—§ 9.4, n. 10.
State of (see name of state)
State Realty Co. of Boston v. MacNeil Bros. Co.—§ 4.31, n. 7; § 5.28, n. 42.
State Sav. Bank of Anderson v. Harbin—§ 10.14, n. 10.
State Sav. & Loan Ass'n v. Kauaian Development Co., 445 P.2d 109—§ 12.9, n. 4, 41, 43; § 13.3; § 13.3, n. 19, 32.
State Sav. & Loan Ass'n v. Kauaian Development Co., Inc., 613 P.2d 1315—§ 12.9, n. 41; § 13.3, n. 20.
State Securities Co. v. Daringer—§ 3.32, n. 20.
State Tax Commission v. Shor—§ 13.6; § 13.6, n. 20.
Statland Holliday, Inc. v. Stendig Development Corp.—§ 12.9, n. 9.
Stava v. Stava—§ 6.19, n. 5.

Stavrides v. Mellon Nat. Bank & Trust Co.—§ 4.19, n. 6.
St. Clair Sav. Assn. v. Janson—§ 10.13, n. 15.
St. Clair Supply Co., Inc., In re—§ 10.2, n. 12.
St. Cloud Tool & Die Co., Matter of—§ 10.9, n. 14.
Steadman v. Foster—§ 5.33, n. 33.
Stearns v. Porter—§ 2.4, n. 7.
Steckelberg v. Randolph—§ 3.4, n. 10.
Stedman v. Georgetown Sav. and Loan Ass'n—§ 12.3, n. 18.
Steel Suppliers, Inc. v. Ehret, Inc.—§ 12.4, n. 41.
Stegeman v. First Missouri Bank of Gasconade County—§ 5.33, n. 1.
Stein v. Blatte—§ 8.3, n. 41.
Stein v. Nellen Development Corp.—§ 8.1, n. 1; § 8.3, n. 41.
Stein v. Simpson—§ 6.7, n. 2.
Stein v. Sullivan—§ 5.34, n. 29.
Steinert v. Galasso, 69 A.2d 841—§ 5.9, n. 5.
Steinert v. Galasso, 63 A.2d 443—§ 5.3, n. 3.
Steinhoff v. Fisch—§ 3.32, n. 5.
Stemper v. Houston County—§ 4.12, n. 21.
Stempler v. Frankford Trust Co.—§ 12.11, n. 8.
Stenehjem v. Kyn Jin Cho—§ 12.9, n. 23; § 12.10, n. 35.
Stenger v. Great Southern Sav. and Loan Ass'n—§ 5.22, n. 14; § 5.24, n. 118.
Stephans v. Herman—§ 7.22, n. 37, 38.
Stephens v. Clay—§ 10.11, n. 15.
Stephens, Partain & Cunningham v. Hollis—§ 7.21, n. 70.
Steptoe v. Savings of America—§ 11.5, n. 28.
Sterling Steel Treating, Inc., In re—§ 4.47, n. 14.
Stern v. Great Plains Federal Sav. and Loan Ass'n—§ 12.4, n. 14.
Stern v. Itkin Bros., Inc.—§ 2.1, n. 9; § 5.31, n. 8.
Sternberger v. Sussman—§ 10.13, n. 30.
Stern & Son, Inc. v. Gary Joint Venture—§ 12.4, n. 35.
Stevens v. Brown—§ 4.2, n. 14.
Stevens v. Dogoli—§ 6.6, n. 27.
Stevens v. Miner—§ 7.4, n. 12.
Stevens v. Rock Springs Nat. Bank—§ 5.30, n. 6.
Stevens v. Smathers—§ 4.4, n. 7.
Stevens v. Turlington—§ 4.1, n. 13.
Stevens v. Wilson—§ 3.33, n. 4.
Stevens Const. Corp. v. Draper Hall, Inc.—§ 13.3, n. 38.
Stevenson v. Black—§ 5.3, n. 3.
Stevenson v. Owen—§ 3.29, n. 32.
Stevenson v. Stevenson—§ 5.6, n. 1.
Steward v. Bounds—§ 12.3, n. 48.
Steward v. Good—§ 7.20, n. 14.
Stewart v. Brown—§ 7.21, n. 22.

TABLE OF CASES

Stewart v. Crosby—§ 5.27, n. 8; § 6.6, n. 9, 10, 12.
Stewart v. Fairchild-Baldwin Co., 108 A. 301—§ 4.3, n. 3; § 4.21, n. 7.
Stewart v. Fairchild-Baldwin Co., 106 A. 406—§ 4.38, n. 3.
Stewart v. Gardner-Warren Implement Co.—§ 12.5, n. 3.
Stewart v. Gurley—§ 8.14, n. 20.
Stewart v. Smith—§ 9.1, n. 4, 6, 13, 19.
Stewart v. Thornton—§ 5.29, n. 15, 20.
Stewart, United States v.—§ 11.6, n. 56.
Stewart B. McKinney Foundation, Inc. v. Town Plan and Zoning Com'n of Town of Fairfield—§ 11.5, n. 18.
Stiles, In re—§ 8.15, n. 54.
Stiles v. Resolution Trust Corp.—§ 11.7, n. 15.
Stimson Mill Co. v. Braun—§ 12.5, n. 3.
Stimson Mill Co. v. Nolan—§ 12.5, n. 3, 4, 8.
Stinemeyer v. Wesco Farms, Inc.—§ 3.29, n. 1.
Stingley v. City of Lincoln Park—§ 11.5, n. 17.
Stitt v. Rat Portage Lumber Co.—§ 3.23, n. 3; § 3.24, n. 7.
St. James Bank and Trust Co. v. S & H Enterprises, Inc.—§ 10.2, n. 1.
St. Louis Globe-Democrat, Inc., In re—§ 8.14, n. 2.
St. Louis Nat. Bank v. Field—§ 4.21, n. 5.
Stockton v. Dundee Manufacturing Co.—§ 6.7, n. 6.
Stockton v. Lucas—§ 13.6, n. 17.
Stockwell v. Lindeman—§ 12.9, n. 17.
Stockyards Nat. Bank v. Capitol Steel & Iron Co.—§ 12.8, n. 12.
Stokes v. Stokes—§ 10.14, n. 11.
Stolk v. Lucas—§ 3.7, n. 2.
Stone, In re—§ 12.8, n. 10.
Stone v. Jenks—§ 3.3, n. 2.
Stone v. Pitts—§ 13.3, n. 35.
Stone v. Tilley—§ 4.31, n. 14.
Stonebraker v. Zinn—§ 3.27, n. 5; § 3.32, n. 2.
Stonecrest Corp. v. Commissioner—§ 3.34, n. 16; § 9.8, n. 35.
Storer v. Warren—§ 10.7, n. 12.
Stotts v. Johnson—§ 5.6, n. 1.
Stouffer v. Harlan, 114 P. 385—§ 4.24, n. 13.
Stouffer v. Harlan, 74 P. 610—§ 4.24, n. 13, 19.
Stouffer Hotel Co. v. Teachers Ins. and Annuity Ass'n—§ 5.22, n. 42.
Stoughton v. Pasco—§ 2.4, n. 2.
Stow v. Tifft—§ 9.1, n. 10, 18.
Stowe Center, Inc. v. Burlington Sav. Bank—§ 7.10, n. 4.
Stowell v. Pike—§ 4.4, n. 7.
Stowers v. Stuck—§ 5.7, n. 16.
St. Paul at Chase Corp. v. Manufacturers Life Ins. Co.—§ 12.3, n. 44, 50, 53.

St. Paul Federal Bank for Sav. v. Wesby—§ 13.5, n. 17, 20.
St. Paul Fire & Marine Ins. Co. v. Ruddy—§ 4.14, n. 2.
St. Paul Missionary Public Housing, Inc., United States v.—§ 4.33, n. 1, 7; § 4.35, n. 9; § 11.6, n. 85.
Straeffer v. Rodman—§ 12.7, n. 10.
Strand v. Griffith—§ 7.17, n. 12.
Strand v. Mayne—§ 3.29; § 3.29, n. 36.
Strang v. Allen—§ 4.27, n. 17.
Strange v. Maloney—§ 5.6, n. 2.
Strangis v. Metropolitan Bank—§ 7.22, n. 3, 8.
Stratford v. Boland—§ 12.4, n. 14.
Stratford Financial Corp. v. Finex Corp.—§ 5.35, n. 47.
Strause v. Dutch—§ 8.5, n. 6.
Strawberry Commons Apartment Owners Ass'n 1, Matter of—§ 7.21, n. 7; § 7.24, n. 8.
Street v. Beal—§ 7.3, n. 2.
Streets & Beard Farm Partnership, In re—§ 8.19, n. 9, 11.
Stribling v. Splint Coal Co.—§ 5.27, n. 10.
Strike v. Trans-West Discount Corp.—§ 5.27, n. 1.
Strobe v. Downer—§ 7.14, n. 9.
Strock v. MacNicholl—§ 2.2, n. 7, 8.
Strode v. Parker—§ 3.1, n. 12.
Strohauer v. Voltz—§ 5.7, n. 11, 12.
Stroh-Mc Investments v. Bowens—§ 9.8; § 9.8, n. 12.
Strom, In re—§ 5.25, n. 6.
Strong v. Jackson—§ 5.34, n. 29, 35.
Strong v. Manufacturers' Insurance Co.—§ 4.13, n. 3.
Strong v. Merchants Mut. Ins. Co.—§ 7.6, n. 4.
Strong v. Stewart—§ 3.15, n. 8.
Strong v. Stoneham Co-Operative Bank—§ 9.4, n. 14.
Stroop v. Southern Life Ins. Co.—§ 7.7, n. 4.
Strouss v. Simmons—§ 12.4, n. 24, 25.
Strulowitz v. Susan B. Anthony Bldg. & Loan Ass'n—§ 6.7, n. 1.
Strutt v. Ontario Sav. and Loan Ass'n—§ 4.25, n. 3.
Stuart v. American Sec. Bank—§ 7.21, n. 85.
Stub v. Belmont—§ 2.2, n. 1.
Stubbs, State ex rel. LeFevre v.—§ 5.1, n. 4; § 5.3, n. 4, 8.
Stuchin v. Kasirer—§ 3.1, n. 14.
Stump v. Martin—§ 7.17, n. 5.
Stump Home Specialties Mfg., Inc., United States v.—§ 11.6, n. 84.
Sturtevant v. Sturtevant—§ 3.16, n. 8.
Stutsman County Implement Co., United States v.—§ 10.13, n. 2.
Stuyvesant v. Hall—§ 10.15, n. 2.
Stuyvesant Security Co. v. Dreyer—§ 10.11, n. 15.

Suarez v. Rivercross Tenants' Corp.—§ 13.6, n. 16.
Suber v. Alaska State Bond Committee—§ 8.3, n. 22.
Suchan v. Rutherford—§ 3.32, n. 6.
Suitt Const. Co., Inc. v. Seaman's Bank for Sav.—§ 12.3, n. 26.
Sukut–Coulson, Inc. v. Allied Canon Co.—§ 12.2, n. 32.
Sullivan v. Federal Farm Mortg. Corporation—§ 7.21, n. 39.
Sullivan v. Rosson—§ 4.35, n. 23, 31; § 4.43, n. 5, 7, 9.
Sullivan v. Saunders—§ 6.17, n. 11.
Sulzer, In re—§ 8.15, n. 91.
Sumitomo Bank of Cal. v. Iwasaki—§ 12.2, n. 26.
Sumitomo Bank of California v. Davis—§ 7.12, n. 5.
Summerlin v. Thompson—§ 12.5, n. 3.
Summers v. Consolidated Capital Special Trust—§ 9.8, n. 6, 7.
Summers v. United States—§ 12.11, n. 39, 50.
Summit Land Co., In re—§ 3.33, n. 27.
Summit–Top Development, Inc. v. Williamson Const., Inc.—§ 12.4, n. 11.
Sumner v. Enercon Development Co.—§ 8.3, n. 45, 47.
Sumner v. Sumner—§ 7.5, n. 1, 23.
Sunbelt Sav. FSB, Dallas, Tex. v. Amrecorp Realty Corp.—§ 5.29, n. 32, 34.
Sunbelt Sav., FSB, Dallas, Texas v. Cashin Const. Co., Inc.—§ 5.31, n. 8.
Sunbelt Sav., FSB Dallas, Texas v. Montross—§ 5.29, n. 35.
Sunchase Apartments v. Sunbelt Service Corp.—§ 11.7, n. 24.
Sun Country Sav. Bank of New Mexico, F.S.B. v. McDowell—§ 8.5, n. 18.
Sundance Land Corp. v. Community First Federal Sav. and Loan Ass'n—§ 12.10, n. 6.
Sun First Nat. Bank of Orlando v. R. G. C.—§ 7.3, n. 1.
Sunflower State Refining Co., In re—§ 12.7, n. 6.
Sunset Bay Associates, In re—§ 12.9; § 12.9, n. 6, 34, 35; § 12.10, n. 17.
Sunshine Meadows Condominium Ass'n, Inc. v. Bank One, Dayton, N.A.—§ 13.3, n. 39.
Superior Court of Kittitas County, State ex rel. Montgomery v.—§ 4.24, n. 13.
Superior Court, State ex rel. Gwinn, Inc. v.—§ 4.2, n. 18.
Superior Financial Corp. v. Haskell—§ 13.6, n. 22.
Surety Building & Loan Ass'n of Newark v. Risack—§ 7.10, n. 16; § 7.15, n. 26.
Surety Life Ins. Co. v. Rose Chapel Mortuary, Inc.—§ 2.3, n. 7.
Suring State Bank v. Giese—§ 7.16, n. 32.

Surrey Strathmore Corp. v. Dollar Sav. Bank of New York—§ 4.18, n. 9.
Sutor v. First Nat. Bank of Palco—§ 7.10, n. 17.
Sutton, Matter of—§ 8.14, n. 20.
Sutton v. Atlantic Bank and Trust Co.—§ 12.8, n. 15.
Sutton Investments, Inc., Matter of—§ 7.7, n. 25.
Svalina v. Saravana—§ 3.13, n. 3.
Swaggart v. McLean—§ 3.32, n. 16.
Swaine v. Perine—§ 10.3, n. 4.
Swallow Ranches, Inc. v. Bidart—§ 3.17, n. 7.
Swan v. Yaple—§ 5.28, n. 15.
Swansea Concrete Products, Inc. v. Distler—§ 12.6, n. 27.
Swanson v. United States—§ 4.12, n. 5.
Swarb v. Lennox—§ 3.30, n. 10; § 7.26; § 7.26, n. 2.
Swarthout v. Shields—§ 5.7, n. 13.
Swasey v. Emerson—§ 5.34, n. 13.
Swearingen v. Lahner—§ 7.6, n. 15.
Sweatte, In re—§ 2.4, n. 7.
Sweeny v. Patton—§ 2.2, n. 8.
Sweet v. Luster—§ 3.6, n. 1; § 3.8, n. 11.
Sweetwater, In re—§ 8.14, n. 40.
Swenson v. Ramage—§ 9.1, n. 19.
Swift v. Kirby—§ 7.1, n. 7.
Swindell v. FNMA—§ 6.9, n. 3; § 6.10, n. 9.
Swindell v. Overton—§ 7.20, n. 17; § 7.21, n. 37.
Swinerton & Walberg Co. v. Union Bank—§ 12.6, n. 18.
Swinton v. Cuffman—§ 5.27, n. 10.
Sybron Corp. v. Clark Hospital Supply Corp.—§ 6.9, n. 22.
Syracuse Sav. Bank v. Merrick—§ 5.34, n. 31, 42.
Syracuse Trust Co. v. First Trust & Deposit Co.—§ 5.3, n. 3, 7; § 5.19, n. 23.
Syring v. Sartorious—§ 12.6, n. 42.
Szczotka v. Idelson—§ 5.31, n. 11.
Szenay v. Schaub—§ 9.8, n. 31.

T

Tabasso Homes, Inc., State v.—§ 12.5, n. 3, 6.
Tabor Enterprises, Inc. v. Illinois—§ 8.13, n. 33.
Tackett v. First Sav. of Arkansas, F.A.—§ 5.28, n. 4.
Taddeo, In re—§ 8.15; § 8.15, n. 25.
Tahoe Nat. Bank v. Phillips—§ 3.38; § 3.38, n. 10.
Taintor v. Hemmingway—§ 5.10, n. 8.
Takach v. Williams Homes, Inc.—§ 12.10, n. 53.
Tallahassee Associates, L.P., In re—§ 8.14, n. 87.
Tallahassee Bank & Trust Co. v. Raines—§ 5.35, n. 29.

TABLE OF CASES

Tamiami Abstract & Title Co. v. Berman—§ 5.28, n. 42.
Tampa Chain Co., Inc., In re—§ 10.9, n. 7.
Tamplen v. Bryeans—§ 7.6, n. 10.
Tan v. California Federal Sav. and Loan Ass'n—§ 6.5, n. 2.
Tanner v. Shearmire—§ 8.1, n. 1.
Tapia v. Demartini—§ 12.7, n. 7.
Taras, In re—§ 8.15, n. 56.
Tarbell v. Durant—§ 10.3, n. 8.
Tarleton v. Griffin Federal Sav. Bank—§ 7.20, n. 15.
Tarrant Land Co. v. Palmetto Fire Ins. Co.—§ 4.14, n. 15, 18, 19.
Tatum v. Holliday—§ 7.21, n. 24.
Taurus Leasing Corp. v. Chalaire—§ 8.11, n. 4, 6.
Tax Investments, Ltd. v. Federal Deposit Ins. Corp.—§ 11.7, n. 19.
Taylor, In re—§ 8.15, n. 41.
Taylor, Matter of—§ 8.15, n. 45.
Taylor v. American Nat. Bank of Pensacola—§ 5.34, n. 37.
Taylor v. Bell—§ 4.23, n. 3.
Taylor v. Brennan—§ 4.35; § 4.35, n. 28, 29, 31; § 8.18, n. 4.
Taylor v. Dillenberg—§ 7.4, n. 11.
Taylor v. Jones—§ 10.3, n. 5; § 10.10, n. 5, 6, 10; § 10.9, n. 23.
Taylor v. Luther—§ 3.15, n. 8.
Taylor v. McConnell—§ 4.4, n. 24.
Taylor v. Quinn—§ 4.3, n. 2; § 6.11, n. 14.
Taylor v. Roeder—§ 5.33, n. 2; § 5.29, n. 6.
Taylor v. Short's Adm'r—§ 10.15, n. 6, 8.
Taylor v. Taylor—§ 6.6, n. 20.
Taylor Woodrow Blitman Const. Corp. v. Southfield Gardens Co.—§ 12.6, n. 25.
TCF Mortg. Corp. v. Verex Assur., Inc.—§ 11.2, n. 58.
T.D. Bickham Corp. v. Hebert—§ 12.9, n. 47, 59.
Teachers Ins. and Annuity Ass'n of America v. Coaxial Communications of Cent. Ohio, Inc.—§ 12.3, n. 1.
Teachers Ins. and Annuity Ass'n of America v. Oklahoma Tower Associates Ltd. Partnership—§ 4.35, n. 25.
Teachers Ins. and Annuity Ass'n of America v. Ormesa Geothermal—§ 12.3, n. 1.
Teal v. Walker—§ 3.4, n. 4; § 4.2, n. 18; § 4.22, n. 5; § 4.34, n. 19.
Teas v. Republic Nat. Bank of Dallas—§ 5.27, n. 7.
Tech Land Development, Inc. v. South Carolina Ins. Co.—§ 4.13, n. 1, 2, 3; § 4.14, n. 10; § 4.16, n. 3.
Tedesco v. Bekker—§ 5.33, n. 13; § 6.6, n. 24.
Tedesco v. CDC Federal Credit Union—§ 6.6, n. 29; § 12.8, n. 17.
Temple Zion, In re—§ 8.14, n. 76.
Ten Eyck v. Craig—§ 4.31, n. 11; § 4.45, n. 1, 9.
Tennant v. Hulet—§ 6.11, n. 21.

Tenneco Oil Co. v. Clevenger—§ 6.6, n. 17, 20.
Tennery v. Nicholson—§ 3.3, n. 5.
Tennessee Chemical Co., In re—§ 8.13, n. 22.
Tennessee Farmers' Mut. Ins. Co. v. Rader—§ 10.1, n. 14.
Ter-Hoven v. Kerns—§ 12.7, n. 16.
Terrell, In re—§ 8.19, n. 9.
Terrell v. Allison—§ 7.12, n. 2, 13.
Terry, In re—§ 8.15; § 8.15, n. 35, 77, 79.
Terry v. Adams—§ 7.27, n. 17.
Terry v. Born—§ 5.22; § 5.22, n. 36, 37, 38.
Terry v. Fitzgerald—§ 7.21, n. 24.
Texas American Bancshares, Inc. v. Clarke—§ 5.29, n. 28; § 11.7, n. 7.
Texas Bank & Trust Co. v. Lone Star Life Ins. Co.—§ 12.3, n. 3.
Thacker v. Hubard & Appleby—§ 5.5, n. 1.
Thatcher v. Merriam—§ 5.28, n. 3.
Thauer v. Smith—§ 5.34, n. 17, 44.
Thayer, In re—§ 8.13, n. 1.
Thayer v. Mann—§ 6.11, n. 14.
Theodore v. Mozie—§ 2.1, n. 2, 4.
The Praetorians v. State—§ 4.31, n. 14.
Thielen v. Strong—§ 7.2, n. 9; § 8.5, n. 4.
Third Nat. Bank in Nashville v. McCord—§ 4.44, n. 1; § 7.31, n. 1.
T-H New Orleans Ltd. Partnership, In re—§ 4.35, n. 41.
Tholen v. Duffy—§ 3.1, n. 37.
Thomas v. Armstrong—§ 4.41, n. 2.
Thomas v. First Federal Sav. Bank of Indiana—§ 11.5, n. 18, 19, 28.
Thomas v. Hartman—§ 2.1, n. 9.
Thomas v. Home Mut. Bldg. Loan Ass'n—§ 5.5, n. 1; § 5.4, n. 7.
Thomas v. Klein—§ 3.32, n. 3; § 3.29, n. 70.
Thomas v. Klemm—§ 3.8, n. 1; § 3.15, n. 14.
Thomas v. Ogden State Bank—§ 3.18, n. 1.
Thomas v. Reeves Southeastern Corp.—§ 13.3, n. 65.
Thomas v. San Diego College Co.—§ 7.17, n. 7.
Thomas v. State Mortg., Inc.—§ 5.29, n. 11, 19; § 5.31, n. 7; § 5.34, n. 33.
Thomas v. Stewart—§ 7.2, n. 20.
Thomas v. Thomas—§ 7.16, n. 18.
Thomas, United States v.—§ 7.7, n. 42.
Thomas v. Wisner—§ 10.14, n. 6.
Thomas A. Cary, Inc., In re—§ 12.5, n. 19, 25.
Thomasson v. Townsend—§ 3.1, n. 37.
Thom, Inc., In re—§ 8.13, n. 31.
Thompson, In re, 18 B.R. 67—§ 8.17, n. 13.
Thompson, In re, 17 B.R. 748—§ 8.15, n. 45.
Thompson v. Allert—§ 8.3, n. 96, 102.
Thompson v. Chicago, etc. Ry. Co.—§ 4.12, n. 16.
Thompson v. Glidden—§ 2.2, n. 6, 7.
Thompson v. H & S Packing Co., Inc.—§ 5.29, n. 14.
Thompson v. Menefee—§ 7.12, n. 14.

TABLE OF CASES

Thompson v. Miller—§ 5.10, n. 2.
Thompson v. National Fire Ins. Co.—§ 4.13, n. 4.
Thompson v. Ruda—§ 3.28, n. 7.
Thompson v. Skowhegan Sav. Bank—§ 3.33, n. 7.
Thompson v. Smith—§ 12.7, n. 13.
Thompson v. Thomas—§ 10.15, n. 9.
Thompson, United States v.—§ 12.3, n. 7.
Thompson v. Willson—§ 5.19, n. 11.
Thompson Elec., Inc. v. Bank One, Akron, N.A.—§ 12.10, n. 53.
Thomson McKinnon Securities, Inc., In re—§ 5.35, n. 25.
Thormahlen v. Citizens Sav. and Loan—§ 12.10, n. 34.
Thorp v. Croto—§ 4.13, n. 17.
Thorpe v. Helmer—§ 9.2, n. 3.
Thorp Sales Corp. v. Dolese Bros. Co.—§ 12.8, n. 10.
3C Associates v. IC & LP Realty Co.—§ 6.3, n. 1, 2.
Threefoot v. Hillman—§ 7.14, n. 11.
366 Fourth Street Corp. v. Foxfire Enterprises, Inc.—§ 4.35, n. 7.
Thrift Funds of Baton Rouge, Inc. v. Jones—§ 6.9, n. 17.
Thunder v. Belcher—§ 4.1, n. 7.
Tibbetts v. Terrill—§ 10.7, n. 8.
Tidd v. Stauffer—§ 3.29; § 3.29, n. 57.
Tidrick, In re—§ 8.3, n. 57.
Tierce v. APS Co.—§ 5.22, n. 14, 17, 21.
Tierney v. Spiva—§ 7.12, n. 18.
Tifton Corp. v. Decatur Federal Sav. and Loan Ass'n—§ 7.21, n. 43.
Tighe v. Kenyon—§ 12.4, n. 11.
Tighe v. Walton—§ 5.10, n. 2, 16; § 5.15, n. 10.
Tilden v. Beckmann—§ 10.1, n. 15.
Tillery, In re—§ 8.15, n. 5.
Tillinghast v. Fry—§ 7.3, n. 9.
Tilton v. Boland—§ 5.33, n. 5, 6, 33.
Timberland Design, Inc. v. First Service Bank for Sav.—§ 5.29, n. 28; § 11.7, n. 22.
Timken v. Wisner Estates, Inc.—§ 4.46, n. 5.
Timmermann v. Cohn—§ 7.17, n. 9.
Timmreck v. Munn—§ 12.11; § 12.11, n. 18.
Tincher v. Greencastle Federal Sav. Bank—§ 4.13, n. 19.
Tindall v. Peterson, 99 N.W. 659—§ 10.3, n. 9.
Tindall v. Peterson, 98 N.W. 688—§ 10.3, n. 9.
Tinley Park Bank v. Phelps (In re Kokkinis)—§ 8.15, n. 35, 45.
Tinsley v. Kemp—§ 11.5, n. 18.
Tipton, United States v.—§ 11.6, n. 74.
Tirrill v. Miller—§ 8.6, n. 28.
Title Guarantee & Trust Co. v. Monson—§ 8.3; § 8.3, n. 69.
Title Guarantee & Trust Co. v. Mortgage Commission—§ 5.35, n. 11.

Title Guar. & Trust Co. v. Bushnell—§ 5.15, n. 14.
Title Guar. & Trust Co. v. Wrenn—§ 12.5, n. 3.
Title Ins. Co. of Minnesota v. I.R.S. of United States—§ 8.4, n. 17, 18.
Title Ins. & Trust Co. v. California Development Co.—§ 4.34, n. 8, 14.
Title & Mortgage Guaranty Co. of Sullivan County, In re—§ 5.35, n. 15, 16.
Titley v. Davis—§ 7.3, n. 3.
Titsworth v. Stout—§ 7.2, n. 12.
Titus, In re—§ 12.8, n. 13.
TMIC Insurance Co., Inc., In re—§ 11.2, n. 57.
Tobin v. Tobin—§ 6.6, n. 14.
Tobler v. Yoder & Frey Auctioneers, Inc.—§ 7.31, n. 1.
Toby v. Oregon Pac. R. Co.—§ 8.2, n. 2.
Todd v. Todd—§ 3.8, n. 1.
Todd's Ex'r v. First Nat. Bank—§ 10.3, n. 9.
Toledo v. Brown—§ 4.4, n. 18, 26.
Toler v. Baldwin County Sav. and Loan Ass'n—§ 5.10, n. 2; § 10.2, n. 2; § 10.11, n. 2.
Toler v. Satterthwaite—§ 13.3, n. 36.
Tolzman v. Gwynn—§ 5.19, n. 50.
Tomkus v. Parker—§ 5.3, n. 2.
Tomlinson v. Thompson—§ 4.7, n. 4.
Toms v. Boyes—§ 4.44, n. 2.
Toney Schloss Properties Corp. v. Union Federal Sav. & Loan Ass'n—§ 12.7, n. 30, 44.
Tonkel v. Shields—§ 6.7, n. 8.
Toolan v. Trevose Federal Sav. and Loan Ass'n—§ 11.6, n. 25.
Toole v. Weirick—§ 4.29, n. 9; § 7.4, n. 3.
Toomer, Sykes & Billups v. Randolph—§ 4.27, n. 5, 14.
Toomes v. Conset—§ 3.1, n. 3; § 3.15, n. 14.
Torcise v. Perez—§ 3.29, n. 18.
Torkko/Korman/Engineers v. Penland Ventures—§ 12.4, n. 14.
Torres Lopez, Matter of—§ 8.15, n. 70.
Torrey v. Deavitt—§ 5.34, n. 14.
Torrey Pines Bank v. Hoffman—§ 8.3, n. 53.
T.O. Stanley Boot Co., Inc. v. Bank of El Paso—§ 12.3, n. 1.
Toston v. Utah Mortg. Loan Corp.—§ 6.16, n. 16.
Totten v. Harlowe—§ 4.34, n. 4, 6.
Toucey v. New York Life Ins. Co.—§ 7.14, n. 14.
Toulouse v. Chilili Co-op Ass'n—§ 3.8, n. 4.
Touroff v. Weeks—§ 4.38, n. 17.
Tousey v. Barber—§ 5.19, n. 33.
Tower Grove Bank & Trust Co. v. Weinstein—§ 8.18, n. 5.
Towers Charter & Marine Corp. v. Cadillac Ins. Co.—§ 12.3, n. 1, 48.
Towerson v. Jackson—§ 4.22, n. 9, 24.

TABLE OF CASES

Town Concrete Pipe of Washington, Inc. v. Redford—§ 12.6, n. 20, 27, 40.
Towne Realty, Inc. v. Edwards—§ 13.5, n. 15.
Town of (see name of town)
Townsend v. Barlow—§ 12.4, n. 45.
Townsend v. Provident Realty Co. of New York—§ 6.17, n. 7.
Townsend v. Ward—§ 5.8, n. 5.
Townside Partners, Ltd., In re—§ 4.35, n. 14.
Tracy v. Wheeler—§ 6.11, n. 40.
Trane Co. v. Randolph Plumbing & Heating—§ 12.6, n. 20.
Trannon v. Towles—§ 4.1, n. 6.
Transamerica Ins. Co. v. Barnett Bank of Marion County, N.A.—§ 12.2, n. 44.
Trans-Bay Engineers & Builders, Inc. v. Hills—§ 5.30, n. 11; § 12.6, n. 31, 34.
Transohio Sav. Bank v. OTS—§ 11.1, n. 8.
TransOhio Savings Bank, F.S.B. v. Patterson—§ 7.31, n. 10.
Trans West Co. v. Teuscher—§ 3.32, n. 26.
Trapp v. Tidwell—§ 12.8, n. 10, 18.
Trask v. Kelleher—§ 4.22, n. 4, 14.
Trauner v. Lowrey—§ 5.3, n. 2, 9; § 7.1, n. 7.
Travelers Indem. Co. v. First Nat. State Bank of N. J.—§ 12.6, n. 35.
Travelers Ins. Co. v. Bullington—§ 8.14, n. 108; § 8.16; § 8.16, n. 25, 27, 28.
Travelers Ins. Co. v. Thompson—§ 7.17, n. 6.
Travelers Ins. Co. v. Tritsch—§ 4.34, n. 12.
Travelli v. Bowman—§ 6.11, n. 35.
Travelstead v. Derwinski—§ 11.2, n. 49.
Travis v. Schonwald—§ 4.27, n. 7.
Treasure Valley Plumbing and Heating, Inc. v. Earth Resources Co., Inc.—§ 5.6, n. 2.
Tremblay, In re—§ 4.10, n. 4, 5.
Trent v. Johnson—§ 6.13, n. 2.
Triano v. First American Title Ins. Co. of Arizona—§ 7.21, n. 91.
Tri-County Bank and Trust Co. v. Watts—§ 6.16, n. 17.
Trident Center v. Connecticut General Life Ins. Co.—§ 6.2, n. 3.
Trigg v. Vermillion—§ 9.2, n. 3.
Tri-Growth Centre City, Ltd., In re—§ 8.14, n. 20.
Trimm v. Marsh, 3 Lans. 509 (1874)—§ 4.2, n. 12.
Trimm v. Marsh, 54 N.Y. 599, 13 Am.Rep. 623 (1874)—4.2, n. 12.
Trina-Dee, Inc., In re—§ 8.14, n. 20.
Trinity County Bank v. Haas—§ 7.6, n. 7.
Triple J Cattle, Inc. v. Chambers—§ 8.1, n. 1, 2, 3.
Tripler v. MacDonald Lumber Co.—§ 2.3, n. 23.
Triplett v. Davis—§ 3.29, n. 1.
Tritten's Estate, In re—§ 5.10, n. 10.
Troj v. Chesebro—§ 12.9, n. 2, 23.
Tropical Inv. Co. v. Brown—§ 4.23, n. 3.

Tropic Builders, Limited v. United States—§ 12.4, n. 35.
Trout's Investments, Inc. v. Davis—§ 12.7, n. 42.
Trowbridge v. Malex Realty Corp.—§ 7.6, n. 15.
Truesdale v. Brennan—§ 9.2, n. 10.
Truitt, In re—§ 2.4, n. 2.
Trull v. Skinner—§ 3.3, n. 2.
Trusdell v. Dowden—§ 5.17, n. 3.
Trustees of C. I. Mortg. Group v. Stagg of Huntington, Inc.—§ 12.7, n. 14.
Trustees of C. I. Mortg. Group v. Stagg of Huntington, Inc. (D. C. Goodman & Sons, Inc.)—§ 12.7, n. 26.
Trustees of Old Alms-House Farm of New Haven v. Smith—§ 6.13, n. 2.
Trustees of the Washington-Idaho-Montana Carpenters-Employers Retirement Trust Fund v. Galleria Partnership, 819 P.2d 158—§ 8.3, n. 6.
Trustees of the Washington-Idaho-Montana Carpenters Employers Retirement Trust Fund v. Galleria Partnership, 780 P.2d 608—§ 8.3, n. 12.
Tuchman, In re—§ 8.15, n. 41.
Tucker, In re—§ 8.14, n. 9.
Tucker v. Gayle—§ 6.7, n. 1.
Tucker v. Lassen Sav. and Loan Ass'n—§ 5.21, n. 32.
Tucker v. Pulaski Federal Sav. & Loan Ass'n—§ 4.18, n. 9; § 5.22, n. 19; § 5.24, n. 87.
Tucker Door & Trim Corp. v. Fifteenth St. Co.—§ 12.5, n. 19, 25.
Tucker Federal Sav. & Loan Ass'n v. Alford—§ 5.21, n. 33.
Tucker's Estate, In re—§ 10.14, n. 11.
Tucson Federal Sav. & Loan Ass'n v. Sundell—§ 13.3, n. 21, 23, 24, 25.
Tucson Indus. Partners, In re—§ 8.18, n. 46.
Tukey v. Reinholdt—§ 7.5, n. 4, 15.
Tuller v. Nantahala Park Co.—§ 2.3, n. 19.
Tully v. Harloe—§ 2.4, n. 7; § 12.7, n. 10.
Turk v. Page—§ 4.30, n. 2.
Turley v. Ball Associates Limited—§ 12.3, n. 51.
Turner, In re—§ 8.16, n. 17.
Turner v. Blackburn—§ 3.30, n. 4, 5, 10, 11; § 7.24; § 7.24, n. 8, 12; § 7.25; § 7.25, n. 3, 4, 19, 23, 24; § 7.26; § 7.26, n. 8, 9; § 7.27; § 7.27, n. 2, 4.
Turner v. Boger—§ 3.1, n. 37.
Turner v. Domestic Inv. & Loan Corp.—§ 2.1, n. 5.
Turner v. Houston Agr. Credit Corp.—§ 12.7, n. 11.
Turner v. Impala Motors—§ 7.27, n. 14.
Turner v. Johnson—§ 4.30, n. 1.
Turner v. Lytton Sav. and Loan Ass'n—§ 12.7, n. 36, 46.
Turner v. Mebane—§ 4.6, n. 6.
Turner v. Porter—§ 2.3, n. 19.

Turner v. Powell—§ 6.13, n. 2.
Turner v. Superior Court of Kern County—§ 4.34, n. 22; § 4.35, n. 49; § 4.41, n. 14.
Turner v. Turner—§ 7.4, n. 10, 12.
Turner Coal Co. v. Glover—§ 4.9, n. 2.
Turney v. Roberts—§ 10.5, n. 10.
Turrell v. Jackson—§ 4.4, n. 14, 18; § 4.5, n.15.
Tuscaloosa Housing Development Corp. v. Morrow—§ 5.26, n. 5.
Tuscarora, Inc. v. B.V.A. Credit Corp.—§ 12.9, n. 1; § 12.10, n. 7, 33.
Tuthill v. Morris—§ 6.7, n. 12.
Tuttle v. Burgett's Adm'r—§ 2.2, n. 10.
Tuxedo Beach Club Corp. v. City Federal Sav. Bank—§ 11.7, n. 14.
Tweitmann v. Lampman—§ 4.36, n. 1.
Twin City Bank v. Verex Assur. Inc.—§ 11.2, n. 58.
Twin City Federal Sav. and Loan Ass'n v. Zimmerman—§ 11.2, n. 52.
Twin Const., Inc. v. Boca Raton, Inc.—§ 11.7, n. 19.
266 Washington Associates, In re—§ 8.14, n. 27, 96, 100.
220 West 42 Associates v. Ronbet Newmark Co.—§ 12.9, n. 56.
200 Woodbury Realty Trust, In re—§ 12.6, n. 33; § 12.7, n. 42.
2550 Olinville Ave., Inc. v. Crotty—§ 6.4, n. 31.
2140 Lincoln Park West v. American Nat. Bank and Trust Co. of Chicago—§ 5.22, n. 23.
Tyler v. Butcher—§ 12.7, n. 10, 39.
Tyler v. Equitable Life Assur. Soc. of United States—§ 6.2, n. 3.
Tyler v. Granger—§ 4.2, n. 16.
Tyler v. Wright—§ 2.1, n. 4.
Tynan, Matter of—§ 8.13, n. 33; § 8.17, n. 4.
Tyson v. Masten Lumber & Supply, Inc.—§ 12.5, n. 39.

U

Ulander v. Allen—§ 3.32, n. 12.
Ulen v. Knecttle—§ 5.33, n. 33.
Umdenstock v. American Mortg. & Inv. Co. of Oklahoma City—§ 4.19, n. 6.
Underhay v. Read—§ 4.22, n. 24.
Underwood v. Jarvis—§ 12.8, n. 17.
Unger v. Shull—§ 2.4, n. 2.
Unico v. Owen—§ 5.29, n. 21.
Unifirst Federal Sav. & Loan Ass'n v. Tower Loan of Mississippi, Inc.—§ 5.24, n. 54.
Union Bank v. Anderson—§ 8.3, n. 102.
Union Bank v. Dorn—§ 8.3, n. 52.
Union Bank v. Wendland—§ 8.3, n. 110; § 12.8; § 12.8, n. 1, 22.
Union Bank of Brooklyn v. Rubinstein—§ 5.19, n. 48.

Union Bank & Trust Co., N.A. v. Farmwald Development Corp.—§ 12.9, n. 7.
Union Central Life Ins. Co. v. Cates—§ 10.-11, n. 6.
Union Central Life Ins. Co. of Cincinnati, Ohio v. Codington County Farmers Fire & Lightning Mut. Ins. Co.—§ 4.14, n. 10.
Union Dime Sav. Bank v. 522 Deauville Associates—§ 4.40, n. 4.
Union Elec. Co. v. Clayton Center Ltd.—§ 12.4, n. 33.
Union Mut. Life Ins. Co. v. Hanford—§ 5.11, n. 2; § 5.19, n. 5.
Union Mut. Life Ins. Co. v. Kirchoff—§ 7.3, n. 7.
Union Nat. Bank of Chicago v. International Bank of Chicago—§ 5.17, n. 12.
Union Nat. Bank of Little Rock v. Cobbs—§ 7.7, n. 30.
Union Nat. Bank of Little Rock v. First State Bank & Trust Co. of Conway—§ 12.7, n. 37; § 12.8, n. 10.
Union Sav. Bank of Patchogue v. Dudine—§ 10.5, n. 6.
Union Trust Co. v. Biggs—§ 2.1, n. 5.
Union Trust Co. of Rochester v. Rogers—§ 5.9, n. 18.
United Accounts, Inc. v. Larson—§ 13.3, n. 29.
United Bank of Lakewood Nat. Ass'n v. One Center Joint Venture—§ 6.16, n. 14, 15.
United Bonding Ins. Co. v. Donaldson Engineering, Inc.—§ 12.2, n. 22.
United California Bank v. Prudential Ins. Co. of America—§ 12.3, n. 5, 41.
United Companies Financial Corp. v. Davis—§ 8.15, n. 54.
United Companies Financial Corp. v. Mellon Financial Services Corp. No. 7—§ 7.24, n. 27.
United Home Loans, Inc., In re—§ 5.27, n. 11; § 5.28, n. 6.
United Housing Foundation, Inc. v. Forman—§ 12.3, n. 58; § 13.6, n. 15.
United Masonry, Inc. v. Jefferson Mews, Inc.—§ 13.3, n. 46.
United Nat. Bank of Miami v. Airport Plaza Ltd. Partnership—§ 5.29, n. 3, 5.
United of Omaha Life Ins. Co. v. Nob Hill Associates—§ 12.3, n. 1, 40.
United Oklahoma Bank v. Moss—§ 7.16, n. 25, 26, 29.
United Orient Bank v. Lee—§ 6.6, n. 37.
United Pacific Corp. v. Commissioner—§ 3.34, n. 16.
United Plumbing v. Gibraltar Sav. & Loan Ass'n—§ 12.6, n. 28.
United Sav. Ass'n of Texas v. Timbers of Inwood Forest Associates, Ltd.—§ 8.14; § 8.14, n. 17, 27, 109; § 8.16; § 8.16, n. 14.
United States v. _____ (see opposing party)

TABLE OF CASES

United States Bank of Washington v. Hursey—§ 7.15, n. 1, 7, 23.
United States Bond & Mortg. Co. v. Keahey—§ 5.17, n. 3.
United States By and Through I.R.S. v. McDermott—§ 9.1, n. 28.
United States Cold Storage of California v. Great Western Sav. & Loan Ass'n—§ 12.9, n. 36; § 12.10, n. 28.
United States Fidelity & Guaranty Co. v. Borden Metal Products Co.—§ 12.2, n. 35.
United States Fidelity & Guaranty Co. v. Leach—§ 12.2, n. 44.
United States Fidelity & Guaranty Co. v. Long—§ 10.13, n. 2.
United States Fidelity & Guaranty Co. v. Lowe—§ 5.10, n. 2.
United States Fidelity & Guaranty Co. v. Maryland Cas. Co.—§ 10.1, n. 7, 16.
United States Finance Co. v. Jones—§ 5.29, n. 17, 19, 20.
United States Financial v. Sullivan—§ 4.5, n. 15, 16.
United States Nat. Bank of Portland v. Holton—§ 5.34, n. 34.
United States Sav. Bank of Newark v. Schnitzer—§ 7.10, n. 16.
United States Savings Bank of Newark, N. J. v. Continental Arms, Inc.—§ 7.6, n. 1, 13, 15.
United States Steel Homes Credit Corp. v. South Shore Development Corp.—§ 10.1, n. 1; § 10.2, n. 4.
United States Truck Co., Inc., In re—§ 8.14, n. 81, 99, 101.
United States Trust Co. v. Miller—§ 4.31, n. 1.
United Virginia Bank/National v. Best—§ 5.22, n. 14.
Universal Title Ins. Co. v. United States—§ 10.6, n. 10.
University Sav. Ass'n v. Springwoods Shopping Center—§ 7.22, n. 34.
University State Bank v. Steeves—§ 5.3, n. 8; § 5.9, n. 3; § 10.2, n. 3.
Upham v. Lowry—§ 4.15, n. 2.
Upjohn v. Moore—§ 7.14, n. 16.
Upson v. Goodland State Bank & Trust Co.—§ 6.6, n. 1.
Uransky v. First Federal Savings & Loan Association—§ 12.8, n. 20.
Uransky v. First Federal Sav. & Loan Ass'n of Fort Myers—§ 12.8, n. 12, 18.
Urban Systems Development Corp. v. NCNB Mortg. Corp.—§ 12.6, n. 38.
Urquhart v. Brayton—§ 5.6, n. 1.
Urrey Ceramic Tile Co., Inc. v. Mosley—§ 12.4, n. 37.
Usery v. Turner Elkhorn Min. Co.—§ 5.24, n. 47.
Utah Cooperative Ass'n v. White Distributing & Supply Co.—§ 3.36, n. 3.
Utah Mortg. and Loan Co. v. Black—§ 8.2, n. 2.
Utah Sav. & Loan Assn. v. Mecham—§ 12.7, n. 42.

V

Vahlco Corp., United States v.—§ 5.20, n. 5; § 11.6, n. 82; § 12.8, n. 13.
Vail v. Derwinski—§ 11.2, n. 44; § 11.6, n. 71.
Valairco, Inc., Matter of—§ 12.6, n. 5.
Valentine v. Portland Timber and Land Holding Co.—§ 7.12, n. 5; § 7.13, n. 3, 5.
Valinda Builders, Inc. v. Bissner—§ 8.3, n. 35, 51.
Vallely v. First Nat. Bank of Grafton—§ 3.12, n. 1.
Valley Development at Vail, Inc. v. Warder, In and For Eagle County—§ 7.25, n. 3.
Valley Intern. Properties, Inc. v. Brownsville Sav. and Loan Ass'n—§ 4.24, n. 1.
Valley Nat. Bank of Ariz. v. Avco Development Co.—§ 7.17, n. 17.
Valley Nat. Bank of Arizona v. Insurance Co. of North America—§ 4.14, n. 10.
Valley Sav. & Loan Ass'n, State ex rel. Bingaman v.—§ 5.22, n. 13, 19.
Valley Trust Co. of Palmyra, PA v. Lapitsky—§ 8.1, n. 9.
Valley Vue Joint Venture, In re—§ 10.2, n. 11.
Valparaiso Bank and Trust Co. v. Royal Trust Bank, N.A.—§ 10.9, n. 7; 10.11, n. 5; § 10.13, n. 2.
Vanderkemp v. Shelton—§ 7.14, n. 5; § 7.15, n. 10, 12.
Vanderslice v. Knapp—§ 4.6, n. 4; § 4.7, n. 4.
Vanderspeck v. Federal Land Bank—§ 10.-11, n. 6.
Vandeventer v. Dale Const. Co.—§ 12.3, n. 49.
Vandever Inv. Co., Inc. v. H. E. Leonhardt Lumber Co.—§ 10.13, n. 15.
Van Dusseldorp v. State Bank of Bussey—§ 6.6, n. 37.
Van Dyke v. Grand Trunk Ry. Co. of Canada—§ 4.8, n. 2.
Vanjani v. Federal Land Bank of Louisville—§ 7.16, n. 17.
Vann v. Marbury—§ 5.34, n. 13.
Van Pelt v. McGraw—§ 4.4, n. 11; § 4.5, n. 15.
Van Schaick v. Lawyers' Mortg. Co.—§ 5.35, n. 15.
Van Senden v. O'Brien—§ 7.16, n. 12.
Van Stone v. Stillwell & Bierce Mfg. Co.—§ 12.4, n. 4.
Van-Tex, Inc. v. Pierce—§ 5.30, n. 11; § 12.6, n. 25, 34.
Van Valkenburgh v. Jantz—§ 5.2, n. 5.
Van Vlissingen v. Lenz—§ 7.6, n. 7.

Van Vronker v. Eastman—§ **4.30, n. 7**; § **4.32. n. 6**.
Van Woerden v. Union Imp. Co.—§ **6.16, n. 16**.
Varco–Pruden Bldgs. v. Becker & Sons Const., Inc.—§ **7.18, n. 3**; § **7.19, n. 4**.
Varga v. Woods—§ **5.20, n. 5, 7, 11**.
Vargas v. Nautilus Ins. Co.—§ **4.14, n. 2**.
Vaughan v. Crown Plumbing & Sewer Service, Inc.—§ **12.8, n. 18**.
Vaughan v. Mansfield—§ **6.13, n. 1**.
Vaughn & Co., Ltd. v. Saul—§ **12.8, n. 13**.
Vawter v. Crafts—§ **7.3, n. 11**.
Vecchiarelli v. Garsal Realty, Inc.—§ **4.43, n. 5**.
Vega v. First Federal Sav. & Loan Ass'n of Detroit—§ **4.19, n. 33**.
Venable v. Harmon—§ **3.29**; § **3.29, n. 45, 51**.
Venable v. Payne—§ **5.31, n. 3**.
Vend–A–Matic, Inc. v. Frankford Trust Co.—§ **7.16, n. 25**.
Ventura–Louise Properties, In re—§ **4.35, n. 14**.
Venture Properties, Inc., In re—§ **12.4, n. 29**.
Verde Capital Corp. v. Gutierrez—§ **6.13, n. 6**.
Verdugo Highlands, Inc. v. Security Ins. Co. of New Haven—§ **12.2, n. 28**.
Verex Assur., Inc. v. AABREC, Inc.—§ **7.16, n. 26**.
Verex Assur., Inc. v. John Hanson Sav. and Loan, Inc.—§ **11.2, n. 58**.
Vermont Fiberglass, Inc., In re—§ **5.34, n. 30**.
Vermont Toy Works, Inc., In re—§ **10.9, n. 7**.
Verna, In re—§ **8.17, n. 33**.
Verna v. O'Brien—§ **7.7, n. 7, 9**.
Vernon v. Bethel—§ **3.1, n. 16**.
Vernon v. Resolution Trust Corp.—§ **5.29, n. 38**.
Victor Gruen Associates, Inc. v. Glass—§ **10.9, n. 15, 16**.
Victor Hotel Corp. v. FCA Mortg. Corp.—§ **11.7, n. 22, 37**.
Victory Highway Village, Inc., United States v.—§ **7.7, n. 42**; § **11.6**; § **11.6, n. 68**.
Victory Highway Village, Inc. v. Weaver—§ **8.3, n. 45**.
Viele v. Judson—§ **5.33, n. 21**.
Vienna Park Properties, In re, 976 F.2d 106—§ **8.18, n. 46**.
Vienna Park Properties, In re, 120 B.R. 332—§ **4.2, n. 1**.
View Crest Garden Apartments, Inc. v. United States—§ **4.35, n. 10**.
View Crest Garden Apts., Inc., United States v.—§ **11.6**; § **11.6, n. 49**.
Village of (see name of village)
Village Properties, Ltd., Matter of—§ **4.35, n. 31**; § **8.18**; § **8.18, n. 12, 15, 20, 23, 53**.
Villers v. Wilson—§ **7.21, n. 64**.

Vincent v. Garland—§ **5.3, n. 8**; § **5.9, n. 3**.
Vincent v. Moore—§ **4.31, n. 14, 15**.
Vincent E. Webb v. Commissioner—§ **3.34, n. 18**; § **9.8, n. 37**.
Vines v. Wilcutt—§ **10.9, n. 19**.
Vinquist v. Siegert—§ **3.8, n. 10**.
VIP Motor Lodge, Inc., Matter of—§ **8.14, n. 66**.
Virginia Beach Federal Sav. and Loan Ass'n v. Wood—§ **8.18, n. 53**.
Virgin Islands Nat. Bank v. Tyson—§ **7.18, n. 4**.
Voechting v. Grau—§ **3.1, n. 37**.
Vogel v. Pardon—§ **4.4, n. 32**; § **4.11, n. 2, 3**.
Vogel v. Troy—§ **5.34, n. 22**.
Volpe Const. Co., Inc. v. First Nat. Bank of Boston—§ **12.6, n. 26**.
Voltin v. Voltin—§ **10.10, n. 6**.
Vonk v. Dunn—§ **7.6, n. 3**.
Von Oehsen v. Brown—§ **3.4, n. 4**.
Voss v. Multifilm Corp. of America—§ **8.1, n. 10**.
Vreeland v. Dawson—§ **3.25, n. 5**.
Vrooman v. Turner—§ **5.15, n. 6**; § **7.12, n. 16**.
Vulcraft, a Div. of Nucor Corp. v. Midtown Business Park, Ltd.—§ **12.4, n. 10**.

W

Waddell v. Dewey County Bank—§ **5.35, n. 25**.
Waddell v. Roanoke Mut. Building & Loan Ass'n—§ **5.17, n. 16**.
Waddilove v. Barnett—§ **4.22, n. 24**.
Wade v. Hannon—§ **8.15**; § **8.15, n. 77, 82, 85**.
Wade v. Hennessy—§ **4.12, n. 19**.
Wadleigh v. Phelps—§ **4.30, n. 2**.
Wadsworth v. Lyon—§ **5.2, n. 5**; § **10.2, n. 4, 6**; § **10.10, n. 8**.
Waff Bros, Inc. v. Bank of North Carolina, N.A.—§ **10.9, n. 7**; § **10.13, n. 2**.
Wagar v. Stone—§ **4.23, n. 1**; § **4.34, n. 17, 18, 19**.
Wager v. Link—§ **5.15, n. 6**.
Wagner v. Benson—§ **12.11, n. 28**.
Wagner v. GMAC Mortg. Corp. of Iowa—§ **5.27, n. 1**.
Wagoner v. Brady—§ **5.19, n. 33**.
W.A.H. Church, Inc. v. Holmes—§ **7.32, n. 9**.
Wahl v. H. W. & S. M. Tullgren, Inc.—§ **7.16, n. 34**.
Wahl v. Southwest Sav. & Loan Ass'n—§ **12.6, n. 28**.
Waible v. Dosberg—§ **4.43, n. 5**.
Wakefield v. Day—§ **6.6, n. 14**.
Wakefield v. Dinger—§ **7.20, n. 13**.
Wakey, In re—§ **8.18, n. 6**.
Waldo v. Rice—§ **7.5, n. 1**.
Waldorff Ins. & Bonding Inc. v. Eglin Nat. Bank—§ **13.3, n. 21**.
Waldron, In re—§ **8.19, n. 9**.
Walgreen Co. v. Moore—§ **4.39, n. 5, 9, 10**.

Walker v. Boggess—§ 7.22, n. 4.
Walker v. City of Hutchinson—§ 7.24, n. 6.
Walker v. Community Bank—§ 8.2, n. 9, 12; § 8.3, n. 58, 129.
Walker v. Dement—§ 5.35, n. 11.
Walker v. First Pennsylvania Bank, N. A.—§ 12.1, n. 32; § 12.3, n. 19.
Walker v. Houston—§ 6.7, n. 11.
Walker v. Nunnenkamp—§ 3.32, n. 17, 21.
Walker v. Queen Ins. Co.—§ 4.14, n. 10.
Walker v. Schreiber—§ 7.10, n. 15.
Walker v. Schultz—§ 7.5, n. 4.
Walker v. Valley Plumbing, Inc.—§ 13.3, n. 31.
Walker v. Warner—§ 7.5, n. 4, 15; § 7.12, n. 13.
Walker v. Whitmore—§ 12.8, n. 18, 20.
Walkup v. Cushing—§ 6.16, n. 27.
Wallace, In re—§ 8.15, n. 43.
Wallace v. Hammonds—§ 5.18, n. 4.
Wallowa Lake Amusement Co. v. Hamilton—§ 6.6, n. 16; § 6.7, n. 1.
Walmer v. Redinger—§ 5.33, n. 18, 25, 33.
Walser v. Farmers' Trust Co. of Indianapolis, Ind.—§ 5.15, n. 14.
Walsh v. Glendale Federal Sav. & Loan Ass'n—§ 6.9, n. 2.
Walsh v. Henel—§ 7.6, n. 15.
Walsky v. Fairmont Arms, Inc.—§ 7.31, n. 12.
Walter v. Calhoun—§ 4.27, n. 3; § 4.28, n. 9; § 4.30, n. 8; § 4.32, n. 3.
Walter v. Kressman—§ 9.2, n. 10.
Walter v. Marine Office of America—§ 4.15, n. 2.
Walter E. Heller Western, Inc. v. Bloxham—§ 8.3; § 8.3, n. 123.
Walter Harvey Corp. v. O'Keefe—§ 12.3, n. 1; § 12.7, n. 29.
Walters v. Patterson—§ 3.8, n. 1.
Walters v. Walters—§ 10.3, n. 5.
Wansley v. First Nat. Bank of Vicksburg, Vicksburg, Miss.—§ 7.21; § 7.21, n. 75, 82.
Ward, In re—§ 8.12, n. 13.
Ward v. Carey—§ 9.1, n. 8.
Ward v. McGuire—§ 6.7, n. 3.
Ward, United States v.—§ 6.11, n. 18.
Ward v. Yarnelle—§ 12.4, n. 31.
Waring v. Cunliffe—§ 3.1, n. 21.
Waring v. Loder—§ 4.13, n. 16; § 4.14, n. 15.
Waring v. National Sav. & Trust Co.—§ 4.44, n. 13.
Warner v. Rasmussen—§ 3.29, n. 39.
Warner v. Tullis—§ 3.22, n. 1.
Warner Bros. Co. v. Freud—§ 8.5, n. 9.
Warren v. Government National Mortg. Ass'n—§ 7.28; § 7.28, n. 6.
Warren v. Lovis—§ 3.4, n. 8.
Warren v. Rodgers—§ 3.36, n. 7.
Warren v. Yocum—§ 3.28, n. 9.
Warren Mortg. Co. v. Winters—§ 9.1, n. 22.
Warrington 611 Associates v. Aetna Life Ins. Co.—§ 5.22, n. 40; § 6.5, n. 3.

Warth v. Seldin—§ 7.24, n. 26.
Warwick v. Hammell—§ 4.41, n. 8.
Wasco Creamery & Const. Co. v. Coffee—§ 4.2, n. 16.
Washer v. Tontar—§ 5.20, n. 2.
Washington v. Davis—§ 11.5, n. 18.
Washington Federal Sav. and Loan Ass'n v. Schneider—§ 13.3, n. 51.
Washington Federal Sav. and Loan Ass'n of Miami Beach v. Balaban—§ 11.6, n. 20.
Washington Fire Ins. Co. v. Cobb—§ 4.14, n. 8.
Washington Homes Ass'n v. Wanecek—§ 5.4, n. 1.
Washington Mut. Sav. Bank v. United States—§ 8.3, n. 22.
Washington Nat. Building & Loan Ass'n v. Andrews—§ 5.17, n. 8.
Washington, State of v. Time Oil Co.—§ 4.47, n. 16.
Waterman v. Curtis—§ 4.30, n. 7.
Waterman v. Matteson—§ 4.6, n. 3; § 4.4, n. 8.
Waters v. Bossel—§ 7.14, n. 11.
Waters v. Crabtree—§ 3.4, n. 4.
Waters v. Wolf—§ 12.5, n. 3.
Waterson v. Devoe—§ 4.45, n. 3.
Waterville Industries, Inc. v. Finance Authority of Maine—§ 4.48, n. 10.
Watkins v. Kaolin Mfg. Co.—§ 4.8, n. 2.
Watseka First Nat. Bank v. Ruda—§ 7.7, n. 1.
Watson v. Hunter—§ 4.7, n. 4.
Watson v. Pathway Financial—§ 11.5, n. 18, 20.
Watson, State ex rel. v. White—§ 4.10, n. 1.
Watson v. Tromble—§ 7.17, n. 12.
Watson v. United American Bank in Knoxville—§ 7.21, n. 6.
Watson Const. Co. v. Amfac Mortg. Corp.—§ 12.6, n. 27; § 12.7, n. 14.
Watt v. Wright—§ 6.12, n. 14.
Watts v. Synes—7.2, n. 4.
Watt's Adm'r v. Smith—§ 4.38, n. 17.
Wavetek Indiana, Inc. v. K.H. Gatewood Steel Co., Inc.—§ 12.4, n. 21, 39.
Wayne Bldg. & Loan Co. of Wooster v. Yarborough—§ 12.7, n. 14; § 13.3; § 13.3, n. 18, 34.
Wayne International Building & Loan Ass'n v. Beckner—§ 5.7, n. 11, 13.
Wayne Sav. & Loan Co. v. Young—§ 7.1, n. 5.
Weadock v. Noeker—§ 4.46, n. 3, 20.
Weast v. Arnold—§ 5.28, n. 6.
Weatherby v. Smith—§ 3.1, n. 37.
Weathersbee v. Goodwin—§ 4.24, n. 2.
Weatherwax v. Heflin—§ 12.7, n. 11.
Weaver v. Tri City Credit Bureau—§ 3.38, n. 15.
Webb v. Hoselton—§ 5.31, n. 13.
Webb v. Southern Trust Co.—§ 6.2, n. 9.

Webb v. Superior Court (New West Federal Sav. and Loan Ass'n)—§ 11.7, n. 23.
Webb v. Verville—§ 4.44, n. 7.
Webber v. King—§ 4.42, n. 17.
Webster v. Wishon—§ 7.31, n. 1, 3.
Weidner v. Thompson—§ 10.7, n. 13.
Weigell v. Gregg—§ 5.33, n. 33.
Weikel v. Davis—§ 2.1, n. 9.
Weiman v. McHaffie, 470 So.2d 682—§ 5.24, n. 87.
Weiman v. McHaffie, 448 So.2d 127—§ 5.24, n. 40.
Weimer v. Uthus—§ 7.16, n. 34.
Weinberger v. Weidman—§ 6.13, n. 12.
Weinstein v. Investors Sav. and Loan Ass'n—§ 6.4, n. 2.
Weiss v. Brentwood Sav. & Loan Ass'n—§ 12.10, n. 7.
Weiss v. Karch—§ 13.6, n. 17.
Weiss, Dreyfous & Seiferth v. Natchez Inv. Co.—§ 12.10, n. 46.
Welch v. Beers—§ 10.11, n. 6.
Welch v. Cooper—§ 3.29, n. 1.
Welch v. Graham—§ 2.1, n. 4.
Welch v. Priest—§ 5.28, n. 12.
Welch v. Thomas—§ 3.7, n. 1.
Wellenkamp v. Bank of America—§ 5.21, n. 32; § 5.22, n. 19, 20; § 5.23, n. 10.
Wells v. American Mortg. Co. of Scotland—§ 7.14, n. 14.
Wells v. Flynn—§ 2.1, n. 9.
Wells v. Harter—§ 6.11, n. 26.
Wells v. Kemme—§ 4.3, n. 1.
Wells v. Lincoln Co.—§ 7.15, n. 2.
Wells v. Ordway—§ 7.8, n. 3.
Wells v. Van Dyke—§ 4.29, n. 17, 20.
Welsh v. Griffith-Prideaux, Inc.—§ 3.23, n. 3; § 3.25, n. 4.
Welsh v. Lawler—§ 7.16, n. 5.
Welsh v. Phillips—§ 5.28, n. 12.
Welton v. Tizzard—§ 3.12, n. 1.
Wenning v. Jim Walter Homes, Inc.—§ 5.30, n. 6.
Wensel v. Flatte—§ 3.3, n. 6.
Werner v. Automobile Finance Co.—§ 9.4, n. 14.
West v. Middlesex Banking Co.—§ 4.24, n. 13.
West v. Treude—§ 4.4, n. 4.
Westage Towers Associates v. ABM Air Conditioning and Refrigeration, Inc.—§ 13.3, n. 40.
Westberg v. Wilson—§ 3.18, n. 4.
Westbrook State Bank v. Anderson Land and Cattle Co.—§ 2.3, n. 16, 17.
Westchase I Associates, L.P., In re—§ 4.35, n. 25, 27.
Western Bank, Santa Fe v. Fluid Assets Development Corp.—§ 7.15, n. 1, 15, 23.
Western Coach Corp. v. Rexrode—§ 10.1, n. 16.
Western Federal Sav. & Loan Ass'n v. Heflin Corp.—§ 8.3, n. 72.
Western Federal Sav. & Loan Ass'n v. Sawyer—§ 8.3, n. 137, 138.

Western Insurance Co. v. Eagle Fire Insurance Co.—§ 7.14, n. 5.
Western Life Ins. Co. v. McPherson K.M.P.—§ 5.24; § 5.24, n. 133; § 5.26, n. 6.
Western Loan & Building Co. v. Mifflin—§ 4.2, n. 18.
Western Mortg. Loan Corp. v. Cottonwood Const. Co.—§ 12.7, n. 13; § 12.10, n. 47.
Western Pennsylvania Nat. Bank v. Peoples Union Bank & Trust Co.—§ 12.7, n. 11.
Western Sav. and Loan Ass'n v. Diamond Lazy K Guest Ranch, Inc.—§ 5.29, n. 24.
Western Sav. Fund Soc. of Philadelphia v. Goodman—§ 7.31, n. 1.
Western & Southern Life Ins. Co. v. Smith—§ 11.2, n. 30.
Western States Finance Co. v. Ruff—§ 3.38, n. 5.
Westesen v. Olathe State Bank—§ 12.3, n. 46.
Westfair Corp. v. Kuelz—§ 3.36, n. 4; § 3.32, n. 18.
Westfour Corp. v. California First Bank—§ 12.4, n. 37.
Westinghouse Credit Corp. v. Barton—§ 8.3, n. 52.
Westland Homes Corp. v. Hall—§ 12.10, n. 47.
Westlund v. Melson—§ 7.7, n. 4.
Westmoreland Manganese Corp., United States v.—§ 9.3, n. 1.
Westnau Land Corp. v. SBA—§ 11.6, n. 76.
West Point Corp. v. New North Mississippi Federal Sav. & Loan Ass'n—§ 5.3, n. 4; § 5.11, n. 6; § 5.19, n. 42.
West Portland Development Co. v. Ward Cook, Inc.—§ 6.3, n. 3; § 6.6, n. 3.
Westside Galvanizing Services, Inc. v. Georgia–Pacific Corp.—§ 12.4, n. 37.
West Side Trust & Savings Bank v. Lopoten—§ 4.22, n. 2, 12.
Weyand v. Park Terrace Co.—§ 6.7, n. 22.
Weyh v. Boylan—§ 5.32, n. 3.
Weyher v. Peterson—§ 3.29; § 3.29, n. 35, 38.
Whalen v. Ford Motor Credit Co.—§ 12.3, n. 9.
W.H. Dail Plumbing, Inc. v. Roger Baker and Associates, Inc.—§ 13.3, n. 38, 46.
Wheat v. Rice—§ 5.18, n. 15.
Wheatley's Heirs v. Calhoun—§ 9.1, n. 18, 19.
Wheaton v. Ramsey—§ 12.2, n. 23.
Wheeler, In re. 34 B.R. 818—§ 8.15, n. 5; § 8.17; § 8.17, n. 7, 13, 15, 72, 73, 74.
Wheeler, In re, 5 B.R. 600—§ 8.18, n. 19.
Wheeler v. Reynolds—§ 3.24, n. 11.
Wheeler v. White—§ 12.3, n. 25.
Whelan v. Exchange Trust Co.—§ 12.7, n. 10.
Whipple v. Edelstein—§ 7.14, n. 9.

TABLE OF CASES

Whispering Bay Campground, Inc., In re—§ 8.13, n. 33.
White, In re, 41 B.R. 227—§ 8.14, n. 55, 56.
White, In re, 22 B.R. 542—§ 8.15, n. 40.
White v. Berenda Mesa Water Dist.—§ 12.2, n. 15.
White v. Brousseau—§ 3.29, n. 74.
White v. Costigan—§ 8.5, n. 9.
White v. Eddy—§ 6.7, n. 26.
White v. First Nat. Bank of Emporium, Pa.—§ 4.31, n. 18.
White v. Ford—§ 3.6, n. 1, 8; § 3.7, n. 2; § 3.8, n. 9, 11, 15.
White v. Gilliam—§ 5.29, n. 27.
White v. MacQueen—§ 7.12, n. 22; § 7.21, n. 59.
White v. Melchert—§ 7.13, n. 1.
White v. Mid–Continent Investments, Inc.—§ 5.31, n. 1.
White v. Moore—§ 3.14, n. 2.
White v. Polleys—§ 10.14, n. 10.
White v. Rittenmyer—§ 7.12, n. 18.
White v. Schader—§ 5.7, n. 11, 13; § 5.10, n. 11.
White v. Shirk—§ 7.31, n. 6.
White, State ex rel. Watson v.—§ 4.10, n. 1.
White, United States v.—§ 3.30, n. 5; § 7.24, n. 27; § 7.26, n. 8, 12.
White & Bollard, Inc. v. Goodenow—§ 12.9, n. 24.
Whitehead v. American Security and Trust Company—§ 5.33, n. 3, 6.
Whitehead v. Derwinski—§ 11.6; § 11.6, n. 65.
White Lakes Shopping Center, Inc. v. Jefferson Standard Life Ins. Co.—§ 12.3, n. 19.
Whitestone Sav. & Loan Ass'n v. Allstate Ins. Co.—§ 4.16, n. 7, 9, 13.
Whiteway Finance Co., Inc. v. Green—§ 12.8, n. 6.
Whitfield v. Parfitt—§ 3.4, n. 9.
Whiting v. Gearty—§ 5.18, n. 5.
Whiting v. New Haven—§ 4.12, n. 16.
Whiting Pools, Inc., United States v.—§ 8.18, n. 45.
Whitley v. Barnett—§ 4.25, n. 5; § 4.28, n. 6.
Whitley v. Challis—§ 4.41, n. 1.
Whitlow v. Mountain Trust Bank—§ 7.20, n. 11; § 7.21, n. 59, 70, 71, 72, 76, 77.
Whitman v. Transtate Title Co.—§ 7.21, n. 6.
Whitney v. Adams—§ 4.29, n. 1.
Whitney, United States v.—§ 11.2, n. 43; § 11.6, n. 89.
Wichita Eagle & Beacon Pub. Co., Inc. v. Pacific Nat. Bank of San Francisco—§ 10.2, n. 12.
Wickard v. Filburn—§ 5.24, n. 12, 14.
Widmann v. Hammack—§ 7.8, n. 3.
Widmayer v. Warner—§ 3.24, n. 9, 11.
Wiemeyer v. Southern Trust & Commerce Bank—§ 6.7, n. 11.

Wierzbicki v. Alaska Mut. Sav. Bank—§ 12.11, n. 12.
Wiesel v. Ashcraft—§ 7.16, n. 26.
Wiggin v. Lowell Five Cent Sav. Bank—§ 4.11, n. 4; § 4.31, n. 10.
Wiggins v. Freeman—§ 4.43, n. 14.
Wilcox v. Allen—§ 5.35, n. 17.
Wilcox v. Campbell—§ 10.10, n. 8; § 10.11, n. 1, 2, 6, 9, 11.
Wilder's Ex'x v. Wilder—§ 10.3, n. 9.
Wile v. Donovan—§ 3.7, n. 3.
Wiley, Banks & Co. v. Ewing—§ 7.2, n. 17.
Wilkin v. Shell Oil Co.—§ 8.8, n. 14, 15.
Willamette Production Credit Ass'n v. Day—§ 12.7, n. 11.
Willard v. Worsham—§ 5.13, n. 1; § 5.18, n. 6.
Willcox Clinic, Ltd. v. Evans Products Co.—§ 5.18, n. 6.
William H. Metcalfe and Sons, Inc. v. Canyon Defined Ben. Trust—§ 10.13, n. 2.
William J. Morris, Inc. v. Lanzilotta & Teramo Const. Corp.—§ 12.2, n. 27.
Williams, In re—§ 8.15, n. 24.
Williams v. Baldwin—§ 12.2, n. 35.
Williams v. Chicago Exhibition Co.—§ 4.10, n. 3.
Williams v. Fassler—§ 6.2; § 6.2, n. 7, 21.
Williams v. First Federal Sav. and Loan Ass'n of Arlington—§ 5.21, n. 11, 33.
Williams v. Matthews Co.—§ 11.5, n. 16.
Williams v. Moniteau Nat'l Bank—§ 2.4, n. 2.
Williams v. Robinson—§ 4.34, n. 2.
Williams v. Roundtree—§ 3.4, n. 10.
Williams v. Rouse—§ 4.29, n. 3.
Williams v. Townsend—§ 4.45, n. 3.
Williams v. Vestman—§ 12.9, n. 5.
Williams v. Williams—§ 3.10, n. 3; § 3.4, n. 5, 7.
Williams Const. Co. v. Standard–Pacific Corp.—§ 5.30, n. 10.
Williamson, In re—§ 12.4, n. 30.
Williamson v. Field's Executors & Devisees—§ 7.12, n. 22.
Williamson v. Floyd County Wildlife Ass'n, Inc.—§ 3.11, n. 1.
Williamson v. Magnusson—§ 3.32, n. 7.
Williamson v. Wanlass—§ 3.29, n. 1; § 7.7, n. 22, 23, 24.
Williams Plumbing Co. v. Sinsley—§ 3.29, n. 26.
Williams & Works, Inc. v. Springfield Corp.—§ 12.5, n. 19.
Willis, In re—§ 8.15, n. 5; § 8.17, n. 13.
Willis v. Community Developers, Inc.—§ 6.9, n. 21.
Willis v. Miller—§ 8.5, n. 9.
Willis v. Nowata Land and Cattle Co., Inc.—§ 4.14, n. 10.
Willis v. Rabun County Bank, 291 S.E.2d 715—§ 12.8, n. 15.
Willis v. Rabun County Bank, 291 S.E.2d 52—§ 6.6, n. 28.

Willowood Condominium Ass'n, Inc. v. HNC Realty Co.—§ 12.3, n. 25.
Willow Tree Investments, Inc. v. Wagner—§ 11.7, n. 23.
Wills, In re—§ 5.29, n. 19.
Willsey v. Peoples Federal Sav. and Loan Ass'n of East Chicago—§ 6.6, n. 19.
Willson v. Burton—§ 10.7, n. 6.
Wilmarth v. Johnson—§ 4.28, n. 4.
Wilson, Ex parte—§ 4.21, n. 8.
Wilson, In re, 144 B.R. 318—§ 8.15, n. 52.
Wilson, In re, 58 B.R. 164—§ 8.15, n. 50.
Wilson, In re, 11 B.R. 986—§ 8.15, n. 40.
Wilson v. Adams & Fusselle, Inc.—§ 8.3, n. 20.
Wilson v. Commonwealth Mortg. Corp.—§ 8.15, n. 56, 66, 70, 71.
Wilson v. European & North American Railway Company—§ 4.12, n. 19.
Wilson v. Fisher—§ 3.2, n. 1; § 4.29, n. 21, 33.
Wilson v. Gadient—§ 4.45, n. 14.
Wilson v. Maltby—§ 4.5, n. 13, 14.
Wilson v. McLaughlin—§ 4.2, n. 16.
Wilson v. Pacific Coast Title Ins. Co.—§ 5.34, n. 4.
Wilson v. Ripley County Bank—§ 12.7, n. 14.
Wilson v. Russell—§ 2.1, n. 15.
Wilson v. Steele—§ 5.31, n. 2; § 5.29, n. 9; § 5.31, n. 13.
Wilson v. Stilwell—§ 5.10, n. 13.
Wilson v. Tarter—§ 7.3, n. 8.
Wilson v. Vanstone—§ 6.17, n. 11.
Wilson v. Vaughan—§ 2.4, n. 2.
Wilson v. Wallace—§ 5.35, n. 11.
Wilson and Herr v. Hayward—§ 5.35, n. 9.
Wilson Bros. v. Cooey—§ 5.32, n. 10, 28.
Wilton-Maxfield Management Co, In re—§ 8.3, n. 51.
Wimpfheimer v. Prudential Ins. Co. of America—§ 7.2, n. 17.
Winchell v. Coney—§ 12.7, n. 10.
Windle v. Bonebrake—§ 5.34, n. 12.
Wingert v. Brewer—§ 6.7, n. 8.
Winick Corp. v. General Ins. Co. of America—§ 12.6, n. 9.
Winklemen v. Sides—§ 8.2, n. 5; § 8.3, n. 36.
Winnett v. Roberts—§ 6.6, n. 2; § 6.7, n. 9.
Winnisimmet Trust v. Libby—§ 4.22, n. 4.
Winshall Settlor's Trust, Matter of—§ 8.17, n. 29.
Winslow v. Clark—§ 7.12, n. 13.
Winslow Center Associates, In re—§ 4.35, n. 14.
Winter v. Kram—§ 6.13, n. 2.
Winterburn, United States v.—§ 3.27, n. 5.
Winters, In re—§ 8.17, n. 73.
Winters v. Sami—§ 6.6, n. 1.
Winters v. Winters—§ 7.20, n. 9.
Winthrop Towers, United States v.—§ 7.7; § 7.7, n. 34.
Wisconsin Cent. R. Co. v. Wisconsin River Land Co.—§ 4.2, n. 16.
Wisconsin Inv. Bd., State of v. Hurst—§ 12.9, n. 21.
Wisconsin League of Financial Institutions, Ltd. v. Galecki—§ 4.19, n. 29; § 11.6, n. 26, 46.
Wisconsin Mortg. Assur. Corp. v. HMC Mortg. Corp.—§ 11.2, n. 58.
Wise v. Layman—§ 4.29, n. 7; § 4.31, n. 7, 12.
Wisner's Estate, In re—§ 10.2, n. 7.
Witczinski v. Everman—§ 12.7, n. 10.
Witt v. Trustees of the Grand Grove, U. A. O. D.—§ 4.29, n. 22.
Wittenburg, In re—§ 5.28, n. 34.
Wohlhuter v. St. Charles Lumber & Fuel Co.—§ 5.20, n. 5.
Wolcott v. Winchester—§ 5.28, n. 14.
Wolfe v. Lipsy—§ 7.21, n. 91.
Wolfe v. Murphy—§ 5.19, n. 5, 16.
Wolford Enterprises, Inc., In re—§ 8.14, n. 21.
Wolkenstein v. Slonim—§ 4.43, n. 8; § 4.34, n. 9.
Women's Federal Sav. and Loan Ass'n v. Nevada Nat. Bank—§ 5.35; § 5.35, n. 23, 52.
Women's Federal Sav. Bank v. Akram—§ 8.1, n. 19.
Women's Federal Sav. Bank v. Pappadakes—§ 7.1, n. 1, 2.
Wonder Corp. of America, In re—§ 8.14, n. 41.
Wonderly v. Giessler—§ 6.16, n. 27.
Wong v. Beneficial Sav. and Loan Ass'n—§ 12.8, n. 2, 10.
Wood v. Babb—§ 6.7, n. 2.
Wood v. Barnes—§ 13.3, n. 31.
Wood v. Goodfellow—§ 6.12, n. 7, 9.
Wood v. Gulf States Capital Corp.—§ 5.33, n. 1.
Wood v. Lafleur—§ 5.4, n. 7.
Wood v. Parker Square State Bank, 400 S.W.2d 898—§ 12.8, n. 14.
Wood v. Parker Square State Bank, 390 S.W.2d 835—§ 12.7, n. 23.
Wood v. Rabe—§ 3.24, n. 13.
Wood v. Sparks—§ 5.34, n. 37.
Woodall v. Citizens Banking Co., 507 N.E.2d 999—§ 12.10, n. 34.
Woodall v. Citizens Banking Co., 503 N.E.2d 427—§ 12.10, n. 8, 34, 51.
Woodard v. Bruce—§ 5.29, n. 14.
Woodbridge Place Apartments v. Washington Square Capital, Inc.—§ 12.3, n. 19, 22.
Woodbury v. Swan, 59 N.H. 22—§ 4.44, n. 11; § 4.45, n. 12.
Woodbury v. Swan, 58 N.H. 380—§ 10.2, n. 3.
Woodcock v. Putnam—§ 6.13, n. 1.
Woodcrest Apartments, Ltd. v. IPA Realty Partners Richardson Palmer, 3rd Investment KG—§ 5.24, n. 87.
Wooden v. First Sec. Bank of Idaho, N.A.—§ 12.10, n. 57.

TABLE OF CASES

Woodhurst v. Cramer—§ 6.17, n. 12.
Woodmen of the World Life Ins. Soc. v. Sears, Roebuck & Co.—§ 4.2, n. 3.
Woodruff v. California Republic Bank—§ 8.2, n. 4.
Woods v. Monticello Development Co.—§ 3.29, n. 1.
Woods v. Wallace—§ 3.4, n. 11.
Woodside v. Lippold—§ 6.17, n. 14.
Woodson v. Veal—§ 3.10, n. 3.
Woodstone Ltd. Partnership, In re—§ 5.29, n. 31; § 11.7, n. 10, 43.
Woodward v. Brown—§ 5.19, n. 37; § 10.15, n. 2.
Woodward v. Phillips—§ 4.29, n. 3.
Woodworth v. Redwood Empire Sav. & Loan Ass'n—§ 12.10, n. 31.
Wooldridge Const. Co. v. First Nat. Bank of Arizona—§ 12.4, n. 27.
Woolley v. Holt—§ 4.23, n. 1.
Worcester, In re, 811 F.2d 1224—§ 7.22, n. 17.
Worcester, In re, 28 B.R. 910—§ 8.15, n. 5; § 8.17, n. 15.
Wordinger v. Wirt—§ 7.8, n. 10.
Work v. Braun—§ 8.7, n. 13.
Workmon Const. Co. v. Weirick—§ 3.6, n. 1.
Worley v. Worley—§ 7.22, n. 47.
Worth v. Hill—§ 10.13, n. 33, 34.
Wortman & Mann, Inc. v. Frierson Bldg. Supply Co.—§ 12.7, n. 36.
Wright, In re—§ 8.15, n. 58, 59.
Wright v. Anderson—§ 5.3, n. 1, 10; § 6.16, n. 17, 18, 22.
Wright v. Associates Financial Services Co. of Oregon, Inc.—§ 7.27, n. 2.
Wright v. Bank of Chattanooga—§ 5.6, n. 6.
Wright v. Estate of Valley—§ 10.2, n. 3.
Wright v. Home Beneficial Life Ins. Co.—§ 12.9, n. 46, 47.
Wright v. Howell—§ 7.2, n. 14.
Wright v. Johnston—§ 8.3, n. 102.
Wright v. Lincoln County Bank—§ 12.8, n. 15.
Wright v. United States—§ 12.11, n. 13, 23.
W. R. Kuhn Co., In re—§ 4.22, n. 14.
Wuchter v. Pizzutti—§ 7.24; § 7.24, n. 29, 31.
Wunderle v. Ellis—§ 10.3, n. 5.
Wuorinen v. City Federal S & L Ass'n—§ 4.35, n. 31.
W-V Enterprises, Inc. v. Federal Sav. & Loan Ins. Corp.—§ 12.3, n. 43.
WWG Industries, Inc., In re—§ 13.3, n. 31.
Wychoff v. Scofield—§ 4.38, n. 16.
Wyman v. Roesner—§ 6.6, n. 2.
Wynnewood House Associates, In re—§ 8.18, n. 54.
Wyoming State Farm Loan Bd. v. Farm Credit System Capital Corp.—§ 9.7, n. 3.
Wyser v. Truitt—§ 4.2, n. 16.

Y

Yager v. Rubymar Corp.—§ 5.4, n. 3.
Yale Exp. System, Inc., In re, 384 F.2d 990—§ 8.14, n. 112.
Yale Exp. System, Inc., In re, 362 F.2d 111—§ 5.10, n. 2.
Y Aleman Corp. v. Chase Manhattan Bank—§ 3.30, n. 12; § 7.27, n. 2.
Yankee Bank for Finance & Sav., FSB v. Task Associates, Inc.—§ 11.6, n. 79.
Yarbrough v. John Deere Indus. Equipment Co.—§ 7.12, n. 25, 26.
Yarlott v. Brown—§ 6.11, n. 21.
Yasuna v. Miller—§ 5.1, n. 4; § 5.8, n. 9.
Yazell, United States v.—§ 11.6; § 11.6, n. 50.
Yelen v. Bankers Trust Co.—§ 5.24, n. 54.
Yerkes v. Hadley—§ 4.44, n. 2.
Yingling v. Redwine—§ 4.2, n. 17.
Yoelin v. Kudla—§ 4.43, n. 5.
York Associates, Inc. v. Frenchman's Creek Investors, Ltd.—§ 5.26, n. 8.
Yorkshire Bank v. Mullan—§ 4.40, n. 1.
Yost-Linn Lumber Co. v. Williams—§ 12.7, n. 14.
Young, In re—§ 8.15, n. 35, 41.
Young v. Brand—§ 7.17, n. 17.
Young v. Chicago Federal Sav. and Loan Ass'n—§ 5.35, n. 55.
Young v. Clapp—§ 7.13, n. 13.
Young v. Hawks—§ 5.1, n. 1; § 5.33, n. 30.
Young v. Morgan—§ 10.7, n. 2, 7; § 12.7, n. 10.
Young v. Ridley—§ 7.25, n. 18; § 7.26, n. 7; § 7.27, n. 1.
Young v. Weber—§ 7.16, n. 34.
Young Men's Christian Ass'n of Portland v. Croft—§ 5.14, n. 10; § 5.15, n. 7.
Youngs, In re—§ 8.15, n. 91.
Youngs v. Trustees for Support of Public Schools—§ 5.18, n. 9.
Yu v. Paperchase Partnership—§ 3.35, n. 2.

Z

Zablonski, In re—§ 8.15, n. 55.
Zachery v. Treasure Lake of Georgia, Inc. (Ga.)—§ 12.11, n. 20.
Zachman Homes, Inc., In re—§ 13.3, n. 44.
Zaegel v. Kuster—§ 7.2, n. 5.
Zajac v. Federal Land Bank of St. Paul—§ 7.7, n. 51.
Zandri v. Tendler—§ 4.44, n. 3, 7.
Zapata v. Torres—§ 10.4, n. 1.
Zastrow v. Knight—§ 5.3, n. 1, 8; § 5.9, n. 3, 13; § 5.19, n. 24, 25.
Zeballos v. Zeballos—§ 7.18, n. 3.
Zeeway Corp., In re—§ 4.35, n. 39.
Zeligman v. Juergens—§ 4.33, n. 2.
Zellerbach Paper Co. v. Valley Nat. Bank of Ariz.—§ 10.13, n. 2.

Zellmer, Matter of—§ **8.15, n. 89.**
Zellner v. Hall—§ **5.19, n. 49.**
Zimmern v. People's Bank of Mobile—§ **4.22, n. 1.**
Zions First Nat. Bank v. United Health Clubs, Inc.—§ **2.3, n. 19.**
Zirinsky v. Sheehan—§ **3.32, n. 26.**
Zisman v. City of Duquesne—§ **4.25, n. 6;** § **4.26, n. 1.**
Zisser v. Noah Indus. Marine & Ship Repair, Inc.—§ **7.16, n. 26, 28.**
Zoll v. Carnahan—§ **6.12, n. 9.**
Zorn v. Van Buskirk—§ **5.34, n. 17.**
Zuege v. Nebraska Mortg. Co.—§ **4.44, n. 16.**
Zumstein v. Stockton—§ **3.32, n. 17.**
Zuni Const. Co. v. Great Am. Ins. Co.—§ **12.2, n. 28.**

Index

References are to Sections

ABSOLUTE DEED AS MORTGAGE
Burden of proof, 3.7.
Conditional sale, 3.17.
Creditors of grantee, 3.12.
Effect between parties, 3.9.
Factors establishing mortgage intent, 3.8, 3.19.
Fraudulent conveyance, 3.13.
Grantor's rights upon grantee's sale, 3.11.
Language negating mortgage intent, 3.19.
Oral understanding of defeasance, 3.5.
Parol evidence rule, 3.6, 3.15.
Parol trust distinguished, 3.16.
Reasons for use, 3.5.
Recordation, 3.14.
Restatement approach, 3.8.
Sale and leaseback, 3.19.
Separate instrument of defeasance, 3.4.
Statute of frauds, 3.15.
Title of grantee, 3.10.

ACCELERATION
See also Due–On Clauses.
Agricultural Credit Act of 1987, 7.7
Bankruptcy, 8.15.
Clauses, 1.1, 7.3, 7.6, 7.7, 8.15.
Limitations on, 7.7.
UCC, 7.7.

ACQUISITION OF TITLE IN BREACH OF DUTY
By mortgagee, of tax title, 4.45.
By mortgagor, 4.4.
Tax payment by junior mortgagee, 4.46.

ADJUSTABLE RATE MORTGAGES, 11.4

AFTER–ACQUIRED PROPERTY CLAUSES, 9.3

AGRICULTURAL CREDIT ACT OF 1987, 7.7, 8.16

ALTERNATIVE MORTGAGE INSTRUMENTS, 11.4

ALTERNATIVE MORTGAGE TRANSACTION PARITY ACT OF 1982, 11.4

AMORTIZATION, 1.1

ANACONDA CLAUSE, 12.8

ANNUAL RESTS
See Mortgagee In Possession.

ANTIDEFICIENCY STATUTES
California scheme, 8.3.
Deficiency judgments, 8.1.
Fair value, 8.3.
Guarantors, 8.3.
Legislation, 8.3.
Mixed collateral, 8.3.
One-action rule, 8.2.
Power of sale prohibition, 8.3.
Purchase-money prohibition, 8.3.
Uniform Land Transactions Act, 8.3.
Waiver, 8.3.

ASSIGNMENT BY MORTGAGEE
See Transfer By Mortgagee.

ASSIGNMENT OF RENTS
Bankruptcy, 8.18.
Federal law, 8.18.
Restatement approach, 4.35.
State law, 4.35.

BANKRUPTCY
Absolute priority rule, 8.14, 8.16.
Assignment of rents, 8.18.
Avoidance powers, general, 8.13, 8.16.
Bifurcation of home mortgage, 8.15.
Chapter 11, 8.14.
Chapter 12, 8.16.
Chapter 13, 8.15.
Constitutional problems, 8.14, 8.16.
Cramdown concept, 8.14.
De-acceleration, Chapter 11, 8.14.
De-acceleration of home mortgage, 8.15.
Equity, defined, 8.13, 8.14.
Fraudulent conveyance, foreclosure sale as, 8.17.
Fraudulent conveyances, generally, 8.13.
Installment land contracts, 8.19.
Lien stripping, 8.13.
Modification of home mortgage, 8.15.
Pre-bankruptcy foreclosures, 8.17.
Preferences,
    Generally, 8.13.
    Foreclosure sales as, 8.17.
Relief from stay, 8.13, 8.14, 8.15, 8.16.
Rents in bankruptcy, 8.18.
Reorganization plans, 8.14, 8.15, 8.16.
Statutory redemption, 8.13.
Stays, 8.13, 8.14.

INDEX

References are to Sections

BANKRUPTCY—Cont'd
Straight bankruptcy, 8.13.
Trustee abandonment, 8.13.

BOARD OF GOVERNORS OF THE FEDERAL RESERVE SYSTEM
See Federal Reserve Board.

BONDS, CONSTRUCTION, 12.2

BUY-DOWNS OF MORTGAGE INTEREST, 11.4

CERCLA
See Environmental Liability.

CIVIL RIGHTS ACTS, 11.5

CLOGGING THE EQUITY OF REDEMPTION
Adjustable rate mortgage, 3.1.
Deed in escrow, 3.1, 3.31.
Deed in lieu, 3.3, 6.18, 6.19.
Definition, 3.1.
Due-on clauses, 3.1.
Graduated payment mortgage, 3.1.
Options as clogs, 3.2.
Restatement approach, 3.1, 3.2.
Shared appreciation mortgages, 3.1.
Subsequent transactions, 3.3.
ULSIA, 3.2.

CLOSE-CONNECTEDNESS DOCTRINE, 5.29

COLLATERALIZED MORTGAGE OBLIGATIONS, 11.3

COMMERCIAL BANKS
Generally, 11.1.
Construction lending by, 12.1.

COMMITMENTS, MORTGAGE LOAN, 12.3

COMMUNITY REINVESTMENT ACT OF 1977, 11.5

COMPTROLLER OF THE CURRENCY
Alternative mortgage instruments, 11.4.
Discrimination in mortgage lending, 11.5.
Due-on clauses, 5.23–5.25.
Preemption of state law, 11.6.
Regulation Q, 11.4.
Regulatory authority, 11.1.

CONDITIONAL SALE
See also Absolute Deed as Mortgage.
Establishing as mortgage, 3.18.
Extrinsic evidence, 3.18.
Factors establishing as mortgage, 3.19.
Language negating mortgage intent, 3.19.
Restatement approach, 3.19.
Sale and leaseback as mortgage, 3.19.

CONDOMINIUMS
Generally, 13.1.
Construction financing, 13.3.
Conversion of rental buildings, 13.4.

CONDOMINIUMS—Cont'd
Financing, 13.2, 13.4.
Mortgage rider, 14.11.
Priority of mechanics' lienors, 13.3.
Priority of unit purchasers, 13.3.
Special declarant rights, 13.3.
Taxation, 13.1.

CONSENT STATUTE, 11.7

CONSIDERATION
See Obligation.

CONSTRUCTION CONTRACTS AND BONDS, 12.2

CONSTRUCTION DEFECTS, LENDER LIABILITY, 12.11

CONSTRUCTION LOANS
Generally, 12.1.
Commitments, 12.3.
Condominium, 13.3.
Disbursement, improper, 12.10.
Documentation, 12.1.
Lenders, institutional, 11.1.
Liability for defective construction, 12.11.
Priority, 12.7.
Priority as to fixtures, 9.7.
Subordination to, 12.9.
Underwriting, 12.1.

CONTRACT FOR DEED
See Installment Land Contract.

CONTRACTS, CONSTRUCTION, 12.1

CONTRIBUTION, 10.3
See also Subrogation.

CONVERSION TO CONDOMINIUM OR COOPERATIVE, 13.4

COOPERATIVE APARTMENTS
Generally, 13.1.
Conversion of rental buildings, 13.4.
Federal Housing Administration, 13.6.
Financing, 13.2, 13.6.
Taxation, 13.1.

CUT-OFF NOTICE, 12.7

DEBT
See Obligation.

DEED
As assignment of mortgage, 5.28.
As mortgage, 3.7–3.19.

DEED IN LIEU OF FORECLOSURE
Clogging the equity of redemption, 3.3.
Pitfalls for mortgagee, 6.18, 6.19.
Reasons for use, 6.18, 6.19.

DEED OF TRUST
Generally, 1.1.
Forms, 14.3, 14.7, 14.12, 14.16, 15.9.
Trustee's duties, 7.21.

DEED OF TRUST—Cont'd
Trustee's wrongful acts, effect on assignee, 5.34.

DEFICIENCY JUDGMENTS
See also Antideficiency Statutes.
FHA and VA loans, 11.2.

DISCHARGE
See Payment.

DISCOUNTS ON FHA OR VA LOANS, 11.2

DISCRIMINATION IN MORTGAGE LENDING, 11.5

D'OENCH, DHUME DOCTRINE, 5.29, 11.7

DRAGNET CLAUSE, 12.8

DUE–ON CLAUSES
See also Transfer By Mortgagee.
Case law, pre-Garn Act, 5.22.
Concealment of transfer, 5.25.
Extension of window period, 5.24.
Forms, 14.3, 14.13, 14.15, 14.16, 14.17.
Garn–St. Germain Act, 5.24.
Increased interest on transfer, 5.21.
Installment land contracts, 5.21.
Mortgagee's duty to respond, 5.24.
Office of Thrift Supervision regulation, 5.24.
Policy arguments, 5.26.
Prepayment penalty enforceable, 6.5.
Reasons for use, 5.21.
Release of original mortgagor, 5.6, 5.24.
State legislation, 5.22, 5.24.
Wraparound mortgage, effect on, 9.8.

DUE PROCESS OF LAW
Bankruptcy plans, 8.14, 8.16.
Installment contract forfeiture, 3.30.
Judicial foreclosure, 7.12, 7.13, 7.15.
Mechanics' liens, 12.5.
Power of sale foreclosure, 7.24–7.30.
Receivership, 4.36.
Strict foreclosure, 7.10.

EMINENT DOMAIN
Rights to award, 4.12.
Uniform eminent domain code, 4.12.

ENTRY WITHOUT PROCESS
See Strict Foreclosure.

ENVIRONMENTAL LIABILITY
CERCLA, 4.47, 4.48, 4.49, 4.50, 4.51.
Deed in lieu, 4.48, 4.49.
EPA regulation, 4.49.
Foreclosure, 4.48, 4.49.
Forms, 14.3, 14.17, 15.9, 15.16.
Indicia of ownership, 4.48, 4.49.
Lien for cleanup costs, 4.50.
Loan documentation, 4.51.
Mortgagee participation in management, 4.48, 4.49.

ENVIRONMENTAL LIABILITY—Cont'd
Post-foreclosure mortgagee liability, 4.48, 4.49.
Safe harbor, 4.49.
Security interest exemption, 4.48, 4.49.
State legislation, 4.50.
Title theory, 4.48, 4.49.

EQUAL CREDIT OPPORTUNITY ACT, 11.5

EQUITABLE LIEN, 12.6

EQUITIES, PATENT AND LATENT, 5.32

ESCROW
Installment land contract fulfillment, 3.31.
Purchasers' deposits, 13.3.

ESCROWS FOR TAXES AND INSURANCE
Constitutional problems, 4.19.
Constructive trust theory, 4.18.
Description, 4.17.
Express trust theory, 4.18.
Form, 14.3.
Miscellaneous theories, 4.18.
Office of Thrift Supervision regulation, 4.19.
Pledge theory, 4.18.
Requirements by mortgagees, 4.17.
RESPA, 4.19.
Resulting trust theory, 4.18.
Statutory regulation, 4.19.

FAIR HOUSING ACT, 11.5

FARMERS HOME ADMINISTRATION, 7.17, 7.24, 7.28, 8.16

FEDERAL DEPOSIT INSURANCE CORPORATION,
Defenses of borrowers against, 11.7.
Holder in due course status, 5.29.
Regulatory authority, 11.1.
Savings Association Insurance Fund, 11.1.

FEDERAL HOME LOAN BANK BOARD
See Office of Thrift Supervision.

FEDERAL HOME LOAN BANKS
Assignments of mortgages to, 5.28.
System operation, 11.3.

FEDERAL HOME LOAN MORTGAGE CORPORATION
Generally, 11.3.
Adjustable rate mortgages, 11.4.
Condominium loan purchases, 13.2, 13.5.
Due-on clauses, 5.22, 5.23, 5.24.
Foreclosure by, constitutionality, 7.28.
Forms, 14.2–14.12, 14.16.
Late payment fees, 6.10.
Participation certificates, 5.35.
Preemption of state law, 11.6.
Prepayment fees, 6.4.
Recordation of mortgage assignment, 5.34.

FEDERAL HOUSING ADMINISTRATION
Amortized loans encouraged by, 1.1.

INDEX

References are to Sections

FEDERAL HOUSING ADMINISTRATION
—Cont'd
Commitments, 12.3.
Condominium program, 13.1, 13.5.
Construction loans, 12.1.
Construction defects, liability, 12.11.
Cooperative apartment program, 13.6.
Federal National Mortgage Association purchases, 11.3.
Foreclosure guidelines, 7.7.
Foreclosure sale, constitutionality, 7.28.
Late payment fees, 6.10.
Mortgage forms, 14.13, 14.14.
Mortgage insurance programs, 11.2.
Negligent inspection by, 12.11.
Preemption of state foreclosure law, 11.6.
Prepayment fees, 6.4.

FEDERAL HOUSING FINANCE BOARD, 11.3

FEDERAL NATIONAL MORTGAGE ASSOCIATION
Generally, 11.3.
Adjustable rate mortgages, 11.4.
Commitments, 12.3.
Condominium loan purchases, 13.2, 13.5.
Due-on clauses, 5.22, 5.23, 5.24.
Foreclosure by, constitutionality, 7.28.
Forms, 14.2–14.12, 14.16.
Late payment fees, 6.10.
Notice of mortgage assignment, 5.33.
Preemption of state law, 11.6.
Prepayment fees, 6.4.
Recordation of mortgage assignment, 5.34.

FEDERAL RESERVE BOARD, 11.1
Regulation Q, 11.4.

FEDERAL SAVINGS & LOAN INS. CORP.
Defenses of borrowers against, 11.7.
Holder in due course status, 5.29.
Regulatory authority, 11.1.

FINANCIAL INSTITUTIONS REFORM, RECOVERY, AND ENFORCEMENT ACT OF 1989 (FIRREA), 11.1, 11.3, 11.6, 11.7

FIXTURES
Generally, 9.5.
Construction mortgages, 9.7.
Forms, 15.7.
Pre–UCC law, 9.6.
Prior real estate mortgages, 9.7.
Remedies, 9.7.
Subsequent real estate mortgages, 9.7.
UCC law, 9.7.

FNMA
See Federal National Mortgage Association.

FORECLOSURE
Acceleration prior to, 1.1, 7.6.
Chilled bidding, 7.21.
Constitutionality, power of sale, 7.23–7.30.

FORECLOSURE—Cont'd
Defects, in power of sale, 7.20, 7.21.
Installments, 7.8.
Joinder, 7.12, 7.13.
Judicial, 7.11–7.18.
Leases, 7.12.
Mortgagee purchase, 7.21.
Multifamily Foreclosure Act of 1981, 7.19.
Omitted parties, 7.15.
Parcel or bulk sales, 7.16, 7.21.
Parties, necessary and proper, 7.12.
Place of sale, 7.21.
Power of sale, 7.19–7.30.
Purchaser's position, 7.17, 7.21, 7.22.
Reforms suggested, 7.30, 8.8.
Remedies for defective sale, 7.22.
Sale, conduct of, 7.16, 7.21.
Sale price, 7.16, 7.21.
Senior interests, effect on, 7.14.
Strict, 7.9, 7.10, 7.15.
Surplus, disposition of, 7.31, 7.32.
Title stability, 7.18.
Trustee purchase, 7.21.
Uniform Land Transactions Act, 7.19.

FORFEITURE
See Installment Land Contract.

FORMS
Adjustable rate note, 14.7.
Assignment of rents, 14.17, 15.11.
Attornment, 15.12.
Condominium development, 15.3.
Construction loan agreement, 15.2.
Deed of trust, residential, 14.3, 14.4, 14.15.
Deed of trust, multifamily, 14.16, 14.17.
Estoppel statement, 15.13.
FHA, 14.13, 14.14.
Graduated payment note, 14.8.
Growing equity note, 14.9.
Guaranty, 15.10.
Lease, shopping center, 15.16.
Leasehold mortgage, 15.14.
Mortgage, residential, 14.5, 14.6.
Mortgage, multifamily, 14.17.
Mortgage, commercial, 15.8.
Mortgage, subdivision, 15.9.
Promissory note, 14.2, 14.7, 14.8, 14.13, 15.6, 15.8.
Subordination, 15.4, 15.12.
Subdivision development, 15.9.
Veterans Affairs, 14.15.

FRAUDULENT CONVEYANCE
Absolute deed as, 3.13.
Foreclosure as, 8.17.

FUTURE ADVANCES, 12.7

GARN–ST. GERMAIN DEPOSITORY INSTITUTIONS ACT
Due-on-sale clauses, 5.24.
Lending powers of regulated institutions, 11.1.
Preemption of state law, 11.6.

GOVERNMENT NATIONAL MORTGAGE ASSOCIATION
Mortgage-backed securities, 11.3.

GRADUATED PAYMENT MORTGAGE, 11.4

GROWING EQUITY MORTGAGE, 11.4

HAZARDOUS WASTE
See Environmental Liability.

HISTORICAL DEVELOPMENT
Clogging the equity of redemption, 3.1.
Common law, 1.2.
Equity of redemption, 1.3.
Principal American theories, 1.5, 4.1, 4.2.
Variants from normal mortgage,
    Deed of trust, 1.6.
    Installment contract, 1.7.

HOLDER IN DUE COURSE, 5.28–5.32

HOME EQUITY CONVERSION MORTGAGE, 11.4

HOME MORTGAGE DISCLOSURE ACT, 11.5

INCOME TAX, FEDERAL
Cooperative housing projects, 13.1.
Installment sale, wraparound mortgages, 9.9.
State housing agency bonds, 11.3.

INDEXED MORTGAGE, 11.4

INSTALLMENT LAND CONTRACT
As a mortgage substitute, 1.7, 3.26.
Bankruptcy of vendee, 3.33, 8.19.
Bankruptcy of vendor, 3.33, 8.19.
Constitutionality of forfeiture, 3.30.
Cooperative apartment sale, 13.2.
Damages, 3.32.
Deeds in escrow, 3.31.
Due-on clauses, 5.21, 5.22, 5.24.
Election of remedies, 3.32.
Equity of redemption, 3.29.
Federal tax liens, 3.33.
Foreclosure as mortgage, 3.29, 3.32.
Forfeiture clause, 3.26, 3.27.
Forfeiture—judicial limitations, 3.29.
Income tax treatment, 3.34.
Judgments against vendee, 3.36.
Judgments against vendor, 3.36.
Mortgage of vendee's interest, 3.35.
Mortgage of vendor's interest, 3.37.
Notice to junior interests, 3.35.
Recordation, 3.34.
Remedies, 3.27, 3.28, 3.29, 3.31, 3.32.
Restitution, 3.29.
Restrictions on vendee transfer, 5.21, 5.22, 5.24.
Soldiers and Sailors Civil Relief Act, 8.10.
Specific performance, 3.29, 3.32.
Statutory regulation, 3.28.
Strict foreclosure, 3.29, 3.32.
Title problems, 3.33, 3.34.

INSTALLMENT LAND CONTRACT—Cont'd
Vendee's remedies, 3.28, 3.29.
Vendor's remedies, 3.32.
Waiver of forfeiture, 3.29.

INSTALLMENT LAND SALES, 3.34

INSURANCE
See also Mortgage Insurers.
Application of proceeds, 4.14, 4.15, 4.16.
Effect of foreclosure, 4.16.
Escrow for insurance, 4.13, 4.17, 4.18, 4.19.
Forms, 14.3, 14.15, 14.16, 14.17, 15.7, 15.9, 15.14, 15.16.
Interests of parties, 4.13.
Loss payable policy, 4.14.
Mortgagee failure to pay premiums, 4.13.
Policy types, 4.14.
Restoration of premises, 4.15.
Standard mortgage policy, 4.14.

INTEREST RATES
Alternative mortgages, 11.4.
Mortgage affordability, 11.4.
Payments, effect on, 1.1.

INTERMEDIATE THEORY, 1.5, 4.3

INVERSE ORDER OF ALIENATION, 10.9

JUDICIAL FORECLOSURE
See Foreclosure.

LATE PAYMENT, 6.8–6.10
See also Payment.

LEASE, PRIORITY, 12.9

LEASEHOLD MORTGAGE, 15.14, 15.15

LENDER LIABILITY
Commitment, failure to meet, 12.3.
Construction defects, 12.11.
Construction loan disbursement, 12.10.
Stop notice, 12.6.

LENDING INSTITUTIONS
    Generally, 11.1.
Construction lending by, 12.1.
Insolvent, resolution of, 11.7.

LIEN THEORY, 1.5, 4.2, 4.23

LIENS, MECHANICS'
See Mechanics' Liens.

LIFE INSURANCE COMPANIES, 11.1

LIS PENDENS, 7.13

MARSHALLING
    Generally, 10.9.
Assumption, effect of, 10.11.
By debtor, 10.14.
Gift conveyances, 10.12.
Inverse order of alienation, 10.9.
Release by mortgagee, 10.15.
Second mortgages, 10.13.
Two funds doctrine, 10.9.

References are to Sections

MECHANICS' LIENS
Generally, 12.4.
Condominiums, priority as to, 13.3.
Constitutionality, 12.5.
Equitable lien, 12.6.
Priority, 12.4.
Stop notice, 12.6.

MERGER
Generally, 6.15.
Between mortgagor and mortgagee, 6.16.
Deed in lieu, 6.17, 6.18, 6.19.
Intervening interests, 6.17.

MODIFICATION OF SENIOR MORTGAGES
Generally, 9.4.
Extensions of time, 9.4.
Increases in interest, 9.4.
Increases in principal, 9.4.
Optional future advances, relation to, 9.4.

MORTGAGE BANKERS, 11.1

MORTGAGE INSURERS, 11.2
See also Federal Housing Administration.

MORTGAGE LOAN COMMITMENTS, 12.3

MORTGAGEE IN POSSESSION
Generally, 4.24
Accounting by, 4.27, 4.28.
Annual rests, 4.32.
Compensation for services, 4.30.
Improvements, 4.29.
Liability of mortgagee to third party, 4.26.
Maintenance and improvements, 4.29.
Taxes and insurance, 4.31.
What constitutes possession, 4.25.

MUTUAL SAVINGS BANKS, 11.1

NEGATIVE COVENANT AS MORTGAGE
See Negative Pledge As A Mortgage Substitute.

NEGATIVE PLEDGE AS A MORTGAGE SUBSTITUTE, 3.38

NEGLIGENCE IN CONSTRUCTION LOAN DISBURSEMENT, 12.10

NEGOTIABLE NOTES, 5.28–5.29

NO–BID CLAIMS, VA LOANS, 11.2

OBLIGATION
Assignment of, 5.27.
Consideration, 2.3.
Description in mortgage, 2.4.
Nature of, 2.2.
Necessity for, 2.1.
Non-recourse loans, 2.1.
Support mortgages, 2.2.
Transfer of, 5.27.

OFFICE OF THE COMPTROLLER OF THE CURRENCY
See Comptroller of the Currency.

OFFICE OF THRIFT SUPERVISION
Alternative mortgage instruments, 11.4.
Cooperative apartment loans, 13.6.
Discrimination in mortgage lending, 11.5.
Due-on clauses, 5.23–5.25.
Late payment fees, 6.10.
Preemption of state law, 11.6.
Prepayment fees, 6.4.
Regulation Q, 11.4.
Regulatory authority, 11.1, 11.6.

ONE–ACTION RULE
See Antideficiency Statutes.

PARTICIPATION AGREEMENTS, 5.35

PAYMENT
Acceptance, 6.6.
By grantee, subrogation, 10.7.
Condemnation, 6.3.
Insurance proceeds, 6.3.
Involuntary payment, 6.3.
Late payment fees, 6.8, 6.9.
Prepayment fees, validity of, 6.2.
Prepayment fees-due-on enforcement, 6.5.
Regulation of prepayment, 6.4.
Right to prepay, 6.1.
Tender, 6.7.
To assignor as a defense, 5.33.

PLEDGE
Of note, as mortgage assignment, 5.28.
Tax and insurance escrow accounts, 4.18.

POWER OF SALE FORECLOSURE
See Foreclosure.

PREEMPTION BY FEDERAL LAW, 11.6

PREPAYMENT
See Payment.

PRICE LEVEL ADJUSTED MORTGAGE 11.4

PRIORITY
Alternative mortgages, 11.4.
Among participants, 5.35.
Between mechanics' liens and vendees, 13.3.
Effect of modification, 9.4.
Fixtures, 9.5–9.7.
Foreclosure, 7.11–7.15.
Purchase-money mortgages, 9.1–9.2.
Subordination agreements, 12.9.
Wraparound mortgages, 9.8.

PRIVATE MORTGAGE INSURANCE, 11.2

PURCHASE AND ASSUMPTION TRANSACTIONS, 11.7

PURCHASE MONEY MORTGAGES
Generally, 1.1, 9.1.
Deficiency judgments, 8.3.
Priority, 9.1.
Recording, 9.1.
Subordination of, 9.1.

PURCHASE MONEY RESULTING TRUSTS
Contract or option to purchase, 3.24.
Prior ownership in borrower, 3.23.
Security agreements, 3.21.
Statute of frauds, 3.22.
Statutory abolition in some states, 3.24.

RACIAL DISCRIMINATION, 11.5

REAL ESTATE INVESTMENT TRUSTS, 11.1

REAL ESTATE MORTGAGE INVESTMENT CONDUITS (REMICS), 11.3

REAL ESTATE SETTLEMENT PROCEDURES ACT (RESPA)
Escrows for taxes and insurance, 4.19.
Preemption of state law, 11.6.

RECEIVERSHIPS
Advantages of, 4.33.
Agreements for rents and profits, 4.35.
Basis for appointment, 4.34.
Collusive leases, 4.42.
Constitutional problems, 4.36.
Ex parte receiverships, 4.36.
General or equity receivership distinguished, 4.41.
Imputed rent, 4.40, 4.41.
Leases, effect on, 4.37.
Milking by mortgagor, 4.42.
Mortgagor conducting business, 4.41.
Mortgagor in possession, 4.40.
Priorities among mortgagees, 4.43.
Rents, effect on, 4.37, 4.38, 4.39.
Sweetheart leases, 4.42.

RECORDING
Absolute deed, 3.14.
Mortgage assignments, 5.34.
Purchase money mortgages, 9.2.
Subordination agreements, 12.9.

REDEMPTION
Amount to be paid, 7.3.
Bankruptcy, 8.13.
Equitable vs. statutory, 1.3, 1.4, 7.1.
Federal statute, 11.7.
From mortgage, 7.1.
Laches, 7.5.
Limitations on right, 7.5.
Omitted parties, 7.15.
Procedure, 7.4.
Revival of liens, 8.6.
Statutory, 7.1, 8.4, 8.5, 8.6.
Who may redeem, 7.2, 8.5.

REDLINING, 11.5

REFORMING THE FORECLOSURE PROCESS, 7.30, 8.8

RELEASE OF MORTGAGE
See also Payment.
Assuming grantee, 5.18.
Effect on marshaling, 10.15.

RENTS
See also Assignment of Rents; Receiverships.
Agreements for rents and profits, 4.35, 8.18.
Bankruptcy, 8.18.
Definition, 4.35, 8.18.
Lease before mortgage, title states, 4.21.
Lien states, 4.23.
Milking, 4.42.
Mortgage before lease, title states, 4.22.
Priorities among mortgagees, 4.43.
Rights in general, 4.20.

REPLACEMENT MORTGAGES, 9.4

RESOLUTION OF INSOLVENT FINANCIAL INSTITUTIONS, 11.7

RESOLUTION TRUST CORP.
Generally, 11.7.
Defenses of borrowers against, 11.7.
Holder in due course status, 5.29.

REVERSE ANNUITY MORTGAGE, 11.4

SAVINGS AND LOAN ASSOCIATIONS, 11.1
See also Office of Thrift Supervision.

SECURITIES ACTS
Mortgage loan commitments as within, 12.3.
Mortgage participations as within, 5.35.

SECURITIZATION OF MORTGAGES, 11.3.

SERVICING OF MORTGAGES, 5.33, 11.1.

SEVERED PROPERTY
Injunction against removal, 4.7.
Mortgagees' rights, 4.6.

SEX DISCRIMINATION IN MORTGAGE LENDING, 11.5

SHARED APPRECIATION MORTGAGE, 11.4

SHARED EQUITY MORTGAGE, 11.4

SOLDIERS AND SAILORS CIVIL RELIEF ACT
Generally, 8.9.
Default judgments, 8.11.
Installment land contracts, 8.10.
Mortgages and Deeds of Trust, 8.10.
Stay provisions, 8.9, 8.10.
Taxes, 8.9, 8.10.

STANDBY LOAN COMMITMENTS, 12.3

STATE HOUSING FINANCE AGENCIES, 11.3

STATUTES OF LIMITATIONS
Bankruptcy, 8.13, 8.14, 8.17.
Extension, effect on junior interests, 6.12.

STATUTES OF LIMITATIONS—Cont'd
Extension by grantees or junior interests—effect on mortgagor, 6.13.
Marketable title legislation, 6.14.
Obligation and mortgage distinguished, 6.11.
Soldiers and Sailors Civil Relief Act, 8.9, 8.10.
Statutory trends, 6.14.

STOP NOTICE, 12.6

STRICT FORECLOSURE
Generally, 7.9, 7.10.
Constitutionality, 7.10.
Miscellaneous foreclosure methods, 7.10.
Omitted parties, 7.15.
Use for, 7.10.

SUBORDINATION AGREEMENTS, 12.9
By vendees, 13.3.
By vendors, 12.9.
Conditional, 12.9.
Forms, 15.4, 15.12.

SUBROGATION
Generally, 10.1.
Assignment, compelling, 10.8.
Grantee, payment by, 10.7.
Grantor, payment by, after grantee assumes, 5.9.
Grantor's liability when grantee assumes, 5.13.
Loan to pay mortgage, 10.5.
Payment to protect an interest, 10.3.
Surety, payment by, 10.2.
Taxes, payment by subsequent mortgagee, 4.46.
Volunteer, payment by, 10.4.

SUPPORT MORTGAGES, 2.2

SURETYSHIP
Assumption of mortgages, 5.1–5.20.
Construction bonds, 12.2.
Liability of surety for noncompletion of construction, 12.10.
Marshaling, 10.9.
Mechanics' liens, effect on, 12.4.
Subrogation upon payment as surety, 10.2.

TAX–EXEMPT BONDS, 11.3

TAX TITLES
See Acquisition of Title in Breach of Duty; Bankruptcy.

TENDER OF PAYMENT, 6.7

TITLE INSURANCE ON PARTICIPATION INTERESTS, 5.35

TITLE THEORY, 1.5, 4.1, 4.21, 4.22

TOXIC WASTE
See Environmental Liability.

TRANSFER BY MORTGAGEE
Assignment of mortgage alone, 5.28.
Deed by mortgagee, 5.28.
Holder in due course doctrine, 5.29–5.33.
Latent and patent equities, 5.32.
Methods of transfer, 5.28.
Nature of transfer, 5.27.
Negotiability of obligation, 5.29.
Negotiation by mortgagee, 5.29.
Non–HDC assignees, 5.32.
Partial assignments, 5.35.
Participation agreements, 5.35.
Payment as a defense, 5.33.
Recording acts, effect of, 5.34.
Statutory and regulatory limitations, 5.30.
Subrogation, as compelling assignment, 10.8.

TRANSFER BY MORTGAGOR
Assumption of mortgage, 5.4.
    Deed provisions, 5.5.
    Implied assumption, 5.8.
    Parol evidence rule, 5.7.
    Statute of frauds, 5.6.
Due-on clauses, 5.21–5.26.
Extension or modification by mortgagee,
    Effect of UCC, 5.19–5.20.
    Effect on liability of mortgagor, 5.19.
Methods of transfer, 5.2.
Rights of mortgagee against grantee,
    Generally, 5.11.
    Assuming second mortgagee, 5.16.
    Grantee's defenses, 5.17.
    Miscellaneous theories, 5.14.
    Subsequent discharge or modification between grantor and grantee, 5.18.
    Successive grantees, 5.15.
    Suretyship subrogation, 5.13.
    Third party beneficiary theory, 5.12.
Rights of transferor,
    Assuming grantee, 5.10.
    Non-assuming grantee, 5.9.
Transfer subject to mortgage, 5.3.
Transferability of interest, 5.1.

TRIPARTITE SECURITY TRANSACTIONS
See Purchase Money Resulting Trusts.

TRUST DEED MORTGAGE
See Deed of Trust.

TWO FUNDS DOCTRINE, 10.9

UNIFORM COMMERCIAL CODE
See also Acceleration; Fixtures; Power of Sale Foreclosure; Transfer by Mortgagee; Transfer by Mortgagor.
Holder in due course under, 5.28–5.32.
Pledges of mortgage notes, 5.28.

UNIFORM COMMON INTEREST OWNERSHIP ACT, 13.1, 13.5

UNIFORM CONDOMINIUM ACT, 13.1, 13.5

UNIFORM CONSUMER CREDIT CODE, 5.30

USURY
Federal preemption, 11.6.
Prepayment fees, 6.2.
Wraparound mortgages, 9.8.

VETERANS AFFAIRS, DEPARTMENT OF
    See also Federal Housing Administration.
    Generally, 11.2.
Forms, 14.15.
Liability for construction defects, 12.11.

VOLUNTEER RULE, 10.4

WASTE
Covenants against, 4.11.

WASTE—Cont'd
Damages, 4.4.
Defined, 4.4.
Financial, 4.11.
Impairment of security, 4.4.
Injunctions against, 4.10.
Taxes, failure to pay, 4.11.
Tortious injury by mortgagor, 4.4.
Tortious injury by third parties, 4.5, 4.6.
Voluntary vs. permissive, 4.11.

WRAPAROUND MORTGAGES
    Generally, 9.8.
Assumption by second mortgagee, 5.2, 5.4, 5.16.

WRIT OF ENTRY OR POSSESSION
See Strict Foreclosure.

†

0-314-02434-4

90000

9 780314 024343